Marketing

CONCEPTS AND DECISION MAKING

Marketing

CONCEPTS AND DECISION MAKING

Charles W. Gross
University of New Hampshire

Robin T. Peterson
New Mexico State University

WEST PUBLISHING COMPANY
St. Paul New York Los Angeles San Francisco

Copyediting Sonsie Carbonara Conroy
Artwork Reese and Deborah Thornton
Art direction Wendy Calmenson
Composition Parkwood Composition Service
Photo/advertisement research Natalie Goldstein
Cover design Delor Erickson, Studio West

Library of Congress Cataloging-in-Publication Data

Gross, Charles W.
Marketing: concepts and decision making.

Includes index.
1. Marketing—Decision making. 2. Marketing—Management. I. Peterson, Robin. II. Title.
HF5415.135.G76 1987 658.8′02 86-26676
ISBN 0-314-85242-5

Photo/Advertisement Credits

Contents **vii** Courtesy Visual Arts Press. Creative Director: Silas Rhodes; Designer: Bill Kobasz; Illustrator: Marvin Mattelson; Copywriter: Dee Ito; **ix** Courtesy Volkswagen United States; **xi** Courtesy CIGNA Corporation; **xii** Courtesy Johnston & Murphy and Weitzman, Dym & Associates, Inc.; **xx** Courtesy AT&T Communications and N W Ayer Incorporated

Chapter 1 **3** Naoki Okamoto/Stock Market; **4** Courtesy Sears; **9** Rocky Widner/Retna Ltd.; **11** Courtesy McDonald's; **14** Courtesy Avant Salon, formerly 7th South 8th for Hair, and Fallon McElligott, Inc.; **16** Courtesy Porsche and Chiat/Day. Television commercial produced by Coppos Films.; **17** Courtesy Eastpak and ClarkeGowardFitts. Copywriter: Jon Goward; Art Director: Jim Fitts.

Chapter 2 **21** Courtesy Visual Arts Press. Creative Director: Silas Rhodes; Designer: Bill Kobasz; Illustrator: Marvin Mattelson; Copywriter: Dee Ito.; **22** Courtesy The Professional Golfers' Association of America; **29** Courtesy Apple Computer, Inc.; **31** Courtesy Coors, Mark Harmon, and Foote, Cone & Belding; **34** Courtesy Sony Corporation of America; **39** Courtesy Bloomingdale's Food Division; **42** Courtesy Gold Toe Socks/Great American Knitting Mills and Baron & Zaretsky

Chapter 3 **48** Courtesy St. Andrews Development Company of Boca Raton, Inc.; **49** Courtesy My Child's Destiny, San Francisco; **52** Courtesy The Stride Rite Corporation, Cambridge, MA; **53** Courtesy Johnson & Johnson; **59** Courtesy Karastan Rug Mills, 1984 Communication Arts Award of Excellence, 1985 Clio winner for the best single print ad: The Fan-tailed Dove.; **62** Courtesy BMW of North America, Inc.; **64** Courtesy Royal Caribbean Cruise Lines and McKinney Silver & Rocket. Art Director: Larry Bennett; Writer: Harriett Frye; Photographer: Barbara Bordnick

Chapter 4 **69** Courtesy *The Wall Street Journal*; **70** Courtesy Chrysler Corporation; **72** Philip Jon Bailey/Stock, Boston; **75** Geoffrey C. Clifford/Wheeler Pictures; **78** Courtesy Amtrak and DDB Needham Worldwide, Inc.; **84** Courtesy IBM

Chapter 5 **91** Steven E. Sutton/Duomo; **92** Courtesy Fisher-Price; **99** Courtesy Minstar, Inc.; **107** Courtesy Volkswagen United States; **111** Courtesy American Cancer Society; **115** M. W. Peterson/The Image Bank; **116** Courtesy The Quaker Oats Company and Batten, Barton, Durstine & Osborn, Inc.

Chapter 6 **120** A. Keler/Sygma; **121** Ken Karp Photography; **128** Courtesy Shade and Fallon McElligott, Inc.; **134** Courtesy Owens/Corning Fiberglas and Ogilvy & Mather; **139** Courtesy American International Group; **142** Courtesy Nevamar Corporation and Lord, Sullivan & Yoder, Inc.; **148** David Hiser/The Image Bank

Chapter 7 **153** Frank Siteman/EKM-Nepenthe; **154** Courtesy Wendy's International, Inc.; **159** Courtesy Interline Communication Services, Inc., and Fallon McElligott, Inc.; **161** Wolf Winkler/The Image Bank; **162** Courtesy *Rolling Stone*/Straight Arrow Publishers, Inc., and Fallon McElligott, Inc.; **167** Courtesy Schenley Industries, Inc., ©1984 and Leo Burnett Company, Inc.; **172** Dan McCoy/Rainbow

Chapter 8 **181** Walter Bibikow/The Image Bank; **182** Stanley Rowin/The Picture Cube; **183** Courtesy People Express; **184** John Maher/EKM-Nepenthe; **194** Courtesy Super Wernet's; **198** Courtesy Wienerschnitzel and Blake, Walls and Associates; **203** Courtesy CIGNA Corporation

Chapter 9 **207** Courtesy Primo Angeli Inc.; **208** Courtesy *Los Angeles Times*; **210** Courtesy Waterford Crystal and Ammirati & Puris, Inc.; **211** Courtesy Coleman Company and Fallon McElligott, Inc.; **219** Courtesy Chanel Inc. and Doyle Dane Bernbach Inc.; **220** Courtesy Brunswick Corporation

Chapter 10 **228** Courtesy Primo Angeli Inc.; **229** Grafton M. Smith/The Image Bank; **233** Courtesy General Foods and Y&RNY; **239** Courtesy Ralston Purina Company and Bartels & Carstens. Creative Director: Donn Carstens; Writer: Donn Carstens; Art Director: Marijo Bianco; Photographer: Jon Bruton; **242** Courtesy The Coca-Cola Company; **244** Courtesy The Procter & Gamble Company; **246** Courtesy Jewel Food Stores, ©1986

Chapter 11 **252** Cliff Feulner/The Image Bank; **253** Courtesy Heath Company; **255** Courtesy Dexter Shoe Company; **260** Milton & Joan Mann; **262** Courtesy Burlington Northern Railroad; **267** Courtesy Curtis Mathes Corporation, ©1986; **273** Courtesy Pillsbury and Leo Burnett U.S.A. Creative Director: Gerry Miller; Art Director: Wayne Johnson

Chapter 12 **278** Arthur d'Arazien/The Image Bank; **279** Courtesy ENRON Corp.; **282** Courtesy Hyster Company; **285** Courtesy Rapistan, A Lear Siegler Company; **290** Courtesy Santa Fe Railroad; **291** Courtesy Flying Tigers and HCM; **294** Courtesy of Federal Express

(Credits continued following index)

Contents in Brief

PART FOUR Marketing Mix Elements 205

PART FIVE Special Topics in Marketing 483

Contents

To be good
is not enough,
when you dream
of being great.
SCHOOL OF VISUAL ARTS

CHAPTER 2 The Strategic Marketing Decision Process 21

CHAPTER 3 Market Segmentation 48

It's hot in California.
On the freeways. By the beaches. In the valleys. From Malibu to Monterey. Volkswagen Convertibles are as popular as hot tubs. And not only in sunny California. They're popular wherever people know fun when they drive it. Maybe it's our German engineering.
A new 1.8-liter high-performance engine. And a new close-ratio five-speed transmission.
Fuel injection. Front-wheel drive. Sport suspension.
A body made at the Karmann Coachworks in Osnabruck, West Germany, where human hands still outnumber machines.
Or maybe it's just that the top goes down.
It caught on in Kansas. It's popular in Pennsylvania. It could even get hot in Alaska.
The Convertible.
It's not a car.
It's a Volkswagen.

CHAPTER 5 Understanding Consumer Behavior 91

CHAPTER 6 Understanding Industrial and Other Organization Buying Behavior 120

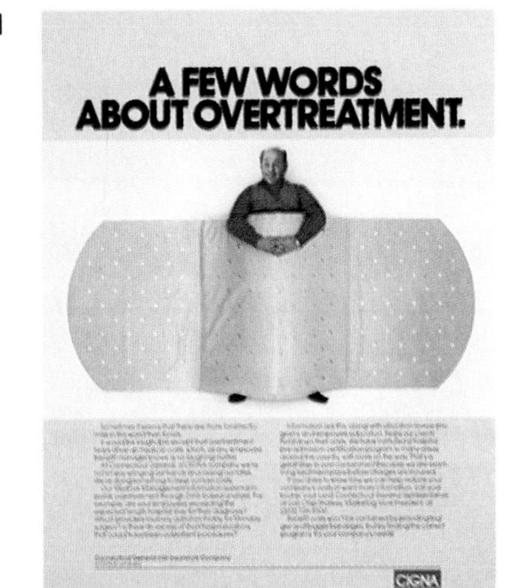
A FEW WORDS ABOUT OVERTREATMENT.
CIGNA

Unmistakably
Meet Our Maker.
See a fascinating demonstration of hand-shoemaking.
A J&M tradition since 1850. Ask inside for details.
Johnston & Murphy.

CHAPTER 13 Intermediaries: Retailers 297

CHAPTER 14 Wholesaling and Intermediary Buying Behavior 323

"We'll eat pizza and birthday cake, then we'll all sleep over in the garage. Wanna come, Uncle Bill?"
You can say it all for less with AT&T's Special Discounts
AT&T
Reach out and touch someone.
AT&T

Preface

Introduction

Increasing world trade interdependence, technological change, demands by special interest groups, competition from abroad, changing consumer values, and a maturing population are just some of the many challenges facing managers in the late 1980s. Each of these challenges poses potential threats to some businesses, but also opens doors to new opportunities.

Marketing is the dynamic and exciting function that links a society's needs and production activities, thereby enabling businesses to meet the challenges that they face. And its role in modern business is increasing. Through marketing decision making, organizations sense their place in an ever-changing world and set their destinies. The 1980s have been termed the "marketing decade" by some business executives, educators, and others because of the realization of the importance of this field.

We have attempted to create a vehicle through which the reader can gain a solid understanding of marketing. The objectives of this book are oriented toward that mission, and will

- Cover the essential areas of the discipline. The text deals with those components of marketing that students should master in order to be well versed on the subject. An understanding of the topics presented will prepare students for jobs in industry, whether they assume marketing positions or serve some other functions in business and directly or indirectly interrelate with those in marketing.
- Provide a marketing decision-making perspective to students. Today's students are tomorrow's practicing managers. As such, they should learn the discipline in a way that will be of value for managerial purposes.
- Provide the conceptual underpinnings of the field in an integrated framework.
- Illustrate important concepts with practical examples. It is difficult for students to gain an understanding of the field solely through the study of abstractions and theory. This text contains numerous examples of how businesses have used (and misused) marketing to nurture reader insight into the field.

- Stress marketing decision making that is useful to all types of organizations, including large and small business, marketers of services, and not-for-profit organizations. Throughout this book, examples provide insights into how marketing methods can be employed by any institution, regardless of its nature or size.

Highlights and Features

Marketing: Concepts and Decision Making began by conducting several sessions with key executives and middle managers of various businesses, diverse in scale and scope. The idea was to discover what business students should know about the field from those who will eventually hire them. Many discussions were then held with marketing academics covering the same topics. The final product represents a melding of what both groups had to say about what the content of such a book should be, along with the authors' own ideas.

The text has several major distinguishing highlights. One of these is the strong decision-making perspective. The initial foundation chapters pave the way for the succeeding chapters that contain more applications and actual decision-making tools and methods.

This book is integrative in nature. The various chapters and sections are tied together with an overall managerial perspective in terms of the need to emphasize decision-making strategies and to synthesize concepts and means of analysis.

The book also contains several areas that have expanded in significance to today's marketers and deserve in-depth treatment. For example, analytical techniques used by businesses for market opportunity analysis are presented, such as net present value analysis and modern forecasting techniques. Coverage of these topics is considered essential in a day (especially since the advent of PCs and spreadsheets) when most marketing decisions are based upon analysis using such tools. We have also included separate, comprehensive treatments of direct marketing, the marketing of services and not-for-profit marketing, industrial buying behavior, wholesaling, and transportation.

Many realistic examples appear throughout the text. Care was taken to select the examples from a blend of not-for-profit organizations, small and large businesses, service organizations, and industrial marketers in order to represent each of these key marketing action areas.

While the book has a definite decision-making focus, it provides strong treatment of essential principles, theories, and societal/ethical considerations. An attempt has been made to arrive at a proportional, but in-depth, coverage of each.

In order to achieve the objectives of the text, certain components appear in each chapter, including

- Objectives to set the stage for the material to be covered.
- An opening Marketing Success or Failure (in vignette form) experienced by some organization that is related to the content of the chapter. The Successes and Failures illustrate how various principles mentioned in the chapter can be utilized (or not utilized).
- Marketing Briefs that are interspersed throughout the text. These aid in generating student interest, understanding of real world problems, and providing insight into constraints that confront managers. The Briefs illustrate what some of the theories and principles actually mean.
- Relevant photographs, figures, and illustrations that have been carefully designed, selected, and interwoven into the narrative discussion.
- A summary and questions that serve to reinforce major points.

- Key terms that assist students in developing a marketing vocabulary. They have been defined in the margins as well as at the end of the book in a Glossary.

Contemporary Cases that can be used with a number of different chapters appear following the Appendixes. They present decision-making situations where students provide advice to management regarding the best course of action to pursue. Forty-six Cases are included to allow for wide application of the marketing concepts.

We think that we have accomplished our mission to cover and integrate topics that both academics and business managers feel are appropriate as we head toward the twenty-first century. The verdict from practitioners is decisive, and perhaps best summed up by the president of one international company, who said: "This marketing book covers exactly what students should be learning to enhance their business careers." Encouraging to us is the fact that key academic reviewers echoed these same thoughts.

Supplementary Materials

Various supplementary materials complement the textbook and are designed to aid student learning. A Student Study Guide is available that provides meaningful discussions of each chapter's coverage. An Instructor's Manual was prepared by the authors to assist in class coverage of the materials. Sets of transparency acetates and masters have been prepared to assist with presentation of the material. These include both key figures from the text plus additional supplementary materials. A Test Bank available in printed form and on computer disk has been prepared to facilitate testing and questioning parallel with the text. Finally, other materials are being prepared and are expected to be offered in the near future to make the package even more comprehensive.

Contributors

The authors are indebted to numerous individuals without whose assistance this book could never have been constructed. Above all, we are indebted to our families, who have tolerated us during the development of this book and have had to put up with our countless hours of absence, midnight tossings and turnings, and walking into walls while mumbling something like "principle #24 is . . ."

West Publishing company personnel, including Denise Simon, Executive Editor, Theresa O'Dell, Developmental Editor, and Barbara Fuller, Senior Production Editor, were all instrumental in the production and showed interest and competence much beyond the call of duty. The authors are indebted to M. Dean Martin, Western Carolina University, who developed the student Study Guide, and Eric Pratt, New Mexico State University, who constructed the Test Bank. We also wish to thank Francisco Coronel, Loyola Marymount University, for advice and selected materials for Case development.

A special thanks is given to the business practitioners who gave us insight and encouragement in the development of this text. These include Mr. John Day, Vice President—Beatrice Foods Inc.; Mr. Jack Edwards, Vice President—Household Finance Corporation; Mr. Richard Elliot, Vice President—Addressograph Multigraph Corp.; Mr. William Guerra, President—Duty Free Shoppers Group Ltd.; Mr. Bruce Jordan, Marketing Manager—Motorola Corporation; Mr. Larry Luther, Vice President—Ball Corporation; Mr. James Proebstle, Marketing Director—Xerox Corporation; Mr. Curt Richards, Consultant—Independent; Mr. Joseph Ruegg, Sales Manager—Levi Strauss & Co.; Mr. Joseph Shidle, Marketing Manager—Motorola Corporation; Mr. Barry Simpson, Vice President—Barrett Paving International; Mr.

Charles Skillman, President—Skillman Group (Advertising); and Mr. Richard Smith, Buyer—Sears, Roebuck & Co.

In addition, the following academic reviewers contributed hours of intense effort analyzing individual chapters and providing constructive comments.

Charles A. Bearchell	California State University, Northridge
William E. Bell	California State University, Fullerton
William G. Browne	Oregon State University
Randi S. Clark	North Harris County College, Texas
Barbara Coe	North Texas State University
William A. Cohen	California State University, Los Angeles
Edmund A. Cotta	California State University, Long Beach
James M. Cupello	Utah State University
M. Wayne DeLozier	University of South Carolina
Dennis J. Elbert	University of North Dakota
John Farah	University of Wisconsin, Green Bay
Wallace Feldman	Suffolk University, Boston
Charles W. Ford	Arkansas State University
Harold W. Fox	Pan American University, Texas
Joyce L. Grahn	University of Wisconsin, Eau Claire
Harrison Grathwohl	California State University, Chico
Robert F. Gwinner	Arizona State University
G. E. Hannem	Mankato State University
Robert R. Harmon	Portland State University
Nathan Himelstein	Essex Community College, Maryland
Robert F. Hoel	Colorado State University
Frederick B. Hoyt	Illinois State University
Kathleen A. Krentler	San Diego State University
Richard C. Leventhal	Metropolitan State University, Minnesota
Jeff W. Lindberg	Central Michigan University
Leslie E. Martin, Jr.	University of Wisconsin, Whitewater
M. Dean Martin	Western Carolina University
Gary F. McKinnon	Brigham Young University
Charles P. Morgan	University of Wisconsin, La Crosse
Mark Moriarty	University of Iowa
James A. Muncy	University of Oklahoma
Joyce F. Noon	San Diego State University
Thomas S. O'Connor	University of New Orleans
William Renforth	Western Illinois University
Edward A. Riordan	Wayne State University, Michigan
Kenn L. Rowe	Arizona State University
William S. Sachs	St. John's University, New York
Joel Saegert	University of Texas, San Antonio
Steven D. Shipley	Governor's State University, Illinois
Bob E. Smiley	Indiana State University
Allen E. Smith	Florida Atlantic University
Paul C. Thistlethwaite	Western Illinois University
James B. Wiley	Temple University, Pennsylvania
Leland Wilson	Southwest Texas State University
Gene C. Wunder	Ball State University, Indiana

Marketing
CONCEPTS AND DECISION MAKING

Part One

Marketing Decision Making: The Framework

Chapter 1

Marketing: An Overview

Objectives

After completing this chapter, you should be able to demonstrate a knowledge of:

- The origins of marketing, which arise from specialization and the separation of production and consumption
- The major functions of marketing
- The major participants in the marketing system: producers, buyers, and marketing intermediaries
- The meaning of the terms *macro marketing* and *micro marketing*
- The major orientations organizations can take toward customers and why adopting the "marketing concept" is preferred
- The marketing mix: the decision tools employed by marketers striving toward their goals

MARKETING SUCCESS

A New Direction in Financial Services

"We knew what consumers wanted when we built our financial network," according to Edward R. Kuby, vice president of marketing of Chicago-based Allstate Insurance Group, Sears, Roebuck and Co. "The old marketing maxim that explains why people buy . . . drill bits also pertains to financial services. . . . They don't really want . . . quarter-inch drill bits; what they want is quarter-inch holes. Consumers don't want insurance companies or stock brokers, they want their financial affairs handled efficiently and professionally—and with the full assurance of security," he said.

In reality, Sears began offering financial services over 80 years ago. Since 1911, generations of Americans have been able to finance their purchases through Sears' credit operations, and insurance has been offered by the company since it opened Allstate in 1931. The company also opened Sears Savings Bank in 1958. But the move into full financial services—the creation of Sears Financial Network—began in 1981, with the company's purchase of Dean Witter (securities) and Coldwell Banker (real estate).

Contrary to early predictions by financial analysts, Sears Financial Network has gained widespread consumer acceptance. According to Kuby, "performance is up for each of the member companies." For example, Sears Savings Bank now has assets of $6 billion, which ranks it as the twenty-first largest savings and loan association in the U.S. For Dean Witter, 35 to 40 percent of its new accounts are opened through the Financial Network Centers, and "80 percent of these accounts are either first-time brokerage accounts or reactivated dormant accounts," Kuby added.

"This performance supports what our research has told us all along—there is a vast middle market that is being overlooked by traditional financial service institutions. We are reaching this new investor and bringing new capital to the market," he said.

Another financial service that Sears is adding to its line is its new Discover card, which provides consumers a line of credit at service establishments nationwide. This card "is the glue that pulls together our banking, insurance, real estate, and investment products," according to Kuby. "It offers the opportunity to save and invest. Card members can take advantage of a savings plan that pays tiered money-market rates based upon the level of their deposits. They also can earn real dollar dividends on their purchases." Also important to the company, "as the card matures in the national market, other deposit, lending, and investment features will be added."

SOURCE: Adapted from "Knowing What Consumers Want Aids Sears' Financial Enterprises," *Marketing News*, April 11, 1986: 19–20.

A Practical Perspective

This book is about marketing: a dynamic activity that demands decision-making attention by managers in every business and most nonbusiness organizations. While many people have some idea of what comprises marketing, most are uninformed about the pervasiveness of this vital activity. Some say that marketing is what farmers do after a harvest, or what people do when they go to the supermarket. Others believe that marketing and advertising are one and the same. These activities are only a part of the marketing process, which begins with a concept of the product and the market and covers every facet of satisfying customer and organizational needs.

The word *marketing* is derived from Latin roots. To the ancient Romans, the verb *mercari* meant "to trade" and the corresponding noun *mercartus* meant "marketplace." These Latin words provide a general, though imprecise, indication of the nature of modern marketing. Before further exploring definitions, though, it is useful to gain a flavor of modern marketing by looking at an example of a Marketing Success: a short case describing the actions of one firm, Sears Financial Network. Similar cases and briefs are also used elsewhere in this book to illustrate various concepts.

Notice that management of Sears Financial Network makes a decided effort to satisfy the needs of a particular group of customers: the "middle market." Management designed its product offerings to appeal to this group, featuring full financial services including banking, real estate, brokerage, insurance, and credit cards. Its locations and operating hours are attuned to the preferences of many people to enable one-stop shopping. In other words, this company is profitable because it satisfies an otherwise unfilled need. The next section relates the various activities of Sears Financial Network and other organizations to a formal definition of marketing.

A Formal Definition of Marketing

A widely accepted definition of marketing is that "**marketing** is the process of planning and executing the conception, pricing, promotion, and distribution of ideas, goods, and services to create exchanges that satisfy individual and organizational objectives." [1] Notice that marketing is a rather comprehensive area, involving many activities and all types of organizations.

Marketing
The process of planning and executing the conception, pricing, promotion, and distribution of ideas, goods, and services to create exchanges that satisfy individual and organizational objectives.

Basically, *marketers must decide which customers to serve.* Then, they carry out plans and actions relating to

- Products, services, or ideas to offer
- Prices to charge
- Promotional activities to communicate with the selected market
- Places where the items will be sold or offered.

Marketing is not altruistic; it is a set of activities designed to help an organization attain its goals. This definition of marketing certainly fits the actions of the managers of Sears Financial Network. The firm chose a group of customers (the "middle market")—termed a *target market*—and made decisions about what products to offer, prices to charge, promotional activities to use, and the location and design of outlets. Marketing managers at Hallmark (gifts and greeting cards), Oneida (silver products), American Airlines, and a host of other companies and organizations make similar types of decisions.

Many nonbusiness organizations also use marketing concepts; some very intensively. For example, the United States Army employs marketing when it attempts to enlist inductees. Churches, charities, schools, and social cause organizations such as the National Organization For Women also use marketing to advance their objectives. All of these make decisions concerning their markets, products or ideas to promote, when to schedule events, prices to charge, and distribution activities to implement.

A final point to consider is that marketers often focus their efforts at multiple parties, called *publics,* in addition to buyers (customers). For example, it is common for large, publicly held firms to spend considerable money and effort telling stockholders and the investment community how well the company performed. Frequently, firms also direct marketing activities toward the work force to attract skilled workers, especially in hard-to-fill fields. Thus, managers can employ marketing to advance all of an organization's objectives concerning important external and internal groups.

Marketing Perspectives

Micro marketing
Marketing decision making within a firm.

Macro marketing
Marketing from the perspective of the overall economy. It includes the nature of marketing institutions and their interplay within a socioeconomic system.

Students of marketing can study either of two basic perspectives of the field. The first involves an overall view of the institutions involved and their interplay within the socioeconomic system. This is the *macro marketing* view, which looks to understanding marketing's underpinnings and its relationship to society at large.

The more common view, and the one that is most useful to decision makers, is **micro marketing:** marketing decision making within a firm. This book takes the micro focus, since its orientation is toward managerial decision making. The next section briefly examines the macro perspective and sets the stage for the remainder of the book.

Macro Marketing

In a **macro** sense, marketing takes on the perspective of the economy at large. It involves all business activities that link production of goods and services to satisfying needs and wants of buyers.[2] It also includes the institutions, as they evolve over time, that perform these activities.[3] The processes of specialization and exchange are at the root of marketing.

Exchange
A process whereby two parties trade goods, services, or claims to goods and services (such as money) with one another for profit.

Specialization and Exchange Marketing developed because of specialization and exchange. As Adam Smith pointed out long ago in *The Wealth of Nations* (1776), specialization and its resulting efficiency can benefit everyone. Specialization leads to efficiencies. For example, BIC manufactures pens in quantity and sells each at a nominal price. This is much more efficient than if we all were to try to produce our own pens. Everyone can benefit from specialization, providing that exchange takes place.

The problem is that **exchange** does not automatically follow specialization. Because of specialization, consumption and production are separated. The 3M company, for instance, makes Scotch® tape in St. Paul, but relies on a host of institutions and users around the globe to distribute and consume this product. Because of specialization, a gap emerges between producers and end-users of a product, as indicated in Figure 1.1. The greater the specialization, the greater is this gap. Exchange will not occur unless the gaps are successfully bridged.

Gap between producers and consumers (end users)
A break, caused by specialization, in the linkage between buyers and sellers.

Utility
A product's total value for producing satisfaction.

Gaps between Producers and Consumers Gaps between producers and consumers have several dimensions, each of which is related to one of the five components of a product's total value or **utility** to potential buyers: form, awareness, place, time, and possession.[4] Producing and distributing a Bruce Springsteen recording is useful to illustrate the utility concepts.

- *Form utility* refers to the physical properties that result from production. Bruce Springsteen recordings appear in several forms, such as records and cassettes. The greatest value exists when the specific forms match buyer wants. Records with the "right beat," minimal background noises, and clear tonal qualities provide the greatest music satisfaction for fans.

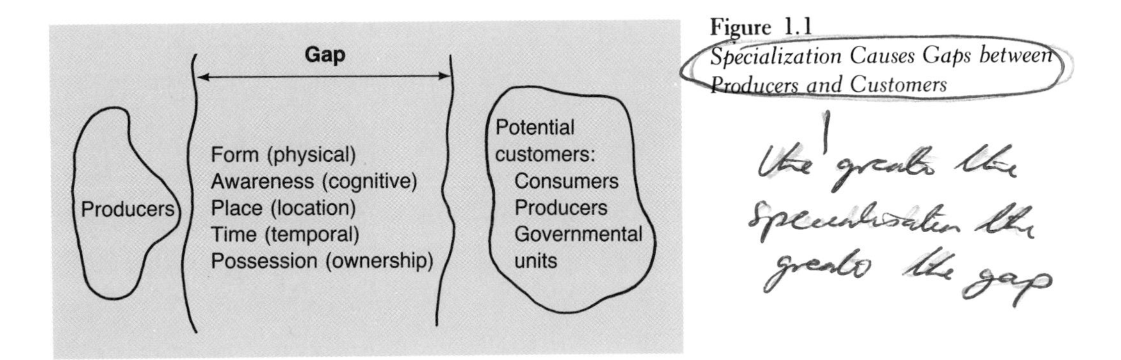

Figure 1.1
Specialization Causes Gaps between Producers and Customers

the greater the specialization the greater the gap

- *Awareness utility* involves the extent to which customers learn about the existence and nature of a product and how it might satisfy their wants. Music buffs must become aware of both Bruce Springsteen and a particular song of his before they will buy it.
- *Place utility* relates to product availability at locations where customers expect to find them for sale. Springsteen's records must be distributed around the world and located in numerous music stores to result in sales.
- *Time utility* means that products (like Springsteen records) must be stocked at the right places and times, that customers must be made aware of their presence when they are available, and displays must be placed at the right time for sales to result.
- *Possession utility* results from activities designed to facilitate purchase, such as providing credit and accepting charges, implementing return policies, providing instructions for use and installation, and making arrangements to transfer title. A guarantee against defective workmanship, for instance, increases the value of a Springsteen record and facilitates possession.

In order that marketing managers can develop the exchange process to its fullest potential, they must design a *total product*—the mix of all utility dimensions—to satisfy customer needs. Production plays an important role in this process by converting resources into forms wanted by users, but there are other equally important functions required to bridge gaps between producers and customers, as Figure 1.2 illustrates.

The Marketing System A system is a set of interdependent components, where a change in any one of them affects the status of the others as well as the entire set.[5] A marketing system's components are of two types: the functions to be performed and the specialized participants that emerge over time to perform them. The functions are considered first.

Functions to Bridge Gaps Collectively, marketers need to perform several functions to develop exchange. There are three broad categories of marketing functions: merchandising, distribution, and facilitative, each having subfunctions as follows:

MERCHANDISING

- **Buying**—bringing together (assembling) collections of goods and services (e.g., H & R Block buys forms and equipment, rents office space, hires people, and so on to be able to offer tax services).

Buying
Bringing together or assembling collections of goods and services.

Figure 1.2
An Overview of the Marketing System

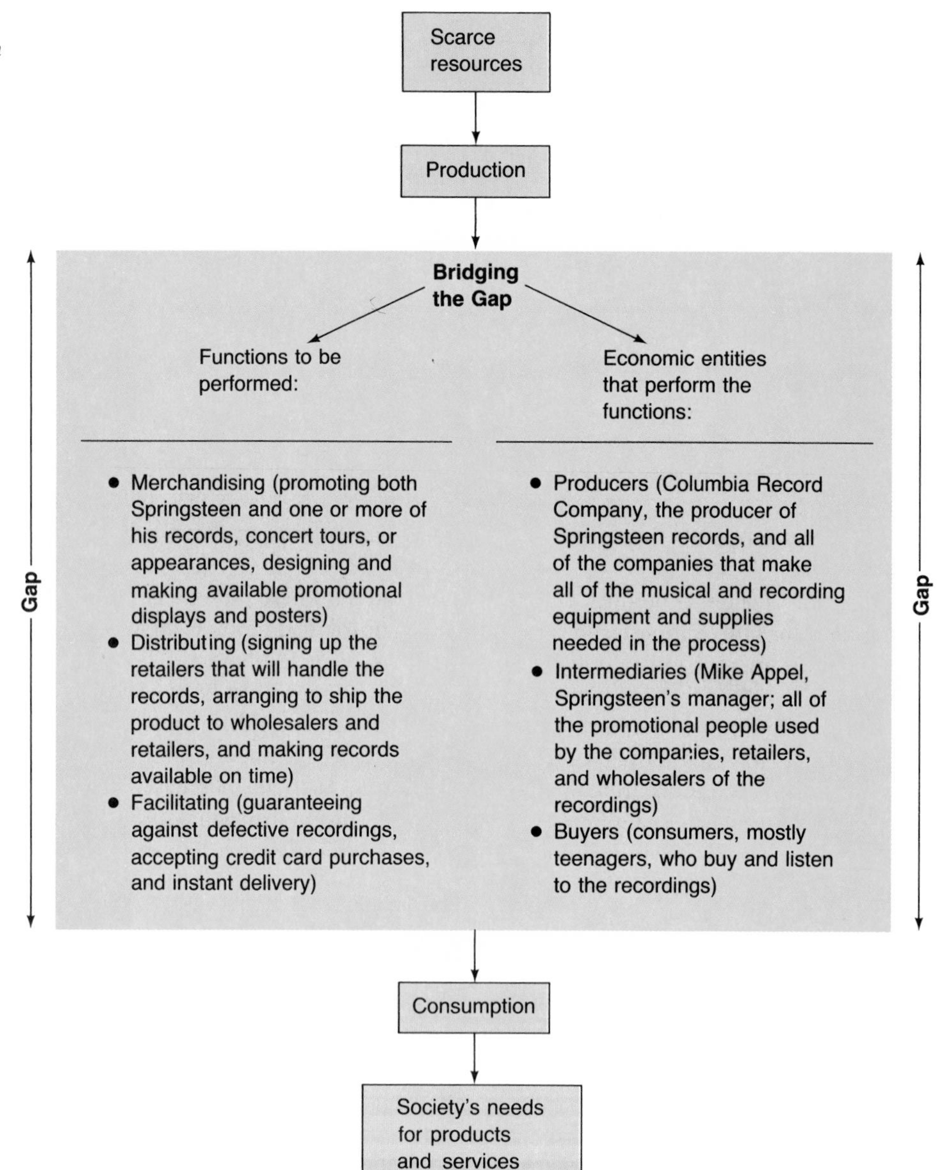

Standardizing and grading
Categorizing products according to a system of types and measures such as weights, sizes, colors, names, etc.

Branding
Giving a unique name to a particular product or class of products offered by a firm.

Pricing
Setting prices high enough to cover costs and earn a profit, yet low enough to attract buyers.

Promoting (promotion)
Communicating with potential buyers about an item's existence and uses to stimulate sales.

- **Standardizing and grading**—categorizing items such as shoes, canned foods, and meat. **Branding** products (naming them) also relates to this function as it serves to identify product offerings.
- **Pricing**—setting prices high enough to cover costs and earn a profit, yet low enough to attract buyers.
- **Promoting**—communicating with potential buyers about an item's existence and uses (e.g., Springsteen ads and other promotional messages informed rock fans and those in the music business about his performances and records. See the accompanying Marketing Brief.)

MARKETING BRIEF

Many Entertainers Have Benefited from Solid Marketing Support

His first album in 1972, "Greetings From Asbury Park, N.J.," sold less than 50,000 copies. "He was already a dead artist who bombed out on his first album," said Clive Davis, then president of Columbia Records. And his second album, "The Wild, The Innocent & the E Street Shuffle," sold even less than his first. The bottom came in the mid-1970s; while on tour with the then-popular group "Chicago" he was nearly booed off the stage.

But Bruce Springsteen did not give up, nor did Mike Appel, his promotionally aggressive manager. "The hype began before I ever even sang a note," said Springsteen. Appel continued his promotional blitz by contacting disk jockeys, personalities, and practically anyone who could help Springsteen's career. Turning his attention back to live performances in relatively small clubs where he was a smash hit, the performer (already popular in his home town on the New Jersey shore) also began to build a loyal following in towns like Phoenix, Austin, Philadelphia, and Cleveland.

His big break came in April 1974—while he and his band were earning only $50 a week—when Jon Landau, the highly respected record editor in *Rolling Stone*, wrote an emotional article for the *Real Paper* stating, "I saw rock and roll's future and its name is Bruce Springsteen."

Columbia's marketing experts cannily noticed the article and used it in an effort to repromote the second album—and critics began to take notice. It was the first time a record company used the prestige of a rock critic to push an artist so hard, and sales climbed back up the charts.

Within six months he had completed "Born to Run," his third album, and Columbia's marketing department was ready. Booking, and then purchasing 980 of the 4,000 seats at the Bottom Line club in Greenwich Village for media tastemakers, Springsteen opened a week before the album was released. Everyone who was anybody in the business from around the country was brought in for the performance at Columbia's expense. Over $250,000 was spent on promoting the album by the end of the year, including an intensive media campaign, the distribution of "Born to Run" buttons, and even billboards. The promotional effort was the biggest of its type for any album, ever. The rest is history. The "Born to Run" album sold over a million copies and earned Columbia millions of dollars per week.

By 1985—four albums, several hit singles, and several transcontinental concert tours later—Springsteen had become the biggest rock star since Elvis. His "Born in the U.S.A." album sold over 13 million copies—the all-time best seller in Columbia's history. During his tour in 1985, Ticketron sold over 236,000 of the $17.50 tickets for his New York performance in one day—breaking the all-time record for any type of performance in history. In Washington, D.C., some 236,000 tickets sold out in an hour, another record. In Chicago, dozens of people moved into the streets to camp out in line for days on the mere *rumor* that Bruce Springsteen tickets *might* be available. While "The Boss" is a good, solid performer with plenty of talent and drive, one critic summed up the marketing of the superstar this way: "Hypes are as American as Coca-Cola so perhaps—in one way or another—Bruce Springsteen is The Real Thing." [*The Real Thing* was a slogan used by Coke for many years.]

SOURCE: Adapted from Maureen Orth, Janet Huck, and Peter S. Greenberg, "Making of a Rock Star," *Newsweek*, October 27, 1975: 57–60; Bill Barol, Mark D. Uehling, Nikki Finke Greenberg, and Shawn Doherty, "He's On Fire," *Newsweek*, August 5, 1985: 48–54; "Springsteen: The Merchandising of a Superstar," *Business Week*, December 1, 1975: 53–54; and Jay Cocks and Cathy Booth, "Round the World, A Boss Boom," *Time*, August 26, 1985: 68–71.

Transporting (transportation)
Moving a product from one location to another, as by truck, rail, boat, or plane.

Storing (storage)
Collecting a quantity of an item at various places, such as a store or warehouse.

Facilitating functions
Specialized activities that aid marketers in performing particular functions.

Marketing research
Systematically obtaining and analyzing information about a market, such as what buyers want, need, think, and feel.

Consumers
People, acting as individuals or groups, who buy items for personal use.

Intermediaries
Specialists who typically perform similar marketing activities for several producers or other intermediaries.

PHYSICAL DISTRIBUTION

- **Transporting**—moving items from one place to another, as by truck or rail.
- **Storing**—collecting a quantity of the item at various places, such as a stock of Springsteen records in a music store or a warehouse.
- **Material handling**—transferring items from transportation to storage facilities and vice-versa.

FACILITATING FUNCTIONS

- **Financing**—arranging for purchase, such as through consumer or trade credit
- **Risk bearing**—taking risks due to errors in judging needs, theft, obsolescence, and so on. (Many people argue that assuming these risks justify profits.) [6]
- **Obtaining information**—learning about user needs (often referred to as **marketing research.**)

The need to perform all of the marketing functions for exchange to take place is inherent in every type of economic system, whether it be capitalism, socialism, or communism. The functions are inherent characteristics of exchange, and how well marketers perform them is reflected in the total value of products and services to buyers.[7] Successfully carrying out all of the functions results in a total product or service, composed of all utility dimensions, being developed to its full economic potential.[8] All have a direct impact on a total product's various utility dimensions, as Table 1.1 illustrates.

McDonald's corporation is very effective in delivering the five different kinds of utility by providing satisfaction to all members of the family. This is illustrated in the accompanying Marketing Brief.

Table 1.1 Relationship between Functions and Types of Utilities*

Marketing Function	Primary Utility(ies) Affected
Merchandising	
Buying	place, form
Standardizing and grading	form
Pricing	all forms of utility
Promotion	awareness, possession
Physical Distribution	
Transportation	time, place, possession
Storage	time, form
Facilitative	
Financing	possession
Risk bearing	place, possession, form
Obtaining information	all forms of utility

* While all functions relate to each type of utility either directly or indirectly, this table illustrates the utilities most directly affected by the activities within each of the functions.

McDonald's is very good at developing all forms of utility that it offers customers.

Marketing System Participants The second arm of the marketing system consists of the entities that perform the functions: buyers, producers, and **intermediaries.**

BUYERS

- **Consumers**—the 230 million people in the U.S. who collectively spend over $2.5 trillion a year on items for personal use. Also, consumers around the world are comprising increasingly attractive markets.
- Government units—federal, state, and local bodies who, together, buy about $1 trillion of goods and services per year, from Air Force bombers to green beans.
- Industrial and other product buyers—all 10 million of them, who collectively buy every imaginable item so that they can perform their organizations' tasks. Included are profit-seeking firms like IBM, and not-for-profit organizations such as St. Mark's Methodist Church.

PRODUCERS—who play a dual role of buying and resource conversion.

INTERMEDIARIES—specialists who perform marketing activities for several producers.

- Selling intermediaries—retailers and wholesalers who generally buy and resell items. Sears Roebuck buys from many sources and resells items at convenient locations and through its catalogs.
- Facilitative intermediaries—companies that specialize in performing particular functions for others, such as advertising and public relations firms, marketing research firms, transportation firms, and banks.

The study of macro marketing, therefore, focuses on the institutional and work relationships among entities in an economic system. The focus of this book is on micro marketing: the major thrust of the discipline.

MARKETING BRIEF

Hamburger Wars Heat Up— With Lettuce and Tomatoes

McDonald's Corporation, one of the most successful fast-food chains in the world, has become a master at enhancing the utility it offers customers. The company, which pioneered fast food by featuring a take-it-or-leave-it menu at bargain prices, recently announced a new menu item to bolster business: the McD.L.T.— The McD.L.T. is a hamburger that comes with lettuce and tomato. A twin-bay foam container separates the meat from the lettuce and tomato until the customer puts the parts together.

According to Donald Lupa, a restaurant analyst, "McDonald's has a red-hot property." Priced 10 to 20 cents more than the $1.49 or so for a Big Mac, the McD.L.T. appears to be an instant best seller. Nearly a quarter of all customers ordered the new item during its first month, according to estimates, which translates to about 12 percent of total company sales.

SOURCE: Adapted from "The Lettuce and Tomato Wars," *Fortune*, December 9, 1985: 10–11.

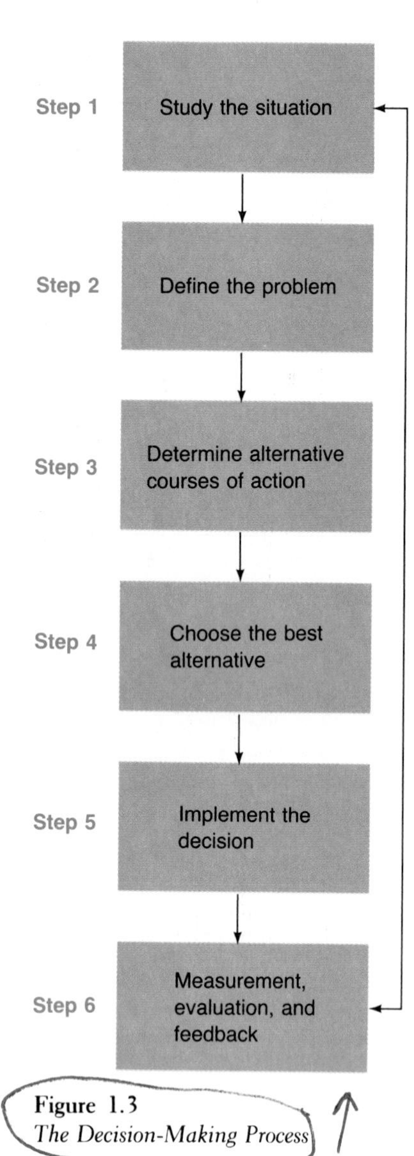

Figure 1.3
The Decision-Making Process

Micro Marketing and Decision Making

Micro marketing consists of the marketing activities carried out by particular companies. This perspective focuses attention on managerial decision making, within a competitive environment, to attract customers and enable a firm to attain its objectives.

Decision Making Decision making is a vital input for successful micro marketing. There are no hard and fast rules to follow to assure that management will make a correct decision in a given circumstance. In fact, the appropriate decision may be different from situation to situation even though the scenarios may be quite similar. In one case, for example, raising prices may be very desirable, while in another similar case this decision may be inappropriate. Thus, decision making tends to be an art rather than a science.

However, there is a logical and systematic process that a manager can follow in decision making, as illustrated in Figure 1.3. Following this process helps increase the chances of making good decisions. First, managers study the decision-making situation in order to gain overall awareness of its major dimensions. Then they define the problem that is preventing the firm from achieving its goals. Next, managers determine alternative courses of action that they might take to overcome the problem. Following this, they select what appears to be the best of the alternatives. Then, they put the decision into effect. Finally, they measure the progress and refine the decision strategy as needed to accomplish the intended results. This means that the decision-making process is an evaluative one—allowing for possible updating of the decisions as needed.

While the major emphasis in this book is on decision making within profit-seeking firms, nonprofit organizations can use the same concepts. Most marketing ideas are directly applicable to all social and economic units that seek to attain their objectives by satisfying some group of constituents.[9] The United Farm Workers, as illustrated in the accompanying Marketing Brief, is one of the many nonprofit organizations that have adopted marketing concepts to advance their causes.

A primary task of management is to find a match between what the company offers and what enough customers want to buy to enable the firm to meet its objectives; that is, management's task is to improve a firm's exchange relationships with potential customers. Management can adopt several different philosophies to accomplish this.

Philosophies of Business Long-run success requires that an organization find and maintain some type of *differential advantage* over its competitors.[10] There are three managerial orientations, or *business philosophies*, that suggest how managers can develop this: a production orientation, a sales orientation, and a marketing orientation. Figure 1.4 presents an overview of each.

Production Orientation A **production** (or product) **orientation** holds that the key to business success lies in solving technological problems. Managers who embrace this philosophy may insist on product quality, but they do so from a technical perspective, seeking products that are viewed as useful or important by engineers and other specialists. They stress standardization and place little emphasis on designing the right product to meet unique customer needs. They also de-emphasize the importance of promoting the product, securing the right distribution, and other marketing activities.

Production orientation
A perspective holding that the key to business success lies in solving technologically related problems (also called *product orientation*).

Sales orientation
An emphasis on persuading potential customers to buy the firm's products.

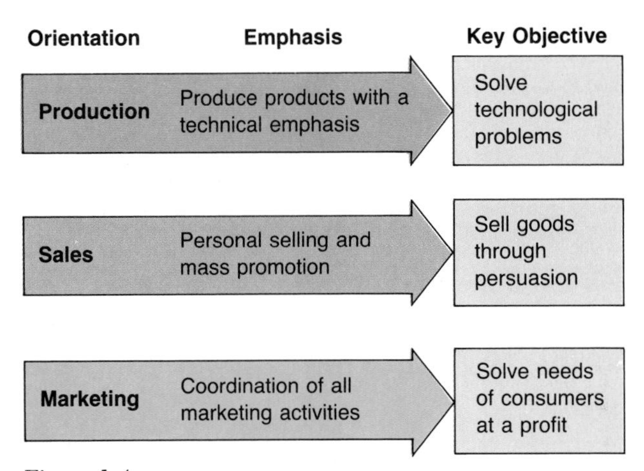

Figure 1.4
Alternative Philosophies of Business

Essentially, the philosophy assumes that good items will sell themselves. To a large extent, the managerial views of the Chrysler Corporation reflected this philosophy until the early 1980s. The company's top management was generally engineering-oriented. The threat of bankruptcy forced a change in management and the adoption of a marketing orientation in the 1980s, enabling the company to reverse its situation and become quite profitable.

Sales Orientation A **sales orientation** is the second guiding business philosophy. Based upon substantial personal selling and mass promotion activities, its emphasis is on persuading potential customers to buy the firm's products. As with a production orientation, management does not tailor products to meet unique customer needs.[11] Instead, the thrust is on convincing as many prospects as possible that the company's items are what they want. Some used car dealers adopt an extreme form of this philosophy by exaggerating—even lying—to obtain sales.

It may be evident that a sales orientation shares some of the defects of a production orientation. Both are myopic, focusing on the needs of the seller rather than on the needs of the buyer. Retail managers who embrace either philosophy, for example, are likely to carry easy-to-handle products and schedule their store's hours and services for ease of management instead of customer convenience. Thus, both are risky strategies, indeed, since long-run success is based upon building lasting customer relationships where both the firm and its customers are satisfied.

Marketing Orientation A **marketing orientation** (often called the *marketing concept*) is a relatively new philosophy of doing business, but an increasingly important one. A firm that advocates this orientation attempts to attain its objectives by organizing and integrating all activities around satisfying its customers' needs. Management realizes that customer satisfaction is crucial or else the company will not achieve its objectives.

General Electric was the first major company to publicly announce this philosophy. Its 1952 annual report stated that:[12]

MARKETING BRIEF

The United Farm Workers—Adopting Marketing Instead of Picketing

More than a decade after they first boycotted lettuce, the United Farm Workers have abandoned their picket signs and have begun to pick up computer surveys of consumers. "Times have changed," according to Frank Ortiz, second vice-president of the migrant workers union. "While we continue to boycott lettuce, it's different now. It's high tech," says Ortiz. In fact, Ortiz does not call it boycotting anymore, referring to the 100,000-member union's activities as "social marketing."

The union studies demographics from census polls and chooses areas that are most likely to support the union position. People living in those areas are then sent letters signed by Cesar Chavez, who founded the union in 1962. "At 3,000 shoppers per store, we can now hit 90,000 people with our message instead of 12,000 or 15,000 with us manning the picket lines," says Ortiz.

SOURCE: Adapted from Kerry Luft, "Lettuce Boycotters Pick a New Tactic: Marketing Replaces Supermarket Picketing," *Chicago Tribune*, August 15, 1985: Sec. 2, p. 3.

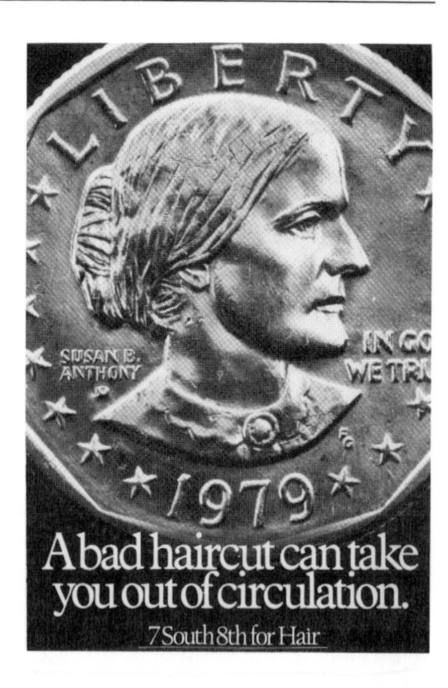

A production orientation diminishes customer satisfaction.

Marketing orientation
A firm's emphasis on attaining its objectives, usually including profit, by organizing and integrating all activities toward satisfying the needs and wants of a selected group of customers (often called the *marketing concept*).

1. Marketing is at the beginning, not the end of the production process.
2. The needs of customers are to be established through studies and research conducted by marketing. Establishing what the customer wants is fundamental.
3. Products will be designed in accordance with what the customer wants in a given product.
4. Marketing is to make decisions about a product's price, its distribution, its sales, its inventory levels, its servicing, and overall timing.
5. Marketing has the responsibility of planning and scheduling products.

In short, the marketing concept (orientation) means giving customers what they want.[13] The accompanying Concept Summary contrasts management attitudes and activities under the three orientations.

While the marketing concept makes intuitive sense, not all companies have adopted it.[14] Some hold fast to a production or a sales orientation for several reasons. Organizations are sometimes slow in changing their ways of operating. They adhere to what worked well in the past. Daily operating pressures may emphasize the short run and de-emphasize long-run customer needs. Also, some managers, especially those with technical backgrounds, feel uncomfortable looking outward toward customers and favor looking inward at production.

Despite these obstacles, there is a growing trend among companies to adopt the marketing concept.[15] This trend should continue since the philosophy increases the firm's chances for success.

Social orientation
Striving to satisfy various publics, such as society at large, employees, and minorities, in addition to target customers (also called *societal orientation*).

Worth noting is that the marketing literature sometimes suggests the emergence of a fourth orientation, called the **social** (or societal) **orientation.** In this orientation, management strives to satisfy various publics (such as society at large, employees, and minorities) in addition to target customers. This text takes the view that this orientation is an extension of the marketing concept; it is compatible with this philosophy.

CONCEPT SUMMARY *Differences in Outlook between the Marketing Concept and the Production and Sales Orientations**

Attitudes and Activities	Production and Sales Orientations	Marketing Orientation
Attitudes toward customers	They're fortunate that our products exist. If they only knew how hard it is.	We're fortunate that they exist. Their needs dictate to us.
Role of marketing research	Used only to determine customer reactions if used at all.	Utilized to determine customer needs and how well they are being satisfied.
Interest in innovation	Technology and cost-cutting procedures are emphasized.	Both locating new opportunities and cost savings are important.
Product offering	The firm sells what it can make.	Firm makes what it can profitably sell.
Role of the sales force	Sell the customer, do not worry about coordinating activities with the rest of the company.	Coordination with other firm activities is important. Helping customers to satisfy their needs is essential.
Emphasis in company advertising	Product features, quality, and perhaps how items are made.	How a product or service satisfies a need.
Transportation	Emphasizes minimum cost.	Viewed as a customer service.
Inventory levels	Set with production requirements in mind.	Besides cost, customer needs receive primary emphasis.
Role of packaging	To protect products.	Useful as a selling tool, but with customer convenience in mind.
Attitudes toward offering customer credit	Seen as a necessary evil.	Viewed as a customer service that enhances product value.

*Adapted from R. F. Vizza, T. E. Chambers, and E. J. Cook, *Adaption of the Marketing Concept—Fact or Fiction* (New York: Sales Executive Club of New York, Inc., 1967):13–15.

Marketing Management

Organizations must manage marketing, like all other functions. In turn, **marketing management** is the analysis, planning, implementation, and control of those business activities designed to facilitate desired exchanges between an organization and its selected group of buyers. It is the process of managing and controlling all dimensions of a total product offering—its form, price, promotion, and place—to reflect the needs of a selected group of customers for the purpose of better enabling the firm to attain its objectives.[16]

A key element in this definition is the selected group of customers. This group is called a **target market**, or alternatively, **target customers.**

The concept of selecting a group of customers to target is based on recognizing the different needs that exist in the marketplace due to the great variety of values and lifestyles. A company risks failure if it tries to become "everything to everybody" because people's needs differ substantially.

Marketing management
Analysis, planning, implementation, and control of all of those business activities that are designed to facilitate desired exchanges between a firm and its selected group of customers.

Target market
A set of customers that the firm is attempting to satisfy (also called *target customers*).

Porsche focuses on satisfying its target market.

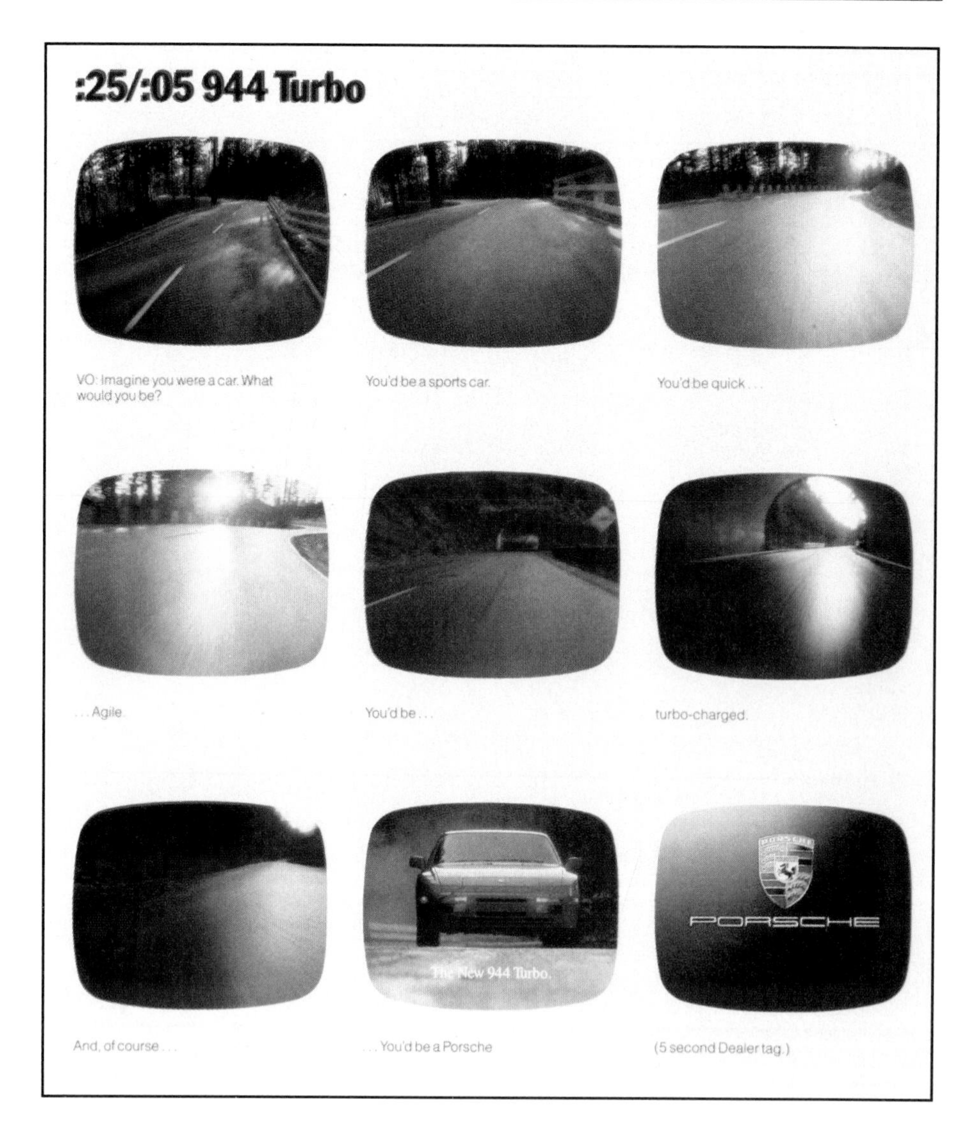

To illustrate, W. T. Grant—once the sixth largest retailer in the U.S.—failed because it tried to appeal to all and did not offer a distinctive identity to consumers.[17] In contrast, Lord & Taylor and K mart are both highly successful, yet they are distinctively different kinds of stores in the minds of most people. This is to the credit of each company's management. Each has focused its efforts on satisfying unique groups of prospective customers. In part, both companies are successful because they target specific market segments. W. T. Grant, on the other hand, tried to compromise and appeal to everyone and lost.

The process of integrating and coordinating all of a company's activities around the selected target's needs is fundamental.[18] When management formulates plans, prices, and other marketing activities around the needs of the target market, all of the actions complement each other for a greater total effect. Neiman Marcus (department store), for example, appeals to affluent people. The store carries high-quality, prestige items. Company promotions emphasize exclusiveness and good taste, and the company

A carefully designed marketing mix focuses all activities around a target's needs.

has integrated distribution strategies to appeal to those desiring convenience and prestige. This is a well-coordinated program.

The Marketing Mix

Focusing efforts on target customers involves blending all controllable activities (those internal to the firm) into an integrated **marketing mix** aimed at a target market's needs, as Figure 1.5 illustrates.

Marketing mix
The various marketing activities used by a given firm to serve a target market.

Most of the marketing literature distinguishes four major groups of variables that can be controlled by managers: product, place, promotion, and price.[19] For convenience of recall, they are often called the *four-Ps of marketing*. This text adds planning, a fifth P, as it is crucial to success and connotes a potential payoff for superior management.[20] The implementation of all decisions on variables that a company

Figure 1.5
The Marketing Mix

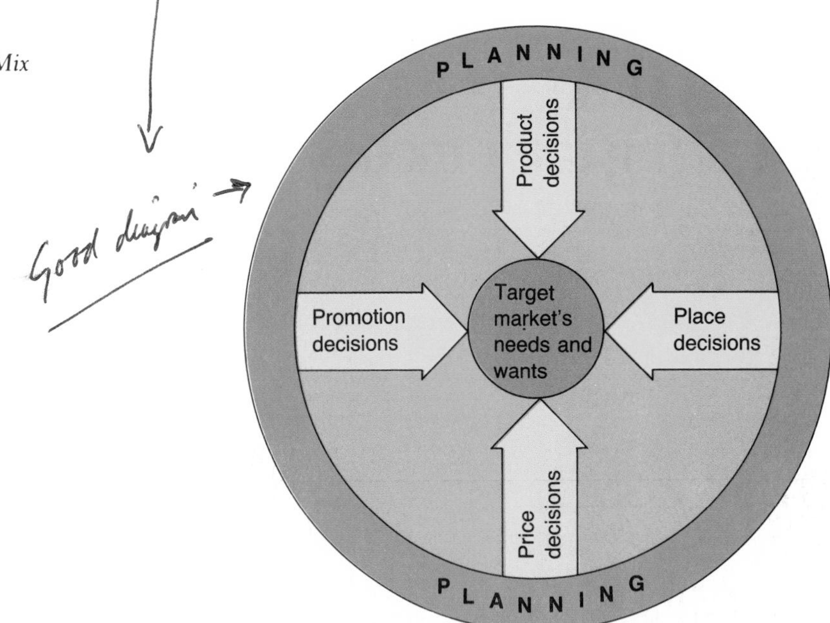

makes defines its total product offering. Each mix element is discussed here only briefly, as all of them will be covered fully in later chapters.

Planning. The need for effective planning permeates all company activities, including marketing. Good planning involves developing the right products at the right time (today's word processors are yesterday's typewriters), placing promotions at the right time (flower ads prior to Mother's day), getting products to the right places on time (an adequate stock of Bruce Springsteen's new release on retailer shelves), and pricing items correctly.

Product decisions. It is marketing's responsibility to coordinate its activities with production so that items match the needs of the target customers. Decisions cover both tangible (color, size, performance specifications, etc.) and intangible (warranties, guarantees, image, etc.) aspects of products.

Place decisions. This involves selecting and maintaining a channel of distribution: a specific collection of intermediaries through which products flow as they move toward final customers. It also involves the formulation and operation of physical distribution systems to handle the physical movement and storage of products.

Promotion decisions. Organizations must effectively communicate messages to target customers when they coordinate all promotion activities, including advertising, personal selling, and sales promotion.

Price decisions. Besides covering costs and generating a profit, prices should be set to reflect the needs of the market.

Marketing Decisions Must Be Coordinated

In a sense, all marketing decisions counterbalance, or act as tradeoffs to, each other. Typically, unclaimed freight stores are situated in low-rent districts of major cities, for example, but are able to attract shoppers through rock-bottom prices. Customers sacrifice convenience and prestige shopping locations for low prices. Similarly, the

MARKETING BRIEF

Laker Airways: The Rise and Fall of a "No-Frills" Marketer

During the 1970s, Laker Airways, headed by Sir Freddie Laker, was very prosperous and was continually mentioned in magazine and newspaper feature stories. The concept was simple: Move passengers across the Atlantic at a low fare and offer few frills. The airline excluded many services, such as advance ticketing, cabin attendant service, and extra space for luggage. In fact, this austere service was featured as "no frills" in Laker advertisements.

The concept worked while traffic across the Atlantic was heavy. In fact, other airlines were content to let Laker take the cheap fare trade while they concentrated on the higher-fare passengers where the required load factors (percentage of the plane filled) were not so critical.

But when the Atlantic traffic declined, other airlines reduced their rates in an effort to increase their passenger loads. Laker, which had always advertised price and not service in its ads, had no strong consumer image with which to attract business flyers and other higher-fare-paying customers who demanded greater services. In 1982 Laker was forced into bankruptcy and the turmoil created within the industry did not end until 1986 when the final court suits were settled in Washington. The settlement entitled travelers who flew to London between March 1, 1982 and March 31, 1984 to a partial discount on a future flight on Pan American, TWA, or British Airways to compensate them for low-priced fares promised by Laker Airways.

SOURCE: Adapted from Howard Sharman, "Laker Got Caught in No-Frills Trap," *Advertising Age* 53, no. 7 (February 15, 1982): 3, 83; and "Sir Freddie Laker's Final Blessing," *Newsweek*, January 20, 1986: 44.

use of very aggressive wholesalers (which are usually costly) can make extensive advertising unnecessary and thereby keep total marketing costs down.

There is a need to coordinate all marketing mix decisions to yield a total product offering that satisfies a selected target market's needs at a profit. The evidence to date indicates that this process definitely increases an organization's chances for success in the marketplace. Stressing only one portion of the marketing mix and assigning low priorities to the others can lead to ill-designed marketing decisions, as illustrated by the experience of Laker Airways.

Chapter Summary

This chapter presents an overview of the marketing field. Marketing is formally defined as the process of planning and executing the conception, pricing, promotion, and distribution of ideas, goods, and services to create exchanges that satisfy individual and organizational objectives. Marketing is rooted in specialization and the accompanying separation, or gap, between production and consumption.

In all economies, the marketing system must perform key functions to close this gap, including merchandising, physical distribution, and exchange-facilitating activities. These functions may be performed by any of the economy's participants, but they must be performed for exchange to take place. Producers and buyers are two of the vital participants in a marketing system, but they are not the only ones. Also included are intermediaries—retailers and wholesalers—who emerge over time as specialists to perform certain important functions. The composite of a marketing system's functions and institutions is termed macro marketing.

Micro marketing is marketing viewed from an individual firm's perspective. Management can adopt a production or a sales orientation in its decision-making stance toward customers, but these are short-sighted perspectives since they result in indifferent attitudes toward customer needs. A better approach, especially in an affluent environment with widely diverse needs, is to adopt the marketing orientation as a guiding philosophy. Its emphasis is the attaining of an organization's goals by coordinating all items in the marketing mix—those activities involving product, price, promotion, and place decisions—around profitably satisfying the needs of a selected target market. Adopting this philosophy increases a company's chances of attaining its objectives.

Questions

1. Explain in your own words what marketing is.
2. Explain how, by personally adopting the marketing concept, a student can develop his or her own career both in school and afterward.
3. Many argue that production is the most important aspect of economic development. Comment.
4. Why is it important for the marketing system to perform all of the functions in developing total utility? Are some of the functions more important than others in some instances?
5. Some critics contend that the U.S. is too marketing-oriented. In their view, socialism or communism is preferred because they are less marketing-driven. Comment.
6. Some retailers feel that marketing and merchandising are synonymous. Are they?
7. Until the energy crises of a few years ago, many utilities encouraged increased consumption of energy. Was this compatible with the marketing concept? Should utilities encourage reduced consumption of energy?
8. Many consumer advocates argue that the marketing activities of many companies are a waste. For example, some contend that all aspirin is alike, but some brands such as Bayer cost more. What do you think? Try to support both pro and con arguments.
9. What is macro marketing? Micro marketing? What is the difference?
10. Identify the marketing activities of your college or university. Were any of the school's efforts effective in causing you to attend? What were they?
11. What is meant by the term "marketing mix?" Why is coordination needed?
12. How can adopting the marketing concept help a church? A retailer? A manufacturer? The United Auto Workers? A hospital?

Chapter 2

The Strategic Marketing Decision Process

Objectives

After completing this chapter, you should be able to demonstrate a knowledge of:

- The steps in the strategic marketing decision process, which are oriented toward establishing a successful market niche for a firm
- Reaffirming the company's mission, objectives, and goals
- Interpreting the environment and deciding broad areas of opportunity
- Assessing opportunities against the organization's capabilities, using the concept of synergy as a guide
- Identifying segments within a market
- Deciding on an appropriate market target after considering competitor strengths
- Determining the basic marketing strategy to use
- Developing, implementing, and controlling the organization's marketing actions

MARKETING SUCCESS

Using Marketing Concepts to Expand Professional Golf Tournaments

Almost since its beginnings, the Professional Golf Association (PGA) catered to players and not to fans. Golf courses were sanctioned for tournaments by considering only how well the game could be played. Onlookers had to fend for themselves to get views of their favorite pro in action—scrambling, pushing, and shoving among trees, hills, and other fans, and, in the process, maintaining a quiet decorum while the players readied their shots.

"No more," said Dean Beman, who was named Golf Commissioner of the prestigious PGA a decade ago (but only a matter of months in the perspective of the slow-to-change game that was invented centuries ago at St. Andrews, Scotland). At that time, the anemic PGA had assets of $730,000 and a paltry income of $3.9 million—all from the sales of TV rights. Concerned that the association's destiny was held solely in the hands of the networks, Beman said, "the PGA is going to make every effort to satisfy the interest of fans—as well as the players." He added, "some day there will be so many delivery systems (networks, cable, and so on) that any one of them could not gather a big enough audience to support a major endeavor like a golf tournament."

Grass has not grown under the energetic Beman's feet since he took office. Today, the association is proud of its current $41.6 million asset base and total revenues of $48.3 million—only 34 percent of which has been earned from the sale of TV rights.

Among the changes, the PGA, under Beman's direction, invented the "stadium golf course," a new concept in golf course design involving constructed spectator mounds along the links at strategic points and earthen mounds (natural grand stands) near the first tee and eighteenth green. As could be expected, some golfers objected to the changes. "Next we are going to offer to pick them [fans] up at home with a limo," said one critical professional.

But others realized that fan revenues contribute to prize monies and fully supported the changes. "It's about time we consider the interests of fans," said another traveling player. "We have been the only professional sport that has ignored fans and our salability," he added, "I'm 100 percent behind Beman—so long as we do not get carried away and make the game impossible to play properly."

The changes have worked and more of them can be expected in the future. Point Vedra, Florida—a course newly designed under Beman's criteria—is a case in point. The 1986 Tournament Players Championship held there attracted 50,000 paying fans a day, a record and more than double the normal attendance at such a match. Besides added ticket revenues, parking fees, and concession sales, the tournament organization realized a bonanza in greater commissions from retailers who rented tents to sell various memorabilia, trinkets, and other products—another of Beman's ideas.

As a result of the wider appeal, prize monies have increased significantly, almost doubling over a couple of years alone. According to Hughes Norton, corporate vice president for golf at International Management Group, the giant sports marketing firm, 79 men earned at least $100,000 in 1985 from the rapidly expanding pots.

To keep costs down, Beman has pioneered new approaches. With the stadium courses, for example, the PGA has entered into several successful joint ventures formed with real estate developers, which work in the following way. An interested developer planning construction of high-priced homes and condominiums around a golf theme contacts the

PGA for advice. The developer then hires a golf course architect who works with the PGA in the design. After construction, the courses are jointly run with the PGA. This process provides the PGA with tour control of a professional tournament-quality PGA course without having to pay for the land or course construction. For the developer, the PGA course offers a tremendous marketing advantage.

These changes have enabled the PGA to provide a more attractive package to fans. And the additional revenues are important to corporate tournament sponsors, charities who often benefit from the proceeds, as well as the players.

SOURCE: Adapted from "How the PGA Is Staying Out of the Rough," *Business Week*, April 7, 1986: 96, 98.

Introduction

Effectively differentiating a company's total product offering from those of competitors helps to establish a strong niche in the market—a "beachhead," or position of strength from which to make further penetrations and to resist any counterthrusts by competitors.

The objective of embracing a marketing orientation is not to create differentiated products for their own sake; it is more self-serving. A marketing orientation helps a company increase its chances for success. The now booming Professional Golf Association (PGA), this chapter's opening Marketing Success, illustrates how a marketing orientation can help drive an organization into a very healthy position. The way for management to bring this about is to identify the company's market alternatives and then try the most promising of these. Dean Beman of the PGA did this before charting the organization's moves and the dividends paid off handsomely.

Consider Figure 2.1. It presents a seven-step strategic marketing decision process that helps management to systematically narrow potential market alternatives down to the one(s) most likely to succeed for the firm.

This chapter presents an overview of this process, while later chapters furnish added detail for topics requiring more thorough treatment. Thus, Figure 2.1 provides a rather rough outline of this book, as well as marketing decision making in general.

Society's Needs for Goods and Services

To society, business exists for the express purpose of providing goods and services to satisfy needs. While there are far too many needs for any single business to meet, a firm is destined to fail if it does not provide enough satisfaction to generate sufficient sales to cover costs and produce a profit. This is the primary purpose of the strategic marketing decision process: to narrow the field of possible alternatives until management finds one or more where the firm has a differential advantage and there are a sufficient number of prospects having such needs to sustain required sales and profit levels.

The Firm's Objectives and Goals

The first strategic marketing decision step is to reaffirm the firm's intended overall direction.[1] As one executive states, "If you do not know where you want to go, any road will take you there." Experience proves that management cannot expect effective results from its actions without first determining what end is desired. "Why not spend $2 million on advertising?" or "How about adding wholesalers to the distribution

Figure 2.1
The Strategic Marketing Decision Process

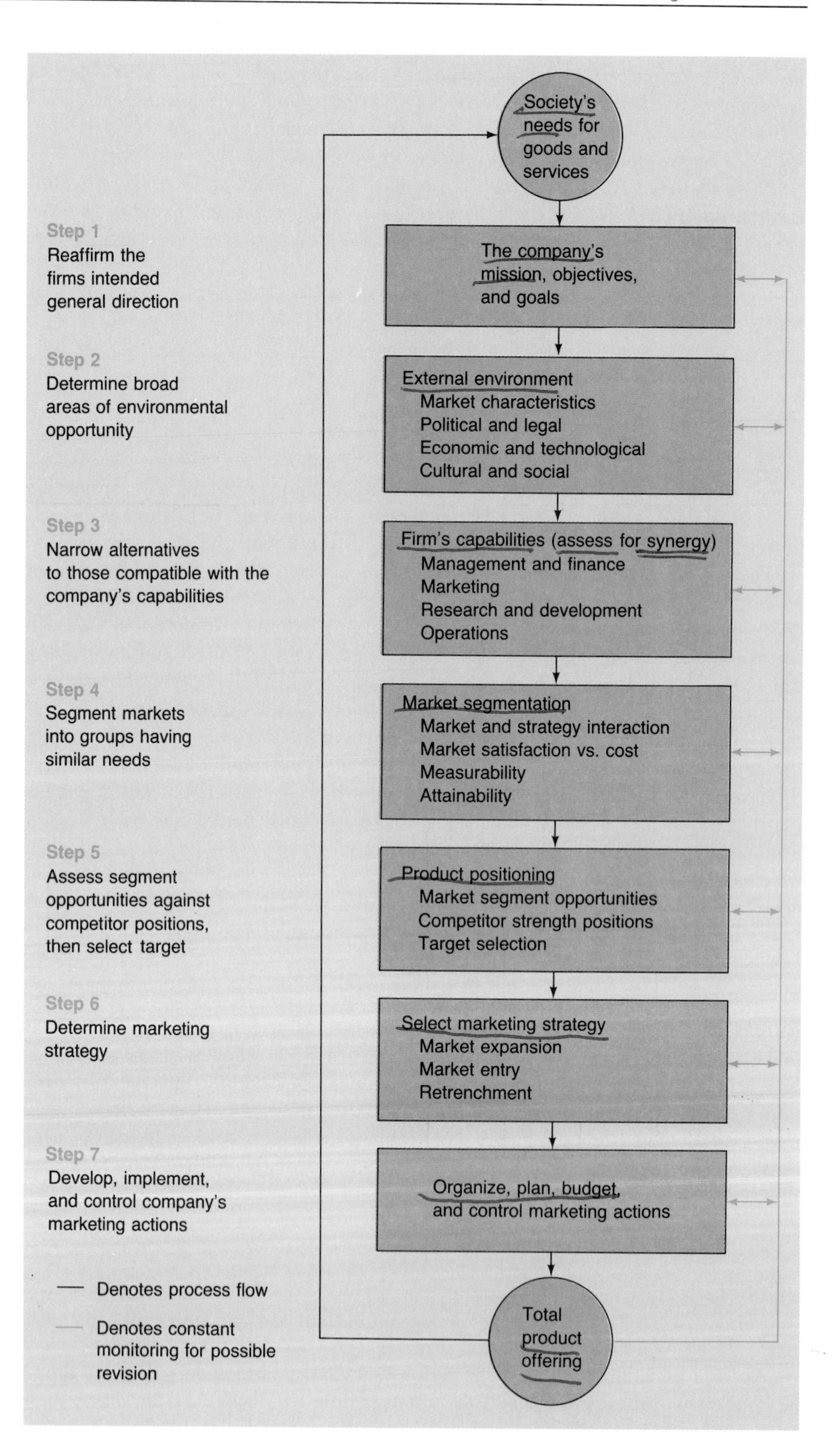

channel?" Managers cannot intelligently answer these and similar questions about each marketing decision without the help of a realistic mission and a set of goals and objectives as a guide.

The Company Mission

A company's **mission** establishes the general direction it intends to take in the marketplace. A mission statement answers the questions "What is our business?" and "What ought it to be?"[2]

Mission
A statement that establishes the general direction a firm intends to take in the marketplace.

- Hyundai's mission is to provide an economical means of transportation.
- General Motors' mission is to provide vehicles to satisfy surface transportation needs (cars, trucks, railroad diesels, buses, etc.)
- Gulf Oil's mission is to satisfy energy needs.
- A small retail grocer's mission is to furnish food and related items to neighborhood consumers.

A company's mission should be neither too narrow nor too broad.[3] Too narrow a definition unduly restricts action and results in lost opportunities. If Gulf Oil, for instance, defined its mission as only supplying petroleum products, management would likely overlook key alternative energy opportunities. On the other hand, too broad a mission fails to furnish much direction to management in decision making. If Gulf Oil stated its mission as providing combustible items to society, that mission would not provide a strong focus for management.

A company's mission should also focus on long-run opportunities. Sustained success does not come from frequently changing missions. A sufficient time span should be devoted to the firm's mission to enable it to develop expertise and create a niche—a position of strength—in the marketplace. However, management should also continually monitor environmental shifts to assure that the mission is not outdated.[4] Impending petroleum shortages, for instance, suggest that recreational vehicle manufacturers like Winnebego consider redefining their missions toward oil-efficient products some time in the future.

Goals and Objectives

Management should establish specific objectives and goals, within the general framework of the company mission, that relate to where the organization wants to be at the end of a particular time period, in concrete and measurable terms, and should not be in conflict with one another.

Some management experts see a technical difference between goals and objectives.[5] **Objectives** are broadly defined statements of the company's intended status, usually within a long-range time span. Profitability, for instance, is usually one of a company's objectives. **Goals** are generally more concretely defined and measurable targets, and they typically span a shorter time period. A 10 percent return on investment next year, for instance, is a possible goal.

Objectives
Broadly defined statements of the company's intended status, usually encompassing a long-range time horizon.

Goals
More concretely defined, measurable statements of the company's intended position, usually with a shorter time span than objectives.

Regardless, goals and objectives serve four specific functions for management: they define the organization in its environment, they establish a means of coordinating company actions, they provide standards for measuring results, and they communicate to employees what the organization strives to accomplish.[6]

What is the specific objective of business? It depends on the particular company. Traditionally, many scholars have argued that it is, or should be, maximum profit.

However, most modern business and economics experts cite ample evidence that many other factors are included as basic objectives of business.[7] Some of the more important include:

- Survival: To stay in existence for the long run.
- Profit: Stated as some return on investment, often 15 percent to 25 percent.
- Growth: To grow at some specified rate; i.e., on the basis of sales, assets, employees, etc.
- Stock valuation: To obtain some particular price/earnings ratio for shares traded on the stock exchanges. This is a function of many variables, including dividends and company profit growth.
- Technical and market leadership: Stated as so many new products per year and as a percentage of market share.
- Social responsibility: This is a relatively new goal, but it is often stated as the number of dollars committed to community development, or to antipollution programs such as product testing, etc.

Coordination and Control Mechanisms

Goals serve to coordinate the efforts of all employees toward desirable standards of behavior. Often, personnel in various functional areas of a business are at odds with each other. Production managers often desire to operate at a constant volume, financial managers desire restrictive credit practices, and sales managers often want just the opposite.

Effectively communicated goals and objectives serve to balance the interests of each of the functional areas in terms of spelling out what is best for the entire organization. Once established, a firm's goals serve as boundaries to which each of the functional areas should conform.

A reasonable question is: "Who should set the objectives?" In large firms, an executive committee made up of managers of various functional areas accomplishes this task. However, the chief marketing manager should be one of the key members involved in formulating an organization's objectives. *Companies simply fail if they do not satisfy their customers' needs*. Because the marketing process ties the firm to potential customers, the chief marketing executive should play an important role in setting objectives.

Objectives are useful in yet another respect: they provide measures which management can use to evaluate performance. If performance is inadequate, management can take any corrective action that may be necessary before it is too late for remedy. This is related to the principle of *management by exception*, which states that management should direct its efforts toward those areas that are not meeting expectations.[8] In turn, objectives serve to establish those expectations.

External Environment Variables

The second step in strategic marketing decision making involves the process of examining and assessing a firm's external environment—those variables over which management does not have direct control.[9] They constitute a framework of constraints within which the firm must operate, and they shape its opportunities. Environmental variables may be classified into five categories: market characteristics, political and legal factors, economic variables, technological variables, and cultural and social factors.

Source	Composition
Mission	Overall purpose of the organization.
Objectives	Broadly defined statements of the organization's intended position, usually encompassing a long-range time horizon.
Goals	More concretely defined, measurable, and having a shorter time span than objectives.

CONCEPT SUMMARY

Sources of Major Guidelines for the Organization

Market Characteristics

Certainly the types of buyers making up a target market, as well as the products and services they purchase, are important market variables that management should consider. An examination of the dimensions of current markets provides considerable insight into future potential opportunities. Let us consider types of customers and then types of products as starting points.

Types of Buyers In this context, "buyers" are both those who engage in purchasing and those who utilize goods and services. Essentially there are four major types of buyers of products and services: consumers, government buyers, industrial buyers, and intermediaries. Chapter one discussed the last two groups as one in order to simplify the exposition. This and subsequent chapters treat them separately because of differences in their characteristics and buying behavior.

Each type of buyer is somewhat different, both in individual members' motivations for purchasing and the way in which they make decisions. The first group, consumers, buy to permit personally desirable activities such as eating nutritious food and driving economical automobiles. Their decisions are directly related to personal choices. Conversely, industrial buyers and governmental units buy items that enable them to produce goods and services for the publics they serve. (The term "institutional buyers" is sometimes used to include all those potential and actual customers who are not consumers.) Their decision making is generally more systematic, involves a greater number of people, and depends somewhat less on personal desires. Intermediaries primarily buy items for resale. They purchase merchandise they believe will satisfy their customers' needs.

Successful marketing requires insights into buyer motivations and the processes buyers use to make purchase decisions. Accordingly, future chapters focus in depth on the behavior of various types of buyers.

Types of Products The members of each buyer category purchase a wide variety of products and services. Figure 2.2 depicts the proportions of consumer spending for various goods and services in the United States. It is apparent that food, beverage, and tobacco products account for the greatest proportion of all consumer dollars. In contrast, personal care items absorb only about 4 percent of the total.

Compilers and publishers of data, including the Conference Board and the Bureau of the Census, report buying patterns in considerable detail for both individual product and buyer classifications.[10] Managers who analyze aggregate expenditures by product class and examine trends over time are able to narrow potential opportunity areas down to those showing the most promise.

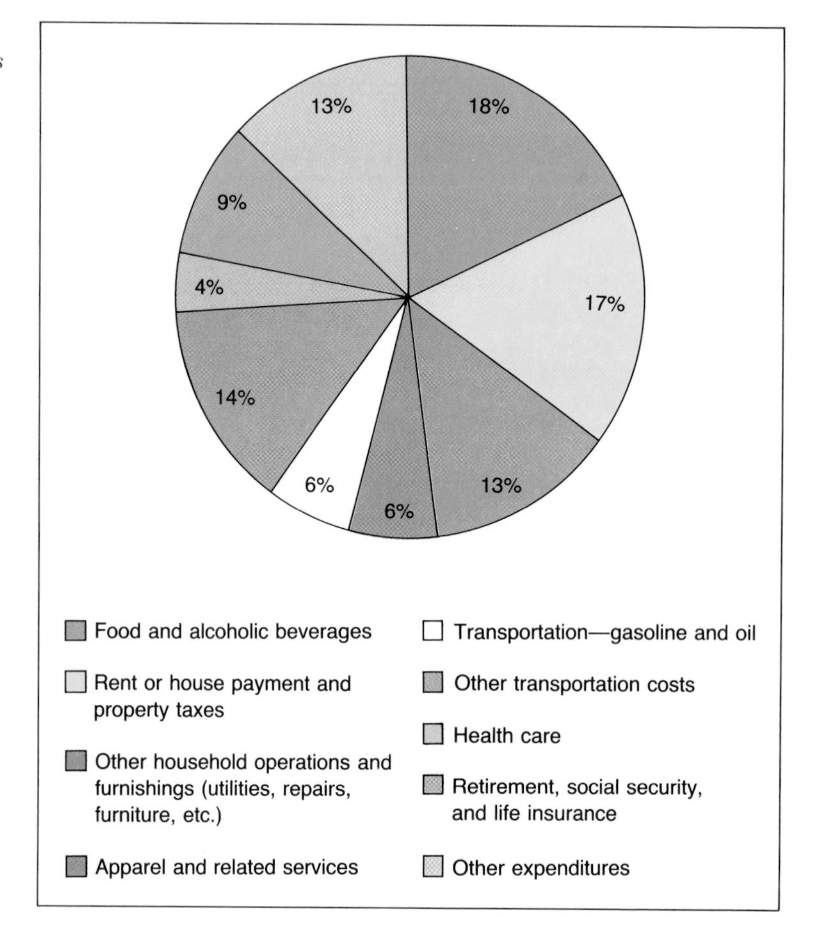

Figure 2.2
Percentages of U.S. Consumer Dollars Spent on Various Products and Services (SOURCE: *Statistical Abstract of the United States* (Washington, D.C.: U.S. Government Printing Office, 1986), 106th ed.)

To illustrate, increasing consumer expenditures for heating signaled to the management of Lennox Heating Systems that a significant opportunity existed for more energy-efficient furnaces. Hence, management considered several alternative products such as specially built chimneys, dampers, alternate insulation packages, and solar heating. The firm eventually developed an energy-efficient furnace that can cut heating costs up to 50 percent for many homes located in northern states. While the new furnaces have been very successful, the main point is that management was able to develop several desirable alternatives by focusing on buying trends for broad types of products.

Political and Legal Environment

Both the political and legal environments in which a firm operates are important determinants of its long-run success. The political environment reflects government attitudes toward business, including pending or future legislation that may affect business opportunities and related decision making. To illustrate, in 1984 the U.S. Department of Transportation issued a ruling requiring passive restraints in automobiles beginning with the 1988 model year. The rule would take effect unless at least 75 percent of the states enacted mandatory seat belt laws like the one in New

Technological breakthroughs have a tremendous impact on market opportunities.

York. Such legal requirements considerably benefit producers of air bags and seat belts.

In another vein, shifts in governmental expenditures can either hinder or aid marketers. The recent redistribution of federal expenditures from social programs to national defense has reduced opportunities for marketers of such things as basic foodstuffs and educational materials.

Today, many statutes and court decisions specifically govern business actions. While managers do have wide-ranging discretion over most of their activities, they must comply with all applicable laws. If they do not, negative publicity, court orders to stop certain actions, substantial fines, and even jail sentences for key decision makers can result. Because of their importance, future chapters discuss political and legal variables more thoroughly.

Economic and Technological Factors

Economic and technological factors are of great concern to marketers. Economic variables affect buyers' ability to purchase items, and include consumer income and savings. The values of alternative opportunities are, to a large extent, a function of a target's economic posture. To illustrate, marketers of new homes constantly monitor savings deposits, population trends, and employment data. Because these variables affect the demand for new housing, monitoring them enables builders to identify pockets of opportunity throughout the United States. The Eaton Company suffered considerable losses during the early 1980s, partially because truck sales were low. Eaton supplies 80 percent of the heavy-duty truck transmissions in the United States.[11]

Similarly, management should consider technology when evaluating general opportunity alternatives. To begin with, technology enables research and development personnel to develop new products. To illustrate, many consumers have a need to prevent tooth decay. A tremendous opportunity would result if a gum producer was able to develop the technology for making a pleasant-tasting chewing gum that actually prevented tooth decay.

The Eastman Kodak Company utilizes technology very effectively in conjunction with the introduction of new products. In 1982 it introduced a faster, more efficient Ektroprint Xerographic Copier, the 250-F, that made a strong penetration in a market once dominated by Xerox. The new product was aimed directly at the market to which Xerox's high volume 900 models appealed. In 1986, the firm switched its new product emphasis to biotechnology.[12]

Second, technology affects the cost of producing items, and this has a bearing on opportunity. For example, General Electric's sales of microwave ovens soared in 1984 when the firm was able to reduce retail prices so they were below $150. The price decreases were made possible by reduced costs because of improved technology.

Technological factors are not entirely external to a firm, since company research and development departments often produce innovations. Polaroid uses the technology it developed for consumer markets to expand its offerings of professional and industrial products, selling such items as specialty chemicals and wafer-shaped batteries to industrial buyers.[13]

Cultural and Social Factors

Cultural and social variables are the final major category of environmental factors that significantly influence general market opportunity. These two classes of variables strongly influence both the types of needs buyers have and the types of products and services they demand to satisfy these needs.

Tremendous cultural and social changes have emerged in the United States over the past quarter century. Birth control, reduced population growth, civil rights, women's liberation, gay liberation, health consciousness, and many other changes have made an indelible mark on society. According to one source:

> The two-child suburban family may still be important [to establishing market opportunity], but so are [the] 49 million single adults, 20 million gay people, 3 million cohabitators, 7 million single parents, and 2.5 million couples purported to be involved in social sexuality, open marriage, or swinging.[14]

In other words, nearly half of the U.S. population does not fit a family behavior mode traditionally considered to be "normal." Similar changes also have emerged in religious beliefs, leisure activities, work ethics, and planned parenthood. Each changing value influences buyer needs and the resulting opportunities. For example, opportunities have emerged for prepaid ambulance services because of increasing concentrations of retirees settling in the warm climates of Florida, Arizona, and California.

One may not agree that society will benefit as a result of any of these changes; nevertheless, their effect on opportunity is clear. A need for particular products and services accompanies each change.

Considering Opportunities

The first two steps of strategic marketing enable managers to delineate broad areas of market opportunity and to initially screen these opportunities for their compatibility

Solid marketing builds upon a firm's unique strengths.

MARKETING BRIEF

Solid Marketing Is Based Upon a Company's Capabilities

Once the darling of the breweries, Adolph Coors Co. of Golden, Colorado faced difficult times in the late 1970s and early 1980s. Despite being distributed in 23 more states, company sales of the suds remained flat from 1977 through 1984.

Coors began a plan to bounce back in 1985. Operations were aggressively expanded into New England and Chicago. The company also launched its first national advertising campaign, featuring actor Mark Harmon, judged the sexiest man of 1986 by *People* magazine, who explained why Coors—brewed with Rocky Mountain spring water—tastes "better." The new marketing focus appears to be working, as Coors sold 14.7 million barrels last year, up 12 percent over 1984.

SOURCE: Adapted from "Coors Comes Bubbling Back," *Fortune*, March 17, 1986: 51–52.

with the attainment of company objectives. Management identifies areas that offer the greatest potential for success by examining buying patterns, political and legal factors, economic and technological variables, and cultural and social forces. Company goals and objectives, especially the firm's mission, help in narrowing the array of potential opportunities down to a few broad areas offering promise, but management needs to take further steps to determine the best alternatives to consider further.

Capabilities of the Firm

The third step of the strategic marketing decision process consists of assessing a firm's unique strengths and weaknesses.[15] The Coors Company, for example, conducted an extensive analysis of its strengths and weaknesses before embarking on its aggressive marketing thrust in 1985 (see the accompanying Marketing Brief). The objective of this step is to evaluate the company's ability to efficiently and effectively carry out the work that each of the alternatives would require. Then, management can select for further consideration those alternatives for which the company is most capable of performing the needed functions.[16]

Some managers develop grand ideas about what the market needs. But they may lack the ability to produce and/or market the product or service required to satisfy those needs. To illustrate, a bright young inventor recently came up with an idea for a new type of lock for sliding doors. The lock was a good idea, at least conceptually. It did not require a key and could be operated easily by a child. Several police and fire departments tested a model and found it to be far superior to other locks being marketed. But the inventor did not know how to market the product. Every lock company he contacted thought it was a good idea, but they would not buy his patent rights. He attempted to interest several large national retailers, without success. He was at a complete loss, lacking the necessary skills to assess the market for this lock and to design a sales strategy accordingly.

If it is to be effective, strategy must reflect a firm's resources and capabilities. Because a firm's capabilities are a function of both its own characteristics and the tasks necessary to follow through on an alternative, management should assess each opportunity separately. It is possible to classify all of a firm's tasks into one of four functional categories: general management and finance, marketing, research and development, and operations.

General Management and Finance

A rule of thumb in political elections is that the odds are heavily slanted in favor of the incumbent. There are several reasons, including name familiarity, access to campaign funds, and publicity.

Certainly, the advantage of being an incumbent is not limited to political elections. Managers and other employees of all organizations gain expertise in their fields of specialization. Executives of Procter & Gamble, for instance, become thoroughly knowledgeable about the consumer products industry by the time they rise to higher echelons. Consequently, the firm has a strong experience base among its managers from which to draw when considering new consumer items. The firm put this expertise to use in 1982 when it purchased the Morton-Norwich pharmaceutical business. Procter and Gamble know-how was invaluable in marketing Morton-Norwich products such as Pepto Bismol and Unguentine. Similarly, Yamaha relied on its managerial expertise to successfully introduce motor scooters into the U.S. market in 1984.[17] Managers who possessed insights on selling motorcycles were able to transfer this capability to the new product line in a very effective manner.

Many organizations cannot pursue opportunities because of a lack of capital. It may cost several hundred million dollars to build a modern steel plant, for example. Few companies besides those already established in the steel industry, such as U.S.X., Bethlehem, and Jones and Laughlin, have the ability to obtain such funds. Capital lending markets heavily favor existing enterprises with extensive experience and large size.

Marketing Capabilities and Reputation

The advantages accruing to an incumbent are perhaps most dramatic in the area of marketing. Sony, for example, has a quality image among customers and a proficiency at reading consumer needs. Accordingly, there is a low probability that a new TV set marketed by the company would be a financial disaster. The firm has both a well-established dealer system and strong loyalty among customers. These give Sony a definitive advantage over companies commanding less marketing strength. This does

CONCEPT SUMMARY

External Environmental Variables

Variables	Composition
Customers and market characteristics	Buyers and users of goods and services engaged in personally desirable activities or producing goods and services for their various publics.
Political and legal environment	Governmental attitudes toward business, some of which is reflected in legislation, plus governmental expenditure patterns.
Economic and technological factors	Variables that enable buyers to purchase items to satisfy their needs and variables influencing new products and the means of producing them.
Cultural and social factors	Broad values, attitudes, perceptions, and behaviors held by large aggregates of individuals.

not mean that other electronics producers cannot succeed in the television market. Instead, it signifies that they must be especially careful in defining their targets and in selecting a strategy in order to obtain a marketing advantage.

As the example of the sliding door lock illustrates, distribution channel marketing experience is often a critical ingredient to success. Some people naively believe that intermediaries are anxious to accept virtually any new item. Such a belief is totally unfounded. To the contrary, sales representatives of many firms barrage wholesalers and retailers in an attempt to get them to carry new or revised products, but shelf and inventory storage space is a limited resource and getting intermediaries to handle an item is no easy task. If a firm already has established a good distribution channel, this simplifies obtaining distribution for a new but similar item. The existence of well-established distribution channels was extremely valuable to the Swanson Company when it introduced its frozen breakfast waffles (for microwave cooking) in 1982.

Research and Development

A firm's capability to obtain and maintain appropriate levels of technology is of primary importance in evaluating some potential market opportunities. Many apparently promising opportunities are really available only to a handful of firms that possess or can obtain the necessary technology. For example, nuclear, solar, and oil shale energy sources are potential future opportunities, but their complexity precludes all but a few firms (such as Occidental Petroleum, Commonwealth Edison of Illinois, and Exxon) from succeeding.

Research and development (R & D) activities do not pertain solely to physical technology but include all areas of technical and specialized knowledge. The ability to conduct market research and forecasting, along with knowledge of buyer behavior, are important factors to consider in assessing whether or not a company has a differential advantage in a particular field.

Sony's past successes contribute to its future chances for success in consumer electronics.

Operations

An organization's current structure of operations sometimes restrains decision making. Organizations, especially large ones, become bureaucracies with established and often rigid rules, procedures, and policies for the conduct of business. These restraints are desirable in order to attain current goals and to achieve efficiencies in operations, but they can inhibit making the changes needed to effectively tackle a new opportunity.[18]

Small firms frequently do not labor under such burdens. One small company located in the Southwest, for example, successfully dropped its ailing skateboard product line and substituted a line of hang gliders in less than a month. Managements of large organizations, however, should generally avoid drastic shifts from routines and standards. The greatest competitive advantages for these firms is generally found in areas where the new operations are similar to the old ones.

Synergy Helps Assess Strengths and Weaknesses

A company should not enter a market unless it has a strong potential for developing a favorable differential advantage over competitors and establishing a long-run market niche.[19] General Foods, for instance, tried to tap the iced tea market a few years ago with Kool-Aid iced tea. But the company was unable to develop a significant advantage over well-entrenched competitors, such as Lipton, among any of the market's segments. Failure was the natural result. The Readers Digest Association had a similar experience. It introduced *Families* magazine in 1981 and was forced to discontinue the publication in 1982. The company did not design *Families* in a manner that appealed to target consumers to the extent that competitors' magazines did.[20]

The concept of **synergy** is useful when management is assessing the potential for differential advantage offered by various opportunity alternatives. Companies attempt to integrate various activities to produce an organized effort. *Synergy exists when, because of the combination of activities, the value of the combined effort is greater than the value of the sum of the parts.* For example, if the value of one activity is 2 units and the value of the second activity is 2 units, synergy exists when 2 + 2 = 5.

Synergy
A situation that exists when, because of a combination of activities, the value of the combined effort is greater than the value of the sum of the parts.

To illustrate, Radio Shack has an established reputation for selling moderately expensive electronic equipment and components to hobbyists. Expanding into personal computers was a natural synergistic opportunity for the company. In another instance, the Boeing Company offers a number of management development programs for executives in other companies. It developed the expertise needed to produce these programs in the process of conducting training programs for its own employees.

The typical view of synergy is that it is either zero (nonexistent) or positive (present). When choosing strategy, though, management is well advised to view synergy along a negative-to-positive continuum, i.e., 2 + 2 might equal 3, 4, or 5, depending on the circumstances. For instance, both Radio Shack and Boeing would likely experience negative synergy in producing and marketing cashew nuts. Each operation (electronics and development programs, and cashew nuts) would contribute little, if anything, to the other, resulting in added overhead and a probable detraction of effort from both. From this perspective, a company is likely to attain positive synergy in only a few areas.

Figure 2.3 illustrates a conceptual means of evaluating the potential synergy of a proposed market opportunity. Note that each row identifies an area of a company's capabilities and each column reflects a synergy component. The next section examines in depth the various synergy components.[21]

Symmetry Effects

Symmetry effects refer to synergy resulting from relationships between current activities and activities required for a proposed new venture. In effect, when management looks for symmetry effects, it dissects an alternative into its functional activity components, then compares the components with existing functions the organization already performs. Synergy may appear in any or all of the functional activity categories.

Symmetry effects
Synergy resulting from relationships between current activities and activities required for a proposed new venture.

There are three types of symmetry effects to consider within each activity category. First, management should assess a proposed new venture's potential contribution to the parent. The "parent" is a firm's existing product offering. Or, in the case of the acquisition of another company, the term "parent" means the buying firm. A new product entry may benefit its parent in many ways. It may provide access to new markets for existing products, new technology that can be transferred to existing

Functional area	Effects due to pooling of competences / Symmetry effects	Startup economies: Investment	Startup economies: Operating	Startup economies: Timing	Operating economies: Investment	Operating economies: Operating	Expansion of present sales	New product and market areas	Overall synergy
	Contribution to parent								
General management and finance	Contribution to new entry								
	Joint opportunities								
	Contribution to parent								
Research and development	Contribution to new entry								
	Joint opportunities								
	Contribution to parent								
Marketing	Contribution to new entry								
	Joint opportunities								
	Contribution to parent								
Operations	Contribution to new entry								
	Joint opportunities								

Figure 2.3
Conceptual Means for Evaluating Synergy (SOURCE: H. Igor Ansoff, *Corporate Strategy: An Analytic Approach to Business Policy for Growth and Expansion* (New York: McGraw-Hill, 1965).)

products, prestige for the parent, and new management or operating skills. The Chrysler Corporation, for example, gained a new market segment for its marine engines when it began to manufacture and sell boats. It subsequently realized favorable synergy for its traditional offerings.

The second type of symmetry effect is the contribution the original product offering can make to a new entry. Management skills, financial capabilities, technological knowledge, marketing, and operating skills may present a meaningful contribution to a new opportunity. For example, past experiences with its SX-70 cameras and film helped Polaroid develop and market its Spectra System cameras and complementary films. Sanders Associates, Inc., uses expertise gained in producing electronic weapons for the government for basic patents that it licenses to the videogames industry.[22]

MARKETING BRIEF

Synergy Adds to the Attractiveness of an Opportunity

Already locked into an intense "cola war" with Coca-Cola Co., PepsiCo unleashed a major salvo against the cola giant by announcing that talks had been successfully completed with Philip Morris, Inc. (PM), for the acquisition of Seven-Up Co., International—one of PM's holdings. Pepsi is betting that it can turn around Seven-Up, a losing proposition for PM since it acquired the company in 1978 for $525 million. Despite Seven-Up's 53 percent of the lemon-lime drink market, PM has generally lost money on the company.

As it turns out, Seven-Up's woes were partly caused by its new owner. Pepsi introduced lemon-lime Slice to the market a couple of years ago, and the juice-based drink quickly captured 12.5% of the lemon-lime market. Almost all of those sales came at Seven-Up's expense.

The Pepsi/Seven-Up combination could help both companies significantly through synergy. Seven-Up will be able to use Pepsi's strong bottling network and marketing clout. In turn, Pepsi will be able to expand its distribution of Slice. Originally, Pepsi intended to buy the worldwide rights to Seven-Up for $380 million, but the agreement was disallowed by the Federal Trade Commission. The new agreement to acquire Seven-Up International will cost PepsiCo $246 million in cash.

Overseas, noncola drinks account for two-thirds of the lucrative soft-drink market. The move will put PepsiCo in a strong position to intensify its battle for international market share leadership, where the company recently trailed Coke by nearly a 2-to-1 margin. Seven-Up holds a particularly strong market position in several key markets, including Canada, Mexico, the Netherlands, Argentina, and the Phillipines.

SOURCE: Adapted from Scott Scredon and Amy Dunkin, "Pepsi's Seven-Up Deal: Shaking Up the Soft-Drink Wars," *Business Week*, February 3, 1986: 31; and John Gorman, "PepsiCo Has to Go Overseas But Finally Manages to Buy Some Seven-Up," *Chicago Tribune*, July 15, 1986, Sec. 3, p. 4.

Joint opportunities, the final symmetry effect, occurs in situations where both existing products and the proposed new venture assist each other. To illustrate favorable synergy in this case, consider a grocery store that sells both ground meat and hamburger buns. Such a store undoubtedly sells more of each item than if it stocked only one of them. Ground meat sales are helped by the buns, and vice versa. Synergy from joint opportunities was the rationale behind PepsiCo's acquisition of Seven-Up International, as illustrated in the accompanying Marketing Brief.

Pooling Effects

The effects of combining competences is an aspect of synergy with which management should be familiar. There are four aspects of **pooling effects:** startup, operations, expansion of present sales, and new product and market areas.

Pooling effects
Synergy resulting from combining competencies.

Startup economies are those that occur in conjunction with the initial costs of becoming involved in a new opportunity. There are investment, operating, and timing startup costs to consider. Investment costs arise because of the need to obtain necessary equipment, plants, patent rights, and other capital expenditure items. For example, prior to AMF's introduction of a new line of scuba gear, the firm invested considerable money in machines, tools, equipment, supplies, and labor to make production facilities ready for operation. Operating startup costs include money spent in gaining initial customer acceptance and the diseconomies associated with small initial production test runs and faulty decision making until management gains experience. Finally, timing startup costs involve expenses incurred because of disruptions in normal operations during the startup period.

Operating economies take place in conjunction with the costs of a new endeavor once it becomes an ongoing operation. Included are the cost levels associated with normal production, added capital requirements to sustain operations (e.g., working capital and new capital investment), and reductions in the unit costs of all products resulting from spreading overhead over a greater number of items.

Operating and startup synergies are generally highly correlated. A residential builder, for instance, is likely to experience favorable startup and operating synergy by expanding into the construction of small commercial buildings, since both types of operations are highly compatible. But this is not always the case. A producer of processed potatoes might experience large startup costs if it added another processed vegetable such as corn, as this could require the purchase of new equipment. But its operating synergy would likely be quite favorable; the same channels of distribution and similar marketing expertise would be applicable, and perhaps the new cash flow pattern would offset current seasonal sales fluctuations.

Synergy related to expansion of present sales is the impact on current product sales resulting from expanding into a new field. In some instances, entry into a new market greatly expands sales of current products. For example, a dairy is likely to experience an increase in sales of whole milk if it adds other types of milk-related products such as cheese and whipped cream. Access to certain retailers is possible with a full line of dairy products. Further, customer awareness of the dairy is likely to increase, creating a larger consumer demand for all of its products. Also, a more favorable image created from expansion might increase sales of current products. Selling $20,000 diamonds, for instance, helps Tiffany's sell its $500 rings.

New product and market area synergy involves the anticipated future benefits to the firm's objectives that the proposed new opportunity creates. The firm may derive these benefits from sales revenues, profits, added management experience, cash flow assistance, and technical knowledge. But trying to gain synergy from new products and market areas is risky, since management is not able to draw on its past experiences.

Exxon management, for example, became concerned with the almost inevitable long-term decline of petroleum due to depletion.[23] Accordingly, the company entered the office machine market in the mid 1970s by introducing the Quip—an image-transmitting machine designed to compete with similar devices marketed by Xerox. Later, the company tried to gain synergy by springboarding off of the Quip and into the Qyx (pronounced "quicks")—a newly designed electronic typewriter containing programmed memory features. Sales of the Qyx were more promising than those of the Quip, but eventually the company withdrew from the office machine market altogether because of poor sales performance. The negative synergy between this market and Exxon's basic business was too great to be offset by any new product and market area synergy.

In a more successful move, the Canteen Corporation, the top caterer to U.S. factories, suffered reduced sales in the early 1980s because the "smokestack industries" (its main customer base) were mired in a recession. This led the firm to pursue faster growing opportunities such as health care, office complex food service, and concessions. The switch was successful; the firm gained 415 new customers in 1982.[24]

Most markets are comprised of distinctive segments.

Overall synergy is the summation of all the values in each row in Figure 2.3; it is the composite synergy from pooling all competency effects. Appendix A presents a way to assess the potential synergy associated with a proposed new venture. Management should consider only those opportunities with a potential for strong favorable synergy and may decide to employ a strategy called market segmentation for those opportunities.

Market Segmentation

A common characteristic of modern markets is that they are comprised of buyers with heterogeneous needs and wants. Management should study various subsets or segments of a market so that it can identify targets that it has a high probability of reaching.[25] The fourth step in strategic marketing decision making, therefore, involves segmenting the markets associated with the remaining opportunity alternatives being considered.

Market segmentation involves dividing a total market into two or more groups of potential buyers so that each group reflects customers having similar needs, but so that the needs of each group differ from other groups.[26] Then management decides which (if any) of the groups to serve. It can be dangerous to attempt to serve all groups in a market with the same marketing mix because the groups may differ in important respects. Management designs different strategies for each submarket served. The following chapter describes this strategy in depth.

Market segmentation
Dividing a total market into two or more groups of potential buyers so that each group reflects customers having similar needs, but so that the needs of each group differ from other groups.

Product Positioning

Beyond identifying segments in the market, management must carefully consider competition strengths and weaknesses. This is the **product positioning** task—strategic marketing decision making's fifth step. In essence, product positioning extends segmentation. After management has identified potential customer clusters, it determines competitor strengths and weaknesses among the various segments. Next, it selects a target, consisting of one or more market segments where the firm is most likely to have a competitive advantage. Then management designs a marketing mix to appeal to these designated segments. The strategic plan includes placing the product uniquely in the minds of consumers relative to rival offerings.[27] Many retailers are strongly committed to positioning, realizing that it is a useful means of making inroads on the sales of competitors.[28] Similarly, many consumer products are carefully positioned by their manufacturers, as illustrated by the accompanying Volkswagen Marketing Brief.

Product positioning
Placing the product uniquely, in the minds of customers, when compared to rival offerings.

MARKETING BRIEF
VW Attempts a Repositioning

Facing an upward drift in its product line over the years, Michigan-based Volkswagen of America announced in early 1986 that plans were underway to reposition itself within a year toward the lower end of the auto market by introducing a new car imported from the company's Brazilian operations. Still code-named "Project 99," the new car will come in four-door sedan and station wagon versions and will be priced under $6,000 to compete with the Yugo, Hyundai Excel, and other models in the growing under-$7,000 segment.

"The car will be aimed at both the entry-level 18-to-30-year-old market of first new car buyers and as a second or third car for older families who remember owning or riding in Beetles," said James Fuller, vice president in charge of VWUS, the sales arm of Volkswagen of America. "It's not only an ideal second car for 2 million former or current VW owners, it's an 'appetizer course' for first-time buyers who will buy an average of 16 new cars in their lives," Fuller added.

The company announced that it will use 15-second television spots in the fall of 1986 to change its image. Richard Marcy, the company's marketing director, added that "we will . . . show off a wide variety of products this spring and build awareness that Volkswagen is not a one-car company." Additional plans are also underway for upgraded versions of other company models.

SOURCE: Adapted from Jesse Snyder, "VW Trying to Shake its One-Car Image," *Advertising Age*, February 24, 1986: 77.

Market Segments

In an often quoted study, Johnson asked a sample of beer drinkers to name those attributes by which they judged various brands of beer.[29] Two attributes emerged as most important: the degree of mildness and the degree of lightness, which appeared to be independent of each other. Thus, the research suggested that brewers might successfully segment beer drinkers on the basis of these two variables.

Johnson also asked the sample to indicate where an *ideal brand* of beer would stand with respect to mildness and lightness. This procedure enabled the researchers to identify nine separate segments of beer drinkers. Figure 2.4 presents the results. The size differences among the circles reflect the numbers of drinkers in each segment.

Competitor Positions

Data on total potential sales within particular segments can be misleading. Segments 1 and 2 of Figure 2.4, to illustrate, appear to be the most promising because they are the largest. A brewery manager might conclude that the firm should market a moderately mild beer midway on the light-to-heavy spectrum. In this way it might capture both segments and the market's biggest sales share. But these segments might also be where all or most of the firm's competitors are focusing their efforts. Thus, another position could offer greater promise. Perhaps no firm is targeting on segments 3, 5, or 8, which means that a moderately light and slightly bitter beer might provide a greater competitive advantage and a larger sales potential.

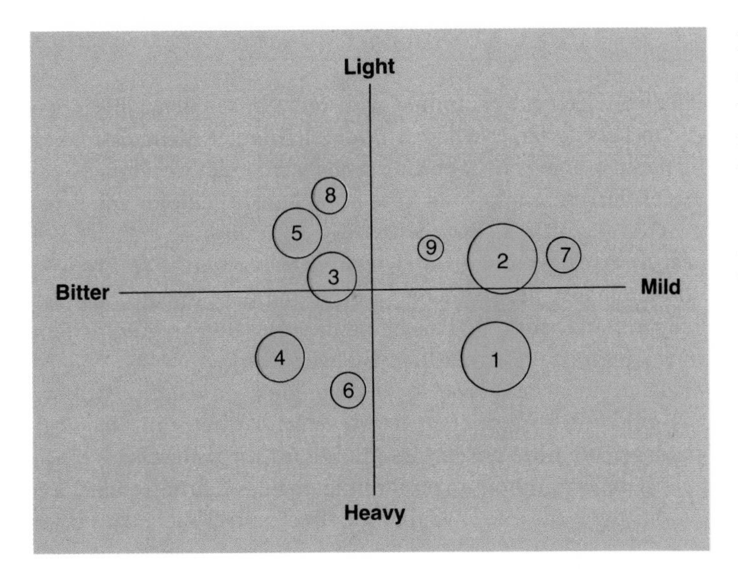

Figure 2.4
Market Segments for Beer, Based on Ideal Points along Two Important Dimensions (SOURCE: Based on Richard M. Johnson, "Market Segmentation: A Strategic Management Tool," *Journal of Marketing Research* 8, no. 1 (February 1971): 16.)

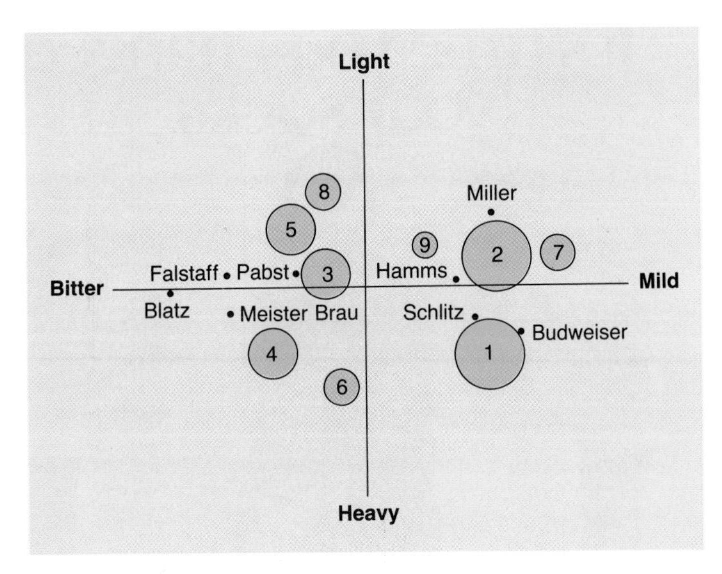

Figure 2.5
Competitor Positions among Various Market Segments for Beer (SOURCE: Based on Richard M. Johnson, "Market Segmentation: A Strategic Management Tool," *Journal of Marketing Research* 8, no. 1 (February 1971): 16.)

To get a fix on competitor positions, Johnson asked the sample to rate each popular brand of beer on scales of mildness and lightness. Figure 2.5 sets forth the resulting brand ratings, as well as the market segments from Figure 2.4 for comparison.[30]

None of the popular brands possessed the actual attributes that any of the segments perceived to be ideal. Schlitz and Budweiser were close to that which segment 1 desired, although these customers preferred a slightly heavier beer. Miller, Pabst, and Hamms were also close, but still deviated from the location of any one cluster. The remaining brands were quite a bit off the mark of any segment. This study, then, indicated where various firms might place their offerings in light of market segment size, consumer preferences, and the offerings of competitors.

Market niche
A position of market strength among one or more segments of a market.

Selecting a Target

Once management is familiar with relevant segments and competitor positions, it is able to select a target where a favorable **market niche** can be created. Since none of the popular brands in Johnson's study were exactly on target, all of the segments were possible targets but it would have been very difficult for any firm other than Budweiser or Schlitz to attain great success in penetrating segment 1. Both of these firms had great marketing strengths and they were positioned relatively close to the segment. On the other hand, segments 5, 8, 4, and 6 represented significant segments that no popular brand satisfied. This being the case, these segments were prime target market candidates for firms other than Budweiser or Schlitz.

Management can repeat the decision procedure outlined above for each opportunity it is still considering. Then it can select as the prime target that alternative which appears to offer the greatest contribution toward the firm's objectives. The important point here is that product positioning enables a firm to select a target for which it has a competitive advantage so that a lasting market niche can be established.

Positioning is comprised of choosing a target market after considering competitor positions.

Selecting Marketing Strategies

Once the firm has selected a target, management's task is clear: to attain the firm's goals and objectives through satisfying the target's needs. The sixth step in strategic marketing decision making is to select the most appropriate strategy to accomplish this task. Market expansion, market entry, and retrenchment are three major strategies a firm may select. The following discussion presents an overview of each.

Market Expansion

Market expansion
Attempting to more fully penetrate an existing target, as opposed to selecting new or additional ones.

Market expansion is generally the safest and most conservative of the strategies that this section discusses. It is based upon trying to improve company performance by more fully satisfying an existing target, as opposed to selecting new or additional ones. Budweiser, to illustrate, might have made its beer slightly less mild and a bit heavier than it was (see Figure 2.5). If successful, the firm would likely have gained a greater share of segment 1's sales at Schlitz's expense. Because this strategy would have involved attempting to improve performance in an area in which the firm had experience, its potential for positive synergy was greater than that of other strategies. It should be noted that market expansion is only effective to a point. Further growth becomes difficult, if not impossible, once a segment's needs become saturated. Management needs another strategy once this happens.

Market Entry

Market entry
Attempting to improve company performance by expanding the scope of operations through penetrating an additional market.

Product development
Attempting to further satisfy a current target through major modification of a total product offering.

With **market entry**, a firm attempts to improve its performance by expanding the scope of its operations. As Figure 2.6 illustrates, product development, market development, and diversification are the principal market entry strategy modes.

Product development involves attempting to further satisfy a current target through major modification of a total product offering. Speidel, for example, added watches to augment its well-known line of watch bands. "Let us extend all the way around your wrist," the company told its target market in its introductory theme. Companies do not always add new items when they practice product development, however. They might also change existing products significantly. Hills Brothers, for instance, introduced High Yield coffee, a natural blend specially processed so that 13 ounces yield

Target market \ Product	Present	New
Present	Market expansion	Product development
New	Market development	Diversification

Market entry strategies

Figure 2.6
Major Performance Expansion Strategies (SOURCE: Adapted from H. Igor Ansoff, *Corporate Strategy: An Analytic Approach to Business Policy for Growth and Expansion* (New York: McGraw-Hill, 1965): 109.)

ANSOFF model

the same number of cups as a pound of regular type, but at a lower price to reflect the three fewer ounces. Thomas J. Lipton, Inc., introduced a 97 percent caffeine-free tea.[31]

Market development
Trying to satisfy new markets with essentially the same product as is used to satisfy old markets.

When an organization tries to satisfy new targets with essentially the same product as it uses to serve old markets, the strategy is termed **market development.** IBM, for instance, positions its typewriters almost exclusively for heavy duty commercial use. The company could undertake a market development strategy by expanding into the consumer market. Such a strategy might involve some changes in the firm's total product offerings. Certainly IBM would redirect some of the advertising effort to new media such as consumer magazines and perhaps it would offer a stripped-down version, or last year's commercial model at a lower price.

Diversification
Entering new markets with new types of product offerings.

Finally, **diversification** involves entering new markets with new types of product offerings. Facing the threat of a declining cigarette market, for example, American Brands spent over half a billion dollars to acquire nearly a third of the ownership of Franklin Life Insurance Co.[32] IBM began producing and selling industrial robots in 1982.[33] This type of market entry is usually the least desirable because it involves moving into an area in which the company has neither operating nor marketing experience. The chances for positive synergy are consequently quite low.

Companies can accomplish market entry in several ways: *Internal development,* which relies on the company's own staff to develop the offering (which can be time-consuming); *acquisition,* the buying of another company that has the ability or experience to deal with the intended offering (which can be costly); and *joint venturing,* forming a partnership with another firm to produce and market the new offering. The appropriate strategy to use, of course, depends upon the costs involved, the timing implications, and the capabilities of the company.

Retrenchment

Retrenchment
Withdrawing from peripheral market segments to a position where the firm has its strongest niche.

Retrenchment is the last strategy considered in this section. Most gardening buffs know that they must sometimes prune an infected limb to save a tree's life. Similarly, in business management it is sometimes necessary to withdraw from unprofitable or cash-draining market segments. Retrenchment is a strategic effort to withdraw from peripheral market segments to positions where the firm has its strongest niche.

To illustrate, American Motors withdrew from its unprofitable line of full-sized cars by dropping its Ambassador. Historically, the firm's strength had been among economy-minded buyers of smaller cars. By retrenching, AMC was able to improve its financial posture through focusing all its efforts on its core market. A less extreme form of retrenchment is to reduce promotion expenditures for a product but continue to offer it. This can increase cash flow when a product is not doing well in a market. After a firm is stabilized, it may again be in a position to expand.

Organizing, Planning, and Controlling

The seventh and final step in strategic marketing decision making requires making decisions to implement, or carry out, strategies discussed earlier. This includes organizing personnel, choosing specific activities and funding them, and establishing control procedures to assure that satisfactory progress is being made.

Organization

In a nutshell, **organizational decisions** determine the interactions among people within a company. Besides establishing who reports to whom and the authority and responsibility of each employee, these decisions strongly influence how well different individuals and departments coordinate their activities with one another.

Organizational decisions
Determining the formal structure of the work interactions among people in an organization.

A wide variety of organizational structures is possible. Some structures grant considerable importance to sales activities and treat other marketing functions as essentially supportive to sales. In this case, a sales manager directs personal selling endeavors and nonsales functions are often under the authority of a director of marketing services. In other firms, sales, advertising, distribution, and other marketing areas are generally organized in separate departments that all report to one manager, typically a vice president of marketing.[34]

Even among companies coordinating all marketing activities in one department, considerable organizational differences remain, but basically the patterns fall into one of three types: functional, market structures, and product-centered organizations. Companies offering relatively few types of products or services, such as American Airlines, typically subgroup marketing activities by function underneath the vice president of marketing. This results in a simple organizational structure and helps to develop expertise among function-based personnel such as those in sales or advertising.

Companies targeting widely divergent market segments, like Xerox (selling to customers ranging from small businesses to commercial printers), use functional specialists but also appoint market managers to be responsible for coordinating the marketing mixes for their respective assigned markets (made up of types of customers).[35] The Mountain Bell Telephone Company, for instance, has executives that specialize in serving specific industries with telephone service. Some, for instance, service hotels and motels, while others specialize in working with educational institutions.

Finally, companies offering many different products to similar market segments, such as General Mills, usually appoint product managers to develop and coordinate a marketing mix for their assigned products. This organization plan helps to assure that functional specialists will allocate their attention to all products, not just the best sellers.

Each organization structure has a number of strengths and weaknesses. In turn, the optimum form for a company depends upon its unique circumstances. In essence, though, management should organize the marketing department to reflect the company's overall strategies.

Planning and Budgeting

An important characteristic that distinguishes many successful businesses from unsuccessful ones is the considerable attention that the former devote to careful **planning.** Detailed plans describe the activities a company will use to accomplish its goals as well as how funds will be used to implement them.

Planning
Determining the activities intended to accomplish a company's goals as well as the utilization of the funds needed to implement them.

Good plans specify detailed goals for each marketing activity as well as the means to attain the goals. A company's strategies provide very useful guides for goal setting. For example, suppose a regional candy producer like Saunders of Detroit decides to enter the national candy market. Several goal directives would be apparent, such as establishing national distribution and utilizing heavy advertising to develop consumer awareness. Beyond just providing direction, goals should spell out the specific tasks that each activity should accomplish. For example, one goal might be to expose 30 percent of the target market to company advertising within one year. Another might be to get 300 new gift shop retailers to handle Saunders' candy.

Plans also spell out specific actions that the company should undertake in each activity along with a timetable for accomplishing them. Saunders' management should specify details of media advertising (how many and what kind of TV ads to sponsor), sales force activities (the amount of time which sales representatives will spend in developing a certain number of new accounts), and other related marketing actions. Management should coordinate all actions so that they complement each other in an integrated effort centering on profitably servicing the selected target market.

Budgeting
Expressing plans in financial terms, forming the basis for control.

Finally, formal planning requires **budgeting,** which expresses plans in financial terms and forms the basis for control.

Control

Controlling
Measuring performance against goals and objectives and taking remedial action when performance is not adequate.

Changes in technology, competitor actions, consumer needs, and environmental conditions are among the many factors affecting performance and opportunity. Consequently, a firm's initial plans often do not result in achievement of its goals. To combat falling off the intended mark, management must periodically engage in **controlling** and revising company activities—often as important as the initial planning itself.

A company's overall objectives and goals, along with specific marketing goals, serve as a basis for controlling ongoing efforts. They represent guidelines against which management can compare actual performance. In turn, significant variances from planned results signal the need to evaluate problem areas. For example, if a 5 percent growth in annual sales is a marketing goal, the firm should seek to determine whether or not a problem exists if sales are stagnant during the first quarter. Perhaps the goal was unrealistic, possibly the marketing activities were inappropriate, or the firm's overall strategy may need revision due to faulty design or recent environmental changes. With proper control measures, however, the firm can develop revised programs before it is too late to keep operations on track.

By following the seven steps in the strategic market planning decision process, management is in a position to increase its chances of attaining success. Selecting the most promising opportunity leads to a consideration of market needs, a firm's abilities, and competitor actions. Once the firm has selected a target, it is in a position to integrate all efforts around profitably satisfying target customer needs. This process is the essence of what marketing is all about.

Chapter Summary

Among the most important decisions that management makes are those that relate to strategically positioning a company's product offerings in the marketplace. Following the seven-step marketing decision process presented in this chapter can help a manager assure that critical factors are considered and decided upon in a logical, sequential order when making strategic marketing decisions. The steps are:

1. Assess the firm's mission, objectives, and goals.
2. Examine external environment variables to determine broad areas of environmental opportunity.
3. Assess the firms capabilities, using the concept of synergy as a guide.
4. Segment the market.
5. Determine the firm's intended position in the market.

6. Identify the general way, or strategy, of attaining that position.
7. Organize, plan and budget, and control all marketing activities.

Essentially, the process focuses management's attention on environmental opportunities, the company's capabilities, and competitive positions in the marketplace. If followed, the strategic marketing decision process serves to narrow the field of possible activities down to one or a few where the firm has the greatest potential for success.

The strategic marketing decision process serves as a framework for integrating the materials in the remainder of the book. A detailed examination of the market segmentation process follows.

Questions

1. Why should management analyze historical buying patterns when considering external variables? After all, the future is of concern and not the past.
2. Should an organization's goals and objectives direct the environmental search, or should the process be reversed? Can managers perform steps one and two simultaneously?
3. In the words of one executive, "There are planners and doers. We do not waste our valuable time putting a lot of fancy gibberish on paper around here, and we've done pretty well." Comment.
4. The text states that there is a reluctance to change because it destroys past accomplishments. Do you agree? Can you see evidence around you in school? At work? In other institutions?
5. What does synergy mean? How does it come about? Why is synergy related to differential advantage?
6. Is the concept of synergy effective in evaluating diverse types of opportunities? Is this form of measurement basically subjective? Why not forget about the chart presented in Figure 2.3 and simply subjectively evaluate each total project?
7. Is market segmentation possible with every market? Will competing companies identify the same segments of a market?
8. Why is it important to consider possible strategy when defining segments?
9. What is product positioning? Why is it important?
10. Compare and contrast market entry and market expansion as strategies.
11. In the words of one executive: "All we do is make what we know how the best that we can, spend as much as we think we can afford on advertising, hire quality salespersons, and price at comparable competitive prices. Our formula for success is hard work and we've been successful." Comment.
12. How are marketing goals and activities related to an organization's goals and objectives? What roles do control and revision play in the process?

Chapter 3

Market Segmentation

Objectives

After completing this chapter, you should be able to demonstrate a knowledge of:

- The meaning of the term "market segmentation"
- The major advantages of segmentation
- The major disadvantages of segmentation
- How to determine whether to segment the market
- How to carry out segmentation strategies
- How to use the important criteria in segmenting

MARKETING SUCCESS

Selling Upscale Children's Items

"Julie is unique and she deserves the best," says Anne Beser talking about her daughter. Beser is a regular customer of "My Child's Destiny"—a unique store selling upscale children's items right-off of San Francisco's equally trendy Union Square. Like most of the store's regular customers, Ms. Beser is a "contemporary success-oriented woman," holding a degree from a prestigious Eastern school and backed-up with a law degree from The University of California.

"Don [her husband] and I waited for Julie a long time and she is special," she says. Like many of her counterparts, Beser postponed having children until mid-life, paying closer attention to her career at first. "My career still means a lot to me," says the 37 year-old partner of a San Francisco law firm. "But Don and I realize there is more to life."

My Child's Destiny contains several stores-within-a-store, laid out in a series of boutiques that feature everything from clothes and hair styling to books and computers. Total earnings from catering to the pampered set in 1985 were roughly $7.5 million and growing rapidly. Inside the store are toddler-height counters, low handrails, and free diapers in the restrooms. "It is the ultimate baby store," says Beser.

One of the store's success secrets is what it does not carry—there are no sex-typed toys on the shelves, each book in inventory is screened for violence, and all violent toys and books containing violence are banned. The store only carries clothes with natural fibers and carries the city's widest selection of European shoes.

The store is exclusive in its target selection, focusing on customers similar to Beser. "These people have the money and want to buy the best," said a company source.

SOURCE: Adapted from "A Boutique Born to Be the Ultimate Baby Store," *Business Week*, April 22, 1985: 65.

Introduction

A product manager for a running shoe marketer has decided to introduce a new offering called the "Jet." In order to determine what kind of shoe runners prefer, the manager has asked the marketing research department to conduct a study of consumer preferences. The company researchers complete the inquiry and produce the following findings:

> Numerous runners like a shoe that is heavily padded. This provides protection to the feet while running. On the other hand, there is a large group that prefers minimal padding, in order to make the shoes light in weight for races. The marketing manager decides to compromise and produce shoes that have intermediate levels of padding.
>
> Consumers with weak arches want shoes with substantial arch support. On the other hand, those with a pronation problem (tendency to run on the inside of the feet) want only moderate arch support. The manager strikes a balance between the two and constructs shoes with some but not too much arch support.
>
> Runners who commonly run on certain surfaces (such as grass, ice, and snow) prefer a heavy tread on their shoes. Conversely, others have no use for tread and even believe that it is a cause of undue physical stress and injury. The product manager does not

want to antagonize either group, and arranges for the production of a shoe with a light tread.

Some consumers are willing to pay high prices for a running shoe, based on the assumption that they will receive a premium product. Others seek bargains. The product manager compromises on this, as with other issues, and sets a mid-level price on the shoes.

The company introduced the product with great fanfare, but the results were dismal. A postmortem analysis revealed the following information.

A college student did not buy the shoes because she felt that the padding was too heavy to enable her to run sufficiently fast in ten-kilometer races, but a computer programmer did not like the shoes because they did not have sufficient padding to absorb the shock to his feet (which had been injured several months before in an overly-zealous marathon run).

A retail store executive with fallen arches did not buy the shoes because they had inadequate arch support. He bought a competing brand. A bank teller with "runner's knee" also avoided the company brand, but his reason was that the shoes provided too much arch support.

A construction worker who had suffered several injuries while falling during running did not buy the shoes because he wanted a make with more tread. Conversely, another construction worker who was accustomed to running on desert sand was not interested in the shoes because of what he felt was excessive tread.

A housewife who wanted only the "very best" shoe avoided the brand because she felt that a shoe with such a low price could not be of high quality. In contrast, a librarian would not consider this brand because he felt it was overpriced.

None of these consumers purchased the product manager's new item. Instead, all of them acquired competing brands. In an attempt to satisfy all, the product manager compromised and satisfied none. Every consumer found a competing brand that he or she felt was superior to the company's new entry. The product manager would have benefited by pursuing a strategy of market segmentation—the subject matter of this chapter.

The Meaning of Market Segmentation

Market segmentation is a strategy in which management produces and carries out programs designed for groups of potential buyers that the organization is able to satisfy. Rather than trying to satisfy everyone, management aligns its efforts toward the unique needs and characteristics of particular groups.[1] My Child's Destiny (see the Marketing Success) stores aim at upscale consumers, for instance. A target market for Citicorp (a large bank) is small- and medium-sized firms in Europe.[2]

Market segmentation
Dividing a total market into two or more groups of potential buyers so that each group reflects customers having similar needs, but so that the needs of each group differ from other groups.

Firms that use market segmentation strive to serve target markets that they are *able* to satisfy, not just any group of buyers that seems to represent a sizeable market. The Coca-Cola Company might experience difficulty in attempting to serve buyers who want automobiles. On the other hand, it has been quite effective in meeting the needs of consumers who desire frozen orange juice through its Minute Maid product.

The appropriate segments of any market are not automatically apparent; management needs to identify them. The results of the identification process can vary dramatically, depending on managers' judgments of the heterogeneity or homogeneity of potential customer needs. Figure 3.1 illustrates several possibilities for a simple example involving ten hypothetical consumers.

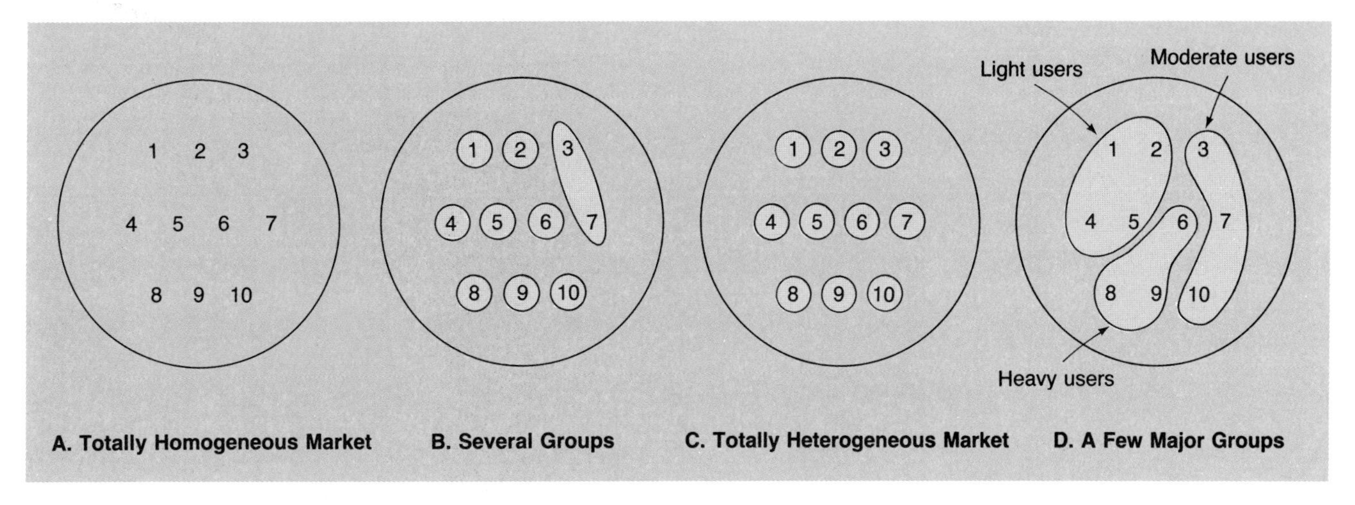

Figure 3.1
Possible Segments

The Extent of Segmentation

At one extreme, management can consider all of a total market's potential customers as belonging to one segment. Figure 3.1A illustrates this extreme—where management presumes that there are no important differences in needs between customers.

Typically, customers have divergent needs for particular items and the marketing strategy should recognize these differences. Some production- and sales-oriented executives naively assume that all needs are alike, whereas managers embracing the marketing concept do not. They look for specific needs around which to focus their marketing mixes so that lasting niches can be developed.

At the other extreme, management could define every potential buyer as a separate segment requiring a custom-made product.[3] This condition is termed "market atomization." Figure 3.1C illustrates this case, where the marketer believes that needs are completely heterogeneous. Such a scheme is common when marketing custom-designed products and services, such as office buildings or hair styling.

Suppose that the ten potential buyers of Figure 3.1 comprise a sample of coffee pot buyers who differ in their preferences for coffee pot size. Perhaps only two of the sample's members wish to brew the same number of cups per pot, while each of the remaining eight wants a different number. In this instance, groups of potential customer needs, based on desired coffee pot size, would appear as in Figure 3.1B.

However, identifying nine distinct segments and designing a marketing mix for each (nine different pot sizes) would be prohibitive in terms of cost. Further, most consumers are probably willing to buy a pot slightly larger or smaller than their ideal. Research might indicate that an acceptable compromise scheme is to identify three groups: light (small pot), moderate (medium-sized pot), and heavy (large pot) users, as Figure 3.1D illustrates.

This segmentation scheme could reasonably satisfy the needs of all three of the customer groupings and also enable the firm to keep its costs under control. Three coffee pot models (say a four-cup, an eight-cup, and a twelve-cup version) could be compatible with the brewing habits of all buyers, as opposed to one version that would not be acceptable to any.

There are a number of guidelines to help managers in making effective segmentation decisions. Some of these relate to the advantages and disadvantages of segmentation to the firm.

Success often depends upon marketing products to meet particular needs.

Advantages of Segmentation

The advantages of segmentation are of sufficient magnitude to lead numerous marketers to pursue this strategy. Segmentation results in the creation of a specific marketing mix for each subgroup of potential buyers that the organization intends to satisfy. Management's goal is to produce goods and services that furnish substantial satisfaction to selected specific groups of potential buyers.

When it is successful, segmentation leads to high customer loyalty for the brand and/or the company. Rivals will experience difficulty in winning away the patronage of target customers. Those marketers who have carved out particular portions of the market and who serve these portions well are in a relatively secure position.

Industrial marketers often find segmentation to be desirable. Companies in basic, old-line manufacturing industries such as steel and mining find it necessary to develop new strategies for profitability and even survival. Many of these firms see their future in switching from basic commodities into faster-growing, higher-margin specialty products aimed at particular segments. In these cases, then, segmentation can provide a means of escaping an industry environment where profits are very difficult to attain.[4]

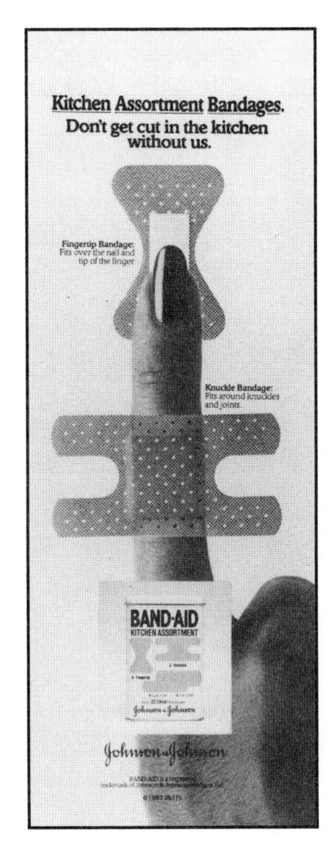

Segmentation is desirable for many products.

Disadvantages of Segmentation

Like any other strategy, market segmentation has its drawbacks. It leads management to a position where it directs the marketing effort to only a portion of the population and neglects other portions. A radio station that broadcasts rock music and attempts to appeal to teenagers, for instance, will not be effective in reaching the 40-and-older group. Similarly, My Child's Destiny does not appeal to parents with limited incomes who are highly price-conscious.

A second disadvantage of market segmentation is that it may increase the company's costs. A firm that pursues two or more segments normally has to develop and offer two or more different marketing mixes. If the company appeals to two different segments, for instance, it may have to design two individual products or services, physical distribution systems, channels of distribution, price structures, advertising programs, personal selling programs, and sales promotion programs.

Economies of scale can result when a firm produces and markets large numbers of units, since the cost per unit is less than if output is small. However, the duplications mentioned above can prevent the firm from realizing these economies.

Major Segmentation Decisions

Two major decisions confront managers in connection with segmentation.

1. Management must determine whether or not the company should identify segments in the market and target certain ones.
2. If management decides to target certain segments in the market, it must then determine how it should structure the marketing mix.

In practical applications, managers cannot readily separate these two decisions; rather they undertake both simultaneously.

Requisites for Segmentation

The firm must fulfill four conditions in order to implement a profitable segmentation program:

1. There must be subgroups of potential customers whose anticipated reactions to marketing efforts are similar but different from those in other subgroups.
2. The subgroups must be reachable through either promotion media or channels of distribution.
3. The marketer should be able to acquire information that determines the subgroup to which each potential customer belongs.
4. Segmentation must provide an adequate profit return.[5]

MARKETING BRIEF
Selling High-Quality Clothing to Professional Women

Carson Pirie Scott & Co. operates Corporate Level, a high-quality clothing store-within-a-store in downtown Chicago. It used to be a dingy basement where shoppers rummaged through piles of bargain-priced clothing, but in 1985 management transformed the 40,000 square foot room into a colorful mirrored space resembling an exclusive shop in Beverly Hills.

The objective of the store is to capture the cream of the shopping masses: professional women who have departed from department stores in search of high-quality products and services.

What makes Corporate Level different is that almost everything that a customer wants is in one place. Designer outfits are steps away from shoes and accessories. A woman can have her shoes repaired and her hair styled, drop off dry cleaning, and eat a meal. For $50 annually she gets extra services, such as check cashing and the assistance of a fashion consultant.

Corporate Level opens two hours earlier and closes two hours later than the rest of the store. It even has a private entrance with a doorman.

The operation is very successful. Sales per square foot are running about 40 percent higher than in the rest of the store. Also, Corporate Level has provided the store with an image boost. It has attracted numerous consumers who once patronized other Chicago stores.

SOURCE: Adapted from "One-Stop Shopping for the Woman on the Go," *Business Week*, March 18, 1985: 116.

If all potential customers will react the same, there is no point in designing a unique marketing mix for each one. In the computer field, for example, departments of large corporations react differently than do small businesses, so they are separate segments.[6]

For successful segmentation, management must reach target customers through either promotion media or channels of distribution that have direct customer contact. For instance, management can contact children through Saturday morning television. Or they may elect to use distribution channels, as when producers of clothing for petite women sell dresses through special small-size stores. If promotion media or channels cannot be used to reach a segment, there is little point in choosing it as a target market.

A prerequisite to segmentation is that management is able to identify the subgroup to which each target customer belongs. The identification of subgroups is not difficult when they are easily located, as when the members of one group reside in a particular city and the members of a second group live in another city. Problems arise in the identification process, however, when the firm employs variables such as behavioral characteristics of potential buyers as a basis for developing subgroups.

Some brewers, such as Olympia and Anheuser-Busch, attempt to appeal to subgroups based upon consumer attitudes toward the intoxicating effect of beer. They have introduced low-alcohol brews (Olympia Gold and LA Beer) to appeal to such consumers.

In order to plan and implement a market segmentation program for low-alcohol beer, management must be able to isolate those segments that might want to purchase this product and to tabulate the numbers in these segments. This is a difficult process, however. It may require a large-scale research project, one which identifies the attitudes of consumers toward alcohol content in beer and also isolates the various segments to which the consumers belong.

A fourth requisite for segmentation is that it yields a higher level of profits than is the case without segmentation. To some degree, management can forecast anticipated profitability by discovering the number and the volume of purchases that potential buyers in each segment make. If, for instance, a particular subgroup has only a moderate number of small buyers, a marketing mix designed specifically for that group may not be justified.

The organization must make a *tradeoff* between satisfying diverse market segment needs and controlling its costs. On the one hand, catering to the specific needs of a market segment increases customer satisfaction and willingness to buy. On the other hand, management must weigh the costs associated with designing a separate marketing mix for each segment. At one extreme, if the firm constructed a unique product for each customer, substantial satisfaction would materialize. For most firms, however, this would be a prohibitively costly strategy.

If potential customer needs are largely homogeneous, management should pursue only one or a few segments. Should there be more than one cluster of needs, then the number of clusters is important and so is the magnitude of potential demand within each segment. A particular grouping of needs is only worth considering as a separate segment if it has a large enough sales potential to cover the costs, plus a profit, for any specialized efforts designed for that segment.

The company's cost situation is also critical. Some small, highly flexible companies have low cost structures that enable them to service small segments. For example, a firm located in El Paso, Texas profitably produces two-way radio systems for small building contractors. The company's success is due to its low overhead and minimal investment, which enables it to keep prices lower than those of most other two-way radio producers. The small segment that this company serves is not large enough to attract the interest of large companies catering to mass markets.

Segmentation of two or more groups of customers is generally more expensive than when the firm targets only one group, because it must design a different marketing mix for each segment. This leads to duplication of efforts and an inability to take advantage of economies of scale. In recent years, inflationary pressures have forced some firms to decrease the number of segments served in order to reduce expenses.

Evaluating the expected profitability of segmentation involves estimating both the resulting volume potentials and the related costs. This is illustrated in the hypothetical example of Tricon Photomatics Corp., which manufactures and markets high-quality photocopying machines to institutional buyers under a nonsegmentation strategy. Troubled by company sales lagging behind others in the industry, Mr. Jason Cooke, Tricon's marketing manager, studied whether the company should adopt a segmentation strategy rather than treat the selected target as a common group.

The following list of benefits are generally used by all photocopier customers in evaluating which brand to buy: quality of reproduction (clarity), speed of reproduction, capacity (ability to produce many copies), operating costs, purchase price, durability (long life), and ease of operation.

Two segments within Tricon's target differed on the basis of benefits sought. Businesses and defense agencies desire quality, speed, capacity, and durability. In contrast, state and local governmental agencies and nonprofit organizations typically seek low operating costs, low initial price, and ease of operation.

If segmentation on the basis of benefits sought were followed, therefore, the marketing strategies would be as follows. One strategy would be directed at businesses and defense agencies: Tricon would offer three machines that produced high-quality copies at a fast rate. The machines would be very durable and their prices would be roughly 10 percent higher than industry averages to cover the added costs.

A second strategy would be directed at state and local governmental agencies and nonprofit organizations: The company would alter three existing models to permit selling them at a competitive price and they would be capable of performing at a low operating cost.

Since the membership of each subgroup is not difficult to establish and each can be reached through a separate marketing effort, Mr. Cooke decided to measure the expected profitability. Several governmental publications were of value in estimating the number of the organizations within each of the two segments, such as the *Census of Manufacturers*, *Census of Business*, and the *Census of Governments*. These indicated that 290,000 business and defense organizations were of sufficient size to be considered as potential customers. The other segment was comprised of 173,000 state and local government agencies and nonprofit organizations large enough to warrant buying high-quality copiers.

The next task was to forecast the sales in each of the segments under the two strategies (forecasting techniques are covered in Chapter 8). Segmentation was estimated to yield sales of $36.2 million versus a sales forecast of $31.2 million under the current strategy, or a $5 million increase. Regarding costs, Tricon's chief cost accountant estimated that the expected marketing, production, administrative, and other expenses resulting from segmentation would run $3.9 million more than the present strategy, meaning a $1.1 million ($5.0–$3.9) additional profit.

Accordingly, Cooke's recommendation to senior management was for Tricon to develop the related products and to engage in the segmentation strategy—a strategy which reversed Tricon's sales dilemma. In reality, the analytical techniques used may be quite complex—forecasting, analysis, and calculating the present value of future cash flows. Nonetheless, the principles are the same. Segmentation makes sense when the expected profitability from the action warrants such a decision.

Characteristics Used for Market Segmentation

Marketers employ a variety of variables or bases for segmenting markets. Whether or not they utilize a particular variable depends upon its success in meaningfully discriminating one group of targeted buyers from others. If each resulting group has different needs and motivations, then such a variable is *relevant*. Consider Figure 3.2, which illustrates a segmentation of the housing market. The figure depicts only three variables for simplicity; however, management should consider all variables reflecting different customer needs, purchasing behavior, or some other characteristic having a strong effect on demand. The major segmentation characteristics include the following:

1. Buyer and product type
2. Demographic characteristics
3. Geographic location
4. Lifestyle differences
5. Behavioral characteristics (buyer benefits, volume, and marketing attributes)

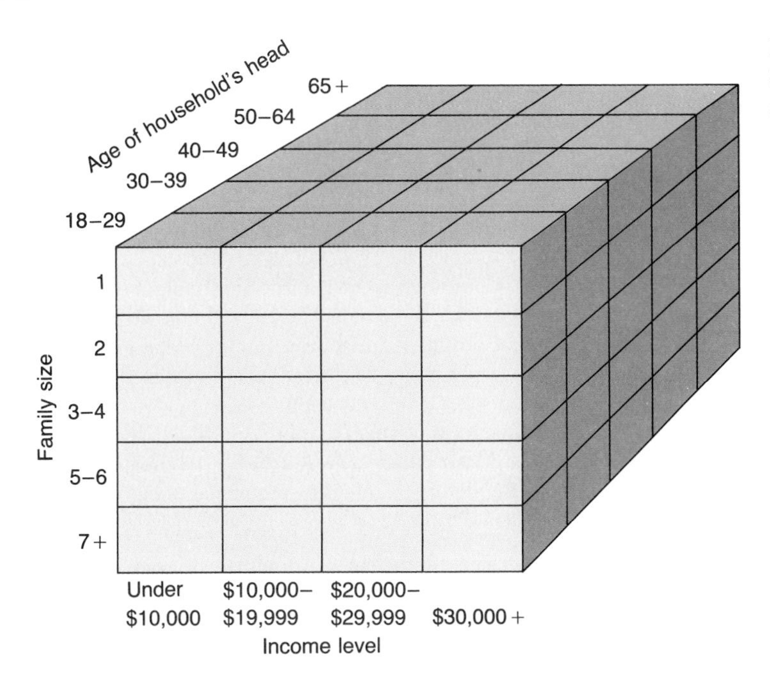

Figure 3.2
Segmentation of the Housing Market by Three Demographic Variables

Buyer and Product Type Characteristics

The needs and motivations of broad types of buyers vary. Further, both the buying expectations and the buying efforts displayed in each category depend upon the type of product being considered. Table 3.1 lists the broad consumer and product classifications generally used by marketers.

These segmenting variables are useful for products that many types of purchasers acquire. Consider personal computers, for example. To most consumers, PCs are shopping goods, meaning that price, the seller's reputation, the machine's size, speed, available programs, and compatibility with other machines are among the important attributes. The average student will compare several PCs on these dimensions, rather than purchasing the first one.

Business and governmental buyers, however, purchase most PCs primarily for office use. Most office PCs function as accessories, frequently requiring semicustom features to meet specialized needs (memory capacity, special characters, and the capability to connect with communications devices). Consequently, a firm may need a different marketing mix to penetrate each segment. Students and office users respond favorably to different product varieties, prices, advertising and personal selling strategies, and distribution arrangements.

Demographic Characteristics

Demographic characteristics Objective and measurable characteristics of human populations, such as age, sex, race, and so forth.

The field of demography deals with objectively measurable characteristics of human populations. Market segmentation by **demographic characteristics** utilizes demographic data to subdivide the market. Some examples of demographic factors are age,

Table 3.1 Types of Final Buyers and Products

Each major category represents a type of buyer, while each subcategory represents a breakdown in types of products.

A. Consumer buyers—consumers ultimately use the product. These are classified by the way consumers purchase or use the item.
   1. Convenience goods. Consumers spend little effort on buying and seek ease and speed in purchasing. Examples are cigarettes, gum, and candy.
   2. Shopping goods. Consumers spend considerable effort in comparing the price and quality of various offerings. These include TV sets and refrigerators.
   3. Specialty goods. Consumers insist on a specific brand and are willing to expend considerable effort to obtain it. Examples include Rolls Royce automobiles and Curtis Mathes television sets.
   4. Services. The product is intangible, such as legal advice and dry cleaning.
   5. Unsought goods. Most consumers will not seek out the product and must be convinced to purchase it through high-intensity promotion methods. These goods include life insurance and dental care.

B. Industrial buyers—buyers ultimately use products for production. These are classified by how industrial buyers use the good or service.
   1. Installations. Major capital items. Examples are buildings and blast furnaces.
   2. Accessory equipment. Capital items of lower cost, such as presses and lathes.
   3. Raw materials. Natural and farm products such as wheat and iron ore.
   4. Components. Goods that are more fully processed than raw materials. Examples include integrated circuits and electric motors.
   5. Supplies. Items not part of the final product but required for maintenance, repair, and operations, such as lubricants and cleaning supplies.
   6. Services. Performance that buyers purchase.

C. Government buyers—the same categories as industrial goods.

CONCEPT SUMMARY

Characteristics Used for Market Segmentation

Characteristic	Nature of Characteristic
Buyer and Product Type	Needs and motivations of buyers and types of products
Demographic	Objectively measurable characteristics of human populations
Geographic	Location of potential buyers
Lifestyle	Psychographic characteristics (attitudes, interests, opinions, activities)
Buyer Behavior:	Conduct of buyers
Benefits	Benefits buyers seek
Volume	Extent to which individuals use the product
Marketing attributes	Attraction to similar elements of the marketing mix

Karastan segments on the basis of home ownership.

income, occupation, education, family size, sex, nationality, social class, and race. For companies who sell industrial goods, some demographic characteristics are customer type, customer size, and customer location.

Universities, governmental agencies, trade associations, foundations, and other organizations acquire and publish considerable amounts of demographic data. Other information exists in internal organization records. If demographic information is not readily available, managers can produce it through marketing research projects. In most instances, researchers can obtain this data more readily than they can other types of segmentation information.

The examples of demographic segmentation are numerous. Helena Rubenstein successfully launched a line of cosmetics called Madame Rubenstein to meet the special needs of women over age 50. The publishers of *Working Woman* aim at female executives. Metaphor Computer Systems, Inc. specializes in custom-designed computerized work stations for particular sizes of companies.[7] Eastman Kodak orients its two major office automation systems to *Fortune 1500* companies.[8]

Demographic segmentation has proven to be valuable to numerous organizations. Research suggests that demographic variables are useful in explaining what subgroups are likely to purchase a particular product or service and which are not. According to one source, demographics are easily obtained and inexpensive to use, are a way to better understand consumers and markets, and can help marketers formulate market strategies.[9]

Overall, marketers are not completely satisfied with the results of demographic segmentation. Some firms have discovered that demographic data do not adequately cluster the market into subgroups with similar reactions to marketing efforts. Using geographical variables may be useful in this regard.

Geographic Characteristics

Management may decide to segment the market by geographic region. This requires subdividing the market into geographic areas and orienting the marketing mix to those potential buyers located in each area.

Geographic segmentation
Subdividing the market into geographic areas and orienting a marketing mix to those potential buyers located in each area.

The full potential for **geographic segmentation** is most obvious for those companies that market their offerings in two or more different countries with dissimilar cultures. Some toothpaste manufacturers, for instance, sell a product that is effective in brightening teeth in some countries. In other nations a different product is made available because local consumers actually value discolored teeth.

Within the market that it serves, the company may employ different marketing mixes for different regions. This reflects such variables as local intensity of competition and consumer preferences. Hence, management may find that competition is quite intense in some states, necessitating low prices and extensive market coverage on the part of sales representatives. It may find in other states that competition is limited, permitting higher prices and less extensive personal selling.

There are a number of marketers who employ the U.S. Postal Service's ZIP codes for market segmentation purposes. Those individuals and families who share the same ZIP code live in close geographic proximity and frequently have relatively similar occupations, social classes, incomes, and values. This being the case, they are good potential market segments.

There is a considerable volume of ZIP code information available. These codes identify more than 35,000 different geographic areas. Further, various governmental agencies collect data about consumers in different ZIP categories, such as occupation, age, education, race, and other variables. A number of marketing research companies also furnish breakdowns of consumer characteristics and behavior by ZIP code variables.

Segmentation by ZIP code has a number of advantages, often uncovering subgroups that react similarly to marketing efforts. The codes furnish data that allows the marketer to determine the subgroup to which each target customer belongs. Finally, marketers can approach the subgroups through unique marketing mixes made possible by direct mail advertising, by choosing other media that cover the desired segments, and by using retailers located near the desired segments.

Lifestyle Characteristics

Lifestyle segmentation
Segmentation by psychological and sociological differences in the patterns of a person's way of life (also called psychographic segmentation).

Lifestyle (or psychographic) **segmentation** involves utilizing subgroups that share certain psychological characteristics such as consumer attitudes, opinions, behavior, interests, activities, or a combination of these. Some examples of characteristics that marketers often employ are given below.

1. Activities: work, social activities, hobbies, entertainment, vacation, shopping.
2. Interests: job, family, community, home, fashion, food.
3. Opinions: personal, social issues, business, politics, products, the future.

Those firms employing lifestyle segmentation seek subgroups with common attitudes, interests, opinions, or behavioral characteristics. Then they are in a position to construct a marketing mix to meet the needs of each subgroup. Frequently, marketers discover that some subgroups are heavy users of the product or service, whereas other subgroups are light or average users. For Scotch whiskey, for instance, heavy users

MARKETING BRIEF
Upscale Pasta

Priced from $1.29 to $1.49 for a 10-oz. box (about 60¢ above standard spaghetti brands) Prince Co. recently announced the introduction of President's Silver Award gourmet pasta. The effort is seen as an attempt to create a niche in the increasingly segmented $1 billion dry pasta market. The timing is right for this move, according to industry analysts. The average American now eats 10.8 lbs. of pasta per year, up 60 percent from 1977.

Views toward pasta have changed dramatically, according to Tina Freeman, marketing director for the Lowell, Massachusetts-based Prince. "There is a definite trend toward pasta among the trendy, and in particular among the nation's best restaurants to treat pasta as a gourmet food," she said. This follows the trend away from heavy consumption of red meats and shows consumer interest in research indicating that pasta is a healthy food to eat. The product is aimed toward the upscale market, according to company officials, although "you don't have to mortgage your BMW to buy it," according to Freeman.

It is interesting to note that in the 1960s, Prince's ads urged the average American family to make Wednesday "Prince spaghetti day." Now the emphasis is on the upscale market segment due to changes in the market around the nation. The new brand is made of different ingredients than the standard brands of pasta, and will come in six varieties ranging from angel hair to spinach fettuccini.

SOURCE: Adapted from Patricia Winters, "Prince Tries Pasta for Gourmet Market," *Advertising Age*, February 24, 1986: 80.

tend to be urban businesspeople, active achievers, older urban sophisticates, and pleasure-seekers. As illustrated in the accompanying Marketing Brief, the Prince Co. recently decided to use a market segmentation strategy in the pasta market to reach consumers with affluent, "upscale" lifestyles.

Segmentation according to lifestyle does have an edge over demographic and geographic segmentation, in some instances. The lifestyle method focuses on those with common patterns of behavior, inducing the marketer to build a consumer-oriented program. Demographic and geographic segmentation do not necessarily yield a marketing mix aimed at those with common desires or common reactions to marketing efforts. Management of a department store, for instance, could aim the marketing mix to affluent consumers. The strategy could involve stocking expensive merchandise, employing chic salesclerks, featuring jet-set individuals in store advertisements, and playing light classics over the audio system. These devices might appeal to some affluent consumers, but not to others. In fact, some of the affluent reject status appeals and might not be attracted to the department store.

The store might avoid this problem through a lifestyle strategy. Management could aim the department store marketing mix at individuals with a particular self-image, such as "upward bound urban professional," rather than at a particular demographic or geographic group.

Of course, lifestyle segmentation has its drawbacks. Sometimes it is difficult to obtain information enabling the marketer to determine the subgroup to which each target customer belongs. Management requires research to ascertain how many customers are members of each lifestyle subgroup. In contrast, they can find out demographic and geographic characteristics very easily.

BMW is one company that segments on the basis of benefits.

Buyer Behavior Characteristics

There are several characteristics relating to the conduct of potential buyers. This section on buyer behavior covers the major segmentation methods that employ these characteristics.

Segmentation by Benefits Marketers can subdivide potential buyers by assigning them to subgroups comprised of those who want particular benefits from the product or service in question. Some individuals, for instance, buy toothpaste to brighten their teeth. Others, however, purchase the product to prevent decay, because of its low price, or because it has a pleasant flavor.

Benefit segmentation
Segmentation based upon the types of benefits sought from a product.

Benefit segmentation makes considerable sense, because the benefits are the major reason why individuals purchase the product. It seems logical that those who desire similar benefits would respond in a similar manner to a particular marketing program. Other methods of segmentation do not necessarily have this advantage.

The beverage industry has witnessed considerable benefit segmentation. Diet Pepsi and other diet drinks provide a low-calorie beverage to those who are weight-conscious. Fruit drinks furnish a natural, nonchemical thirst quencher for those who are concerned about good health. Noncarbonated drinks promise a means of avoiding that "too-full" sensation.

Benefit segmentation requires undertaking research to reveal the benefits that customers desire. Researchers construct segments by assigning persons who have the same sets of desired benefits to common subgroups.[10] Then, researchers are able to determine the demographic, geographic, or lifestyle characteristics of each. An example of benefit segmentation is the Tricon case presented earlier in this chapter.

Segmentation by Volume In the case of **volume segmentation,** marketers group customers according to the extent to which they use the product in question. During a typical time period, some potential buyers use the product a great deal, others frequently, others sparingly, and still others not at all. This being the case, marketers can create groups based upon the amount of use; for example, heavy users, average users, light users, and nonusers. In a segmentation study for professional basketball, the categories included nonattenders, low attenders, and high attenders, based upon the frequency of games viewed.[11] After the membership of the usage groups has been ascertained, the demographic, geographic, and/or lifestyle characteristics of each can be compiled and a search begun for differences in these characteristics between user groups.

Volume segmentation
Segmentation according to the extent to which customers use a particular product.

The data required for volume segmentation may come from surveys, company records, and other sources. Frequently, managers obtain it from consumer panels—groups of consumers assumed to be typical of the general population at large, who agree to record their purchases and allied information in booklets called diaries. Periodically the panelists submit the diary pages to the panel administrators. Oftentimes the panel administrators are independent marketing research companies who sell the information they acquire to marketers. For purposes of volume segmentation, the records of the products and the brands are of value. A breakdown of the demographic, geographic, and lifestyle information by user groups provides a profile of the members of each group.

Segmentation by Marketing Attribute In the case of **segmentation by marketing attribute,** management places potential buyers into subgroups comprised of those individuals who are attracted by the same element of the marketing mix. Potential buyers in some subgroups judge goods and services according to the level of their price, while those in other subgroups evaluate offerings according to their perceived quality. Still others purchase because a sales representative or an advertisement persuaded them or because of some other marketing mix element.

Segmentation by marketing attribute
Placing buyers into groups based on who is attracted by the same element of a marketing mix.

This segmentation technique involves research to indicate the most influential elements of the marketing mix in inducing potential buyers to purchase the offering. The marketer assigns to the same segment those potential buyers who are influenced by common elements of the marketing mix. Like other methods, it requires estimates of the expected profitability of aiming the company's efforts at one or more of these segments.

A bakery might discover that several marketing mix elements could be useful in forming segments. For instance, elements could include ingredients of the product, price, and advertising. The bakery could produce a bread with all natural ingredients or one that is low in calories for a segment based upon the ingredients element, it could offer an inexpensive product to satisfy price-conscious buyers, and make use of image-building advertising to appeal to those who find advertising persuasive.

Royal Caribbean segments on the basis of attributes.

Selected Examples

Canon Inc. The Canon Company is one of the largest producers of copiers in the world, despite the fact that it was unknown in this industry until the 1970s. This firm specializes in making products for small copier users. Before it introduced its personal copier in 1982, existing machines were too expensive, too big, and subject to too many breakdowns to satisfy small customers. However, Canon copiers are inexpensive and easy to use—ideal for the personal copying market.

Bankamerica. In 1985 BankAmerica restructured its marketing staff into three teams, each focusing on a particular market segment: individual customer accounts, personalized service for customers with more sophisticated needs, and small business customers. Previously the firm served all three with one large 220-person marketing staff operation but failed to adequately serve their needs, leading to a decision to create the new structure.

True Delight. L'eggs Corporation's True Delight pantyhose are designed specifically for the needs of larger women. They fit properly in the waist, hips, thighs, and calves. The firm sells this product through direct mail to a carefully developed list of heavy women. Advertisements appear in magazines and depict attractive larger women who experience difficulty finding comfortable pantyhose.

G.U.M. The Butler Company produces the G.U.M. 411 toothbrush, which it has designed to prevent periodontitis and help cure those afflicted with this gum disease that affects millions of young and old people and strikes three out of every four adults over age 35. Research at the University of Michigan indicates that this toothbrush can effectively reduce the incidence of the disease. The product receives good word-of-mouth publicity from dentists and hygienists. It is widely available in supermarkets and drug stores and is extensively advertised.

Chapter Summary

This chapter has dealt with market segmentation, an important competitive weapon in management's marketing decision-making arsenal. Market segmentation is a decision process whereby management identifies segments within an overall market, where each has unique needs relative to the other segments.

There are several major advantages to this process, especially when the market is highly competitive. The principal benefit is that segmentation enables a company to focus especially well on serving the needs of at least one group of customers, as opposed to trying to appeal to everyone. There are disadvantages to be considered, however, particularly the fact that segmentation often involves neglecting a part of the market and that it can add to costs.

Several practical issues concerning segmentation must be considered, beginning with whether or not to segment in the first place. Once the decision to segment is made, management must consider the practicality of the variables used in the process. Buyer and product type, demographic, geographic, lifestyle, and other behavioral characteristics are the most useful variables to use.

The examples cited in this chapter illustrate how the concept can be useful to managers in increasing the effectiveness of their marketing decisions.

Questions

1. Provide, in your own words, a definition of market segmentation.
2. Give three examples of market segmentation, other than those appearing in this chapter. How effective have these strategies been, in your opinion?
3. In what ways do the following practice market segmentation:
   a. The Chrysler Corporation
   b. Holiday Inns, Inc.
   c. IBM
   d. A typical radio station
4. What are the major advantages of market segmentation?
5. What are the major disadvantages of market segmentation?
6. In what ways can market segmentation increase a firm's costs?
7. How do the following practice market segmentation:
   a. A hospital in your college or home community
   b. The Christian Children's Fund
   c. Your college or university
   d. The Salvation Army
8. How can marketers develop subgroups for the purpose of market segmentation?
9. How might you develop subgroups for market segmentation, in the case of:
   a. Lipton Onion Soup Mix
   b. Hellmann's Mayonnaise
   c. Tab
   d. Winchester 30–06 rifles
   e. Maybelline Long-Wearing Lipstick
10. How can marketers estimate the profitability of segmentation?
11. What is geographic segmentation? Provide an example of this strategy.
12. Would you recommend demographic segmentation for Burger King? Why or why not? If yes, what demographic variables would you recommend?
13. What is lifestyle segmentation? Why do some marketers find it superior to demographic and geographic segmentation?
14. Provide an example of benefit segmentation. Do you believe that this is a profitable strategy? Why or why not?
15. Define volume segmentation. Why would marketers practice it?
16. What is marketing attribute segmentation? Would it be applicable, in your opinion, for:
   a. Book of the Month Club
   b. Band Aids
   c. National Van Lines
   d. The American Cancer Society
   e. St. Joseph Children's Aspirin

Part Two

The Firm's Environment

Chapter 4

An Overview of the Firm's External Environment

Objectives

After completing this chapter, you should be able to demonstrate a knowledge of:

- The impact of competitive conditions
- The effect of political variables
- What technological considerations mean to decision makers
- The effect of economic factors
- How specific market factors affect the decision-making process

MARKETING SUCCESS

Governmental Assistance When Times Were Tough

A new and improved relationship between government, management, and labor was at the heart of the resurgence of the Chrysler Corporation in the early 1980s, according to Leo Arthur Kelmenson, president of a major investment trust company. For the first time, the adversary relationship that usually exists between unions and management and between management and Washington was thrown out.

The Chrysler experience provides an example of solving a major problem with the U.S. economy, according to Kelmenson. Americans must learn to sublimate individuality enough to allow teamwork to come into play. The Japanese have known for a long time that teamwork produces success.

When Lee Iacocca joined Chrysler in 1978, its future was uncertain. The firm's costs were running to $4 million per hour and its cash position was very weak. Matters became worse when oil became scarce, interest rates escalated, GNP growth slowed, and new car sales began to fade. In the meantime, the imports' share of the U.S. auto market went from 18 percent to 30 percent in four months.

This untenable situation called for an almost total reorganization and restaffing of the marketing department and all departments dealing with internal and external communications. Chrysler acquired loan guarantees from the federal government and designed ad campaigns with very straightforward messages so that they would appeal to government officials and the financial community in addition to car buyers. Iacocca himself appeared in commercials, first announcing the "New Chrysler Corporation" and later describing new warranty policies.

Government assistance and Chrysler's marketing actions transformed the firm from a failure to a success. Profits, share of markets, and sales jumped to levels far exceeding the expectations of both management and Congress.

SOURCE: Adapted from "Teamwork Spurs Resurgence of Chrysler," *The Marketing News* 17, no. 13 (June 24, 1983): 1, 16.

Introduction

The Chrysler Corporation example is but one of many showing that management cannot make effective marketing mix decisions if it restricts its attention to the company and ignores the outside variables making up the firm's environment. Many phenomena (the actions of rivals, interest rates, and consumer values) are beyond management's control yet they strongly influence the firm's opportunities. As this chapter demonstrates, effective decision making takes both present and anticipated future uncontrollable variables into account when developing marketing strategy. The firm can achieve success only by shaping its efforts so that they are compatible with external environment demands. This chapter considers the nature of this environment and its component variables.

The External Environment Determines Opportunity

Essentially, the firm's mission and its external environment determine the potential opportunities available for exploitation. As Figure 4.1 illustrates, there are five categories of environmental variables:

1. **Competitive conditions**—variables related to the intensity and nature of rivals' strategies and tactics. Examples of these variables are the number of competitors, their goals, their strengths and weaknesses, and their market positions.
2. Political variables—those created by actions of governmental authorities. Examples are the nature of government regulations, loan guarantees and other financial assistance programs, policies adopted with regard to imports from abroad, and steps taken to improve public attitudes toward business.
3. **Technological considerations**—variables related to scientific advancements in providing goods and services to society. Examples are industrial robots for assembly plants, computer technology, communications by satellite, and lightweight steel alloys.
4. **Economic factors**—variables related to the material welfare of society such as interest rates, employment levels, amounts of personal savings, and availability of borrowed capital.
5. **Specific market factors**—the characteristics of a particular market related to the unique needs, buying habits, and motivations of its members.

Competitive conditions
Variables related to the intensity and nature of rivals' strategies and tactics (also called *competitor actions*).

Technological considerations
Scientific advancements and their effects on markets.

Economic factors
Variables related to the material welfare of society.

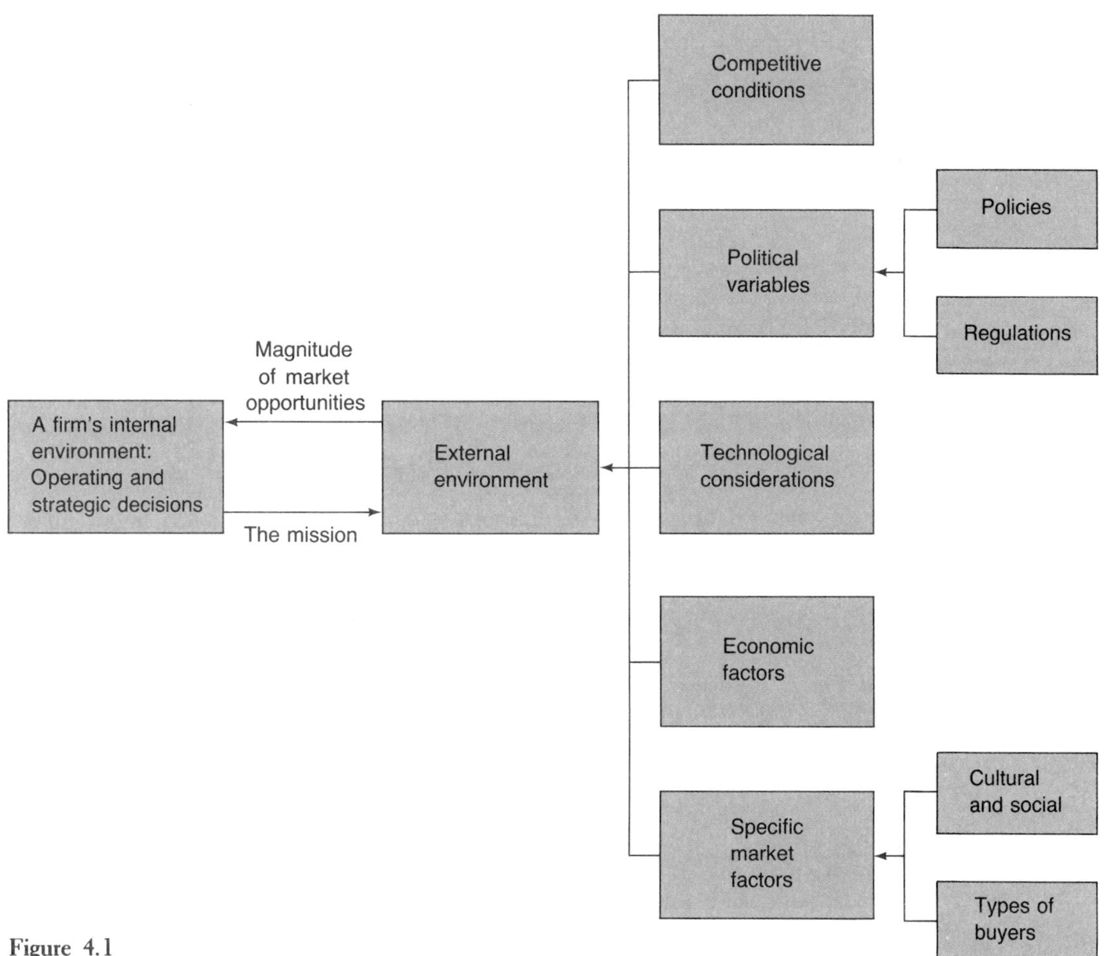

Figure 4.1
The External Environment as a Determinant of Potential Opportunities

Specific market factors
Unique characteristics relating to a particular market.

To a large extent, the environment determines the size and nature of a firm's potential opportunities. Logically, then, success in the marketplace depends upon management's ability to recognize opportunities and to position the firm's offerings to best take advantage of them. Hence understanding the environment is a prerequisite to effective marketing decision making.

This chapter focuses on competitive conditions, political variables, technological considerations, and economic factors. The remaining chapters in this section detail specific environmental factors relevant to consumer, industrial, and government markets.

Competitive Conditions

Disney World has caused a boom to central Florida.

It is vital that expected competitor actions be considered when developing a marketing strategy. To illustrate, Miami Beach's "Gold Coast," once heralded as this country's premier vacation spa, has lost much of its glitter largely due to the success of Disney World.[1] Located in Florida's central region city of Orlando, about 200 miles north of Miami, Disney World has become one of the nation's newest and most popular tourist meccas.

Besides Disney World, the region (sometimes called the "Golden Girdle") contains such popular attractions as Busch Gardens, the Kennedy Space Center, Sea World, and Circus World. To Miami, the Golden Girdle is proving to be a Pied Piper—luring winter-weary northerners and their cash away from Miami. Declining tourism in southern Florida placed some of the most prestigious hotels like the 1,200-room Fontainbleu, along with the smaller Monte Carlo and the Allison, into receivership. In short, central Florida's booming tourism industry effectively dislodged Miami Beach from its once-enviable market niche.

Of course, many factors contributed to Miami's decline, including aging tourist facilities and a reputation for social unrest. But a major cause was the failure of the Miami Beach Tourist Development Authority (an association of businesses catering to tourists) and other city planners to realize the competitive threat of the Golden Girdle soon enough.

In all probability, Miami's business leaders could have taken action to effectively slow or stop mid-Florida's threat. For instance, they could have encouraged the development of new tourist-oriented attractions aimed at vacationers and conventions. Perhaps they could have persuaded the Disney company to build its facilities near Miami, even if tax breaks and other financial incentives would have been necessary to swing the deal. But the Miami business leaders did not take these actions, leaving a significant and growing market segment for the Golden Girdle to penetrate.

Competition has a major role in affecting the decision making and fortunes of many companies. To illustrate:

- Producers of personal computers, such as IBM, have been forced into aggressive price competition by the rigorous pricing strategies of firms such as Apple and Tandy.
- Coca-Cola was successful in replacing Dr. Pepper with Cherry Coke in Hardees restaurants as a result of a well-designed personal selling program.
- Pride Air, a full-service transcontinental airline, was launched in 1985. It does not serve popular hub cities such as Dallas, long dominated by major carriers that are caught up in fare wars. Instead, it serves cities such as Sacramento and Jacksonville, where competition is much less intense.

- AT&T designed its Merlin Communication System for small businesses—a segment that management believed was neglected by other firms. The system allows conference calling, speed dialing, intercom service, and programming for individual phones—all at a price well below that for large business phone systems.
- Quiet World analgesic/sleeping aid is both a pain killer and a relaxant. It was designed when research disclosed that many consumers were dissatisfied with currently-sold products because they provided one but not both of these benefits.
- The Travelers Insurance Company developed a specific life insurance policy for the 7.7 million women who are sole heads of households. It did this because no other company was serving this segment.
- Bruce Seat Lift chairs are recliners that allow physically impaired persons to stand and sit down without pain. These seats are very popular because they perform very well and are inexpensive in relation to the offerings of competitors.

Competitor actions are key environmental forces that must be taken into account for effective strategy development. The status and actions of rivals is a key input into marketing decision making.

Political Variables

Governmental actions can have a large impact on the marketing opportunities facing all organizations. Figure 4.2 depicts the U.S. political/economic system, major ways that government bodies exert their influence, and the relational flows between the various entities. This section considers some of the major effects on marketing decision making.

Political actions are like coins: each has two sides. While each government decision may serve to constrain some marketing activities, it also creates opportunities for others. Several years ago, for instance, the U.S. Food and Drug Administration banned the sale of swordfish meat because of its high mercury content. While the ban played havoc with those fleets unable to switch their operations to other fish, it generated opportunities for fishers of salmon, tuna, and other species. Both the overall policies of government and specific legislative acts affect market opportunities.

Government Policies

Government policies have many far-reaching implications for marketing managers. This section concentrates on several of these areas.

Overall Attitudes toward Business One of the most important of the political variables is government's and society's overall attitude toward business. In general, if both are reasonably satisfied with the performance of the business sector, the resulting favorable **business climate** tends to offer a large number of marketing opportunities. On the other hand, if there is public displeasure, businesses face the threat of punitive or restrictive legislation and regulation.

Business climate
A governmental unit's overall attitude toward business.

The overall U.S. business climate during the past decade can best be described as mixed.[2] Legislators have passed a vast number of bills deepening government's control over business activity. One need only review recent issues of the *Wall Street Journal*, *Fortune*, or *Business Week* to understand the extent of this legislative involvement.[3]

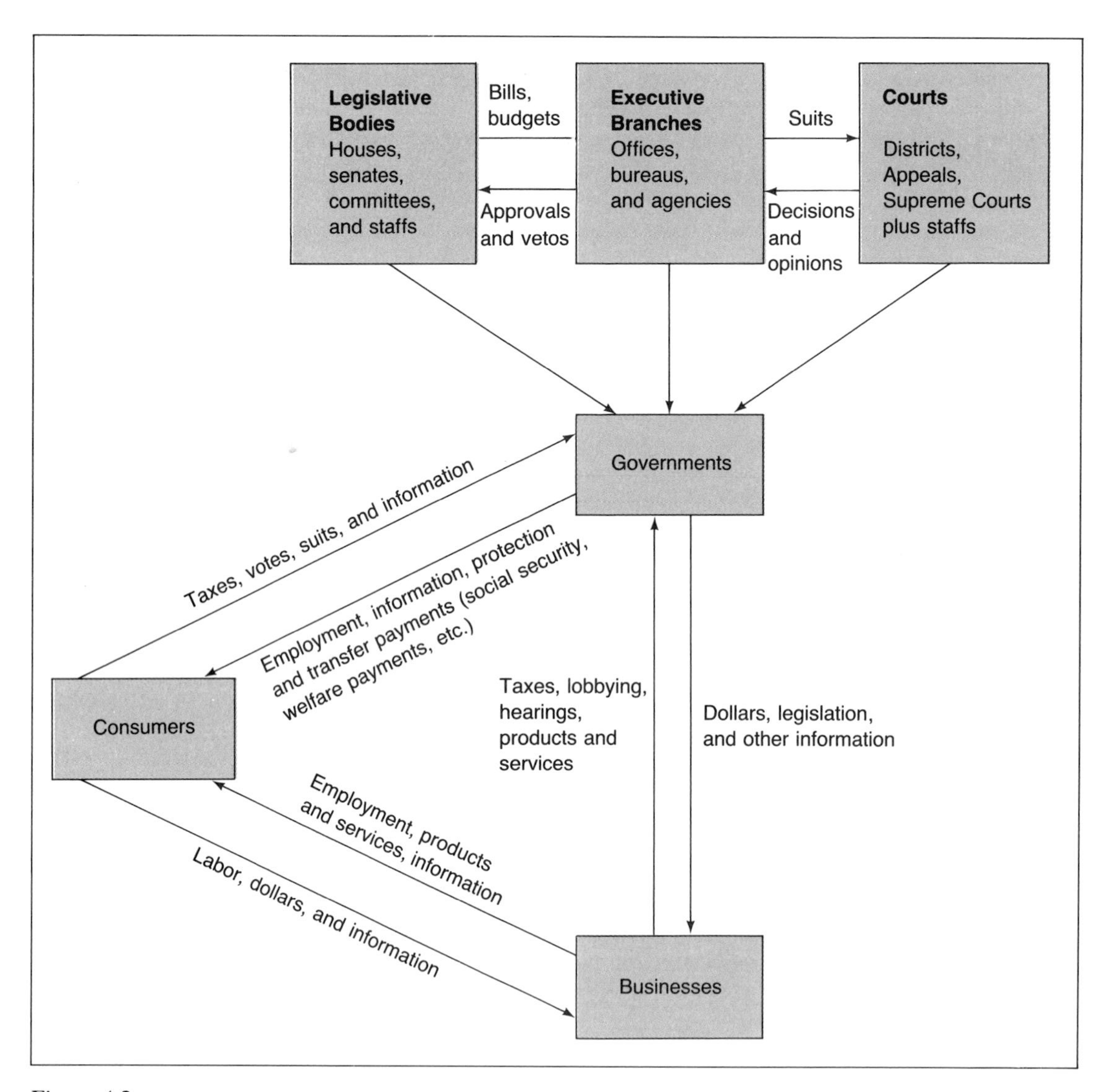

Figure 4.2
An Overview of the U.S. Political/ Economic System

At the same time, the federal government has deregulated some industries that it once closely controlled.[4] Still, the overall pattern is one of greater governmental control.

There are several reasons for this trend. First, a small number of businesses have engaged in unethical and shoddy practices. Illegal political campaign contributions, misleading ads, unsafe products, and hidden or difficult-to-understand clauses in warranties are but a few examples that have raised the ire of both government and consumers alike.

Second, production- and sales-oriented managers often generate ill feelings among customers by using high-pressure selling techniques. Afterward, buyers press their elected representatives to pass legislation to police business. Many states and the federal government, for instance, have passed legislation that grants consumers the right to

The actions of legislative bodies can greatly affect market opportunities.

cancel certain buying contracts from door-to-door salespeople due to frequent complaints about high-pressure tactics.

Third, some market segments are simply too small for marketers to serve profitably. For example, there is a tremendous unfilled need for emergency health services in rural areas, but these segments are relatively small and lack enough buying power to enable medical businesses to serve them profitably. The fact that businesses do not serve such segments creates a negative image among consumers, who often demand that government force companies to serve their needs.

The media have, to some extent, also contributed to an unfavorable image of business. A study by the Media Institute, a nonprofit research organization, has examined the portrayal of business executives in television programs. The analysis showed that most business executives were depicted as foolish, greedy, or criminal, and not being socially concerned.[5]

Finally, many people feel that businesses earn exorbitant profits. According to one survey, the general public feels that businesses earn over 30 percent profit on sales, but that a 10 percent profit would be considered to be fair. In reality, the profits for the businesses studied were less than 5 percent of sales.[6] Business managers have not been successful in informing the public about how they really do not "rip-off" the public.

Treaties and Trade Agreements Treaties and trade agreements also enter the political environments of many marketers. **Treaties** are formal statements of alliance between two or more countries. While they may have mutual defense as their underlying rationale, they also may serve to benefit the economies of the allies. Treaties usually have an impact on a broad number of items, both political and economic. **Trade agreements,** on the other hand, are typically narrower than treaties and cover only economic issues. Their effect is to regulate intercountry trade, usually by establishing tariffs or quotas (or offering relief from them). **Tariffs** are taxes that governments set

Treaties
Formal statements of alliance between two or more countries.

Trade agreements
Narrower statements than treaties, covering only economic issues; their effect is to regulate intercountry trade.

Tariffs
Taxes on imports or exports.

Quotas (trade)
Limits on the quantity or value of goods that can be imported into or exported from a country.

on imports or exports, and **quotas** are limits on the quantity or value of imported or exported goods.

Certainly, both treaties and trade agreements can dramatically affect market opportunities.[7] For example, the opening of trade between the U.S. and China created many untapped markets because of China's population of almost one billion people.[8] In West Germany, demand for Levi Strauss and Lee blue jeans has been so strong that the firms have not been able to produce enough inventories, resulting in a large black market and extensive brand counterfeiting.

But both kinds of agreements can also negatively affect a firm's ability to compete. Agreements with Taiwan and Brazil, for instance, have dramatically altered the U.S. shoe industry. Inexpensive imports made with poorly paid labor have practically wiped out the chance for U.S. companies to compete for any but the expensive domestic shoe segment. Thus, managers must constantly monitor and be ready to react to the opportunities created by emerging treaties and trade agreements.[9]

License
A permission granted by competent authority to engage in business, occupation, or activity otherwise restricted.

Patent
Rights secured to the inventor of an item granting exclusive control over the item for a period of years.

Copyright
The exclusive legal right to reproduce, publish, and sell the matter and form of a literary, musical, or artistic work.

Trademark
Legally protected words, numbers, letters, and pictorial designs relating to specific brands that are legally protected for the holder.

Licenses, Patents, Copyrights, and Trademarks The government has designed several policies to protect the general public and existing businesses by restricting the right to undertake certain business activities. A **license** is required, for example, to operate a tavern or plumbing firm or practice law or medicine. Licensing is usually required when the public needs special protection. Other protections include **patents,** which grant the holder 17-year exclusive rights to a particular product or process; **copyrights,** which provide lifetime exclusive rights to the creator of original literary, musical, and artistic works; and **trademarks,** which are essentially the same thing as copyrights, but protect brands (including words, numbers, letters, and pictorial designs of specific items).

These protections restrict competitors from copying the results of a company's efforts. Violating protected rights can produce significant penalties such as refunding all related profits plus punitive damages. Thus, these regulations encourage firms to incur the high cost—sometimes running into millions of dollars—of developing new products, ideas, and artistic works. Polaroid, for instance, was able to become a major competitor against Kodak because of the instant film it was able to patent.

Social Welfare Both the federal and state governments are heavily involved in a variety of social welfare programs that provide assistance to low-income consumers. This involvement has grown dramatically in recent decades, as Table 4.1 illustrates. Today, various agencies allocate about 20 percent of the GNP to such programs.

Many managers are opposed to these programs because they see mainly negative features—higher taxes and costs. But they also create business opportunities. Welfare programs provide the required financial resources to market segments otherwise unable to afford certain items, including food, clothing, housing, and education.

Government Assistance to Business The government directly assists businesses in three fundamental ways. Perhaps most important, it is the single largest buyer of goods and services in the country. Further, the government sometimes enters into partnerships with private enterprises to help them initiate and even complete certain projects. Finally, federal and state authorities create special programs to enable firms to earn profits when serving key market segments.[10]

Partnerships In some cases where profitability is very uncertain or capital requirements are excessive, the government enters into partnerships with businesses to induce

Table 4.1 Total Government Expenditures (Federal and State) on Social Welfare and Welfare Services in the U.S. (in billions except percents)

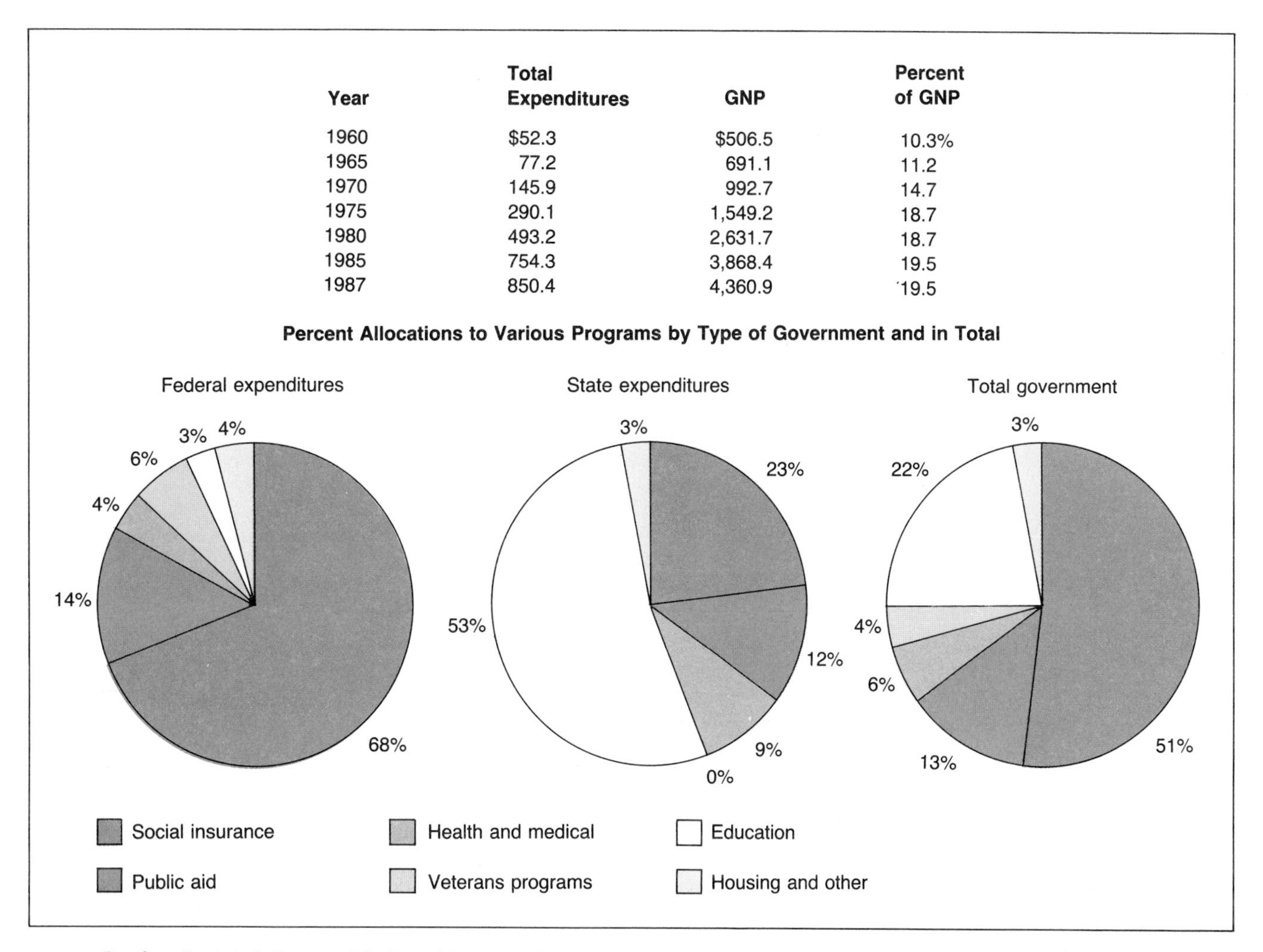

Year	Total Expenditures	GNP	Percent of GNP
1960	$52.3	$506.5	10.3%
1965	77.2	691.1	11.2
1970	145.9	992.7	14.7
1975	290.1	1,549.2	18.7
1980	493.2	2,631.7	18.7
1985	754.3	3,868.4	19.5
1987	850.4	4,360.9	19.5

SOURCE: Based on *Statistical Abstract of the United States* (Washington, D.C.: U.S. Government Printing Office, 1986), 106th ed., and authors' projections.

the undertaking of key projects. Several of these arrangements exist. Among the more popularly known are:

- The Federal Loan Bank, which provides special farm loans
- The Federal Savings and Loan Insurance Corporation (FSLIC), which guarantees savings and loan deposits
- The Federal National Mortgage Association, which guarantees Federal Housing Authority (FHA) home mortgages ("Fannie Mae")
- The Communications Satellites Corp., which rents user time to private communications companies
- Export Import Bank (EXIM Bank), which helps develop and stabilize international monetary exchange.

Amtrak has benefited from the federal government's support.

In special cases, even acts of Congress are used to aid large businesses in financial trouble. The Lockheed Corp., for example, received $250 million in loan guarantees to avoid bankruptcy, which appeared to be sufficient to enable management to correct the situation.[11]

All businesses may benefit from specific programs, even if not directly. To illustrate, since floor covering sales depend upon new construction which, in turn, depends on favorable interest rates, sales of floor coverings by Armstrong, Corp. are affected by FHA lending policies.

Special Programs Governmental bodies also sponsor many special programs that provide marketing opportunities. Among these are:

- Marine subsidies
- Railroad subsidies
- Highway construction subsidies
- Extractive industry depletion allowances
- Farm subsidies for acreages planted (or not planted) in certain crops
- Tax credits on investments in machinery and equipment
- Provision of information through special publications (such as a census)

The Small Business Administration (SBA), a federal agency designed to assist small businesses, carries out one of the most widely available special programs. Section 202 of the Small Business Act (1953) states ". . . the Government should aid, counsel, assist . . . [and] insure that a fair proportion of the total purchases . . . for the Government [are placed] with small business enterprises . . ."

Small businesses can obtain marketing advice, marketing research, and production assistance from this agency. Consulting to help small businesses is also sponsored through universities and a corps of retired executives. The agency also arranges for government-guaranteed low-interest loans from lending institutions and direct loans from the SBA. Further, the SBA and other agencies can help small businesses obtain government contracts. Since such special programs have direct marketing implications, astute managers carefully monitor them when planning their marketing programs.

Local Influences The political environments generated by state and local government units are also critical to marketing opportunities. Some locations of the U.S. are very eager to attract new businesses and have been quite successful in their attempts. To illustrate, Houston has become second only to New York City in housing *Fortune 500* headquarters, with 21 corporations located there.[12] Favorable tax rates, a reasonably priced educated labor force, and other factors prompted these companies to choose Houston as their home. Syracuse, New York, also has been successful in attracting new firms through extensive advertising campaigns featuring the quality of life, low costs, and excellent business opportunities.[13]

Several lures have been successful. South Carolina adopted a pioneering system of vocational and technical schools wherein the state trains local labor to meet the needs of incoming businesses. Puerto Rico offers "tax holidays"—periods of time when it does not assess new businesses.

Local programs can affect marketers in two ways. First, they generally increase local demand. A program that increases an area's employment, for instance, directly magnifies its overall demand for goods and services, such as in booming regions, especially those in the Southwest and the Coastal East.[14] Second, such programs may affect a firm's ability to compete. Tax breaks, for instance, lower a company's costs and improve its ability to compete with rivals located elsewhere.

Regulation of Business Even a brief examination of legal history reveals that the U.S. government is dedicated to preserving competition.[15] In 1986, the Interstate Commerce Commission voted to reject a proposed merger between the Santa Fe and the Southern Pacific railroads, which cast doubt on the future of the latter because of its poor financial condition.[16] The reason was a fear that the merger would create a monopoly. In 1982, the American Telephone and Telegraph Company agreed after lengthy court hearings to divest itself of $87 million in assets, including all local operating systems (such as Mountain Bell, Southern Bell, etc.). This was the largest monetary victory ever won by the U.S. Justice Department, which was convinced that AT&T was monopolizing the telephone industry.[17]

As it pertains to marketing, regulation consists of five major categories: antimonopoly, antiprice competition, consumer protection, laws regulating certain industries, and other legislation. The following discussion is intended to provide only an overview, since a thorough examination is beyond our scope.

Antimonopoly Laws The U.S. is unique in that no other country in the world has adopted such a complete array of legislation to protect open competition and avoid monopoly.[18] Appendix B highlights the major antimonopoly acts (also called **antitrust** acts).

Antitrust (antimonopoly) **laws** Laws to inhibit monopolizing and restraining trade.

Precedents for antimonopoly legislation are traceable to early seventeenth-century England, when the "Case of the Monopolies" (1602) attacked monopolies granted by the Crown. But the real attention in U.S. legislation came after the Civil War and the subsequent rise of big businesses and *trusts*. Trusts were combinations of enterprises with a single legal structure where stockholders gave up shares of stock to managing trustees in return for dividend-paying trust certificates.

The Road Tar Case Challenged the Rule of Reason

In *United States* v. *Koppers Corporation*, the Court found that two firms, Koppers and Dosch-King, divided the state of Connecticut on an equal basis from 1968 to 1975 for the sale of road tar on 169 municipality and four state road maintenance bids. That is, each firm agreed to allow the other to win bids in its half of the state. In this case the court found that both companies were in violation of the Sherman Act for participating in an illegal conspiracy to fix prices.

The court indicated that under this law the government need only prove that the activity occurred. There are no other elements that the prosecution must prove and no allowable defenses that the accused firms can raise to vindicate themselves. The Sherman Act does not make unreasonableness an element of the offense. The activities were illegal *per se*, regardless of the intent of managers of the companies.

SOURCE: Adapted from Ray O. Werner, ed., "Legal Developments in Marketing," *Journal of Marketing* 46, no. 2 (Spring 1982): 126.

By organizing as a trust, managers were able to control many enterprises as one, even if they did not hold the majority of actual ownership. Trusts were common in several industries, including oil, whiskey, sugar, railroads, and banking. The aggressiveness of many trust managers earned them the nickname "robber barrons," who would stop at nothing—even murder in some cases—to gain further wealth. Interestingly, while trusts were only one type of monopoly that raised the public's ire, the term "trust" developed as an acronym for all types of monopolies, which became thought of as enemies of society.

In 1890, Senator John Sherman sponsored the first of a series of antitrust acts (the Sherman Act) to prevent such monopolies.[19] To help strengthen the fight, Theodore Roosevelt, the first U.S. president (1901–1909) to become active in this area, launched a major antitrust drive. In 1903, the Justice Department established its Antitrust Division, which still exists today as the major federal antimonopoly enforcement agency. This organization, and support from the Roosevelt administration, enabled the successful breakup of most of the major monopolies in court. This earned Roosevelt the nickname "Trust Buster."

Congress passed the Clayton and Federal Trade Commission acts in 1914. The former strengthened the Sherman Act by declaring specific types of activities illegal and by stating that actions that *tended* to produce a monopoly might be prohibited. The Federal Trade Commission Act established the Federal Trade Commission (FTC) as a separate agency of the federal government given the authority to investigate and prosecute "unfair practices"—both unethical and deceptive.

Initially, courts decided that a "rule of reason" should prevail in deciding whether a company's size was in violation of the legislation. For example, U.S. Steel was found not to be in violation under this "rule" despite its huge market share because there was no evidence that it abused its power.[20] Later, this "rule" was relaxed.[21] Today, as illustrated in the "Road Tar Case" Marketing Brief, a company is likely to be held in violation of the legislation regardless of the intent of management.

Antitrust legislation was also directed toward large retailers, who as they grew in the 1920s and 1930s began to flex their muscles by forcing manufacturers to grant them price concessions. In response, Congress passed the Robinson-Patman Act, which essentially prohibits buyers from inducing or sellers from granting preferential prices for any intermediary unless the favorable prices can be defended in specific ways as provided by law. Included in the legislation are basic prices themselves, as well as preferential promotional or other allowances (such as advertising allowances). Also prohibited is the establishing of dummy brokerage firms by large retailers—which act as wholesalers in name only to obtain lower prices from manufacturers.

There has been an increase in antimonopoly cases over the past decade, with prosecutors taking aim at giants like IBM, Xerox, General Motors, and several oil companies. All managers should be aware of such actions. One implication is that they may shape market opportunities facing other firms, as illustrated by the rash of communications activity since the breakup of AT&T. Another implication is that a violation is of no small concern to the company charged, carrying fines up to $1 million and possibly jail terms for management.

While all managers should be concerned, this is especially true for those in marketing. As one source indicates, salespeople are the most likely to violate these laws, often by accident.[22]

Antiprice Competition Laws Largely due to pressures by smaller retailers, the government enacted legislation to stop large and growing chain stores from discounting prices. Many manufacturers also supported this legislative move because they felt that they were losing control of their marketing programs to the powerful chains. This legislation was called *resale price maintenance*, or popularly termed **fair trade.**

Fair trade
A legally enforceable agreement that restricts an intermediary from selling an item below a certain price set by the manufacturer or agreed upon by another intermediary.

Fair trade worked this way: If a manufacturer or wholesaler contracted with an intermediary to sell an item at a certain price, or not less than a certain price, *no* competing intermediary could cut the product's price unless it was conducting a legitimate sale or fell under special circumstances (for example, it was going out of business). In the absence of special laws to the contrary, such agreements would be held illegal under antitrust legislation because they would represent collusion.

Because these laws were self-serving of the inefficient, they were repealed in 1975. Even though fair trade is nonexistent today, managers should not forget it. Many independent retailers and some manufacturers remain in strong support and from time to time attempt to pressure legislators into reenactment of the provisions.

Consumer Protection Appendix B presents a summary of selected major **consumer protection acts** affecting a wide array of consumer goods companies.[23] The reason for this legislation is clear—some business practices have been appalling.

Consumer protection legislation
Laws to promote the well-being of consumers.

Turn-of-the-century hucksters sold ordinary tap water as cure-alls for ailments ranging from arthritis to pneumonia. One firm sold laudanum—a mixture of opium and alcohol—as a curative. Perhaps the most notable critic of the food industry was Upton Sinclair who, in his book *The Jungle*, described the then-deplorable meat packing industry:

> Men, who worked in the tank-rooms full of steam . . . fell into the vats; and when they were fished out, there was never enough of them left to be worth exhibiting—sometimes they would be overlooked for days, 'til all but the bones of them had gone out to the world as Durham's Pure Leaf Lard![24]

The Mail Fraud Act of 1892 was the first corrective step taken by the government. The laws of 1906 enabled the government, acting through the Food and Drug Administration, to police meat packing and drugs. Later, Congress strengthened and broadened these laws to cover many other types of products. In 1938, legislators broadened the role of the FTC to include policing deceptive advertising and other promotional methods.

There has been considerable legislation enacted by the federal and state governments since the mid-1960s to further protect consumers on a broad front, including the extension of consumer credit, safe toys for children, smoking health hazards, making untruthful product and warranty claims, and protection of the environment.

The Consumer Product Safety Commission, established by the Consumer Product Safety Act of 1972, has the potential for great future impact on marketers. The commission has the power to set safety standards for consumer products and, through federal courts, have those items not meeting the standards removed from the market. Beyond this, there has been a tremendous surge in product liability suits by consumers over the past several years—sometimes justified, sometimes ill-founded—which has caused problems even for completely ethical companies.

Many other pieces of legislation have been proposed, are pending, and are likely in the future. The FTC has also increased its efforts to police deceptive advertising practices. For example, the agency recently litigated its first landmark case containing a corrective advertising order.

Beginning in 1921 and continuing until the late 1970s, Warner-Lambert advertised

CONCEPT SUMMARY

Key Ways in Which the Federal Government Affects Marketing

Source of Influence	Probable Impact
Treaties and trade agreements	New market opportunities; also could place restrictions on the firm's market opportunities
Licenses, patents, copyrights, and trademarks	Protection for the firm's innovations; restrictions on using the creations of other firms
Social welfare programs	Creation of new markets and strengthening existing ones
Government assistance to business	Aid to marketers in addressing important problems
Antimonopoly laws	Restrictions on practices that could create monopolies and hinder competition
Antiprice competition laws	Restrictions on certain kinds of pricing practices that could injure rivals or consumers or others
Consumer protection	Restrictions on practices which could harm the well-being of consumers
Regulated industries laws	Provision of monopoly power to certain firms deemed to be public utilities

that its Listerine mouthwash helped prevent colds, sore throats, and their symptoms. Expert testimony revealed that the product could only kill bacteria, not viruses—the causes of these ailments. The FTC ordered that the firm must cease advertising this theme and ordered the company to correct the impact of past deceptions by including the following statement in future ads: "Contrary to prior advertising, Listerine will not prevent colds or sore throats or lessen their severity." [25]

A related issue is the FTC's advertising substantiation program, which requires that firms document advertising claims based upon tests or clinical studies. The agency designed the program to prevent such claims as Firestone's, that its tires "stop 25% faster" or General Motors', that "Vega handles better" without proof of the claims.[26]

The FTC is also concerned about misleading advertising. For example, it convinced PepsiCo and Seven-Up to halt advertising that implied that their soft drinks were sweetened with only NutraSweet and that saccharin had been removed, unless that is the case.[27]

A good starting place for marketers to keep abreast of related legislation is to read the "Legal Developments in Marketing" section in each quarterly issue of the *Journal of Marketing*. It summarizes the most important court decisions and proposed legislation relating to marketing.

Laws Regulating Certain Industries There are also many laws governing the operations of certain industries. To illustrate, most utilities have been exempted from antitrust legislation, but have specifically designed laws governing their regulation.

Other important regulation includes the vast body of commercial law bearing on contracts, sales, debts, and other matters. Prudent marketing managers rely on legal advice from experts in guiding them to establish policies regarding pricing, contracts, product claims, and other important issues before implementing them.

Finally, the restrictions on marketing decision making are sometimes voluntary. Many in the business community support *Better Business Bureaus* to advise consumers about the reputations of particular businesses. Trade associations within an industry often set standards for products, such as package sizes and strength of materials. Astute marketing managers consider these factors as they relate to their specific companies and industries.

Technological Considerations

Technology has affected practically everything in modern life. Synthetic fibers for clothing, new ways of printing books, the advent of television news, the invention of the VCR, and the ever-widening influence of the computer are but a few examples of items technology has made possible. Because technology is like a mist penetrating every stratum of culture, marketers should be constantly alert to its change.[28]

Technological breakthroughs often have far-reaching implications for marketing opportunities. Laser beams, for instance, have altered dramatically telecommunications, certain metal workings, surgical procedures, defense systems, and many other processes. In the 1980s, many small high-tech firms in industries such as bioengineering,[29] electronics, computers, and health science appeared almost overnight, producing significant innovations—and the technologies at the hearts of many of these companies can be traced in some way to the space exploration efforts of NASA. Some experts, in fact, are calling NASA's space shuttle the key to opening the next industrial revolution.[30]

Technological change can affect virtually every marketing mix element. To illustrate, RCA and other firms sell space on direct-broadcast satellites to television programmers; "scratch-and-sniff" chemicals have brought aromas into advertising. Toll-free telephone numbers have created a free business communication network for consumers. Electronic funds transfer technology (the remote transfer of funds from one account to another) has the potential to dramatically change retailing and create a cashless society. The list is almost endless. Companies that do not adjust their marketing mixes to reflect this rapidly changing technology are often destined for failure.

The Rate of Technological Change

Technological change is occurring at an unprecedented rate. Alvin Toffler's *Future Shock* gives a feeling of its pace:

> If the last 50,000 years of man's existence were divided into life-times of approximately 62 years each, there have been about 800 such lifetimes. Of these 800, fully 650 were spent in caves . . . only during the last six lifetimes did masses of men ever see a printed word. Only during the last four has it been possible to measure time with any precision. Only in the last two has anyone used an electric motor. And the overwhelming majority of all the material goods we use in daily life today have been developed within the present, the 800th lifetime.[31]

Of importance to marketers is the fact that the pace of this change is not abating.[32] Within the past century, the incubation period required to bring ideas from technical

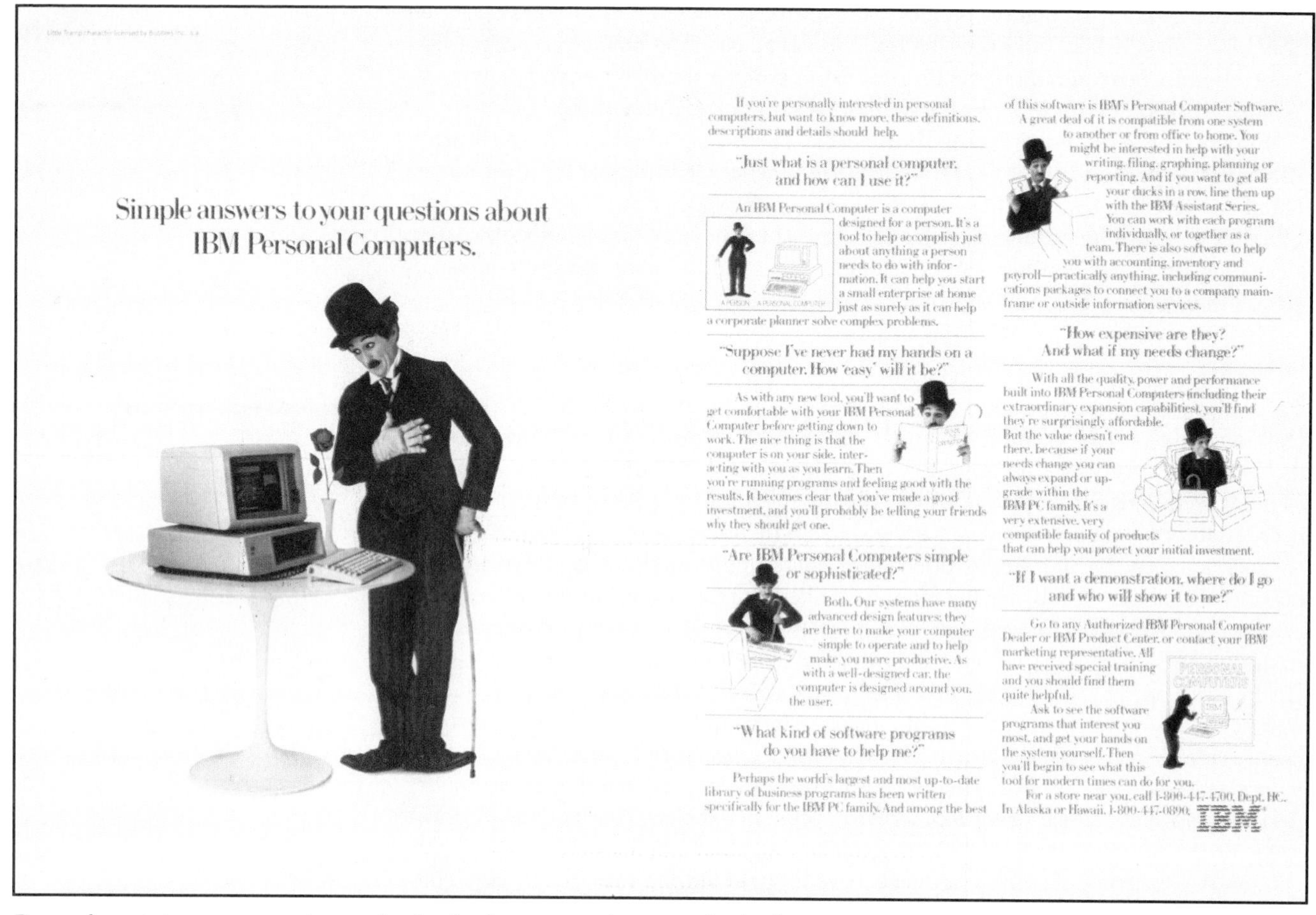

Personal computers are a recent example of technology penetrating many levels of society.

feasibility to commercial potential has dropped from an average of seven years to only five.[33]

Two factors account for this acceleration. First, as in a nuclear reaction, technological developments tend to accelerate due to the self-feeding nature of technology. As a greater base of technology becomes known, ideas interact and provide a basis for still further research as well as practical applications. Second, this country's commitment to research has been expanding dramatically, as depicted in Figure 4.3. As a result, today's managers are faced with a changing technological environment requiring some adjustment in the firm's marketing mix. Those unable to adjust are likely to be left behind.

Technological Forecasting

As the experience of Learjet illustrates (see the accompanying Marketing Brief), management must anticipate future technology in a timely fashion—when both market opportunities and capabilities develop. Digital Equipment Corp. is an example of a company that has done quite well in this regard.

Digital began on a shirt-sleeve basis in 1957 when a computer filled an entire room and cost millions of dollars. The company developed the first mass-produced mini-

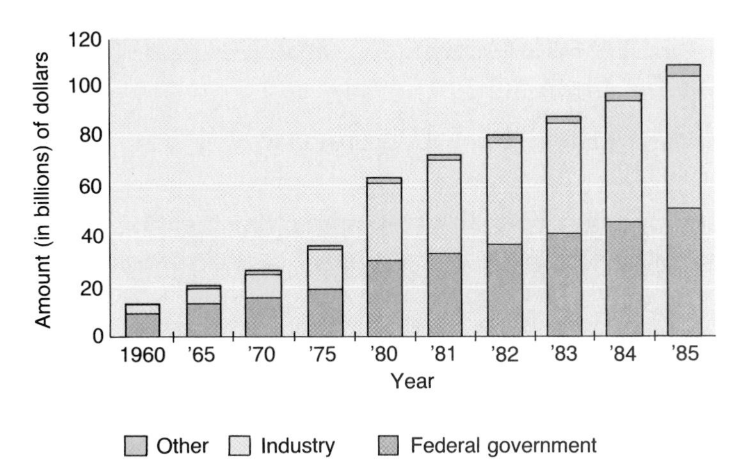

Figure 4.3
U.S. Expenditures on Research and Development, Selected Years, 1960–1985 (SOURCE: Based on *Statistical Abstract of the United States* (Washington, D.C.: U.S. Government Printing Office, 1986), 106th ed., and authors' projections.)

computer, allowing it to become the second largest computer producer and posing a threat to industry giant IBM. In turn, the 1980s witnessed the growth of personal computers and office automation systems introduced by new competitors such as Apple. Managers who are able to forecast such changes have a clear advantage over competitors.[34]

Forecasting technological change is by no means a simple task. Technological developments are usually the domain of physicists, electronic engineers, and other technical experts and many marketing managers are unfamiliar with these fields. To complicate matters, experts in the technical areas are generally unfamiliar with the marketability of new or potential developments. Consequently, an integrated, closely coordinated effort involving both marketing and research and development personnel is essential to the successful development and introduction of new offerings.

Exploratory (technological) forecasting Forecasting future developments in technology by examining anticipated future production capabilities.

A carefully integrated effort meshes smoothly with the two basic approaches to technological forecasting. The first of these, **exploratory forecasting,** is technique-oriented. With this procedure, forecasters make estimates concerning developments by examining expected future production capabilities. Technical experts conduct analyses of new patents, project recent trends in production capabilities, study research findings, and, based on these sources of information, estimate future production capabilities. Based on these estimates, they produce forecasts of technological developments. Managers then assess the expected impact of the technology on market opportunities. For example, guided by progress in genetic research, General Electric's scientists have created a "super-bacteria" capable of digesting crude oil. This breakthrough could significantly improve the world's ability to clean up oil spills. Once informed of such capabilities, marketers should try to assess the potential market opportunities as well as the anticipated effects on current marketing mixes.

Normative (technological) forecasting Forecasting future developments in technology by examining needs, under the assumption that they will trigger new developments.

The second approach, termed **normative forecasting,** is to identify current and expected future needs with the assumption that these needs will trigger new technological developments for fulfillment. Following this procedure, managers critically appraise how well needs related to their firm's overall mission are currently being satisfied. For instance, impending natural gas shortages and residential heating needs represent a field for the natural gas industry to consider. Needs are then discussed with company technical experts so as to direct their future research. With close coordination between marketing and technical personnel, the firm can direct research and development specifically toward bright future market opportunities.

MARKETING BRIEF
Technology Can Be a Critical Factor in Success

William P. Lear, Sr. rolled out the first small jet aircraft for business travel in 1963, but the Wichita pioneer's booming vision for his fledgling company did not last long. He was forced to sell out to Gates Corp. four years later, largely because of financial considerations.

Under new ownership Gates Learjet Corp. dominated the market, holding nearly a 27 percent share of the business segment. The company's planes were considered by many to be the leader in the field of nine competitors.

But beginning in the late 1970s, Learjet began to lose ground. By 1986 its stock had slumped to below $6 per share. It only delivered 33 planes in 1985, which represented a paltry 14 percent of the market.

Many of Learjet's problems were from the company's own makings. Instead of spending research dollars on a new generation of jets, the company gambled on a risky diversification into propeller-driven aircraft. In 1983, the company joined forces with Italian plane manufacturer Rinaldo Piaggio in a $100 million venture to build an advanced turboprop craft. The plane was supposed to reach near-jet speeds but use 35 percent less fuel. With declining oil prices and market trends, Learjet was forced to scrap the project, losing $40 million in the deal. The company's problems have been greatly compounded by the cash drain caused by this failure, and it is now facing stiff competition. With neither an advanced jet nor the funds to develop one, the company's future may be in peril.

SOURCE: Adapted from Mark Ivey, "For Learjet, Merger May Be the Only Answer," *Business Week*, March 17, 1986: 87.

But technological forecasting has its limitations. Both exploratory and normative techniques are rather subjective, using the opinions of various experts as primary inputs.[35] Since this is the case, the optimism or pessimism of the analysts easily can influence the results. Further, forecasters have difficulty in estimating the current status of technology. Companies are not eager to share their private research findings with others, for obvious reasons, and try to conceal them. Accordingly, completely unnoticed breakthroughs can and do occur, frequently catching managers off-guard.

Finally, some identified opportunities may be out of a company's reach because of limited resources. The profitable extraction of petroleum from oil shale is becoming technically feasible, but attempting such a venture will fail if it is beyond a particular firm's capabilities. This is not a technological forecasting weakness *per se*; accurately forecasting the future does not guarantee success, it only points the way.

Economic Factors

Obviously, demand can be greatly affected by economic conditions. Fluctuating prices for home fuel, for instance, have altered the market for products such as home insulation, storm windows, solar water heaters, and solar space heaters.

Astute managers carefully follow economic trends and shape their decisions accordingly. Recent energy shortages, for example, have influenced research efforts in many industries. Lockheed has shifted scores of engineers from its once-active helicopter studies into researching windmills and ocean heat conversion and storage. All indications are that firms will continue this energy research in the future.[36] There were oil and natural gas surpluses in the early 1980s but major shortages are forecasted for as early as 1988.[37]

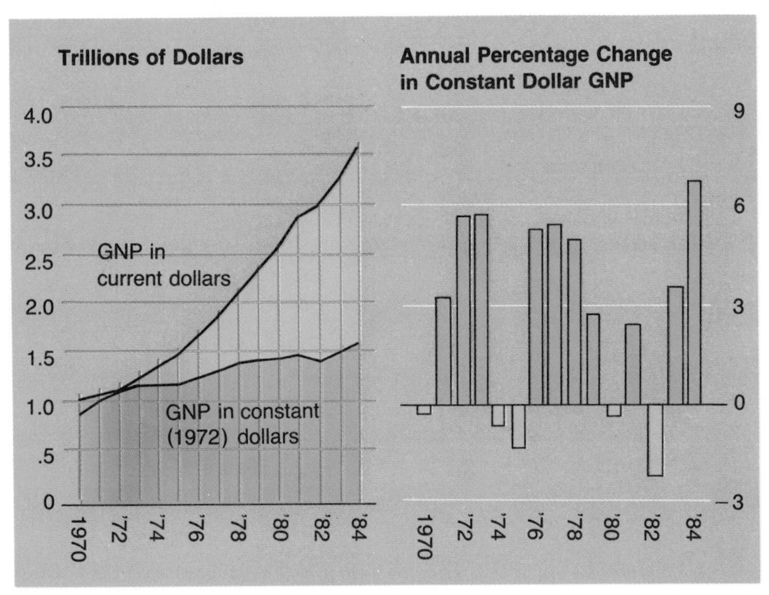

Figure 4.4
Gross National Product and Economic Growth, 1970–1984
(SOURCE: *Statistical Abstract of the United Staes* (Washington, D.C.: U.S. Government Printing Office, 1986), 106th ed.)

Measures of Economic Activity

The U.S. has the largest gross national product (GNP) of any country.[38] At nearly $4 trillion, the level is about four times that of Germany or Japan—making the U.S. the world's largest market for goods and services.[39] American per-capita GNP is about $7,000. In contrast, the African country of Tanzania has a per-capita GNP of only a little over $250.[40] Market potentials, especially for items other than basic necessities, are obviously very limited there. Significant differences, though not so dramatic, exist within each region, state, county, and city of the U.S. Marketers should take these differences into account when assessing opportunities.

Economic fluctuations are just as important to decision making as the levels themselves. Change patterns affect future demand. As Figure 4.4 illustrates, U.S. economic expansion has been running at a rate between 3 and 6 percent per year. If past growth trends continue, therefore, future GNP increases should be in the $40 to $60 billion range for each of the next several years.

All managers should be aware of the relationships between the growth rate of the nation or a particular region and trends within their own companies. Sales in the forest products industry, for instance, typically follow overall patterns in GNP. During the recession of the late 1970s and early 1980s, sales suffered severe setbacks due to large declines in the demand for new homes and paper products.[41] Other industries, such as those providing home entertainment and motion pictures, find the reverse to be true, with booms during economic slowdowns and declines during periods of expansion.

Knowledge of the relationship between company sales and economic fluctuations can help management plan marketing actions. Even otherwise sound strategies may fail if a firm launches them at the wrong time.

Economic measures such as GNP do provide clues to important trends, but they are affected by inflation and can be misleading. To illustrate, one naïve manager recently reported, "Last year was great. Sales were up 6 percent." But inflation was 8

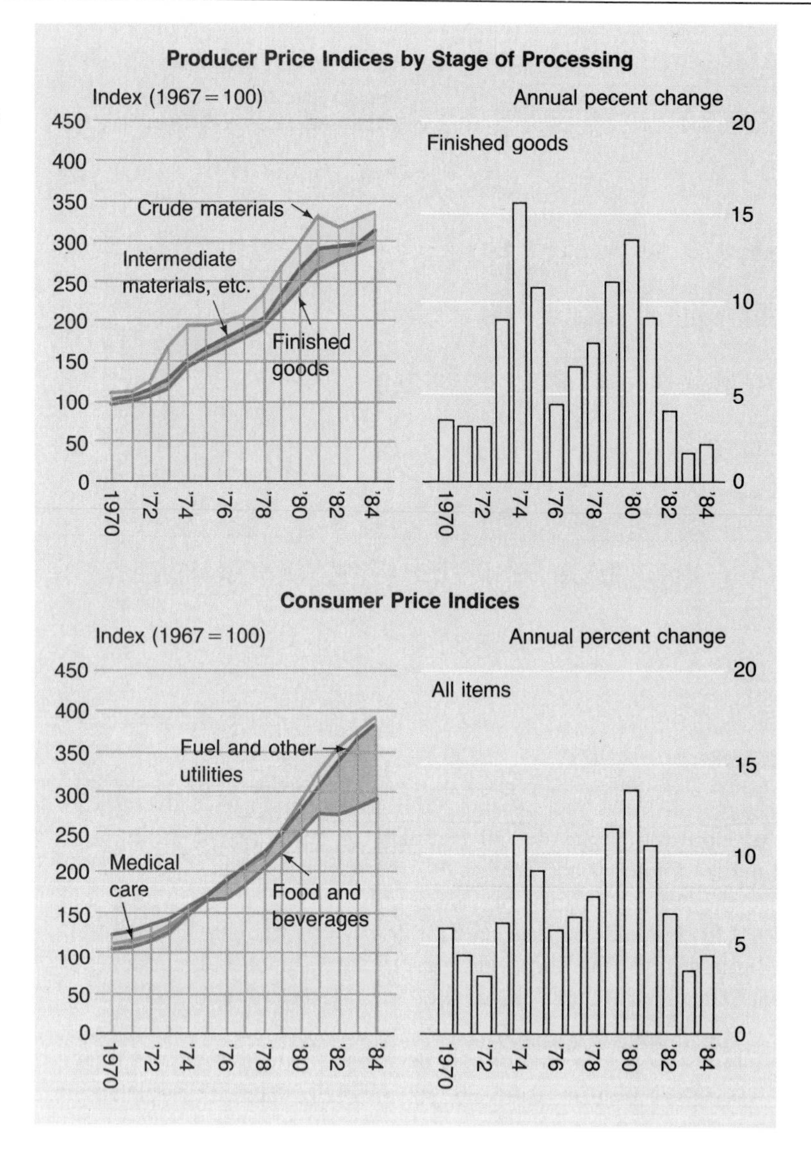

Figure 4.5
Price Indices, 1970–1984
(SOURCE: *Statistical Abstract of the United States* (Washington, D.C.: U.S. Government Printing Office, 1986), 106th ed.)

percent for the year, meaning that sales were actually down by 2 percent. Fortunately, price indices are available to correct monetary values for inflation and give "constant dollar" amounts. Calculating *deflated* (termed *real*) prices helps managers in two ways. First, a more consistent analysis of events from one year to another is possible. Second, real prices enable more accurate portrayals of any relationships among various economic measures. Figure 4.5 presents historical consumer and producer price indices for the U.S.

Fiscal and Monetary Policies

The importance of government's policies cannot be understated. Approaching $1 trillion, total government spending is about 25 times larger than it was in 1940.

Further, the federal government controls the money supply. Decisions over both of these variables can greatly affect market opportunities.

Fiscal policy includes all government spending and taxing actions, both to buy operating items and to bring about economic stability. Changes in fiscal policy directly affect specific marketing opportunities. To illustrate, if Congress allocates increased funding to urban renewal, construction firms in major cities benefit considerably. Likewise, oil depletion tax credits affect the profitability of industries related to oil exploration and regions where these activities take place.

Fiscal policy
Government spending and taxing activities to buy operating items and to bring about economic stability.

In contrast, **monetary policy** is the deliberate exercise of the government's power to *expand or contract* the money supply. In the U.S., this authority rests primarily in the hands of the Federal Reserve Board, a separate federal agency.[42]

Monetary policy
Deliberate exercise of the government's power to expand or contract the money supply.

While fiscal policies directly affect specific marketing opportunities, monetary policy's impact tends to be more widespread and indirect. When the Federal Reserve Board tightens the money supply, for instance, this tends to raise interest rates. Higher interest rates, in turn, produce greater borrowing costs, which affect businesses and consumers alike. As a consequence, practically all industries may experience a slowdown. Generally, marketers should remain alert to patterns of fiscal spending and proposed changes in the money supply so that they may be in a position to make appropriate adjustments in the marketing mix.

Do Managers Need to Be Economists?

Of course, considerable technical training is required to be able to fully assess fiscal and monetary policies, but managers do not need to be formally trained economists in order to make the required assessments. Some organizations do employ professional economists who are experts in analyzing the outcomes of anticipated policies. These companies make their predictions and suggestions available to managers for only a nominal fee. Major banks like Chase Manhattan and Wells Fargo provide projections to their commercial customers. Likewise, some trade associations and universities, as well as the Federal Reserve Banks themselves, also provide professional forecasts.

But this does not mean that managers can afford to sit idly by and wait for economics experts to tell them what the future holds. Managers can combine easy-to-acquire information inputs with their own judgments. Sources like *Business Week, Wall Street Journal*, and business sections of major newspapers like the *New York Times* print anticipated governmental policy changes. Past experience and a basic understanding of federal policy and what its effects can be expected to be should enable managers to better prepare for influences on their target market and marketing mix.

Specific Market Factors

The final set of environmental variables consists of specific market factors: unique needs, motivations, and buying habits of the buyers in each market. Compared to producers, for instance, consumer buyers have more numerous, but less explicit, objectives and their decision making is less formal and systematic and is more often influenced by social relationships and personalities.

A sound grasp of buying patterns and the factors influencing these patterns is important in understanding specific market factors. The remaining chapters in this section focus on the decision-making habits of ultimate buyers: consumers and industrial and governmental purchasers.

Chapter Summary

This chapter provided an overview of the external environment of marketing. Understanding this environment is vital for marketing decision making because it sets the stage for all business successes or failures. The environment, in effect, establishes the magnitude of the opportunities a firm faces.

Competitive conditions have an effect on marketing decision making, as the dynamics of intracompany rivalries affect the ease of penetrating certain markets. Political variables, both policies and regulations, establish the overtones of the business climate in general and create constraints on certain activities. Major antimonopoly, antiprice competition, and consumer protection regulations and certain other laws are among the political factors affecting the business community. It is worth noting, however, that legislation should be viewed as a two-edged sword, since each prohibition also establishes another opportunity.

Technological change also can be a major factor affecting the opportunities a firm faces, both by reducing the significance of some products and increasing the potential of others. Similarly, overall economic factors are very important determinants of the magnitude of the opportunities that a firm faces.

Since these environmental factors are centrally important to all business actions, marketing managers must be intimately familiar with the environment of business when making decisions.

Questions

1. Many marketers argue that the government only interferes with opportunity. What do you think?
2. How do political policies affect a market's opportunity? Provide an example.
3. How can programs like welfare services create opportunity? After all, they are financed through taxes on hard-earned profits. Do you think such programs are desirable?
4. "Patents only serve to reduce competition and opportunity for others." Comment.
5. What is the Sherman Act? Why was it necessary to amend it with the Clayton Act?
6. Explain the Robinson-Patman Act.
7. Are consumer protection laws and the marketing concept opposed to each other? Would such laws (or so many of them) be necessary if more firms adopted the marketing concept?
8. What is technology and why is it important to marketers?
9. How do overall economic factors influence opportunity?
10. Find out about two pending federal, state, or local spending programs that will affect your local economy in some way. (Check business information sources in local newspapers, ask the Chamber of Commerce, or check with the business librarian.) Then, pick a local retailer, a manufacturer, and a firm offering a business service. What impact could the programs have on the firms you selected? If you were a marketing advisor to each of the three firms, what advice would you give them? Why?
11. Does the government sponsor programs to assist business in your local community? What are the programs?
12. Several fast food restaurant chains have recently argued that the food stamp program should be extended to allow take-out food to be covered. What do you think and why?

Chapter 5

Understanding Consumer Behavior

Objectives

After completing this chapter, you should be able to demonstrate a knowledge of:

- The meaning of the term "consumer behavior"
- Major trends in U.S. consumer purchase behavior
- The major variables that have an impact on consumer behavior
- The ways in which variables interact to influence consumer behavior
- How marketers can utilize insights into consumer behavior in order to devise marketing strategies and tactics

MARKETING SUCCESS

Birthrate Surge Leads to Heightened Competition in Toys

Facing a steady decline in birthrates since the late 1970s, Fisher-Price Toys (FP), the world's largest maker of infant and preschool toys, cut back its advertising programs. But then in the mid-1980s, the preschool market suddenly became much more attractive due to a resurgence in the birthrate: the "baby boomers" of the 1950s were beginning to have children. As it has in the past, FP astutely is tailoring its marketing strategies to meet these trends, which accounts for its market leadership.

Aggressive marketing efforts by several giants, including Hasboro, Kenner Products, and Mattel, and entry into the preschool segment by others, such as Matchbox Toys, Schaper Mfg. Co. (Tendertoys) and Walt Disney (Gummi Bears), have made this segment one of the most hotly contested in the entire toy industry.

There are several aggressive moves being planned by FP. With at least 50 new toys presented at the February 1986 Toy Fair trade show in New York, Robert Moody, FP's director of advertising, predicted that 1986 "promises to be a very bright year for Fisher-Price." To augment the new line of products, "We have increased our advertising budget by 90 percent to $50 million for 1986," added Mr. Moody.

SOURCE: Adapted from Judith A. Biltekoff, "Fisher-Price Stuffs Ad Budget," *Advertising Age*, February 24, 1986: 62.

Introduction

Consumers are at the focus of most companies.[1] In this regard, profitably satisfying consumer needs is at the heart of successful marketing.[2] Understanding why consumers purchase certain items, avoid others, and how they make their purchase decisions is of vital interest to marketing managers.[3] This chapter paints an overview of consumer buying and presents an integrated approach to understanding this process from a marketing perspective.

Who Are Consumers?

Consumers
People, acting as individuals or groups, who buy items for personal use.

Consumers are people, acting as individuals or in small groups, who buy goods and services for *personal* purposes—to satisfy personal desires—in contrast to industrial buyers who buy and use items for commercial purposes. While users and buyers of consumer items are sometimes different people (wives buy some items for husbands, for example), this chapter emphasizes buying, not consumption *per se*. Thus, it refers to consumer buyers as consumers.

Many consumer characteristics are important for marketing decision making. The following is a sampling.

Population. A diverse group of individuals and small groups, with nearly 240 million of them in total in the U.S. of all shapes, sizes, colors, intellects, ages, abilities, fears, frustrations, needs, and purchasing patterns.[4] Trends in population have a great affect on marketing decisions.[5, 6] To illustrate, many colleges and universities have begun to market continuing education programs to adults to offset declines in high school graduates.[7] Similarly, a resurging birthrate has lead to increasing competition in the toy market for Fisher-Price, as indicated in the Marketing Success. Exhibit 5.1 presents a sampling of selected significant population trends in the U.S. today.

Exhibit 5.1
Selected Significant U.S. Population Trends

The population in the U.S. has changed significantly over time, affecting the opportunities faced by marketers. This exhibit highlights several of the key population trends emerging in the U.S. today. [All figures are based on the *Statistical Abstract of the United States* (Washington, D.C.: U.S. Government Printing Office, 1986), 106th ed.]

Total U.S. Population by Age Group, Actual and Projections

Percent: 0, 10, 20, 30, 40
0–4, 5–17, 18–24, 25–44, 45–64, 65+
Age group
1960, 1970, 1980, 1990, 2000

U.S. Citizens by Highest Education Level

Percent: 0, 10, 20, 30, 40
Elementary or less, Some high school, High school graduate, Some college, College graduate or beyond
Education level
1975, 1980, 1985

U.S. Household Income Classes

Percent: 0, 5, 10, 15, 20, 25
$0–3, $3–5, $5–7, $7–10, $10–15, $15–25, $25+
Household income, in thousands of dollars
1972, 1980, 1985

Percent of Women in the U.S. Labor Force

Percent: 0, 10, 20, 30, 40, 50
Total women, Married women
Women in the labor force
1950, 1960, 1970, 1980, 1985

U.S. Population Distribution by Region, Actual and Projected

Population, in percent of U.S. total: 0, 10, 20, 30, 40
Northeast, North central, South, West
Region
1950, 1960, 1970, 1980, 1990

Marital Status of U.S. Population, Standardized by Age Distribution

Percent: 0, 10, 20, 30, 40, 50, 60, 70, 80
1960, '65, '70, '75, '80, '85
Single, Widowed, Married, Divorced

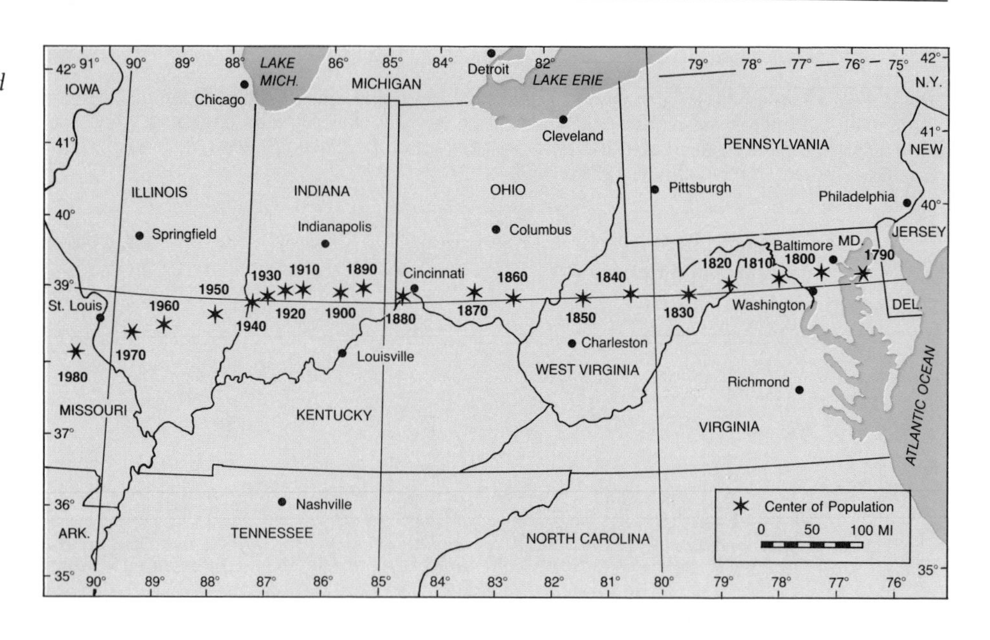

Figure 5.1
Western Population Migration, Based on Center of Population during U.S. History (SOURCE: From *Statistical Abstract of the United States* (Washington, D.C.: U.S. Government Printing Office, 1986), 106th ed.)

Geographic Patterns. The U.S. population is continuing to heed Horace Greeley's words, "Go west, young man," as Figure 5.1 indicates, providing new opportunities for marketers who adjust to these shifts. For example, the ski industry has boomed with the population growth in the Rocky Mountain region over the past 20 years. Naturally, such changes in trade areas affect marketing opportunities.[8]

Metropolitan statistical areas (MSAs) Integrated social and economic units having 50,000 or more inhabitants in an identifiable city or area.

Marketers generally use **metropolitan statistical areas (MSAs),** which are detailed breakdowns of Census Bureau reporting units, to monitor trends within specific areas. An MSA is an integrated social and economic unit having a large population nucleus. It is an urban area including at least one city with 50,000 or more inhabitants, or a U.S. Census Bureau-defined urbanized area of at least 50,000 inhabitants and a total MSA population of at least 100,000 (75,000 in New England). In all, there are about 260 MSAs in the U.S., including Puerto Rico, and collectively they account for nearly 75 percent of the population and 16 percent of the nation's land mass.[9] The remaining areas are considered nonmetropolitan, and many of the residents feel the need to travel to an MSA for shopping to assure variety and reasonable prices.[10]

Consumer Expenditures. In total, consumers in the U.S. spend a staggering amount—about $2.5 trillion a year—on a bewildering array of items from soup to nuts, from pencils to vacations in Hawaii. And the trend is upward, having nearly quadrupled since 1970 (see Figure 5.2).

As one might suspect, there are literally thousands of items included in the composite data. In the face of such big numbers, it is easy for managers to overlook the fact that each consumer is somewhat different. Some are loyal to certain brands, some buy items to impress their friends, some buy only after lengthy deliberation, others are impulsive. In short, consumers have heterogeneous characteristics, needs, and life styles, and buy products accordingly.

Managers have the task of creating order and understanding out of the seeming hodgepodge of differences within consumer markets.[11] This leads to the study of consumer buying profiles.[12]

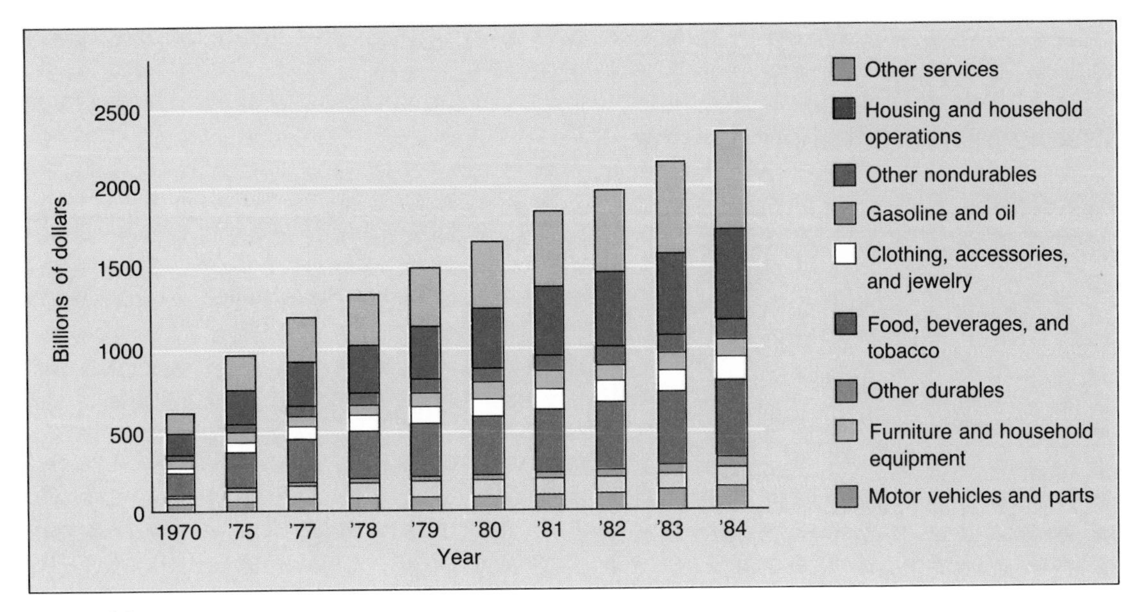

Figure 5.2
Personal Consumption Expenditures in the U.S. for Selected Years

Buying Profiles. Because of the large numbers involved, most marketers of consumer items focus their attention on groups of people, rather than individuals, when developing strategies. To illustrate, one study revealed that over 30 percent of "service-oriented" bank customers earned over $20,000 per year, or 1.5 times as much as "convenience-oriented" bank customers.[13] The two classes of customers also differed along several other dimensions, including their occupations, whether or not both spouses were employed, and ages. This knowledge enabled bankers to develop marketing strategies centered on catering to the needs of a selected group of consumers. Most marketers of consumer goods and services use these techniques in developing their marketing programs.[14]

However, these **buying profiles**—especially those based upon demographics alone—do not explain all consumer buying behavior. In order to gain greater insight for decision making, managers must have a sound grasp of the "Why?" of buying.[15] The remainder of this chapter focuses on examining the wide field of consumer buying behavior.

Buying profiles
Listings of characteristics of a firm's customers.

Consumer Buying Behavior

Behavioral scientists and marketing researchers have for years devoted considerable effort to understanding why consumers behave as they do, but the subject matter is very complex. Most restricting is the fact that unlike the physical scientist's world of precise measurement, a consumer behavior analyst cannot accurately measure or observe mental processes directly.[16] Instead, he or she must formulate inferences about the causes of behavior, as Figure 5.3 illustrates, and these inferences are subject to error.

This figure identifies stimuli—the input variables that trigger individual behavior. Many stimuli can be important to buying decisions, including an item's physical

MARKETING BRIEF
Debunking a Myth (?) about Leisure

There are many terms for it: the "rat race," the "merry-go-round," the "time famine." They all mean the same thing. Whatever it is called, many workers in the U.S. are living an extraordinary paradox: despite all the rhetoric, the proliferation of labor-saving devices and unmatched wealth, true leisure remains elusive. "We have the material necessities, but we pay for it with a frantic lifestyle," says Geoffrey Godby, a Pennsylvania State University professor.

The 40-hour workweek, protected by federal law for 50 years, is a pure fiction for many wage earners. Professionals and managers work an average of 45 hours a week, while manufacturing employees put in an average of 43 hours. And they have less vacation time—an average of two weeks a year—than do workers in every industrial country except Japan. Despite vacation credits of three or four weeks, many industry managers seldom take more than three or four days off a year, with true leisure being reserved for retirement.

The new emphasis is on making leisure activities "efficient." The leisure industry promotes, and the public is buying, the drive to perform. There are three-day getaways for vacationers who won't take a full week away from work, racquetball is promoted "because it takes less time than golf or tennis," even everyday activities like walking are marketed as trendy sports requiring just the right equipment. A new magazine for recreational walking, for example, promises advertisers that "the more walking people do, the more they want to learn about . . . places to walk, clothing to walk in, equipment to tune walking muscles." More is being spent on "leisure activities," however defined, as illustrated in the accompanying graph.

SOURCE: Adapted from Jolie Solomon, "Working at Relaxation: In Spite of Unprecedented Affluence, Americans Labor to Find the Time for Leisure Pursuits," *The Wall Street Journal*, April 21, 1986, Sec. 4, pp. 1D–3D.

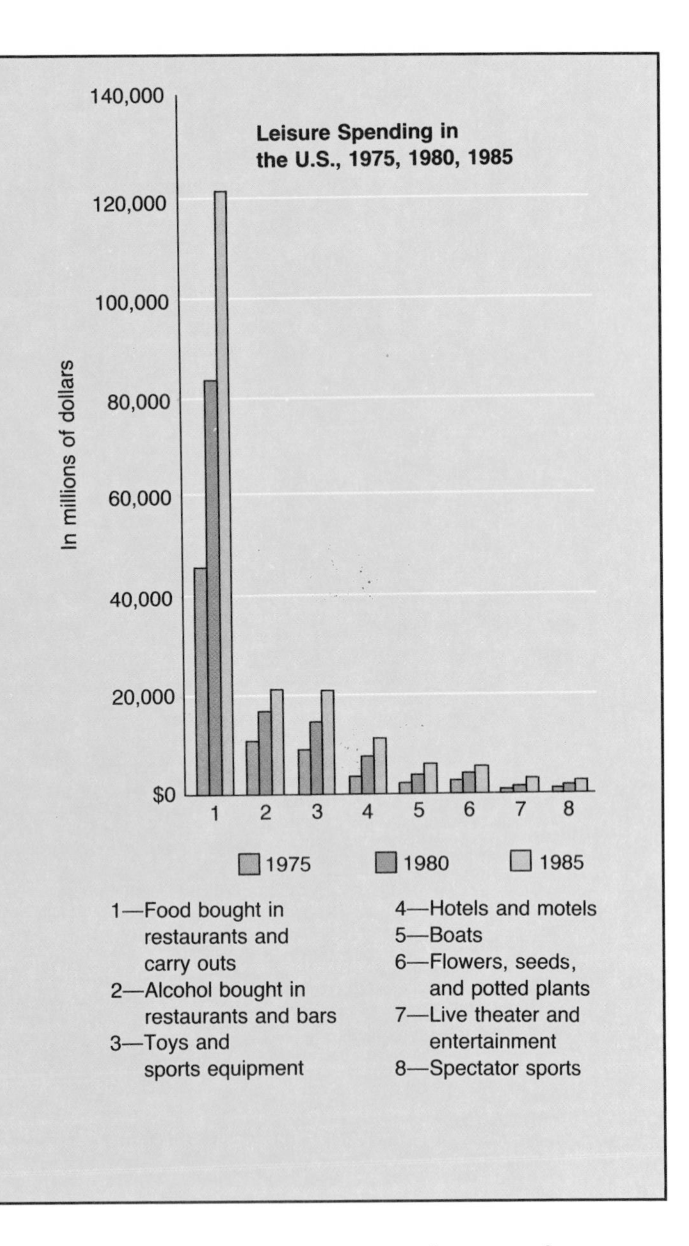

attributes and price, the person's needs, and advertisements the person has seen or heard. In turn, stimuli trigger mental activity, resulting in a particular type of behavior such as the purchase of a diskette in a computer store. Both conscious and subconscious mental processes stand between stimuli and behavior and they are hidden from direct observation. Hence, behavior analysts sometimes describe the mental processes as being within an unobservable "black box."

Models of Consumer Behavior

Explorers of consumer behavior have proposed a number of models describing buying processes and how these processes develop. A **model** is simply an abstraction of the phenomenon it is intended to represent. In effect, it specifies the essential elements within the black box that the analyst deems to be important, represents the interrelationships between them, and spells out how behavior results from these elements. While no consumer behavior model is perfect, models offer several advantages making them worth using: They provide *frames of reference* for analyzing variables related to consumer behavior and the interrelationships of these variables. They furnish a *means of fitting together information* in a meaningful way. They serve as *guides for future research*. Models also provide *guides for establishing marketing plans and actions.*

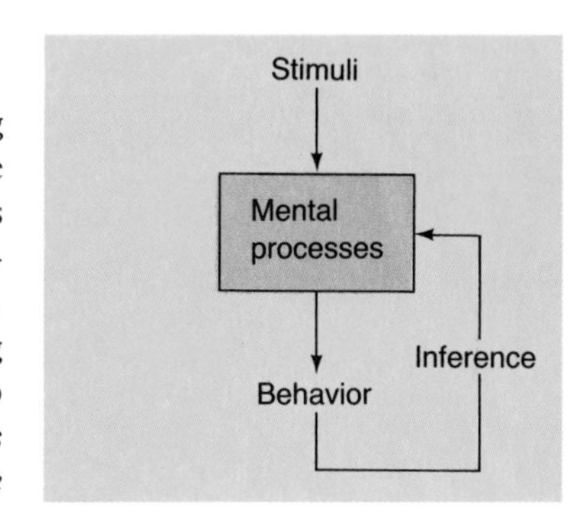

Figure 5.3
The "Black Box" of Consumer Behavior

Marginal Utility Economists have called the first model of consumer behavior covered in this section the **"marginal utility model"** (also called the "economic man" model). It uses three factors to explain decision making: consumers' perceived utility of each item, the price of each item, and consumers' budget levels. More specifically, the model states that individuals buy items to maximize the benefits they receive from a given budget level. That is, the model asserts that people allocate their incomes so that the benefits derived from (marginal utility/price) all items is equal.[17] If any good or service offered less utility relative to price, consumers would increase the total satisfaction from a given budget by purchasing less of that item and more of some other.

Model
An abstraction of the phenomenon that it intends to represent.

Marginal utility model
A hypothetical consumer who chooses between alternatives in a manner that is consistent with evaluations of how the alternatives will affect the consumer's self-interest (also called the *economic man model*).

There are several problems with this model. For one, it devotes little attention to *why* and *how* consumers develop and change utility structures. Another problem is that the model points out ways people *should* behave, not necessarily ways they *do* behave. It omits from consideration the fact that habits, the subconscious, social forces, and psychological pressures exert a strong influence on consumer behavior.[18]

These problems do not mean that the model is wrong or useless. It does stress the fact that people pursue their own self-interest, which is one insight that is important in understanding market behavior. The model may be fine for economists, who emphasize the "big picture" and how things "ought to be," but it has certain deficiencies from management's perspective. Managers need to know why and how consumer preferences develop in order to make marketing mix decisions that result in strong preferences for company products.

A Comprehensive Model In the past, marketers mainly borrowed behavioral models from other disciplines, especially sociology and psychology.[19] Until the 1960s, these approaches were splintered; they failed to recognize and account for the full array of variables that should be considered, and they lacked a decision-making orientation from the perspective of marketing managers. Then in the mid-1960s, three major, though somewhat different, new models appeared in the literature. All three integrated behavioral concepts from various disciplines into conceptual systems fully representing the overall process of consumer decision making.

Nicosia proposed the first such model in 1966.[20] The Engel, Kollat, and Blackwell[21] and the Howard and Sheth[22] models followed in 1968. These models, coupled with previous research, laid the foundations of an interdisciplinary approach to formally study consumer behavior from a marketing perspective.[23]

All three models have considerable merit and receive frequent citations in the literature. However, many marketing experts consider the Howard and Sheth model

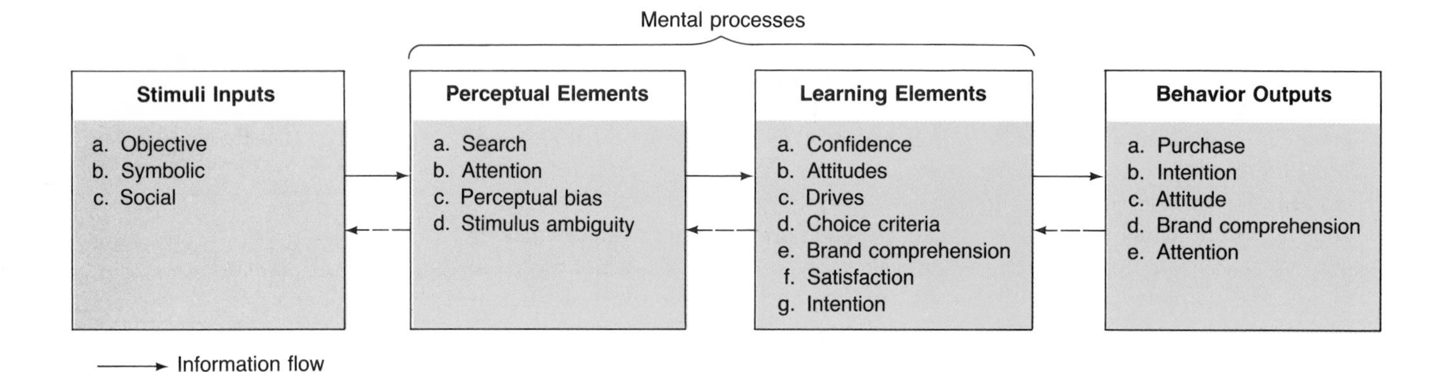

Figure 5.4
Major Elements in the Howard/Sheth Model of Consumer Behavior
(SOURCE: Adapted from John A. Howard and Jagdish N. Sheth, *The Theory of Buyer Behavior* (New York: John Wiley & Sons, 1968): 30.)

to be the most comprehensive of the three, and this section focuses on it. Figure 5.4 illustrates the model's major components.

The left side of the model depicts **stimuli** inputs, consisting of information originating from three sources outside the individual. The first, **objective stimuli,** are the real attributes of a particular marketing mix. G.E. refrigerators, for example, are available in certain stores, are advertised in specific media with definite messages, and have set dimensions and operating characteristics.

Stimuli
Entities that trigger a person's mental processes.

Objective stimuli
The real attributes of an object, such as a product.

Symbolic stimuli
A person's subjective perceptions, either real or imagined, of an object's attributes, such as a product.

Social stimuli
Information a person receives from other people concerning the attributes of an object, such as a product.

Second, **symbolic stimuli** are those relating to a person's subjective perceptions—either real or imagined—of a product's attributes. Each product or service stands for something beyond its physical characteristics. For example, a firm could create an affluent, prestigious image by bottling a wine in a cork-sealed container, adding an elegant label, and advertising it in a luxurious apartment served as part of a candlelight dinner for an attractive couple dressed in fashionable clothing. Harvey's Bristol Cream promotions create such an image.

Finally, **social stimuli** include all the information a person receives from his or her family, friends, reference groups, social class, and others. Unlike the limited model of "the economic person," therefore, the Howard and Sheth model recognizes the importance of social variables.

Stimuli serve to trigger a person's mental processes. The first of these is perception: the process of becoming aware of stimuli. The exact nature of a perception depends upon the clarity of the information received, how much attention the receiver gave, the extent of his or her search for information, the degree to which other stimuli competed for attention, bias in perception, and ambiguity in the stimuli. The learning subsystem mentally processes perceptions further. Personal confidence, attitudes, drives, criteria for making decisions, understanding the nature of a brand, satisfaction derived from brand use, and future intentions are among the learning subsystem's elements.

The model specifies various kinds of behavioral outputs. Foremost in managers' minds is a consumer's decision to buy or not to buy. However, managers should consider other behavioral outputs. Focusing exclusively on the purchase decision can be misleading.

A manager who is positioning a new detergent to compete against Procter & Gamble's highly successful Tide might consider an ad ineffective if it did not immediately increase sales. But the ad could have been quite successful, in fact, even if it did not attain this end. Perhaps attitudes toward the new detergent became very

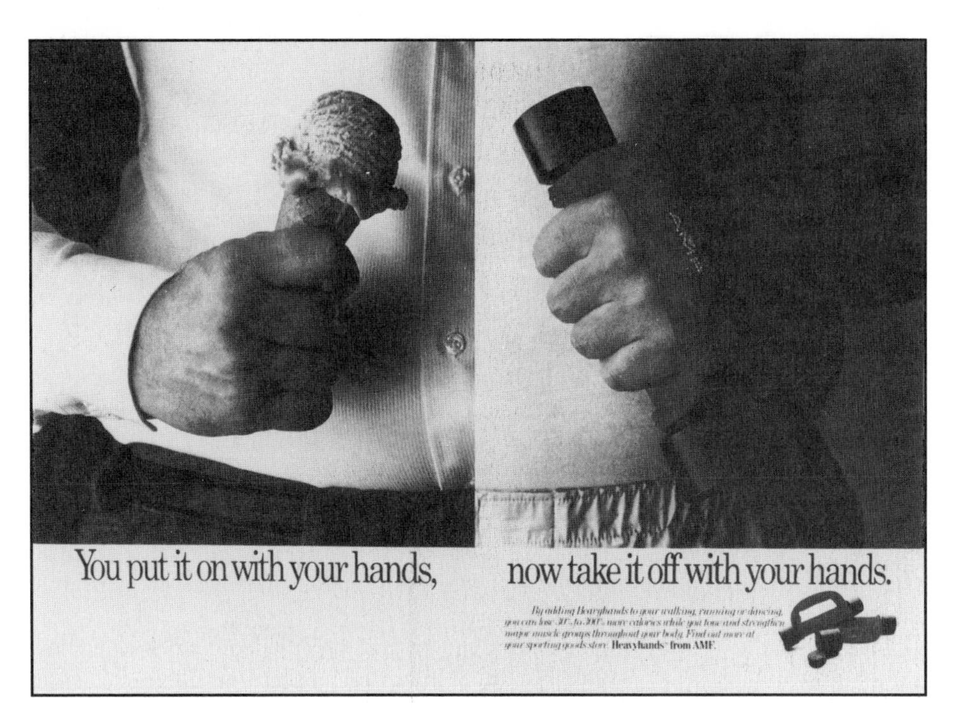

There is a definite health trend in the United States.

favorable after the appearance of the ad; if the firm continues the advertising a little longer, it may break some existing Tide brand loyalty. Other behavior outputs that marketers may choose to analyze are the degree of attention prospective consumers pay to a marketing effort, their understanding of the product's attributes, and their intention to purchase at some future time.

Finally, the model illustrates that behavioral outputs feed back to affect an individual's mental processes. When consumers buy Florsheim shoes, for instance, they evaluate the derived satisfaction, resulting in adjustments to their attitudes and to other behavioral elements such as feelings toward Florsheim and other brands. These adjustments, in turn, influence future consumer perceptions, the degree of information they seek before buying the next new pair of shoes, and future buying decisions.

Researchers have devoted considerable effort to studying consumer satisfaction, dissatisfaction, and the implications for managers.[24] Many dissatisfied buyers of an item will not repurchase it. One study indicated that from 30 percent to over 90 percent of the dissatisfied consumers did not plan to repurchase the brands in question.[25] Another consequence of dissatisfaction is negative word-of-mouth, in which the consumers tell friends and associates about their bad experiences with a brand. When consumers are only moderately dissatisfied, their responses do not often result in negative word-of-mouth. However, when consumers are seriously unhappy with a product, they complain to others regardless of any actions marketers take to remedy the ill-will. It is at moderate levels of dissatisfaction that management policy may have the most impact. For instance, if retailers encourage complaints they have a chance to remedy legitimate grievances and win back customers who may also make positive reports to others, thus increasing goodwill.[26]

In summary, the Howard and Sheth model presents a comprehensive overview of the many variables involved with the "black box" of consumer behavior. This classic

CONCEPT SUMMARY

Major Elements of the Howard and Sheth Model

I. *Stimuli inputs*—Information originating from three sources outside the individual.
   A. Objective stimuli—the real attributes of a particular marketing mix
   B. Symbolic stimuli—subjective impressions of a particular marketing mix
   C. Social stimuli—information a consumer receives from others

II. Perception—The process of becoming aware of stimuli.

III. Learning elements—Mental activities that follow perceptions. These include personal confidence, attitudes, intentions, drives, choice criteria, the ability to understand a product's features and uses, and satisfaction with the product.

IV. Behavioral outputs—Consumer conduct resulting from mental processes. These include purchases and outputs relating to intentions, attitudes, brand comprehension, and attention.

and widely-cited model has been utilized in a variety of research contexts. It performs a valuable function in pulling together the many factors that bear on consumer behavior.

The remainder of this chapter expands upon many of the important behavioral concepts originating from a number of disciplines. One of these, psychology, focuses mainly on people's mental activity. Those influences on consumer behavior originating within an individual can best be understood through psychological factors.

Psychological Influences

Vast differences in behavior from one individual to another are common. Grasping why people behave the way they do can help in developing effective marketing strategy.[27] Figure 5.5 presents a rudimentary model of individual behavior from a psychological perspective. This section considers each component of the model.

Need
Physical or mental state arising within a person resulting from some felt deficiency.

A **need** is a physical or mental state arising within a person resulting from some felt deficiency. In turn, the individual is motivated to satisfy this deficiency. At some time or another, everyone senses deficiencies involving hunger, thirst, security, affection, achievement, and other elements.

Certainly, some needs are greater than others and some people feel certain needs more or less strongly. There are individuals, for instance, who have a strong need to display evidence of their financial success. They buy expensive homes, cars, clothing, or yachts even though more modest purchases would adequately meet their basic requirements. Others have a need to feel helpful to others and contribute effort and money to charities. An example of a company targeting on needs is Richardson-Vicks, Inc., which discovered through research that there are more young adults in the U.S. who have skin blemishes than there are teens with this problem. The firm addressed this need with its Clearasil Adult Care cream.[28] At this point, it is useful to examine how needs relate to other psychological constructs. This can be done by considering what is called the "cognitive structure."

Cognitive processes
Mental activities that are geared toward thought processes.

Cognitive Structure Needs are neither behavioral acts nor intentions to act. Rather they are tensions that trigger mental activities, collectively termed **cognitive processes,** which in turn are geared to alleviating a sense of deficiency. Once the individual senses a need, the mind works much like a computer scanning a series of data banks

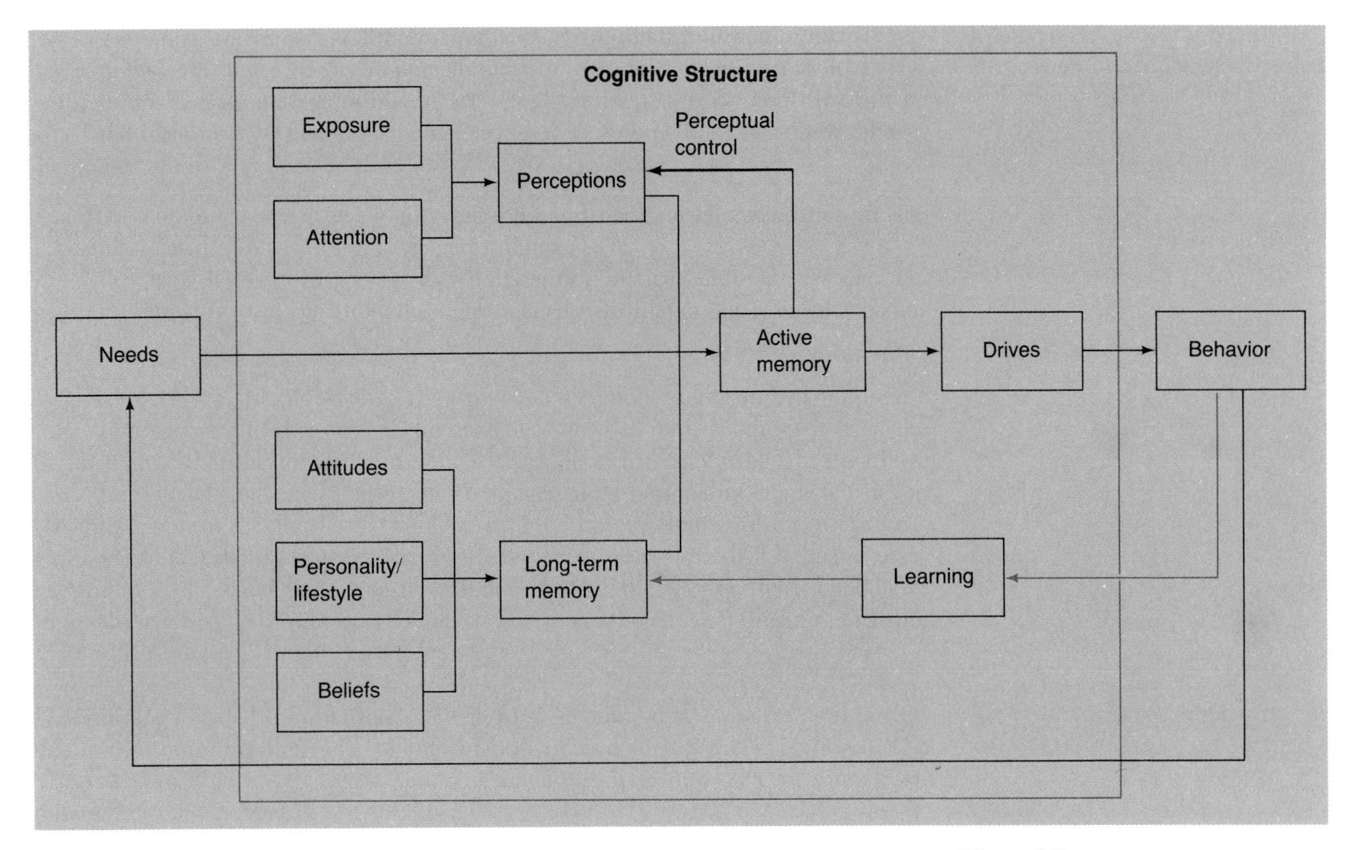

Figure 5.5
Individual Behavior from a Psychological Perspective

for information. It scans the person's memory and sensory inputs, makes interpretations, and chooses the appropriate behavior to achieve satisfaction.[29]

For instance, suppose a consumer feels a need to buy a new pair of slacks. Cognitions interpret the relative importance of this need in relation to all others, and then determine some preferred way to reduce the tension. One means of handling the situation is to realize that other needs are more pressing or that finances are inadequate. In this case, the person reduces tension by attempting to satisfy other needs.

But if other needs are not too pressing and if finances are adequate, the consumer evaluates various cognitions of pant styles, brands, and stores selling pants in an attempt to develop a concept of the slacks that will best satisfy the need. Perhaps the individual will conduct a shopping trip that includes browsing and additional perceptions of various pant selections, or possibly this person will search magazine or newspaper ads for more information. Marketing's task is to relay promotional communications in some way so that consumers consider the company's product offering before buying decisions are finalized. Further discussion of various elements of the cognitive structure is necessary in order to point out the various alternatives open to marketers.[30]

Memory Past experiences become part of consumers' psychological makeups and influence their cognitions and their resulting future behavior. Individuals often become loyal to certain brands and buy them each time a certain need arises. As one source indicates, analyzing memory should be considered as one of the highest priorities of consumer research.[31]

Memory has two distinctive features: active memory for use while thinking, and long-term retention.[32] Upon recognizing a need, the active memory gathers information available in long-term storage, collects incoming sensory stimulations, and processes the information so that it is available for making decisions. Much of the information the senses gather is very short-lived and is lost before it can be transferred to memory. Further, only a portion of long-term memory is available for use within active memory. Marketers have the task of trying to keep information about their company's offerings in the active memories of their target consumers.[33]

Two factors seem to determine whether or not individuals can retrieve information stored in long-term memory. One is the depth to which they originally analyzed the information. The more extensive the analysis, the greater the chance that they can retrieve it. While marketers cannot fully control how extensively consumers analyze their products, they can design promotions to help consumers retain messages. For instance, the Kellogg Company recently ran a highly successful advertising campaign to tell consumers that Kellogg's All-Bran was rich in fiber. The campaign appeared not long after considerable mention in the press that fiber is an essential ingredient to good health.

The other factor affecting long-term memory is the frequency of use. As Figure 5.6A illustrates, people tend to forget over time what they previously learned.[34] This is a special concern to marketers of infrequently purchased products and services.

Organizations can monitor memory decay rates through research to determine when they should run promotional messages to offset the decay. Properly timed promotion messages can keep the images of a product or service fresh in the memories of a target, as Figure 5.6B depicts. Members of IBM's sales force, for instance, routinely call on past customers to make sure that they are not experiencing data processing and other computer-related problems. At the same time, they inform customers of new company models, improved software, and other developments. This helps to keep the company readily in the minds of customers when they are considering replacements.

High-involvement situations
A decision setting where the outcome is considered to be of great importance and there is heavy personal involvement.

Traditional marketing research has focused on cognitive structures under situations where consumers were heavily involved in the purchase (**high-involvement situations**), as when they are considering a new home or automobile. However, consumers make the majority of purchase decisions under conditions of low involvement, where they do not view the product or service in question to be highly important and their identification with the product is not strong.

Figure 5.6
Memory Decay

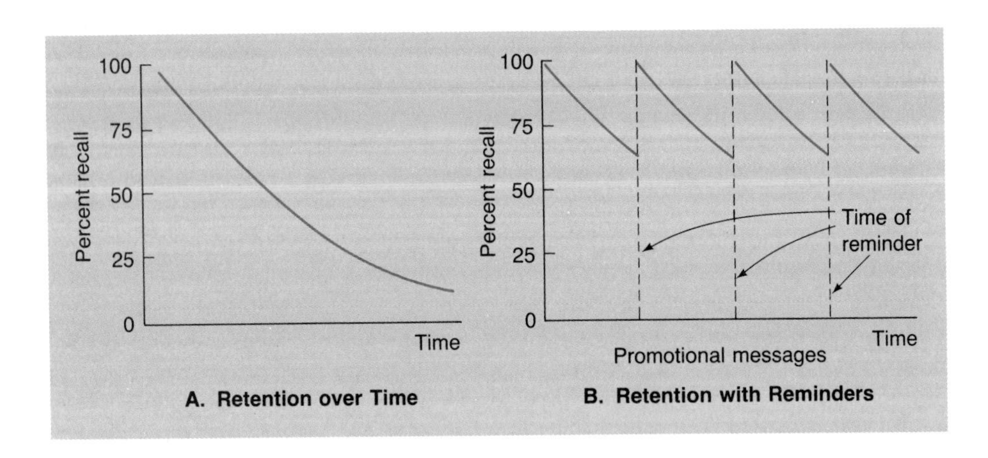

Memory formation in **low-involvement cases** produces passive learning, which has been the focus of recent study. In the case of television viewing, for example, many consumers are in relaxed states and do not pay much attention to commercial messages.[35] They do not closely associate the message with their brand beliefs, past experiences, and needs. Further, they retain information on a random basis because the message is repeated numerous times. Hence, they can recall many commercials, but their attitudes toward particular brands are not heavily influenced.

Low-involvement cases (situations)
A decision setting where the outcome is not considered to be of great importance and there is little personal involvement.

Low-involvement consumers do not actively seek information on the merits of various brands. Rather, they are passive receivers. They may not resist messages not conforming to their prior beliefs. They may purchase some brands without really consciously thinking about them. In addition, they do not extend themselves in making comprehensive searches for the best buy, believing that the time and energy required for such a search is not worth whatever reward might follow. All types of consumers, without reference to their beliefs, personalities, attitudes, and other traits, may purchase particular brands because the messages do not challenge strongly held feelings.

Low-involvement situations, then, are significant in their impact on memory formation. They also can temper management's views of other psychological variables, such as attitudes and beliefs.

Attitudes and Beliefs **Beliefs** are emotionally neutral cognitions that a person holds about some object's attributes which form as the person receives information over time. Beliefs reflect a person's defined set of attributes about an object, which may be real or imagined. To illustrate, many people imagine that snakes have slime on their skins, which is untrue, but they operate as if the belief were true. Thus, beliefs reflect what people "know" to be true about a product's attributes. For example, most people "know" that San Francisco is located on a bay, is hilly, has a scenic bridge, and cable cars, yet they may have never visited the city.

Beliefs
A person's set of emotionally neutral cognitions about an entity, real or imagined.

In contrast, **attitudes** are emotional evaluations of beliefs, having a positive or negative affective dimension. They reflect, for instance, whether or not a particular individual finds San Francisco's hills and other attributes to be appealing. Attitudes may be neutral (indifference) or they may be either positive or negative in varying intensities. Research indicates that attitudes have a directive influence on behavior.[36] Hence, a person liking San Francisco's attributes may consider visiting the city on a vacation.

Attitudes
Emotional evaluations of beliefs, having a positive or negative affective dimension.

An attitude develops for each belief about a product. Because beliefs about multiple attributes may materialize, some attitudes relating to a product may be positive, others negative, and still others somewhere in between. For instance, a person might like San Francisco's scenery but not its traffic congestion. Most research points to attitudes as being *compensatory* for most individuals, meaning that a negative attitude on one belief offsets positive feelings on others.[37] That is, consumers form an overall attitude toward a specific product by balancing all of the attitude/belief combinations.

The Fishbein model is a widely adopted means of explaining how the balancing comes about, as follows: [38]

$$A_o = \sum_{i=1}^{N} B_i a_i$$

where: A_o = the overall attitude toward buying an object
B = strength of the belief that an attribute is related to the object
a = value of this attribute to the consumer
N = the total number of beliefs

For illustration, assume that a consumer is ready to buy a new TV set and is evaluating various brand alternatives. Assume further that "picture clarity," "dependable operation," and "price" are the significant attributes used in comparing brands. Some statements of belief, therefore, could be as follows:

The set has a crisp, clear picture with vivid colors.
The set has a low frequency of needed repair.
The set costs $400 or less.

A marketing research project could then measure attitudes toward a particular brand, say Sony, by asking the following questions:

Sony has a crisp, clear picture with vivid colors.
(B_1) Probable _____ _____ _____ _____ _____ Improbable
(A_1) Good _____ _____ _____ _____ _____ Bad
Sony has a low frequency of needed repair.
(B_2) Probable _____ _____ _____ _____ _____ Improbable
(A_2) Good _____ _____ _____ _____ _____ Bad
Sony will cost less than $400.
(B_3) Probable _____ _____ _____ _____ _____ Improbable
(A_3) Good _____ _____ _____ _____ _____ Bad

After measuring various other brands according to the same pairs of questions, the analyst is then able to estimate an individual's overall attitude toward buying each of the measured brands. This is done by multiplying the (B_i) and (A_i) components for each belief and then summing across the total number of beliefs. The brand having the greater A_o score is the one that the individual is most likely to buy.

Management can use attitude information in conjunction with a segmentation strategy to select target markets. Sales- and production-oriented managers tend to concentrate marketing efforts on advertising and personal selling to favorably influence customer attitudes toward their products. While managers can use promotion efforts in this way, it is generally much more efficient for them to alter a marketing mix to reflect a target's existing attitudes.[39]

Personality
That which establishes and maintains a consistency of attitudes and beliefs that characterize a person's unique behavioral orientations.

Personality **Personality** is a cognitive component that is closely related to attitudes. While the individual forms attitudes toward specific objects, the personality develops as his or her general orientation toward objects and life in general. It establishes and maintains a consistency among a set of attitudes and beliefs that characterize a person's unique nature. Furthermore, personality affects the development of attitudes. For instance, a person who likes outdoor sporting activities (a personality trait) is likely to have favorable attitudes toward games such as golf and tennis.

Three factors are instrumental in shaping a person's personality.[40] First, *inborn potentials* such as body type and mental capacity are influential. The most dedicated five foot adolescent with slow reactions, for example, could not realistically expect to play in the National Basketball Association. Personality must develop in light of a person's innate abilities. Second, cultural values to which one is exposed, such as feelings about work, cleanliness, and promptness, serve to affect personality. Finally, the unique experiences a person encounters influence personality development.

One may be able to understand some important aspects of personality by examining the two dimensions forming a paradigm illustrated in Figure 5.7. First, stable people are those whose emotions are not easily aroused. They are calm, reliable, and even-tempered. At the other extreme, unstable persons are anxious, moody, restless, and

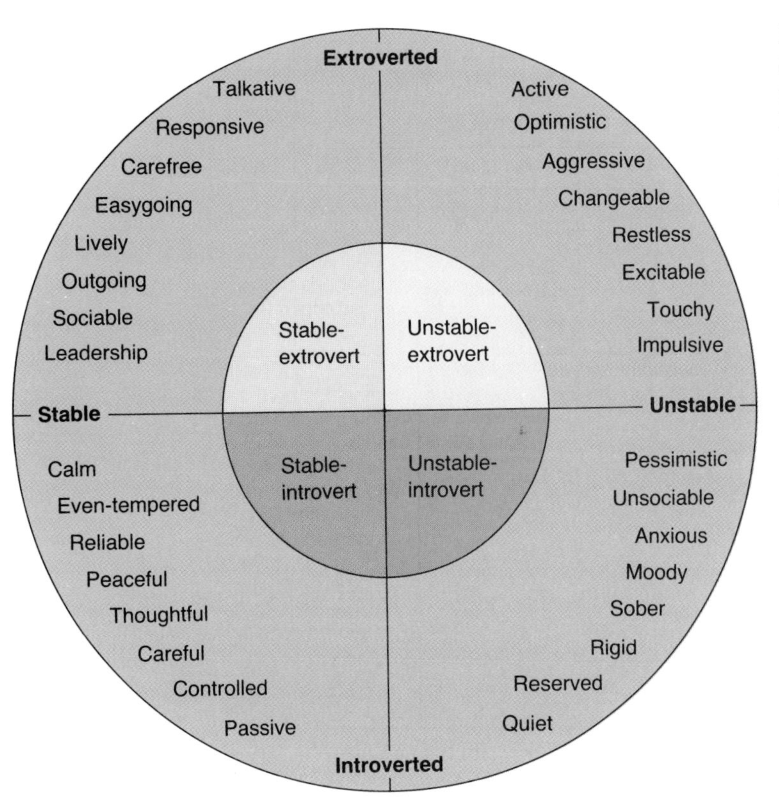

Figure 5.7
Personality Dimensions
(SOURCE: Adapted from H. J. Eysenck and S. B. G. Eysenck, *The Eysenck Personality Inventory* (San Diego: Educational and Industrial Testing Service, 1963).)

touchy. Along the other dimension, extroverts tend to be very sociable, outgoing, and relate well with others. Finally, introverts are withdrawn, shy, prefer to work alone, and experience difficulty and stress in socializing.

Some marketers feel that personality is an important behavioral influence and use this concept when they are designing marketing programs. The AT&T promotional theme, "Reach Out and Touch Someone" focuses on stable, extroverted people; those who are outgoing, sociable, and lively. But the real effect personality has on buying is not clear; research has generated conflicting evidence. For example, one study found that significant relationships exist between personality and purchasing convenience items.[41] The bulk of the research evidence, however, does not support the utilization of personality concepts as a major means of understanding consumer behavior.[42]

Lifestyles An important extension of the personality is an individual's **lifestyle.** Some people, for instance, like to dress casually, spend considerable time at home, and avoid flashy styles. Others prefer to dress fashionably, attend parties, and drive prestigious automobiles. Ample evidence does exist to indicate that lifestyle dimensions can help explain buying behavior differences.[43] In one study, for example, researchers found that the lifestyles of credit card users differed considerably from nonusers.[44]

Lifestyle
Everyday behaviorally oriented facets of people's activities, as well as their feelings, attitudes, and opinions.

As one authority puts it, "lifestyle deals with everyday behaviorally oriented facets of people as well as their feelings, attitudes, and opinions. Further, it answers questions like 'What do women think about the job of housekeeping? Are they interested in contemporary fashions? Do they participate in community activities?' "[45] Exhibit 5.2 illustrates some typical areas for lifestyle, also called **psychographic** research.

Psychographic (factors)
Another term for *lifestyle variables*.

Exhibit 5.2
Typical Lifestyle Dimensions

Activities	Interests	Opinions	Demographics
Work	Family	Themselves	Age
Hobbies	Home	Social issues	Education
Social events	Job	Politics	Income
Vacation	Community	Business	Occupation
Entertainment	Recreation	Economics	Family size
Clubs	Fashion	Education	Dwelling
Community	Food	Products	Geography
Shopping	Media	Future	City size
Sports	Achievements	Culture	Life cycle stage

SOURCE: Joseph T. Plummer, "The Concept and Application of Life Style Segmentation," *Journal of Marketing* 38, no. 1 (January 1, 1974): 34.

Psychographic studies play a major role in the marketing research efforts of many firms.[46] For example, in a classic study of users and nonusers of bank charge cards, psychographic analysis revealed profiles of segments that other approaches could not detect. The study indicated "that users of commercial bank charge cards, in contrast to nonusers, exhibit a 'contemporary state of mind' and a rejection of conservative traditional concepts." [47] Such knowledge is valuable to management in segmenting markets and in designing promotional messages.

Perception
The act of becoming aware, through the senses, of objects, qualities, and relationships existing in the environment.

Perception Consumers utilize both new information and that contained in long-term memory when making buying decisions. They use perception in acquiring information. **Perception** is the act of becoming aware, through the sense organs, of objects, qualities, and relationships existing in the environment.

Theoretically, all stimuli that cause sensory activity enter the memory,[48] but consumers quickly forget many perceptions. For example, only 44 percent of those exposed to the thousands of print ads analyzed by the Starch readership research service say they notice a particular ad, about a third say they recall enough to identify a brand, and merely a tenth say they recall most of an ad.[49] Marketers should devote considerable effort to learning about target customer perceptions and other information processing elements so they can design effective promotion messages.

Both exposure and attention are necessary for perceptions to register in a person's memory. An operational difficulty confronting managers, however, is that consumers control their own perceptual processes. Experience with TV's "All in the Family" illustrates this fact. CBS introduced the show in the early 1970s and it satirized Archie Bunker as a narrow-minded bigot, yet many viewers saw Archie as a hero.[50]

Selective perception
Perception that is controlled by a person's desires and other cognitions, causing control of his or her perceptual attention and exposure to stimuli.

Control over perception begins with a person's exposure to information. This **perception** is **selective,** as people choose to whom they talk, what they read, to which TV and radio programs they expose themselves, and other inputs. They may control which commercials they see by switching TV set channels when unwanted commercials appear—a practice advertisers call "zapping." [51]

Effective communication of marketing messages begins when management precisely identifies the right target audience. Next, the manager must determine the types of media that actually reach target consumers. Which magazines do they read? Which television programs do they watch? Which newspapers do they receive? After learning

California is legend for setting lifestyles.

the answers to such questions, a manager can deliver marketing messages to potential customers.[52] This logic is illustrated by Tyndale House Publishing Company's choice of the Christian Broadcasting Network to advertise "The Book," a 1,285 page easy-to-read Bible.[53]

Individuals also selectively control their attention to stimuli. Some promotional messages register either a negative impression or no impression at all on many of the people exposed to them.[54] This is not surprising, as consumers normally attempt to maintain consistency among their attitudes and this affects the way in which they attend to messages.[55] For example, Chevrolet's Vega had engine cooling problems during its early years. Surveys revealed that many people associated the Vega engine problems with all of GM's small cars. They believed that the Chevette had similar defects despite two facts: the firm had largely corrected Vega's technical problems, and GM made the Chevette's motor of cast iron, a material not susceptible to the same difficulties as the Vega's aluminum engine.

The most logical strategy is for management to direct marketing efforts to those consumers already having neutral or positive attitudes toward the firm and its products. When this is accomplished, consumers are more likely to perceive messages in the manner intended by the marketer. The chances of changing the minds of those who are negatively disposed are so small that such actions are usually not worth the effort.[56]

But sometimes a company has no choice except to appeal to those who are negatively disposed. This is common in the life insurance industry. Experience suggests that the best way to overcome the problem of selective attention from negative consumers is through a technique called controlled exposure.[57] This method involves placing prospects into situations where they have little choice but to give their undivided attention to company-sponsored messages. A number of time-share resort real estate marketers, for instance, invite prospects to exclusive restaurant facilities, provide them with dinners and free overnight accommodations, and then present hard-sell promotions about their properties. These marketers select and arrange rooms so that there are few distractions such as windows and pictures.

Drives
Mental elements that incite a person's behavioral acts.

Drives and Behavior **Drives** are the mental elements that incite a person's behavior. They are internal states of tension that require relief. After sensing a need, a person's active memory evaluates its importance and calls upon stored information as well as new perceptions to develop alternative ways of finding satisfaction. A drive, also called a motive, directs behavior toward satisfying needs.

Reinforcement
The effects of behavior on need satisfaction.

Learning
An outcome of reinforcement that changes the probability that a behavior will recur the next time that the need arises.

Cognitive processes again come into play once consumers have made a purchase. Now, however, the purpose is to evaluate how well the purchase satisfied the individual's needs. The term **reinforcement** refers to the effects of behavior on need satisfaction.[58] **Learning,** the outcome of reinforcement, changes the probability that a behavior will recur the next time the need arises.

If the reward is positive, as when a can of Sprite satisfies thirst and tastes good, the likelihood of repeat purchase increases. Conversely, if the reward is negative, the probability of repeat purchase is likely to decline. These observations provide support for the marketing concept. They suggest that the long-run success of the organization depends on its ability to satisfy customer needs, not just on getting initial purchases.

Some managers make a major mistake by assuming that sales are finished when buyers obtain their goods or services. However, purchasers often experience doubt after a buying decision. The academic literature calls this "cognitive dissonance," where recent purchasers undergo considerable self-questioning over whether or not they made the correct decision.[59] Marketers of expensive items should take steps to reduce postpurchase conflict so that reinforcement will be as positive as possible. Astute realtors, for instance, often call back on recent purchasers to help them adjust smoothly to their new surroundings. Informal visits to answer questions about shopping, schools, and community activities even after home buyers move in can be important in generating customer satisfaction.

Cognitive dissonance
Lack of equilibrium between two cognitive elements, often relating to a postpurchase decision.

Trials
The number of repetitions involving a need and a resulting behavior response.

Dissonance takes place when two or more cognitive elements are not in equilibrium. These elements are beliefs, opinions, and knowledge. If one element is contrary to another, **cognitive dissonance** occurs, and the consumer is motivated to seek equilibrium. Hence, a recent purchaser of an Oldsmobile Firenza might experience dissonance after reading a comparative ad pointing out that Plymouth Horizons are superior to Firenzas. It is in Oldsmobile's self-interest to prevent and dispel such beliefs. Management can accomplish this through such devices as sponsoring advertising that praises Firenza quality and performance and having the salesperson call new car buyers several days after purchase to reassure them.

The number of repetitions, termed **trials,** with a need and a resulting behavior response also directly effects learning. The learning curve in Figure 5.8 illustrates this.[60] For example, the more times customers dine in a certain restaurant and receive positive reinforcement, the greater the chance of their returning again. Marketers are well advised to utilize learning curves as guides to decisions. For instance, some managers spend their entire advertising budget on only a few advertisements, but these make a small impact on consumers' memory because of low repetition. A more desirable approach may be to reduce the size but to increase the number of ads. This could result in a far greater probability of purchase because of greater repetition.

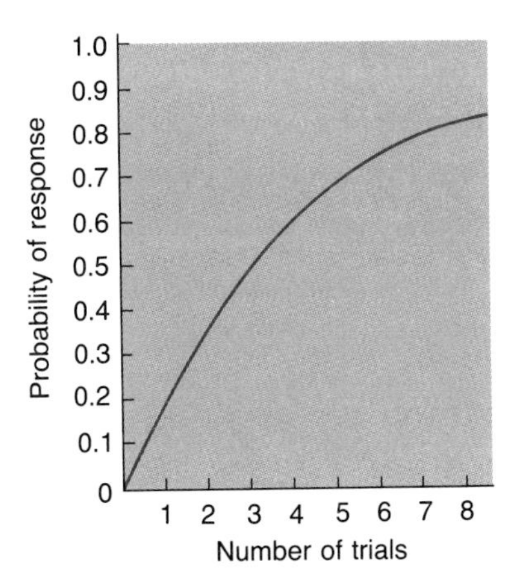

Figure 5.8
Learning Curve for a Hypothetical Product

Sociological Influences

Few consumers live in social isolation. Rather, most learn patterns of behavior from others and this influences their buying habits. For instance, business executives who live in the West often dress more casually than those in the East. Most college students wear clothing similar to that of other students. Figure 5.9 presents an overview of the major social influences on consumer buying.

Culture Many people use the term **culture** to identify symphonies, art, plays, and museums—"the finer things in life." While the humanities are part of culture, the concept is really much broader. Childrearing, marriage, laws, and all other activities that are repeated more or less consistently among a given population are part of its culture. Culture is very important to marketing decision making, as illustrated in the accompanying Marketing Brief.

Culture
All activities that are repeated somewhat consistently among a given population. Its three components are the normative, action, and symbolic and material products systems.

All three of culture's major components influence consumer decision making.[61] First, the *normative* system instructs people on how they are supposed to behave. It

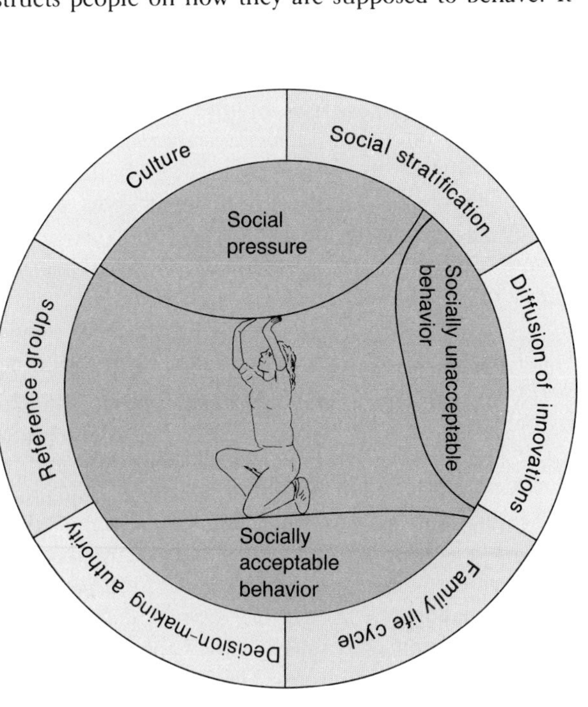

Figure 5.9
Individual Behavior from a Sociological Perspective

MARKETING BRIEF

Shaping Products to Reflect Social Forces

Mother Jones (MJ), the controversial San Francisco–based, left-leaning muckraking magazine, is looking for new readers, according to Don Hazen, the publication's new publisher. There have been considerable sociological changes in the U.S., according to Mr. Hazen, since the days of President Carter. "People are not as responsive to political magazines," he said. "We want people to know *Mother Jones* has kept pace with the times."

The magazine plans to remain involved with social issues, but there will be a definite reduction in the political involvement of the publication. An example of a potential feature for the magazine's new launch in September 1986 involves the cultural differences between singles, couples, and those with families. Another example of this new type of story is a feature that ran in December 1985 concerning natural versus hospital childbirth. They will not alienate their current readers, though. They will continue to publish satires on government officials and other politicians.

SOURCE: Adapted from Kevin Brown, "Times Are A-Changin' at 'Mother Jones,' " *Advertising Age* (January 13, 1986): 40.

spells out the duties, responsibilities, and privileges of society's membership. Norms range from the informal behavioral codes of lovers to the formal legal codes governing complex organizations like governmental bodies or corporations.

Second, the *action* system spells out specific acts society encourages or frowns upon. A "good father" in a particular society may be one who provides for his family, attends to certain household duties, but does not develop a questionable track record at the local bar.

Finally, the system of *symbols and material products* impinges upon buyer behavior. Educational institutions, modes of transportation, means of communication, housing, and other elements all influence cognitive processes and the resulting behavior. Through their culture, consumers become accustomed to associating certain products and meanings with certain needs.

Because of their common experiences, members of cultural groups develop somewhat similar cognitive structures. In addition, there are subcultural differences within a broad population. Most Americans, for instance, enjoy pork products. But many Jewish and Arabic Americans avoid them because of subcultural pressures. Blacks, Puerto Ricans, Mexican Americans, Catholics, Mormons, northerners, and city dwellers are among the extensive list of subcultures residing within the U.S. All of these groups have slightly different cognitive structures that might dictate the direction of effective marketing strategy.

Failure to properly recognize cultural differences can lead to major marketing blunders.[62] Colgate-Palmolive, for instance, raised the ire of many citizens when it introduced Cue Toothpaste into French-speaking countries. This is because in French, "cue" is an off-color word. Similarly, a canned fish producer sponsored a commercial aired in the Quebec market depicting a woman in shorts, golfing with her husband, and then serving the canned fish for the evening meal. The product failed because all three activities violated the culture's norms.[63]

In the past, cultural change was relatively slow, but rapid technological advancement and consumer mobility have accelerated today's changing values and ideas. Women's liberation, birth control, equal rights, and the growing demands of senior citizens have all had a dramatic impact on market opportunities. This means, of course, that managers must monitor cultural factors more closely than ever before.

Several business-sponsored research groups study and report changing values and how they impact on consumer choices; *Monitor* is perhaps the most comprehensive of them. Yankelovich, Skelly, and White, Inc. produces *Monitor*, an annual survey of 2,500 people from across the U.S. that focuses on identifying social change behavior.[64] All managers, especially those who market consumer products, should keep abreast of these changes.

Social Stratification Patterns of **social stratification** mark all societies, differentiating members of various groups from those in other groups. In the U.S., some people live in the "right" neighborhoods while others live "on the other side of town." In the Soviet Union, apartment size and location along with summer home ownership are dependent upon and define one's status.

A person's birth may form the basis for a stratification system, as in the now-defunct caste system in India, but stratification usually is less rigid and is termed *social class*. As one source states, "those who interact in the social system of a community evaluate the participation of those around them . . . and . . . members of the community are explicitly or implicitly aware of the ranking and translate their evaluation of such social participation into social class rating. . . ."[65]

There is emerging a strong antismoking normative system in the U.S. culture.

Social Classes in the U.S. Various social scientists have proposed several different class breakdowns for the U.S. Research tradition in marketing generally has followed a six-class system, as Exhibit 5.3 sets forth.[66] This categorization is based upon a classic study of nearly 4,000 households.[67] According to the study, social class is a function of three demographic variables:

Social stratification
Systems whereby members of various groups are differentiated from other groups, often relating to economic position.

1. occupation—laborer, skilled trade, managerial, professional, etc.
2. source of income—salary, investments, etc.
3. housing type—style, location, size, etc.

Exhibit 5.4 presents two more-recent breakdowns of social class. In general, both present categorization schemes similar to that set forth in Exhibit 5.3.

Some marketers find that social class helps to explain many buying decisions. For instance, those in higher classes make most purchases of luxurious vacations, while those in the low to middle classes often take family car trips. One study indicated that middle-class adolescents were better able to manage consumer finances than their low-class counterparts.[68] However, the relationship between income and social class may cloud the picture. Income and social class are typically closely related, with those earning high incomes also belonging to high classes, and several studies indicate that income can be more important as a predictor of purchase behavior than social class.[69] Further, within each social class are "privilege groups," made up of individuals who have more income and wealth than others in the class. Privilege group members purchase many luxury goods.[70]

Exhibit 5.3
Traditional Social Class Categories

Class	Description
Upper-upper	It is comprised of those with established family backgrounds and inherited wealth. They are the "pillars of the community," active in social organizations such as charities and represent a small but significant market for the most expensive jewelry, homes, antiques, etc. (This class represents less than 1 percent of the population.)
Lower-upper	These are the newly-arrived wealthy due to exceptional success in business and in the professions. Their ambition is to be accepted by the upper-uppers. Their consumption is conspicuous, with frequent purchases of yachts, cars, expensive homes, and other status symbols. (About 2 percent of the population are in this category.)
Upper-middle	Many lawyers, college professors, physicians and managers fall into this category. They represent a sizeable market for quality items such as furniture, appliances, good homes, clothing, and automobiles. They seek to entertain and make social contacts with "the right people." (About 12 percent of the population.)
Lower-middle	These people are the "silent majority" who obey the law, attend church, follow cultural norms, and work conscientiously. They buy nice homes and conventional furnishings. Much of the work around the home they do themselves and spend a lot of time shopping for good buys. Most "white collar" workers (office workers) and "gray collars" (firepersons and police) fall in this category. However, some of the skilled trade workers do too, such as tool and die journeymen, plumbers, electricians, etc. (About 30 percent of the population.)
Upper-lower	These persons lead acceptable, but dull lives. Life is often repetitive, and they are the most brand-loyal. Most have manual jobs and only moderate education. (About 35 percent.)
Lower-lower	They are at the bottom of society and include slum dwellers. Unfortunately their consumption is marked by minimal planning for buying, heavy reliance on credit, and paying more than necessary to purchase items. (About 20 percent.)

Reference groups
Groups to whom individuals refer in setting standards of proper conduct.

Reference Groups In general, people adjust their behavior to meet the formal and informal standards of groups to which they belong or aspire to belong. These groups are called **reference groups** because individuals refer to them in setting standards of proper conduct. Their influence can affect behavior tremendously. For example, most business administration students aspire to belong to a loosely knit group of "managers" upon graduation. Accordingly, they learn and use the vocabulary of managers, enroll in courses of study they feel will help them gain entry, buy interview clothing that makes them appear to belong, and subscribe to the *Wall Street Journal* or similar publications.

Generally, a reference group is a collection of people that influences the behavior or attitudes of others. However, a reference group can also be a single individual, like a rock star or a popular person at school. Many types of reference groups exist. *Primary* groups are those with few enough members to allow intimate, face-to-face communication.[71] Families, friendship groups, golfing partners, and some teams of workers are of this type. In another major category, *secondary* groups, interpersonal face-to-face interactions are not possible because too many members exist. For many consumers, religious organizations and trade unions are of this variety.

Reference groups may be formal or informal. *Formal* groups have an established organization, such as the employer, the church, and the Elks Club. On the other hand, *informal* groups are voluntary associations of persons with similar interests.

Exhibit 5.4
Contemporary Versions of American Social Classes

The Gilbert-Kahl New Synthesis Class Structure	The Coleman-Rainwater Social Standing Class Hierarchy
Upper Americans 1. *The Capitalist Class* (1%). These individuals' decisions shape the national economy. Their income is mostly from assets and earned/inherited. They have considerable prestige and university connections. 2. *Upper Middle Class* (14%). They are upper managers, professionals, and medium businessmen. College education. Their family income runs nearly twice the national average.	*Upper Americans* 1. *Upper-Upper* (0.3%). They are distinguished by inherited wealth, aristocratic names, and high society. 2. *Lower-Upper* (1.2%). They are the newer social elite, drawn from current professional and corporate leadership. 3. *Upper-Middle* (12.5%). They are the rest of the college graduate managers and professionals. Their lifestyle centers on private clubs, causes, and the arts.
Middle Americans 1. *Middle Class* (33%). They are middle-level white-collar, top-level blue-collar. Their education is past high school. Their income is somewhat above the national average. 2. *Working Class* (32%). They are middle-level blue-collar and lower-level white-collar. Their income runs slightly below the national average. Their education is also slightly below average.	*Middle Americans* 1. *Middle Class* (32%). They are average pay white-collar workers and their blue-collar friends. Live on "the better side of town," and try to "do the proper things." 2. *Working Class* (38%). They are the average pay blue-collar workers. They lead a "working class lifestyle" whatever the income, school background, and job.
Marginal and Lower Americans 1. *The Working Poor* (11–12%). They are below mainstream America in living standard, but above the poverty line. They include low-paid service workers and operatives, and have some high school education. 2. *The Underclass* (8–9%). They depend primarily on the welfare system for sustenance. Their living standard is below the poverty line. They are not regularly employed and lack schooling.	*Lower Americans* 1. *"A lower group of people but not the lowest"* (9%). They are working and not on welfare. Their living standard is just above poverty. Their behavior is judged as "crude," and "trashy." 2. *"Real Lower-Lower"* (7%). They are on welfare, visibly poverty-stricken, usually out of work (or have "the dirtiest jobs"), and include "bums," and "common criminals."

SOURCE: Adapted from Richard P. Coleman, "The Continuing Significance of Social Class to Marketing," *Journal of Consumer Research* 10, no. 4 (December 1983): 48–59.

Bridge clubs, car pools, and cliques are examples. Two kinds, primary and informal groups, exert the most influence on consumer behavior.

Such groups, especially informal ones, do not readily lend themselves to analysis by marketers or to treatment as separate segments.[72] Two factors account for this. First, the groups generally contain too few members to warrant the firm's creation of unique marketing mixes. Second, and perhaps more important, they generally are neither attainable nor measurable for strategic purposes (see the requisites for segmenting markets in Chapter 3).

Many formal and secondary reference groups, on the other hand, are large, visible, and measurable. In many cases, a membership roster with mailing addresses and other means of contacting members exists. Such bodies as the American Bar Association and the American Association of Manufacturers are practical groups for segmenting markets.

The Family The family exerts perhaps the most influence of all the reference groups when it comes to consumer behavior. While each family has somewhat different buying habits, all tend to pass through stages that influence their consumption patterns.[73]

1. Bachelor Stage—young, single people away from parents' home
2. Newly Marrieds—young, no children
3. Full Nest I—youngest child under 6 years
4. Full Nest II—young marrieds, youngest child over 6 years
5. Full Nest III—older marrieds, dependent children
6. Empty Nest I—older marrieds, no dependent children, household head in labor force
7. Empty Nest II—older married, no dependent children, retired
8. Solitary Survivor I—spouse deceased, still in labor force
9. Solitary Survivor II—spouse deceased, retired

Both needs and desires on the one hand, and incomes on the other, tend to change with the passage of each stage. The Bachelor stage, one that is growing, is the prime market for singles apartments and rental furniture. Conversely, Full Nest I accounts for the core of the baby food, clothing, and furniture market. Empty Nest I is the stage with the greatest discretionary income and is the prime market for expensive vacations and retirement homes. The family life cycle paradigm is very useful to marketers for segmenting markets and for formulating strategy because it describes the conditions under which consumers are interested in many different kinds of products.

Decision-Making Authority Another aspect of family influence on consumer behavior is the concept of decision-making authority: which member(s) of the family have the authority to make product selections. Many parents are ***gatekeepers*** for children and for each other. Gatekeepers filter information about products and services, deciding what to pass on and what to withhold and also make purchases of products for others to consume. They are the principal decision makers for many products, particularly gifts. Gatekeeping is especially predominant within families, as parents typically buy clothing, toys, food, and most other products that their children (and also their spouses) consume. Some marketers miss their targets by aiming promotion efforts at product users rather than gatekeepers. Most cereal and toy companies, for instance, advertise heavily during Saturday morning children's cartoon programs. These marketers might be wise to orient advertising to parents rather than to children.

Decision-making authority within families varies widely. Research indicates four family decision-making molds.[74]

1. *Autonomic*—equal number of different decisions made by each partner
2. *Syncratic*—most decisions made jointly
3. *Husband-dominance*—the husband dominates most decisions
4. *Wife-dominance*—the wife dominates most decisions

All modern societies exhibit some of each pattern of decision making. In the U.S., however, there is a trend toward increasing numbers of syncratic and autonomic families. This may be due to higher levels of education and the women's movement.

Another way of classifying families is according to the strategies employed by

The trend is toward syncratic and autotomic families in the U.S.

individual spouses in making joint decisions. One researcher revealed six influence strategies: [75]

1. *Noninfluencers*—people who influence their spouses very little, except when they have direct expertise concerning the purchase.
2. *Light influencers*—people who influence their spouses somewhat, but are generally timid and often state reasons beyond their control, such as "the other brand is out of stock," when it really is available.
3. *Subtle influencers*—people who rely on a reward/referent strategy, which means that they offer subtle rewards to their spouses for adopting their views.
4. *Emotional influencers*—people who sway their partners through emotional displays, such as shouting or crying.
5. *Combination influencers*—people who make moderate use of all of the strategies.
6. *Heavy influencers*—people who play a heavy hand in trying to exert dominance over the decision.

The relative power of each spouse and the way in which he or she exerts this power differs considerably from one influence strategy grouping to another. This provides guidelines to the marketer in deciding which promotion media and messages to utilize.[76]

Diffusion of innovations
The time sequence through which various groups (innovators, early adopters, early majority, late majority, and laggards) in a population adopt an innovation.

Diffusion of Innovations A concept that is closely related to reference group influence is the **diffusion of innovations.**[77] All consumers do not immediately adopt new products, even if they are far superior to those they replace. It may take months or even

Young people serve to demonstrate the workability of some products.

years before a new offering effectively can penetrate a market. Consider the introduction of drip coffee makers into the United States. Drip-brewed coffee makers, which pass hot water over ground coffee beans only once, have been popular in Europe for many years. North American Systems refined and improved the drip principle and introduced Mr. Coffee to the U.S. market in the early 1970s. While the firm made dramatic sales gains, it did not accomplish them overnight. By 1976,

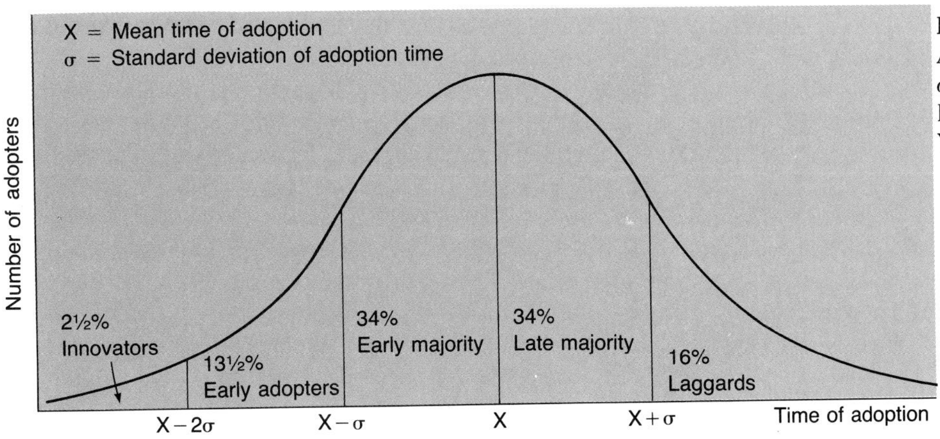

Figure 5.10
Adopter Categories and Relative Time of Adoption (SOURCE: Everett M. Rogers, *Diffusion of Innovations* (New York: The Free Press, 1962): 162.)

U.S. consumers had purchased nearly eight million automatic drip makers, with Mr. Coffee holding over half of the market share.[78] Likewise, sales of frozen breakfast foods remained stagnant for many years until the late 1970s and early 1980s, when microwave ovens became popular and manufacturers brought out new offerings such as Kellogg's Eggo waffles and Pet's Downy Flake.[79]

Many researchers have studied society's patterns of adopting innovations. A major synthesis of over 600 separate studies revealed that adopters of new innovations fall into one of several different categories distinguishable on the basis of relative times of adoption. The study also showed that each category has social characteristics that distinguish it from others.[80] Figure 5.10 illustrates the concept, which is discussed in the remainder of this section.

Adopter Categories As the figure indicates, there are five **adopter categories** explained by the area under the normal curve: innovators, early adopters, early majority, late majority, and laggards.

Adopter categories
Groupings of individuals based upon their relative time of adopting an innovation: innovators, early adopters, early majority, late majority, and laggards.

Innovators are the first 2.5 percent of those who ever adopt a new idea (or product). They tend to be venturesome, worldly, and are on the fringe of the social system. They are considered both by others and by themselves as deviants from society's norms and standards of behavior. Innovators are mobile, traveling considerably and changing jobs, residences, and other arrangements frequently. These individuals are "social guinea pigs," demonstrating the practicality, workability, or desirability of an innovation to others. Early hippies and beatniks, for example, were innovators of dress styles later adopted by straight people.

Early adopters are the next 13.5 percent to adopt the new idea or product. Unlike innovators, they are not deviants from the social system; they conform more closely to society's norms and values.[81] However, they are often among the better educated and more financially successful members of society. They are generally respected by other members of society, tend to be young, and are frequently considered to be *opinion leaders*. Successful professionals, wealthy entertainers and some members of high society were the next to adopt the beads and embroidered denim worn by the early hippy innovators.

The *early majority* are the next 34 percent to adopt the idea or product. Their primary function is that of sanctioning the use of an innovation. They may be eager to embrace new ideas but are often unsure of themselves and wait for sufficient social approval and for the early adopters to try out the innovation. Middle executives, aspiring professionals, and others next adopted fancy denim for casual wear.

The *late majority* are the next 24 percent to finally adopt after 50 percent of the others have already done so. They tend to resist change but are tied to the society and adopt when an innovation becomes inevitable. Often they succumb to social pressures to accept a new idea, reluctantly changing past patterns. Middle-class consumers next adopted less-expensive denim.

Laggards are the final 16 percent to adopt. They cling to past behaviors, norms, and values. Like innovators they are deviants in some respects, but at the opposite end of the social spectrum. In general, laggards are older members of society and are often on the verge of departing into some new population. Older persons and those in lower social classes finally adopted denim as acceptable dress.

Stages of adoption
Mental states that people pass through before adopting a new innovation: awareness, interest, evaluation, trial, and adoption.

Stages of Adoption Research reveals that people pass through a series of mental **stages** before they adopt a new innovation: [82]

1. *Awareness*. The person becomes cognizant of the existence of a new idea, but not fully informed about it.
2. *Interest*. The person develops the motivation to seek information about the innovation.
3. *Evaluation*. This is the decision stage, where the person determines whether or not he or she should try it.
4. *Trial*. The person tries the innovation, but does not make any lasting commitment to use it again.
5. *Adoption*. The person decides to make regular use of the innovation.

The stage that most consumers are in helps the marketer design the marketing mix for a new offering. For example, if the bulk of the target market is in Stage 2, management could offer free samples of the new product as a means of inducing consumers to try it. On the other hand, if the bulk of the target is only in Stage 1, management might feature an extensive informational advertising program to provide information about the innovation.

A working knowledge of the adoption process can be a big help to managers in designing effective marketing strategy. For example, later members of adopter categories tend to rely on information from other members of the same social group to help them make their decisions. The marketer can expedite the adoption process by using testimonials by people appearing to be similar to those in the target. Pepsi's taste tests, for instance, picture a wide array of people with whom practically any prospective customer can identify. In addition, some firms find diffusion concepts to be useful in forecasting sales.[83] The chapters focusing on marketing mix decisions later in this book provide examples of further implications of these concepts.

Chapter Summary

Consumer markets are diverse and quite confusing at first glance. The manager's task is to identify order and understanding out of the complexity so that he or she can make more effective marketing decisions.

Consumers are dynamic and reflect this in their buying. Determining trends and developing demographic and psychographic customer profiles is a good start toward identifying order in consumer buying. In addition, managers should acquire as much information as possible about why consumers develop particular purchase patterns.

The task is not easy, since consumer behavior is complex. A tangled web of psychological, sociological, and economic factors shapes it. A model of consumer behavior helps managers understand how and why particular behavior occurs and can be changed.

The needs of individuals, as well as their cognitive structures, are very important determinants of their conduct. Each person has a different set of needs, past experiences, attitudes, beliefs, lifestyle, and motivations that shape purchase decision making.

But people are not islands, as social interactions influence their product choices. More specifically, consumers' cultural environments, social position, and the pressures exerted by reference groups for conformity all play a role in influencing their product choices.

While understanding consumer behavior aids managers in making more effective decisions, it also helps them to identify important information they lack about target customers. This leads to more productive marketing research and even better subsequent decisions. The next chapter probes producer and government buying, building on the framework established here.

Questions

1. When people move long distances, they frequently need to purchase a new set of products and services unfamiliar to them, including housing, new stores and schools, etc. Why is it important for certain marketers to contact these people rapidly? How can they do this?
2. Speculate on the categories of items that consumers will buy in greater quantities if overall affluence continues to increase. What do you base your comments on?
3. What is meant by lifestyle research? How does it relate to marketing?
4. How do demographics help the marketer evaluate opportunities for existing types of products? What about new ones?
5. What are the weaknesses of the "economic man" model of consumer behavior? What are its strengths or good points?
6. Name three products, the demand for which is separately affected by the following demographic variables:
   a. sex
   b. age
   c. occupation
   d. ethnic origin
   e. geographical location
   f. wealth
7. Develop a demographic profile of your class. How does it compare with the rest of society? Some critics of higher education contend that it develops a group of elitists. What do you think?
8. Explain what is meant by the concept of cognitive structure.
9. How does knowledge of perception help marketers? If marketers truly understand perception and other cognitive processes, some critics argue that they could control consumers. What do you think? What are some of the ethical implications?
10. Think of your own experiences. Are there instances where you have observed social class to be a factor in explaining differences in behavior?
11. What is the adoption process? How does it relate to marketing?
12. At which stages of adoption are marketers' influences most effective?
13. Explain the family life cycle's influence on consumer behavior, using your own family as an example.
14. Explain the Howard and Sheth model of consumer behavior in your own words. What are the difficulties that you see for marketers attempting to employ it? What are its strengths?
15. How are conflicting attitudes toward a product resolved? How can marketers research the process?
16. What are gatekeepers? What is their significance?
17. What impact will the following have on future consumer buying:
    a. the women's movement
    b. inflation
    c. a four-day work week
    d. increasing levels of education among consumers
    e. a recession
    f. high interest rates

Chapter 6

Understanding Industrial and Other Organization Buying Behavior

Objectives

After completing this chapter, you should be able to demonstrate a knowledge of:

- The meaning of the terms "industrial" and "governmental" markets
- The economic significance of these markets to marketing decision makers
- The characteristics of industrial goods markets
- The buying procedures used by organizations in these markets
- Major governmental buyers and the requirements they have developed for marketers

MARKETING FAILURE

ITT Drops Out of Digital Telephone Switching

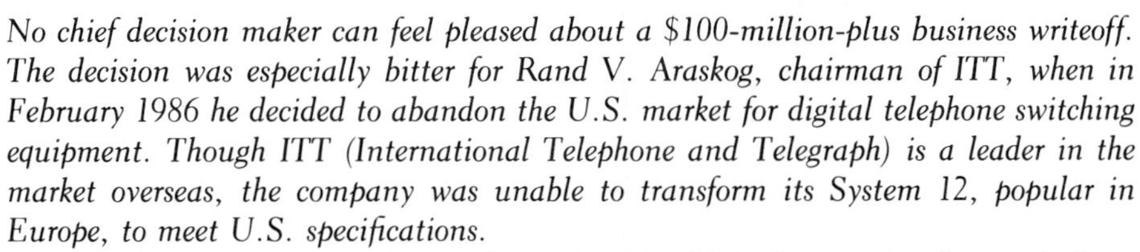

No chief decision maker can feel pleased about a $100-million-plus business writeoff. The decision was especially bitter for Rand V. Araskog, chairman of ITT, when in February 1986 he decided to abandon the U.S. market for digital telephone switching equipment. Though ITT (International Telephone and Telegraph) is a leader in the market overseas, the company was unable to transform its System 12, popular in Europe, to meet U.S. specifications.

Digital equipment is in heavy demand in the U.S. because it allows telephone companies to offer cash-generating services such as call forwarding, call waiting, and especially Centrex—the equivalent of a private telephone system for business customers. The equipment can also transmit data along with voices. AT&T's older analog switching system can handle Centrex, but it cannot move data as efficiently as a digital system.

Mr. Araskog indicated that ITT failed because of bad timing. "Our strategy was to establish a leadership position in Europe and then bring the product to the U.S.," he said. "As it happened, we came in too late." Fred Baker, an assistant vice president of Atlanta-based BellSouth, which was to be ITT's first Bell system customer, agrees: "They just ran behind. Their window in this market was 1987–88. They had to be ready to go then, and they weren't going to be."

The loss means more than the $105 million writeoff to the company. It puts ITT in a vulnerable position against hard-charging competitors in the rest of the world.

SOURCE: Adapted from Michael Brody, "ITT's Wrong Number in the U.S.," *Fortune*, March 17, 1986: 40–42.

Introduction

Far too many people envision marketing as solely relating to the glamorous arena of consumer products; firms such as Helena Rubenstein, Charles of the Ritz, Jordache, and Yardley of London. To some, marketing consists of Madison Avenue sales tactics, martinis at lunch, attractive models, and exotic products that make consumers look, smell, and feel better as they strive for some higher order of existence.

Certainly, marketing does apply to consumer products (although it involves more than nice lunches). But consumer items represent only a portion of the total picture. Institutions such as American Airlines, ITT, and the U.S. Army account for more dollar purchases than do consumers, for two reasons: First, intermediaries purchase practically all consumer items before they sell them to consumers. Second, manufacturers design and sell products to satisfy the needs of producers and governmental institutions involving products such as coal, cement, nails, pig iron, and forklift trucks. This chapter focuses on industrial and government purchasers, who buy items to be used in producing other goods and services. A later chapter examines intermediaries—institutional members of a channel of distribution who buy items for resale to others.

The cost of failure can be incredibly high, as illustrated in this chapter's Marketing Failure. Using solid marketing concepts and decision making can help reduce the chances of such losses when serving industrial markets. Many of the strategies relating to consumer marketing are equally appropriate for industrial buyers, so this chapter will concentrate on theories and concepts that focus on marketing to industrial and governmental institutions.

Industrial Buyer Purchasing

Industrial buyers
Institutional purchasers that buy items so that they can perform their major organizational tasks.

Industrial buyers (sometimes called business buyers or institutional buyers) seek ways of attaining their objectives by producing goods and services and selling them to others. In turn, they buy goods and services to enable them to operate. Industrial buyers are manufacturers of products, such as FMC Corp., National Cash Register (NCR), and Honda; also they are firms providing services, like Kemper Insurance Company, American Airlines, churches, and racetracks. Government units also are producers in the sense that they too create and distribute services, but this chapter treats them separately as their buying practices are somewhat unique. Many industrial buyers are profit-seeking. Others, like Blue Cross/Blue Shield and charitable organizations such as The United Fund, are termed not-for-profit since they seek only to generate enough revenues from their products or services to cover their costs of operation.

All producers are also buyers—they must purchase items that enable them to operate. American Airlines, for instance, buys airplanes, computers, fuel, pens, food, and a vast array of different items. In total, there are over 10 million producers in the U.S. who collectively generate over $1 trillion dollars in revenue and employ about 25 percent of the total population. Obviously, producer markets are gigantic and represent sought-after targets for many companies. Those firms that sell to industrial buyers are called industrial marketers.

Industrial Buyer Characteristics

The major categories of industrial buyers include:

1. Agricultural producers (farming, forestry, and fishing)
2. Service companies (for consumers, such as hospitals, travel agencies; for business, such as CPA firms, office cleaning services)
3. Construction firms (commercial and residential)
4. Extractive firms (mining, quarrying, and drilling)
5. Financial institutions (banks, insurance, and real estate)
6. Manufacturing firms (auto makers, airplane manufacturers)
7. Not-for-profit institutions (churches and charities)
8. Public utilities (electric, telephone, and radio)
9. Transportation firms (airlines, railroads, buses, and taxis)

As a group, industrial buyers have behavioral characteristics different than purchasers of consumer goods and marketers should be aware of these differences when designing their strategies. While all industrial buyers have unique needs, each of them utilizes a similar buying approach. This section discusses them as a single class of buyers.

Available Information Fortunately for marketing decision makers, federal and state governments and trade associations collect substantial detailed data relating to industrial buyers. These organizations publish and make available to managers much of

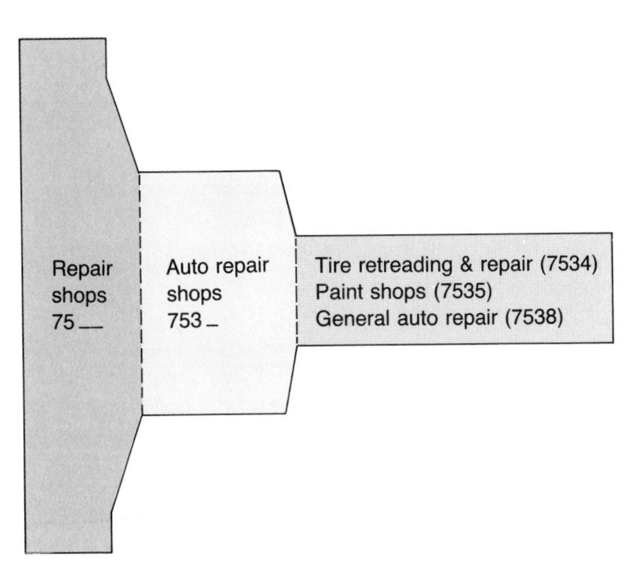

Figure 6.1
Standard Industrial Classification Codes

this information.[1] They report on the number and type of establishments, their sales volume, numbers of employees, cost structures, and other important variables for a large number of industry groups. Most often, the reported data are broken down into **Standard Industrial Classification (SIC) Codes,** which categorize producers by the types of products they manufacture.

Standard industrial classification (SIC) codes
Means of categorizing industrial buyers by the types of products they produce.

Breakdowns of sales and other data by SIC categories are useful to industrial marketers in locating market opportunities. The codes utilize a four-digit number, where the first two digits identify a particular industry, such as machinery or apparel. The code 75__ refers to repair shops, for instance. The last two digits signify subdivisions of the industry. 753_, for example, refers to all automobile repair shops. To illustrate, 7534 identifies tire retreading and repair, 7535 means paint shops, and 7538 is used for general auto repair shops. See Figure 6.1 for this example.

Governmental and other organizations collect and report many types of composite data for all companies within each classification. A major concern is concealing the identity of an individual company. A breakdown is not reported if it would contain such a small number of competitors that data relating to a particular firm could be determined. Thus, SIC-coded data reflect composite categories and not particular firms.[2]

Unfortunately, the SIC categorizes companies on the basis of the primary type of product or service they create and not on the basis of the types of items they buy. However, marketers sometimes can infer industrial buyers' needs by studying the types of items they produce. For example, hospitals with cardiac wards constitute the primary target for certain technical heart monitoring and stimulating equipment, while wheat farmers need wheat seed and particular kinds of fertilizer. Consequently, SIC-coded data are extremely useful in at least initially segmenting producer markets.

Concentration Industrial buyers are more highly concentrated in particular geographic locations than are consumers. To illustrate, roughly 50 percent of the 1.8 million manufacturing and service firms in the U.S. are located in eight eastern and midwestern states plus California.[3] Within individual industries, concentration is even greater in terms of both geography and size. Most of the rubber industry, for example, is located in Ohio; many steel plants are situated near Pittsburgh; and Detroit is the site for numerous automobile producers. As for size concentration, nearly half of all value added by manufacturing is accounted for by the largest 200 companies.[4]

Concentration of the market has two important implications for marketers. First, a single potential buyer is usually more important to an industrial marketer's success than is a single consumer to a marketer of consumer goods. This is because sales to a producer are generally much larger in dollar volume than sales to a single consumer. DuPont's success in the paint industry, for instance, has been attributed largely to supplying practically all of General Motors' paints. In cases such as this, marketers often segment markets on the basis of individual potential customers and adopt a very flexible approach to each.

Second, because of industrial buyer concentrations, mass promotion campaigns are often unnecessary. Television ads, for instance, extolling the virtues of Jones & Laughlin ¼ inch anodized cold rolled steel in four-ton rolls are not likely to excite either a South Dakota farmer concerned about wheat blight or a small machine shop owner. Instead, because of concentrations, personal selling is generally much more efficient.

Informed Purchasing One of the key factors distinguishing industrial buyers is their informed and skillful buying.[5] When consumers buy a faulty product, say a toaster that burns toast, they are likely to become upset; but the consequences are not often monumental. On the other hand, if an industrial buyer makes a multimillion dollar mistake, it could mean major losses or even bankruptcy. To illustrate, assume that a Chris Craft Corporation buyer mistakenly purchases a fiberglass resin that breaks down after two years and many customers' boats suddenly sink. The boat producer might not ever recover from the resulting negative image and possible lawsuits.

Many factors such as favorable terms of sale, freight charges, dependable rapid delivery, and price are all critical to an industrial buyer's success.[6] A price only a few cents per ton lower on steel, for example, could result in added profits of a million dollars or more to a large company such as General Motors. Certainly, effective buying can provide a competitive edge for a firm.

Accordingly, industrial buyers devote a great deal of time and effort to purchasing. Most are aware that they must remain current on all information about items which might fill their needs. In fact, many are actively involved in informing potential suppliers about their existing needs as well as those anticipated in the future. Further, numerous industrial buyers employ purchasing specialists whose jobs entail aggressively seeking information about products, services, and suppliers.

Types of Products Purchased Industrial buyers purchase all sorts of products, including pencils, steel, integrated circuits, electricity, buildings, lasers, industrial robots, and janitorial services. Exhibit 6.1 sets forth a classification scheme for industrial offerings based upon their use by industrial buyers. Installations, accessories, supplies, and services do not become identifiable portions of an industrial buyer's output (goods and services sold). In contrast, raw materials and components do become identifiable portions of the final product. When managers are making decisions, they should consider the category within which an offering falls because this provides clues as to the expected buying process.[7] Note that Exhibit 6.1 includes examples of each category as well as associated marketing decision implications.

Exhibit 6.1
Major Categories of Industrial Goods

Not Part of the Final Product	Examples	Major Marketing Implications
1. *Installations*—Long-lived, expensive, manufactured products that affect the scale of the buyer's operation.	Buildings, major computers, major equipment such as large presses, kilns, airplanes, etc.	Each sale is very important because of its size. Generally a salesperson and supportive technical staff work closely and for long periods of time with customers in developing specifications. Each item is generally tailor-made.
2. *Accessory items*—Capital items of lower importance and cost. A single item does not affect a producer's scale of operations.	Office equipment and machines, small power tools, washroom fixtures, etc.	Generally standardized products not made to specification. Salesperson may be very active for large orders. Smaller orders may be handled by intermediaries. Promotional activities can be effective.
3. *Supplies*—Items used for maintenance, minor repair, and to facilitate operations *(these are often called MRO items).*	Fuel oil, electricity, oil and lubricants, cleaning products, pencils, stationery, etc.	Products are very standardized with wide distribution. Intermediaries are generally used and price competition is very important. These items are usually the first to be cut in a slowdown period.
4. *Services*—Items used for business advice and to facilitate operations.	Certified Public Accounting, legal advice, marketing and other business consulting, window washing, elevator and air conditioning maintenance, etc.	Services are very specialized. Professional services are marketed on the basis of reputation and contacts, and price can be critical. Also, advertising can be effective with other services. Location is often important for both types of services.
Part of the Final Product	**Examples**	**Major Marketing Implications**
1. *Raw materials*—Items that receive no processing other than what is necessary for protection while handling or for transportation economy.	There are two types: those found in natural states (minerals, forest products, sea products), and agricultural products (corn, rice, wheat, livestock, and animal products).	These products are generally in restricted supply, are highly standardized and graded, and are often perishable. Contracted prices are often established far in advance and transportation is critical.
2. *Components*—These items receive processing before delivery. Some are identifiable in the final product and some receive substantial further processing.	Tires on new automobiles, pig iron to be processed into steel, flour for pies and cakes, cloth for slacks, etc.	Generally, price and a timely supply are important. Sometimes orders are placed one year or more in advance. Large orders are characteristic, and direct salesperson contact is important. For those items identifiable on the final product, branding and consumer advertising may be important.

The Marketing Concept for Industrial Firms

Many sellers of producer items historically have not used the marketing concept. According to Corey, three basic reasons account for this neglect.[8] First, many such firms were traditionally product-oriented and have continued to keep this orientation. Second, industrial buyers pull many goods and services into existence, leaving marketers with a dangerous misconception that all they have to do is produce items that sellers request. Industrial buyers are active in describing their needs to suppliers and even place considerable pressure on them to provide needed items. For instance, about 20 companies are currently conducting experimental research with electric-powered vehicles. Their experiences have led them to place considerable pressure on manufacturers to develop improved batteries.

Finally, numerous industrial items tend to be technical in nature. In the past, many marketers lacked sufficient knowledge in chemistry, metallurgy, and other technical fields to fully grasp the nature of specific industrial buyer needs. This situation is changing today. One reason is that many engineers and other technical specialists are obtaining advanced degrees in marketing. Another is that many companies have learned that a strategy of waiting for customers to point out their needs does not lead to establishing a lasting market niche, especially in today's competitive environment.[9] The discussion that follows explores the rationale for this line of reasoning.

Selling Producer Items

Exchanges in a chain (chain of exchanges)
An interwoven web of exchanges beginning with a set of resources and ending with the production and sale of some final good or service.

Chain of Exchanges As the previous chapter has indicated, consumer buying is complex, but the process of industrial exchange can be even more complicated. It is based on an interwoven web of **exchanges in a chain** that begins with a set of resources and ends with the production and sale of some final consumer good or service. Further, each exchange in the chain depends on all others in the web.

To illustrate, consider the manufacture of this book. Somewhere, perhaps in Ontario, Canada, a mining company obtained iron ore and sold it to a steel producer, which marketed the steel to machinery manufacturers who, in turn, made printing presses and equipment for lumbering. A saw mill, possibly in Maine, logged a tree with this equipment in order to produce paper. A printer commissioned by the publisher purchased both paper and press. Finally, bookstores bought copies and sold them to students. This example shows only a few of the many links in the chain resulting in the production and sale of the book you are reading. It is sufficient, nevertheless, to portray the complexity of producer market structures involved with producing just one consumer good. Each link in the chain contributes a small but important part of some final product and each exchange involves strategic marketing decision making.

Derived demand
Demand that is predicated upon what the customers of producers (and eventually consumers) seek for need satisfaction.

Inelastic
A condition where the demand for a product is not very sensitive to a price change; when a reduction in price does not cause total revenue to appreciably increase (or an increase in price does not cause total revenue to decline appreciably).

Demand Is Derived and Inelastic There is a fundamental difference between consumer and industrial buyer demand for products and services. First, consumer demand is direct because consumer goods and services provide personal need satisfaction. On the other hand, industrial buyer demand is indirect. Industrial buyers do not purchase products to obtain satisfaction from using them. Instead, they use purchased items to produce goods and services for their customers and thereby earn profits.[10] Demand for industrial items, then, is predicated upon what the customers of producers (and eventually consumers) seek for need satisfaction. Industrial buyer demand is consequently **derived.** If student demand for books were to diminish, for example, so would the demand for trees, printing presses, and all other products in that exchange chain.

The derived property also means that the total demand for a type of industrial product tends to be relatively **inelastic,** as Figure 6.2 indicates.[11] Thus, price changes bring about smaller increases or decreases in quantity demanded than would be the case if demand were relatively elastic (e.g., as change from Q_O to Q_I as opposed to Q_O to Q_E).

Cause of Demand Inelasticity The value of each link in the chain of exchanges depends upon consumer demand for the end product. Since each link contributes only a fraction of the value of a total final offering, the impact of a change in price at one link is diminished by the overall effect of the other links. Consider the fact

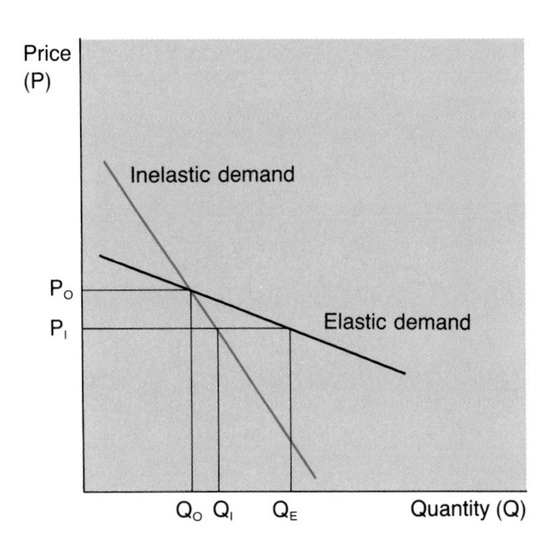

P_O = Original price
P_I = New price
Q_O = Original quantity
Q_I = Quantity generated by new price when demand is inelastic
Q_E = Quantity generated by new price when demand is elastic

Figure 6.2
Relative Inelasticity of Producer Demand

that the cost of any consumer product is made up of various component costs. A price increase or decrease of any one element brings about a far smaller result at the end of the chain.

For illustration, reconsider the example of this text. Suppose that timber mills cut the price of a log used for paper by $5. Because wood contributes only one portion of the total cost of a finished book, the end product would show only a small reduction in price, perhaps 10¢ (or a 10¢ increase in profits). Consequently, the quantity of texts demanded would not materially change. Since the demand for pulp wood is derived from demand for texts and for many other products, the price cut would not significantly increase the total quantity of wood demanded. A similar rationale applies to the other elements of the marketing mix.

Industry vs. Company Demand The discussion on price elasticity refers to total industry demand for an industrial product. An individual company's demand, on the other hand, can be very elastic. This is because many items that competing producers sell are physically similar, sometimes even identical. A pine tree harvested by Weyerhaeuser in Washington, for example, is physically the same as one taken by an independent tree harvester in Wisconsin. Coal, iron ore, steel, wheat, and even most machinery are similar between competitors. This means that price differences can have a large impact on selective demand, despite the industry's relatively inelastic total demand, as Figure 6.3 illustrates. (More will be said about calculating elasticity in Chapter 19.)

Often inelastic industry demands but elastic company demand (because of competitors)

Employing the Marketing Concept A pattern of relatively inelastic industry demand coupled with very elastic company demand has some very significant implications for firms selling producer items. Lowering prices, for example, may initially stimulate company sales but at least some competitors are likely to follow suit, driving company prices still lower. All companies are likely to experience declining revenues and profits as a result of this scenario.

Employing the marketing concept is generally more profitable than competing solely on the basis of price. By differentiating its offerings, a firm is able to develop a niche among industrial buyers if it is able to satisfy a segment's needs more fully than competitors. It may accomplish this through any element or combinations of

Figure 6.3
Relative Elasticity of Demand for an Individual Industrial Product

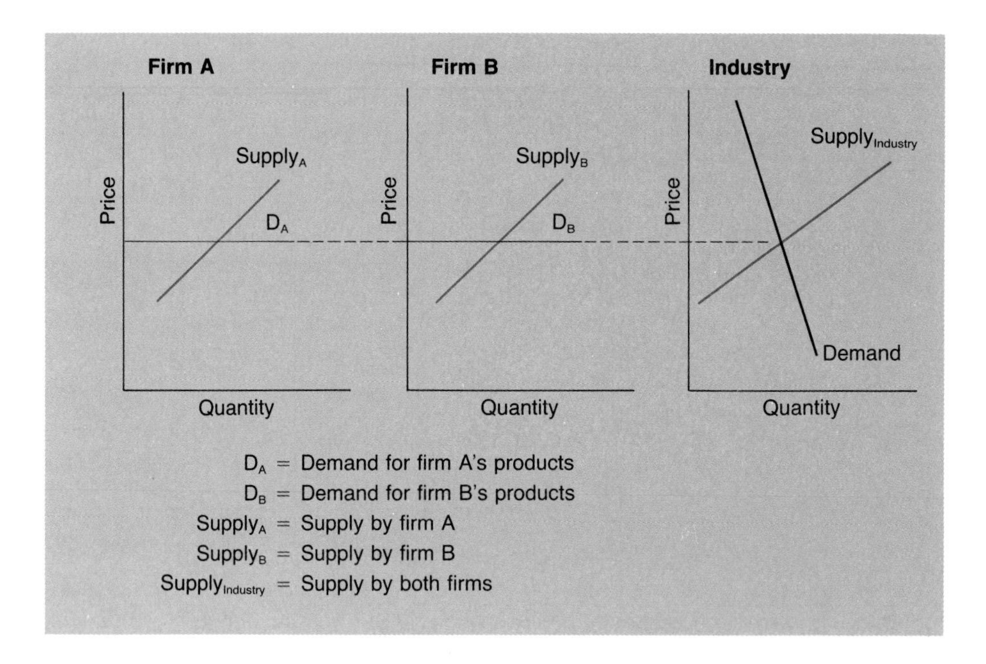

Differentiation is possible for most products, even commodity-type industrial-oriented ones.

elements in the marketing mix, provided that such action brings the firm's offering closer to the needs of a specific market segment.

For example, Gulfstream Commander business jets are very fuel-efficient and have luxurious facilities for passengers. These features satisfy the needs of numerous buyers, who are willing to pay a premium price for the airplane. The firm has gained a lasting marketing niche by tailoring its marketing mix around the needs of a specific and viable target.

The overall process of segmenting markets, providing a differential advantage, and

Exhibit 6.2
The Importance of Marketing Functions for Consumer Markets and Producer Markets

Marketing Functions	Consumer Markets	Producer Markets
Planning	Very important; emphasis on diversity of consumer needs, style is very important	Very important; emphasis on technical differences rather than style
Buying (the selling company's buying role)	Moderately important; appropriate quality, durability, and supply	Very important; often compete on objectively measured differences in quality, a break in supply could mean a major account lost forever
Merchandising:		
Standardizing and Grading	Some products are standardized and graded, but most are not; branding is often used to signal some type of standard	Many products are standardized and graded; products must often meet rigid specifications
Pricing	Pricing is important, but often not as critical as in producer markets	Pricing can make or break a company because of the many standardized products
Selling:		
Advertising	Very important; there often exist very low levels of awareness; persuasion is often very effective; images important	Frequently not too important; relatively easy to obtain potential customer awareness but persuasion through advertising is difficult
Sales Promotion	Very important; in-store displays and other features are often critical to gaining a strong foothold	Important, but only as they assist the salesperson in performing duties (pictures, durability tests, etc.)
Packaging	Very important; eye appeal, ease of opening, attractive colors, etc., are often critical	Very important for product protection, but beyond this not too important
Publicity	Very important; a dollar's worth of favorable publicity can mean more than many paid advertisements	This is very important, but largely stems from past performance of other marketing functions
Personal Selling	Very important for some durables, but generally not too critical; often uneconomical	Critical; many sales are dependent upon a superior relationship with potential customers
Physical Distribution:		
Transporting	Very important to get the product in the right retailer's hands, but consumer buyers generally assume responsibility for future transporting	Critical; dependable transportation that matches buyer's timing needs is essential; late shipments may mean customers lost forever; the cost of transportation is often an overwhelming factor
Storing	Important, the right goods must be available at the right time	Very important; some sellers may even need to construct warehouses near major clients as a condition of obtaining business
Facilitative:		
Financing	Growing in importance as more consumers utilize credit, especially important with durables	Critical; trade credit, leasing, etc., are standard practices of doing business; also, sizeable inventories often necessary
Risk Bearing	Very important, especially because of consumerists' emphasis on warranties, class action suits, and so forth	Important, especially with regard to the threat of carrying obsolete inventory but generally not as risky with respect to class action claims, etc., due to buyers being better able to determine technical aspects
Obtaining Information	Very important. Shifts in consumer preferences and competitor actions are centrally important to strategic marketing	Extremely important. Success is often found by being one step ahead of competitors. Because buyers are well-informed, any firm lagging behind others is very likely to rapidly lose sales

integrating all company efforts around profitably satisfying the needs of selected target markets is essential for sellers of both industrial and consumer items.[12] However, because of the difference in the nature of their markets, industrial items generally require slightly different marketing mix emphases than do consumer items, as Exhibit 6.2 illustrates.

MARKETING BRIEF

Focusing on Satisfying Unfilled Needs Can Offer a Distinctive Competitive Advantage

"We don't believe that service should be a bargaining tool," says Dave Armstrong, vice president of marketing for Herman Miller, Inc. With 1985 sales topping the scales at a half billion dollars, Miller is one of the nation's largest and most progressive producers of office furniture and equipment for health care, lab, office, and industrial installations. Less than a year ago the company launched a highly successful "customer satisfaction" program that is unparalleled in the industry and is sounding sweet music to Miller's stockholders—to the tune of a 20 percent sales increase in six months.

Cornerstones of the company's programs involve offering product warranties, guaranteed move-in dates, and quality audits (examinations of installations for projects to assure that the appropriate equipment is used) for all customers, not just the largest ones who negotiate these advantages into their contracts. "The industry has become lazy in the offering of these services," says Armstrong.

"Our customers deserve these things on a regular basis," he added. "Customers buy from us to help them in performing a service for their customers. It's our job to make sure that an application that we sell does the job properly."

SOURCE: Adapted from "Customer Service Key to Office Furniture Strategy," *Marketing News* 20, no. 10 (May 9, 1986): 10.

Considerable testing is undertaken by Miller to assure that the products chosen do, in fact, meet customer needs. These quality audits are routinely made for all contracts of $50,000 (a small contract in the industry) or more. Miller also performs a second quality audit between 6 and 12 months after installation of all contracts of $1 million or more. Company representatives then discuss the results of these audits with clients and answer any questions or concerns.

It is no surprise that Miller is an industry marketing leader. The company's management programs were recently lauded in both *A Passion for Excellence* and *The 100 Best Companies to Work for in America*—quite a feat for the relatively small company, one that has hardly become a household word when compared to well-known U.S. giants.

In another whirlwind—but well-thought-out—marketing first, Miller has taken the industry by storm with a new program that offers compensation for relief if shipments are incorrect, deliveries delayed, or if other company-caused problems emerge. "We tailor compensation to the individual needs of the client," says another company official. "This really helps to reduce any customer anxiety after making a purchase from us," she added. This policy is expected to carve another notch in Miller's "cut-above-the-rest" market advantage.

Notice that all of the marketing functions apply to both types of markets but assume different levels of importance. Certainly advertising, packaging, style, and sales promotion are very critical elements of the consumer marketer's strategy mix. On the other hand, industrial marketers tend to place more emphasis on technical features, buying skills, pricing, personal selling, transportation, financing, and storage. For them, close personal contact with sales personnel and receptiveness to specific buyer needs are often keys to success. Despite these differences, both producer and consumer marketers should follow a common policy of employing the marketing concept and concentrating on buyer needs, not just technical features.

To illustrate, IBM has experienced phenomenal growth over the past 30 years, but its success is not solely a function of technological excellence. The firm does produce high-quality products, but many technical experts contend that competitors like Control Data, Digital Equipment, and Prime Computer have equipment that is superior. However, IBM has succeeded by focusing on buyer needs and has designed its strategies to fulfill them. The company has devoted considerable attention to software programs, the ability to add more components when needed, and on providing service capabilities, applications advice, and financing plans suited to buyer needs. By attending to buyer needs, IBM has developed sizeable niches in its markets while some production-oriented competitors have not.

Identifying Industrial Buyer Needs

One way of learning about industrial buyer needs is to study their past purchases, as much organizational buying is highly repetitive. A better way, however, is to attempt to identify and fill unmet needs, as does the management of Herman Miller, Inc., one of the nation's most highly successful producers of furniture and office equipment (see the accompanying Marketing Brief). As with Miller, this strategy offers the marketer opportunities to differentiate itself from the competition.

A key to this approach is the concentration on a potential customer's link in its related exchange chain. To illustrate, Figure 6.4 centers around one of a hypothetical marketer's potential customers—customer A, which is in competition with its rivals to establish a solid market stronghold. Now if this marketer recognizes unfilled needs in A's relationships, either in buying or in marketing, and is able to offer means of strengthening A's position with respect to competitors, it is likely to win A's patronage and loyalty. For example, if A cannot provide rapid and dependable deliveries to customers, and if the marketer can adjust its mix to offer something to overcome this weakness, the marketer may have found the key to winning A's patronage. Assisting A could include faster transportation, more warehouse space, or automated order processing. By assisting its customers in establishing sound niches in their markets, an industrial marketer also establishes its own niche.

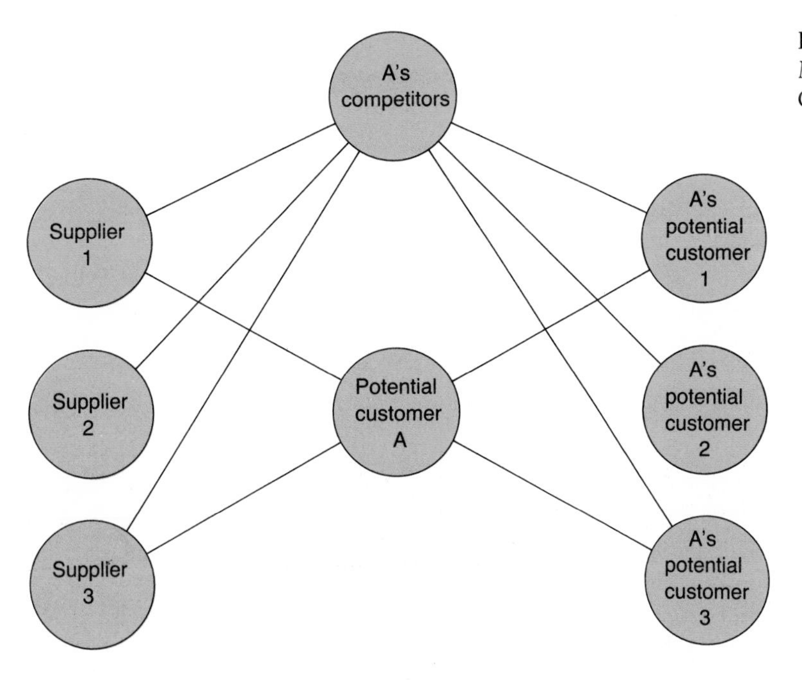

Figure 6.4
Need Relationships in Potential Customer Exchange Chains

Industrial Buying Behavior

It is important for marketers of producer items to become familiar with the behavioral aspects of industrial buying. This is because understanding behavioral processes can lead to more effective marketing strategy and tactical decision making. This chapter considers some important behavioral elements of industrial buying behavior, beginning with the role of the purchasing agent.

Buying Specialists

Most producers devote considerable attention to the buying process. This is because it can be critical to maintaining their competitive position and because they often acquire large volumes and varieties of items. Consequently, most employ one or more buying specialists usually called *purchasing agents*, who serve as the company's acquisitions experts.[13] Understanding producer buying, therefore, should begin with trying to comprehend the functions and operations of these buying experts.

The Role of the Purchasing Agent The nature and scope of a purchasing agent's responsibilities vary from one organization to another and depend upon many factors. These include the organization's size, the variety of products acquired, whether or not purchased items are standardized or specialized, the technical complexities of the products, and whether or not the firm has purchased similar items before. Some small companies, in fact, do not employ purchasing agents—owners do the buying, or the job is another responsibility of an office manager, accountant, or engineer. Larger companies generally hire specialists whose sole jobs consist of purchasing. Ordinarily they are organized to include a complete department of purchasing agents, sometimes headed by a manager at the vice presidential level.[14]

Professional purchasing agents differ in many respects from consumer buyers. The main difference, however, is that they are much better informed. In this regard they are responsible for aggressively seeking pertinent information about both new and existing goods and services. Sometimes they are so proficient at their jobs that they know more about a certain supplier and its products than that supplier's poorly trained sales force.[15]

Because purchasing agents are avid information seekers, industrial marketers generally place their promotion emphasis on top-quality personal selling as opposed to mass advertising. Highly competent sales personnel who are knowledgeable about their own company's and competitors' offerings and who have expertise in identifying buyer needs are valuable information sources for purchasing agents. Professional buyers will listen to knowledgeable people.

This does not mean that advertising and other impersonal promotional methods are unimportant. On the contrary, these methods are often the most efficient means of rapidly informing many purchasing agents of new product introductions and improved features of old products, especially for standardized items. But because they are professionals, purchasing agents generally extend their selective perceptions to seeking out, receiving, and actively evaluating product-related information more than consumers do. Marketers generally need less emphasis on establishing basic product awareness among these buyers.

Systematic Buying Most industrial buying specialists adopt a systematic approach to buying; one that is both purposeful and methodical. The complexity of the systems they employ depend upon their employer's particular needs. The more important

Element	Importance
1. Industry demand is derived and inelastic	Industrial goods demand originates from consumer goods demand so price changes bring about relatively small changes in quantity demanded.
2. Company demand can be elastic	Price changes can bring about relatively large changes in company demand when competing producers sell items that are similar.
3. Employing the marketing concept is important	Attempting to achieve customer satisfaction can be more effective than competing solely on the basis of price.
4. Certain marketing functions assume major importance for many industrial goods	Industrial marketers tend to place strong emphasis on technical features, buying skills, pricing, personal selling, transportation, financing, and storing.
5. Industrial marketers can determine buyer needs by analyzing exchange chains	Marketers can ascertain buyer requirements by recognizing unfilled needs in customer relationships, either in buying or in marketing.

CONCEPT SUMMARY

Some Vital Elements in Marketing Industrial Goods

elements of the systematic approach are a reference library, approved supplier lists, multiple suppliers, and advanced buying procedures.

Reference Library Most purchasing agents maintain a well-stocked library of reference materials containing information on goods and services and on suppliers. They have catalogs, specification books, price sheets, notes on past experiences, and many other detailed documents on file. These assist buyers in initially evaluating specific items and their prices. Many buyers also maintain Dun & Bradstreet or other financial ratings of companies with which they might do business; few are willing to place sizeable orders with suppliers who are on the verge of bankruptcy.

To marketers, the existence of reference libraries means that they should periodically supply potential customers with updated information such as price lists, descriptions of new products and services offered, delivery schedules, and replacement part numbers. By keeping purchasing agent files current, marketers have an opportunity to promote their offerings and can avoid serious misunderstandings before orders are placed.

Approved Supplier Lists Like consumers, industrial buyers do not comprehensively evaluate every possible supplier on each purchase occasion. Instead, they develop loyalties to certain suppliers, also termed *vendors*, especially for frequently purchased items. Consequently, industrial buyers generally maintain **approved supplier lists** from which they select specific vendors for particular purchases. Firms included on these lists are there because of favorable past evaluations. Once the buyers have identified

Approved supplier lists Lists of potential suppliers used and maintained by industrial buyers.

While personal selling is the mainstay, advertising may also be important when selling to industrial buyers.

NB. Particularly to get a new product or old one with new modifications quickly known

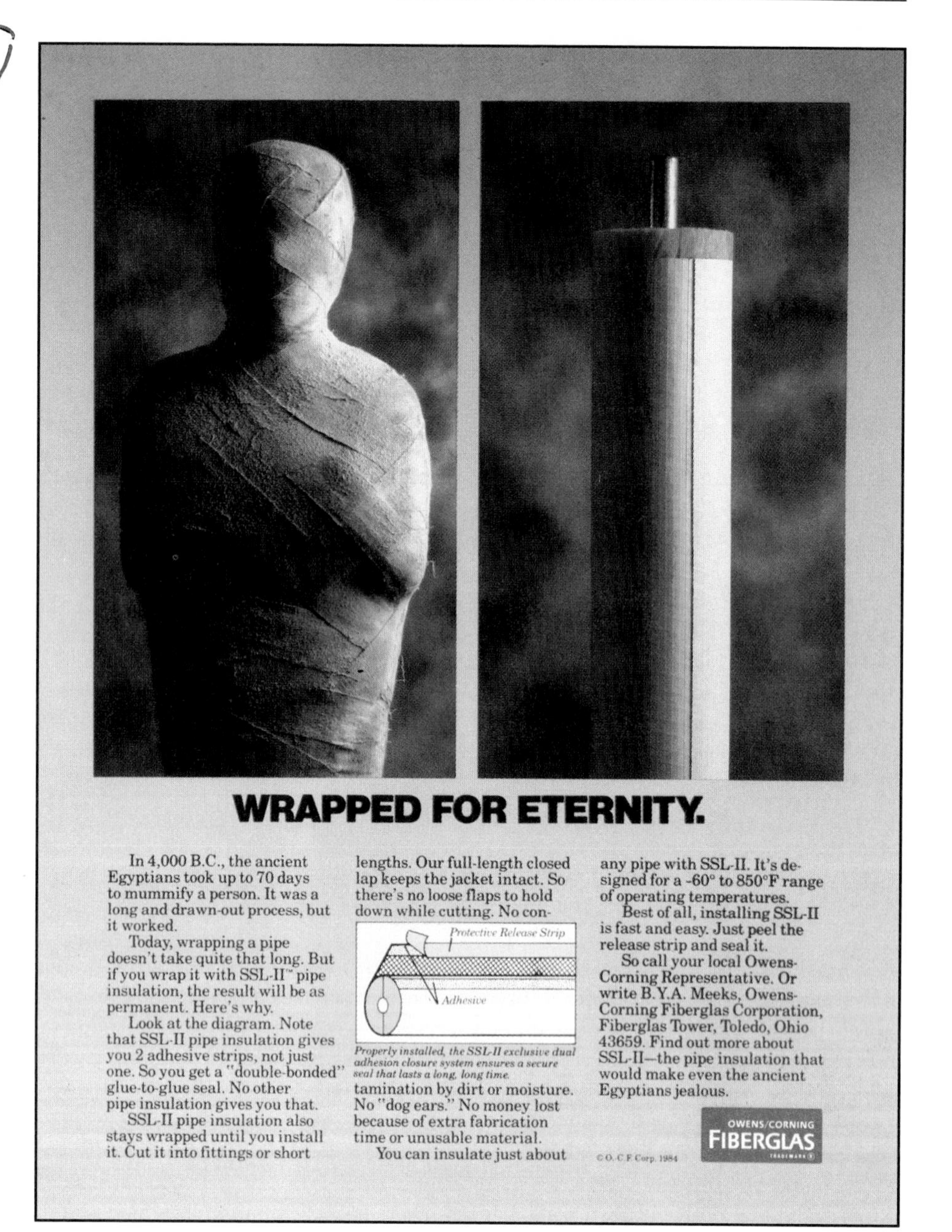

a repetitive product need, they restrict their selection of suppliers to firms named on the list.

The operations of some industrial buyers have become so automated since the computer revolution that many routine purchases are handled automatically. These buyers have computers that monitor inventory levels and when supplies are sufficiently low, the computer automatically prints a purchase order and the name of a supplier chosen from an approved list.

Needless to say, marketers not included on an approved list cannot expect to receive an order. Fortunately, buyers do not make all purchases in such a routine fashion.

Further, they revise approved lists periodically. Therefore, marketers should direct their efforts toward the long run; developing a marketing mix that will fulfill the needs of the buyer.

The marketer's battle is not over when the company is selected for inclusion on an approved supplier list. U.S. Leasing International, which purchases office and other equipment and leases it to industrial customers, has a supplier list that includes approximately twenty firms. However, the bulk of its purchases are from only three. Getting on an approved list, therefore, only means that a company has earned a chance to bid on purchases.

Similarly, continued aggressive marketing is warranted even after an approved vendor receives some orders. Perhaps the company can increase the size of orders for its merchandise. If American Motors could convince Avis or Hertz to increase its number of AMC built cars from 5 to 10 percent of its fleet, for instance, the change would represent a 100 percent sales increase to AMC. In the same vein, suppliers receiving large shares of a buyer's orders should not sit idly by and assume that their status is guaranteed. They can only remain on top by being as aggressive, if not more so, than less successful suppliers.

Multiple Suppliers Industrial buyers are naturally reluctant to restrict their buying of any single item to only one source. The possibility of supply shortages due to strikes, fires, etc., would pose a great risk. Consequently, many organizations frequently acquire items from at least two or three vendors. If the buyer experiences a problem with one, he or she can easily shift orders to another with which the buyer has good working relations. The Goodyear Company developed a tire capable of delivering between 3 and 8 percent better gasoline mileage than radials. The tire also required a new type of wheel. But because multiple suppliers were unavailable, automobile producers did not order the innovation.[16]

This practice of purchasing from multiple sources also affords leverage to buyers in demanding favorable terms from suppliers. It forces the latter to be on their competitive toes to continually satisfy buyer needs. To illustrate, consider the example of the vice president of purchasing for New York's Rheingold brewery, who buys cans for its beer. Using the leverage of hundreds of millions of cans a year, like many other buyers, he takes punitive action when one company slips in quality or fails to deliver. "At one point American started talking about a price rise," he recalls. "Continental kept its mouth shut. . . . American never did put the price rise into effect, but anyway, I punished them for talking about it." For a three-month period he cut the percentage of cans he bought from American.[17]

Advanced Buying Procedures Most professional buyers continually seek improved procedures in their buying endeavors.[18] Hence, producer marketers should remain fully aware of new developments in the field. Reading the *Journal of Purchasing and Materials Management* is a good start, since it explores new techniques and buying models. Also, the National Association of Purchasing Managers is active in informing its members about new buying situations, procedures, and techniques. The NAPM disseminates ideas by sponsoring meetings where buyers exchange ideas and by publishing literature designed to improve buying effectiveness. Further, many professional buyers read a variety of articles in their field and attend seminars on materials management. Some of the topical areas are quite quantitative; for example, many buyers employ some version of a technique called **Economic Order Quantity** (EOQ) to determine order sizes for repeated purchases. The basic EOQ model is a means of

Economic order quantity (EOQ) An amount calculated by formula which represents the number of units of an item that should be ordered at a time to maintain an inventory in the most economical way.

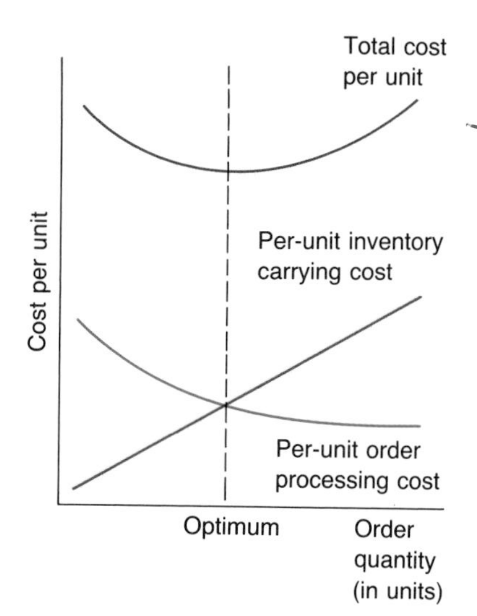

Figure 6.5
Basic Economic Order Quantity (EOQ) Model

calculating how many units of an item the firm should purchase in order to minimize inventory costs, as Figure 6.5 illustrates. There are two fundamental cost categories associated with an inventory: holding costs and ordering costs. Holding costs consist of interest, storage facility charges, and other expenses associated with maintaining an inventory. In general, the larger an inventory, the larger the holding costs. For a given sales level, bigger inventories require more space and the firm holds items longer because they turn over slower (the sales/inventory ratio is smaller). Conversely, ordering costs tend to be lower when the firm places large orders. Buyers can take advantage of quantity discounts and more economical shipping costs to reduce ordering expenses. The most economical quantity of a repetitively purchased item to order, therefore, is the one which balances these two types of cost and thereby minimizes total costs.

Figure 6.5 is not a totally realistic presentation of how firms employ EOQ. Those which utilize EOQ use complex calculus-based mathematical equations and computer simulations much beyond the scope of this book. Generally, the equations take into consideration such factors as expected fluctuations in demand, interest effects (present value) of capital tied up in inventory, and quantity discounts.[19] Other procedures include break-even analysis, net present value analysis, and tax analysis. (Break-even analysis and net present value analysis are covered in Appendix C).

Industrial marketers should be familiar with these and other widely-used methods to increase the effectiveness of their decisions. First, they are a way of doing business for most progressive buyers. Second, effective marketing strategy for less advanced buyers might include helping them to reduce their inventory costs by assisting in developing and implementing such models. Helping to provide buyers with insights on how they can more effectively carry out their functions can be the ticket for developing very positive and lasting relationships.

Buying Situations

As was suggested earlier, producer buyers do not devote equal amounts of attention to each purchase. Instead, different situations demand different amounts of time and effort. This section considers some of the different situations.

New tasks (buying)
Buying situations that are original experiences.

Straight rebuy
A repetitive buying situation where a reorder is simply made to a past supplier.

Modified rebuy
A repetitive buying situation where moderate effort is made to evaluate new supply sources.

Classes of Situations There are three major classes of buying situations.[20] First, some purchases represent **new tasks**, in that buyers lack experience with a product or service they have not purchased before.[21] These situations are the most complex. Of all the classes, new tasks require the greatest amount of information search, evaluation, deliberation, and advice from others. As a result, they offer the greatest opportunity for a marketer to obtain new accounts. Buyers are open to advice from sales representatives in these situations. A representative can make a mark by helping to reduce uncertainty through providing needed information about how the firm's offerings can help solve the customer's problems.

The opposite of this class is the situation termed a **straight rebuy**, where an organization conducts buying automatically by computer or by exclusive use of an approved supplier list. The only decisions to be made are how much and what kind of items to buy. Realistically, there is little chance of obtaining new accounts in these situations. Experienced sales representatives learn the art of detecting these low-potential customers and finding more promising prospects.

Finally, there is a broad group of situations between the two extremes, termed **modified rebuy**, where buyers are willing to consider new information, new sources

CONCEPT SUMMARY

Systematic Buying by Industrial Buyers

Element	Description
1. Reference Library	Buyers maintain an extensive library of reference materials containing information on goods and services and on suppliers. These assist buyers in evaluating items and their prices.
2. Approved Supplier Lists	Buyers maintain lists of suppliers from which they select specific vendors on particular purchase occasions.
3. Multiple Suppliers	Many buyers frequently acquire purchased items from at least two or three vendors.
4. Advanced Buying Procedures	Most professional buyers continually seek improved procedures in their buying endeavors. They are active in seeking new techniques and ideas.

of supply, and slightly different products or services. Those on approved supplier lists are most likely to obtain eventual orders, but there is some degree of opportunity for astute marketers capable of zeroing in on unsatisfied needs.

Most straight-rebuy situations periodically slip into modified-rebuy ones. This gives buyers the opportunity of reconsidering their acquisitions at some desired regularity. Marketers need to be alert to these opportunities and be ready to respond quickly. Further, existing suppliers also need to be ready to respond, in order to take steps to avoid the loss of customers. Marketers should develop potential alternative strategies ahead of time in anticipation of altered buyer needs, so that they are ready to respond rapidly and effectively. Frequent contacts with customers are useful as a means of detecting when buying situations may change.

Phases of Commitment Closely related to the three situations are eight **phases of commitment** to a decision, as the left side of Figure 6.6 illustrates. It can be seen that organizations begin the buying phase with the recognition of a need and end it with postpurchase evaluation.[22] Buyers become progressively more committed to a decision as they pass through each phase. Many marketers find that a successful strategy is to assist buyers in identifying their exact needs and in establishing a general means of fulfilling them. In fact, some astute marketers help buyers identify needs for items not even sold by their firms. This helping process establishes trust, which encourages the buyer to consider items the company does sell.

Phases of commitment
Stages that industrial buyers go through in the purchasing process, ranging from need recognition to performance feedback and evaluation.

The right side of Figure 6.6 relates buying phases to each of the three types of buying situations. Notice that the greatest amount of time and effort are needed for new task buying. The upper left portion of the figure identifies situations where there is the largest opportunity for obtaining new customers.

Need Awareness

Perhaps the most critical phase of buying is anticipating and recognizing the firm's needs. Buyers go about this in several ways. First, others often make them aware of

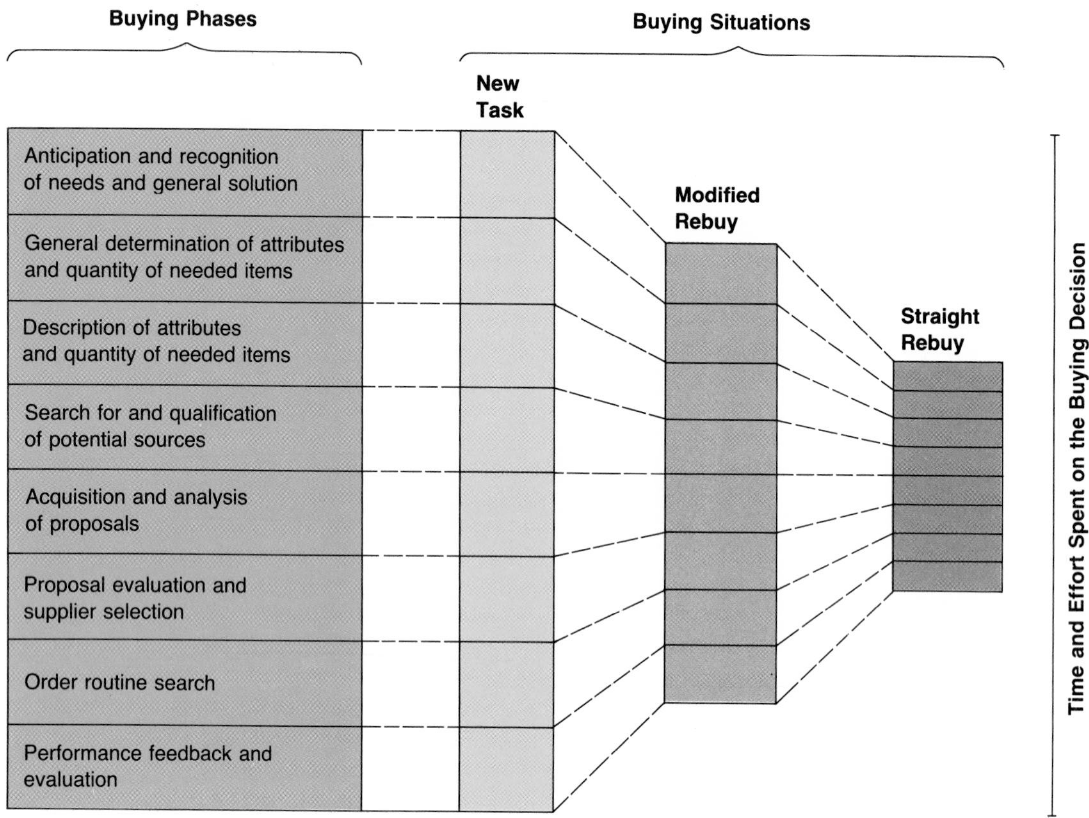

Figure 6.6
Buying Phases and Situations (SOURCE: Adapted from Patrick J. Robinson, Charles W. Faris, and Yoram Wind, *Industrial Buying and Creative Marketing* (Boston: Allyn & Bacon, Inc., 1967): 14.)

their firm's needs. Many companies have set procedures for requisitioning purchases. After receiving notification (usually in the form of a document called a purchase requisition) from designated persons within the organization, purchasing agents set out to locate the most appropriate vendor of a product or service. Further, marketing efforts of suppliers (such as advertisements or calls by sales representatives) often point out a need for some item. Second, many progressive purchasing agents have extended the scope of their role by employing a procedure termed *value analysis,* which is geared toward actively identifying needs.

Value analysis
An approach used by institutional buyers to reduce costs by carefully analyzing components of items to see if they can be standardized, redesigned, or made by less expensive means.

Value analysis, originally developed by General Electric, is a procedure that attempts to reduce costs by carefully analyzing components of items to see if they can be standardized, redesigned, or made by less expensive means.[23] The approach requires that purchasing agents become knowledgeable in areas such as production, physical distribution, and engineering. By understanding the technical aspects of their purchases, they are often able to more efficiently specify their company's needs. Essentially, there are five steps associated with the procedure, as follows:

1. Determine if a standard item can be used instead of some specially ordered one. For example, can standard sized nuts and bolts be used rather than custom ones, as per engineering's specifications?

Focusing on needs is critical for success in marketing to industrial buyers.

2. Determine if a product can be slightly redesigned to include standardized parts. To illustrate, can the product be reduced in weight to enable using standard shipping containers rather than specially built ones?
3. Determine if the number of parts can be reduced by combining two or more into one. For example, can a door handle be combined with a lock?
4. Determine if a less expensive substitute material can be used. To illustrate, is it possible to replace a brass part with one made of aluminum or plastic?
5. Ask suppliers if parts can be made for less by tooling or production changes and/or by ordering larger quantities. For example, ask supplier A if it would buy a larger machine and cut its price if a greater share of the business were directed its way.

A survey reported that, as far back as 1962, 48 percent of the purchasing agents sampled used value analysis.[24] Today this figure is likely to be far greater as more and more buyers recognize its merits. Industrial marketers can use value analysis as an effective means of guiding their efforts. By carefully assessing buyers' purchases through an examination of their particular value analysis methodology, a firm can more effectively shape its offerings around satisfying potential customer needs. This aids the marketer in developing a tailor-made marketing program for particular buyers and potential buyers.

Buyer Objectives

Consumers are often driven to purchase by their emotions and psychological needs. Image, self-esteem, personal preferences, and other noneconomic factors are often instrumental. In contrast, economic motives largely direct industrial buyers. Costs, profits, and being better able to maintain their market niches are overriding factors.

This does not mean, however, that emotional considerations are absent from buyers' mind sets. One needs only to observe the plush offices of many executives to realize that they are concerned with noneconomic factors. Emotions drive even purchasing agents in basic industries like steel and coal. Personal likes, dislikes, free lunches, seller images, and other noneconomic factors are important considerations. Some companies pride themselves on owning the most prestigious office locations and hiring well-known CPA firms. Moreover, purchasing agents are interested in protecting their own careers. Unless they can envision substantial benefit by purchasing from a new vendor, many avoid the risk associated with change. But all this is simply saying that organizations consist of humans.[25] Effective marketing takes these factors into account.[26]

Model of Industrial Buyer Behavior

how to segment the market

Managers estimate market segments for industrial goods in much the same way as for consumer items. Economic, demographic, and geographic factors are as important in segmenting producer as they are in consumer markets. Of course marketers measure different variables, reflecting the fact that the target market is made up of firms rather than individuals. Industrial marketers use company size, SIC codes, and other pertinent variables in lieu of variables such as social class and family income; nevertheless, the general approach is essentially the same. In fact, most methods of analysis and theories used for consumer products remain applicable.

The conceptual model describing behavior within segments, however, should be different from those utilized by consumer goods marketers. As Sheth points out, the Howard and Sheth model (as well as other models of consumer buyers) has certain emphases. More specifically, it stresses individual cognitive processes, avoids group decision making, and is not oriented toward aggressively seeking information.[27] Hence, it is most applicable to consumer goods purchase behavior.

For small organizations, where one person "handles the show," the Howard and Sheth model is probably appropriate. For medium and large buyers, this is not the case because the assumptions underlying the model are unrealistic. Accordingly, Sheth has proposed a more suitable model to conceptualize industrial consumer buying. Figure 6.7 presents its major elements. There are five major parts to the model: inputs, psychological factors, conditions causing joint decision making, the process of joint decision making, and outputs. This section briefly examines each major part.

Inputs

Note that there are two major types of input factors. First, industrial buyers obtain specific information about particular firm's offerings from sources such as sales representatives and **trade shows**. Second, situational factors or "happenings" also serve as information. Included are various specific conditions or events that prompt or have an influence on buying decisions. For example, if a buyer learns that a supplier is going to raise prices by 10 percent in one week, this might prompt an immediate large purchase.

Trade shows
Periodic meetings of an industry's members to display new product offerings and to learn trends in the business.

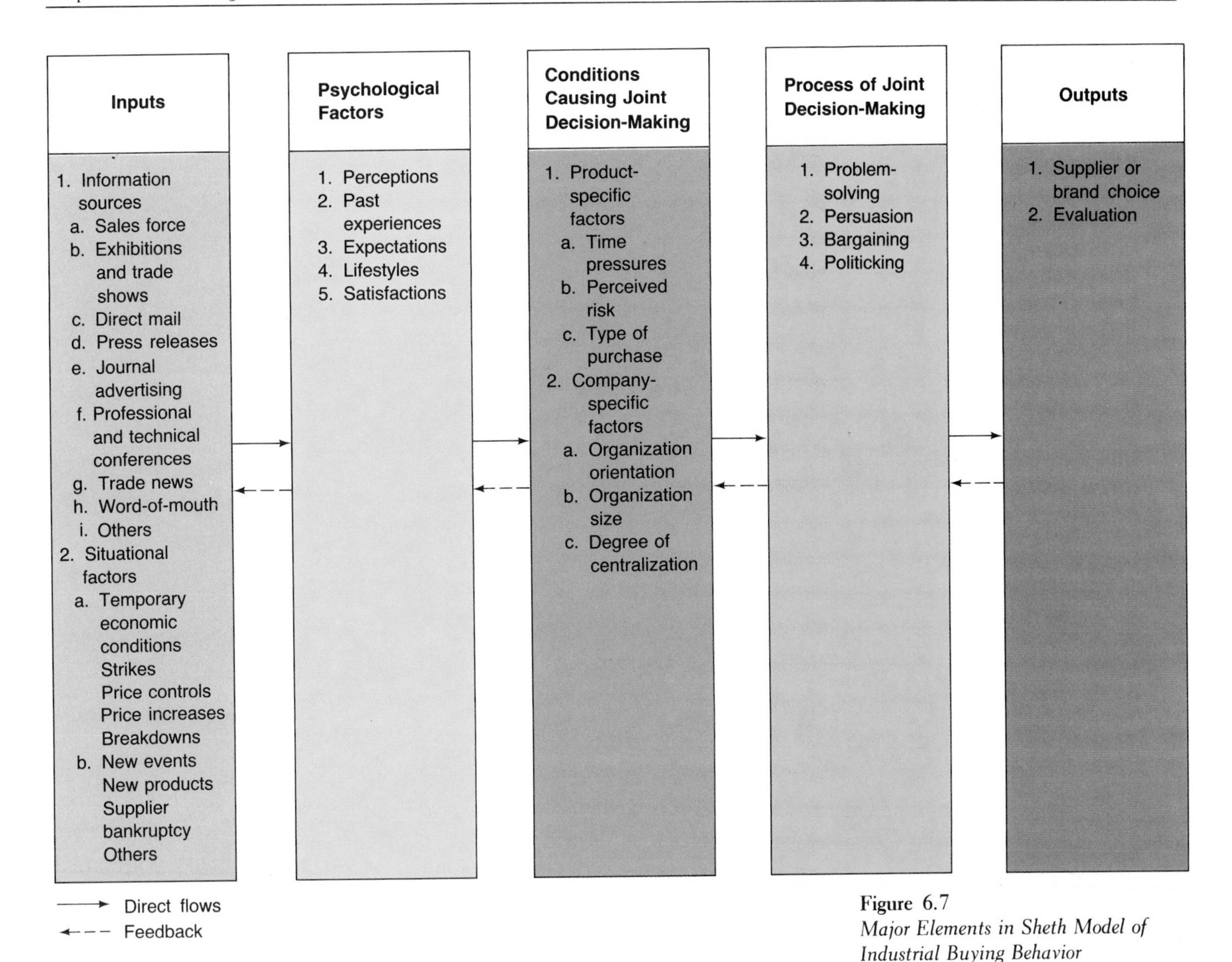

Figure 6.7
Major Elements in Sheth Model of Industrial Buying Behavior
(SOURCE: Adapted from Jagdish N. Sheth, "A Model of Industrial Buying Behavior," *Journal of Marketing* 37, no. 4 (October 1973): 50–56.)

Psychological Factors

The perceptions, past experiences, expectations, lifestyles, and other psychological factors of the individuals in a purchase decision can be instrumental in industrial buying. In this regard, there are two differences between this model and the Howard and Sheth consumer model. First, the model explicitly considers the backgrounds of all participants in the decision. Second, it emphasizes their technical training and the roles that they serve in the organization.

Conditions Causing Joint Decision Making

Purchasing agents are generally responsible for placing orders, but they are seldom solely responsible for making buying decisions, especially major ones. Instead they make **joint decisions** with others.[28]

Joint decisions
Buying decisions that involve two or more persons.

Like consumers, industrial buyers may also be influenced by creative approaches.

The degree of joint decision making involved with a specific purchase is the result of both specific product and company factors. A heavy emphasis on joint decision making is most likely when time pressure is not great, there is a high degree of risk, the product is a new task purchase, and it is a major item such as an installation. Similarly, if the company emphasizes task force decision making, is a small organization, and if it decentralizes authority, there is likely to be a high degree of joint influence.

Consider the complexities involved in a typical computer purchase. The purchase decision process might begin with the inventory control manager, who recognizes that the department has a need for a new computer. The manager informs the purchasing agent of this need and the latter begins initial discussions with sales representatives of three computer companies. Sales representatives then meet with the inventory control manager, who makes a tentative decision to buy from supplier C. The associate research director, research director, plant engineer, controller, and finally the corporate director of purchasing evaluate the decision, and the approval of all of these managers is required before the firm places an order. The whole process—from need recognition until order—is likely to take many months, perhaps even years.

Of course, not all decisions are so complex. But as a rule, several people are typically involved, in one way or another, in the buying task. A complex buying decision situation can involve four, five, or more departments of the organization in one way or another.[29] Users, engineers, the head of buying, financial experts, and many others may be participants.

Of course, multiple buying influence complicates a marketer's task. Salespeople may be denied direct access to some group members, including those with the greatest influence. Further, formal titles and behavior in the presence of outsiders do not always reveal each person's relative importance. A secretary who reports to a major executive may be a critical barrier to a computer purchase. Consequently, it is necessary to anticipate the concerns and reactions of all potential influences on a purchase and to obtain as much information as possible about each one. Effective marketers first learn important buying relationships within the organizations of each key current and potential customer and then adjust their marketing mixes accordingly.

Process of Joint Decision Making

Attempts at joint decisions sometimes result in conflict. Figure 6.7 indicates that members may engage in problem solving, persuasion, bargaining, and politicking (or some combination of these) to resolve this conflict. The more autonomous a decision, the more rapidly is this stage completed.

Outputs

The output of the model consists of the act of selecting a specific supplier or brand. Once the industrial buyer has selected and used the product or service, it evaluates the purchase. This, in turn, affects the degree of satisfaction with past purchases and the decision-making processes that produced them. This is important to marketing managers, since it may result in their companies being placed on the approved supplier lists for future purchases. Consequently, once the organization has made a purchase, the marketer should initiate appropriate followup procedures designed to assure customer satisfaction.

Basic Exchange Approaches

The Sheth model brings together many of the facets of industrial buyer decision making; however, yet another factor must be considered. A buyer may elect one of four approaches to evaluating suppliers and entering into exchange, as follows:

Inspection
A procedure of examining each item upon delivery of a purchase.

Sampling (shipments)
Inspecting a portion of a total order.

Description (buying)
Ordering items on the basis of specifications, grades, or brands.

Negotiated contracts (buying)
Purchasing in a way so that the specifications may be changed during production, usually relating to major capital items.

- **Inspection,** which involves thoroughly examining each item being considered. Buyers often use this process for nonstandardized items such as livestock, machinery, buildings, and airplanes.
- **Sampling,** which is the inspection of a portion of a total order. Buyers may use sampling when a large number of items are involved, some of which may have perished in transit, such as farm produce.
- **Description** involves simply ordering items on the basis of specifications, grades, or brands. It is based on trust when quality is not likely to vary and when the supplier is known to be reputable.
- **Negotiated contracts** are usually entered when exact specifications have not been drawn up by the buyer. To accommodate design changes, buyers award contracts where suppliers work on some negotiated profit margin.

Marketers should make themselves aware of both prevailing exchange practices and existing buyer expectations in developing strategies for particular buyers. Marketing success is often based on developing and furthering the trust relationships required to simplify the target's buying and making it as trouble-free as possible.

Government Buying

Many firms have learned that a marketing orientation can help in developing favorable exchanges with government buyers. The remainder of this chapter is devoted to government buying.

Total Size

Total government spending is gigantic. Federal, state, and local agency purchases lumped together account for nearly a quarter of the country's GNP. The federal sector alone spends two-thirds of this amount, or nearly $450 billion per year. This makes Uncle Sam the largest single buyer of goods and services in the U.S., and the government buys almost every conceivable item. Besides missiles, tanks, and naval vessels, it purchases products as diverse as food, clothing, education, pencils, uranium, and even illicit drugs for research purposes. The *Statistical Abstract of the United States* reports that all governmental units spend about $265 billion for defense, $175 billion for education, $640 billion for social welfare, and $37 billion for highway construction.[30] In addition, they buy for hundreds of other purposes.

Consequently, many marketing managers pay considerable attention to governmental needs. Just one contract for a very small portion of what the government buys can mean the difference between success and failure for even a large company. Seattle, for example, experiences periodic booms and busts as a result of Boeing Corp. employment fluctuations when it wins or loses major government contracts.

Because the risks are so great and the opportunities so substantial, many companies, both large and small, are recognizing the importance of employing the marketing concept to direct their orientation to obtaining governmental business. This trend is likely to continue as expenditures are rising both in total and as a percentage of GNP. Consequently, opportunities are expanding but competition is becoming more difficult as a greater number of companies are actively seeking government buyers. The *National Journal* is an interesting source of information for the nation's top decision makers, as indicated in the accompanying Marketing Brief.

MARKETING BRIEF

Targeting "Movers and Shakers" in the U.S. Government

At $3,900 for a full-page ad and with a total circulation of only 5,000 copies, the *National Journal* is probably the most expensive magazine advertising buy in the world. Its purchase price is no bargain either, at $546 per year for the weekly publication.

On the other hand, the *National Journal* is no *National Enquirer*. Boasting a subscription unparalleled among other publications, it includes 500 senators and congressmen, and 100 paid copies are delivered to the White House. More than 40 percent of its circulation is within the "Washington Beltway," with the balance shipped to corporate executives, media people, and ad agency executives. A 1984 study revealed that the mean read time (the average amount of time a reader spends reading an issue) was 68 minutes—practically unheard of, especially considering the decision-making power of the audience.

Further, 61 percent of *National Journal* readers pass an issue on to someone else to read, 95 percent are college grads, 61 percent own stock, and their mean 1983 personal income was $48,293. According to estimates by publisher John Fox Sullivan, who worked at *Newsweek* before joining the *National Journal*, each copy is read by eight people, which makes the cost per thousand people reached equal to $780, versus $20 for an ad in the *Washington Post*.

The *National Journal* has had no trouble selling its ad space. In December of 1985, for example, the House of Seagram formally ended its cable and print campaign for alcohol equivalency (ratings), but not in the *National Journal*. "We're trying to reach decision makers with our message," said Rick Conner, Seagram's director of government affairs in Washington. Like Seagram's ad, most advertising in the publication relates to political issues. In the January 18, 1986 issue, one of the eight annual four-color covers that break away from the magazine's normal drab brown fronts, there were ads from the Times-Mirror Corp., Goodyear Aerospace, the Catholic Health Association, Wang Computer, Rockwell International, and General Motors Defense. In total, there were nearly $2 million in ad revenues for 1985.

SOURCE: Adapted from Steven W. Colford, "Movers and Shakers Buy 'National Journal'," *Advertising Age*, February 24, 1986: 43.

Demand Characteristics

As is the case with industrial buyers, the government's demand for goods and services is derived; however, it is derived not from consumers but indirectly from voters through their elected representatives.

Further, total governmental demand is very inelastic. Mainly, this stems from the way money is appropriated for expenditures. Governmental budgeting procedures are different from those employed by private businesses. Administrative action determines the budgeted amounts. The various spending agencies consider all items, including capital expenditures, to be expenses during the year incurred, rather than as investments (as in private business).

Similarly, since government is a not-for-profit organization, authorities appropriate money with the intention that it will be spent. Usually, administrators cannot exceed their budgets, but they are not normally rewarded for spending less than their budgeted amounts. In fact, they are sometimes penalized in later years for spending less, because future budgets are often based on previous expenditures. Consequently, once monies are appropriated, the administrator is motivated to spend all of it. Total demand, therefore, tends to be very inelastic.

The budgeting process does not mean that government is unconcerned about price. In fact, price may be the government's primary criterion in the selection of a particular supplier. This is especially the case when agencies employ competitive bidding. However, it does have several implications, as follows:

- Expenditures must fit into the budget's appropriations. Marketers may have to develop lease arrangements for expensive capital items, for example, to enable the agency to acquire items too expensive to fit in one year's budget.
- Developing good relationships with government buyers can help marketers identify budget categories in which funds are available for purchases.
- Lobbying (the use of paid representatives to interact with government officials) can be useful to learn what the government is planning as well as shifting opportunities in favor of a company. Effective but ethical lobbying can gain the support of sympathetic officials who can make decisions in favor of the sponsoring company or industry.[31]

Who Buys?

Some companies avoid dealing with the government because of the apparent complexity of the process. This section indicates how complexity can be reduced by analyzing major types of purchasers and their buying processes. The major categories of buyers are the federal government, and state or local governments. The discussion below highlights each of these.

ws Central

Federal Government Buying The federal government's buying organization and procedures look overwhelmingly complex to the uninitiated, but it is actually quite uncomplicated. Essentially, all buying is divided into two major sectors, civilian and military, as Figure 6.8 illustrates.

The General Services Administration (GSA) plays a dominant role in the civilian sector by serving as a purchasing agent for standard items, such as supplies and stationery. Perhaps more important, the GSA develops purchasing procedures for the rest of the civilian sector to follow.

The Defense Logistics Agency (DLA) is the military equivalent of the GSA. Further, it attempts to identify and develop standardized equipment, such as weapons, that all military branches can use. There is a large turnover of personnel within these buying groups, complicating the marketing process and necessitating continuous advertising and personal selling to educate buyers on the merits of a particular company's products and services.[32]

To be sure, Washington, D.C., is the haven of federal government buying, but it also takes place throughout the country, in cities as large as New York and Los Angeles and in towns as small as West Yellowstone, Montana and Arco, Idaho. Practically every government office and post throughout the world buys many local products and services such as food and fuel. This means, of course, the small local firms also can effectively penetrate part of the government market.

Further, the government is committed to the concept of distributing purchases among various suppliers. To assist potential sellers, it provides substantial information to interested parties, as follows:

- *Commerce Business Daily* (U.S. Printing Office) lists all proposed defense purchases of $10,000 or more and civilian purchases over $5,000.

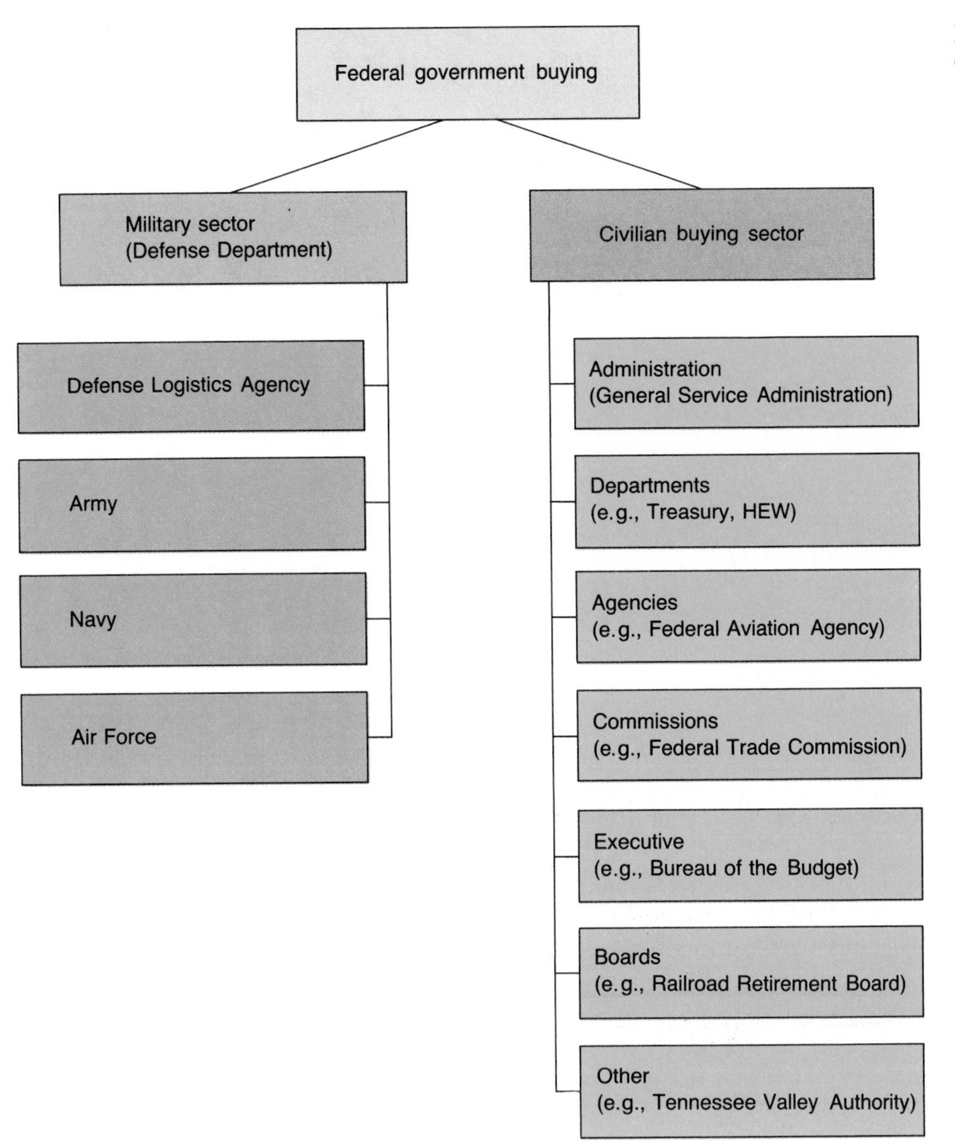

Figure 6.8
Government Buying Units

- *U.S. Government Purchasing, Specifications, and Sales Directory* (Small Business Administration) lists thousands of the most commonly purchased items and the government units buying them.
- GSA offices are maintained in several large cities to provide instruction on buying procedures and to recommend steps for potential buyers to follow.
- Mailing lists of interested suppliers are maintained by most buying agencies. By requesting to be included on such a list, companies are mailed announcements of intended purchases.

State and Local Government Buying Marketing opportunities are not restricted to federal agencies; each state and local government also engages in buying activity. Education activities account for a large proportion of the total dollars spent. For

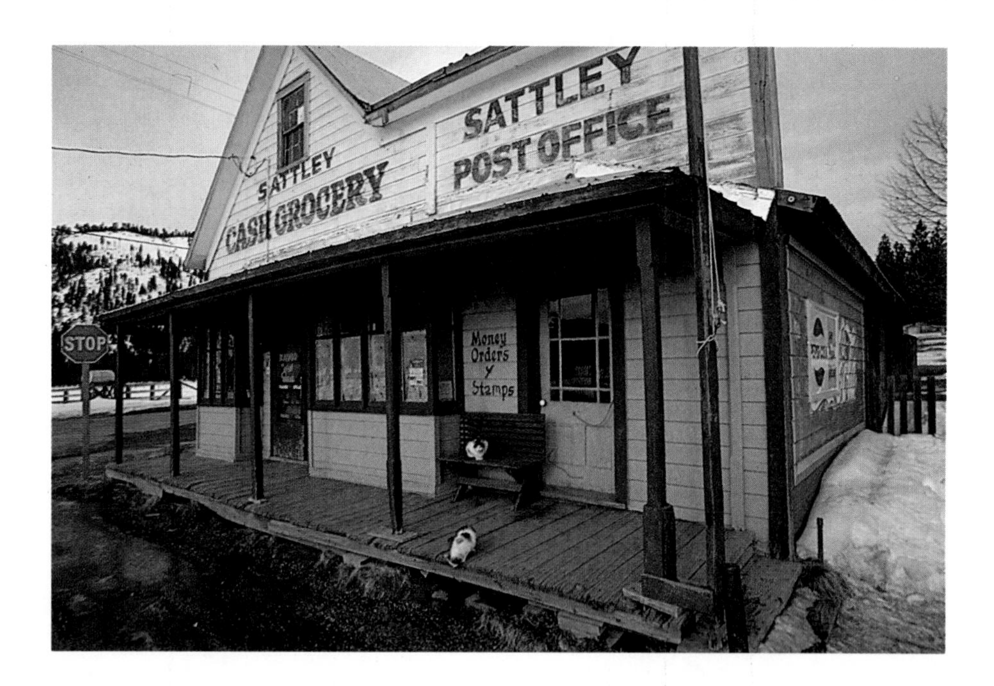

Much of the federal government's buying is decentralized around the country.

example, Michigan allocates approximately 70 percent of its property tax receipts to primary, secondary, and community college education (about $10 billion per year). On top of this is an allotment of over a half billion dollars to higher education. In addition to education, state and local governments fund many other projects such as roads, parks, trash removal, hospitals, and a host of other items. State and local units sometimes supplement their funds with federal money, as when they employ Federal Highway Trust Fund money to construct roads. Revenue-sharing programs also provide substantial assistance to many cities and localities.

Individual states generally decentralize buying responsibility. That is, individual school boards, road commissions, hospital boards, water and sewer boards, and similar units make the bulk of all procurement decisions. Thus, managers of even small firms in less-populated cities and towns have an opportunity to compete for a piece of the action.

Buyer Behavior

Government buyers sometimes make their acquisitions through negotiated contracts when a particular supplier's products are uniquely desirable.[33] The normal approach, however, is through description and competitive bidding. Generally, the lowest bidder receives the contract, unless the low bidder is not considered "responsible or responsive to the terms of the solicitation." This means that buyers may consider a company's reputation, financial solvency, and past experience.

The Sheth model of industrial buyer behavior, mentioned earlier in this chapter, effectively describes the governmental buying decision processes. As in the case of industrial buying, marketers have substantial opportunity to shape their strategies around the target customers' needs. In fact, as with industrial buyers, an astute marketer frequently helps in identifying the government agency's needs.

Chapter Summary

Organizational buying presents a very significant opportunity, often the largest one, for many marketers. This chapter examined industrial and other organizational buying behavior, as understanding this phenomenon is vital for making effective marketing decisions concerning these markets. Employing the marketing concept when attacking these markets is important for success.

There are many different varieties of industrial and governmental buyers who, in total, buy every conceivable type of item for a myriad of uses. In general, their demand for goods and services is relatively inelastic and dependent upon their relationship to others in the chain of exchanges. Nevertheless, the demand for a particular firm's offerings tends to be very elastic. This means that deciding on an appropriate marketing mix is critical to the success of suppliers.

In contrast to consumers, industrial and governmental buyers are generally better informed. This is because these organizations usually employ buying specialists who are aggressive in their search for information about products. This means that particular elements of the marketing mix often require a different relative emphasis than for consumer markets, with personal selling often receiving the greatest weight.

Most of the buying specialists employ systematic buying procedures. Further, several people are often concerned with making a buying decision. While emotional motives are involved, they are usually less instrumental than in consumer purchases.

Finally, the chapter provided a slightly altered (from consumer buying) model of the buying process to guide a manager's understanding of this process. This model is useful in understanding the dynamics of institutional buying, which leads to improved decision making concerning these markets.

Questions

1. Why is the marketing concept important for industrial marketing? After all, the buyers are specialists who cannot be tricked by advertising and other marketing gimmicks. What about governmental buyers?
2. What are the various categories of items purchased by industrial buyers? How do they differ from each other and from consumer items?
3. Does categorizing items only serve to describe buying, or does it help the marketer's understanding? Why?
4. Explain the importance of considering derived demand.
5. In the words of one entrepreneur, "The key to selling industrial buyers is technological advancement and price. The rest of that stuff is just plain garbage." Comment.
6. How does the chain of exchange concept assist marketers in defining needs?
7. How do purchasing agents differ from consumer buyers?
8. What is value analysis?
9. How is a new task buying situation different than a straight or modified rebuy?
10. "Close contact with industrial or governmental buyers is unnecessary. After all, numerous persons are instrumental in making decisions and the buyer is really just a clerk." Comment.
11. Explain the differences between the industrial and consumer buying behavior models.
12. Is lobbying ethical? What purposes does it serve?
13. Compare competitive bidding and negotiated contracts. Which is better?

Part Three

Marketing Opportunity Analysis

Chapter 7

Marketing Research and Information Systems

Objectives

After completing this chapter, you should be able to demonstrate a knowledge of:

- Why marketing managers need detailed information about the marketplace for effective decision making
- The components of marketing information systems
- How marketing information systems can be designed and operated
- The meaning of the term "marketing research"
- The seven stages of the marketing research process: initial observation, hypothesis formulation, determination of needed information, development of a data collection instrument, data acquisition, analysis and interpretation, and specific follow-up procedures

MARKETING SUCCESS

Marketing Research Paves the Way to Prosperity in Fast Food

The 1970s and early 1980s marked the rapid expansion of the fast-food business, with overall industry sales growing at an annual compound rate of 10 percent during the period. Several companies set the pace. McDonald's, the largest, sustained a decade-long 30 percent annual jump in both sales and profits despite the company's already large base of 4,200 outlets and sales of over $3 billion. Wendy's International was another leader. The number of its retail outlets jumped from 9 to 520 during the late 1970s, with company sales mushrooming 100 times to $180 million and profits to over $7 million. Growth was not universal within the industry, however. Several companies, even some large ones, lost considerable ground throughout the period: examples include Kentucky Fried Chicken, Burger Chef, and Pizza Inn, all of whose sales fell precipitously during the period.

A major characteristic separating the winners and losers was the former's dedication to the diligent use of carefully gathered and analyzed market information. For instance, McDonald's management learned through research that it could greatly expand profits by adding breakfast entries such as Egg McMuffins. Another finding was that locating stores near where people gathered, such as in shopping malls, hospitals, and school cafeterias, could significantly increase total business as opposed to locating just near where people live. The company also began to improve the effectiveness of its advertising and other promotion campaigns based upon research findings.

In contrast, the managers in many of the companies that lost ground continued to make their decisions on the basis of intuition. Their performances suffered as a result. Simply put, they were not in touch with their markets.

SOURCE: Adapted from Richard Kreisman, "Big Mac Ads Hit Back at BK," *Advertising Age* 53, no. 46 (November 1, 1982): 58; "The Fast-Food Stars: Three Strategies for Fast Growth," *Business Week*, no. 2473 (July 11, 1977): 56–57; and Scott Hume, "Research Ignores Preteens: Big Mac Exec," *Advertising Age* 57, no. 22 (March 17, 1986): 28.

Introduction

Management can adopt one of three styles of using information when making decisions, relying primarily on intuition, on informally collected data, or on information collected in a systematic and objective way.

The experience of Gino's, an Eastern fast-food franchise, illustrates the result of relying on blind intuition. Through insight and without any market testing, management introduced the "heroburger," a rectangular sandwich instead of the customary oval-shaped one. Management was so convinced of its salability that all other sandwiches were pulled from the company's menu. As Gino's chairman later lamented, "We shot ourselves out of the water with that one." [1]

Informally collected information can also be used, as when a butcher asks regular customers how they enjoyed their last roast. While it is a step in the right direction because it at least asks customers what they think, such informal data can also lead to poor decisions because of the inherent personal bias involved. Who qualifies as a regular customer? Are these people representative of the market at large?

Finally, management may pursue a systematic and objective style, like that practiced at Wendy's and McDonald's (as illustrated in this chapter's Marketing Success). This style is much more likely than the other two to result in a solid decision because it is founded on obtaining needed, accurate, and unbiased information about the firm's environment. While intuition and judgment will always be valuable, decisions based on systematically and objectively collected information significantly increase a company's chances for success.

This chapter explores why and how much information an organization should collect, it provides an overview of marketing information systems, and finally, it examines the components of marketing research.

Collecting Marketing Information

Why Collect Information?

As Table 7.1 illustrates, most major companies systematically collect and analyze many forms of marketing information. There are several reasons for this.

First, many companies are geographically separated from the bulk of their markets. Kohler Co., for example, manufactures premium plumbing fixtures in Wisconsin but relies for sales on customers around the globe. Collecting information about these distant markets is essential so that management can make intelligent decisions about what is needed in far-away places.

Second, important information is seldom obvious.[2] Why do some people buy Amway detergents from in-home representatives, for example, while others buy competitive items in supermarkets? Accurate answers to important behavioral questions may be essential in deciding effective strategy, yet the answers may be difficult for management to answer without conducting research.

Executive isolation is a third reason for collecting market information. Highly paid, well-educated top managers have needs, activities, and desires far removed from all but a few market segments.[3] Relying on collected market information enables them to make effective decisions relating to all target markets.

Finally, accurate and carefully researched information is needed because of the high cost of making a mistake. A plant expansion might cost $250 million or more, or a large-scale advertising budget might exceed $200 million per year.[4] Management cannot afford to risk making a wrong decision on the basis of mere hunches or guesses.

How Much Information Should Be Collected?

Too little information results in needless risk, but attempting to collect too much information involves excessive costs. Therefore, it is prudent for management to make a tradeoff between the cost of collecting and analyzing additional information, and the expected cost of making a wrong decision if the information is not collected. Decision theory concepts are helpful in assessing whether or not the collection of information is warranted.[5] Appendix C presents a discussion and illustrations of the use of decision theory concepts for this purpose.

Table 7.1 Percentage of Industrial and Consumer Companies Doing Selected Types of Research

Type of Research	Percent	
	Industrial companies	*Consumer companies*
Advertising Research		
a. Motivation research	26	67
b. Copy research	37	76
c. Media research	43	69
d. Studies of ad effectiveness	47	85
Business Economics and Corporate Research		
a. Short-range forecasting (up to 1 year)	96	90
b. Long-range forecasting (over 1 year)	96	87
c. Studies of business trends	97	79
d. Pricing studies	93	88
e. Plant and warehouse location studies	84	76
Corporate Responsibility Research		
a. Ecological impact studies	52	40
b. Studies of legal constraints on advertising and promotion	80	64
Product Research		
a. New product acceptance and potential	93	94
b. Competitive product studies	95	93
c. Packaging research	85	83
Sales and Marketing Research		
a. Measurement of market potential	97	97
b. Market share analysis	97	96
c. Determination of market characteristics	97	92
d. Sales analysis	97	96
e. Distribution channel studies	87	86
f. Consumer panel operations	30	80
g. Test markets, store audits	43	83
h. Promotional studies of premiums, coupons, sampling, etc.	32	73

SOURCE: Abstracted from Dik W. Twedt, ed., *1978 Survey of Marketing Research* (Chicago: American Marketing Association, 1978): 41–44.

Marketing Information Systems

Management's need for information is ongoing and ever-increasing. If sales suddenly dip in a territory, if customer complaints surge, if a competitor is planning a new product line, or if conflicts with intermediaries emerge, management needs to be informed soon enough to plan timely corrective action. A marketing information system (a subset of a management information system) can supply such information.

What Is an MIS?

Most progressive companies have a formal system of collecting and reporting market information.[6] The major feature of this arrangement, termed a **marketing information**

system (MIS), is that the firm systematically collects and reports data in such a way that they are of major value in assisting decision making.[7] For example, General Electric has installed a computer-assisted MIS called "World Wide Marketing Screen."[8] At its heart is a central computer that key managers can access with desktop terminals located in their offices. The memory contains millions of information pieces, such as the names of 46,000 potential business customers worldwide, all planned construction projects worldwide that amount to $1 million or more, and 20-year economic forecasts of 160 countries. At the touch of a button, executives can acquire product sales forecasts, define target markets, and even plan future sales efforts. Foremost-McKesson, the largest wholesaler in the United States, has an equally extensive system. It shares much of the information it collects with retailer-customers.[9]

Marketing information system (MIS) A formal system (usually part of a general management information system) for routinely collecting and reporting information to aid marketing decision making.

MIS Composition

Figure 7.1 gives an overview of an MIS. Because of the vast quantity of potentially useful data, the advancement of computer technology has greatly enhanced the development of these information systems.

Developing an MIS

There are four critical steps in developing an MIS: determining the types of information managers need for decision making, collecting the information, manipulating the data, and reporting information to appropriate managers.

Determining Needed Information The starting point of MIS development is determining what types of information management needs. The primary criterion to use in this regard is its usefulness for decision making. Usually, the goal of collecting information for an MIS is to obtain it from existing sources and integrate it in a central location so that it can be readily reported and accessed by management as needed.

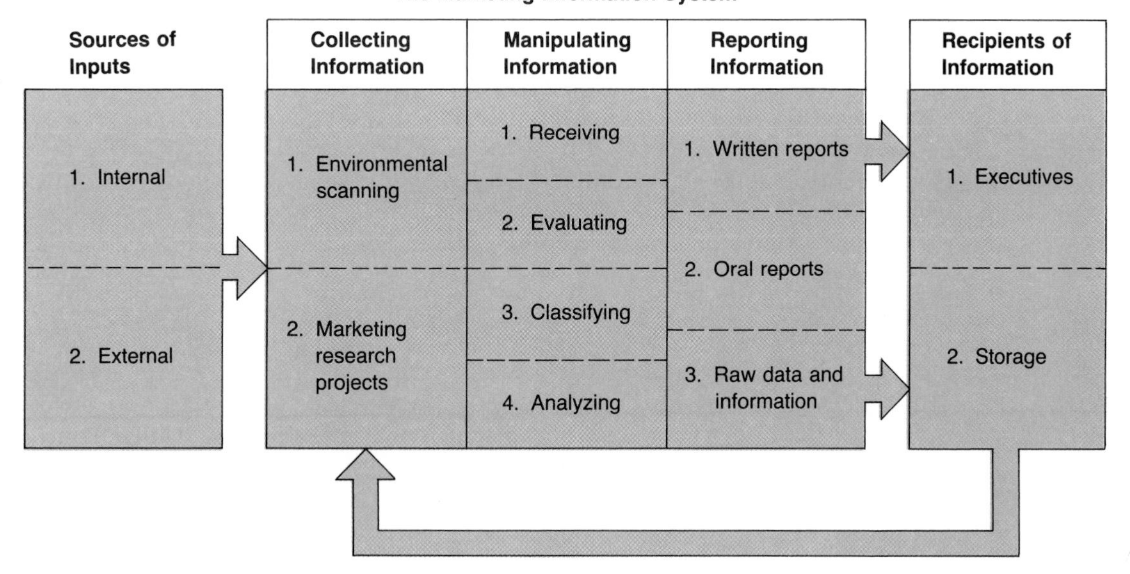

Figure 7.1
Overview of a Marketing Information System (MIS)

Data
Pieces of information.

Primary data
Data originated for a particular study.

Secondary data
Data already existing and collected for some other purpose, often by some other party.

As a point of clarification, **data** generally may be classified into two types: primary and secondary.[10] **Primary data** are originated for a particular study, as when *Reader's Digest* collects statistics on sales generated by a new promotional brochure. In contrast, **secondary data** already exist and were collected for some other purpose, often by some other party. An example is *Reader's Digest* monitoring of population migration as reported by the U.S. Census Bureau. The information collected in an MIS, therefore, consists primarily of secondary data.

The specific information needs of managers vary from company to company. Thus, it is difficult to be specific about the types of data that should be included in an MIS. But in general, there are two sources of information inputs: internal and external. The first arises from within the company and consists of such sources as sales records, warranty cards, past research studies, shipping records, and other company accounting records. If the firm has not already set up adequate records to help in decision making, marketers should recommend that they be established. They may suggest, for instance, breaking sales data down by product class, customer type, or geographic area.

An MIS differs from an accounting system in that it also includes the integration of information originating outside of the firm. All data important to management for decision making is collected, wherever the origin. There are two major sources of such external secondary data: government publications and private publications and reports. Federal, state, and local government documents are especially useful sources of relevant MIS data. These can be obtained from the Government Documents sections of major public and college libraries, Department of Commerce offices, regional governmental agencies such as regional Federal Reserve Banks, universities, and Chambers of Commerce.

Many private sources of secondary information are also invaluable. Professional publications such as the *Journal of Marketing Research*, are useful for a variety of topics. The National Industrial Conference Board and various trade associations publish reports of general interest such as information about consumer market trends.[11] The A. C. Nielsen Co. and Market Research Corporation of America report retail sales of products by classes. Far too many sources of secondary data are available to be covered extensively here. Appendix D lists several of the most generally useful secondary sources for marketing information.

Collecting Information Integrating both internally- and externally-generated information into one source represents a big step forward in providing management with needed decision-making information. An MIS is designed to collect information from selected sources. One means of collection is environmental screening. This is continuous monitoring of the environment through multiple sources such as sales reports, trade journals, and published government statistics. Another source includes past marketing research projects the firm has initiated from time to time to yield specific primary data.

Aggregating data (data aggregation)
Reduction of detailed data to summary measures.

When developing an MIS data base, though, the firm should avoid **aggregating data** (reducing detailed data to summary measures). Facts should be stored in as much detail as possible. Aggregation lessens management's ability to later search for causes and relationships. Detailed facts are needed to answer such questions as "Have profits eroded because sales have declined? For which products? Which territories? Which kinds of customers? What time of year? Which day of the week?" Aggregation only serves to conceal underlying influences.[12]

Effective MIS development means tailoring the information communicated around the individual needs of decision makers.

Manipulating Data Soaring computer technology has greatly advanced the development of the MIS. Third- and fourth-generation mainframes, desktop terminals, and user-friendly software have enabled companies to maintain, analyze, and report more information than they could ever even dream about in the past. And the proliferation of this technology will spur future MIS development.[13]

Schenley Industries (a liquor producer), for example, has installed a very modern system that enables key managers to retrieve figures on current and past sales along with inventory levels for all brands and package sizes for each of 400 distributors. Computer terminals allow the information to be retrieved at a moment's notice.

Smaller companies should also consider using an MIS, even if an advanced system is beyond their financial reach. Smaller companies simply must be more selective about the kinds and volume of information included. Then too, tumbling prices and the continuing evolution of microcomputers make relatively complex systems affordable to all but the very smallest of companies.

Reporting Information The final step in developing an MIS consists of reporting information to key decision makers. There are three types of information an MIS reports to managers: control information, planning information, and information needed for marketing research.[14]

3 types of info:

Control information
That which permits continuous monitoring of marketing activities.

Control Information This type of information permits continuous monitoring of marketing activities. It allows managers to spot trends, symptoms of problems, and even market opportunities before it becomes too late to take needed action.[15]

As an example, the Federal Mogul Corp.—a supplier of many parts to the auto industry—maintains a comprehensive MIS system. Through the system, management can use desktop computer terminals to gain access to many important pieces of information such as sales of any part, current inventory levels, the complete status of any assembly using a particular part, sales orders, orders to suppliers, current sales forecasts for any part, and other similar information. The system enables management to anticipate potential problems before they arise and take timely corrective action.

Planning information
Information used for developing marketing strategy.

Planning Information A well-designed MIS contains information that is useful for the effective development of marketing strategy.[16] Like GE's system, the information includes characteristics of target markets, market positions of the company's as well as competitors' products, emerging environmental trends, and other inputs useful in sound strategy formulation.

Research information (basic)
A base of information, generally secondary, that provides a springboard or starting point for marketing researchers for their studies.

Research Information An MIS also provides information to serve as a springboard of knowledge for marketing researchers. This is especially important during the initial phases of the research process.

The specific ways an MIS reports information to management varies from company to company, depending upon needs and the system's capabilities. Most systems include some combination of both regularly printed reports and various means of handling special information requests. Computers dramatize some reports, often in color and with graphics.[17] With terminal-accessed systems, such as at G.E. and Schenley, it is usually possible for management to readily access and process information as the need arises. User-friendly software such as LOTUS 1–2–3 has greatly expanded this capability.

Experience indicates that at least one thing is clear: reports should not consist of ream after endless ream of computer printout. Too much, as well as not enough, information is the antithesis of solid systems. When too much information is reported, managers eventually fail to notice even important items.

Management by exception
A style of management that involves focusing attention primarily on troublesome areas; the reporting of information concerning troublesome areas that interfere with the attainment of company goals.

Here is where the principle of **management by exception** is relevant: only the information that management needs for problem solving should be highlighted. Focusing on troublesome areas enables managers to pinpoint their efforts. Interestingly, research indicates that line managers are quite likely to use information gathered through an MIS when their organization is decentralized and there are few formal procedural rules that they must follow.[18]

Consequently, data processing specialists need to work hand-in-hand with line managers in pinpointing the exact types of information needed. In doing so, both should answer the following questions:

1. What types of decisions do you regularly make and what information do you need for them?
2. What types of special studies do you need?
3. What types of information would you like to get that is currently unavailable?
4. How should the information be reported, in terms of both form and frequency?
5. What improvements in information would you like to see?

While a well-conceived MIS can provide an invaluable data base for decision making, the data collected is not always sufficient to solve particular decision problems and additional data collection is required. Miles Laboratories, for example, learned from research that many consumers objected to the smell of ammonia contained in the popular glass-cleaning products. Following this opportunity, the company developed and introduced Glass Works, a vinegar-based glass cleaner, in early 1986. Whenever information is collected and analyzed for a particular decision problem, the process is termed **marketing research,** which is part of an MIS.

Marketing Research

Good marketing research generates directional information for decision making.

Marketing research consists of planning for, obtaining, analyzing, and interpreting all the facts necessary to make an intelligent decision concerning a particular problem.[19] It involves systematically obtaining and analyzing information about a market, such as what buyers want, need, think, and feel. While the involvement in this function varies from one company to another, practically all firms of any size do some marketing research.[20] Typically, management budgets around 1 percent of sales for this activity, and about 60 percent of all companies have formal marketing research departments. Other organizations rely on consultants, advertising agencies, and independent research agencies to conduct research for them. Even those companies with formal research departments spend, on average, about half their budgets on contracted work.

Marketing research
Systematically obtaining and analyzing information about a market, such as what buyers want, need, think, and feel.

In point of fact, performing marketing research is itself a big business. In 1985, for instance, A. C. Nielsen—the largest of the marketing/advertising research firms—billed clients more than the $340 million that Young & Rubicam (the largest of the ad agencies that year) grossed in advertising revenue.[21]

By itself, though, simply spending money on research is no guarantee of useful results. Some studies merely verify the obvious; others are performed haphazardly. Ford Motor Company's experience in researching the Edsel, probably the most heavily researched car of its time, is a classic example. After ten years and millions of dollars of research into images, names, and other features, the research failed for several reasons. The company did not relate what the research discovered about product images to product attributes, and the data did not reflect the market at the time of introduction. While many other factors also contributed to the Edsel's failure, this illustrates that research is no guarantee of success.[22]

Whether the research is done internally or contracted from outside sources, in all cases it is management's responsibility to be in a position to assess a research project's usefulness and to judge whether or not it represents a quality piece of work. This is accomplished by understanding the nature of objectivity and the scientific method.

Objectivity and the Scientific Method

Quality research yields results that are both valid and reliable.[23] **Validity** refers to the extent to which a study measures that which is intended. **Reliability,** in contrast, corresponds to its repeatability: whether or not the results are from random fluctuations or if, in fact, they are consistent with the underlying phenomena being measured. Research on the Edsel lacked validity because it no longer matched market conditions at the time of introduction. It also failed in reliability because the image measures varied and did not relate to the car's actual attributes.

Validity
The extent to which a study measures what is intended.

Reliability
The degree to which study results are consistent with the underlying phenomena being measured; repeatability.

The best way to assure valid and reliable results is to follow the scientific method, which is a systematic and objective procedure.[24] The scientific method involves a sequence of activities which, when combined, produces what is called the marketing research process: initial observation, hypothesis formulation, determining needed information, developing a data collection plan, data acquisition, analysis, interpretation.

MARKETING BRIEF

Aggressive Competition with a New Product

Miles Laboratories introduced Glass Works, a vinegar-based glass cleaner, in 1986. The company objective was to overcome the two brands that dominated the market—Windex, with a 58 percent market share, and Texize's Glass Plus, with 22 percent of industry sales.

Both Windex and Glass Plus are ammonia-based. Miles, acting upon research that showed consumer dissatisfaction with the smell of ammonia, brought out Glass Works with a vinegar base. A $7 million advertising campaign promoted the new offering. Since Miles was new to the glass cleaner category, Glass Works ads contained the legend "From the makers of S.O.S." [soap pads].

"It will be interesting to see how Glass Works does," says Betsy Donovan, an analyst with Charles Kline & Co. of Fairfield, N.J. "Most glass cleaners are also promoted for their other cleaning uses as well." Consequently, only time will tell how well the strategy used for Glass Works will fare.

SOURCE: Adapted from Laurie Freeman, "Miles Sees Window of Opportunity," *Advertising Age* 57, no. 25 (April 7, 1986): 3, 95. Also see Stewart Alter, "Stewart to Creative Top Spot at DDB," *Advertising Age* 57, no. 22 (March 17, 1986): 2, 106.

Carefully designed marketing research breaks through stereotypes and provides valid information about a target.

and establishment of follow-up procedures.[25] This formal process can be quite time-consuming, involving much searching for information and analytical work. But as the accompanying Campbell Soup Marketing Brief illustrates, this task has become much more streamlined and efficient with the advancement of computers and software.

Figure 7.2 illustrates the marketing research process. While the procedures may vary a bit, companies successfully using marketing research follow the basic process that is illustrated.

Initial Observation Marketing research's first step is initial observation, where researchers learn the fundamentals relating to a particular decision problem. This enables them to set a realistic direction for the entire research effort. The activities of awareness, fact finding, and problem definition are parts of this step.

Awareness Gaining a basic understanding of the characteristics of the decision environment is essential before attempting to tackle a research project.[26] Awareness is somewhat vaguely defined, as an overall understanding of a decision's environment depends upon the particular situation. If the company plans research to learn why many customers do not repeat their purchases of a particular brand, such as Cheer, the researchers should first become familiar with the nature of detergents, the target market's makeup, the competitive setting, the consumer decision-making process, and related factors.

Though the need for awareness might be obvious at first glance, inexperienced researchers and those trying to cut corners sometimes try to collect data before they first understand the situation and what management expects from the research. The Edsel's researchers erred in this regard. They left some 800 stylists with the problem of determining what a car should look like to portray the intended image and personality,[27] but they did not extend the research to learn if the design actually created the desired personality in the eyes of consumers.

Fact Finding In fact finding, analysts construct a list of facts to later consider as symptoms of underlying causes.[28] The symptoms may be that sales are falling, that there is a low awareness of the product among consumers, the morale of the sales force is poor, or intermediaries are not spending their advertising allowances. Some research projects uncover literally hundreds of symptoms.

While fact finding, researchers are like auditors who investigate company documents such as warranty files, sales records, and accounts receivable to gain useful insights. Fact finding can also include talking with company representatives, executives, distributors, customers, and examining past research reports. No attempt should be made to explain the facts during this stage, only to uncover them—both the "good ones" and the "bad ones."

Problem Definition Before collecting any primary data, the researchers should carefully define the problem. Exploratory research—small-scale studies that examine various directions and different probable solutions and implications—is sometimes desirable. For example, many factors relating to salespeople (personality characteristics, salary structures, and education) might be looked at to learn if they relate to performance. Here the intent is to narrow the direction of future research. But generally, the research should be focused directly toward helping to solve a specifically defined problem. A distinction exists between *basic* and *applied* research. The former is largely exploratory, having widespread application to many types of businesses and decisions. Most research conducted by universities and foundations is of this type. Applied research deals with a particular decision faced by a specific company. Most research conducted by companies is of this type.

There is a difference between a *decision problem* and a *research problem*. The former is one that managers must resolve, such as "How can we increase camera and film sales?" or "How can we improve our sales force's performance?" A research problem, on the other hand, specifies precisely what information the research should provide. It is both specific and limited in scope. Good research consists of chipping away at the unknown, rather than trying to learn everything in one study.[29]

For example, marketing researchers have for a long time searched for the variables that affect a salesperson's performance. In this realm, management's decision problem is "How do we get more out of the sales force?" Researching all the ways would not be cost-effective even if it were possible. Defining a researchable problem involves first identifying a theory that is consistent with the symptoms uncovered and then testing to see if it does explain the facts. One study, for instance, theorized that personality differences influence sales performance.[30] The research problem was "Do personality characteristics affect a salesperson's performance?" The research problem related directly to the decision problem, but it was sufficiently specific and limited in scope to produce meaningful research results.

Hypothesis Formulation Formulating hypotheses is second on the marketing research agenda. Sometimes formally identifying a problem is sufficient to enable management to make an intelligent decision; the solution to the problem is obvious. But in many cases, the best course of action is not clear and further research is needed.

Dealing with theories is tricky. They often are complex and not directly testable. For example, the theory that "personality influences a salesperson's performance" is

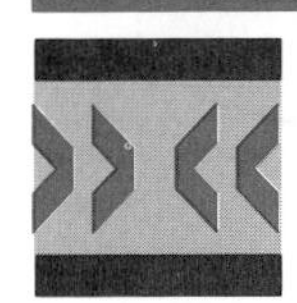

MARKETING BRIEF

Computers Integrate Marketing Research into Management Decision Making

Nearly overwhelmed with data from consumer research, the Philadelphia-based Campbell Soup Company recently adopted a new software program called Acustar and marketed by Metaphor Computer Systems, Inc. to manage its extensive data bases. According to a Campbell's spokesman, "Acustar is a powerful data management system capable of handling large-scale data bases and manipulating them in a very user-friendly way."

Campbell has also allowed its advertising agencies to access the data. A case in point is Hal Riney & Partners, the Philadelphia agency that develops Campbell's advertising for Swanson's frozen dinners. "The system has really helped us in identifying key attributes of target audiences," say officials. "It allows us to focus on message development and creative aspects, rather than trying to find data."

SOURCE: Adapted from "Riney & Partners Opens Campbell's Tin of Information" *Advertising Age* 57, no. 28 (April 28, 1986): 55.

Figure 7.2
The Marketing Research Process

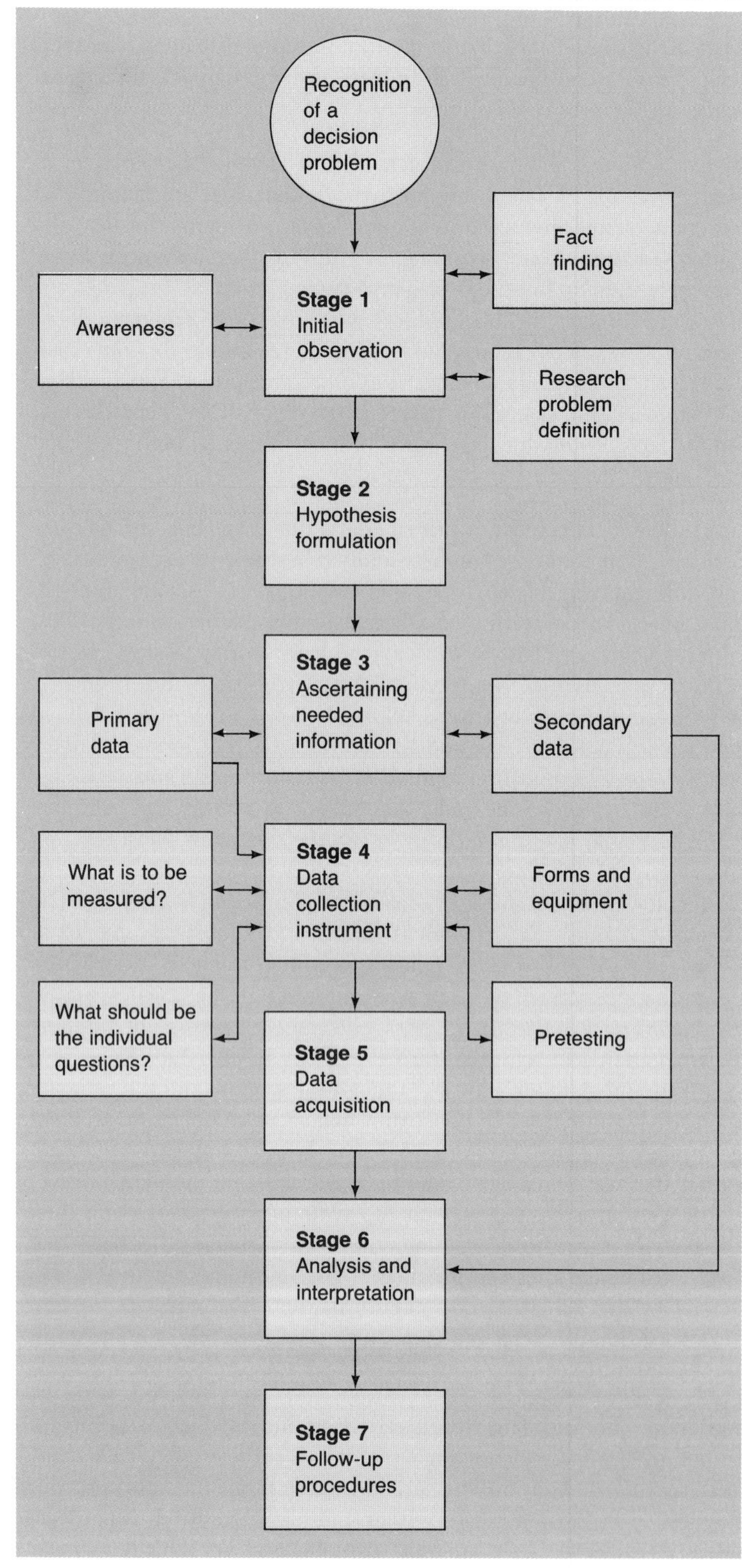

too all-encompassing to permit direct testing. To get around this difficulty, researchers use hypotheses to test a theory's applicability to a particular decision problem. **Hypotheses** are operational extensions of a research problem theory, and they can be tested and measured.[31] The following hypotheses were among those used in the above-mentioned study.[32]

Hypothesis
An operational extension of a research problem theory that can be tested and measured.

1. "The combined set of personality variables and personal characteristics are significantly related to measures of sales performance."
2. "Increasing levels of the personality traits of dominance, endurance, social recognition, empathy, and ego strength are associated with higher levels of sales performance."

Hypotheses are useful because they provide direction to researchers—they are something concrete to measure. If the evidence shows that a hypothesis is true, the implication is that the theory from which it was derived is applicable. In the above case, the research indicated that if sales managers used personality characteristics in screening applicants, sales levels would probably improve, but until the researchers created testable extensions of the theory, there was no way to see if it helped explain performance. To avoid unnecessarily complex studies, the least complex hypotheses should be assessed first. Managers should stay on top of the research direction to assure that the least costly solution can be found.

Determining Needed Information The third stage of the marketing research process involves determining the types of information needed to test the hypotheses. The researchers may decide that data from a secondary source, new data, or some combination of both is needed.

Data from a Secondary Source Marketing research projects produce *primary data*—the information analysts collect for the specific purposes of a particular study.[33] But researchers also use data originating in **secondary sources.** For instance, if Lever Brothers collects demographics from published sources to determine who buys particular kinds of detergents, the data originates from a secondary source.

Secondary sources (of data)
Places where existing data already collected may be obtained (also see *secondary data*).

Some impatient researchers and managers believe that they must rush out and gather new data through some sort of survey whenever management needs new information. As one source has accurately stated, "a good operating rule is to consider a survey akin to surgery—to be used only after other possibilities have been exhausted.[34] Since it is foolish for researchers to try to "reinvent the wheel," they should always begin by discovering if the appropriate data can be found in the company's MIS or in other secondary sources.

Data Generated by the Primary Source Frequently the data obtained from secondary sources do not provide all the information needed for a particular research project. The units of measurement or classifications used in reporting the data may be wrong for the current study's purposes, the data may be obsolete or incomplete, or new areas of inquiry may be originated.[35] Researchers must then resort to collecting original data, termed **primary source generated data.** Management should be concerned with both the sampling process and the means used to collect primary data.

Primary source generated data
The primary data generated for a particular study.

The Sampling Process Researchers should take painstaking care in collecting primary data since the quality of the information acquired is dependent on it. Practically all primary data collection efforts in marketing research gather information from repre-

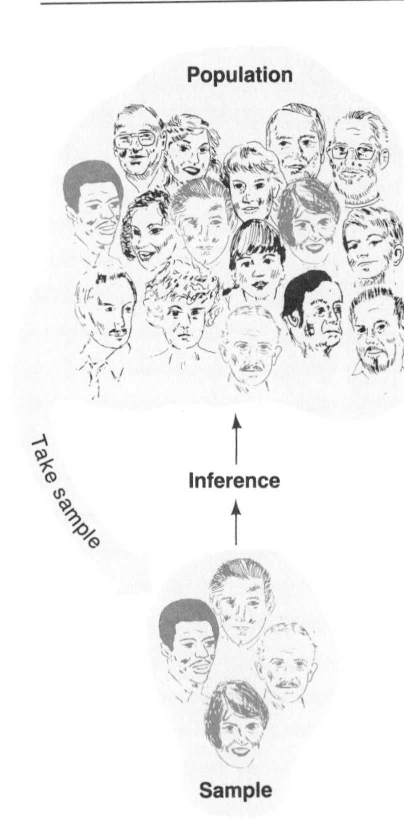

Figure 7.3
The Sampling Process

Population
The complete set of a defined group, including all members, people, or objects of that group.

Sample
A subset of a population that is examined in a study and used to make inferences about the entire population.

sentative samples of existing or potential customers which researchers use to make inferences about all existing or potential customers. Figure 7.3 illustrates the overall process. Three steps are critical in gathering all types of primary data: defining the population, determining the sampling selection procedure, and setting the size of the sample.

Population A **population** refers to all persons or objects about which a research team would like information; they may be customers, trucks, warehouses, retail stores, salespeople, or any other group. For example, if a marketing researcher for a political candidate wishes to predict voting behavior during an upcoming election, the population probably includes only registered voters in the election district.

Sometimes students get the impression that the relevant population is obvious, but that assumption can be dangerous. To illustrate, consider the case of a dog food producer

> . . . who went out and did an intensive market study. He tested the demand for dog food, he tested the package size, the design, the whole advertising program. Then he launched the product with a big campaign, got the proper distribution channels, put it on the market and had tremendous sales. But two months later, the bottom dropped out—no follow-up sales. So he called in an expert, who took the dog food out to a local pound, put it in front of the dogs—and they would not touch it. For all the big marketing study, no one had tried the product on the dogs.[36]

Defining the relevant population in marketing research is not always simple. Gatekeepers pose one problem, as the discussion above illustrated. Another results from naively assuming that people listed in directories such as telephone books, city directories, partially complete or dated mailing lists, and the like, make up an entire population. Such directories often exclude many potential prospects.

Sample Selection Procedure When populations are very small, a complete enumeration (termed a *census*) of all members is generally the most appropriate procedure. Hughes Aircraft, for instance, obtains information about military helicopter purchase intentions by directly contacting all potential buyers. A census is feasible and desirable in this case because there are only a relatively few potential buyers and the dollar volume of each potential order is large enough to justify the expense of contacting each of them.

In contrast, most companies find it uneconomical to contact every member of a population. For example, millions of people buy soap from Procter & Gamble each year. The very large number of customers plus the relatively small purchase price make a census economically impossible. In such cases the procedure is to examine a portion of the population (termed a **sample**) to make inferences about the entire population.

Two major categories of sampling designs are available: probability and nonprobability samples.[37] In the case of the former, each population member has a known, nonzero chance of being sampled. Random selection determines whether or not a particular population member is included; researcher biases do not influence whether or not a certain subject is chosen.

Probability samples conform to the laws of large numbers—the bases of probability theory and modern statistics.[38] Accordingly, they are the only type that researchers theoretically should use for statistical inference. All statistical techniques assume a probability sample, since this is the only type that statistically represents an intended

Carefully defining the target market is essential for good marketing research results.

population. Firms should base formal marketing research projects on probability samples so long as cost, time, and other constraints do not prohibit their use.

Nonprobability samples allow personal judgments of researchers to determine which members of the population will be included. As a result, biases may enter into the selection and render the results unrepresentative of the population. Nonprobability samples can lead to correct inferences, though, under certain circumstances; for instance, if very little variance exists in subject responses. But because response variability is seldom known ahead of time, researchers should avoid nonprobability samples whenever possible.

However, nonprobability samples are very useful for pretesting (discussed later in this chapter) and in cases where management must have immediate information. In some emergency situations, poor information is better than that which is accurate, but late.

Exhibit 7.1
Survey Types Based on Different Sampling Designs

Type of Probability Samples:	Description	Advantages	Disadvantages
1. Simple Random Sample	Each member of a population has an equal chance of being selected as part of the sample. Also, the probability of any member's inclusion is not affected by whether or not any other particular member is chosen (e.g., if A is selected first, B's chance of being selected next is unaffected).	Follows the laws of large numbers, thus enabling the use of statistical theory, and is relatively simple in design. This is a very common design in marketing research, for all members of a population have an equal chance of affecting results.	Can be costly to administer since consideration is not given to geographical distances between selected sample members. Further, all members of a population may not be of equal concern.
2. Systematic Random Sample	A random start is used to select the first sample member, then a *predetermined* system is used to select the remainder. As examples, the third household in a neighborhood might be randomly selected, then every eleventh thereafter, or the twenty-eighth name in a telephone book selected randomly then every one-hundredth thereafter.	Simplicity in selecting subjects is the major advantage of this type of sample. Assuming that an underlying bias does not exist in the predetermined selection system for those selected after the random start, results approximate a simple random sample.	The principle disadvantage of this method is that an underlying bias may exist. For example, every eleventh house might be a residence at an intersection. Thus, results could be distorted.
3. Stratified Random Sample	A procedure that allows population groups that are more important to testing a hypothesis to have a greater probability of being included in a sample. For example, heavy and medium cola drinkers might be more important to a decision than all soda drinkers. Thus, a greater proportion of heavy and medium drinkers are included. Stratification may be based on one or more of several variables such as geography, product use, or demographics.	This method is very desirable when vast differences exist between subgroups within a population. It enables information to be gathered to reflect these differences.	Sample selection procedures and data collection are made more difficult. Also, a researcher must first know that differences exist so that the design may be constructed ahead of time. Therefore, a pretest is usually necessary as a first step.
4. Cluster Sample	Subjects are divided into groups. For example, each block within a city might be defined as a cluster, or perhaps each census tract. Then every subject in a random selection of clusters is surveyed.	The simplest and least costly of the probability sampling designs and thus used frequently in marketing research studies.	One problem is that subjects in one or a few clusters may have significantly different characteristics from others and thus bias may be introduced.

There are several sampling design subcategories. Exhibit 7.1 describes the types commonly encountered in marketing research and their advantages and disadvantages.

Sample Size The third step of the sampling process involves determining the sample's size. It is the variability among a population, not its total size, that is the key in determining how large the sample should be. If all people consumed exactly the same number of cups of tea per day, a sample size of one person would be perfectly adequate to determine the average number of cups consumed by everyone. In reality differences almost always exist, making the procedure more complicated.

Exhibit 7.1 *(Continued)*

Type of Nonprobability Samples:	Description	Advantages	Disadvantages
1. Convenience Sample	Subjects are selected on the basis of ease of contact by the researcher. All students in a marketing class, for example, might be sampled for some purpose. Or the first 50 shoppers in some supermarket might be selected.	The simplest and least costly to administer of the sampling designs.	Samples taken in this manner are seldom representative of the population. Thus, results are likely to be biased.
2. Quota Sample	Numerical objectives for responses are set, then subjects are selected by convenience until the objectives are met. They differ from the above, however, in that they are stratified on the basis of some variable. To illustrate, it might be known that 40 percent of the population is made up of men. For a total sample of 300, quotas are set for 120 men and 180 women. Once either quota is met, additional subjects are eliminated unless they fall in the remaining category.	Enables stratification and is relatively simple to administer.	Since subjects are not selected at random, responses may not be representative of the population.

Several equations are available for determining the proper sample size, depending both on the type of information sought and the sample design.[39] The main point is that researchers can extract much information with a high degree of precision from relatively small samples. Too small a sample, of course, provides unreliable results. But too large a sample wastes money and does not generate more reliable information.[40] The A. C. Nielsen Company, for instance, uses only about 1,600 television viewing residences to generalize about the television viewing habits of the entire U.S. population.

Means Used to Collect Primary Data Selecting an appropriate method for collecting primary data is as important as choosing a correct sampling design. In fact, according to one study, nonsampling error contributes more to total survey error than does sampling error.[41] The principal methods employed by marketing researchers are observation, surveys, experiments, and in-depth probes.

Observation Sometimes researchers can best collect needed data simply by observing and recording the actual behavior of consumers. McDonald's, for instance, built a mathematical model for locating restaurants largely by observing customer and other traffic patterns. License plate numbers (indicating where individuals reside) recorded at McDonald's restaurants revealed how far patrons were willing to venture from home for a Big Mac. Observing their activity patterns after dining at McDonald's also revealed that other attractions like shopping malls, tourist attractions, and related facilities help draw restaurant customers.

Observation has many other applications, such as for measuring shopper reaction

Exhibit 7.2
Observation Techniques for Collecting Primary Data

Type	Description	Examples
Simple Direct	Observation is made of the desired activity in its *natural* setting. An observer typically acts as another shopper to detect buying behavior, watch which brands are purchased, and so forth. In all cases, subjects remain unaware that their behavior is being observed and recorded.	Observing which brands of breakfast cereal are purchased, detecting how long customers will wait in line to buy items, and observing traffic flow.
Mechanical	Mechanical devices are used to record information. Perhaps the most notable of such devices is the audimeter used by the A. C. Nielsen Company to record when radio and TV sets are turned on and to which stations. Others include cameras, tape recorders, and computers that measure traffic.	Monitoring television and radio station listening habits, counting passing vehicle traffic, and observing in-store shopping behavior.
Contrived	An artificial but realistic situation is created so that the observer can record results. To illustrate, an observer may pose as a potential customer for a new home to learn how a salesperson handles prospects. It is essential for the subject to believe that the observer is a real shopper.	Learning how salespeople react to customers, learning how customers react to personal persuasion, and observing treatment of customers returning merchandise.

to in-store displays, monitoring in-store traffic patterns to design store layouts and merchandise placement, determining customer difficulties in following product instructions and in opening packages, and evaluating sales force performance. Several different types of observation methods are available.[42] Exhibit 7.2 presents the three most widely used in marketing.

The chief advantages of observation are that it is typically inexpensive on a per-response basis, it can be very objective (free from the subjectivity sometimes associated with interviews), subject cooperation need not be sought, and subjects may be monitored in a totally realistic setting. The subjects may not even know that the researchers are observing their behavior.

On the other hand the chief disadvantages of observation are that it can be time-consuming (observers might have to wait a long time for subjects to do "it") and the sample may not be a probability type. Consequently, the results can be inaccurate and misleading. It also is quite difficult to infer motivations, perceptions, and other psychological variables. Many clothing shoppers might stop to carefully examine test garment styles, for example, which could lead to the conclusion that the fashions were attractive to them. But a more comprehensive examination might reveal that the subjects stopped for a closer look because they "never saw anything so silly."

Surveys Surveys are one of the most widely used methods for obtaining opinions and attitudes.[43] Hardly a week goes by without the news media reporting the results of some opinion survey about national issues like gun control, abortion, and the popularity of various political candidates. Organizations such as Gallup, Robinson, and the University of Michigan's Institute for Social Research have turned the U.S. into a country better informed about resident opinions than any other major nation in history. Surveys provide information to define target markets, develop strategy, plan promotional mixes around media exposure habits, and develop distribution channels to satisfy target customer needs.

There are five major types of surveys: personal interviews, telephone interviews, direct mail, panels, and focus groups.[44] Exhibit 7.3 describes each type. The most

Exhibit 7.3
Survey Types Based on Data Collection Methods

Type	Description	Major Advantages	Major Disadvantages
Personal Interviews	Interviewers directly contact respondents face-to-face, soliciting their cooperation and asking their responses to various questions.	The interviewer is able to explain the meaning of unclear questions, observe a person's reactions, and reduce the number of those refusing to cooperate. Also, flexibility exists so that additional information may be sought that was not thought of when originally designing questions.	Very costly, especially if sample is geographically dispersed; highly trained interviewers are required so as to reduce bias, and extensive supervision is usually required to ensure against faked responses.
Telephone Interviews	Similar to personal interviews, except that telephones replace face-to-face contact.	Using telephones enables large, geographically dispersed samples to be taken. Other advantages are the same as personal interviews except that subject reaction cannot be visually observed.	Many desired subjects may have unlisted telephones (up to 30 percent of the phones in major cities are unlisted), refusals to cooperate are high (some simply hang up their phones), and the length of the interview and responses to questions must be relatively short or cooperation may be lost.
Direct Mail	Printed questionnaires are mailed to subjects to fill out and return.	Least costly of the survey methods on a per-subject-contacted basis, especially effective for large samples covering widely dispersed areas and more detail and potentially embarrassing questions may be asked (e.g., toilet paper consumption, drug use, and personal hygiene).	Response rates are low, sometimes only 10 to 20 percent (this can be improved by recontacting subjects and offering rewards for returning data, such as discounts on a future purchase), and there is no way to clarify questions or ask further ones.
Panels	A number of individuals, such as consumers or retailers, who agree to provide information to the sponsoring organization over time. Some firms maintain panels to sell general information about brand usage, while others maintain them for their own use (e.g., one European cigarette manufacturer maintains a panel to evaluate all new brands).	They enable researchers to obtain *longitudinal* data; i.e., successive measures over time, which enables trends to be spotted and the impact of changing any of the marketing mix variables to be evaluated.	Panels are costly to maintain. Subjects often require monetary remuneration or free merchandise. Also, panel members may start to evaluate as if they are taste and quality connoisseurs after repeated trials, thus making them nonrepresentative of the population.
Focus Groups	An interviewer questions a number of respondents, usually between 10 and 15, simultaneously and as a group. Respondents are allowed to discuss the merits of a product with other group members before stating responses. This method is growing in importance and use.	It allows for group interactions, which represents the interaction between reference groups that are so important in influencing the purchase of some products such as lawn fertilizers, boats, and vacations.	They are time-consuming and expensive. Substantial training is necessary before an interviewer can effectively lead a group. Further, many hours of interacting may be necessary. Also, many subjects are reluctant to answer potentially embarrassing questions in such a context.

appropriate type of survey to use depends upon the nature of the information sought, the required sample size, and the location of subjects. *Direct mail* is probably the most common type, since it permits economical surveying of widely dispersed subjects from one central point. *Personal and telephone interviews,* in contrast, permit far greater persuasion in gaining subjects' cooperation, flexibility in answering their questions, and in learning unanticipated information. *Panels* are useful for obtaining

Taste test experiments are often performed in a laboratory setting.

longitudinal measures over time, which enables management to detect trends. Finally, *focus groups* are of value in measuring the influence of group interactions on behavior, which is somewhat analogous to a reference group talking over a product's merits. In the give-and-take of focus group discussions, consumers often reveal attitudes and perceptions that they would not make evident through other data collection modes.

Experiments Experiments comprise a third major category of techniques used in gathering primary data.[45] They differ from the other collection techniques because of their greater scientific precision. Experimentation requires the careful control of variables related to the desired information, and consequently allows for the specific measurement of causal relationships.

An experiment tests a group of representative subjects on a dependent variable (such as favorable attitudes toward a brand). Then the same subjects are exposed to a treatment (such as reading an advertisement featuring the brand). After the treatment, the subjects are tested again. The assumption is that any difference between the posttreatment and pretreatment scores is due to the treatment, provided that the researchers have controlled extraneous variables. Often experimenters compare the performance of subjects in test groups to that of control groups, who do not experience the treatment.

Researchers may conduct experiments either in a laboratory or in a field setting. Laboratory tests offer the greatest precision because all variables can be monitored in a tightly controlled environment. Also, labs may employ special equipment that is useful in measuring such variables as interest levels in advertising messages by using machines to measure pupil dilation, breathing rates, skin temperatures, and related responses.[46] However, lab experiments in marketing may be unrepresentative of the marketplace because of the inherently sterile environment. This being the case, re-

Exhibit 7.4
Major Types of Marketing Experiments

Type	Description	Advantages	Disadvantages
Laboratory Test	An experiment conducted in a relatively sterile environment where all variables may be controlled so as to focus on the effects one or more of them cause on the variable of interest.	Allows for a high degree of control precision so that the causal effects of a change in the tested variable can be carefully measured.	Can be very costly, especially if expensive equipment is required. Highly trained researchers are usually necessary. Further, laboratories do not represent subjects' normal environments, which may distort results.
Field Test	An experiment conducted in a realistic buying or consuming location, such as a person's home. For example, subjects might be asked to prepare several food products then indicate their preferences. A control group receives regular items and an experimental group receives items where one of the products has been altered. Stated preferences are then compared.	Represents a more realistic setting than a laboratory, but still enables causality to be estimated.	Less control of all variables is possible than in the lab setting. Like lab tests, field tests are costly and difficult to administer, but their ability to estimate causality may be worth the price.
Test Market (the most common type of field test)	A section of some market (geographical or by retail outlet) wherein an experiment is conducted in an actual market situation. For example, a new version of some product (in terms of any or all elements of a marketing mix) may be developed. Normal marketing procedures are followed in the control areas. The new marketing mix is offered in the test area for a period of time, then results are compared to learn if the new version increases profits.	Represents the ultimate environment that marketers are concerned about: actual market settings. The true test of a proposed change is its impact on sales, which can be estimated in this manner.	It is difficult to find locations in which to run test markets. An ideal city is one that is large enough to represent all types of buyers, but secluded enough to be relatively free from surrounding influences. In New York, for example, subjects would be bombarded by marketing efforts in surrounding metropolitan areas, distorting results. Cities like Denver are ideal but are tested frequently, which may also distort results. Further, competition can easily distort results by running special sales or increasing or even decreasing advertising. Also, test markets are very costly to run. Finally, conducting test markets eliminates the possibility of surprise. Competitors may even develop similar items and introduce them first.

searchers often use field tests to reflect market realism and permit experimentation in a more natural setting. Test markets—special types of field tests—are the most widely used of this type. They are especially useful in assessing whether or not a new product or a promotional mix change has commercial feasibility.

For instance, the Cargill Company tested "Country Cut Beef," four-to-a-pound boneless beef sections in vacuum bags. It conducted the test in Memphis and Oklahoma City.[47] By testing the new product line under real competitive settings, management was able to get a good fix on the line's appeal to target consumers. The Pet Company is another firm that regularly uses market tests to assess the salability of new products, including frozen breakfast foods. Exhibit 7.4 describes the types of experiments used in marketing and also examines their advantages and disadvantages.

The Use of Multiple Methods By its very nature, marketing research requires making assumptions and imposing limitations on findings. Because these may be unrealistic, experienced researchers have learned to base their interpretations and conclusions on multiple methods when possible. For example, instead of using one large survey to research a problem, they may employ a smaller survey augmented by a separate panel study to gain more trustworthy results. If both inquiries suggest roughly the same course of action, there is considerable research credibility.

The Data Collection Instrument The fourth stage of the marketing research process consists of developing a vitally important tool: the data collection instrument. This might be a questionnaire, a diary of purchases for consumers to fill out, a record of visually observed shopper reactions to an in-store display, or whatever is appropriate to the study. Basically, the nature of the instrument determines what information is to be collected and how it is to be measured. This stage is extremely critical, as numerous errors can result from poorly designed instruments.[48]

To complicate matters, standard instruments are uncommon in marketing research. Because researchers collect so much nonstandardized data in behavior research, fully standard instruments are difficult to develop.[49] The following section looks at the processes involved.

What Is to Be Measured? The first task in building an instrument is to define what types of information are necessary to test the study's hypotheses. Basically this task involves clearly defining those variables that are logically important for analysis.

Univariate analysis
The study of one variable at a time; also called monovariate analysis.

Some studies attempt to analyze one variable at a time. These are termed *monovariate* (also **univariate**) analyses. These studies are also called *descriptive* because they seek to describe the nature of a chosen variable such as its mean, standard deviation, and frequency. Descriptive studies are helpful in gaining an understanding of the dimensions of some important variable. For instance, an appliance producer might track retailer prices to see what actually is charged for some item such as a slow cooker. Having this information handy can help considerably in making future pricing decisions.

Multivariate analysis
The study of two or more variables at a time and their interrelationships.

Most marketing research projects, however, involve *explanatory* studies where analysts examine two or more variables. This is called **multivariate** analysis. The intention is to evaluate the relationships between a primary variable of interest such as sales, and secondary variables of interest such as group memberships, income, and advertising levels. The former are termed *dependent* variables, whose values are presumed to be functions of the secondary variables of interest. The latter variables are *independent* because their values are presumed not to be functions of the dependent variables. Income, for example, is not a function of the purchase of a stereo, but the reverse may be true.

Dependent relations imply causality. That is, if one variable depends upon others, the latter must surely cause the values of the first. While only carefully controlled experiments prove causality in theory, an analyst often has no other operational choice but to use judgment in assuming that causality exists. Thus, if it is discovered that other related studies suggest causality, or if logic suggests this condition, it is often assumed that the dependent/independent relationship holds true (this assumption then becomes a candidate for future study).

Researchers may measure dependent variables either directly or indirectly, depending upon the nature of the particular project in question. To illustrate, assume that Sony is attempting to define the profile of its stereo buyers. Answers to the question of whether or not a subject has bought a set is directly measurable. But suppose management seeks to measure the effectiveness of company advertising. This variable cannot be measured directly. Consequently, *surrogate indicators* would be used, such as attitudes, levels of advertising awareness, or purchase intentions of the intended audience.

It is necessary that the researchers identify appropriate independent variables. They often consider elements of the marketing mix and economic, demographic, and psychographic variables in this regard. The specific variables about which they should collect information are identified on the basis of past studies, experience, logic, and intuition. The analysis phase of the marketing research process reveals which of those are truly significant. Unlike dependent variables, the analysts should select independent variables so that direct measurement is possible, permitting simplified analysis and interpretation.

Types of Questions The second task of building a data collection instrument is to formulate the questions to be asked. Here is where instrument development is more an art than a science.[50] Beyond initial training, analysts need substantial experience and creativity to construct meaningful questions. Essentially, there are two major parts of this task: determining the type of questions to use and establishing the question sequence.

"Would you like to buy this product?" "Why would you like to own one of these items?" "Rank the following products in the order of most to least desirable to you." These are only a few examples of the types of questions that marketing researchers ask. Obviously, the questions must relate directly to the variables about which information is sought, but beyond this, researchers must determine the type of question that is most likely to reveal useful information. Four basic types of questions are used: open-ended, structured, indirect, and semantic differential questions. Exhibit 7.5 presents a brief description of each.[51]

Typically, questionnaires have three major sections: basic information sought, classification information, and identification information.[52] Basic information includes questions about opinions, attitudes, and intentions to purchase. Classification information enables an analyst to group subjects into meaningful categories, such as by demographics. Finally, identification information tells who the respondent and/or the interviewer is; often it consists of questionnaire and interviewer numbers. Generally, researchers can improve response rates by informing respondents that they will hold individual responses in confidence.

It is important that opening questions gain the respondent's interest. Initial questions should be relatively easy to answer and should not cover potentially embarrassing topics. Each subsequent section then asks for information of declining subject interest. Usually it is better to first ask general questions, then more detailed queries on a subject of interest. When asking about past behavior, it is useful for researchers to follow a chronological sequence, first asking about events taking place in the distant past and then moving toward more recent events. Specific questions should be worded as simply as possible so as to avoid confusion. A common mistake is to ask too many questions. Relatively short questionnaires result in higher response rates, are simpler to analyze, and are more likely to yield accurate responses.[53]

Above all, questions should not suggest appropriate answers. For example, answers to the question "Would you like to buy one of these items?" are influenced by preceding questions that describe product advantages or disadvantages. Questions referring to a particular product are usually placed at the end of the questionnaire to avoid this

Exhibit 7.5
Major Types of Questions Used in Marketing Research

Types of Questions	Examples	Advantages	Disadvantages
1. Open-Ended	Why did you buy a Cross pen and pencil set? Which features of the Florsheim shoes do you like? Which aspects of American Airlines service do you like least?	These types of questions are good for starting a survey because they introduce the subject. Answers are not influenced by answer categories from which subjects are to select. They open the way for further research.	The variety of answers obtained are often extreme and unpatterned, making analysis difficult because machine tabulation may not be possible. These questions also bias responses toward those who are more literate. Also, they may result in an interviewer bias when recording personal or telephone interviews.
2. Structured (two or more preestablished response choices—also termed closed-ended)	Do you like your new Seiko watch? Yes ____ No ____. How often do you buy Sealtest milk? Never ____, Sometimes ____, More than other brands ____, Always ____. What is your age? 10–19 yrs. ____, 20–29 yrs. ____, 30–39 yrs. ____, 40 or older ____.	Questions may be answered faster, reducing subject boredom. Tabulation is simplified. Interviewer bias is reduced.	They restrict subject answers to predetermined categories. Also they suggest logical answers that may not be correct. Further, the order of responses can bias results.
3. Indirect (used for measuring attitudes)			
a. Thurstone Scales (also termed "method of equal appearing intervals")	The use of eleven statements related to an attitude, ranging in a continuum from one extreme to another, and subjects are asked to check all that they agree with, e.g.: 1. All cigarettes should be banned by law. ____ 2. Smoking cigarettes is a complete waste of time. ____. . . 11. Cigarette smoking is the best thing ever invented ____.	While people may not be able to attach a quantitative measure to an attitude, they should be able to indicate which statements relating to the attitude they agree with.	These scales are very difficult to construct, statement positions are subject to researcher bias, and evaluation is difficult. It is difficult to compare individuals marking one response and those marking two or more.
b. Likert Scales (most widely used indirect type in marketing research)	Like Thurstone Scales, Likert scales involve structured choices. Instead of checking those statements with which they agree, however, subjects are asked to indicate the degree of agreement or disagreement with a statement, e.g.: The Dodge Aspen has a sleek style. Agree very strongly ____ Agree ____ Undecided ____ Disagree ____ Disagree very strongly ____	Likert scales have the same advantages as Thurstone scales, plus they are simpler to construct and evaluate.	Because only certain statements are presented, they may omit relevant dimensions of an attitude. Further, because questions are asked, subjects may answer them even if they seem meaningless.
4. Semantic Differential (especially useful for brand and company image studies)	A set of bipolar scales to rate an item of interest: Rate RCA television sets: Well-known _ _ _ Little-known; Reliable _ _ _ Nonreliable; Durable _ _ _ Undurable; Clear picture _ _ _ Poor picture	Can easily be used to compare products or companies. For example, the same set of statements could be used for Zenith, then patterns of similarities and differences can be identified. Simple to use and administer and is sensitive to small differences.	The major disadvantage is that important factors may be omitted. Because of their strengths, semantic differentials are used in many studies.

CONCEPT SUMMARY

Major Steps in Marketing Research

Step	Composition
Initial Observation	Awareness, fact finding, and problem definition to learn the fundamentals of a particular decision problem to set the direction for the research effort.
Hypotheses Formulation	Develop untested theories that can be assessed by the research process.
Obtain Needed Information	Determine the types of information that are needed to test the hypotheses.
Develop the Data Collection Instrument	Construct an overall plan for the collection of data needed in the research project.
Data Acquisition	Collect the data specified in the plan.
Analysis	Break the data down into meaningful categories and study differences and relationships between these categories.
Interpretation	Informing management what the research uncovered and the meaning of the research to management.
Establish Follow-up Procedures	Anticipate potential changing conditions or incorrect conclusions that may have been drawn because of erroneous assumptions and related causes.

problem. Also, many researchers use several forms of a questionnaire, with the questions in each one appearing in a different order. In this way, they can control the effects of positioning.

Forms and Equipment The third task of building a data collection instrument consists of reproducing necessary forms and obtaining appropriate equipment. This task is relatively straightforward, but keep in mind that it is important to get forms printed and have traffic counters, movie cameras, or whatever equipment is necessary to collect data available ahead of time.[54]

Pretesting Pretesting is the fourth and final task involved in building a data collection instrument. Some neophyte researchers are prone to develop instruments and then rush directly into collecting data. The experience of the Anderson Elevator Service Company illustrates the problem with this approach. This firm maintains and services elevators in a large midwestern community. To learn about attitudes toward the company, it commissioned a research firm to survey area building maintenance managers. However, the questionnaire used marketing jargon—terms such as "promotional strategy," "differential advantage" and "product mix,"—which were not understood by the maintenance people. Consequently, management was unable to use the results for decision making.

The researchers could have avoided this problem had they pretested the measuring instrument by administering it to a small group of subjects and then determining if any problems existed in interpreting the questions or in other areas. Furthermore, pretesting often indicates that the researchers can discard some of the independent variables originally thought to be important. After pretesting, considerable streamlining is often possible.

Data Acquisition Data are acquired in stage five of the marketing research process. This can be very time-consuming; Liggett & Myers, for example, test marketed two new cigarette brands (L&M Superior and Dorado) for six months in Albuquerque and Dallas.[55] Direct mail surveys typically take up to two months for responses to be returned.

The research instrument, the sampling design, and the information needs of management dictate the procedures to follow in this stage.[56] Some firms use part-time help to collect the data because of the cost economies. Students, teachers, housewives, and retirees are relatively inexpensive to hire for this task. On the other hand, part-timers usually require considerable training and supervision to assure that procedures are followed accurately and consistently. For this reason, most companies hire good field research firms who maintain professional staffs of competent and fully-trained interviewers to collect data.

Nevertheless, problems still may emerge when firms contract out personal interview field work to a specialty firm. Field personnel often receive their pay on a piecework basis, sometimes without close field supervision, and interviewers may "cut corners": violate instructions in order to speed up the survey process, or even fabricate ficticious interviews and turn in counterfeit measuring instruments. Most reputable field research firms verify collected information by having editors recontact a sample of a study's respondents (usually 10 percent) to assure that they were in fact surveyed and that instructions were followed.

Analysis and Interpretation Researchers analyze and interpret the data in stage six of the research process. Computers are especially useful in performing this part of the job.

Analysis
Breaking data down into meaningful categories and studying the differences and relationships between these categories.

Analysis **Analysis** involves breaking data down into meaningful categories and studying differences and relationships between them. It includes selecting and applying some type of mathematical model to test a study's hypotheses. The objective is to uncover relevant variable parameters (such as means and standard deviations) and associations between variables. There are two major categories of mathematical models researchers use in marketing: statistical models and management science (also termed operations research) models.

Dependent variable
A variable, usually one of primary research interest, whose value is presumed to be a function of specific independent variables.

Independent variable
A variable that presumably affects the value of a dependent variable.

Statistical models are used most often in marketing. Multivariate statistical analysis is used extensively with survey information in order to calculate how much of a **dependent variable's** fluctuation can be explained by fluctuations in the values of the **independent variables.** Statistical procedures including multiple-regression analysis, discriminant analysis, cluster analysis, and factor analysis are used for this purpose.[57]

With the passage of time, marketing researchers are also increasingly called upon to solve problems of optimization. Determining optimal allocations of advertising dollars among various media, the best sales force territory assignments, and the most efficient shipping routes are examples of problems that cannot be solved using statistical

MARKETING BRIEF
Sponsoring Sporting Events and Appealing to Customers

The John Hancock Mutual Life Insurance Company was the sole sponsor of the Boston Marathon in 1986. The firm believed that it would obtain visibility among runners, who tend to be young, married, college-educated, healthy, and upper-middle class. In short, they are good clients for a financial services company. Marketing research indicated that sponsoring sporting events is an efficient way to reach a specific group.

Hancock believes that publicity received from sponsoring the race has resulted in several million dollars worth of press coverage. In return, it has pledged $10 million to the race over 10 years. By the end of the period, it will have benefited many times over the amount paid for the event, according to company studies.

The Boston Marathon has been virtually rescued from extinction by this firm. It is the oldest and most prestigious of the U.S. marathons; however, other races began offering prizes and appearance money to attract top runners while Boston clung to its pure amateur status and awarded only medals and olive wreaths. Thus, world-class marathoners avoided the race. Hancock reversed this process, offering valuable prizes and coverage by ESPN (the cable sports network). The Marathon survived and Hancock received substantial publicity and generated goodwill among target consumers.

SOURCE: Adapted from "Money Talks, Nobody Walks in Boston," *Business Week*, April 21, 1986: 51; and J. Warner, "Hancock and Hill, Holliday Reshape Marathon," *Advertising Week*, April 21, 1986: 27, 62.

procedures. Linear programming, integer programming, and a group of similar specialized techniques are used for such purposes.[58]

Interpretation After the analysis, it is the responsibility of the research team to **interpret** the data for management. This consists of informing management, usually in both oral and written reports, what the study uncovered and the meaning of the research to management. Included should be a discussion of both accepted and rejected hypotheses, assessment of their meaning, and a clear explanation of the assumptions of the analysis. The statement of assumptions is extremely important, and unfortunately is sometimes forgotten by naive and technique-oriented researchers.

Interpretation (in research) Determining and reporting the meaning of particular research to management.

It should be kept in mind that the purpose of practical research is to assist management in decision making and nothing more. Esoteric research and interpretations are not needed. John Hancock's management, for example, relied on simple surveys of sports enthusiasts in its decision to sponsor the Boston Marathon and the results have been enormously successful for the firm.

Follow-up Procedures A research project should not be forgotten upon completion; in the final stage, the analysts should specify follow-up procedures. Perhaps they should perform a future study to determine if conditions change over time or test some of the assumptions to learn if they were appropriate. Proper follow-up procedures anticipate changing conditions or incorrect conclusions that may have been drawn because of erroneous assumptions or other reasons. By performing follow-up studies, possible trouble spots may be uncovered before it is too late to take corrective action.

Chapter Summary

This chapter provided an overview of the process of obtaining marketing information for decision making. The geographic separation between producers and markets requires that certain information be collected about buyer needs and processes. Beyond this, though, critical information should be collected about buyers and markets since important factors such as motivations are seldom obvious and must be researched to be learned. Further, research is needed to overcome the problem of "executive isolation," which could greatly hamper sound decision making.

The need for solid marketing information is ongoing for routine and daily marketing operations. In order that appropriate information is available when it is needed for decision making, installation of a marketing information system is recommended. Such a system collects, integrates, and reports information summaries as required by management for normal activities. Taking steps to ensure that sufficient detail is recorded so that evaluation and reevaluation is possible is a key to the development of such systems. While advanced computers have greatly contributed to the development of such information systems, even managers of the smallest businesses can benefit greatly by developing marketing information systems.

Additional specific information is often required for making particular marketing decisions. This is the realm of marketing research. Objective, and therefore very useful, information is best obtained by following the marketing research process, which involves following seven steps: becoming familiar with the area and specific definition of the research problem, developing testable hypotheses, determining the specific information that is needed to test the hypotheses, developing the data collection instrument, acquiring the data, analyzing the data, and establishing follow-up procedures.

Questions

1. What is marketing research? Why is it important to management?
2. Describe the various phases of the observation stage of the marketing research process.
3. Describe the ways to obtain primary data.
4. How do surveys and experiments differ? Which is better?
5. What major tasks are involved when building a data collection instrument?
6. Describe the various kinds of samples.
7. One manager recently stated, "So much improvement has been made in research that speculative judgments are no longer required." Comment.
8. What is an MIS?
9. What steps are involved in developing an MIS?
10. Describe how small businesses can benefit by MIS. What economic implications are there for smaller firms?

Chapter 8

Analyzing Market Opportunity

Objectives

After completing this chapter, you should be able to demonstrate a knowledge of:

- The process of analyzing market opportunity
- How a firm's environment, internal characteristics, synergy potential, competitive advantage, and segmentation possibilities can lead to the identification of a potential market opportunity
- Some of the basic forecasting methods and how firms can utilize them to generate sales estimates
- The use of break-even, net present value, and payback period analyses in evaluating potential opportunities
- How analyzing market opportunities lays the groundwork for developing marketing plans

MARKETING FAILURE

Polaroid's Unsuccessful New Projects

The Polaroid Corporation, plagued by falling sales and profits, embarked on a program of acquiring new projects in the 1980s. It attempted to diversify into video equipment, computer products, and electronic imaging, but these projects proved to be less than successful.

In 1982 the firm paid $2.5 million for a stake in Image Resource Corp. (IRC), a small producer of color printers that can photograph images from a computer screen. Despite this investment, management then decided to develop a new printer from scratch. The IRC printer was a low-cost one and management felt that Polaroid could develop a much higher-quality model. To fund the development, Polaroid sold its stake in IRC for less than one-third of its original investment.

In 1983 the company paid $6 million for 1984 Inc., a fiber optics research and development company with one employee—its founder. When this individual quit the company, 1984 Inc. was dismantled.

In the videotape market, Polaroid has positioned its product at the high end of the market, selling for premium prices. The result was a 1985 market share of less than 1 percent and a loss of roughly $10 million. Consumers simply refused to pay extra for high-quality videotape. The company also has been unsuccessful in attempting to sell high-quality floppy discs at premium prices.

It may be that this firm will have to return to its roots in amateur instant photography in order to restore lost sales and profits. To date, the move into new ventures has not worked well.

SOURCE: Adapted from "A Troubled Polaroid Is Tearing Down the House That Land Built," *Business Week*, April 29, 1985: 51–52.

Introduction

All the products listed in Table 8.1 have one thing in common—they failed to meet or even come close to the profit goals that their producers set for them. Practically every major company has had at least one (and sometimes many) losing products, as illustrated by Polaroid's diversification experiences (see the Marketing Failure). Making such mistakes can be very expensive. Pioneer Electronics, for instance, lost over $13 million in attempting to market videodisk players for TV sets.[1]

Generally, product failures stem from one of two basic mistakes: poorly implemented marketing or production plans, and selecting target markets that lack sufficient potential for the product. Poorly conceived marketing programs and poor production performances account for the first mistake. As to the second, a product is destined for failure, regardless of how well plans are implemented, if too small a market potential exists to support the effort.

In fact, even too large a potential for the company to effectively handle can cause problems. Frontier Airlines, for example, bit off more than it could chew when it expanded nationally from the Rocky Mountain West in 1978, the firm's historical stronghold, when Congress deregulated the airlines industry. Fierce national competition forced management to retreat back to the west in 1983 to recoup its losses.[2]

Table 8.1 Products That Failed to Meet Their Profit Goals

Best Foods: Knorr soups	Gillette: Nine Flags cologne
Bristol-Myers: Resolve analgesic, Serosol Ipana toothpaste	Helene Curtis: Everynight shampoo
Campbell Soup Co.: Red Kettle soups	Hunt-Wesson: Supreme Spaghetti Sauce
Colgate-Palmolive Co.: Cue toothpaste	Lever Bros.: Vim tablet detergent
Eli Lilly & Co.: Oraflex antiarthritic drug	Rheingold: Gablinger's beer
General Foods: Post Cereals with freeze-dried fruit	Sambo's: Fast food restaurants
Displayphone: Telephone/personal computer work station	Scott Paper: Babyscott Diapers
	DeLorean: Luxury automobile
	Warner Lambert: Reef Mouthwash

After this, the company was acquired by People Express, a company that also attempted to take on the national market with discount prices. This effort also failed, when People Express suffered severe financial setbacks in 1986. The result of this over-aggressiveness was that People attempted to sell off its assets, including its Denver-based Frontier operations, to United and other strong national carriers.[3]

Evaluating a market's potential is called the process of **analyzing marketing opportunity**, and is the subject of this chapter. A detailed example involving one particular firm is used to illustrate the process and the interrelationships between the various steps.

Analyzing market opportunity The process of evaluating a particular market's potential.

The Process of Analyzing Market Opportunity

Carefully analyzing a proposed market's potential before jumping in with both feet is important to a company's success—and even its survival. Figure 8.1 illustrates what is involved.

The process begins with recognizing potential opportunities, both new and existing ones, upon which the firm might be able to capitalize. New opportunities might

As People Express learned, capturing a significant share of a market segment is no simple matter.

originate from developments within the firm, such as a breakthrough in the R & D lab. Or they might arise from researching unfilled customer needs. Factors explored in earlier chapters, such as the firm's mission, environment, prospects for synergy, differential advantage, and market segmentation are all important to consider when searching for product ideas.[4]

After identifying potential target markets, it is important to judge their profit potentials. Those opportunities that offer the greatest potential of contributing toward the firm's goals are the ones selected for targeting.

Following the process helps in the development of successful plans. Some projects may, of course, fail to meet their expectations and must later be abandoned. Nonetheless, carefully following the process of evaluating potential opportunities helps to keep the firm on track toward goal achievement. The example of Midwestern Climate Control is extensively used here to illustrate the process.

Midwestern Climate Control: An Example of Market Opportunity Analysis

Midwestern Climate Control Corp. manufactures various climate control devices, such as room thermometers, air humidifiers, and dehumidifiers. This example is abstracted from a real situation; however, both the names and data have been disguised to protect confidentiality. Because of the uncertainty of fuel prices, Americans have become increasingly concerned about fuel conservation since the mid-1970s and have paid considerable attention to cutting their bills for heating and cooling. Besides investing in insulation devices, people have been encouraged to develop the habit of dialing down their thermostats at night and while away from home to cut their bills even further.

Midwestern's thermostat timer was designed to control an existing residential thermostat.

A New Product Opportunity Idea

William Smith, Midwestern's marketing manager, wondered how strongly consumers were motivated to conserve fuel. To learn the answer, he conducted a small survey of 200 households, which indicated that practically everyone was concerned with saving on heating bills. Most also stated that they actually did lower their thermostats below their customary settings. But the research also revealed that practically no one dialed their thermostats down at night. While most people were in agreement with the principle, they did not want to wake up to cold rooms.

After some thought, Smith concluded that this unfilled need might present potential for the company. By developing some type of timer to control thermostat settings, Midwestern might be able to satisfy this need.

This potential opportunity was worth Midwestern's attention for three major reasons. First, it appeared that widespread unsatisfied demand existed. Second, the opportunity was within the firm's overall mission. Finally, the company already sold some climate control items with timers, such as special types of space heaters. Therefore, from a synergy perspective, such a project appeared to be desirable.

Defining the Target Market

Figure 8.2 illustrates what Smith felt were the major segments in the market. Of the overall climate control device market (some segments were omitted for simplicity), the general segment that he was considering was thermostats used to control heating.

While timer-controlled thermostats might have future air conditioning application possibilities, he considered such a use to be secondary. The survey revealed that residential users of air conditioning were not too interested in changing temperature settings throughout the day. Thus, initially at least, Smith considered potential applications to heating as the primary potential target.

The next step was to further assess differences in needs within the "Thermostat for heating" total segment. All types of buildings were within the overall segment, but Midwestern's ability to compete for use in public and commercial buildings was not strong. Using the concept of synergy as a guide, Smith omitted all but residential housing from consideration. Public and commercial buildings would require technologically complex equipment beyond Midwestern's capabilities. Further, the company had no marketing experience in these segments. Therefore, any effort directed toward these targets would only result in a competitive disadvantage.

The residential housing segment was made up of two major divisions, as Figure 8.3 illustrates. The new construction segment was the smallest, but perhaps the most promising. With approximately 1.3 million new housing units being constructed each year, a strong demand probably existed for timers in this segment. However, management also considered the firm's competitive position. Historically, Midwestern specialized in distributing products through retailers. It had no experience in marketing through contractors or building supply wholesalers. Further, Smith was aware of seven companies who were planning to introduce integrated time-controlled thermostats for newly constructed homes currently or in the immediate future. Major firms with established reputations in this segment, such as Honeywell, were among these seven. To a large degree these well-entrenched companies could be expected to dominate the new construction market.

Smith concluded that if Midwestern were to have a chance, it must be within the existing construction segment of residential housing. After checking with company engineers, he learned that the units being introduced by the seven competitors probably would not highly satisfy this segment. These units required rewiring at an estimated electrician cost of nearly $75 plus a minimum retail price of $50. Some do-it-yourselfers would no doubt convert their own thermostats, but experience with projects requiring wiring indicated that the majority of homeowners would not do so and a total cost of $125 or more would be excessive for many homeowners in this segment. (Rewiring was not necessary for new construction, so the cost was estimated at around $50 for the unit itself.)

Additional research indicated that two potential competitors had models specifically designed for existing structures. Both were powered by batteries, thus avoiding rewiring. One was a complete unit with a thermostat that would replace an existing heat control mechanism. However, its price was above $85, which Smith believed was too costly. The second competitor's product, priced at $49.95, was essentially an adapter attached to existing thermostats. Midwestern's engineers tested this product and found that it was difficult to install, only fit a few types of units, and did not have an accurate timer. Further, the manufacturer was a newcomer to the field and was just beginning to establish distribution networks. Therefore, management concluded that this segment represented the general market that Midwestern should pursue if enough opportunity existed.

The next step was to confer with company design engineers to learn if they could develop a product to meet this segment's needs. Before conducting the consumer survey mentioned earlier, Smith had discussed the concept of a thermostat timer with Midwestern's chief engineer. As a result, the technical staff had begun considering

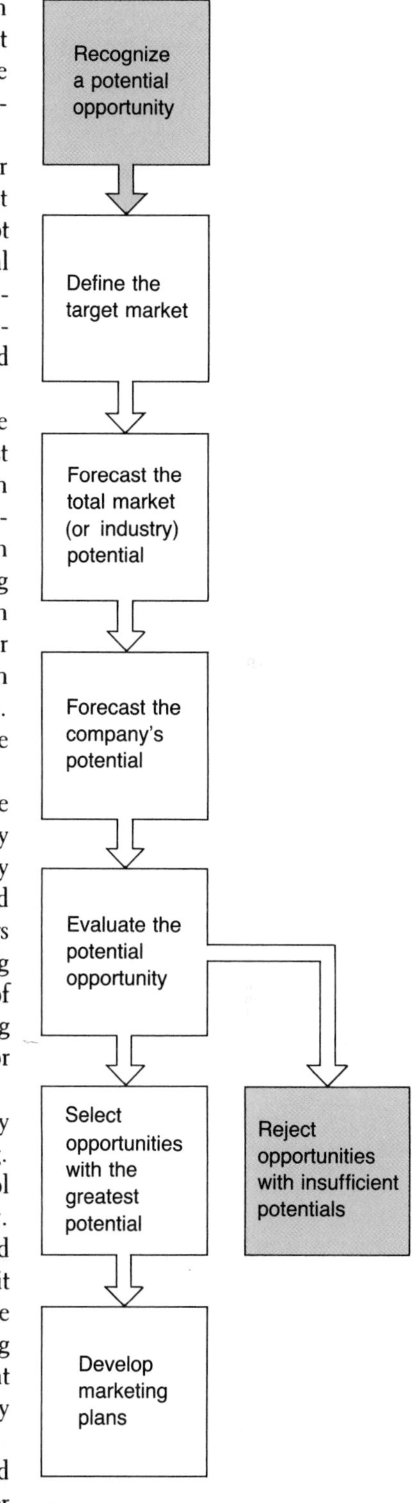

Figure 8.1
Analyzing a Market Opportunity

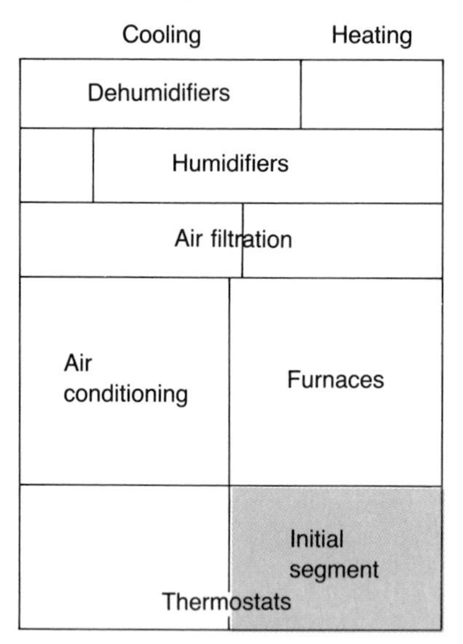

Figure 8.2
Initial Segmentation

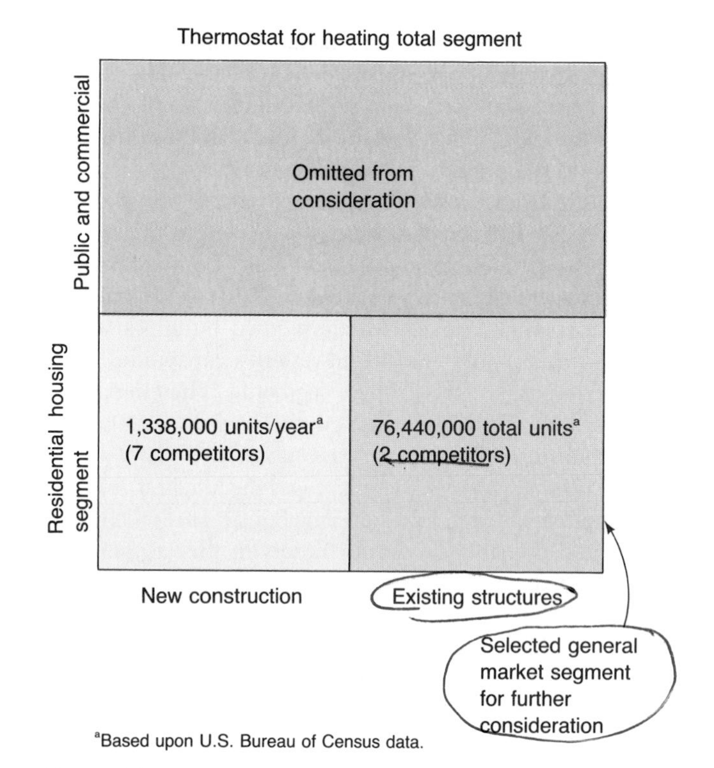

Figure 8.3
Heterogeneous Needs within the Total Segment

possible product types. The refined target market's product specifications added further direction to the staff's development efforts. Within two months, the chief engineer reported that the firm could develop an attachment-type unit with specifications far superior to the direct competitor's offering.

The proposed climate control device would feature five distinctive attributes:

- Timer accuracy. A supplier had developed an extremely accurate clock.
- Compact size. The unit used two penlight batteries instead of the competitor's two size D dry cells.
- Low cost operation. The batteries needed replacement only once each season versus two or three times for the competitor's model.
- Simple installation. The product did not require special wall fasteners, as did the competitor's.
- Wide application. The attachment fit any round thermostat because of several adapter rings to be included with the package. (Shapes other than round could not be fitted, but the adapter rings fit more brands than the competitor's unit.)

Management's next task was to more precisely refine the target's definition. Rough cost estimates indicated that a price of at least in the $25-to-$35 range would be necessary for the project to be economically worthwhile. Smith conducted another survey, and after fairly extensive analysis concluded that the potential primary target's profile was as presented in Table 8.2.

Table 8.2 The Potential Primary Target for Thermostat Timer Control Devices

1. Residences having round thermostats.
2. Residents of the following geographic regions:
   New England (Maine, New Hampshire, Vermont, Massachusetts, Rhode Island, Connecticut)
   Middle Atlantic (New York, New Jersey, Pennsylvania)
   East North Central (Ohio, Indiana, Illinois, Michigan, Wisconsin)
   Residents of these regions comprise the heaviest users of fuel (within densely populated areas) and therefore are most interested in cutting fuel bills.
3. Year-round housing units. People were not interested in buying units for vacation homes.
4. Owner-occupied households. Renters did not appear interested in buying a permanent attachment for thermostats.
5. Male heads of households. While sales to women would be encouraged, the survey indicated that primarily men would be interested in installing such a unit.
6. Households with one central thermostat. Those with separate heat zones did not appear interested in such units.
7. A family income range between $10,000 and $25,000. Lower-income households did not seem interested because of the unit's cost and higher-income families did not seem to be interested in altering their lifestyles.
8. Those in the age group of 21 to 64. Other age groups did not seem interested even if they were the heads of households.

Management would focus on the residences associated with the eight characteristics listed in the table if the firm marketed the product. Figure 8.4 visually illustrates this segmented target.

Forecasting Total Market (or Industry) Potential

Finding out which target market offers the greatest potential and determining whether or not a particular project is desirable are two separate issues. A large enough potential market might not exist even if management has identified the best target. For example, eccentric millionaires might be the best target for a $1,500 high-quality pocket camera but there may be too few of these individuals who demand such a camera for it to be a profitable venture. The next step in analyzing a potential market opportunity, therefore, is to **forecast** its sales potential. The general principles of forecasting will be covered before their application to Midwestern Climate Control is discussed.

Forecast
An estimate of the future value of some variable or the occurrence of some event.

Forecasting Fundamentals

Levels of Forecasts Essentially, there are three levels of forecasts about which managers should be familiar: [5] overall magnitudes of economic activity, industry magnitudes, and firm magnitudes. A frequent practice is to translate forecasts of overall levels into industry forecasts and to use these to generate company forecasts.

Figure 8.4
Potential Core Market for Midwestern's Proposed Thermostat Timer

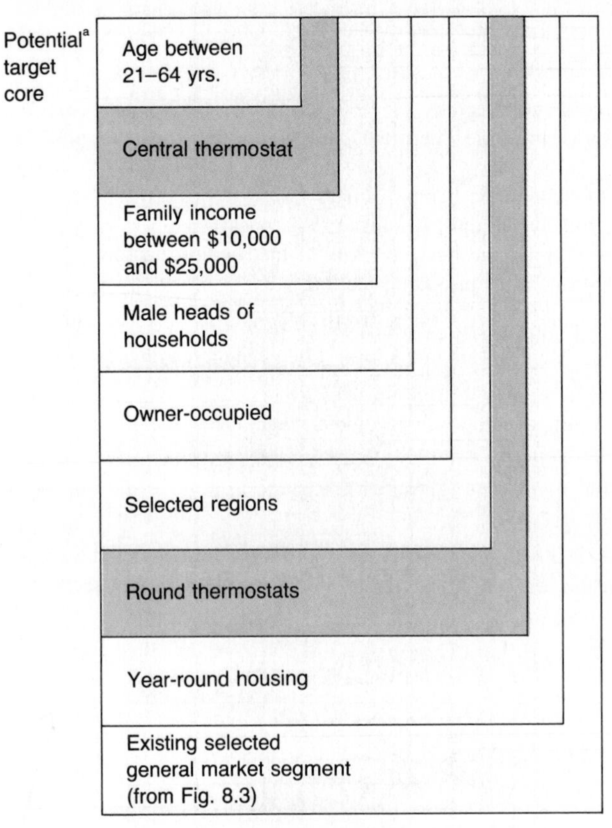

[a]The potential target core consists of all those individuals having all the identified characteristics.

Forecasts of Overall Levels of Economic Activity Broad economic fluctuations affect the sales of almost all companies and management should consider the forecasts of these when making decisions. Levels of GNP, investment, unemployment, prices, income, and population are but a few of the many variables of concern. Which aggregate measures are important and what impact they have depends on the particular company and situation. To illustrate, movie attendance tends to increase during recessions, whereas the demand for housing works just the opposite way.

Macro forecasts
Forecasts of broad levels of economic activity, such as gross national product.

Fortunately, companies do not have to forecast broad levels of economic activity (termed **macro forecasts**). The federal government, through the Departments of Treasury, Commerce, and the Federal Reserve System, employs many professional econometricians (mathematically trained economists that specialize in macro forecasting) to prepare such forecasts. So do large banks (such as the Bank of America) and universities (such as the Wharton School of Business at the University of Pennsylvania). Businesses can acquire these forecasts, usually for a small fee compared to what it would cost to prepare them from scratch. Of course, each company must determine any relationships to its own sales and the extent to which the forecasts might be in error.[6]

Industry Forecasts While general macro forecasts may be useful, specific industry forecasts are often even more important to managers for decision making. To illustrate, the sales of durables are generally inversely related to interest rates, yet over the past several years sales of computers have soared even when interest rates have increased.

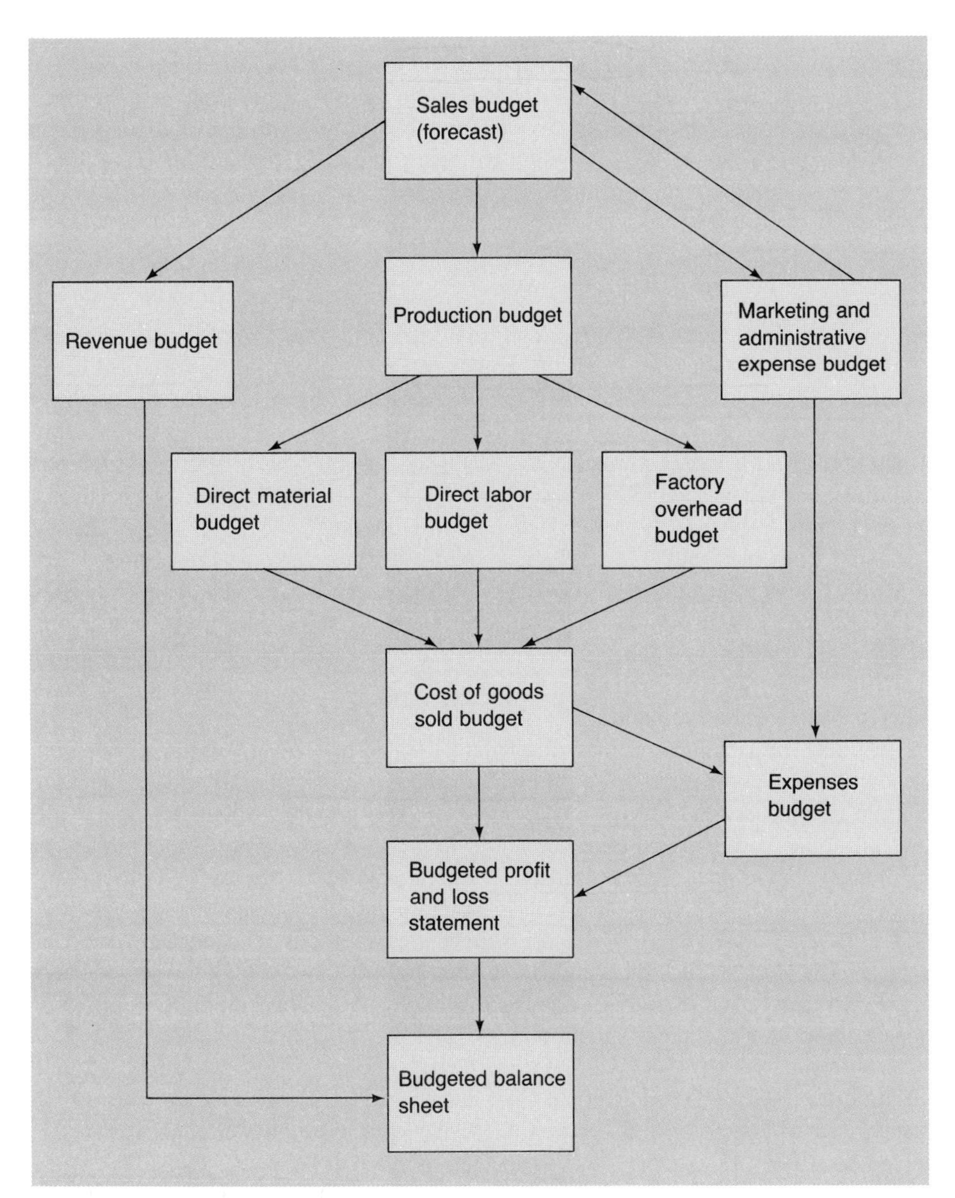

Figure 8.5
The Relationship of Forecasting Among Budgets (SOURCE: Adapted from C. W. Gross and R. T. Peterson, *Business Forecasting*, 2d ed. (Boston: Houghton Mifflin, 1983), p. 17.)

Some companies prepare their own industry forecasts, while others do not. Sometimes industry trade associations employ professionals to prepare industry forecasts and provide them to members. Other organizations also prepare industry forecasts in some cases. For instance, the Supermarket Institute underwrites forecasts of trends within its industry. Boston-based Arthur D. Little Co., a consulting firm, prepares sales forecasts for makers of computer-controlled energy management systems for commercial buildings.[7] Similarly, professional forecasting services such as Morton Research Corp., Predicasts, Inc., and American Sports Data, prepare forecasts for several separate industries.[8]

Micro forecasts
Forecasts of company sales, either in total or for particular categories (product groups, geographic areas, types of customers).

Firm-Level Forecasts To managers, forecasts of company and product sales, called **micro forecasts,** are the most important of all, as they form the basis for all budgeting and planning.[9] Figure 8.5 illustrates the budgeting process of a typical manufacturer.

Notice that all budgets hinge upon the sales budget, which is a forecast. The same is true for service companies. The sales forecast is the cornerstone of all planning.

Each company should produce its own micro sales forecast since reliable ones generally are unavailable from other sources. Also, only a company's management knows for sure what marketing actions are being planned, and the affects of these actions on sales should be considered in the forecast.

Forecasting Techniques

Far too many forecasting techniques exist to allow more than a brief overview here.[10] However, they all fall within one of two categories: those requiring historical data, and those useful in new-opportunity situations, where historical data are unavailable.

Techniques Requiring Historical Data Typically, some type of statistical extrapolation is made when adequate historical data exists. In effect, this type of forecasting is "an attempt to foresee the future by examining the past." [11]

Many companies routinely use such methods in their periodic forecasting. Even when the results indicate that improved procedures might be desirable, as with MEDICASTER for medical supplies (see the accompanying Marketing Brief), projections into the future represent a good starting point in the forecasting process. This is because many of the methods are relatively easy and inexpensive to use, especially if computerized models are available.

A number of useful techniques are available and all of them involve analyzing past trends in one way or another. Of these, *exponential smoothing* is perhaps the least complicated to use. Ease of use makes these models desirable when there are many forecasts to be made, as in the case of wholesalers and retailers who handle thousands of products.[12] Despite their simplicity, research has demonstrated that smoothing models can yield forecasts as accurate as far more complex procedures.[13] *Regression and time series analyses* are two more widely used methods requiring an historical data base to work with.[14,15] Exhibit 8.1 presents an overview of these methods and also lists their advantages and disadvantages. Which approach is best to use, of course, depends upon the particular situation.

New Op. Situ.

Techniques Useful When Historical Data Are Unavailable When analyzing a new product, or when the historical patterns are expected to change dramatically in the future (as when a new competitor is expected to enter the market), four major types of forecasting approaches can be used. They are indexes, surveys, test markets, and expert judgment.

Index
A percentage determined by the proportion that one entity has to another entity, such as a target market characteristic in proportion to that characteristic in the overall population.

Indexes An **index** is a percentage. Its value is determined by the proportion that the target market possesses of some characteristic relative to the overall population. For instance, Washington State accounts for roughly 1.7 percent of the total personal income in the U.S. If the sales of some product, say diamonds, are totally dependent upon personal income, then one might forecast that diamond sales in the state would be 1.7 percent of their total U.S. sales.

Indexes may be simple, as in the above illustration, or complex, involving many interactive percentages, with each referring to a different important characteristic. For example, income, population size, age group identification, and accumulated savings might all be linked through a series of indexes; a procedure that is called the *chain-ratio technique*. This technique is illustrated for Midwestern Climate Control later in this chapter.

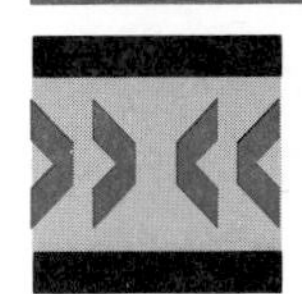

MARKETING BRIEF
A Forecasting Methodology for Medical Products

"Forecasting medical supplies has been a real problem," said Mark Hammond, a Chicago-based securities analyst. "Industry suppliers face a myriad of forces, including physicians who change their approaches to treatments, patients who have differing views, changing coverages by insurance carriers, and many other factors which cause nightmares for companies," he added.

"No more," say executives of National Analysts, an economics research division of the consulting giant Booze, Allen & Hamilton, Inc., that has recently introduced MEDICASTER, a forecasting system designed specifically for medical products. "Sellers of medical supplies need to forecast sales and market shares when they consider introducing new products," state executives of National Analysts, "and we've designed our system for that purpose."

Standard forecasting techniques have not proven very successful when used by producers of medical supplies. Complicating the issue is that specialized skill and knowledge are required to capture the decision processes of physicians, their characteristics, patient characteristics, and other salient market information. All of these factors interact uniquely in this market and are difficult to capture.

MEDICASTER is designed to take these factors into consideration, using estimated utilities and market information combined in a predictive model, and has demonstrated significant improvements over the standard forecasting techniques. The system is designed for nondurable medical products for which the physician is the principal decision maker. It analyzes the unique interactions among predictor variables, including interactions among patients and physicians, and not just judgments of doctors.

In a demonstration study of ethical drugs, MEDICASTER identified three major market segments (patients) and generated quite accurate forecasts for each of them. It also revealed the major characteristics of the patients in each segment—information that is critical in formulating marketing strategies. The forecasting program also indicated how physicians would react to various combinations of drug attributes such as side effects and the increasingly important issue of cost-per-day to patients. Finally, MEDICASTER generated estimates of the expected sales impacts of advertising, sales force sizes, and dates of product introduction.

SOURCE: Adapted from Carl Finkbeiner, "Tool Aids Forecasts for Medical Products," *Marketing News* 20, no. 1 (January 3, 1986): 40.

Census data are useful in providing index values for demographic and economic variables. *Sales and Marketing Management* magazine also is valuable because it annually publishes a "Survey of Buying Power." The survey furnishes accurate economic indexes for various populations such as counties and SICs (Standard Industrial Classification codes) by region within the U.S.[16]

Indexes offer the advantage of being relatively simple to obtain and use. Besides being useful in situations where historical data are lacking, they also enable management to draw analogies from one product to another. For example, management might expect that a new deluxe version of a successful product would sell 10 percent as many units as the basic model, based upon experience with other products in similar markets. But there are drawbacks to using indexes since they offer only crude approximations and do not consider the uniqueness of a given situation.

Surveys and Test Markets Surveys and test markets may be useful in forecasting sales. The management of American Airlines, for example, was able to determine from surveys that the company's overall market share could be materially improved by targeting on older travelers (see the accompanying Marketing Brief). Similarly, test

Exhibit 8.1
Historical Data-Based Forecasting Techniques

Methods	Basic Mathematical Models	Advantages	Disadvantages
1. *Exponential smoothing* is an autoregressive technique, meaning that the forecast variable itself is the primary means of making future forecasts. Differences between past forecasts and actual values are used to prepare the next forecast.	$F_{n+1} = \alpha A_n + (1-\alpha)F_n$ where F_{n+1} is the forecast for period $n+1$, the next period, α is a smoothing constant between the values of 0 and 1.0, A_n is the actual sales value for period n, and F_n is the old forecast of A_n	Highly complex formulas are avoided, only a minimal number of computations are needed, and above all, historical data need not be reevaluated every time a forecast is made. Especially useful when many forecasts are needed, such as in a department store handling thousands of items. Results are often as accurate as is possible with much more complicated methods. The basic model can be modified to adjust for linear and quadratic trends and for seasonal influences.	Attention is not explicitly paid to seasonal fluctuations, and other variables are ignored. Thus, causal variables such as income could change and not be detected by the model.
2. *Regression analysis* is a method of statistically measuring the relationships between a dependent variable (like sales) and independent variables (like advertising, income, and the number of target customers). The equation is found with the least-squares procedure, a way of defining the function that minimizes unexplained variations. Values of the independent variables are used to forecast the dependent one.	$Y = a + b_1x_1 + b_2x_2 + \ldots + b_nx_n$ where Y is the forecast of the dependent variable, a is a constant, b_1 is a slope coefficient stating Y's relationship to values of x, x_1 is a specific independent variable used in forecasting Y (like income), and n is the number of independent variables that are found to be significantly related to Y	The mathematical precision conforms to statistical theory, it allows for the explanation of variance in the forecast variable, it is increasingly simple to use because of growing computer availabilities, and the method can lead to very accurate forecasts.	It assumes that a causal relationship exists between the variables that cannot be proven by the analysis and historical relationships that might not hold in the future. Further, complex analysis is needed for nonlinear relationships and when the independent variables are interrelated.
3. *Time series analysis* is a means of dissecting an historical series of observations over time into seasonal, cyclical, long-range trend, and erratic components. In effect, a separate forecast is made of each component and then all are combined to yield the projection of the forecast variable.	$Y = S \times C \times T \times E$ where Y is the forecast variable of interest, S is the seasonal index, C is the cyclical index, T is the forecast of a long-range trend, and E is an erratic, or random, component	Enables the identification of various time-related components that typically exist in the case of sales. For instance, toys have their peak selling season prior to Christmas.	Numerous computations are needed and underlying conditions might change in the future. While hybrid models are available, the basic model itself does not take into account influences of variables other than time.

markets also enable management to make sales estimates for the company's intended overall trade area. Chapter 7 covers test markets in depth.

Judgments of Experts Using the judgment of experts is another means of forecasting when historical data are unavailable. Helene Curtis Industries, for instance, relied heavily on the judgment of its executives when they forecasted that Finesse hair

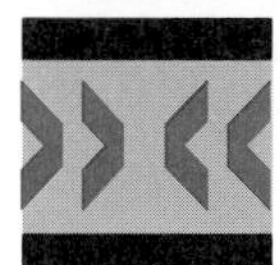

MARKETING BRIEF
"Yuppies" Are Out—"Grey" Is In

In an ever-expanding search for new market segments to penetrate, passenger air carriers have in the past targeted various groups: business travelers, the wealthy, middle-income families, "baby boomers," and, more recently, even "yuppies." American Airlines is one company whose marketing research has recently uncovered another segment—the ranks of older Americans.

"Our research indicates that people over 50 years old vacation far more extensively than any other group," said American's Michael W. Gunn, senior vice president for passenger marketing. "And when they do, they spend up to 30 percent more than younger travelers," he added. "We aim to get their business."

As a result of American's research, management developed marketing strategies to target the "greying" group. Special vacation programs to exotic spots such as Tahiti were developed with tie-ins to hotel accommodations, side trips, and tours; "the whole works to make vacationing easy," said management. Also, special fares were initiated involving 10 percent discounts to all those 65 years and older to encourage them to fly. "This group currently accounts for 7 percent of all of American's customers," said the company spokesman, "and it is the fastest-growing age group in the country."

American used television, newspapers, and magazines extensively to spread the word of their focus on seniors. The investment in advertising has paid handsome dividends to American, with its share of this segment increasing by over 10 percent in a matter of months.

SOURCE: Adapted from "Last Year It Was Yuppies—This Year It's Their Parents," *Business Week*, March 10, 1986: 72.

conditioner would generate healthy sales if introduced, and they were right; Finesse has become a very profitable product for the company.

Identifying the most appropriate experts is one challenge with this approach. Executives, salespeople, intermediaries, and a mixed group of specialists (including county agricultural extension agents, officers of trade associations, and medical researchers) often are used. Of course, which experts to use depends upon the situation.

Another challenge with using experts is to get them to use their best judgment when making their estimates. Several techniques are of value in extracting good estimates.[17] One of these is a PERT-related weighting scheme and another is the Delphi technique.

PERT stands for Program Evaluation and Review Technique—a procedure developed for estimating completion dates for major projects—and it has been found useful in forecasting. The method asks experts to make three estimates: optimistic (O), pessimistic (*P*), and the most likely (*L*). A broad spectrum of experience indicates that O, *P*, and *L* combine as follows:[18]

$$\text{Forecast} = \frac{P + 4(L) + O}{6}$$

with a standard deviation of:

$$S = \frac{O - P}{6}$$

The aging of America has presented emerging opportunities for several astute companies.

To illustrate, assume that a company's sales force estimates that a new toothpaste brand's sales will be \$2.5 million if the product has broad appeal to consumers, \$1.5 million if the marketing efforts are rather unsuccessful, and \$2.1 million if an average response is generated. The forecast would be calculated as follows:

$$\text{Forecast} = \frac{\$1.5 + 4(\$2.1) + \$2.5}{6} = \$2.07 \text{ million}$$

with a standard deviation of:

$$S = \frac{\$2.5 - \$1.5}{6} = \$0.17 \text{ million}$$

Combining these calculations with statistical approximations allows statistical confidence intervals to be estimated. Assuming that a 95 percent confidence level is desired, the confidence range for the example would be estimated using two standard deviations

$= \pm 2$ SD

(from the normal curve in statistical theory). That is, the forecast confidence interval would be estimated as the range of \$2.07 million ± 2(0.17) = \$1.73 million to \$2.41 million.

The Delphi technique is another useful judgment-based method. Popularized by the Rand Corporation's "Think Tank," the procedure aims at having a group of experts make initial forecasts and then modify their judgments in accordance with other experts.[19]

Instead of using one estimate from each expert, the firm uses a series of them in the following way. First, an initial-round questionnaire is used to elicit individual forecasts from each expert. The mean and standard deviation of these first forecasts are then calculated and presented to the experts along with a second-round questionnaire asking them if they would like to change their estimates. Only composite estimates are presented to the experts, which means that the identity of other individual forecasters is concealed. The procedure continues until responses stabilize. The aggregate mean and standard deviation are then used for the final forecast.

The concealment of individual identities is a major feature of the Delphi technique. In this way, personality, organizational position, and other similar factors are less likely to influence the results. Thus, the forecasts are not influenced by group dynamics. This has resulted in quite successful results in many situations, especially those involving long-range prediction.[20]

Many firms use judgmental forecasting. At Lockheed Aircraft, for example, executives role-play as specific major customers, evaluate attributes of the firm's and competitors' products, and then estimate which planes buyers will choose.

Judgmental methods have several major advantages. For one, no other realistic choice may be possible when historical data are unavailable. Another is that the results can be obtained rapidly. Finally, they explicitly allow changing market conditions to be incorporated because the experts can take them into account when making their estimates. These forecasts do inject personal bias into the process, however. Salespeople, for instance, often make their estimates low so as to keep their sales quotas down and make them easier to attain.

A Combination of Techniques Is Best Because of the mathematics that are often involved, forecasting intimidates some managers to the point that they accept projections at face value. Instead, they should question all results since forecasting is an art, not an exact science. Each forecasting technique requires many assumptions, any one of which may result in considerable error. The mid-1970s oil embargo, for instance, led to gasoline shortages and price increases that substantially curtailed vacationing. The result was that the historical-data–based methods that had been used for forecasting led to considerable error.[21]

A good way to attempt to validate forecasting results is to use multiple methods. This is particularly appropriate in cases where large losses are possible if a poor forecast is used as the basis for decision making. In addition to its executive-judgment–based estimates, Lockheed also uses various statistical extrapolations and combines them into an overall forecast. When several estimating procedures are used in this way, additional examination of their assumptions becomes warranted if considerable discrepancies exist between them. This might involve, for instance, commissioning a customer survey.

Now that key forecasting topics have been covered, let us apply them to the Midwestern Climate Control example.

Forecast of the Thermostat Timer's Market Potential

Midwestern's proposed thermostat timer was a new product, which meant that there was no sales history. Consequently, Smith, the company's marketing manager, focused his attention on forecasting procedures that did not rely on historical data. After considering the alternatives, he decided to forecast the target's industry-wide sales potential with a combination of survey results, the chain-ratio index method, and expert judgment. The survey results refined the target's eight relevant characteristics, as Table 8.2 showed. Smith relied upon census and trade association data for determining appropriate indexes.

Table 8.3 presents the resulting calculations. The data for the first five columns come from the Census of Housing. In any such application, it is essential to select proportions on the basis of *conditional events.*[22] To illustrate, examine Table 8.3's entry in column 2 for New England. The 0.61 refers to the proportion of owner-occupied year-round housing units. Simply using the proportion of all housing units and multiplying it times the number of year-round housing units would distort the results because some owner-occupied homes are not year-round units. The key is to use the proportion that reflects only those housing units having all of the target's characteristics. In Table 8.3, this means that each successive column must also satisfy the characteristics of previous columns. Column 5, to illustrate, is stated in terms of column 4, which is stated in terms of column 3, and so on.

Data for columns 6 and 7 come from the industry's trade association. Unlike the figures in columns 2 through 5, however, they are not based upon conditional events. Rather, they reflect all types of housing, not just those that are owner-occupied, with male heads of households, plus the other characteristics. Fortunately the trade association previously had conducted a study indicating that the existence of central thermostats in residences was relatively independent of the other important variables in Midwestern's case. Further, according to Smith's judgment, the incidence of round thermostats was also independent of the other variables. Therefore, he made the assumption that the proportions for all households could be considered to be representative of the target market. This assumption could be tested with further research, but the need to make some reasonable assumptions is almost always necessary when estimating market opportunity.

Table 8.3 Calculation of Total Market Potential from Midwestern's Identified Target Market

	Year-round housing units (in thousands)	Proportion of col. 1 that is owner-occupied	Proportion of col. 2 with male household head	Proportion of col. 3 with household head within age range	Proportion of col. 4 with income within range	Proportion of households with central thermostats	Proportion of households with round thermostats	Combined (mult. all columns—in thousands)
New England	4,278	0.61	0.78	0.78	0.55	0.67	0.58	339
Middle Atlantic	13,724	0.57	0.77	0.78	0.55	0.71	0.61	1,119
East North Central	14,589	0.68	0.76	0.76	0.57	0.69	0.60	1,352
Total potential								2,810

Thus, based on the calculations in Table 8.3, management concluded that there was a maximum potential of approximately 2.8 million total units that could be sold to the target market. This figure did not represent an annual volume potential; instead, it meant a total saturation of the entire target. Once saturated, only replacement business would materialize. Further, this potential volume was for the entire industry, not just that portion Midwestern could expect to attain.

The next step was to estimate **industry sales potential** on an annual basis. This task was not as straightforward. Smith used both past experience and the survey of interests. Roughly 20 percent of those surveyed had indicated that they would be very eager to buy a control timer if one were available. Management's experience with marketing other climate control equipment, however, suggested that such a high proportion would be overly optimistic.

Industry sales potential (forecast) Estimate of future total sales in an industry.

There are a number of factors that tend to inhibit initial sales. It takes months for a firm to fully establish a distribution network, some potential buyers have early doubts and wait to learn about performance characteristics, and some remain unaware of a new product's existence. Past experience suggested to Smith that annual sales of climate control devices were generally about a quarter of the proportion of target consumers who indicated that they were very eager to buy one. Therefore, he estimated that roughly 5 percent of the total market (¼ × 20 percent) were likely to purchase a control device each year. This percentage also was comparable to the ratio of annual sales to total saturation levels for other products successfully marketed by the firm in the past.

Consequently, Smith estimated annual industry sales at 140,500 units from the selected target (2,810,000 × .05). This estimate was admittedly somewhat subjective; however, in marketing as well as in all areas of business, sound judgment is a major input in managerial decision making.

Forecasting Midwestern's Potential Once management had forecasted the industry's total potential market, the next step was to estimate Midwestern's specific **market potential.** Since two direct competitors existed, Smith took both into account in this process. In addition, he considered the expected impact of the firm's anticipated marketing mix along with those of all potential competitors, including the seven firms who specialized in construction of new units.

Market potential Estimate of a total market's volume.

Smith reasoned that since the product would be of high quality but priced below $50, the company should have a clear price and quality advantage. Also, Midwestern had an established distribution system at the retail level in each region. Further, the firm was in a position to promote the item, if introduced, at a level commensurate with the competition. Accordingly, management estimated that Midwestern should be able to penetrate between 50 and 60 percent of the industry potential (defined in terms of the proposed target as above). Thus, estimates were that sales should be between 70,250 and 84,300 units per year (140,500 × .50 and 140,500 × .60), assuming that the firm's marketing effort would be relatively effective.

Evaluation of Potential Opportunity

The next step in market assessment is to evaluate whether sufficient potential exists to warrant market entry. Firms most frequently use three techniques in such evaluations: break-even analysis, net present value, and payback period analyses. (Appendix C provides a brief overview of each technique for readers unfamiliar with them.[23])

Segmentation strategy has a bearing on market potential, such as in fast foods.

Each of the three methods has distinctive advantages and disadvantages, as listed in Exhibit 8.2. Conceptually, the net present value approach is superior to the others but because of the difficulties in forecasting future periods over a proposed project's life, many analysts (especially those in fast-moving industries) prefer the payback or break-even methods.

Since all of the methods have slightly different emphases, strengths, and weaknesses, it is recommended that managers use all three methods in evaluating a potential opportunity's desirability. By doing this they will gain additional insight into any project. All three approaches often yield the same rejection or acceptance solution. In instances where they do not, management should consider such factors as expected environmental changes, the nature and intensity of competition, and the firm's objectives when sifting through each solution to determine which appears to be the most reasonable. The following discussion applies each of the techniques to the Midwestern Climate Control example.

Break-even analysis
Determining the volume or price that will result in covering total costs.

Break-Even Analysis Smith required additional information to perform a **break-even analysis**—a better fix on both the thermostat control device's price and its costs. Regarding price, management predicted that Midwestern's primary competitor, the one currently selling a unit for $49.95, would reduce its price to around $30 if Midwestern entered the market. Smith felt that price was an important consideration to buyers, and therefore assumed that the company should price competitively (which he estimated should be at a level of $30 per unit). If this price proved to be potentially profitable, he felt confident that the timer's superior quality and ease of installation

Exhibit 8.2
Techniques for Evaluating Potential Opportunity

Method	Advantages	Disadvantages
Break-even analysis. Several forms of analysis are possible. Costs are first separated into fixed and variable components. Unit variable costs are then subtracted from the revenue per unit to yield the unit contribution. Next, fixed costs are divided by the unit contribution to determine the volume required to break even. This volume, finally, is compared to the potential volume to assess the desirability of a project.	Simple to use, reflects the fact that costs and profits must be considered and not just sales. It specifically stresses the relationship between volume and profitability.	It can be difficult to accurately separate fixed and variable costs. It assumes that linear cost relationships exist. An assumption about marketing effectiveness must be made. The emphasis is on a single year of operation and ignores any value differences between future versus present dollars.
Net present value analysis. All revenues and costs, both initial and future, are determined. Then, compounded interest factors are used to equate all cash flows with today's dollars.	The entire duration of a project is emphasized, the method accounts for the present values of future monies, it is a good means of comparing projects, and it emphasizes return on investment.	Many future forecasts are needed (costs, sales, etc.) for all future periods of a project's life. Forecasts may contain substantial error, especially those involving distant periods, particularly in dynamic settings.
Payback period analysis. Costs in future periods are subtracted from anticipated revenues. Then, the number of years that it will take for the contribution margin to recover all related investment is calculated. The number of periods is then compared with a predetermined cutoff criterion. If fewer years are required, a project is considered desirable.	This method is simple to use. It stresses the need to recover all costs rapidly, which is especially important in dynamic, fast-paced industries. The results can be almost identical to methods emphasizing return on investment for some projects.	A project's total life is not emphasized, meaning that a potentially profitable project in the long run could be mistakenly turned down. It does not specifically emphasize the present value of money. It is difficult to interpret when additional future investment is required or when cash flows are periodically uneven.

Table 8.4 Midwestern Climate Control Cost Estimates for Proposed Thermostat Timer

Variable Costs per Unit	
Clock	$1.75
Gears	2.50
Adapter rings	0.75
Assembly	0.95
Other production costs	1.05
Shipping, handling, and other variable marketing costs	0.75
Total variable costs per unit	$7.75
Total Annual Fixed Costs	
Equipment depreciation[a]	$100,000
Building depreciation[a]	50,000
Other production fixed costs	75,000
Advertising expense	200,000
Administrative salaries	40,000
Total annual fixed costs	$465,000

a. Since this represents a new project, it is assumed that the related investment will only be made if the project is approved. Because this represents marginal cost, the depreciation must be considered to reflect these costs in break-even analysis.

would result in a strong leadership position for the company. Midwestern's channel members required a total markup of 40 percent. Consequently, the company's effective selling price would be $18 ($30 × 0.6).

Midwestern's chief engineer, its cost accountant, and Smith estimated the timer's production and marketing costs (presented in Table 8.4). Smith made the following calculation to determine the break-even point in units (see Appendix C).

$$\text{Break-even volume} = \frac{\$465{,}000}{\$18.00 - 7.75} = 45{,}366 \text{ units per year}$$

Recall that the annual sales potential was 70,250 to 84,300 units. Thus the volume required to break even was equivalent to less than two-thirds of the predicted volume potential. Hence, the project appeared to be desirable from a break-even perspective. Even if Smith had substantially overestimated Midwestern's potential, the firm should have been able to attain at least a break-even volume.

Break-even analysis also is useful when assessing profit potentials. If Midwestern succeeded in attaining its sales volume potential, the profit would be in the range of $255,000 to $399,000 per year, calculated as follows:

	at 70,250 units	*at 84,300 units*
Sales ($18.00 × volume)	$1,264,500	$1,517,400
Less costs		
Variable ($7.75 × volume)	544,438	653,325
Fixed	465,000	465,000
Total costs	1,009,438	1,118,325
Profit potential	$ 255,062	$ 399,075

If break-even analysis was the only technique used, management would compare this profit potential with that anticipated from other alternatives and then choose the one offering the greatest potential profit. In Midwestern's case, however, management also considered both net present value and payback period analyses.

Net present value analysis
A method of using compound interest calculations to discount future cash flows to equal their current financial worth.

Net Present Value Analysis Midwestern's management made the following estimates:

1. *Capital outlays.* Smith conferred with the company's chief engineer and accounting staff and found that Midwestern would need an initial investment of $1.5 million for plant and machinery. They believed that no other capital investment would be needed over the proposed project's life. Because such an investment would require an immediate cash outlay, its present value was $1,500,000 (1.00 × $1,500,000). The value was negative since it represented a cash outlay, not an inflow.
2. *Projected sales volume.* Management assumed that the calculated minimum potential of 70,250 units was a conservative but reasonable forecast for each year. Further, it felt that a ten-year life for the project was realistic. The assumption was that the venture could perhaps last longer, but that the firm would have to make many changes in product styling and machinery by the end of that period. Thus, the time horizon was limited to ten years.
3. *Cost and price levels.* To simplify the calculation, management assumed that costs and prices would remain constant over the project's ten-year life. If desired, changes in costs and prices in future years can also be handled by this method. Specific values for each year must be specified and then multiplied by each year's appropriate discounting factor instead of treating the problem as an annuity, as is done here. For net present value, depreciation must be excluded from the fixed costs presented in Table 8.4. This is because net present value only considers cash flows when they occur. Since the capital investment is considered at the onset, it is excluded in future years. Hence, the fixed cash costs become:

$465,000	(Total fixed costs in Table 8.4)
− 150,000	(Depreciation in Table 8.4)
$315,000	Annual fixed cash costs

4. *Salvage value.* Midwestern's management believed that it could salvage $10,000 from the proposed project's related machinery and equipment at the end of ten years.
5. *Interest rate.* Management should establish a minimum acceptable rate of return in relation to both the project's degree of risk and the firm's cost of capital.[24] Midwestern's management required a minimum 20 percent return on investment before it would accept a project, indicating a moderate degree of perceived risk and cost of capital. Table 8.5 presents the net present value calculations required for the Midwestern analysis. The present value for the proposed thermostat timer was positive, signaling that the opportunity was a desirable one. A 20 percent return on investment, the firm's acceptable minimum, appeared to be likely. If the calculations produced a negative net present value, of course, management would deem a project undesirable.

Payback period analysis
A method of estimating the number of periods, usually years, that it will take to recover the investment cost of a venture.

Payback Period Analysis Midwestern also calculated the time period required to pay back the capital investment for the project. Using the conservative estimate of sales potential, the following analysis was made:

Table 8.5 Midwestern Climate Control Net Present Value Analysis

	(a) $Amount	(b) Present Value of $1.00	(c) Net Present Value (a × b)
Initial capital outlay	(1,500,000)	1.00	($1,500,000)
Future cash flows:			
Sales ($18 × 70,250 units per year)	1,264,500	4.193[a]	5,302,049
Variable costs ($7.75 × 70,250 units/year)	(544,438)	4.193[a]	(2,282,829)
Fixed costs per year (cash outlays)	(315,000)	4.193[a]	(1,320,795)
Salvage value	10,000	0.162[b]	1,620
Net present value			200,045

a. From Table C.1 of Appendix C. For simplicity, the calculations assume that all funds are received at the end of each year. Interest rate is 20 percent at 10 years.
b. From Table C.1 of Appendix C, at a 20 percent interest rate.

Sales ($18.00 × 70,250 units per year)		$1,264,500
Less costs (from Table 8.4)		
Variable ($7.75 × 70,250)	$544,438	
Fixed (cash flows only)	315,000	859,438
Contribution per year		$ 405,062

Thus, it would take $\frac{\$1,500,000}{\$405,062} = 3.70$ years ($1,500,000 ÷ $405,062) to recover the initial investment, ignoring any salvage value. Management's predetermined payback period cutoff was 6 years or less. Hence, the thermostat timer appeared to be desirable from an investment payback perspective.

Selecting the Best Alternative and Developing Marketing Plans

The final stages of the process include first selecting the best alternative and then developing a set of preliminary marketing plans. In Midwestern's case, all three analyses suggested that the firm should introduce the proposed thermostat timers. Furthermore, the projected profitability appeared to be greater than other projects being considered. Accordingly, management decided to market the timers.

What Happens When an Opportunity Is Rejected? It turned out that Midwestern's evaluation of the thermostat timer was favorable. But what if one or more of the analyses suggested that the opportunity was undesirable? Suppose, for instance, that the project's net present value appeared negative or the payback period was excessive?

Management's initial response may be to scrap a proposed project entirely; such a decision may be inevitable if the evidence against it is very strong. But the reason for

CONCEPT SUMMARY

Analyzing Market Opportunity

Steps	Activities Involved
1. Recognize a potential opportunity	Identify new and existing opportunities upon which the firm may be able to capitalize.
2. Define the target market	Determine which target customers will be the focus of company efforts.
3. Forecast the total market (or industry) potential	Obtain sales forecasts for the economy at large and for the specific industry. These forecasts are prepared largely by organizations outside the company.
4. Forecast the company's potential	Estimate future sales levels of the firm's product offering. Some techniques require historical data and some do not.
5. Evaluate the potential opportunity	Assess the opportunity using techniques such as break-even, net present value, and payback period analyses.
6. Select opportunities with the greatest potential	Select the alternative that appears to be superior to the others, based on the previous evaluation.
7. Reject opportunities with insufficient potential	Reject alternatives that are inferior to the chosen one. Study rejected alternatives for possible adaptation in the future, however.
8. Develop marketing plans	Develop a marketing mix specifically tuned to the needs of the target market.

the negative evidence may indicate that management has defined a target market too narrowly or too broadly. Perhaps it should expand the target by adding another geographical region, or narrow the target definition.

In the process of redefining a target, management should reevaluate both internal and external variables to the company. Internally, the costs of approaching alternative segments are of different magnitudes. To illustrate, accepting a smaller segment might enable Midwestern to cut advertising and the scale of operations, leading to reduced expenses. Ligget and Myers found this to be the case when it introduced the Eve 120mm cigarette. The 120mm category represented only 2 percent of the total cigarette market. The firm was able to acquire the dominant share of this market with only a small advertising budget. Conversely, a more broadly defined target might easily increase costs and the level of competition. Nevertheless, because of a larger total target size, such segmentation might prove desirable.

Taking all of this into account, it is evident that management should make a decision to scrap a proposed project only if the opportunity appears undesirable under all target definitions.

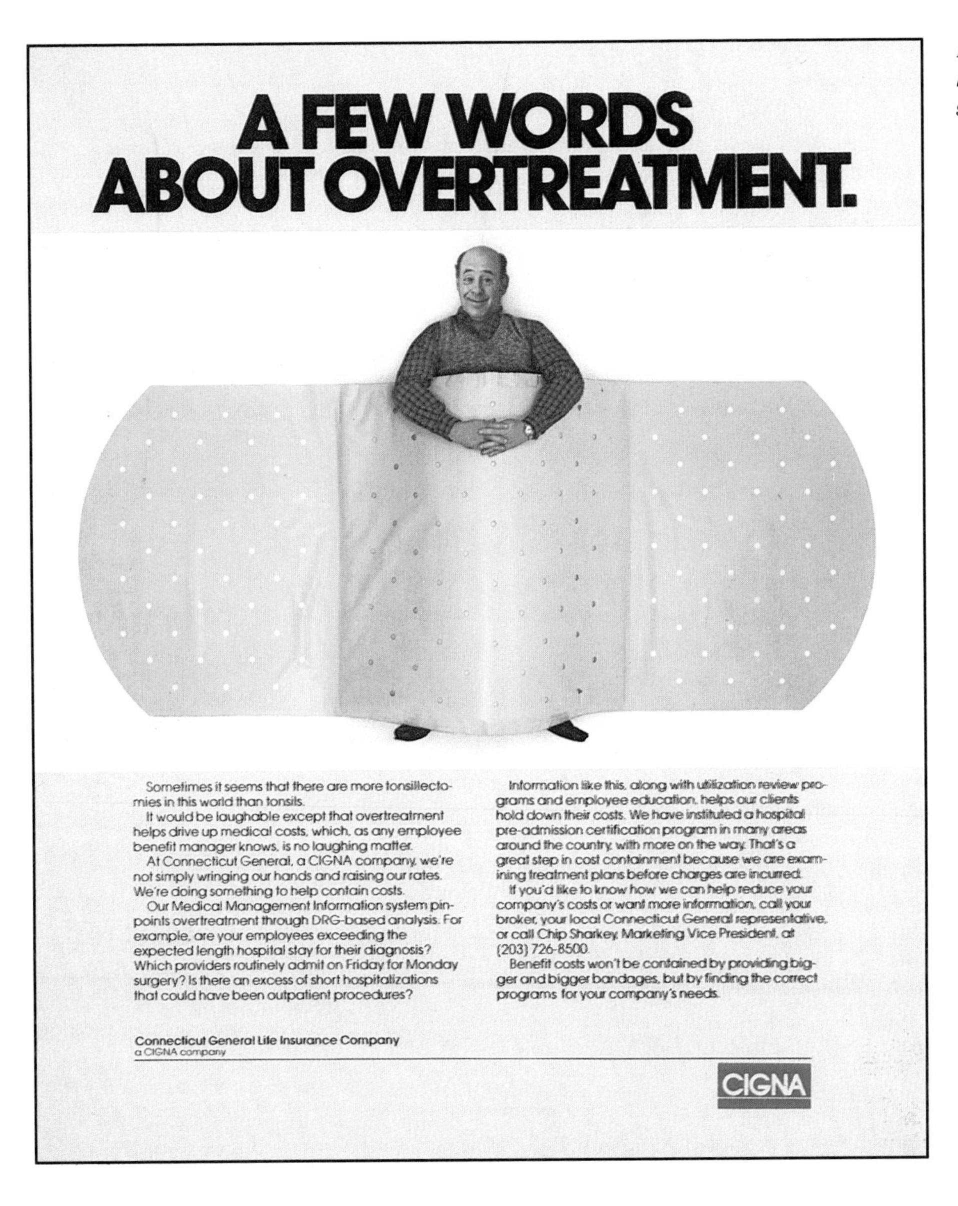

Helping business to manage rising health costs has become a significant service opportunity.

Chapter Summary

This chapter examined the process of analyzing market opportunity, which is a major cornerstone of effective marketing decision making. Management can identify potential market opportunities through considering the firm's environment, its internal characteristics and potential for synergy, competitive advantages, and possibilities for segmenting the market.

Being able to forecast market potential is an important part of the process of analyzing market opportunity, and market potentials at both the industry and firm levels must be considered. The techniques of break-even, net present value, and payback period are used to evaluate market opportunity.

Analyzing marketing opportunity lays the groundwork for deciding detailed marketing plans and actions. The next section focuses on decisions concerning elements of the marketing mix.

Questions

1. The text states that several factors are important when defining a potential target. Among them are internal characteristics and the potential for synergy. Shouldn't a firm define targets exclusively on the basis of market-related factors?
2. What role does judgment play in defining a target? Why not eliminate judgment entirely and rely completely on marketing research?
3. In the words of one entrepreneur, "All that forecasting is a bunch of bunk. After all, all those fancy techniques are based on guesswork. You guess potentials, marketing effort and effectiveness, and just too many things. Using those techniques only makes you feel like the numbers have real meaning, rather than being detailed assumptions. We simply judge a potential opportunity on the basis of whether we think its a good idea." Comment.
4. The same entrepreneur states: "Judging opportunity on the basis of break-even is silly. We're in a business to make a buck, not to cover costs." Comment.
5. Assess the desirability of using net present value analysis.
6. What about the payback period technique? Is it useful? After all, many experts say it is conceptually foolish because it does not take into consideration the present or future value of money.
7. What are the various levels of forecasts that are important to marketers? Which level is most important and why? Does this mean that the other levels are unimportant?
8. Why is forecasting important?
9. Explain the role of forecasting in planning.
10. What are the advantages and disadvantages of exponential smoothing? Of regression? Of time series analysis?
11. Why are such techniques as the Delphi process needed for obtaining expert judgment?
12. Are expert judgments and guesses the same?
13. Why do firms often use more than one forecasting technique?
14. Describe what should be done when an evaluation of a potential opportunity is negative.
15. The Amherst Company is considering a new venture. Its potential market is estimated to be 5,000 units per year for each of the next ten years, which is based upon 10 percent of the industry's potential. Amherst expects to realize a selling price of $5.00 per unit. Total variable costs are estimated at $4,500 for a volume of 3,000 units. The total investment required is estimated at $26,000. Further, the financial manager indicated that an 18 percent return is the minimum that the company can accept. Usually, the company expects to recover its investment in 5 years. With this project, salvage is estimated at $0.
    a. What is the break-even point in units? In sales dollars?
    b. What is the net present value?
    c. What is the payback period?
    d. What should the company do?
16. A firm is evaluating a project with an optimistic estimate of $6 million, a pessimistic estimate of $2 million, and a most likely estimate of $3 million. Estimate sales and standard deviation using the PERT method explained in this chapter.

Part Four

Marketing Mix Elements

Chapter 9

Product Decisions: An Overview

Objectives

After completing this chapter, you should be able to demonstrate a knowledge of:

- The meaning of the terms *product, product mix,* and *product line*
- The concept of an optimal product mix, which serves as an important guideline in making strategic product decisions
- The basic strategies companies can implement when the contribution from product offerings appears to fall short of established goals, a condition termed *contribution gap.* But a market expansion strategy should receive considerable attention, because it is most likely to result in favorable synergy
- The product life cycle. Like living organisms, products have life cycles consisting of introduction, growth, maturity, and decline. Understanding the product life cycle can assist managers in making strategic product decisions
- The meaning of product portfolio analysis and how management can use it as a guide in strategic product decision making

MARKETING SUCCESS

Using Research Inputs to Design a New Magazine

"We are not going to be outdone by those Eastern newspapers—or anyone else, for that matter," said a spokesperson for the Los Angeles Times, *the leading newspaper in the West, at least in circulation count. And the* Times *recently has taken significant strides to outpace the competition. "Our goal is to be the best—in news coverage, in special features, in editorials—in all!"*

An indication of the paper's commitment to excel is the whopping $400,000 and two years it recently spent on research—the largest marketing research project ever undertaken by the firm—to create a new publication, the Los Angeles Times Magazine *(LATM), a thick, colorful, interest-oriented supplement to the paper's Sunday edition. According to Donald F. Wright, president, the project was undertaken to replace the outmoded* Home *supplement, the former magazine that had outlived its readers' interest. "Our goal was to attract more male readers and additional advertisers," said Wright, "and we have succeeded." "The . . . [LATM] . . . is fresh, new, and full of interesting features that fit into the lifestyles of Southern California."*

A variety of research topics were studied. Target audience lifestyles, values, and attitudes led the list of the research interests. When copy formats were narrowed down to two heavyweight contenders, samplings were used to determine which had the greatest punch. The focus was on two especially important, highly divergent market segments revealed in the research: "outer-directed achievers," and "inner-directed societally conscious." The final decision was to design the magazine to include features relevant to societally-conscious readers and also features with a human relations perspective. All of this effort has led to a highly successful new publication that is being read by the target, according to followup research, and advertisers have taken note, with revenues increasing dramatically over the outdated Home.

SOURCE: Adapted from "Huge Research Effort Guided Newspaper's Magazine Launch," *Marketing News* 20, no. 1 (January 3, 1986): 50, 54.

Introduction

As in the case of the *Los Angeles Times* in the chapter's opening Marketing Success, managers recognize that a major key to long-term success is making effective decisions relating to the company's product offerings. There are two important and related types of decisions to be made.

First, managers must monitor existing product performance and change strategy when necessary. This is what the management of the *Los Angeles Times* did when it recognized that its old *Home Magazine* supplement was not reaching the market and replaced it with the updated *Los Angeles Times Magazine.*

Second, developing new products—ones other than those currently sold—is important in product decision making. New products account for somewhere between 10 and 20 percent of current revenues to firms in general.[1] Companies such as Jovan, Inc. owe much of their success to management's informed judgment and carefully conceived research into new products.[2]

Thus, effective product decisions encompass both strategically managing existing products and developing new ones.[3] This chapter explores decision-making concepts for existing products or services. Chapter 10 considers decision making for new products.

Important Product Concepts

Before examining specific product decisions, it is logical to begin the discussion with several important marketing concepts relating to products or services. These include attributes, levels of product abstractions, product lines, and the idea of an optimal product mix.

Attributes

To marketers, a product is an entity that has certain attributes such as color, size, weight, quality, reliability, and taste. For instance, Tabasco pepper sauce is a red, easy-to-pour, concentrated hot sauce for seasoning foods. People evaluate products by deciding if acquiring the attributes of a given product will enable them to accomplish their intended life activities. People make a purchase when they believe that an item's attributes suit their needs better than the attributes of other products.[4] People seeking a hot, spicy flavor are likely to buy a bottle of Tabasco sauce, for example, if they feel that it creates a more desirable flavor than would competing brands, such as A.1. Steak Sauce. To marketers, therefore, the concept of a product is viewed in terms of the item's ability to fulfill customers' desires.

Level of Product Abstraction

Buyers also view products at three levels of abstraction: a generic product, a specific product, and a total product. At the broadest level, a **generic product** is a type or class of item designed to satisfy some basic need, such as the refrigeration of food. The underlying intention of most purchases is the satisfaction of one or a combination of basic needs. People do not buy refrigerators for their own sake—because they have sophisticated electrical devices or attractive hinges and handles—they buy them to preserve food.

Generic product
A type or class of item designed to satisfy some basic need.

A **specific product** is a subclass of a generic product. Specific products have distinguishable attributes that set them apart from other items within the same generic class. Because of differing attributes, however slight they may be, General Electric, Westinghouse, and Frigidaire refrigerators differ from each other. In general, consumers perceive up to five characteristics that distinguish specific products from each other:

Specific product
A subclass of a generic product with distinguishable attributes that set it apart from other items within the same generic class.

1. physical attributes (size, capacity, power source, and ease of operation)
2. style (shape, color, and fashion)
3. quality (durability, operating costs, and life expectancy)
4. brand (an identity for similar groups of identical products, such as General Electric, Amana, and Kenmore)
5. package (a specific container that protects the product and may display information about its use as well as promotional messages). For some products such as refrigerators, the package (a quickly discarded crate) serves only a protective role. For other items such as detergents and perfumes, the package also contains attributes and helps customers to distinguish between brands.

Attributes and benefits are what people seek when they buy products.

The specific product attributes satisfy secondary needs. While people buy refrigerators to preserve food (a primary need), secondary needs such as color coordination, durability, and styling generally determine which specific product they will buy within a generic class. An important task of most marketers is to see to it that their company's products satisfy the secondary needs of the selected target.

Total product
A set of specific product physical attributes, plus all other elements of the marketing mix.

Total consumption system
All buyer-related needs, not just those pertaining to physical attributes.

Finally, buyers evaluate a **total product.** This includes all the elements of a marketing mix, not just physical attributes. Instructions for use, retailer locations, advertising messages, and all other marketing mix decisions serve to shape a total product. By including K mart in its list of appliance distributors, for instance, General Electric changed its total product offering. The notion of a total product leads marketers to examine a buyer's **total consumption system**—all buyer-related needs—when developing a marketing mix.[5]

Coleman offers a broad line of outdoor products.

Product Lines

Few companies rely solely on a single product. There are several reasons for this. The risks are too great to rely on one item, average overhead costs can be reduced by spreading the total over several products, and distributors and other customers often expect companies to handle several items.[6] Large companies such as Sears, IBM, and Ford rely on thousands of products. And while most smaller companies begin with a single product, they usually branch out rapidly into new items. A product line and a product mix are terms used to describe multiple product situations.[7]

A **product line** is a group of closely related products that are offered for sale by a company. Product lines may be related because they are substitutes, complements, sold to the same target market, distributed through the same channel, or are within the same price range. To illustrate, Zenith offers several TV models that vary in size, style, and color. All of them are part of the company's television set line.

Product line
A group of closely related products that are offered for sale by a company.

In contrast, a **product mix** is the complete set of products that a company offers for sale and involves one, two, or more product lines. Zenith, for instance, sells TVs, radios, and other electronic product lines. Holiday Inns' product mix also includes institutional furniture manufactured by a company division and other products, in addition to its lodging line.

Product mix
The complete set of products offered for sale by a company.

Figure 9.1
Product Mix and Goals: The Concept of a Contribution Gap

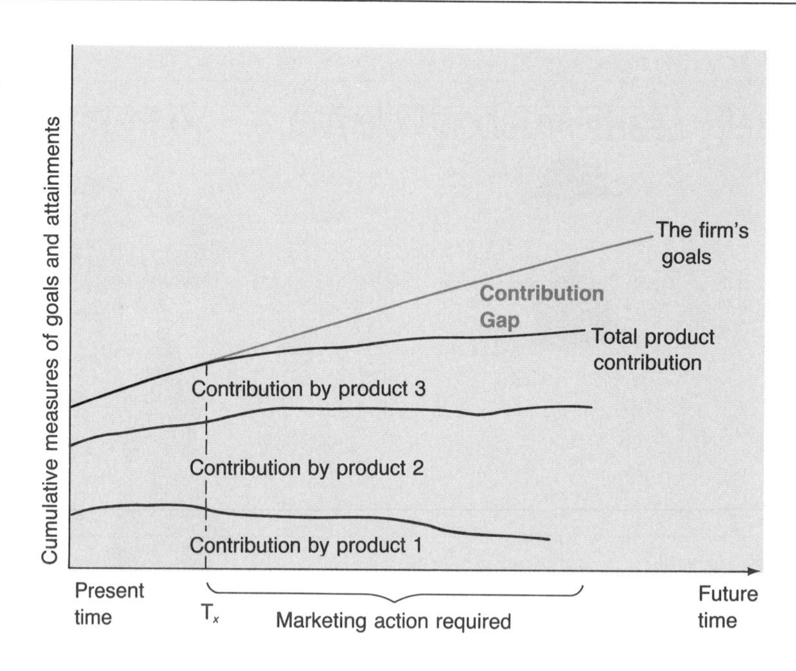

The Optimal Product Mix and Contribution Gap

Another useful idea is that of the optimal product mix, which is the one that best allows an organization to reach its goals. The idea is illustrated in Figure 9.1. Each item in a product mix makes some contribution toward a firm's goals. In turn, the organization's goals serve as yardsticks by which management can measure performance and the need for some type of action.[8] Management makes product decisions to close the gaps between goals and achievements.

Contribution gap
The difference between a firm's goals and the potential of a product mix toward achieving them.

Such a **contribution gap** is shown in Figure 9.1. The existence of a gap beginning at time period T_x suggests that actions must be undertaken ahead of time if the business is to keep on its intended track. Of course, such a gap could result if management sets goals too high, meaning that expectations should be revised downward. A contribution gap also occurs when the organization needs new product strategies.

This was the case for the R. P. Scherer Corp. in 1986 (see the accompanying Marketing Brief). Unexpectedly plagued by the Tylenol tragedy, management had little choice but to make alternative product decisions. All ended well for the company because management was prepared for such contingencies. The story could have had a different ending, however, had management not done its homework.

Market expansion
Attempting to more fully penetrate an existing target, as opposed to selecting new or additional ones.

As Figure 9.2 illustrates, there are two fundamental product decision strategies for management to make. The first, **market expansion,** involves fine-tuning the marketing mix for one or more existing products in an attempt to squeeze a greater contribution from the product mix toward company goals. The second strategy is to develop and market new products—change the product mix—to generate the additional contribution. The concept of synergy is useful in assessing the relative merits of these strategies. Market expansion is explored in the remainder of this chapter, while new product development is discussed in Chapter 10.

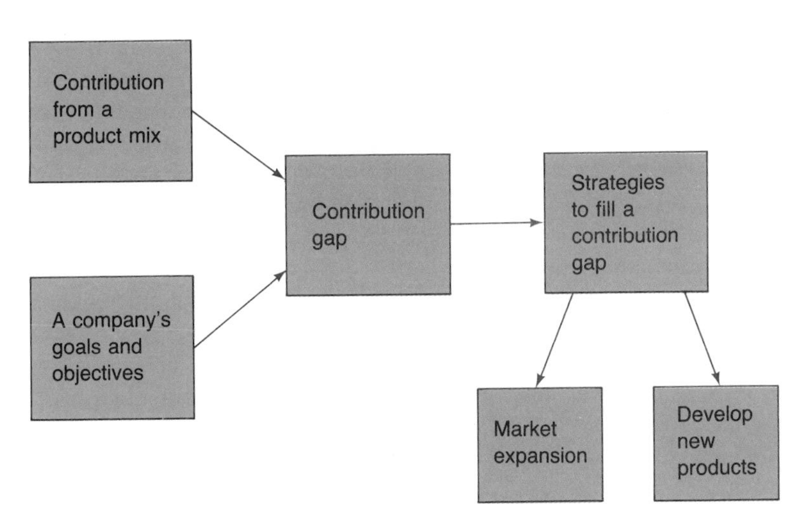

Figure 9.2
An Overview of the Product Decision Framework

MARKETING BRIEF

Events Can Trigger the Need to Have New Products at the Ready

"They were sailing along smoothly, then their ship all but sank," said one securities analyst. "Ironically, the public was not even aware of their dilemma, though I guess they weren't concerned, either," he added.

The company is Troy, Michigan-based R. P. Scherer Corp., one of the world's largest producers of capsules for pharmaceuticals, and one of their major accounts was Johnson & Johnson Co.'s Tylenol division. Supplying two-piece dissolving capsules for Tylenol and other drug manufacturers amounted to a major slice of Scherer's bread and butter. But the market for the easy-to-fill hard-shell capsules softened considerably when Tylenol suffered severe setbacks in early 1986 from its second major poisoning scare in as many years. Like Johnson & Johnson, the bottom fell out of Scherer's stock and company phone lines were tied up with inquiries from reporters, concerned citizens, and stockholders during the ordeal.

The management of Johnson & Johnson made the decision to switch to soft-shell caplets, a choice that involved adding to product cost because of the greater difficulty in filling them. But, the decision made sound marketing sense (not to mention its product liability implications), for the soft-shell variety was much more difficult to tamper with. Other over-the-counter pharmaceuticals were expected to make the same decision to switch rather than buck the trend.

Fortunately, Scherer's management had been experimenting with the soft-shell caplets ahead of time, though the fortuitous event was happenstance more than insight into potential safety risks. Intensive competitive pressures had caused prices to fall in the hard-shell capsule market during the past year. Declining profits accompanied the downward pricing spiral.

The new caplets also offer a greater profit potential because Scherer itself fills the soft-shell pills and helps develop drug formulations needed to make the process work. "We don't want to take advantage of a tragic situation," said Peter R. Fink, Scherer's president and chief executive officer, "but a soft-shell caplet is very hard to tamper with." Accordingly, management has made a commitment to pursue other products, such as antacids and also prescription drugs. The company also has developed and readied for market a freeze-dried tablet process that enables the contents to dissolve in the mouth in less than two seconds. This new process is expected to have wide appeal for children, the elderly, and in veterinary applications.

SOURCE: Adapted from "Scherer is Ready to Try New Medicine," *Business Week*, March 10, 1986: 58, 62.

Market Expansion Strategies

Because a planned marketing mix is seldom perfect, improving the impact of management's actions provides an opportunity to close a contribution gap within an existing product mix. In effect, this strategy involves expanding the market for an existing product and it offers the greatest potential for synergy. This is because it involves emphasizing activities related to the firm's existing experiences. Before considering the introduction of new products, therefore, management should first consider making improvements in the planned product, price, promotion, and place mixes of each item in the current product mix.

To illustrate, making an item slightly larger, smaller, of different quality, or changing the package might generate a greater contribution. As examples, Procter & Gamble used such a strategy for Gleem toothpaste by slightly changing its attributes to include a "New Burst of Flavor," and Sony improved the clarity of its VCR pictures. All planned marketing activities offer the potential of improvement. The concept of a product life cycle provides a convenient way of discussing various types of market expansion strategies.

Product Life Cycles

Product life cycle
An orderly pattern over time of a product's introduction, growth, maturity, and decline in sales and profits.

The sales and profitability levels of products typically change over time in an orderly manner, termed the **product life cycle.** Many examples serve to illustrate these cycles. Products as diverse as streetcars, trains, piston-powered commercial airplanes, manual typewriters, hand-crank telephones, and many others have experienced a fluctuation from rapid growth to decline, as shown in Figure 9.3. The shape of the curve is dependent upon the number of customers who purchase the product, the number of units purchased on each shopping trip, and the magnitude of repeat purchase.[9]

The time it takes for a life cycle to be completed differs from one product to another. Fad items such as Pet Rocks and clothing styles typically have very short life cycles, perhaps only weeks or months. At the other extreme, products like sheet steel and gasoline have lengthy cycles spanning decades. There is evidence that the average length of product life cycles is shortening over time.[10] Management has the task of distinguishing between fads and true underlying trends, of course, as trends are more lasting and have general marketing planning implications.

Several guidelines are useful in distinguishing fads from trends: [11]

1. The new development must fit with basic changes in lifestyles and values for it to be a trend. An example is the changing roles of women.
2. The number of sources and types of information that are associated with the new development indicate its importance. For example, the increasing consumption of fish and poultry as opposed to red meat is associated with reliable sources of information on health, weight loss, economy, and concern for the family. This suggests that the direction is a trend.
3. A new development is more likely to endure if different people can modify or express it in different ways. Fads are relatively rigid, whereas trends are flexible. For example, not many people could wear hairstyles such as the "punk" look, which means that this style is probably a fad.
4. If very credible people are early adopters of the new development, there is a greater chance for it to endure. If President Reagan began wearing bow ties, for instance, they might become more of a trend than when they were adopted by PeeWee Herman.
5. Basic themes are more enduring than their particular manifestations. Physical fitness is a trend, while roller skating and pumping iron are probably fads.

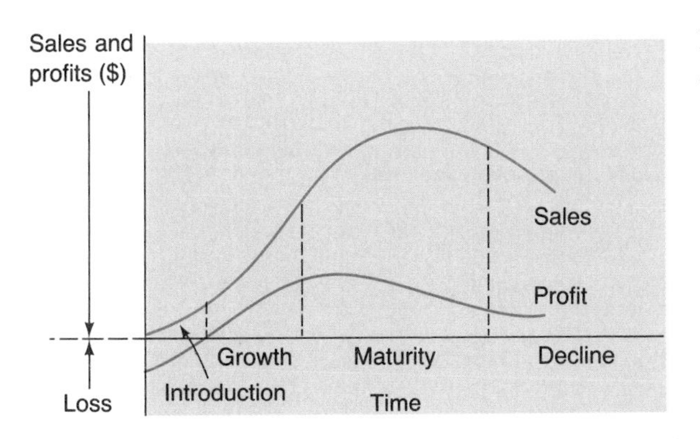

Figure 9.3
Stages of the Product Life Cycle

6. A new development is more likely to be a trend if other related trends support it. Not smoking is a trend because it is supported by trends toward health, physical fitness, and stress management.

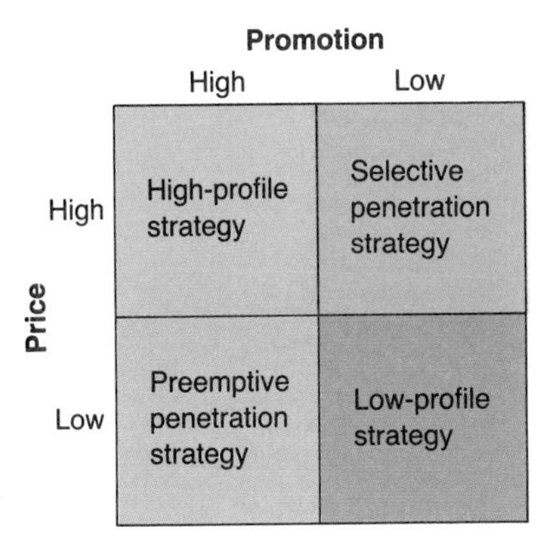

Figure 9.4
Marketing Strategies During Product Introduction

Regardless of its length, a life cycle's overall pattern is quite similar, consisting of four stages: introduction, growth, maturity, and decline. The notion of a life cycle is meaningful for all levels of a product (generic, specific, and total) and the variations do not necessarily correlate. In 1985, for instance, the U.S. auto industry was in the mature stage of its life cycle, while the Yugo (a new car imported from Yugoslavia) was a popular newcomer to the market and in its infancy.

However, the life cycle concept is probably most useful to managers in helping to shape company strategy during a generic product's life. While the specific points of demarcation between stages are somewhat arbitrary and difficult to pinpoint, successive stages on the continuum usually suggest that changes in strategy are in order.[12]

Exhibit 9.1 lists various market expansion strategies that are appropriate for the life cycle stages. The following discussion applies the concepts to decision making.

Introduction Stage The **introduction stage** occurs when a company introduces a new product to a market. As Figure 9.3 indicates, this is a period usually marked by low sales and losses instead of profits, because introduction generally requires a heavy financial investment in marketing to create product awareness, and investments in other areas such as production and research and development. Some new products, such as industrial robots, diffuse very slowly into their potential markets, while other products virtually bypass this stage.[13]

Introduction stage
Initial stage of the product life cycle.

There are four basic strategies management should consider during a product's introductory stage, encompassing combinations of price and promotion levels, as Figure 9.4 illustrates. For a particular firm, the most promising strategy, of course, depends upon its objectives and the nature of its market environment.

High-Profile Strategy Managers who pursue a **high-profile strategy** introduce a product with a substantial promotion expenditure as well as a high price in order to recover as much cost and profit as is possible in a short time period. Marketers of new appliances often employ this strategy. Trash compacters, one-minute burger makers, popcorn poppers with automatic buttering features, and hand-held hair dryers have been introduced with a high-profile strategy. It is most effective when a large portion of the target market is unaware of the item, price is relatively unimportant to the target

High-profile strategy
A strategy of high levels of promotion and high price, especially during product introduction.

Exhibit 9.1
Market Expansion Strategies for Life Cycle Stages

Life Cycle Stage	Strategies	Definition
1. Introduction	A. High-profile	• High promotion expenditure and high price
	B. Preemptive penetration	• High promotion expenditure and low price
	C. Selective penetration	• Low promotion expenditure and high price
	D. Low-profile	• Low promotion expenditure and low price
2. Growth	A. Strive for early profitability	• Moderate promotion budget and initial high prices
	B. Invest in marketing for future opportunity	• High promotion budget and other initial investment with initial low prices
3. Maturity	A. Any means of differentiating product from rivals	• Activities designed to make product meaningfully different from its competitors
	B. Marketing mix modification	• Altering one or more elements of a marketing mix for growth potential
	C. Brand extension	• Find new uses for marketing the product
4. Decline	A. Recycle	• Heavy promotion effort to bring offering out of decline
	B. Status quo	• Retain same marketing mix that was used during maturity
	C. Retrenchment	• Withdraw from weak segments to enable concentration on strong segments
	D. Milking	• Cut costs to a minimum and sell as long as revenues cover variable costs
	E. Pruning	• Abandon the product

market, and the firm wants to develop strong preference for its brand because extensive competition is expected in the future.[14,15]

There are some very good reasons for pursuing a high-profile strategy. Heavy promotion levels can inform target customers of an item's existence. A high price can both help to build an item's prestige image and generate funds to pay for the extensive promotion effort.

Preemptive penetration
A strategy of high levels of promotion and low price, especially during product introduction.

Preemptive Penetration **Preemptive penetration** requires a heavy promotional expenditure accompanied with a low price. Managers adopting this strategy believe that target customers are largely unaware of their product's existence, price is relatively important to them, a large potential market exists with economies of scale possible from large sales volumes, and substantial competition is expected.

Low margins and high sales volumes tend to discourage competitors from entering a market, while scale economies are expected to help profitability. Tract housing developments and tour travel packages are two examples of products that managers frequently introduce through a preemptive penetration strategy. Campbell Soup Co. used this strategy when it introduced its highly successful Great Starts frozen breakfasts in 1984. The Chrysler Corp. also used preemptive penetration to introduce its Dodge Mini Ram vans in 1984.

Selective Penetration **Selective penetration** consists of pricing a product relatively high while keeping promotional expenditures at a moderate level. Firms typically introduce prestige items like furs, diamonds, and high-fashion attire in this way. Selective penetration can be a good decision when numerous target customers are aware of an item, customers are willing to pay a high price, a relatively small potential market exists (substantial economies of scale are unlikely), and little future competition is expected.

Selective penetration
A strategy of low promotion and high price, especially during product introduction.

Once the high-price market is saturated, management may decide to lower prices to entice new customers into making a purchase. The old Bell System used selective penetration for many new products such as push-button and decorator telephones.

Low-Profile Strategy This strategy combines a small promotional budget with a low price. Marketers introduce many producer items with a **low-profile strategy,** such as lubricants and cleaning and office supplies. It is most effective when many target customers are aware of a product, a large, price sensitive market exists, and a significant level of competition is expected.

Low-profile strategy
A strategy of low promotion and low price, especially during product introduction.

Growth The second stage of the product life cycle is that of **growth,** which is marked by increasing profits and sales. Because rapid growth in sales and increasing profits signal the existence of opportunity to other firms, increasing competition from other items in the same generic class often evolves as the stage progresses. Rapidly expanding demand may be sufficient, however, to enable several competitors to maintain prices and earn good profits.

Growth (stage)
Second stage of the product life cycle; marked by rapid expansion of sales and profits.

Managers need to make a strategic tradeoff between two fundamental and opposing strategies during this stage. First, they may opt to earn as much short-run profit as possible by holding prices up and spending only moderate sums on marketing efforts. Time Computer Co. selected this strategy for its Pulsar digital watches. Rather than investing in marketing to aim for future profits, the company assessed high prices (as much as $2,500 for a gold model), utilized exclusive distribution, and engaged in only limited product development and promotion.

Other organizations choose to reinvest profits into substantial marketing efforts in order to build a strong market position for future profitability. MCI Communications did this with its new postal service, MCI mail. Firms electing to pursue this alternative emphasize some combination of large-capacity production facilities that will bring about greater scale economies, changes in quality, adding more intermediaries, and heavy promotional efforts to build brand preference.

The first strategy, that of stressing profitability during a growth stage, can bolster a firm's financial posture over the short run but it can also weaken a product's market strength during future stages. Time Computer, for instance, withdrew from digital watches in the late 1970s in the face of declining sales and profits. Conversely, overly heavy emphasis on the future is also risky, as a strong market position might never be secured despite the fact that the firm invests in marketing programs. Consequently, the appropriate strategy depends upon management's assessment of the long-run market potential, the degree of expected future competition, and the firm's ability to build brand loyalty through investing in marketing activities.

Maturity (stage)
Third stage of the product life cycle; marked by stagnating sales and mixed profits.

Maturity A marked change occurs during **maturity.** At the start, sales increase but at a declining rate, eventually peaking and then declining a bit. Profits also begin to fall. This is the status of many basic U.S. industries today, including steel, automobiles, and home construction.

Several factors account for the sales deceleration. For one, customer awareness of the product has generally reached a high level by this stage. For another, the product may be losing its appeal; perhaps new substitutes have emerged. Finally, competition tends to be greater than during any other stage of the product's entire life, reflected in some firms' heavy price cutting.

Effective differentiation is very important to a company's success during maturity, as when Audi developed a five-cylinder engine for its cars to provide both performance and economy. Beyond this, there are two major strategies that are especially useful: market mix modification and brand extension.

Marketing mix modification strategy
A strategy of locating new segments, changing the marketing mix to stimulate growth, or product modification, especially during product maturity.

Marketing Mix Modification Strategy Altering one or more of the elements of a product's marketing mix is called a **marketing mix modification strategy.** It may involve seeking new segments to pursue, stimulating greater usage of company brands by current customers, modifying products, or repositioning the product entirely.

Sometimes a firm can locate new segments of customers. To illustrate, many companies initially market consumer items on the East and West Coasts, the Midwest, and in the Southeast because of high population densities, adaptive cultures, and high incomes. As these segments mature, they then develop strategies to penetrate other, less-populated states. Deciding to enter foreign markets to gain access to new segments is another example.

Modifying the marketing mix to stimulate greater usage by existing customers is another way of generating increased sales. Burger King and other fast food retailers, for instance, use contests and coupons to promote increased consumption. Packaged food companies provide free recipes using their products for the same effect.

Product modification
A strategy of slightly changing the product to tap new market opportunities.

Product modification is another technique that involves making slight style and feature improvements. The Coca-Cola Company, for example, introduced Diet Coke on a worldwide basis in order to appeal to health- and weight-conscious consumers. The annual style changes in the fashion and auto industries are another example. Some critics of marketing contend that this amounts to "planned obsolescence," and is inherently undesirable. Although, it can be argued that if the improvements satisfy some unfilled need, the companies are doing what they should be doing: providing items to satisfy customer needs. Of course, to be successful, the changes must satisfy some need.

Finally, a marketer might decide to reposition a product altogether. Research might indicate, for instance, that all age groups are buying an item in moderation, revealing an unclear image among customers. To counter this, management might focus its efforts on those segments where the greatest opportunity exists. PepsiCo repositioned Pepsi Light in 1983 to appeal to men, a segment that management felt soft drink producers were largely ignoring. As another example, Wang Labs was unable to completely reposition itself as a full computer supplier by 1985, after two years of attempts.

Brand extension
A strategy of finding new uses for a product.

MARKETING BRIEF

Wang Laboratories Is Unable to Effectively Reposition Itself

Wang Laboratories, Inc., suffered a disastrous fiscal year in 1985. The firm laid off 1,500 workers and reported a $109 million fourth-quarter loss. Much of the problem was due to lack of marketing expertise, particularly in the product planning field.

In 1983 the firm noted that its word processing machines were being supplanted in the office market by IBM Personal Computers. These PCs could send electronic mail and process data as well as perform word processing tasks. Intent on becoming more than just a word processor producer, Wang decided to become a full-service computer company.

The company has not been able to fulfill that strategy. Many customers rely on Wang for word processing expertise but rely on firms such as IBM for sophisticated office systems. Wang has suffered from demand for a "connectivity" among diverse computer systems. Only recently did it make its machines compatible with IBM PCs, but Wang machines still connect poorly with Digital's products.

Further, Wang's machines are vulnerable to replacement because there is only a limited amount of good software for them. The firm did develop systems to merge word processing, spreadsheets, and electronic mail into one package, but customers report that the software is riddled with bugs.

SOURCE: Adapted from "The Revolving Door to Wang's Executive Suite," *Business Week*, April 21, 1986: 29.

Brand Extension Strategy **Brand extension** is another major strategy that can be helpful during maturity. It involves finding new uses for a product. DuPont Inc., for instance, originally developed nylon for military uses (parachutes, rope). Later it extended the brand to include an expanding market, consisting initially of women's hosiery and later expanding to tires and fabrics. Similarly, Arm & Hammer has promoted its baking soda as an odor inhibitor for refrigerators, cat litter boxes, and thermos bottles. Many software producers have moved from developing video games to educational programs for home computers.[16] Successful brand extensions can enable marketers to break away from mature markets and into growth opportunities.[17]

A word of caution is in order. Brand extension usually involves substantial marketing costs because it is similar to bringing out a new product and requires a high initial investment. Consequently, management should pursue it only if the extension actually produces substantial benefits to a significant market segment that was previously unsatisfied.

Chanel has extended its line into the men's market.

Decline The fourth and final life cycle stage is **decline.** It can occur rapidly, perhaps within weeks or months after the introduction as in the case of fad items, or it might not set in for decades with products such as asbestos insulation. Research shows that industrial goods tend to have a longer product life cycle than do consumer goods.[18] Life cycle theory proposes that all products eventually will enter into a decline stage.[19]

Decline (stage)
Final stage of the product life cycle; marked by declining profits and sales.

More and more customers purchase less or stop buying the item as the stage progresses. Automobiles have replaced horse-drawn wagons and hand-held calculators have supplanted slide rules. As sales begin to fall, the least profitable firms begin to abandon the market because they are forced out of business or they pursue other

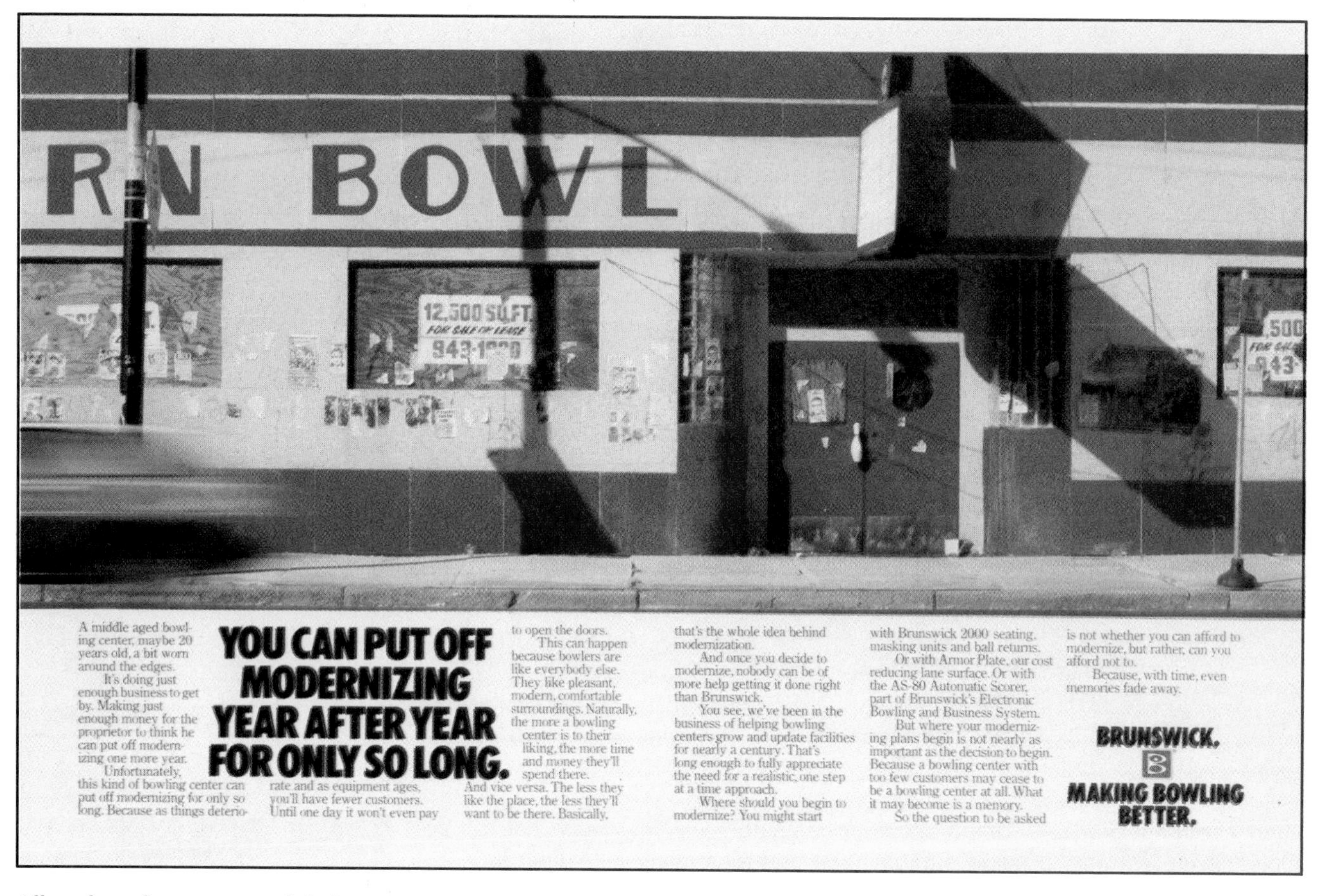

All products face an eventual decline.

opportunities. Many remaining firms lower their prices to inhibit further losses. Also, they often cut promotion expenditures due to restrictive budgets and high levels of product awareness among target members.

Five basic strategies are available during a decline stage: recycle, maintain the status quo, retrench, milk the product, or prune it. The most appropriate strategy depends on management's assessment of the expected size of the remaining market, anticipated competitor actions, and available alternative opportunities.

Recycle (strategy)
An attempt to restimulate demand through heavy promotion.

Recycle Strategy A classic study of the pharmaceutical products industry revealed that a heavy promotional effort during a product's decline stage can result in a **recycle,** as Figure 9.5 illustrates. To rationalize such a strategy, one should look for two factors. First, sales during a decline stage might still be sufficient to exceed the levels of the first two stages of a product's life. Sales may be falling, but this does not mean that they are dead. Second, fewer competitors typically are in operation than was the case during earlier stages. This means that competitor counteractive strategies are less likely. Hence, any successful effort to stimulate sales is likely to be quite profitable to a remaining firm.

Seagram Co., Ltd., successfully employed a recycle strategy. Plagued by a declining liquor market as consumers began switching to wine and other light alcoholic beverages, management ignored conventional wisdom and doubled its advertising budget to $40 million.[20] Sales results suggested that Seagram had generated a very successful recycle; one that is much like those found in pharmaceuticals. If a firm has sufficient financial strength and if management is confident that a heavy promotional push will revitalize interest in a product, a recycle strategy can lead to handsome payoffs. This was the case with Right Guard deodorant, which completed a successful recycle in 1983.

Even if a company is successful with a recycle strategy, it is likely to experience further decline at some future date. Then management should consider one of the four remaining decline stage strategies. These are not market expansion strategies, *per se*. That is, they do not attempt to stimulate a larger market for a product. However, one may classify them under the umbrella of market expansion because they are geared toward improving a firm's financial picture, thus providing resources for developing other opportunities.

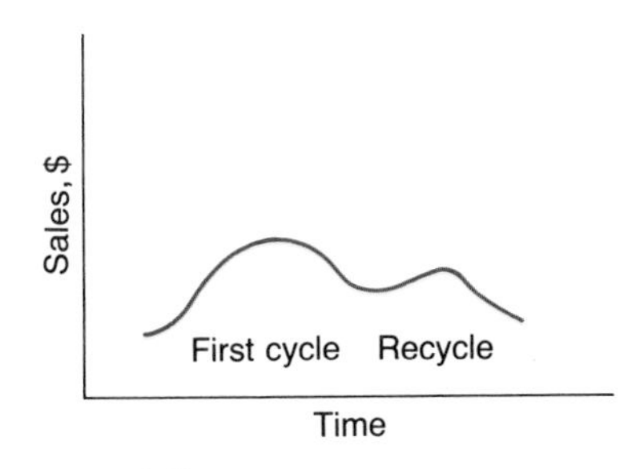

Figure 9.5
A Recycle After a Heavy Promotional Effort During the Decline Stage

Status Quo Strategy Under a **status quo strategy,** the firm retains the same marketing mix that it employed during maturity. This is especially appealing to companies that once held significant consumer loyalty within specific market segments. As a market begins to decline, it often does so through a peeling away of the outer segments distant from its core. However, those firms with an established niche at the heart of the market may be able to maintain profitability by continuing their current strategies. To illustrate, many commuters continue to ride trains to and from work without apparent effort on the part of railroads to attract them. Abbott Laboratories has maintained a status quo strategy with its infant formula Similac. It is able to do this because the brand is very well known among physicians.[21]

Status quo strategy
A strategy of continuing the marketing thrust as usual.

Retrenchment Strategy **Retrenchment** takes place when a firm withdraws from weak market segments to enable concentration on those segments where it has greatest strength. It is based on the "80–20 principle": 80 percent of a company's sales are often derived from 20 percent of its customers. Similarly, 20 percent of a company's products often account for 80 percent of its sales.

Retrenchment makes cost reductions possible and allows concentration of marketing efforts in the most promising arenas. The firm can stimulate profitability as a result. The Korvette discount chain followed a retrenchment strategy by selling its six Chicago retail outlets. Afterward, management concentrated its efforts on its eastern stronghold, where it owned most of the 52 remaining stores.[22] Once a firm has successfully retrenched, it can again attempt to expand its operations once it has regained its financial strength.

Retrenchment
Withdrawing from peripheral market segments to a position where the firm has its strongest niche.

Milking Strategy A **milking strategy** is roughly analogous to salvaging a sinking ship—a firm cuts all costs to a bare minimum and continues to sell the product so long as revenues cover all variable costs. This strategy makes sense when it appears certain that a product's death is close at hand. To illustrate, most publishers stop all promotion efforts for books with sales that have dropped below a certain volume but they continue to sell the books until either existing inventory is depleted or orders disappear.

Milking strategy
A strategy of cutting all costs to the bone, including marketing.

Pruning The final strategy is one of **pruning,** or abandoning a product. Unfortunately, many managers hold on to products which once were popular and perhaps contributed substantially to establishing the company's market position. However, outdated successes are not part of a marketer's realm. Therefore, once forecasts of opportunity no longer justify continued efforts, the firm should drop a product so that it can devote efforts to more promising ventures.[23]

Pruning
The elimination of a product from the product mix.

CONCEPT SUMMARY *Market Expansion Strategies and Life Cycle Stages*

Stage and Strategy	Definition	Useful When
Introduction		
High-profile	High promotion and price	a. Target is unaware of the item b. Price is relatively unimportant c. Brand preference is desired because strong future competition is expected
Preemptive penetration	High promotion, low price	a. Target is unaware of item b. Price is relatively important c. Large potential market and economies of scale are possible d. Substantial competition expected
Selective penetration	Low promotion, high price	a. Target is aware of the product b. Price is relatively unimportant c. Relatively small market exists d. Little future competition expected
Low-profile	Low promotion, low price	a. Target is aware of the product b. Price sensitive market c. Significant competition expected
Growth		
Strive for early profits	Moderate promotion, high initial price	a. High degree of competition b. Company is relatively weak
Invest in marketing for future opportunity	High promotion and other investments, low prices	a. Large potential market is promising b. Company is in strong position to capitalize on the future market

The Life Cycle Concept Is No Panacea

The concept of a product life cycle is not a panacea for operating managers who are responsible for deciding marketing strategy. Some critics contend that too many life cycle variations exist for the concept to be a reliable decision guide.[24] Consider the case where management mistakenly interprets a seasonal or cyclical drop in sales as entry into a decline stage and, as a consequence, cuts marketing efforts. Of course, this action could bring about a premature sales decline. In other words, management can unwittingly kill a product's chances of attaining its potential through actions suggested by misinterpreted sales fluctuations.

Such criticism does have some merit. Nevertheless, the product life cycle notion is quite useful as a conceptual guideline for collecting and interpreting marketing information to devise marketing strategy and tactics. If sales begin to level off or decline, managers should search for the underlying reasons for this behavior. Marketing research, for example, might signal that buyer preferences are shifting toward competitive items. If other evidence supports this conclusion, managers should consider that a decline has begun and take appropriate action. Perhaps the firm should launch a recycle attempt, but if such an endeavor appears to be unsuccessful then a more appropriate decline stage strategy is in order.

CONCEPT SUMMARY *(Continued)*

Stage and Strategy	Definition	Useful When
Maturity		
Differentiation	Make product particularly different from rivals'	• Useful throughout stage, emphasizes examining segment needs
Marketing mix modification:		
Locate new segments	Find pockets of opportunity	• When untapped needs can be found
Modify marketing mix to stimulate use	Finely tune marketing efforts to stimulate sales	• When demand can be stimulated by various means
Product modification	Make slight style and feature changes	• When demand is sensitive to style and feature characteristics
Brand extension	Find new uses for the product	• When some modification can be made to enable the product to penetrate a slightly different market
Decline		
Recycle	Heavy promotion effort	• When interest in the product can be revitalized
Status quo	Use historical marketing mix	• When the firm is already positioned at the market's core
Retrenchment	Withdraw from weak segments and concentrate on strengths	• When firm is strong among certain segments and not others
Milking	Cut costs to the bone	• When the future no longer looks promising
Pruning	Eliminate product	• When variable costs can no longer be covered

If executed properly, market expansion can bring about two very important accomplishments. First, it may increase a product's contribution toward the attainment of company goals. As Figure 9.6 illustrates, successful market expansion can play a role in reducing an emerging contribution gap. Second, market expansion enables an extension of the time by which management must rely on new product development to meet the company's objectives. In Figure 9.6, notice that because of effective market expansion, management can delay necessary action from time T_x to time T_y. The added time permits more thorough new product planning and development, and increases its likelihood of success.

Product Portfolio Analysis

Many companies use the market expansion strategies discussed earlier in making product decisions. In addition, many have recently begun to integrate strategies for an entire product mix. This is called the **product portfolio** approach.

Firms who offer a variety of goods and/or services, such as General Mills, may be in a position to benefit from product portfolio analysis. This procedure is based upon the principle that if management considers all product strategies in conjunction with one another, the company is more likely to benefit than if individual product decisions

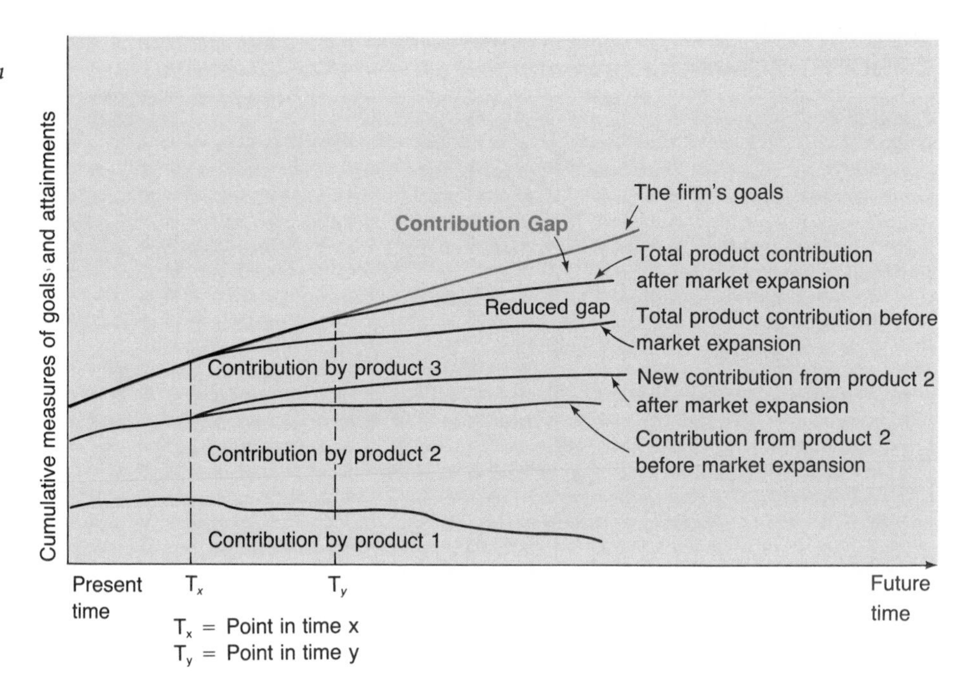

Figure 9.6
The Impact of Market Expansion on a Contribution Gap

Product portfolio
The categorization, for strategic marketing purposes, of products according to current or expected market growth rate and market share.

are made independently.[25] This approach is analogous to the investment portfolio strategies adopted by various individual investors and companies. They attempt to maintain some balance in their investments in order to attain diversified goals such as income and capital growth.

The Concept

A widely adopted form of portfolio analysis involves categorizing products along two dimensions: current or expected market growth rate and market share. Consider the grid in Figure 9.7, which shows products arrayed along these dimensions.

Often market growth rate is stated relative to the change in gross national product, providing an index that is relative to all products and services. Another modification is to state market share as a percentage of the firm's largest competitor, a logical transformation because the strategies that are appropriate for a given market share could differ, depending upon the market share of the largest competitor.

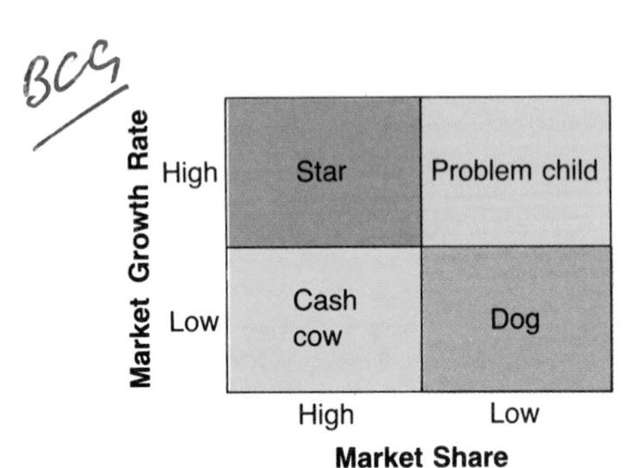

Figure 9.7
Product Portfolio Quadrants

Users of the product portfolio concept often arrange company operations into *strategic business units* (SBUs). These are divisions that offer one or more products to a particular market and that resemble separate firms. The truck division of Navistar Corp. (International Harvester), for example, is a strategic business unit.

With product portfolio analysis, the entire firm is viewed as a portfolio of SBUs or individual products. This requires that each SBU has a clear-cut strategy and serves a well-defined segment of the market. In turn, management should develop the strategies of the SBUs in a manner that promotes overall company goals, resulting in balanced growth in various products' sales and earnings and in the overall asset mix.[26] Much of the work with product portfolio analysis follows the pioneering effort of the Boston Consulting Group, a consulting firm that developed a number of the strategic concepts.[27]

Market share and market growth are, of course, interrelated. During times of substantial market growth, consumers and intermediaries are not locked into rigid purchase patterns and a firm can acquire additional market shares at reasonable expense. Conversely, when the growth rate is low (as it is during later points in the product life cycle), the firm finds it is more difficult to increase market share; consumers and intermediaries have developed entrenched purchase patterns and competitors can be expected to react intensely when their market share is threatened. For instance, the Carborundum Company found it was very difficult to increase its market share for abrasives in the late 1970s; competitors such as 3M and Norton fought off every attempt to advance Carborundum's share.

Using Product Portfolio Analysis

Breaking down SBUs (or individual products) into the four quadrants identified in Figure 9.7 can provide numerous strategic prescriptions.

Low Growth, High Market Share (Cash Cows) Products in this category are profitable and tend to generate large amounts of cash. The firm can retain its market share without expending substantial resources. Hence, the best strategy is to take steps to ensure that the company maintains its high market share without taking extreme measures such as price cutting or developing many related new products. The firm can use funds generated from **cash cows** to support research, promotion, and product development activities for other SBUs. The VF Company has followed this procedure: utilizing funds earned from its cash cow Lee Jeans to develop other products such as lingerie.

Cash cow
A product with a high market share and a low market growth rate.

High Growth, High Market Share (Stars) In the case of **stars,** the SBU enjoys both high growth and high market share and requires substantial amounts of cash in order to maintain growth. Management can accomplish this through market extension, research and development, increased promotion, and reduced prices. These, of course, tend to drain cash resources, as evidenced by the experience of General Electric, which invested substantial amounts in the early 1980s in efforts to maintain its high market share in semiconductor chips.

Star
A product with a high market share and high market growth rate.

Low Growth, Low Market Share (Dogs) Products which are in the low growth and low market share category are termed "**dogs,**" and pose problems for the firm. These SBUs often do not generate much in the way of cash or profits and opportunities for future growth are limited because the markets are not growing. Given this background, a milking or pruning strategy is probably called for. Fairchild Industries, for instance, pursued what was essentially a milking strategy during the early 1980s for its executive airplane business.

Dog
A product with a low market growth rate and a low market share.

High Growth, Low Market Share (Problem Children) Products with high growth and low market share are termed "**problem children.**" As any parent will agree, this situation calls for substantial amounts of cash in order to maintain the growth and avoid a "dog" status. The firm may consider strategies such as repositioning, product modification, or brand extension, or might decide that the costs of maintaining problem children are just too high and get out of the business.

Problem child
A product with a high market growth rate and low market share.

Exxon maintained a problem child with its office systems division (producers of word processors and related products) for several years. Confronted with substantial competition from well-established rivals, it invested substantial sums in an effort to expand market share. Eventually, the firm dropped out of the business in 1986 because the huge investment really never lived up to its expectations.

Composite Strategy As with any investment portfolio, a firm should strive for a condition of balance among the various categories. If the product portfolio is characterized primarily by dogs and problem children, strong remedial action is required. Management should aim for a situation where there are some products producing profits and cash and others utilizing cash as a means of providing future growth. Hence, cash cows and stars are desirable targets.

In some cases there are opportunities for beneficially converting a product's status from one category to another. For instance, the company can use funds from cash cows to develop problem children into stars so that when the problem children's growth rate slows, the next generation of cash cows will be replaced. Management should be on the alert for such strategic modifications.

Utilizing the Concept Product portfolio analysis does not provide useable answers to all strategic product questions. There are several problems with the approach, including the following.[28]

1. Classifying SBUs into the different categories is imprecise. Standard procedures that lend themselves to all situations are unavailable, causing measurement problems.
2. Variables other than market share and market growth are also important to consider.

CONCEPT SUMMARY *Product Portfolio*

Category	Characteristics	Cash Effects	Recommended Strategy
1. Star	High market share, high growth rate	Consumes considerable cash	Maintain growth through means such as market extension, research and development, increased promotion, and reduced prices.
2. Cash Cow	High market share, low growth rate	Generates considerable cash	Take steps to maintain market share without taking extreme measures such as price cutting or developing large numbers of new products. Use funds generated from cash cows to invest in other projects.
3. Problem Child	Low market share, high growth rate	Consumes cash to avoid "dog" status	May require cash investments, repositioning, product modification and brand extension. Sometimes, when costs are too high, pruning is appropriate.
4. Dog	Low market share, low growth rate	Does not generate much cash or profits	A milking or pruning strategy is appropriate.

3. The focus is on internally generated and used cash. Management should also consider other sources of cash, including the financial markets.
4. The focus is on the short run. Long-run implications should also be evaluated.

While there are weaknesses, the major advantage of the approach is that it stresses achieving a balance among all of a company's products. In this sense, product portfolio analysis forces management to integrate its efforts.

Chapter Summary

This is the first of several chapters that examine individual elements of the marketing mix. The discussion expanded the definitions of a product, a product mix, and a product line and explained the concept of an optimal product mix. This concept is useful as a guide in making strategic product decisions. There are several basic strategies that managers can decide to use when the contributions from product offerings appear to fall short of established goals, a condition termed "contribution gap."

In general, market expansion strategies should receive major attention whenever a contribution gap is expected, since they are most likely to result in favorable synergy. The particular market expansion strategy to use depends on many factors; however, the concept of the product life cycle is useful as a means of sorting out which strategy to use and when.

Finally, product portfolio analysis allows the marketing manager to view an entire mix of products simultaneously while making decisions. Although the method has several drawbacks, it does offer the advantage of integrating product decision making by a company.

Questions

1. What is a product? (Use your own words.)
2. Distinguish between generic and specific products.
3. What is a total consumption system? Provide an example based on your own experience.
4. Distinguish between product mix and product line.
5. What is a contribution gap? What are the major ways of overcoming it?
6. What is the difference between market expansion and new product development? What circumstances justify each?
7. What is the product life cycle? Define the various stages.
8. Briefly describe each strategy.
   a. High-profile
   b. Preemptive penetration
   c. Selective penetration
   d. Low-profile
   e. Marketing mix modification
   f. Brand extension
   g. Status quo
   h. Retrenchment
   i. Milking
   j. Pruning
9. What is portfolio analysis?
10. Describe the four product categories used in product profile analysis. What strategic implications exist for each category?

Chapter 10

New Product Development

Objectives

After reading this chapter, you should be able to demonstrate a knowledge of:

- The importance of new product development to marketing managers
- The four fundamental types of new product strategies: rounding out existing lines, and adding market-related lines, adding technology-related lines, and adding unrelated lines
- The conditions under which each of the four fundamental types of new product strategies is appropriate
- The stages of new product development and how companies use these in bringing out new offerings
- How management can employ branding and packaging as means of implementing product strategy
- Various forms of organization that firms can employ for new product development

MARKETING FAILURE

Not Knowing What Products to Offer Can Be Fatal

Ailing Cleveland-based Midland-Ross Corp., a diversified manufacturing concern, remained in agony in 1986 after a six-year bout with anemic sales and even worse profits. "They just haven't been able to get their act together," said one security analyst. The one-time manufacturing giant continued to suffer almost singlehandedly the Rust Belt's deep recession during the early 1980s despite almost total recovery by other firms in the area. "Their problems go much deeper than location," said the source. "Simply put, they do not seem to know which products to offer." Unlike other Rust Belt concerns, Midland-Ross seemed unable to find a suitable mix of new products to sell in the economy's transition away from a smokestack base.

Between 1981 and 1986, Midland-Ross wrote off $97 million for closed and distress-sale businesses. The company's historical strength came from serving the railroad business but its entire railroad castings operation, once a contributor of 40 percent of the company's revenues, was unloaded on the trading block in 1984 after this industry nearly collapsed. The chosen replacement was electrical connector products, which contributed about a third of company sales in 1986.

"They shot themselves in the foot with that one," smirked a disgruntled former company executive. "No sooner had the company moved into those products than the market softened and competition grew tough," he said. "They were once a major auto parts supplier, but got out of that business, too—just before the auto industry recovered with record sales!"

Company management continues to look for a business in which to become a major factor, but has not been able to come up with the solution. In the meantime, the transitions have caused considerable pain. Seven vice presidents have left since 1982 to seek their silver linings elsewhere. The company's assets continue to erode and its debt continues to climb—to about 35 percent of its capital. "Management simply does not know which products to add and which to drop," said another source.

SOURCE: Adapted from "Can Midland-Ross Climb Out of the Rust Bowl?" *Business Week*, April 29, 1985: 58.

Introduction

A big risk is taken when marketing a new product, as the management of Midland-Ross Corp. discovered. There are two major hurdles to overcome. First, introducing a new product is usually quite expensive, with the initial development and marketing costs of even relatively simple items exceeding $1 million. Second, new products have an enormous failure rate, causing many companies to shy away from the prospect if possible. Failure rate estimates vary from study to study, ranging from 30 percent to 93 percent depending upon the definition of "failure."[1] Some researchers define a failure as a discontinued product, whereas others adopt a broader definition that involves not meeting management's pre-set objectives.

There is evidence to indicate that more successful introductions result when management takes a long-run rather than a short-run view when deciding whether or not to introduce new products.[2] In any case, the failure rate is discouraging to most managers and has contributed to the reduction in the number of new products introduced to the market over the past several years.[3]

Despite the cost and risk, management may have no other choice but to introduce a new product. Usually, market expansion alone cannot fill a contribution gap in the long run. This chapter examines the new product development process.

New Product Strategies

There are four fundamental types of new product strategies, as Figure 10.1 illustrates; three of them involve developing new product lines. Each strategy differs on the basis of a new product's similarity to the marketing and production characteristics of a firm's existing products.

Rounding Out Existing Lines

Depth (product line or mix)
The number of substitutes that a company offers within a line.

Substitute products
Closely related products, such as in a line, that serve as alternatives to each other.

The first new product strategy involves intensifying the **depth** of an existing product line, termed *rounding out* a line ("depth" refers to the number of **substitutes** or variations a company offers within a line). When management rounds out existing lines, similar customers, marketing skills, and technology are involved; the firm stays on familiar ground. After Country Time's initial success with regular lemonade, for example, General Foods succeeded in rounding out the line to include pink lemonade. Coca-Cola introduced Minute Maid reduced-acid frozen orange juice in 1983 and "New Coke" in 1985.

After expanding a line, the firm may be better able to meet the needs of target customers. Companies such as IBM and Gillette are masters at rounding out. Figure 10.2 illustrates that each thrust into a significant new market segment can turn a line's stagnant market into one of growth opportunity.

Rounding out usually offers the greatest potential for synergy of the four new product strategies.[4] This is because the company can take advantage of its current marketing strengths: image and awareness among customers, channels of distribution, and so on. Similarly, the strategy usually takes advantage of the company's current production

Figure 10.1
New Product Development Strategies

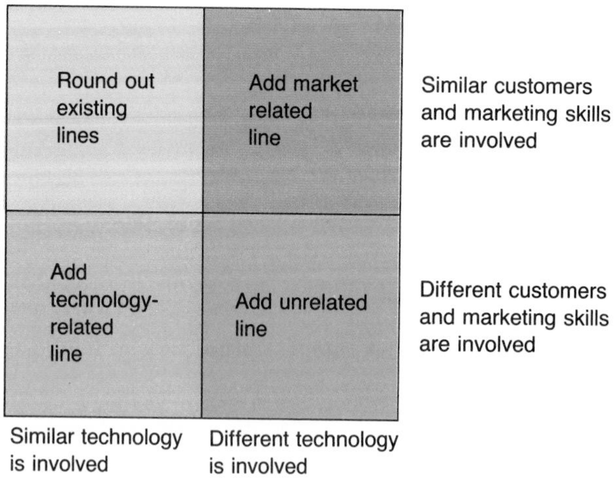

	Similar technology is involved	Different technology is involved
Similar customers and marketing skills are involved	Round out existing lines	Add market related line
Different customers and marketing skills are involved	Add technology-related line	Add unrelated line

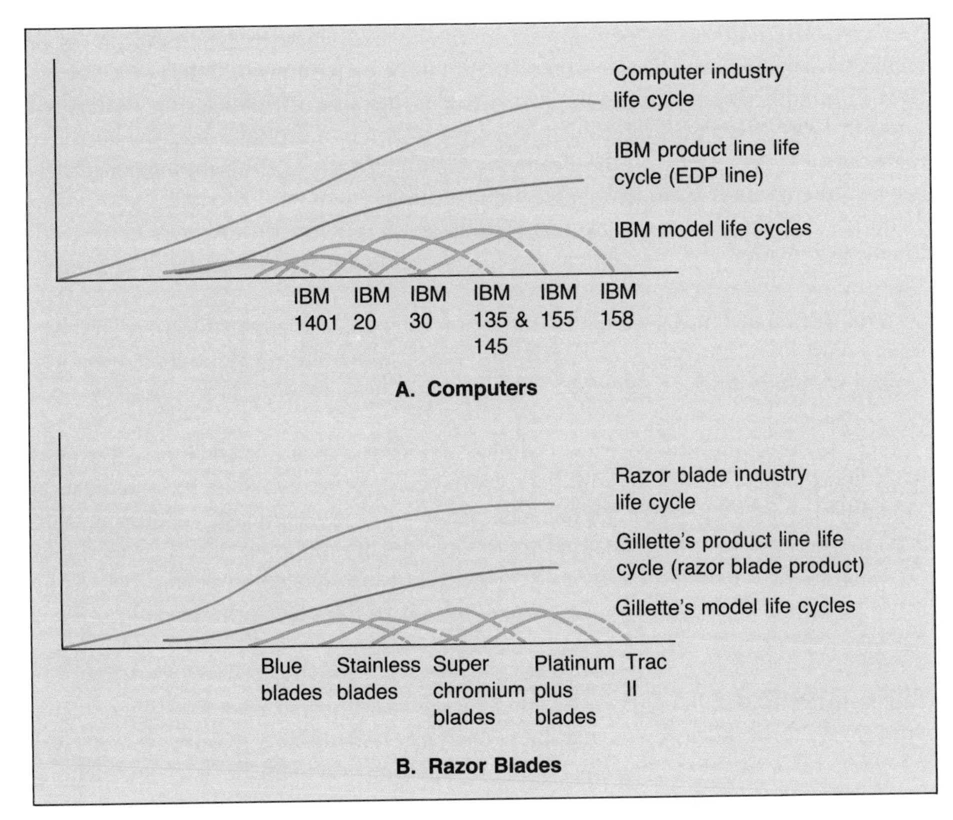

Figure 10.2
Product Modification and the Product Life Cycle (SOURCE: Adapted from John A. Weber, *Growth Opportunity Analysis* (Reston, Va.: Reston Publishing Co., 1976): 227.)

expertise because the products are similar, keeping down the associated development costs.

Success in filling out a line depends largely on how divergent are the needs of various segments, as well as what size they are. Companies seeking to attract the patronage of many segments adopt a *full-line* strategy. Maxwell House, for instance, markets a full line of coffee drinks, including Mellow Roast—a lost-cost coffee and grain beverage.

On the other hand, smaller firms are often forced to adopt a *limited-line* strategy and target one or several segments that industry leaders have bypassed. Some coffee service firms provide their own blends of coffee to offices located in major cities. While their coffees are typically unavailable to the general public, these firms seek their niches in segments bypassed by large competitors.

Creating New Lines

The **breadth** of a product mix refers to the number of lines a firm offers. To illustrate, general hospitals typically have six or more lines of service, including maternity, surgery, extended care, cardiac treatment, outpatient care, and emergency treatment.

Breadth (product mix)
The number of product lines offered by a firm.

The second new product alternative is the creation of new lines to fill a contribution gap. By so doing, a company is able to expand its potential opportunity by channeling a portion of its efforts into new types of products and new markets. There are three possible expansion strategies that a firm can take: adding market-related lines, adding technologically related lines, or introducing unrelated lines.

Market-Related Lines A new line is market-related when its target customers or required marketing activities are very similar to those of existing customers or activities. Bacardi Imports, Inc., for example, introduced its first line of products outside distilled spirits in 1986—Bacardi Tropical Fruit Mixers, frozen nonalcoholic drinks. This move was designed to capitalize on the strong association already existing among consumers between the name Bacardi (rum) and tropical drinks, such as piña coladas and frozen daiquiris. The new product line was introduced as a joint venture with Coca-Cola Foods, Inc., which had experience with frozen drinks due to ownership of the Minute Maid brand.[5]

Complementary products
Two or more products whose use is strongly related, such as hamburgers and buns.

A market-related line is often a substitute for other items in an organization's product mix. To illustrate, Dairy Queen added Slim Stuff, a line of low-calorie frozen yogurts. **Complementary** items are also possible, however; Kodak, for instance, markets both cameras and film.

Next to rounding out an existing line, adding a market-related line is the most likely new product strategy to result in positive synergy, since it enables the organization to capitalize on its marketing expertise.[6] After gaining experience in dealing with certain types of customers, channel members, and promotional efforts, a company management team is better able to exert its expertise in related areas. Further, if the new line fails, it may not damage the reputations of the older lines because of their separate identities.

Technologically Related Lines Another means of achieving favorable synergy is to expand into technologically related lines. As a result of engaging in ongoing technical activities, managers and operatives develop expertise in certain fields of production, research and development, financial planning, and organizational skills. This knowledge may provide the necessary differential advantage for expanding into technically related fields.

For example, before the turn of the century the Coors brewery was forced to make its own porcelain products required for brewing beer. The firm was isolated near the mining camp of Denver; wagon-delivered imported German porcelain fixtures were broken in transit and hence almost impossible to obtain. Out of necessity the company became skilled at making its own porcelain—so skilled that today it is one of the finest industrial porcelain manufacturers in the U.S.

While expanding into technologically related lines can be synergistic, many production-oriented managers neglect one important element: assessing market opportunity.[7] A company may have a production-related competitive advantage only because the potential market for an offering is so small that other firms are not willing to enter. Management should consider any new product strategy only if it offers sufficient profit opportunity to warrant incurring the inherent risks and the company has both the marketing and production skills required for successful introduction.

Unrelated Lines A third possible strategy for broadening a product mix is to expand into unrelated lines, sometimes termed *special situations*. As Figure 10.1 indicates, unrelated lines are those that are neither market- nor technologically related to a firm's existing lines.

Some organizations regularly pursue special situation strategies; some job-shop manufacturers go after virtually any type of business they can get. Other companies expand into unrelated lines when competition becomes too fierce or demand declines in established industries.

Expanding into market-related lines can be a good new product development strategy.

Adding an unrelated product line is the strategy least likely to succeed because a company can neither capitalize on its marketing ability nor its technological experience. The Boeing Company, for instance, once built streetcars for Boston's Massachusetts Bay Transportation Authority. In 1977, four years after the company secured the contract, the enterprise had delivered only 32 of the 175 cars ordered, and only 16 of the 32 ran. A well-known transportation consultant summarized the situation by stating that "every time an American aerospace company has gotten into surface transportation, the result was a financial disaster. It's apparent that technological solutions and markets in surface transportation are far different." [8]

Thus, management should usually consider expanding into unrelated lines only as a last resort. In most instances, it makes far better sense to engage first in market expansion, then move on to some related line (depending on the market opportunity and the firm's competitive advantage), and then start another round of market expansion.

Cannibalization and Trading Up

Cannibalization
One company product that takes sales away from another, more profitable, product in a line.

Any type of expansion through new product introduction can do more damage than good, even if the offerings are, by themselves, very successful. If a new product contributes less to the company's objectives than those it displaces and if it caters to essentially the same target, the result may be **cannibalization.** Cannibalization takes place when more profitable items do not sell in sufficient volume because consumers purchase a new but less profitable product.

Successful new product strategy is often a function of obtaining *conquest* sales—those taken away from competitors' products. The Almay Company did just that in the early 1980s with the introduction of Colorplus lipstick, aimed at consumers aged 16–34. Cannibalization did not occur because this age group was younger than the typical Almay user.

Trading up
Developing substitute products that are more desirable and profitable than others in a line, and convincing customers that they should purchase the more profitable ones.

However, successful new product strategy does not always require conquest sales. Instead, the firm can **trade up** customers to an item yielding a greater contribution. Trading up involves developing additional products that are slightly more desirable to buyers (and also more profitable to the company) and then convincing consumers that they should purchase the more profitable ones. For example, Sears offers several models of most major appliance lines such as washers. Each successive model has additional features and is accompanied by a price increment of perhaps $30 to $50. Because Sears' cost for an added feature is usually nominal, margins are larger for the more expensive models. In a similar fashion, General Electric has been able to trade consumers up (particularly young adults) to digital-control appliances (refrigerators, ranges, and dishwashers) without eroding sales and profits.[9]

Bait-and-switch
Advertising a low-priced item, then exerting undue pressure on customers to buy a more expensive one. This is an illegal practice.

Management must exercise caution when attempting to trade up customers. Sears, for instance, once promoted bottom-of-the-line appliances at prices near company cost as a means of generating store traffic. Then the sales force would exert undue pressure on consumers to buy more expensive models. If the company exerts too much pressure to trade up or if low-priced items are unreasonably shoddy or purposefully made unavailable, the practice is termed **bait-and-switch,** which is illegal. In 1976, the Federal Trade Commission ruled that Sears exerted too much pressure and was guilty of practicing bait-and-switch. Accordingly, the commission issued a restraining order against these acts.[10]

New Product Development

Figure 10.3 presents an overview of the new product development process. Management must carefully coordinate the entire process with the intended strategy to ensure a high probability of success.[11] Further, secrecy is of paramount importance in the process, as illustrated by the Schechter Group's development of New Coke's package, because leaks can give competitors the upper hand.

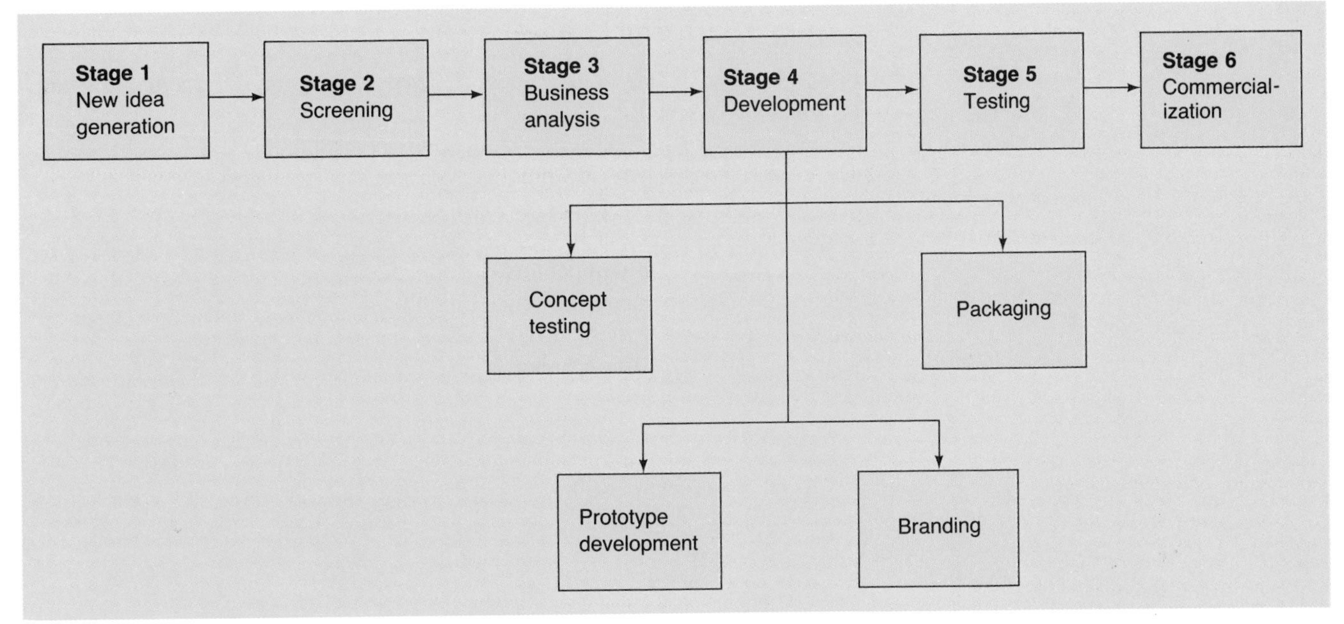

Figure 10.3
Overview of the New Product Development Process

MARKETING BRIEF

New Coke Packaging Developed Under a Veil of Secrecy

The Schechter Group, Coca-Cola's packaging design firm, went to extreme lengths to prevent premature leaking of the New Coke introduction in 1985. Security measures more appropriate for the MX missile project than a soft drink were instituted.

The firm was involved in a ten-day round-the-clock marathon to design the perfect package, characterized by private meetings, isolation, and utter secrecy. Only the president and a few of his directors were privy to the reformulation of Coca-Cola. The designers involved in the project were segregated from the rest of the staff, sometimes behind locked doors, and were told only that Coke was to get an updated package as part of its centennial celebration.

It might appear that these cloak-and-dagger tactics were excessive, but the secrecy was essential. Even some Coca-Cola directors (and the bottlers) had not been consulted about the plan to change Coke's formula. A press leak could have wiped out the whole project.

The Schechter Group carried out its task successfully—word did not leak out to the press, competitors, bottlers, or even Coca-Cola's own directors. The firm had managed to keep a very important trade secret confidential.

SOURCE: Adapted from Lynn G. Reiling, "New Coke Packaging Designed in Secret Marathon," *Marketing News* 19, no. 21 (October 11, 1985): 1.

New Product Development Stages

This section considers each of the steps involved in new product generation and discusses how to avoid failure.

New Idea Generation There are many sources of new product ideas. Monitoring technological breakthroughs; brainstorming; eliciting concepts from company R & D specialists, customers, sales personnel, channel members, and other company employees; and even spying on competitors can provide ideas for new products.

In the idea generation stage, the objective should be to produce a large number of new ideas but not to test them. Management can screen out poor ideas at a later time. Generally, the larger the number of new ideas, the greater is the likelihood of finding a good one.[12]

Product Development (a newsletter for R & D executives) obtained survey responses from 52 percent of its 600 subscribers as to what products they felt could be expected to emerge in the future. The results appear in Table 10.1. Note that the respondents were fairly optimistic about very innovative products and services appearing during the next hundred years.

Table 10.1 New Products or Services That May Be Available in Future Years

Product or Service	Percentages of Respondents				
	5 Years	*10 Years*	*25 Years*	*100 Years*	*Beyond that*
1. Artificial human organs, excluding the brain	35	43	21	0	0
2. A car-less means of transportation, perhaps an individual flying machine	0	13	63	22	0
3. A drug that will cure or prevent cancer	31	26	22	13	8
4. A drug that will cure or prevent the common cold	39	21	20	6	7
5. A personal telephone, no larger than a cigarette pack, that can be used from any location	43	45	12	0	0
6. In-home/in-office receipt of routine mail and publications via wire or radio transmission	30	48	13	8	0
7. A vehicle that will run for a year on atomic power at a cost of 10¢ per mile or less	0	4	61	26	8
8. Solar and/or wind power will completely replace oil as a major energy factor	0	0	48	35	17
9. Health technology that will extend the average lifespan to 100 years	0	8	43	22	26
10. All materials used around humans will be fireproof	0	13	22	35	30
11. Manufacturing will be 90 percent automated	0	9	30	43	16
12. A pocket-sized personal/business computer that will answer all questions put to it	4	30	39	13	14
13. Clothing that can be cleaned by placing it in a cleaning chamber for a few minutes	13	39	35	8	5
14. A synthetic material that will replace wood	22	43	17	13	5

SOURCE: "Survey of New Product Developers Offers 25-year Innovation Forecast," *Marketing News* 15, no. 5 (September 4, 1981): 4.

Exhibit 10.1
Checklist for Product Screening

Product Characteristic	Rating				
	Excellent	Good	Fair	Poor	Very Poor
1. Differential advantages over rivals	___	___	___	___	___
2. Consumer need fulfillment	___	___	___	___	___
3. Can be produced economically	___	___	___	___	___
4. Can be marketed economically	___	___	___	___	___
5. Compatible with company image	___	___	___	___	___
6. Company personnel have the expertise to produce and sell it	___	___	___	___	___
7. Company personnel have the time needed to produce and sell it	___	___	___	___	___
8. Will not consume excessive funds	___	___	___	___	___

They were also relatively accurate in looking five years into the future—a period which has since passed. The artificial heart has already been tested, a number of drugs have been marketed that can arrest the spread of certain cancers, personal telephones (though larger than a cigarette pack) are now available for remote use, and many substitutes for wood have been used in many applications.

Screening The first critical test of an idea's merit occurs at the **screening** stage. Like separating the wheat from the chaff, screening involves separating new product ideas into those worthy of further consideration and those warranting immediate rejection. The concept of synergy is useful for making such distinctions; those ideas that do not fit in with the firm's strengths and experience from both market and internal capability perspectives are logical candidates for rejection.[13]

Screening
Separating new ideas into those that warrant further consideration and those that deserve immediate rejection.

Some managers use checklists for screening.[14] These embody a listing of various desired product attributes and a scale for assessing each product idea on each attribute. Exhibit 10.1 shows one such checklist.

Business Analysis The third stage, **business analysis,** involves estimating the magnitude of market opportunity for a new idea, the competitive situation, potential sales, costs, investment requirements, and rate of return. This phase, then, utilizes financial data in great quantity.

Business analysis
Estimating the magnitude of market opportunity for a new idea, the competitive situation, potential sales, costs, investment requirements, and rate of return.

Knowledge of the adoption process can help in estimating potential sales and marketing costs, and sometimes in predicting how rapidly competitors will enter the market. The speed at which a new consumer product is adopted is a function of five variables.[15] Exhibit 10.2 outlines these.

Various techniques exist for carrying out the calculations required in business analysis. These include net present value analysis, break-even analysis, and Bayesian decision theory.[16] But the primary test is whether or not a new idea is likely to contribute above an acceptable minimum to narrowing a contribution gap.[17]

Development (new product)
Engaging in concept testing, prototype construction, branding decisions, and packaging decisions.

Development The fourth stage, **development,** is possibly the most critical because it usually involves substantial investment. Further, this is where management learns whether or not it can turn an idea into a technical reality. There are four phases of

Exhibit 10.2
Variables Influencing Product Introduction Speed

1. *Relative advantage.* Customers adopt new ideas that will clearly lead to better achievement of their needs at a faster rate than those having only a minor advantage.
2. *Compatibility.* Customers adopt products that are compatible with their cognitive sets more rapidly than widely divergent products. Some managers, for instance, do not comprehend computer fundamentals and feel computers pose a threat to their job security. Because of this cognitive conflict, some managers resist computerized information systems.
3. *Complexity.* Customers are slower to adopt new ideas that are very complex and difficult to use than relatively simple ones. It took many years for computers to begin their boom. Likewise, large numbers of customers are slow to accept new types of insurance.
4. *Divisibility.* Customers readily adopt items they can use on a limited basis, such as where they can purchase a small quantity rather than making a major commitment. For example, allowing customers to buy single cans of a new soft drink should result in more rapid adoption than if only 24-container cases are sold.
5. *Communicability.* Product innovations that are highly visible or that become subjects of conversations are adopted more rapidly than low-key products. For example, women adopt certain personal hygiene products at slow rates because of the social stigma attached to discussing them with friends.

the development stage: concept testing, prototype development, branding decisions, and packaging decisions.

Concept testing
Assessing potential buyer reactions to a new product idea beginning in the early stages of idea development.

Concept Testing **Concept testing** assesses potential buyer reaction to an idea.[18] It usually involves working with a panel of customers who are representative of an intended target. Typically, concept testing begins by verbally (or in writing) describing a product concept. For example:

> It is a lightweight, four-person tent somewhat similar to a pup tent but larger. It is made of nylon fabric colored international orange and includes a detachable rainfly. Construction is fairly simple, with two collapsible shock-corded aluminum poles and eight tiedown cords. It can be used by backpackers, and, when folded, it fills approximately two-thirds of a standard size mountain backpack. Its total weight, with poles and stakes, is roughly four pounds (see the enclosed sketch).

Panel members are then asked questions about the overall concept and its attributes.[19]

1. Are the potential uses for this tent understandable? What are they?
2. Does the product have favorable features compared to pup tents? Cabin tents? What are they?
3. Would you be interested in buying this product? Why or why not?
4. What are your needs for tents? For this particular type of tent?
5. What improvements or additional attributes do you think are necessary?

Britannica Collins used concept testing to develop a mail-order product for helping workshop hobbyists.[20] Working with a panel, management was able to determine the kinds of information do-it-yourselfers needed and the most convenient means of information access and storage. The result was Britannica's Fix-It-Fast card reference files, which it successfully sold by direct mail.

Prototype
A model of a new product, used in testing, that exhibits the features of the version that will later be produced in quantity.

Prototype Development Once a concept is clearly defined, the next step is to build a **prototype:** one or a few units of an actual product, created to be used and tested. In many cases a prototype is a skeletal product, not a working model, showing the

Solid product strategy takes into account market segment differences.

essential distinguishing features of the new offering. In the appliance industry, for example, companies produce tools and dies to build a prototype. They hand-make many assemblies and, since they have not yet acquired production experience, unit production costs may be very high.

A frequent danger in developing a prototype is that engineers and other technicians may attempt to incorporate their own personal preferences into a product. For example, a West Coast food processor embarked on a program designed to develop an improved frozen french-fried potato. Researchers using concept testing found that most consumers preferred french fries about four inches long. A technician, however, developed various items that were about three inches in length because he liked shorter fries. Obviously, management must insist that consumer preferences be adhered to in the absence of contradictory marketing research.

MARKETING BRIEF
Fighting Off Competition in the Cookie Market

Procter & Gamble (P & G) made an error in moving into the ready-to-eat cookie market with a product that now has no real advantages over rival offerings. The firm entered the market with an item based on new technology, namely a cookie that was soft on the inside and crunchy on the outside. This would appear to be a major advantage, but Nabisco and Keebler came up with the same type of cookie even before P & G's market testing period was over. This left P & G with a "me-too" product.

In the cookie market, firms can easily copy new innovations; the manufacturing process is such that rapid emulation is possible. This happened to P & G—competitors quickly duplicated the firm's cookies. Management was not aware that competitors were about to enter the market, so the firm was not ready to fend off competitive inroads.

The outcome of the cookie introduction was that P & G received much lower sales and share of market from its new cookies than management had expected. This turned out to be just another phase of the "cookie wars"—intense competition that has characterized the industry in recent periods.

SOURCE: Adapted from Nancy Giges and Laurie Freeman, "Wounded Lion?" *Advertising Age* 56, no. 58 (July 29, 1985): 1, 51.

Branding and Packaging Development The third phase of development involves making choices on branding and packaging alternatives. Because branding and pack aging can be just as important as the development of the physical product, these topics are examined in depth later in this chapter.

Testing (product)
Assessing an actual prototype, along with its planned package and brand.

Testing In the fifth stage of new product development, **testing,** the company assesses an actual prototype along with its planned package and brand. Management may use several types of testing. Durability tests, such as driving new cars on test tracks, are important to assure that the product meets acceptable performance standards. Safety tests are also important, such as those revealing whether product use and packaging can result in personal injury. The marketability of the item might also be tested. This may involve test marketing, panels or other kinds of surveys, or possibly introducing the product on a limited basis but with greater effort than for test marketing.[21]

To illustrate, Church & Dwight Co., makers of Arm & Hammer, successfully conducted market tests for Dental Care, a plaque-fighting tooth powder in 1984 in Madison, Wisconsin prior to the brand's national introduction. While Dental Care could cut into Arm & Hammer sales (some people use that product as a dental powder), management was not too concerned because it would amount to trading up customers and felt that baking soda sales were flat anyway.[22] Whenever testing is used, though, management must be cautious about revealing its hand to competitors. To illustrate, Procter & Gamble showed its cards to competitors when it market tested soft-on-the-inside, crunchy-on-the-outside cookies in 1985. Before the tests were completed, both Nabisco and Keebler had beaten P & G to the market with their own brands.

Commercialization
The stage where a new item is actually introduced to the market.

Commercialization If all previous stages show positive results in terms of enabling a firm to close its contribution gap, the **commercialization** stage begins. In this stage the company actually introduces the new item to the market. Accordingly, product introduction should be timed to coincide with the period when a contribution gap is expected to materialize. Planning techniques such as the Program Evaluation and Review Technique (PERT) or the Critical Path Method (CPM) are both useful in attaining the necessary activity coordination.[23]

Branding and Packaging

The physical development of a product does not complete a marketer's retinue of important product decisions. Selecting an item's name and its package can be equally important to the success of a new offering.

Branding Decisions Appropriately naming products can be critical to their success. Brand names such as Clairol, White (trucks), Pinkerton (Security Systems and private investigators), and Comtrex are valuable property.[24] They are so valuable that some unethical managers produce counterfeit products, such as when a rival of Jordache jeans breaks the law and places the Jordache label on its products. The process of naming and otherwise designating products is termed **branding.**

Branding
Giving a unique name to a particular product or class of products offered by a firm.

Technically, there are several major aspects of a brand, as follows:[25]

- *Brand.* A brand is a name, term, symbol, design, or some combination of them intended to identify the goods and services of one seller or group of sellers and to distinguish or differentiate them from those of competitors.
- *Brand name.* This is a more limited concept. It refers to words, or that part of a brand that can be vocalized or spoken. Coke, G.E., Maybelline, and Old Spice are four of the many products having familiar brand names.
- *Brand mark.* This is the part of a brand that can be recognized, but cannot be verbalized. Examples include distinctive shapes (e.g., McDonald's golden arches) and colors or lettering (e.g., a publisher's symbol on the spine of a book).
- *Trademark.* A brand or part of a brand that is granted legal protection, giving the holder exclusive rights to use the brand name or mark. The first user of a mark or name may register it with the U.S. Patent Office for 20 years with renewable rights.[26]

CONCEPT SUMMARY *New Product Development Stages*

Stage	Description
New Idea Generation	Developing ideas for new products.
Screening	Separating new ideas into two groups: those warranting further consideration and those deserving immediate rejection.
Business Analysis	Estimating the magnitude of market opportunity for a new idea, the competitive situation, potential sales, costs, investment requirements, and rate of return.
Development	Concept testing, prototype development, branding decisions, and packaging decisions.
Testing	An actual prototype along with its planned package and brand are assessed. May include safety, durability, and marketability tests.
Commercialization	A new offering is actually introduced to the market.

Coca-Cola's bottle has evolved into Coke's distinctive mark.

However, to ensure that its rights are not lost, a company must protect itself by identifying a trademark as such on all advertising, labels, and wherever else it may appear.[27]

Why Brand Some Items and Not Others? A fundamental decision is whether or not an organization should brand an item. In general, branding helps in establishing a total product's distinctive identity. Firms cannot effectively differentiate their products unless potential buyers are able to distinguish between items within a generic product class.

Because of brands, buyers are able to discriminate among the products of different companies, enabling them to select the particular item offering the greatest promise of satisfying their unique needs. Branding, however, is not always desirable for the firm. If it cannot maintain quality, for instance, a brand can signal to buyers that a particular item should be avoided in the future.

Exhibit 10.3 presents the major reasons for and against branding, along with a brief discussion of each. Determining whether or not a particular company should brand an item, of course, depends upon the situation.

Brand Strategies Once a manager decides that branding is desirable, the next decision is to select the most appropriate strategy. Figure 10.4 illustrates the four major possibilities.

The mid-1970s witnessed the appearance of a trend that was to gain momentum in the early 1980s: generic brands. (Generic brands do not have a brand name. The package merely identifies the product and the marketer.) Many consumers found that they could buy generic packaged and canned groceries, paper products, and even

Exhibit 10.3
Reasons For and Against Branding Products

	Reasons For Branding
1. Identification	Branding can help to establish an item's identity. A brand enables buyers to form attitudes about an item, which simplifies shopping. To illustrate, many experts argue that Idaho potatoes are no different than other Russet Burbank potatoes grown elsewhere, yet many potato lovers are willing to pay a premium price for them. With a brand, promotional efforts may be geared around developing selective demand ("Eat Idaho Potatoes") versus primary demand ("Eat Potatoes"). Brands also help to identify items in storing and shipping.
2. Quality	Branding serves to indicate a consistent level of quality. Bausch & Lomb binoculars, for example, are recognizable as being of good quality because of their brand. Even lower-quality, lower-priced items may be identified, such as Motel 6 and Budget Inns. The point is that knowledge of a brand suggests a level of quality to buyers, which may then be evaluated against needs to simplify purchasing.
3. Legal protection	Branding enables marketers to protect unique features of products. Protection allows an investment in marketing efforts to stimulate selective demand and gain market share. Loyalty to a brand may result from satisfactory experience and familiarity with an item.

	Reasons to Avoid Branding
1. Inability to Identify	Only items which can be identified in some real or psychological way from others in their generic class should be branded. Some marketers go to great lengths to brand items, such as Sunkist (stamping a brand on fruit) and meat packers (placing a brand inside a wrapper). But if a brand cannot be identified or if an item cannot be distinguished from substitutes, other marketing actions are likely to be more effective in stimulating demand. For example, lower prices or expanded distribution could be more effective than branding for items such as top soil, copper, fish, and so forth.
2. Inability to Maintain Quality	Inconsistent quality can ruin a brand. If quality control steps cannot weed out poor items, branding only serves to mark items that buyers seek to avoid in the future. Assuring consistent quality with some items such as produce can be almost impossible.
3. Nonexistent or very small market segments	Branding serves as a means of differentiating one item from others, which implies that it is a means of targeting on segments of needs. However, if segments of needs are nonexistent or if existing segments are too small to warrant segmentation efforts, branding is not likely to be justifiable from a cost-efficiency perspective. Branding should only be considered when stimulating selective demand is desirable.
4. Irregular availability	If a customer begins to use a brand, it should be regularly available for future use. Its absence only serves to negate past efforts. Branding should be avoided if a marketer cannot assure a steady supply.

cigarettes at lower prices than if they bought branded items. Generic brands, of course, directly compete against branded items.[28]

Individual Brands **Individual brands** (such as General Mill's Bacos), which are unique names given to individual items, have two distinct advantages. First, a firm does not tie its image to the success or failure of a single item. Second, a firm can introduce a lower-prestige item without harming the image of existing successful products.

Individual brands
Unique names given to individual items.

There are two major individual brand strategies. The first is to use a completely separate brand for each distinct offering. Lorillard is one of many companies that use such a scheme, termed a *multibrand strategy* (e.g., Virginia Slims, Old Gold, and

Figure 10.4
Classes of Brand Strategy

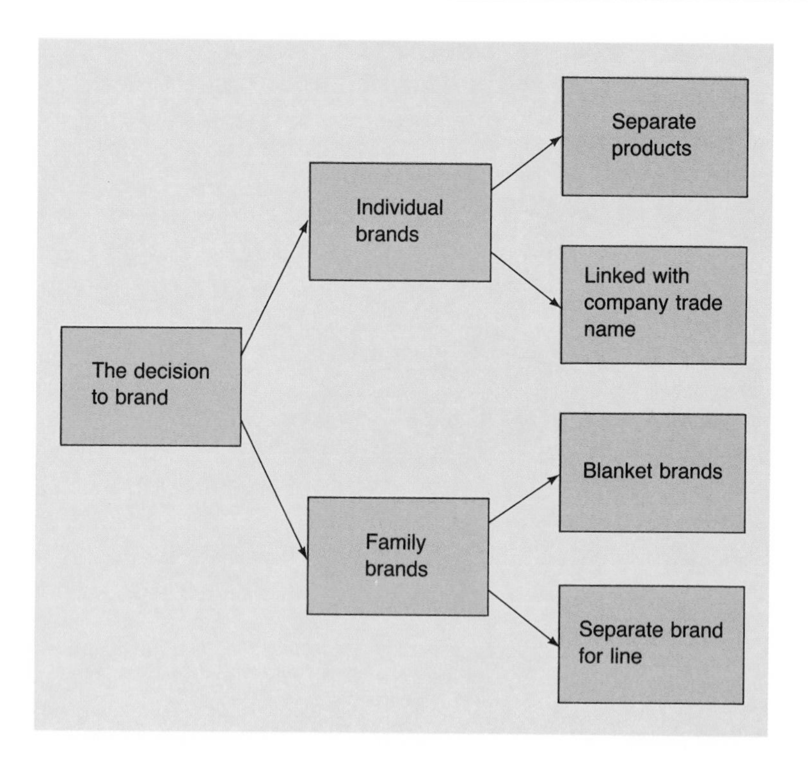

Procter & Gamble has chosen a strategy of using individual brands for its products.

Kent). This makes sense when the firm is appealing to completely different segments with different items. Also, offering separate brands can help a company capture a greater share of a market.

However, offering separate brands can present some major difficulties. This arrangement may require large separate promotional budgets since promotion efforts are independent and not combined, and a new brand name does not benefit from the "halo effect" (acquiring an identity from a familiar name).

The second individual brand strategy is for management to link a new product's identification with the company's name, even though it still employs individual brands. Kodak disc cameras and Kodachrome film are illustrative. This strategy makes sense when a company has an established and favorable reputation in a generic product area. The firm thus is able to take advantage of the positive halo effect but can still retain enough separate identity to appeal to individualized market segments.

Family Brands A **family brand** exists when more than one of a firm's products have the same name. Examples are Fisher-Price toys and Wish Bone salad dressings. There are two fundamental advantages to a family brand strategy. First, it aims directly at capitalizing on the halo effect, which often helps in promoting initial sales for new products. Second, the costs associated with introducing a new product are generally lower than for individual brands. The firm need not spend sizeable funds for creating brand recognition with this strategy.

There are two general types of family brand strategies. The first is to use a ***blanket brand***—a common name for all of a company's offerings. General Electric, for instance, applies the G.E. brand to every one of its products, from multimillion dollar turbine generators to 29-cent light bulbs. A blanket brand can be very functional due to the halo effect, but each item carrying the brand should be of comparable quality, as inferior goods may impair the reputation of other offerings.

The second strategy is to use a different brand for each line of products in order to maintain a separate identity. Swift, for instance, produces both packaged meats for human consumption (Premium brand) and a line of fertilizers (Vigoro). Naturally, a separate identity is desirable for each line.

Family brands
Where more than one of a firm's products have the same name.

Naming Brands The naming of brands is an important function not to be taken lightly. Ford Motor Company management considered nearly two thousand names, for instance, for the firm's new car introduced in 1957. Several research firms surveyed numerous consumers in various parts of the country. The researchers asked the respondents what the various proposed brand names meant to them. Management eventually selected "Edsel," in honor of Henry Ford's only son, despite the fact that consumers felt this name had negative associations, including "pretzel," "diesel," and "hard sell." [29]

Marketing research firms use elaborate procedures to test proposed names, including brainstorming, free-association tests, learning and pronunciation tests, and memory tests. [30] Although the name Edsel was not the only reason for the Ford offering's well-publicized failure, the example illustrates the impact of making an error in this field. Exhibit 10.4 presents four characteristics of good brand names that can be used as guidelines to avoiding similar failures.

The fourth characteristic listed in the exhibit, "should be legally protectable," needs elaboration. [31] Historically, companies have lost successful brand names to generic usage. For example shredded wheat, cellophane, linoleum, and aspirin were once protected brand names belonging to individual firms and not available to others. But that protection was lost ironically due to marketing success: over a period of time buyers commonly used the names as being synonymous with generic classes. More recently, a U.S. Appeals Court ruled that Miller could not retain sole use of the word "Light" despite the fact that the firm registered the name, as "Light" has become a generic word for low-calorie beer. [32]

To guard against losing a protected brand to generic use, many firms such as Eastman-Kodak link their company name with popular brands. In addition, they purposefully use the symbol "R" with all printed material to show a trademark is registered, such as Cheerios®.

Exhibit 10.4
Four Characteristics of a Good Brand Name

1. *It suggests the desired image.* Frigidaire refrigerators, Bisquick baking mix, Spic and Span, Mr. Coffee, and Mustang fulfill this criterion.
2. *It is easily recognized, with simple pronunciation and memorability.* The pronunciation of "Audi" presents problems to many English-speaking people. Is it *Awdee?* Or *Owdi?* This is a particular problem in international markets, but can also be important domestically. Some easy-to-recognize brand names are Karo Syrup, Golf (Volkswagen auto) and Centurion bicycles.
3. *It is relatively short and inoffensive.* Management chose Exxon, for example, for many reasons when changing the firm's name from Enco. One reason was that in Japanese, Enco means "stalled car." Other examples are Ragu Spaghetti Sauce and Eve cigarettes.
4. *It should be legally protectable.* The Lanham Act (1946) states that a firm cannot protect a name that is the generic word for a type of product. Bobbie Brooks, to illustrate, could not protect "sportswear" as its own brand name.

Jewel is one company that has developed its own set of branded products.

Who Brands? In a sense, producers have the ultimate authority as to whether or not a specific product is to be branded. This is because they have the final say as to whether or not they will manufacture the product. However, this position is quite misleading. In fact, both manufacturers and intermediaries engage in branding.

Manufacturer Brands Manufacturer brands are those owned by the producer of the goods. Historically, manufacturers have dominated branding. Today, many companies such as IBM, General Foods, and Kohler (plumbing fixtures) continue to produce practically all of their output under their own names.

Manufacturer brands offer various advantages. For producers, they allow the opportunity to closely control all aspects of a marketing effort, including advertising campaigns, packaging, and transportation. Also, producers can pull offerings through nonaggressive and ineffective dealers by building final customer demand with promotion. Manufacturer brands can also offer advantages to intermediaries. If the producer has heavily promoted an item, demand may be established and lower inventories may be possible.

Distributor Brands Over time, more intermediaries are engaging in branding their own products.[33] Nearly 90 percent of the items Sears sells, for example, carry the firm's own labels. Practically all retail chains now brand at least some of their products, and many wholesalers also carry their own brands.

There are some advantages to distributor brands, mainly that managing the brand is placed nearer final customers, meaning that needed changes caused by market trends and pressures can be more readily implemented. There are fewer channel layers to go through. To illustrate, Sears often works through its own design studios (company-owned and contracted) to develop products to meet market needs. This enables the retailer to develop new designs faster than if it were to depend upon manufacturers to do the job. It also frees manufacturers to pay exclusive attention to production. Further, producers sometimes are able to sell surplus inventory under a distributor's brand.

However, branding by distributors can cause conflict within channel systems. Manufacturers lose an element of control over their destinies in the process, and manufacturers frequently have more at stake in the success of a given item since intermediaries can readily handle some other product if one fails. Manufacturers cannot so easily convert their facilities.

The "Battle of the Brands" The conflict between manufacturers and intermediaries for the control of brands is sometimes called "the battle of the brands." Some intermediaries, especially large retail chains, attempt to displace producers from their historically dominant role of control over branding decisions. Intermediaries have various weapons to deploy in this war. Many consumers feel confident in buying distributor brands because they know that intermediaries usually take special care in assuring consistent quality. Further, many intermediaries pay particular attention to the promotion of their own brands and often give them premium shelf locations. In addition, retailers sell many products at low prices because they have not invested large sums in advertising.

The upshot is that producers may be forced into accepting distributor branding. Distributors may exert pressures on manufacturers to divert advertising budgets toward higher trade allowances, improving quality, extended credit, and other actions in return for allowing desirable shelf space. Once the process begins, manufacturers have fewer funds available for promotion, and their brand images may decline accordingly.[34]

To illustrate, Koepplinger's Bread Co., a Midwestern producer of premium breads, refused to cave in to such pressures. Retailers cut shelf space allocated to the company to about half and sales fell proportionately.[35] A producer facing such a dilemma has three options available:

1. Succumb to the pressures, temporarily easing the condition, and live in fear of another round of pressure at some future date. Warwick Electronics, for example, sells its entire output under distributor brands.
2. Sell only a portion of its output under this arrangement, but maintain a separate channel for its own brands. For instance, Whirlpool produces appliances under both its own name and under the Sears Kenmore brand.
3. Intensify the marketing of its own brands to stimulate final customer demand, which can alleviate the distributor pressures. Management of Koepplinger's, for example, more than doubled its advertising budget, and developed "Sunny Honey," a new high-fiber bread, which it promoted heavily. Because the company appreciably stimulated consumer demand, retailers eventually returned lost shelf space.

Measuring Brand Acceptance Consumers generally develop a set of brands from which they make selections when they buy a generic class of product. This set, which is a subset of all brands available, is sometimes called the **evoked set,** meaning the set of brands considered when making a decision. For instance, one man might generally choose from Brut, English Leather, and British Sterling when purchasing an aftershave, and not consider other brands. Collectively, this concept implies the degree of brand acceptance that the market affords a given product. There are four stages of brand acceptance:

Evoked set (of brands)
A subset of brands within an overall set of a generic product class that buyers choose when making a related product buying decision.

1. *Brand unfamiliarity*. Most members of the target are unaware of a product's existence.
2. *Brand recognition*. Most members of a target are cognizant of a brand.
3. *Brand preference*. Most potential buyers favor a particular brand.
4. *Brand insistence*. The objective of all marketers. Most of a target will search for and accept only a particular brand.

Research can assist managers in determining a brand's degree of acceptance. In turn, this knowledge helps to develop appropriate strategy. To illustrate, if most potential customers are unfamiliar with the brand, a strong promotional effort is probably needed to create recognition. On the other hand, if numerous customers recognize the brand but few prefer it, some type of repositioning might be in order. Perhaps certain physical attributes such as style or quality need modification. Reminding consumers about the offering and taking steps to ensure that it is readily available in distribution outlets are often keys to success when brand preference exists. Finally, a strong distribution system and an emphasis on consistent quality are necessary to maintain brand insistence.

Packaging Decisions Developing a good physical product and brand name are necessary steps in generating a strong product mix, but these do not constitute the whole of product decision making. Marketers must also pay close attention to packaging. Packaging costs for foods and beverages average about one-third of the value of the goods they protect.[36] *The Modern Packaging Encyclopedia and Planning Guide* indicates that firms spend over $40 billion annually in the United States on packaging materials, and these expenditures are advancing rapidly.

Packaging Functions Packages can perform a number of functions. "Packaging is more than just the container. It is a system in which the product is the focal point." [37] In other words, the package can help cultivate a product's worth to buyers. Exhibit 10.5 presents eight possible package-related functions by which management may accomplish this.

There are a number of specialized packaging companies that aid producers. These specialists are of value when the producer needs a new package for a test market. Also, specialists can package seasonal products, eliminating the necessity for manufacturers to contend with idle packaging equipment during the off-season. Finally, if a new product is successful, the specialists can aid the marketer in jumping into the national market with new packages before rivals do.[38]

Each of the eight packaging functions is not equally important for all products. Some products such as tent stakes, need little protection, while others, such as personal computer diskettes, are very delicate. Borden, Inc. was the first major U.S. food producer to utilize aseptic packaging, which removes all contamination through sterilization and allows fruit juices to be stored without refrigeration.

Cost considerations are important in packaging decisions. Generally, the greater the extent to which the firm attempts to provide for each of the functions, the larger the total packaging cost. Additional costs constitute waste unless they are associated with a necessary function.

In summary, the most appropriate mix of functions for a package is dependent on the nature of the product, the needs of the intended market, and cost factors.

Organization for New Product Development

There are four ways to organize a firm to accomplish new product development efficiently: product managers, new product staffs, new product committees, and new product teams.[39]

Product managers, also called brand managers, are people assigned to a particular product or line and charged with the responsibility of setting and implementing marketing objectives and strategies. They are also often responsible for developing new products. Product managers are often found in industries where marketing accounts

Exhibit 10.5
Eight Package Functions

1. *Protection.* Probably the most fundamental function is to secure a product from the point of its manufacture to the point of use. A product can become damaged while in transit, storage, or sitting on a customer's shelf while waiting to be used. Protective packages are a major feature of Pringles potato chips, keeping the contents fresh and unbroken until they are consumed.
2. *Containment.* Packages serve to hold products. Imagine trying to handle a month's supply of toothpaste without a tube. Without packages, marketers could not distribute and handle many items such as liquids, loose solids, and corrosive and gaseous products.
3. *Sanitation.* Packages provide various sanitary functions, including spoilage reduction and reducing nutrient loss. Further, disposable packages can sometimes offer better sanitary protection than containers that need washing before reuse.
4. *Communication.* Packages enable marketers to communicate information about contents, handling requirements, and use to prospective final customers as well as to channel members. Further, properly designed packages can serve as a means of promotion, capturing prospective customers' attention and interest as they pass an item on a retailer's shelf.
5. *Unitization.* Packages permit marketers to combine a number of individual packages into collections that represent an efficient entity for buyers. For example, manufacturers wrap candy bars individually, then place 24 bars in a box, then transmit 12 boxes into a shipping carton, and further unitize cartons on a pallet for shipment.
6. *Protection against pilferage.* Pilferage (on the part of customers and employees) from retail stores exceeds $9 million per day. Packaging can help to reduce such theft. For example, a blister-pack fitted over a product with an oversized cardboard backing makes items like razor blades or cassettes difficult to steal.
7. *Apportioning and dispensing.* Packages enable buyers to apportion and dispense items to facilitate need satisfaction. For example, safety caps prevent children from consuming certain dangerous over-the-counter prescription drugs, and instant coffee is available in easy-to-reclose jars.
8. *Utility for reuse.* Producers design some packages to provide buyer utility (reuse). Decorator glasses, plastic margarine tubs, and designer perfume dispensers all can increase a product's total worth by making the packages themselves useful to buyers.

for a substantial portion of the product's cost and value, such as in cosmetics, detergents, and health and hygiene. Product managers formulate prices, advertising budgets, packaging and branding decisions, and help to motivate sales personnel. Procter & Gamble, General Mills, and numerous other companies employ this organizational form.[40] (Product management is treated in greater detail in Chapter 21.)

Another common arrangement is to have a separate staff responsible only for developing new products. In many organizations this staff has direct access to the president or to an executive vice president. Its responsibility is to manage the development of new offerings from their inception until they reach the testing stage. After testing, the staff turns new items over to others for commercialization. New product staffs have the advantages of having top management visibility and specialized skills.

Many companies utilize a group of high-level executives from various functional areas such as marketing, finance, production, and R & D to evaluate new product proposals. These committees supervise the new product development process and approve decisions relating to it. However, committee members often find that responsibilities in their normal functional areas are very time-consuming and they have only limited time available for committee work. Consequently, a new product committee may not be sufficient by itself to carry out the functions needed in dynamic industries.

The final type of arrangement is that of new product teams, consisting of groups specially formed from several operating departments for the express purpose of developing a new offering or a new business. Once a new idea is developed, the team is dissolved. The advantage of this concept is that the change of pace usually instills the excitement of entrepreneurship and creativity among team members, increasing their efforts and producing excellent results.

The most appropriate form of organization in a particular case depends upon the specific company, its personnel, the type of products offered, and other organizational arrangements. The most important guidelines to keep in mind, however, are to recognize the importance of new product development and allocate appropriate resources to this function, and furnish personnel with sufficient time to break away from daily operations so that they are able to plan for the future.

Chapter Summary

This chapter focused on decision making concerning new product development strategies and steps involved in the process. While new product development is a necessity for most marketing managers, the associated risk of failure is quite high. Thus, it is imperative to carefully plan each step when making these decisions.

There are four fundamental types of new product development strategies for management to consider. These are rounding out existing lines, adding market-related lines, adding technologically related lines, and adding unrelated lines. Each of these may be appropriate in a given situation, but the concept of synergy should be considered when evaluating which to use.

The chapter also discussed the stages of new product development. Management must carefully coordinate all stages ahead of time so that a new product may be offered to the market as soon as a contribution gap is expected to materialize.

This chapter also examined branding and packaging decisions, which are important considerations whenever a new product is developed. Finally, organizational forms to assure that new product development receives adequate attention were also considered. Ensuring that adequate time and personnel are made available is the most important criterion when selecting an organizational form.

Questions

1. What is meant by depth and breadth when referring to the goods and services offered by a marketer?
2. Define the strategy of rounding out a product line. Provide an example of rounding out that you have observed.
3. Describe a full-line strategy and a limited-line strategy. Give an example of each.
4. A marketing manager for an industrial goods producer has stated that adding market-related lines is likely to result in considerable synergy. Do you agree or disagree? Why?
5. Why would a firm choose to add a technologically related line?
6. What are the shortcomings of adding an unrelated line?
7. In your opinion, how successful would the following firms be in adding the indicated new product lines:
   a. The Ford Motor Company adds a bicycle line.
   b. An insurance company adds mutual funds to its offerings.
   c. Burger King adds a line of dietary fast foods such as low-calorie sandwiches.
   d. Nabisco adds a frozen vegetables line.
8. Provide an example of cannibalization that has taken place recently.
9. What is the possible legal danger in a trading-up strategy?
10. Assume that you have been asked to come up with new industrial product ideas for IBM. Where would you get your ideas? Give five possible new industrial product ideas for this firm.
11. Why do firms screen new product ideas? Can't this step in new product evaluation often be skipped?

12. How important is business analysis in new product evaluation? Support your answer.
13. How might a museum use concept testing to help determine if it should add a new wing featuring antique art?
14. What is a prototype? Of what value is it in assisting new product development?
15. What is the difference between market testing and commercialization?
16. Differentiate between brand, brand name, brand mark, and trademark.
17. What are the advantages of individual brands over family brands?
18. Are the following good or bad brand names in your opinion? Support your answers.
    a. Fram (auto and truck maintenance supplies)
    b. Fiber One (cereal)
    c. Sanka (coffee)
    d. Delco Freedom batteries
    e. Moisture Drops (eye drops)
19. Why would a retailer such as Sears use distributor brands?
20. What major functions do the packages for the following items provide?
    a. Revlon lipstick
    b. Book of the Month Club books
    c. Del Monte spinach
    d. Sara Lee frozen dinners
21. What are the four major means through which firms organize themselves for new product development? Which of these four means do you favor? Why?

Chapter 11

Channels of Distribution

Objectives

After reading this chapter, you should be able to demonstrate a knowledge of:

- The meaning of the term "channels of distribution"
- The contributions of wholesalers and retailers to manufacturers' marketing efforts
- How the overall strategy for channels of distribution is formulated
- How detailed decisions on channels of distribution, such as determining which activities to delegate to wholesalers and retailers (or manufacturers), are carried out
- How the leader in the channel of distribution operates to coordinate all organizations involved in the channel

MARKETING SUCCESS **Heathkit®**

Distributing Robots to Consumers

One of the first personal robots to be marketed commercially is the Hero 1, a practical domestic robot manufactured and marketed by the Michigan-based Heath Company, a division of Zenith, Inc. "We introduced a breakthrough here," said a company spokeswoman. "Though limited in capabilities compared to R2D2 of Star Wars, Hero 1 can perform useful functions—not just 'whirr around' beeping with lights flashing and looking silly after the first 10 minutes of use," she said.

Unlike industrial robots that are limited-function production machines performing repetitive tasks such as welding or bolt tightening, the Hero 1 can be programmed by owners to perform different simple household tasks such as turning off the TV set and serving drinks. It also comes equipped with an internally built home security function—a built-in ultrasonic ranging system that can detect prowlers and activate a synthesized voice to scare them away.

Heath sold over 10,000 Hero 1 units by the beginning of 1984. "At a $2,499 price for an assembled unit and $1,500 for an unassembled kit, that's not bad," said the company source. "While the market is ripe for a robot," said one securities analyst, "No one expected them to sell over 5,000 units a year," said Thomas Pringle, an analyst with Chicago-based Barton and Weise Securities, Inc. The typical buyer is 35 to 45 years old, college-educated, and economically upscale. "High in the ranks of buyers are technicians, computer experts, and professionals."

Heath made a conscious decision to avoid marketing the Hero 1 through department, computer, or hobby stores as some of its competitors did. "We did not feel that they could adequately service customers and answer their questions," said the company spokeswoman. Instead, management decided to distribute the innovative product through the company's 65 Heathkit Electronic Centers located around the country, Heath's mail order catalog, and through the Diner's Club gift catalog.

The strategy has been very effective to date. Heath sold out its first year's production run in three months. "We felt that we could best exercise control over the distribution this way," said the company representative. "We are confident that we will gain greater market share in the long run with this strategy," she said.

SOURCE: Adapted from Bernie Whalen, "Upscale Consumers Adopt Home Robots, But Widespread Lifestyle Impact Is Years Away," *The Marketing News* 17, no. 24 (November 25, 1983): 5.

Introduction

After ordering a new sofa from a furniture store, a typical customer's first question is "When will you deliver it?" While final delivery is of concern to consumers, it is only part of the distribution picture. Marketers devote considerable attention to managing activities designed to make their products available to customers when and where their needs arise, whether they be for furniture or personal robots.

Like the Heath Co., Chesebrough-Pond's (cosmetics) and several other concerns opened several company-run stores in the mid-1980s to ensure adequate distribution.[1] As a former insecticide industry executive stated, "brand loyalty is mainly a matter of what's available at the store . . . [consumers] take whatever's on the shelf." [2] While his comment is an overstatement, it does highlight the importance of effectively managing distribution.

Channel of distribution
A network of organizations that arranges for changes of title to goods as they move from manufacturer to customers.

Management makes two types of distribution decisions: First, it establishes interorganizational arrangements, termed **channels of distribution,** which are networks of organizations that arrange for changes of title to goods as they move from manufacturers to final customers. Heath's management needed to establish the company's contractual relationship with Diner's Club, for example. Second, management seeks a means of physically distributing items to customers. This chapter examines the elements of the first type of decision.

The Need for Channels

Because producers and final customers are separated from each other due to specialization, the gap between them necessitates the development of delivery systems to permit exchange. This delivery is not only in terms of physically moving items, but also in the sense of all economic transactional flows, as Figure 11.1 illustrates.

Consider Miles Laboratories, for instance. While located in Elkhart, Indiana, the company sells Alka Seltzer around the world. Accordingly, management must cultivate several arrangements to facilitate transactional flows, including becoming aware of consumer needs, arranging for distribution around the world, making potential customers aware of Alka Seltzer's availability and performance, transferring ownership to buyers, and obtaining funds for supplying the product.

In other words, managers undertake activities to develop the needed flows to bring together buyers and sellers in the marketplace. The activities may be grouped into nine key marketing functions that need to be performed: [3]

- buying
- selling
- financing
- standardizing and grading
- transporting
- risk-bearing
- pricing
- storing
- obtaining market information

Let us examine how this is related to channels of distribution decision making.

Channel Structures

Simply put, channels of distributions are the sets of institutions and agencies that are used to make a product or service available to customers.[4] The set of institutions used for a particular product is called its channel system, which is responsible for collectively performing all of the needed functions to bring buyers and sellers together.[5]

Some producers attempt to perform for themselves all or most of the needed marketing functions, resulting in rather simple channel configurations: direct from the producer to final customers.[6] Companies such as AT&T, U.S.X., and Metropolitan Life Insurance follow this mold, relying exclusively on company marketing personnel to perform the work.

In contrast, most producers rely upon other businesses that are functional specialists to perform many of the needed marketing tasks. Panasonic, for instance, develops physical products, adds the brand, establishes warranties, and determines prices to charge wholesalers. Then it uses importers to maintain large inventories in the U.S., advertise, and develop regional distributors. The regional distributors maintain inventories, provide delivery service, and sell to retailers. Finally, retailers advertise, use

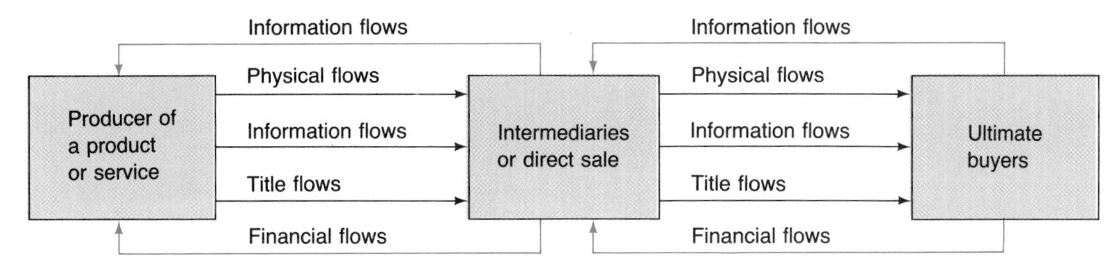

Figure 11.1
The Concept of a Distribution Channel

personal selling, maintain display models, arrange for consumer delivery, and arrange for credit if needed. As is apparent, distribution channels can become quite complex because several businesses become involved.

Retailers, wholesalers, and transportation companies are the three principal types of specialists that producers call upon to help in performing major distribution functions. They are called intermediaries because they represent intermediate steps linking producers and final customers. The first two, retailers and wholesalers, are **selling intermediaries**—they directly engage in making sales. Transportation companies are **shipping intermediaries.** Their shipping expertise and transportation services can be important in facilitating sales.

Selling intermediaries
Those who engage in making actual sales, thereby linking producers and final customers.

Shipping intermediaries
Those who engage in transportation.

Channel Systems

While the institutions involved in a channel system are important, what is even more important are the functions that they perform.[7] Thus, a channel system can be thought of as both the institutions and the work that they do. A new channel system results, then, when there is a change in either the institutions or their functions. For example, a new distribution system results when a shoe manufacturer either adds a new retailer, such as Kinney, to those that handle its shoes, or if there is a change in the work that the retailer performs, such as having Kinney suddenly handle advertising. Decisions affecting a channel system are warranted when the firm introduces new products or drops old ones, competitive or other environmental factors make an existing system obsolete, or an existing channel does not enable the firm to attain its objectives.[8]

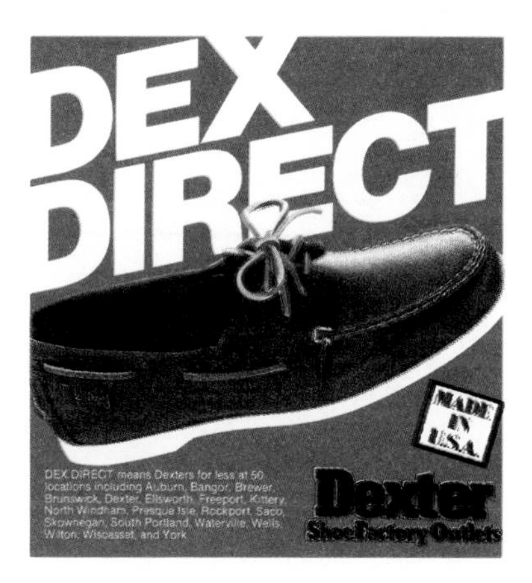

Dexter Shoes is a company that has aggressively developed a direct distribution system targeting on consumers.

Channel Attributes

Some channels are lengthy, involving several different types of intermediary specialists. This is especially the case when marketing in certain foreign countries, such as Japan, where this is the customary way to do business. Other channels are short, with producers contacting customers directly. Some channels are difficult to change over time, while others are capable of responding rapidly to emerging environmental conditions.[9]

Like products, distribution channels have various attributes that define their structures. Exhibit 11.1 presents the six most important channel attributes.

The number of channel levels determines its length, as illustrated in Figure 11.2. The simplest, a two-level channel (also called **direct distribution**), is where a producer sells directly to final customers. A three-level structure includes one selling inter-

Direct distribution
A producer that sells its output to final customers with no intermediaries involved.

Exhibit 11.1
The Six Most Important Attributes of a Distribution Channel

1. *Length.* The specific number of channel levels employed. Each different type of selling intermediary adds another level to a channel.
2. *Width.* The number of channel participants used at each level.
3. *Tasks.* Specific sets of functions to be performed by each channel member.
4. *Adaptability.* The ability of a channel to change according to its environment.
5. *Specific participants.* The type, number, and specific set of members that are part of a channel.
6. *Conflict.* The degree of competition among members of a channel and between competing channels. Included is the resolution of intrachannel conflict by a member assuming leadership control over the channel.

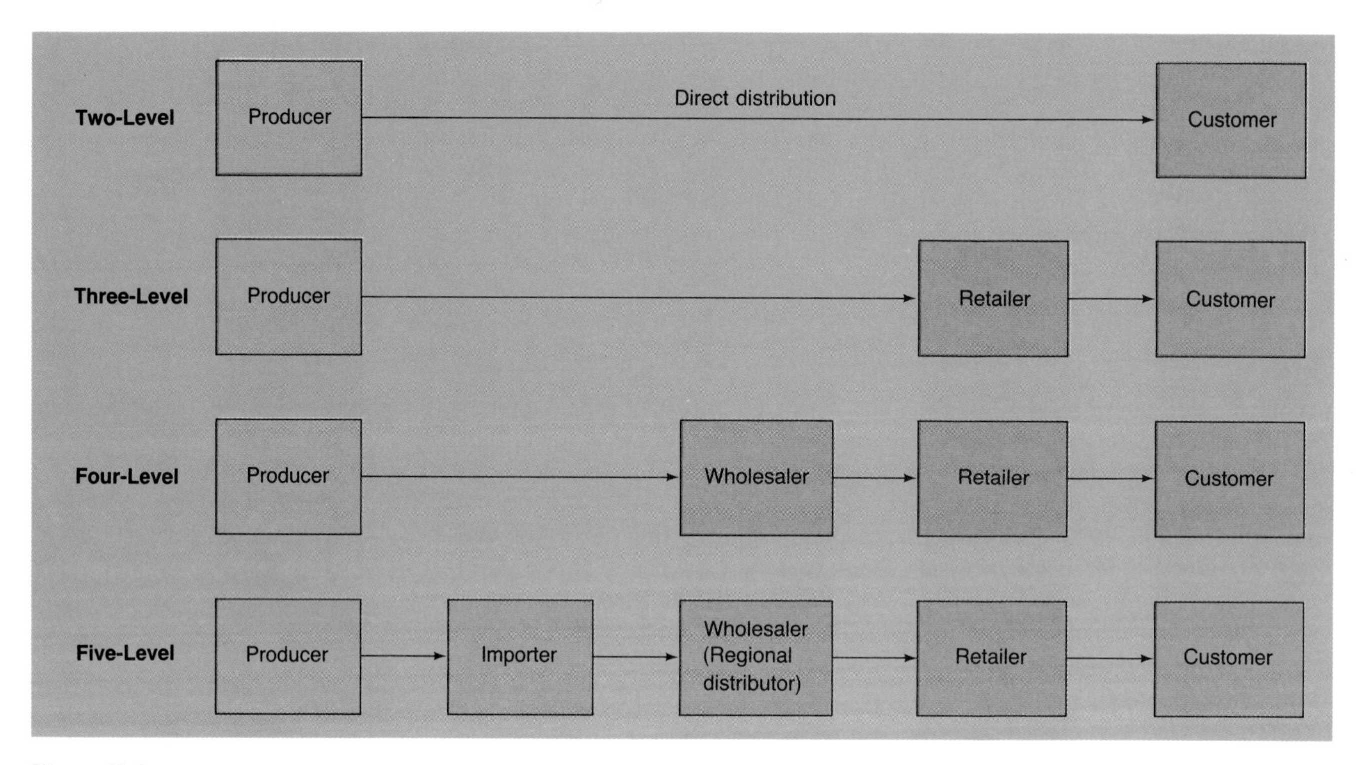

Figure 11.2
Different Channel Levels

mediary, either a retailer selling to consumers or a wholesaler selling to institutional buyers.

The Agricultural Division of the Upjohn Co. (see the accompanying Marketing Brief) uses a two-level system by selling directly to veterinarians and a three-level distribution system by selling to other markets through distributors. (Using a system involving more than one set of levels is called dual distribution, and is covered later in the chapter.) Direct distribution allows a producer the greatest control over the distribution system's marketing efforts. In Upjohn's case, management felt that this control was essential for reaching veterinarians and gave the company a competitive advantage, since most competitors used lengthier channels for this market segment.

Four-level channels include two selling intermediaries. In consumer markets, this

MARKETING BRIEF
Changing a 20-Year-Old Channel of Distribution

"Our previous 20-year-old channel of distribution served us well in the past, but it outlived its usefulness," said Norm Braksick, executive director of the agricultural marketing division of Kalamazoo-based Upjohn Co. "The company had been working with two completely different sales forces that distributed three different product lines." Due to the confusion, the situation had become unworkable, with excessive costs and lost sales in over-the-counter, feed additives, and animal health products. "We wanted to make the distribution system more efficient and more responsive to the marketplace," he said.

A twelve-person task force, chaired by Mr. Braksick, led the company's six-month study of alternatives. The basic procedure followed in the deliberations, laid out by Braksick at the onset, involved:

- Developing a list of performance characteristics of the old distribution system (and why it had to change)
- Developing a list of objectives and criteria for selecting channel systems
- Refining a set of weights to be assigned to each objective to reflect its relative importance
- Producing a list of possible channel alternatives, including variations of a mix of company salespeople and outside distributors
- Evaluating each channel configuration against each criterion and assigning a scaled number from 1 to 10 based on how well the task force judged the fit
- Multiplying each assigned alternative channel/criterion weight by the weight assigned the corresponding objective, and adding the results
- Evaluating the total scores for each alternative achieved in the process

The system chosen was the one yielding the highest numerical score: a dual distribution channel where Upjohn sells directly to veterinarians and through distributors who cover other markets. While relatively new, the dual distribution system appears to be fully satisfying management's expectations, according to Mr. Braksick.

SOURCE: Adapted from Linda Daly, "Coaching Helps Revitalize Distribution System," *Marketing News* 20, no. 8 (April 11, 1986): 6, 26.

usually amounts to a wholesaler and a retailer, such as when Pillsbury Co. sells flour to a wholesaler who, in turn, resells it to retailers. With institutional markets, the two intermediaries might be two different wholesalers. A five-level system is common in importing, with an importer, wholesalers (regional distributors), and retailers all helping to perform the needed marketing tasks. Sometimes even more than five levels exist, although this is not very common.

Why Should a Producer Align Itself with Intermediaries?

Producers give up some control over their destinies by aligning themselves with intermediaries, who naturally expect to be compensated for their efforts. Since producers could market directly if they chose to, why do many opt for affiliating themselves with intermediaries?

The answer lies in the fact that intermediaries can substantially enhance a channel's overall performance. They might add to a channel's efficiency (ability to do the work at lower cost), its effectiveness (ability to do the work well), or both. Then too, many producers lack the capital that it would require to go direct. The Ford Motor Co.,

Figure 11.3
Required Transactions Are Reduced by Intermediaries

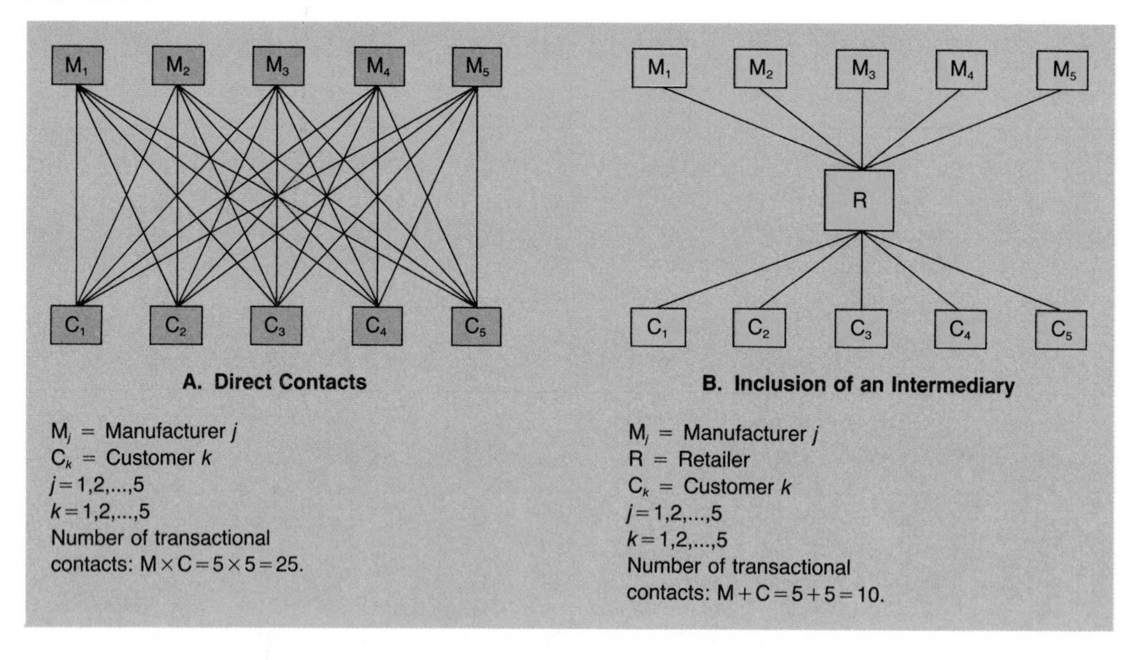

for example, uses about 8,000 independent dealers worldwide. The total investment for Ford to accomplish distribution directly would run $100 billion or more—enough to break its treasury despite its being among the top ten largest manufacturers. Ford has better alternatives for spending its money—just being competitive with new cars and trucks demands enormous investment—than tying it up in bricks and mortar for showrooms.

Another reason to affiliate with intermediaries is that they facilitate the buying process for many customers by building assortments, or bundles, of items in one location that customers believe are related.[10] Grocery shoppers, to illustrate, prefer to buy soup, meat, canned goods, vegetables, and household items in one location, rather than from the Campbell Soup Store, and from the Lettuce Store and so on.

Finally, intermediaries can substantially reduce the total number of transactional contacts and related costs between producers and final customers, as Figure 11.3 illustrates. Five different manufacturers must establish separate contacts with five customers in Part A of the figure, which depicts direct distribution. The total number of required contacts is calculated by multiplying the number of customers by the number of manufacturers, or $5 \times 5 = 25$ for the illustration. Part B of the figure illustrates the impact of just one retailer. Now the total number of contacts is calculated by adding the numbers, or $5 + 5 = 10$ contacts. For an entire economy such as in the U.S., with hundreds of millions of consumers and hundreds of thousands of producers, the contact efficiencies are astronomical when intermediaries are brought into the picture.

Many critics of marketing point to the profits of intermediaries as being exorbitant, but they fail to grasp the idea that intermediaries can actually reduce costs and prices. By specializing, they can often perform the same functions for different producers at a lower total cost and they significantly cut the number of transactional contacts required between producers and users. It is true that intermediaries charge a markup for their services, but it is also true that intermediaries can clearly cut costs.

Strategic Channel Decisions

Strategic channel decisions may be grouped into three categories: determining needed marketing activities to be performed, selecting overall channel strategy, and choosing from among interorganizational and structural alternatives, as Figure 11.4 illustrates. Of course, like all elements of a marketing mix, channel decisions should reflect a company's objectives and its selected target market.

All channel decisions are interrelated. The needed activities determined by management depend in part upon the capabilities of all available channel members. Similarly, the unavailability of channel members can affect which market target is most promising, and consequently the marketing activities to be carried out. Thus, management should consider all channel decisions as being simultaneously related. For discussion, however, we will consider channel decisions independently as they appear from left to right in Figure 11.4. This illustration views channel decision making from the perspective of a producer who is a channel's principal decision maker.

Determine Needed Marketing Activities or Functions

Just what constitutes an optimal channel system depends upon the particular environment confronting the firm.[11] The best set of channel attributes for steel is quite different than that for ice cream, for instance. But an optimal channel's characteristics

Figure 11.4
Key Strategic Channel of Distribution Decisions

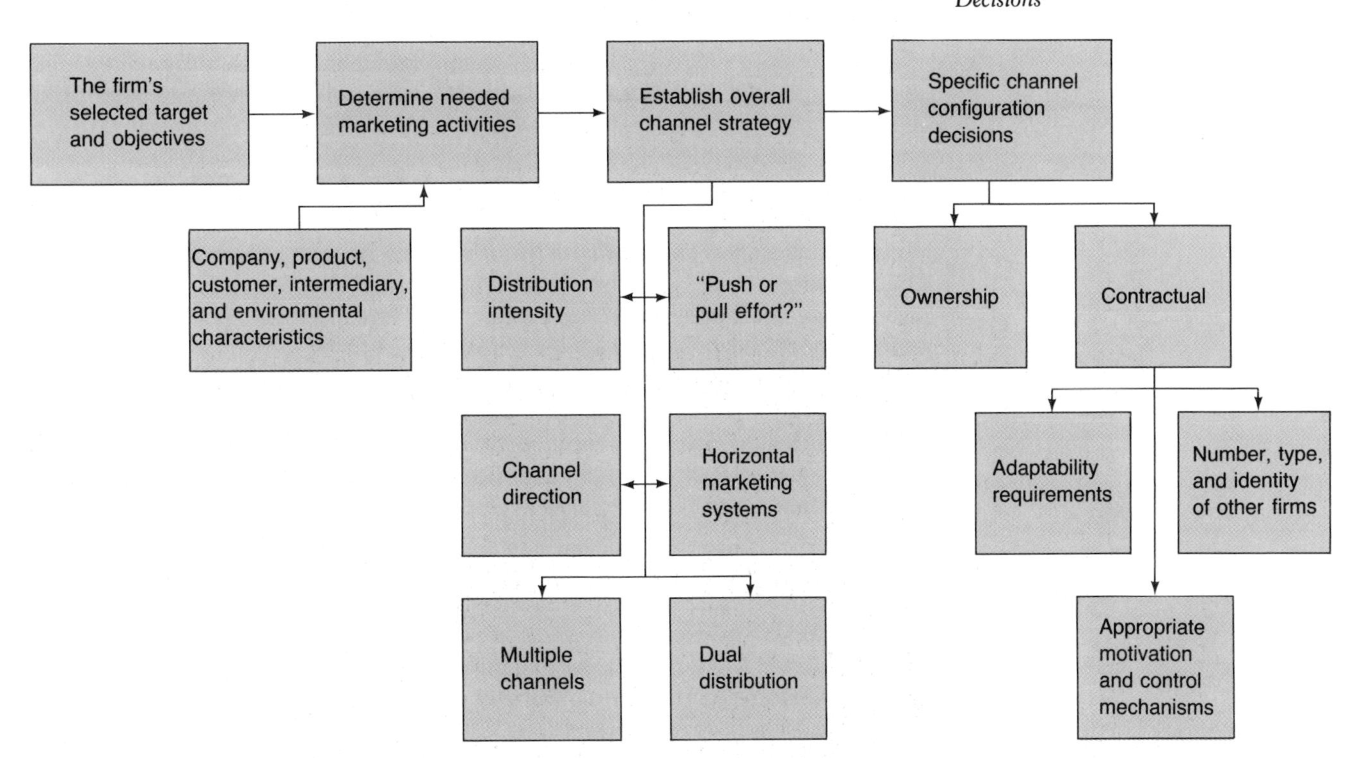

Wholesalers perform many important functions in the distribution of some products.

may also vary among firms within the same industry. Different target markets, different objectives, and a host of other factors can bring management to place varied emphases on particular marketing functions. In turn, these factors affect the desirability of including certain intermediaries in a channel.

There are five major categories of factors to consider when attempting to determine the marketing activities that a channel should accomplish. Figure 11.5 depicts them visually.

Target Customer Characteristics Probably the single most important class of characteristics influencing a channel system's design are those relating to target customers. When there are numerous customers, each purchasing small quantities on a frequent basis, producers tend to develop rather lengthy channel systems that are also quite broad—that is, with many intermediaries at each level. This is especially true when customers are widely dispersed geographically.

In contrast, producers tend to develop short and narrow channels when there are only a few geographically concentrated target customers, especially when large purchase quantities are involved. These conditions favor direct distribution. U.S.X., for example, markets directly to companies within the metal-working industry because of their geographical concentration and large potential orders.

Product Characteristics Product characteristics also play a major role in the design of a channel system. In general, the greater the value of an item, the shorter should be the channel for two reasons. First, expensive products usually require a heavy personal selling effort (as in the case of mainframe computers).[12] Short channels have greater flexibility when it comes to meeting individual customer needs such as specially arranged deliveries, financing, and instructions for use. Second, short channels can

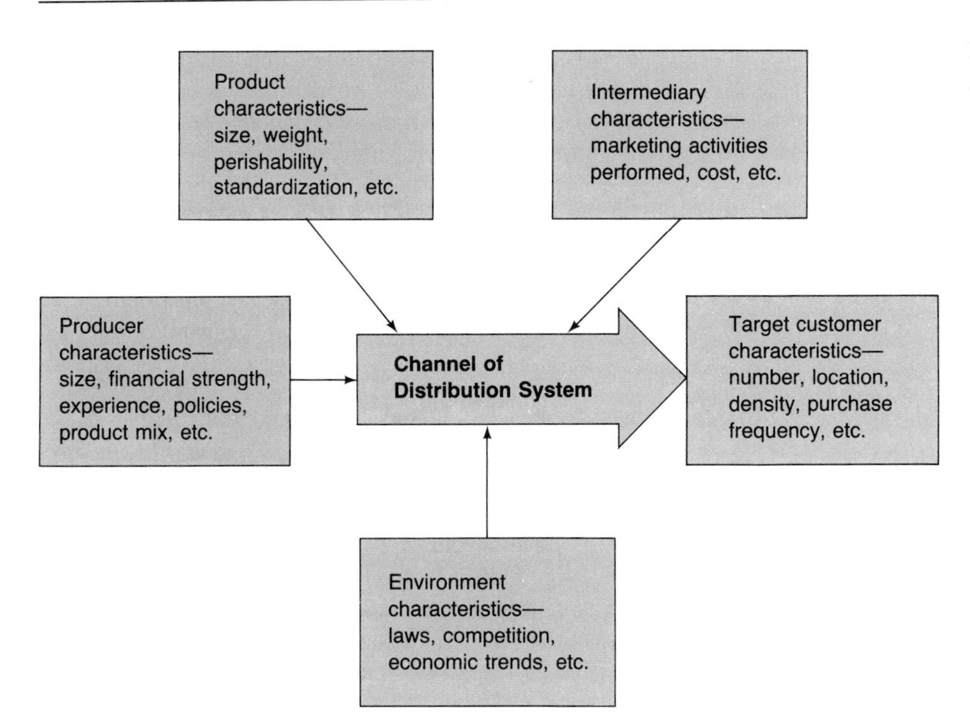

Figure 11.5
Factors Affecting Channel Design

reduce an entire system's total inventory and related carrying costs. If numerous intermediaries besides retailers stored fur coats, for instance, inventory carrying costs would mushroom dramatically.

A product's bulk and weight are also important. Large items cost more to store, ship, and handle; the greater these costs are compared to an item's unit value, the greater is the need to emphasize efficient handling and transportation. Thus, bulky and heavy items with low unit values tend to have longer channels.

Perishable items deteriorate over time; from decay (aging food) or from style deterioration (many types of fashion clothing). Highly perishable items usually require shorter channels so as to speed delivery to market. Milk typically has a shorter channel than canned vegetables. Similarly, fragile items typically have short channels.

Further, if items are custom-made to buyer specifications, a short channel is usually necessary. In contrast, highly standardized offerings such as jars of peanut butter can be efficiently handled by functional specialists. Thus, longer channels tend to be used. The degree of required servicing, such as adjustments and installation, is also a consideration. Products that require extensive servicing typically move through short channels, as is the case with central air conditioners.

Intermediary Characteristics Intermediaries vary in their ability and desire to perform various marketing functions such as storing, advertising, and personal selling. Producers should take these differences into account when designing interorganizational arrangements.

For example, large retailers such as major department stores can provide extensive exposure for a product because of their ability to draw heavy shopping traffic. On the other hand, smaller specialty stores might offer greater sales potentials. While small units typically attract fewer shoppers than department stores, their customers often are

An item's bulk is a factor in determining the optimal channel system.

more focused. A sporting goods store might not attract a large total number of shoppers each day, but those that do enter are predisposed toward buying sporting goods. Further, the relative promotion emphasis that a particular product receives is likely to be greater in a small store than in a large one.

Environmental Characteristics Various characteristics of the environment also have an impact on a channel's design. Rapid economic expansion might require the selection of intermediary members that would otherwise be unacceptable; or a recession could mean that management would need to terminate some channel members.

Legislation also has direct implications. The Robinson Patman Act, for example, disallows granting price concessions to certain intermediaries and not to others and the Clayton Act disallows some tying and exclusive dealing contracts. Intelligent managers seek advice from legal experts before attempting to enter into major contractual arrangements with channel members to avoid future legal problems.[13]

Similarly, managers should consider competitors' systems when designing a channel. Producers seeking to penetrate closely related markets may develop channel systems that display their products next to competitive brands. Lancome, Revlon, and Estée Lauder products, for instance, often sit side-by-side in cosmetic sections of department stores.

Company Characteristics Finally, various company characteristics play an important role in influencing channel system development. Large, financially strong producers are sometimes able to attain scale efficiencies as specialists because of their size. Accordingly, they often perform many needed channel functions for themselves. For instance, IBM uses a well-trained and motivated sales force to sell personal computer software to retailers.[14]

Smaller firms, in contrast, usually rely upon intermediaries to gain efficiency. Most personal computer software companies rely on wholesalers to feed their products to retailers and cannot hope to provide these stores with the same level of support as IBM can.

Channel design decisions should also reflect a company's past experiences. While General Foods is large, it has a history of using wholesalers to distribute its products. Trying to contact retailers directly could place the company at a disadvantage since it lacks experience in such matters. In a similar vein, marketing policies can influence the type of channel needed. To illustrate, the policy of "a maximum three-day delivery deadline for 90 percent of our customers" requires certain types of intermediaries to permit implementation.

Channel design is also influenced by the completeness of a producer's product mix in relation to the target market's desired bundle of items. Consider the case of an insurance company that writes only life insurance. If it chooses a target that has relatively few needs for other types of insurance, then a simple channel configuration may be appropriate. A direct distribution channel might be appropriate if it targets graduating college students, for example, since most of these prospects do not yet have needs for home, annuity, and other forms of insurance.

In contrast, consider the same life insurance carrier trying to penetrate a target of families that also have home, retirement, and many other types of insurance needs. Since it only handles life insurance, its product mix only presents a small portion of a complete insurance package to these buyers. Consequently, a more complex channel is warranted, as Figure 11.6 illustrates. By working through independent agents who handle all other types of insurance from different carriers, the life insurance specialist can arrange to become part of an overall package of insurance coverage that represents a complete bundle of products to the target.

Establish Overall Channel Strategy

Finely tuned channel strategy decisions provide for strong armaments in a company's arsenal of competitive weapons. Consider the history of the Formica Corporation, which had a mission of selling plastic laminated sheets for use in construction.[15] One use was in the making of doors. During the early 1960s, the company operated its own door manufacturing plant that used the plastic sheets on the door exteriors. Company personnel handled all distribution and promotion activities; this did not work very well, resulting in poor sales performance.

By the 1970s, the company switched to using wholesalers to handle its doors, but again this arrangement did not work well because the company's mission was to sell the plastic sheets, not doors. Later in the 1970s the company developed 25 independent door manufacturers as "approved Formica sources," which helped expand sales of the plastic sheets. By the 1980s, the company had expanded the concept of "approved Formica sources" to cabinet makers, building supply outlets, and home improvement

Figure 11.6
The Relationship between a Producer's Offering and a Desired Bundle Has a Bearing on an Optimal Channel

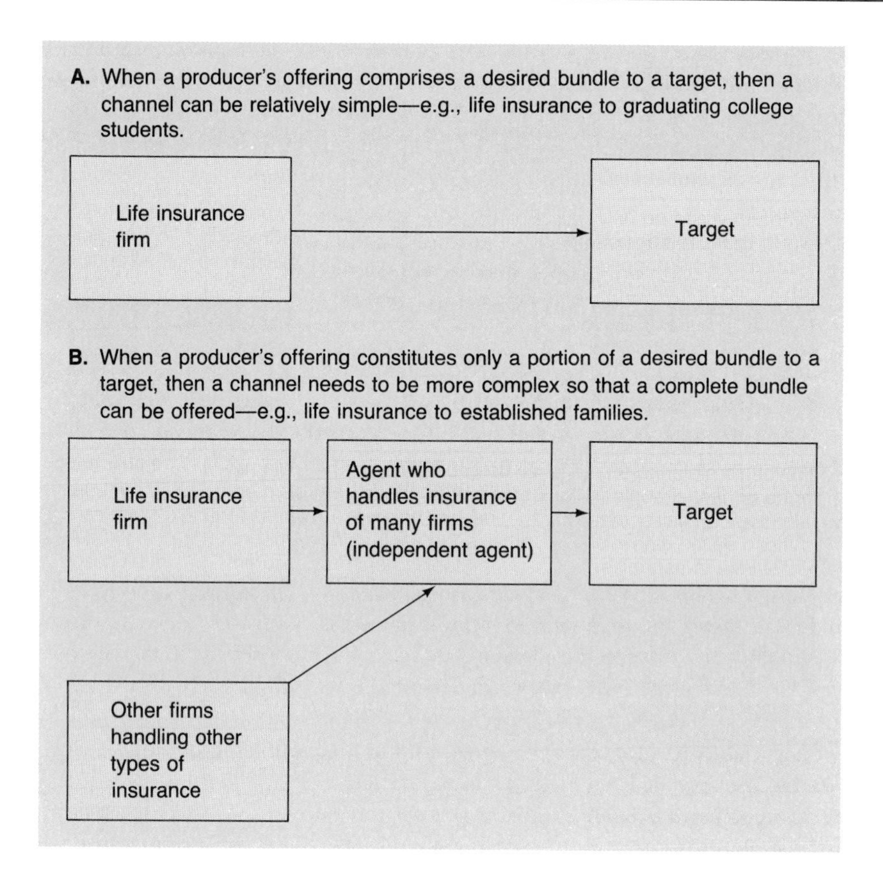

centers, turning the company into a very profitable operation. Relying on intermediaries turned the company around. This example illustrates that channel strategy has important implications for attaining a company's objectives.

Intensity (distribution)
The width of a channel, referring to the scope of the market served.

Distribution Intensity **Intensity,** the width of a channel, is a cornerstone of distribution strategy. Several degrees of intensity are possible, as Figure 11.7 illustrates. While intensity is a continuum, it helps to think of three discrete alternatives: intensive, selective, and exclusive.

Intensive distribution
Making an item available at all locations where customers expect to find it.

Intensive Distribution **Intensive distribution** is the strategy of making an item available at all locations where customers expect to find it. It is especially appropriate for consumer convenience items such as gum and candy bars, and for certain producer supplies such as common lubricants, floor-cleaning products, and other commodity items that face heavy direct competition. Intensive distribution is common for low-priced items.

Many buyers of such products accept substitutes if their favorite brand is unavailable. Hence, intensive distribution is important whenever a convenient location is a critical factor to buyers and when a high level of competition exists between brands. If consumers cannot find convenience items in their favorite shopping location they will simply buy a competitor's product. Because numerous locations are required, intensive

CONCEPT SUMMARY

Major Factors Influencing Channel Length

Factor	Influence
Target Market Characteristics	In the case of numerous customers who each purchase small quantities on a frequent basis (especially when they are spread geographically), lengthy and broad channel systems with intermediaries are likely.
Product Characteristics	Inexpensive items that are bulky and heavy, those that are not perishable, and those that are not custom-made tend to have longer channels.
Intermediary Characteristics	The existence of strong and efficient intermediaries tends to promote long channels.
Environment Characteristics	All elements of the environment—economic, social, technological, political, and competitive—can influence channel length.
Company Characteristics	Small firms, those that lack experience in wholesaling and retailing, and those with a limited product mix tend to use long channels.

distribution almost always necessitates the use of many intermediaries. All intermediaries where target customers shop should be included. All retailers for a paint brush manufacturer, for instance, might mean all paint, hardware, and department stores.

Selective Distribution **Selective distribution** requires being a bit more discriminating about which organizations are to be included in the channel. Shopping goods are typical products for selective distribution. Customers are usually willing to search longer and travel more than for convenience items so that they can compare competing brands. Thus, convenient locations are less important than for convenience items and fewer intermediaries become necessary.

Selective distribution
Stocking an item in a relatively small number of outlets.

While fewer intermediaries are needed, the objective of selective distribution is not based upon numbers. Customers do not buy items because they are offered in fewer places. Instead, the goal is high-quality performance. Because few channel members exist, less intrachannel competition is involved and the producer can expect more from intermediaries.

Further, selective distribution enables the producer to exclude marginal dealers such as those with low sales, bad credit ratings, and small orders. Therefore, when customers are willing to seek out a product beyond the nearest convenient location and when a moderate marketing effort by intermediaries is required, selective distribution is likely to be appropriate.

Exclusive Distribution The most restrictive strategy regarding a channel's breadth is **exclusive distribution.** With it, selected channel members receive an agreement granting them sole rights to sell a product line in a certain territory.

Exclusive distribution
Providing channel members with exclusive rights to sell a product line in a certain territory.

Figure 11.7
Distribution Intensity, Assuming One Major Trading Area

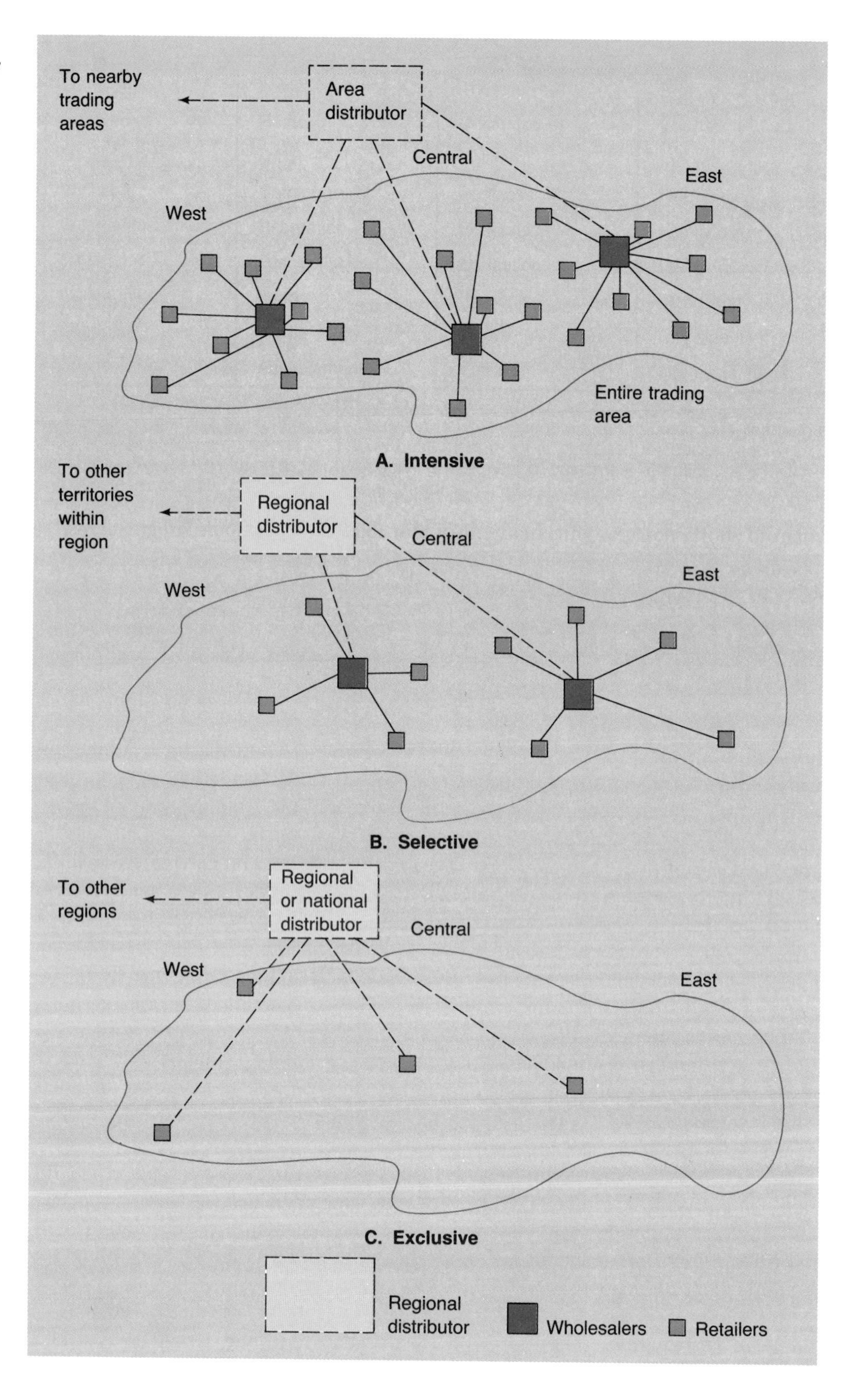

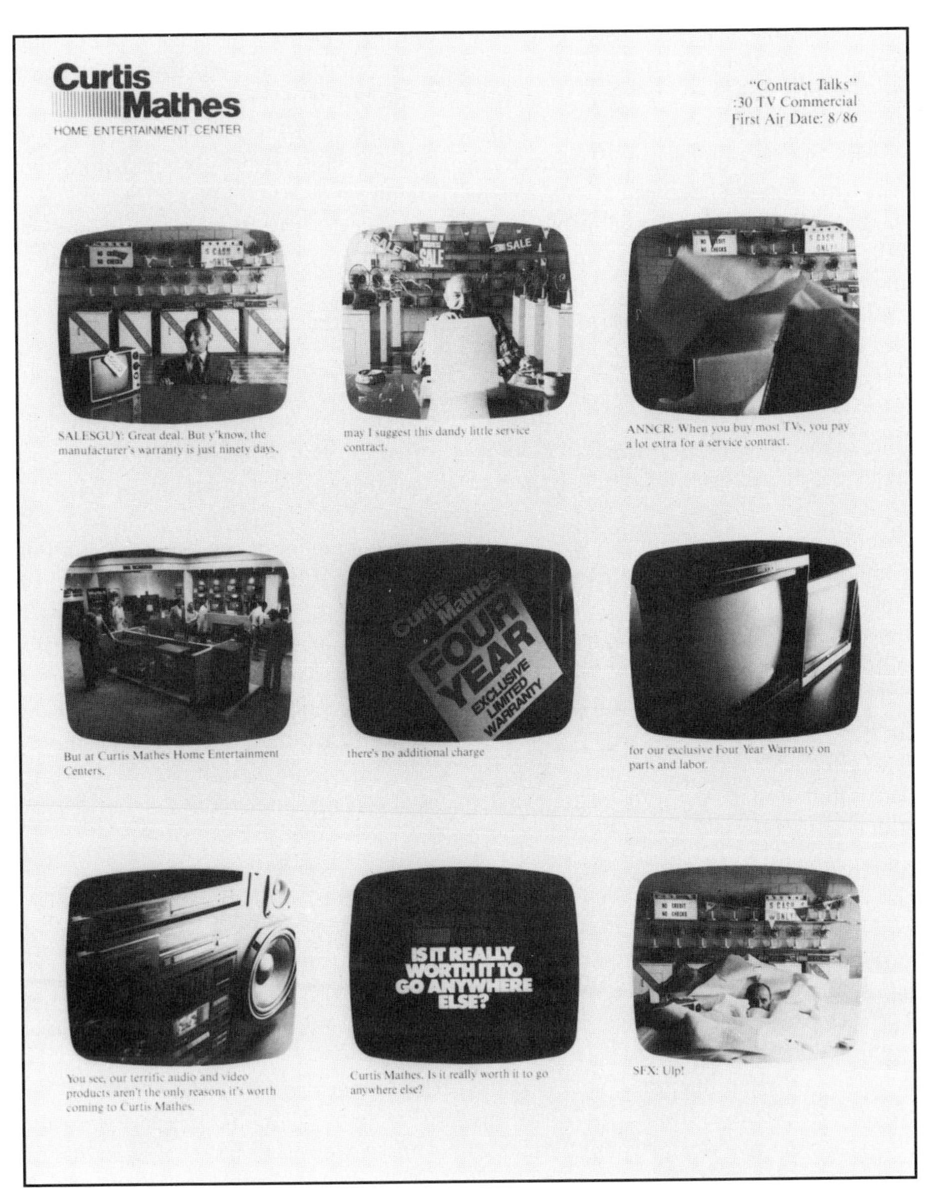

Curtis Mathes is one company that has chosen an exclusive distribution strategy.

Producers of consumer specialty items and of parts and equipment sold to producers frequently employ exclusive distribution. To illustrate, NEC Corp. uses exclusive distribution for its television sets, as does McDonald's with its restaurants. Only one retailer exists within a certain trading area.

The advantage of exclusive distribution to producers is that they can expect chosen channel members to effectively perform many of the needed marketing functions. For example, successful selling of top-quality skis and boots typically requires salespeople who are both skiing and equipment experts and sources of customer advice. Retailers who have exclusive distribution are more willing to hire experts at premium salaries to help customers satisfy their unique needs.

To intermediaries, exclusive distribution means that they have less direct competition. There may be others who handle the same line in nearby regions; however, the territories are usually large enough to avoid substantial direct competition.

New or small producers may not have a choice over the intensity strategy they employ. Established intermediaries may demand exclusive distribution before they will carry a product. By obtaining exclusive rights, they can reap a greater share of the benefits of helping to establish a successful product. This may bring about vigorous intermediary efforts for a producer, but it may also result in lost control. Therefore, management must exercise extreme care in assuring that distributors are capable of both serving the identified target and helping the producer to attain its objectives in the long run.

Channel Direction The second fundamental distribution strategy question deals with how management will direct the channel relative to competing products. There are two basic alternatives: a frontal strategy or one of bypass distribution.

Frontal strategy
Using a channel system configuration paralleling those of leading competitors.

Frontal Strategy A **frontal strategy** consists of using a channel system configuration paralleling those of leading competitors. For instance, Philip Morris and American Tobacco compete head-on in their attempts to capture similar targets with similar tobacco products. Both firms use wholesalers and retailers and both employ intensive distribution. In fact, many intermediaries carry competitive products of both producers. While a firm may use the same intermediaries as rivals do, this is not necessary. So long as it employs the same type of channel structure as competitors, a frontal strategy is in effect.

A frontal strategy makes sense when a producer is working from a position of strength, such as:

1. When the same intermediaries as competitors use are eager to handle a competitive product because the intermediaries can capture a new segment (Chanel perfume competes for a different enough segment from Coty to interest an intermediary in handling both), the producer offers higher profit margins than do competitors,[16] or evidence exists that customers prefer the new product over those the intermediaries formerly handled.
2. When the producer has had favorable past relationships with similar or the same channel members as those which rivals use. If Procter & Gamble, for example, were to add a new product to compete directly against Clorox's Formula 409, it would require only limited effort to get grocery stores to handle the product because of P & G's past successes with detergents and cleaners.
3. When similar, but different, intermediaries that a producer's competitors have avoided seek to compete in the same or a closely related market. Burger King, to illustrate, has employed a frontal strategy against McDonald's, with independent businesses not holding the latter's franchise.

Bypass distribution
Using a channel system configuration that differs from those of leading competitors.

Bypass Distribution In the case of **bypass distribution,** the producer employs a different distribution structure than its competitors. K-tel, for example, has successfully pursued this strategy. Bypassing the industry's mold of using record wholesalers and retailers, K-tel advertises heavily on TV and radio and uses direct mail for delivering telephone and mail orders.

Bypass distribution is often necessary when rivals have blocked access to key intermediaries. Strong intermediaries may be tied to competitors or unwilling to place needed special emphasis on critical marketing mix elements, such as advertising, personal selling, or in-store displays.

Multiple Channels Another strategy choice pertains to whether a firm should develop a single- or **multiple-channel system.** A single channel is often insufficient when the company is marketing its product line to highly divergent market segments. To illustrate, both consumers and government buyers purchase meat from Swift & Company. Swift needs different channels for each segment. Whenever a producer pursues a segmentation strategy to capture a position in two or more distinct market segments, it should consider installing a separate channel for each.

Multiple-channel system
Using a separate channel in each of two or more market segments.

As in the electric wire and cable industry, which Figure 11.8 illustrates, multiple channels can become quite complex, adding considerably to administrative costs. But by developing separate channel systems for each major segment, a company can effectively tailor its offerings to meet the unique needs of each.

Dual Distribution Closely related to multiple channels is **dual distribution,** where a producer markets a product to the same segment through two or more competing channel structures. The term also includes distributing two or more brands of similar products (such as two different manufacturer brands or an intermediary and a manufacturer brand) through different channels.[17] Unlike a multiple channel arrangement, the channels under a strategy of dual distribution compete directly with each other. To illustrate, a producer may distribute a product to both wholesalers and directly to large retailers within the same trading area.

Dual distribution
Marketing a product to the same or a closely related market segment through two or more competing channel structures.

When sufficiently large market segments exist that permit all channel members to attain their goals, or when significant enough differences exist between segments so that competition between channel members does not get out of hand, dual distribution can lead to effective market penetration. The major danger is that competition among channels can escalate into warfare, alienating channel participants and reducing overall effectiveness. Some intermediaries may feel that competitors have cut them off from profitable customers. Others may feel that producers are charging them excessive prices; large department stores, for instance, may seek the same prices as wholesalers pay.

Congress has examined dual distribution and found it not to be illegal *per se* under antitrust legislation, but maintaining sufficient price differentials to prevent substantial injury to competition was recommended.[18] Further, courts have ruled that when a producer has monopoly power over a product, it must preserve independent distributors if it once used them. Producers may replace distributors if necessary, but cannot enter into competition with intermediaries and destroy them in the process.[19]

Horizontal Marketing Systems Another possible distribution strategy is a **horizontal marketing system,** which is comprised of an alliance between two or more companies to jointly tap a market opportunity. Despite Pillsbury's success in grocery stores, for example, it lacked the ability to distribute refrigerated doughs for biscuits, cookies, and rolls. Merchandising these products required special refrigerated display cases. Pillsbury was not set up to distribute refrigerated products, but Kraft Foods was because of its cheese products. Accordingly, the two firms entered into an arrangement where Pillsbury produces and advertises its refrigerated dough line while Kraft handles the personal selling and distribution functions.

Horizontal marketing system
Alliances between two or more companies to jointly tap a market opportunity.

Also termed *symbiotic marketing,* horizontal marketing systems make sense when one firm is incapable of providing sufficient capital, marketing, or production expertise

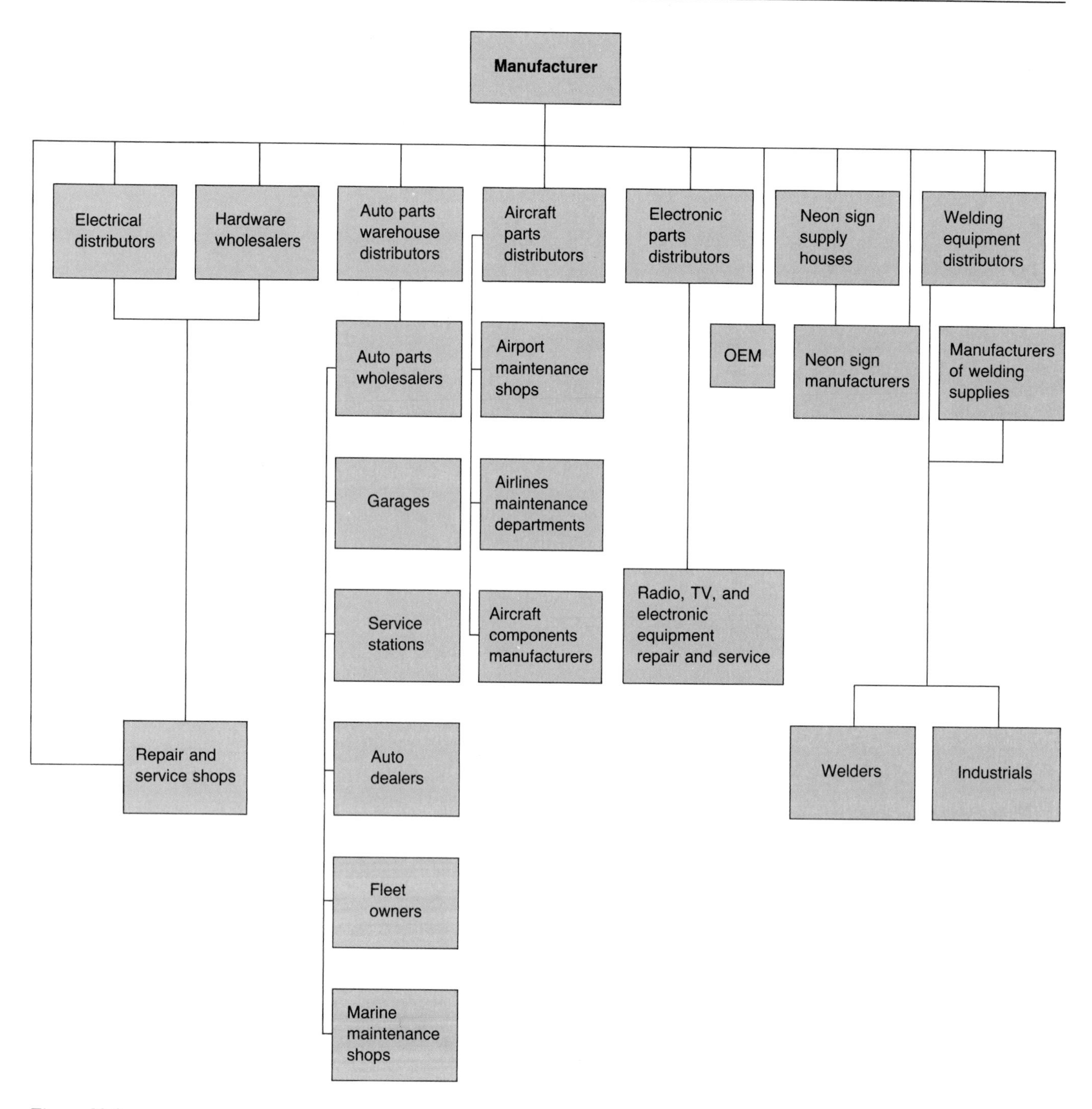

Figure 11.8
Multiple Channels of Distribution for a Major Manufacturer of Electrical Wire and Cable

to capitalize on a market opportunity by itself; or when substantial synergy is expected from the proposed relationship.[20]

Push or Pull? The final aspect of distribution strategy to consider is whether a producer should "push" or "pull" a product through a channel. **Pulling** an item through a channel is based upon initially developing demand among final customers who, in turn, exert pressure on their suppliers to stock the item. To illustrate, some new product ads suggest to consumers, "If it is not available in your favorite store, ask the manager when it will be." This is an overt or explicit pulling strategy. Through a pulling strategy a producer might gain access to otherwise uninterested intermediaries by building demand among final customers.

Pulling an item
Developing strong demand among final buyers, who exert pressure on their suppliers to stock the item.

A covert pulling strategy is also possible. As in an overt case, the producer extends heavy promotion efforts. Once it can demonstrate that there is widespread awareness and interest within a target, intermediaries are more eager to listen to sales efforts oriented toward getting them to join a channel.[21]

Pushing consists of concentrating promotion efforts on intermediaries, who are then expected to promote the item to ultimate customers. Strongly entrenched producers such as Heinz and Philip Morris often use a pushing strategy by exerting pressure on other channel members to accept a new product. Industrial marketers are strong proponents of pushing.[22]

Pushing an item
Marketing efforts to intermediaries, who are then expected to promote the item to final customers.

Legally, a firm cannot force others into carrying an item, as the Clayton Act disallows tying contracts. Nevertheless, the producer can exert some pressure. Intermediaries know that producers can withdraw support for other items short of breaking the law. For example, if stock-out conditions develop among intermediaries, a noncooperative channel member might be the last firm to be restocked.

Sometimes weak firms find pushing to be a useful course of action. Instead of brute force pressure, however, they emphasize finesse through higher margins and allowances than those of competitors. Because of the substantial profit potentials, other channel members may become interested.

Specific Channel Configuration Decisions

Once producers have decided upon an overall strategy, it remains necessary for them to make specific channel attribute decisions. The overriding set of criteria to use as guidelines consists of the marketing activities that must be performed to permit effective market penetration. Two major alternatives exist, ownership or contractual arrangements.

Ownership The first question to be addressed is whether the firm should farm out marketing tasks to intermediaries or carry them out itself. When a company desires to perform tasks for itself that are not normally thought to be carried out on its level in a channel (e.g., a producer also serving as a wholesaler to retailers), the process is termed **vertical integration,** or a vertical marketing system.[23] In other words, vertical integration involves expanding a firm's activities to other channel levels.[24]

Vertical integration
Purchasing firms located either forward or backward in a channel.

Forward vertical integration means that operations are expanded toward target customers. For example, Singer integrated its operation forward by opening company-owned retail sewing centers. This method's chief advantages are that the firm can maintain control of marketing activities and capture a greater profit margin.

Integration of a channel can also extend away from target customers, toward the source of supply. Termed backward vertical integration, the strategy may involve a producer who manufactures rather than buys parts and supplies. Another form is where a retailer performs wholesaling or manufacturing activities. Sears, to illustrate, integrated backward to the point that it does most of its own warehouse activities and even holds ownership in several manufacturing facilities. Del Monte owns a plantation in central America to grow pineapple for U.S. markets.[25] Backward vertical integration can offer the advantages of assuring a steady supply, quality and price control, and the potential to retain a large percentage of an item's profit margin.

Integration is not an "all-or-nothing" proposition. A fully integrated firm is one that extends all the way from raw materials to ultimate buyers. Many service firms are fully integrated, but those involved with manufactured products seldom are because of investment requirements and other more favorable opportunity alternatives. Once a company establishes how far it wishes to vertically integrate, if at all, it must then address the question of establishing contractual arrangements with other firms.

Administered (channel) **systems** Informal channel arrangements between independent members of a channel system.

Contractual Arrangements Contractual arrangements set the agreements between independent firms at different levels of a channel.[26] These arrangements may be formal and relatively permanent, as in the case of franchise organizations and wholesaler-sponsored chains, or they might be less formal and permanent (**administered systems**) as when Kroger Supermarket decides to buy dairy products from Borden.

Three types of decisions are relevant in entering into these arrangements: adaptability requirements, appropriate motivation and control mechanisms, and the number, type, and identity of other firms needed.

Adaptability Before establishing a channel, management is wise to consider the long-range prospects that could require future changes. Technological developments, changes in a product's life cycle, economic and legal developments, and competition can cause a particular channel to become dated.

Apple Computer, for example, found it necessary to drop wholesalers and to sell its personal computers directly to retailers via its own 350-person sales force, as a means of more fully coordinating efforts with retailers.[27] Thus, before attempting to establish formal and relatively permanent contractual arrangements with other firms, successful managers first attempt to estimate future conditions.

Appropriate Motivation and Control Mechanisms All efforts of a channel's members should interact in harmony for a marketing program to attain its maximum impact. In fact, some experts argue that intermediaries and producers are well advised to see themselves as partners by coordinating their efforts for their mutual benefit.[28] However, while a carefully coordinated effort is a desirable goal, a harmonious relationship is not automatic. All channels, especially those involving contractual arrangements, contain some degree of conflict that strains relationships and can weaken performance.[29]

Conflict is inherent in channels because of nonparallel goals among channel members. For example, Winnebago chose to install Renault engines in its RVs a few years ago to get better fuel mileage. This alienated many dealers because their mechanics were not trained to work on Renault motors.[30] More recently, in 1986 General Motors made the decision to raise prices by 2.9 percent to improve future cash flow, despite company sales being down at the time. In turn, dealers were concerned about their own cash flow problems as inventories climbed. These types of decisions strain channel relations.

Conflict also stems from competition within the channel itself. Intermediaries are often competitors with each other, putting stress on the whole system. If one Mobil station cuts the price of its gas, for example, it raises the ire of other nearby Mobil dealers. Similarly, large intermediaries often seek to gain favorable prices or delivery schedules, which upsets smaller firms. For example, Lever Brothers found that many

By joining forces with Kraft, Pillsbury was able to gain market access with refrigerated products.

full-retail-price druggists removed Pepsodent (the best selling toothpaste at the time) from their shelves because large discounters began to cut its price.

Finally, intermediaries are usually a part of multiple channel systems. Marshall Field's, for example, handles both Apple and IBM computers. Naturally conflict may develop in their relationship with a given manufacturer since they attempt to balance their efforts on the lines they carry and even attempt to play one against the other in striking better deals.

A moderate degree of conflict can actually increase a channel's effectiveness by helping to reduce apathy.[31] But too much is counterproductive. To strike a balance, management should work on developing an equitable system of motivating and controlling an integrated channel effort, including appropriate marketing plans, intermediary training sessions, margins and allowances, quotas, delivery schedules, and other moves designed to motivate members and to spell out the activities for which they are responsible.[32] This should be done before the system is formed, so that all parties know what is expected of them and what may be done in the event of noncompliance.

Managing conflict can be especially troublesome during periods of economic stagnation and decline. Manufacturers and wholesalers often demand larger minimum orders and more rapid payment when distribution costs rise and markets shrink.[33] The proper incentives, leadership, and consistency are needed to hold conflict to a tolerable

MARKETING BRIEF

General Motors Strategies and Tactics Surprised Its Dealers, But They Remained Loyal

The General Motors Corporation made some marketing decisions in 1986 that surprised and even dismayed some of its dealers. The firm's sales were off, yet it raised its prices by 2.9 percent. Many of the firm's dealers were baffled, especially since company auto sales were down by 6 percent from a year before. In the face of this, dealers had inventories that were 30 percent above normal. Joseph E. Meyers, president of Collins Oldsmobile, Inc., in Indianapolis related, "they just couldn't resist the temptation to reach out and grab the bucks."

The dealers expected GM to launch new sales incentives eventually, but probably not until inventories dropped. Then, they predicted that the firm would roll out cash rebates. In the meantime, many dealers were suffering from the double crunch of large inventories and reduced sales.

Many firms would experience reduced dealer performance under such conditions. However, General Motors has built up a high degree of motivation and a cooperative arrangement with dealers. Many were optimistic in 1986 that the company was doing the right thing, despite the unfavorable signs. Charles R. Hutton, general manager of a dealership in Memphis, indicated that he had accumulated large inventories to take care of the expected large surge in sales later in the year. In addition, the company offered rebates and low-interest financing on some slow-selling models to help alleviate its inventory problems.

SOURCE: Adapted from J. K. Teahen, Jr., "GM Raises Prices 2.9 Percent; Estimated Average Is $400," *Automotive News* (March 31, 1986): 3.

level under these circumstances and to lead to lasting channel relationships. A flashy representative of a film producer once said to a Chicago theater owner, "If you make money on this deal, I'm not doing my job right." [34] Like the representative, such a position results in eventual failure. Long-run success is best achieved when all members of a channel benefit from affiliating with the channel.

Number, Type, and Identity of Other Firms Finally, management needs to make specific decisions about the number and type of other firms to include in a channel, including the number of trade areas to cover, the number of representatives in each trade area, the channel level best able to service each area, and the specific firms to include.[35] Economic factors, along with needed marketing activities, are the primary criteria for guiding such decisions. Break-even analysis is a useful technique in evaluating proposed channel alternatives, as Exhibit 11.2 illustrates.

XYZ Company currently employs a three-level channel, including retailers, to distribute items to consumers. Per-unit revenue, cost, and profit data appear at the left of the exhibit. This structure has a break-even of 10,000 units.

Data for a proposed four-level channel (representing the addition of wholesalers) appear at the right of the exhibit. Wholesalers require a markup of $10 per unit as incentive for handling XYZ's line. In return, wholesalers perform certain marketing activities, thus reducing XYZ's variable and fixed marketing costs. Consequently, adding the fourth channel level results in a break-even of 8,000 units—a 20 percent reduction. Assuming that wholesalers would adequately service retailers—so long as unit sales would not fall by 20 percent or more—their addition to the channel would increase profitability.

Exhibit 11.2
Break-Even Analysis Used to Evaluate Proposed Channel Alternatives, XYZ Company

Existing Channel (including retailers):		
Unit data		
Sales price (retail)		$80.00
Retailer profit margin (markup)		30.00
XYZ's unit receipts		$50.00
Variable product costs		
labor	$5.00	
materials	5.00	
marketing (shipping, storing, etc.)	10.00	20.00
Unit contribution margin		$30.00
Fixed costs (overhead, production, and marketing)		$300,000
Break-even: $300,000 / $30/unit = 10,000 units		

Proposed Channel (wholesalers added):		
Sales price (retail)		$80.00
Retailer profit margin (markup)		30.00
Wholesaler unit receipts		50.00
Wholesaler profit margin (markup)		10.00
XYZ's unit receipts		$40.00
Variable product costs		
labor	$5.00	
materials	5.00	
marketing (shipping, storing, etc.)	5.00[a]	15.00
Unit contribution margin		$25.00
Fixed costs (overhead, production, and marketing)		$200,000[a]
Break-even: $200,000 / $25/unit = 8,000 units		

a. These costs are lower because wholesalers would perform certain marketing activities, thereby reducing XYZ's costs (perhaps a company-owned warehouse could be eliminated).

Ultimately, management must decide which particular firms to include in a channel and what their tasks are to be. Ideally, they should select channel members whose strengths most closely match task requirements. This involves considering inventory policies, advertising ability, personal selling efforts, return and allowance policies, pricing practices, and the entire array of marketing activities. For example, certain retailers have prestige images, such as Bloomingdale's in New York, Neiman-Marcus in Dallas, and May D & F in Denver. If the producer selects a prestige-oriented target consumer, then it should include such retailers.

This selection process can be the most difficult part of channel decision making, as the most desirable intermediaries may already be committed to competitors' products. For example, a new appliance manufacturer would have extreme difficulty in getting prime retailers to handle its products because General Electric, West Bend, and other established producers have already secured the best ones. Accordingly, management may find it necessary to accept less-than-ideal channel members.

Channel Leadership

To this point it has been assumed that producers are the developers and prime coordinators of the channel. In a sense, producers have the ultimate decision-making power because they can always decide whether they wish to produce an item or not. But short of this extreme, producers are not always the principal channel decision makers.

In each channel system there is one firm that assumes a leadership position in determining who is to perform which functions. This firm is the channel's leader or **captain**—the principal decision maker within a channel system. A product's manufacturer most often fills this role, but sometimes it is an intermediary.

Captain (channel)
Primary decision maker (leader) in a channel.

Who Becomes a Channel's Leader?

A producer is always the leader in a direct channel since no intermediaries are involved. The leader of a lengthier channel might instead be a wholesaler or retailer. Usually the strongest member of a channel system emerges as its leader.

Factors Favoring Producers as Leaders Producers tend to be the leaders when large-scale expenditures are required for the marketing, production or technological development of a product line. Examples include industries such as soft drinks, patent medicines, and automobiles. The major factors leading to a producer channel control is that a large expenditure is required for marketing, production, or both; the items are targeted for mass markets in multiple geographic areas; and the products are likely to be highly differentiable from others within their generic product classes.

In general, intermediaries do not have the single product capabilities, sufficient capital, or sufficiently large markets to develop products requiring large-scale efforts. Developing a new TV set, to illustrate, might cost Quasar in excess of $50 million. Larger markets than those serviced by intermediaries are typically necessary for such an investment to be financially feasible. Since producers can distribute through numerous intermediaries, large investments become more feasible.

Factors Favoring Intermediaries as Leaders An intermediary is likely to be a channel's leader when one of three factors exist. First, strong intermediaries may have to assume leadership when producers are too weak to do so. Sears, to illustrate, is the channel leader for most of the items that it sells. By contracting with weaker manufacturers to provide items sold under Sears' own brands, both the retailer and its affiliated producers benefit. Sears is able to control the entire marketing effort of its products and manufacturers obtain access to large markets they would otherwise be unable to penetrate.

Second, strong intermediaries can develop leadership roles by helping to differentiate otherwise similar basic commodities. To illustrate, many shoppers think of cans of corn as being pretty much alike despite their production origins. Reasonable quality is important in determining which brand they select, but so is price. Intermediaries can and do develop their own brands, like Kroger's "Golden Corn." In this case the Kroger name provides an assurance of reasonable quality.

Finally, when producers experience difficulty in forecasting or stimulating demand in local areas, intermediaries are in a good position to become channel leaders. This is largely the case for fashion-oriented apparel and household items. The "in" clothing in New York is different from what is found on the West Coast or in Kansas City. Local intermediaries generally are in the best position to judge what consumers will demand in their trade areas. Accordingly, they generally assume channel leadership.

In short, whichever channel member is in the best position to absorb risk is best able to assume control. When adjusting to local conditions is critical, retailers or wholesalers are often in the best position. When a larger scale is required, producers generally assume channel leadership. It is the leader's responsibility to develop an effective channel system and to see that it functions properly.

Tasks of Channel Leaders

Channel leaders seek to accomplish the following major objectives:

1. To develop an integrated and effective marketing program
2. To develop a smooth-running channel system relatively free of interorganizational conflict
3. To control inventories for customer service and corporate costs
4. To provide adequate service to ultimate customers and other channel members

In order to accomplish these objectives, leaders must realize that all participants, including themselves, tend to adopt a comparative profit approach when determining the extent of their involvement in a particular channel.[36] That is, the degree of support that a channel member is willing to provide is in direct proportion to the profit that it can expect by so doing. Thus, the captain should see that adequate financial incentives are available for all channel members. Beyond this, interpersonal leadership and a sound marketing program are necessary for channel member support.[37]

Finally, some researchers propose that large firms should utilize a channel manager to coordinate channel decisions. The firm would receive benefits such as coordination and control and full-time attention to the channel's field. Further, this would ensure that the company affords channel decisions as much attention as decisions in areas such as product planning and advertising.[38]

Chapter Summary

This chapter examined decisions about channels of distribution. Channels involve the sets of institutions and agencies used to make products and services available to customers. Producers typically lack the expertise, finances, and operating scale needed to both effectively and efficiently perform all marketing activities needed to fully develop a marketing mix's place component, especially for consumer products. Consequently, manufacturers generally rely on economic relationships with intermediaries to develop a distribution system for product marketing.

Three basic types of major channel decisions are involved. First, management must identify needed marketing activities, based upon target customer, product, intermediary, environment, and company factors. Second, management should select an appropriate overall channel strategy. This involves determining the desired distribution intensity, channel direction, and whether multiple channels, dual distribution, horizontal marketing systems, and a pushing or pulling effort are most appropriate. Finally, management needs to make specific channel configuration decisions, consisting of determining which activities the firm itself should perform, which should be contracted out, and which intermediaries should be used.

Producers are generally responsible for overall channel development and coordination, but not always. Selling intermediaries—wholesalers and retailers—sometimes assume channel leadership roles. It is the responsibility of channel leaders to develop a channel's structure and to motivate members to provide an aggressive, integrated effort without excessive conflict within the system.

Questions

1. A noted business leader once said, "Flows, shmos—the only important thing is to have stuff available when people want it." Comment.
2. Are channels of distribution likely to increase or decrease in importance in the future? Why?
3. What is meant by a product bundle? What does a channel have to do with this?
4. What is meant by the concept of a channel's attributes? Which factor should be considered when identifying a channel's desirable attributes?
5. It has been said that "Since the best intermediaries are not always available, it's foolish to enter into idle speculation about desirable channel parameters. Selling to the right intermediaries is the key to success, not discussing which activities are needed on paper." Comment.
6. What are horizontal marketing systems? When are they desirable?
7. Compare and contrast a pulling and pushing strategy. When is each most appropriate?
8. What decisions must be made when designing a channel?
9. Compare and contrast various types of vertical integration.
10. What is a channel leader? What functions does the leader serve? Who becomes a channel leader?
11. Compare and contrast intensive, selective, and exclusive distribution.
12. What is bypass distribution?
13. What are the advantages and disadvantages of dual distribution?

Chapter 12

Physical Distribution Decisions

Objectives

After completing this chapter, you should be able to demonstrate a knowledge of:

- What is meant by the term "physical distribution"
- What the systems concept is and how management can employ it in physical distribution decision making
- The components of the two major areas of administrative authority in physical distribution: materials management and transportation management
- The major kinds of decisions management must make in the materials management field
- The characteristics of the major modes of transportation and the rates and services associated with each
- How marketers can coordinate physical distribution decisions

MARKETING SUCCESS

Formulating a Huge Pipeline after Deregulation

With a broad scythe cutting a wide swath of reform under President Reagan, many industries (including airlines, trucking, and communications) have been competitively trimmed through deregulation—the elimination of price (and other) controls. Another business to be affected is the pipeline industry, mainly a shipper of bulk natural gas and petroleum products.

The reforms were intended to bring down prices, and they have worked, proving to be a Grim Reaper for many of the weakest companies. Others have managed to merge and avoid becoming one more fatality.

Enron Corporation is one such company, despite being saddled with a huge debt—$4.3 billion worth—acquired in the conglomeration process. Formerly known as HNG/InterNorth, the new company, made up of both the former InterNorth and Houston Natural Gas companies, was put together by Kenneth L. Lay, Enron's chairman, who used all of his skills as a seasoned industry executive and the education provided by his Ph.D. in economics to bring about the deal.

Despite the residual debt, most analysts feel that Enron will emerge from the whole process as one of the strongest contenders in the industry, "A real heavy-weight," said one. Under Mr. Lay's leadership, the company has assembled an impressive 37,000-mile coast-to-coast pipeline network—one of the industry's largest. Equally important is its access to the nation's fastest-growing gas markets—Southern California and Florida. When coupled with the company's availability to the cheap, unregulated Texas natural gas, Enron is well positioned to stave off any future competitive threats. "I am convinced that Enron will be the brightest star in the industry," said the analyst. "Lay has succeeded in putting together all of the pieces."

SOURCE: Adapted from "The 37,000-Mile Deal," *Time*, May 13, 1985: 55.

Introduction

Physical distribution (PD), also called logistics, is an important function that is closely related to channel management. PD refers to a broad range of activities involving the efficient and effective movements of products.[1] PD also involves the many ways to move items, from trains to ships, from planes to pipelines. And it involves several companies that specialize in performing the work, from Flying Tiger Airlines to Union Pacific Railroad, and from Pacific Intermountain Express truck lines to Enron Corporation pipelines, highlighted in the chapter's opening Marketing Success.

PD itself relates to the flow of products across space and time from producers to customers. In contrast, PD management involves the design and implementation of systems to control this flow. PD management is related to, but distinct from, channel management. On the one hand, channel management is concerned with who is to participate in a channel structure as well as all of the flow relationships between the participants. On the other hand, PD management focuses on the efficient and effective movement, storage, and handling of items.

Physical distribution
Activities involved in efficiently and effectively moving products across space and time from producers to customers.

More specifically, PD management seeks to attain efficiencies in the mechanical problems of [2]

1. *Warehousing and storing*—how much inventory should be stored and where
2. *Transportation and handling*—what is the best means of moving goods from one point to another
3. *Order processing*—what is the most efficient and effective means of processing and placing orders
4. *Location selecting*—where should warehouses, stores, inventory stocks, and other elements be located

Historically marketers have not granted as much attention to PD as they have to the activities of locating customers and motivating them to buy, but today this is changing. With rapidly rising transportation, storage, and handling costs, marketers are increasingly treating PD as a last frontier for gaining efficiency. PD functions historically have accounted for nearly half of a firm's total marketing costs, or about 14 to 30 percent of sales.[3] Consequently, a relatively modest improvement can bring about startling rewards, as illustrated in the following examples.

Foremost-McKesson (the world's largest wholesale distributor) has automated and computerized systems in all 72 of its chemical warehouses. This allows the firm to streamline ordering, delivering, invoicing, and developing customer profile data. The computer system makes it possible for one warehouse to serve an entire region rather than only one local market.[4]

One of UNICEF's fundraising programs is the sale of gifts and cards through catalogs. Buyers receive both the material they order and the knowledge that they have contributed to this cause. UNICEF has utilized computerized inventory control methodologies borrowed from industry, allowing it to cut inventory costs substantially.

Sophisticated computer analytic techniques showed General Electric that an annual savings of nearly $3 million was possible by redesigning the PD system of just one subsidiary with sales of $50 million—a profit improvement of 6 percent of sales. To appreciate the size of this savings, consider the fact that business profits generally average about 6 percent of sales.[5] Thus, business profitability would double if all firms could gain the same relative improvement by carefully controlling PD activities.

The Systems Approach

Systems approach to physical distribution
Minimizing total PD costs, subject to enabling the channel system to maintain a desired level of service.

A **systems approach to physical distribution** is especially useful when making decisions about various physical movement alternatives.[6] The overriding objective is to minimize total PD costs while maintaining a desired level of service.

When making PD decisions, management should first establish the level of service that it seeks to offer customers to attract their business. Some firms, like Pillsbury, define their delivery goals as "third morning delivery anywhere in the U.S." Others define their goals as a percentage of customers who should get their order in a particular number of days. Still others think of holding out-of-stock conditions down to a certain level.[7] To customers, service takes several forms: [8]

1. Time from order receipt to order shipment
2. Order size and assortment restrictions
3. Percentage of items out of stock
4. Percentage of orders filled

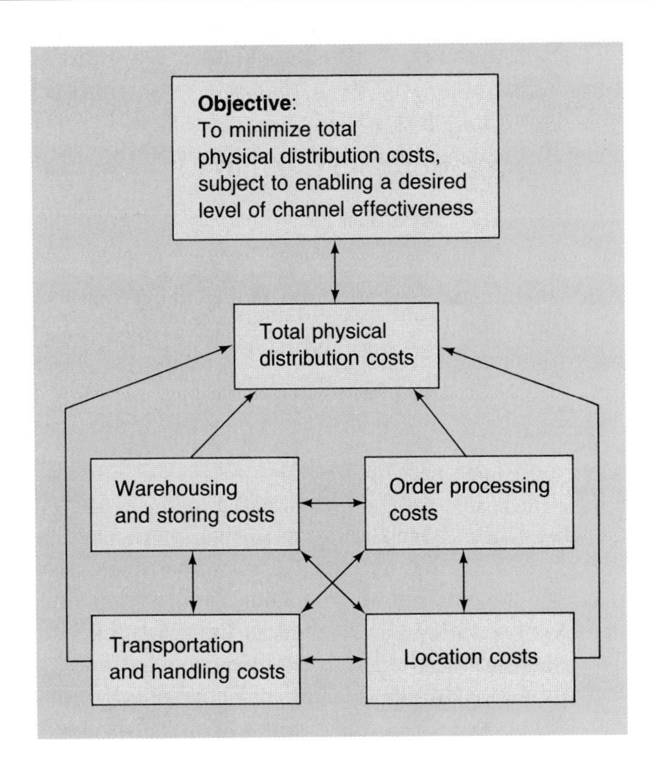

Figure 12.1
The Physical Distribution System

5. Percentage of orders filled accurately
6. Percentage of orders filled within a reasonable number of days
7. Percentage of orders that arrive in good condition
8. Time from order placement to order delivery
9. Ease and flexibility of order placement
10. Consistency of delivery times

In general, the greater the service level, the higher the PD costs. Conversely, lower service levels involve smaller PD costs, but sales tend to drop as the service level falls so management should not lower the level of service too far.

Determining the appropriate level of service to offer is one of the most difficult tasks in marketing.[9] Each situation is unique. In essence, the appropriate level of service should reflect current competitors' services as well as estimated customer and competitor reactions to alternate levels of service. Even rough estimates are useful in learning the impact of PD alternatives.[10]

The costs of a PD system include warehousing and storing, order processing, transportation, handling, and operating the facilities in given locations. The objective is to minimize the total of these costs while providing a desired level of service.

As Figure 12.1 illustrates, all of a PD system's components are interactive, meaning that management must make tradeoffs when attempting to minimize costs. Adding another warehouse means larger associated costs but could also result in a less expensive means of shipping goods and fewer lost sales due to out-of-stock conditions. Because PD should be thought of as a system, total costs and their overall implications on channel effectiveness are the important evaluative criteria, not the individual costs of any single component.[11]

Gathering information in a systematic way is a must for the systems concept to work.[12] Computers and model-building techniques such as simulation provide workable tools for managers to use in making decisions for particular components, based upon their impact on the overall PD system.[13]

Components of a Physical Distribution System

As a systems perspective suggests, intelligent decision making considers all PD activities as totally interactive. Consequently, extensive coordination is required. But for organizational convenience, we shall consider PD decision-making activities as falling into one of two categories: materials management and transportation management.

Materials Management

Materials management is an important part of physical distribution.

Generally, firms have a need to maintain inventories and physically move items from one place to another for effective operation. This involves receiving and storing raw materials for continuous production, and storing finished goods and then moving them in a way that allows efficient transportation and satisfies uneven sales levels. The administration of these activities is called **materials management.** Let us first consider materials management issues pertaining to inventories.

Inventory Decisions Inventories are held for two reasons: to enable relatively even production levels over time despite sales fluctuations, and to take advantage of the most economical means of transportation, which usually means bulk shipments. If sales were always constant, say 1,000 units per day, and if transportation, ordering, and handling costs were the same per unit regardless of the size of the batch, then maintaining inventories would be economically wasteful. Production would be set at 1,000 units per day and inventories would be eliminated.

But these costs do vary per unit, with larger quantities usually resulting in lower average ordering costs. And if sales are lost because of not having an adequate stock on hand, termed a **stock-out** condition, the customer may be lost forever.[14] Firms generally try to maintain some inventory level in reserve, called **safety stock,** to enable them to meet unexpected demand. Thus, inventories facilitate sales and enable efficiencies in shipping, handling, and ordering. Figure 12.2 illustrates these relationships.

Notice in panel A of the figure, the firm produces goods until it has accumulated an amount, called the *optimal shipment level*, which permits efficient transportation. Then it arranges for a shipment and inventory falls to zero. This process is repeated over time, permitting both even production runs and low-cost transportation. In panel B, a marketing intermediary has goods on hand that are gradually depleted by sales. Once inventory falls to a desired safety stock level (for emergencies such as surges in demand and late shipments) shipment 1 arrives, providing items to be made available for sale over the next phase of the inventory cycle. This process continues with shipment 2 and subsequent shipments.

Holding an inventory is costly because of

1. the cost of capital (interest costs from tying up funds)
2. opportunity costs (the inability to use funds for other purposes)
3. theft, spoilage, obsolescence, and breakage of items being stored[15]

Materials management
Receiving and storing raw materials for continuous production and storing finished goods and then moving them in a way that allows efficient transportation.

Stock-out
Lost sales because finished goods are not on hand when customers want them.

Safety stock
Inventory levels maintained in reserve to meet unexpected demand.

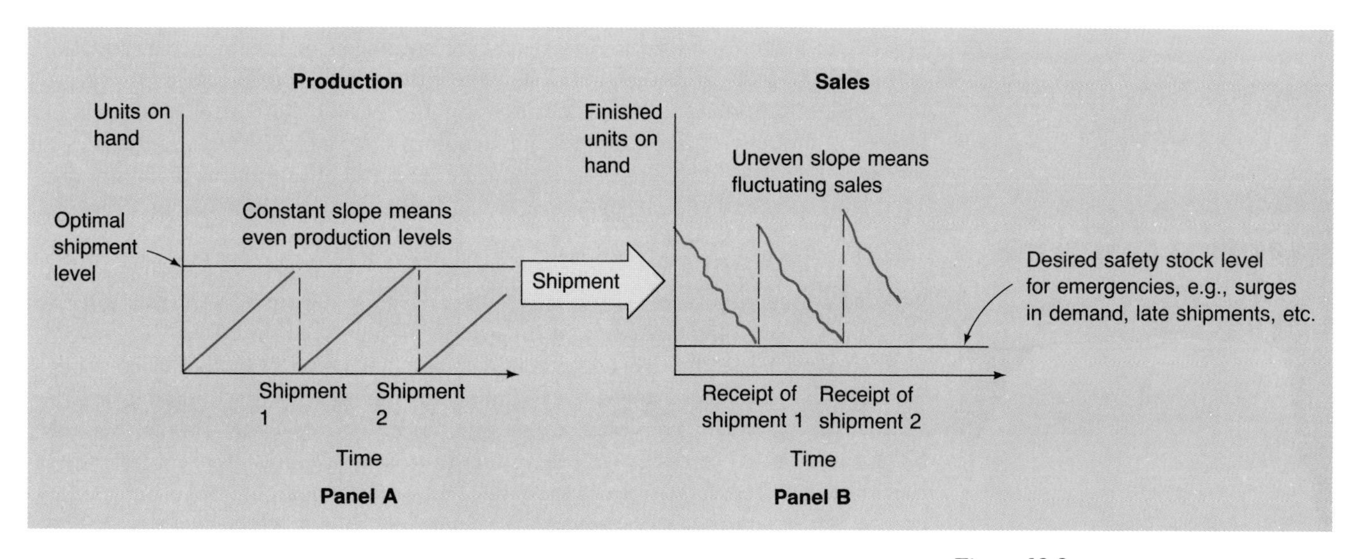

Figure 12.2
Inventories Help Generate Efficiencies and Also Supply Fluctuating Demand

But not holding adequate inventory (attempting to place or fill small orders) is also costly because of

1. lost sales due to stock-outs
2. excessive overhead caused by placing and filling small orders
3. not being able to take advantage of quantity discounts, both for purchases and for reduced large-lot-size transportation rates and handling costs

Properly managing an inventory consists of attempting to minimize total inventory costs, both the out-of-pocket types and those related to not being able to service customers (i.e., stock-out costs) as Figure 12.3 illustrates. The figure shows that total inventory costs per unit first fall to an optimal inventory size level, then rise as the total number of units of inventory increases.

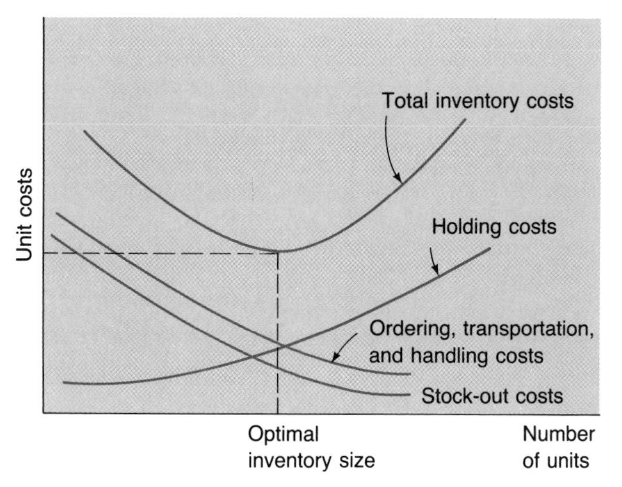

Figure 12.3
Optimal Inventory Level

MARKETING BRIEF

Champion Spark Plug Has a Difficult Inventory Situation

The Champion Spark Plug Company produces spark plugs for new automobiles, trucks, and other vehicles and as replacement parts (the aftermarket). In recent years, its physical distribution problems have increased dramatically.

Aftermarket parts remain in stock for a long time. The Model T Ford has not been made since 1927, for instance, yet in 1982 Champion produced 17,649 Model T spark plugs. Recently, the number of new spark plugs needed to keep in inventory has increased substantially because of the influx of imported vehicles and older vehicles still on the road.

SOURCE: Adapted from "Automotive Aftermarket Is Confronted with Turbulent Times," *The Marketing News* 17, no. 4 (February 18, 1983): 24.

The components of total inventory cost are holding costs; ordering, transportation, and handling costs; and stock-out costs. The first, holding costs, rise as inventory is increased—the more goods that are in stock, the greater the cost of holding them. However, ordering, transportation, and handling costs fall as the quantities ordered increase. Likewise, stock-out costs decline as the number of units in inventory rises. This is to be expected, as larger inventory levels lessen the chances that potential buyers will not be served.

The complexities of managing inventories can be staggering. Keeping track of hundreds, even thousands, of different types of items is common, as illustrated by Champion Spark Plug Company in the accompanying Marketing Brief.

Technological advances in computers, software, and complex mathematical models have greatly expanded management's ability to manage inventories and determine optimal stock levels for even extensive product lines.[16, 17] A few years ago, for example, Montgomery Ward invested over $40 million in an advanced inventory control system. Electronic cash registers tie directly into the firm's central computer to record all sales. In a matter of seconds, management can determine exactly which items are selling, current inventory levels, when to order new stock, and how many units should be ordered. The resulting cost and efficiency improvements have been remarkable. Even the smallest of firms, however, can attain efficiencies through hand-tabulated information systems that carefully control inventories.

Warehousing Decisions Inventory and warehousing decisions are closely related. Warehousing is the storing, housing, and handling of goods from the time they are produced to the time they are sold. Included are all activities from the time items arrive at a warehouse until they leave for shipment to customers. Warehousing is required for accumulating and storing items in assortments and breaking large quantities into smaller ones for allocation to customers at the appropriate time. Two types of decisions are needed: determining the number of warehouses and selecting their locations.

Number of Warehouses Maintaining a large number of warehouses makes very effective servicing of customers possible, especially if the warehouses are situated near clusters of customers. When inventories are located nearby, stock-out conditions are less likely to occur. Further, a larger number of warehouses may reduce shipping costs since part of an item's movement can be in large batches from the point of production toward final buyers. Conversely, a greater number of warehouses drives up inventory costs, as larger total inventories and more handling is usually required. As a result, deciding the appropriate number of warehouses to use involves making a cost tradeoff, as Figure 12.4 illustrates.

As shown in the figure, total distribution costs per unit first fall and then begin to rise as the firm adds warehouses. A greater number of warehouses lowers transportation and lost opportunity costs, but drives up inventory carrying costs. The net effect of these counterbalancing costs is that there is an optimal number of warehouses that a firm should use to minimize total costs.

There are a number of analytical methods that can help in calculating the appropriate number of warehouses, especially with the use of modern computers, that are beyond the scope of this text.[18] It should be noted that complex techniques are not always required for decisions of this type. If management carefully audits company cost relationships and imposes judgment, a close approximation of the appropriate

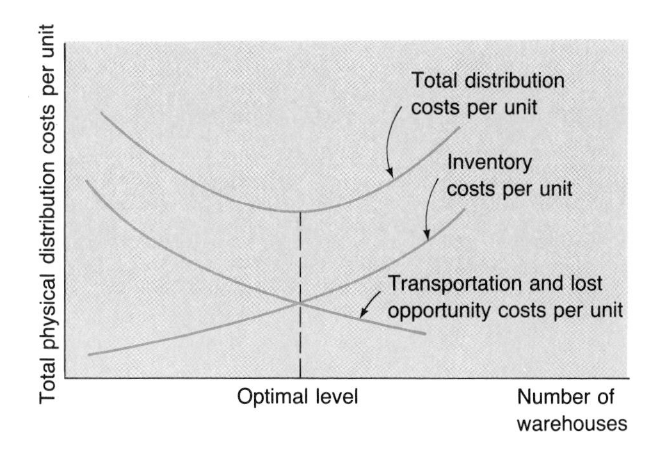

Figure 12.4
Optimal Number of Warehouses

Modern warehouses are designed for efficiency.

number of warehouses can often be made. Even small and uncomplicated firms can take advantage of well-conceived decisions in this area.

Locating Warehouses In essence, firms have two choices when deciding where to house inventories. First, they may hold an inventory at a central point in or near the firm's production facilities. Loads are then shipped to customers as orders are received. Nabisco and Keebler both successfully move cookies and related products in this manner.[19] The second choice is to transport goods to storage points near customers and then reship them to fill orders. For example, assume that a producer in Ohio sells many of its items in California and the east coast. Instead of storing items in Ohio, it may be more desirable to maintain inventories on both coasts.

Centrally located storage has the advantage of tying up less capital in inventory since the firm requires fewer items to be held. Random fluctuations in sales within regions tend to offset each other, thus necessitating smaller safety stocks. However, centrally located inventories may result in higher transport costs if shipments to customers are so small that the firm incurs costly transportation rates. Further, central storage may result in a longer time being required to fill orders, which can produce stock-outs and lost sales.

Regionally located inventories, on the other hand, usually permit rapid servicing of customers and efficient transportation, at least to the point of storage. But a firm's total inventory level can be substantial, resulting in large holding costs. Consequently, management's deliberations on which, if any, locations to select as storage points are based on tradeoffs between costs of central versus regional storage.[20]

Figure 12.5 illustrates distribution through direct shipment in panel A and break-bulk through a warehouse in panel B.[21] A manufacturer of small electric appliances such as electric can openers, blenders, and knives distributes through three retail chains: retailer 1, retailer 2, and retailer 3. In the case of panel A, the company fills their orders through direct shipments from the factory to each retail warehouse. Under the alternative posed in panel B, the firm ships large quantities of goods to a company warehouse where shipments are received and broken down into quantities that meet retail order sizes.

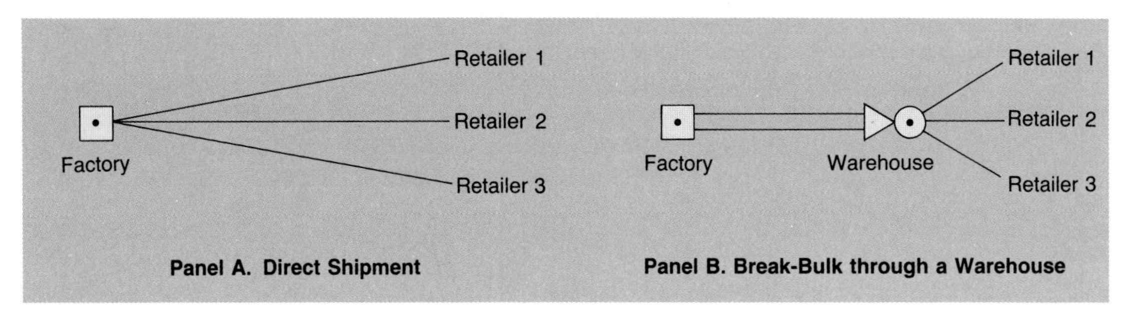

Figure 12.5
Direct Shipment and Break-Bulk through a Warehouse

The break-bulk arrangement has two advantages for the manufacturer. First, it is less costly than direct shipment. Transportation carriers such as railroads and trucking firms charge lower per-unit rates for large than for small shipments. The break-bulk alternative, then, allows the manufacturer to ship large quantities of goods at low rates to the warehouse. The shipments at higher freight rates in smaller volume units from the warehouse to the retailers are for very short distances. As a result, the total cost of the arrangement in panel B could be considerably less than for panel A.

The panel B arrangement enjoys another cost advantage. A large volume of merchandise flows through a warehouse whose size is sufficiently large to justify specialized personnel and automated equipment. This also permits very efficient distribution.

Finally, alternative B may allow the manufacturer to serve retailers adequately. The specialized personnel and automated equipment allow the company to reduce the incidence of errors such as late deliveries and incorrectly filled orders. Further, since the warehouse is located near the retail warehouses, the manufacturer can provide fast delivery. Overall, then, the break-bulk procedure can offer substantial cost reductions and customer service advantages.

Marketers generally have three choices when considering regional storage. First, management may add a level to an existing distribution channel. A wholesaler with adequate facilities may be the answer to regional storage needs, for instance. Second, public warehouses may be used, which are independent firms that rent space for storage. In fact, some provide almost as many services as do wholesalers. Further, management can use items stored in them to obtain warehouse receipts as collateral for loans. There are many types of specialized public warehouses, such as cold storage, grain elevators, and bonded warehouses (for specially taxed items such as imports and liquor). By using bonded warehouses, the company need not pay excise taxes until the items are released for shipment.

Finally, some firms buy or build their own private warehouses. General Motors, for example, maintains company-owned parts warehouses in several key locations around the world. Sufficient volume to justify each location and the ability and need to more rapidly service customers are prerequisites for this option. Generally, warehouses are costly to maintain and operate efficiently.

Transportation Management

Transportation management
Administration of the physical movement of goods from point of origin to point of destination.

Transportation management, the administration of the physical movement of goods from point of origin to point of destination, is the second arm of PD that is particularly important to today's managers. In 1973, the 500 largest industrial firms spent nearly $70 billion to move their products to market, which was nearly double the amount spent a decade before.[22] In the early 1980s this figure was $214 billion and growing steadily.[23] Consequently, managing these costs is becoming a major concern to businesses. In 1985, for instance, General Motors located its Saturn production plant in Tennessee primarily because the location offered the potential of lowering the company's transportation costs. Managers are faced with the need to make two key groups of decisions regarding transportation: when to ship, and the mode to use.

When to Ship Should marketers send goods to customers as soon as they receive orders? Sales managers are tempted to answer "Yes!" They know that stock-outs can lead to lost sales, and therefore seek to make rapid shipments. When asked the same question, cost-oriented managers are tempted to answer "Wait until we can assemble a large enough lot for shipment to the same destination at lower rates." They know that handling costs are smaller with large orders and that transportation rates are lower too. Carload lots (40,000 to 100,000 pounds) and truckload lots (15,000 pounds) have the lowest rates. Shipments of smaller sizes cost significantly more per pound.

All physical distribution decisions are characterized by the necessity for cost trade-offs. Thus, knowing when to ship depends upon the characteristics surrounding a particular firm: factors relating to its customers and the nature of its product, and upon management's strategies. Management should make an attempt to minimize both out-of-pocket and opportunity costs.

The Mode to Use A closely related decision is the selection of the specific mode of transportation. Modes are classified in two ways: by customers and by type of equipment.

Customer Type Transportation companies, termed *carriers*, exhibit three types of customer usage patterns. **Common carriers** are those which accept shipments from all customers requesting their service, even on the same vehicle. Most railroads, air carriers, and some motor carriers are of this type. Though this has changed to an extent (discussed later in this chapter), common carriers remain regulated as to routes, time schedules, and rates by the Interstate Commerce Commission (ICC) for railroad, motortruck, and inland waterway carriers; the Federal Power Commission (FPC) for pipelines; and the Federal Maritime Commission (FMC) for ocean-going water carriers.

Contract carriers lease or rent their services to individual shippers. Usually their rates are negotiable and, unlike common carriers, can adjust routes and schedules to fit the needs of shippers. Due to this flexibility, they can offer a great advantage over common carriers to large shippers and to those requiring shipping speed.

Finally, some large shippers maintain their own fleets of transportation equipment. These are called **private carriers.** Safeway, for instance, owns a large motortruck fleet. This alternative is often most desirable for shippers who require rapid speed and very flexible routes. Also, privately owned fleets can reduce total transportation costs for large shippers. If initial equipment, maintenance, and operating costs, plus the cost of tied-up capital, are less than the rates a firm would pay for commercial carriers, then a firm is wise to consider operating its own fleet.

Type of Equipment The type of equipment that a carrier uses is also a variable to consider in making channel decisions. Table 12.1 illustrates historic freight traffic

MARKETING BRIEF

GM Considered Transportation as the Major Factor in New Plant Location

GM decided to locate its new Saturn automobile manufacturing plant in the small Tennessee town of Spring Hill, near Nashville. The major reason for selecting the location was geography.

The site is close to GM's suppliers and within 500 miles of 76 percent of the U.S. population. Three interstate highways crisscross Nashville, and there is a rail attachment to the 234-mile Tennessee Tombigbee Waterway, a barge canal that connects with the Gulf of Mexico. This means low freight costs for the company.

SOURCE: Adapted from "Why a 'Little Detroit' Could Rise in Tennessee," *Business Week*, August 12, 1985: 21.

Common carriers
Transporters that accept shipments from all customers; highly regulated.

Contract carriers
Transporters that make contracts with shippers for their services; less regulated than common carriers.

Private carriers
Shippers who maintain their own fleets of transportation equipment.

Table 12.1 Historical Intercity Freight Traffic

	1965		1975		1984	
Type of Equipment	*Billions of Ton-Miles Carried*[a]	*Percent of Total*	*Billions of Ton-Miles Carried*[a]	*Percent of Total*	*Billions of Ton-Miles Carried*[a]	*Percent of Total*
Railroads	709	43.3	759	36.7	936	36.6
Motor Vehicles	359	21.9	454	22.0	602	23.6
Inland Waterways	262	16.0	342	16.6	404	15.8
Oil Pipelines	306	18.7	507	24.5	605	23.7
Airways	2	0.1	4	0.2	7	0.3
Totals	1,638	100.0	2,066	100.0	2,554	100.0

a. Defined as one ton carried one mile.
SOURCE: From *Statistical Abstract of the United States* (Washington, D.C.: U.S. Government Printing Office, 1986), 106th ed.

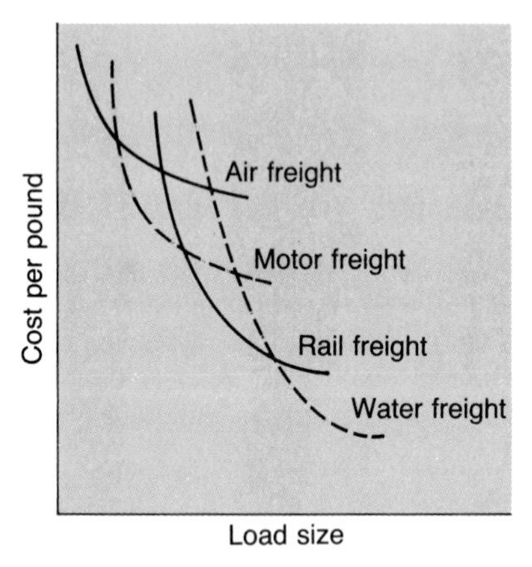

Figure 12.6
Shipping Costs Related to Weight, by Equipment Type

patterns over a 20-year period. While declining in relative terms, railroads remain the leading carrier of items handled on the basis of weight. This is because they are especially suited to handling heavy loads such as coal and iron ore. Also, railroad rates are relatively low. In general, rates are lower for slower means of transportation, as Figure 12.6 illustrates. However, rates also vary significantly within a particular mode of transportation.

Other factors besides the rate charged can be instrumental when management is selecting a particular mode of transportation. A fast and dependable means of transportation may be best despite high rates. Rapid delivery means that inventory sizes can be minimized, thereby freeing up capital. Consequently, firms such as IBM and Control Data often use air freight for expensive parts. Exhibit 12.1 compares transportation modes by characteristics. Consistent with all physical distribution decisions, the appropriate mode to use should be the one that helps to minimize a firm's total distribution costs.

Railroads All but a few of the smallest railroads in the United States are classified as common carriers. They are very competitive in the movement of bulky and heavy commodities over long distances at low costs. Most shippers find that if they ship goods by motortruck rather than by rail, the unit costs of transportation for smaller shipments tend to be lower. As firms increase shipment sizes they eventually reach a point where rail transport equals and then is less than motortruck rates. Shippers of such commodities as cement, bulk salt, lumber, coal, grain, and quarried rock use rail freight.

There are a number of disadvantages associated with railroad shipment. It is slower than air and many truck carriers, and some railroads have spotty records for damaging goods in transit and for unreliable delivery. In addition, service is available only in those areas where tracks exist.

Piggyback
Truck trailers that are loaded, placed on railroad flatcars, transported, and driven to the final destination by truck (also called *trailer on flatcar* or *TOFC*).

Railroads provide many services to shippers, although it should be noted that other transportation modes also offer many of these services. In the case of **piggyback** shipment (or TOFC—trailer on flatcar), truck trailers are loaded, placed on railroad flatcars, carried by rail to a terminal near the shipper, and then driven to the final destination by a truck. The advantage is a lower total cost and time consumed than for shipment by motor freight.

Mode	Characteristics				
	Cost per pound	Speed	Reliability	Specialized services	Ability to reach all destination points
Rail	Low	Poor	Poor	Superior	Poor
Pipeline	Very Low	Moderate	Excellent	Moderate	Poor
Motor Vehicle	Moderate	Moderate	Moderate	Excellent	Excellent
Water	Very Low	Poor	Poor	Moderate	Poor
Air	High	Excellent	Excellent	Good	Excellent

Exhibit 12.1
Transportation Mode Characteristics

Railroads assess two categories of rates, based upon the quantity moved. **Carload rates** apply to some minimum shipment size, such as 40,000 pounds, for a particular commodity. These are substantially smaller than rates for less-than-carload lots and such shipments normally move much faster. In the trucking industry a similar situation exists for truckload (**truckload rates**) and less-than-truckload shipments.

Carload rates
Lowered transportation rates that apply to a shipment size that occupies a full railcar.

Many small shippers do not move substantially large amounts of goods to qualify for carload rates. They can compensate for this by utilizing mixed car or pool car services. When they employ mixed car service they can move two or more different goods (such as work benches and tool boxes) in the same car. The railroad will bill this shipment at the rate which is the highest for any of the goods moved. By combining two or more goods the shippers may be able to qualify for carload rates. Several shippers may combine their products in order to qualify for reduced rates and fast delivery times in the case of pool car arrangements.

Truckload rates
Lower transportation rates that apply to a shipment size that occupies a full truck trailer.

Railroads provide another service called **diversion-in-transit.** This allows the shipper to move carloads that are in the process of transit to a destination that it did not specify when it originally turned over the goods to the carrier. Assume that an orange-growing cooperative is moving a shipment of oranges from southern California to Denver, where it intends to sell the fruit. In the process of transit, however, the price for oranges increases substantially in Omaha, until it is much higher than the Denver price. This induces the cooperative to change the destination from Denver to Omaha. It can do this and pay only the rate that applies for shipments to Omaha, plus a diversion fee. This rate is cheaper than shipping from southern California to Denver and then on to Omaha. The railroads permit diversion only when the new destination is in the same direction as the original one.

Diversion-in-transit
A privilege granted by carriers where the point of destination is changed while the shipment is in transit.

Some shippers prefer to process their goods after they have loaded them at the point of origin and before they reach the destination point. Firms may want to fatten livestock or mill flour, for instance, at locations between the origin and the destination. Railroads make available a **processing-in-transit** privilege, which allows shippers to stop their goods for processing at an intermediate point and then move them on to the destination at a lower rate than if the firms moved the goods to the intermediate point in one shipment and then on to the destination in another.

Processing-in-transit
The privilege of processing goods while in transit at a lower rate than if the goods were unloaded, processed, and then moved to the point of destination.

Railroads have undertaken a number of innovations, all designed to improve their competitive position. They have obtained specialized cars such as those employed for

Piggyback service has helped to speed shipping by railroad.

TOFC and large refrigerated tank cars. They have adopted computerized equipment that can sense damaged tracks and hence prevent accidents. Further, through sophisticated computer programs they can efficiently route and schedule the utilization of cars. These and other improvements have permitted railroads to compete more effectively.

Railroads do face some major problems, despite their innovations. Their labor costs are advancing rapidly. Some of the cars and trackage are in need of major repairs. Many rail rates are so high that they are noncompetitive. An example is in the coal industry, where high rates from mine to port have made U.S. coal very expensive in some foreign markets.[24] In addition, rivals, particularly air and motor carriers, are becoming more aggressive in seeking business. Nonetheless, railroads continue as the major mode of transportation for many shippers.

Motor Carriers Motor transportation is superior to railroad shipping under certain circumstances. Motortrucks have a competitive rate advantage in conveying small shipments over short distances. They can reach areas that are not accessible to rail, such as rural sites, and can pick up goods at loading docks and transport them to receiving docks without the necessity of reloading. Distributors of Mountain Valley Bottled Water (the largest selling brand in the U.S.) deliver water directly to homes, offices, and factories by trucks.[25] For short distances, trucks are faster than railroads. Damage in transit is less of a problem than it is with rail freight.

Congress designed The Motor Carrier Act of 1980 to aid in deregulating the trucking industry through fewer restrictions on setting rates, deciding which products to carry, and determining what routes to serve. Experience in the early and mid-1980s, however, indicated that the Interstate Commerce Commission still imposed substantial authority over these functions. The ICC indicated that before it would allow carriers to offer a new service they had to prove a need for the service and their ability to provide it.

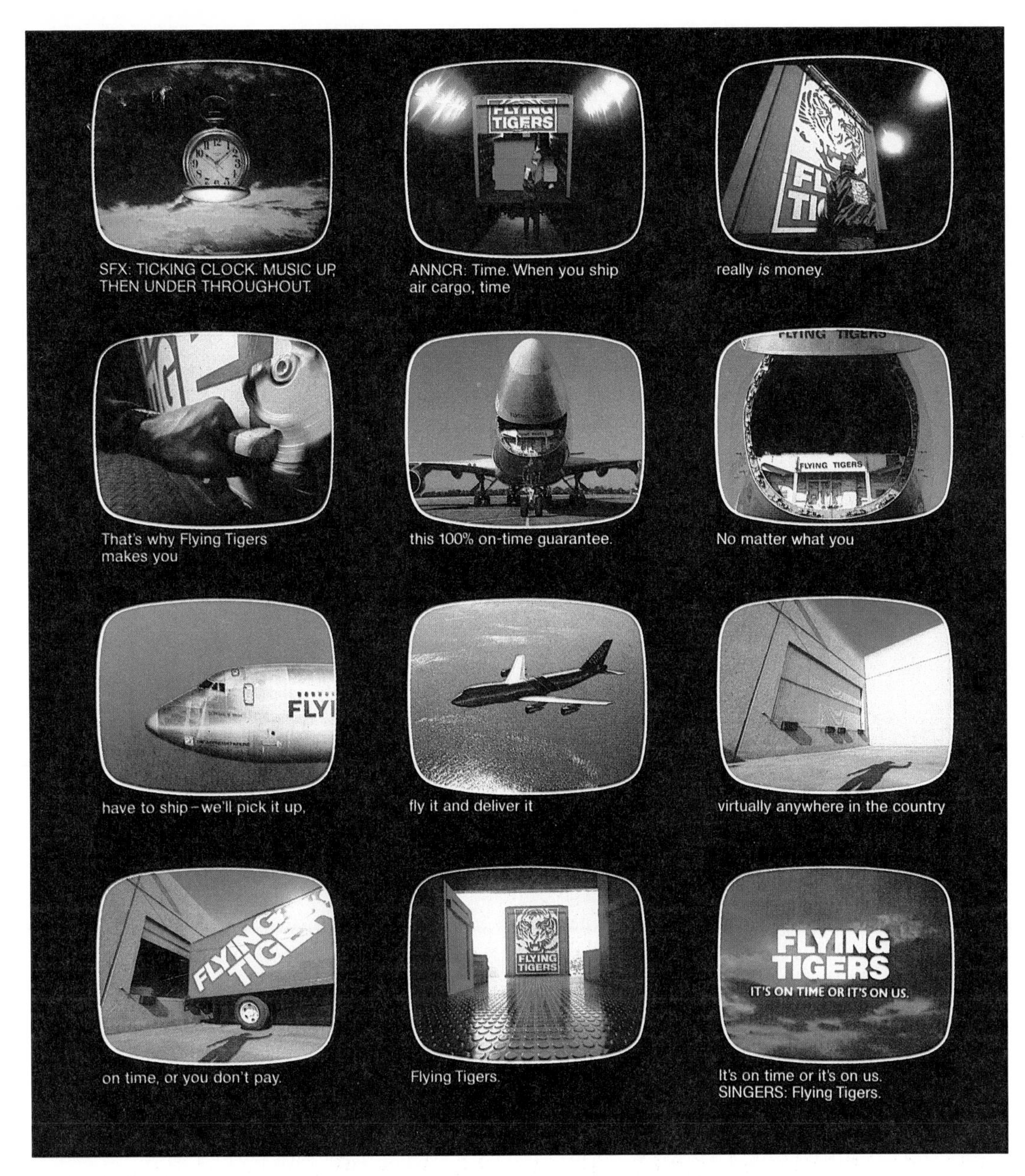

Air freight has been a growing means of shipping products.

Further, the agency denied a large number of rate change requests on the grounds that they were discriminatory in that they unduly benefited large shippers.[26] In short, despite the deregulation of 1980, motor carriers remain heavily regulated. What deregulation has accomplished is to allow many new firms to enter the industry, thereby making it much more competitive.[27]

Airlines Speed is the major advantage that airlines enjoy. For many shippers this advantage more than compensates for the high freight charges. They can achieve inventory reductions and consequent savings on warehousing costs as a result of rapid transportation. Generally, airlines have good records for minimal damage in transit. In addition, they can reach difficult-to-access areas such as parts of Southeast Asia, Africa, and Alaska, where roads and railroad trackage are nonexistent or in very poor condition.

In the main, shippers have employed air transport historically to move perishable goods, goods of high unit value, and emergency shipments to take care of important orders that they could not readily fill out of existing inventory. Today, however, shippers of numerous types of commodities utilize air freight.

Technological advances in air transit now permit the carriers to furnish some very attractive services to industry. The Flying Tiger airline, for example, has discovered that the giant Boeing 747 is a profitable vehicle for conveying air freight. United Airlines offers a computerized control system that allows shippers to determine by telephone exactly where their goods are and who possesses them. Further, United offers a small package dispatch, where it can direct important small shipments to 113 cities within 24 hours. Eastern Airlines has invested heavily in capital improvements designed to make it more competitive in this area.[28] Nonetheless, airlines accounted for only about 3 percent of the total revenue received from shippers in 1986. However, future growth can be expected due to the personal selling and advertising programs of the air carriers. Numerous campaigns emphasize the possibility of lowering total costs through air transport, even though the rates are higher than for other modes.

Congress's deregulation actions in the 1980s created considerable rate competition among airlines, particularly as a result of new low-rate carriers who challenged the traditional giants of the industry for both passenger and freight traffic. Profits fell and some carriers, such as Braniff and World Airways, were forced into bankruptcy or significantly curtailed services.[29] Some industry experts, however, predict that the eventual outcome of deregulation will be a stronger industry, one that operates in a more competitive environment that is not propped up by artificially high rates.[30]

Water Carriers The oceans and inland bodies of water such as the Great Lakes and the Mississippi River are where water carriers operate. In some parts of the country, such as Hawaii, transportation by water carrier plays a dominant role in the economy, as illustrated in the accompanying Marketing Brief. In general, though, water transport is a slow, low-cost method of conveying bulky and heavy commodities such as lumber and sand. One obstacle is ice that closes some passages during winter periods; shippers must transport their goods while the harbors are open, or utilize other modes during the winter.

On inland waterways, barges are a common vehicle. For oceangoing transportation, carriers utilize a variety of vessels. These include large tankers that carry petroleum and other liquids, and general merchandise freighters that hold a variety of cargos, including machinery, equipment, packaged goods, and automobiles. A new trend is the effort on the part of governments and shipbuilders to develop automated nuclear-powered vessels. While environmentally controversial, these are capable of very low cost operation.

Pipelines Pipelines are very specialized carriers that move natural gas and liquid petroleum. They transport crude oil from individual wells to treatment and storage centers. From here, the pipelines carry the liquids from large trunk lines to various refineries.

MARKETING BRIEF

Emphasizing Customer Service in an Industry Characterized by Tough Competition

American President Cos., a large water carrier, is considered to be the innovator in its industry. Both sales and earnings have grown rapidly during recent years despite a sales slump in the industry, which is marked by overcapacity and price wars. These wars reduced the number of U.S. operators from thirteen in 1975 to seven in 1985, despite the fact that the federal government furnishes U.S. carriers with heavy subsidies.

American has been successful in avoiding price wars by providing premium service. The firm has been able to charge more and maintain better margins than rivals even during down cycles. The firm invested $50 million in computer systems, including one to link up with U.S. customs. Customs officials can see a list of each APC shipment, its contents, and its location, which speeds inspections. This pleases customers very much.

The firm has been instrumental in the development of double-stacked railcars, which carry two containers instead of one. Management developed a ten-year contract with Union Pacific to provide APC with more rail service. To help keep APC containers filled, the company spent $60 million to buy the largest U.S. shipping agent, National Piggyback Services, which books cargo onto trains and trucks.

SOURCE: Adapted from "A Once-Stodgy Shipper Sets Sail for the Future," *Business Week*, October 14, 1985: 71.

The pipelines are a reliable and low-cost mode of transportation that can move large quantities of liquid or gas from one location to another. Oil producers own and operate most of the larger pipelines. Exxon, for example, owns and operates the Service Oil Company (a carrier).

Rate Structures Shippers and contract carriers engage in negotiations over the rates shippers will pay. However, the law stipulates that common carriers publish their rates in documents called "tariff books." These publications are very lengthy and complex and quote three kinds of rates: class, exceptions, and commodity rates.

Class rates
Shipping rates for related groupings of items; high cost in comparison to exception rates.

The transportation carriers have classified goods with similar transit characteristics into classes. These characteristics include value, density, difficulty of loading or un loading, perishability, and other indexes of the value and cost of transit. Each class has a specific **class rate** per 100 pounds. The objective of the classification is to simplify computations of the cost of transit. Since the carriers transport tens of thousands of individual products in any given year, they find it much simpler to base assessments on a small number of classes than on a large number of individual products.

Shippers initiate the calculation of transportation costs by determining the class the carrier has assigned to the product. This is available in a rating book the carrier furnishes. Next, the shipper looks up the rate basis, which reflects the distance that the goods will move. The longer the distance, the higher the rate basis. Finally, shippers consult the tariff book, which sets forth the rate per 100 pounds for a product with specific class and rate basis designations. Shippers multiply the rate per 100 pounds by the number of hundredweights in the shipment to arrive at total freight cost.

Modern service is the key to success for transportation companies.

Since class rates are higher, shippers usually attempt to have the carrier designate their items for commodity or exception rates. Only a small proportion of shipments move under class rates. Those that do are so small in size that shippers are not strongly motivated to bargain with the carriers.

Exception rates
Negotiated reductions in shipping rates from class rates.

The common carriers base class rates on the average demand and cost characteristics of the items in each class. Conversely, they base **exception rates** on differences between the demand and cost attributes of individual products. Shippers endeavor to convince carriers that exceptions are justified because the shipper is experiencing rigid competition, pays more than the costs of transportation dictate, wants to penetrate new markets, is a loyal customer, or for some related reason. Shippers calculate exception rates through tariffs in the same way as they do class rates.

Commodity rates
Lowered shipping rates for particular commodities and points.

Commodity rates are for particular products moving from a specific origin to a specific destination. The carriers do not group items into classes, nor do they establish rate bases for them. Rather, they base the commodity rates on the cost and demand characteristics of particular items and markets, rather than on average demand and cost characteristics.

In most cases, commodity rates exist for companies and industries where the volume of shipment is sufficiently large to justify differences from average rates. Examples are the movement of Montana coal to the Northeast and of Iowa corn to food processing centers in Minnesota. As with exception rates, commodity rates normally come about as a consequence of negotiations between the shipper (or shippers, in the case of an industry trade association that bargains over rates) and the carrier. The bulk of the freight that common carriers transport is assessed commodity rates. Since transportation rates have an effect on pricing decisions, more will be said about them in Chapter 20.

Organizing Physical Distribution Decision Making

Before concluding this chapter, it is important to point out that PD is not usually the sole responsibility of the marketing department; rather, PD decisions should reflect the concerns of production and finance in addition to marketing managers. For many firms this poses a problem. Individual executives often make decentralized decisions about various components of a firm's PD system. For instance, inventory managers may derive optimal inventory levels purely from a storage and handling perspective. Transportation managers may set shipping schedules solely on the basis of the least-cost routes and modes. Independent decisions concerning individual components are likely to lead to suboptimization of an overall PD system. Carefully coordinated decisions should be made for all components.

To combat the problem of coordinating PD decisions, companies have tended to take one of two courses of action.[31] Some have organized PD committees made up of representatives of several functional areas. Meeting periodically to set policy, these committees can coordinate PD activities throughout a firm for overall system efficiency. Other companies have reorganized to centralize PD responsibility into one department. For instance, Burroughs created a distribution services department, a subunit of its marketing department, to make all PD decisions. H. J. Heinz, on the other hand, created a separate department headed by a vice president of distribution. Equal in authority to production and marketing, this department is responsible for making coordinated PD decisions. The specific organizational configuration, however, is not as important as that managers recognize sizeable cost savings and service improvements are only possible through carefully coordinated PD decision making.

Chapter Summary

This chapter focused on decision making involving physical distribution—the movement of goods from producers to customers over time and space. The PD function should be studied intensively, as it offers many ways of achieving differential advantages for a firm.

The systems concept provides a useful means of focusing on PD. This enables consideration of many variables simultaneously, along with their interactions, as the goal should be to enable the channel system to maintain a desired level of customer service at a minimum cost.

There are two main areas of administrative concerns with a PD system. One involves materials management, which refers to inventory management and warehousing. The second involves transportation management, or the physical movement of items from their points of origin to their destinations. The major decisions here involve when to ship and the modes to use.

Five major transportation modes are available: rail, truck, air, pipeline, and water. Each has various advantages and disadvantages, depending upon the product and the intended market.

There is considerable room in most companies to improve PD decisions. A major improvement is possible in many cases by centrally coordinating all PD-related activities within the company. Establishing a PD department is often the most effective way to bring about the desired efficiency and effectiveness, although a PD committee often represents a good start in this direction. The important point is that all PD activities should be coordinated with the overall marketing mix, as PD is as important as other mix elements.

Questions

1. Define the term *physical distribution*. How does it differ from channels of distribution?
2. Why is physical distribution important to marketing managers?
3. What physical distribution problems might each of the following companies face?
   a. Chrysler Corporation
   b. Good Humor (ice cream bars)
   c. Topps chewing gum
   d. A producer and marketer of precision machine tools
   e. The U.S. Army commissary system
4. Describe the systems approach to physical distribution. Why is it useful?
5. What are the major costs of holding inventory? Which of these would be most important for
   a. Nabisco crackers
   b. Borden's ice cream
   c. A small convenience store
   d. A hospital
   e. U.S.X. (steel)
6. Why would a manufacturer decide to utilize direct shipment to customers, rather than break-bulk through a warehouse.
7. How do common carriers differ from contract carriers?
8. What are the relative advantages of
   a. Railroads
   b. Trucks
   c. Air carriers
   d. Water carriers
   e. Pipelines
9. Describe each of the following:
   a. Trailer on flatcar
   b. Mixed cars
   c. Pool cars
   d. Diversion-in-transit
   e. Processing-in-transit
10. Distinguish between class, exception, and commodity rates.
11. Why is decentralization in physical distribution decision making a problem? How can this problem be overcome?

Chapter 13

Intermediaries: Retailers

Objectives

After completing this chapter, you should be able to demonstrate a knowledge of:

- The characteristics of retailers and what differentiates them from other marketing intermediaries
- The major decisions retailers make in carrying out marketing responsibilities
- The extent to which retailing is dynamic and changing
- The major classification schemes for retailers
- The major components of the retailer's offering: the location, product or service, supplementary customer service, image, and price mixes, and the major decisions required for each

MARKETING SUCCESS

Price Club—Making New Inroads into the Retailing Arena

One of the more recent explosive breakthroughs in retailing has been the growth of so-called "wholesale clubs" in the United States. Despite the name, these outlets are really retailers. They operate on a cash-and-carry basis and typically have 100,000–square-foot operations, which are registering net profits of over 3 percent.

The wholesale club concept was introduced in the 1970s by Price Club, based in San Diego. Currently the firm has 20 outlets, most of them located in California and Arizona. Individual outlets average $60 million in annual sales. They draw customers from a trading area extending 50 miles or more.

Price Club outlets operate on a bare-bones status, with few services or store niceties for customers. The stores offer a broad but shallow selection of goods at prices that actually are price-competitive with wholesalers, let alone other retailers.

Companies such as Price Club are growing rapidly. Some analysts believe that they will realize sales of $15 billion by 1990. Others foresee them capturing a 13 percent share of the apparel market by that time. Some department stores, fearing competition by wholesale clubs, have sold as much as three-quarters of their goods at markdown prices.

SOURCE: Adapted from Kevin T. Higgins, "Retail Strategies Always Evolving," *Marketing News* 20, no. 3 (January 31, 1986): 6.

Introduction

Sandi and Fred Johnson began to relax after dinner, both being exhausted after their typically difficult day. Just as Fred eased into his favorite chair, Sandi said, "It's your turn to do the grocery shopping. I did it last week." "I'll do it tomorrow, you slave driver," responded Fred. "No!" said Sandi. "The Smiths are coming tomorrow and we need to get everything now. Besides, you promised." Somewhat begrudgingly, Fred said "O.K., I may as well."

With a few yawns and a stretch, he stood up, strolled to the TV set and turned it on. He then started the family's computer and activated a program that controlled the TV. He eventually came to Channel 19's program, "Your Shopping Basket." Passing time unraveled the show's drama. "Carrots . . . 50¢ per bunch . . . No. 49517; Celery . . . 75¢ a bunch . . . No. 49518; Hunts 16 oz. catsup . . . 89¢ . . ." Every so often, Fred punched one of the numbers into the computer. In about an hour, Fred said "Done! I'm exhausted. I don't know what we'd do without our umbilical cord."

The scenario above depicts a hypothetical futuristic shopping scene. Using special cable TV hookups, computers or other remote devices, and special programs, Americans may someday do much of their shopping from within their family rooms. Coupled to computers, orders will be placed remotely, funds electronically transferred from checking accounts for payment, and delivery arranged for those who do not want to pick up their goods.

Originally forecast to be widely operational by the end of the 1970s, such systems have been slow in coming, largely because of technical problems.[1] But some limited systems are here today on a test basis,[2] and others have been experimented with to iron out the wrinkles. For example, Warner Systems, the U.S.'s largest cable TV company, extensively tested such a system in Columbus, Ohio in the late 1970s and early 1980s.[3]

Such systems may have a dramatic impact on the way consumers buy products in the future.[4] But, in a sense, this is not surprising. Successful retailing requires an evolving set of facilities and services to match changing lifestyles and favorably differentiate a firm from its rivals. By specializing their offerings, retailers attempt to carve out their niche in the market and outdo their rivals. The Price Club is an example of a retailer that has experienced rapid growth by emphasizing low prices, minimal services, and broad selections.

This chapter examines types of retail specialization. It also discusses marketing peculiarities faced by retailers as they seek to establish their respective niches in the market.

Why Are Retailers Important?

Retailers
Intermediaries who receive the majority of their sales from consumers, not businesses or other organizations.

Retailers comprise all organizations that receive the majority of their sales from consumers, not business or other organizations. Excluded from this category are all manufacturers and all intermediaries who never or only occasionally sell directly to consumers. Retailers are specialists. They build assortments of products, typically from numerous producers, to match target consumers' needs for a bundle of goods and services at a certain time and place.[5]

In total, there are about 1.6 million retailers in the U.S. who collectively account for total sales of around $1,300 billion per year.[6] One would have to spend nearly a million dollars a minute, 24 hours a day, seven days a week to equal this sum. In a word, retailing is gigantic![7]

But all retailers are not gigantic, nor are they all alike. They comprise a broad mix of entities of almost every conceivable size. For every large retailer in the U.S. there are approximately 80 small entities.[8]

The main reason retailers are important is that they facilitate exchange. From a consumer's perspective, they create assortments of goods and services and make them available at the time and place people want them. Because of retailers, consumers in Wisconsin are able to buy Florida oranges and Iowa corn as near as their closest grocery store. But even more than this, retailers enable consumers to compare the prices and quality of various items.

Retailers are vital components of many channels of distribution. They enable producers to concentrate their activities in certain parts of the country for efficiency, but without losing access to markets across the nation or even the world. A New York garment manufacturer, for example, has the ability to sell in Topeka as well as Vancouver. Accordingly, producers are able to attain economical scale efficiencies, locate near resource or labor supplies, and concentrate on manufacturing. Without a healthy retail network, producers would have to locate near consumers with small-scale operations, resulting in substantially higher costs and prices.

Competitive Characteristics

The most distinguishing feature of retailers is that they are dynamically competitive. Montgomery Ward must compete with a host of firms, including Sears, K mart, and Woolworth. Supermarkets that carry Planters Peanuts must compete with other supermarkets and with convenience, discount, and other stores that carry the same brand.[9]

Retailers are constantly seeking ways to fine-tune their offerings to outpace their competitors. Montgomery Ward & Co., for example, recently began an experiment of leasing marginally profitable space to other retailers in a store-within-a-store mini-mall setting called "Sidetrips." Many other retailers are expected to follow Ward's lead with similar concepts. As one source indicated, ". . . retailers are constantly probing the empty sectors of competitive strategy, with many failures. Until one arrives at the right time, the merchant prince's skill may be in judging opportunities rather than in originating techniques." [10]

Volatility

Competition among retailers is best described as fierce and volatile. The survivors make it only because they satisfy consumer needs better than their competitors. They can be successful by offering the right assortments of products and services. But they can also fail miserably by making a single mistake. Rapid change is characteristic of retailing. In 1984, to illustrate, there were around 16,000 retailers that entered business, but there were also about 12,000 failures.[11]

Turbulence is not confined to small retailers. The 1970s and 1980s saw giants like K mart expanding rapidly. Others, like W. T. Grant, moved into bankruptcy. As stated in *Business Week*, Grant's banks wrote off approximately $234 million in bad debts and its suppliers $110 million in receivables, 1,073 retail stores were closed, and 80,000 people were put out of work.[12] This dramatic change occurred just three years after a profit level of $38 million, when the company achieved the rank of the seventeenth largest retailer in the U.S. Other retailers, such as Allied Department Stores, significantly changed their modes of operation. Allied vastly increased its offerings of furniture, appliances, and sporting goods, and enjoyed excellent profit gains.[13]

One study of retail survival rates in Illinois showed that farm equipment dealers, motor vehicle dealers, and lumberyards were the most likely types of firms to remain in business. Conversely, fruit stores, candy, nut, and confectionary stores, and eating places had small survival rates.[14] Yet, this drastically changed in the recession of the early 1980s, with many of the former suddenly going bankrupt.

Why is retailing so volatile? A complete answer is complicated. One reason is that consumers want change. Today's "in" item is often tomorrow's memory. Pity the entrepreneur entering the video arcade business in 1984 when its popularity fell through the floor. At the same time, other firms such as Jordan Marsh profited from the trend toward physical fitness by starting "active wear" departments, which sell clothing for sports and recreation.[15] Any environmental change can dramatically shift consumer wants. Retailers must anticipate what tomorrow's consumer desires will be when they order their goods today.

Another reason for volatility is that entry into retailing is relatively simple. Long training periods, hard-to-get licenses, and large amounts of capital are not required. Though skill is needed for long-run survival, the field is open for those who think they have a better idea. For example, after being laid off from Chrysler Corp. during

MARKETING BRIEF
A New Store-within-a-Store Strategy

To first-time customers, Sidetrips looks like a trendy new mini-mall, with shops selling fresh-baked cookies, silk flowers, fashionable costume jewelry, and recycled-paper greeting cards, and even a few ferns here and there to make the "fern bar" crowd feel at home. But the self-contained retail gallery is really quite different: It is Montgomery Ward & Co.'s new design to deal with a growing problem, oversized stores. Located in Ward's operation in suburban Chicago's Randhurst Mall, one of the region's first malls, Sidetrips was developed by management as a solution to dealing with 15,000 square feet of excess floor space.

In an era of cost consciousness, "downsizing"—retail jargon for reducing the size of stores—has become a real trend among many retailers in the mid-1980s as they scramble to get rid of excess capacity. "There's a lot of it going on, because stores built 10 or 15 years ago just have too much space," said William Davidson, the one-time Ohio State University professor and current president of Management Horizons, a leading retail consulting firm and a division of prestigious Price Waterhouse.

Solutions vary among companies and locations. Other ways of dealing with the problem, including leasing departments such as furs, electronics, and cosmetics, have been around for years, but are coming back among belt-tightening retailers. And when all else fails, some retailers have simply sealed off entire floors, saving energy and maintenance costs.

"We plan to roll out 20 variations of this gallery by the end of the year," said Bernard Brennan, Ward's chairman. Sidetrips, a 17-shop mini-mall designed and leased (licensed) by company management teams in five months, cut the company's Randhurst store from 125,000 square feet to 110,000. It also meant the elimination of much of the store's marginally profitable lawn and garden lines.

"I think that we'll see a lot more of these mini-malls being built," said Davidson. "Many retailers, particularly department stores and general merchandisers, will begin imitating Montgomery Ward's mini-mall concept, if only because they're comfortable with licensed operations."

Sidetrips is an example of several stores within a store.

SOURCE: Adapted from Janet Key, "Big Stores Become Too Much of a Good Thing," *The Chicago Tribune*, July 6, 1986, Sec. 7, pp. 1, 4.

a recent recession, an energetic entrepreneur started Anton's, an upscale men's store, on borrowed funds from family and friends. Through hard work, an eye on market needs, a willingness to expand, and luck, he became a multimillionaire in a couple of years. Though not the norm, such success stories occur frequently enough to keep all retailers on their toes.

Another cause of volatility is that there are more retailers—one for about every 100 residents in the U.S.—than any other type of business. This fact places considerable competitive pressure on all of them to survive. Even Marshall Field & Co., a landmark Chicago-based department store, felt the competitive pinch in the late 1970s and early 1980s, with steadily eroding profits and sales. Among the causes was the fact that the firm's many elegant marble and mahogany fixtured departments catered to a dying breed of traditional customers, and that the company was very restrictive in granting credit.[16] In effect, the chain was being outdone by its rivals. Fortunately for its owners, management instituted massive changes that enabled the firm to turn its situation around. Retailers must constantly strive for new and better ways to operate—ways that reflect emerging customer needs and competitor actions—if they wish to survive.

Innovation among retailing institutions has been the subject of careful study. Research shows that, like products, retail institutions have life cycles.[17] New types emerge and grow rapidly, accompanied by high profits during initial stages of development. As an example, supermarkets experienced rapid growth in the 1930s and catalog showrooms mushroomed in importance during the late 1960s. Both sales and profits begin to level as the institutions mature because competition becomes keener and markets become saturated. Many fast-food restaurants, for instance, are currently facing stagnating sales and profits. Eventually retailing institutions enter a decline stage where sales and profits begin to fail.

Geographic Dispersion

Retailing is the most geographically dispersed form of business. This is because consumers seek outlets that are conveniently located. For the past forty years, marketers have studied the distances people will travel to shop. The results of an early research effort became known as *Reilly's Law of Retail Gravitation.*[18] According to William J. Reilly, the pioneer researcher, two cities attract retail trade from any intermediate city or town (or area) in the vicinity of the breaking point—approximately in direct proportion to the population of the two cities and in inverse proportion to the squares of the distances from these two cities to the intermediate town. Mathematically, this may be expressed as

$$\frac{R_a}{R_b} = \left(\frac{P_a}{P_b}\right)\left(\frac{D_b}{D_a}\right)^2$$

where

a, b = the two retail centers being compared
R_i = The proportion of retail trade from an intermediate location attracted to area i
P_i = The population of area i
D_i = The distance from an intermediate point to area i

Consider the case where cities with populations of 100,000 and 20,000 located 20 miles apart, attract business from a city that is 5 miles from the second city.

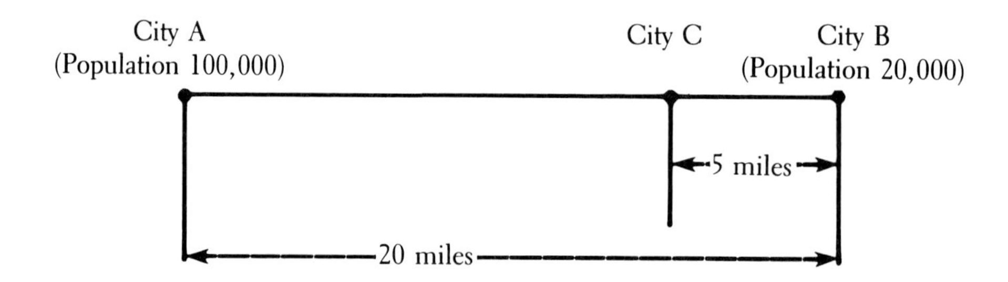

The calculations are as follows:

$$\frac{R_a}{R_b} = \left(\frac{100{,}000}{20{,}000}\right)\left(\frac{5}{15}\right)^2 = \frac{5}{9}$$

Reilly's law predicts that City B will obtain almost twice the retail trade of City C as City A will.

More recent studies indicate that other variables affect intercity trade. Transportation availability, communications, other attractions, and promotional intensity are among the important ones. Another is the economic environment.[19]

The point is that there is a definite limit to the distance that consumers are willing to travel when they shop. Population expansion and migration create new opportunities for retailers. Sears, for example, owes much of its current success to accurately predicting suburban sprawl. Lagging behind Montgomery Ward in sales through the early 1950s, Sears rushed to the suburbs ahead of Ward's and was able to secure the best sites for growth. Sales soared, paralleling urban expansion, while Ward's remained behind in stagnating major cities.[20] It took over a decade for Ward's to reverse its downward sales trend by expanding to suburbs that were even further away from cities.

Types of Retailers

Since retailers are so varied, many classification schemes are available to describe them. The principal types of items that they sell, the size of their operations, and their ownership are three of the most common means.

Items Sold and Scale

The Department of Commerce generally reports data about retailers according to the principal types of items they sell, as Figure 13.1 illustrates. Knowledge of the number of stores in each category, their aggregate sales volumes, and trends in these areas can prove valuable to managers in making and evaluating channel decisions. The proportion of the 52,000 drug and proprietary stores in the U.S. carrying PhisoHex skin

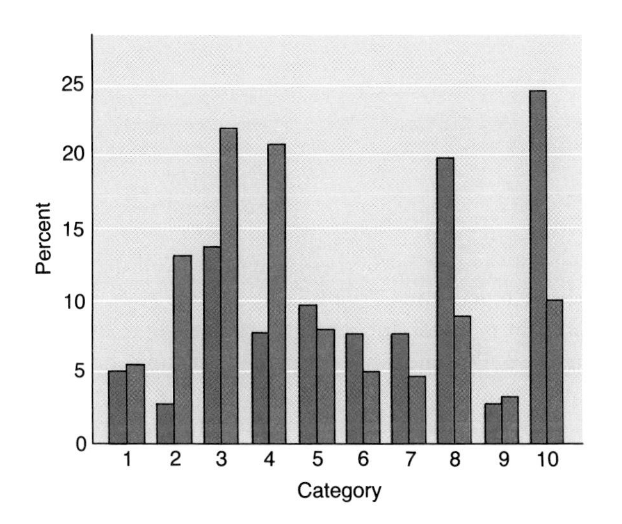

Category:
1 Building materials, hardware, garden supply, and mobile home dealers
2 General merchandise stores
3 Food stores
4 Automotive dealers
5 Gasoline service stations
6 Apparel and accessory stores
7 Furniture, home furnishings, and equipment stores
8 Eating and drinking places
9 Drug and proprietary stores
10 Miscellaneous retail stores

Percent of total number

Percent of total sales, $

Figure 13.1
Retail Establishments by Principal Type of Item Sold
(SOURCE: *Statistical Abstract of the United States* (Washington, D.C.: U.S. Government Printing Office, 1986), 106th ed.)

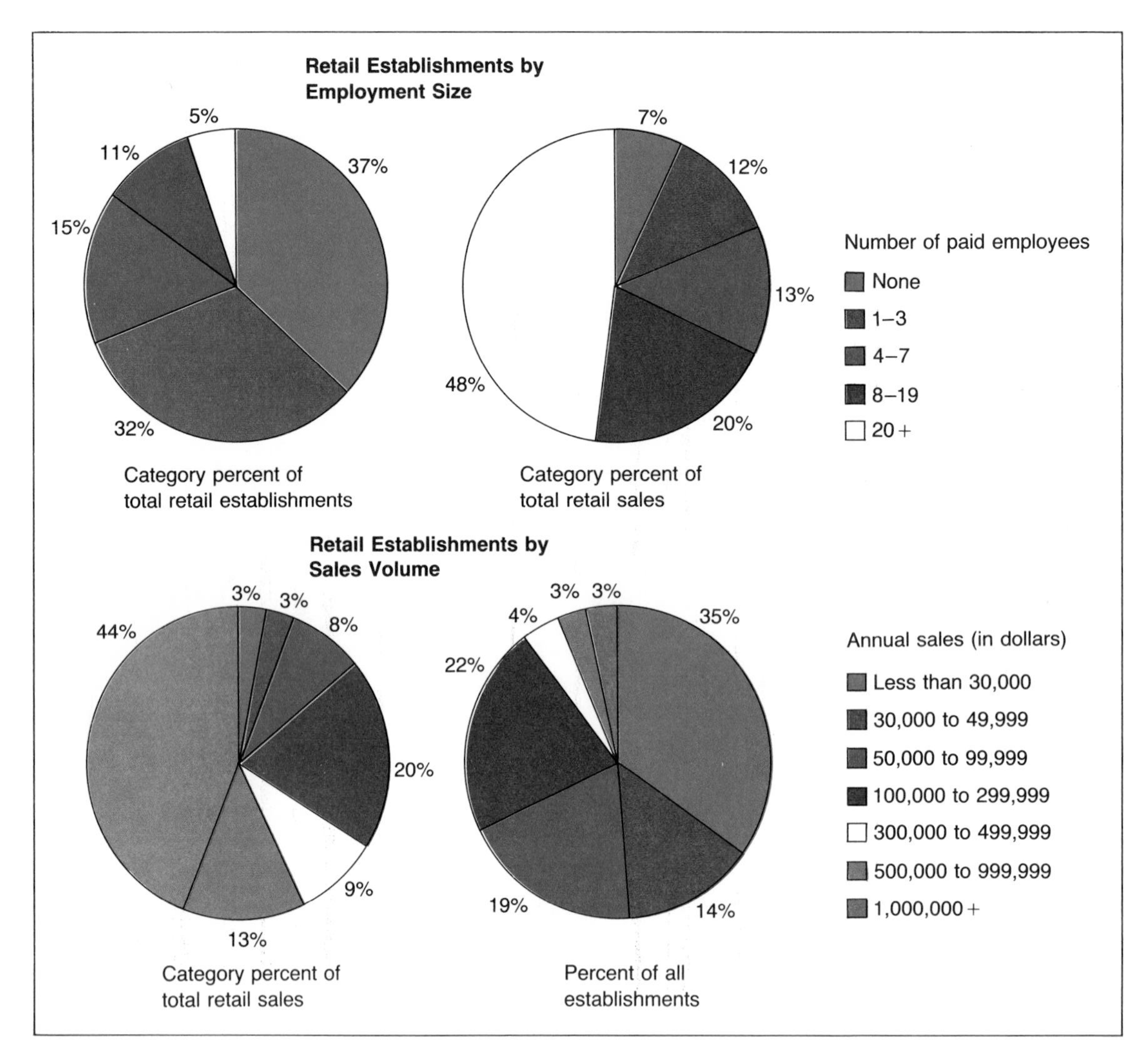

Figure 13.2
Retail Establishment Scale Diversity
(SOURCE: Based on *The Census of Retailing*, 1982 (Washington, D.C.: U.S. Government Printing Office, 1982).)

cleanser, for example, can tell the management of Sterling Drug how well the company's channel development efforts have performed.

The size of retail establishments also is important. In total, retailers employ over 14 million people,[21] but as Figure 13.2 illustrates, only 5 percent of them have 20 or more paid employees. Perhaps more important, only about 3 percent of all retailers account for more than 40 percent of all retail sales dollars. Obviously, gaining access to high-volume retailers can be critical to successful channel decisions.

Ownership

Ownership is another key descriptive variable for retailing. There are four fundamental categories: independent, chain, cooperative, and franchise.

Independent Retailers **Independent retailers** are single operations that are not affiliated with other units in the same or similar types of business. They represent the bulk of all retailers, approximately 87 percent of the total number. The majority of the independents are small, as evidenced by the fact that they only account for about half of total retail sales.[22]

Independent retailers
Single operations that are not affiliated with other units in the same or similar type of business.

Chain Stores **Chain stores** are characterized by common ownership of two or more separate retail units. In some chains all the units have the same name, but in others the stores (or subchains) have different names. For example, the Federated chain includes among its 18 divisions Abraham Straus, Burdine's, Foley's, Levy's, I. Magnin's, and Shillito's.[23]

Chain stores
Organizations characterized by common ownership of two or more separate units.

Only about 12 percent of all retail units in the U.S. are members of chains, but they account for nearly half of total retail sales. There are several reasons for this, but most relate to synergy. First, chains are able to hire very competent managers because of their large scale of operation. Second, they benefit from common advertising. Third, many perform their own warehousing and are able to avoid wholesaler profits without a loss of efficiency. Finally, many are able to take advantage of price reductions for quantity purchases.

Cooperatives To more efficiently battle chains, some independents have consolidated with others into **cooperatives.** Sometimes the resulting organizations consist of a loosely knit group of retailers banding together to perform joint wholesaling, advertising, and other marketing activities for their mutual benefit. Or a group of independent retailers may associate itself with a wholesaler for mutual benefit. Even consumers themselves have banded together to act as their own retailers. Exhibit 13.1 explains the three types of cooperative arrangements.

Cooperatives
Independent firms that consolidate their operations in one organization.

Cooperative and voluntary chains have grown dramatically over the past few decades. One of the major reasons for their success is the "clarity of total offering" made possible by consistent programs for all members. After seeing a store's affiliation, usually displayed on a sign, consumers can clearly understand the retailer's marketing orientation: its product and brand mix, services provided, and store atmosphere.

Franchising **Franchising** is a kind of business ownership situation, usually involving retailers, that falls somewhere between chain and independent operations.[24] In 1985 there were 481,200 franchise establishments in the U.S., with annual sales of $529 billion.[25] This arrangement incorporates a central business organization—a franchisor—that grants privileges to independently owned outlets called franchisees. The privileges may include the rights to sell the franchisor's products or to use its name, symbols, trademarks, architecture, or operating methods. Usually a written contract spells out such terms as the size of the business area and the time period in which the rights are granted.[26] While many forms of franchising exist, there appear to be five basic types of systems:[27]

Franchising
A form of organization where a central business organization—a franchisor—grants privileges to independently owned outlets called franchisees.

1. *Manufacturer-manufacturer franchises.* In this case, one manufacturer grants another a franchise to produce its products. The agreement may allow national or

Exhibit 13.1
Types of Cooperative Retailing Organizations

Type of Cooperative Retailing Organization	Description
Cooperative Retail Chains	Retailer-sponsored voluntary organizations that set up their own wholesaling operation. The driving force for cooperation comes from the retailers, who establish a democratically run wholesaling unit to service member firms. Consisting of small retailers who obtain the bulk of their products from a common production source, these cooperatives are typical in the grocery field. Some prime examples are Associated Grocers and Certified Grocers.
Voluntary Retail Chains	Wholesaler-sponsored organizations. Typically the wholesaler is responsible for developing marketing programs. By banding together, members can provide products and support services more effectively and efficiently than if they acted alone. Probably the best known voluntary retail chain is the Independent Grocers Alliance (IGA). Members achieve economies of scale through promotional synergy, being able to hire expert merchandisers, developing intermediary brands, and being able to manage large-scale storage and handling equipment and facilities.
Consumer Cooperatives	Consumer cooperatives have never been a major force in the U.S. They consist of consumers banding together to purchase large quantities at low prices. Generally they operate on a not-for-profit basis with voluntary or poorly paid management. Most end in failure because of membership turnover and the nominal savings compared to the amount of work required. Further, most have very poor managers, typically volunteers with little or no business training.

even global distribution when transportation rates and inadequate capital for diversified operations would otherwise preclude such distribution by the franchisor acting alone. Sealy mattresses are produced in this way.

2. *Manufacturer-wholesaler franchises.* Coca-Cola, Pepsi Cola, and Seven-Up are three soft drink manufacturers who provide syrups to franchised wholesalers that bottle and distribute products to retailers. Many beer companies such as Coors, though typically performing their own bottling, distribute through a similar franchise arrangement.
3. *Manufacturer-retailer franchises.* The automobile companies distribute through this type of link with automobile dealers.
4. *Wholesalers-retailer franchises.* Rexall and Sentry Drug stores are two examples where wholesalers secure retailers by granting franchises.
5. *Service sponsor-retailer franchises.* Avis Car Rental, Kentucky Fried Chicken, McDonald's, Holiday Inns, Midas Muffler, AAMCO Transmissions, and Kelly Girl exemplify this arrangement.

As Figure 13.3 illustrates, franchising is a large and diverse field involving many products and services ranging from automobiles to motels, and the field is still growing because it can provide substantial advantages to both franchisors and franchisees. With it, franchisors are able to expand operations without having to provide all the capital and other resources and bear all the risks. Franchisees can also benefit from gaining consumer recognition, marketing and operating advice, and typically better market and financial information than if they were to go it alone.

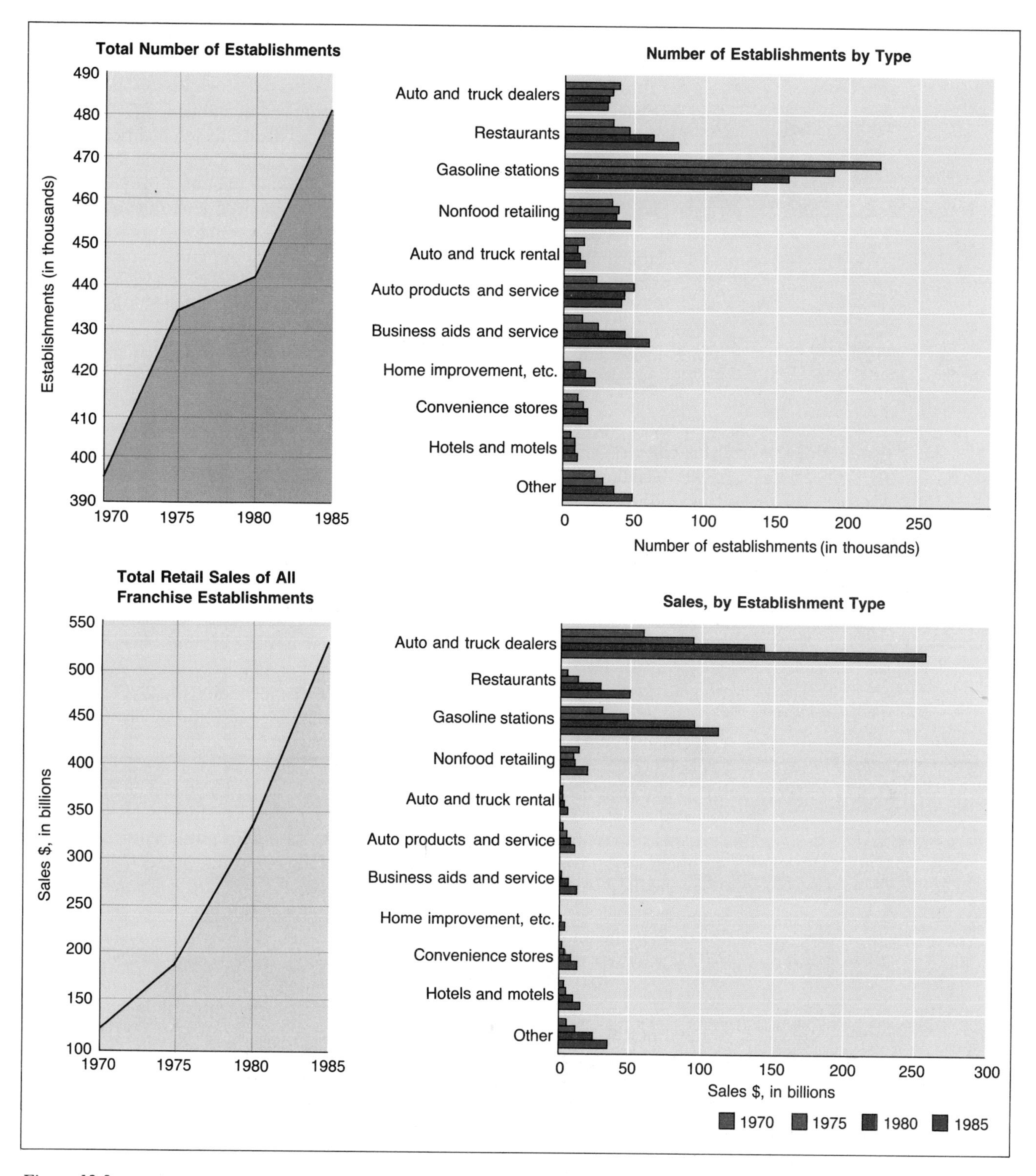

Figure 13.3
Franchising and Total Retail Sales for Selected Years (SOURCE: *Statistical Abstract of the United States* (Washington, D.C.: U.S. Government Printing Office, 1986), 106th ed.)

Franchise terms vary widely, but in general franchisees are expected to develop and maintain a market for a franchisor's product or service. In return a franchisor is expected to differentiate its offerings from competitors' through image-building promotions and to maintain consistent product quality and quantity.

Franchisors provide both initial and continuing services to their franchisees.[28] Initial services include market information, site selection, facility design and layout, lease negotiation and financial advice, operating manuals, and training programs for managers and employees. Continuing services include field supervision to assure consistent performance, promotional programs, additional training, centralized purchasing, market data, auditing and record keeping, reports, and group insurance plans.

Similarly, franchisees are required to do certain things. They report key information on sales, profits, local advertising, and employee turnover to their franchisors monthly. Also, they are expected to follow prescribed operating procedures. For example, McDonald's franchisees must only sell certain meals, utilize particular signs and architecture, and furnish employees with approved uniforms.

For the right to the specified privileges, franchisees pay fees to their franchisors. The exact level and type of fees vary, but there are six typical sources of fees. Initial franchise fees, although they are sometimes as small as $5,000, can be quite expensive. McDonald's and Holiday Inn franchises, for instance, cost over $100,000 just for the right to use the name and to obtain the initial services. Land, building, and fixture costs are extra. Royalty fees are also common as a percent of sales, a flat monthly fee, or on a per-unit basis (such as a fixed amount per hotel room). Sometimes franchisors own the buildings and equipment and charge a lease fee. They also may assess license fees, especially in manufacturer-manufacturer franchises, for the right to use a trademark and various production processes.

Many franchisees are required to purchase certain products from their franchisor. Coca-Cola, for instance, sells syrup to its bottlers and Holiday Inns owns furniture and carpeting manufacturing facilities to supply associated inns. Finally, fees may be charged for management reports and continuing training. Of course, many franchisors also derive sales revenues from nonfranchise elements of their businesses. Figure 13.4 illustrates the relative importance of the principal sources of their revenues.

Franchising can be a conflict-provoking arrangement.[29] Franchisees often complain that they receive inadequate assistance in dealing with operating problems and are restricted to selling within certain territories and at uniform prices. Also, some franchisors own and operate outlets that compete with their own franchisees. McDonald's, for instance, owns nearly half of its stores. The Federal Trade Commission has examined many of the complaints and is likely to control franchising activity more closely in the future.[30]

But perhaps the biggest complaint against franchisors has been unethical recruiting techniques. For example, nearly three-quarters of all franchisees earn profits below the minimums projected by the pro-forma income statements used during franchise sales presentations. In response, most states have passed statutes to clean up the misrepresentations, and the remainder are likely to follow suit.

Despite its weaknesses, franchising is here to stay, and with a flourish.[31] It benefits franchisors by enabling them to expand the scale of their operations on a limited capital budget. Once attained, larger operations permit economies in advertising, buying, information systems, and other activities. For franchisees, the system provides relatively small, weak independents the opportunity to associate with a large organization and gain identity, information systems, and other benefits that they could not

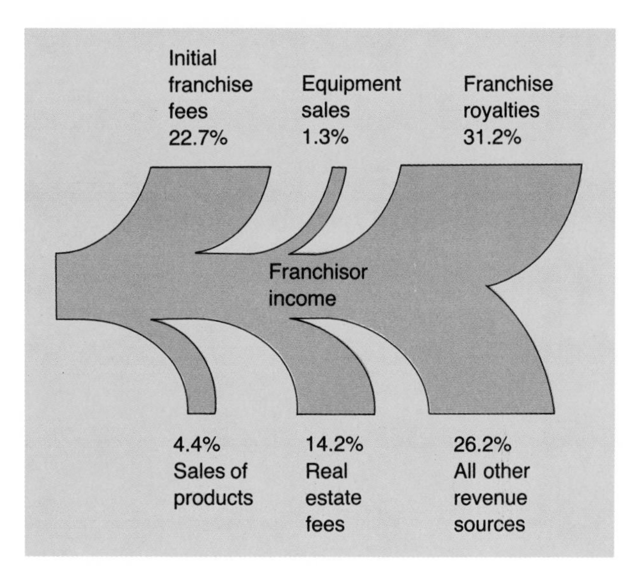

Figure 13.4
Relative Importance of Principal Sources of Franchisor Revenue
(SOURCE: Adapted from E. Patrick McGuire, *Franchise Distribution* (New York: The Conference Board, 1981): 20.)

otherwise obtain. One classic study showed that half of all franchisees would not be self-employed were it not for franchising.[32]

A Retailer's Total Offering

Some retailers are successful and others are not. An interesting question for marketers to ask is, "Why do consumers shop at one store and not at another?"

Several studies have been done of why shoppers choose a particular retailer, termed **patronage motives.** One such classic study, which frequently appears in the literature, revealed that shoppers fall into one of four patronage-motivated groups, as follows:[33]

Patronage motives
Reasons why shoppers choose a particular retailer.

1. *Economic shoppers.* About a third of all consumers are very sensitive to prices, quantity, and the variety offered by a retail outlet. Large discount operations such as K mart, Wal-Mart, and Price Club owe their success to these shoppers.
2. *Personalizing shoppers.* Nearly a quarter of all shoppers choose retailers with "people-oriented" atmospheres. Traditional stores such as Marshall Field's and Lord & Taylor that offer a full range of customer services—friendly sales clerks, delivery, layaway, and liberal return policies—appeal to these shoppers. Research indicates that women whose self image is "feministic" tend to be of this type.[34]
3. *Ethical shoppers.* Nearly 20 percent of all shoppers buy from certain small or locally-owned retailers because they feel that "they should have the business." Local retailers in ethnic communities often rely on ethical shoppers for their survival.
4. *Apathetic shoppers.* The remaining consumers dislike the process of shopping, but do it out of necessity and with minimum effort. When in a rush, they may shop in mass-merchandising stores because convenience is a key.[35] Quick entry and exit units such as 7-Eleven and Pic-Quik, along with mail order and door-to-door retailers, also cater to this group.[36]

The products a retailer carries are important to attract consumers, of course, but so is a store's return policy. The quality of items handled is a factor, but so is the

Some retailers, such as 7-Eleven, rely on convenient locations for their success.

store's atmosphere. Many factors, then, influence consumer patronage decisions. Essentially, all of the variables over which a retailer has control fall into one of five separate mixes, or categories, as follows: location mix, product (or service) mix, image mix, price mix, and supplementary customer service mix.

Figure 13.5 presents a conceptual model of a retailer's total offering. It incorporates both customer needs and retailer strategic decision variables into the model so as to place each marketing component into perspective. We shall further examine each of the components.

Location Mix

Location refers to the place where a retailer offers items for sale. Basically, there are two broad alternatives from which to choose: in-store and non-store retailing.

Non-store retailing
Where the seller's operation is not confined to the fixed premises normally associated with retailing (also called *direct marketing*).

Non-Store Retailing With **non-store retailing,** also called *direct marketing*, the seller's operation is not confined to the fixed premises normally associated with retailing. There are six major types of direct marketers: direct mail, catalogs, magazines, newspapers, radio and TV, and telephone. Direct marketing is one of the fastest-growing segments of retailing in the U.S., largely due to changing American lifestyles.

In general, non-store retailing is most successful when consumers desire a high level of convenience. For instance, Canteen Corporation, the U.S.'s largest in-house supplier of food for plant and office workers, generates over a quarter billion dollars in annual sales from its vending division, simply because workers can buy items without having to leave their work premises.[37] Because of the rapid growth and important future of direct marketing, Chapter 18 separately examines the field in depth.

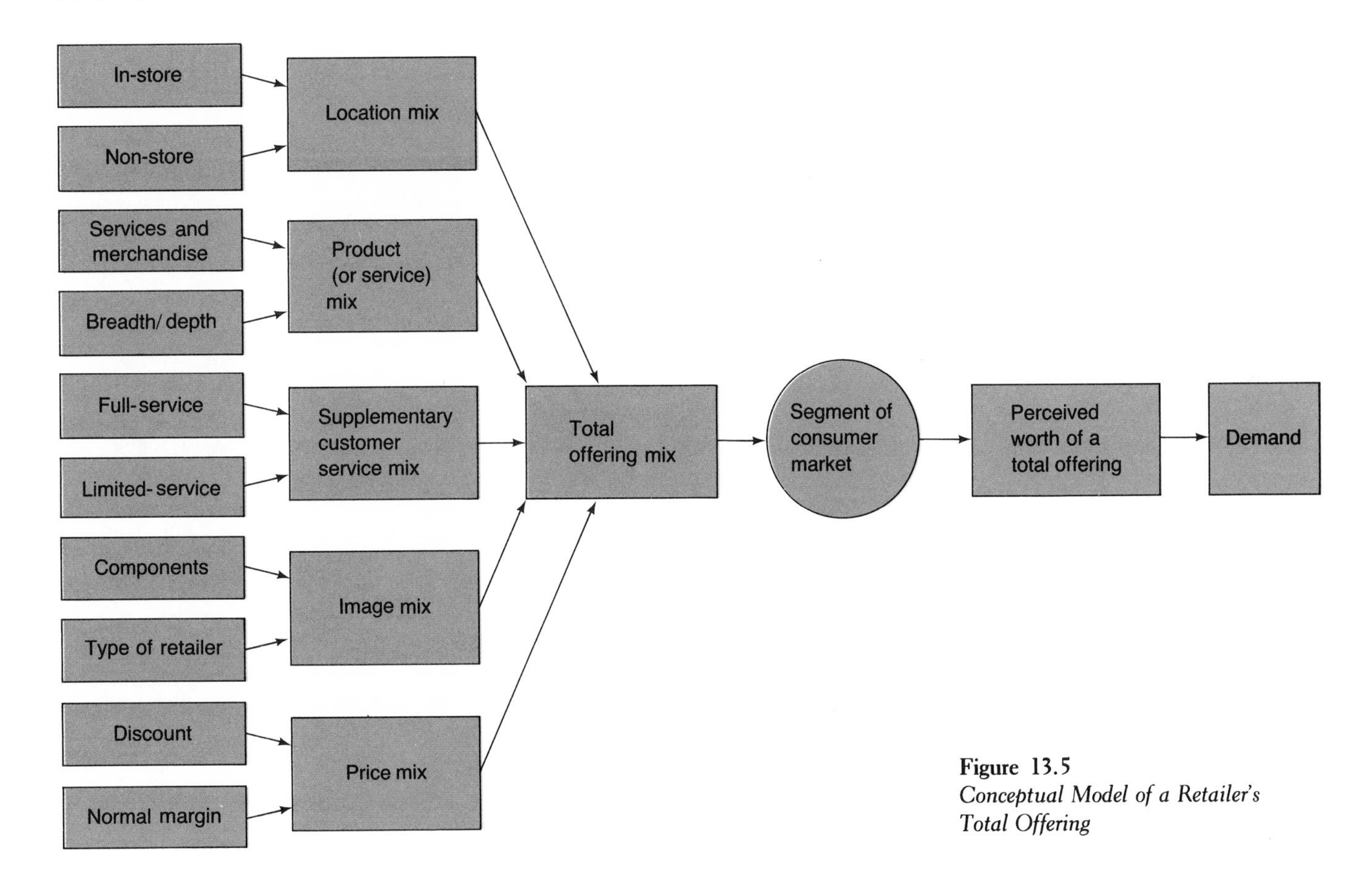

Figure 13.5
Conceptual Model of a Retailer's Total Offering

In-Store Retailing The vast majority of retailing takes place within stores, where consumers visit a retailer's place of business to buy items. There are five types of **in-store retailing** locations: independent locations, central business districts, various types of shopping centers, strings, and clusters. Each has advantages and disadvantages; Exhibit 13.2 presents a discussion of these.

In-store retailing
Where consumers visit a retailer's place of business to buy items.

Location It is obvious that retailers should devote considerable attention to selecting a proper location for their operations. Franchisors like Burger King often spend tens of thousands of dollars on building site location models to help identify the best places. These models usually include many variables for calculating optimal sites. Among them are such factors as the following.[38]

- surrounding economic conditions
- population
- complementary businesses
- parking
- growth
- potential competition
- costs
- pedestrian and auto traffic
- aesthetics of the surroundings
- potential area changes

Exhibit 13.2
Types of In-Store Retailer Locations

Types of In-Store Retailer Locations	Description
Independent Locations	Some retailers are able to draw customers from considerable distances and locate their establishments away from competitors. Included are some large retailers such as K mart and Six Flags amusement parks, and several smaller specialized businesses including medical and dental offices. While most retailers rely heavily on close proximity to other retailers and the resulting heavy shopping traffic, these retailers may pick independent locations because shoppers seek them out for business. Another reason is that they locate very near customer needs and offer extremely convenient locations. Examples are 7-Eleven convenience stores and gasoline stations located along expressways.
Central Business Districts (CBDs)	CBDs are the downtown business areas of towns and cities. Most contain department stores, banks, and stores dealing in specialty items (e.g., sporting goods and luggage shops). While many CBDs have deteriorated over the past several decades, some cities have successfully revived them. San Francisco's Union Square and Riverfront Plaza in Louisville are examples.
Shopping Centers	These are planned groups of retail stores in one location. Generally, one party owns the facilities and leases space to the stores. They usually provide ample free parking. Newer centers are often designed as malls and provide enclosed facilities for climate control. There are four major types of shopping centers, based upon the size of the market they serve: 1. *Convenience centers* contain three to six stores, perhaps a branch bank, a dry cleaner, and a drug store. Generally, one of the units carries high-volume items to attract traffic. These centers primarily serve local shoppers. 2. *Neighborhood centers* are usually similar to convenience centers, but are larger (about 14 or 15 stores) and have more traffic. Usually a chain supermarket is included, and perhaps a barber shop or beauty shop. 3. *Community centers* are still larger (about 16 to 30 stores), and usually include a small department store, a supermarket, and quality clothing stores. They are able to draw from several neighborhoods because they offer a variety of merchandise. 4. *Regional centers* are large centers with more than 30 stores. Large ones include more than 100 separate retailers and more than a million square feet of space. An example is Lakeside Center, located north of Detroit. Included are four theaters, an indoor skating rink, several restaurants, two candy stores, and three department stores. The department stores in these centers are called "anchors" because they attract customers to the center and cause people to walk between each of them and be exposed to other stores. All of the stores are accessible from within an enclosed mall area with trees, fountains, gardens, and terraces. Such centers often draw people from a distance of 30 miles or more, even in large cities where there are many shopping alternatives. These centers are very popular with shoppers as the wide variety of merchandise and outlets are synergistic, attracting more customers for all of the retailers than if they located in smaller centers.
Strings	These are groupings of retailers located along major thoroughfares without centralized planning. Shopping center managers plan for a certain variety of stores. In contrast, these strings develop without such planning, as the individual retailers see fit. They usually develop along high-traffic areas where there exists nonrestrictive zoning. Auto dealers and fast-food outlets are often successful in these strings.
Clusters	This configuration generally exists around high-density areas such as in or near large apartment complexes and office buildings. Clusters usually lack centralized planning and include stores that specialize in a small variety of prestige items, such as florists, delicatessens, gourmet restaurants, office supply stores, and boutiques. Most have quite limited floor space, rely on heavy floor traffic, and cater to specialized needs.

Producers of consumer goods are also concerned about retailer locations. It is the selling establishment's location that buyers consider when evaluating a product's place component of the marketing mix. To illustrate, a producer trying to penetrate the Edmonton, Canada consumer market must pay attention to establishing distribution through retailers located in the West Edmonton mall because the mall captures 25 to 28 percent of the Alberta community's market for department store merchandise.

Product (or Service) Mix

The mix of products or services offered for sale is a cornerstone of a retailer's total offering. In determining which items to handle, management bases the decision on the potential synergy it creates by combining a particular item with others in the mix. This occurs if a particular item is part of the target customers' desired assortment bundle and if it is likely to contribute to the firm's objectives. Stores that appeal to do-it-yourselfers, for example, carry a broad line because these buyers usually seek stores that carry a wide array of complementary products and services.[39] Some IBM PC computer dealers also carry Apple products to provide customers with alternatives.[40]

Some retailers specialize in carrying a small mix of products. For instance, yard-care appliance dealers normally handle only one or two brands of lawn mowers, garden tractors, and snow blowers. Others, such as Sears, carry thousands of products—from lawn mowers to warm cashew nuts.

Retailers, then, vary in the ways they assemble their product mixes to meet their target market needs. Understanding the various retail product mix strategies is useful for managers of all consumer goods firms. It helps them develop overall retail marketing strategies and assess the degree of fit between their strategy and the needs of the overall channel system.

The various retail product strategies can be identified by considering two dimensions of the product mixes: breadth and depth. **Breadth** refers to the number of *noncompeting* products carried. J. C. Penney, for instance, handles a broad product mix, including several lines of clothing, appliances, and housewares, that attracts customers having a wide variety of needs. In contrast, other retailers specialize in trying to attract a limited range of consumer needs by carrying a narrow mix of products. A fast-food franchise is an example.

Breadth (product mix)
The number of (noncompeting) product lines offered by a firm.

The **depth** of a mix concerns the number of *competing* types of products handled. A deep line involves many substitutes within a generic product class. A major appliance store, for example, usually carries three or four competing brands of television sets, with several models of each brand. This product mix strategy is useful when the firm is seeking to attract all portions of a highly segmented market. In contrast, a shallow line makes more sense when a retailer is trying to penetrate a relatively unsegmented market. Door-to-door encyclopedia salespeople, for instance, carry a very shallow line since they offer only one item to prospects.

Depth (product mix)
The number of substitutes that a company offers within a line.

As Figure 13.6 illustrates, these two variables, breadth and depth, may be used to classify retailers according to their product mixes. Using breadth and depth as criteria, Exhibit 13.3 identifies the major classes of retailers in the U.S. today.

The Retail Accordion Theory A consideration of the depths of historical product mixes highlights the evolutionary character of retail institutions. As one source observed, "domination by general-line, wide-assortment retailers alternates with domination by specialized, narrow-line merchants."[41] Termed the *retail accordion* theory,

MARKETING BRIEF
A Modern-Day Prairie Oasis

Amidst ashen wheat fields burned down by blustery winter temperatures below −40°F and further stripped of life by penetrating chinook winds gusting up to 80 knots per hour, rises a 13-story structure where monkeys play, Siberian tigers roam, 544 different kinds of trees over 12 feet tall grow, four submarines prowl a 438-foot-long lake, couples are wed on an exact-scale replica of Christopher Columbus's Santa Maria, and hockey superstar Wayne Gretzky practices with the Edmonton Oilers.

This "new Phoenix" is none other than the West Edmonton Mall, thus far a $640 million complex, that is the biggest shopping center in the world—half again as big as the next biggest, located in Los Angeles. Opened in 1981, the project—developed by the Iranian immigrant Ghermezian brothers (Eskander, Raphael, Nader, and Bahman)—is not even yet completed. Scheduled for opening soon is a water park as big as five football fields, where surfers will ride six-foot waves 360 feet across and visitors can tan themselves despite the blustery outside weather under a giant artificial sun. Also rising is the planned $35 million, 380–room Fantasyland Hotel with themes for some of the suites. Guests in the Polynesian rooms, for example, will float on warrior-catamarans-turned-into-beds, and cowboys-for-the-day can sleep in beds sculpted from a pickup truck.

Supporting the complex are 817 stores generating $360 (Canadian) revenue per each of the mall's 3.8 million leasable square feet. This compares to the $240 average of other Canadian malls. To some critics, though, the mall is too large, especially compared to Edmonton's half-million population. According to Phillip Boname, president of Urbanics, a Vancouver-based retailing consultant, "You're going to see some turnovers and closures in the future."

The Ghermezians do not see any doom ahead. The multimillionaires have earned their huge wealth (they own several major properties in Alberta and throughout Canada) by their investment shrewdness. "We do not enter a project unless it generates a 16 percent minimum return on investment," says Eskander. "Most projects earn 20 percent to 25 percent."

Attracting tourists is a goal of the Ghermezians, who see the project eventually drawing 8 million visitors a year or more—rivaling Disneyland and Disney World's 10+ million draw. If enough are attracted to the mall, which also encloses an amusement park to entertain children while parents shop, the project should reap a bonanza for the Ghermezians, as well as Edmonton—which provided $20 million in tax breaks for the project.

The next step in the Ghermezians' plan is to expand their mall concept south of the border. In early 1986, Michael O'Laughlin, the mayor of Niagara Falls, N.Y., dropped by to sell the brothers on choosing his city for the $1.5 billion U.S. imitation. "I'm willing to make the Falls the equivalent of a mall decoration if it means tourists will stay in town longer," he said.

SOURCE: Adapted from Douglas Martin, "A Shoppers' Paradise on the Prairie," *The New York Times*, February 23, 1986, Sec. 3, pp. 1, 28; and Linda Matchan, "The West Edmonton Mall, 'Wow!'," *The Boston Globe*, November 9, 1986, pp. B37, B40.

the hypothesis is that dominant retail institutions in the U.S. have oscillated between the two product line breadth extremes.

General stores dominated early retailing and handled very broad merchandise assortments. Later, limited-line retailers prevailed as populations moved into burgeoning cities during industrialization. Department stores followed, again turning the tide back toward broad product mixes. Then in the early-to-mid–1960s, the tide reversed once more toward narrow lines with fast-food merchandisers, furniture showrooms, and other specialists. Today the trend is again in favor of broad lines, such as those carried by mass merchandisers. While each oscillation tends to result in a new type of dominant institution, the general evolutionary pattern is strong. Thus, the

The West Edmonton Mall is the largest in the world.

retail accordion theory should help marketers in anticipating future retail institutional evolution.

Supplementary Customer Service Mix

A third dimension of a retailer's total offering involves supplementary customer services. These are specific intangibles that a retailer offers customers to attract their patronage. Table 13.1 presents a listing of major supplementary services. Those retailers offering most of the services on the list are called **full-service stores.** Retailers offering few of the services are called **limited-service stores.**

Full-service stores
Retailers offering numerous supplementary customer services and generally high margins.

Limited-service stores
Retailers offering very limited supplementary customer services and generally lower margins.

Figure 13.6
Examples of Retailers According to Breadth and Depth of Line Mix

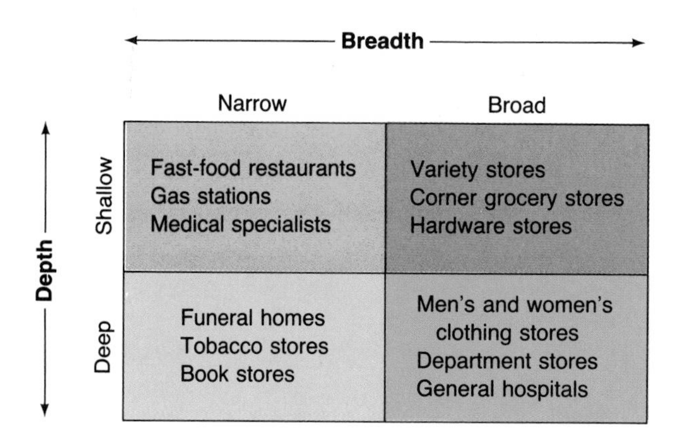

Table 13.1 Supplementary Customer Services

Alterations	Gift wrapping
Appliance installation	Lay-away
Check cashing	Merchandise returns and allowances
Complaint department	Parking
Credit	Repair facilities
Delivery	Technically knowledgeable sales personnel
Extended hours (evenings or Sundays)	Telephone and/or mail orders

Generally, retailers can attract additional shoppers by offering supplementary customer services, but customer services are costly to offer.[42, 43] Therefore, management must be sure that they help to favorably differentiate the firm from competitors for them to be worthwhile. Usually the greater the number of services offered, the larger the margin needed on each sale to maintain profitability. Thus, more services usually mean higher prices.

Wheel of retailing
New types of retailers make their initial inroads by offering low prices with few services. Later they increase their services to attract more customers, resulting in higher prices and leaving room for a new breed of retailer to enter.

The Wheel of Retailing The evolutionary character of retailing is further evidenced by historical patterns in supplementary customer services. Early department and limited-line stores became known as *full-service stores* because they offered a full line of supplementary services.

Later, the early volume merchandisers displaced the popularity of full-service stores, such as the first supermarkets, by cutting these services to the bone and lowering prices. Such stores became known as *limited-service stores*. This change in service mix may be explained by the wheel-of-retailing theory.[44]

According to the **wheel-of-retailing** theory, new types of retailers make their initial inroads by being "lean"—that is, by offering low prices with few services. Later, to expand their horizons, they increase their services to attract more and more customers. Because they upgrade their services, they then leave room for a new breed of retailer to enter with low prices and bare-bone services.

K mart, for example, began its meteoric rise as a stripped-down mass merchandiser offering few services and low prices. But it has begun a major move to upgrade its image and services to attract new market segments.[45] McDonald's is another example.

Exhibit 13.3
Retailers Classified by Breadth and Depth of Product or Service Mix

Type of Retailers	Description
General Stores	(or trading posts) have their roots in the early development of rural America. They carry an extremely broad but shallow line of merchandise, from staple foods to nails. While most have disappeared, a few remain today.
Limited-Line Retailers	specialize in one or a few separate lines of items such as fabrics (e.g., Minnesota Fabrics). Within the lines handled, the selection is very deep.
Specialty Retailers	(or specialty shops) usually handle exclusive items that "average" retailers do not carry and feature expert salespeople. These include prestige stores in fashionable areas (e.g., high-fashion dress shops). They usually handle a limited line.
Department Stores	offer both a wide and deep product mix, organized by departments coinciding with major product lines (e.g., Sears, Roebuck, J. C. Penney, and Macy's). They usually provide extensive supplementary services and are generally large, with annual sales over $10 million and sometimes much more.
Discount Sellers	offer reductions from the full list prices on the merchandise they handle. These stores are usually independents, and the discounts offered are flexible—often through negotiation. Examples include many appliance, tire, and furniture stores. Sometimes the seller offers discounts only to groups, such as to members of credit unions or to teachers. Others operate open showrooms (open to everyone) where dealers and public alike can buy below list price.
Discount Houses	sell items at posted prices reduced from list to all customers and usually handle hard goods and jewelry. Examples include Service Merchandise, E. L. Rice, and W. Bell & Co. Some have developed their own private brands to give them control over price.
Supermarkets	are large discount houses that specialize in grocery and household items. Examples include Safeway, Jewel, and Kroger. According to the Super Market Institute, a trade association that does research and disseminates information on the industry, there are about 3,000 of these in the U.S., and they account for about two-thirds of all grocery sales (despite the fact that they represent about one-seventh of all grocery stores).
Convenience Stores	are small retailers specializing in convenience items such as soft drinks, snacks, staple drugs (e.g., aspirin), and so forth. They are located near major traffic routes and some are affiliated with self-serve gasoline stations. Examples include 7-Eleven, Pic-Quik, and AM-PM.
Mass Merchandisers	are a cross between supermarkets, discount houses, and department stores. They are large stores, usually organized by departments (limited in number), and handle fast-moving items. Examples include K mart and Venture. These retailers emphasize self-service, free parking, and many cash registers in the store's front.
Hypermarkets	are mammoth self-service mass merchandisers that sell an even broader line of merchandise, including groceries, small appliances, clothing, fast-moving auto supplies, and practically anything that has a large potential volume. The stores are very large, often 75,000 square feet or bigger—about 50 percent larger than a supermarket, or more. These stores have made a big dent in retailing in Europe. Hugo Mann, a West German entrepreneur, has built a billion-dollar empire with over 20 such stores in West Germany. While some U.S. merchandisers have developed small hypermarkets (e.g., Price Club and Safeway), most have been reluctant to enter in force because of greater discount competition than in Europe.

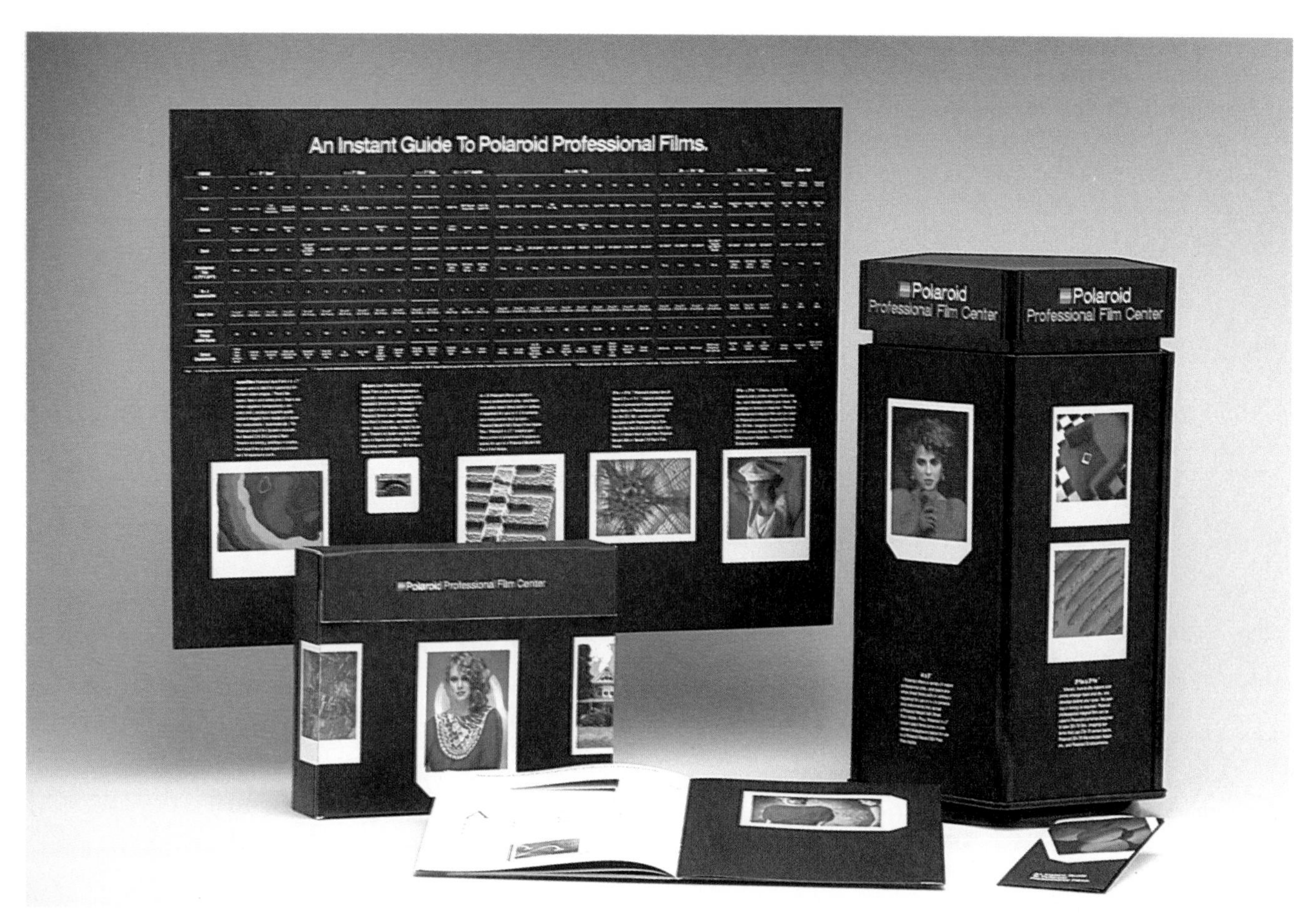

The use of point of purchase (POP) displays can be quite effective in stimulating retail sales.

Its first store in Des Plaines, Illinois (now a museum) was a take-out, drive-in hamburger stand offering only hamburgers for 15¢, cheeseburgers for a little more, fries, and drinks. As the firm grew, it upgraded both its services (rest rooms, dining rooms, and attractive stores) and menus to expand into additional market segments. As these retailers expand and become "fat," they open opportunities for a new type of "lean" retailer that offers low prices and limited services, thus beginning a new round of the wheel.[46]

While the "wheel" pattern does explain some of the shifts in retailing, other retailers have managed to shift to meet emerging customer needs without becoming excessively "fat." Many have drastically cut their supplementary customer service mixes by dropping items such as gift wrapping and switching from free or nominal-charge service to accepting major credit cards (at a cost of between 3 and 6 percent of the sale).[47] Others have simply cut their prices across the board.[48]

Image Mix

The retailer's image is a fourth component of its total offering. One source views a store's image as "the way the store is defined in the shopper's mind, partly by its functional qualities and partly by an aura of psychological attributes."[49] As a Neiman-

Revitalized downtown shopping malls have reversed the erosion of downtown shopping areas in many parts of the country.

Marcus senior vice president once related, "Our name is the most important merchandise we sell. . . . A gift from Neiman-Marcus should be special simply because it was purchased here." [50]

To illustrate, people feel uncomfortable in some stores—as if they do not belong. Perhaps the facility's layout or merchandise seems shoddy.[51] Or some people might feel uneasy in a high-fashion women's store having thick carpets, unmarked prices, and seemingly arrogant sales clerks. Such feelings come from the store's image.

Shoppers seek retailers with images that are compatible with their own self-images, personalities, and lifestyles.[52] Wealthy consumers, for instance, might feel comfortable in the high-fashion women's store described above. There are two interrelated ways to view retailer images: in terms of a classification scheme that considers why consumers shop at a particular type of store, and in terms of a detailed analysis of specific image components.

Type of Retailer From the first perspective, all retailers fall into one of three categories in the perceptions of consumers, as follows:

1. *Convenience stores*, where the primary benefit is shopping ease, with convenient locations, easy entry and exit, and quick service. Examples include 7-Eleven and

Pic-Quik. Currently, these stores account for about 3 percent of all retail food sales, and there are about 30,000 of them with a growth rate of about 15 percent a year. Prices range up to about 15 percent higher for the same items sold in other stores.[53]
2. *Shopping stores* are stores that shoppers perceive as being ideal for browsing. Most stores that offer a broad product mix are of this type, such as Macy's, Lord & Taylor, and Sears.
3. *Specialty stores* are stores that develop a great deal of loyalty among their customers, who are often willing to travel long distances to shop. These stores usually offer a deep product mix. Examples include Eddie Bauer, Inc. (an international sporting goods store) and Minnesota Fabrics (sewing shops).

This classification scheme refers to the stores themselves, not necessarily to the types of merchandise that they carry. Each type of store might specialize in convenience, shopping, or specialty items.[54] For example, a limited-line furniture store located in a small town might serve its target's needs through a convenient location. Customers would not have to go "into the city" to shop.

Retailer Image Components Image extends beyond the above classifications. Different stores within each class have different images. Sears and Saks are both department stores, yet are viewed quite differently by consumers. Bullock's and Hartmax are looked upon as places where people who have succeeded in business can reward themselves.[55, 56]

All of the components of a marketing mix can have an impact on a store's image. As for specifics, a study of department store images isolated 12 significant image components, as follows:[57]

- advertising
- price levels
- supplementary services
- store atmosphere (decor, displays, types of customers, waiting lines)
- assortment and brands of merchandise
- quality of merchandise
- fashion of merchandise
- location convenience
- sales personnel
- attitude about returns and allowances
- sales promotions (special sales, teen themes, fashion shows)

The importance of each of these components depends upon the specific retailer and its intended target. Evidence indicates that consumers draw relatively consistent conclusions about a retailer, however, even when they have only limited information about the store. In a classic study, researchers tested ads for a leading Kansas City store in two locations. Figure 13.7 illustrates the results. Groups in both locations gave practically identical image ratings despite the fact that the Atlanta residents had no association or familiarity with the store other than the test ads.

For the best results, advertising and all other elements of a store's intended image should be blended around the needs of the target group of customers. To illustrate, management of Curtis Supermarkets, located in the coastal town of Hingham, Mass., selected wealthy residents and summer resort vacationers as the company's target. As the company's president stated, "We have to compete in price, but the key to our success . . . is our strong service image. I would say that's our top drawing card."[58]

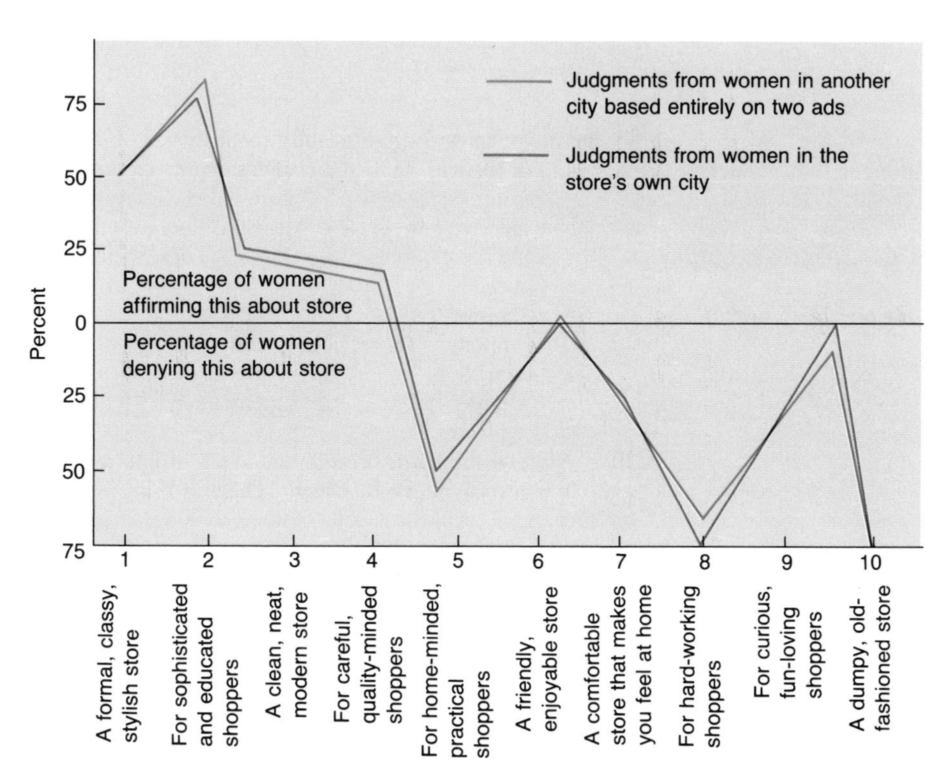

Figure 13.7
Identical Determination of Department Store Image by Different Groups of Shoppers in Kansas City and Atlanta (SOURCE: Adapted from Pierre Martineau, "Social Class in the Buying Environment," in Britt, Stuart Henderson, ed., *Consumer Behavior and the Behavioral Sciences* (New York: John Wiley & Sons, 1966): 420.)

Price Mix

The final mix retailers manage is price. There are two tracks that are usually followed. One group tends to adopt a traditional pricing philosophy, using standard markups for all items. The second group tends to stress lower markups and lower prices, reduced services, and greater volume to generate profits. Sears, Neiman-Marcus, and Lord & Taylor are among the first group.[59] Volume merchandisers, such as K mart and Venture are among the second, although all retailers tend to increase their markups to a high level for items that are in heavy demand, such as Cabbage Patch dolls when they were first introduced.[60] As with other marketing mix elements, the appropriate price mix depends upon the target market, and no element, including price, is more important than the others.

Chapter Summary

This chapter focused on intermediaries, with special emphasis upon the marketing decision components of retailers. It is important for all marketers to understand the decision processes of intermediaries, including producer marketers, because intermediaries often represent a vital link in the entire channel system. Understanding their decision processes and motivations can be crucial to making good marketing decisions even by producers.

As an institution, retailing is dynamic and volatile. Retailing is constantly evolving to meet the changing needs of consumers. While many classifications exist for retailers, probably the most useful for marketing decision making is to consider the elements of the total offering, based on the mix of location, product (or service), supplementary customer service, image, and price. Each mix represents a critical decision area for a retailer, and the results can have a dramatic effect on an entire channel system.

Questions

1. What is a retailer? Why is retailing so volatile?
2. Many critics of the business system argue that retailers only serve to gouge customers for added profits. What do you think?
3. How can you account for the fact that retailers are so geographically dispersed?
4. Small retailers are as important as big ones. Comment.
5. What are cooperative retailers?
6. In your opinion why do consumers select the following stores in preference to others?
   a. Safeway Stores
   b. Neiman Marcus
   c. Western Auto
   d. Sears, Roebuck and Co.
   e. Computerland
7. What do retailers offer to their customers?
8. What are the kinds of shopping centers? If you were to open a retail store, in which type of center would you try to locate (in your town) if the establishment were a
   a. full-service gasoline station
   b. men's quality clothing store
   c. expensive gift shop
   d. discount store
   e. fast-food restaurant
9. How important are services to customers of:
   a. bridal shops
   b. toy stores
   c. computer stores
   d. supermarkets
   e. drug stores
10. What do the terms breadth and depth of line refer to?
11. In the words of one manager, "The only thing important for success in retailing is selling items at lower prices than competitors." Comment.
12. What are convenience, shopping, and specialty stores? Provide an example of each.

Chapter 14

Wholesaling and Intermediary Buying Behavior

Objectives

After reading this chapter, you should be able to demonstrate a knowledge of:

- What wholesalers are and the major ways they differ from other marketing intermediaries
- The roles performed by wholesalers for manufacturers and retailers
- The dynamics of the wholesaling decision environment
- The major types of wholesalers, based upon the functions they perform
- The nature of intermediary buying decision making (for both retailers and wholesalers), including who makes the decision, their objectives, and their buying styles

MARKETING SUCCESS

Selling Office Furniture through a Video Catalogue

New York-based Showroom Online (SO), a wholesaler of office furniture division of the privately held $1.5 billion international conglomerate TBG, has generated wild enthusiasm among interior designers for its innovative computer-based marketing system.

"Until now, the catalogue has been the manufacturer's major link with the designer," said SO's president Burton Schwartz. "While they are still vital to the marketing and product search processes, catalogues can slip out of date, be cut up, carried off, torn up, become dog-eared, or misplaced," he added.

"The over $3 million development cost of the system was money well spent," said Schwartz. The software and hardware visually links designers and manufacturers of equipment through screens tied to SO's centrally located Denver-based system, which can store and retrieve over 400,000 images from thousands of interior furnishings catalogues. "The beauty is that it can do an exhaustive search in minutes and can be updated overnight," Schwartz added.

Users of the easy-to-use system push a few buttons on a typewriter-like keyboard to identify a type of furniture. The computer then provides information on item specifications, colors, special features, prices, sizes, manufacturers' names and phone numbers, plus a video image of products that appears on nearby twin video screens.

SO's suppliers are drawn from the lists of furniture manufacturers, fabric mills, producers of floor and wall coverings, lighting makers, and other office furnishing companies from throughout the U.S. and Canada. A manufacturer pays a $13,500 fee for its product line to be included in the system. Also paying a fee to tap into SO's system are the design and architectural firms that use the service—to the tune of $6,000 each per year.

"The system greatly broadens our product choices," says John Lijewski, managing principal of Neville Lewis Assoc., one of the nation's largest industrial design outfits. "It is well worth the fee because it greatly expands our horizons and greatly reduces the time and energy required to search hundreds of different products to match our specifications."

SOURCE: Adapted from "Video Catalogue Provides Product Data for Companies Seeking Office Furniture," *Marketing News* 19, no. 11 (May 24, 1985): 51.

Introduction

This chapter first examines **wholesalers,** specialists that are positioned between producers and final buyers in a channel-of-distribution system, as illustrated in Figure 14.1. It then looks at the buying behavior of intermediaries in general, both retailers and wholesalers.

One should not confuse the terms wholesaling and wholesaler. Wholesalers are institutions, whereas wholesaling refers to the functions performed by a channel-of-distribution system. Management may eliminate wholesalers from a channel system,

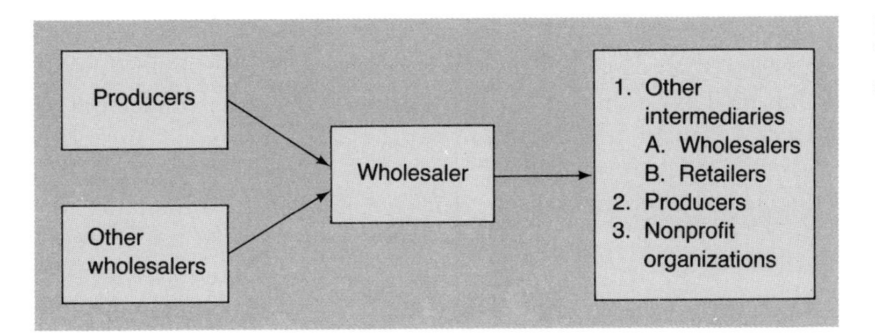

Figure 14.1
Wholesalers Link Producers with Other Organizations

but not the functions themselves. For example, Marshall's, the nation's largest retail chain of off-price clothing, performs its own wholesaling activities. In other cases, producers rely on independent wholesalers, such as Showroom Online, to perform the wholesaling functions because they are better able to do the required work. In both cases similar functions are required.

This aspect—relying upon other firms to perform certain marketing duties—causes many marketing novices to question the value of using wholesalers. Because they buy goods, do not alter them physically, and then resell them at a profit, some feel that their efforts are mere duplications. But the work that they perform would have to be done anyway—by producers, retailers, or final customers themselves. By specializing, companies such as Showroom Online are often able to become more efficient or effective at the required tasks. No single producer would be able to economically support a program such as Showroom Online's system. Thus, a wholesaler's services may be cost-justified despite its markups.

Wholesalers
Marketing intermediaries that receive the bulk of their revenue from producers, other wholesalers, retailers, or nonprofit organizations.

Characteristics of Wholesalers

In total, there are about 416,000 wholesalers in the U.S. with combined annual sales of about $2,000 billion, or about $8,300 for each person in the country.[1] Their concentration, functions performed, types, and their evolutionary nature are important decision concerns to management.

Concentration to Gain Efficiencies

Wholesalers are more concentrated geographically than are retailers, but less so than manufacturers. Around half of all wholesaler sales, for example, take place in the 15 largest Metropolitan Statistical Areas. Figure 14.2 illustrates the regional geographic dispersion of wholesalers and distribution by sales volumes throughout the U.S. There is also a graph of the population within each region for comparison. The Middle Atlantic states, for instance, comprise 11 percent of the population but account for 21 percent of all wholesale activity.

Notice in the figure that many wholesalers are also situated in small cities and towns, such as in the mountain states. This allows producers to maintain distribution in areas where there are fewer people. By representing several producers, wholesalers can efficiently service smaller populations, an economic impossibility for many producers if they were to go it alone.

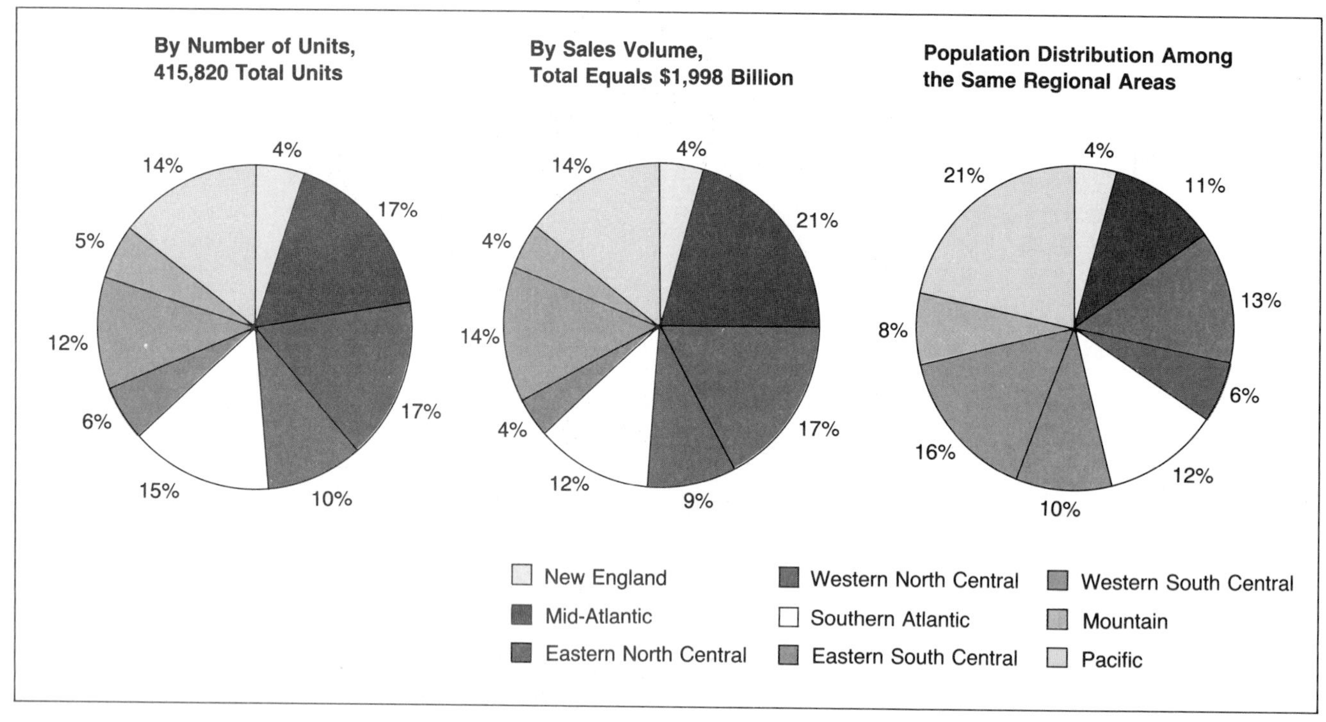

Figure 14.2
Dispersion of Wholesalers by Geographic Area (SOURCE: Adapted from U.S. Bureau of the Census, *1982 Census of Wholesale Trade;* and *Statistical Abstract of the United States, 1986,* 106th ed.)

Wholesalers Perform Various Functions

Wholesalers owe their existence to performing marketing, especially distribution activities, more efficiently than other channel members. For example, the Sysco Corporation, a large food distributor, is often able to deliver better control over foodstuffs than would be possible if its restaurant clients were to try to do this job. The firm operates with enough volume to be able to dictate quality terms to its suppliers. Sysco is also noted for its exceptional effort to satisfy delivery schedules, a must for many of its clients.

Wholesalers are especially expert at helping retailers build desired assortments of products from many different sources.[2] Many can also handle a producer's entire set of transporting, selling, storing, financing, and other distribution activities.

Gaining operating efficiencies through specialization are a wholesaler's key to success. One wholesaler, for example, handles all of G. D. Searle's sales of Equal sweetener to food service firms that provide meals to groups such as college students in cafeterias. It also sells a complete bundle of food items from other food producers to efficiently service its client food service firms.[3] Because of specialization, the firm is able to perform similar marketing functions for all of the producers at an overall net savings to each one and to customers.

Figure 14.3 illustrates the activities that a wholesaler might perform for both customers and suppliers. Some wholesalers are capable of performing all of the activities, while others specialize in only a few of them.

Of course, wholesalers charge a fee for their services. Their markups range from a low of only a few percent to as much as 50 percent, depending upon the activities

Wholesalers serve to sort, accumulate, allocate, and assort bundles of items, which facilitates smooth exchange between producers and final users.

MARKETING BRIEF
Outdoing Competitors in Food Distribution

Sysco Corporation is the largest food distributor in the United States. It supplies restaurants, schools, hospitals, and other institutions with food products. During 1985 the firm's earnings rose 12 percent and its sales grew twice as fast.

The firm's founder, John F. Baugh, expanded his frozen food distribution business in 1970 because he expected that people would eat more meals away from home, which turned out to be the case. The firm has purchased more than 40 small distributors, making economies of scale, bargaining ability with food processors, and the ability to provide consistent quality for some 8,000 items possible.

The firm has high quality standards. Tuna sold to Sysco must be caught on lines so there are no struggle marks from nets, and the firm once turned away three truckloads of ham that contained too much water. Samples from every product lot are carefully tested. Many buyers pay a bit more for Sysco quality and service than they will pay competitors. Recently a chef at the Petroleum Club of Houston changed the evening menu at 2 P.M. A Sysco man jumped into his car and personally delivered 24 pounds of wild rice—attesting to the service level of this firm.

SOURCE: Adapted from "Food Distribution: The Leaders Are Getting Hungry for More," *Business Week*, March 24, 1986: 106, 108.

Figure 14.3 *Wholesaler Functions*

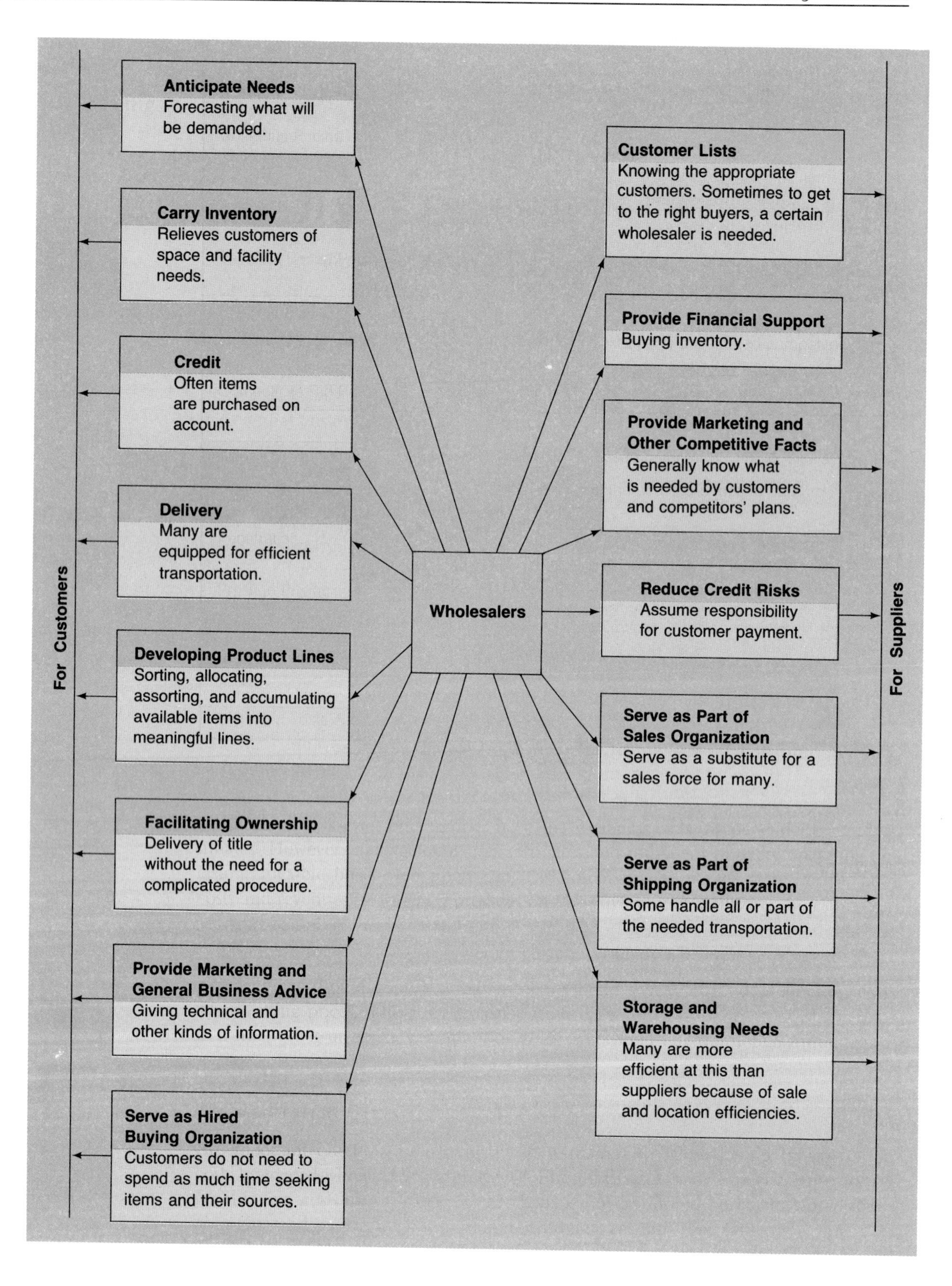

they perform. On the average, though, markups range somewhere between 5 percent and 20 percent. Naturally, the greater the number of activities they perform, the greater is their markup.

Wholesaler Functions for Customers Wholesalers provide a number of functions for their customers. The major ones are as follows.

Anticipating needs. Because of their wide contacts and expertise, wholesalers are often able to anticipate brands, styles, models, and quantities of items that will be demanded in the future, which helps their clients in decision making.

Carrying inventories. Many wholesalers carry inventories, relieving customers of the need to devote space, equipment, and other resources to this vital function. Representing many customers, wholesalers can employ more modern facilities, equipment, and systems such as the newest trucks, most modern warehouses, computer systems to track stock, and storage and retrieval equipment, than their customers could individually afford, resulting in an overall savings to all.[4, 5]

Credit. Most wholesalers grant trade credit to their customers, which frees up their clients' capital for other purposes. Some will also arrange credit to the customers of their clients, which stimulates sales.

Delivery. Most wholesalers will arrange delivery to their customers and to final buyers. Specialization and large scale enables them to use the most advanced equipment, making the process more efficient.

Developing product lines. Wholesalers are involved in sorting, allocating, assorting, and accumulating available products, often from different producers, into meaningful lines to customers. **Sorting** involves receiving bulk shipments from different suppliers and grouping them into bundles of related items; brass fittings from several producers are sorted by size and purpose. **Accumulating** is building an adequate stock of the items that a wholesaler handles; 5,000 brass fittings, 3,000 washers, and so on. **Allocating** is determining the quantity of each item to ship to each customer; how many ½–inch brass fittings to ship to Jones Plumbing, Inc. **Assorting** is where the wholesaler assembles a set of heterogeneous goods to meet the needs of customers; brass fittings, pipe, and faucets meet the needs of plumbing contractors.

Sorting
Receiving bulk shipments from different suppliers and grouping them into bundles of related items.

Accumulating
Building an adequate stock of the items that an intermediary handles.

Allocating
Determining what quantity of items to supply each customer.

Assorting
Collecting a set of heterogeneous goods that will meet the needs of customers.

Facilitating ownership. Wholesalers can streamline the delivery of title to customers. Because they are in close contact with clients, they are often in a better position than producers to judge their creditworthiness and competency.

Providing marketing and other business advice. Wholesalers can provide their customers with expert advice on product policy, technical aspects, advertising, and other important business activities.

Serving as a hired buying organization. In many respects, wholesalers serve as hired buying organizations for their customers, much like a staff of purchasing agents. This makes up-to-date ideas and procedures available to even the smallest businesses.

Wholesaler Functions for Suppliers Wholesalers also perform several functions for their suppliers. The more important ones are as follows.

Providing customer lists. By affiliating with a wholesaler, producers have immediate access to a customer base through an established channel system.

Providing financial support. By purchasing goods for inventory, wholesalers provide financial support to their suppliers and free funds for production and other activities.

Providing marketing and other competitive information. Wholesalers are able to provide a wealth of information about customer needs and competitor activities that

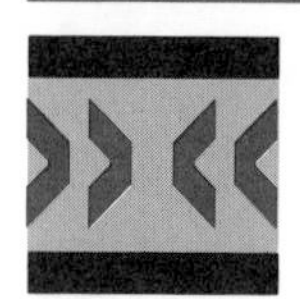

MARKETING BRIEF

Wholesaler Pressures to Raise Prices of High-Cost Items

Bottlers of Coca-Cola and Pepsi-Cola exerted considerable pressure on the beverage producers in 1986 to raise the prices of drinks containing NutraSweet and fruit juice. General Cinema Corp., PepsiCo, Inc.'s largest independent bottler, led the move to abolish uniform pricing, which led to resistence from PepsiCo. The bottler charged retailers ten cents more for six-packs and jumbo size bottles of its diet and Slice sodas. Several Coca-Cola bottlers made similar demands.

Bottlers favor price differentials because diet drinks and juice-based products cost more to make than sugared soft drinks. The bottlers had absorbed the added costs in the past but decided that this was no longer acceptable. In the meantime, Coca-Cola and PepsiCo executives were worried about higher retail prices. Locked in a bitter fight for market share, neither one wanted to increase prices. Still, both yielded to the pressures imposed by their bottlers and allowed the price increases to go into effect.

SOURCE: Adapted from "Fancy Soft Drinks—With Prices to Match," *Business Week* (April 7, 1986): 41; and "General Cinema Plans a Premium Soft-Drink Line," *The Wall Street Journal* (November 18, 1985): 17.

is vital for a marketing information system. Wholesalers of Coca-Cola and Pepsi-Cola, for instance, recently put pressure on the producers to increase the price of diet drinks. The wholesalers were in a good position to initiate the price changes because they had a better feeling for competitive reaction than the producers.

Reducing credit risks. By assuming responsibility for customer payment, wholesalers reduce the credit risks to their suppliers.

Serving as part of the sales organization. Wholesalers serve as sales representatives for their suppliers.[6] This may be the only way for smaller firms to penetrate foreign

IGA is an example of a wholesaler-sponsored voluntary chain.

markets.[7] Still other producers augment their own sales and marketing staffs with wholesalers.

Serving as part of the shipping organization. Wholesalers may serve as an extended transportation department for their suppliers.

Providing storage and warehousing services. Using wholesalers can substantially reduce the need for storage and warehousing facilities for producers' finished goods.

Types of Wholesalers

It is customary to group wholesalers into categories on the basis of the functions they perform. There are four major categories: merchant wholesalers, exchange facilitators, manufacturers' sales branches, and other specialty types. Figure 14.4 illustrates these, along with their major subclasses.

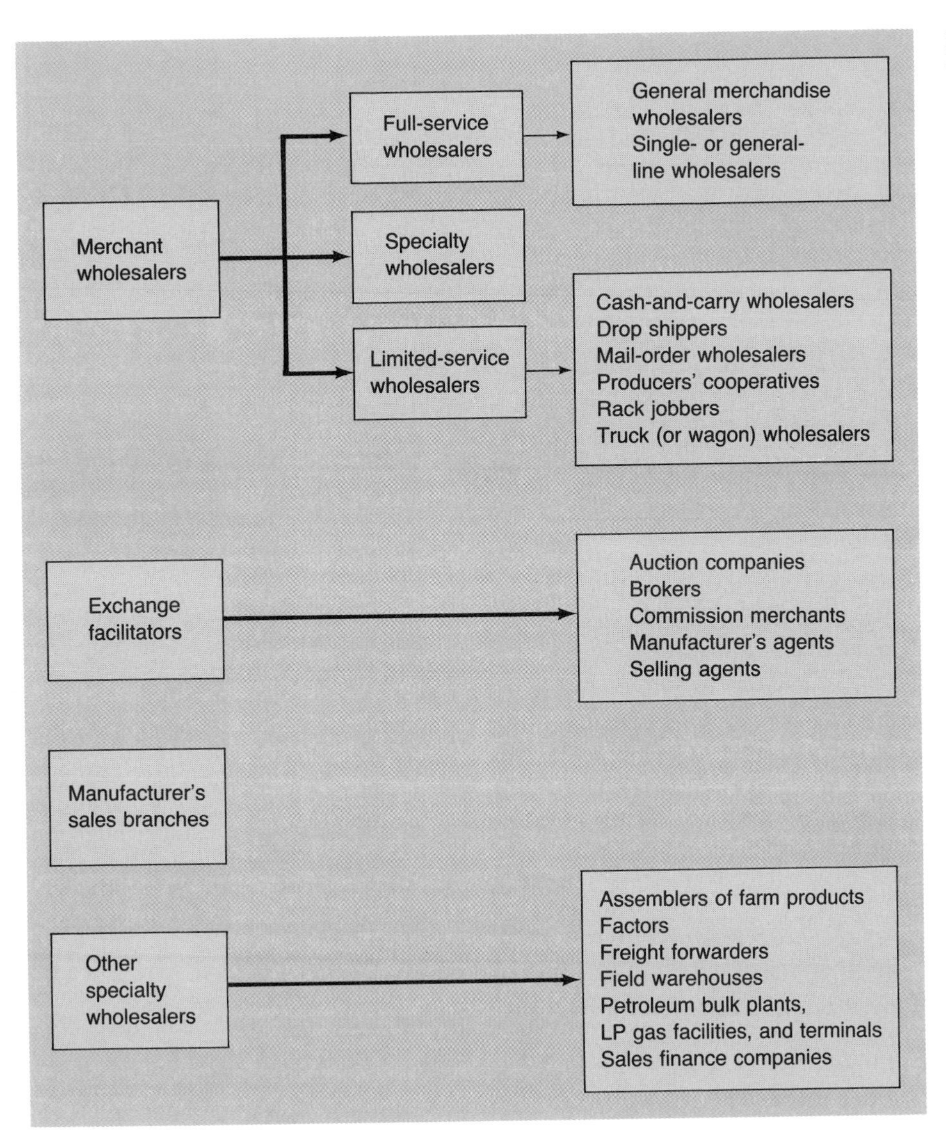

Figure 14.4
Types of Wholesaling Intermediaries

Exhibit 14.1
Functions Performed by Major Wholesaler Types

Functions Performed	Merchant Wholesalers									Exchange Facilitators		
	Full Service			Limited Service						Agents and Brokers		
	General Merchandise	Single-Line	Specialty Merchandise	Rack Jobbers	Cash and Carry	Drop-Shippers	Truck Jobbers	Mail-Order	Producers Cooperatives	Manufacturer's Agents	Selling Agents	Brokers
Transactional Functions												
Buying	Y	Y	Y	Y	Y	Y	Y	Y	Y	N	N	N
Sales calls on customers	Y	Y	Y	Y	N	Y	Y	N	Y	Y	Y	Y
Risk-taking (takes title)	Y	Y	Y	Y	Y	Y	Y	Y	Y	N	N	N
Logistical Functions												
Creates product assortments	Y	Y	S	Y	Y	N	Y	Y	N	S	N	Y
Stores products (maintains inventory)	Y	Y	Y	Y	Y	N	Y	Y	Y	N	N	S
Sorts products	Y	Y	Y	Y	Y	Y	Y	Y	Y	N	N	N
Transports products	Y	Y	Y	Y	N	N	Y	N	Y	S	S	S
Facilitating Functions												
Provides credit	Y	Y	Y	Y	N	Y	N	N	S	N	S	N
Provides market information and research	Y	Y	Y	S	N	S	N	N	S	S	S	Y
Grading	Y	Y	Y	S	N	S	N	S	S	N	S	Y

SOURCE: Adapted from Joel R. Evans and Barry Berman, *Marketing,* 2d ed. (New York: Macmillan, 1985), p. 382; Thomas C. Kinnear and Kenneth L. Bernhardt, *Principles of Marketing* (Glenview, IL: Scott, Foresman, 1983), pp. 374–375; and Louis W. Stern and Adel I. El-Ansary, *Marketing Channels,* 2d ed. (Englewood Cliffs, NJ: Prentice-Hall, 1982), pp. 147–151.

KEY: Y, Yes; N, No; S, Sometimes

The two major groups are merchant wholesalers and agents and brokers. They perform the bulk of the wholesaling work. Exhibit 14.1 presents a comparison of the functions performed by the principal types within each category.

Merchant wholesalers
Organizations that take title to the goods they sell. They may be full-service or limited-service firms.

Merchant Wholesalers **Merchant wholesalers** are the workhorses. In total, they account for over $1.36 trillion in sales—nearly 70 percent of all wholesale sales. Figure 14.5 pictures the breakdown of these sales by types of goods. Merchant wholesalers differ from the other types in that they actually buy (take title) to goods, which means that they run a far greater risk if a product is not successful. Accordingly, they tend to charge a relatively high markup for their services. There are two major groupings of merchant wholesalers: full service and limited service.

Full-Service Wholesalers Full-service wholesalers offer a wide range of services for their suppliers and customers. Many are capable of performing all of the distribution

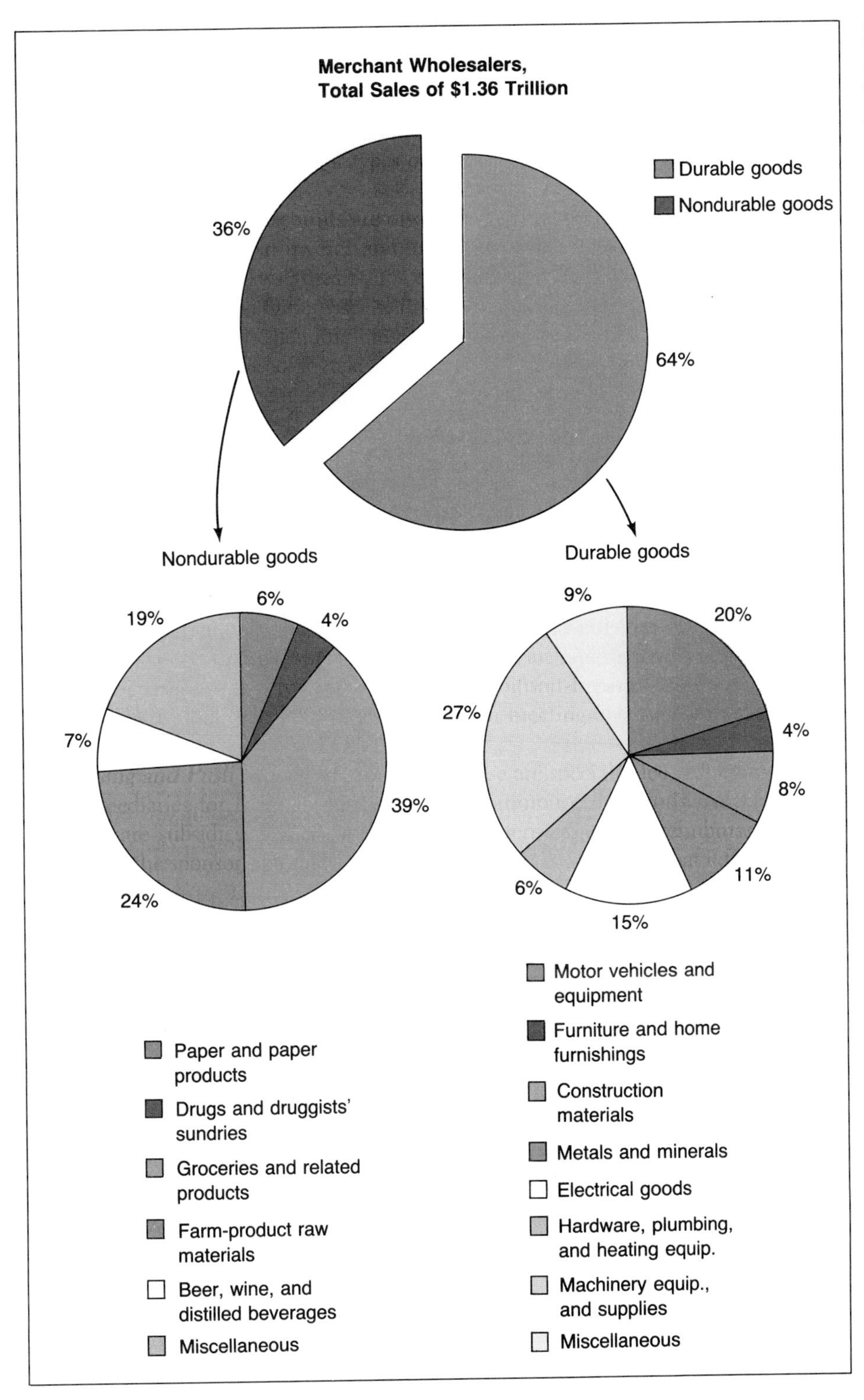

Figure 14.5
Sales of Merchant Wholesalers
(SOURCE: Adapted from *Statistical Abstract of the United States, 1986,* 106th ed., p. 784.)

and transportation functions required by producers. There are several types of full-service wholesalers.

General merchandise wholesalers carry a broad mix of lines, such as hardware, sporting goods, kitchen appliances, electrical supplies, patent drugs, and paint. They usually service hardware stores, small department stores, general stores, and similar outlets that handle broad but shallow lines.

Single- (or general) line wholesalers carry a narrow, but deeper line than general merchandisers. They specialize in one or a few lines, such as general sporting goods. They usually serve single- and limited-line retailers or industrial buyers by providing specialized service such as overnight delivery.

Specialty wholesalers carry a very narrow, but very deep line, such as tennis equipment and supplies. They specialize in carrying a full range of items in a line, some of which might require technical knowledge and special handling capabilities, such as highly carcinogenic (cancer producing) or corrosive materials.

Limited-Service Wholesalers Limited-service (sometimes called limited-function) wholesalers specialize in performing only certain of the channel functions for suppliers and customers.

Cash and carries are similar to general merchandise wholesalers, except that they service small retailers who buy only limited volumes on a cash-only, no-delivery basis. Many auto parts wholesalers operate on this basis and service small auto repair shops.

Drop-shippers (sometimes called "desk jobbers") deal in bulky items, such as lumber, coal, oil, and chemicals. They differ from other wholesalers in that they buy items but *do not take delivery*. They specialize in locating items, often from several producers, to fill a given order.

Mail-order wholesalers conduct their business by mail thus cutting the cost of a sales force. Some sell to retail customers too, but they offer significant discounts to businesses who buy in volume. They are a vital source to retailers operating in small towns, enabling them to obtain items nationally, such as jewelry, clocks, and furniture.

Producers' cooperatives often operate much like full-service wholesalers except that their profits are returned to cooperative members. Two examples are the Sunmaid Raisin Growers Association and the California Fruit Growers Association. Generally, they adopt stringent standards and engage in promotional activities to benefit all members. They do not build assortments of items, however, nor do they represent nonmembers.

Rack jobbers provide and stock nonfood, high-volume items to grocery stores and supermarkets. The dry-cell batteries, gum, candy, and magazines found near the checkout stands of supermarkets, for example, are often provided by rack jobbers. They maintain the stacks of items, replenish stocks, and are paid for the items sold (typically on a consignment basis).

Truck or wagon wholesalers operate from trucks that are stocked with items (often perishable) such as potato chips, soft drinks, or bread, and are delivered at the time of sale. They are the descendents of the wagon wholesalers that helped settle the American West by serving general stores.

Exchange facilitators
Organizations that do not take title to goods. They serve to bring about purchases by acting as a go-between among buyers and sellers.

Exchange Facilitators Several intermediaries perform a variety of functions that facilitate the exchange process and enable a channel system to operate smoothly. Called **exchange facilitators,** these organizations usually provide fewer services than do merchant wholesalers and often limit their risks by not assuming title to items.

Auction companies represent one important type of exchange facilitator.

Essentially, they serve as go-betweens for buyers and sellers and provide a helping role in bringing about exchange. There are several types of these companies.

Auction companies furnish a meeting place for buyers and sellers when it is important that goods be inspected, such as fruit, livestock, tobacco, and fur. They generally are located near transportation centers and they charge a small fee for their service.

Brokers represent either the buyer or the seller for one or a series of transactions, but do not take title or possession of the goods. Their function is to locate either buyers or sellers and to negotiate a deal. Some brokers, especially in food, have expanded operations to become almost like a full marketing department for sellers. Many small producers use brokers until their volumes climb to the point that they can support their own marketing staff, as did Ore-Ida a few years ago.[8]

Commission merchants are often used by food and textile producers that wish to avoid local auctions by shipping directly to large cities where goods are then sold at market, presumably at higher prices.

Manufacturer's agents act much like a manufacturer's sales force on a commission basis. They usually cover a specific territory with noncompeting lines. However, a manufacturer can obtain wide geographical coverage by using many agents. Their specialty is having close contacts with buyers and may be the only realistic way of penetrating a new market.[9]

Selling agents, also called "sales agents," may virtually assume the entire marketing function of a manufacturer, including the setting of prices and terms of sale. They sometimes handle competing items and may provide financial backing for manufacturers. But, because of their total domination of the marketing function, the manufacturer is often at their mercy.

Manufacturer's sales branches
Sales branches that are owned and operated by manufacturers. The Bureau of the Census reports them as wholesalers.

Manufacturers' Sales Branches Some manufacturers operate their own sales branches in high-sales areas where it is economically desirable to do so. IBM, for instance, owns IBM product centers in major cities to sell IBM computers, software, and other products to individuals, small businesses, and professionals.[10] Company-employed sales representatives operate out of these offices. If the facility carries an inventory it is called a sales office; otherwise it is called a **manufacturer's sales branch.**

Sales branches and offices enable a company to exert an aggressive selling effort on major market segments. They also help to promote the company's identity in the area and enable the producer to exert a greater degree of control over the marketing activities.

Other Specialty Wholesalers There are several other specialty wholesalers that should be mentioned because they perform key functions for several companies, especially in certain industries.

Assemblers of farm products specialize in sorting and assembling the outputs of many farms within a particular geographic region and gain economies of scale in storage and transportation.

Factors provide working capital to businesses by buying accounts receivable, though their service is generally quite expensive—charges of 30 percent or more are possible, depending on the risks associated with collection and whether or not the factor is to be held responsible for defaulted accounts.

Freight forwarders accumulate many small shipments from different shippers and arrange to transport them in bulk at much lower transportation rates.

Field warehouses segregate and physically control part or all of a company's inventory on the company's own premises. The field warehouse company issues a receipt that the company can use as collateral on a loan from a financial institution.

Petroleum bulk plants, LP gas facilities and terminals provide specialized handling and storage facilities for companies engaged in the petroleum industry.

Sales finance companies mainly provide consumer credit, but they also finance inventories for retailers (which is called *floor-planning*). Auto, truck, and appliance dealers often use the services of sales finance companies.

The Evolutionary Character of Wholesalers

Like retailers, wholesalers have evolved dramatically over time to meet new needs, technologies, and competitive conditions. Their unique position in the middle of channel systems places them under considerable pressure to adjust to constant changes in the entire marketplace.[11] They have thrived in the face of competition from producers, retailers, and institutional customers trying to take over their functions. To

Many display racks located near supermarket checkout counters are stocked by rack jobbers.

survive, wholesalers must be flexible in the services that they provide and capable of adapting to emerging changes among producers and institutional buyers.[12]

According to one source, the three most significant sources of pressures on wholesalers are the increasing trend of multinational companies to perform importing and exporting activities on their own, the fact that producers have grown in scale and in product line breadth (meaning that many of these producers can develop their own assortments of products to customers), and the growth of chain retailers and mass merchandisers who perform their own wholesaling activities.[13] Despite these threats, wholesalers must have adapted quite well indeed. Since 1975 their numbers have increased by about 20 percent and their sales have more than doubled.[14]

Intermediary Buying Behavior

Those firms that sell through retailers and wholesalers need insights into their buying behavior. The remainder of this chapter looks into this topic.

Selling through Intermediaries

Sellers face a twofold problem when they decide to distribute products through wholesalers and retailers. In the first place, getting and maintaining those intermediaries having the desired characteristics to handle the output of the producer is no simple task. Supermarket managers, for example, are typically offered between 15 and 25 new items each week but accept only about 10 percent of these.[15] Motivating them to effectively market these new products to their customers can be another problem.

Intermediaries buy items for two reasons. A small portion of their purchases is for operating items such as display facilities and maintenance supplies. For these acquisitions, their buying behavior parallels that of industrial buyers.[16] But the bulk of their total purchases are items to be resold. This discussion considers the buying behavior for these products.[17]

Figure 14.6
Organization of the Buying Function of the Typical Retailer

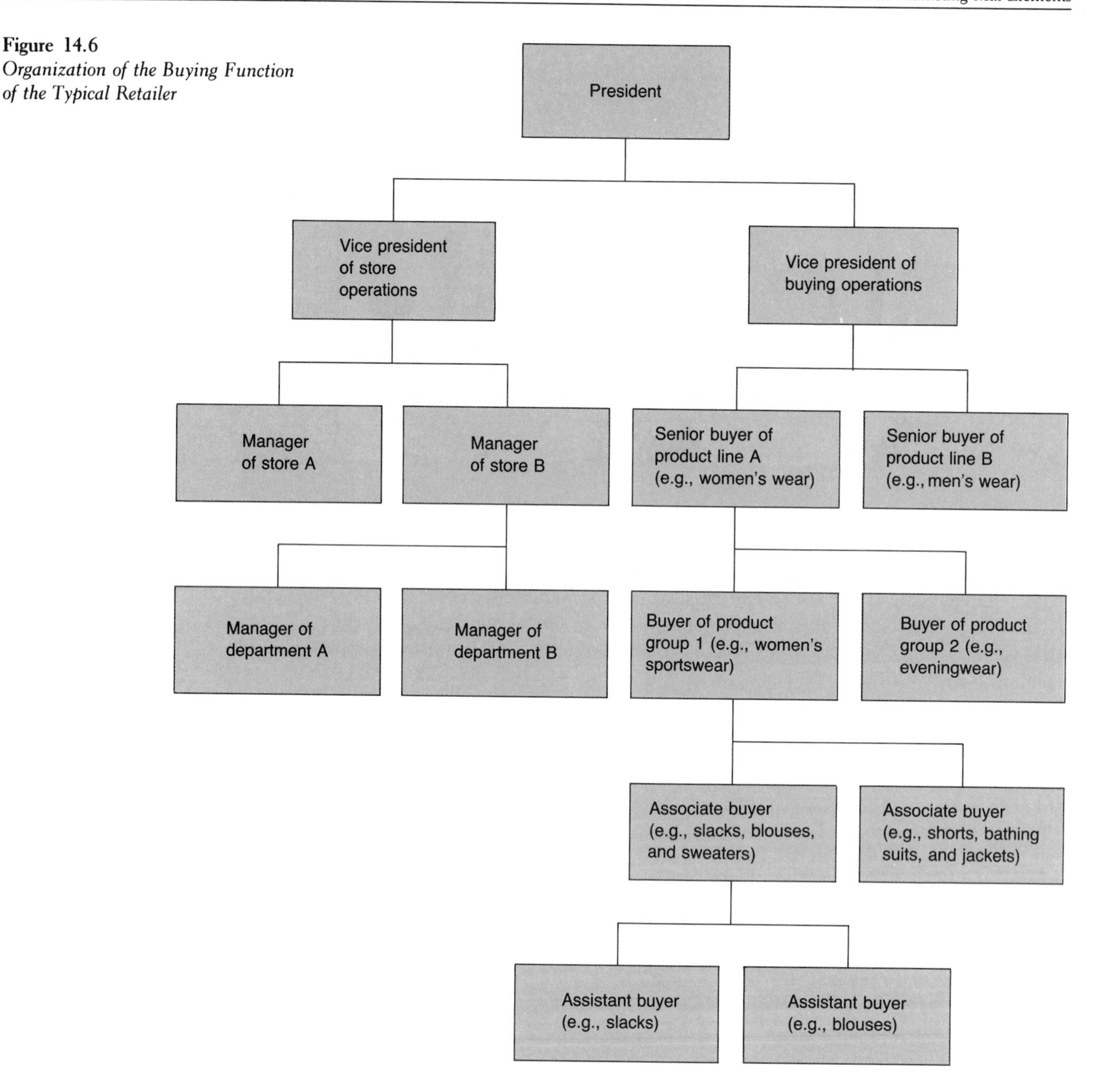

Who Makes Buying Decisions?

The decision-making process of intermediaries is varied, depending upon the firm, the product involved, and the situation. In general, though, the buying function is formally organized in a buying department that is organizationally separated from operations, as illustrated in Figure 14.6. Normally, the buying department has the responsibility for making decisions over which items will be handled by the firm, while the operations area is responsible for selling those items and running the stores.

Chicago's Merchandise Mart, containing the equivalent of 97 acres of floor space, is the world's largest wholesale buying center.

Buyers usually get their ideas about which items to handle by visiting various producers and from calls made by sales representatives. Usually, their decisions are made somewhat autonomously, although they do reflect the advice of operating management.

An important exception is that several mid-sized and smaller retailers rely upon independent buying organizations (another intermediary) called **resident buyers.** These companies perform the buying for multiple retailers, which cuts the cost of staffing this function for their customers. Most resident buyers also offer other services such as legal advice, marketing surveys, store planning, personnel screening, and advice on computer use.[18] Most resident buyers operate from central locations (New York, Los Angeles, and Chicago) where there are important trade markets to display the wares of many producers.

Resident buyers
Independent buying organizations, located in major wholesale markets, that make purchases for multiple customers—normally small retailers.

Chicago's Merchandise Mart is one such important center. A huge building—the largest in the world before the construction of the Pentagon—the Merchandise Mart houses the selling offices of hundreds of producers of many types of products. Open only to commercial buyers, it enables buyers to shop conveniently for the appropriate products for their needs. Across the street from the Mart is located the Apparel Center, another gigantic building, that serves the same purpose but is devoted to clothing and related goods.

Most large chains also centralize their buying near these centers, such as Sears (Chicago) and Ward's (New York). But other chains, such as Allied, decentralize their buying so that decisions will more closely reflect local market conditions. As illustrated in Figure 14.6, large buyers usually assign a separate buying specialist with responsibility for each line. Because they may organize product lines differently from producers, salespeople often have to call on several buyers to service one account.[19]

While buying specialists, sometimes called merchandising managers, may have full authority to make decisions, in some companies they must make proposals to their organization's buying committee—made up of the head of buying and representatives from operations—before an item is accepted. Regardless, the buyer is the key to a successful sale, as representatives are usually excluded from buying committee meetings. Therefore, the buyer screens the information that the committee will consider.[20]

It is also wise to consider the roles of store managers. While most do not play an important role in deciding which items their company chooses to handle, they are important in deciding which items from this set that they will stock, in what quantity, and with what type of shelf exposure. Estimates vary, but one source indicates that only a third of all items are "forced" on individual store managers of a chain.[21] IBM, for example, found it essential to use its sales force to enlist the support of individual franchisees of its computers in addition to buyers at the headquarters of major customer prospects.[22]

What Are Their Objectives?

Profit Profit is the overriding motivation of intermediaries in their buying decisions. Since their floor and shelf space is their most precious commodity, most intermediaries translate their profit goals into a per-square-foot basis. If a currently stocked item is missing this target, management is likely to drop it to make room for others, although some items might be handled to enhance the company's image.[23] Many department stores, for instance, carry silver goods at a loss to build their image among consumers. Grand Union Supermarkets carry gourmet items as image-builders.[24]

Surrogate Indicators of Profit Since the profitability of new items is difficult to forecast, most buyers rely on surrogate indicators of potential profitability when deciding whether or not to stock an item. One study of supermarket buyers revealed 18 variables that they might use.[25] Exhibit 14.2 describes the 9 most important of these. While other products might be handled in some cases, those with positive profit indicators are the most likely to be selected in intermediary buying decisions.

Adopting a Buying Style

Like producers, intermediary buyers face two basic buying situations: new orders and repeat purchases. Both situations tend to be more simplified for intermediaries than for producers, however. Producers often enter into extensive research to determine which item will best suit their needs. In contrast, few intermediaries will tinker with items that are selling well. For new items, the decision is also simplified because it generally involves only a "go" or "no-go" choice. If an item does not sell, it will be replaced at a future date by some other item.

In general, intermediary buyers tend to adopt one of seven buying styles.[26]

Exhibit 14.2
Important Surrogate Profit Indicators Used by Supermarket Buyers

1. Competition. If the competition carries an item, buyers are more likely to handle it.
2. Packaging. The more favorable the subjective rating for the package (label, size, protection, stackability, etc.) the more likely it is to be taken on.
3. Category volume. The greater the volume of similar items (e.g., other floor cleaners or spices), the greater the likelihood of purchase.
4. Sales presentation. Better presentations are more likely to result in purchases.
5. Cost. Items priced low relative to close substitutes are more likely to be carried.
6. Newness. Items with no close substitutes are more likely to be carried.
7. Private label. Items that would not compete with a store's own brands have a greater chance.
8. Shelf space. If stores have available space for the type of item, purchase is more likely.
9. Introductory allowances. Allowances such as free cases, discounts, and other deals increase the likelihood of acquisition.

Together, these variables accounted for nearly 90 percent of all decisions to accept or reject an item.

SOURCE: See David B. Montgomery, "New Product Distribution: An Analysis of Supermarket Buyer Decisions," *Journal of Marketing Research* 12, no. 3 (August 1975): 257.

1. Loyal buyers, who buy from the same suppliers year after year.
2. Opportunistic buyers, who develop an approved buying list and then buy only from those on the list from whom they can get the best terms and arrangements.
3. Best deal buyers, who choose the best deals available from any source at any given time.
4. Creative buyers, who attempt to build unique product mixes. For example, Sears maintains its own design studios for many of its products, then arranges to have the items produced by suppliers.
5. Advertising buyers, who make decisions on the basis of the best advertising allowances available.
6. Chiselers, who constantly attempt to negotiate price concessions.
7. Nuts-and-bolts buyers, who are most concerned with quality, durability, and other physical features, sometimes even more so than with salability.

An important step in getting desired intermediaries to handle a firm's products is determining the styles of their buyers and then developing an appropriate marketing mix to interest them. For example, a sales representative might offer additional advertising allowances to advertising buyers and lower prices to best-deal buyers to get them to buy.[27] The margins to the seller might be the same in both cases, with each buyer believing that it obtained a better deal.[28]

Chapter Summary

This chapter examined wholesalers, the second set of marketing intermediaries. Wholesalers are very vital members of the distribution channels of many products. Even when they are not used, however, the functions that they perform must be accomplished by either producers or retailers. Since omitting wholesalers completely usually is an option, the existence of wholesalers indicates that they are able to perform their functions more efficiently than can others in the distribution system.

Wholesaling is a very dynamic field. The kinds of wholesalers, as well as the activities they perform, change and evolve over time to better meet the needs of producers, other channel members, and end users.

While there are several classification schemes useful to describe wholesalers, the most useful of these for marketing decision making is according to the major functions wholesalers carry out. This classification scheme involves merchant wholesalers, exchange facilitators, manufacturers' sales branches, and other specialty wholesalers.

The chapter also examined intermediary buying behavior for both wholesalers and retailers. Important variables for managers to consider include who makes the buying decisions, buyers' objectives, and buying styles. This chapter completes the detailed examination of intermediaries. The next four chapters consider promotional activities.

Questions

1. What are wholesalers? How do they differ from retailers?
2. Explain why each of the following would logically use or not use wholesalers.
   a. The Coca-Cola Company
   b. Jeno's Inc., for frozen pizza
   c. Procter & Gamble, for High Point coffee
   d. Clorox Co., for bleach
   e. Apple Personal Computers
3. The terms "wholesaler" and "wholesaling" refer to different things. Comment.
4. "If wholesalers were eliminated, marketing costs, and thereby prices, would be reduced." Comment.
5. Where do wholesalers tend to locate? What are the implications for producers?
6. What are some of the major functions that wholesalers perform for their customers and for their suppliers?
7. Differentiate between each of the following:
   a. Merchant wholesalers
   b. Exchange facilitators
   c. Manufacturers' sales branches
   d. Other specialty wholesalers
8. How do general merchandise wholesalers differ from single- or general-line wholesalers and specialty wholesalers? Explain why general merchandise wholesalers might be useful in selling
   a. Hardware to hardware stores
   b. Over-the-counter drugs
   c. Groceries
   d. Clothing
9. Describe each of the following:
   a. Drop-shippers
   b. Rack jobbers
   c. Brokers
   d. Manufacturer's agents
   e. Selling agents
10. "Many wholesalers have instituted changes allowing them to survive and to prosper, despite predictions to the contrary." What are some of the major changes they have created?
11. Who makes buying decisions for small intermediaries and for large intermediaries?
12. What is meant by an intermediary buying style? Provide an example.
13. What are the implications of intermediary buying styles for producers?

Chapter 15

Promotion Functions and Sales Promotion and Publicity Decisions

Objectives

After completing this chapter, you should be able to demonstrate a knowledge of:

- The meaning of the term "promotion"
- The importance of promotion to marketing decision makers
- The various levels of promotion objectives and the usefulness of each to marketers
- An overall view of the communications process, involving receivers, channels, messages, sources, and feedback
- The makeup of the promotion mix and how balance is usually achieved in advertising, personal selling, publicity, and sales promotion
- The various factors that influence the composition of the promotion mix
- The nature and extent of sales promotion
- The function of publicity in marketing

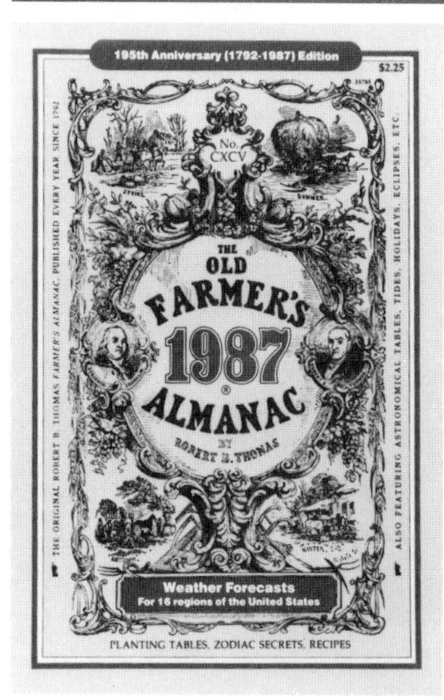

MARKETING SUCCESS

Selling the *Old Farmer's Almanac*

With 195 years of consumer exposure, it might be thought that the venerable Old Farmer's Almanac *would practically sell itself. However, point-of-purchase displays, advertising, press releases, and publicity have been found essential for maintaining the publication's viability.*

In 1979 Yankee Publishing Co., the producer of the almanac, started a point-of-purchase (POP) floor stand display program for the 1980 edition that is still used today. Sales during the first year were 43 percent larger than those in control cities where the firm did not use the displays. Subsequent studies produced increases of 202 percent in Tucson, 212 percent in Savannah, Ga., 599 percent in Houston, and 445 percent in Peoria. Unit sales in 1980 were 1.6 million, increasing to 2.1 million in 1983.

The firm has used some consumer ads for the Old Farmer's Almanac, *but press releases, interviews, and extensive free publicity are the backbone of the promotion program. The almanac receives mention in newspaper wire services, network news programs, recorded editorial segments aired by more than 1,000 radio stations, and literally thousands of quotations of the almanac's anecdotes, recipes, humor, and features by commentators throughout the U.S.*

The success of the almanac is not attributed to chance. "Marketing strategy has played a big role in the Old Farmer's Almanac's *success," according to B. Michael Kukulka, director of retail marketing for Yankee Publishing.*

SOURCE: Adapted from "20,000 P-O-P Displays Help Sell 2.2. Million Copies of Venerable *Old Farmer's Almanac,*" *Marketing News* 17, no. 11 (May 27, 1983): 8.

Introduction

Did you know that Rex gravel bed filters—a product of Rexnord, Inc.—can remove up to 99 percent of the air pollutants from cement and lime plants? Or that by using krypton—Superman's old nemesis—Sylvania's 93-watt Super Saver light bulbs can illuminate as well as ordinary 100-watt lamps, but at a significantly lower operating cost?

Undoubtedly, few readers are aware of these two products, and it may be just as well, since few, if any, have a need for gravel bed filters. Most readers are not too concerned about light bulbs either, relying on the decisions of others to buy them. Nonetheless, many people do have needs for some products about which they are unaware, and there is a corresponding gap in information when this occurs, resulting in diminished demand for those products and unsatisfied needs. One of the essential tasks of marketing is to communicate with target customers—to provide them with information about available products—for demand to reach its potential. This is the critical task of the promotion function, which is essential for new products and even those nearly 200 years old, such as Yankee Publishing's *Old Farmer's Almanac.*

This is the first of four chapters devoted to promotional activities. An overview of promotion is presented here, with following chapters keying on:

- advertising, the primary means used to communicate with mass audiences
- personal selling, the basic means of individually communicating with customers and
- direct marketing, a specialized and growing field that heavily relies on promotional activity.

Scope of Promotion

Many organizations allocate substantial resources to **promotion,** which is the communication with potential buyers about an item's existence and uses to stimulate sales. Consider the following:

Promotion
Communication with potential buyers about an item's existence and uses to stimulate sales.

- Total advertising expenditures in the U.S. were nearly $90 billion in 1984 and were estimated to grow to nearly $140 billion by 1988.[1]
- Together, the five largest advertisers—Procter & Gamble, General Motors, Sears Roebuck & Co., Beatrice Foods Co., and R. J. Reynolds—spend nearly $4 billion on advertising alone in an effort to tell their stories.[2]
- Stroh Brewery Co., a large company with a big ad budget, but not large enough to place the firm on the list of 50 largest advertisers, allocated $10 million for its national introduction of Signature beer in 1986.[3]

The list is almost endless. Political candidates, not-for-profit institutions such as Blue Cross/Blue Shield, and even doctors and lawyers engage in some kinds of promotional activities, including TV and radio ads, signs, business cards, newspaper ads, and Yellow Page insertions.[4] The role of promotion in these and other firms is considered next.

The Overall Promotion Objective

All promotional activities have the general objective of changing the behavior of potential buyers—to turn them into *actual* buyers of a particular product, service, or idea. In its simplest form, management might promote a product by simply telling people about its existence. One example is the signs that one sees along highways that call out "Food Ahead" or "Five Miles to Hal's Family Restaurant."

More often, however, promotional activities extend far beyond this by involving persuasion—attempting to convince people that the sponsor's product, service, or idea is better than others. For instance, through promotion, marketers can persuade some customers to believe a brand is "favorable."

To illustrate, many studies have indicated that in blindfold taste tests (where people are asked their preferences when the brand names are not revealed, as with the "Pepsi Challenge"), most consumers cannot distinguish between brands of cola, beer, turkey meat, cigarettes, and many other products.[5] Yet, largely due to promotional themes such as "We bring good things to life" (General Electric), most consumers have decided preferences for many items. Consumers who place a high value on time tend to be brand-loyal, for instance.[6] Presumably they have neither the time nor inclination to experiment with different brands. Promotion campaigns help to develop and maintain such preferences.

TV ads, contests, and sweepstakes, as companies such as *Reader's Digest*, Coca-Cola, and Philip Morris can attest, are among the many promotional techniques that can help to position a product and develop its link with needs and social acceptance.

One objective of promotion is to inform people about the existence of an item.

This does not mean that false promises lead to lasting marketing relationships; lasting relationships depend on delivering products which do, in fact, satisfy needs. But promotion efforts can help to bring this about. TV commercials, for instance, can inform consumers that the *Old Farmer's Almanac* is entertaining and informative, and as a result they can be instrumental in building sales. If the publication is not entertaining or informative, however, the ad effort could be wasted.

Secondary Promotional Objectives

While fundamentally geared toward influencing behavior, management may have any of several secondary objectives in mind for a given promotional activity. It is important to identify these ahead of time so that more effective promotions can be designed. While many objectives are possible, they essentially fall into one of three categories: stimulating demand, building an organization's image, or reinforcing past behavior.

Stimulating Product Demand The most widely adopted purpose for engaging in promotion is to directly stimulate the demand for a product, service, or idea. This might be accomplished through attempts to stimulate primary demand (for a generic type of item) or selective demand (for a brand).

Stimulating *primary demand* focuses on building the demand for a generic type of item; for example, artificial sweeteners. The aim is to get people to choose the generic type over a substitute product such as sugar. Using this focus in designing promotions makes sense in three circumstances.

■ *To help build a market for a generic product that is in the early stage of its product life cycle.* For example, G. D. Searle used this strategy in the early 1980s with its newly developed aspertame, a sugar/saccharin artificial sweetener substitute. A TV and print campaign was used with the theme "You can't buy it but you're gonna love it." Later, when soft drinks, hot cocoa mixes, cereal, and chewing gum products containing aspertame were introduced (produced by other companies), demand became so great that Searle was hard-pressed to produce enough of the additive.[7]

■ *When the collective efforts of all competitors can be mustered together to battle against sellers of substitutes.* For example, the Florida Tourist Council (an association of Florida tourist businesses) advertises heavily in northern states during cold months to attract tourists to the "Sunshine State." Tourist councils, trade associations, agricultural commissions (e.g., the California Iceberg Lettuce Growers Association), and shopping center associations are useful for this purpose.

■ *When the sponsoring company has a dominant market share in an industry.* Campbell Soup Co., for example, markets more than 90 percent of the canned soup in the U.S. It stresses "soup for lunch" in some of its ads to build primary demand for soup.

Most promotion activity, however, is oriented around building *selective demand* for a particular brand. Attempting to build selective demand is especially prevalent among companies with products in the later stages of their life cycles. The focus is to stress actual, or even psychologically perceived, differences in brand attributes. Aspirin, for instance, is a widely known, long-used remedy for headaches and other ailments. Because significant increases in primary demand are unlikely, it makes sense for producers such as Bayer to stress their own brand in promotional messages, as they all fight for market share.

Breakfast cereal is another product in a later stage of its life cycle. To establish a differential advantage, the Kellogg Co. promotes All-Bran by linking its fiber content to fighting cancer. The result has been a substantial sales increase for the brand.[8]

Institutional Image Building Promotional activities also are used to improve an organization's overall image. This, in turn, helps the sponsor to attain its objectives, such as sales, higher stock prices, or whatever. Goodyear, for example, promoted its progress in developing an elliptical radial tire designed for better gas mileage. The tire was not yet ready for sale, but telling people about the company's R & D leadership helped in selling other company tires. Similarly, much of the advertising Nike sponsors for its running shoes is designed to build the company's quality image.[9] Its sales representatives stress the same image.

Promotional activities are also used to offset negative public opinions generated by pressure groups such as consumerists.[10] Many environmentalists, for example, have condemned tree harvesting in certain wilderness areas. In response, Weyerhaeuser has placed ads showing how modern harvesting techniques can actually enrich both forests and animal life. Chevron sponsors institutional image-building promotions in regions of the U.S. where public attitudes toward the company are negative. These promotions help to sway public support to favor an organization's activities.

Reinforcement Finally, memory decay causes people to forget about products over time, especially those they purchase infrequently (such as major durables) and those involving low levels of personal involvement in the decision (such as convenience items). Promotional activities may be used to remedy this by reinforcing past learning and brand loyalty.

To illustrate, many credit unions and savings and loan associations send their members monthly or quarterly newsletters to remind them of the financial rewards made possible by making regular deposits. Similarly, Chevrolet publishes *Friends*, a magazine it sends monthly to past new car buyers. Featuring interesting travel articles,

Some promotion is directed toward building the image of the sponsor.

CONCEPT SUMMARY

Some Important Promotion Objectives

Objective	Description
Overall objective	Changing the behavior of potential buyers or some other key group
Stimulating generic demand (for a generic product)	Building greater acceptance of a generic product or class of products
Stimulating selective demand (for a particular brand)	Improving an organization's image among general or specific groups
Reinforcement	Eliminating loss of memory about the product or service through reinforcing past learning

MARKETING BRIEF

Point-of-Purchase Displays Can Be Effective in Reinforcing Purchase Behavior

A significant development in point-of-purchase displays was announced by Portland, Oregon-based Marketplace Communications Corp. in early 1986: permanent audio-visual units. Early use of similar displays was abandoned due to the poor durability of the original units. Their portability and poor construction resulted in their being knocked down by customers and stock clerks. Repairs became a nuisance, causing most retailers to remove the units entirely.

Audio-visual POPs were originally developed and tested for six months in a Canadian market during 1983. The units used filmstrip projectors coupled with product displays to test the effects of selling 13 products in the automotive, hardware, and housewares areas for two weeks each. Two mass merchandisers were used in the tests.

Retailers positioned the audio-visual units at the ends of aisles. Heat sensors in the units detected the presence of people when they came within nine feet of a unit. Though some customers were startled when the units began working, sales results were dramatic. Sales gains ranged from a high of 2,695 percent for a $4.39 windshield cleaner to 120 percent for auto headlights. According to Point-of-Purchase Advertising Institute vice president John M. Kawula, "For some products, sales increases of more than 1,000 percent after the use of this kind of device is not unusual."

The announcement of the permanent units that overcome the problems with the original units is expected to rekindle retailer interest in these units. The cost of these units is also much lower on a per-person basis than many other types of promotion, including TV advertising and shopping cart advertising. Consumers began to see the units in supermarkets and mass merchandisers during the summer of 1986.

SOURCE: Based on "Sales Skyrocket in Six-Month Test Using End-Aisle Displays and A-V Presentations," *The Marketing News* 17, no. 17 (August 19, 1983): 9; and "P-O-P Display Units Capture POPAI Awards; Outstanding Merchandising Awards Presented to P-O-P Manufacturers," *Product Marketing—Cosmetic & Fragrance Retailing* 15 (January 1986): 22.

the publication also contains considerable narrative praise about company products. Chevrolet reinforces past buying behavior through this medium, enhancing the likelihood of repeat purchases. Small companies sometimes sponsor local softball teams. The name of the sponsor appears on the uniforms and serves to reinforce past patronage of the company. Further, point-of-purchase displays can be very effective in achieving reinforcement, as indicated in the accompanying Marketing Brief.

Promotion and the Communications Process

Once a company's objectives are set, management is ready to design a promotional program. When designing the program, much can be gained by keeping the findings of communications researchers in mind. Figure 15.1 presents a conceptual model of the communications process. The model helps identify key principles that help managers make more effective promotional decisions. The model's five components are considered next.

Receivers

Receivers
Members of the group that intercept a communication message (also called *audience*).

Effective promotion begins with learning as much as is possible about the intended **receivers,** also called intended *audience*, as is practical. This group is usually composed

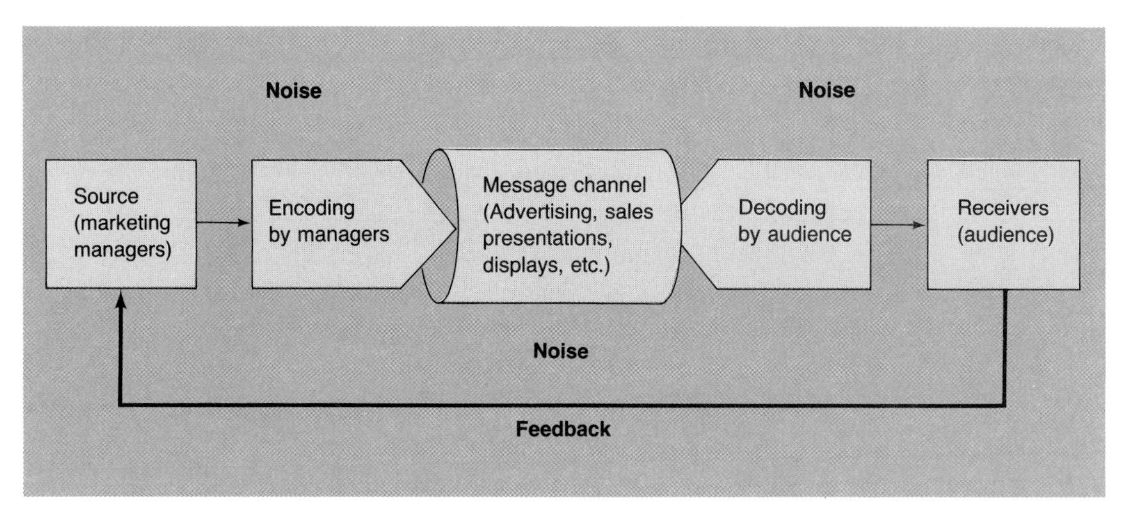

Figure 15.1
Model of the Marketing Communications Process
(SOURCE: Adapted from Wilbur Schramm, "How Communication Works," in *The Process and Effects of Mass Communications*, ed. W. Schramm (Urbana: Univ. of Ill. Press, 1965): 4.)

of the target market. Management's knowledge about the market is useful here, but marketing research is often necessary to assure that their inherent biases do not cloud the impressions. Insights into the intended audience's media consumption habits, brand preferences, and attitudes toward the product, company, and competitors help managers in recognizing what information should be available, how it should be used, and how it should be presented to yield maximum results.[11]

It is especially important not to overlook key attitude information. Research might indicate that prospective customers are confused about certain of a product's attributes. Promotional messages can then be designed (or encoded) to overcome this difficulty. To illustrate, Apple Computer recognized that many people were unaccustomed to, and even intimidated by, the use of personal computers. Accordingly, it featured several Macintosh ads centered around the machine's user friendliness—a computer for "the rest of us." In contrast, Kimberly-Clark had difficulty in selling its Averts facial tissues, which were treated with cold and flu remedy chemicals. Its promotional messages did not convince people of the brand's cold and flu aversion properties.[12]

There are many possible attitudes and perceptions to be concerned about. Those which best help in building an overall positive orientation toward the product should, of course, be identified. Avis, for example, capitalized on dissatisfaction among competitors' customers with its theme "We try harder." Thus, learning about current attitudes, ambiguities, and beliefs enables management to focus its promotional activity on the areas where they will do the most good.

Communications channels
Means of carrying messages to receivers.

Advertising
Any paid form of nonpersonal promotion of ideas, goods, or services by an identified sponsor.

Channels

Communications channels are means of carrying messages to receivers. There are many types of promotional channels available, as indicated in Table 15.1. Essentially, all of them fall into one of four categories:[13]

1. **Advertising**—any paid form of nonpersonal promotion of ideas, goods, or services by an identified sponsor.

Table 15.1 Major Promotional Methods Available to Marketers

Brand publicity	Posters
Catalogs	Premiums (introductory offers, cents-off coupons, special gifts, etc.)
Contests	Sales conferences
Demonstrations	Sale prices
Endorsements	Sales brochures
Films	Sales presentations
Firm identification programs	Searchlights
Firm publicity	Space advertising (magazines, newspapers, billboards, bus and cab signs, etc.)
Free samples	Speeches
In-house publications (house organs)	Spot advertising (radio, television)
Loudspeaker advertising	Trade exhibits
Mailings	Trading stamps
Packaging	
Point-of-purchase displays	

2. **Personal selling**—personal communication with one or more prospective buyers for the purpose of making sales.
3. **Publicity** (and *public relations*)—nonpersonal promotion of a product, service, or business unit resulting from planting commercially significant news about it in a published medium or by obtaining favorable unpaid-for presentation of it on radio, television, or stage.
4. **Sales promotion**—promotional activities, other than personal selling, advertising, or publicity, that stimulate customer purchasing and dealer effectiveness, such as displays, packaging (sometimes considered a separate category), demonstrations, and various nonrecurring selling efforts not in the ordinary routine.

Personal selling
Personal communication with one or more prospective buyers for the purpose of making sales.

Publicity
Nonpersonal unpaid promotion resulting from planting commercially significant news in a published medium or on radio, television, or stage.

Sales promotion
Promotional activities other than personal selling, advertising, or publicity that stimulate customer purchasing and dealer effectiveness.

Each promotional channel has unique characteristics.[14] These are described and compared in Exhibit 15.1.

Message

The most important aspect of developing effective **messages** is for management to grasp the intended audience's mental frame of reference. Audiences interpret (**decode**) communications from their own perspectives, based upon past experiences, needs, and interests. The problem is that managers tend to design (**encode**) messages from their perspectives, which are likely to differ significantly from that of the audience.[15] Studies indicate that perhaps 30 percent or more of all messages tend to be misinterpreted because of this problem.[16] For example, DayFlo, Inc., a producer of computer software, promoted one of its products as a "fluid format, personal information manager." Most people, including the authors, had no idea what this meant, and the promotional expense was wasted.[17]

Message
A communication that is encoded by managers and decoded by an audience.

Encode
The source's transformation of ideas into messages.

Decode
The receiver's transformation of messages into meaning.

Exhibit 15.1
Major Features of Promotion Categories

	Description	Personal versus Impersonal	Efficiency per Contact	Risk
Advertising	A broad category, including methods as diverse as broadcasts on radio and TV to posters on the backs of bus stop seats; from magazine ads to signs displayed on hot air balloons.	Impersonal standardized messages presented to mass audiences. This means that message presentation is inflexible but can be repeated over and over.	Usually quite inexpensive on a per-contact basis.	Because messages can be carefully controlled and tested, the risk of alienating an audience can be quite low.
Personal Selling	Taking orders over telephones, industrial selling, door-to-door selling, etc. Any activity where a salesperson is being paid to present messages and make sales.	Very personal, meaning that messages can be tailored to an individual receiver's needs. It is also flexible, meaning that a presentation can be adjusted for each situation. Further, it enables a continuing effort to build rapport between a receiver and a message sender.	Very expensive per contact, but also very effective. For mass consumer markets, effectiveness is often offset by the high cost of making individual contacts.	There is a risk that receivers will become alienated, especially consumers who often do not want to be bothered. Also, because of flexibility, a salesperson can commit a firm to unfavorable prices or delivery schedules. Intense control is usually needed.
Publicity	Media-sponsored promotion of a product or a firm, such as editorials, listings in *Consumer Reports,* "Helpful Hints" columns, news stories, etc.	Impersonal with standardized messages presented to mass audiences.	Publicity does not cost a firm directly. However, many firms maintain publicity departments to send information to newspersons about a firm's activities. Such staffs can be costly, as maintaining contacts is essential.	This is very risky, as message contents cannot be fully controlled. Since publicity is independent, it is very believable. A negative story can do much damage, but a favorable story may be worth millions of dollars of advertising.
Sales Promotion	A broad category of other types of promotion. Included are cents-off coupons, trading stamps, free samples, in-store displays, buying allowances, and contests.	Sales promotion materials are impersonal, being designed to appeal to many receivers as a group, rather than as individuals.	Usually quite inexpensive per receiver contacted.	Can be risky. If used improperly or overused, it may suggest to buyers that a product cannot sell on its own merit. If special deals become expected, they are no longer special, but they can be effective as a sales catalyst. A temporary special deal can break traditional behavior.
Packaging	A specialized category that relates to a physical product. One function of packaging is to protect the product. The other is to present promotional messages to prospects.	Impersonal, as any message is directed to a group of people, rather than being personalized.	Very inexpensive, since the package usually needs to be designed anyway.	Can be risky if the wrong message is displayed, but is normally quite safe. The promotional aspect of packaging may be particularly important for convenience items, where attracting attention is important for generating sales.

Effective communications requires encoding messages in a way that they can be interpreted properly by the audience.

Designing effective messages requires that management become intimately familiar with the target audience's needs, experiences, attitudes, language, and other factors that affect meaning.[18] Yale University, for example, recently had some difficulty in attracting good students. A naïve promotional approach probably would have involved messages telling people about the school's solid reputation, but this would have been inappropriate; the school's reputation was already known. The problem stemmed from the school's high tuition. Accordingly, the school's administration developed a program for tuition loans to be repaid by students after graduation on a scale adjusted to earnings. Promotions for this program were very effective in reversing the declines, since they focused on the key problem restricting the applications.

Ads featuring *fear appeals* for certain products also illustrate the point of emphasizing key perceptions.[19] For example, breath freshener ads that ask, "Will he be able to smell my breath?" focus on key social cognitions and are effective as a result.

Other important message ingredients to consider are timing of the important points to be mentioned and whether or not both sides of the issue should be mentioned.

Research indicates that the major points should be mentioned first when it is necessary to capture the audience's fleeting attention. Statements such as "Carson, Pirie, Scott drastically cuts the price of . . ." and "What if you want to improve your cash flow . . ." are often desirable.

Further, *one-sided arguments* (avoiding any mention of negatives) tend to be best when the audience's attitudes are already positive. *Two-sided* arguments, on the other hand, tend to be more effective when the message conflicts with existing cognitions.[20] To illustrate, antidrinking ads probably would be more effective if they also acknowledged the realistic pleasures that drinkers do receive from consuming alcohol.

Source

Above all, the source should be perceived as *credible*, which means that receivers perceive it as being expert, trustworthy, and likable.[21] The media itself can impart a degree of credibility. Favorable publicity from news columnists, for instance, offer an advantage here, and business ads appearing in *Fortune* and *Forbes* connote trustworthiness. Likewise, firms located in certain countries (such as Japan) have more credibility than those headquartered in others (such as Italy).[22]

To build credibility, firms often hire spokespersons to tell their stories, such as Bill Cosby's endorsement of Coca-Cola.[23] But this can be very costly, involving $20,000 or more just for the initial fee, with royalties to follow.[24] Further, studies indicate that in many situations what is most important is a moderate level of credibility; not necessarily notoriety.[25]

Consequently, some firms have avoided the use of celebrities because of the high cost. Miles Laboratories, for example, successfully uses past customers for its long-running Alka Seltzer Plus ads. To gain credibility, though, it used ordinary people from Buffalo, N.Y.—a city widely known for its bitter winters.

Feedback

Feedback
Getting information about how messages were received by an audience.

Finally, **feedback**—getting information that messages were received as intended by the audience—is important for communication to be effective. The entire communications process is laced with noise, or interference, which may lessen the message's impact, including conflicting messages by competitors, poorly selected channels, and poorly designed messages. Thus, it is important to assure that the messages were received by the audience as intended.

Personal communications methods are superior in this regard because feedback can be elicited during the presentation. Accordingly, many companies, such as Xerox, provide salespeople with extensive training in listening. With nonpersonal communications, marketing research is needed to provide the feedback.

The Promotion Mix

Promotions mix
The combination of promotion types used by a firm.

It is generally best to use a mix of promotional channels (termed a **promotions mix**) to communicate messages. This is to achieve promotional synergy, where each type of promotion used complements each other. For example, General Mills introduced its Circus Fun children's presweetened cereal in 1986 with a $24 million promotional budget spread among television, radio, and print advertising plus the distribution of 273 million coupons.

Management makes two fundamental types of decisions when designing a promotion mix: deciding how to integrate each of the promotions (the campaign), and determining the relative emphasis to place on each medium (the mix).

Campaign

A promotional program is integrated through a **campaign**—a unified, organized series of promotional messages which has one theme or central idea. For example, Charmin tissue focused on the "Squeezably Soft" campaign theme for several years, making Mr. Whipple something of a celebrity. Within a campaign, management integrates advertising, package design, point-of-purchase displays, and dealer incentives around the central theme to gain a cumulative impact.

Campaign
A unified, planned, and organized series of promotion messages.

The appropriate duration of a campaign depends upon its success and whether or not its theme becomes stale to the audience. An unduly long running time results in lost impact. For instance, finding that the audience was tiring of its "Peter Pan can" campaign, Swift & Co. switched to a theme of "Is Peter Pan calling you?"[26] A new campaign may be just the ticket for restimulating excitement about messages among customers, management, and dealers.

Mix Composition

Regarding the mix of promotional vehicles to use, there are five factors which are centrally important.

The Target The nature of the target audience is an important factor to consider in choosing particular media to use. Consumers, for instance, are widely dispersed geographically, tend to buy in modest quantities, and are quite varied in many ways. A general promotion aimed at a large number of consumers, therefore, is typically weighted heavily toward mass communications media such as TV. In contrast, specialized markets such as an industry group (steel mills, for example) tend to be localized, relatively few in number, buy in larger quantities, and tend to select suppliers on the basis of how well they can adjust their marketing mixes to meet the group's particular needs. Consequently, sales representatives may be a better choice than mass media for such a market. Thus, companies such as Digital Equipment extensively use salespeople for their promotions. However, as Figure 15.2 illustrates, personal and nonpersonal communications tend to be used for both consumer and industrial items, though in different proportions.

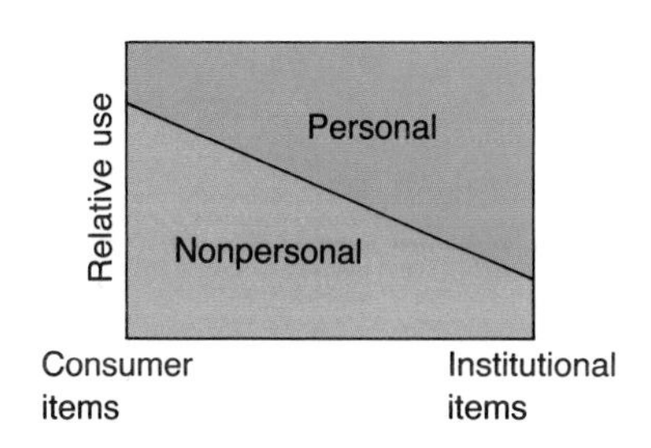

Figure 15.2
Relative Uses of Personal and Nonpersonal Promotional Methods by Type of End User

The Budget The size of the company's budget has an effect. Mass media campaigns are usually inexpensive on a per-person-contacted basis, but expensive in total. Just one minute's worth of prime-time TV, for instance, can cost nearly three-quarters of a million dollars. A full-page ad in a popular magazine such as *Time* or *Newsweek* can cost over $100,000.[27] And many ads are usually needed, as each one only makes a limited contribution by "nudging the consumer along the path of adoption."[28] Consequently, many companies are forced to select promotional tools within their financial reach.[29]

The Competition Companies sometimes use promotion as a principal weapon in their competitive battles. Thus, management must anticipate the promotional efforts

FRANK: Hello. This is Frank Bartles speaking to you from New York City.

As many of you know, the Bartles & Jaymes Premium Wine Cooler is not only perfect as a refreshment, . . . but with meals as well.

Ed says it even goes with these big doughnuts they like to eat here.

I personally would not have thought Bartles & Jaymes and doughnuts would go together, much less doughnuts and fish.

But I have tried it myself, and once again, Ed is right.

So please continue to enjoy Bartles & Jaymes with all kinds of food, and we thank you once more for your support.

Some campaigns run a long time, but most are limited in duration.

of competitors when making its promotion decisions. But relying on promotions to offset product vulnerability is a mistake.

The analgesic industry provides an interesting illustration.[30] Aspirin substitutes were unheard of prior to the mid-1970s. McNeilab, Inc., makers of Tylenol, led the aspirin substitute charge into the adult market through heavy advertising expenditures and sales soared at the expense of the old-line pain relievers, who, in turn, increased their promotional budgets. Anacin, for example, bumped up its budget and claimed that it contained an ingredient (aspirin) which could help reduce swelling due to rheumatism and other inflammatory diseases. The response was totally ill-conceived, as a U.S. District Court judge ruled that it was misleading and therefore illegal. The only way the aspirin in Anacin could help such swelling was if the product were taken in quantities far in excess of the recommended dosages. A more logical strategy would have been for the old-line analgesic firms to add a nonaspirin product as well—a solid rounding-out strategy. Thus, promotions should not be considered an alternative to a poor marketing strategy.

The Product The characteristics of the product should be considered when developing a promotional program. Consumers carefully deliberate over expensive items before they make a purchase. Consequently, personalized messages may be very important to answer questions, arrange delivery, and handle other details. The complexity of the product is also a consideration. If lengthy messages are needed, such as for computers, print is probably a better choice than TV or radio if mass communications are used. In contrast, frequently purchased durables that are simple to understand and are aimed at large markets, such as a new deodorant, can probably be best promoted through rapid-paced mass communications such as TV or radio.

Media Cost Finally, the cost of each medium should be considered when determining a promotional program. Ideally, the budget should be allocated in a way that the marginal benefit divided by the marginal cost of each is equal. In reality, this is impossible to measure. All promotional efforts interact with each other, and with other marketing mix elements, in a unique way for each company and each promotional objective. Thus, selecting a particular mix tends to be more of an art than a science. (More will be said about selecting media in Chapter 16, which focuses on making advertising decisions.)

Each channel has both strengths and weaknesses that make it advantageous to use in certain situations (see Exhibit 15.1). Figure 15.3 illustrates how managers involved with marketing different types of goods perceive the relative importance of various promotional channels. As indicated, advertising and personal selling are considered to be the major means of promoting all types of products. Accordingly, these topics are considered in depth in the next two chapters. The remainder of this chapter examines sales promotion and publicity, which are also important means of getting the firm's messages across to an audience.

Sales Promotion

Sales promotion activities are often considered supplemental ingredients of a promotional mix. This is because they are generally used to supplement advertising and personal selling programs. While they are not always as visible as advertising and personal selling, they are important armaments in a full promotional arsenal. Sales promotion

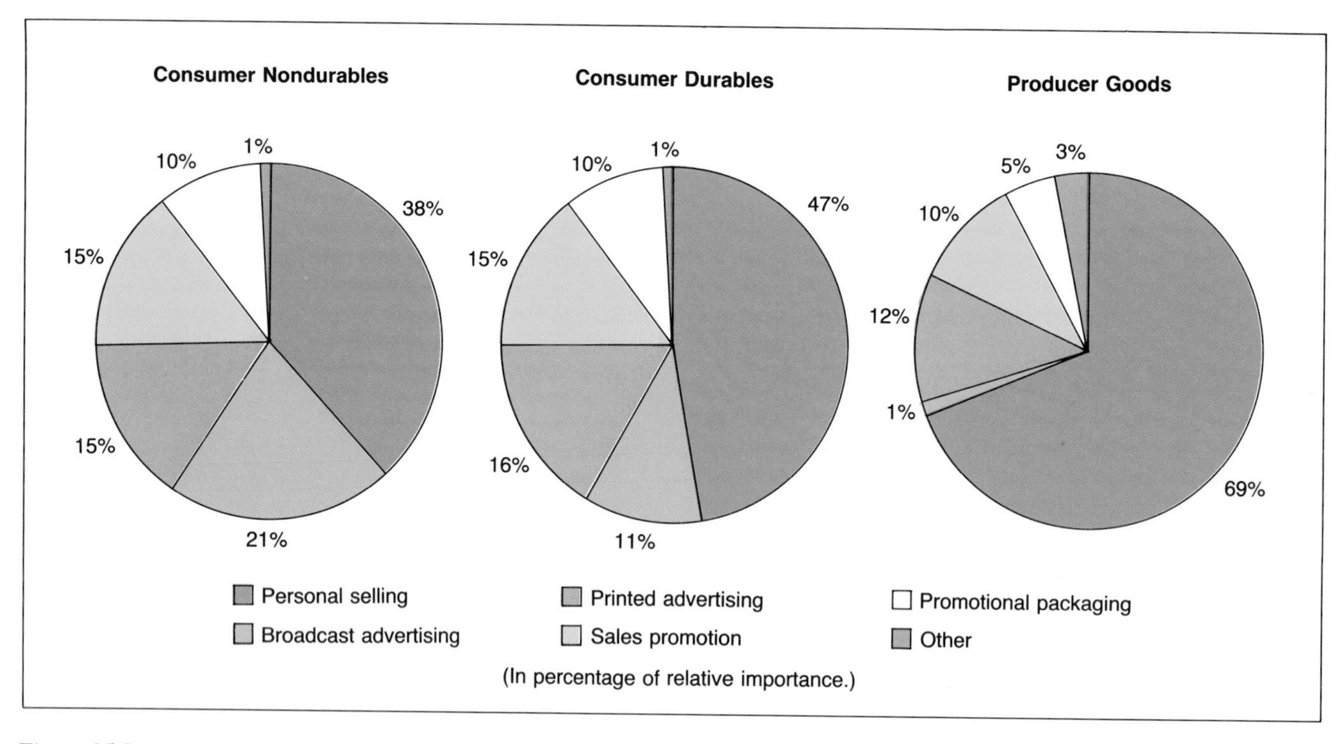

Figure 15.3
Perceived Importance of Promotional Channels by Producers of Three Types of Items (SOURCE: Adapted from Jon G. Udell, "The Perceived Importances of the Elements of Strategy," *Journal of Marketing* 32, no. 1 (January 1968): 38.)

activities are quite varied and their use depends upon the situation, but all of them attempt to get customers or dealers to use or handle the product.

In effect, sales promotion is usually thought of as a sort of middle ground between advertising and personal selling. This is because it is usually not focused at as large an audience as advertising, but is designed to reach a much larger group than personal selling. However, sales promotion is by no means considered an afterthought in the minds of most marketing managers.

Scope of Sales Promotion

While an accurate count of how much is spent on sales promotion is not available, estimates indicate that in total, companies spend a little over half again as much on all sales promotion activities as on all advertising programs.[31] This translates to about $70 billion per year.[32] In terms of growth, sales promotion expenditures have been increasing at around 13 percent per year on average over the past six years, while advertising has climbed about 10.5 percent per year during the same period. However, the widespread use of cash rebates over the past several years, especially in the auto industry, has affected these figures considerably.

Sales promotion activities are diverse and are aimed at both end users of a product or service (mostly consumers) and at intermediaries and other members of a distribution channel, including the company's own salespeople. Further, sales promotions are designed to reach a diversity of target audiences and to achieve a wide set of objectives, including

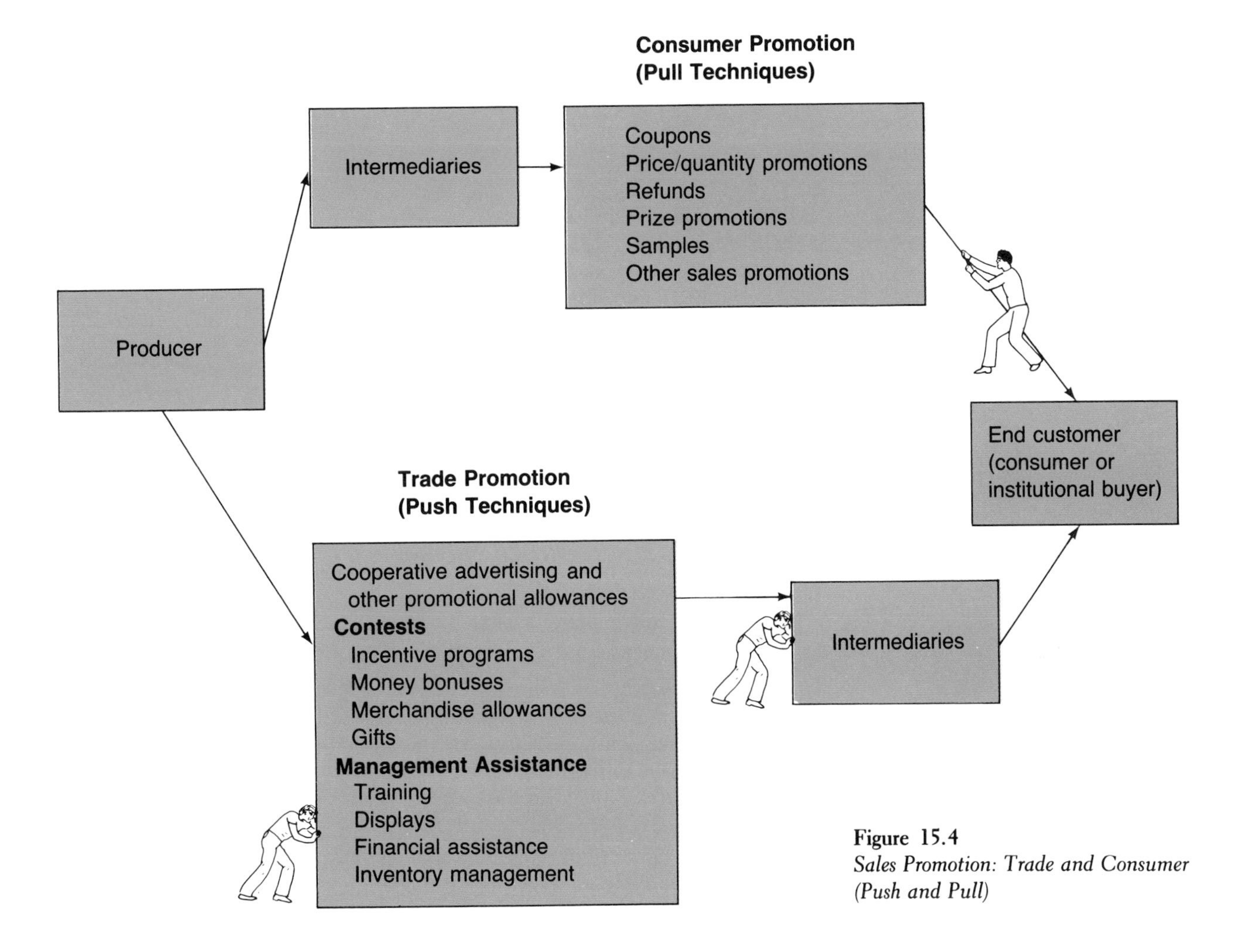

Figure 15.4
Sales Promotion: Trade and Consumer (Push and Pull)

- getting customers to try new products (free samples)
- gaining more shelf space with retailers or wholesalers (promotional, special handling, and special display allowances)
- identifying sales leads (trade shows)
- increasing market share (special multipacks offering two for the price of one, or a prize such as a free T-shirt with a purchase)
- reducing price cutting

Figure 15.4 illustrates the two major categories of sales promotion: trade promotion and consumer promotion, along with various types of each. These are discussed next.

Consumer-Oriented Sales Promotion As indicated in Figure 15.4, consumer sales promotion is directed at **pulling** a product through a distribution system. This means that the marketing activities are directed toward consumers in an effort to build sufficient demand to cause intermediaries to handle more of the product, and thus the name "pull."

Pulling (an item)
Developing strong demand among final buyers, who exert pressure on their suppliers to stock the item.

The use of consumer sales promotion is widespread. As to the types used, one study examined 7,000 consumer-oriented sales promotions and found the following [33]

Type of Promotion	Frequency of Use
Coupons	66
Price/quantity promotions	11
Refunds	10
Premiums	8
Prize promotions	4
Samples	1
Total	100 percent

Coupons Coupons, like those offered by Burger King in an effort to entice consumers, are sales promotions that usually offer a discounted price to the consumer to encourage purchase or trial. An astounding number of coupons are distributed to each household in the U.S.—more than 1,400 of them.[34] In total, over 100 billion are distributed annually, with redemption rates varying from 2 percent to 25 percent. Generally, coupons distributed through direct mail have the greatest redemption rates and are therefore the most effective.[35]

For products in the mature stage of their lives, couponing may only reduce gross revenues from already loyal customers. There also have been problems with misredemption of coupons. Coupons are refunded by retailers who later get reimbursed by the producer or an independent redemption center paid to handle the burden by the manufacturer, and some of them have taken liberties by making false claims.[36] This causes additional auditing burdens on the part of producers. Nonetheless, the use of coupons has nearly doubled in the past five years.

Price/Quantity Promotions Many producers have used special price/quantity deals in their sales promotions. These are usually short-term price reductions or "bonus packs" that offer an additional quantity to induce trial or to retaliate against a competitor's actions. For example, if a competitor introduces a new bar of soap, the company responds with a "two packages for the price of one" deal. The short-term promotion makes the competitor's introduction more difficult.

Refunds and Rebates Special temporary refunds and rebates have become an increasingly popular way for dealers to clear excess inventories. While many producers use refunds or rebates, the practice has become especially common in the auto industry. A distinctive advantage of refund and rebate programs is that the manufacturer retains control of the situation. Another advantage is that many customers do not claim the refund for small amounts, thus reducing the program's cost.

Premiums Premiums are often used to stimulate consumer sales and involve offering merchandise free or at substantially reduced prices over retail. This latter type of premium is often called *self-liquidating*, since the amount charged to customers covers the cost of the item. There are many examples of premiums. McDonald's offered drinking glasses picturing Snoopy and the crew from Peanuts, with weekly visits being required to collect the set; John Deere offered special caps with the company's logo at a nominal price; and Merit cigarettes offered special, free sailcloth wallets to customers who bought specially wrapped packs of two at the normal price.

MARKETING BRIEF
Free Samples Gain Access to College Markets

Beginning over 20 years ago, New Jersey–based MarketSource Corp. developed almost an institution: Campus Trial Pak, one of the most effective means of gaining entry to the college market. Campus Trial Pak is a cooperative sampling program that puts company products into the hands of young consumers who are in the process of forming long-term brand loyalties. Many manufacturers of consumer staple items are convinced that including their products in this sample package is one of the best ways to reach college students and tap into this $4.5 billion market.

The Campus Trial Paks are distributed to students each fall at over 400 colleges and universities, generally through bookstores. There is usually no charge to the students, which makes the packages especially attractive. Many students make special trips to their bookstores to receive them, and studies show that they are an effective means of influencing these young buyers. Products sampled are reported to show a dramatic increase in usage, brand awareness, and purchase intent. Enrollment in the program buys the following for manufacturers: 1.2 million Paks distributed (700,000 female, 500,000 male), controlled distribution to students (students must present a coupon with name and I.D. to receive a Pak), a comprehensive market research study, and trade support services to ensure that participating brands are stocked in college stores.

While the Fall Pak represents the dominant share of the Trial Pak business for MarketSource, the firm also offers Spring Campus Trial Pak (distribution of 500,000 Paks) and an Ethnic Campus Trial Pak (distribution of 100,000 Paks) delivered through 50 schools with large black and Hispanic enrollments. This is especially useful for reaching the ethnic student market.

SOURCE: Based on a MarketSource advertisement appearing in *Advertising Age*, February 10, 1986: 25.

Prize Promotions A fifth type of sales promotion is the use of prizes, or contests. The *Reader's Digest* annual contest is probably the best-known of these and features millions of dollars in prizes to winners. In some of the contests, like the *Reader's Digest* sweepstakes, contestants are required to do nothing except respond to have a chance at winning. In others, contestants must take an active role, such as completing a jingle, filling in a drawing, completing a sentence, or some other action. Response to these contests and other prize sales promotions is usually very heavy.

Samples Another common sales promotion is sampling, which involves offering the product free or at a greatly reduced price. This sales promotion method is usually reserved for new products with the aim of putting the item in consumers' hands to induce future purchases. A trial size is usually smaller than the regular package size—generally equal to about half the normal purchase cycle.[37] For example, toothpaste is generally purchased once a month, and a sample would generally contain about a two-week supply. In this way, if the sample is liked, the consumer will remember to buy the new brand on the next shopping trip. Sampling is best used for products that are bought frequently, have a low unit price, and are new. Care must be taken to assure that the product has a noticeable differential advantage or the sample could stimulate negative word-of-mouth discussion among consumers.[38]

Other Sales Promotions There are also other types of consumer-oriented sales promotions. Demonstrations are sometimes staged to illustrate the use of a product, such

POP displays can be effective for industrial as well as for consumer products.

as Teflon-coated frying pans, in a supermarket or department store. These are relatively expensive to perform, so there must be considerable traffic to justify the expense. Trading stamps also are sometimes issued, although their use has diminished over the years. All of these sales promotions have a common objective: to induce consumers to purchase (or try) the product.

Pushing (an item)
Marketing efforts to intermediaries, who are then expected to promote the item to final customers.

Trade-Oriented Sales Promotion As indicated in Figure 15.4, trade-oriented sales promotions also are used to bolster the effectiveness of advertising and personal selling, though they are aimed at intermediaries. In this case, the promotions are labeled **pushing** techniques, as they have the effect of providing incentives to intermediaries to handle the product. The idea is to push items along toward end-customer purchase.

Trade promotion is widely used, and there are several possible types. The most common of these are listed below.

Cooperative Advertising (promotional allowances) This involves manufacturer rebates for all or a part of the cost of advertising the company's product by an intermediary, usually a retailer. An example is when Black & Decker reimburses Ace Hardware stores for ads that the latter runs in local papers for the former's power tools. This topic is covered in the next chapter dealing with advertising decisions.

Contests Contests are also run for distributors (and the company's sales force) to encourage additional support of a company's promotional campaigns. These involve some award, such as a trip, if dealers order or sell a quantity of units beyond a certain minimum. An equipment manufacturer such as Caterpillar Tractor Co. might offer a vacation to Hawaii or Tahiti as an incentive to dealers to push sales during a traditionally slow period. These contests are often very effective in gaining enthusiasm, as one might expect.

Incentive Programs These involve money bonuses, special prices on merchandise, and gifts such as watches or personal computers to enlist the support of dealers and their sales forces.

Management Assistance Finally, sales promotion activities also involve various additional programs to help dealers perform better jobs. Training is often helpful, especially for technical products such as computers. Special in-store displays help retailers induce consumers into buying. Financial assistance is sometimes useful. In the auto industry, for example, most manufacturers pay for the carrying costs of new inventory for a period of time, such as 15 to 20 days (called *floor planning*). Also, assistance might involve helping dealers to use advanced concepts—often mathematical in nature—to better manage their inventories.

Public Relations and Publicity

Public relations
Function of evaluating public attitudes, identifying the policies and procedures of an individual organization with the public interest, and executing a program of action to earn public understanding and acceptance.

Public relations and publicity are another means of promoting a company and its products to mass markets. **Public relations** "evaluates public attitudes, identifies the policies and procedures of an individual or an organization with the public interest, and executes a program of action to earn public understanding and acceptance." [39] The public involved may be consumers, employees, stockholders, the investment community, government administrators, suppliers, or the community at large. An organization's public relations role involves the use of many communications paths, including institutional advertising, personal selling by senior corporate executives, and publicity—an activity that strongly supports public relations, but has a role extending much beyond this. Since the first of these topics is covered in later chapters, publicity is considered below.

Publicity is a form of promotion that is not paid for directly, but there are costs involved pertaining to staff and for creating opportunities to generate media coverage of the message. News releases have to be prepared and sent. Media representatives may have to be entertained in the hopes of getting a favorable story. Photo packages have to be released. All of these factors contribute to the cost. As more and more companies attempt to obtain publicity in this era of increasing skepticism, many companies have turned to hiring public relations directors to help gain effectiveness and credibility.[40]

The Tools of Publicity

There are several publicity tools available to a public relations director. Most companies active in developing publicity use the news release, which is an announcement regarding changes in the company, its product line, or the company's position regarding some recent news event. The intent is to inform a newspaper, radio station, TV station, magazine, or other mass communications vehicle of the change.

A news conference is another tool. Representatives of the media are invited to a meeting by sending advance materials regarding the content of the conference. This is a powerful tool, as it generates the undivided attention of the media, but the news had better be perceived as "newsworthy" by the media or they will not attend the conference.

Nonprofit organizations rely heavily on public service announcements, which are free time or space donated by the media. For example, the charter of the American Red Cross does not allow the organization to advertise. Consequently, to induce people to donate blood, local chapters must rely on such announcements to get their message out to mass audiences.

Managing Publicity

Effective publicity depends upon interweaving a campaign into the total promotional program of the organization. The Xerox Corporation, for example, has found that sponsoring marathon runs is very effective in gaining publicity and getting the company's name in front of people without spending large sums.[41]

A carefully coordinated campaign enables all of the organization's promotional elements—advertising, personal selling, publicity, and sales promotion—to complement each other. For all of these activities, objectives need to be set, budgets determined, media targeted, and performance evaluated. All of these activities are powerful, but their total impact is much greater when they are carefully coordinated.

Another example involving Tylenol illustrates this point. Johnson & Johnson overcame financial disaster in early 1986 when confronted with the company's second poisoning tragedy within three years. In a rapid response practically unheard of in the industry, the company pulled its advertising for Tylenol from the air on February 11, one day after a New York woman died after taking cyanide-tainted capsules of the brand's Extra-Strength remedy. Next, the company scheduled several news conferences to inform the media of the company's quality control procedures, actions that it was taking to isolate the cause, and other facts related to the situation, such as how the company would work with investigators to locate the problem. In the meantime, management rapidly prepared a new TV ad in which Johnson & Johnson's McNeilab, Inc. division president appeared on February 19, asking consumers to trade in their Tylenol capsules for Tylenol caplets. Facts later revealed that this was another case of tampering with the product after it had been sold. During the entire crisis period, the company provided a full-time staff of representatives to furnish information to investigators and to the press.

The pain reliever remained the subject of public scrutiny for several weeks as capsules were removed from store shelves across the country and replaced by caplets. After it was learned that the cause was beyond the company's control, brand advertising resumed on March 7, featuring testimonials from contented users. An interesting phenomenon was that despite all the editorials and press surrounding the tragedy, Tylenol came through without major damage to its image. In fact, studies indicated that advertising awareness was boosted afterward, largely because the company responded in a sound, coordinated way.[42]

Chapter Summary

This chapter began a detailed examination of promotion activities. These activities comprise an organization's communication mechanism to influence prospects into buying a particular product, service, or idea. Promotion can have various motives, but essentially all promotions are geared toward stimulating either primary or secondary demand. This may take the form of attempting to stimulate product demand directly through reinforcement, or indirectly through institutional image building.

Promotional efforts are made more effective when promotional decisions are developed with the theoretical communications process in mind. This process involves receivers, noise, channel, message, source, and feedback. Understanding the relationships of all of the components can lead to better promotional messages.

The chapter next examined the promotions mix. Effective promotion is based on a carefully coordinated blend of advertising, personal selling, publicity, and sales promotion. Organizations accomplish this through major programs termed campaigns. Among the major factors influencing the promotions mix composition are the target customer, the promotion budget, the competition, and the product.

Finally, the chapter looked at decision making concerning sales promotion and publicity. Sales promotions are considered by many to be supplementary to personal selling and advertising, despite the fact that some firms spend more on them than other promotional channels. There are two major uses. Coupons, price/quantity promotions, refunds, premiums, prize promotions, and a few other types are frequently used to attract consumer purchases. For institutional sales, cooperative advertising, contests, incentive programs, and management assistance are used.

Public relations and publicity, in contrast, are oriented toward gaining unpaid promotions of a product, firm, or idea. Publicity can be managed through news releases, news conferences, and possibly public service announcements. Regardless of the techniques used, promotions are most effective when they are coordinated in a campaign to spread the company's story.

Questions

1. "Promotion is undertaken mainly by the larger companies, such as IBM and Coca-Cola." Comment.
2. Compare and contrast the distinctive characteristics of advertising, personal selling, publicity, and sales promotion.
3. What, in your opinion, might some of the major promotion objectives of the following companies consist of?
   a. Firestone Tire & Rubber
   b. Raleigh Cycle Company (bicycles)
   c. Wal-Mart stores
   d. Dr. Pepper Company
4. Locate an ad in a consumer magazine that is apparently designed for institutional image building. Is the ad effective in building the image of the organization in your mind? Why or why not?
5. The national trend toward physical fitness probably could benefit obese people most, yet many health club managers report that few overweight people enroll in fitness programs. Assess the promotional program of a widely known health club to see if some improvements could be made to attract this market segment.
6. In your next conversation, attempt to locate the major sources of "noise" in the communication process. How could the "noise" be mitigated?
7. "Ideally, the promotion budget for a consumer good should emphasize advertising over personal selling." Comment.
8. Develop a set of themes that consumer products companies might follow in promoting various deodorants to different target markets segmented on the basis of age, sex, and income.
9. Railroad companies largely use personal selling to promote their services. Do you think that advertising, publicity, and sales promotion should play roles in their efforts?
10. The management of Hi-C was pleased when market research showed that many people thought the drink was nutritious and reasonably priced. Should they have been?
11. Should marketers of personal computers stress advertising, personal selling, or sales promotion in their campaigns?
12. "Cabbage Patch" dolls benefited substantially from publicity during the 1983 and 1984 Christmas seasons. Newspapers, magazines, radio, and TV all carried extensive pieces on the dolls. Consumers literally battled with one another in retail stores to acquire this product. Should the firm have ceased all advertising efforts, since the dolls were extensively promoted through free publicity? Why or why not?
13. How does the level of the promotion budget affect the composition of the promotion mix?

Chapter 16

Advertising Decisions

Objectives

After completing this chapter, you should be able to demonstrate a knowledge of:

- What is meant by the term "advertising"
- The importance of advertising to marketers
- A seven-step advertising decision process designed to provide guidance for advertising decision making: defining goals, the target, the budget, messages, selecting media, appropriate timing decisions, and evaluating past performance
- The nature and operation of advertising agencies
- Some major criticisms of advertising and how these criticisms can be overcome

MARKETING FAILURE

Herb the Nerd Failed to Sell Burgers

Burger King scrapped its $40 million "Herb" campaign in March of 1986 because it failed to build sales, win significant numbers of new customers, or clearly position the No. 2 hamburger chain's image, according to company president Jay Darling.

The campaign was an expansive one, involving several promotional facets. The character Herb was a nerd according to his father, another character used in several of the advertising spots. "Herb never did anything right," his dad lamented to Herb's mom. In order to build suspense, Herb was not introduced to the public for over a month, but there were plenty of ads about him. The audience learned that Herb was the only American who had never been into a Burger King, which triggered his dad's cutting remarks. In another series of ads, Herb's friends also poked fun at how he was always out of step. All the while, the audience was asked if it knew where Herb was, implying that he was lost again.

Herb was finally introduced to the audience during the Super Bowl in 1986. You guessed it—Herb was a bespectacled, plaid-jacket-and-white-socks-wearing oddball. Accompanying the advertising was a fifty-state promotional tour of company stores by Herb and prizes of up to $5,000 to the first person to recognize him in one of the restaurants.

But the hoped-for sales did not materialize from the campaign. At best, industry sources indicated that company sales were up only 1 percent, clearly not enough to offset the lavish campaign's cost. The Herb campaign was the company's second disappointment in a row. In 1985, its $32 million drive for a reformulated Whopper also led to lackluster results although the entire industry was in the doldrums. According to Darling, the Herb campaign did create greater awareness of Burger King, but it did not "work hard enough extolling the virtues of our products."

SOURCE: Based on a series of articles in *Advertising Age*, *The Wall Street Journal*, and the *Chicago Tribune*, various dates, March 1986.

Introduction

Advertising is probably the most controversial element of the marketing mix. To some people, it represents a twentieth-century form of true art expression. As for film prizes at Cannes, or Oscars and Emmys, industry insiders gather annually in New York to honor advertising's creative best with Clio awards. To others, advertising is pure evidence of capitalistic decadence, insulting to the audience's intelligence, dehumanizing people by creating stereotypes, and unnecessarily costly.

The truth is at neither extreme. "Good" ads are not necessarily those that win awards; they are ads that help their sponsors achieve their promotion goals. To illustrate, Burger King's "Herb" ads (see the opening Marketing Failure) were creative, but they did not sell the product. In contrast, MAACO car painting ads will never win awards, but they do their job.

This chapter emphasizes the key elements of advertising decision making from the perspective of a marketing manager. First, it examines the scope of this key function and then moves on to important strategic and tactical decision-making implications. Finally, it considers advertising's criticisms.

The Scope of Advertising

Advertising dates back to ancient times. Archaeological digs in Pompeii, for example, unearthed, among graffiti and political slogans, walls also blanketed with signs promoting the wares of local merchants. By the early twentieth century in the U.S., lavish printed displays dotted both city and countryside alike with billboards and painted barn signs.[1]

Early ads were a far cry from what the public is exposed to today. The producer of Kennedy's Medical Discovery, for example, heralded a remedy that "cured any skin disorder, including scrofula, erysipelas, scaldhead, scurvey, pimples, canker, and every disease of the skin of whatever name or nature." Of course, today's ads are not so deceptive, as truth-in-advertising laws and enlightened self-interest on the part of advertisers have curtailed such flagrant claims.

But advertising's importance has mushroomed dramatically over the past few decades. Figure 16.1 shows that about $110 billion was spent on advertising in 1986, or a 160-percent increase over the 1978 level.

The advertising budgets of some companies are also staggering, as Table 16.1 indicates. The leader, Procter & Gamble, spends nearly 70 times more on advertising than the average manufacturer has in total sales dollars. In 1985, the Tokoi Company (of Japan) conducted the most ambitious ad campaign for disposable lighters (Scripto brand) in several years. It spent $5 million on the campaign, exceeding the combined ad spending for the entire disposable lighter industry for the past six years.[2] In general, though, companies allocate less than 2 percent of their sales dollars to advertising, which is a modest fraction of their total operating expenses.

Advertising is by no means a tool only of large companies. To the contrary, organizations of virtually every size use it in some way. Advertising is not a tool

reserved just for businesses, as organizations diverse as the Red Cross, Christian Children's Fund, Save the Children Africa Emergency Fund, The American Cancer Society, the armed forces, political candidates, foundations, and some churches utilize this vital promotional vehicle. Even professionals such as lawyers and dentists use advertising to tell their stories, as indicated in the accompanying Marketing Brief.[3]

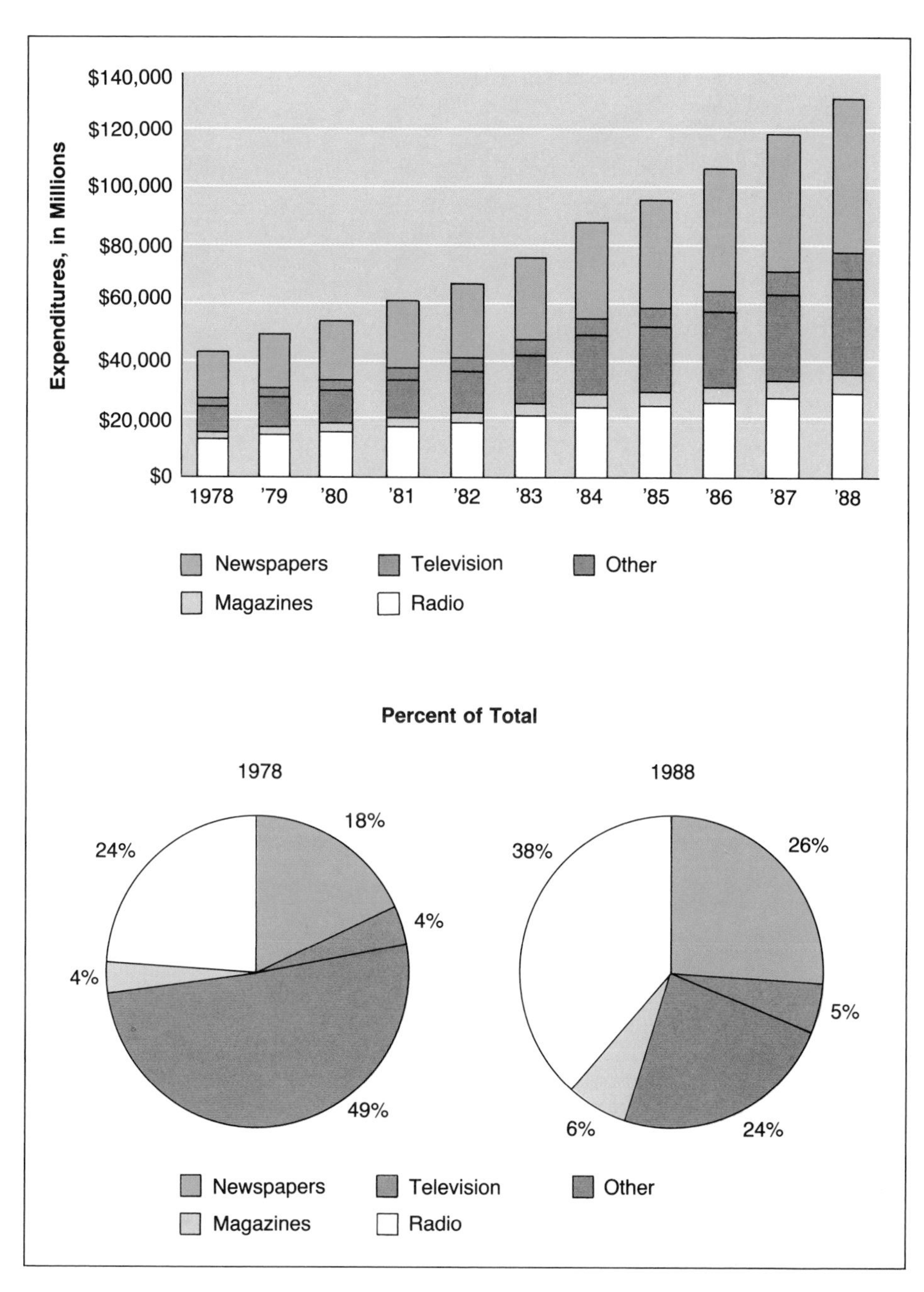

Figure 16.1
U.S. Advertising Expenditures 1978–1988, Actual and Authors' Forecasts (SOURCE: Adapted from *Statistical Abstract of the United States*, 1986, 106th ed.)

Professionals Also Use Advertising

GreatTeeth Dental Centers poised for the launching of three new Twin Cities offices (Minneapolis/St. Paul) in early 1986 with a quarter-million-dollar media blitz. The dental firm, which already operates one successful office in a mall, rents space from Sears and is planning to expand to additional Sears facilities.

The campaign features an animated 30-second TV spot, focusing on women and family members, which will run during early morning and evening time slots in the Twin Cities area. GreatTeeth will also use print and outdoor (billboard) support and direct mail sent to Sears' credit card customers. Sears operates an additional 34 outlets in the upper midwest where GreatTeeth plans future openings if this expansion goes as expected.

SOURCE: Adapted from Bob Geiger, "Sears Opens Wide for Dental Centers," *Advertising Age*, February 10, 1986: 62MW.

Table 16.1 Leading National Advertisers

Rank	Company	Expenditure (Ad dollars in thousands, 1984)
1	Procter & Gamble Co.	$872,000
2	General Motors Corp.	763,800
3	Sears, Roebuck & Co.	746,937
4	Beatrice Cos.	680,000
5	R. J. Reynolds Industries	678,176
6	Philip Morris, Inc.	570,435
7	American Telephone & Telegraph	563,200
8	Ford Motor Co.	559,400
9	K mart Corp.	554,400
10	McDonald's Corp.	480,000
11	J. C. Penney Co.	460,000
12	General Foods Corp.	450,000
13	Warner-Lambert Co.	440,000
14	Ralston Purina Co.	428,600
15	PepsiCo. Inc.	428,172
16	American Home Products	412,000
17	Unilever U.S.	395,700
18	International Business Machines	376,000
19	Anheuser-Busch Cos.	364,401
20	Coca-Cola Co.	343,300
21	Nabisco Brands	334,977
22	Pillsbury Co.	318,473
23	Chrysler Corp.	317,400
24	Eastman Kodak Co.	301,000
25	Johnson & Johnson	300,000
26	U.S. Government	287,807
27	American Cyanamid	284,410
28	General Mills	283,400
29	Dart & Kraft	269,200
30	Colgate-Palmolive Co.	258,731
31	Bristol-Myers Co.	258,440
32	Sara Lee Corp.	258,362
33	RCA Corp.	239,400
34	H. J. Heinz Co.	227,286
35	Kellogg Co.	208,800
36	Revlon Inc.	205,000
37	General Electric	202,400
38	Tandy Corp.	190,000
39	Nestle Enterprises	186,848
40	Warner Communications	181,749
41	CBS Inc.	179,800
42	Mobil Corp.	172,500
43	American Express Co.	172,100
44	ITT Corp.	168,000
45	Sterling Drug Co.	166,600
46	Gillette Co.	165,673
47	Nissan Motor Corp.	164,200
48	Richardson-Vicks	163,500
49	Quaker Oats Co.	161,300
50	Gulf & Western Industries	149,249

SOURCE: R. Craig Endicott, "P & G Retains Ad Spending Crown," *Advertising Age* 56, no. 71 (September 26, 1985): 1.

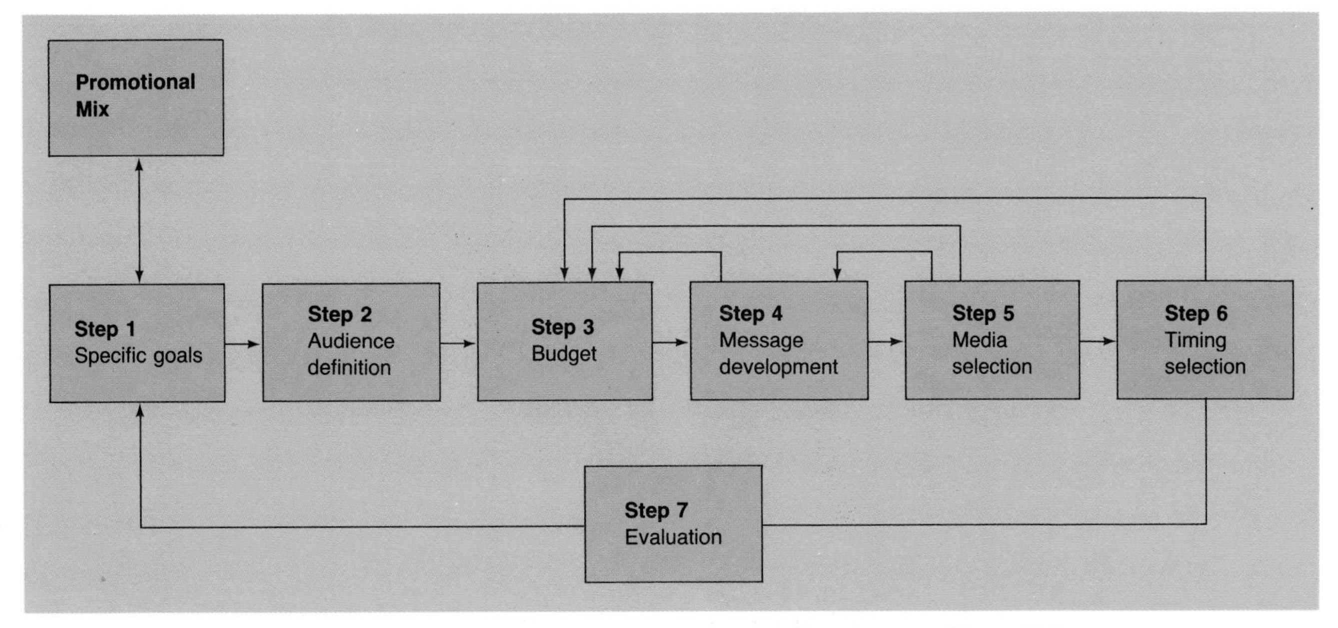

Figure 16.2
The Advertising Decision Process

The Advertising Decision Process

Though creativity is an essential input, consistently effective advertising comes about because of well-founded decision making. Marketers can achieve positive results by organizing advertising's seven key decision areas as a sequential process, as illustrated in Figure 16.2. The discussion that follows examines each of these steps.

Specific Goals

Marketers should set specific goals for each promotion mix component, including advertising. These serve as focal points around which budgets may be formulated and also provide a means of evaluating performance. To develop realistic goals, managers are forced to critically examine what they know and do not know about their intended customers, how well past advertising efforts performed so that needed corrections can be made, and what types of messages are needed.

Rather than general statements such as "increase sales," it is best if the stated advertising goals are specific about both the time involved and audience cognitions. The following illustrate several possible concrete advertising goals:

- "An increase in target brand awareness from 30 to 35 percent in three months."
- "A shift in the proportion of target customers having a preference for our brand from 12 to 14 percent by Christmas."
- "A reduction from 50 to 40 percent of all target customers who do not know that our landscaping service costs less than our competitors in the same area by this coming March."

Besides attainability, an important criterion for judging the reasonableness of advertising goals is their compatibility with the company's overall promotion objective.

Because one of its objectives is promoting a high-quality image for its brand, Weber barbecue grill ads state "available at better stores."

Two-step flow of communication The process of using formal communications techniques to influence opinion leaders who, in turn, influence others through conversations and other informal means.

Further, experienced marketers try to design advertising goals so that they augment other personal communications promotional efforts, especially personal selling. To illustrate, the Beatrice Foods Co., a large food and other consumer product conglomerate, uses ads to create name recognition for the parent company, making it easier to place the company's new products in retailers' stores.[4]

Another possible link to personal communications is through the **two-step flow of communications.**[5] This concept holds that opinion leaders in reference groups can be turned into a company's unpaid sales force. The way it works is by influencing opinion leaders through directed advertising, who in turn talk up the product to others in their reference group. For example, Fabergé has successfully used the two-step flow idea for its Organics brand of shampoos, by stating, "You'll tell two friends, and they'll tell two friends, and so on and so on."

While the Organics ad was an obvious case, interpersonal interaction can be stimulated in more subtle ways. As one source indicates, firms can stimulate personal influence by[6]

1. Providing opinion leaders with items on attractive terms
2. Designing advertising to feature conversations between those readily identified as leaders (e.g., movie stars, sports figures, etc.) and others
3. Developing advertising that is high in conversation value, that is, worth talking about

Opinion leaders are typically early adopters of a product or an idea.[7] Once identified, messages may be directed to them to get them to spread the word to the vast majority of adopters. Identifying opinion leaders is not a simple task, since they tend to be product-specific and differ over time.[8] Nonetheless, gaining their help through the two-step process can well be worth the effort.

It may be necessary for management to change the company's advertising goals over time as strategies or environments change. K mart ads, for example, emphasized the fact that the company was upgrading its stores in 1984. Then in 1985, the ad objective was to stress low prices.[9] Thus, like all marketing activities, the advertising goals selected should mesh with all other components of the firm's marketing mix.

Target Audience

Step two of the advertising decision process is to define the target audience. This process is critical to developing successful ad programs, as illustrated in the accompanying Marketing Brief. The process parallels that of defining a target market, as the members of the target market and audience are generally one and the same. Demographic and lifestyle variables are useful for this purpose. For example, Midway Airlines targeted its 1985 ad campaign for frequent travelers, featuring comfort and prestige, to upper-income achievers—people who are upwardly mobile.[10]

It is important to learn as much as is practical about the audience: its needs, when the needs arise, and the types of media that are most likely to reach members during need arousal.[11] This helps to develop better messages and to select the most appropriate advertising vehicles to reach the intended audience. The goal is to send messages when the selective perceptions and exposures of audience members are "tuned in."

- The Banker's Trust Company's target includes large multinational corporations and advertises accordingly in major financial publications such as *The Wall Street Journal*. Small town banks, in contrast, target consumers and smaller businesses and promote in local papers and through local civic programs, such as sponsoring a little league baseball team.
- Mattel spends the bulk of its television ad budget for toys on Saturday mornings, when viewing by children is at its peak.

MARKETING BRIEF
Defining the Target Audience Is Critical

Detroit-based Stroh Brewery Co. decided to introduce its Signature superpremium beer without using television, an unusual move in the hotly contested U.S. beer market. Instead of the normal TV exposure, the company announced that it would spend almost all of its $10 million roll-out budget on an eight-page "advertorial" insert in 15 to 20 magazines, beginning in May 1986.

Stroh introduced Signature to regional markets in spring, 1982, and sold about 150,000 barrels in 1985 in Michigan, Illinois, Ohio, Indiana, West Virginia, Maryland, and Washington. Originally, the company had planned a national introductory campaign for late 1984 or early 1985 using TV and picturing bearded men who rejected corporate life to go into business for themselves. But the campaign was delayed because American premium beers were losing market share to European imports due to their low prices, bolstered by the strength of the U.S. dollar. With the dollar's decline, Stroh now feels that the timing is right.

SOURCE: Adapted from Raymond Serafin, "Stroh Signature Signs Off TV for Launch," *Advertising Age,* March 17, 1986: 92.

Out is the use of TV, however. Said J. Wayne Jones, executive vice president for marketing. "The group that we want to appeal to watches TV relatively less and reads magazines relatively more." Initial ads will profile Richard Konkolski, a Rhode Island sailor who has made two solo voyages around the world. After Konkolski, the role model campaign will continue with other rugged, independent males—a skier, pilot, photographer, and mountain climber—although they will not be real characters. The eight-page spreads were scheduled for *Sports Illustrated* and *Time* in mid- to late 1986 and several specialty magazines, such as *Skiing* and *Runner*, shortly thereafter.

A concurrent magazine campaign will position Signature as an alternative to imports and will stress the theme "Born in America of European Heritage." The message "100 years experience in Europe and 100 years experience in the U.S." will be featured, emphasizing the Stroh family heritage. "The character of a European beer and the drinkability of an American beer" will be the tag line in the ad and also will be on the label.

- A high-rise apartment complex increased its occupancy dramatically. Recognizing that commuters hate traffic, management wisely switched from newspaper ads to a lighted billboard along a nearby highway that stated, "If you lived in the Whittier, you'd be home by now."

The purpose of defining the target audience is not to select specific media, as this comes later in the process. Nonetheless, management should begin to think about how to most effectively reach the selected audience as early in the process as possible.

Budget

The third step in the advertising decision process consists of setting the budget. There are various techniques used for this task, including assigning some percentage of anticipated sales, setting an amount to create a level of parity with competitors, basing the decision upon the amount of funds available, and using the "task build-up" method. The latter method is recommended because it requires building the budget around clearly defined goals and the tasks needed for their attainment.[12] Budgeting is

Cooperative advertising helps to stretch an ad budget.

fully covered in Chapter 18, but cooperative advertising which affects budget decisions will be discussed here.

Cooperative advertising Where two or more firms, often vertically related in a channel system, combine their advertising efforts.

Cooperative Advertising **Cooperative advertising**—where two or more firms combine their efforts—is an important way to stretch an advertising budget. Most cooperative advertising takes place among companies vertically related in a distribution channel. Cannon Mills, for example, offers its retailers an incentive to advertise its towels, sheets, and bedspreads by reimbursing 50 percent of the related costs. While many consumer product companies have similar programs, their particular arrangements vary.[13] Some reimburse 50 percent, like Cannon, and others a different percentage. The idea is to get the entire channel supporting the promotional effort.

Besides stretching the budget, cooperative advertising offers several advantages, including favorable media rate structures for ads placed by a local firm (local retailers can place more ads for the same budget), the fact that intermediaries are more likely to aggressively support a product if they have shared in its promotional cost, and retailers are in a better position to adjust messages to coincide to local conditions and events, such as festivals, sporting events, parades, and fairs.

There are some disadvantages, however. Some retailers crowd the ads of several producers into one, causing audience recognition difficulties. Also, producers must carefully monitor the process to assure that reimbursement claims are valid and must train their sales force (or others) to make sure that retailers understand the co-op plan and use it effectively.[14] Despite these difficulties, cooperative advertising is very useful to many producers and retailers.

Worth noting is that cooperative advertising is sometimes used by horizontal members of a channel system. Retailers often pool their efforts by jointly sponsoring ads to stimulate shoppers into visiting their trade areas, such as particular malls or downtowns, special sidewalk sales, "midnight madness" sales, and so on. Like co-op advertising within a channel, combining efforts can have a favorable synergistic impact on the sales of all participants.

Message Development

Developing a promotional message is next on the advertising decision-making agenda. Several factors should be considered. Later decisions (such as media to be used) should be anticipated so that messages can be designed to fit those characteristics. For example, the use of billboards implies that relatively simple messages are most appropriate. The time of year is also important, as in the case of Christmas, because messages should also be designed around these seasons. Most important, ample evidence indicates that effective advertising messages coincide with the needs of the target audience.[15]

Message development involves making decisions about an ad's three basic components:

Theme
Overall information to be conveyed by advertising.

Copy
An ad's pictures, words, and symbols used to present the theme.

Format
Advertising layout specifications.

Theme (the overall information to be conveyed). Themes are essentially appeals the ads make to potential buyers. For example, Jazzercise (exercise classes) emphasizes "the best workout my body ever had"; becoming fit and having fun in the process.

Copy (an ad's pictures, words, and symbols used to present the theme). For example, Van de Kamp Lights (breaded fish fillets) feature a "yuppie" woman in a grocery store puzzling over what to buy for dinner.

Format (the layout specifications, including specific colors to use, the length of a TV or radio spot, the space for print, type sizes, specific actors, and so on). Walgreen's drugstores use a "bargain" format, listing large numbers of products and prices in one ad.

The AIDA Model Creative copy and presentation can greatly increase an ad's impact.[16] Thus marketers usually rely on specialists, designers and illustrators formally trained with creativity in mind to actually develop the ads. Nonetheless, management should be familiar with guidelines for generating favorable audience response so that it can evaluate the messages suggested by such experts.

All ads have a common purpose: to bring about the desired response from the audience. Essentially, there are three stages of response possible: establishing knowledge, changing an attitude, or creating an actual behavioral change.[17] Normally, members of an audience pass through each stage in succession before making a purchase.

AIDA model
Acronym for Attention, Interest, Desire, and Action.

Figure 16.3 presents three alternative models of viewing audience response stages. Differences between the models are largely semantic, since they all view audience members as having the same essential response stages. Since the **AIDA model,** an

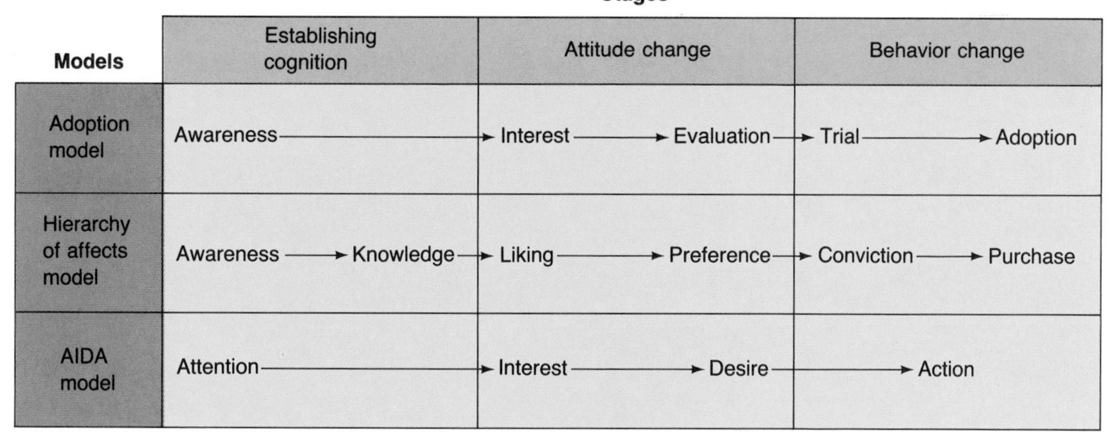

Figure 16.3
Audience Response Models
(SOURCE: Adapted from Philip Kotler, *Marketing Management: Analysis, Planning, and Control*, 3rd ed. (Englewood Cliffs, N.J.: Prentice-Hall, 1980), p. 319.)

acronym made from the first three letters of each component, is the oldest and most widely recognized of the three, it is explored further.

Attention To be effective, advertising must first get and then hold the audience's attention. Color, loud voices, humorous lines, or something to "grab" the audience is necessary.[18] To illustrate, consider the humorous copy used by Life cereal: "Let Mikey try it." The ads featured children who were fussy eaters and used Mikey, the youngest of the group, to try new foods because "Mikey won't eat *anything*." Well, he liked Life cereal, and captured viewer attention in the process. This campaign ran for several years and continued to attract attention. Contrast that campaign with another possibility, one where a commentator would simply say something like "Life cereal is good for kids." Children would probably go to the refrigerator for a cold drink instead of watching the message.

Using popular celebrities is another technique used to catch an audience's attention. For example, the "contract for life" campaign sponsored by the liquor industry was highly successful. Featuring Dallas Cowboy wide receiver Drew Pearson, the ads appeared on 400 TV stations, 1,000 radio stations, and various print media and resulted in a "noticeable reduction in teen-age highway deaths."[19] Many advertisers use such celebrities in their ads. However, their fees are often so high that only very large advertisers can afford them.[20]

Interest Effective commercials stimulate interest in both the ad and the product. Some ads stimulate interest, but not in the product. Picturing a sexy man or woman, for example, might stimulate interest in the ad, but it would be ineffective unless it also developed interest in the product.

One very successful ad program promoted "power for living" religious books and featured such notables as Dallas Cowboy coach Tom Landry, singer Pat Boone, and former White House aide Charles Colson. The ads generated thousands of calls per day.[21] CBS software "whodunnit" computer ads built interest in games designed for the family by showing mom, dad, and the kids dressed in classic detective clothing and peering around an old mansion with magnifying glasses—a humorous approach.

Grabbing the audience's attention is essential in advertising.

Desire Ads should generate desire among the audience to try the product. This can be quite difficult because it requires a thorough knowledge of the audience's motivations and needs. Desire can be built by showing how an item can satisfy these needs. The above mentioned "power for living" ads, for example, created desire by showing how religion could add meaning to people's lives. U.S. Postal Service Express Mail ads describe the speed, reliability, and economy of the service. Sometimes ads that favorably compare the company's brand with those of competitors can be very useful in building desire.[22]

Action Finally, the ultimate test of a message's effectiveness is whether or not it effects the action desired. Sales can best be stimulated by offering a need-related incentive for buying. Crest offers the possibility of reducing tooth decay. Fram oil filter ads show a mechanic working on an engine, stating "either pay me now [for a filter] or pay me later [for a major engine repair]." The Chrysler Corp. promises automatic transmissions at no extra cost for its Plymouth Reliant Super K. Effective

Effective advertising stimulates the audience's interest.

advertising messages capture an audience's attention, develop interest in buying the product, and stimulate sales.

The AIDA model does not imply that silly or cute ads are necessarily effective. Rather, messages should state something desirable about a product in terms of needs, something unique or exclusive about a brand compared with close substitutes, and the statements should be believable.

Media Selection

The fifth step of the advertising decision process involves selecting specific **media**—the communications channels. Two types of decisions are needed: how much to spend on various media types and what specific media to use.

Media
Communication channels (or vehicles) to use in advertising, such as television and newspapers.

Types of Media to Use Conceptually, an advertising budget should be allocated to various media in proportion to their potential for effectively conveying the intended message. The target audience's media consumption habits and the characteristics of both the product and the message are important factors to consider in making this decision. The discussion below considers two pharmaceutical products: one that requires a physician's prescription, and another designed for over-the-counter use.

Physicians, acting as gatekeepers, make the product decision in the first instance and therefore comprise the target audience. Physicians generally rely on medical journals, information that drug companies provide about recent product tests and developments, and personal contacts by pharmaceutical reps and peers to keep them abreast of product performances. Consequently, ads appearing in medical journals and direct mail pieces are useful in influencing these gatekeepers.

Over-the-counter medical products are usually best advertised over mass media such as TV, radio, and newspapers. Billboards can also be very effective in reaching some mass markets, particularly if the message is received at the time of need, such as to sell gasoline or sunscreens near recreational areas.[23]

Specific Media Vehicles After determining the types of media to use, management's next task is to choose specific media variables (i.e., *Cosmopolitan* or *Playboy?*, *CBS Evening News* or NBC's *Tonight Show?*). Sometimes, as illustrated in the Citizen Watch Marketing Brief, it is desirable to use relatively new media. In other cases, media used in the past work best. It is useful to focus on four elements when making the decision concerning the particular media to use: advertising objectives, media circulation, media costs, and the type of message to be conveyed.

Advertising Objectives The objectives to be accomplished through advertising are key when evaluating specific media. Suppose, for instance, that the objective is to make upper-income people aware of the luxury features of the Jaguar Vanden Plas (including walnut veneer dash, swivel-based reading lamps, and sports car performance). Full-page ads in magazines that focus on the wealthy are most appropriate, such as *Avenue*, *Parkway*, and *Ultra*.[24] Or, the objective might be to get owners of small businesses to call the Canon Co. for a demonstration of its latest copier. Here an ad in *Inc.* magazine (which appeals to small and medium businesses) is probably a good choice. An objective of convincing preschoolers that they should ask their parents to buy a brand of breakfast cereal should be advertised during a popular Saturday morning television cartoon series, such as "Smurfs." Advertising objectives, then, are instrumental in choosing specific media vehicles.

Media Circulation Media are chosen on the basis of whether or not their readers, viewers, or listeners comprise market targets for the product. For example, *Better Homes and Gardens* is a logical choice for Campbell's soup ads urging homemakers to use the company's tomato soup in meat loaf recipes because many housewives read the magazine. Likewise, NFL football telecasts are good vehicles for Miller's beer commercials because many males aged 21 to 36 (the largest target group for beer) watch these games.

Media companies acquire and make available data on their audiences, often categorized by income, geography, age, occupation, and sometimes ownership of durable goods. The Hartford *Courant's* Sunday magazine, *Northeast*, for example, reports that its audience is middle-income and higher, active, mobile, and takes frequent vacations.[25] While the reported data may not be fully complete for each marketer's needs (e.g., psychographic variables may not be reported, although this is an increasing trend), they provide a good indication of the audience's general characteristics.

MARKETING BRIEF

Surprise Tactics Can Be Important in Planning Advertising

In a stunning move, Citizen Watch Co. of America broke its 1986 $15 million U.S. advertising campaign in an unusual arena, at least for watches—ABC-TV's Wide World of Sports. Even though more women than men purchase wristwatches, the company decided in favor of network sports events for at least $4 million worth of the ads. "Research showed that sports programs tested better [in terms of audience recall] than prime-time shows," said Tony DeGregario, senior vice president and associate creative director of Citizen Watch. "We are convinced that our ads will stand out among the rest because the others are sponsored by makers of such products as beer, razors, shaving cream, and cars."

The new campaign marks more than selecting another advertising vehicle for the company. It introduces Citizen's new thrust into the midpriced watch market in the U.S., the fastest growing, most profitable segment of the business, according to several industry analysts. "We are watching Citizen's moves with keen interest," said Chicago-based R. James Beers, of the securities firm of Hinkley and Salzberg, Inc. "Their new strategy should pay off handsomely," he added.

Directed by Steve Horn, named *Advertising Age* Director of the Year in 1985, the ads featured several of the company's new line of watches being worn by several attractive, active men and women getting dressed for evening dates. In the background, an Al Jolson imitator sang the 1920s hit "About a Quarter to Nine," while the people hurried to change their sporting outfits and checked their Citizen watches frequently to keep on schedule.

Levine, Huntley, Schmidt, and Beaver, the ad agency handling the account, performed extensive preliminary testing before the ads were scheduled. "The ads tested out well in image impact studies for the midprice market," said a spokeswoman. "While the preliminary results of the actual ads look good, we are anxious to see their final impact," she said.

SOURCE: Adapted from Lisa E. Phillips, "Citizen Elects Midprice Niche," *Advertising Age* 57, no. 28 (April 28, 1986): 68. Also see "People to Watch: John Witt [vice president of marketing for Citizen Watch of America]," *Fortune* 113 (May 12, 1986): 110.

Making media selection more precise is the fact that increasing specialization is taking place. At one time, most media tried to appeal to the masses. Today, media are focusing more on audience segments. Magazines such as *M—The Civilized Man*, *Couponing*, *Games*, and *Computer World* all specialize in particular segments. Even the national media have tended in this direction. *Time* and *The Wall Street Journal*, for example, publish regional editions to appeal to local interests.

Media Costs Media cost is an important criterion in choosing particular media. One measure is total cost. This is one of the reasons why smaller companies often use low-cost media, such as local radio and newspapers. Cigar manufacturers also have moved into low-cost vehicles and away from TV because of cost considerations.[26]

Cost-per-thousand (CPM) Price of a single message divided by circulation size in thousands.

Another cost factor to consider is the cost-per-person of reaching the target audience. This is typically measured in **cost-per-thousand (CPM),** which is calculated as follows:

$$\text{Cost per thousand (CPM)} = \frac{\left[\begin{array}{l}\text{Price of a single message}\\\text{(space or time insertion)}\end{array}\right]}{\left[\begin{array}{l}\text{Circulation size}\\\text{(in thousands)}\end{array}\right]}$$

For example, assume that an ad would cost $10,000 and the circulation of a medium is 50,000 people. The CPM for this vehicle, then, would be:

$$\text{CPM} = \frac{\$10{,}000}{50} = \$200$$

The Standard Rate and Data Service, Inc. provides circulation and rate data to advertisers (for a fee) which can then be used to calculate CPMs for various media of interest. But there are weaknesses in the CPM approach. Total circulation figures may be misleading for a couple of reasons. For one, readership or viewership is often far greater than circulation. In the case of print, to illustrate, the circulation refers to the number of copies sold. *Time*, for example, has a circulation of about 4 million, but over 21 million read the magazine as more than one person reads an individual copy. For another, circulation does not reflect exposure to the target audience. For example, *Time* may be cheaper per person contacted than *Boating*, but the latter is less expensive for advertising by a yacht manufacturer per target audience member contacted.

CPM also does not consider the effects of image. To illustrate, *Playboy* has a large circulation, even among churchgoers, but is not likely to be the most effective medium in which to run ads for bibles. Nor would *Police Gazette* be a good choice for Porsches or industrial chemicals.

Finally, CPM does not consider the effects of exposure duplications. To illustrate, Figure 16.4 pictures an audience's exposures to three media: A, B, and C (say NBC's *Today* show, ABC's *Nightly News*, and a UHF channel's reruns of *All in the Family*). Since A and B have the largest exposure rates, an advertiser might select these two vehicles even though they duplicate exposure to the same audience. C might only be considered as an afterthought, and only if there is a healthy budget. While research indicates that repetitive exposures by an audience are often effective, management may wish to generate as broad an exposure as possible.[27] If so, then either A and C or B and C would be a better choice than A and B.

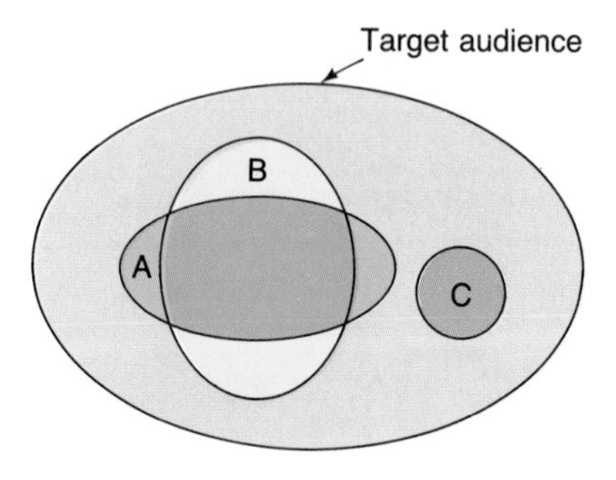

Figure 16.4
Media Vehicle Selection and Duplication of Audience Exposures

Type of Message to Convey The character of the media chosen should be compatible with the advertising message. If management wishes to create interest and excitement in a new product offering, for instance, television may be useful since its combination of auditory and visual cues carries an impact among consumers. In contrast, if the objective is to convey detailed information about a product's specifications, such as for a new type of computer, then a print medium would probably be better, since television is not suited to long, detailed messages.

Timing Selection

The sixth advertising decision step involves determining when ads should be placed. Suppose, for instance, that it is decided that six ads should appear in *Newsweek* during the third quarter of the year. The question to be answered is, "How should the six ads be spaced?" One way would be to evenly space them throughout the period; for example, every two weeks. Another way would be to bunch them together, all within one month, with some issues containing two insertions.

Many timing alternatives are possible, but they tend to fall into four basic patterns,[28]

Ralph Lauren ads appear in prestigious media consistent with the label's upscale image.

as illustrated in Figure 16.5. There are several factors to consider when determining which pattern is best in a particular situation, including the following.

Periodic patterns in purchasing. For example, consumers buy most beer near the end of the week for weekend consumption. Accordingly, breweries usually follow a continuous, unevenly spaced pattern, with peaks coinciding with heavy buying days. La-Z-Boy follows an intermittent, unevenly spaced pattern in advertising chairs heavily to coincide with Father's Day, its peak selling period.[29]

Forgetting rates. The more rapidly the audience forgets about a brand, the more evenly spaced should the pattern be to reinforce past learning. Fast-food companies such as Wendy's follow evenly spaced patterns to continuously remind people about their stores.

Competitor advertising patterns. Ideally, the firm should space ads in such a way as to help ward off attitude inroads made by competitor ads. For example, the Hershey Foods Corp. decided to move advertising for its Hershey Kisses into prime-time TV, on an intermittent unevenly spaced basis to coincide with holiday buying, because its competitors were using that time and attracting large audiences.[30]

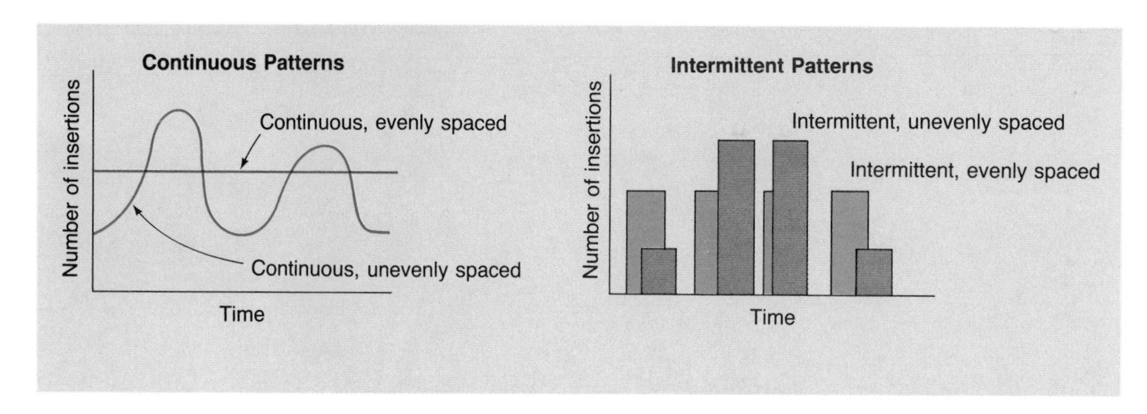

Figure 16.5
Major Timing Alternatives

Pulsing
An advertising tactic where very large amounts of money are spent during a short time period followed by an absence of advertising (also called *flights*, or *waves*).

A common practice is to use *flights* or *waves* (called **pulsing**), where the advertiser follows an intermittent pattern (see Figure 16.5) by concentrating large expenditures in a short time period followed by an absence. There are two reasons for using pulsing. First, research indicates that people retain in memory longer information that is learned rapidly than information they learn slowly.[31] This increases advertising's impact. The second reason is that it is less costly. Fewer ads need to be placed to have the same impact as continuous advertising.[32]

Evaluation

The final advertising decision process step involves evaluating advertising's effectiveness. Historically, organizations did not spend much time and effort in trying to do this.[33] But spiraling advertising costs, more intense competition, and advancements in computer technology both increase the need and enable the application of sophisticated mathematical analysis.

Analyzing advertising's effectiveness is tricky, however. This is especially the case for corporate advertising.[34] On the surface, the job appears easy. One might think that simply measuring the change in sales after the advertising would be a good test, but it is not. Many factors affect sales—not just advertising. Further, advertising tends to have a long-run cumulative impact: it nudges the audience toward buying. Today's Oldsmobile buyer may be acting upon a lifelong exposure to the company's ads.

Because of the complexities, measuring advertising's impact will probably never be an exact science, but management can gain considerable insight by researching its effects. Essentially, marketers use two types of advertising effectiveness research: message research and impact studies. These are considered next.

Message Research Message research involves determining if the audience perceives, comprehends, and remembers ads. There are two types.

Pretests
Assessments of whether or not intended messages will be effective.

Pretests involve doing the testing before the ad campaign is run. After exposing a sample from the target audience to proposed ads, subjects are then tested on a number of measures, including which ads they like best, their reactions to messages, whether or not they found them confusing, and so on. Sometimes physiological responses are

CONCEPT SUMMARY

The Advertising Decision Process

Key Decision Area	Description
Goal Setting	Establish specific goals for the campaign
Audience Definition	Determine who the advertising is aimed at
Budget Determination	Decide the total amount of funds that will be allocated to advertising
Message Development	Design the advertising theme, copy, and format (the AIDA model is useful for this process)
Media Selection	Determine what media are to be employed to carry the message(s)
Timing Selection	Determine when advertisements are to be placed
Evaluation	Assess the effectiveness of advertising

measured. A pupilometer might be used, for instance, to measure pupil dilation elicited by an ad. Or a machine to register pulse rates might be used. The assumption is that ads which evoke the greatest reactions are the best for attracting audience attention.[35]

Posttests involve estimating how well an audience has received ads after they have been run. There are a variety of approaches used, but they all involve sampling. In recall tests, subjects are instructed to indicate which ads they recall appearing in a particular medium. For example, Drexel Furniture Co. might place an ad in *Better Homes & Gardens* and later ask the sample if they recall seeing the ad. Frequently questions about certain details of the ad are asked to assure that subjects are telling the truth about their recollections. In attitude tests, measurements are obtained, such as on a semantic differential, to learn if the audience's attitudes changed as hoped after being exposed to an ad. In this case, it is necessary to have measures of the same attitudes prior to the ad for comparison.

Posttests
Assessments of how well advertising messages were received by an audience after the fact.

Sales Impact Studies While these measures are not precise, management can gain insight into the advertising-sales relationship through regression, time series, and similar kinds of statistical techniques.[36] Another measure is to use market share as a criterion.[37] Nabisco Brands, for example, decides if it will continue to use a certain ad agency on the basis of whether or not market share improvements have met stated goals.[38] Some firms run their ads and then compare sales before and after in an informal manner. However, this practice should be avoided because it does not isolate advertising's effects.

Some firms have also developed experimental methods whereby they try advertising in a controlled segment of the market. For example, Seattle might be isolated and exposed to the ad. Then management can measure the impact, using other cities not exposed to the ad as comparisons. Nabisco, for example, developed a computerized technique called *Probe* based upon this principle. Through it, management learned that the best way to advertise company products was through a **blitz** tactic, which is a form of pulsing. Under a blitz tactic, the advertiser uses pulsing and also rotates geographical areas to receive the heavy expenditures over time. This enables an even cash flow on overall advertising spending, but also makes more efficient the overall budget. By following a blitz tactic, Nabisco's management was able to substantially

Blitz
A form of pulsing that also involves rotating the geographical areas that receive the pulses.

increase sales of some old established brands such as Ritz Crackers. Because of such successes, an increase in both the number and the sophistication of similar tests is likely in the future.

Advertising Agencies

Advertising agencies
Specialists in preparing and placing advertisements that serve advertisers, who are their clients.

Advertising agencies are specialists in preparing and placing ads. They are service firms that help their clients—the advertisers. Agencies are capable of providing various services for clients, designing entire campaigns, determining objectives, selecting and contracting development with media, designing themes and appeals, and copy design.

Figure 16.6 identifies the top ten agencies in size (as of the end of 1985), the growth of agencies over the past ten years, and the proportion of agency incomes by world source. Selected major accounts of these agencies are listed in Exhibit 16.1. Several major mergers took place in mid-1986, especially the Omnicom Group (BBDO International, Doyle Dane Bernbach, and Needham Harper Worldwide) and Saatchi & Saatchi/Bates, which will likely affect the relative sizes of many agencies.[39] Along with this, however, came a rash of account realignments which continued well after the mergers. Consequently, it may take years for the eventual effects of the mergers to be fully known.[40] Nonetheless, advertising agencies clearly play a dominant role in the advertising scene.

Figure 16.6
Top Ten Advertising Agencies and Relative Sizes of Top 25 and Top 500 Agencies (SOURCE: Adapted from "U.S. Advertising Agency Profiles, 1986 ed.," *Advertising Age* special issue (March 27, 1986).)

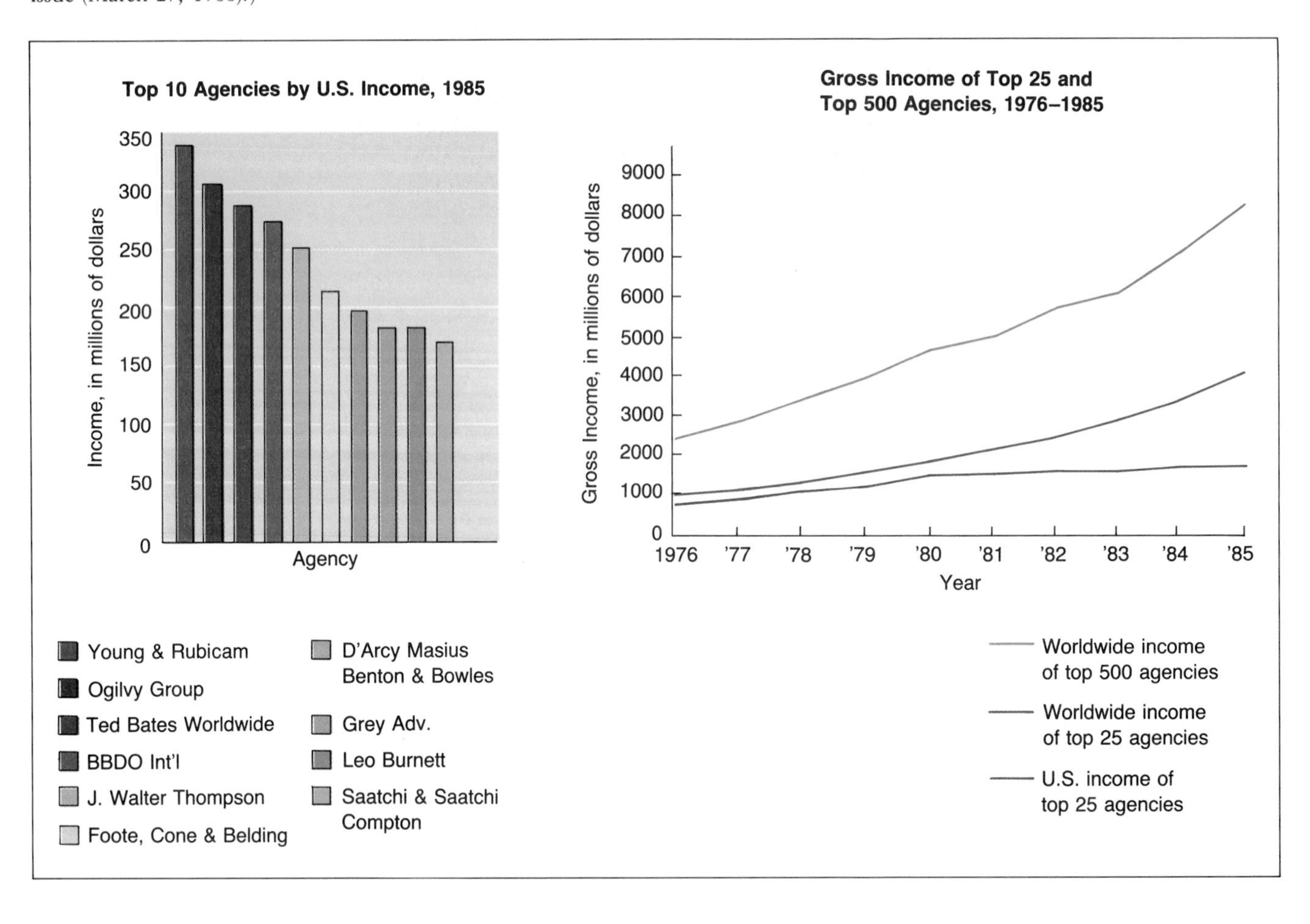

Exhibit 16.1
Selected Major Accounts Gained by the Largest 10 Advertising Agencies in 1985

Firm	Percent Increase 1985	Selected Major Accounts
Young & Rubicam	24	Disney Operations; American Greeting Cards; Union Carbide, Prestone, Simonize, STP; Colgate-Palmolive, Ultra Brite; AT&T Opportunity Calling; Kraft, new products, Adidas; Gillette, new product assignments
Ogilvy Group	14	Seagram, gin, vodka, 7 Crown, and others; General Foods, Tang; Hardee's Food System; Ansa Corp., Management Information Services; Covidea
Ted Bates	10	Avis Rent-A-Car, Commodore Business Machines; Warner-Lambert; Panasonic
BBDO Int'l.	11	Visa; Lorillard, Kent cigarettes; Polaroid; Household International; Kupenheimer Mfg. Co.
J. Walter Thompson	16	Emery Worldwide; Sears, Discover Card; Burger King, Miller Brewing Co., Eckerd Drug Store; Fisher-Price; Jacuzzi Whirlpool Bath; Marineland Amusement Park
Foote, Cone & Belding	6	Colgate-Palmolive, Ajax line; AT&T consumer marketing; ConAgra, Supercuts, Armour Banquet Foods
D'Arcy Masius	−6	MCI; A&P; Southern Electric; Wilson Sporting Goods; General Motors; ConAgra, consumer frozen foods; Dow Chemical, corporate advertising; Weyerhaeuser.
Grey Advertising	16	U.S. Dept. of Treasury, commemorative coins; Humana; Red Lobster; Mitsubishi; International Playtex; General Mills Restaurant Group; BankAmerica
Leo Burnett	7	Pillsbury, Totino's, Jeno's; United Airlines; Seven-Up; McDonald's Operators (Chicagoland and Northwest Indiana)
Saatchi & Saatchi	31	McDonald's; Citibank, IBM word processors; British Rail; Campbells; Nissan cars; Sands Hotel Group

Large agencies such as Ogilvy and Mather, J. Walter Thompson, and Leo Burnett employ staffs of expert specialists in each of these and related fields. Smaller agencies do not specialize so intensively, of course, but can also offer needed services to clients, especially in the creative areas.

Many agencies furnish a wide range of services beyond straight advertising help. Many can offer assistance in designing products, pricing them, designing packages, developing channel of distribution strategies, conducting marketing research studies, and related functions. Agencies that perform such activities have become marketing specialists or consultants. In fact, some companies virtually turn planning and directing of their marketing programs over to agencies.

In contrast to full-service agencies described above, there are limited-service agencies called "space sellers." They provide only very basic advertising functions, such as placing ads in media, and charge smaller fees than do full-service firms. As might be expected, space sellers appeal to the cost-conscious segment of the market.

Successful advertising stimulates desire and action on the part of the audience.

Agencies receive their compensation from commissions and fees. Commissions result from buying media space or time. A media firm, such as a television station, grants a commission (often 15 percent) for national ads that an agency places. The agency charges the client the full fee for the ad, but deducts the commission upon paying the medium.

Some advertisers prefer fees over commissions, so that they end up paying only for the services that they receive. Further, fees are usually necessary for additional services such as marketing research. These fees are often negotiable, but advertisers usually get what they pay for. There has been a strong move toward fee structures rather than straight commissions for an agency's services.

There is a decided advantage for a local firm such as a retailer to place ads directly with the media, since there is usually a significant discount granted to local advertisers. National agencies cannot purchase these ads at the same reduced price. Figure 16.7 compares national and local advertising in the U.S. in relative terms. However, some firms recognize strong advantages in using agencies and ignore the local discounts. Further, many firms pay fees for agency help then place the ads themselves to get the lower rates.

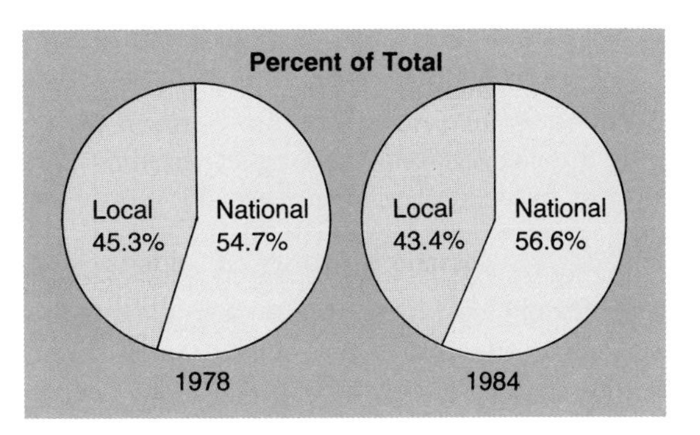

Figure 16.7
National and Local Advertising as a Percent of Total Advertising, 1978 and 1984 (SOURCE: *Statistical Abstract of the United States, 1986,* 106th ed.)

Agencies offer several distinct advantages to advertisers. Because they are specialists, they usually employ professionals with far greater capabilities than one advertiser could afford. These experts are able to effectively work on several accounts, thereby minimizing the cost to a single client. A second advantage is that they usually have a sound grasp of the various media characteristics. This puts them in a very strong position to plan an effective advertising program. Finally, they provide a competitive means of obtaining new advertising ideas. Association with an agency is voluntary and many vie for a company's business. Consequently, advertisers can select the one with the best approach. If the firm is dissatisfied, it can replace an existing agency with a new one.

As is the case with any outside supplier, conflict often develops in firm-agency interrelations.[41] Managers typically want substantial results with low budgets, and agencies like to see large budgets and fees. Nonetheless, due to their expertise, agencies are generally advantageous for national advertisers, who can avoid most of the potential problems by spelling out precisely the way in which agency performance will be evaluated at the start of a relationship. But since ultimate responsibility for advertising lies with the sponsoring firm, managers should be intimately familiar with the decision process the agency uses so that they can effectively control the program.

Criticisms of Advertising

Advertising is the most controversial component of marketing. The criticisms vary, but most serious ones fall into one of three categories: deception, the power to influence values, and advertising's cost and effect on prices.

Deception

Deception
Misleading customers by making false claims.

Many critics argue that advertising uses **deception,** or purposely misleads customers through false or deceptive claims. In some cases, these criticisms are justified. Since the Wheeler-Lea amendment to the Federal Trade Commission Act (see Appendix B), the FTC has been active in policing deceptive practices. It has placed particular emphasis on requiring substantiation of claims, assuring that advertised items are made available, and deterring other forms of deception. The general rule is that it is unfair (and thereby illegal) to present a claim without having a reasonable basis for doing so. Unfairness may exist even if the claim is true but it is not substantiated with prior

Bait-and-switch
Advertising a low-priced item then exerting undue pressure on customers to buy a more expensive one. This is an illegal practice.

evidence.[42] Similarly, the FTC has found some companies to be guilty of advertising a low price then either not making a reasonable supply of the item available or trying to **bait-and-switch** customers into buying a more expensive item.

Such practices do not make good marketing sense. To begin with, they are illegal and can result in significant fines and costs to run required corrective ads. At one time, Warner-Lambert advertised Listerine as a means of preventing colds. But, as testimony by experts proved, the alcohol in Listerine could not touch viruses—the cause of colds. To rectify the misleading ads, the FTC ordered Warner-Lambert to spend $10 million in advertising to inform consumers that "Listerine will not help prevent colds or sore throats or lessen their severity."[43]

Research supports the idea that corrective ads can be very effective in overcoming past deception.[44] But a company must bear the cost of the ads simply to right any past wrongs, and research also indicates that such corrective advertising does have a significant negative impact on a company's image.[45]

Moreover, deception does not help in developing market niches. Advertising, like all other elements of marketing, is most effective when it is geared to establishing a mutually beneficial long-term relationship with a target. Deception is counterproductive over time. Consumers and legitimate marketers alike should be upset about deceptive advertising. Fortunately, companies, industry associations, and governmental agencies are making vast improvements to eliminate these unscrupulous methods.

Power to Influence Values

Many critics argue that the real threat of advertising is its ability to manipulate consumer values. Vance Packard was among the first to advance this notion, and various scholars have similar views.[46] According to Galbraith, advertising results in ". . . a control of consumer reactions which, though imperfect and greatly complicated by the rivalry, is still far more secure than would be the ungoverned responses of consumers in the absence of such effort."[47]

In one sense, the thrust of these arguments is correct. Advertising can cause people to buy items they might otherwise pass over. But all information about products, regardless of the source, has the same effect. No evidence exists to indicate that behavior is altered by anything but free choice. Instead, the evidence suggests that advertising does not shift cognitions except in directions desired by the audience. Therefore, the solution the critics suggest presupposes ignorance (a lack of information about products due to limited advertising) to be a desirable state. Such a position is difficult to defend, as making good buying decisions requires adequate information, not a lack of it.

Closely related is the charge that some advertising engenders dehumanizing, or antisocial values. To illustrate, does the theme "ring around the collar" suggest that others should judge a housewife's worth by the brightness of her wash? Or do the many drug ads suggest that consumers can cure all their problems by taking a pill? Similarly, does real "gusto in life," as a beer commercial implies, instead mean unhealthy livers and acute alcoholism?

Undoubtedly, there is some merit in this criticism of advertising. Society has not yet established guidelines to limit advertising's impact on social values. Perhaps it is impossible to do so because society itself has difficulty defining which values are desirable. The Federal Trade Commission, however, has decided to address itself to such matters.[48] The full scope of the FTC's actions, however, remain to be seen. Many marketers will diligently follow the next several years of FTC rulings because they could result in definite advertising standards.

A final criticism of advertising's value-influencing power is its alleged use of subliminal advertising, messages that sponsors flash on a movie screen that are below conscious perception to induce consumers to buy treats, or similar messages in some other medium such as TV. There is no credible evidence that such advertising is effective. Consumers may not perceive below-threshold stimuli or if they do perceive them they might misinterpret the ads, leading to the purchase of competing brands.[49] Consequently, this form of influencing consumers is certainly not recommended.

Higher Prices

Perhaps the largest group of critics have addressed the issue of advertising's impact on prices. Being learned adversaries, economists have traditionally led the charge by arguing that heavy advertising builds brand loyalty, presents barriers to competition, and results in higher prices. Many contemporary economists and journalists hold similar views.

Several well-known researchers, such as economist Phillip Nelson, have furnished research evidence indicating just the opposite.[50] This group argues that heavily advertised brands are generally the best buys. First, their research suggests that such offerings tend to be of higher quality than less-advertised items. It would be catastrophic to heavily promote shoddy items, for this would only create greater negative visibility and lost sales. Second, advertising contributes needed information to consumers, enabling them to make better choices.[51] Without such information, prices tend to be higher as a result of monopolies created out of ignorance. Advertising serves to create awareness, which broadens the number of brand choices that consumers perceive and take into consideration.

In addition, some evidence indicates that heavily advertised items reduce prices by placing pressure on markups demanded by intermediaries. In the toy industry, for example, studies demonstrate that heavily advertised items do in fact have lower prices and smaller intermediary unit margins.[52]

Despite its criticisms, advertising is a necessary ingredient in the overall marketing mix. And like a chain, a total marketing effort is only as strong as its weakest link.

Chapter Summary

This chapter focused on advertising decision making, which is a very important element of the promotion mix for many organizations. A wide variety of profit and not-for-profit organizations rely on advertising as the major vehicle for conveying their messages to their intended audiences.

A seven-step advertising decision process includes carefully defining specific goals, the target audience, an appropriate budget, messages, media, timing, and evaluating past performance. Following this process helps management assure that a systematic approach is taken when making advertising decisions, which helps to improve results.

The chapter also considered the role of advertising agencies. These specialists can prove invaluable in helping to develop effective messages and campaigns.

Finally, the chapter viewed the criticisms of advertising. Since advertising is one of the most visible elements of the marketing mix and it is obviously biased, it has received considerable criticism over the years. Such criticisms tend to fall into one of three categories: deception, the power to influence values, and the effects of advertising on price. Each of these criticisms was analyzed.

Questions

1. Provide an example of a specific goal that might be used in advertising for
   a. Florida orange juice
   b. "Bubble Yum" bubble gum
   c. The U.S. Army (in recruiting)
   d. The Red Cross
   e. Honeywell Corporation
2. What are the characteristics of good advertising goals?
3. What is cooperative advertising? What are its advantages? Its disadvantages?
4. Define advertising themes. Provide an example of a theme that you recently have heard or read. Do you think it was appropriate?
5. What is advertising copy? What is the format?
6. Indicate how advertising can attain
   a. Attention
   b. Interest
   c. Desire
   d. Action
7. What, in your opinion, are appropriate advertising media for:
   a. A radiator repair shop
   b. Folger's Coffee
   c. A legal firm
   d. Wendy's
   e. Cabbage Patch dolls
8. What are the strengths and weaknesses of using the cost-per-thousand criterion as a means of selecting media?
9. Dissect four popular television commercials (two "good" and two "bad"), using as much of the chapter's materials as possible. What are the commercials' strengths and weaknesses?
10. A candy company is trying to decide which of two copy versions of a commercial to use. The first shows a youth walking to a store, deliberating over the brand to buy, fishing in his pocket for the money, and finally eating the candy in a park near a lake. The second version stops once the brand is selected. Which version do you think is best and why?
11. Why would advertisers use pulsing (flights, or waves)? What kinds of firms might use this tactic?
12. What are advertising agencies? Why do clients utilize these firms, rather than handling all of the advertising decisions themselves?
13. Provide an example of an advertisement that you believe to be deceptive. Indicate why it could be deceptive. How could it be changed so that it did not have this feature?
14. "Advertising has a strong influence on the values of the average citizen." Critique this statement.
15. In your opinion, does advertising lead to higher prices than would be the case with no advertising? Justify your answer.

Chapter 17

Personal Selling Decisions

Objectives

After reading this chapter, you should be able to demonstrate a knowledge of:

- The meaning of the term "personal selling"
- The importance of personal selling as an element of the promotion mix, including the decision tradeoff necessary because of its high cost
- The elements of the personal selling process: presale preparation, prospecting, route planning, sales presentation, and postsale activities
- One class of sales force decisions that managers make, involving development: determining sales force size, recruiting, structuring, assigning people, and compensating them
- The other major class of sales force decisions, involving supervising: training, motivating, directing, and evaluating

MARKETING SUCCESS

One, Two, Three—"You're Hot"

In all the hype about computer high tech, the stellar performer recognized by most experts as being the industry's super nova is the little-known, Minneapolis-based Cray Research, Inc.—maker of the Cray, the high-powered Ferrari of all computers. Big, fast, and expensive, with price tags of up to $20 million each, Crays are the most powerful computers available, and are used for the most complex jobs, including weather forecasting, automotive design, basic research, and oil exploration.

The pace-setting racehorse among Cray's marketing stable is Zellers C. West, the company's leading salesman. During 1985, West made "only" three sales, but they amounted to $33 million, or about 10 percent of total company sales in the same year. At $60,000 West's base salary is respectable, though it pales in comparison to his $250,000 total compensation, including commissions. "Not bad," mused the 57-year-old, mild-mannered West with a chuckle.

Mr. West began selling computers—with Univac Division of Remington Rand—in 1956 after earning his degree from Penn State. In 1960 he moved to Honeywell, then on to Control Data in 1966. He took a 50 percent pay cut, at a base of $50,000 per year, to join Cray in 1977 because of the new company's exciting potential—a decision he has never regretted. "I enjoy being associated with the most advanced product and dealing with knowledgeable technical people," he says.

His initial assignment was to cover the northeastern U.S. He had no secretary, no office, and little marketing support: "Nothing behind me but my rear," he recalls with a grin. After only three months on the job, he stunned management by landing an $8.5 million contract. John Rollwagen, current chairman of Cray recalls, "I insisted that the customer was a poor prospect [AT&T Bell Labs in Murray Hill, N.J.], but he got the account anyway."

Unusual in his profession, West does not rely on expensive lunches, dinners, or tickets to performances to attract customers. When Bell Labs bought its second installation from him, he arranged a small party that featured a cake shaped like a cylindrical Cray computer. Normally, when Cray ships a machine, it sends a lone case of beer along, and nothing more.

West is a believer in the "soft sell"—he knows his clients well and knows that "hard sell" will not work. "Besides, that's not my style," he adds. Unlike many salespeople in the industry, he does not bother prospects when they are busy. Once he identifies a prospect with a need and the finances, he searches for a person who will champion Cray computers within that organization. Then he concentrates on supplying as much technical and other information as needed for that person to support the decision to choose Cray.

SOURCE: Adapted from "Where Three Sales a Year Make You a Superstar," *Business Week*, February 17, 1986: 76, 77.

Introduction

Few professions have borne the brunt of as much stereotyping as sales and few are so widely misunderstood. Some people have a negative view of the profession. This stems largely from a general confusion about salespeople and what they do.[1]

Essentially, many sales representatives, also called **"reps,"** are highly trained problem solvers, such as those found at Xerox, U.S.X., IBM, and many more companies, large and small alike. Mr. Zellers West of Cray Research, Inc. is such a rep (see the chapter-opening Marketing Success). He focuses on identifying customer needs and on helping them solve their computing problems.

Reps
Salespeople.

Most companies rely on a **sales force** for their promotions mix mainstay. Thus, marketing managers should become familiar with this important activity. This chapter defines personal selling, identifies key aspects of the personal selling process, and focuses on important decision areas involving sales force management.

Sales force
A company's set of salespeople.

Importance of Personal Selling

About 6.75 million people are employed as **salespeople** in the U.S., or about 7 percent of the total work force. This is around 14 times as many as are employed in advertising.[2] Comparing expenditures, personal selling expenses generally run about 8 to 10 percent of a company's sales, whereas advertising budgets seldom exceed 5 percent.[3] As a further indication of the recognized importance of this vital activity, most firms do not reduce personal selling expenditures during economic downturns.[4]

Salespeople
People hired to stimulate customer sales through personal communication. Successful ones are usually problem solvers. (Also called *salesworkers*, *sales representatives*, and *reps*.)

While some people mistakenly assume that all sales jobs and people are pretty much alike, this is far from the case. There are at least seven types of positions that vary from one another according to their degrees of "professionalism" and promotional involvement, as indicated in Exhibit 17.1.

Exhibit 17.1
Seven Types of Sales Positions

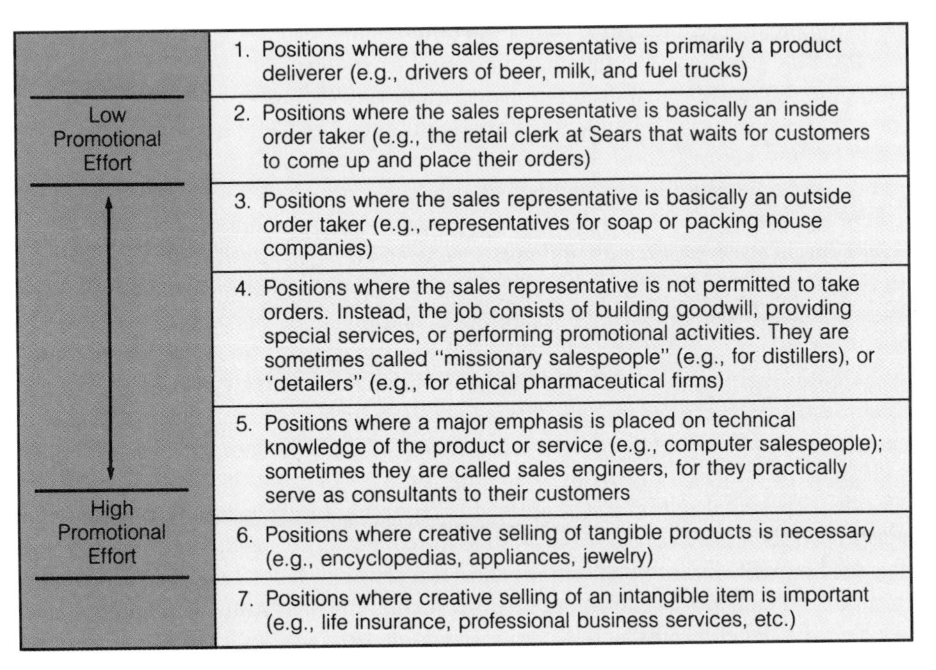

Low Promotional Effort	1. Positions where the sales representative is primarily a product deliverer (e.g., drivers of beer, milk, and fuel trucks)
	2. Positions where the sales representative is basically an inside order taker (e.g., the retail clerk at Sears that waits for customers to come up and place their orders)
	3. Positions where the sales representative is basically an outside order taker (e.g., representatives for soap or packing house companies)
↕	4. Positions where the sales representative is not permitted to take orders. Instead, the job consists of building goodwill, providing special services, or performing promotional activities. They are sometimes called "missionary salespeople" (e.g., for distillers), or "detailers" (e.g., for ethical pharmaceutical firms)
	5. Positions where a major emphasis is placed on technical knowledge of the product or service (e.g., computer salespeople); sometimes they are called sales engineers, for they practically serve as consultants to their customers
High Promotional Effort	6. Positions where creative selling of tangible products is necessary (e.g., encyclopedias, appliances, jewelry)
	7. Positions where creative selling of an intangible item is important (e.g., life insurance, professional business services, etc.)

Personal selling is very effective because of its one-on-one nature.

Promotional Value

It is important to realize that a salesperson is unique among the employees of a firm. To many customers, a sales representative *is* the company—the person who transforms the inanimate object, the "firm," into flesh and blood; a real person who may or may not offer products that solve the customer's problems. The salesperson answers questions, promises delivery, handles complaints, quotes prices, and provides other services. The sales force is also invaluable in gathering important marketing information about customers and competition.[5] Whether or not a marketing effort is successful often depends upon the sales force's ability to satisfy customer needs.

Personal selling is a powerful weapon in a marketer's promotional arsenal. This is largely due to its *flexibility*, its principal characteristic. Because it uniquely involves direct feedback from customers through interaction, personal selling enables messages to be individualized for specific circumstances and potential customers. Astute salespeople are able to "read" their audiences through questions, listen to their concerns, and monitor their gestures for nonverbal communication. This enables them to instantly adjust their presentations to the situation, which increases effectiveness. For this reason, PepsiCo used its senior management to help penetrate the China market, as illustrated in the accompanying Marketing Brief.

Further, personal selling can increase the flexibility of an overall marketing mix. Salespeople often have considerable latitude in making adjustments in delivery schedules, credit terms, promotional allowances, and prices to tailor-make an offering for a prospect. In fact, salespeople are often instrumental in configuring the product itself, as where a Digital Equipment Corp. salesperson presents a customized proposed package of computer hardware, software, maintenance, and support to a customer.

MARKETING BRIEF
Pepsi's Board Sells China

A potential new market of 1 billion people is enough to make any mass marketer salivate. The reality recently came one step closer for PepsiCo, which aims at relieving thirst in China, the world's most populous nation. Better yet for PepsiCo, Coca-Cola does not yet dominate the market.

To set the deal in January, 1986, Donald Kendall, PepsiCo's chairman, paraded his board of directors through China on an eight-day, four-city tour that cost more than $400,000 to make. The tour had all the pomp and complexity of an official state visit. Armed with a letter of introduction from former President Nixon, the PepsiCo high-class traveling salesmen wound up sipping Pepsi with Premier Zhao Ziyang—from among the 130 cases of the product they brought along on the visit.

Coke got to China first, in 1978, by entering into what it thought was an exclusive contract. In the Chinese language agreement, however, the word "exclusive" became interpreted as "priority." This opened the door for Pepsi, especially when, under Deng Xiaoping, local and provincial governments were given more control and autonomy. Pepsi began building bottling plants in Shenzhen and Guangzhou that will provide at least as much capacity as Coke's four plants. To sweeten the deal, Kendall talked about opening an unspecified number of additional bottling plants and a factory to make cola concentrate, now being imported from Ireland. Estimates for the investment ranged to $100 million.

At 13 to 15 cents per 12-ounce bottle, the Chinese can afford a lot of product. Coke charges about the same for 6.5 ounces. Kendall also talked to Chinese officials about selling PepsiCo's Frito-Lay snacks in China and building Pizza Hut restaurants.

Kendall's high-level hard sell has earned him a reputation for being a master at entering tightly controlled Communist markets. He used the same kind of sales diplomacy to successfully enter the Soviet Union in the early 1970s.

SOURCE: Adapted from Louis Kraar, "Pepsi's Pitch to Quench Chinese Thirsts," *Fortune*, March 17, 1986: 58–64.

This flexibility means that personal selling is generally far more effective in conveying messages than other promotional forms. It is not the only means used, however, as it is not always the most efficient method. While personal contacts by salespeople can cost companies like Xerox and Bristol-Myers hundreds of dollars per call, the cost of reaching target customers with mass promotion may only be a few dollars each. Thus, management must make a tradeoff of efficiency versus effectiveness when deciding how much of each type of promotion to use.

Exhibit 17.2 presents eight factors that favor personal selling over other promotional methods. Each factor should be considered as a continuum. The more these eight statements characterize a product, the greater is the need for personal selling. Notice that most consumer products score low among the factors, meaning that nonpersonal communication tends to be relatively important. In contrast, items marketed to organizations tend to score high, which favors personal selling.

Successful Sales Representatives Are Problem Solvers

Despite the stereotypes, there is really little room in personal selling today for hucksters. Buyers are becoming more sophisticated and increasingly are seeking the advice of expert salespeople as problem solvers. For example, a producer of sandpaper does not

Exhibit 17.2
Eight Factors that Favor Personal Selling

1. The product is relatively *complex* (computers and automobiles), thus requiring extensive individualized information, demonstrations, and/or instruction either for users or intermediaries.
2. The purchase represents a *major commitment,* such as expensive products (refrigerators and machinery) and those requiring substantial lifestyle or operating style changes (toupees or a new line of items for an intermediary).
3. Advertising and other nonpersonal means of communication do not *effectively convey the message,* such as for unsought items (encyclopedias and cemetery plots), items where the marketing mix needs adjustment for unique needs (professional business services and major equipment) and where prices are negotiable (construction and appliances).
4. A *"pushing" strategy* is adopted to get items through the channel.
5. *Margins are relatively high* and enable the cost of personal selling to be absorbed (diamonds versus candy).
6. The *market's size is relatively small* and thus does not enable efficiencies from mass communication (most industrial items).
7. *Order sizes (measured in dollars) are high,* enabling the firm to cover the costs of sales calls.
8. *Promotion messages must be customized* for individual potential buyers.

really sell sandpaper in the eyes of customers. Instead, it sells the means of smoothing a surface. Successful sales representatives analyze potential customer problems, then attempt to sell the solution. Similarly, effective computer sales reps do not peddle computers. They analyze the data processing needs of clients, then attempt to solve customer problems—hopefully with a computer of the kind that their company markets. By concentrating on customer needs, modern salespeople are able to establish a lasting relationship based upon trust.

Thus, a new breed of sales representatives is emerging, better able to assess customer needs than their past counterparts. They seek lasting customer relationships, not simply a few easy sales then off to the next city. To fill this role they must be well educated, analytical, knowledgeable, and often familiar with technology to be able to solve customer problems.[6] IBM, for instance, hires top graduates from major business schools for sales positions. Before letting them call on customers, however, the company spends over $150,000 per person training them to be very familiar with data processing so that they may be able to assess customer needs.

Moreover, firms are increasingly supporting their sales forces with competent marketing research and technical staffs to help them with the most difficult problems.[7] In other words, modern salespeople are increasingly becoming professional and oriented toward ethically helping customers solve their problems.[8]

Personal Selling Process

To make better general marketing decisions, all marketing managers should be at least familiar with the orderly process that effective salespeople take in performing their jobs. Figure 17.1 presents a general five-step model of this process. While all of the steps are not applicable to all sales positions (e.g., retail clerks at Meyers Jewelry do not travel routes), the model does illustrate the steps used by most highly successful salespeople. These steps are as follows.

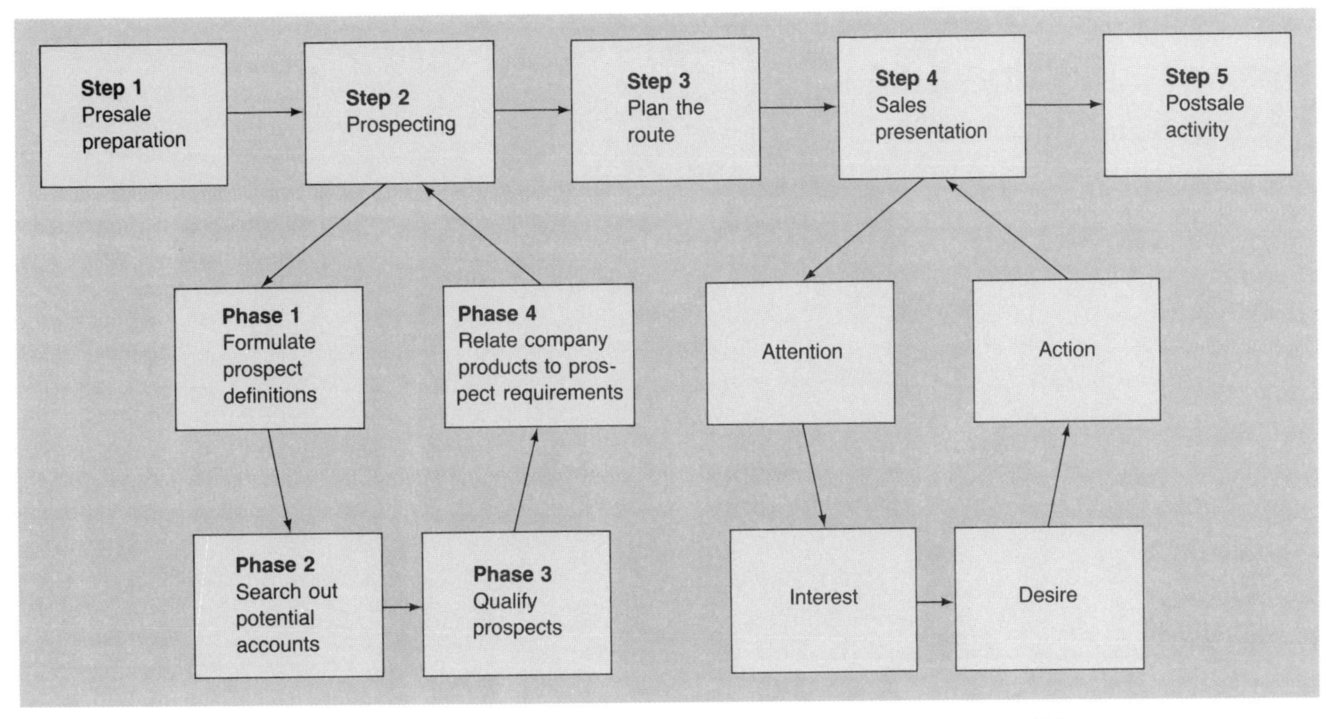

Figure 17.1
The Process of Personal Selling

Presale Preparation

Presale preparation involves becoming intimately familiar with the company's (and competitors') products so that customer problems can be effectively solved by the salesperson. Company training programs and personal study of new developments by each salesperson are essential for effective performances.

Presale preparation
Sales reps becoming familiar with the company's and its competitors' products, as well as learning about customer needs and how well they are being met.

Prospecting

Prospecting involves developing a list of names of potential customers who are most likely to purchase. The idea is to minimize wasted time calling on those having little or no probability of purchase.[9] There are four phases of prospecting.[10]

Prospecting
Developing a list of potential customers to contact who, because of their needs and abilities, are most likely to become converted to customers.

Formulating prospect definitions, which involves developing demographic (and sometimes psychographic) profiles of those who are likely to buy, which is often determined from past experience.

Searching out potential accounts, which involves developing a list of potential customers who meet the prospect characteristics definition. Some companies go one step further. To illustrate, the Rank Xerox Corp. (French) uses professional prospectors who call potential prospects and acquire prospecting information directly from them.[11] This phase provides a tentative list of likely prospects for the sales force to contact.

Qualifying prospects, involving evaluating each prospect along a set of predetermined criteria to establish the likelihood that they will make a purchase. The key criteria are: Does the prospect need the product or service? Does the prospect have

MARKETING BRIEF
Standardized Sales Approaches Work Well for Some Firms

Sales representatives for *Marketing & Media Decisions*, an advertising trade magazine, use a novel tool in their trade. When they make a major sales call to sell advertising in their magazine, they hand out to the prospect neatly bound and carefully researched written sales presentations running from 10 to 20 pages.

The written documents include not only the material the representatives will cover in the oral presentations, but also embody details about the magazine, including circulation figures and documented comparisons showing why it is more effective as an advertising medium than the competition.

Written presentations reinforce a company's selling points. Also, they force the writer (sales representative) to be specific about diagnosing a prospect's needs and demonstrate that the sales representatives have done their homework. The written presentations of *Marketing & Media Decisions* helped create $3.9 million in advertising sales in 1982, a 30 percent increase in a year. The organization is fully committed to this form of selling and will continue to utilize it.

SOURCE: Adapted from Carol Rose Covey, "Put Your Pitch in Writing," *Inc.* 5, no. 3 (March 1983): 113–114.

the financial means to make a purchase? Does the prospect have the authority to make the purchase?

Relating company products to prospect requirements, attempting to solve the prospect's particular problems with company products. For example, successful real estate salespeople qualify prospects for needs (for the number of bedrooms and such) and financial ability (income) and then screen house listings according to a prospect's needs and abilities. Then, those houses meeting the criteria are shown to the prospect. This is much more effective than simply showing any or all houses to the prospect.[12]

Establishing a Route

Route
Sales rep's itinerary schedule for calling on customers.

The third step in effective personal selling is establishing a **route** to follow. Rather than waste time aimlessly calling on prospects, effective salespeople carefully plan their calls and make appointments ahead of time to reduce wasted time.

Sales Presentation: CANAPE

Sales presentation
The process of delivering a sales message to a prospective customer.

The fourth step is the actual **sales presentation** itself. There are many approaches used, with some being very individualized according to the salesperson's own personality and situation. Others are standardized, as illustrated in the accompanying Marketing Brief.

In all cases, the emphasis should be on solving the customer's problems rather than trying to push a particular item. Beyond this, the presentation should be structured such that the promotional message is effectively communicated.

Effective sales presentations can be modeled with the CANAPE (an acronym for

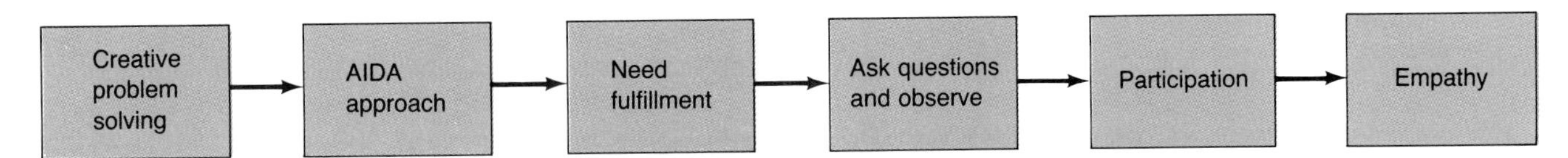

Figure 17.2
The CANAPE Personal Selling Method

the first letter of each step) approach, developed by the authors and outlined in Figure 17.2. The steps should be thought of as being simultaneous rather than sequential.

Creative Problem Solving. Creativity in identifying new, previously unrecognized, solutions to prospects' problems is essential to a successful sales effort.

AIDA. Another acronym. All promotional messages, including personal selling ones, should be designed to capture the prospect's *a*ttention, *i*nterest, *d*esire, and (purchase) *a*ction. The AIDA model was covered in Chapter 16 (Advertising Decisions). It is essential for sales messages to develop each aspect of the model to be effective.[13] To illustrate, one classic study indicated that less than half of all sales reps actually ask prospects to place an order (*a*ction). This is despite the fact that those who do ask for orders average about three times more sales than those who do not.[14]

Need Fulfillment. This means that salespeople are most effective when they are committed to fulfilling the needs of the prospective customer. Ideally, the prospect and the sales rep work closely together in identifying and fulfilling the need.

Ask Questions and Observe. Effective salespeople listen to prospects to learn about their needs. This involves asking questions and observing the customer's operations as well as his or her body language (nonverbal communication conveyed by gestures, posture, and so on).

Participation. Getting the prospect to participate in the sales presentation is much more effective than presenting a message to a passive audience. Having the prospect try the product, such as a personal computer, is much more effective than merely describing its virtues.

Empathy. Finally, CANAPE requires that salespeople mentally place themselves in the place of the prospect. This helps to gain an understanding of the prospect's perspective and leads to more effective presentations.

Of course, some prospects expect to be entertained by salespeople. Some also expect gifts and other personal favors. (Some may even expect bribes.) Research indicates that in some industries, gifts and entertainment are the norm and essential for building rapport with customers.[15] However, salespeople should not overuse them and must be cautious about ethical and even legal issues. The main weapons of sales reps, however, are their own abilities and the resources of their companies.

Sales kits and other tools are often useful for gaining prospect attention.

Postsale Activity

The final step of the personal selling process involves **postsale activity.** Sales reps do not discharge their responsibilities when they take an order. A host of postsale activities are almost always needed to assure full customer satisfaction. At the minimum, orders should be followed up to ensure that deliveries arrive on time. Other actions include making sure that proper product installation is made, that the right items are received in good condition, and that the right quantities arrive. Many of the most successful salespeople even contact customers after they have used the items for a while to make sure that they are satisfied.

Postsale activities
Activities performed by a sales rep after a sale to nurture full customer satisfaction.

CONCEPT SUMMARY

The Personal Selling Process

Step in the Process	Composition
Presale Preparation	Becoming familiar with the company's and competitors' products and learning about customer needs and how well they are being met.
Prospecting	Developing a list of names to contact who, because of their needs and abilities, are most likely to become customers.
Establishing a Route	Developing an itinerary for calling on customers.
Sales Presentation	A problem-solving session where the sales representative contacts the prospect and engages in problem solving, in order to acquire an order or attain some other goal.
Postsale Activities	Carrying on customer service and related activities to promote customer goodwill after the sale.

Postsale activities are important for two reasons. First, successful selling—in the long run—typically is based on repeat business. Follow-up activities reduce a customer's cognitive dissonance and build loyalty. Second, satisfied customers often provide leads to other prospects.

One Lincoln-Mercury new car salesman in Denver, for example, calls past customers during his slow periods to see if they are satisfied with their cars. If not, he personally schedules an appointment with the service department and later calls the customer back to make sure that the problems have been resolved. Because his customers feel that they have someone to turn to, someone who cares, most would not think of buying a replacement elsewhere. And about half of his new business comes through customer recommendations to friends. As his reward, he is highly respected in the community and earns over $200,000 per year in commissions.

Contrast the example with the typical "car peddler" who only seeks a fast buck and ignores customers after they are hooked. Success in selling is clearly based upon establishing a solid market niche—one where the salesperson serves as a catalyst in satisfying the customer's needs.

Sales Force Development Decisions

While sales work often provides an excellent background for a person to later move into management, many managers will progress in a different direction. All managers, nonetheless, must be concerned about the effectiveness of personal selling. Perhaps more importantly, most successful managers will eventually be exposed to sales force development and training decision making, either directly or indirectly, at some point in their careers, making this activity of vital interest to all.

Essentially, management makes two types of decisions relating to a sales force: those that involve force development and those concerning supervising it. The remainder of this chapter focuses on each of these decisions.

The decision to develop a sales force means that five types of subsequent decisions are needed, as illustrated in Figure 17.3. While each of these is discussed sequentially, they are all interrelated, as the figure depicts, and should be considered simultaneously.

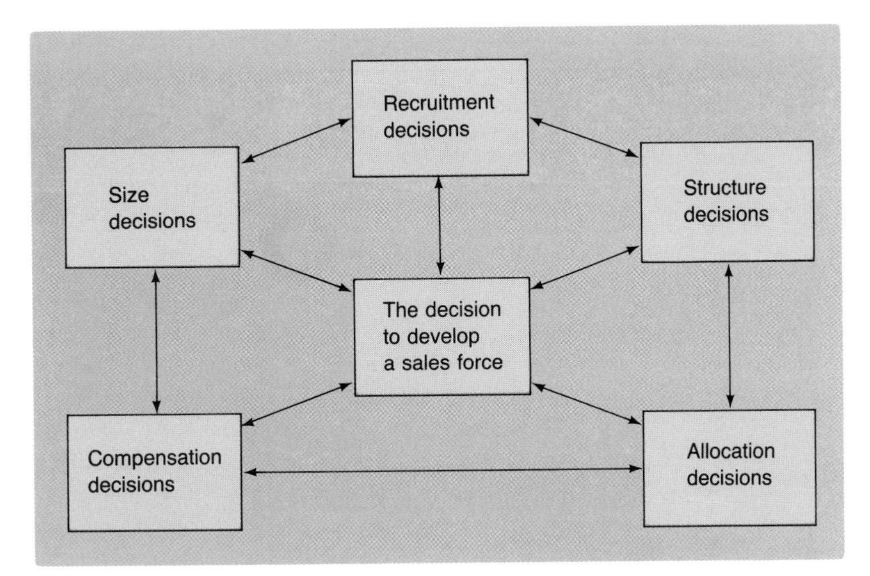

Figure 17.3
Sales Force Development Decisions

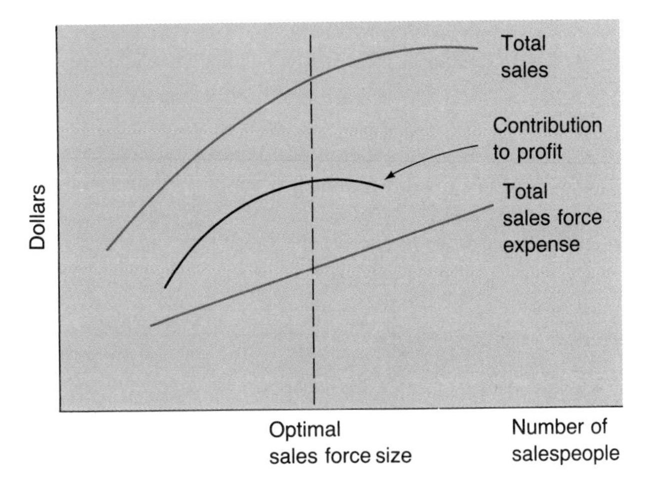

Figure 17.4
The Concept of an Optimal Sales Force Level

Size Decisions

Determining size clearly is an important decision for management to make. Too small a force results in sales that are too low, too large a force results in excessive costs. Conceptually, the process is relatively straightforward, as Figure 17.4 illustrates.

While relatively simple in concept, however, actually determining the appropriate number of salespeople to use can be relatively difficult. The problem lies in estimating the sales impact from additional salespeople. Essentially, there are two popularly used methods: the market potential method and the workload approach.[16]

Market Potential Method In a classic article, Semlow illustrated that examining the productivity of a company's existing salespeople is a useful means of calculating a sales force's optimal size.[17] Called the market potential approach because it focuses

Table 17.1 Actual and Potential Sales for 25 Salespersons in Separate Territories

Territory	Territory's Percent of Total Potential	Actual Sales per Territory (thousands of dollars)	Actual Sales per 1% of Potential
1	11.9	$351	$ 29
2	9.5	300	31
3	7.7	244	32
4	6.4	179	28
5	6.1	393	65
6	4.8	200	42
7	4.7	192	40
8	4.6	312	67
9	4.6	169	37
10	4.1	187	45
11	3.8	218	58
12	3.4	210	61
13	3.3	151	45
14	3.1	186	60
15	2.7	234	89
16	2.6	235	90
17	2.6	194	76
18	2.5	398	160
19	2.2	208	97
20	1.9	344	185
21	1.8	288	158
22	1.8	140	78
23	1.4	252	177
24	1.3	346	250
25	1.2	257	206
	100.0		

SOURCE: Adapted from Walter J. Semlow, "How Many Salesmen Do You Need?," *Harvard Business Review* 37, no. 3 (May–June 1959): 128.

on the relationships between actual and potential sales in assigned territories (geographical areas), the method is also sometimes termed the *sales representative productivity approach*.

Semlow observed that sales reps in territories considered to have the greatest sales potential do in fact tend to produce the highest total sales, as Table 17.1 illustrates. However, examine the last column of the table. Notice that sales per 1 percent of potential (actual sales/territory potential) tend to be far greater in those territories with the smallest relative potential.

Semlow then plotted the data on a graph and developed a "best fit" curve, as Figure 17.5 depicts. The "best fit" curve is that which minimizes the vertical deviations from the curve's individual observations at each given value of the independent variables. The "least squares" procedure of regression analysis, for example, is a commonly used application of best fit. This curve allowed him to average different performances by various sales representatives at each level of territory potential.

The second part of the approach involves determining the optimal number of people using the curve relationship estimated from Figure 17.5. One must make an

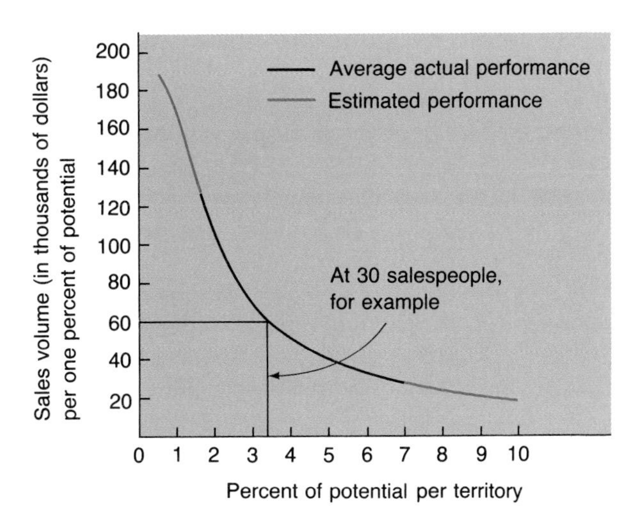

Figure 17.5
Relationship between Sales Volume per One Percent of Potential and Percent of Potential per Territory (SOURCE: Adapted from Walter J. Semlow, "How Many Salesmen Do You Need?," *Harvard Business Review* 37, no. 3 (May–June 1959): 129.)

initial assumption about territories. Both the data in Table 17.1 and Figure 17.5 imply that *all territories should be of equal potential.* If some large ones exist, their total sales should exceed those of smaller ones but their proportional sales will likely be less. Therefore, all territories should be roughly equal in potential.

Consequently, if management uses 30 territories (which also means 30 sales reps in this example), each would have about 3.33 percent of the firm's total potential. Figure 17.5 indicates that each territory, therefore, would average (\$60,000 sales/1% of potential) × (3.33% of potential) = \$200,000 in sales. Assuming 30 equal-sized territories, therefore, would mean total company sales of \$200,000 per territory × 30 territories = \$6 million. Total company sales would then be estimated in a similar manner for other sales force levels. This procedure enables estimating the total company sales response to various numbers of salespeople.

The next step in this procedure is to figure in costs. This is done in two parts. First, operating profit (sales less operating costs) excluding the sales force costs is subtracted from each sales level. Then, the cost of the sales force at various levels is estimated. Subtracting the costs from the operating profit yields the estimated profit levels of the sales force at various sizes.

A number of criteria may then be used to choose the best sales force size. One would be the level that maximizes profit. Another would be the rate of return, which Semlow favored (a 22 percent return with 65 people for the example). Any criterion that management normally uses in its decision making can be used in conjunction with this approach.

Of course, the approach is not without its weaknesses. It requires the availability of historical data, and does not take into consideration different geographical sizes of the various territories.

Nonetheless, the method does enable quantitative analysis of the number of territories to use. This makes it a useful managerial tool in decision making.

Workload Approach The second and most widely used method of determining the appropriate number of salespeople to use is the workload approach. It is based upon equalizing the workload of all sales reps rather than analyzing sales potentials of territories. Therefore, this method is applicable when historical data are not available.

This method, originally proposed in the literature by Talley, requires the following steps to be taken.[18]

Step 1. Group customers into size classes according to their annual sales volume, profitability, needs, or some other measure that results in equal workloads within each class.

Step 2. Determine the intended selling effort, usually defined as call frequency per year, for each class of customer. Both management's own judgment and that of the sales force should be used in this step.

Step 3. Multiply the number of accounts in each class by the call frequency (or other measure) to yield the firm's total annual sales force workload.

Step 4. Determine the average number of calls that each sales representative can make, taking into consideration geographical dispersion, the average time per call, waiting time, and other time-consuming factors. Usually reps can make a different number of average calls to each class.

Step 5. Calculate the number of reps needed by dividing the annual workload by the average number of calls. Exhibit 17.3 illustrates a brief example of the workload approach. Note that the firm in the example needs 88 reps (87.3 rounded up).

Whichever approach is most appropriate depends upon the specific circumstances which the company faces. The market potential approach is most desirable when the various territories are similar in geographic dispersion and in the number of accounts. Generally, though, firms use the workload approach because it takes into consideration differences in the above factors.[19] Further, other factors must be considered. In 1983, Olympia Brewing Co. needed to hire numerous new reps to allow for training and attrition even though the company only intended to expand the size of the sales force by three people.[20]

Recruitment Decisions

The difference between a poor or even average sales performance and a good one can be dramatic. One study, to illustrate, revealed that less than 30 percent of all sales

Exhibit 17.3
Using the Workload Approach to Determine Sales Force Size

Customer Class and Definition	Number in Class	Intended Annual Call Frequency	Total Calls Needed per Class	Average Calls per Salesperson within a Class per Year	Salespersons Needed per Class[a]
1. annual sales over $10 million	200	52	10,400	500	20.8
2. sales between $5 million and $10 million	600	26	15,600	600	26.0
3. sales between $1 million and $5 million	1,700	12	20,400	800	25.5
4. sales below $1 million	2,500	6	15,000	1,000	15.0
TOTAL NEEDED	5,000		61,400		87.3

a. Since partial persons are not possible, whole numbers are required. Rounding indicates that 21 and 26 salespersons are required for classes 1 and 3, respectively. Therefore, 88 salespersons are needed.

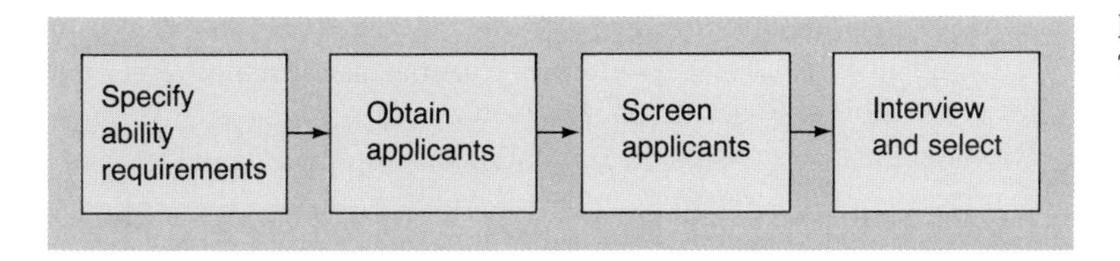

Figure 17.6
The Recruiting Process

representatives account for over half of a typical company's sales. There is strong motivation, then, for management to recruit the best-qualified people once they have determined a sales force's size.[21] Successful **recruiting** is best accomplished by following a four-step process, as shown in Figure 17.6.

Recruiting
Determining which persons to hire and convincing them to join the organization.

Step 1 Determine the specific abilities that good candidates should have. Many studies have focused on identifying the characteristics of successful salespeople. Tobin, for instance, isolated 19 attributes.[22] Among the most important were: ability to ask questions and stimulate answers that develop their points of view, enthusiasm, a sense of humor, human relations leadership, optimism, and above all, persistency. Selling is not a job for quitters. Many sales do not materialize until the fourth, fifth, or even later calls. In another study, unsuccessful sales reps were identified as unmotivated, materialistic, insecure, unaggressive, and unimaginative.[23]

Beyond these generalities, managers need to specify factors such as education, maturity, and experience. For example, many technical companies such as Motorola Corp.'s Communications Division require that candidates have formal schooling in technical subjects. In other companies, such as Procter & Gamble, a degree in business administration is required so that candidates can help solve their customers' general business problems.

Step 2 Obtaining applicants is the second step in recruiting. The task is often quite difficult, especially for entry-level positions, as some people feel that sales work is low in prestige.[24] Many college graduates, for example, would rather take a 9-to-5 routine job with limited advancement potential so that they will be labeled as a "junior executive." Personal selling, in contrast, offers considerable freedom, with each person, in effect, running her or his own business. Further, there is often considerable turnover in sales positions, especially in low-level jobs where the compensation tends to be modest, such as in Avon and Mary Kay cosmetics.[25] Consequently, many managers feel that recruiting is an ongoing, continuous activity.

In large companies, personnel departments usually handle the matter of locating applicants after working with the head of sales to determine the types of people to seek. Operating management usually must get involved in the process in smaller companies. Applicants may be located in a number of ways, including newspapers, college campus interviews, and from employee references. For senior and mid-level positions, many companies such as General Motors have a policy of hiring from within the organization. Many experts argue, however, that outside sources should also be considered.[26] And it seems that most companies do look outside, as many are filling even the topmost positions from outside sources.[27]

Step 3 The third recruiting step is screening and hiring applicants. The annual turnover rates (resignations and dismissals combined) in some successful companies approach a low of 5 percent. This largely results from carefully designed, formalized means of screening and hiring applicants. Specific procedures vary, but often include the use of detailed application forms, formal assessments of experience, reference checks, and formally evaluated interviews.

Some companies use psychological exams (aptitude, intelligence, and personality inventories) in the screening process.[28] While costly to use and evaluate, many organizations, including E. F. Hutton, are avid users of such tests because they can provide insight into a candidate's motivation. But interpreting the tests requires highly trained experts.

A common mistake during screening is to have several persons vote, as a committee, on who should receive an offer. While several people, such as supervisors, other managers, and personnel officials, should talk to candidates, the successful candidate's immediate supervisor should be the one to decide on the candidate if he or she is to ultimately be held responsible for the department's operations.

Step 4 Finally, once a candidate is selected, the firm should be marketed to the person. Good candidates are likely to be attractive to other companies as well, and this effort is necessary to solidify their interest. This can be done by portraying the person's role in the company, remuneration possibilities, benefits, and other highlights. Managers must take care in "not using too much paint while drawing the picture," however. An honest appraisal of what the candidate can expect is the best long-run policy. Further, follow-up procedures should be used once the candidate comes aboard, involving introducing the person to others, making sure that all forms are properly filled out, and getting to know the new employee. Lasting impressions of a company are often formulated by employees during their first few days.

Structure Decisions

Sales force structure
Deciding how sales reps should be deployed among potential accounts.

A third crucial development task involves deciding the **sales force structure**; that is, determining how to deploy individuals among potential accounts.[29] Three factors are considered here: territory design, territory shape, and other structure decisions.

Territory design
The method of assigning prospects to sales representatives.

Territory Design The simplest way of deploying a sales force is to structure it around exclusive geographical territories. **Territory design** requires assigning each person a particular territory to cover along with the responsibility of representing all of the company's products to every current and potential customer located in that area. Moreover, each representative is restricted to selling exclusively within an assigned territory.

This structure has several advantages. For one, it encourages the development of strong customer/representative interpersonal ties. Particular sales representatives know who their customers are and can work to build lasting relationships. Another is that it simplifies the problem of evaluating performances, as management can easily determine who is to receive credit for which sales. Finally, the structure encourages coverage of all sizes of customers. If Wrangler's salespeople were free to sell anywhere, for example, most would concentrate in major cities like Los Angeles and forget about prospects in smaller locations.

Territory Shape Territories really represent the sum of smaller units such as counties, which, when combined, comprise a desired sales potential or workload. Sales managers combine the smaller units after considering several factors, such as the location of

Effectively designing sales territories is a critical sales force development task.

natural boundaries, transportation ease between prospects, and city locations. Companies typically try to achieve a certain geographical shape for each territory, as this can influence the cost of covering prospects, ease of calling on them, and the sales force's overall morale. The cost of territorial coverage can be substantial. A survey conducted by *Sales and Marketing Management* magazine revealed that the mean costs for a sales representative's monthly travel was $641.00. This consisted of $225.75 for auto, $240.25 for lodging, and $145 for meals.[30] Figure 17.7 illustrates four commonly used territorial shapes.

Headquartering representatives at the center of a circular territory helps to reduce wasted travel time. If reps follow a circular pattern of calling on accounts, they lose little time when backtracking to the office. Moreover, representatives are headquartered as near as possible to all customers, which helps in expediting any special trips.

A cloverleaf pattern is quite similar because it divides the total territory into smaller circles. If the leaves are of the right size, representatives can cover each in a circular

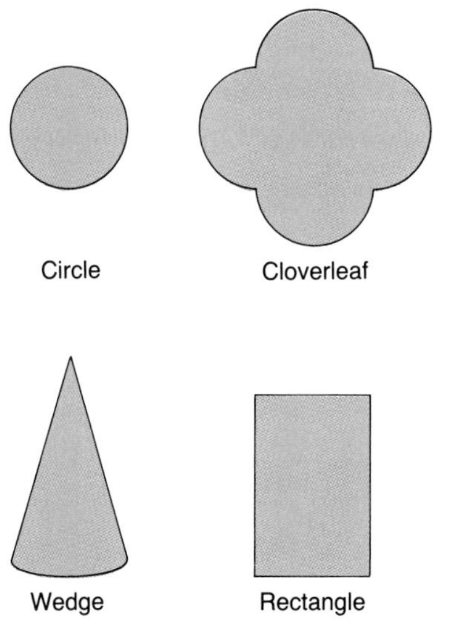

Figure 17.7
Commonly Designed Territory Shapes

pattern in a week of travel. In a month, they can cover all accounts with minimal backtracking by penetrating successive leaves each week.

Firms often employ a wedge shape in metropolitan areas too large for one sales representative to handle. Its virtue is in balancing urban, suburban, and rural accounts among all representatives in the area. But each salesperson becomes headquartered a greater distance from some accounts than with other shapes, resulting in greater wasted time in backtracking.

Finally, companies sometimes utilize a rectangular territory, especially in rural areas where highway and other travel routes tend to parallel latitudinal and longitudinal coordinates. Sales managers use this shape to conform to natural boundaries.

Other Sales Force Structures Structuring a sales force solely around geographical territories works best when a company markets a relatively narrow product mix to relatively homogeneous prospective customers. But consider Westinghouse, which literally sells thousands of items (from light bulbs to electricity generators) to many different types of customers (from small retailers to large utilities). It would be impossible for a single sales rep to know much about all company products and all customer needs in one geographical area.

Therefore, whenever large differences exist between customers and/or products, it is usually best for management to structure the force around predominant groups of similarities, such as by major customer type or major product group, or both.

There are two major disadvantages to nongeographic sales forces, however. Some travel may overlap, leading to additional costs, and two or more salespeople could call on one account for different items. St. Regis Paper Co., for example, had separate reps calling on the same customers for packaging and multiwall (several ply) products. If customers think of both sets of items as being part of the same line, the structure is undesirable as it can lead to confusion and lost sales. Like other elements of a marketing mix, the appropriate sales force depends on both market and cost factors.[31]

Assignment Decisions

Closely related to deciding which structure should be used is deciding which representatives to assign to specific territories. Most companies classify territories according to levels of importance and difficulty. Auto companies, for example, generally use the following three classes: Rural territories (comprised of small dealers with low potential sales volumes), city territories (mostly consisting of medium-sized dealers in moderately-sized towns with greater potential volumes), and metropolitan territories (made up of the largest potential volume dealers because of high population densities in their trade areas).

For all companies, each representative's experience, ability, and motivation should be the prime factors management considers when assigning specific people to specific territories. Metropolitan dealers are of the greatest importance to auto companies because of their large volume potentials. Also, these dealers face the greatest competitive pressures, therefore justifying more calls than their smaller counterparts by the most experienced and able sales representatives.

Rural dealers, in contrast, usually have small potential volumes and they face less intensive competitive pressures. Moreover, travel time between them can be substantial. Thus, they provide a good training ground for newer representatives. The point, of course, is that sales managers should assign the best people to the most critical and difficult tasks.

Compensation Decisions

One of the most fundamental of the sales force development decisions relates to compensation.[32] Essentially, there are three major compensation methods to choose from: straight commission, straight salary, and a blend of the two.

Straight Commission Under a straight **commission** plan, sales reps are paid a percentage of their sales dollar volumes. The plan might be a simple one, where the percentage is applied to sales dollars, or it might be more complex, where a percentage is applied against the related contribution margin (sales less variable costs). While requiring more recordkeeping, the latter is usually better because it bases commissions on profits generated, not simply revenue.

Commission
Payment, usually to sales reps, as a percentage of their sales volume.

Commission plans are the norm in many industries such as security brokerage, textiles, and insurance. The plan has several advantages. It is especially attractive to aggressive salespeople as it rewards them for their efforts, and it alleviates much of the sales force's fixed costs.

There are disadvantages, though. Salespeople are likely to resist directives by management, such as filling out forms and developing new accounts and territories, as time spent on these activities might negatively affect earning commissions. Also, commission structures do not reward, at least in the short run, servicing accounts, such as helping with product installation. Thus, there is a real potential to slide over postsale activities.

Straight Salary At the opposite extreme are straight salaries, which are fixed amounts regardless of volume. This plan offers several advantages, but most significant is that it offers management the greatest ability to direct people. Because the plan does not tie compensation to sales volume, management can easily insist that great attention be placed on things like postsale activities and developing new accounts or territories.

But, there are disadvantages with the payment scheme, especially that it does not offer as much incentive for extra effort as does a plan involving commissions. Consequently, aggressive salespeople with high promotional ability tend to avoid such positions. Therefore, straight salary plans should be used in situations where management wishes to highly control the activities of its people and where aggressive efforts are not required. Inside order takers and missionary salespeople, for instance, are usually paid a straight salary, and so are large-scale computer system sales specialists.

Combination Plans A combination plan offers both a base salary and a commission or bonus on volume. The idea is to enable management to control the sales force, yet to provide incentives for good performance.

The base portion of a combination plan sometimes takes the form of a fixed monthly salary with commissions paid above some specified volume. The Signode Corp., for example, developed a plan where no bonuses are paid until a representative reaches 80 percent of quota. Above that threshold, however, the plan doubles the average bonus in the industry.[33] Another scheme is to offer a **draw,** which is something like a loan in slow periods against future commissions. Exhibit 17.4 illustrates how a draw plan works.

Draw
Payment to a sales rep as a loan against forthcoming commissions.

As the exhibit shows, Jane Doe received $100 against draw in January to bring her pay up to the $600 guaranteed base. She earned $900 commission in February against which management charged the draw, resulting in her receiving $800 for the month. She again fell behind the minimum in March, resulting in a $150 subsidy from her draw account to be applied against future commissions. Management generally has

Exhibit 17.4
Illustration of a Draw Plan

Salesperson: Jane Doe				
Month	Sales	Commission	Draw	Monthly Salary
January	$10,000	$ 500	$100	$ 600
February	18,000	900	(100)	800
March	9,000	450	150	600
Quarter totals	$37,000	$1,850	$150	$2,000
($600 monthly draw, 5% commission on sales dollars earned)				

the option of cancelling any amounts in arrears as an additional incentive. Thus, a draw is much like a loan, but also has characteristics similar to a salary.

Which Plan Is Best? Three objectives are central to determining which compensation method is appropriate. It should attract and keep desired people, keep expenses under control, and help in attaining company objectives. In general, the greater the control desired over the individuals and the lower the promotional abilities they need, the greater should be the tendency to pay straight salaries. The greater the need for aggressive promotional efforts, in contrast, the more important is a commission. The right plan, therefore, depends upon the situation. A comprehensive study of manufacturers revealed that roughly 30 percent of them paid straight salaries, 6 percent straight commissions, and the remaining 64 percent paid a combination of salary plus commission or bonus.[34]

Other Compensation Decisions Two additional compensation issues must be addressed before leaving this topic. The first involves the general pay scale structure to be used. In general, the scale should provide enough incentive to attract and retain good people, but it should also remain competitive to scales for jobs of similar importance within the firm. Determining the general level, though, can be difficult. Accordingly, large companies employing highly professional people (such as Levi Strauss) are increasingly turning to management consulting compensation specialists (such as Hay & Associates) to periodically update their compensation packages.

House accounts
Customers that are handled by management rather than by a sales rep.

Another important issue is the handling of **house accounts.** These accounts are typically very large customers, such as K mart, which management, rather than a salesperson, serves—usually because of the large volume. At Worthington Industries (a heavy metals producer), for instance, the chairman of the board takes on some house accounts.[35] The question is, "should the salesperson assigned the territory be given credit for such sales?"

The answer is "It depends." If a sales representative never had anything to do with the account, then logically he or she should not receive credit. But some managers turn large customers into house accounts just to avoid paying hefty commissions. Management should avoid this practice, as it is sure to alienate good salespeople. Several years ago, for example, a Chicago-based Wrangler salesman lost an important account to the house after he developed the business from scratch. He now sells for Jordache and took many clients with him. The best practice is to bring in house accounts when the company promotes, transfers, or terminates a person. Then it can design territories to treat all salespeople equitably.

Sales Force Supervision

Once management has developed a sales force, its task is to engage in supervising the activities to accomplish the firm's goals. This evokes the final set of ongoing, interrelated decisions to be considered in this chapter. They are illustrated in Figure 17.8.

Training

It is in the company's best interest to sponsor good training programs. At the minimum, management should make new recruits familiar with company products, policies, procedures, and important documents for reporting key information. Moreover, salespeople should receive as much information as possible about leads, prospective customer profiles, competitor activities, company plans, new products, and ways to improve presentations. Some firms even train their customers' sales representatives. For example, Hyster, a large forklift producer, provided training for an established dealer's sales force to the point where they were materials handling specialists.[36] In general, all sales training programs have the following objectives:

- To inform trainees about company developments
- To explain responsibilities and procedures
- To provide information about customers and competitor actions
- To help improve sales presentations

Motivating

Motivating the sales force is another key management activity. Compensation and sales **quotas** (formally defined sales volume goals) are one important motivation.[37]

Quota (sales)
A formally expressed goal for a sales rep, stated either in dollars or in units.

Management should extend beyond compensation to motivate people, however.[38] Pep talks, contests, meetings to build enthusiasm, and other related techniques are all important.[39] One source, however, reveals that the single best way to motivate salespeople is for management to clearly and formally define exactly their expected tasks and how they will be evaluated.[40] The design of the sales job itself is a factor in motivating reps.[41] One study, for instance, suggests that considerable job satisfaction is likely if salespeople feel that their jobs encompass considerable variety and allow them autonomy.[42]

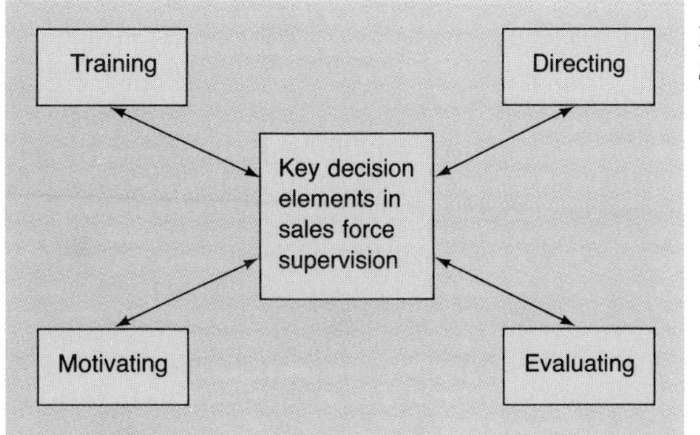

Figure 17.8
Sales Force Supervision Decisions

Training of the sales force is an important investment in a company's assets.

Directing

Providing leadership is another key responsibility of management. An important element of this leadership is provided through effective organization and clerical assistance. (Chapter 21 discusses organizing and controlling marketing activities.) Another important part is to help representatives in planning calls and routes and in allocating efforts across products over time.

Several quantitative techniques are available to help in designing routes in a way to minimize wasted time and effort. One method, called CALLPLAN, is specially designed to consider travel and call times, account profitability, and call frequency.[43] Other methods include shortest path analysis and other forms of mathematical programming.[44] While computers are often needed to perform the calculations, some small territories can be analyzed by hand.[45]

It is also important for management to assure that all items in the product line receive attention by sales reps. Many companies, such as Ford Motor Co., use incentives and contests to assure that slow-moving or new items receive attention. Another way is to vary bonuses and commissions according to how fast a particular item moves. In many more advanced companies, commission structures are based

Contests can be an effective means of motivating a sales force.

upon unit contribution margins (selling price less variable cost). This method encourages salespeople to focus on items that contribute the most toward company profits.[46]

Evaluating

The final concern of supervision consists of evaluating the sales force's performance.[47] Regular evaluation enables the early identification of deviations from plans, which allows management to initiate corrective action before it is too late for remedy. It also fosters the identification of star and poor performers early, which helps to develop a better sales force in the future.

Evaluation is particularly critical when the sales force handles multiple products or product lines. To illustrate, Exhibit 17.5 presents data on Availon Manufacturing Co., which sells three products. It is apparent that the company made only 98 percent of its sales goal. The problem stems from failing to achieve the goals for products 1 and 2.

Exhibit 17.5
Availon Manufacturing Evaluation of Overall Sales Effort

	Sales			Contribution Margin			Effort
Products	Annual Sales Quota (thousands of dollars)	Actual Sales (thousands of dollars)	Percent of Quota	Contribution Margin (thousands of dollars)	Percent of Sales	Percent of Total Contribution Margin	Percent of Total Sales Calls
1	40	37	92.5	7.5	20.3	68.2	49.3
2	58	62	106.9	3.2	5.2	29.1	31.5
3	15	12	80.0	0.3	2.5	2.7	19.2
TOTAL	113	111	98.2[a]	11.0	9.9[a]	100.0	100.0

a. Does not add.

The last two columns are the most revealing. Product 1 provided nearly 70 percent of the firm's contribution margin, but the company directed only 50 percent of its selling effort to this item. Conversely, 20 percent of the selling effort went to product 3, which accounted for less than 3 percent of the contribution margin. On the surface, at least, management should consider shifting future sales efforts toward product 1. Of course, other strategic factors may still favor emphasizing product 3; for example, it may be a new product. But by objectively analyzing results, management forces itself to think through various alternatives.

Similarly, management should spend time to regularly evaluate the individual efforts of salespeople. Formal individual reviews work best because they let people know exactly how they measure up and what the company expects of them in the future. When reviews are done frequently, such as monthly or quarterly, they help management increase their control and results. There are a number of criteria to evaluate, including:

- sales volume
- new accounts
- service calls
- batting average (successful orders/calls made)
- percent of quota
- lost accounts
- contribution margin
- number and size of orders
- selling expenses
- calls per week

Qualitative factors, such as customer relations, eagerness, attitude, and knowledge of both the product line and customer needs should be evaluated as well.[48] Management should also consider comparisons of sales reps against company averages and also against previous-year results, as illustrated in Exhibit 17.6.

Notice that Tony Jones exceeded quota, whereas Mary Jacobson did not equal the expectation (line 6). However, both did a better job than in 1985. Of interest is that their contribution margin percentages were roughly the same (line 14), despite the fact that Jones' expenses were greater (line 11). This suggests that Jones worked harder to cover his territory, which is supported by the market share data (lines 20 through

Decision Area	Components of Decisions
Size	Determine the optimum number of sales representatives to employ, based upon methods such as the market potential or workload approach
Recruitment	Specify sales representative ability requirements, obtain applicants, screen applicants, and interview and select those to be hired
Structure	Determine territory type and shape
Assignments	Determine which sales representatives are to be in charge of each territory
Compensation	Determine the amount and type of plan for compensation of sales representatives, including payments for expenses

CONCEPT SUMMARY

Sales Force Development Decisions

Exhibit 17.6

Evaluation Form for Two Sales Representatives

Line No.		Sales Representative			
		Mary Jacobson		Tony Jones	
		1985	1986	1985	1986
1	Net sales—product 1	$127,500	$135,400	$192,600	$201,700
2	—product 2	230,100	242,700	245,000	246,300
3	Total net sales	$357,600	$378,100	$437,600	$448,000
4	Percent of quota—product 1	84.3%	87.6%	93.7%	98.5%
5	—product 2	93.6	95.4	109.6	107.2
6	Total	90.1	92.5	102.0	103.1
7	Contribution margin before direct selling expense				
8	—product 1	$28,050	$29,788	$42,372	$44,374
9	—product 2	46,020	48,540	49,000	49,260
10	Subtotal	$74,070	$78,328	$91,372	$93,634
11	Less: Direct selling expenses	18,050	20,378	20,420	22,600
12	Contribution margin generated:				
13	—Total (in dollars)	$56,020	$57,950	$70,952	$71,034
14	—as a percent of sales	15.7%	15.3%	16.2%	15.9%
15	Territory:				
16	Total estimated market in sales				
17	—product 1	$350,000	$ 375,000	$ 425,000	$ 450,000
18	—product 2	600,000	650,000	700,000	750,000
19	Total	$950,000	$1,025,000	$1,125,000	$1,200,000
20	Market share—product 1	36.4%	36.1%	45.3%	44.8%
21	—product 2	38.4	37.3	35.0	32.8
22	Total market share	37.6	36.9	38.9	37.3
23	Customers:				
24	Average number of customers	230	240	280	305
25	Number of new customers	25	20	30	42
26	Number of lost customers	20	20	10	17
27	Average sales per customer	$1,555	$1,575	$1,563	$1,469
28	Average contribution margin generated per customer	$243.56	$241.46	$253.40	$232.90

22), the number of customers (line 24), average sales per customer (line 27), and contribution margin per customer (line 28).

Such analysis helps in evaluating the performances. Perhaps Mary was new and still learning, or greater competition may have existed within her territory. Another possibility is that she focused too heavily on large customers and did not spend enough time on new accounts. In contrast, Tony appears to be performing well. However, he may be spending too much time on prospecting for new accounts and handling small customers, as suggested by an $11,000 increase in sales with only a $1,000 increase in contribution margin and a reduction in average order size. If Tony's market shares are above all other sales reps (lines 20 through 22), it would mean that he is covering his territory as well as management could hope. However, if management feels that additional penetration is possible, perhaps it should break up the territory to increase sales coverage.

While a total evaluation would require additional information, the exhibit illustrates how formal analysis can be beneficial in evaluating performances and in pinpointing what steps management might take to increase future performance. Above all, management should communicate the results of an evaluation to the individual. The primary reason for an evaluation is to improve future performance. Management cannot accomplish this by concealing facts and opinions until it decides to fire someone.

Chapter Summary

This chapter examined key decisions involving personal selling, one of the most important ingredients of a promotions mix. It pointed out that personal selling can be one of the most effective means of promoting an item, though it may not be the most efficient due to its expense relative to other promotional vehicles.

All marketers should be aware of the personal selling process, since almost all companies rely on personal selling to some degree. Further, buyers tend to perceive sales representatives as being the company. This means that marketing managers should be aware of the personal selling process in order to make more effective decisions. Presale preparation, prospecting, route planning, sales presentation, and postsale activities are the five steps in the process.

The chapter also examined sales force development decisions, which involve the first half of management's sales force-related decision-making responsibility. Particular development decisions involve determining a sales force's size, recruitment, structure, assignment, and compensation.

The chapter also examined the second half of management's sales force decision making responsibility, which involves supervising a salesforce. The particular decisions concerning supervision include training, motivating, directing, and evaluating performance. As the chapter indicated, it is critical to be as analytical as possible and to look for causes when evaluating performances, or else premature conclusions may be drawn. Both developing and supervising a sales force effectively are essential for a solid marketing program.

Questions

1. Why is personal selling the most effective means of sales promotion? Is it always most important? Why or why not?
2. In the words of one well-seasoned sales representative, "Selling means getting out there and finding some sucker. All that's necessary is to have the gift of gab and a little larceny in your heart." Comment.
3. Explain the need for each of the steps of the personal selling process in your own words.
4. Compare and contrast the market potential and the workload approaches for determining the optimal size of a sales force. Which do you think is better? Why?

5. When does a straight commission compensation plan make most sense? A straight salary plan? What is a draw?

6. In the words of one executive, "All that training stuff is a bunch of garbage. Experience is the best teacher. Get new people out into the field and let results separate the wheat from the chaff." Comment.

7. What role does the quota play in motivating sales representatives? The text states that results can be increased by having sales representatives take part in setting their quotas. Why? Suppose they try to set them too low?

8. The text presents some generalities about attributes of good sales representatives. Describe a research plan that enables a company to identify the attributes that are particularly important for its own sales force.

9. The management of one company would like to know how many accounts its sales representatives should call on each month. Describe an experiment that will help to find the answer.

10. Sam Sellmore, sales manager of Ace Widgets, wants management to cut the company's advertising budget by $30,000 to hire one more sales representative. Sam's reasoning is that the amount would only buy a few ads in *Newsweek* anyway, and surely another sales representative would generate more sales than a couple of half-page ads. Comment.

11. What abilities and characteristics would salespeople representing the following companies need, in your opinion?
   a. Apple computer (selling to computer stores)
   b. Mutual of Omaha (selling life insurance to consumers)
   c. Century 21 (selling real estate to consumers)
   d. MCI (selling telephone systems to businesses)
   e. Mack Trucks (selling large trucks to trucking companies)

12. Should each of the following compensate their representatives primarily by salary or by commission? Substantiate your answer.
   a. Kodak (selling copiers to small businesses)
   b. Dale Carnegie & Associates (selling motivation classes to consumers and businesses)
   c. A Ford auto dealer (selling Ford automobiles and light trucks to consumers)
   d. Royal Business Machines, Inc. (selling copiers to business and nonbusiness organizations)
   e. The Ford Motor Company (selling Fords and Mercurys to Budget and other car rental companies)

13. What would be the more important postsale activities for the following, in your opinion?
   a. Rockwell International (selling B-1 bombers to the U.S. Air Force)
   b. IBM (selling personal computers to consumers)
   c. U.S. Steel (selling steel plating to producers of water, gas, and crude petroleum tanks)
   d. A Maytag dealer (selling clothes washers and dryers to consumers)

Chapter 18

Direct Marketing Decisions

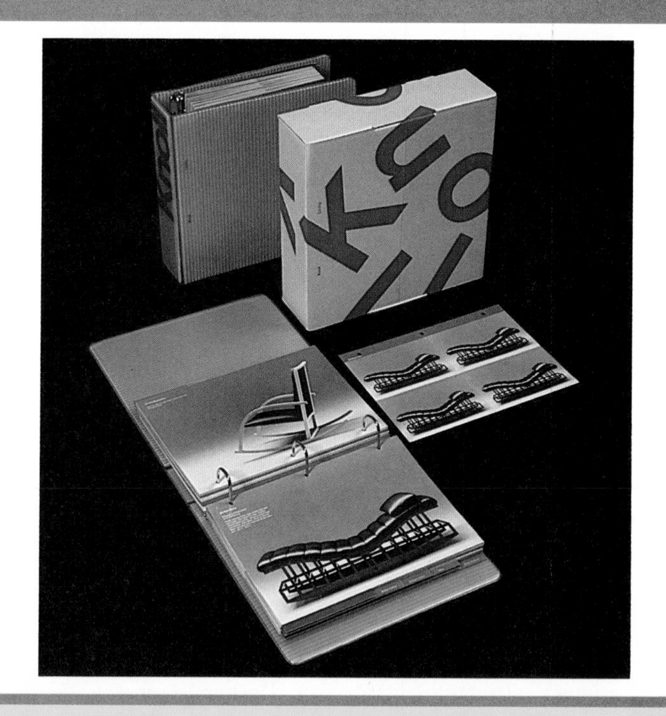

Objectives

After completing this chapter, you should be able to demonstrate a knowledge of:

- The meaning of the term "direct marketing"
- Why social and economic trends favor the growth of direct marketing
- The applications of direct marketing and the directions that it is taking
- The nature of the major media used by direct marketers and the advantages and disadvantages of each
- How managers can employ each of the major direct marketing media as a means of fulfilling marketing strategy
- Indicators of the future of direct marketing

MARKETING SUCCESS

Selling Expensive Fragrances by Mail

In 1979 Jim Roth and David Horner left the Max Factor Company and decided to start a firm that would market perfumes for small companies. They approached Fred and Gayle Hayman, co-owners of Giorgio, the glitzy Beverly Hills Rodeo Drive store, with the idea of creating a new fragrance that would be sold only through their store and by direct mail. The Haymans liked the idea and eventually made Roth and Horner senior vice presidents of the resulting company, Giorgio Parfum, Inc.

The firm conducted considerable research to develop a product with a "sensual romantic floral fragrance," positioned to compete with popular signature fragrances such as De la Renta and Yves St. Laurent. Management tested 140 fragrances before coming up with one that appeared to embody the "Beverly Hills lifestyle." One of the scents turned out to be a hit among women selected at shopping malls and among trend-setting groups. Management decided to price the product at $150 per ounce.

Roth and Horner accomplished what had never been done before. They produced a mail order business for a costly fragrance by inserting scented order forms in magazines appearing in large cities. During the first year the firm's sales were $1.5 million, 80 percent of which was a result of the magazine order forms, letters to the Beverly Hills headquarters, and calls to a toll-free 800 number. By 1985, the team had parlayed the company's sales to nearly $100 million. While in mid-1986 Gale Hayman set off on her own and developed Gale Hayman, Inc.—a design studio for skin care products, fragrances, and makeup—there appeared to be no decline in Giorgio's meteoric growth.

A key advantage of this mail order business is that order forms come directly to company headquarters so management can bank the money the next day. This is in contrast to waiting from 90 to 120 days to receive payment from a department store. Most products are delivered five or six days after the order arrives at company headquarters.

SOURCE: Adapted from Eliot Tiegel, "Eau de Entrepreneur," *California Business*, September 1983, pp. 117–20; and "A Founder of Giorgio Tries a Solo Venture," *New York Times*, May 27, 1986, p. D2.

Introduction

Unrest prevailed in both the North and the South following the U.S. Civil War. While carpetbaggers, land reform, and the abolition of slavery dramatically undercut the social and economic structure of the South, at the same time high costs and low crop prices plagued the North, causing similar problems. In response, many farmers organized themselves into the National Grange, a form of cooperative, whose main slogan was "eliminate the middleman."

Seizing this opportunity, Aaron Montgomery Ward of Chicago published and distributed his first catalog in 1892, which he headlined "Original Wholesale Grange Supply House." [1] By so doing, he greatly reduced the prevailing distribution system—eliminating country stores and other intermediaries. Richard Sears began his mail order business in 1886. Both were aided by the rapid growth of the railway system, the post office, and the advancements in mass production that allowed an increasing quantity, quality, and variety of products to be included in the catalogs.

Montgomery Ward ushered in the start of the modern era of direct marketing.

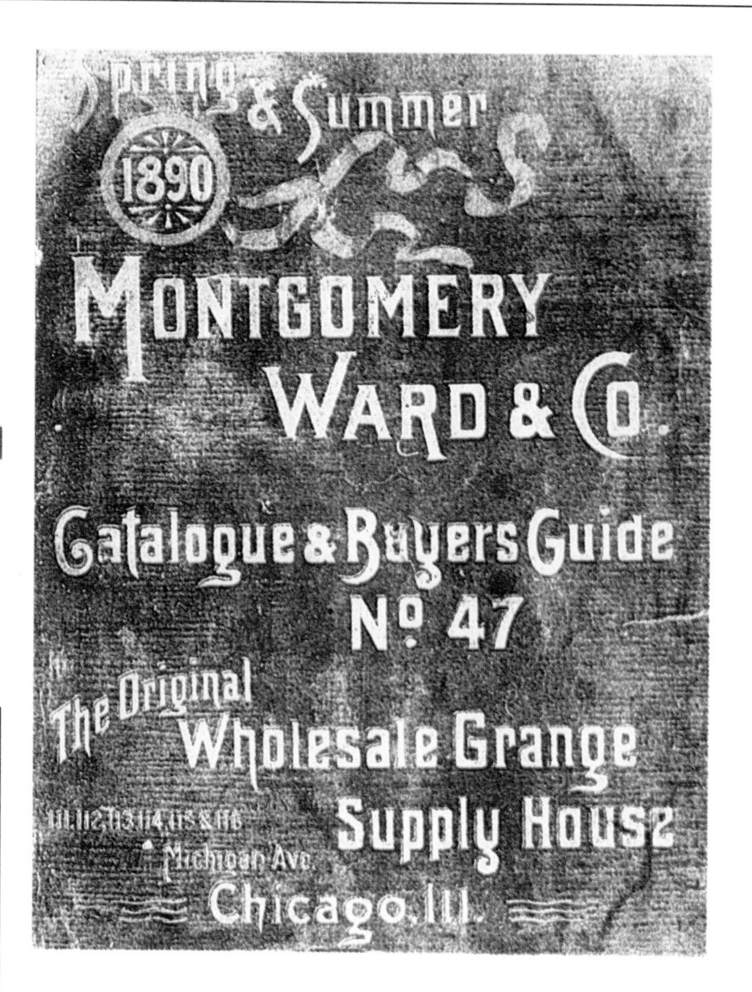

MARKETING BRIEF

Hospital Chain Uses Direct Marketing

HCA West, a hospital chain, has successfully used direct marketing to maintain market share for 13 of its hospitals, while its competitors have faced declining admissions and deep financial trouble. In an innovative move, HCA sent a mailing to 250,000 residents in an area from Alabama to Utah, with each containing six promotional pieces, including a form that consumers could use to preregister with a local HCA hospital.

Once registered, the people are sent a plastic credit-type card to expedite admission, either to an emergency room or for a scheduled stay. The envelopes also contained useful information on drug/food interaction and 10 tips on stress management.

SOURCE: Adapted from Julie Franz, "Rx for Hospitals: Targeted Information Mailings," *Advertising Age* 54, no. 50 (November 28, 1983): M–48.

Ward and Sears ushered in the modern era of direct marketing. While initiated over 100 years ago, this marketing form has experienced tremendous growth over the past two decades. Companies large and small and dealing in all types of merchandise (even perfumes, such as Giorgio Parfum, Inc.) are discovering that direct marketing is useful to either supplement or substitute for traditional ways of doing business.

One source defines **direct marketing** as: "Direct marketing is the total of activities by which products and services are offered to market segments in one or more media for informational purposes or to solicit a direct response from a present or prospective customer or contributor by mail, telephone, or other access."[2]

Direct marketing can include **direct distribution,** where a producer sells to customers directly (such as when Whirlpool sells directly to Sears without using wholesalers), and direct mail, where products are ordered through a catalog or other means and shipped to customers directly. Both of these are parts of direct marketing, but they by no means represent the whole field. Direct marketing is a broad activity that involves many media and activities. Further, it is a dynamic field, adapting rapidly as media evolve into new forms,[3] and it embraces many different industries.[4] Even hospitals, such as HCA West, have benefited from using direct marketing (see the accompanying Marketing Brief).

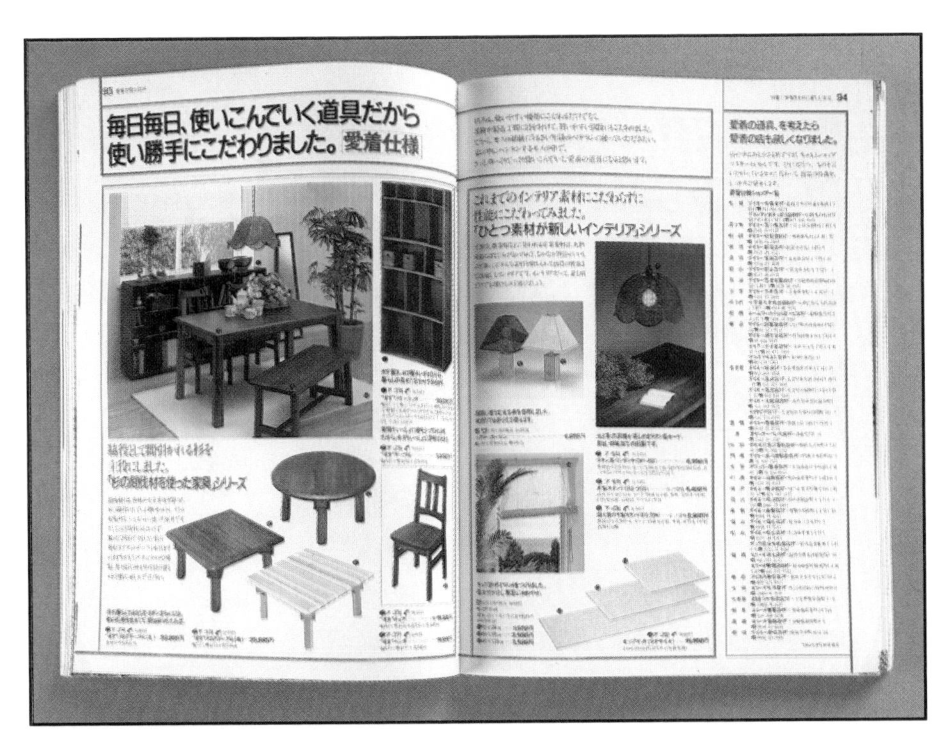

Catalogs are very popular around the world.

Scope of Direct Marketing

A large and growing number of companies are involved with direct marketing. While a complete list is not available, there are about 2,400 company members of the Direct Mail/Marketing Association, Inc.[5] In total, there are probably about five to six thousand firms associated with this field, and the number is growing each year. Overall, it has been estimated that the total dollar amount of goods and services purchased in the U.S. through direct marketing is over $100 billion.[6]

At one time or another, almost all businesses and civic, political, religious, and other organizations use direct marketing in some manner.[7] Many small businesses rely on direct marketing. But as the examples of Sears and Spiegel attest, this form of marketing is by no means limited to small companies.

Direct marketing exists, in one form or another, in every country around the globe. Fingerhut, Inc., the largest direct mail distributor in the world, sells a wide variety of goods in the United States, Canada, Europe, and Asia. Direct marketing is about a $2.5 billion industry in Japan, with department stores generating about 20 percent of the total.[8]

As with any human activity, the unscrupulous have used direct marketing to deceive consumers. Some fly-by-night operators have been involved, selling substandard or nonexistent goods. According to Jonah Gitlitz, president of the Direct Marketing Association (DMA), the industry must counter the "few disreputable companies (that) are a blight on any business and are capable of doing great harm." [9] In this regard, the DMA is working closely with the U.S. Office of Consumer Affairs, the National Association of Consumer Agency Administrators, and the Special Advisor to the President of the U.S. on Consumer Affairs to resolve this problem.

Still, most direct marketing firms are very reputable. This is evidenced by the statistics: about 40 percent of the population buys at least some items from direct marketers on a repeat basis.[10]

Direct marketing
The total of activities by which products and services are offered to market segments in one or more media for informational purposes or to solicit a direct response from a present or prospective customer or contributor by mail, telephone, or other access.

Direct distribution
A producer that sells its output to final customers with no intermediaries involved.

Exhibit 18.1
Representative Companies in Direct Response Marketing

Consumer Books & Magazines
American Heritage Publishing Co., Inc.
Better Homes & Gardens
Book-of-the-Month Club, Inc.
Encyclopaedia Britannica
Harper's Magazine
Ms. Magazine
Newsweek
New York Magazine
The Reader's Digest Association, Inc.
Southern Living
Sports Illustrated
Time-Life Books, Inc.
U.S. News & World Report

Business Books, Magazines, & Services
American Management Associations
Barron's
The Dreyfus Corp.
Fortune
Harvard Business Review
Merrill Lynch Pierce Fenner & Smith
Money Magazine
Wall Street Journal

Consumer Catalogs & Merchandise
Aldens
Collector's Guild, Ltd.
Fingerhut Corp.
The Franklin Mint
Hallmark Cards
The King Size Co.
L. L. Bean, Inc.
J. C. Penney
RCA Records
Spencer Gifts
Spiegel

Business Merchandise
Baldwin-Cooke Co.
Commercial Optical Co.
Elin Uniform Manufacturing Co.
Jensen Tools and Alloys
Pitney Bowes, Inc.
Weber Marking Systems
Xerox Corporation

Specialty Foods
Alamo Fruit, Inc.
House of Almonds
Omaha Steaks International
Swiss Colony
Wisconsin Cheesemakers Guild

Credit Cards
American Express
Carte Blanche
Diners Club
Gulf Oil Co.
Master Charge/InterBank
Mobil Oil Co.
VISA

Trade & Professional Associations
AFL-CIO
Aircraft Owners & Pilots Assn.
American Bar Association
Democratic National Committee
National Restaurant Association
Republican National Committee

Civic, Charitable, & Other Groups
A.S.P.C.A.
Alaska Division of Tourism
American Civil Liberties Union
American Foundation for the Blind, Inc.
Billy Graham Evangelistic Association
Boys' Clubs of America
CARE, Inc.
Disabled American Veterans
Fordham University
National Geographic Society
Public Broadcasting System
Salvation Army
Save the Children Federation
Smithsonian Magazine

Industrial Companies
American Airlines
American Telephone & Telegraph Co.
Bell & Howell
Colgate-Palmolive Co.
Dow Chemical
E.I. duPont de Nemours and Co., Inc.
GTE/Sylvania
Gillette
International Business Machines Corp.
Stauffer Chemical Co.
Texaco
Union Carbide
United Steel Corp.

Insurance
Bankers Life & Casualty Co.
Commercial Travelers Mutual Insurance Co.
Mutual of Omaha
National Liberty Marketing, Inc.
United Equitable Life Insurance Co.

The types of merchandise and services which direct marketers offer is quite varied. The Franklin Mint specializes in collectible coins and plaques. The Book-of-the-Month Club specializes in books. Sears has a general catalog of over 1,000 pages of full-line merchandise, and L. L. Bean focuses upon clothing and outdoor items. Exhibit 18.1 presents a representative list of well-known firms that are involved in direct marketing.

Another measure of direct marketing's magnitude is evident in Figure 18.1, which compares direct marketing advertising expenditures for 1979 and 1983 (the most current categorical data available). As is evident, advertising expenditures are the greatest in the direct mail and telephone categories. Another indicator is the growth in the use of advertising agencies. In total, direct marketers spent over $2 billion in advertising with ad agencies that handle direct marketing during 1985—a 32 percent increase over the previous year.[11] Figure 18.2 depicts direct marketing gross billing comparisons for 1985 and 1984 for ad agencies that specialize in direct marketing and those that also handle other types of accounts.

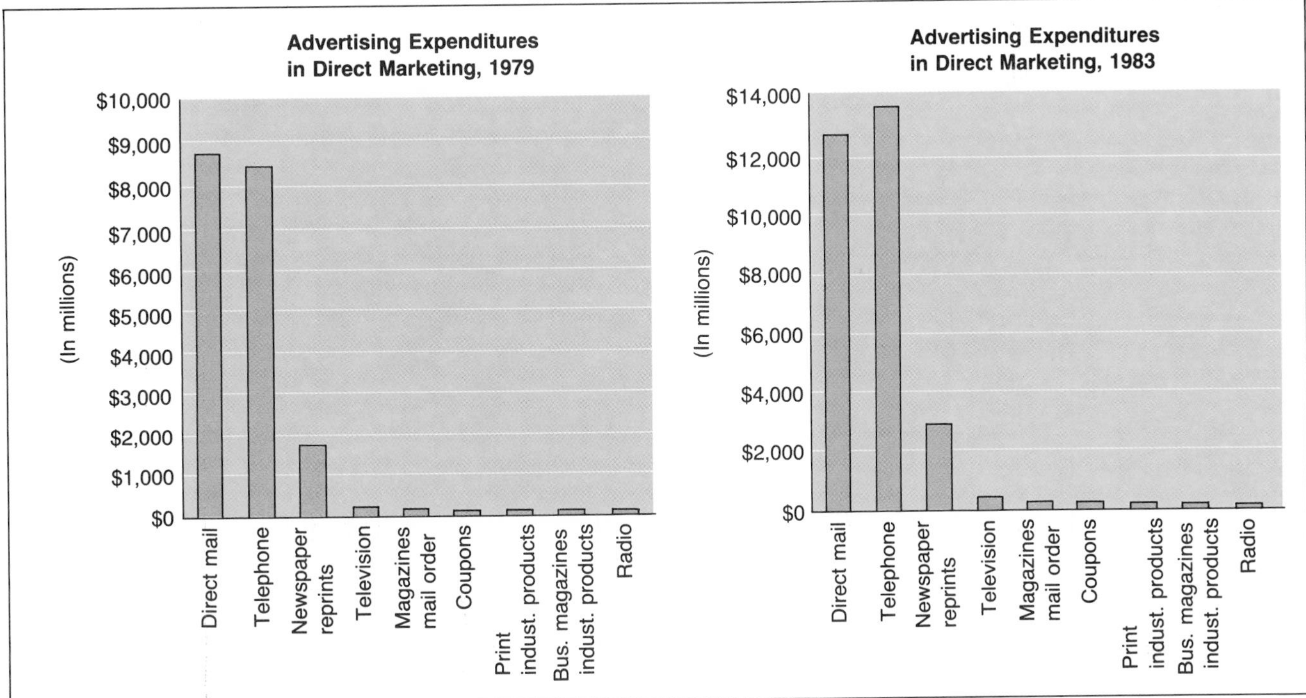

Figure 18.1
Relationships of Advertising Expenditures in Direct Marketing Categories (SOURCE: Adapted from *1981 Fact Book on Direct Response Marketing (Statistical Update)* (New York: The Direct Mail/Marketing Association, Inc., 1981); and "Direct Marketers Outline Goals, Troubles," *Advertising Age* 55, no. 17 (April 16, 1984): M–10.)

Direct marketers have not been assured of success by any means, as illustrated in the accompanying Videotex Marketing Brief. But many direct marketing companies have experienced explosive growth over the past decade, with overall revenues from direct marketing expanding by as much as 16 times during the period.[12] For instance, Chicago Health Clubs—a division of Bally Manufacturing—recently generated renewed interest in its otherwise stagnant health club business in Chicago with a direct marketing campaign aimed at corporate executives. Featuring 12,000 direct mailings with each containing a pair of men's size 60 undershorts and a printed story of "how to reduce corporate waist," the campaign was successful in generating a 5 percent positive response rate, with each new membership costing between $400 and $500.[13]

Direct marketing is different from other marketing forms. According to one source, there are four key factors that distinguish this field from others.[14]

1. *Advertising and selling are combined.* With direct marketing, advertising and sales functions both are covered in a single ad, mailing, or commercial.
2. *Built-in results feedback.* Reply cards, coupons, and phone calls provide a built-in means of measuring every element of a marketing program.
3. *Services add to product value.* Free home trials, delivery to the door, and other services add value to the total product offering.
4. *Action-oriented for impulse sales.* Impulse purchases can be stimulated when needs arise; placing an immediate order is made easy.

While direct marketing uses many of the principles of other marketing forms, these differences cause many to think of it as a new marketing discipline.[15]

Figure 18.2
1985 and 1984 Billings of Direct Marketing Advertising Agencies
(SOURCE: Adapted from Paul L. Edwards, "Links with General Shops Boosts DM Agency Billings," *Advertising Age* (March 24, 1986): 100.)

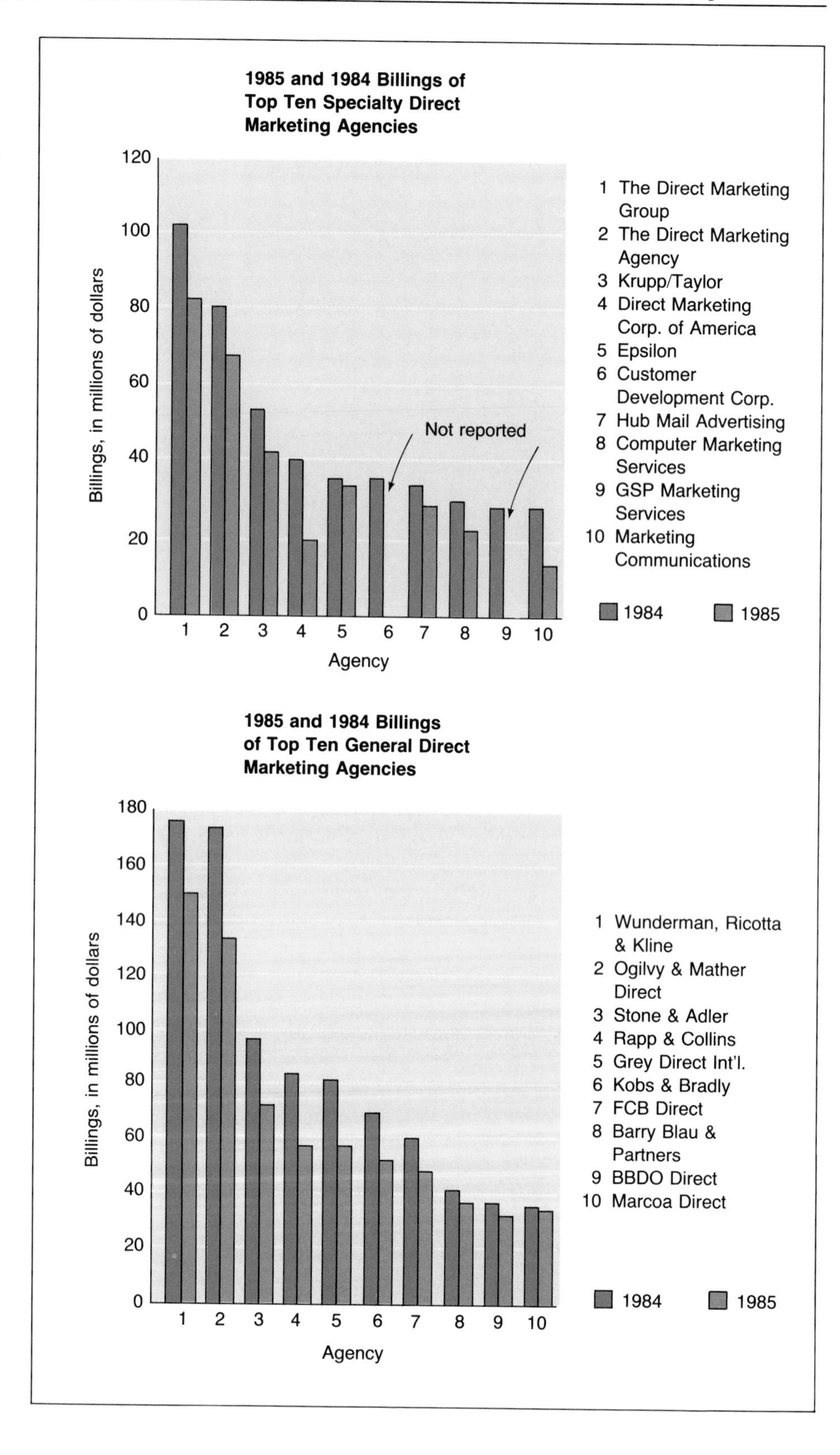

MARKETING BRIEF

Despite Promise, Videotex Fails to Materialize

In 1983, videotex—computerized electronic banking and shopping—was heralded as the most promising new direct marketing vehicle since the catalog. Some even said that it would rewrite the rules of the field. The system had considerable capability and appeal. Enabling individuals to handle nearly all of their banking needs with their home computers, the system also allowed electronic catalog shopping from home and provided several free video games to play as well.

Several heavyweight media and high-tech companies began to pour millions into market tests, confident that the pot of gold lay at the end of the videotex rainbow. While these companies bit the dust quickly, newer and even stronger firms entered the market. By 1986 none of them had earned any money, with most pulling out as wounded casualties.

Miami-based Knight Ridder folded its $50 million Viewtron service in March of 1986, which it had launched in three South Florida counties in late 1983. Initially requiring users to pay $600 for the terminals plus a $35 per month subscription fee, the charge was cut to a flat $40 per month within months. Prior to withdrawal, the company tried to sell the service nationwide to 250,000 owners of personal computers, but only achieved a 10 percent penetration. Los Angeles-based Times Mirror scrapped its Gateway videotex service in the same month at an estimated cost of more than $15 million. Charging users $29.95 a month, Gateway only attained 3,000 customers, far shy of the company's stated goal of 60,000 to 400,000. Other videotex systems were suffering similar setbacks, but those remaining in the game, such as New York-based Trintex, a venture between CBS, IBM, and Sears, Roebuck, expressed resolve to hang on for the long run and evolving growth.

SOURCE: Adapted from Brian Moran, "Videotex Continues to Be Hostile Frontier," *Advertising Age*, March 24, 1986: 4, 119; and "Brighter Picture Is Appearing for Business Videotex," *Communications News* 22 (August 1985): 42–46.

While videotex systems have not yet lived up to expectations, many people feel that they face a strong future.

The Causes of Direct Marketing Growth

Several factors have affected direct marketing's increasing popularity. These involve marketing to both consumers and institutional buyers. For consumers, two forces—demographic shifts and changing attitudes—have made direct marketing increasingly popular and this trend will likely continue.

Women in the labor force. As Figure 18.3 illustrates, about 50 percent of all adult women are now in the labor force, turning their attention away from shopping, which is a time-consuming activity.

Rising affluence. Closely related is a rise in household income, as pictured in Figure 18.4, which places a premium on convenience and specialty items, both of which are especially suited to direct marketing.

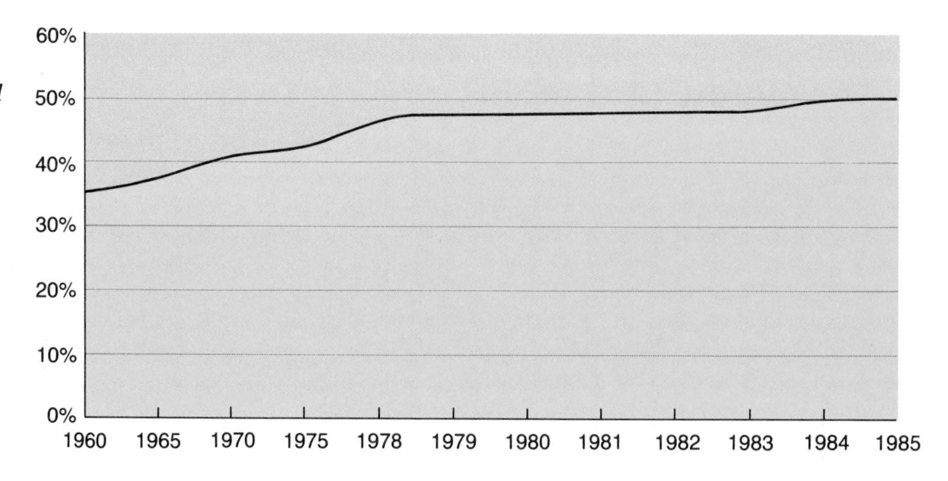

Figure 18.3
Percent of Women in the Work Force, 1960–1985 (SOURCE: From *Statistical Abstract of the United States* (Washington, D.C.: U.S. Government Printing Office, 1986), 106th ed.)

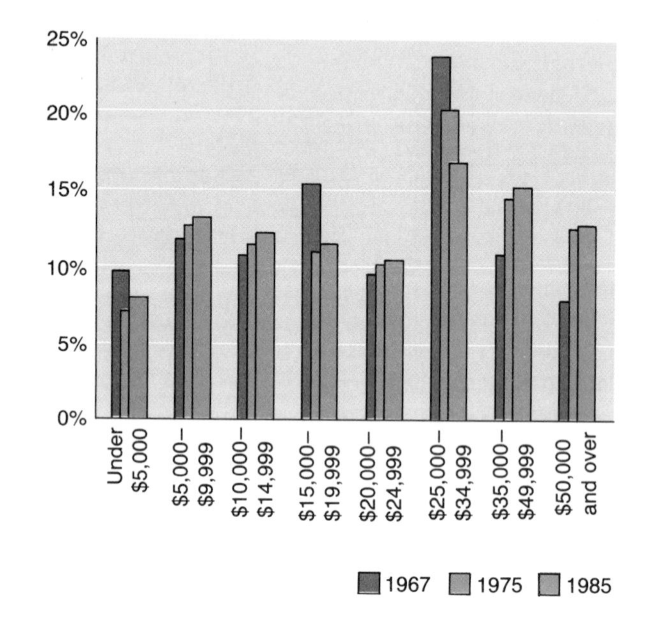

Figure 18.4
Percent Distribution of Household Income for Selected Years, in Constant 1984 Dollars (SOURCE: Adapted from *Statistical Abstract of the United States* (Washington, D.C.: U.S. Government Printing Office, 1986), 106th ed.)

Rising education. The number of college-educated adults in the U.S. has nearly doubled in the past 15 years. Direct marketers generally target on better-educated market segments.[16]

The aging of the population. The "Graying of America" has an effect. Currently the 50+ age group accounts for about 27 percent of the population and will grow to more than 30 percent by the year 2000. Discretionary incomes rise as people age, which favors the buying of specialty items.

The move away from large cities. There is a population trend toward smaller towns, especially in the sunbelt and northeastern states, and away from large cities. Direct marketing offers consumers a greater choice in these locations.

Direct marketing is perceived to be an attractive option to in-store shopping. Studies show that at least a third of all people who buy items by mail do so because of the convenience and variety available.[17]

Consumers open and read nearly two-thirds of the direct marketing literature sent to them, and about a half of the population want to receive such material.[18]

The popularity of direct marketing is also increasing among institutional buyers. Total direct marketing sales to these buyers has been increasing by over 15 percent per year since the mid-1970s.[19]

There are several reasons for the increase. For one, studies indicate that two-thirds of the executive group find that direct marketing is time-saving and efficient and it generates high recall rates among buyers. For another, the cost of alternatives favors direct marketing. To illustrate, the cost of an industrial sales call was about $230 in 1985.[20] In contrast, the cost of an average business letter is around $6.[21] This means that a direct marketer can contact about 38 customers for every 1 contacted by a salesperson.

Direct Marketing Media

Essentially, direct marketers use one or more of six types of media. These are direct mail, catalogs, magazines, newspapers, radio and television, and telephone.

Direct Mail

With **direct mail,** some form of printed material is sent through the mail to a group of prospects. Many organizations, large and small, use this technique for both consumer and industrial items. The advent of word processors and automated letter addressers has enabled the efficient preparation of standardized letters that appear to be individually designed. There are three general types available: traditional format, self-mailer, and the catalog.

Direct mail
Where products are ordered through a catalog or other form of advertising media and shipped to the customer by mail.

In a *traditional* format, the marketer sends letters, brochures, samples, and other material. The 3M Company, for instance, distributes a brochure describing 3M's products with audio-visual applications. Metropolitan Life provides an emergency first aid chart that will adhere to a wall or cabinet. There are a number of articles that can be enclosed, including tokens, pop-ups, simulated telegrams, and stamps—virtually anything that an envelope will hold. This is a very versatile format, which makes it widely used.

The *self-mailer* format uses a combination letter and envelope, where the letter is folded and the address placed on its backside. These tend to be less costly and less versatile than the traditional format variety.

Finally, *catalog* formats constitute soft-cover books ranging from a few to several hundred pages in length. Catalogs are considered later in this chapter.

The **mailing list** used is a vital ingredient in a direct mail program.[22] If it does not adequately cover the right grouping of target customers, is dated (some lists contain incorrect addresses and names of deceased people), or contains other similar defects, an entire direct mail campaign may be doomed.

Mailing list
List containing names and addresses of individuals who are to receive direct mail.

One good mailing list source is company records of past customers. Allstate, for example, ran a very effective campaign for its new motor club by sending brochures as billing inserts to its auto insurance customers.[23] Another source is from one of many outside organizations that provide lists for a fee. **Mailing list brokers** are companies that specialize in renting such lists. Most can provide specialized categories of customers. The MMS company, for instance, provides lists of medical personnel, such as AMA physicians, dentists, and medical students. Another, Direct Media, Inc.,

Mailing list brokers
Specialists in renting mailing lists.

Mailing list brokers can provide lists of names for almost any group of interest.

specializes in business lists. Lists may also be built from city directories, telephone books, auto registrations, and trade association membership directories.

Merge/purge
Combining two mailing lists and eliminating duplicated names.

In an effort to improve lists, some companies use "**merge/purge.**" This procedure involves computer analysis of several lists to eliminate, or "purge" any duplications.[24]

Direct mail marketers soon learn that a key success ingredient is the production of the mailing pieces.[25] Good relations with vendors and keeping good records on competitive costs of printing, mailing, and other services aid in keeping expenses down. Getting quotes from at least three printers is useful in this regard. Savings also result from a careful choice of paper, using two rather than three or four colors, and sometimes the direct purchase of paper stock.

Advantages The use of direct mail offers several advantages. Mailings can be custom-designed for each prospect and management can be very selective about who receives them. This means that focused targeting is possible. For example, the U.S. Army directs its recruiting toward high school juniors, seniors, recent graduates, and college students. This generates about a half million prospects from the 18 million pieces of literature sent out each year.[26] While a mammoth job, the direct marketing approach minimizes wasted circulation to the wrong groups.

Direct mail also tends to monopolize the reader's attention. People open mail with the intention of reading the contents. This is not the case with TV or radio, for example, where the audience often ignores commercials. To further grab attention, several direct marketers offer free premiums or free trial offers. For industrial goods, free cost estimates, free surveys of need, free technical service bulletins, and free newsletters have been effective.[27]

Direct mail is very flexible. Marketers can use only one page or a full booklet. Interested prospects may even read very long copy. Choices can be made of color, formats, headlines, and other features. Deliveries can also be made through the U.S. Postal Service or through private carriers such as United Parcel Service (UPS).

Disadvantages Some people view mailings as "junk mail" and summarily trash whatever direct mail they receive. This is becoming an increasing problem as direct marketers proliferate, with some of them indiscriminately sending mail (often addressed to "occupant"), causing many people, especially high-income professionals, to receive an irritating volume.[28] Nonetheless, a surprisingly large number of people read direct mail, even busy professionals such as medical doctors.[29]

Increases in postage rates have also had a major impact on the cost of this medium. In 1983, for instance, mailers had expected a 10 percent to 15 percent increase in rates but were hit with a 21.9 percent boost. Additional rate increases are likely in the future. Finally, some people are reluctant to order products without first examining them.[30]

Catalogs

Catalogs are another very popular direct marketing medium. Many consumers and institutions buy from them.[31] Social phenomena such as working wives, a desire for convenience, and congested streets and highways promote their use. Many successful catalogs serve a well-defined target market. For example, Bissell Healthcare directs its catalogs to over 70,000 disabled individuals, therapists, and other health care professionals. It sells a variety of personal care, self-help products, including dressing aids and kitchen utensils.[32]

Considerable skill is required in designing the physical elements of a catalog: the overall layout, cover, photography, and design. This is no task for the uninitiated and can make the difference between success and failure. Further, the copy must be well-executed—it must be descriptive, interest-inspiring, and creative.

An important question is, "Who should be furnished with a catalog?" If management has not properly defined the target customer, and the cost of producing and distributing the catalogs is small, then the firm might consider mass mailings. In general, however, marketers need to exercise a degree of selectivity to effectively manage the associated costs.

There are three general types of catalogs: wide-line catalogs, retail catalogs, and specialty catalogs.

Wide-line catalogs offer goods in numerous product lines. Large department stores, such as Sears and J. C. Penney issue them. Among the typical services are liberal credit and return policies and strong guarantees. These publications are very costly to produce and, as a result, the marketers usually provide them free of charge only to past customers who have purchases more than a given minimum volume.

Retail catalogs are similar to the wide-line variety except that the diversity of product offerings is less. Some retailers who issue them are Hallmark (cards), Neiman-Marcus, and Dayton-Hudson. The catalogs generate in-store traffic and also build telephone and mail-order sales outside of the trading area. Retailers whose sales are declining often can reverse this trend through the use of catalogs.

Specialty catalogs cover only a limited line of products, such as home renovation supplies. Some very small businesses (literally operating out of their owners' garages) employ catalogs to sell items such as automobile accessories, stamps, gifts, antiques, seeds, and greeting cards. This segment of the industry had been growing very rapidly.

Sears is one company that maintains several specialty catalogs for distinctive market segments.

Advantages and Disadvantages Catalogs tend to be very popular with buyers.[33, 34] Consumers like catalogs because they make shopping trips unnecessary, often carry a wide range of goods, offer strong guarantees, and (in some cases) allow products to be purchased at low prices. Further, catalog narrative and illustrations can describe products in depth. This is especially important to many industrial buyers. In addition, attractively designed catalogs can carry the image of fashion and quality.

There are certain disadvantages to the use of catalogs. One is that these publications can be very costly to produce and (if they are bulky or heavy) to mail. Another is that it is usually expensive to change catalog copy when management desires product or price changes.

Magazines

Many direct marketers use magazines. The medium reaches many consumers and institutional buyers, and has considerable credibility among them.

An important factor to consider when choosing a magazine is its readership—does it coincide with the marketer's target? There are several other critical issues, including:

- *Scheduling*—when and how often should the ads be inserted? The answer is obvious in some cases, such as for seasonal and gift items. But the timing question is more difficult to answer in other cases and may require considerable study.
- *Ad size*—how large should the ad be? Full page ads attract the most attention but are expensive.
- *Positioning*—the placement of an ad in a magazine has an effect on the results. Ads placed near the front and near editorials usually generate the best response, but a tradeoff is required as costs vary with placement.

MARKETING BRIEF

Postal Service Rate Judgment Provides Reprieve for Color Strips

Color strips, the cosmetic industry's answer to the fragrance industry's scent strips, were given a reprieve in April 1986 by a rate ruling by the U.S. Postal Service. Webcraft, Inc., developed the rub-off eye shadow strip inserts that can be used in magazines as samples of eye shadows. The strips can be rubbed off by consumers and used to try various eye colorings. Industry officials hope that the strips will be similar to the scratch-and-sniff strips used by fragrance makers; already Chanel, Christian Dior, and L'Oreal are lined up to use them.

In a postage rate ruling last month, the USPS declared that the strips were actually samples instead of advertising, as is the ruling with the scratch-and-sniff strips. As a result of the former ruling, any magazine using them would have had to pay the third-class postage rates instead of the much cheaper second-class rates. While the strips could still have been used as in-store pull-offs, the postage rate ruling would have increased costs to the point that they would have become prohibitive for use in magazines.

But the reversal on rates—allowing the strips to be considered advertising—has put them back on track in the plans of cosmetic firms that want to put their messages across to consumers through magazine ads. Under the ruling, all of the inserts will have to bear the message: "This is not a product sample but a facsimile or replica of the product, [or words to that effect]" said Scott Hamel, general manager, Postal Service Mail Classification Division. However, plans were also underway to use the color strips for other purposes, such as disposable cosmetics kits that can be used while traveling or dispensed from hotel rooms. "If the color strips are to be distributed and sold or given away like a normal product," said Mr. Hamel, "the USPS would have to take another look at the rate classification on the strips. Samples are not eligible for the favored rate treatment."

SOURCE: Adapted from Pat Sloan, "USPS Reverses Ruling on Color-Strip Use," *Advertising Age*, April 14, 1986: 40; and "USPS Casts Shadow on Color Strips," *Advertising Age*, March 24, 1986: 6.

Besides major general audience magazines, such as *Time*, and *Newsweek*, there are many specialized magazines that reach focused audiences. Examples include the *Ice Cream Journal*, *Water and Waste Digest*, *Working Mother*, *World Tennis*, and *Seventeen*. Several of these have regional editions, permitting targeting on certain geographical locations, but their ad rates tend to be higher with fewer ad placement choices possible.[35]

Card inserts that appear between two magazine pages can be very effective in gaining readers' attention, but as the Postal Service Marketing Brief illustrates, marketers must be careful not to cause postal rates to increase as a result of the inserts.

Magazine copy must be chosen carefully. For example, this sentence appeared in an ad for expensive timepieces: "Gent's two-toned bracelet watch $850.00." The term "gent's" stems from the 1930s and suggests images of old barbershops and spats. It was inappropriate to use for a modern and expensive watch and the resulting sales were abysmal.[36]

Advantages and Disadvantages On the plus side, magazines are capable of reaching many potential buyers, frequently at a reasonable cost. The reproduction quality of many magazines is quite good and they tend to be read, often by multiple consumers at a leisurely pace. Also, magazine ad rates have traditionally increased more slowly than other media.[37]

Many types of products are direct marketed.

Magazines also have their drawbacks. In the case of large-circulation volumes such as *Reader's Digest* and *Time*, advertising is very expensive. Some magazines have long lead times (periods between the submission of the ad copy and the time it appears in print). Further, most magazines are not well suited for reaching local markets such as only one city or trading area. Also, many magazines have lost readership in recent periods, particularly sales of newsstand copies.[38]

Newspapers

Newspapers may be very useful as a medium for reaching masses of people, particularly within a localized area. The medium is flexible in several ways, offering marketers the choice of display and classified advertising. Many papers also offer the use of supplements for advertising messages. Syndicated supplements, such as *Parade*, are useful carriers of ads to national markets. These essentially are magazines and are treated as such.

When the marketer wants consumers to read advertisements in the near future, newspapers can be a valuable medium. Most people read them within a day or two of printing, unlike magazines, which they may not read for some time.

Advantages and Disadvantages Newspapers are useful in extensively covering local markets. Many households subscribe to a newspaper and often several household members read its contents. Because the rates for space are relatively low, the cost per contact is often below that of other printed media. The medium also has a relatively short lead time, enabling new information such as changes in prices to be announced quickly.

There are various disadvantages to the use of newspapers. Direct marketers with a national market may choose not to use them because most represent only local coverage (with a few exceptions such as *USA Today* and *The Wall Street Journal*). Also the reproduction quality is not as good as that available in most magazines, catalogs, and direct mail. Finally, most newspapers are filled with advertising, which lowers the perceptibility and impact of any single insertion.

Radio and Television

Direct marketing through radio and television is rapidly growing. Many organizations use these media to sell products such as facial cream, albums and tapes, cookware, and cutlery. They are also used to develop subscribers to ideas and services, such as Garner Ted Armstrong and his religious programs.

Sometimes marketers use TV and radio to develop inquiries by asking people to call or write for information. In other cases, the intent is to directly sell a product.

The process of selecting particular stations and time slots to use is the same as that involved in choosing all advertising media, as described in Chapter 16.

Advantages and Disadvantages Television and radio reach most homes in the United States. By selecting approximate times of day, programming, and stations, advertisers can hit desired target consumers and minimize wasted circulation. One organization has even formed a radio network (Children's Radio Network) devoted entirely to preteens.[39] In addition, television has prestige value to most consumers and it appeals to both the senses of sight and sound. Each medium can reach either national or local markets.

The major disadvantage of television is its high cost, making it impractical for many small direct marketers. Radio is considerably less expensive. Further, lead times tend to be long for television, but not so long for radio. The message for both media is not as permanent as in the case with catalogs, magazines, and newspapers. Radio, of course, is not effective when a firm needs to present visual messages.

Direct Marketers Even Sell Hamburgers

White Castle System, a Columbus, Ohio-based fast-food chain that sells tiny square 28-cent hamburgers, introduced a national 24-hour telemarketing service in 1983. By calling 1-800-WCASTLE, consumers as far away as Albuquerque, New Mexico (an order of 125,000) and Fountain Hills, Arizona (an order of 10,000 for a chamber of commerce fundraising event) have ordered the burgers, which arrive packed in dry ice.

Management speculated that transplanted Midwesterners, who had bestowed a cult status on the unique hamburgers (affectionately called "sliders" by locals), caused the surge in orders. The telemarketing service generated about 10,000 units per week in the mid-1980s.

SOURCE: Adapted from "Telemarket Drive Nets Meaty Sales for Burger Chain," *The Marketing News* 17, no. 24, Sec. 2 (November 25, 1983): 28; and "Restaurants Take to the Road in Pursuit of New Customers," *The Wall Street Journal*, October 24, 1985: 35.

Telephone (Telemarketing)

The use of telephones for direct marketing, called **telemarketing,** has bloomed in recent years. Total expenditures exceed those for all other direct marketing media (although, the dollars are difficult to interpret because they include the cost of 800 numbers). A separate trade association, the American Telemarketing Association (ATA), is a group that serves as the industry's spokesman, code of ethics champion, and standard bearer.

Technological developments, the high cost of sales force travel, and the flexibility of this medium have promoted its growth. Often, marketers use the telephone in conjunction with other media, as when salespeople call prospects who inquire about a product by mail.[40] To illustrate, several firms use a combination of ads, catalogs, and toll-free phone numbers to sell liquor and wine to virtually every region of the country. An extensive network of affiliated liquor distributors fill the orders that the direct marketers receive. Tele-Wine, Inc., for instance, has been in business for seven years and has a network of 17,000 associated retailers. White Castle, a midwestern and eastern hamburger chain, is another company that has successfully used telemarketing.

Careful selection and training of people who do selling by telephone is essential. Many telephone companies offer free or low-cost instruction programs in telemarketing that can be useful. Some of the tips are listed below.[41]

- Engage in active listening—don't talk too much
- Avoid a high voice pitch
- Practice clear enunciation
- Avoid talking too fast
- Avoid talking with gum, cigarettes, etc., in the mouth
- Smile while talking with customers—this is reflected in the voice tone
- Avoid monotone speaking
- Be well prepared with facts
- Avoid arguing

Some telephone messages are recorded to enable detailed preparation. These may be introduced by a live individual, who informs the customer that a taped message will follow, often from a prominent person. After the tape, the salesperson takes over to close the sale. Several specialized companies also offer their telemarketing services to other firms. An example is WATS Marketing of America, Inc., an affiliate of American Express. These telemarketers have equipment and specialized personnel that their clients do not possess.

Telemarketing
The use of telephones for direct marketing.

Advantages and Disadvantages Centrally located telephoning enables contacting customers who are located many miles from a sales office, prospecting for sales leads, taking orders directly, following up on direct mail programs, and handling inquiries—all at a relatively low cost. Messages may be personalized for particular customers and immediate feedback is possible. Telephones are very effective in persuading people to purchase. Prospects can easily discard a direct mail piece or ignore a commercial, but find that it is more difficult to ignore a telephone call. Further, marketers can deliver messages at the exact time desired.

This medium has its disadvantages. It can be costly (although telephone line services such as AT&T's WATS and Sprint tend to decrease the cost). Some consumers view sales calls as irritants or invaders of privacy.[42] It also is difficult to convey some complex messages over the phone.

The Future of Direct Marketing

The future of direct marketing looks very positive. Continuance of the social trends discussed earlier will undoubtedly increase the size of direct marketing's key segments. Also, the continuing rising cost of direct sales calls will also increase the comparative efficiency to industrial sellers.

Several technological developments are also likely to spur the growth of this field. The following are among the more significant of these.

Electronic funds transfer. Increasing availability of funds to consumers will enhance consumer buying convenience and further simplify the transaction process.

Printing technology. Improvements in computerized typesetting, electronic image processing, and laser printers will enable more elaborate, individualized, and more efficient printed and electronic messages by direct marketers.

Computers. Advances in computer technology, such as elaborate data base networks and communications, will enable access to far greater stocks of goods, people, shipping modes, and information processing, which will greatly expand the effectiveness of this form of marketing.

In many respects, direct marketing may represent the wave of the future for many companies. All marketers should keep abreast of these developments.

Chapter Summary

This chapter examined direct marketing, a rapidly growing marketing area. Many factors account for this, especially changing lifestyles, affluence, and instantaneous communications. Thus, social and economic trends favor the further emergence of this field, which will likely increase its challenge to more traditional means of distribution.

The chapter also looked at the major media used by direct marketers.

Direct mail is a personalized medium. It is very selective, and monopolizes reader attention. It is very flexible, but it is unread by some recipients. Postage advances increase costs. As more firms use it, clutter is produced and it loses credibility and interest value. Some consumers are reluctant to order merchandise without first examining it.

Catalogs make shopping trips unnecessary and carry a wide range of goods. Usually they offer strong guarantees and sometimes low prices and can offer a very wide or a very narrow product line. Products can be described very precisely and in depth. Catalogs can carry an image of fashion and quality. They are very costly to produce and mail, and it is costly to change catalog copy.

Magazines can reach large numbers of customers, often at a reasonable cost. Reproduction quality can be very good and the medium offers targeting to a particular readership. Magazines are read and reread, often by several different readers and at a leisurely pace. Rates have increased slowly, but can be quite expensive. Some have long lead times. Magazines usually are not suited for local markets.

Newspapers extensively cover local markets. Most consumers are exposed to them and cost per contact is low. They are more permanent than broadcast media but less permanent than magazines. Newspapers offer a short lead time. Generally they are not suited for national markets, and reproduction quality is low.

Radio and television reach most homes. Advertisers can be selective. TV has prestige value and considerable impact, appealing to many senses, and can reach both national and local markets. But TV is costly and often requires long lead times. Messages are not permanent. Radio is far less expensive and requires shorter lead times, but is limited in effect due to the lack of visual stimuli.

Telephone sales can personalize messages. Immediate feedback is possible and it is difficult to ignore. Telemarketing is a potentially persuasive medium. It can be delivered at the exact time and to whom desired, but can be quite costly. Some prospects are irritated by calls, and it is difficult to convey complex messages by telephone.

Finally, the chapter considered the future of direct marketing, which looks very bright.

Questions

1. Define direct marketing, using your own words. How does it differ from direct distribution?
2. "All organizations use direct marketing." Comment.
3. In what ways do the following use direct marketing?
   a. The United States Army
   b. Churches
   c. Sears, Roebuck and Company
   d. Book-of-the-Month Club
4. Identify a business in the local community that uses direct marketing. Why do you suppose that the business decided to utilize this strategy?
5. What are the major factors contributing to the growth of direct marketing?
6. Outline the major advantages and disadvantages of utilizing direct mail.
7. How can a marketer obtain a good mailing list?
8. What are the major decisions that marketers must make when they utilize catalogs?
9. Why would a direct marketer elect to utilize magazines to carry promotion messages?
10. What are the major advantages of using radio and television in direct marketing endeavors?
11. What is the future of direct marketing, in your opinion? Substantiate your position.

Chapter 19

Pricing Decisions: Price Theory, Marketing Objectives, and Cost- and Competition-Based Strategies

Objectives

After reading this chapter, you should be able to demonstrate a knowledge of:

- The importance of pricing to the marketing success of a good or service
- Essentials of price theory, centering around marginal analysis
- The concepts of marginal and total revenue and of price elasticity
- Types of costs and their behavior
- Various objectives used by marketers when setting prices
- Cost-based pricing strategies, including markup pricing, cost-plus pricing, target return (on investment) pricing, and payback period pricing
- Competition-based pricing strategies based on existing market rates and competitive bid pricing

MARKETING SUCCESS

Specialty Farmers Command Premium Prices for Their Products

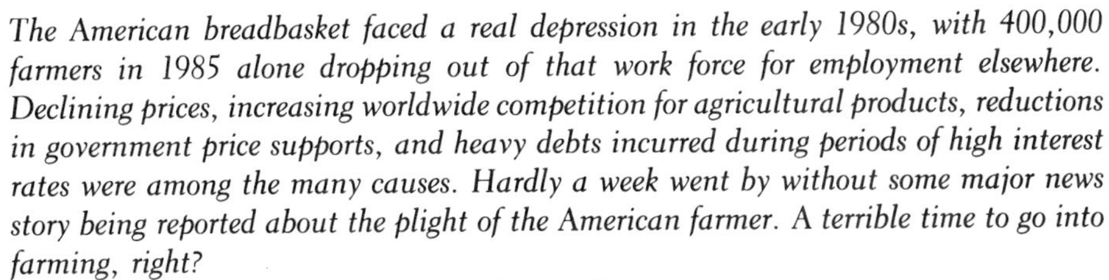

The American breadbasket faced a real depression in the early 1980s, with 400,000 farmers in 1985 alone dropping out of that work force for employment elsewhere. Declining prices, increasing worldwide competition for agricultural products, reductions in government price supports, and heavy debts incurred during periods of high interest rates were among the many causes. Hardly a week went by without some major news story being reported about the plight of the American farmer. A terrible time to go into farming, right?

Wrong! At least not for "specialty farmers."

Eliot C. Clarke, former senior vice president of New York-based Morgan Guarantee Trust Co. and who longed to kick the rat race, is now a deer farmer in Millbrook, N.Y. and his venison is served at the finest restaurants in Manhattan, 75 miles to the south. While all his neighbors are losing money on cattle and sheep, Clarke says "This is the only profitable form of farming I know."

Clarke is one of several thousand specialty, or "boutique," farmers who have carved out a very profitable niche amidst the otherwise very depressed farm market. Supplying specialty fruits, meats, and vegetables, they are cashing in on Americans' increased concern with nutrition, boredom with processed foods, and new tastes for the exotic. They are raising Muscovy ducks and European fallow deer, planting groves of Malaysian carambolas and Chinese lychees and harvesting African eggplants and Japanese cucumbers.

The prices charged for these specialty products routinely run double, or more, those of the standard fare routinely stamped out by agribusiness. Howard Josephs, a former real estate broker, charges $40 a pound for Moulard ducks for foie gras *served in New York's Catskill Mountains. Stephen Swift, president of Nantucket Game Bird Co., charges $10 a pound for pheasant and quail. "The emphasis must be on quality and freshness," he says. And profitability has been very good. Tom Willey barely eked out a living on his 20-acre farm outside of Fresno, Calif. raising zucchini and green beans. But he switched to specialty crops such as baby vegetables and French beans and he now has a gross margin of 25 percent to 30 percent on his business.*

SOURCE: Adapted from Alex Beam, David Kohn, and Marla S. Henken, "Down on the 'Boutique Farm': Lychee Nuts, Fallow Deer, Carambolas," *Business Week*, February 17, 1986: 80–84; and M. Magnet, "A New Crop of Farmland Gamblers," *Fortune*, April 14, 1986: 68–73.

Introduction

Pricing is the final marketing mix decision that this book examines in detail. Here we will present significant pricing concepts from a marketing decision-making perspective.

How Important Is Pricing?

Hardly a week goes by without most people being reminded of the effects of pricing decisions. Newspapers contain regular discussions of farm prices (see the opening Marketing Success), gas stations reflect the vast fluctuations in oil prices,[1] and we have all witnessed the dramatic drop in the price of microcomputers.

On the one hand, pricing is the most important marketing decision that management makes. Too high a price means that the product will not sell, while too low a price dictates low profits or even losses. Yet on the other hand, price tends to be used less as a strategic tool for many companies than other marketing mix elements. Studies indicate that most companies do not try to establish a niche in the market through low prices and focus on other means of differentiating themselves.[2]

Of course, some companies stress low prices to gain a market advantage. Laker Airways, for example, began no-frills, first-come, first-served service in late 1977 between New York and London at a fare of $390—a $360 discount from the regular $626 fare of other airlines. But unlike other solidly developed differentiation strategies, competitors can easily copy low prices to eliminate any competitive advantage. Pan American quickly followed Laker's lead by cutting its price to $256 for the same trip and offered other services, including meals and landings at Heathrow, London's close-in airport. Laker lost its competitive advantage as a result and went bankrupt.[3] Not learning from Laker's mistakes, People Express followed a similar low-price/low-frills strategy in the mid-1980s for both domestic and international travel. By 1986, People also faced the same economic fate.[4] In contrast, the specialty farmers highlighted in the Marketing Success have insightfully used marketing segmentation and positioning strategies to achieve high levels of profitability in an otherwise highly competitive market.

But this does not mean that pricing decisions are unimportant. They are very important for all types of businesses, large and small. Basically, there are three major instances when management makes pricing decisions:

People are constantly bombarded with information about prices.

1. For new products
2. In reaction to competitor-initiated price changes
3. When the firm itself initiates the price changes for some reason

The remainder of this chapter considers major pricing decision-making concepts that apply in all three instances. The discussion begins with an examination of price theory.

Price Theory

The field of economics has contributed heavily to the development of price theory. In this theory, it is generally assumed that companies operate with essentially a single objective in mind: to maximize profits. (In reality, other objectives also come into play, and they are covered later in this chapter.)

A company can achieve maximum profit if it sets its price at the level where marginal revenue (additional) derived from selling the final unit equals the marginal cost of producing that unit.[5] Thus, there are two offsetting entities to consider—revenues and costs—when evaluating the theoretical price that a company should charge for an item.

Revenues

Revenues are clearly important in pricing, since they represent the cash generated to cover the costs of producing and/or selling the product or service, plus any profit. Revenues are a function of the demand for the product; customers balance the cost of acquiring a product (its price) against the anticipated benefits from owning it. Thus, before making a decision on an item's price, marketers must understand the relationship between price and demand. This section considers the price-demand relationship existing in various market conditions.

Pricing in Different Types of Markets The seller's ability to set a price depends a good deal on the type of market in which the product competes. Economists generally distinguish four major types of markets: pure competition, monopolistic competition, oligopolistic competition, and pure monopoly. Each of these presents a different pricing challenge.

Under **pure competition,** the market is composed of many buyers and sellers, all of whom trade in an undifferentiated, homogeneous commodity, such as wheat, soybeans, or financial securities. No single buyer or seller has much impact, if any, on the market's going price. A seller cannot charge more than the market's price since buyers can acquire as much as they want at that rate. Nor would sellers charge less than the going rate since they can sell as much as desired at the prevailing price.

Pure competition
A market that is composed of many buyers and sellers, each of whom has no individual effect on the market, and who trade in an undifferentiated commodity.

Purely competitive markets are characterized by both a high mobility of resources and a high level of information among buyers and sellers. This means that if a company's prices and profits rise over the long term, buyers readily shift to buying from less costly suppliers. Also, new sellers can easily enter the market. The net effect is that sellers in such markets tend to be price-takers, rather than price-setters. If the sellers cannot establish a differential advantage to break out of this market condition, then the role of marketing research, marketing strategy, advertising, and other marketing activities become diminished in importance. But as this chapter's Marketing Success illustrates, marketing strategies often give companies—even farmers—a way

Stocks and commodities are traded in a pure competition setting—with constant price updates to reflect supply and demand.

of differentiating their product offerings to break away from competing in a pure competition market.

Monopolistic competition
A market that is composed of many buyers and sellers who transact over a range of prices because of differentiation.

Under **monopolistic competition,** the market is composed of many buyers and sellers who transact over a range of prices rather than at a single market price. The reason for the price range is that sellers are able to differentiate their offerings to buyers through physical differences, style, physical distribution, or some other marketing mix element. Generally, sellers try to develop differentiated offerings for different market segments and freely use branding, advertising, and personal selling. Because of these differences, buyers will pay different prices.

Through differentiating their offerings, some of the sellers are able to earn a much higher rate of return than others. Their continued success depends upon their ability to establish barriers to entry from other competitors, such as through patents, advertising, goodwill, developing brand loyalty, licensing agreements, high capital requirements, and by keeping one step ahead of the others in developing new products. This makes all marketing activities much more important than in pure competition. But because there are many competitors, each firm is less affected by competitors' marketing strategies than in oligopolistic markets.

Under **oligopolistic competition,** the market consists of a few sellers who are highly sensitive to each other's pricing and other marketing strategies. The product can be homogeneous (steel, aluminum) or heterogeneous (computers, television sets). The reason there are few sellers is that there are high barriers to entry, such as heavy capital costs, control of distribution channels, control over resource supplies, patents, and so on. Each seller is alert to competitor's strategies and moves. If Apple slashes the price of its computers by 20 percent, for example, many buyers will quickly switch to its products. The other suppliers, such as IBM, will have to also change their pricing schedules or change their total offering to make it a better deal by improving services, adding features, or improving performance.

Oligopolistic competition
A market that consists of a few sellers who are highly sensitive to each other's pricing and other marketing strategies.

An oligopolistic company is never sure that it will gain anything permanent through a price cut. But it is also never quite sure that competitors will follow a price increase and cause a retraction. This means that oligopolists must take into account the strategies of competitors when making pricing and other marketing decisions. Further, competition tends to be based most heavily on nonprice means of differentiating products, which greatly elevates the importance of all marketing activities. This is the situation facing most managers in the U.S. today, as most major U.S. industries are oligopolistic.

Under a **pure monopoly** there is only one seller. The seller may be a government monopoly (U.S. Postal Service), a private regulated monopoly (a power company), or a private nonregulated monopoly (Polaroid when it introduced instant photography). Pricing is handled differently in each case.

Pure monopoly
A market that is made up of only one seller.

A government monopoly can pursue a variety of pricing objectives. It might set a price below cost because the product is important to buyers and they cannot afford to pay full cost. Or the price might be set to cover costs or even be quite high to discourage consumption. In a regulated monopoly, the government permits the company to set rates that will yield a fair return on investment—one that will enable the company to maintain and expand its plant as needed. Nonregulated monopolies are free to price at what the market will bear. However, they do not always charge the full price for a number of reasons, including fear of government regulation, desire not to attract competition, and a desire to penetrate the market faster with a low price.

Marginal (and Total) Revenue

The concept of marginal revenue is important in price theory. **Marginal revenue** is the incremental revenue earned from selling one more unit of some item. In the case of pure competition, marginal revenue is the same value, a constant, for all quantities that one producer can sell. This is because each seller has virtually no effect on the market and prices will not fluctuate noticeably with one producer's volume variations. Consequently, the total revenue of a firm in a pure competition market is simply a function of the quantity sold times the established market price. This is illustrated in Figure 19.1.

Marginal revenue
The incremental revenue earned from selling one more unit of some item.

The situation is quite different in the other market conditions, also illustrated in Figure 19.1. Because of differentiation, each producer faces a downward-sloping demand curve and marginal revenue curve. Further, the total revenue curve has a maximum point, also depicted in the figure. This is due to the market's price sensitivity toward the differentiated product offering of a given seller. Price cuts are necessary to stimulate additional sales volumes. But because of the price cuts, some potential revenue is lost on those units which would have sold at a higher price (but at a lower total volume). Beginning at a low initial price, the additional volume more than offsets any such revenue losses. At some point, though the additional volume stimulated at

Figure 19.1
Demand and Average and Marginal Revenue under Pure Competition and Other Competitive Markets

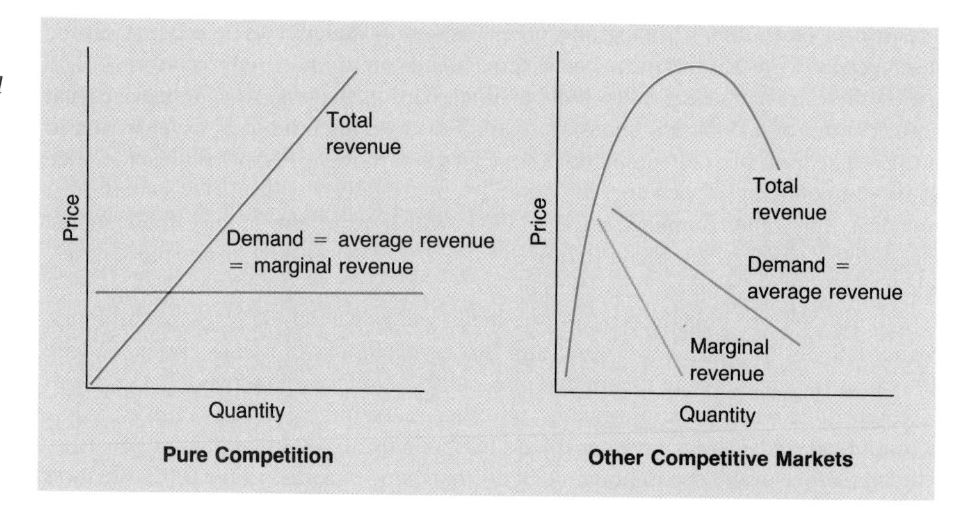

the lower price is insufficient to offset such revenue losses, meaning that the marginal revenue becomes negative.

This situation is the one faced by the vast majority of competitors in the U.S. and all modern economies and, consequently, will be referred to later in this chapter after cost factors are examined. Price elasticity of demand is first considered, however.

Price Elasticity

Price elasticity
The sensitivity of total revenue to a change in price.

Price elasticity is a concept that relates to how responsive demand will be to a change in price. There are two separate graphs in Figure 19.2 which help to illustrate the concept.

Figure 19.2A illustrates two demand curves: one that is relatively elastic and one that is relatively inelastic. Notice that at a price of P_1, the quantity demanded is Q_1 in both cases. If the price is cut to P_2, the quantity demanded increases only to Q_2 in the case of the relatively inelastic demand. In contrast, the same price cut caused the quantity demanded to jump to Q_3 for the relatively elastic demand function. Thus, if demand only changes a small amount when there is a price cut, the demand curve is said to be **inelastic.** If there is a sizable increase in demand, then the demand function is called **elastic.**

Inelastic
A condition where the demand for a product is not very sensitive to a price change; when a reduction in price does not cause total revenue to appreciably increase (or an increase in price does not cause total revenue to decline appreciably).

Figure 19.2B illustrates another elasticity concept. All downward-sloping demand curves (except a vertical one, which is practically never the case) have a relatively elastic portion and a relatively inelastic portion. This relates to the total revenue effects from a price change. The price elasticity of demand is calculated with the following formula:

Elastic
A condition where the demand for a product is sensitive to a price change; when a reduction in price causes total revenue to increase (or an increase in price causes total revenue to fall).

$$e = \text{price elasticity of demand} = \frac{\%\text{ change in quantity demanded}}{\%\text{ change in price}}$$

Because of the normal inverse relationship between price and quantity demanded, the sign of the price elasticity coefficient will usually be negative. As a result, the number reported is often stated as an absolute value (with the negative sign dropped).

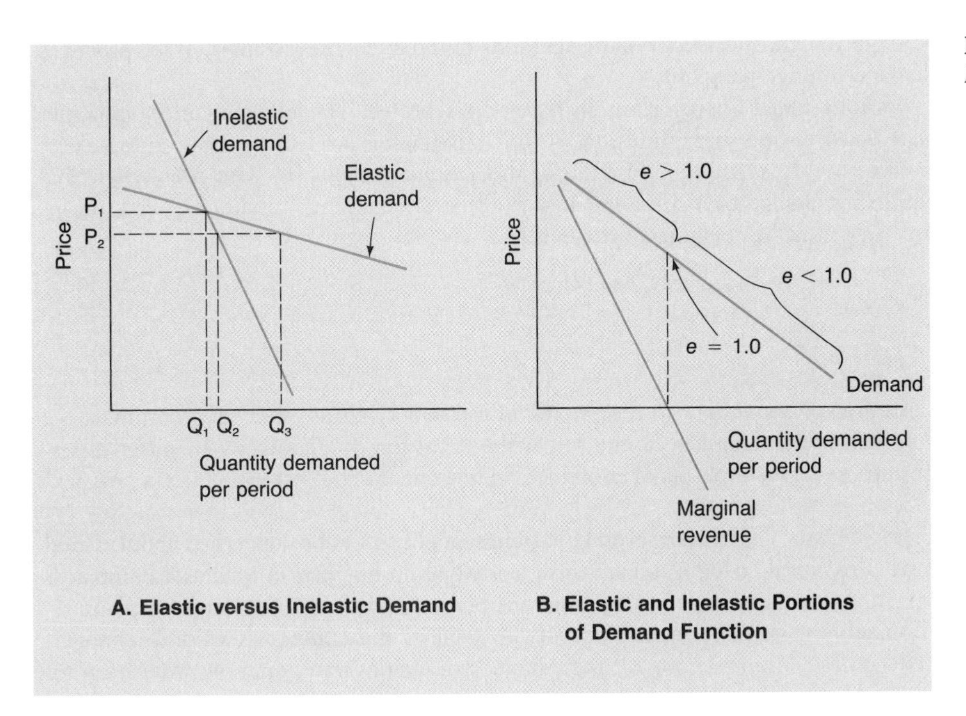

Figure 19.2
Basic Elasticity Concepts

Then, an elasticity coefficient may take on an absolute value from 0 to ∞. Absolute values are the reporting method used in this discussion.

Since the demand function is directly related to total revenue, the elasticity must also be related to total revenue. In fact, the elasticity coefficient becomes less than 1.0 when marginal revenue becomes negative, indicating that further price cuts do not stimulate greater total revenue. At higher prices, the elasticity coefficient is greater than 1.0, indicating that a price cut will stimulate greater total revenue. And at an elasticity of 1.0, called **unitary elasticity,** a price cut will result in an identical total revenue, which is the same as when marginal revenue equals 0. This is also illustrated in Figure 19.2B.

Unitary elasticity
An elasticity coefficient of 1.0; a point in a demand curve where a price cut yields the same total revenue as the original price.

A good question to ask is, "What determines the price elasticity of demand?" The answer is that demand is less likely to be relatively elastic under the following conditions:

- When there are few or no substitutes or competitors, including situations involving highly segmented markets and differentiated products
- When buyers do not readily perceive the relatively higher prices; for example, if items are paid for by third parties (parents, insurance companies, and so forth)
- When buyers are loyal to certain brands and habits and are slow to search for alternatives
- When buyers believe that the higher prices are justified by quality improvements, normal inflation, and other factors

If demand is elastic, sellers will probably consider lowering their prices to increase total revenue. This is logical so long as the costs of producing and selling additional volume do not increase disproportionately. However, many of the activities of marketers are designed to segment the market and position their products in such a way as to increase the inelasticity of the demand. This reduces the sensitivity of the product's demand to price competition.

Various studies of price elasticity have been reported. The following price elasticities were listed in one study: housing = 0.5, refrigerators = 1.07 to 2.06, automobiles = 0.6 to 1.1, cereal = 1.4 to 1.7, and gasoline, about 0.[6] The problem is that elasticities change over time and under different economic conditions. This means that they must be reestimated frequently.

Costs

Costs are very important in the pricing of a product because they set a boundary—a floor below which prices cannot fall without causing the company to suffer losses. Further, profit is simply a matter of the total revenue less the cost to produce a product.

Fixed costs
Those costs which do not vary in total as a company's operating volume changes.

Variable costs
Costs which vary in total in proportion to volume changes.

Total costs
The combination of fixed plus variable costs.

Average costs
The total costs of some product divided by the volume, in units.

Marginal cost
The additional cost involved with producing one more unit of some item.

Types of Costs There are several different types of cost to be concerned about. **Fixed costs** (also called "overhead") are those costs that do not vary in total as a company's operating volume changes. An example is property taxes on the company's plant.

Variable costs, in contrast, do vary in total as the company's volume changes. Kellogg has additional costs for ingredients, packaging, transportation, and so on for every additional box of Special K that it produces.

Total costs are the combination of fixed plus variable costs. Thus they, too, vary in total as the company's volume changes because one of the components—variable costs—varies proportionately with volume.

Average costs are simply the total costs of some product divided by the total number of units considered. Accordingly, average costs tend to decline as the number of units produced increases—at least to some point—because the overhead is spread over a larger base.

Marginal costs are the additional costs involved with producing one more unit of the item being considered.

Cost Behavior Costs may behave in a number of ways, depending upon the conditions. Frequently it is assumed that costs fluctuate as linear functions, as illustrated in the left portion of Figure 19.3.

This situation assumes that, at least for the relevant range being considered, total fixed costs remain at a constant level and that variable costs also remain at a constant amount per unit. This also means that marginal cost equals the per-unit variable cost throughout the relevant range. Thus, marginal costs are depicted by the horizontal line in the graph in the left half of Figure 19.3. Linear cost behavior is a reasonable assumption in most situations, given that decisions are made concerning a realistic range of operations—within normal and usual operating volume levels for a given facility.

Probably a more complete picture of cost behavior is presented in the right half of Figure 19.3, where the cost functions are allowed to become nonlinear. As pictured, the nonlinearity may be due to total variable costs. This would occur if the per-unit variable costs were to vary, depending upon the volume level. Such a condition is possible in several situations, including scheduling overtime at a premium pay rate to allow expanded production, paying a premium price to obtain additional scarce parts or other supplies, and paying commission bonuses to encourage additional sales.

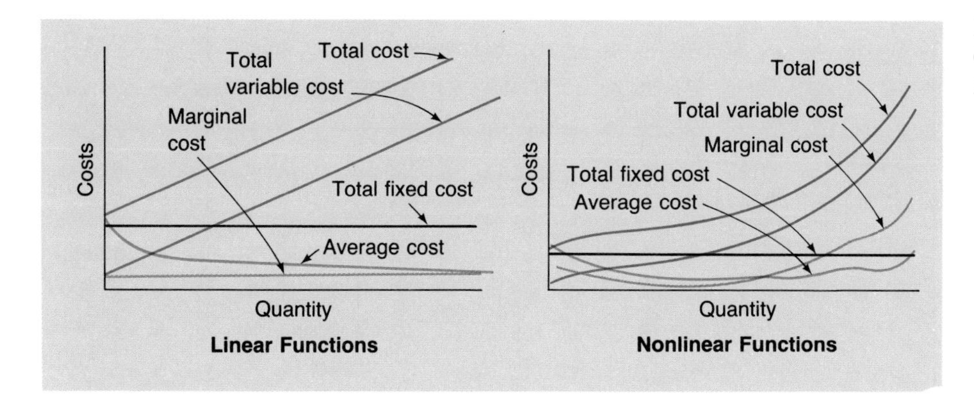

Figure 19.3
Costs As Linear and Nonlinear Functions

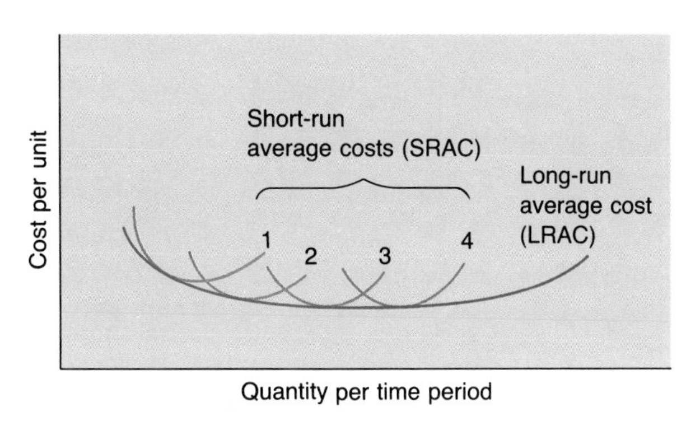

Figure 19.4
Short-Run and Long-Run Average Cost

Fixed costs also might vary with large volume changes (not illustrated, but the results are essentially the same). For example, additional facilities or equipment may have to be rented if volume is to be pushed beyond some level. In both cases—where fixed costs or where unit variable costs rise at some point with volume increases—the net effect is that the average total costs fall to some low point and then begin to rise, as illustrated at the right of Figure 19.3. Also, marginal costs tend to initially fall rapidly, begin to rise and intersect average costs at their lowest level, then start to rise rapidly to reflect the straining of capacity at higher volumes.

Short-Run versus Long-Run Average Costs Finally, average costs also depend on long-term effects, as illustrated in Figure 19.4. In the relatively short run, say up to a year or so, average costs behave as explained above, but in the longer term, average costs may shift to a new plateau, as illustrated in Figure 19.4.

There are two reasons that average costs tend to fall over time as volume increases. First, **economies of scale** tend to lower costs as volume expands over the long term. This stems from being able to acquire and use larger, more efficient plants and equipment, such as heavily automated manufacturing plants and warehousing facilities with robotics. The second reason is the **learning effect** (also called the learning curve effect). The more the experience, the greater is the chance that operations can be

Economies of scale
Reduced costs with increased volumes from being able to use larger and more efficient plants and equipment.

Learning effect
Reduced costs from becoming more experienced with an operation with practice.

Figure 19.5
Example of Total and Marginal Costs and Revenues

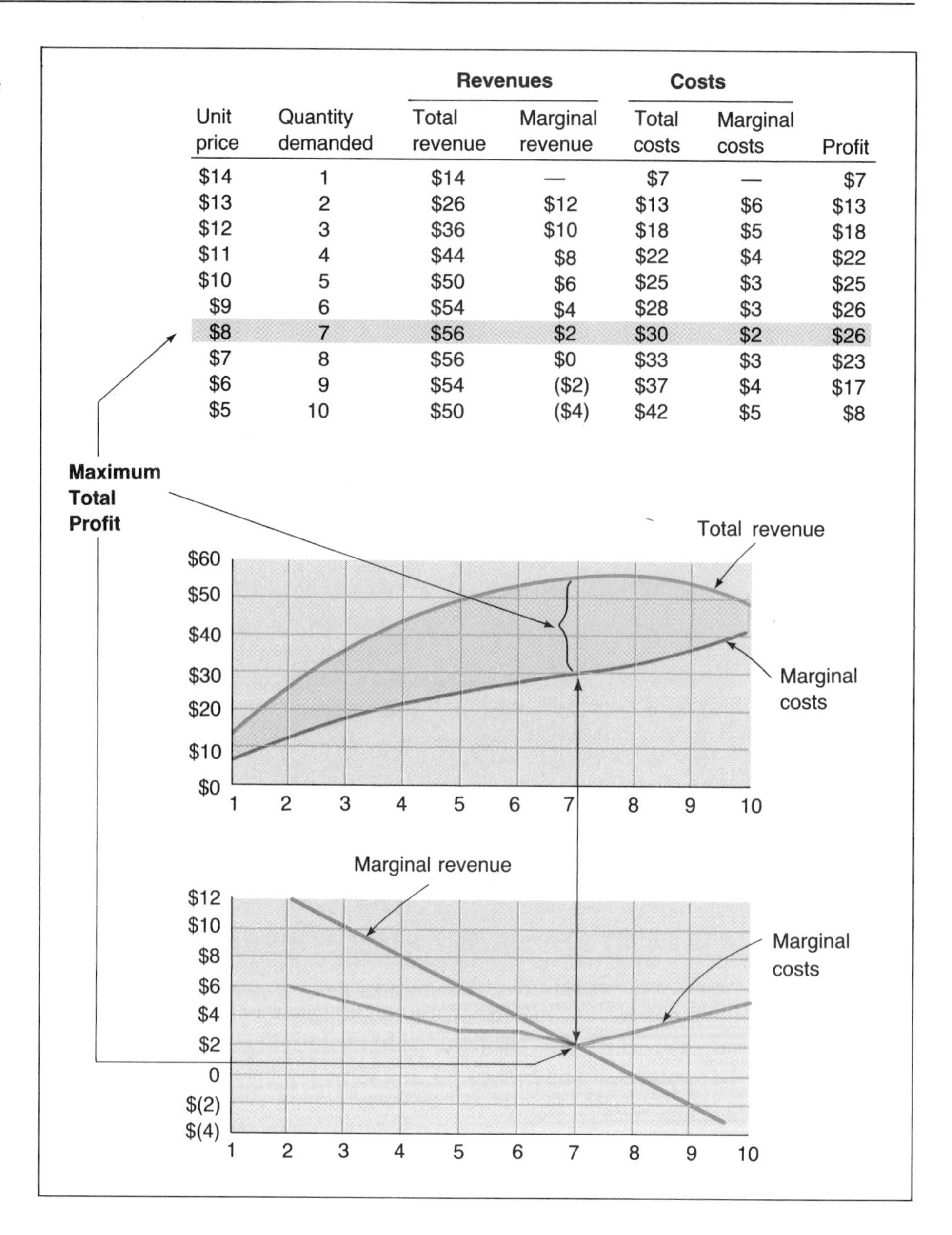

Unit price	Quantity demanded	Revenues: Total revenue	Revenues: Marginal revenue	Costs: Total costs	Costs: Marginal costs	Profit
$14	1	$14	—	$7	—	$7
$13	2	$26	$12	$13	$6	$13
$12	3	$36	$10	$18	$5	$18
$11	4	$44	$8	$22	$4	$22
$10	5	$50	$6	$25	$3	$25
$9	6	$54	$4	$28	$3	$26
$8	7	$56	$2	$30	$2	$26
$7	8	$56	$0	$33	$3	$23
$6	9	$54	($2)	$37	$4	$17
$5	10	$50	($4)	$42	$5	$8

streamlined and be made more efficient due to greater worker familiarity with tasks and management's expanded experience base from which to draw in decision making.

Revenues and Costs Combined

Continuing with this theory, both cost and revenue factors must be considered when setting prices to maximize profits. Figure 19.5 sets forth an example, which is illustrated in both tabular and graph forms. Besides marginal revenues and costs, the figure also depicts total revenues and costs to illustrate the relationships. Significantly, the figure shows that the largest vertical profit distance between total revenue and cost is at the

CONCEPT SUMMARY *Marginal Analysis*

Assumptions	Advantages	Disadvantages
1. The sole objective of management is to maximize short-run profits (or minimize losses) 2. The demand and cost functions are known 3. Price is set at a level where marginal cost equals marginal revenue (this is also the point where total revenue minus total costs is the greatest or where losses are minimized)	1. It focuses attention on the combination of factors that should be considered simultaneously when setting the price 2. It focuses on the immediate concerns of a company	1. Difficult, if even possible, to administer, especially for firms selling multiple products 2. Demand is an ever-changing phenomenon, meaning that measurement would have to be continuous, which is impractical 3. Focuses attention solely on the relatively short run 4. Does not reflect the existence of other very real objectives that management has in setting products

same point where the marginal cost and revenue curves intersect. *Thus, in theory, management should strive to set prices where marginal cost equals marginal revenue to maximize profits.*[7]

Use of Marginal Analysis

While marginal analysis provides considerable insight into pricing, very few firms use the theoretical model as an operational tool in determining prices. This is because they find it to be practically impossible to accurately estimate future costs and demand.[8] Also, demand conditions relate to momentary points in time and change whenever conditions change. This means that conditions would constantly have to be studied and prices regularly adjusted accordingly, as with a security or commodity on a financial exchange. Furthermore, the model assumes that maximizing immediate profit is the overriding objective followed by management, which is not the case in most situations. Generally, there are other goals that management seeks to accomplish.

Nonetheless, managers can benefit from the model by understanding the basic relationships that influence profit from among the major pricing determinants. The next section looks at the major methods that are used by marketing managers to make pricing decisions, but refers to price theory from time to time to evaluate the effectiveness of the operational methods. Before examining the methods, however, the marketing objectives pricing often seeks to accomplish are first examined.

Pricing and Marketing Objectives

Before setting a price, management must decide what it wishes to accomplish with the particular product. If the target market and market position have been selected carefully, then the marketing mix strategy, including price, will be relatively straightforward. For example, auto detailers such as Stephen Marchese, have targeted

MARKETING BRIEF
A Well-Defined Target Can Simplify Pricing

Auto detailing—the super-cleaning of cars—began in Southern California, where "you are what you drive," but it has spread around the country. Beyond the standard hose and sponge, detailers are like "dirt crime fighters," cleansing every nook and cranny with an array of armaments, including toothbrushes, cotton-tipped swabs, waxes, electric buffers, and leather and vinyl cleaners.

A typical tab is $125 to $150, compared to a simple wash and wax job for 20 percent of that price, and many customers have the job done twice a year. "As Americans buy ever more costly cars and keep them longer, detailing helps an owner protect his investment," says Stephen Marchese of Newport Beach, Calif., a pioneer in the business.

While detailing will never replace the corner car wash nor the Saturday afternoon do-it-yourself special, it has boomed in the prestige segment and has even made a mark among owners of Chevrolets and Fords. Marchese expects to add 30 new shops in 1986; his $45,000 franchise fee includes training, operating manuals, and management advice. The small businesses have been very profitable. 25-year-old David Crichton of Johnstown, Penn., for example, recouped his initial $56,000 investment in his first year of operation.

SOURCE: Adapted from "Gold Is in the Details," *Business Week*, February 3, 1986: 79–83.

themselves at the customized, top-quality end of the car cleaning market (see the accompanying Marketing Brief). Accordingly, they must charge a very high price to reflect their time and costs and to portray a prestige image.

At the same time, management may wish to pursue additional objectives. The clearer management is about its objectives, the easier it is to set a price. Several common objectives are survival, current profit maximization, market-share leadership maximization, and product/quality leadership.

Survival

Companies that are plagued with overcapacity, changing consumer demand patterns, or intense competition often set survival as an overriding objective. To keep the plant going and the inventories turning over, companies must set a low price in the hope that the market demand is price-elastic. Profits are less important than survival. For example, in recent years, troubled companies such as International Harvester (Navistar) and AMC's Jeep Division have offered large rebate programs in order to survive. As long as their prices cover variable costs and some fixed costs, they can stay in business—at least for a while. And as the heavy rebates of the once deeply troubled Chrysler Corporation illustrate, the price incentives can provide enough momentum to enable a recovery.

Current Profit Maximization

Some companies try to set a price that will maximize current profits. They estimate the demand and costs associated with alternative prices and choose the price that will generate the largest current profit, cash flow, or rate of return on investment. This

Pricing is rather straightforward when the target market is carefully identified.

objective places emphasis on current financial performance rather than long-run results.

Market-Share Leadership

Other companies want to achieve a dominant market share. They believe that the company owning the largest market share will enjoy the lowest costs and highest long-run profit. They go after market-share leadership by setting prices as low as possible. Albertsons, Inc., a supermarket chain operating in 17 western and southern states, is an example of a company that recently adopted such a strategy (see the accompanying Marketing Brief). A variation of this objective is to seek a specific market-share gain,

MARKETING BRIEF

An Objective of Gaining Market Share Often Leads to Lowered Prices

One thing distinctive about Albertsons, Inc., a supermarket chain operating in the western and southern market, is that the company steadily outperformed the industry for the past five years, achieving an annual sales growth rate of 13 percent, while the industry as a whole grew at about 5 percent. However, the company's growth had been slowing down in recent years—down to a 21.9 percent gross profit margin in 1985 (very high by industry standards).

The firm caught everyone's attention in early 1986 when it closed its Denver stores, and then reopened them with a low-price strategy that touched off a price war among area supermarkets. The strategy, a far cry from the firm's past service-oriented image, was clearly designed to gain further market penetration.

SOURCE: Adapted from Janet Simons, "Albertsons' Discount Strategy Shakes Up Market," *Advertising Age*, April 28, 1986: S-30, 31; and "Traders Shop for Supermarket Chain Stocks Following Dart's Interest in Buying Safeway," *The Wall Street Journal*, June 30, 1986: 53.

such as an increase in market share from 10 to 15 percent in one year. Management will then choose the marketing program, including price, that will accomplish this.

Product/Quality Leadership

Some companies, such as Mercedes Benz, adopt the objective of being the quality leader in the market. This normally calls for charging a high price to cover the high product quality and high cost of R & D. Hewlett-Packard has long been a company following this strategy in the calculator market. It is a leader in introducing new features, emphasizes specially designed products to meet the needs of market segments, and prices its calculators well above others in the market. And because of this leadership, Hewlett-Packard's success has continued throughout the turmoil within the calculator industry, while the "bottom fell out" for most of the other companies.

Other Objectives

Price might also be used to help achieve other specific objectives. Prices might be set low to prevent competition from entering the market or set at the level of competition to help stabilize the market. They might be set at a level to strengthen the loyalty and support of intermediaries, or they might be set to help avoid government intervention. Prices might be temporarily set low to generate customer enthusiasm, or they might be set temporarily high to offset demand for items in limited supply. Further, prices might be set to help the sales of other items in the product line. Thus, pricing may play an important role in helping to accomplish the company's objectives at many levels.

Operational Pricing Approaches

There are several approaches adopted by marketing managers in the pricing decision-making process. In general, these may be categorized into one of three types, as Figure 19.6 illustrates. None of the three explicitly recognizes the conceptual interrelationships between demand and cost to the extent that price theory does. Nevertheless, the approaches tend to be operationally feasible and readily administered.

The remainder of this chapter examines the cost- and competition-based strategies. Demand-based pricing strategies are considered in Chapter 20, along with other pricing considerations.

Figure 19.6
Commonly Used Pricing Strategies

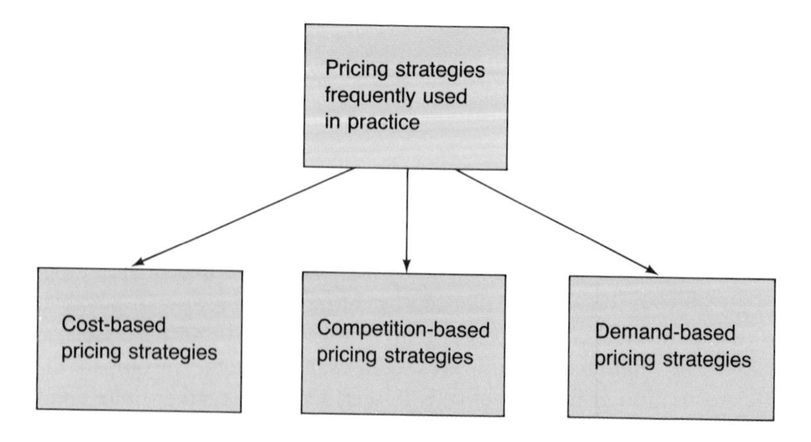

Cost-Based Pricing Strategies

Cost-based pricing strategies are those where management sets prices specifically in relation to costs—that is, heavy emphasis is not placed on factors such as demand and competition. The four major strategies in the category, as illustrated in Figure 19.7, are markup, cost-plus, target return, and payback period pricing.

Markup Pricing

Many organizations mark up products by a fixed percentage over costs. This is especially true for intermediaries. For instance, clothing retailers traditionally apply a markup of 40 percent, while confectionery wholesalers generally use a 10 percent margin. Many producing and service marketers also use **markup pricing.** To illustrate, accounting and law firms normally bill clients at a percentage over labor costs and automobile manufacturers mark up vehicles first in determining their sales prices to dealers, then again to establish a suggested retail price.

Markup pricing
Establishing the price of an item by increasing the amount by a fixed percentage over the item's total cost.

Some companies that market many different items find standard markups to be the only feasible way to set prices. Firms like J. C. Penney sell thousands of different products. One soon realizes that marginal analysis is impractical, despite its conceptual strengths, after multiplying the difficulty of using this form of analysis for a single product by the many items that a firm might handle.

Furthermore, intermediaries generally do not have great incentive to tinker with finding an item's optimal price. With retailers, for example, shelf space is a valuable commodity, and items that do not meet established markup-volume expectations are logical candidates to be dropped and replaced with new product offerings that meet these expectations in an attempt to achieve the organization's overall goals. (Calculating markups is covered in Chapter 20.)

Cost-Plus Pricing

Cost-plus is somewhat similar to markup pricing. Typically, contracts involving custom construction or manufacturing work require **cost-plus pricing** methods. The Martin Marietta Corporation, for instance, billed the federal government on a cost-plus basis for much of its work in building space capsules for the National Aeronautics and Space Administration (NASA). With this method, management does not specify an item's price until it knows all associated costs. Then it adds an agreed upon percentage or a fixed amount, depending upon the contract, to provide a profit.

Cost-plus pricing
Addition of a fixed fee to an item's total cost to establish a price.

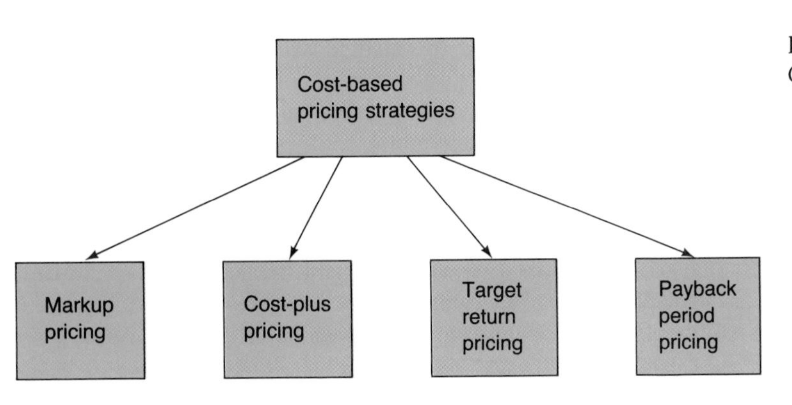

Figure 19.7
Cost-Based Pricing Strategies

Markup pricing is the only realistic means of setting prices when there are many products handled.

While it may not be readily apparent, cost-plus pricing is conceptually much closer to marginal analysis than is markup pricing. This is because management considers demand implications when establishing profit margins to be included in the price. Usually, cost-plus contracts result only after considerable negotiation between buyer and seller. If sellers insist on excessively high margins or overly extensive profits, they may lose contracts to competitors. Consequently, this method indirectly takes both cost and demand characteristics into consideration. Further, it provides sufficient flexibility to both buyer and seller to alter a project, as necessary, practically up to its completion date.

Target Return Pricing

Target return pricing
Setting a price in anticipation of earning a target rate of return on investment.

Another common cost-related strategy is to set prices in an attempt to attain a desired target return on investment. Exhibit 19.1 presents the four steps involved with **target return pricing,** along with an example.

The primary problem with this method is that management must make sales volume estimates before considering price, which is like putting the "cart before the horse." Sales volume usually depends upon price, not the other way around.

Despite the method's shortcoming, some producers—especially those facing strong alternative opportunities—use it to set prices. DuPont and Standard Oil of New Jersey, to illustrate, were among the many firms reported to use this method in a famous Brookings Institute study.[9] In practice the method does not totally ignore demand. Rather, users generally assess the reasonableness of attaining estimated sales volumes at calculated prices. Management may select from two options if it judges that a quantity-price combination appears unreasonable: make revisions and calculate a new

Exhibit 19.1
Target Return Pricing

There are four steps required to determine an item's price under the target return pricing method.

Step 1. Determine the investment required for the item and a target profit. For example, assume that some product requires a total investment of $1 million in plant and equipment. Further, assume that management has a policy of seeking a 20 percent return on investment before taxes on all projects. Thus, the target profit is 20 percent × $1 million = $200,000.

Step 2. Calculate both unit variable and total fixed costs associated with producing and marketing a product. For the example, assume that the variable costs are estimated at $5.00 per unit and fixed costs are $100,000 per year.

Step 3. Estimate a reasonable sales volume. For the example, assume that management feels that 150,000 units should be sold to obtain a satisfactory market penetration.

Step 4. Calculate the price. This calculation is similar to break-even analysis (see Appendix C), as follows:

$$\text{Per-unit selling price} = \frac{\text{Fixed Cost} + \text{Target Profit}}{\text{Estimated Sales Volume}} + \text{Unit Variable Cost}$$

For the example,

$$\text{Per-unit selling price} = \frac{\$100{,}000 + \$200{,}000}{150{,}000 \text{ units}} + \$5.00 \text{ per unit}$$
$$= \$7.00 \text{ per unit}$$

price, or drop the product for an alternative one with more promise of attaining the desired target return.

Payback Period Pricing

Payback period pricing requires calculating the price that will enable the firm to cover all costs and capital investment for an item within a specified time period. Exhibit 19.2 presents the four steps involved, along with an example.

Payback period pricing
Setting a price so that it will enable the covering of all costs and capital investment within a specified time period.

Target return and payback period pricing methods can yield identical prices because the approaches are quite similar. They are also subject to similar criticisms.* However, payback period pricing is especially useful in dynamic industries where substantial environmental change is common. This is true within several industries, including high-tech and consumer-packaged goods—industries where returns cannot be accurately forecast for new products. Rapid change injects uncertainty into decision making, and this approach forces management to realize the need to recover all costs in a relatively short period of time.

To illustrate, electronic digital watches have experienced dramatic technological breakthroughs over the past decade, which means that related investments tend to be

*The payback method will yield the same price as the target return pricing method when the payback period equals the reciprocal of the desired return. For example, 20 percent was used as the target return in the example. Its reciprocal is 1/0.20 = 5.0. Therefore, if the payback period selected were five years instead of four years, a $7.00 price would have been calculated. Prove this for yourself. The only times a considerably different answer will be calculated is if there exists substantial salvage value at the end of the period to be accounted for or if revenues fluctuate significantly from year to year over the project's duration.

Exhibit 19.2
Payback Period Pricing

There are four steps required to determine an item's price under the payback period pricing method.

Step 1. Determine the investment required; assume $1 million. Further, determine the appropriate payback period; assume four years for the example.

Step 2. Calculate unit variable and total fixed costs associated with producing and marketing the product. For the example, assume that the variable costs are estimated at $5.00 per unit and fixed costs are $100,000 per year.

Step 3. Estimate a reasonable sales volume. For the example, assume that management feels that 150,000 units should be sold to obtain a satisfactory market penetration.

Step 4. Determine the price that will cover all costs by the end of the payback period, as follows for the example. (Note: volume for four years is 150,000 × 4 = 600,000 units.)

Total costs for the period

Variable costs (600,000 units × $5.00)	$3,000,000
Fixed costs ($100,000 × 4 years)	400,000
Total operating costs	$3,400,000
Investment costs	1,000,000
Total costs	$4,400,000

Appropriate price

$$\frac{\text{Total Costs}}{\text{Estimate Volume}} = \text{Price}$$

For the example,

$$\frac{\$4{,}400{,}000}{600{,}000} = \$7.33 \text{ per unit}$$

Heavy price competition has caused many firms, especially electronics, to focus on short payback periods.

very short-lived. In order to earn a profit, companies foresee the need to recover all developmental costs within a reasonably short period of time before being confronted with some new breakthrough by competitors. Other pricing approaches, covered in the next section, specifically focus on the prices of competitors.

Competition-Based Pricing Strategies

Competitor prices play a dominant role in influencing the pricing practices of some firms.[10] Generally, the less differentiated items are within an industry, the greater is the need to determine prices in relation to those of competitors. Thus, as personal computers have become increasingly standardized, price has become a strong weapon and cutthroat competition has forced some, such as Victor Technologies, into bankruptcy.[11] At an extreme, the lack of differentiation forces firms to adopt prevailing market prices.

But often there are some differentiation possibilities, such as through delivery schedules, location, or some other variation in the marketing mix. The greater the differentiation, the more a firm is able to price independently of competition. Nevertheless, many companies try to avoid price wars if possible by at least keeping their prices generally in line with competitors. Manufacturers of personal computers have enjoyed little success in this regard, as price competition is severe in that industry. As Figure 19.8 illustrates, there are essentially two types of competition-based pricing models: existing market rates and competitive bids.

Existing Market Rates

The most common competition-based pricing method is that of adjusting a firm's price to reflect existing, or anticipated, competitor prices. In the largely undifferentiated aluminum market, for example, firms such as Kaiser Aluminum, Martin Marietta Aluminum, and Reynolds Metals constantly try to maintain their prices on a par with other firms in the industry, including foreign rivals.[12] Provided that all competitors have similar cost structures, this practice may result in an acceptable profit for all. Common prices tend to favor large companies, since they are generally better able to take advantage of economies of scale. Thus, common prices often give large companies an added potential for substantial profits.[13]

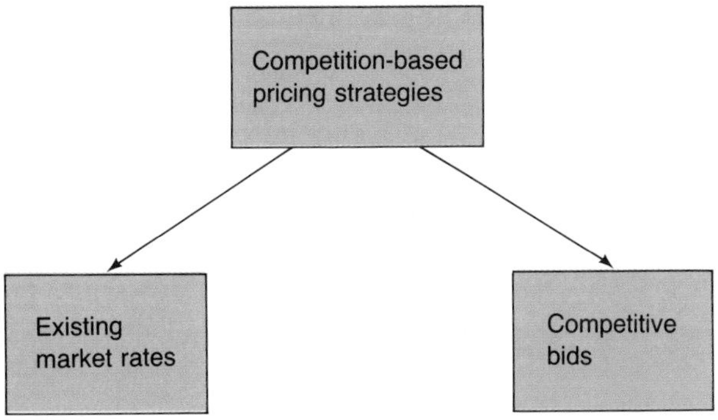

Competition-based pricing strategies

Existing market rates

Competitive bids

Figure 19.8
Competition-Based Pricing Strategies

MARKETING BRIEF
Competition Can Greatly Pressure Pricing Decisions

Back in 1981 when IBM introduced its personal computer for a price of $2,205, few people imagined that even more powerful machines would be selling for less than $500—a price more befitting a color TV set—within five years. But that was the case by the summer of 1986.

Termed "clones," the machines marketed by many competitors are almost identical to the IBM's standard-setting PC, and they are selling well in the mail-order market for as low as $499—about a quarter of the current price of the IBM original.

The clones—made up of an amalgamation of cut-rate parts from Taiwan, Hong Kong, Malaysia, Korea, and Singapore and often assembled in the U.S.—are winning respect in the marketplace. Although IBM spokespeople question the reliability of the low-priced imitations, few analysts doubt that IBM and other large computer makers will have to drastically cut their prices to remain competitive.

Speaking of the cut-rate competitors, "Their quality has improved significantly," said one industry expert. "No longer are they inferior imitations." Adds Stephen Dukker, president of Thomas, Harriman & Edwards Computer Products Ltd. of Chicago, which produces a $506.50 machine, "This is an IBM PC selling for what it should be selling for."

For years, several large makers of computers sold IBM compatibles for 10 percent to 30 percent lower prices, but never before have there been so many small companies selling cloned products for such deep discounts. According to Peter Teige, a microcomputer market analyst for a division of Dun & Bradstreet Corp., "They're having the effect of drawing the whole market down because people are beginning to see behind the veil obscuring how much these things really cost to build." Most analysts also feel that the major computer manufacturers will be forced to cut the prices of their PCs to below $800 before Christmas of 1986 or shortly thereafter.

SOURCE: Adapted from Brenton R. Schlender, "Higher-Quality IBM 'Clones' Put New Pressure on Computer Prices," *The Wall Street Journal*, May 13, 1986: 33.

Precisely where management should price an item in relation to competitive products depends upon the firm's overall marketing strategy. Swensen's Ice Cream Co., Haagen-Dazs, and Baskin-Robbins all price their ice cream at a high level to signify quality and a prestige image. Some mass merchandisers, such as K mart, tend to price lower than competitors, as reduced services at lower prices are part of their marketing strategies. Similarly, Braniff has pursued a no-strings, low-fare strategy.[14]

Regardless of the pricing strategy used, management should maintain some flexibility in its pricing structure to enable reaction to competition. To illustrate, IBM was forced into lowering its prices on the IBM PC because of the aggressive pricing structures of the "look-alike" machines marketed by competitors. This is illustrated in the accompanying Marketing Brief.

Whenever demand is highly price-sensitive, competitors discount willingly, and customers are aggressive bargainers, there is a need to be flexible in pricing to permit price adjustments in response to competitive pressures. The management of American Airlines, for example, felt the need to slash its prices in 1985 by up to 70 percent in more than 2,400 markets because of tight fare competition from discount airlines such as Southwest and People Express.[15]

One way to retain flexibility in pricing is to involve sales representatives in any price changing decision making.[16] They are often in a good position to judge when adjustments in prices are needed to obtain orders. Of course, management must use discretion in evaluating the inputs of sales reps in these decisions, as they are inherently motivated to lower prices to push volume.

Competitive Bid Pricing

Government, custom machinery and equipment, and building construction purchasers often require interested sellers to competitively bid on a contract. These bids are formal proposals made to the buying organizations stating a specific price, terms, product specifications, and other important characteristics of the product offering. Sometimes buyers insist that bidders submit their bids in a sealed envelope, called a *sealed bid*, so that the competitors remain unaware of the prices and terms proposed by each other. Under this practice, the lowest bidder generally receives the contract, although the buyer often evaluates other aspects of a proposal, such as the bidder's ability to deliver, reputation, and factors other than price alone.

The competitive bidding process poses difficult decision choices for a bidder. On the one hand, bidders would like to propose high prices. On the other hand, the higher the price, the greater is the chance that competitors will bid lower, meaning that the contract may be lost. Several quantitative analysis techniques, such as decision theory, have proven useful in helping managers assess these probabilities and potentials for profits in bidding.[17]

Most important for continued success, however, is past experience in bidding against competitors and understanding both their cost structures and pricing practices. Experience provides a manager with "gut feelings" of how badly competitors want a contract and, consequently, what prices they are likely to propose.

Chapter Summary

This chapter was the first of two which look at pricing decisions, which are among the most important that marketing managers make. The importance of pricing is fundamental: too high a price results in poor sales, whereas too low a price results in high volumes at a loss. While most marketing managers attempt to avoid competing on the basis of price and rely on other elements of the marketing mix instead in their competitive battles, pricing is nonetheless important to all managers.

To grasp the essential concepts involved in deciding prices, managers should be familiar with the economics concepts involving an optimal price. The theoretical model emphasizes that both costs and revenues should be considered in the process.

The concepts of marginal revenue and marginal cost are fundamental in this theory. The discussion examined pricing in different types of market conditions, types of costs and their behavior, and the concept of price elasticity.

Next, operationally used pricing strategies were examined, beginning with a look at various objectives that marketers have when making price decisions. Then, the widely used cost- and competition-based strategies were considered. Chapter 20 will examine the demand-based pricing strategies used by managers in decision making.

Questions

1. Why is pricing so vitally important, and yet considered less important than other marketing mix elements by many marketing managers?
2. What are the main advantages and disadvantages of the theoretical pricing model?
3. The following demand schedule relates to some product:

Price	Quantity Demanded per Period
$1.00	600
$2.00	500
$3.00	400
$4.00	300
$5.00	200

   a. Plot the demand curve.
   b. Plot the marginal revenue curve.
   c. Calculate the price elasticity for a change in price from $2.00 per unit to $3.00 per unit. What does the price elasticity that you calculated mean?
4. The following is the cost of production and marketing associated with the demand schedule listed in problem 3 above:

   Fixed costs = $100 per period
   Variable costs = $1.00 per unit

   a. Plot the company's cost structure.
   b. Calculate the optimal price that the company should charge for the item.
5. Assume that a firm is trying to determine the appropriate price for a new product. Its total investment is calculated as $150,000. Fixed costs are $50,000 and variable costs are $2.00 per unit. Estimated sales volume is 50,000 units. What is the appropriate price:
   a. Using a target rate of return of 20 percent.
   b. Using a desired payback of four years.
   c. When would the price under a payback criterion equal that of a target rate of return criterion? Prove this with calculations for the example.
   d. Assess both methods.
6. A first-year economics student has just challenged you in an argument. The student's contention is that a cost-based pricing method is always wrong. After all, "You can't estimate volume unless you first identify the price!" Defend the cost-based methods.

Chapter 20

Pricing Decisions: Demand-Based Strategies; Flexible Break-Even, and Other Considerations

Objectives

After reading this chapter, you should be able to demonstrate a knowledge of:

- The major types of demand-based pricing strategies, including price discrimination, skimming, penetration pricing, prestige pricing, loss-leader pricing, and odd-number pricing
- Flexible break-even pricing—how the method works and how it takes advantage of considering both cost and revenue factors when making pricing decisions
- The pricing implications of transportation costs
- The pricing implications of markups
- Other factors to consider when establishing a price structure

MARKETING SUCCESS

A Dual-Pricing Structure Works for Airlines

To compete with discount airlines and in an attempt to segment the market into two groups—those who are price-sensitive and those who are less price-sensitive—the major full-service airlines began an extensive program of heavily discounting air fares in late 1985. The rate structures differed a bit from company to company, but essentially they followed a similar pattern of allowing a more deeply discounted fare the further ahead a customer was willing to pay for a ticket. In general, an advance purchase could result in the following average savings: 7 days, 20 percent off; 14 days, 40 percent off; 21 days, 65 percent off, and 30 days, 70 percent or more off.

A major concern of management was to effectively distinguish two groups of customers in the pricing structures: business travelers and vacationers. The demand for flights by business travelers was relatively inelastic, whereas that by vacationers was highly price-sensitive. The discount structure was very effective in segmenting the two groups.

To discourage business travelers from filling the discount seats, rather hefty penalties were established for cancelling a flight. Up to 50 percent of the price paid was lost in redeeming a discounted ticket not used as scheduled. Because business travelers usually make travel plans within only a few days of a scheduled trip, this practice helped to curtail business travelers from buying blocks of tickets ahead of time without having firm travel plans and then refunding the unused ones. But the discount rate structures were very successful in stimulating receipts from vacation travelers, who plan their trips far in advance and stick to their schedules.

SOURCE: Adapted from Carol Jouzaitis, "Cheap Airline Seats Getting Costlier to Forfeit," *Chicago Tribune*, May 14, 1986, Sec. 3, pp. 1, 7.

Introduction

This chapter continues to discuss the operational methods used by managers in making pricing decisions.[1] Flexible break-even pricing and other pricing considerations are also covered.

As the chapter's opening Marketing Success illustrates, management is wise to consider all aspects of demand when making pricing decisions. By offering deep discounts for advance purchases, airlines are able to effectively tap two separate markets—business and vacation travelers—and do so by increasing their total profitabilities.

Demand-Based Pricing Strategies

Many managers price products in relation to their perceptions of the prevailing demand conditions in the market. As Figure 20.1 illustrates, there are six major demand-based pricing strategies: price discrimination, skimming, penetration pricing, prestige pricing, loss-leader pricing, and odd-number pricing.

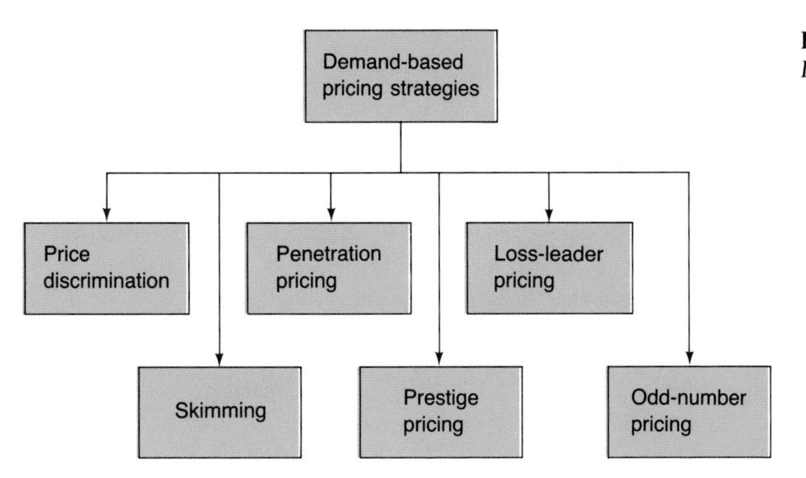

Figure 20.1
Demand-Based Pricing Strategies

Price Discrimination

Price discrimination exists when a marketer charges different prices for items of the same kind and grade to different buyers. The discount fare structures for advance purchases of the major airlines are examples of price discrimination.

Price discrimination
Charging different prices to different buyers for items of the same kind and grade.

This method is generally illegal under the provisions of the Robinson-Patman Act (see Appendix B) for the sales of *goods* to different members at the same level of a distribution channel, unless the firm can raise one of the legally prescribed defenses. However, this law does not prohibit price discrimination involving consumers or the pricing of services.

Further, foreign markets sometimes present an opportunity to charge different prices to channel members, although an increasing number of countries have passed "anti-dumping" laws that prohibit the selling of excess inventories in foreign markets at lower-than-normal prices.

By pricing to meet the demand of each individual buyer, a seller can realize a high average price and total profit. For example, prices for most durables such as automobiles, furniture, and major appliances as listed by retail stores are typically negotiable. This practice enables sellers to increase their overall profits in the process.

Some buyers are willing to pay high prices, as illustrated by P_1 in Figure 20.2. Others are willing to buy only at lower prices, such as P_2 in the figure. Under such a system, each item's marginal cost plus some minimally acceptable unit profit serves as a floor below which the seller is unwilling to sell.

In effect, the objective of price discrimination is to turn consumer surplus into profit for the firm. **Consumer surplus** is the term used to describe the "net savings" that people would accrue by not having to pay the amount they would be willing to pay for an item. To illustrate, under "normal" circumstances, such as if there were pure competition, the price that people would have to pay would be P_e (the equilibrium price illustrated in Figure 20.2). The **equilibrium price** is the price where all buyers and sellers are in equilibrium, meaning that the quantity that buyers are willing to buy equals the quantity that sellers are willing to sell at that price.

Consumer surplus
The sum of the differences in what buyers would have been willing to pay for an item and what they finally pay.

Equilibrium price
The price where the quantity demanded of an item is equal to the quantity supplied at that price.

Some of the buyers would have been willing to pay a higher price for the item but do not have to do so because the market price is lower. The net "savings" for these buyers is called consumer surplus, which is illustrated in Figure 20.2. Thus, under price discrimination, management adjusts its prices to turn this surplus into profits.

Figure 20.2
Price Discrimination Attempts to Turn "Consumer Surplus" into Profits

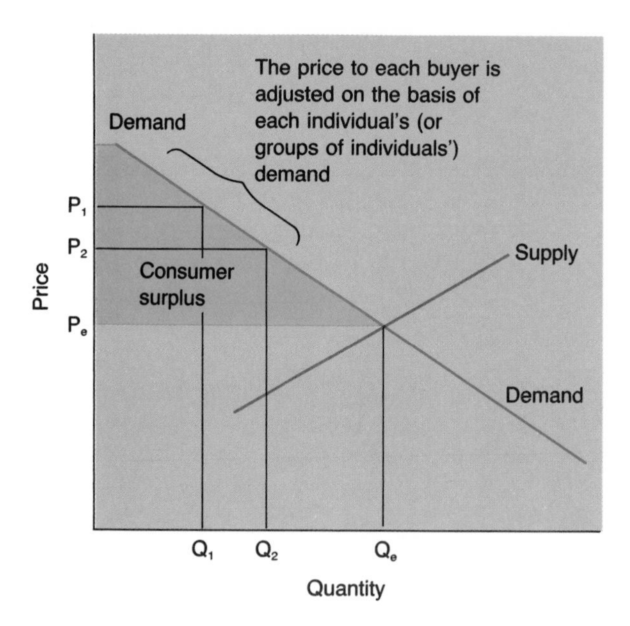

A major problem with a price discrimination system is that it requires extensive control and the ability to "feel out" a buyer's demand through negotiation. Consequently, a price discrimination strategy makes most sense in situations involving substantial personal selling effort and where negotiation is the norm. So long as the lowest price covers the organization's marginal costs, it can result in higher overall profits than if all customers paid identical prices.

Skimming

Skimming
Establishing beginning prices at high levels, and then lowering them over time.

Skimming is another strategy designed to turn consumer surplus into profits. In the case of skimming, management initially establishes high prices and directs the product or service in question to market segments with relatively inelastic demand. As these high-price segments become satisfied, the firm lowers its price to capture additional customers. Successive rounds of price cuts follow until further reductions appear unprofitable.

The old Bell System (before the breakup of AT&T) provides a classic example of skimming. The firm charged a significant premium rate for new items it offered customers, such as extra-long telephone cords, color phones, touch button dialing, and new types of phones. After it satisfied initial demand, Bell usually reduced an item's premium rate to attract additional customers. To bring in still more customers, it lowered prices still further so that any premium was eventually nominal.

Another example of skimming involved the traditional practices of auto manufacturers in the pricing of aftermarket replacement parts (see the accompanying Marketing Brief). The manufacturers zeroed in on the cream of the market, and left the rest to used parts dealers.

There are two major problems with skimming:

- Initial high prices raise the temptation for competitors to market similar items, but at lower prices, resulting in low long-run profits for all. This happened in the auto

MARKETING BRIEF

Skimming Can Be Profitable until Competition Arrives

Historically an overlooked market, auto manufacturers laid claim to a virtual monopoly—the aftermarket for parts. Through the late 1970s, manufacturing and supplying replacement fenders, hoods, bumpers, and other parts was one of the most profitable portions of the business. Body shops were happy to go along with the high prices charged by the companies, as they marked up the inflated parts and generated even greater profits for themselves. Only insurance companies (who were left to hold the bill) and consumers (who paid higher insurance premiums as a result) suffered in the process.

The situation began to change in 1980, when offshore manufacturers, mostly in Taiwan, began to manufacture several of the most commonly used replacement parts, including fenders, bumpers, and hoods for popular cars.

In late 1983, State Farm, the largest U.S. car insurer, entered into the battle. It commissioned Automatic Data Processing, Inc., to develop a computerized repair estimating and parts locating system from a customized data base. The system enabled State Farm to make their estimates for claims using the cheaper "gypsy parts" sold by the copycat companies. It also enabled such parts to be located around the country.

While there were many complaints about the quality of the replacement parts by the auto manufacturers, body shops, and some customers, one thing was clear. The monopoly by the auto manufacturers was broken. Three years before the offshore parts began to arrive, a GM-made replacement fender sold for $152. By 1986, the price was down to $104 to compete with the offshore versions, which sold for as little as $92.

SOURCE: Adapted from Ford S. Worthy, "A War over Parts for Wrecked Cars," *Fortune*, March 17, 1986: 71–73; and "Dry Source," *Automotive News*, May 10, 1986: E.40.

parts aftermarket. Another example of this is the initial high price charged for cordless telephones, which led to intensive competition, falling prices, and eventual poor profit positions for the remaining competitors.

- Cutting prices too often might signal to buyers that something is wrong with the product or the company.

Therefore, a skimming strategy makes most sense in situations where there exists significant barriers to entry by competitors. Further, the strategy should not result in price changes being made too frequently.

Penetration Pricing

A direct alternative to skimming is **penetration pricing** (also called **preemptive penetration** when accompanied by heavy promotion during a product's introduction), which requires setting initial prices relatively low to rapidly penetrate those who seek bargains and are very responsive to low prices.[2] This pricing method is closely related to competition-based approaches, as management intends for it to generate economies of scale before competitors have a chance to enter the market. By successfully obtaining a large sales volume through low prices, a firm might be able to attain low average costs due to the scale of its operation and its experience. This may drive away potential new competitors because entry into a new market is generally accompanied by low volumes and high average costs.

Penetration pricing
Establishing beginning low prices to encourage rapid adoption by the market to get average product costs down.

Preemptive penetration
A strategy of high levels of promotion and low price, especially during product introduction.

Penetration pricing is aimed at generating high volume.

In 1982, for example, Jack Tramiel, then president of Commodore, set the price of the company's model 64 home computer under $200, well below that of all competitors. Sales were so high—attaining a 45 percent market share at Christmas of that year—that the firm could hardly keep up with orders.[3] Following a similar strategy at the helm of Atari, he announced the company's new 1040ST in early 1986 at less than $1,000—or $1,500 below Apple's new Macintosh Plus, a very similar machine.

Penetration pricing does mean that a firm foregoes the opportunity of generating extra profit from first setting high prices to meet high initial demand and then lowering them to capture further customers. But in large, highly competitive markets, such a strategy makes sense; it serves to strengthen a company's long-run profitability.

A high price can add to the prestige of a premium product.

Prestige Pricing

How would consumers perceive Nikon 35mm cameras if they sold at a lower price than Kodak Instamatics? Or if mink coats sold off the rack at a discount store for $99.95?

Many studies indicate that buyer perceptions of quality and prestige are often directly proportional to an item's price.[4] For most products, even aspirins, there are prestige, high-quality market segments made up of buyers who expect to pay more for "the best." The high popularity of Bayer aspirin is an example. When consumers experience difficulty in objectively assessing an item's quality, many use high price as a signal of quality and prestige. **Prestige pricing,** which involves the charging of a premium price for an item, is a strategy designed to capitalize on these perceptions.

Prestige pricing
Selling premium products at high prices to engender prestige for the items.

Figure 20.3 depicts a typical demand curve associated with prestige items. Notice that it is shaped like a traditional curve at relatively high prices. But at some point, lower prices result in smaller quantities being demanded. Price reductions signal that the offerings "must be less desirable."

Marketers seeking to penetrate high prestige/quality market segments should be aware that many buyers expect relatively high prices. Levitz Furniture Corp., for instance, increased its demand by marketing higher priced furniture than it once did. This does not mean that nonprice elements of the marketing mix are unimportant. An item's actual quality must at least meet buyer expectations. Besides increasing its prices, Levitz also began to carry furniture with better materials and workmanship. Similarly, other marketing mix elements such as promotion should be blended with the price mix to augment a high quality/prestige image.

Leader prices
Items sold at reduced prices, but at a slight profit, to attract additional customers, who then might buy other items at regular prices.

Loss leaders
Items sold below cost (resulting in a negative contribution to overhead) for the purpose of attracting additional customers to buy other items that are sold at a profit.

Odd-number prices
Setting prices to end with odd numbers, such as 99¢ and $7.95.

Loss-Leader Pricing

Frequently, retailers sell products at low prices simply to build store traffic. For example, supermarkets feature special rates on milk, coffee, hamburger, and other often purchased staples in order to attract customers. Once in the store, shoppers are likely to buy additional items at normal prices and margins. **Leader prices** are below those of competitors and yield less than normal markup percentages. On the other hand, **loss-leader** prices are below cost.

Some marketers also use loss leaders to gain entry to industrial goods buyers. Once on their approved buying lists, a seller may be able to obtain other orders with higher unit profits. However, industrial goods buyers are apt to simply place orders on loss leaders and purchase other items from regular suppliers. Therefore, the use of loss leaders in industrial markets is quite limited. They serve little useful purpose for items sold to the government. Government buyers seldom hold allegiances for past favors at special prices. Consequently, marketers typically view each government purchase as a completely separate transaction where an acceptable profit is necessary.

Many retailers regularly feature leader prices and loss leaders to build store traffic.

Odd-Number Pricing

Finally, most marketers set prices to end with an odd number, such as 99¢ or $7.95. For items priced below $50, it is customary to set prices at 1¢, 5¢, or 7¢ below an even dollar figure. $7.99, $7.95, or $7.93 are such prices. For items above $50, common practice is to set the price $1 or $2 below an even dollar amount, such as $78 or $79.

Merchants first began such practices many years ago to force clerks to register sales instead of pocketing receipts. **Odd-number prices** required making change, meaning that clerks would need to ring sales on a cash register to gain access to the change drawer. Sales taxes in almost all states today accomplish the same purpose ($1.00 plus 4¢ sales tax), yet the practice continues.

Apparently, many marketers feel that the demand curves for their items contain breaks, as Figure 20.4 illustrates. Such a demand curve would exist if buyers feel that there are price thresholds. Perhaps they perceive 79¢ as being significantly less than 80¢ because it is in the 70¢ range, not the 80¢ range. Nevertheless, odd-number pricing is in widespread use if for no other reason than custom.

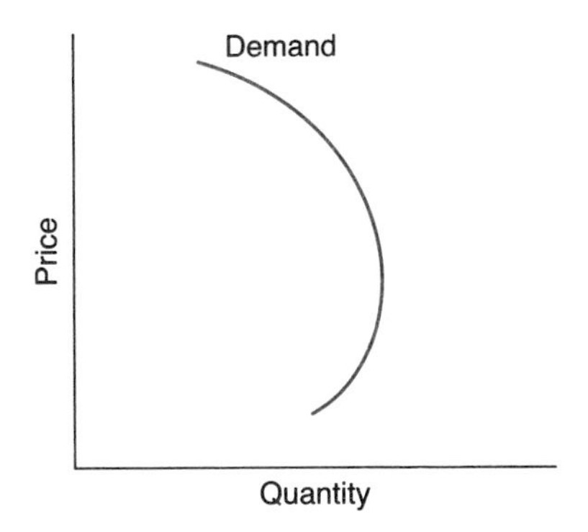

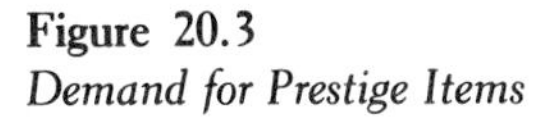
Figure 20.3
Demand for Prestige Items

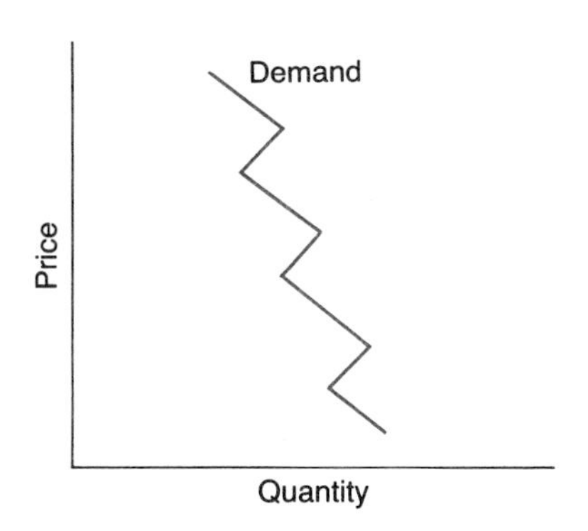

Figure 20.4
Assumed Demand Curve When Odd-Number Pricing Is Used

Multiple Pricing Approaches

Many firms use two or more methods simultaneously to set their prices. For example, a retailer might use markup pricing for all items but then adjust the calculated prices to reflect competitor actions. The retailer might further adjust specific prices to attain customary odd-number amounts. Similarly, management may adjust prices to reflect the product's stage in its life cycle. Most important, management should set prices to coordinate with the firm's overall marketing strategy. One way to accomplish this is through flexible break-even pricing, the topic of the next section.

Flexible Break-Even Pricing

While most organizations use one or some combination of the operational pricing approaches, all of the methods have conceptual weaknesses—they tend to ignore the *combination* of costs and revenue. Another operationally useful method considers both costs and revenue. Termed **flexible break-even pricing**—an extension of **break-even analysis**—the method does not require the very difficult task of accurately measuring the demand functions. (See Appendix C for a discussion of **break-even.**) Estimates of costs and sales volumes are used instead, based on experience and judgment. The following example illustrates how the process works.

Flexible break-even pricing
A combination of break-even analysis with costs and judgment to estimate demand to attempt to determine an optimal price for a product.

Break-even
The point at which revenues equal costs.

Break-even analysis
Determining the volume or price that will result in covering total costs.

The management of Maycrest Co. is attempting to determine the most profitable price to charge for its newly developed "Straightline," a mechanical pencil especially designed for drafting. Straightlines carry a five-year guarantee and are expected to be both durable and somewhat of a status symbol among drafting people and certain commercial artists. Management estimates that Straightlines should sell somewhere in the range of $6 to $12. Market research indicates that a price over $12 would be too expensive. Conversely, a price below $6 would neither result in profitable operations nor connote the desired quality image. Maycrest's accounting department estimates fixed costs to be $500 per month and variable costs at $5.00 per pencil produced.

Table 20.1 presents estimates of Maycrest's unit sales volumes at various prices. Sales representatives, channel members, and marketing managers are excellent sources of expert estimates. Tapping their experience can be quite useful in judging how responsive demand is to an item's price. Using several experts can increase estimate

Table 20.1 Maycrest Company: Estimates of "Straightline" Unit Sales Volume at Various Prices

Selling Price	Estimated Unit Sales Volume per Month	Estimated Monthly Sales Dollars (in Thousands)
$12.00	325	3.900
11.00	450	4.950
10.00	650	6.500
9.00	750	6.750
8.00	800	6.400
7.00	825	5.775
6.00	850	5.100

accuracy. The Delphi technique (described in Chapter 8) is useful for refining initial group member responses in light of other members' opinions, for instance.

Step 1

The first step in flexible break-even analysis is to graph the demand estimates, as in Figure 20.5. Notice in the figure that several total revenue (TR) functions are presented. Each of these picture how much the total revenue would be at a given price per unit times various sales levels. For example, if the price were $12 per unit and Maycrest could sell 1,000 units per month, the total revenue would be $12,000 per month. Thus, the TR function for a $12 price ($TR_{\$12}$) passes through $12,000 at a quantity of 10 hundred (1,000) units per month. Other total revenue functions are plotted in a similar manner, without paying attention to what the estimated demand might be.

Also notice that an estimated total revenue curve is superimposed upon the total revenue curves of Figure 20.5. This curve is based upon plotting the estimated monthly sales dollars of Table 20.1 for the various price levels. To illustrate, for a price of $10.00, it was estimated that a total revenue of $6,500 per month would be generated. Accordingly, the total revenue curve of Figure 20.5 passes through the $TR_{\$10}$ function at $6,500 and a volume of 650 units per month. The other sales estimates of Table 20.1 are plotted similarly in Figure 20.5 to complete the estimated total revenue curve.

Step 2

The second step of the flexible break-even method is to calculate the optimal sales price. This is done after first superimposing the company's cost structure on the total revenue functions and the total revenue curve, as in Figure 20.6. Notice in the figure that the fixed costs and the total costs (both fixed and variable) are plotted.

This information may then be used to estimate the item's optimal price. This is done by locating the greatest profit, expressed as the vertical distance between the estimated total revenue curve and the total cost curve. This is also illustrated in Figure 20.6.

For the Maycrest example, the optimal profit of Straightlines appears to be attainable with a total revenue of approximately $6,800 and a quantity of 710 units per month.

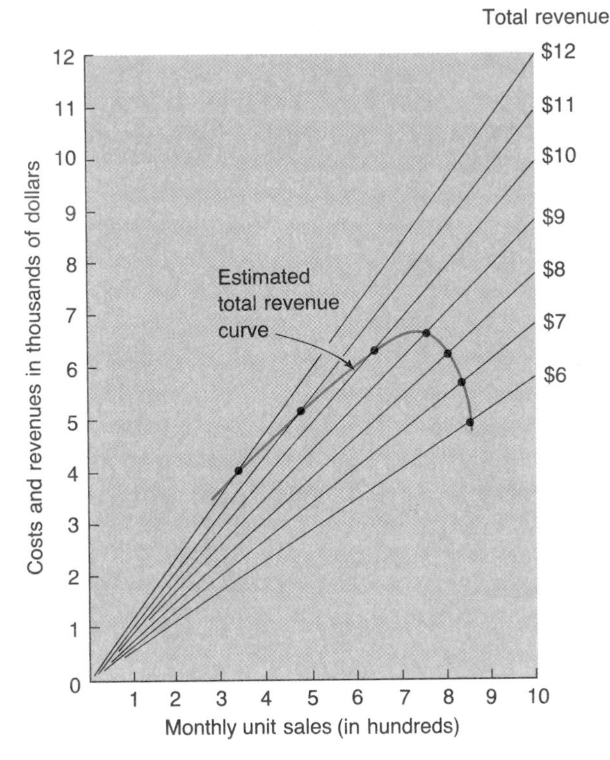

Figure 20.5
Flexible Break-Even for Maycrest Corp.: Total Revenue Functions and Estimated Total Revenue Curve

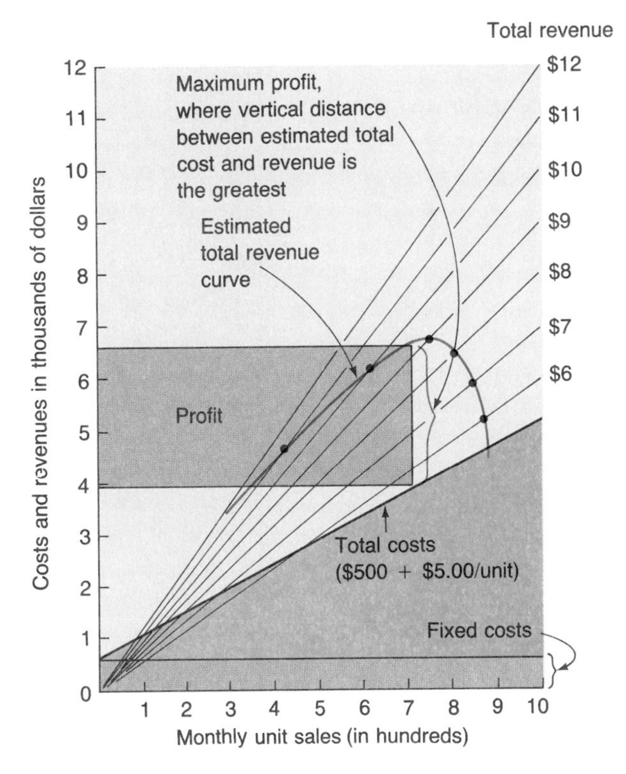

Figure 20.6
Flexible Break-Even for Maycrest Corp.: Optimal Price

This is read in Figure 20.6 by extending the maximum profit point from the total revenue curve to each of the axes. Thus, the optimal price would be approximately $6,800/710 = $9.577 per unit.* If Maycrest's management uses odd-number pricing, the price might be set at $9.59 because prices ending in 9 are more common than those ending in 8.

The approximate monthly profit would be $2,760, which may be read from the graph. This profit can also be calculated as follows:

Total revenue ($9.59 × 710 units)		$6,808.90
Less costs:		
Variable costs (710 units × $5.00 per unit)	$3,550.00	
Fixed costs	500.00	
Total costs		4,050.00
Estimated monthly profit		$2,759.90

*It is not necessary to have a TR line and volume estimate for each possible price. Thus, this method assumes that the estimates of volume at various prices are continuously distributed over all prices. Considering that judgments are used, this assumption is not unrealistic.

CONCEPT SUMMARY

Major Operational Pricing Approaches

Cost-Based Pricing Strategies	
Markup Pricing	Similar types of items are marked up a fixed percentage over costs.
Cost-Plus Pricing	An item's final price is not specified until all associated costs are known. Then an agreed upon percentage or a fixed amount is added for profit.
Target Return Pricing	Prices are set in anticipation of earning a desired target return on investment.
Payback Period Pricing	A price is determined that will enable the firm to cover all costs and capital investment within a specified time period.
Competition-Based Pricing Strategies	
Existing Market Rates	Prices are set to reflect existing or anticipated competitor rates.
Competitive Bid Pricing	Prices are set in anticipation of competitor bids and costs.
Demand-Based Pricing Strategies	
Price Discrimination	Different prices are assessed different buyers for similar items.
Skimming	Establishing high prices, then cutting prices to capture additional customers.
Penetration	Establishing low prices to gain volume and drive down average costs to head off anticipated competition.
Prestige Pricing	Assessing high prices to enhance an item's prestige image.
Loss-Leader Pricing	Selling some items at low prices to build retail store traffic.
Odd-Number Pricing	Setting prices to end with an odd number, such as $9.95.
Flexible Break-Even Pricing	
Expected costs and revenues are estimated and a profit maximizing price is calculated.	

Flexible break-even pricing does have the weakness of being dependent upon estimates. However, management uses estimates and judgment in every operating decision. Flexible break-even pricing at least forces management's attention on *both* costs and revenues. Further, it provides an objective way of analyzing the estimates.

Other Factors to Consider

Management should consider several factors besides demand and production costs when setting prices. These are transportation costs, discounts, prices of other items in a line, other means of changing the price, and other environmental influences.

Transportation Costs

An important question for management to answer is, "How should transportation costs be treated when pricing a product?" Should the company expect a buyer to pay for shipping costs as a separate item? Perhaps buyers should be left to worry about arranging and paying for transportation entirely. Yet, an important way to increase an item's worth to buyers is for management to provide this service to customers and set prices to cover the additional costs. For many companies, the answer to these

Exhibit 20.1
A Sampling of the Rates Used in the Railroad Industry

Besides the distance shipped, carload rates (CL rates), and less-than-carload rates (LCL), railroads might base shipping charges on:

1. *Class rates.* All items have special rates, based upon value and bulk (about 5 percent of all items are shipped under class rates).

2. *Commodity rates.* Special rates for specific commodities, especially bulky, low-value items.

3. *Blanket commodity rates.* Commodity rates that apply over a large geographical area (regardless of the distance shipped) especially for items traded on exchanges, such as wheat and corn. (Both types of commodity rates cover about 85 percent of all railroad shipments.)

4. *Negotiated, or exception, rates.* Specially negotiated rates by a specific shipper, often to meet competition. (Nearly 10 percent of all loads are shipped under these rates.)

5. For *specialized services,* including:

   Containerized rates. For items packed in custom-designed containers of specific dimensions that facilitate rapid loading and unloading.

   Diversion in transit. Where the shipper may change the ultimate destination while en route, provided that the same general direction is maintained. (Useful to shippers that are sending goods to market where prices may vary by location.)

   Fast freight. For express trains.

   Piggyback. A special rate for hauling loaded truck trailers intact, which is a special form of containerized rate. (This is called *fishyback* when the trucks are loaded on boats.)

   Pool cars. A special rate for putting together a CL up to a certain geographic location, then breaking the CL apart to ship further the remainder of the items at LCL rates, but in the same general direction.

   Mixed cars. Similar to a pool car, but for different types of commodities in the same car. (The most expensive commodity rate applies.)

   Transit privilege. A feature that allows items to be shipped, unloaded for further processing, then reloaded for shipment to the final destination, provided it is in the same general direction. (Especially useful for milling and meat processing.)

   Transloading. The shipping of CL lots to the point nearest to all ultimate destinations, then breaking the load into LCL lots for final shipment.

questions is an integral part of establishing marketing strategy and determining the pricing component of the marketing mix.

Transportation rate structures can be very complex, even to experts. Exhibit 20.1 illustrates a sampling of rates used in the railroad industry. While not unique, as other modes have similar structures, train rates provide an illustration of the difficulty confronting traffic managers.

To grasp the complexity of a traffic manager's job, multiply this sampling of rate structures by the various modes of transportation, then by numerous products, and finally by hundreds of thousands of destinations! It is no wonder that some shipments are late, become lost, or are charged the wrong rate.

F.O.B. A frequently encountered term in marketing is F.O.B., which means "free on board." Because quoted prices may or may not include transportation charges (especially for institutional sales), it is often necessary to state the price at a given

F.O.B. (free on board)
The point to which the seller pays transportation costs.

location. To avoid confusion, companies use the term F.O.B. to clarify who is responsible for which portions of the transportation costs. **F.O.B.** identifies the location where the seller's responsibility to cover transportation costs ends. Thus, to make F.O.B. meaningful, one must also name a place. There are several possibilities. Assuming that the seller is located in Kansas City:

1. The seller assumes no responsibility for freight. The term "F.O.B. factory" would be appropriate.
2. The seller pays for loading onto a common carrier, but no more. Terms such as "F.O.B. railhead" or "F.O.B. Kansas City" would describe this situation.
3. The seller assumes freight responsibility up to the nearest large city to the buyer. A term such as "F.O.B. Chicago" or "F.O.B. Los Angeles" would be used.
4. The seller pays for all freight and unloading at the nearest major transportation center, but no more. A term such as "F.O.B. unloaded Atlanta" would be appropriate.
5. The seller pays full freight charges to the buyer's location. Then, terms such as "F.O.B. delivered" and "F.O.B. buyer's warehouse" are descriptive.

There are many such possibilities. Clearly, the specific terms have an effect on the total price that a buyer pays for an item. "F.O.B. factory," for example, means that the buyer also must do the work to arrange transportation and insurance during transit. Thus, transportation costs and terms definitely play a significant role in affecting the price of a product offering.

Uniform delivered price
Charging one common price to buyers of an item regardless of their location.

Uniform Delivered Prices The term **uniform delivered price** means that the seller charges one final price to all buyers, regardless of their location. The seller assumes all costs for transportation. Firms whose shipping costs are relatively insignificant often use uniform delivered prices, which also permits national ads to include a product's price since it is the same for everyone.

Zone prices
Charging uniform prices to all buyers within a stated zone.

Zone Prices **Zone prices** are charged when the seller divides the total market area into separate zones. A uniform delivered price is charged to all customers within each zone, but the prices may vary between zones, depending upon each one's average shipping costs. Sears, for example, uses this technique for its catalog sales.

Freight Absorption The term freight absorption means that the seller pays (or absorbs) some of the transportation costs that customers would otherwise have to assume. With freight absorption, sellers are able to compete on the basis of delivered price in distant locations where competitors are located.

Base-point prices
Where competitors use a common scheme for charging freight from common zones.

Base-Point Prices In some industries such as automobiles and steel a somewhat unusual pricing method has been used at various times: **base-point** (or basing-point) **pricing.** With this system, one or more competitors recognize a particular set of locations as shipping points, or base points. Figure 20.7 illustrates a hypothetical base-point system. A seller charges each customer for freight under this system, but the charge is from the nearest base point regardless of the shipment's origin. Customer C_1, for example, would pay transportation from BP_1, even if the origin was P_A or P_B. Similarly, customer C_2 pays transportation from BP_2, despite the location of the shipment's origin. The number of base points varies from industry to industry.

Single Base-Point Systems In the case of single base-point arrangements, sellers recognize only one location as a common origin. Historically, auto manufacturers have used such a system, with those headquartered in Detroit choosing that location as the base point; even if a car was built in San Jose, a California customer would pay freight from Detroit. Generally, the Federal Trade Commission has ruled that most single base-point systems are illegal.

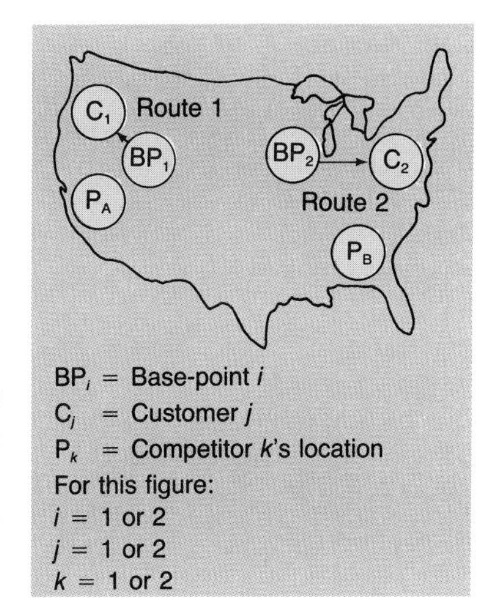

Figure 20.7
Hypothetical Base-Point System

Multiple Base-Point Systems Figure 20.7 illustrates a multiple base-point system, where two or more base points are identified. Such systems are generally legal because they encourage competition between distant manufacturers. However, management must be careful to avoid **phantom freight,** which refers to charging for freight that exceeds actual transportation costs. This practice is illegal. Recall from the discussion of Figure 20.7 that the firms charge for freight from the nearest base point regardless of the shipment's origin. Provided that such systems develop out of good-faith competition, they are generally considered legal.

Phantom freight
Charging for freight that exceeds the actual transportation charge.

Including Transportation Costs in Prices Generally, marketers of most consumer goods assess one price to cover all marketing and production costs, including the necessary transportation to the place of purchase. Notable exceptions include motor vehicles and items sold through catalog outlets, where management levies a separate charge for transportation. In some other instances, separate transportation charges are imposed for consumer items requiring home delivery and setup, such as washers and dryers, depending upon the services mix of the selling retailer. But in general, shipping charges are absorbed in the retail price paid by consumers for most of the items they buy.

In contrast, many items sold to producers, governmental units, and to channel members for resale do not include transportation charges. Manufacturers frequently assess separate charges for shipping, and this charge can represent a major portion of an item's total cost. Therefore, management must be certain to specify which services a price is to cover.

Whether or not prices include transportation usually depends upon several factors, including the prevailing competitive practices, how sizable shipping costs are in relation to total product costs, and the length of the distribution channel.

In general, lengthy channels include transportation as one of the functions intermediaries perform to earn their margins. Accordingly, prices tend to include transportation in such cases. Conversely, short channels often involve separate charges for shipping, although shipping is usually negotiable when sizable orders are involved. Also, including transportation is also often dependent on the desires of major customers. Some companies such as General Motors have extensive transportation departments and sometimes prefer to arrange their own shipping, whereas other companies would rather have the seller assume the tasks.

Discounts

Many producers use intermediaries to perform various portions of the marketing process. The conventional means of paying for their services is through discounts. There are two types: trade and special discounts.

Trade discounts
Price allowances offered to channel members to compensate them for the activities that they perform.

Markup
The margin charged for an item over its cost.

Margin
The difference between the price and the cost of an item, or between revenues and costs.

Trade Discounts **Trade discounts** (also called margins and markups) are the price allowances offered to channel members to compensate them for the activities that they perform. They are discounts from the final purchase price allowed to an intermediary. (See Appendix C for further discussion.)

For example, a manufacturer of an item retailing for $100 and distributed directly to retailers might allow a 30 percent **markup** *on retail* to the retailers for handling the item. Retailers would then pay $70 for each item purchased.

Margins may be stated either on the basis of the final selling price, as in the above example, or on the basis of cost. To illustrate, a 30 percent markup on cost for an item retailing for $100 is calculated as:

$$\frac{\left(\begin{matrix}\text{Intermediary's}\\ \text{Selling Price}\end{matrix}\right)}{\left[1.0 + \left(\begin{matrix}\text{Markup on Cost}\\ \text{Percentage}\end{matrix}\right)\right]} = \frac{\$100.00}{(1.0 + 0.3)} = \$76.92$$

Thus, the differences between the markups allowed can be dramatic, depending on whether the markup is based upon cost or eventual selling price.

Another consideration is when there are several levels of intermediaries involved in the distribution system. Compensation for each level is typically provided through a *chain of discounts*. Exhibit 20.2 illustrates how chain discounts work when they are based upon costs or selling prices.

Markups are generally set at customary or standard levels within an industry. While some intermediaries such as mass merchandisers rely on low margins to generate volume, manufacturers should establish common discount structures for all channel members at the same level. The Robinson-Patman Act (see Appendix B) prohibits charging different prices to different intermediaries at the same channel level.

Exhibit 20.2
Chain Markups on Cost and on Selling Price

Assume that an item sells at retail for $100 and is handled by retailers and wholesalers, in addition to the producer. A 30%, 10% chain is used for markups in this example.

Margins and Costs When Markups Are on Cost

	Selling Price	Cost	Markup	Margin
Retailers	$100.00	$76.92	30%	$23.08
Wholesalers	$76.92	$69.93	10%	$6.99
Producer	$69.93			

Margins and Costs When Markups Are on Selling Price

	Selling Price	Cost	Markup	Margin
Retailers	$100.00	$70.00	30%	$30.00
Wholesalers	$70.00	$63.00	10%	$7.00
Producer	$63.00			

Special Discounts Sometimes producers find it necessary to offer intermediaries added incentives to enlist their aggressive support. Record companies such as Columbia frequently reimburse retailers for money spent to advertise certain popular albums; or manufacturers frequently offer an additional margin to "kick off" a new product campaign. There are three major types of special discounts.

Cash Discounts **Cash discounts** are discounts granted buyers for paying their bill in a short period of time. An invoice amount for $2,000 with the statement "2 percent in ten days, net in 30 days" means, for example, that the buyer pays only $1,960 if the bill is paid in 10 days. Otherwise the full amount is due in 30 days. Some companies have been successful in extending these discounts to consumers as well.[5]

Cash discounts
Offering of a reduction from the posted price for the rapid payment of cash.

Buyers are well advised to take advantage of these discounts when offered by suppliers. Saving 2 percent by paying 20 days sooner amounts to a 36.5 percent annualized finance charge for *not* doing so (365 days/20 days × 2% = 36.5%).

Quantity Discounts Many buyers, especially industrial ones, expect to receive discounts if they buy in large quantities.[6] There are two types of **quantity discounts.** *Noncumulative* discounts are granted on individual orders above a certain quantity, such as for a full carload. Generally, these discounts are legal, so long as they are made available to all intermediaries. *Cumulative* quantity discounts are extended to buyers who purchase a large amount—determined by adding individual orders—over an extended period of time, such as a quarter or a year. Cumulative discounts granted to intermediaries are largely illegal under the Robinson-Patman Act unless the seller can document proof that the cost or competition-meeting defenses of the act apply.

Quantity discounts
Offering discounts from stated prices for sizable orders.

Advertising and Push Money Allowances These are special price reductions offered to intermediaries for them to perform certain promotion functions. **Advertising allowances** are subsidies, full or partial, paid to intermediaries to reimburse them for advertising the sponsor's product, such as when Safeway advertises that it features Prell

Advertising allowances
Subsidies, full or partial, paid to intermediaries to reimburse them for advertising the sponsor's product.

An item's price must reflect the prices of other items in the product line.

Push money
Special payments offered to intermediaries to encourage their aggressive efforts to sell a particular product.

Shampoo. **Push money** consists of additional payments to intermediaries to aggressively sell a particular product. In turn, it is usually expected that the intermediaries will pass along the additional incentive to their sales representatives. Generally, these allowances are legal provided that they do not result in price discrimination. For some items, such as groceries, offering special discounts is almost a prerequisite for getting shelf space for a new product.

Pricing a Product Line

When two or more related products are marketed by a company, the price of each item in the line should be set in relation to the prices of the other items. For example, No Nonsense Fashions markets different brands of panty hose at different price levels aimed at different market segments. In such cases, management must coordinate the price of each item so that the overall line contributes to the company's overall goals.

Cross-elasticity
The relationship of the change in price of one product to the demand effects on another product. A high cross-elasticity means that the products are highly related in this regard, and vice versa.

Cannibalization
One company product that takes sales away from another, more profitable, product in a line.

Related items in a line are usually substitutes for each other, meaning that they have high **cross-elasticities.*** This term means that a change in the price of one item affects the demand for another. A buyer of a 30-watt stereo set, for example, might trade up if a 40-watt set's price is lowered a bit, or trade down if a 20-watt set's price is too close to the 30-watt's price. (This latter condition is termed **cannibalization.**) Thus, if prices are improperly set in relation to market segment differences, there may be cannibalization and a loss in profits. When the prices properly reflect segment differences, however, there is a good possibility of trading up some of the customers. (See Chapter 10 for further discussion of cannibalization and trading up.)

Cross-elasticities present a problem in measuring demand. Because of the operational difficulty, many firms establish *price lines* for groups of products within a line. These are preestablished price levels for items within the line. For example, retailers often sell men's slacks at $19.95, $24.95, $29.95, $34.95, and $39.95. These price levels are based upon what the managers consider to be distinctive price thresholds in the overall market.[7] Once set, the firm then develops or locates products that can profitably be sold at each of the price lines. Using cost as a guide, managers can then concentrate on developing items with the intention of satisfying a particular segment's needs as an objective. Women's clothing, appliances, houses, and even motor vehicles are among the many items companies price in this way.

Other Means of Changing Prices

As exemplified by the airline industry's mileage programs (see the accompanying Marketing Brief), there are other means of changing an item's price besides altering the price tag.

Unit pricing
Posting prices in terms of commonly accepted unit volume measures, such as the price per ounce.

Changing the quantity included. Potato chips, for example, were sold largely in one-pound packages several years ago. Today's large bag costs about the same but is only 8 or 10 ounces. **Unit pricing** laws (where the price-per-unit, such as an ounce, is posted) have been passed in many states, enabling many consumers to better make choices than in the past.[8] Nonetheless, changing the quantity is one alternative to consider.

*Economists call this kind of relationship a positive cross-elasticity. Conversely, negative cross-elasticity exists when the products in question are complements, such as coffee and coffee creamer, and an increase in the price of one tends to decrease the quantity demanded of the other.

MARKETING BRIEF
Frequent Flyer Programs Score a Success

Begun about five years ago as a means of luring well-traveled executives into brand loyalty, frequent flyer bonus programs have become almost essential for airlines to attract the business trade. The programs, offered by all of the major airlines and many affiliated regional carriers, all have a similar theme: fly on the sponsoring carrier's routes a certain number of miles and get free tickets. While the programs are open to everyone, they are targeted at business travelers since they are the group that does the vast majority of the flying.

The perks vary, but include travel to such exotic places as Europe, Hawaii, the Orient—even cruises on ships. "The beauty of these programs is that we get to pick the destinations," according to one seasoned business traveler. The air miles required for a free ticket bonus also vary, from 20,000 miles on Republic to 150,000 miles for two free first class international tickets on United. And there are more benefits possible as well, including free car rentals and hotel accommodations. Even auto rental companies and some hotel chains have climbed aboard by offering a mileage credit on some of the frequent flyer programs, such as 500 or 1,000 miles, to travelers who rent a car from or stay with them while on a trip scheduled with an air carrier.

The programs are in such high demand that many rebelled when some companies tried to get their employees to turn the bonus tickets in for company credit. For instance, the Phoenix Suns basketball players responded by refusing to sign autographs or take part in other promotional programs in protest. "Why should the players [who are corporate executives knocking down $200,000 a year and more] give up one of their perks," says Charles Granthan, executive vice president of the NBA Players Association.

SOURCE: Adapted from "Managers Tug at Frequent-Flyer Bonuses," *Advertising Age*, February 24, 1986: 50.

Giving cents-off coupons or rebates. In effect, the mileage bonuses offered by air carriers offer travelers this type of incentive.

Offering specially reduced financing plans. The auto industry frequently uses this incentive to spur purchases.

Selling items at special prices through nontraditional channels. For example, some ski areas in Utah sell lift tickets at discount prices in major city supermarkets.[9]

In fact, any component of the overall marketing mix might be altered as an alternative to changing the sales tag price of an item.[10] Accordingly, managers should not set prices in a vacuum. All components of the marketing mix must be considered.[11]

Other Considerations

In closing this chapter, it is important to point out that pricing is a complex area of decision making that is affected by competitive and environmental forces. Shifts in economic conditions, resource availabilities, and interest rates are but a few of the many factors that create elements of uncertainty in decisions. But as Guiltinan points out, ". . . pricing policy under uncertainty need not consist solely of defensive, risk aversion alternatives, but can be positive and opportunistic in perspective."[12]

In other words, by carefully analyzing economic, environmental, and market factors and acting on these, a marketer is in a far better position to attain a firm's objectives than is possible by simply following the leads of competitors.[13] "In pricing strategy, the key is advance planning to retain the initiative, rather than be forced to react to competitive moves."[14]

Atlantic Richfield is one company that reduced its credit service to affect a lower price.

Chapter Summary

This was the second and final chapter examining price decisions. It began with a discussion of demand-based operational strategies used by managers in making price decisions. Price discrimination involves the charging of different prices to different market segments. Skimming is initially charging high prices, then lowering them to capture more of the market. Prestige pricing is the charging of high prices to add to the "elite" image of an item. Loss-leader pricing involves selling some items at a loss (or a slight profit, but lower than usual) to attract customers who might then buy other normally priced items. Odd-number pricing is the common practice of setting prices to end in an odd number, such as 99¢.

The chapter then examined flexible break-even pricing. This is a method of setting prices by using break-even concepts to estimate costs and judgment to estimate revenue functions. The idea is to estimate an optimal price for an item.

Next, other factors to consider when setting prices were discussed. These include the issue of transportation costs, discounts, pricing a product line, and other means of changing the price besides altering the ticket amount.

This chapter concludes the section on decision making for individual marketing mix elements.

Questions

1. Explain price discrimination. Why is its use desirable to a firm? What are the risks? What about the legal implications? Ethical implications? Can you think of examples to discuss in class?
2. Explain skimming. What are the risks involved?
3. Compare and contrast prestige pricing with skimming.
4. What do you think of the practice of specifically setting odd-number prices?
5. Explain flexible break-even pricing.
6. Use flexible break-even pricing to find the optimal price for the following:

Fixed costs = $100 per week
Variable costs = $2.00 per unit

Estimates of weekly sales volume at various prices:

Selling Price	Estimated Weekly Volume
$10.00	100
9.00	300
8.00	450
7.00	550
6.00	600
5.00	650

7. A new entrepreneur has just announced, "We will focus on mass merchandisers. They accept a smaller markup, which means more profit for us!" Comment.
8. What are the advantages and disadvantages of a retailer's offering cash discounts to consumers?
9. If a manufacturer receives $50 from each item sold to cover costs and profit, how much will the retail price be if markups are 30 percent to retailers and 20 percent to wholesalers when
   a. Markups are on cost
   b. Markups are on selling prices
10. If an item sells for $200 retail list, how much will the manufacturer receive (assume the same markup percentage as in problem 9) if markups are on:
   a. Cost
   b. Selling price

Part Five

Special Topics in Marketing

Chapter 21

Organizing, Budgeting, and Controlling

Objectives

After completing this chapter, you should be able to demonstrate a knowledge of:

- How marketing organizational structures evolve within an organization
- The major types of marketing organizational structures and their advantages and disadvantages
- The budgeting process as it relates to marketing planning and decision making
- Various means of formulating marketing budgets, including the allocation of some percentage of sales, establishing parity with competitors, funding on the basis of available resources, and the task buildup method
- How managers can employ control measures to assure that a firm is not departing excessively from its intended path
- Major control measures, including comparisons with budgets, industry, and past performance
- The nature and composition of the marketing audit

MARKETING SUCCESS

A Turnaround at Ashton-Tate

Edward M. Esber, Jr. hardly looked like a savior to many analysts, even to some on the Board of Directors of Ashton-Tate, when he took over as the company's chief executive in late 1984. In his former role as software developer, the Harvard MBA engineer had been demoted three times. But take over he did, and with a vengeance. "The 'proof of the pudding' . . ." said one securities analyst.

Ashton-Tate was in the doldrums when Esber took over the helm from David C. Cole, who had become chairman after cofounder George Tate died of a heart attack in August 1984. While charismatic and entrepreneurial, Cole failed to create a well-organized operation. Overly ambitious sales projections and a lack of financial controls caused company earnings to plummet by nearly 60 percent, to $830,000, in the first half of 1985 despite a 70 percent sales gain.

Esber's first goal was to inject Aston-Tate with massive doses of "management 101." He replaced Cole's flamboyant, autocratic rule with a lower-key, more participatory style. He instituted simple but important procedures such as formalized planning and budgeting. The development of new product ideas was also emphasized to enable less reliance on the company's dBASE III® (a popular data-base management program) which accounted for over half of the company's sales. Meetings about new products, once held at the former chairman's whim, are now formally scheduled for every other week. This has led to many new and exciting products on the horizon.

He has also demonstrated a solid understanding of marketing products, according to many company observers. Taking a new tack in promoting FRAMEWORK®, a package that was developed before he arrived at the helm as an "integrated package," he has sold it by stressing that it is a fancy word processing and spreadsheet program and sales have picked up.

The results have been very impressive, indeed. While most of the company's competitors were barely treading water over the past 14 months, Ashton-Tate's profits climbed 146 percent on a 45 percent jump in revenues and the company's stock nearly quadrupled in price, to around $20.

SOURCE: Adapted from Scott Ticer, "The Dark Horse Who Has Ashton-Tate Galloping Again," *Business Week*, February 10, 1986: 89–90.

Introduction

A company's organization is very important to its internal decision-making processes because the structure itself establishes the interactions among positions, and therefore the people. Budgeting and controlling activities are also critical to the success of an organization. These processes serve to formalize the planning and evaluating of functions and people. Who reports to whom, the nature of their authority, the resulting decision-making responsibility, and the degree of participation by others in decision making are all set in part by the organizational structure. And the way people are formally enabled to perform their functions and the evaluative criteria used are set by the budgeting and controlling processes.

The Ashton-Tate Marketing Success points out that skilled managers can create an organizational climate that is conducive to success. In that company formalized planning and control, along with participatory decision making, works very well. Other organizational forms work best in other companies.

This chapter looks at these vital activities within organizations, with special focus being placed upon the marketing function. It stresses marketing organizations within manufacturing companies, as concern for marketing organizations largely emerged within manufacturing businesses. Similar developments are starting to emerge in service and not-for-profit organizations, however. Retailers, banks, mass transit companies, health maintenance organizations and others are learning the value of emphasizing marketing activities and the need to effectively organize, budget, and control them.

Organizing Marketing Activities

The extensiveness of the marketing organization within a company depends, in part, upon the evolution of the marketing function itself within that company. In general, marketing functions become more complex as the marketing work performed expands. Failure to evolve as circumstances dictate can be catastrophic to a firm.[1]

At least three phases are identifiable in the development of marketing departments: a simple sales department, separate "sales" and "marketing" departments, and a contemporary marketing department.[2] The following section traces this evolutionary process.

The Evolution of Marketing Departments

In even very small companies, management should assign the responsibility for at least three key functions to someone: raising and managing capital (finance), producing (operations), and selling output (sales).

A sales department is the simplest marketing organizational form. The person responsible for sales is also often accountable for other functions as well in small firms. But with expansion, a full-time manager is generally made fully responsible for managing the sales force. Other marketing functions such as advertising and marketing research are also part of this manager's responsibility if there is a need for them, but the primary emphasis of the department is on sales.

The marketing departments of most companies historically have centered around their sales departments; and this type of organization still exists today in some enterprises, especially smaller ones and those serving producer and government markets.

As a company expands, marketing functions in addition to sales tend to become more important. Growth usually requires the penetration of new markets. This, in turn, means more marketing information is needed, advertising becomes more important, and so forth. Thus, growth in all of the marketing functions occurs.

Typically during this transition, many companies create two departments to handle the required marketing work, as illustrated in Figure 21.1. Top management assigns all nonsales activities to the "marketing" department and charges the sales department with selling.

Separate "marketing" departments can be effective for some firms, but there is great potential for extensive internal conflict in this organizational form. The head of

Developing an effective organization is essential for any successful marketing effort.

marketing is likely to seek long-run success, whereas the head of sales is more apt to push for immediate results. And both may envision each other as a power threat. Thus, a structure with these "separate, but equal" departments is usually unstable in the long run, and generally represents only a stepping stone in the evolutionary process.

In a contemporary marketing department, all marketing functions, including sales, are organized under one head—typically a vice president of marketing—and such an arrangement complements the adoption of the marketing concept, where management integrates and coordinates all marketing activities around profitably satisfying the target market's needs. Housing all of the marketing functions under one roof helps to assure

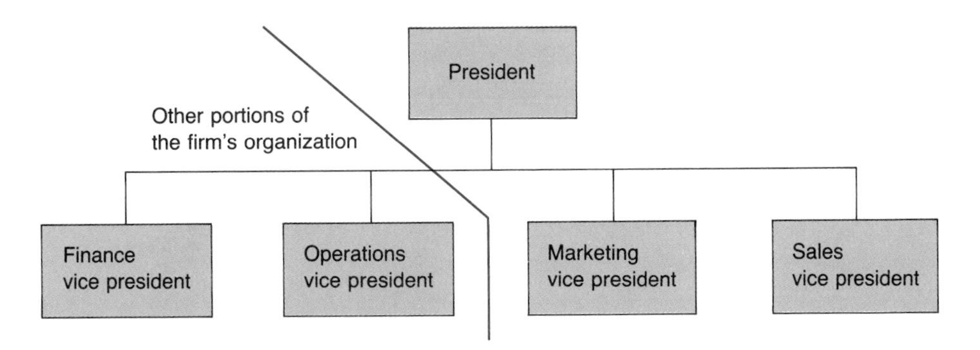

Figure 21.1
The Marketing Organization When Sales and Marketing Are Separate Departments

that no single function will dominate at the expense of the others. And, as the accompanying Marketing Brief discussing the successes of Japanese firms illustrates, it is important for all of the company's marketing activities to be integrated into the company's central decision making.

Not all companies have evolved to the point of organizing their marketing activities in a contemporary way. Nor is it likely, as there are always companies in different stages of evolution. Further, the expansiveness of each of the marketing functions varies within companies. The Electric Boat Division of General Dynamics (makers of submarines), for instance, performs most of its needed marketing functions through engineers and their interplay with government and naval officials. So does the Budd Company, a producer of dies and toolings for industry. But such companies deal with relatively few customers, can focus directly on each, and their success stems largely from solving clients' technical problems.

In contrast, most large organizations, especially those involved with consumer markets, such as Procter & Gamble and Coca-Cola, face numerous customers, fragmented markets, and considerable competition. For these companies, success usually requires carefully coordinating a full mix of marketing activities around chosen targets. A contemporary marketing organization is best suited for bringing about the required functional integration. In the next section, ways of implementing a contemporary marketing department are examined.

Organizing Contemporary Marketing Departments

Contemporary marketing departments tend to be organized along one of three general lines: according to the functional tasks to be performed, around target markets, or around products.

Functional Organizations The term "function" refers to a set of major related activities that need to be performed, such as advertising or physical distribution. Accordingly, the simplest and most common marketing structure is to organize along the various marketing functional specialties, as illustrated in Figure 21.2. In such a **functional organization,** the marketing vice president directs and coordinates all functional managers. In turn, the individual managers supervise and coordinate the personnel assigned to their respective units.

Functional organization
Where all specialists within a given function, such as sales, report to a central position.

MARKETING BRIEF
Molding the Organization around Customers

Legends are made from events like the success of Japanese companies in practically all of the markets they compete. The result has been an onslaught of U.S. business onlookers visiting Japan and her industrial giants, a friendly American invasion of the country unlike the one planned, but never carried out, in the mid-1940s. The goal is to learn from Japanese management's apparent mastery.

Trips by executives of General Motors, Motorola, U.S. Steel, and a host of others have focused on learning management methods, decision-making styles, and worker productivity improvement plans. And many of the differences, such as worker participation in decision making and morning group exercise classes, have been widely reported and copied by some U.S. companies.

Another difference, though less reported and perhaps more fundamental, is that many of the most successful Japanese companies are organized around customers and their needs. Market research is no mere nicety to the "Japanese style," it is an obsession. "We must learn first about the customers," said a key official of Toyota. Beyond this, the organizations are structured around implementing the research findings. "This is a big difference in the way we perform," said an executive of Sony.

The R & D department of most successful Japanese firms is in a very strong position. This is evidenced by that division's department head reporting to the organization's chief executive officer, not the production chief as in most U.S. companies. And the practice is for R & D and marketing to work very closely together, whereas in many U.S. companies the two areas almost do not speak to one another.

The Japanese hold weekly meetings of senior people in R & D, marketing, and production. The purpose is to facilitate rapid adjustments to the marketplace. New products can be developed and introduced in Japan within six months, compared to about two years in the U.S. To many analysts, this is a major contributing factor to the Japanese success story.

SOURCE: Adapted from Frank E. Moroya and James Hance, "Obligation to Customers Key to Successful Marketing," *Marketing News* 19, no. 12 (June 7, 1985): 6.

The organization illustrated in Figure 21.2 is a relatively uncomplicated one. In a large organization such as United Airlines there are many more functional lines established. This may result in a greater number of managers reporting to the vice president of marketing, which could cause difficulty in supervising all functions directly.[3] In such cases, it is common to group the functions into related areas, and then add another hierarchical layer in the organization. To illustrate, among those reporting to the vice president of marketing would likely be a director of planning, whose responsibility would include marketing research, product planning, and perhaps forecasting. Another senior manager, perhaps a director of marketing operations, would also report to the vice president and be responsible for sales, advertising, and customer services.

Functional marketing organizations have two major advantages: They nurture the internal development of experienced specialists, and the organization is structurally straightforward and simplified.

There are major disadvantages, however. The members of each functional group may become myopic and see themselves in competition with other groups for funds. Job rotation—moving people from one department to another—helps here, but also partially offsets the potential benefits of specialization. Also, adequate management of an extensive product mix can become difficult because the specialists tend to

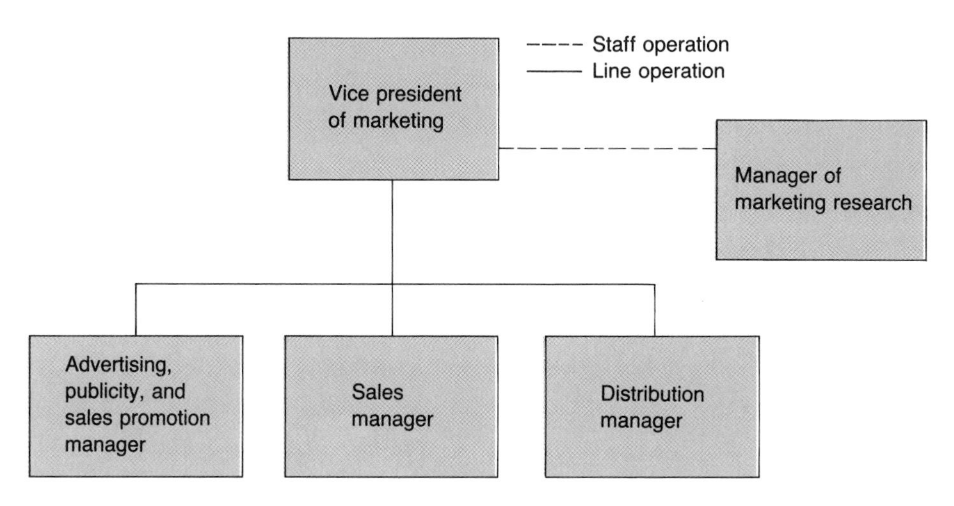

Figure 21.2
Typical Functional Marketing Organizational Structure

concentrate their efforts on high-volume key products, which may lead to neglect of new products and new markets.

Market-Structured Organizations To offset the disadvantages of functional organizations, many companies set up their marketing organizations around the markets themselves. Two types of **market-structured organizations** are distinguishable: decentralized market-based divisions and market-centered organizations.

Market-structured organization
Structuring a marketing department around major target markets.

Decentralized Market-Based Divisions Divisions are major sections of a company, and each operates something like an independent business intent on capturing a separate, unique target market. For example, Levi Strauss has several **decentralized market-based divisions,** including basic denims, fashion wear, and teenage and children's wear. The company utilizes a separate marketing staff in each one. The number of divisions within a company can be quite large; Emerson Electric has 44 and Merrill Lynch has 15. Beatrice Foods, a large conglomerate with many divisions (such as La Choy Chinese foods and Samsonite luggage), has no corporate-level marketing director. Instead, each division has its own.[4]

Decentralized market-based divisions
Where major subunits of an organization are created to operate much like separate companies that focus on different segments or different markets entirely.

Figure 21.3 illustrates a typical divisionalized marketing department, with only two divisions depicted for simplicity's sake. Sometimes the targets of two or more divisions are fairly similar, such as Ford Motor Company's Ford and Lincoln-Mercury divisions. This puts each division into competition with each other as well as with rival companies. Usually, though, completely different segments are the targets of divisionalization, as with Merrill Lynch. In either case, division managers are responsible for developing their own marketing mixes.

Divisionalization means that authority and responsibility are decentralized. **Decentralization** occurs when higher-level managers delegate authority and responsibility to lower-level managers. And through it, management can more readily design separate marketing mixes around different market segments. Beyond this, a classic study of General Motors revealed that divisionalization has several other advantages, including[5]

Decentralization
Where managers formally delegate authority and responsibility to subordinate managers.

- Speed and lack of confusion in decision making
- Fairness in dealing with management and reduced organizational politics
- Informality and democracy in management
- Less organizational distance between top management and lower subordinates

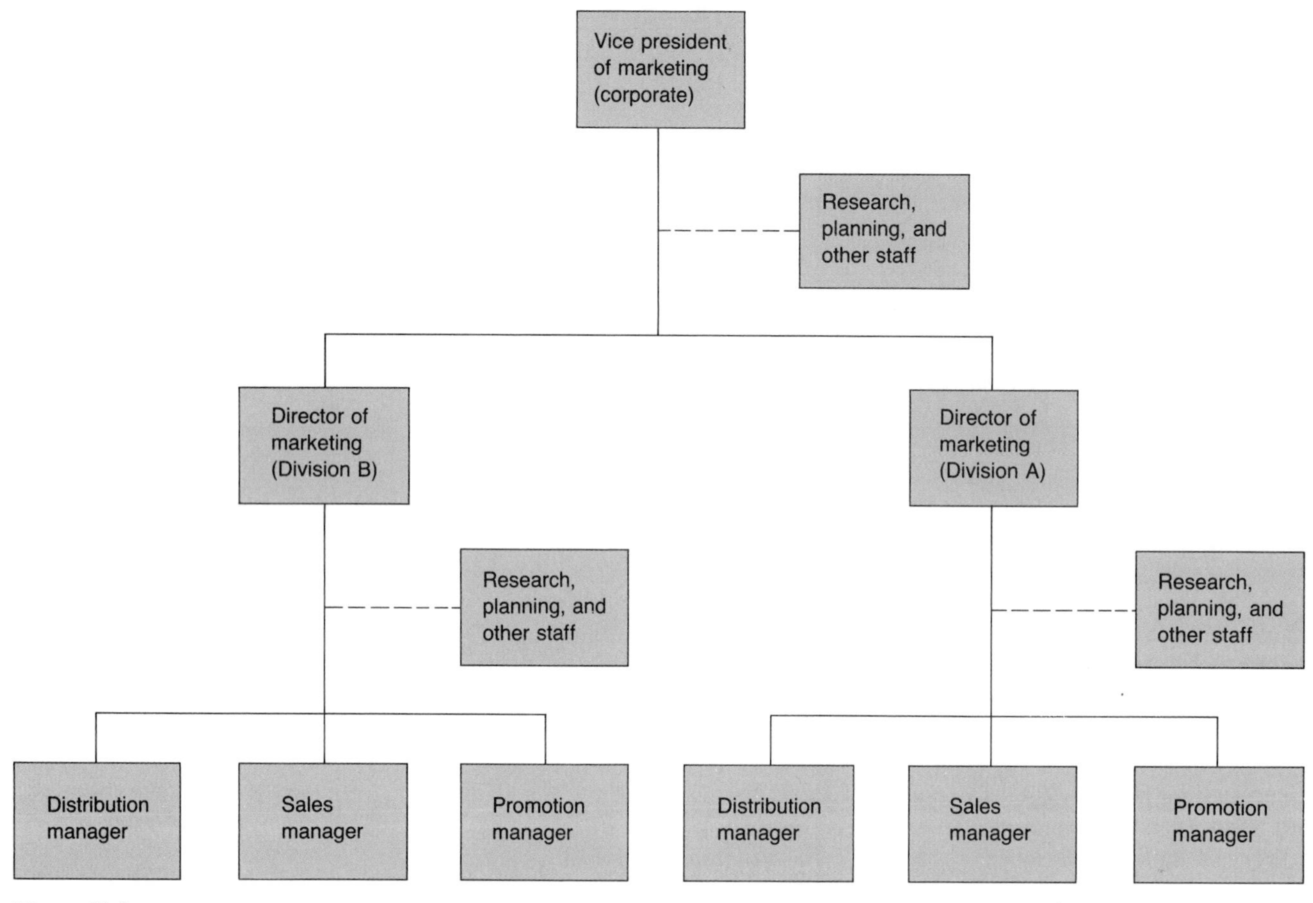

Figure 21.3
Typical Divisionalized Marketing Department

But divisionalization has its disadvantages. The major one is that inefficiencies may result from duplicate positions in the divisions, especially among smaller organizations. Accordingly, many once-divisionalized companies have restructured so that they might benefit from specialization.[6]

Divisionalization is *least* logical when the work required for the items in a product mix is quite similar and *most* logical when each organizational unit will perform different marketing tasks. The activities required to market large electric generators differ greatly from those needed for small electrical home appliances. Accordingly, companies marketing both of these product lines (such as General Electric and Westinghouse) do so through separate divisions. But if the marketing tasks are essentially the same, management probably should avoid divisionalization.

Market-centered organization
Where market managers are created to develop and coordinate specific marketing mixes for each of a company's products being targeted at a particular market.

Market-Centered Organizations Developing a **market-centered organization** is the other means of reflecting differing market characteristics among targets. Figure 21.4 illustrates such an organization.

Most managers in market-centered organizations are responsible for functional activities, such as sales. In addition, the firm utilizes *market managers* to develop and coordinate specific marketing mixes for each product or product group targeted toward a particular market. For instance, consumers on the one hand and contract buyers

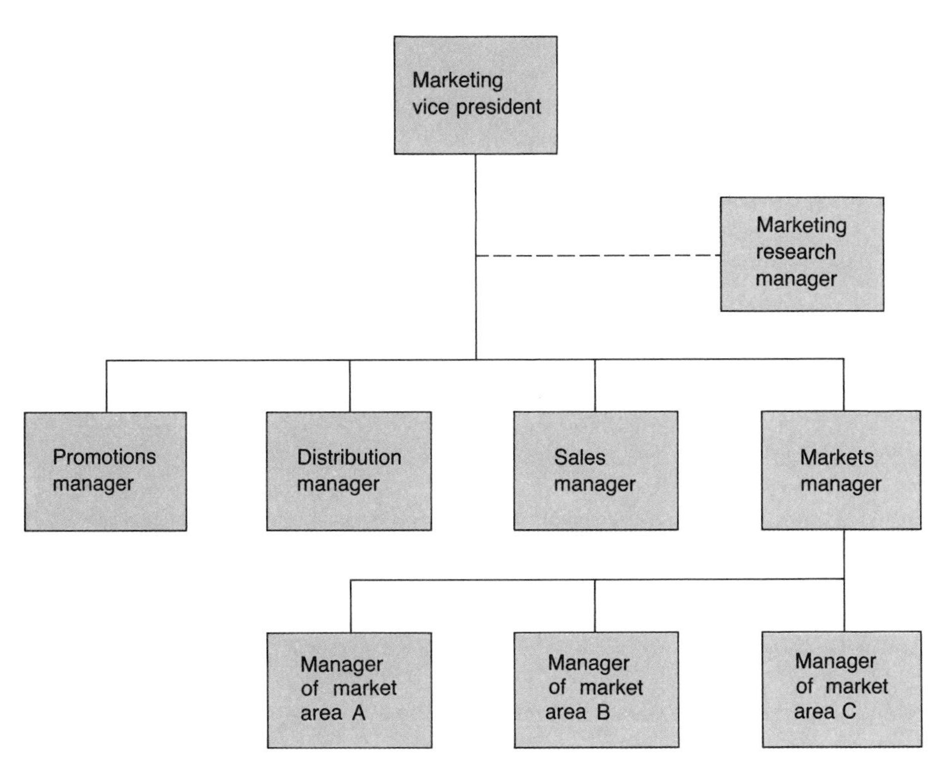

Figure 21.4
Market-Centered Organization

(residential builders and apartment landlords) on the other, represent two distinct markets for home appliances. Under a market-centered organization, a separate market manager would assume the responsibility of developing and coordinating the marketing mixes for all company products aimed at a particular market.

Market managers are responsibility centers for specific markets. They are charged with developing marketing plans and strategies, implementing them, and with earning a profit. If the market is large, the firm may assign some personnel to the market manager to provide assistance. But, usually not for normal functional support, such as sales, as the organization's functional managers provide such expertise. To illustrate, the organization allocates a portion of the sales force's time to selling products to a particular market. Since functional managers have limited resources, market managers compete with one another to enlist functional support.

The structure offers several advantages. It formalizes the process of fine-tuning marketing activities for a particular market segment, it makes someone directly responsible for keeping abreast of changing conditions in a market, and it provides an excellent training ground for marketing personnel.

Yet there are disadvantages. There is a risk of creating considerable internal conflict as the various market managers compete for internal resources while lacking full authority to totally control activity within their areas. A degree of inefficiency may develop, as efforts are duplicated by the addition of more managers performing similar tasks.

Though organizing around markets is relatively new, a growing number of companies are adopting this structure because the advantages offset the disadvantages for them. The Xerox Corp. is a highly visible example.

Product-centered organization
Where authority for a particular product is assigned to a particular manager, called a product manager or brand manager.

Product-Centered Organizations Some companies sell many different products to the same or similar market segments, such as Pillsbury, which markets many processed foods to consumers. Also, Motorola's Communications Division sells literally thousands of electronic items to various producers. A major management concern among these companies is to devote sufficient attention and resources to each of their products. It would be easy for a sales force, for instance, to push fast-moving well-established items and forget about slow-moving new ones. To prevent this from happening, many such companies have found it advantageous to assign responsibility for particular products to a specific manager by developing a **product-centered organization.**[7]

Often called either a *brand-managed* or a *product-managed* organization, product-centered marketing departments are quite similar to market-centered ones, as Figure 21.5 shows.[8] Here, though, the emphasis is on products instead of markets.

Product manager
A manager who is responsible for managing the marketing efforts for one or a group of products (see *product-centered organization*).

The Procter & Gamble Company pioneered the use of **product managers** in the late 1920s. Camay, a new soap at the time, was not selling well. A mid-level executive, who later rose to P & G's presidency, received the exclusive responsibility for developing and implementing a strong marketing plan for the brand. The results were so spectacular that management created additional product manager positions for all of P & G's other products.

Brand manager
Another name for a product manager.

Today's **brand managers** work with many groups when they develop marketing plans, including:

- Marketing research, in monitoring customer profiles, purchasing patterns, attitudes, and the like
- Planning specialists
- Distributors, to track allocated shelf space, turnover, special incentives and promotional programs
- The sales force, to enlist sales support and to learn of any customer resistance[9]
- Advertising agencies, to formulate effective ad campaigns
- Technical experts, to develop new and improved products

Intrapreneurship
An entrepreneurial spirit within large organizations; one where individual effort is not stifled by lengthy lists of rules and procedures.

The advantages and disadvantages of a product-centered organization practically parallel those of a market-centered one. One distinctive advantage for some companies, though, is that the former fosters product champions, people devoted to mustering internal support for a product, which helps to develop each product to its full potential. Another advantage is that the concept helps to foster *intrapreneurship* within large organizations.[10] **Intrapreneurship** is a term meaning an entrepreneurial spirit within large organizations; one where individual effort is not stifled by lengthy lists of rules and procedures. As a result, products, new ones and old ones alike, do not get lost in the crowd among the red tape and lack enough support to generate their potentials.

A disadvantage is that if top management allows product managers to operate very independently, they may pursue goals contrary to corporate objectives. Top management can overcome this through careful control measures. In the Stanley Hardware Division of Stanley Works, for example, top management holds weekly meetings with all product managers to discuss goals and ways to meet them.[11]

Which Structures Do Best? It is difficult to generalize about how best to organize a marketing department, as different structures might be appropriate among even close competitors. The retail giant, Federated Department stores, is comprised of 18 separate chains, including I. Magnin's, Burdine's, and Abraham Straus. Each operates as a

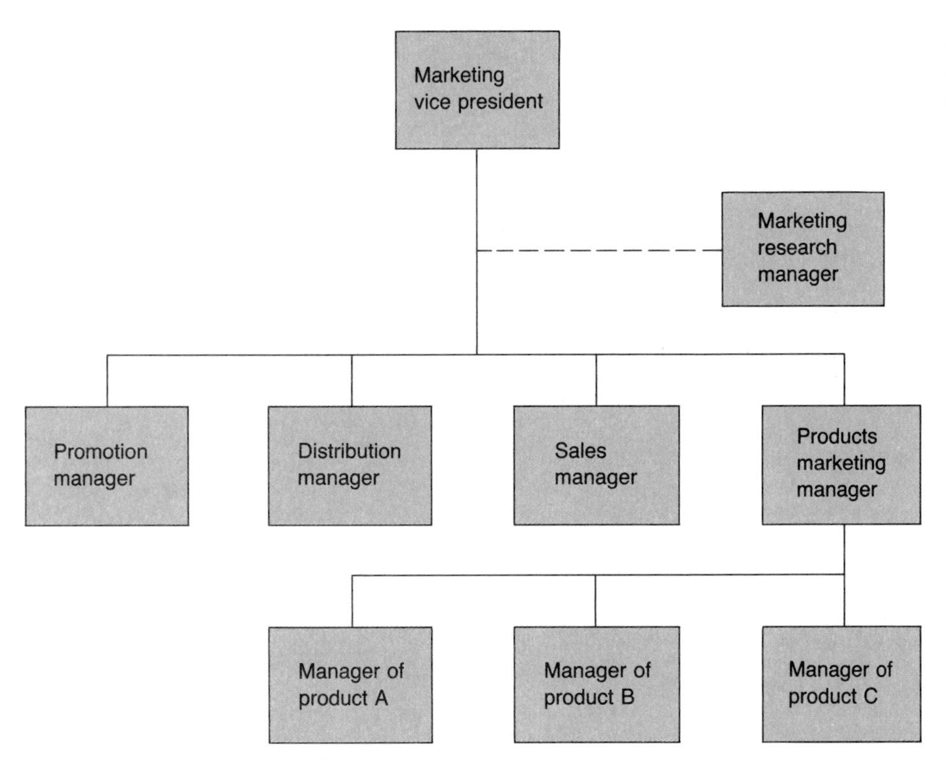

Figure 21.5
Product-Centered Structures (Brand or Product Managers)

separate division with autonomous decision making. K mart, in contrast, tightly administers most decision making from its Troy, Michigan corporate headquarters. Yet both organizations are successful. W. T. Grant was organized similarly to K mart, but the firm failed.

This does not mean, however, that any organizational structure will fit the needs of a particular company. The "best" organization nurtures both efficient and effective supervision of a company's anticipated intermediate and long-run marketing activities. Therefore, management should structure a marketing department to reflect the organization's strategies.[12] Since many variables, such as company strengths, size, and the competitive setting, are important in determining effective strategy, management should consider all of them when choosing an organization form, as illustrated by the accompanying Eastman Kodak Marketing Brief.

Regardless of which form of organization management adopts, effective marketing requires the careful administration of various control functions.

Controlling Marketing Activities

Inflation has had a tremendous impact on marketing activities. TV and newspaper ad rates, for instance, have tripled during the past decade.[13] The effect has been skyrocketing marketing costs for many companies.[14] For example, Procter & Gamble's 1976 bill for domestic advertising set a milestone, almost topping the half-billion-dollar mark—an amount that nearly equaled half of Iceland's total GNP for the same year. By 1985, the firm spent nearly nine-tenths of a billion dollars for the same purpose—a 75 percent increase in nine years![15]

MARKETING BRIEF
An Organization Should Reflect Its Strategies

The beginning of 1986 was greeted dismally by Eastman Kodak's management. On January 9, a federal judge in Washington ordered the company out of the instant photography business for violating seven of Polaroid's patents. A week later, the Rochester, N.Y.-based company dismissed 500 workers. On January 21, the company announced its return to the 35mm camera business after a 17-year absence—with a camera made not in its own once-heralded plants, but in Japan. And in February, the company announced that its earnings would be flat.

These events were startling to a company that once prided itself on technical know-how, manufacturing expertise, management leadership, and solid profitability.

Complacency set in the company during the 1970s and 80s, while others produced the innovations that Kodak was once known for: easy-to-use cameras, better and faster color film, and more efficient processing. Even worse, silver halide photography, the technology that Kodak invented 105 years ago, is slowly being surpassed by electronic imaging.

The company's lethargy was partly caused by its organization along functional lines. This was traditional in the company, "the way George (Eastman) did it." Under Kodak's new leadership of Chairman Colby H. Chandler, things are changing drastically. The photographic business has been completely reorganized to better serve company markets. Chandler has also set three primary goals for the company: to be a leader in the new "imaging" technology, to keep the $11-billion-a-year company among the 25 largest in the U.S., and to boost shareholders' return on equity to 20 percent.

SOURCE: Adapted from Alex Taylor III, "Kodak Scrambles to Refocus," *Fortune*, March 3, 1986: 34–39; and "Kodak Stands Tall with Customers while Demarketing Instant Photo Line," *Marketing News* 20 (January 31, 1986): 1, 27.

CONCEPT SUMMARY

Marketing Department Organization

Method of Organization	Description
Functional Organization	Various marketing functional specialists report to a central position. Functional managers supervise and coordinate the activities of all personnel assigned to their units.
Market-structured Organization	Marketing departments are organized around major target markets. Can be decentralized, with market-based divisions.
Market-centered Organization	Each major market has a manager, who heads functional activities. In addition, market managers are used to develop and coordinate specific marketing mixes for each of a company's products being targeted at a particular market.
Product-centered Organization	Marketing responsibility for a particular product or group of products is assigned to a product (or brand) manager.

Other marketing mix activities have been similarly affected. Adding a salesperson, along with accompanying support, can cost a company $100,000 per year; perhaps more. Building inventory to support a new product can consume $10 million in working capital.

Because of such almost overwhelming costs, and to monitor effectiveness, today's managers are increasingly emphasizing controlling marketing activities, the subject matter of the next section.

Budgeting

Budgeting is a tool to help management with the financial aspect of the planning and controlling functions of a business.[16] Put simply, a **budget** is a formal financial expression of management's plans. Plans specify ways that management intends to accomplish the firm's goals and objectives in the future.[17] Budgets spell out the anticipated cost of implementing a set of plans, as well as the expected financial results.

Budget
The total amount of money to be spent on an activity or activities during a period of time.

Why Budget? Some managers are critical of budgets and budgeting because they are generally used in evaluating performances and take considerable time to prepare. Consequently, there is often a degree of tension among personnel concerning the whole process.

Nonetheless, the budgeting process is generally worth the effort. Budgeting offers several advantages. It helps managers become conscious of the need for effective decision making. Strong budgeting pressures initiated within the Smith Corona Company in 1986, for example, were instrumental in reducing costs and turning losses into profits.[18] Budgeting also forces management to look toward the future in concrete, measurable terms and facilitates planning throughout the organization. It helps to coordinate activities and also provides "blueprints" for others to follow in the event of personnel changes.

In effect, formal planning and budgeting have value for every company, even the smallest.[19] The process is not without problems, however, particularly because of the intraorganizational conflict caused. Such conflict is inevitable because people from various functions view matters from different perspectives. Exhibit 21.1 illustrates the nature of such conflict.

It is senior management's role to moderate the conflicts and to bring balance to the divergent interests among the various units within the organization. If properly managed, budgeting contributes to the well-being of the entire organization, not just to a particular department.

Types of Budgets Companies formally committed to planning typically use several different types of budgets in their operations. The time periods and the activities involved are the two basic ways in which they differ.[20]

The time horizon used in budgeting is usually one year. This parallels the principal accounting report period, allowing sufficient time to enable the continuation of campaigns but focusing on a short enough time to enforce regular evaluation. Within the year, time frames are usually broken down into quarters and months, and sometimes even weeks. Also, many firms, such as Motorola, Inc., use a **continuous annual budget** (also called a "rolling budget"), which is a budget that is repeatedly prepared for 12 months into the future. Thus, at the end of each quarter a new quarter is added for the future. In addition, most companies also prepare longer-term budgets, such

Continuous annual budget
Repeatedly budgeting for one year into the future.

Budgeting formalizes planning in terms of both time and specific actions.

as for three years, but these usually relate to capital planning and are generally not used in operations.

A variety of activities are usually covered in the budgeting process, including marketing expenses, production operations, and capital requirements. Collectively, the separate budgets for the various operating activities of a company make up the *master budget*. Figure 21.6 illustrates typical subcategories for a manufacturer. The master budgets for intermediaries and service companies are similar, except that they omit production. Notice in the figure that a master budget explicitly interrelates all of a company's planned operating activities.

Exhibit 21.1
Typical Interorganizational Conflicts among Departments

Types of Activities	Department			
	Engineering	**Production**	**Finance and Accounting**	**Marketing**
Product Creation	Stresses functional features, long design lead times, and specialty components	Long-run with few model changes, standard orders and components, and large inventories	Standard functions and components, low inventories	Short design and lead times, sales features, large inventories, custom components
Pricing	High prices to allow more product features	Priced for steady order volume	Priced to cover costs in the short-run; tough credit terms	Priced for market expansion; easy credit availability and terms
Promotion	A good product will "sell itself"	Enough properly timed emphasis for steady orders	Strong controls and limited emphasis	Heavy emphasis with few controls for positioning and volume generation
R & D	Strong emphasis on technological development	Emphasis on machinery and systems for efficient production	A necessary emphasis, at best	Strong emphasis on learning unique customer needs and better sales techniques

Developing Marketing Budgets The way managers make decisions concerning planning and budgeting items varies from company to company and from individual to individual along two dimensions: the decision-making style and the techniques used.

Decision-Making Styles In some companies, top management assumes full and total responsibility for setting plans and budgets. In others, middle management plays a far greater role. Essentially, there are three types of basic styles.

"Top-Down" is where top management provides explicit directives to functional managers as to what to accomplish during a forthcoming planning horizon, as well as how much they can spend in the process.[21] The advantage is that the most seasoned executives make the plans. The disadvantage is that it does not reflect the opinions and experiences of the functional middle managers.

"Bottom-Up" is where each manager of a basic business unit in the organization plays a dominant role in the planning and budgeting for that subunit. Superiors must approve any decision, of course, but top management's role in the process is rather passive and reactive.[22] It places the decision making in the hands of those closest to a particular operation, it serves as good training, and it provides incentives to middle managers. The disadvantage is that it places less-experienced people in a dominant role within the process.

"Management by Objectives" (MBO) is a style that falls between the previous two extremes.[23] It begins when top management establishes a range of goals for each organizational unit along with an accompanying budget range. Superiors then meet with subordinates to negotiate a final settlement. The process offers the advantage of training and motivating middle management and still retains much of senior management's control over the process. This style is probably the best means of setting plans and budgets in companies having a highly qualified middle management.

Budgeting Techniques Conceptually, marginal analysis provides the best means of determining a total marketing budget. As Figure 21.7 illustrates, a total budgeted amount should be that which maximizes profit.

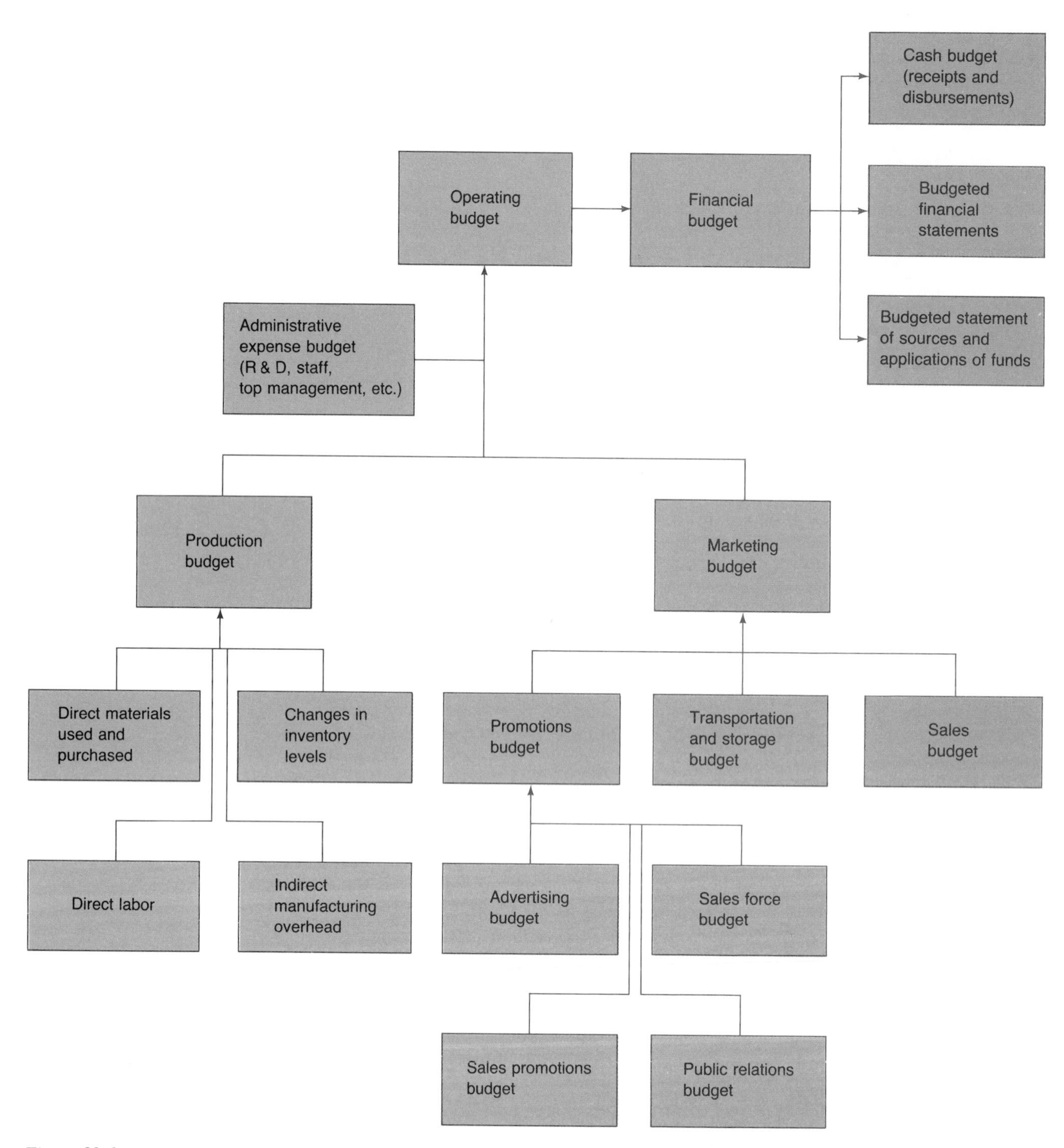

Figure 21.6
Master Budget for a Typical Manufacturer

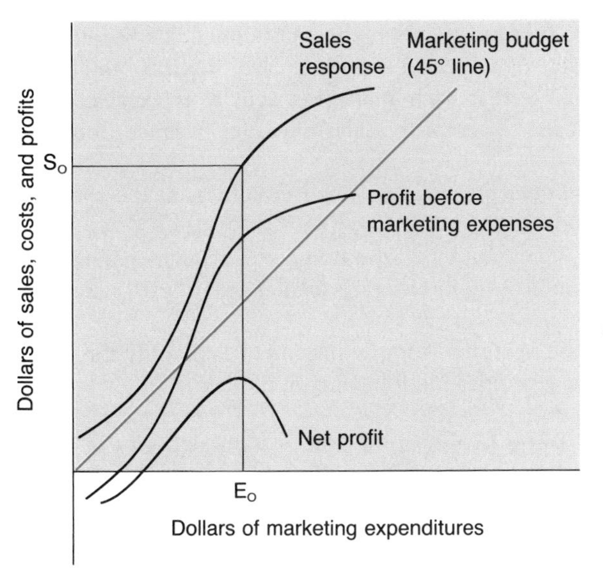

Figure 21.7
Concept of an Optimal Level of Marketing Expenditures

However, while conceptually sound, problems with the marginal approach make it difficult to use. It is hard to measure the responsiveness of sales to various budget levels and to break a total budget down into its various components, considering the tradeoffs between marketing activities.

Accelerating advancements in computer simulation, a technique especially suited to analyzing complex systems of interrelated variables, offer potential promise for future applications of the concept. But until these breakthroughs materialize, the approach is likely to remain more a conceptual overview than an operational technique.[24]

Basically, there are four budgeting methods which are frequently used in organizations today.

Percentage of Sales In this case, some percentage of forecast sales is allocated to each budget activity. While simple to administer, this method is conceptually limiting. At best, the percentages used are arbitrarily derived. Further, the logic is inverted, suggesting that marketing expenses result because of sales, whereas sales are the result of marketing expenses.

Competitive Parity The budget is set according to the expected levels of competition. There may be straight parity, where the same levels of expenditures are set, or market-share parity, where the amounts are adjusted for the relative market shares of each firm. The weaknesses of this method are identical to the percentage of sales method; also, it is based upon the philosophy of mutual survival instead of competition.

Available Resources This approach is based upon subtracting budgeted nonmarketing expenses from forecasted revenue, then apportioning what is left over to profit and marketing expenses. This method also makes little sense, since marketing expenditures should not be considered an afterthought.

Task Buildup This is the most conceptually sound means of setting a marketing budget. As indicated in Figure 21.8, the task buildup process begins with examining the goals that each marketing activity is expected to accomplish during the time horizon. Goals for the sales force, for instance, might include:

1. Contacting existing retail customers at the average rate of 18 times during the period
2. Increasing by 20 the number of retailers handling company products
3. Increasing the average retailer order by 10 percent

The next step is for management to identify the specific tasks needed to attain the goals. Consider the following examples.

- If a firm has a goal of adding 300 retailers to its channel, the required number of sales calls that need to be made to prospective accounts should be determined.
- If a goal is to cover existing accounts at an average rate of 1.5 calls per month, then the total number of contacts needed should be estimated.

Figure 21.8
Task-Buildup Method of Marketing Budget Development

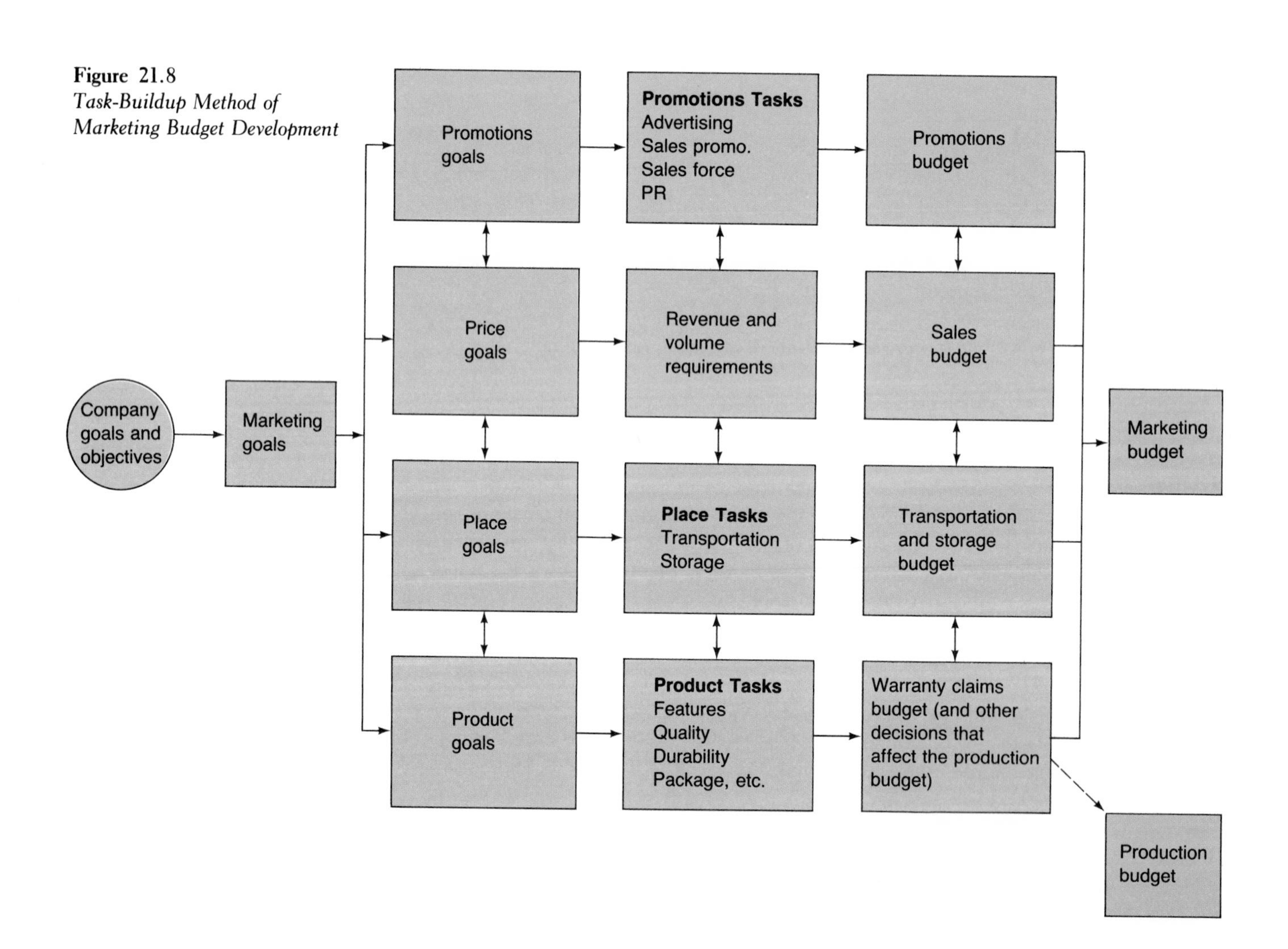

Contingency plans are preparations for times when it is necessary to "bite the bullet" and change directions.

- If an average of two exposures to advertising among target members is a goal, then management should use media consumption habits and the number in the target to determine the needed space or insertions for advertising messages.

Usually, the identified tasks can be accomplished in a number of ways. To illustrate, 20 spots on CBS's "Nightly News," four insertions in *Time*, or 50 local radio spots are among the many ways that ad exposure to a target group may be obtained. Thus, the third step of the task buildup method is to identify the specific set of activities that are the most efficient to use. Several complex quantitative methods can assist in the identification.[25] ADMOD, for instance, is a procedure for identifying optimal media schedules for advertising, based upon costs and expected exposures. Another model, termed CALLPLAN, helps identify the optimal number of calls a sales representative should make.[26]

While mathematical techniques can help in identifying optimal sets of activities, the real virtue of these methods is that they focus management's attention on understanding those activities required to attain goals. Thus, the approaches can be useful even to those firms that do not have extensive historical data to formally analyze.

Contingency plans
Plans written for unforeseen future events.

Contingency Plans Experienced managers have learned that plans and budgets should not be considered as "cast in stone." Unforeseen events may require deviations. A competitor, for instance, might launch an unanticipated promotional campaign for a new product offering. Or, perhaps a product defect might initiate the need for a product recall, thus requiring additional advertising to offset the negative publicity.

Accordingly, most successful firms develop **contingency plans.** Obviously, management cannot fully develop such plans in every detail, for it is impossible to know ahead of time the nature and magnitude of all possible unforeseen events. However, the types of events with major potential impact usually can be identified, such as a major recession. By planning at least initial responses ahead of time, the firm is not likely to be caught totally off guard, as was the Coca-Cola Company in 1985 when many consumers rejected New Coke and management was forced to bring back the old product, labeled as Classic Coke, to avoid large losses in market share.

Control Mechanisms

A large consumer products marketer once invested considerable time and money in a promotion using an inflatable cartoon display character as a premium for supermarkets, but management noticed that there did not appear to be any resulting additional sales activity. A quick survey of retailers discovered that only 2 percent of the stores were actually displaying the premium. The inflatable characters were so attractive that they were being taken home by store personnel for their children and by the marketer's own sales force, thus preventing their display for consumers.[27] This example illustrates the need to control planned marketing activities.

A strong commitment to planning and budgeting is only half of the battle of effectively managing the future of a company. The other half is controlling activities. Whereas planning and budgeting involve developing details of where a company is headed, control assures that the company does not get lost on its way.

A major principle of administration is that management should direct its attention to areas where performance is less than desirable. Termed *management by exception*, the principle holds that management can best improve a firm's performance by focusing attention on trouble spots, such as the example given above.[28] Effective control pinpoints the weak spots so that management can take corrective action before it is too late.

Activity reports
Written reports of work undertaken by functionaries.

Activity Reports and Budget Schedules The first mechanism of control involves the periodic reporting of all marketing activities in formal, routinely prepared reports (called **activity reports**) throughout the budget period. In this way, performance levels may be regularly compared with planned activity schedules, tasks, and budgets to assure that the intended activities are proceeding as expected.

Most firms, to illustrate, require the sales force to complete several reports on a daily or weekly basis. *Call reports* list all prospects contacted during a period. *Customer reports* detail specific actions sales representatives have taken. *Expense reports* detail the expenses incurred. *Order forms* specify an account's purchases. Exhibit 21.2 illustrates several typical forms used to control personal selling activities.

Other members of a marketing team generally prepare similar reports related to their operations, including physical distribution, advertising, advertising allowance, warranty claims, and price change reports, and others. The reporting time period is often a week or a month, depending upon the nature of the activity. A manufacturer

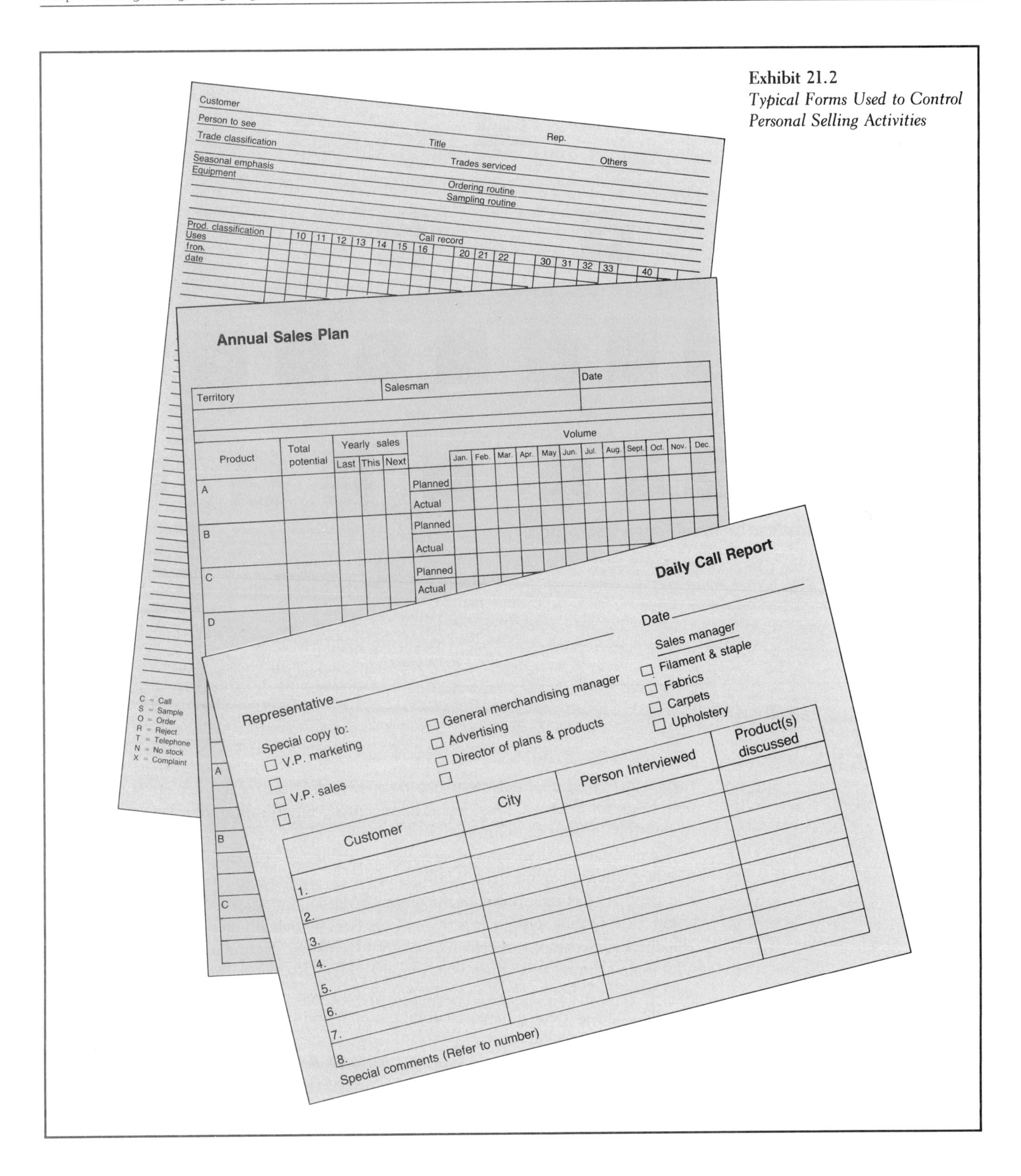

Customer
Person to see
Trade classification — Title — Rep.
Seasonal emphasis — Trades serviced — Others
Equipment
Ordering routine
Sampling routine
Prod. classification
Uses
from
date
Call record
10 11 12 13 14 15 16 20 21 22 30 31 32 33 40

C = Call
S = Sample
O = Order
R = Reject
T = Telephone
N = No stock
X = Complaint

Annual Sales Plan

Territory	Salesman	Date

Product	Total potential	Yearly sales: Last	This	Next		Volume: Jan.	Feb.	Mar.	Apr.	May	Jun.	Jul.	Aug.	Sept.	Oct.	Nov.	Dec.
A					Planned												
					Actual												
B					Planned												
					Actual												
C					Planned												
					Actual												
D																	

Daily Call Report

Date

Sales manager
☐ Filament & staple
☐ Fabrics
☐ Carpets
☐ Upholstery

Representative

Special copy to:
☐ V.P. marketing
☐
☐ V.P. sales
☐
☐ General merchandising manager
☐ Advertising
☐ Director of plans & products
☐

Customer	City	Person Interviewed	Product(s) discussed
1.			
2.			
3.			
4.			
5.			
6.			
7.			
8.			

Special comments (Refer to number)

Exhibit 21.2
Typical Forms Used to Control Personal Selling Activities

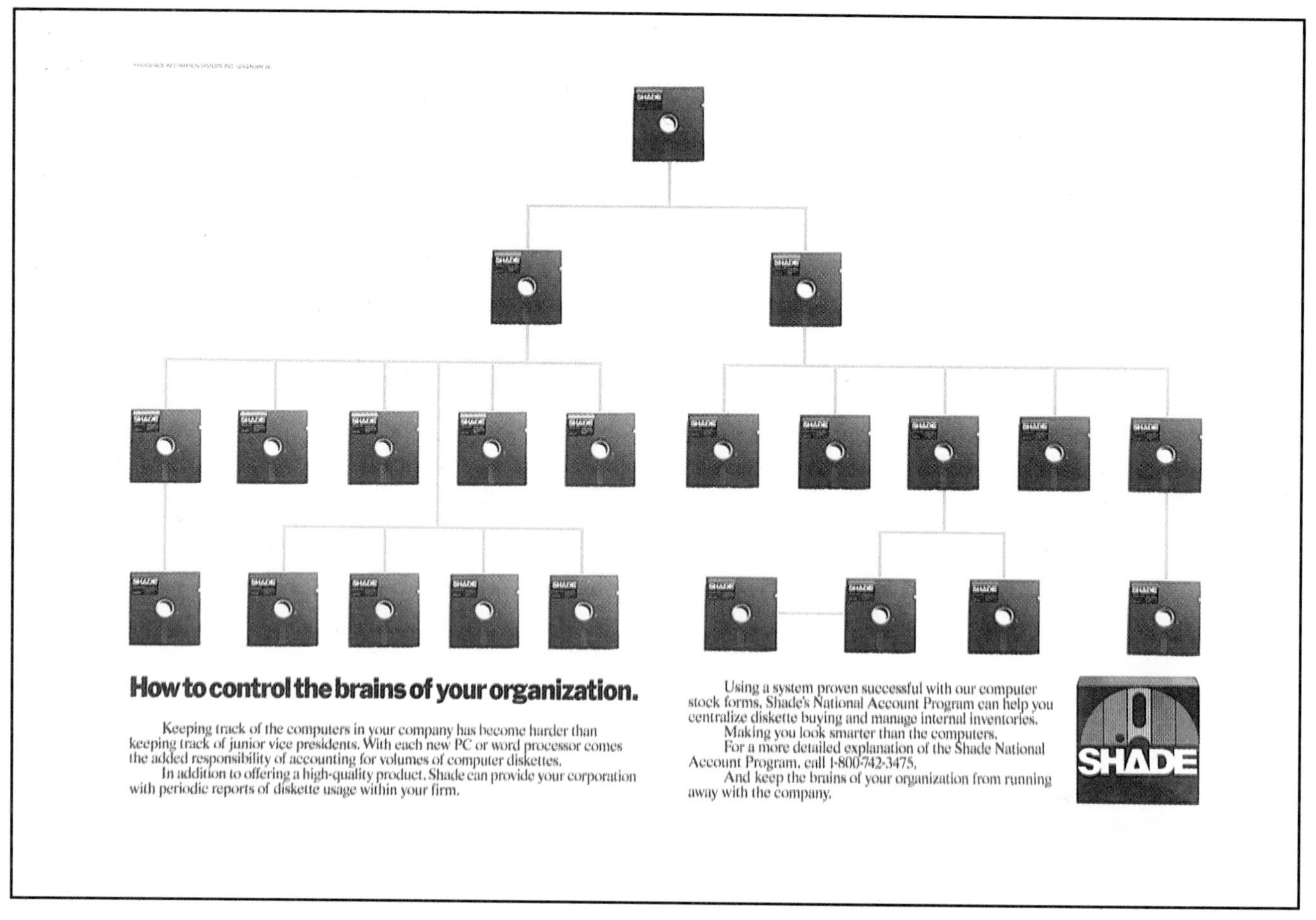

Computer technology has greatly aided the analytical aspects of organizational control.

may even expect channel members to report conditions. Auto dealers and fast-food franchises, for instance, must report financial and other important information weekly or monthly to their franchisors.

Other reporting instruments are also available. A company's financial reporting system is often a key means of learning of budget variances.[29] Another important tool is a good marketing information system. Nabisco, for instance, expanded its computerized reporting system into a "cell system," which divides the entire U.S. into 100 different geographical cells. Company advertising, in-store promotional programs, sales force actions, and other types of marketing activities are entered into the system weekly by cell for analysis. While this system was very expensive to develop and operate, management's increased ability to plan and control the company's marketing activities lowered total costs.

Comparisons with Past Company and Industry Performances A company might be proceeding as planned, but the plans may have been poorly laid. Competitors could be advancing at a faster pace, or results may be below expectations but because of industry downturns, competitors may be falling even faster, signaling relatively good performance. Two control mechanisms are helpful in this analysis.

Market Share Analysis Comparing a company's share (percentage) of the market to the competition over time indicates how well the company is tracking in relation to the overall competitive setting. In 1983, for example, General Electric noted that its industry share of appliance repair revenues had fallen. This led to company efforts to improve its advertising and service quality.[30]

Many companies avidly follow market share data. For example, television networks use ratings (compiled by research companies such as A. C. Nielsen and Arbitron) when deciding which shows to continue and which to drop.[31] The data are important to follow, since a sagging market share implies that a company is losing the competitive battle and may need to develop a new strategy or products.

Ratio Comparisons Financial ratios can also provide useful insights into current and emerging problem areas. Important statistics include profit as a percentage of sales, return on investment, the average age of accounts receivable, accounts receivable turnover (sales/average accounts receivable), inventory turnover (sales/average inventory), and several other ratios that are useful to indicate possible weaknesses.[32]

Strategy Effectiveness Analysis Another effective control technique is to assess company strategies to determine whether or not marketing activities are proving to be successful and whether they should be changed in the future. There are three such techniques.

Sales Analysis **Sales analysis** involves finding out who is buying a company's product offerings.[33] Comparison of buyer profiles (demographics and psychographics) indicates whether or not the intended target is being penetrated.

Sales analysis
Periodic examination of all marketing activities for the purpose of identifying who is buying the company's products.

Attitude Tracking **Attitude tracking** consists of learning whether changes in attitudes are occurring among the target market.

Attitude tracking
Learning whether changes in attitudes are occurring among the target.

Environmental Monitoring **Environmental monitoring** involves keeping track of environmental forces, such as monetary policies of the Federal Reserve Board, employment levels, and other factors that are critical to sales.

Environmental monitoring
Keeping track of environmental forces, such as the government's monetary policies, employment levels, and growth patterns.

The Marketing Audit Perhaps the most comprehensive control measure that marketers can implement is the marketing audit, which is an impartial, rigorous, and systematic review of the entire marketing function in a firm. It is designed to assess the marketing strengths and weaknesses and how effectively the firm is carrying out each portion of the function.

There are generally six phenomena audited as to their appropriateness: objectives, policies, organization, methods, procedures, and personnel. Several different parties may be used for the auditing tasks, including those whose work is being evaluated, outside consultants, staff personnel, and ad hoc committees. The main thing for the success of such an audit is that the personnel used for the auditing should be able to be objective and should have sufficient expertise to make any suggestions meaningful. This means that consultants, staff personnel, and ad hoc committees may be the best choices for such audits.

Search for Problems, Not Symptoms Before concluding this chapter, it is important to point out that managers should guard against prematurely reacting to reported deviations from plans and budgets.[34] Control mechanisms only identify symptoms and

CONCEPT SUMMARY

Control Mechanisms

Mechanism	Description
Activity Report and Budget Schedules	Periodic reports of actual activity during a budget period.
Market Share Analysis	Comparing a company's share of total industry sales relative to its competitors.
Ratio Comparison	Financial ratios such as profit as a percentage of sales.
Sales Analysis	Finding out who is actually buying company offerings—determining sales by various categories such as geographic units.
Attitude Tracking	Assessing changes in target market attitudes toward the company's offerings.
Environmental Monitoring	Careful monitoring of the elements of the environment that might affect marketing performance.
Marketing Audit	Comprehensive and systematic review of the entire marketing function of a firm.

not the underlying problems themselves—the causes of the symptoms. An advertising effectiveness survey, for instance, might indicate that a campaign generated less brand awareness than management had expected. Premature reaction to such a symptom might cause a manager to scrap the campaign, but the real cause of the diminished brand awareness could have been something other than a poor ad campaign, such as increased competitor advertising or new competitive products. The campaign itself might have lived up to expectations under the circumstances.

Thus, management needs a careful analysis of all symptoms to uncover why they developed before it maps out any corrective action. Only then can management be confident of getting a company back onto its intended track.

Chapter Summary

This chapter examined a number of important concepts relating to organizing, budgeting, and controlling marketing activities. Marketing organizational structures typically evolve over time within companies. A sales department is usually the first stage of the process because sales is a necessary function for survival. The next stage is the development of a marketing department, with a separate-but-equal stature compared to sales. Still further growth typically involves the creation of a contemporary marketing department, where all marketing functions are organized under one marketing head for greater coordination capabilities.

Contemporary marketing structures frequently differ in various respects. Some are organized around functions, others focus on market targets, and still others emphasize products. The best form to use depends upon the company and the nature of its target market and product mix interrelationships.

The chapter also examined a number of budgeting and controlling concepts and actions that go hand-in-hand. Plans outline intended future actions and budgets provide financial expressions of the plans. Both force managers to look into the future and to coordinate activities.

Several means of setting budgets are prevalent, including

allocations on the basis of some percentage of sales, competitive parity, available resources, and the task-buildup method. The latter results in funding that is directly related to attaining company goals.

Controlling is as important as planning and budgeting. Comparisons with budgets, the industry, past performances, and evaluation of strategy effectiveness are the major control mechanisms. Many companies, especially large ones, have developed a formal control function by conducting annual marketing audits. Regardless of the controls established, however, managers must be cautious about reacting to deviations from plans. Deviations almost always require further analysis to correctly identify underlying problems.

Questions

1. What are the advantages and disadvantages of a functional organization?
2. Explain the types of decentralization in marketing organizations. What are their advantages and disadvantages?
3. Compare and contrast market-centered and product-centered structures.
4. Discuss the problems that you see in conducting a marketing audit.
5. The ABC Company produces a wide line of consumer products and engages heavily in institutional advertising for the entire line. How should this advertising expense be allocated to each type of item for budgeting and profitability analysis?
6. How can the task buildup method be used in budgeting for marketing research?
7. Why not structure control reports to spell out problems instead of merely reflecting symptoms?

Chapter 22

International Markets

Objectives

After completing this chapter, you should be able to demonstrate a knowledge of:

- The importance of international marketing to the U.S. economy and to individual domestic firms
- The risks involved in international marketing
- How environmental factors, which vary from one country to another, impinge upon marketing strategy
- The process and difficulties of obtaining market information on foreign countries
- The major considerations that determine whether or not to do business in a foreign country
- The process of designing an ongoing marketing strategy in a foreign country
- The nature of various controversies regarding the operation and role of large multinational corporations

MARKETING SUCCESS

Expanding into the West German PC Market

IBM has long been a monumental force in the West German full-size computer market. With a 30 percent market share and a 6,200-person sales force in the country, IBM is the leading force to reckon with in the German $7 billion computer mainframe market. Headed by Hans-Olaf Henkel, vice president in charge of IBM's West German subsidiary, profits soared to $455 million in 1986, up 57 percent over 1985.

Not one to rest on laurels, Henkel recently directed the subsidiary toward expanding the company's sales of PCs, which have not been keeping track with the PC boom in other countries. The problem has not been one of poor sales performance by IBM in particular, but rather the challenge of expanding the PC market in general. As a former German IBM executive put it, "the vast majority [of people] doesn't even have anything like the PC." The reason, he concluded, is that the German public basically "mistrusts computers."

Under Henkel's direction, the company adopted the strategy of penetrating first the technical and engineering market segment. "Our strategy is to gain further entry through technical users who will be able to clearly see the need and are already familiar with computers," said Mr. Henkel. "After their usefulness has been demonstrated, we will move toward general business users and managers."

According to plan, much of the initial thrust was aimed at technicians and researchers. The company's new RT-PC, an engineering work station, provided the major weapon in the company's arsenal. Additional emphasis also was placed on selling to universities. This strategy pitted IBM directly against Digital Equipment Corp., a company that has long maintained a stronghold among technical users.

With a total market potential of 1.9 million units, there remains extensive room for further improvement. Accordingly, IBM has formed alliances with software houses and with other large customers such as automotive and aerospace firms to further break into the engineering and business markets.

"The job will not be easy," said a former IBM official. "The European community has fears that IBM will monopolize the market. That will keep Henkel in the 'hot seat'." But the strategy has worked well in IBM's quest for additional domination. With sales at 64,100 units and a 33 percent market share in 1985, the company doubled its total installed base of them in that year alone.

SOURCE: Adapted from "IBM Tries to Cure Germany's PC Phobia," *Business Week*, May 26, 1986: 126, 128.

Introduction

"A Big Mac, fries, and a beer, please!" Does something sound different? Ordering beer at McDonald's sounds odd to Americans, but not to residents of the West German city of Hamburg. McDonald's operates around 200 restaurants in Europe, which represent only a few of the countries in the firm's worldwide operations (including China).

Like McDonald's, many U.S. companies are heavily involved in international marketing.

- Holiday Inn operates at least one hotel complex in practically every major city throughout the world.
- Hallmark International sells greeting cards in more than 100 foreign countries, with distinctive strategies in many of them. In France, New Year's cards outsell Christmas cards 14 to 1. Latin Americans exchange cards on Kid's Day.[1]
- Weight Watchers International operates more than 200 centers throughout Italy, following a fitness trend in the country.[2]

While most managers would rather focus on domestic targets due to familiarity, many have learned that foreign opportunities can be great. Accordingly, Ford Motor, Nabisco, Nestle, Toyota, and Sony are among the rapidly growing list of multinational organizations that span national boundaries to capitalize on the most promising opportunities wherever they may be located.[3] The opening Marketing Success illustrates how IBM has prospered in West Germany. Not all efforts are successful, however, as witnessed by the experience of Sears, which has suffered losses in Brazil, Belgium, and Mexico.

While the same marketing principles apply, decision making is often more complex in the case of international marketing than the domestic variety. This is because far greater differences exist throughout the world than in the U.S. Thinking that foreign markets are alike or that they are the same as in the U.S. is a sure recipe for failure. This chapter surveys important factors for managers to consider when making decisions concerning multinational marketing.

U.S. Involvement in International Marketing

Most modern countries encourage international trade for several reasons.[4] Countries can economically benefit by specializing in activities in which they have relative advantages. Trade helps nations to overcome resource imbalances, as in Japan, which has relatively few basic commodity resources such as petroleum and ore. Also, trade is often encouraged for political reasons, such as the U.S. trade agreements with Israel.

Given the benefits, it is not surprising that governments attempt to stimulate trade with other countries, as the following section illustrates.

Volume of U.S. International Trade

International markets offer significant opportunities for many companies.

Figure 22.1 depicts exports of U.S. firms from 1966 through 1984. As indicated, the volume is large and growing rapidly. In perspective, the total dollar amount represented about 6 to 7 percent of gross national product throughout the past decade. Because the statistics do not reveal revenues that U.S. firms earn from overseas installations, the total involvement is quite impressive. Further, both large and small companies participate—about 70 percent of all U.S. manufacturing exporters employ fewer than 500 people.[5]

Not surprising is the fact that some products account for a much higher percentage of exports than others. Figure 22.2 pictures these breakdowns for 1984. Clearly, the export of machinery and transportation equipment leads all others in volume, but other categories are significant as well.[6]

The volume of U.S. trade with different parts of the globe varies significantly, as illustrated in Figure 22.3. As indicated, Asia, North America, and Western Europe, together, comprise the destinations for about 85 percent of all U.S. exports. Naturally,

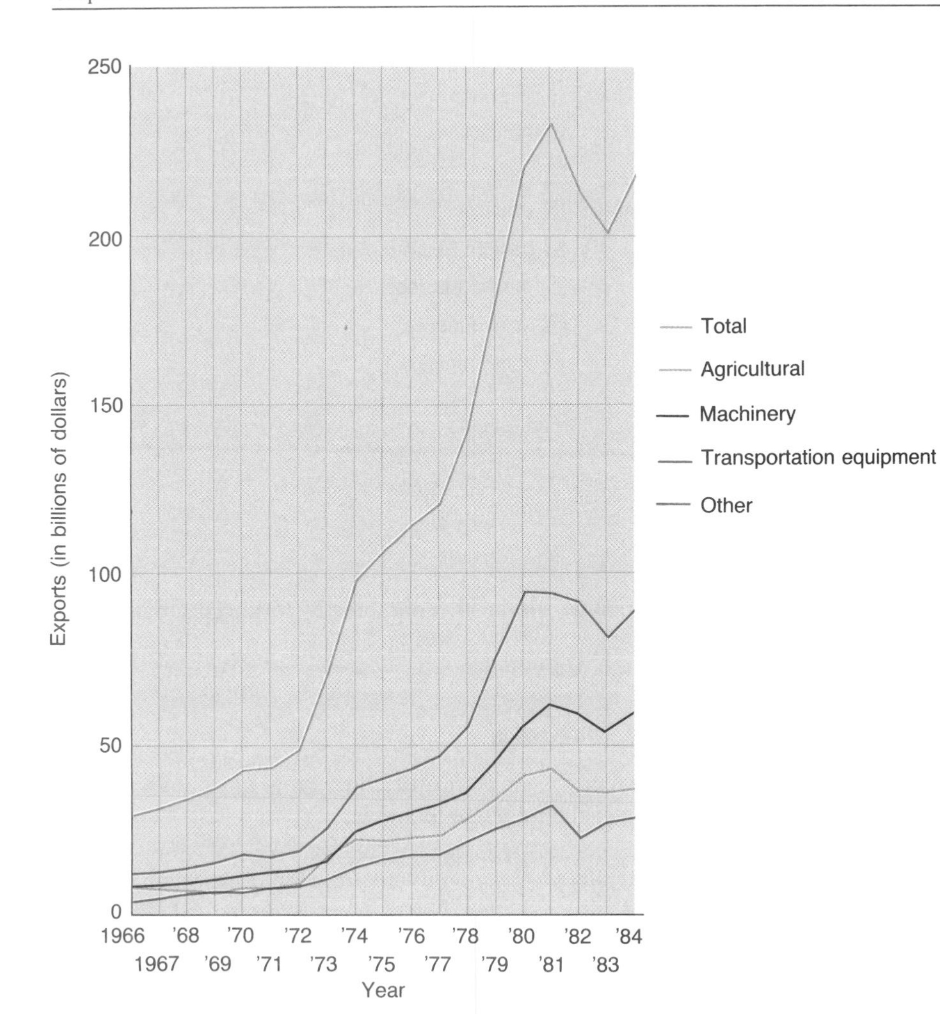

Figure 22.1
United States Exports, Selected Years 1966–1984 (SOURCE: From *Statistical Abstract of the United States* (Washington, D.C.: U.S. Government Printing Office, 1986), 106th ed.)

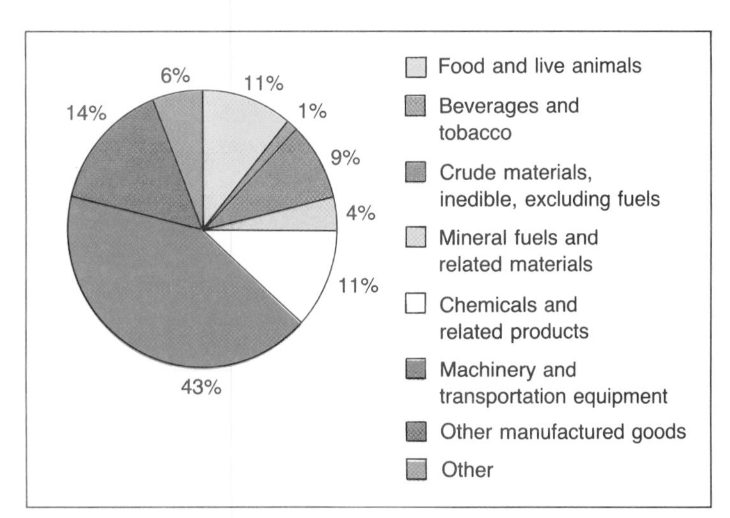

Figure 22.2
Domestic Exports by Selected Commodity Groups (1984) (SOURCE: *Statistical Abstract of the United States* (Washington, D.C.: U.S. Government Printing Office, 1986), 106th ed.)

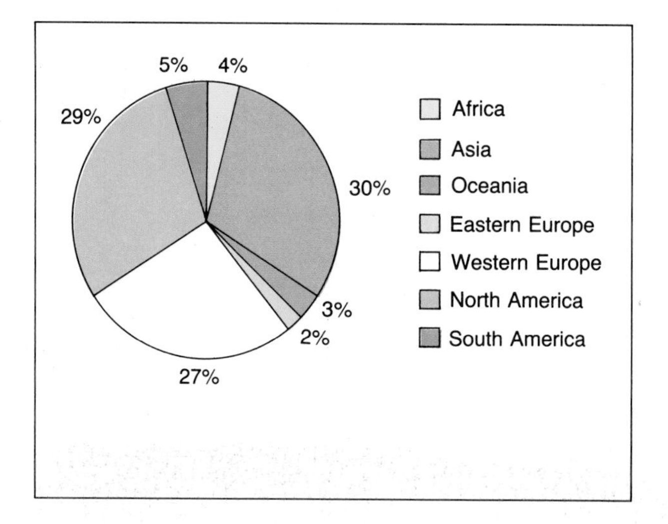

Figure 22.3
United States Exports by Selected Regions (1984) (SOURCE: *Statistical Abstract of the United States* (Washington, D.C.: U.S. Government Printing Office, 1986), 106th ed.)

this is because these regions include the most economically advanced countries in the Free World.

Importance to Individual Companies

Foreign operations are vital to many U.S. companies, and grow more so over time as U.S. markets mature. Consider the following examples.

- The R. J. Reynolds Company relies heavily on international markets which, unlike in the U.S., continue to grow at record rates. The company has reported increasing sales (through licensing agreements) in West Germany, France, Spain, Holland, Italy, the Middle East, Africa, Brazil, and Japan. In fact, the company recently announced agreements to sell two styles of Winston and More 120-mm cigarettes in China—the first extra-length brand sold in that country.[7]
- The Carnation Co. recently announced expanded entry into West Germany through the purchase of Luenebest Dairy, a family-owned German company.[8]
- The Electrolux Corp. (Stockholm, Sweden) earns over 80 percent of its revenues in foreign markets, especially France, Great Britain, and the U.S. Consequently it is one of the two largest vacuum cleaner marketers in the world.[9]
- The H. J. Heinz Co. markets chilled salads, fish marinades, and sauces under the Nadler-Werks name throughout Europe. The company operates 15 manufacturing plants in Germany and sales are expanding very rapidly.[10]
- The Fruehauf Corp. produces and markets truck trailers, bodies, braking systems, wheels for small cars, parts for turbine engines and aircraft, and related products around the world. Its current 25 percent revenue base from foreign operations is growing much faster than in the U.S., a trend that management expects to continue into the foreseeable future.[11]

The Task Is Not Easy

Marketing to foreign countries is not an easy task.[12] U.S. companies face two major difficulties in this regard. First, the U.S. no longer holds the technological advantage

MARKETING BRIEF
Keying in on the Arabian Market

While the oil revenues of the Arabian Peninsular Oil States—Saudi Arabia, Kuwait, Bahrain, Qatar, the United Arab Emirates, and Oman—have fallen drastically, by about half, the oil states remain viable markets. Despite recession, the countries remain relatively strong markets for many goods and services.

The region remains dependent upon imports to supply virtually every item needed by modern societies, with the exception of oil products, base petrochemicals, steel and aluminum bars, many construction materials, and some basic food items. Even with reduced oil prices, Saudi Arabia, for example, is a rich country by world standards. Its markets are open, doing business there is relatively easy, and its society is receptive to new ideas.

But there are major cultural differences. There is a belief that there are certain "right" nations that are better for manufacturing certain types of goods: Germany and the U.S for cars, France for clothes, and Italy for furniture. The established brand is generally assumed to be better, making success almost impossible for new entries unless they offer a genuine advantage. The availability of advertising is diminished, and there is often a feeling that goods that have to be advertised are inferior.

But many marketers have found considerable success in these states. Through adopting the marketing concept in this market, Polaroid, for example, has become the standard for photography and has, in large part, been responsible for breaking down former religious taboos against picture-taking in the Arab world. Polaroid has found that a good way to spread its advertising messages is to put them on videocassettes in some of the countries.

SOURCE: Adapted from several articles in "Special Report: Marketing to the Arab World," *Advertising Age*, January 30, 1986.

over the rest of the world that it once had. When U.S. technology reigned supreme, companies could penetrate foreign markets almost as afterthoughts—places to ship last year's models and items unsalable at home. This has changed, as foreign firms in Japan, West Germany, and elsewhere, have equaled—if not surpassed—U.S. companies in technology. Consequently, such a sales orientation is likely to fail.

Second, worldwide competition has increased dramatically over the past decade. Foreign firms dominate throughout the world in many types of products, such as TVs, radios, steel, and even autos to an extent. And while worldwide competition is increasing, many foreign countries are also attempting to restrict imports to help improve their balance of payments, further complicating the difficulties.[13]

Adopting the Marketing Concept Is the Key

While international marketing is difficult, it is not an impossible task. The key to success lies in adopting the marketing concept, as Polaroid has practiced in the Middle East (see the accompanying Marketing Brief).

Failure often stems from not tailoring a marketing mix to meet the unique needs of the foreign target market. For example, U.S. tableware, dinnerware, and glassware firms consistently have failed to penetrate Japanese markets.[14] Paying little attention to cultural differences, the companies insisted on packaging items in multiples of four, despite the fact that this is considered an unlucky number in Japan. One American retailer even complained to U.S. Commerce Department officials about "excessive" Japanese trade restrictions, stating: "They required labels to be written in Japanese, not English." [15]

In contrast, several U.S. food firms approach foreign targets with a marketing orientation. Pillsbury, Monsanto, Corn Products, and Coca-Cola have successfully recognized the uniquenesses among developing countries and produce special high-protein, low-cost foods to meet these needs. Their efforts result in better diets for the people and return handsome profits.

Even the Russians, perhaps to Marx's dismay, are learning that marketing expertise is needed to succeed. After suffering considerable setbacks under a production orientation, Belarus (makers of inexpensive, durable Soviet tractors) switched to marketing techniques to enable the firm to successfully compete with Massey-Ferguson and John Deere. "Western-styled advertising . . . marketing research . . . and [a hired] 'All-American' sales and marketing corps . . ." was used to turn the company around. [16] Similar techniques were used to turn the Soviet Merchant Marine into one of the world's largest shipping fleets. The next section examines the process of decision making for marketing internationally.

Multinational Marketing Decision Process

Each step in foreign strategic marketing decision making is probably more critical than when dealing with domestic markets. Figure 22.4 presents an overview of the decision-making process. Each of the components is examined below.

Environmental Factors

The environment poses perhaps the greatest difference between marketing to a foreign market and a domestic one. There are many variables over which a marketer has virtually no control that affect the eventual outcome of an entry into a foreign market. Complicating this is that a manager is never quite sure that he or she has all of the needed information to make good decisions. For instance, American Motors relied on misguided marketing research that suggested the name "Matador" meant virility and excitement to Puerto Ricans. But after introducing a car with that name, management learned that the word really ". . . meant 'killer'—an especially unfortunate choice for Puerto Rico, which has an unusually high traffic fatality rate." [17]

While many similar problems exist with domestic markets, their impact is greatly exaggerated in foreign ones. Political unrest, changing trade alliances, new trade barriers, and many other situations cause higher levels of uncertainty. There are four groups of environmental variables to consider: population and geographic, economic, political and legal, and cultural.

Population and Geographic Variables The U.S.'s 240 million people pales in number when compared to the rest of the world; this country comprises only about 5 percent of the world's total population. Figure 22.5 presents several selected statistics about the world's population today and projected into the future. As is evident, foreign populations represent huge market potentials in terms of people, and this will increase with time.

Population densities also vary greatly around the globe. In high-density areas such as the Republic of South Korea, target customers can be easily reached through retailers and mass communication. [18] In low-density countries such as New Guinea, the problems become more difficult because of the population's dispersion and limited size.

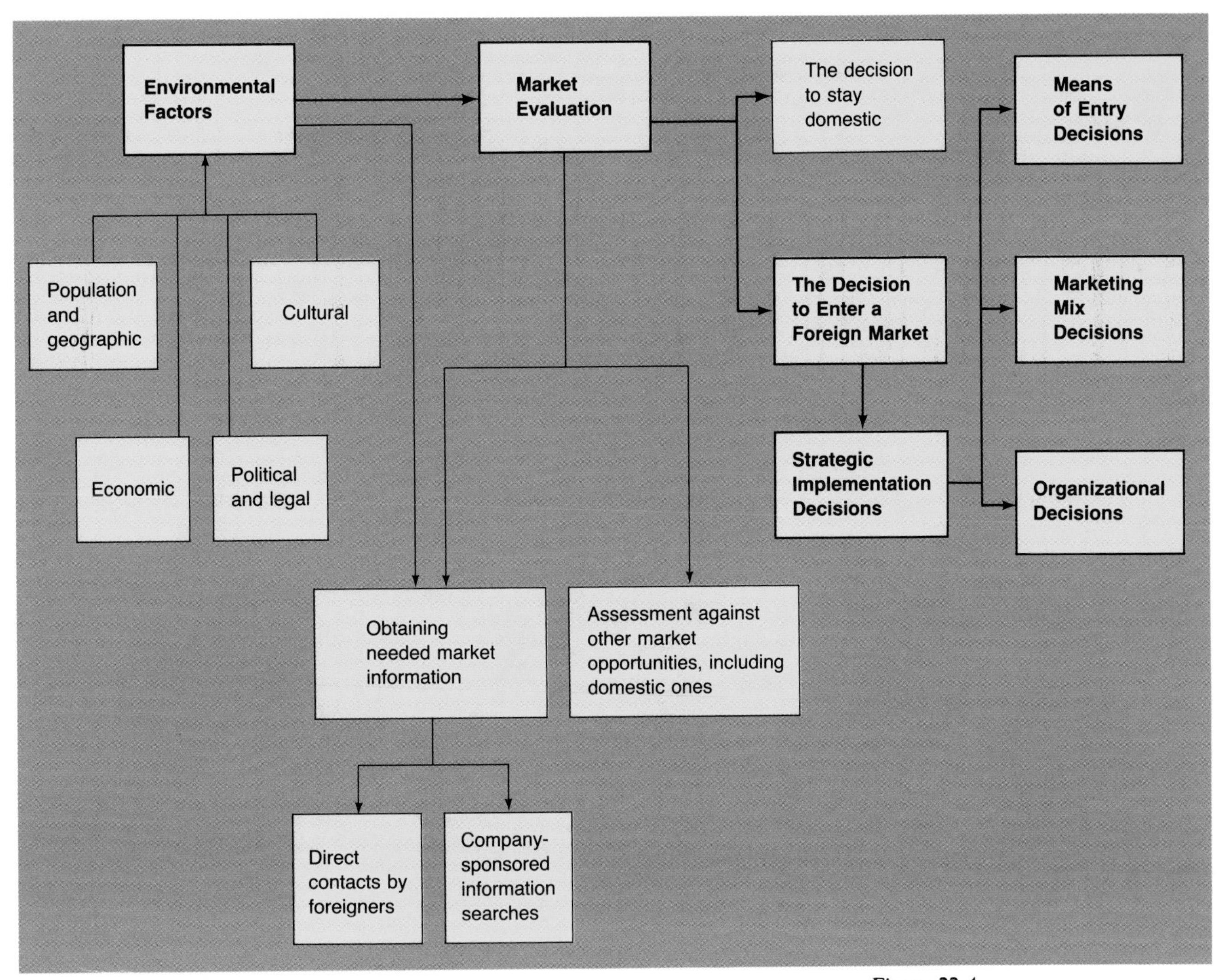

Figure 22.4
The Multinational Marketing Decision Process

Geographical differences can cause major hurdles to foreign marketers. Differing needs due to geographical variations are relatively minor in the U.S., but not in international settings. Extremes of heat, humidity, soil conditions, and altitude can have a major impact on product performance. For example, construction and farm equipment producers such as Massey-Ferguson find that major product design changes are needed for hot sandy environs, as in the Sahara, in contrast to humid jungles or high altitudes where low oxygen robs engines of power.

Even the character of the markets within a particular country may be quite different because of geography. To illustrate, the rugged Columbian mountain chains have resulted in underdeveloped transportation and communication links between cities. As a result, residents are effectively isolated into four distinct population and market centers. Major differences in culture, needs, climate, and lifestyles between the areas force marketers to treat each as a completely separate target. Similar differences are frequently visible throughout South America, Africa, and even parts of Europe.

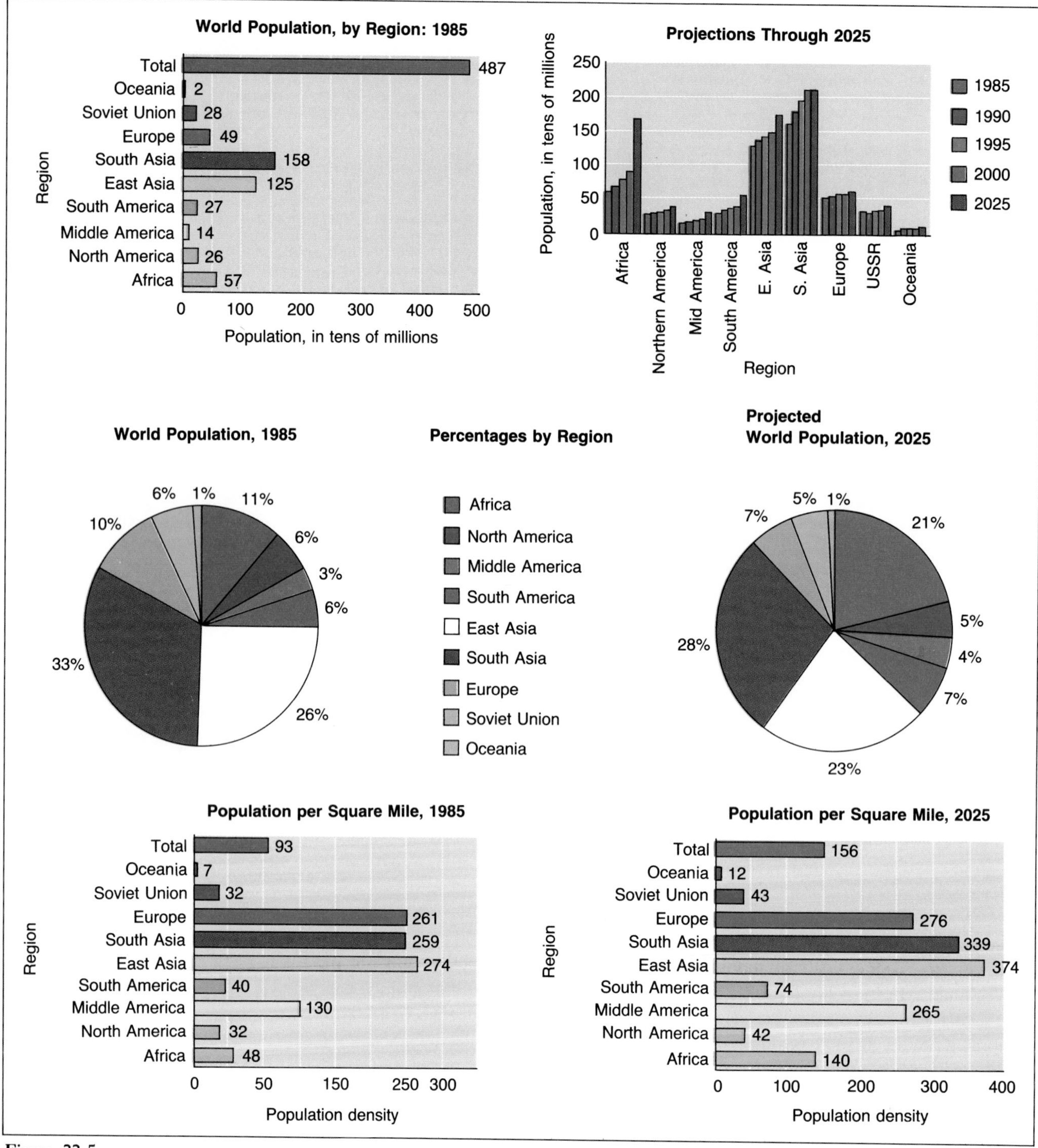

Figure 22.5
Selected World Population Statistics (SOURCE: *Statistical Abstract of the United States* (Washington, D.C.: U.S. Government Printing Office, 1986), 106th ed., actual and projected figures.)

The geography can vary dramatically within many countries.

Economic Factors Economic factors are generally more significant in international marketing than in the domestic variety due to vast variations between countries. A $140 dinner is expensive, but affordable for many Americans on special occasions. In contrast, the same $140 represents an entire year's per-capita GNP to a resident of Tanzania! Accordingly, many foreign markets, even if they are highly populated, do not represent much market opportunity for many items simply because of the economic conditions.

There are five economic dimensions of critical importance for international marketers to consider.

Exhibit 22.1
Five Stages of Economic Development

Stage	Description
Stage 1: The Traditional Societies	The vast majority of people are at a low level of poverty and are illiterate. Companies and government do not systematically apply modern science and technology, which means that they can do little to significantly increase productivity. Parts of Africa, South America, and New Guinea are at this level. They do not represent potential markets for any but a handful of items from advanced economies.
Stage 2: The Preconditions for Takeoff	Agricultural and extractive industries begin to apply science in countries at this stage. Transportation, power, communications, health, and education are the principal public developments. Parts of the Mideast, South America, and Central America fall into this category. Often they have a small percentage of extremely wealthy landowners and a large majority of impoverished persons. There is not much potential for outside firms to sell to mass markets. However, small markets usually exist for luxury items for landowners. These luxury markets can be very lucrative because there is usually an absence of domestic competition.
Stage 3: The Takeoff	Countries in this stage have developed human resources and social overhead such as education and energy facilities to sustain steady future economic growth. Manufacturing consists primarily of the processing of raw materials, and there is an emerging middle class plus a number of foreign advisors and technicians who represent a reasonable market to some foreign firms. Domestic production of luxury items is generally nonexistent, meaning that significant opportunities may exist for some international marketers.
Stage 4: The Drive to Maturity	Nations in this stage seek to extend their developing technology to all types of economic activity in which they choose to become involved. Durable goods manufacture for domestic markets begins in this stage, but heavy reliance is still placed on exporting raw materials. Often such economies attempt to protect their emerging industrial bases with heavy import restrictions. Frequently, foreign marketers cannot compete with domestic producers because of their low labor costs. But because of these lower costs, some firms are active in exporting to other countries.
Stage 5: The Age of High Mass Consumption	Nations in this stage are the industrial leaders who produce all types of items and regularly engage in exporting manufactured items and technical services. These countries place great emphasis on producing consumer goods. A large proportion of the population has significant discretionary income. These countries usually present substantial opportunities for both importing and exporting, but stiff competition from domestic producers often makes market penetration quite difficult.

SOURCE: Based on Walt W. Rostow, *The Stages of Economic Growth* (London: Cambridge University Press, 1960), Chapter 1.

Economic Structure It is useful to think of the local economy's structural development when making international marketing decisions. The most widely used classification scheme for structural development appears in Exhibit 22.1. In general, the model is useful for determining the types of items that are likely to be demanded as well as the degree of existing local competition.[19]

Countries in the first stages are likely to require products to satisfy basic needs, such as hunger and health, whereas countries in stages 2 and 4 are prime candidates for technical products and services. More advanced nations generally contain markets for all types of consumer items.

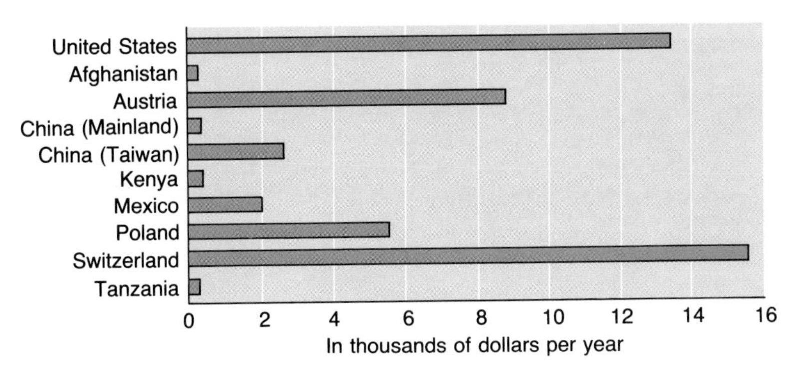

Figure 22.6
1983 Per-Capita GNP for Selected Countries (SOURCE: *Statistical Abstract of the United States* (Washington, D.C.: U.S. Government Printing Office, 1986), 106th ed.)

Progression through each stage generally takes decades and even longer and requires the accumulation of sufficient capital. The Middle East is unusual in this regard due to its massive oil revenues, which have provided tremendous opportunity for multinationals helping to build housing, schools, and industrial bases.[20]

Income Income levels closely parallel the structural development of countries, and there are vast differences between countries as Figure 22.6 illustrates.

A problem confounding international decision making is that per-capita data can be misleading due to income distribution. In general, incomes tend to be distributed among the populations in one of five ways:

1. Very low incomes—where practically all people subsist at the barest of levels, as in the least advanced countries.
2. The majority have low incomes, with a few high incomes (where a small number of families are extremely wealthy and the rest live in poverty; e.g., the Philippines under Marcos).
3. Low, medium, and high incomes—where a middle class exists, usually accompanied by industrialization in democratic societies.
4. Mostly low income, as in the case of industrialized but communistic countries, where the state accumulates the bulk of the capital and wealth.
5. Mostly medium income levels, as in advanced socialistic countries where tax plans are designed to eliminate the wealthy, but material possessions are possible for most citizens due to the high income levels.

Financial Managers also consider financial factors when evaluating foreign markets. As with domestic opportunity evaluation, the anticipated future profitability and the required investment are important factors. Beyond this, there is the issue of currency stability when marketing abroad. The Mexican peso declined by 870 percent against the U.S. dollar, for example, over the past several years. Such declines can occur very rapidly, even overnight; causing sizable losses on contracts and investments. To illustrate, International Telephone recently lost over $48 million as the result of a lira decline.[21] Generally, advice from experts in international finance is suggested before making long-term foreign commitments.

Resources Local resource availability, both natural (water, oil, etc.) and public (education, transportation, health, etc.), can be critical to an international marketer's success. These resources both shape the needs of the country and affect product

Currency stability is a great concern to multinational companies.

performance. To illustrate, the British North Sea oil fields and Bolivian copper mines presented unique needs and opportunities for producers of specially designed extractive machinery. Similarly, advanced computers are useless unless skilled workers are available to run them, many electrical appliances require dependable, nonfluctuating electricity which is unavailable in many parts of the world, and underdeveloped transportation routes in countries such as Thailand, Brazil, and Ethiopia make full penetration into many markets impractical.[22]

Competition Finally, the state of competition within the foreign market is an important economic consideration. J. C. Penney, for example, faced near financial disaster in Belgium with its "Sarma" operations because it was competing with Gb-Inno-Bm, which was three times as large and operated out of most of the choice retail sites.[23] While in some cases there may be a prevalent attitude toward "buying foreign" among the target, such as for French wine and Swiss watches, more often foreign nationals prefer to buy from home-grown companies. This is especially true in Japan. Consequently, exporters must carefully weigh their competitive strengths and weaknesses relative to both current and potential domestic marketers of similar products.

Political and Legal Factors The international political and legal arena can be very perplexing to the uninitiated. These variables tend to fall into one of three groups.

Encouragement of Trade Some countries are antagonistic—even hostile—to outsiders. While recently taking an about-face, China, for example, all but forbade outsiders in the past.[24] Others engage in foreign trade, but are quite difficult to do business with.[25] India and some countries in Africa and South America, for example, insist upon extensive employment of nationals and significant domestic ownership along with extensive regulation and "red tape" (and sometimes bribery of officials is the norm). Japan, for instance, erected barriers against U.S. telecommunications companies by requiring all communications equipment to be certified by various boards—a process that proceeds at a snail's pace.[26]

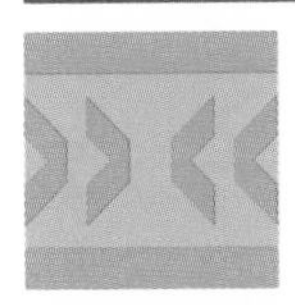

MARKETING BRIEF

Breaking into the Japanese Communications Equipment Market

For decades Japan's Nippon Telegraph and Telephone Public Corporation allowed only a handful of Japanese companies to sell it equipment. In 1983, however, there were signs that NTT was willing to open the procurement door, if only a crack. Florida-based Paradyne Corporation, a data communications manufacturer, won a bid to provide NTT with instruments to transmit computer data over telephone lines (modems).

Hiroaki Kobayashi, managing director of Paradyne's Japanese subsidiary said the NTT purchase should give his company the prestige and exposure necessary to compete in the $5 billion Japanese communications equipment market.

To take full advantage of the growing market, Paradyne entered into a joint marketing venture with Computer Services Corporation (CSK), a fast-growing Japanese software services company. Together they market Paradyne's PIX II system. The PIX II provides a link between a centrally located mainframe IBM or IBM compatible computer and remote terminals. Paradyne expected to sell up to $2 million worth of equipment annually by the mid-1980s and double that amount in subsequent years.

Kobayashi cautioned that Paradyne still has a tough battle ahead. Users in Japan normally buy from companies in their "keiretsu"—family-like business groups linked by cross-ownership of equity. Kobayashi believed that Paradyne's link with CSK is the key that could open the closed doors of the keiretsu system. Although not a member of a keiretsu, CSK does develop software and maintain computers for 510 major corporations across most major keiretsu. Even then, Kobayashi warned, "selling in Japan is not going to get easier. We still have to try harder."

During the next few years, developments in Japan favored Paradyne and other marketers to the telephone industry. Deregulation in the country led to the privatization of Nippon Telegraph and Telephone Co. (altering its status from a governmental to a private organization) in 1986. The same year witnessed a sharp rise in the value of the yen to the dollar, making American goods cheaper, relative to their Japanese counterparts.

SOURCE: Adapted from "NTT Gives Another Inch to the U.S.," *Business Week*, January 24, 1983: 42; and "Will Japan Really Change?" *Business Week*, May 12, 1986: 47–49, 57.

The biggest problem, though, is that foreign regulations often change over time. For example, after years of stable economic relations, the Canadian government initiated a number of steps in the 1970s to keep U.S. firms from expanding into Canada, including hefty taxes on specialty steel, petrochemicals, subway cars, and textiles. After several years, these taxes were dropped to bolster the sagging Canadian economy, but the point is that trade relations between even very friendly countries can change dramatically in time.[27]

On the other hand, some countries go to considerable lengths to aid and encourage foreign businesses. Ireland, for example, offers substantial inducements to foreign companies, including grants of up to 50 percent of the cost of constructing buildings and equipment and 100 percent of the cost of training personnel, low wages, and no taxes on goods produced within and sold outside of the country.

Stability There is nothing like the threat of having sizable investments nationalized or expropriated to give an executive ulcers. **Nationalization** is when a government buys out an operation owned by foreigners, often at a nominal price. **Expropriation** is even worse—it is the seizure of an operation with no remuneration at all. Recent

Nationalization
When a government forcibly buys out an operation run by foreigners.

Expropriation
When a government seizes an investment, with no remuneration at all.

events have included the loss of millions of dollars by oil companies in the Middle East and numerous manufacturers in South America, Africa, and Asia.[28]

Political stability means more than this, however. New trade alliances, import restrictions, and other changes are important to a multinational firm.[29] To illustrate, French-speaking Quebec has threatened to separate from the rest of Canada. Because of the uncertainties, many companies have felt it necessary to pull out their operations and move to Toronto, in Ontario—and even out of the country altogether.

Treaties, Tariffs, and Other Legislation Legislation also looms large in influencing overseas opportunities.[30] The most obvious effect is on the use of products. Italy, for example, levies a hefty tax on the cubic displacement of automobile engines, favoring small motors. In Canada, a tax is charged on autos weighing over 3,000 lbs. and those equipped with air conditioning. Accordingly, a multinational's product offering often must be adjusted to local conditions.

Quotas (trade)
Limits on volumes of goods that can be imported into or exported from a country.

Tariffs
Taxes on imports or exports.

Treaties
Formal statements of alliance between two or more countries.

Trade agreements
Narrower than treaties, covering only economic issues, their effect is to regulate inter-country trade (also called *trade alliances*).

GATT (General Agreement on Tariffs and Trade)
The first modern trade agreement among numerous trading nations.

In a similar vein, countries sometimes maintain **quotas**—which allow only a certain number of items to be brought in from abroad, and **tariffs**—a tax on the importation or exportation of a good. These barriers often greatly favor the domestic producers within the foreign country, as was the case in Japan during the development of its auto industry.

GATT Practically all nations have entered into **treaties** and trade alliances to develop and regulate international trade. The first modern **trade agreement,** the **General Agreement on Tarriffs and Trade (GATT),** became a reality in 1947. By the mid-1960s, membership had grown from 23 originators to over 70 nations, resulting in tariff reductions on thousands of items. Essentially GATT upholds four basic principles:[31]

1. Trade liberalization—it disallows import quotas restricting volumes and types of imports, except under special circumstances
2. Tariff negotiation—it holds that tariffs should be negotiable
3. Nondiscrimination—every member agrees that any tariff concession or trade advantage granted to one GATT member shall also be granted to other members (This is sometimes called the "Most Favored Nation" clause)
4. Consultation—GATT provides a forum for settling disputes among members

Despite its successes, GATT has not produced totally free trade among members.[32] Most world trade, while expanded because of GATT, takes place between particular blocks of nations. North America, Japan, and Western Europe comprise one such block. Another is composed of the Soviet Union, Eastern Europe, and parts of Africa, Asia, and Cuba. Exhibit 22.2 presents the major world trade alliance existing today.

Some of the alliances, such as COMECON, OPEC, and EEC have been strong and have furnished significant advantages to their members.[33] (OPEC has been under considerable pressure due to a glut in world oil supplies of late. However, the eventual outcome is still in doubt.) Others, such as CACM, have not been successful due to border conflicts and political turmoil. In addition, most countries maintain bilateral agreements covering other types of products, such as military equipment.

Cultural Factors One of the biggest differences between foreign and domestic markets is in culture. Foreign places present new social surroundings—places and situations where norms, mannerisms, lifestyles, and even ways of conducting business are dif-

Exhibit 22.2
Major World Trade Alliances

Alliance	Description
OECD (Organization for Economic Cooperation and Development)	This is a consulting group geared toward assisting all members help solve economic problems. It consists of 18 European nations plus Canada, Japan, and the U.S. This agency does not set policy for members, but is often instrumental in influencing trade relationships.
EEC (European Economic Community)	This organization is commonly referred to as the European Common Market. Its objective is to remove all import taxes on industrial products. Full members include Belgium, France, Germany, Ireland, Italy, Luxembourg, The Netherlands, The United Kingdom, Spain, and Portugal, but over 20 other countries of Western Europe and Africa are associate members. By investing in one of these countries, a U.S. marketer of industrial items can gain ready access to most of Europe.
EFTA (European Free Trade Association)	This association is not quite as successful as the EEC, but nevertheless is similar in scope for other European countries such as Austria, Denmark, Norway, and several others.
CACM (Central American Common Market)	Various Central American countries established this group to fill the same role as the EEC. CACM includes Costa Rica, El Salvador, Guatemala, and Nicaragua.
COMECON (Council for Mutual Economic Assistance)	This association is very strong, consisting of the Soviet Union and communistic European nations. Each member nation specializes in producing certain items and exporting a portion of its output to other members.
OPEC (Organization of Petroleum Exporting Countries)	This organization consists of a cartel of oil-exporting states. Included are Iran, Iraq, Kuwait, Libya, Saudi Arabia, Venezuela, and several small Arabian shiekdoms. The cartel was not too effective until 1972, when it reduced production and set prices at four times their previous levels. The alliance does not affect exporters attempting to sell to OPEC markets. Other countries have made similar attempts at cooperation for resources such as copper, but they have been unsuccessful thus far.

ferent from those with which a company's managers are familiar. While there is increasing commonality in this regard, each new cultural setting usually requires adjusting a company's marketing mix for it to be effective.[34]

Influence on Consumers Culture plays a very significant role in shaping the behavior of consumers.[35] Each society tends to develop customs, meanings, and feelings toward words, colors, types of products, and other objects. A marketer who is ignorant of these cultural norms may be in for catastrophe. For example, Radio Shack made a major blunder a few years ago when it mailed its Christmas catalog out to residents of Holland on December 10th. Only after the mailing did management learn that the Dutch give their seasonal gifts to each other on December 7th.

Cultures around the world can be very different. Most Asians, for instance, have a strong sense of national pride, and the marketer must be careful to cater to this

Bargaining over prices is a way of life in many open markets around the world.

feeling by acknowledging the blend of modern and ancient beliefs. In other societies, however, just the opposite can be true.[36] To illustrate, a cigarette manufacturer once successfully exported a brand to Venezuela. Because of strong sales, the company invested heavily in manufacturing facilities in the country, which resulted in total failure simply because the package included the words "Made in Venezuela," as locals preferred foreign brands.

Another classic example of failing to understand the cultural dimensions involves a baby food firm that once failed miserably in a foreign attempt. The world's illiteracy rate is about 26 percent.[37] The particular countries this marketer attempted to penetrate were especially problematic in this regard. The solution derived by this manufacturer was to picture a happy, smiling baby on the product's package without printed words. Management soon learned a lesson: the natives thought that was exactly what was in the product—ground-up babies![38] The obvious solution is for management to become intimately familiar with the foreign culture and then make the appropriate marketing decisions.

Influence on Business Practices Culture also plays a big role in how individuals conduct business in foreign markets. There are many differences. In most less-developed countries, intermediaries expect full commissions but do not expect to emphasize or promote the product. In Mexico, many retailers expect customers to haggle. Asians are not used to saying no. Some South Americans feel insulted if they cannot negotiate face-to-face so closely that their noses almost touch. Many managers in Slavic countries feel insulted if business guests do not consume alcohol. The list is endless.

American managers often become confused, hostile, or even insulting when they are faced with these unfamiliar practices. The idiosyncracies of foreign markets can set the stage for very sizable blunders unless management first recognizes and then adjusts the firm's efforts accordingly.[39]

Environmental Factor	Composition
Population	Overall size and density
Geography	Extremes of heat, humidity, soil conditions, and altitude; natural barriers; differences in culture and style of living
Economic Factors	Stage of economic development, income, anticipated future profitability, currency stability, required investment, local resource availability, and competition
Political and Legal Factors	Encouragement of trade, restriction of foreign trade, possibility of nationalization and expropriation, treaties, tariffs, and other legislation
Cultural Factors	Norms, mannerisms, lifestyles, ways of doing business, and literacy

CONCEPT SUMMARY

Environmental Factors in the Multinational Marketing Decision Process

Market Evaluation

The second set of variables in the multinational marketing decision process relates to evaluating the attractiveness of foreign opportunities. Obtaining needed market information and assessing a particular situation against other market opportunities (including domestic ones) comprise market evaluation's two major components.

Obtaining Needed Market Information Entering foreign markets without first gathering adequate market information is like betting on long shots at a horse track. The chances for lasting success are negligible.[40] Managers can obtain information on foreign opportunities in one of two basic ways: through direct contacts with foreign buyers or by company-sponsored information-gathering activities.

Direct Contacts by Foreigners Sometimes foreign buyers contact a company to meet their needs. Several years ago the Soviet Union contacted both Ford and Fiat to negotiate building and initially operating a truck plant in the U.S.S.R. Partially due to political considerations, Ford dropped out of the negotiations while Fiat went ahead with a successful venture.

Direct contacts are most common in technical manufacturing, construction, and defense industries. Israel, for instance, receives a large proportion of its arms from the U.S. Direct contacts by Israeli officials initiated these sales.[41]

This is the least risky of all possible ways for a firm to enter a foreign market. A good way for management to nurture the development of contacts is to attend international trade shows that are held regularly in major cities throughout the world.

Company-Sponsored Information Searches The most common way for companies to become involved in foreign markets is for management to initiate the search for opportunities. There are no hard-and-fast rules to follow.[42] Marketers can obtain information relating to buyer needs and factors affecting profits from published sources (secondary data) or from original research (primary data) the company sponsors. Most organizations use a combination of both.

Numerous sources of secondary data exist. A good starting place is the *Statistical Yearbook* and its references, which the United Nations publishes annually. It reports many important environmental variables such as population, income, expenditures, and the items various countries historically import and export.

Similarly, published studies by cultural anthropologists, sociologists, nutritionists, and other experts can provide useful insights. Other sources of information include foreign embassies, the State Department, the Small Business Administration, public accounting firms, large banks, and the Department of Commerce. Also, American chambers of commerce located in numerous countries provide data.

Despite the considerable published information, though, marketers often find themselves at a loss for appropriate data.[43] Information is slowly or inaccurately reported in much of the world.

Furthermore, some governments purposefully alter information for political purposes. Apparently, releasing inflated measures of economic activity helps them to remain in power. Hence, managers should exercise caution when interpreting published data. Original marketing research may be even more important in foreign markets than in domestic ones.

Assessment of Market Opportunities As in domestic marketing, multinational managers should follow the strategic marketing process. This, of course, requires screening potential opportunities against a company's objectives, abilities, and competitor strengths among various market segment positions. Regarding ability, marketers should not overlook access to critical supplies as an important criterion. To illustrate, a fast-food fish and chips chain might be expected to bypass England because of the proliferation of domestic competitors. However, a shrinking cod supply has troubled England and a foreign firm with strong access to these fish might have the competitive edge needed for successful market penetration.

Typically, management discovers several foreign markets in which the firm has significant profit potentials. It is then necessary to rank them in order of the most to the least attractive. The procedures described in Chapter 8 are useful for evaluating international opportunities.

Strategic Implementation Decisions

Once a firm decides to enter a foreign market, management's next task is to develop strategies that bring this decision into reality. The means of entry, the marketing mix to use, and the type of organization that is most appropriate are the decisions required.

Means of Entry Gaining entry into a new foreign market can be quite difficult. Basically, there are three major entry strategies to use: export, joint projects, and direct investment.

Exporting
Selling domestically produced output abroad.

Export **Exporting** involves selling domestically produced output abroad. In some cases, the items involved are physically the same as those marketed domestically, although the items may also be altered to reflect different local needs and competition. Exporting is the simplest and least risky alternative because it involves the least investment. There are two variations of exporting to choose from.

Direct export is where the firm itself handles all the details of contacting and shipping to foreign buyers. Its principal advantages are that it allows the exporting firm full control over the process and that the profit yield can be the greatest. This method is generally superior when the firm has expertise in dealing with the specific country or when foreign buyers have initiated the contacts.

Using intermediary export specialists familiar with the intended market is the second means of gaining entry. This avenue is especially useful if management is uninitiated in international trade. There are many domestic merchants, agents, and cooperatives that are geared to marketing goods to foreign buyers around the world. Further, the Webb-Pomerene Act enables U.S. producers to form associations for jointly exporting their products without exposing themselves to antitrust prosecution.[44]

Joint Projects A second entry strategy is to do so through a **joint project** with other investors; a partnership that spreads the risks and can bring in greater expertise.[45] Most foreign nationals are familiar with the business culture and ways of doing business within their own lands, which can greatly help projects succeed.[46] In addition, some countries, such as India and Mexico, require that their citizens become partners in many kinds of foreign businesses. Even when not required, this option should be considered because it reduces the venture's political vulnerability and creates good will.

Joint projects, foreign trade Partnerships between domestic and foreign firms for the purpose of carrying out business operations.

There are disadvantages to joint ventures, however. The greatest risk is that a partner may decide to become a direct competitor after learning the business. Also, disputes may arise if the partners do not share common goals. There are four common types of joint project arrangements: licensing (including franchising), contract manufacturing, management contracting, and joint venturing. Exhibit 22.3 presents a description of each.

Direct Investment **Direct investment** is where the company commits capital to company-owned foreign facilities. Its magnitude is large: over 2,900 U.S. firms have direct investments in Mexico, for instance.[47] Sometimes the facilities are limited, as when only final assembly is handled. For example, U.S. auto companies operate assembly plants in Europe, South America, and Australia. In other cases, the foreign operations cover complete manufacturing processes. Colgate, for example, owns a complete production facility in Italy.

Direct investment, foreign trade Committing capital to developing company-owned foreign facilities.

Direct investment is advisable under certain circumstances. It overcomes many problems involving import restrictions and may gain income tax breaks, lower labor and transportation costs, full control over operations, and the fact that trade secrets are not shared with tomorrow's potential rivals.

There are drawbacks to consider as well. Substantial investment is often required—along with the inherent risks of currency variations, fluctuating interest rates, and nationalization. Also, direct investment creates added managerial complexities due to the distances involved, communication difficulties, and cultural differences. To illustrate, most Americans have difficulty in adjusting to the two or three hour lunches that are prevalent in South America, even though the work day may include the same number of total hours. Such differences in operating styles can easily strain relations.

Marketing Mix Decisions Because each foreign market presents a different environment, management usually needs to adjust the marketing mix to each opportunity pursued.

Exhibit 22.3
Four Joint Project Arrangements in International Marketing

Type of Joint Project	Description
Licensing	The domestic firm (licensor) enters into a legal contract with another firm (licensee), either a manufacturer or an intermediary, within a target locality. Licensees obtain the right to use the company name, patents, technological process, or other valuable elements and the licensor receives a fee or a percentage of sales. Franchising is a form of licensing, although it often involves more completely defined rules of operation than other forms. Its chief advantages include low required investment, potential high rate of return on invested capital, no danger of nationalization, and the potential for entry into noncapitalistic markets. Its principal disadvantages include the threat of a licensee becoming a competitor after learning the business (a disadvantage of all joint projects), limited licensee control over operations, and possible contract renewal problems. Because of its low capital requirements, however, licensing is often a favored choice of small- and medium-sized companies. Some large firms, like PepsiCo. and McDonald's, also use licensing extensively throughout the world.
Contract Manufacturing	A domestic firm retains marketing responsibility in the foreign market, but contracts with a manufacturer to produce items there. It offers the advantages of rapid startup and elimination of the need to operate a plant overseas where work practices might be unfamiliar. Its chief disadvantage is that the marketer relinquishes some control over manufacturing. Large retailers, such as Sears, frequently employ this method. Also manufacturers such as Procter & Gamble often use it in markets where labor costs are significantly lower than in the U.S.
Management Contracting	This arrangement consists of an exporter furnishing management skills to a foreign company that provides capital. The marketer exports management skills in return for fees and often a percentage of the profit. Its primary advantages are the low risk and possibly an option to purchase stock. But the contracts generally prohibit the exporting company from entering into its own directly competing venture. Examples of this method include many of the foreign Hilton hotels. This arrangement is a good way to avoid nationalization in politically unstable economies.
Joint Venturing	This is where an exporter and nationals within a foreign country join together in a business where they are legal partners. Some countries, such as India, require this form of investment by foreigners. It has the advantage of added financial backing and the use of native managers who are knowledgeable about local conditions. But some foreign partners treat marketing as purely selling. Further, many believe in taking profits out of a business rather than reinvesting for further expansion. Nevertheless, this is an increasingly common arrangement.

Product and Promotion Mixes Researchers generally identify five possible product and promotion mix changes when considering a foreign market.[48] Figure 22.7 illustrates these. Straight extension is the least costly, but also the least customized. At the other extreme, product invention is the most individually designed, but also the most expensive. The appropriate strategy, of course, depends upon the nature of the market considered.

Modification of an Existing Product/Communications Blend

		Product mix: Same	Product mix: Altered
Communications mix	Same	Straight extension	Product adaption
	Altered	Communication adaption	Dual adaption

Development of a new product/communications blend

Product invention

Figure 22.7
Five Product/Promotion Strategies for Pursuing a Foreign Target

Price Mix Pricing can be difficult in foreign markets. Many impose extensive regulations and local customs often vary significantly. Retailers in France, for example, tend to avoid discounting and price competition.

Place Mix It is especially important for international marketers to take a comprehensive view of the channel of distribution all the way to the final buyers, as illustrated in Figure 22.8. Many companies have learned that important links may be unavailable. Channels may be nonexistent. Procter & Gamble, for example, resorted to selling door-to-door in the Philippines and several other countries because these areas lacked a sufficient number of retailers. Existing competition may block channels. The United Fruit Co., to illustrate, was forced to buy several distributors to gain access to European markets. Many countries have poor transportation systems and storage facilities, which impacts the physical distribution system.

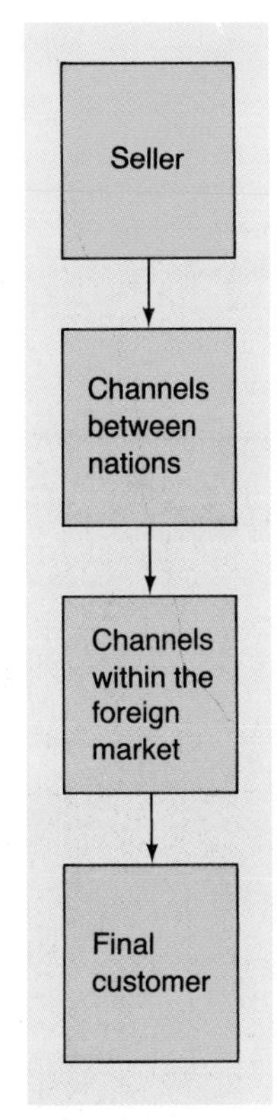

Figure 22.8
Channel of Distribution Concept in International Marketing

Organization Decisions The final implementation decision involves organizing the international marketing effort. Depending upon the scope of its foreign involvement, a firm may be organized in several ways.

Export Department Usually the first step an international marketer takes, the unit operates like a domestic sales department except that its sales are abroad. Major marketing decisions, however, remain the responsibility of the company's marketing group.

International Division A division is usually established when a company attacks several foreign markets and when sales levels become significant. These units are more complex than export departments, often including marketing finance, production, and administrative personnel. They are often located in a foreign country and have major decision-making authority.

Full Multinational Marketing Organizations Some companies attain the status of global marketers. Examples are Ford Motor Co., IBM, Coca-Cola, Eastman Kodak, Toyota, and Nestlé. For these firms, the concept of domestic versus foreign markets is a nonentity because they treat the entire world as their market. Generally, they have several international divisions, each to cover a different geographic region.

The Controversy over Multinational Companies

Both the power of multinational companies (MNCs) and the criticisms levied against them have grown significantly over the past decade or so. Skeptics see these firms as major world threats. The wealth of some MNCs is almost bewildering. ". . . GM is bigger than Iran, Venezuela, and Turkey; Goodyear Tire is bigger than Saudi Arabia." [49] And because of their wealth, such companies could ". . . threaten, if they chose, the sovereignty and viability of the political organization that characterizes the twentieth century, the industrialized nation state." [50] Essentially, the criticisms involve questions of influence on foreign policy, government protection, and citizenship.

Influence on Foreign Policy

A major criticism of MNCs involves their influence on foreign policy. U.S. oil companies, for instance, have convinced Congress to favor their investments abroad, elevating royalty payments paid to foreign governments to the status of a tax and making them eligible for deduction as a foreign tax credit. According to the chief counsel of the U.S. Senate Foreign Relations Subcommittee on Multinational Corporations, the policy has led to vast investment concentrations in OPEC countries and insufficient fuel source investment in the U.S.[51]

Some MNCs have also engaged in bribery of foreign officials. One count of U.S.-based MNCs, for example, revealed that over 250 of them made questionable foreign payments. "These payments and the publicity attached to them have destabilized governments in Italy and Japan and have resulted in criticism of government leaders in a number of less-developed countries." [52] Even the U.S. has not been spared. House investigations revealed that several U.S. politicians accepted bribes from a Korean businessman in return for helping Korean businesses sell in the U.S.

Successful global marketers view the world as a series of segments to penetrate.

The obvious concern is what controls, if any, should governments impose over companies that influence foreign policies for their own self-interest?

Government Protection

Perhaps the most controversial of the MNC issues deals with governmental protection of a domestically-based company's international interests.[53] The activities of MNCs often affect two or more sovereign states and can, at times, lead to considerable tensions between nations.

The most obvious cases deal with matters of legal grievances, such as patent rights and copyrights. For instance, Taiwan has allowed its companies to pirate written works without honoring foreign copyrights. The question is, "How much protection and involvement should a government such as the U.S. provide to help companies who are involved in such cases?"

In another instance, in 1970, International Telephone and Telegraph (ITT) executives admitted trying to enlist several U.S. agencies, including the CIA, in plots to prevent the election of Salvador Allende, a Marxist, as Chile's president. They also admitted to seeking the disruption of the Chilean economy to stimulate concern over communist control. Their objective was to prevent the expropriation of ITT's Chilean subsidiary. The question is, "How much and what kind of assistance, if any, should a government furnish to preserve the interests of multinationals?"

Citizenship

A final concern relates to citizenship. To which country does a multinational really belong? By which country's laws must it abide?

The issue is not trivial. U.S.X. (steel), for instance, must comply with U.S. antitrust legislation in its international operations, yet the Japanese steel industry is allowed to engage in collusion by its government. This arrangement places a great burden on U.S. companies.

Or consider another case. France adopted a policy of protecting the franc by tightly limiting any capital flight out of the country. Yet multinationals beat the system by first investing capital in traded securities and then converting them to other currencies outside of France.[54]

The important questions are, "To what extent must multinationals abide by the conflicting intentions of various nations? Should they be allowed to rise above local statutes because of their worldwide operations?"

The Solution

While the critical questions are clear, the prospects for solution are not. Countries have vested interests in their MNCs and nations have always had conflicts, even wars, over matters relating to trade. Yet rationally, the issues should be resolved.

Many alternatives have been proposed, from leaving the current system alone to imposing tight trade barriers.[55] Some countries, including France and Germany, argue for United Nations involvement. Any eventual solution remains uncertain at this time, but it is likely that the controversy will heighten as MNCs grow in scope.

Chapter Summary

This chapter examined international marketing and the decision process of managers involved with developing foreign markets. As the U.S. and other countries have become increasingly trade-interdependent, international marketing has become much more important. This trend will likely continue into the foreseeable future. As the emphasis on international markets grows, the need to adopt the marketing concept becomes increasingly important for international efforts to succeed.

The international decision process was highlighted in the chapter. It is important to recognize that foreign markets are much more risky than are domestic ones. Environmental factors can vary dramatically from country to country, and can change completely overnight in some cases. Complicating matters, obtaining market information is generally more difficult than for domestic markets. Once the decision is made to enter a foreign market, management must decide upon the most appropriate entry strategy to use, the best marketing mix to use, and make organizational decisions.

The final topic covered was the controversy concerning multinationals. Their growth, sizes, and certain actions have triggered considerable criticism from around the world. Managers involved or concerned with international markets should follow with a keen eye the trends in regulating multinational corporations and other pending legislation, as the success of their efforts may be heavily dependent on these factors.

Questions

1. Some politicians argue that the U.S. should be heavily involved in foreign policy with military and economic assistance playing an important role. Others contend that the U.S. should be more concerned with domestic affairs and lessen its involvement with other countries. What is the potential impact of both views on international marketing? What about on domestic GNP?
2. "U.S. marketers have led the world internationally in adopting the marketing concept as illustrated by the country's leadership in total foreign trade." Comment.
3. Why is the strategic marketing process more important in international marketing than in domestic marketing (which does not mean that it is unimportant at home)?
4. In many countries, bribery is a way of life. What role should U.S. business play?
5. Cultural factors influence consumer needs, but they also influence the way businesses operate. How can customary business practices influence marketing decision making?
6. What is the Common Market? How does its existence hamper a U.S. marketer's ability? Are there ways that it helps?
7. What are the criticisms of multinational organizations? Should they be outlawed or controlled in some way? How?
8. Should the U.S. increase import restrictions against foreign steel or machinery? Why?
9. The U.S. is the largest exporter of food products. Many have argued that these items could be used politically, just as oil has been used. What is your opinion?
10. Describe the "average world consumer."

Chapter 23

Service, Social, and Not-for-Profit Marketing Decisions

Objectives

After completing this chapter, you should be able to demonstrate a knowledge of:

- The nature of services
- The importance of services in the U.S. economy
- Major characteristics of services
- How the marketing concept relates to services
- The process of designing a marketing mix for services
- The meaning of societal, social, and not-for-profit marketing
- The contributions of societal marketing to organizations that use it
- How managers apply marketing concepts in societal marketing decision making

MARKETING FAILURE

IU International Unloads Ryder/PIE

In late 1985 IU International Corporation began steps to sell Ryder/PIE Nationwide, Inc. The latter company, which provided truck rentals and delivery service to its customers, had been consistently unprofitable for several years.

Some of Ryder/PIE's problems were brought about by deregulation, which attracted a number of small competitors who charged lower rates. Most of the problems, however, were a direct result of customer dissatisfaction with the company.

The Interstate Commerce Commission hit Ryder with its biggest trucking fine ever for keeping overpayments customers had made accidentally. The result was the loss of many customers. At the same time, small low-cost nonunion truckers undercut unionized carriers like Ryder/PIE in hauling full loads. This left the firm fighting hard in the less-than-truckload market—picking up and delivering partial loads at several locations. The firm was too big to be a regional carrier and too small to be national.

Firm pricing policies were chaotic. It double-billed some customers and it tried to drive away unprofitable short-haul business with high prices but lost higher-margin long-haul shipments too. Many customers rebelled at company policies. The final result was a decision by IU International to sell off the ailing business.

SOURCE: Adapted from "Getting Rid of Ryder Will Lighten IU's Load," *Business Week*, November 18, 1985: 86, 87.

Introduction

What do medical doctors, lawyers, CPAs, truck rental firms, fitness centers, hair salons, consultants, hospitals, Save the Children African Emergency Fund, the U.S. Postal Service, and IU International Corp.'s Ryder/PIE Nationwide Division have in common? The answer is that they are all involved in societal and/or service marketing—the subject matter of this chapter. The two fields, societal marketing and service marketing, have much in common so they are treated together. Solid marketing decision making is often the key ingredient to success in either of these two fields.

Service Marketing

Services
Intangible goods, such as legal advice and dry cleaning.

Services consist of performances, activities, or acts that a firm provides for customers. Like tangible products, services satisfy buyers' needs but they do so through activities rather than through physical objects (products). United Airlines sells a transportation service, rather than seats on an airplane. The United States Fidelity and Guarantee Company sells insurance protection, not pieces of paper containing printing and signatures. The insurance protection, not the piece of paper, is what the insured pays for. Firms offer many kinds of services to customers. Several examples appear in Exhibit 23.1.

Nature of Services

In truth, it is not always clear whether an offering is really a good or a service. Some would argue that a fast-food restaurant, such as Arby's, sells sandwiches, potatoes,

Consumer Services	Industrial Services
Air transportation	Legal advice
Hotel accommodations	Consulting services
Medical service	Marketing research
Electric utilities	Computer maintenance
Legal advice	Architectural services
R.V. rental	Ad agency service
Hair styling	Accounting services
Banking services	Banking services
Travel agency service	Cleaning services
Motion pictures	Warehousing
Appliance repair	Brokerage services
Tax advice	Industrial laundering
Landscaping	Telephone service
Fitness advice	Business insurance

Exhibit 23.1
Types of Services

salads, and other products. Others view their offerings as services; a convenient relief from home cooking and speedy service. The distinction is not always clear.

Company total product offerings fall on a continuum, ranging from pure goods to pure services. Some items may be purely goods, such as pig iron sold at the plant, and others may be purely services, such as commercial lawn mowing. But most items fall in between the extremes and provide a mix of the two. For instance, buyers of steel look for services too, such as transportation, storage, advice, and attributes other than the purely tangible.

A convenient way to view services is to consider the extent to which they are central to a purchase transaction. A **central service** is one that provides most of the satisfaction when a buyer makes a purchase. Examples are airline travel, hotel accommodations, and accounting services. In other words, buyers acquire these services for their own sake.

Central service
One that provides most of the satisfaction when a buyer makes a purchase (a buyer acquires it for its own sake, see *services*).

In contrast, a **supplemental service** is one that is acquired as an accompaniment to the purchase of a tangible good. When an oil field drilling company buys casing (pipe), for instance, the seller may also arrange delivery, perhaps with a Ryder truck. The buyer of a new computer also receives instruction and installation services. The focus of this chapter is on central services.

Supplemental service
That which is provided to augment the sale of some central service or a tangible good, such as gift wrapping and free delivery.

Importance of Services Marketing

A large portion of expenditures in the U.S. is for services, and the proportion is expanding. Figure 23.1 illustrates the total amounts spent on various service categories over selected years and the percent of national income derived from services. Also note that a separate category called "service industries" is included. This is a special category reported by the federal government and includes hotels and other lodging, personal services (dry cleaning, beauty salons, etc.), business services (consulting, accounting and auditing, etc.), health services, and legal services. When one combines

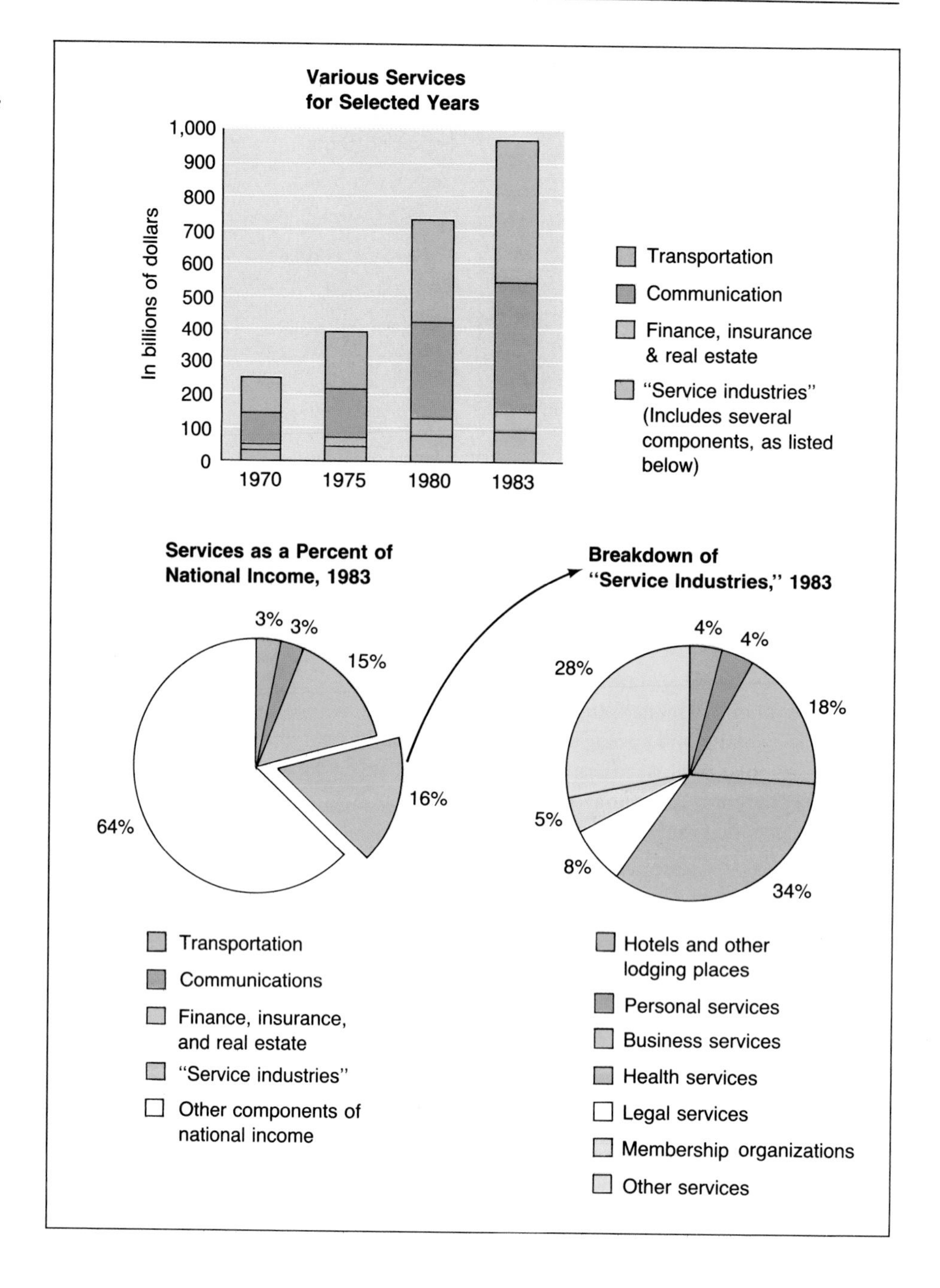

Figure 23.1
Various Services for Selected Years (SOURCE: *Statistical Abstract of the United States* (Washington, D.C.: U.S. Government Printing Office, 1986), 106th ed.)

transportation, communication, finance, insurance, and real estate with this category, about 36 percent of the national income is derived from services. In addition, one could also include government spending, wholesaling, and retailing activities in this total, as these items are also a type of service, making the overall component of the economy that is service-based a very large part.

Several reasons account for the growth of services in the U.S. over recent years. One force has been a rapid rise in the prices of services, which have advanced much faster than those for tangible products (causing them to account for a greater share of

Telephoning is a service that has been heavily marketed.

GNP due to this inflation). Manufacturers have been successful in automating production, but this process is much more difficult for services because services are very labor-intensive and costly to provide. Thus their prices have risen rapidly along with rising labor costs.

Another reason is the rapid infusion of women into the labor force. There is simply much less time available for mom to cook at home, do the laundry herself, and do other things for the household. A greater number of singles have added similar pressures, as many of them rely heavily on personal services.

A related factor has been a rise in personal incomes. Additional money, supported in part by two working household adults, makes available the resources for travel, hired lawn services and household painting and repair, and similar services to make life around the home more enjoyable.

A final cause for the growth of services is that there has been a great proliferation of services being made available. Landscaping, lawn fertilization, computer instruction, bed and breakfast lodging, investment counseling, chimney cleaning, and child care centers are examples of services that were not widely available even a decade ago.

Similar forces have contributed to the advance of business services as well. In addition, the environment has become increasingly complex over recent years, involving regulation, floating monetary rates between countries, and similar forces. This has resulted in a greater need than in the past for consulting, tax, computer application, and legal advice. These forces are likely to continue throughout this century, and the field of services will probably grow even further to meet this need.

Characteristics of Services

Services have certain characteristics that set them apart from goods and also pose particular implications for marketing decision making. The major characteristics are intangibility, inseparability of production and consumption, heterogeneity, and perishability.[1]

Intangibility Because services are intangible, individuals cannot see, taste, touch, or feel them, as they can goods. This means that marketers cannot store their offerings and often find it difficult to promote or display them.[2] Further, they cannot seek patent protection and may experience difficulty in setting prices. Consumers often cannot readily evaluate services before purchasing them and they may find the utility resulting from purchase to be short-lived. All of these phenomena pose problems for service marketers.

Inseparability of Production and Consumption Marketers produce services at the same time that their customers consume them. On the contrary, organizations produce goods first and then sell them for consumption. Consumers must be in contact with producers for many services to take place, so they are actually involved in the production process (as when a customer tells a hair stylist how to do her hair). Services, then, are often highly customized. This very factor, however, usually means that low-cost mass production is not available.

Heterogeneity Services are heterogeneous—they are not as standardized as products. Their nature and quality can vary from one customer to another and can vary over time. Customers, then, cannot assume that what they will buy will be the same or the same quality as what other customers buy or what the customers bought in the past. All these factors make it difficult for marketers to achieve quality control and standardization.

Perishability Services cannot be inventoried. Empty seats at a ball game, for instance, are lost forever. This makes it difficult to bring supply and demand into adjustment. Demand may be too great (as when there is a long line waiting to see a rock concert)

Adopting the market concept is a key to the successful marketing of services.

or supply may be excessive, adding to costs (as when several rooms remain unoccupied in a hotel on the weekends).

These characteristics affect the ways in which service marketers carry out their decision making. Although, research indicates that various service companies are affected differently. The nature of their target customers, the geographic coverage, benefits offered customers, and the need for the customer's presence during the service production are all variables that determine the ways the four characteristics impact upon a particular service company.[3]

Service Marketing Decisions

The Marketing Concept Adopting the marketing concept in service companies is a relatively new phenomena. In the past, many survived—even thrived—under a production orientation because the demand for services exceeded the supply. But the demand/supply situation has been changing rapidly for many services, causing managers to more fully embrace the marketing concept in their decision making. Doctors, lawyers, and hospitals, for example, have had to become more competitive in attempting to attract customers through advertising and other marketing programs.

Managers of service companies have largely been production-oriented because it reflected their training. Home repair specialists, for instance, are trained in carpentry and plumbing and not in marketing. The same is true for CPAs, who are experts in accounting. Small hospital administrators tend to have only a limited knowledge of marketing decision making.[4]

A problem in implementing the marketing concept is that quality is often defined differently by service managers and their customers. To illustrate, customers of service firms reported the following as evidences of high quality:[5]

- Banking customers value privacy or confidentiality during transactions with their bankers
- Credit card users value security features that hinder unauthorized people from using their cards
- Product maintenance and repair customers view the friendly atmosphere of small firms as being important

Managers, in contrast, see services from a technical perspective, such as the type of repair to be done and the length of time it takes for a credit transaction to clear, and they are unaware that customers view the services in a different way.

But much of this is changing, as many managers of service companies are beginning to learn the value of putting the needs of customers first in their decision making. Health maintenance organizations (HMOs), for example, have been very aggressive with marketing concepts that have proved to be very successful despite an overall stagnant health care industry.[6] Many CPA firms have also found that marketing concepts are necessary to attract new clients.[7] Law, dental, and many other firms are also making major inroads by using marketing concepts.

Service Planning The counterpart of product planning in service industries is service planning. Management decides what services to continue, which to drop, which to change, and which to add to current offerings. Management also should consider depth and breadth possibilities in much the same way as do product marketers. Many banks, for instance, have added to the breadth of their services in an attempt to expand business volume. Conversely, other firms find that they can better achieve financial health by concentrating on existing services rather than adding new ones.[8]

CONCEPT SUMMARY

Distinguishing Characteristics of Services

Characteristic	Nature of Characteristic
Intangibility	Consumers cannot see, taste, touch, or feel services as a separate entity
Inseparability of production and consumption	Consumers are involved in the production process because they consume services as they are produced
Heterogeneity	Services are not as standardized as products
Perishability	Neither producers nor consumers can save services

Many types of services are marketed.

The fact that services are intangible, inseparable, heterogeneous, and perishable poses special problems for management. Many customers form their attitudes about the quality of the service based upon such things as the attractiveness of the service firm's office and the professionalism and friendliness of the secretarial personnel. Management can often improve customer satisfaction by locating service facilities in shopping centers and places of work. Possibilities of customized work open up opportunities for differential advantage. Some hair salons, for example, specialize in very professional customized styling of clients' hair, usually at a premium price.

Services pass through a life cycle much like that of products. During introductory stages the firm may be faced with having to absorb losses and probably will have to invest heavily in promotion. A new motel, for example, may find it necessary to spend considerable funds on signs, direct mail, and media advertising in order to generate consumer attention and interest. Later stages in the life cycle require appropriate alterations in this policy.

Pricing Historically, most service firms have relied upon cost-plus pricing. Attorneys, for example, often charge their clients an hourly fee based upon their costs and their expected salaries.

However, prices increasingly are set to reflect supply-and-demand considerations. Increased competition, for instance, has led to lower prices in some instances. To illustrate, karate studios, which once were local monopolies due to the scarcity of their services, were confronted with the need to make significant price cuts as the number of competitors proliferated.[9] Lowering price during periods of slack demand is also a good way to stimulate volume, as when airlines offer special fares for weekend travel. Many lawyers in recent years have advertised lowered, set fees for routine cases such as uncontested divorces and the preparation of wills because of competitive pressures. Many HMOs have found that competitive pricing is a desirable practice.[10]

Service marketers that are able to effectively differentiate their offerings may be

MARKETING BRIEF
Marketing Research Is Important for Services

Chicago Sting soccer club officials gained considerable knowledge about the team's fans through a market survey. In turn, the survey was very useful in designing a marketing strategy.

Prior to the study, officials believed that most Sting fans lived in the suburbs. A survey showed that this was not the case and that a large portion (32 percent) of the fans were residents of the city, not the suburbs. Other questions provided data on fan residence, age, yearly income, occupation, and favorite sports team. Of interest was the fact that many of the respondents were Sting fans only, not sports fans—they were interested in the team but not in sports in general. Only 30 percent had ever attended a Black Hawks hockey game or a Bulls basketball game. In short, the Sting is not reaching many casual "crossover" fans.

The research results were used by team officials to aid in developing a comprehensive marketing strategy. Guided by facts, rather than by guesses, management is in a position to formulate a marketing mix that appeals to the unique needs of its target consumers.

SOURCE: Adapted from "Soccer Survey Shows Surprising Statistics," *Marketing News* 19, no. 19 (September 13, 1985): 54.

able to charge premium prices. Nautilus Fitness Centers, for example, offer unique programs and machines for workouts. Because competitors have not been able to copy the patent-protected equipment, the company is able to charge premium rates to members.

Various other marketing pricing practices are also useful for services. Quantity discounts are sometimes desirable, as when a college offers reduced-rate tickets for a season of theater performances. Medical doctors sometimes use price discrimination based upon a patient's income or insurance level. Geographic pricing policies may be effective, as when a towing service charges a higher fee to travelers stranded in a dangerous area of town.

Promotion Personal selling is very important for most services. The inseparability of producers and buyers often requires this form of communication.[11] Those who provide the service are also the ones who sell it. The person-to-person encounter between seller and buyer—client and provider—is critically important to the overall success of the marketing effort. Many service situations require heavy interaction between the buyer and the provider, such as consulting services, hairdressing, and medical services.[12] This means that those providers who become familiar with personal selling techniques to be used while they perform their services have an edge over their competitors.

Promotion is very important in setting the right image for the service. This is because many customers base their assessment of a service's quality on its image. Insurance ads, for instance, very carefully depict the company's image, such as Prudential with its "rock" (stability) theme.[13] Savings and loan associations and banks are also devoting more attention to image-development programs.[14]

Word-of-mouth publicity also can be a very effective means of building a service market's image, making the views of opinion leaders very important. A travel agency that bends over backwards to serve busy executives, for example, is in a favorable position to develop customer loyalty with the friends of these executives.

Place The major distribution decision to be made concerning services is deciding where to locate the business. Convenience is a factor for many services, such as motels and auto repair shops and ten-minute oil change facilities. In other cases, prestige locations are of primary importance, such as a Chicago lawyer locating so that he has a prestigious Wacker Drive address.

Marketing research may be helpful in uncovering useful information for this decision. To illustrate, research conducted by the Chicago Sting soccer club proved helpful in its decision to remain near the city limits rather than move to a more distant suburb. In fact, marketing research is useful for shaping the entire service mix to be offered customers.

Societal Marketing

Over the past two decades, marketing has increasingly extended to new frontiers by applying its concepts directly to social issues and causes. In this area, termed **societal marketing,** there have been two major fronts: social marketing and not-for-profit marketing.

Social Marketing

One source has reported that "**social marketing** is the design, implementation, and control of programs calculated to influence the acceptability of social ideas and involving considerations of product planning, pricing communication, distribution, and marketing research."[15] Essentially, then, social marketing describes the use of marketing principles to advance a social cause or issue, such as family planning or heart disease prevention. Exhibit 23.2 illustrates other applications.

Social marketing goes beyond **social communication** (the advertising and promotion of social causes). In addition, it uses the following tools.

- *Marketing research,* to learn about the market and the probable effectiveness of alternative marketing approaches
- *Product development*, such as the design of automatic devices to regulate thermostats rather than merely relying on appeals to "dial down" to save fuel
- *Incentives*, such as offering small gifts to people who show up for vaccinations
- **Facilitation,** which means making it easy for people to adopt a new behavior, such as offering conveniently located smoking cessation classes

In other words, social marketing involves using all of the Ps of marketing to advance some cause, such as the finding of missing children. (See the accompanying Marketing Brief.)

Any group or organization can carry out social marketing. Further, management can apply it to any side of an issue, which makes it highly controversial.

Social Responsibility Another aspect of social marketing is to ensure that the results of all marketing decisions have socially desirable consequences. This means that all managers should make decisions that exercise **social responsibility.** Profit should not

Societal marketing
Applying marketing concepts directly to social issues and causes and not-for-profit organizations.

Social marketing
The use of marketing principles to advance a social cause or issue.

Social communication
The advertising and promotion of social causes.

Facilitation
The process of encouraging ways to make it easy for others to adopt some behavior.

Social responsibility
A concept that suggests that businesses have the need to be concerned about the well-being of society in general when they make their decisions, not just the needs of their customers or their own profits.

Exhibit 23.2
Improving the Quality of Life through Marketing Approaches

There are a number of situations where marketing theory, research, and techniques can be applied to social problems. These include:

- Convincing people to boil their water and keep the water supply covered when water supply facilities are primitive in nature.
- Encouraging people to avoid consumption of products that are undesirable or potentially harmful—cigarettes, drugs, and highly refined foods that contribute to lung and heart disease, liver damage, overweight conditions, and other problems
- Convincing people that they should actively take steps to improve their health and that of their family through such means as getting more exercise, losing weight, flossing their teeth, etc.
- Convincing parents to limit the size of their families as a means of inhibiting the population explosion
- Distributing "Helping Smokers Quit" kits, which physicians can employ to help convince patients to stop smoking
- Demonstrating preventative health measures and healthy life habits through hospital workshops

SOURCE: Adapted from Karen F. A. Fox and Philip Kotler, "The Marketing of Social Causes: The First 10 Years," *Journal of Marketing* 44, no. 4 (Fall 1980): 24–33.

MARKETING BRIEF
Industry Pitches in to Find Missing Children

The extensive campaign to help locate lost children began in 1985 by Supermarket Communication Systems, Inc. (SCS). "It has mushroomed into the most extensive effort to date in behalf of finding missing children," said Rochelle Dishon, Director of Public Relations of SCS. "The project represents a joint industry effort, and we are very proud of that," she added. "We are all happy to help in this tragedy." Nestlé Foods led the list of corporate contributors with a $250,000 pledge, and the National Center for Missing and Exploited Children (NCMEC), and regional supermarket chains were big contributors as well.

As many as 90 million people see the "Good Neighbor" in-store message center displays each week, which show photos of missing children that are victims of both parental and stranger kidnappings. Also listed is a toll-free 800 number, staffed by NCMEC, to call with information. The operation serves as a clearinghouse for information about missing children.

Participating supermarkets include Pathmark, A&P, Stop and Shop, Kroger, Jewel, Dominics, Alpha Beta, Lucky, Eagle, Ralphs, and Pantry Pride, with more chains expected to sign on. Several dairies have also joined forces by printing pictures of missing children on milk cartons.

An additional boost was provided by free radio and TV public service announcements. "All of the stations are eager to pitch in," said Ms. Dishon. The TV spots feature famous actors who donated their time for the worthy cause, such as Daniel J. Travanti ("Hill Street Blues"), who has become an unofficial spokesman for the group. Several U.S. senators, including former basketball star Sen. William Bradley, have joined in the battle. "This project is an example of how a direct marketing/literature distribution company can use its resources to affect an important and vital community effort," said Ms. Dishon.

SOURCE: Adapted from "Supermarket Chains Join in Quest for Missing Children," *Marketing News* 19, no. 21 (October 11, 1985): 22.

Marketing has been used successfully in addressing social problems.

be the only motivation when making decisions. Figure 23.2 presents a matrix of a firm's interrelationships with its environment. It indicates that several factors should be considered by management when making decisions. The effects of decisions on employees and suppliers should be considered, since the firm deals directly with them. Also, the effects on the community-at-large should also be considered.

This does not mean that profitability can or should be ignored. What it does mean is that establishing a long-term niche in the marketplace depends, in part, upon the firm being able to satisfy many of society's needs. Selling some product at a low cost while contributing to environmental pollution, for example, only serves to displace the firm from its long-run market niche.

Figure 23.2
Constituents to Be Considered When Assessing Socially Responsible Marketing Actions (SOURCE: Adapted from Robert W. Ackerman and Raymond A. Bauer, *Corporate Social Responsiveness: The Modern Dilemma* (Reston, Va.: Reston, 1976), p. 15.)

Constituencies

Activities	Employees	Customers	Owners	Vendors	Immediate community	Larger community
Products						
Production						
Marketing						
Finance						
Facility location						
R & D						
New business development						
Government relations						
Special programs						

Not-for-Profit Marketing

Not-for-profit marketing
Applying marketing concepts to not-for-profit organizations.

Not-for-profit organizations
Institutions whose mission is to provide some service, but not to earn a profit.

A closely related situation is where managers apply marketing concepts in not-for-profit organizations such as churches, the National Association for the Advancement of Colored People (NAACP), the United Way, colleges, governmental agencies, and a host of similar institutions.[16] **Not-for-profit marketing** is similar to social marketing because both generally involve attempting to advance issues and causes of societal concern. It is different, however, in that not-for-profit marketing involves the advancement of an identifiable organization as well as its causes—often defined directly as a product or service. Like profit-oriented companies, **not-for-profit organizations** can often more readily attain their objectives by adopting marketing principles such as segmentation and logic.[17]

Since social marketing and not-for-profit marketing are closely related, some experts do not distinguish between them.[18] Others, however, see a difference and treat them separately.[19] This text treats them as a common societal entity since the issues, concepts, and concerns are closely aligned.

Focusing on the needs of several segments, not just short-run profit, is a key in becoming socially responsible.

Both social marketing and not-for-profit marketing are also closely related to service marketing. This is because the societal marketing area involves, to a substantial extent, marketing services or ideas relating to services. The material on service marketing, therefore, is very much applicable to this section of the chapter.

Application of Marketing Techniques Not-for-profit organizations use marketing techniques and principles in much the same way as do profit-seeking concerns.[20] The Christian Children's Fund (CCF) serves as an example. This organization's "product" consists of a service whereby individuals and families can become sponsors of children in foreign countries and on American Indian reservations. The sponsors receive letters from their "adopted" children, literature about what the organization does for the needy, and a good feeling about engaging in activities needed by the less fortunate.

The CCF is a nonprofit corporation funded by private sponsors only. This organization charges its sponsors $15 per month that provides for the basic maintenance needs of a child. Beyond this, sponsors are permitted to send gifts or extra funds.

The CCF is active in promotion, particularly in advertising. It features advertisements in magazines that depict the plight of underprivileged children and how sponsors can assist them. Normally the advertising copy is accompanied by emotion-evoking photographs of children who are obviously in need.

Target customers for this organization are families with upper-middle and higher incomes. Many such individuals feel that they have been sufficiently fortunate in life to share a small portion of their incomes with underprivileged children.

Nonprofit organization
A term used interchangeably with not-for-profit organization.

This **nonprofit organization** has been very successful. It has expanded both the number of sponsors and the number of children served at a fast pace. Further, it has set up operations in various countries that it did not serve in the past. At the same time, it has been able to remain solvent. Such organizations do not attempt to earn a profit but do endeavor to keep expenditures and revenues reasonably close to one another, at least in the long run.

Why Is Societal Marketing Needed?

Why do societal organizations need marketing concepts and logic? Why would it not be better to simply "sell" the cause that the organization sponsors?

There are two principal reasons why marketing is important to these organizations: public attitudes and management practices. Both are interrelated.

Public Attitudes Public attitudes are often negative when it comes to strong support of societal causes and institutions. There are more than 330,000 churches in the U.S. alone. Added to these are literally thousands of charitable organizations, local, state, and federal agencies, national organizations of numerous types, educational institutions, and other special-interest groups. And all are more or less competing with one another for public support as well as public impact.

Most Americans are inundated with requests for financial contributions or volunteer help for various causes. Because most people feel flooded with requests, it is very difficult for many societal organizations to succeed.

Essentially, all societal organizations face three major kinds of publics, as indicated in Figure 23.3. First, there are those who consume its services—the people for whom the cause is intended. In the case of shelters for battered women, for example, the consumers are the battered women clients. Second there are those who provide the necessary resources. These include taxpayers and others who donate funds, items, or time. Finally, there are those whose goodwill is important to the organization. For example, managers often solicit movie stars and other celebrities to support causes, such as Jerry Lewis, who raises money for muscular dystrophy. The intention is to attract attention and support of a cause through the goodwill acquired.

Marketing concepts can be conducive to success, especially considering the vigorous level of competition. In turn, designing marketing strategy for social causes requires considering several factors.[21]

1. How involved mentally, both at the specific moment and over time, are the various publics with the issue?
2. What are the available benefits that relate to the issue?
3. What are the costs, both monetary and nonmonetary, of subscribing to the cause in relation to the benefits?
4. What is the level of preexisting demand for the issue?
5. What are the various relevant market segments?

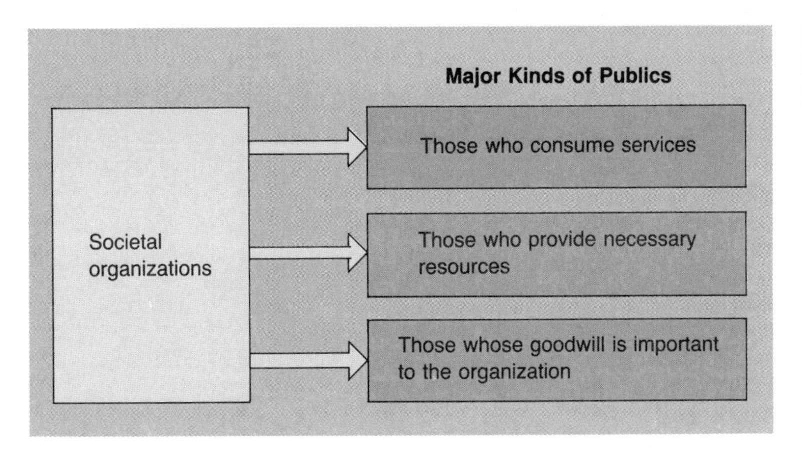

Figure 23.3
Major Kinds of Publics for Societal Organizations

Management is in a position to choose strategic communications alternatives once these questions are answered.

Consider the issue of the 55 mph speed limit, for instance. Several energy shortages and years of governmental regulations and warnings have exerted little impact on many people. Only a moderate preexisting demand to slow down exists, while numerous drivers cling to a lifetime habit of speedy driving using reasons such as "time is scarce" and "large engines are meant for fast driving."

The example also highlights the difficulty of marketing to an entire society. Those people who do comply with the speed limit do not receive reinforcement when they see energy wasted but time saved by the many who do speed.

There is little that marketing communications *per se* can do in such a case. Developing a more favorable cost/benefit relationship, possibly through either higher gasoline prices or rationing, may be the key. Exhibit 23.3 depicts this and three other examples for further illustration. In sum, carefully identifying targets and designing strategies around their needs can best enhance an organization's chances for success.

Management Practices Traditionally, most managements of societal organizations have been production-oriented. Instead of being flexible and adjusting to market conditions, many have been quite rigid—feeling their cause to be absolute, almost holy, and ready to be adopted by all human beings once they understand the implications.

But competitive pressures and rising costs impel many such managers to change. Some experts have predicted, for instance, that as many as 1,500 hospitals will close in the next ten years and several hundred private colleges will do likewise.[22] Other organizations such as churches, opera companies, and charitable groups are facing similar problems.

Management's adaptation of a marketing orientation favors the fortunes of many of these organizations. Flexibility in positioning, for instance, may mean that a hospital should specialize in outpatient care for the aged instead of offering a full line of services. Or a college might offer classes in a company's offices to attract those who work there, rather than expecting adult students to travel to a central campus.

Essentially, a marketing orientation in a societal organization requires integrating all efforts around the needs of the target constituencies.[23] The principles are the same as for profit-seeking firms. Product, price, promotion, place, and timing are all key

Exhibit 23.3
Key Factors Surrounding Four Social Marketing Situations

Case	Situation Involvement	Enduring Involvement	Benefits/ Reinforcers	Costs	Cost/ Benefit	Preexisting Demand	Segmentation	Conclusion
Military Enlistment	Very complex High cost	Little past experience Cultural values	Personal intangibles	Several years of one's life Personal rights	Very good for some segments	Fairly high	Very specific and limited	Marketing communications can have an impact
55 mph speed limit	Low Little interest	Central beliefs	Few personal benefits Weak societal benefits	Time Ego/macho	Poor	Virtually none	All drivers	Low likelihood of marketing communications impact
Antilitter	Low Little interest	Past nonreinforcing experiences	Few personal benefits Moderate societal benefits	Inconvenience	Poor	Low	All members of community	Short-run impact possible Long-run impact difficult
Voting	High to low—depends on political race	Central beliefs Pressure to behave	Good citizenship	Time inconvenient Infrequent/ low	Favorable for voting Less favorable for analyzing issues	Moderate	All citizens over 18 years of age	Short-run impact likely Long-run impact not necessary

SOURCE: From Michael L. Rothschild, "Marketing Communications in Nonbusiness Situations or Why It's So Hard to Sell Brotherhood Like Soap," *Journal of Marketing* 43, no. 2 (Spring 1979): 17.

elements that management should determine and integrate to satisfy the needs of targets and allow the organization to attain its goals. By organizing and controlling the organization's efforts around satisfying the needs of targets, societal groups considerably magnify the chances of succeeding in their efforts.

Implications for Today's Managers

Many societal organizations are beginning to recognize the benefits of the marketing concept.[24] Consequently they will be calling upon marketing specialists more and more to help develop and manage social causes in addition to providing goods and services. By the same token, additional involvement means that more marketers (and marketing as a field) will be on greater public display, raising the following ethical issues.[25]

1. Marketers could be perceived as the propagandists of our society
2. Marketing specialists may acquire considerable social power without concomitant safeguards to ensure that they are responsible to society
3. Marketers have a responsibility to carefully consider the social ramifications of their programs

Marketing has been used effectively for advancing many different types of causes.

Marketers will have made a major contribution to both themselves and to society if they can satisfactorily resolve these issues. If not, "outsiders who are critical of social marketing will increase in number and in their pressure to legally control marketing activities." [26]

Demarketing

Demarketing
Using marketing actions to deliberately restrict demand or shift demand to some other product because of shortages.

The final societal topic that we will consider is that of **demarketing,** or deliberately attempting to restrict demand. In some industries, past marketing has become so successful that demand has outpaced supply, resulting in shortages and inflation. For example, the huge U.S. trade deficit is in large part due to the American public being sold on a lifestyle involving the heavy use of cars and air conditioning. Too much success in marketing such items has overly strained the abilities of the economic system and the natural resource base.

Marketers have three basic choices when facing these situations. First, they can raise prices, which reduces the quantity demanded. But such price rationing can result in a heavy public outcry and federal regulation, as happened in the oil industry in the late 1970s and early 1980s. This only causes companies to lose respect among customers.

The second choice is to somehow restrict demand, such as by intentional cuts in quality or in quantity rationing. This choice also alienates past customers and depletes their loyalties.

The third alternative is to engage in demarketing, which uses marketing tactics to reduce the underlying demand conditions. The tactics center on marketing substitutes that may partially replace the items in short supply.[27] To illustrate, during oil shortages, many oil companies promoted the use of car pools and public transportation. Electricity producers have provided rate incentives for using appliances during periods below peak demand. Included in demarketing is the actual development and marketing of substitutes.[28]

By using demarketing tactics in such situations, companies are able to maintain their positive images with their targets. And by pointing to substitutes, the firm is exercising an ethical concern for their chosen target market's well-being. Through a dedication to the target's satisfaction, the firm and the target are more likely to develop a lasting relationship.[29]

Chapter Summary

This chapter examined service and societal marketing: two closely related topics because they both deal with intangibles, as opposed to goods.

Services are an integral part of marketing and are growing dramatically in the U.S. They have several important characteristics that set them apart from goods, including intangibility, inseparability of production from consumption, heterogeneity, and perishability. These characteristics vary from one class of service to another and have a major influence on the marketing programs that are most appropriate.

The process of marketing services closely resembles the process of marketing goods. The marketing concept is equally applicable to both; product, price, promotion, and place decisions all are necessary.

Societal marketing involves the marketing of social causes and the marketing of not-for-profit organizations. Both of these overlap considerably with marketing services. Further, marketing concepts are equally applicable for advancing the cause of the sponsor.

Questions

1. What are services? What sets them apart from goods?
2. Are the following goods or services?
   a. Meals at Burger King
   b. Insurance policies
   c. Hotel rooms
   d. College football games
3. What is the difference between central and supplemental services? Provide an example of each.
4. Explain why services are important to the U.S. economy.
5. What forces have accounted for the growth in service marketing in the U.S.? How do you expect these forces to behave in the future?
6. What is meant by the phrase "inseparability of production and consumption"? What are the implications for service marketing? For social marketing?
7. Why are services not as homogeneous as are products? What are the marketing implications?
8. Provide an example of the application of the marketing concept in service marketing.
9. How effectively do the following practice the marketing concept?
   a. Medical doctors
   b. Lawyers
   c. Motion picture theatres
   d. Hair stylists
10. What are some of the principles that service marketers should be aware of when engaging in marketing?
11. What characteristics of services pose particular problems to price formulators?

12. What locations are best for the following? Why?
  a. An expensive hair stylist
  b. An inexpensive barber
  c. Automobile rental agencies
  d. CPAs
  e. Consultants

13. What is societal marketing? What are its two major subdivisions? How are they alike? Different?

14. Why is marketing important to societal organizations?

15. Based upon your observations, how effective are the following in marketing?
  a. The Heart Fund
  b. The Salvation Army
  c. A local church
  d. The National Association for the Advancement of Colored People
  e. The Sierra Club

Appendix A

Conceptual Model for Assessing Synergy

Assessing the potential for synergy among alternatives is an important aspect of marketing decision making. While physical measurement is not possible, subjective measures may be used by managers to get an idea of the potential synergy associated with a given alternative. This appendix presents one such subjective model. The idea is for management to subjectively evaluate a potential opportunity along each of the synergy measures, as follows:

Example

A manufacturer of high-precision machine parts is assessing whether or not to enter the market for camera components. There is a great deal of similarity in producing, but not in marketing, the two product lines. The startup economies are evaluated as follows.

Contribution to Parent

- *Investment*—a small amount of capital is needed for new machines, which will have no benefit to the parent and will use capital.
- *Operating*—will take some supervision time away from current production.
- *Timing*—has no effect.

Contribution to New Entry

- *Investment*—less capital is needed than for other opportunities.
- *Operating*—technology is known and experience base is similar.
- *Timing*—minimal delay in beginning production.

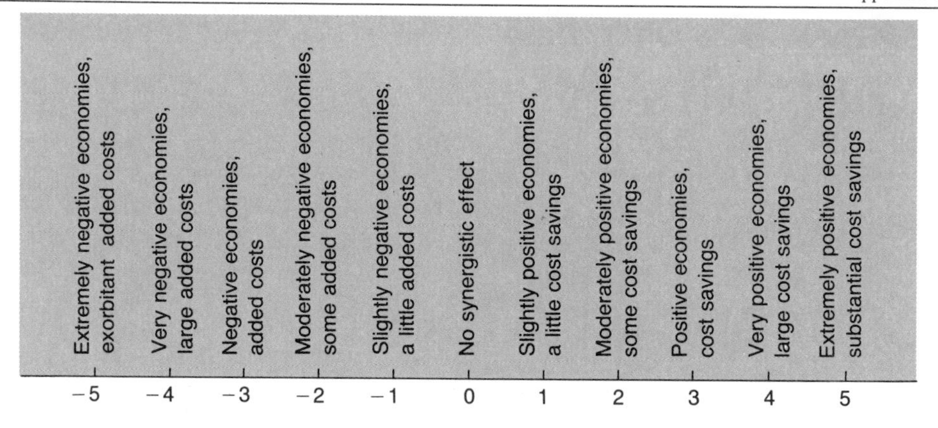

Measurements of synergy are based upon one of three variables: operating costs, sales revenue, or investment requirements. The appropriate variable should be substituted for the term "costs" in the above evaluation response. To illustrate, a weight of −5 is used for extremely low sales and exorbitant additional investment, as well as for exorbitant added costs.

Figure A.1
Subjective Evaluation of Each Measure

Joint Opportunities

- *Investment*—Free training is provided by an equipment supplier, which will upgrade the skills of tool makers. This education is needed in current operations and would otherwise have to be paid for.
- *Operating*—no effect.
- *Timing*—expansion will boost stock values.

Each row and column value in the synergy table (Figure A.2) is subjectively derived in a similar manner. The completed row for operations and assumed subjective values of the final column for this example appear below.

The net value of an opportunity stems from adding all the values in the final column of the table. For the example, an overall score of 32 is computed. Examining the rows reveals that expanding into camera components is beneficial to this company from operations and R & D perspectives, but not from marketing and management views.

The overall effects of one alternative, as above, would then be compared to others. In this manner, all opportunities can be evaluated on a common basis. The opportunity with the highest positive score has the greatest potential for favorable synergy and is often the most logical alternative to select.

Functional area	Effects due to pooling of competencies / Symmetry effects	Startup economies			Operating economies		Expansion of present sales	New product and market areas	Overall synergy
		Investment	Operating	Timing	Investment	Operating			
	Contribution to parent								−3
General management and finance	Contribution to new entry			(Enter appropriate values)					−2
	Joint opportunities								0
	Contribution to parent								3
Research and development	Contribution to new entry			(Enter appropriate values)					2
	Joint opportunities								1
	Contribution to parent								−4
Marketing	Contribution to new entry			(Enter appropriate values)					−2
	Joint opportunities								0
	Contribution to parent	−2	−2	0	2	3	1	0	2
Operations	Contribution to new entry	4	4	5	5	5	0	4	27
	Joint opportunities	3	0	1	1	2	1	0	8
								Total	32

Figure A.2
Example of Evaluating an Opportunity for Synergy

Appendix B

Major Federal Legislative Acts That Affect Marketing Decision Making

There are numerous pieces of federal legislation that have an impact on marketing decision making. This appendix looks at a sampling of the major ones about which all marketing managers should be aware.

Federal Antitrust Legislation

The federal government has enacted legislation that controls certain marketing actions that serve to reduce competition. Several of the major acts follow.

The Sherman Antitrust Act (1890)

This was the federal government's first attempt to effectively control large business monopolies. The following actions were declared illegal.

- *Section 1.* All contracts, combinations, mergers, and conspiracies in restraint of interstate or foreign trade.
- *Section 2.* All monopolies and attempts to monopolize, and all conspiracies (collusion) with others in an attempt to monopolize.

The Clayton Act (1914)

This act was passed to strengthen the Sherman Act. This act declared the following activities illegal:

- *Section 2.* Charging different prices to different intermediary buyers at the same level of the distribution channel for commodities of like quality, grade, and quantity, if the effect is a substantial lessening of competition in interstate or foreign trade.

- *Section* 3. The use of tying contracts, which means sellers cannot lease, sell, or contract for the sale of goods on the condition that the lessee or buyer not use or deal in the commodity of a competitor if the effect is to substantially lessen competition or to monopolize interstate or foreign trade. (For example, a manufacturer of rivets cannot force a retailer to also handle its riveting machines if the result reduces competition.)
- *Section* 7. A corporation cannot buy part or all of a competing corporation's stock (in the same industry) if the effect is to substantially reduce competition.

The Federal Trade Commission Act (1914)

This act was passed to strengthen the Sherman Act and Clayton Act. It also established the Federal Trade Commission (FTC) as an independent agency of the federal government for enforcement. The act declared as illegal:

- *Section* 5. "Unfair methods" of competition, as defined by the FTC, and grants the FTC power to prosecute offenders.

The Robinson-Patman Act (1936)

This act was passed to protect smaller independent wholesalers and retailers and was largely an amendment of the price discrimination clause of the Clayton Act. It declared the following activities illegal:

- *Section* 2*(a)*. Granting price differences to different buyers of commodities of like grade and quality if the effect is a reduction in competition between a seller and its competitors, a buyer and its competitors, or between the customers of a buyer. Price differences may be allowed only if they are made in good faith to attempt to meet the prices of competition, or they can be justified because of cost factor differences.
- *Section* 2*(c)*. Granting brokerage allowances to a buyer or brokerage firm owned by a buyer.
- *Sections* 2*(d and e)*. Granting of allowances or supplementary services to buyers on a basis other than proportionately equal to their buying volumes.
- *Sections* 2*(f)*. A buyer's inducement of a knowingly discriminatory price from a seller.

The Celler-Kefauver Antimerger Act (1950)

This act strengthened the Clayton Act (Section 7) by declaring illegal the purchase of assets as well as stock of another company, if the effect is to substantially reduce competition in interstate or foreign trade.

Major Federal Anticompetition Acts

The federal government has also controlled the extent of competition. The major acts are as follows.

The Miller-Tydings Act (1937)

Amended the Sherman Act to exempt resale price maintenance agreements made between suppliers (usually manufacturers) and intermediaries under fair trade laws. This enabled manufacturers engaging in interstate or foreign competition to sign such contracts.

The McGuire Act (1952)

Amended the above act by providing a nonsigner's clause. This meant that all intermediaries were required to maintain prices if any of them at the same level in the channel signed a resale price maintenance agreement with the manufacturer.

Public Law 94–145 (1976)

This law repealed the above two acts, making any fair trade agreements affecting interstate trade illegal. There remains some pressure to reinstate these laws, however, and they could appear again.

Selected Major Federal Consumer Protection Legislation

Mail Fraud Act (1872)

This act made fraud involving items sent by mail illegal.

Federal Food and Drug Act (1906)

This act made illegal the sale of adulterated and fraudulently labeled foods, drugs, and therapeutic devices used by humans or animals. It also established the Federal Food and Drug Administration (FDA). The act has been strengthened by several subsequent laws, including the Food, Drug and Cosmetics Act (1938), the Pesticide Chemicals Amendment (1954), the Delaney Amendment (1958), which required the FDA to test new food additives before their sale, the Kefauver-Harris Drug Act (1962) requiring the FDA to test drugs and label them with their generic name, and the Color Additive Act (1960), which sets limits on the amount of color used in foods, drugs, and cosmetics.

Meat Inspection Act (1906)

This act provided for inspection of meat sold in interstate commerce and the enforcement of sanitary requirements in meat packing companies. This act was strengthened by the Wholesome Meat Act (1967) and extended to poultry by the Poultry Act (1968).

Wheeler-Lea Act (1938)

This law added to the strength of the Federal Trade Commission Act by broadening the scope of the FTC to include practices that injure the public, such as deceptive advertising and sales practices.

Wool Products Labeling Act (1939)

The first of a series of laws that require truthful description of product contents, their origins, and common names (such as "wood" rather than esoteric ones like "Northwoods Wonder"). Other acts in this series cover fur, textile fibers, and the Fair Packaging Labeling Act (1966), which provides that each industry establish voluntary uniform packaging standards.

National Traffic and Motor Vehicles Safety Act (1966)

This law authorizes the Department of Transportation to set compulsory safety standards for automobiles and tires.

Child Safety Act (1966 and strengthened in 1969)

This act prevents the sale of potentially harmful toys and authorizes the FDA to remove harmful products from the market.

Cigarette Labeling Act (1966)

This act requires that cigarette manufacturers label their products regarding the health hazards they involve.

Consumer Credit Protection Act (1968)

This law requires full disclosure of interest rates and finance charges on consumer loans and credit buying.

The National Environmental Policy Act (1969)

The NEPA and its amendments (the 1970 Clean Air Act and 1972 Clean Water Act) empowered the Environmental Protection Agency to set standards and prosecute for air and water protection.

Appendix C

Marketing Math

There are several mathematical techniques that are especially important as tools in marketing decision making. This appendix discusses several of the most widely used of these. Included are: Bayesian analysis (whether or not to collect more information), break-even analysis, net present value analysis, payback period analysis, and calculating markups and markdowns.

Bayesian Analysis

The decision to conduct marketing research is generally an expensive one, with even modest surveys often costing in excess of $100,000 to conduct and analyze. Thus, management must carefully assess whether or not additional information should be collected prior to undertaking such expenditures. Bayesian analysis, also called decision theory, can help in this assessment. A relatively simple example is used below to illustrate what is involved with this concept.[1]

Example

The marketing manager of Sandcastle Swimming Pools, Inc., is considering whether or not a new line of swimming pools should be introduced. Management is convinced that one of three events will happen: there will be an excellent market, a mediocre market, or a poor market response. Management feels that the probability of occurrence of these events and the associated profits are as follows:

Market Event	*Resulting Profit or (Loss)*	*Probability*
Excellent Market	$800,000	0.2
Mediocre Market	$100,000	0.6
Poor Market	($500,000)	0.2

The above probabilities and profit estimates reflect management's subjective opinions, based upon experience. There are two questions to answer: "Should the new line be introduced?," and "Should marketing research be conducted?" Expected value calculations are the cornerstones to the solution.

Expected Value

Expected value (*EV*) is a technique that helps to determine what is likely to happen if a decision is made. The formula is as follows:

$$EV = \sum_{i=1}^{n} (P_i O_i)$$

where EV = expected value
P_i = probability of occurrence of event i
O_i = outcome of the ith event's occurrence
n = the total number of events possible

Thus, the expected value of the example's new pool line is:

$$EV = (0.2)(\$800{,}000) + (0.6)(\$100{,}000) + (0.2)(-\$500{,}000) = \$120{,}000.$$

Statistically, the *EV* means that if a firm undertakes such projects many times, it will earn, on average, the calculated *EV* each time. While many decisions (such as this example) are a one-time opportunity, since other opportunities are not identical, the assumption is made that if the firm implements only projects with positive *EV*s, it will earn an average of the profits in the long run.[2] Thus, since the *EV* for the example is $120,000, management should introduce the new line.

Research Proposal

Now, suppose that management is concerned about the 20 percent chance of losing $500,000 and is entertaining the possibility of performing a market study. The cost of this study is $20,000 and, while such studies are not always perfect, past experience indicates that there is a 90 percent chance that it will accurately predict the eventual market outcome. (When wrong, it is assumed that the 10 percent error is distributed equally over the other outcomes.) The question to answer is: "What should be done? Should management employ the research?"

Bayesian Decision Theory

Bayesian decision theory, which is closely related to expected value analysis, is useful for answering the above question. The procedure is based upon revising subjective probabilities with new information, such as from research.

For Sandcastle, there are three possible market conditions, termed conditional events (*CE*): an excellent, mediocre, or poor market. If management conducts the survey, two factors will determine whether or not the actual profit associated with a particular market condition will result: the likelihood of the *CE*, and the research forecast. A forecast of either of the first two *CE*s will result in entering the market, while a forecast of the poor market will result in dropping the line. Further, the survey may be wrong, which can be accounted for by calculating the "expected value of the conditional event" (*EVCE*). All *EVCE*s are then evaluated together by calculating their overall expected value. The following calculations illustrate the analysis.

CE_1: An Excellent Market The following are the calculations required for evaluating CE_1.

Survey Forecast	*Resulting Action*	*Probability of Forecast*	*Resulting Profit from Action*	$EVCE_1$
Excellent	Introduce	0.90	$800,000	$720,000
Mediocre	Introduce	0.05	$800,000	$40,000
Poor	Drop	0.05	-0-	-0-
Total		1.00		$760,000

The above calculations assume that the true market condition is an excellent one. If this is so, there is a 90 percent chance that the survey will say so, a 5 percent chance that it will forecast a mediocre market, and a 5 percent chance it will predict a poor market. In the first two cases the line of pools will be introduced, and in the final case it will not, since a loss will be anticipated. The *EVCE* is the sum of the products of the last two columns, which means that if an excellent market exists in fact, the company can earn a $760,000 expected profit (ignoring the cost of the survey, which is considered later).

CE_2: A Mediocre Market The following are the calculations required for evaluating CE_2.

Survey Forecast	*Resulting Action*	*Probability of Forecast*	*Resulting Profit from Action*	$EVCE_1$
Excellent	Introduce	0.05	$100,000	$5,000
Mediocre	Introduce	0.90	$100,000	$90,000
Poor	Drop	0.05	-0-	-0-
Total		1.00		$95,000

Thus, there is a $95,000 *EVCE* if there is, in fact, a mediocre market. Next, the final conditional event is calculated.

CE_3: A Poor Market The following are the calculations required for evaluating CE_3.

Survey Forecast	*Resulting Action*	*Probability of Forecast*	*Resulting Profit from Action*	$EVCE_1$
Excellent	Introduce	0.05	($500,000)	($25,000)
Mediocre	Introduce	0.05	($500,000)	($25,000)
Poor	Drop	0.90	-0-	-0-
Total		1.00		($50,000)

In this case, there is a $50,000 expected loss associated with the conditional event.

The final step is to calculate the overall expected value, as follows:

Conditional Event	EVCE	Probability of Occurrence	Product
CE_1	$760,000	0.20	$152,000
CE_2	$9,500	0.60	$5,700
CE_3	($50,000)	0.20	($10,000)
Total		1.00	$147,700
Less: cost of research			$20,000
Total Expected Value			$127,700

Therefore, for the example, management should pay the $20,000 for the research, since the total resulting expected value is greater than the expected value of introducing the line without doing the research. That is, there is a $127,700 − $120,000 = $7,700 improvement in the expected value from performing the research. Of course, if the expected value were lower than the original, the research proposal would be rejected.

Break-Even Analysis

Break-even analysis is probably one of the most widely used of the quantitative techniques in marketing decision making. Its principal advantage is that it enables a manager to identify the volume necessary to cover all costs related to a proposed venture.[3] The analysis assumes that costs are of two essential types: fixed and variable.

Fixed Costs

Fixed costs are those that do not vary in total as the sales volume fluctuates. Examples include executive salaries, office expenses, depreciation, property taxes, insurance, and budgeted advertising expenditures.[4] Because they do not vary in total, fixed costs are represented by a straight horizontal line as Figure C.1 illustrates.[5]

Variable Costs

Variable costs are the opposite of fixed costs because their total amount does fluctuate proportionately to sales volume. (Nonlinear costs functions also can be figured, but are ignored here for simplicity.) Variable costs are generally assumed to be *constant per unit, but variable in total*. Examples include direct labor, direct materials, sales force commissions, the cost of items purchased for resale, and shipping expenses. Because they vary, total variable costs are pictured as in Figure C.1.

Total Costs

Figure C.1 also pictures total costs, which are the sum of fixed plus variable costs. Total costs also vary with volume since a component (total variable costs) varies with volume.

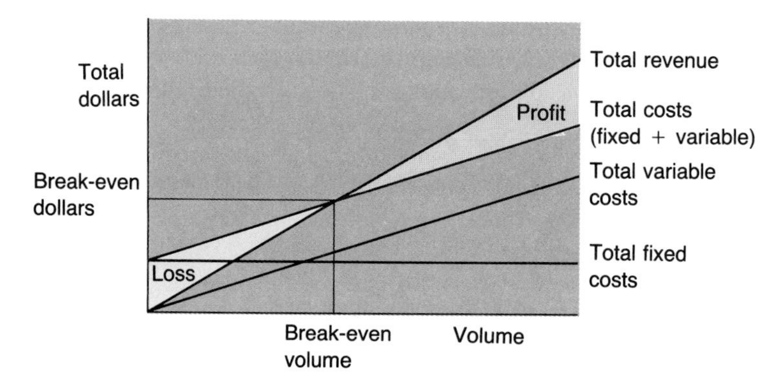

Figure C.1
Relationships of Fixed, Variable, and Total Costs to Volume

Total Revenue and Break-Even

Finally, Figure C.1 shows the break-even point in volume and dollars. It is the point where total revenue equals total costs.

Formulas for Calculating Break-Even

Rather than graphs, formulas are generally used to calculate the break-even point. The formulas are as follows:

$$\text{Break-even in Unit Volume} = \frac{\text{Total Fixed Costs}}{\text{Unit Selling Price} - \text{Unit Variable Costs}}$$

$$\text{Break-even in Sales Dollars} = \frac{\text{Total Fixed Costs}}{\text{Contribution Margin}}$$

$$\text{where: Contribution Margin} = \frac{\text{Unit Selling Price} - \text{Unit Variable Costs}}{\text{Unit Selling Price}}$$

Example A company sells an item at $3.00 per unit. Variable costs are $1.00 per unit and fixed costs are $100,000. What is the break-even in both units and sales dollars?

Solution

In units

$$\frac{\$100{,}000}{\$3.00 - \$1.00} = 50{,}000 \text{ units}$$

In dollars

$$\text{Contribution Margin} = \frac{\$3.00 - \$1.00}{\$3.00} = 0.66667$$

$$\text{Break-even} = \frac{\$100,000}{0.66667} = \$150,000$$

One can easily modify the above equations to determine the sales required to attain break-even plus a target profit. There are two cases: where there is a fixed dollar amount involved, and where a percentage of sales is involved.

Example—Fixed dollar profit goal The company wants to earn an annual 20 percent return on its investment of \$150,000. Thus, a profit of (0.2)(\$150,000) = \$30,000 per year is desired.

Solution

Treat the fixed profit as an addition to fixed costs, as:

$$\text{Break-even} = \frac{\$100,000 + \$30,000}{\$3.00 - \$1.00} = 65,000 \text{ units}$$

Example—Profit as percent of sales The above company wants to earn a 15 percent profit on sales.

Solution

Treat the variable profit as a unit variable cost, as:

$$\text{Break-even} = \frac{\$100,000}{\$3.00 - (\$1.00 + \$0.45)} = 64,516 \text{ units}$$

Net Present Value Analysis

Many financial experts argue that net present value analysis (NPV) is the best means of evaluating a project's desirability.[6] This is because the method uses compounded interest calculations to estimate the present worth (which is a common base) of all future revenues and expenditures. Compounded interest refers to the accumulation of principal and interest over multiple time periods, as a bank account grows—with interest upon interest—over time. To illustrate, \$1,000 deposited today at 10 percent interest, compounded annually, would result in \$1,331 in three years (\$1,000 × 1.10 × 1.10 × 1.10).

Users of NPV discount anticipated revenues and costs for all time periods, current and future, by the compounded interest rate. Two types of techniques are available: calculations determining the present value of fixed amounts at some future time period, and calculations determining the present value of a steady stream of funds over several periods, termed an *annuity*.

Example A company is considering the introduction of a new product. The initial investment required is \$1,000,000. Estimates of annual revenues and expenses are:

Sales ($80 per unit × 10,000 units per year)		$800,000
Less costs:		
Variable costs ($30 per unit)	$300,000	
Fixed costs per year	200,000	500,000
Contribution margin per year		$300,000

The product is expected to sell for five years, after which the firm may decide to abandon the project or substantially reinvest to completely update the production facilities. The present equipment is estimated to have a salvage value of $20,000 at the end of the five years. Senior management will not approve a project unless it can expect at least an 18 percent or better return on investment. What should management do?

Solution The annual $300,000 contribution margin is treated as an annuity. From the top of Table C.1, it is evident that the present value of a $1.00 annuity for five years is 3.127. The present value of the annual contribution margin, therefore, is 3.127 × $300,000 = $938,100.

The salvage will be available at the end of five years. At the bottom of the table one can see that the present value of $1 received in five years at 18 percent interest is $0.437. Thus, the salvage has a present value of 0.437 × $20,000 = $8,740.

This means that the total present value of the future net revenues is $938,100 + $8,740 = $946,840. From this one must subtract the initial $1,000,000 cash investment, which means that the project has a negative NPV of $53,160. This means that the firm should abort the project, since it will not earn the required 18 percent return that management seeks.

Payback Period Analysis

Payback period analysis is another technique that managers frequently use to evaluate projects. In a sense, the method is a cross between break-even and net present value analyses. It is different, though, in that it focuses on determining how long it will take to recover the related capital investment involved in a project.[7]

Example A company is considering whether or not to add a new product to its line. Assume that the initial investment for equipment equals $200,000. The following is the estimate of annual revenues and expenses:

Sales ($10 per unit × 15,000 units/year)		$150,000
Less costs:		
Variable ($5 per unit × 15,000/year)	$75,000	
Fixed, per year	20,000	95,000
Contribution margin per year		$55,000

Solution It would take 3.64 years for the company to recover its investment, calculated as follows:

$$\frac{\text{Required investment}}{\text{Net annual contribution}} = \text{Payback period, in years}$$

$$= \frac{\$200{,}000}{55{,}000} = 3.6364 \text{ years.}$$

Table C.1 Present Value of an Annuity of $1

Period	Interest Rate 8%	10%	12%	14%	16%	18%	20%	24%	28%
1	0.926	0.909	0.893	0.877	0.862	0.847	0.833	0.806	0.781
2	1.783	1.736	1.690	1.647	1.605	1.566	1.528	1.457	1.392
3	2.577	2.487	2.402	2.322	2.246	2.174	2.106	1.981	1.868
4	3.312	3.170	3.037	2.914	2.798	2.690	2.589	2.404	2.241
5	3.993	3.791	3.605	3.433	3.274	3.127	2.991	2.745	2.532
6	4.623	4.355	4.111	3.889	3.685	3.498	3.326	3.020	2.759
7	5.206	4.868	4.564	4.288	4.039	3.812	3.605	3.242	2.937
8	5.747	5.335	4.968	4.639	4.344	4.078	3.837	3.421	3.076
9	6.247	5.759	5.328	4.946	4.607	4.303	4.031	3.566	3.184
10	6.710	6.145	5.650	5.216	4.833	5.494	4.193	3.682	3.269
11	7.139	6.495	5.988	5.453	5.029	4.656	4.327	3.776	3.335
12	7.536	6.814	6.194	5.660	5.197	4.793	4.439	3.851	3.387
13	7.904	7.103	6.424	5.842	5.342	4.910	4.533	3.912	3.427
14	8.244	7.367	6.628	6.002	5.488	5.008	4.611	3.962	3.459
15	8.559	7.606	6.811	6.142	5.575	5.092	4.675	4.001	3.483
16	8.851	7.824	6.974	6.265	5.669	5.162	4.730	4.033	3.503
17	9.122	8.022	7.120	5.373	5.749	5.222	4.775	4.059	3.518
18	9.372	8.201	7.250	6.467	5.818	5.273	4.812	4.080	3.529
19	9.604	8.365	7.368	6.550	5.877	5.316	4.844	4.097	3.539
20	9.818	8.514	7.469	6.623	5.929	5.353	4.870	4.110	3.546
25	10.675	9.077	7.843	6.873	6.097	5.467	4.948	4.147	3.564
30	11.258	9.427	8.055	7.003	6.177	5.517	4.979	4.160	3.569

Present Value of $1

Period	Interest Rate 8%	10%	12%	14%	16%	18%	20%	24%	28%
1	.926	.909	.893	.877	.862	.847	.833	.808	.781
2	.857	.826	.797	.769	.743	.718	.694	.650	.610
3	.794	.751	.712	.675	.641	.609	.579	.524	.477
4	.735	.683	.636	.592	.552	.516	.482	.423	.373
5	.681	.621	.567	.519	.476	.437	.402	.341	.291
6	.630	.564	.507	.456	.410	.370	.335	.275	.227
7	.583	.513	.452	.400	.354	.314	.279	.222	.178
8	.540	.467	.404	.351	.305	.266	.233	.179	.139
9	.500	.424	.361	.308	.263	.226	.194	.144	.108
10	.463	.386	.322	.270	.227	.191	.162	.116	.085
11	.429	.350	.287	.237	.195	.162	.135	.094	.066
12	.397	.319	.257	.208	.168	.137	.112	.076	.052
13	.368	.290	.229	.182	.145	.116	.093	.061	.040
14	.340	.263	.205	.160	.125	.099	.078	.049	.032
15	.315	.239	.183	.140	.108	.084	.065	.040	.025
16	.292	.218	.163	.123	.093	.071	.054	.032	.019
17	.270	.198	.146	.108	.090	.060	.045	.026	.015
18	.250	.180	.130	.095	.089	.051	.038	.021	.012
19	.232	.164	.116	.083	.080	.043	.031	.017	.009
20	.215	.149	.104	.073	.051	.037	.026	.014	.007
25	.146	.092	.059	.038	.024	.016	.010	.005	.002
30	.099	.057	.033	.020	.012	.007	.004	.002	.001

This solution ignores any salvage values, which are often negligible in such projects. After the 3.64 years, any contribution would be actual profit.

Companies using payback period analysis typically predetermine the number of years they use as a criterion to evaluate new projects. In the above example, to illustrate, management uses a four-year payback as a cutoff when considering new projects. Since the one evaluated has a shorter payback than the cutoff criterion, the project likely would be considered desirable.

Markups and Markdowns

Markups and markdowns are common in business, especially among intermediaries. Several traditional markups are presented, and how to calculate markups and markdowns is explained.

Markups

Wholesalers and retailers generally mark up the items they sell by a percentage to establish their selling prices. While different markups may be used from item to item, and from competitor to competitor, depending upon pricing strategies and service mix, the following table gives several traditional markups used by retailers.

Markup Percentage	*Selected Types of Items*
40% +	Furs, jewelry, restaurant and bar items, furniture, bakery items
30 to 39%	Carpets, clothing, gifts, appliances, drugs, automobile parts, heating fuel
20 to 29%	Hardware, sporting goods, filling stations, lumber, general merchandise
Below 20%	Packaged liquor, vehicles, groceries, meats

How to Calculate Markups There are two types of markup methods used: on the basis of selling price, and on the basis of direct cost. Both begin by first establishing the dollar amount of the markup involved, which is the difference between the direct cost of the item and its selling price. The methods differ in the denominator used in the calculation.

Example An appliance costs \$100 and has a retail list price of \$160. Thus, there is a \$60 markup involved.

Markup on Cost The historic way is to calculate the markup on cost (this is also referred to as "*mark-on*"). For the example,

$$\frac{\$60 \text{ markup}}{\$100 \text{ cost}} = 60\% \text{ markup}$$

Calculating markups on cost is used less frequently than in the past.

Markup on Selling Price This is the increasingly common way of calculating markups (also called simply "*markup*"). For the example,

$$\frac{\$60 \text{ markup}}{\$160 \text{ selling price}} = 37.5\% \text{ markup}$$

The increasing popularity of this approach is due to its closer conformity to managerial accounting techniques, which more readily enables break-even calculations.

Conversion from One to the Other Because some intermediaries use both systems, it is essential to be able to convert from one system to the other. This is easily accomplished by using the appropriate formula, as follows.

To convert a markup to a mark-on:

$$\% \text{ markup on cost} = \frac{\% \text{ markup on selling price}}{100\% - \% \text{ markup on selling price}}$$

For the example,

$$\% \text{ markup on cost} = \frac{37.5\%}{100\% - 37.5\%} = 60\%$$

To convert a mark-on to a markup:

$$\% \text{ markup on selling price} = \frac{\% \text{ markup on cost}}{100\% + \% \text{ markup on cost}}$$

For the example,

$$\% \text{ markup on selling price} = \frac{60\%}{100\% + 60\%} = 37.5\%$$

Markdowns

Sometimes items sell below their stated selling price for several reasons, including regular sales, special inventory reductions, and so on. These price reductions are called *markdowns*.

How to Calculate Markdowns The calculation of a markdown is straightforward. To illustrate, assume that the above appliance, which had an initial price of \$160, is reduced to \$130. This translates to a \$30 markdown.

Companies typically calculate markdown percentages on the basis of *actual final (or net) selling price*. The following is the formula for calculating the markdown percentage.

$$\% \text{ markdown} = \frac{\text{Dollar markdown}}{\text{Final selling price}} \times 100 = \text{Markdown percentage}$$

For the example,

$$\% \text{ markdown} = \frac{\$30}{\$130} \times 100 = 23.08\%$$

Most companies keep track of all markdowns granted so that they can reassess their pricing and buying practices. Excessive markdowns may signal too high a pricing practice or the purchase of poorly selling merchandise. Thus, calculating markdowns helps to control these activities.

Appendix D

Secondary Data Sources

Secondary data are invaluable in marketing research. This appendix lists several widely available sources of such data useful to marketing managers. There are three types: company records, government sources, and private sources.

Company Records

Type of Record	*Useful For*
Accounts receivable	Assessing charging practices and developing profiles of those unlikely to pay
Customer complaint files	Learning the extent and patterns of complaints
Inventory records	Determining how well items move, thefts, and damage or spoilage
Markdown reports	To assess pricing, which items are price-elastic and slow-moving
Merchandise return reports	Assessing customer satisfaction with purchases
Research reports	Assessing specific situations
Sales force call performance reports	Assessing sales force and customer buying practices
Sales records	Learning which items sell, trends, how they are financed, etc.
Special sale reports	Learning about the success of special sales
Shipping reports	Assessing customer locations and quantities purchased

Stockout reports	Learning which items move fast
Trade-in reports	To learn which competitors the company has been able to switch customers away from
Warranty registrations	Learning about customer locations, where they bought, why, etc.

Government Sources

- *Business Cycle Developments* (U.S. Government Printing Office)—historical and current cycle-related data.
- *Census of Agriculture* (U.S. Bureau of the Census)—reported each five years; reports numbers and sizes of farms, distribution of crops, employment, value of shipments, value of sales, and so on. (*Agricultural Statistics* and *The Commodity Yearbook* supplement this with additional summary data.)
- *Census of Business* (U.S. Bureau of the Census)—reported each five years; reports income, employment, numbers and sizes of wholesalers, retailers, and service establishments.
- *Census of Governments* (U.S. Bureau of the Census)—reports revenue, expenditures, employment, and other variables relating to municipal, county, state, and federal governmental units. (*The Municipal Yearbook* supplements this.)
- *Census of Housing* (U.S. Bureau of the Census)—reported each ten years; statistics on current housing are reported, such as numbers, structural characteristics, and occupancy, classified by geographical area.
- *Census of Manufacturers* (U.S. Bureau of the Census)—reported each five years; presents value of sales, value added, value of shipments, income and employment data for manufacturers classified by the Standard Industrial Classification system. (*The Annual Survey of Manufacturers* supplements this census.)
- *Census of Mineral Industries* (U.S. Bureau of the Census)—reported each five years; reports statistics on production, employment, income, etc. for various industries.
- *Census of Population* (U.S. Bureau of the Census)—reported each ten years; details populations of various geographical regions in the U.S., including many economic and demographic characteristics. (*Current Population Reports* is a supplement during interim years.)
- *Census of Transportation* (U.S. Bureau of the Census)—reports statistics on movement of passengers and freight and transit mode characteristics.
- *County and City Data Book* (U.S. Bureau of the Census)—This document is much more detailed than the *Abstract*, but is only published every three years. It breaks composite statistics down into geographical detail. Each county and city with a population greater than 25 thousand is reported.
- *Federal Reserve Bulletin* (Board of Governors of the Federal Reserve Board)—presents statistics relating to prices, sales, credit, and national income.
- *Foreign Commerce Yearbook* (U.S. Government Printing Office)—presents statistics for many foreign countries.
- *Guide to U.S. Government Serials and Publications* (U.S. Government Printing Office)—this is a guide to federal publications.
- *Marketing Information Guide* (U.S. Government Printing Office)—this is a guide to federally published materials of major marketing importance.
- *Monthly Checklist of State Publications* (Library of Congress)—this is a guide to some information published by various states.

- *Monthly Labor Review* (Bureau of Labor Statistics)—presents statistics on employment, earnings, etc. for U.S. workers.
- *Quarterly Summary of Foreign Commerce of the United States* (U.S. Government Printing Office)—presents statistics relating to importers and exporters in the U.S. and many other countries.
- *Statistical Abstract of the United States* (U.S. Bureau of the Census)—In about 1,000 pages, this annual publication summarizes data published by both the government and several other sources. Detailed references allow researchers to locate supporting data. A detailed bibliography also classifies references by subject.
- *Survey of Current Business* (U.S. Government Printing Office)—This document is published monthly and reports various economic activity statistics. Also, there are articles on business and economic trends. The publication, however, lacks the detail of other sources.
- *United Nations Statistical Yearbook* (United Nations)—reports statistics relating to foreign trade.

Private Sources

- *American Doctoral Dissertations Index* (Microfilm Library Services)—reports and references U.S. Doctoral dissertations on a widely varied list of subjects, including business.
- *Business Periodical Index* (H. R. Wilson Co.)—references articles by subject from a wide range of business periodicals.
- *Business Week* (McGraw-Hill, Inc.)—presents weekly indices on overall economic activity, production, trade, prices, and financial data; monthly indices on personal income, money supply, wholesale prices, housing starts, plant utilization, and inventories, along with articles on business trends and topics.
- *Economic Almanac* (National Industrial Conference Board)—provides extensive economic related statistics over time of both business and government activity.
- *The Fortune Directory* (Fortune Magazine)—lists sales, profits, assets, and employment of the largest manufacturers, retailers, insurance, banking, utility, and transportation companies.
- *F. W. Dodge Reports* (Dodge Corp.)—presents detailed information regarding the construction industry.
- *Journal of Consumer Research* (Association for Consumer Research)—a quarterly publication of findings and methodological issues related to buying behavior.
- *Journal of Marketing* (American Marketing Association)—a quarterly publication of research findings and concepts especially useful to marketing managers.
- *Journal of Marketing Research* (American Marketing Association)—a quarterly publication of findings and research methodological issues related to all elements of a marketing mix.
- *Market Analysis: A Handbook of Current Data Sources* (Scarecrow Press)—lists many of the widely used sources of marketing information.
- *New York Times Index*—indexes articles (this paper is an excellent source of business information) that appeared in the newspaper.
- *Reader's Guide to Periodical Literature*—references articles by subject from a wide range of all types of periodicals.
- *Sales & Marketing Management*—discusses many topics of importance to marketing managers. Especially useful is its annually published (usually in October) "Survey

of Buying Power" which provides indicators of buying strengths in the U.S. by region detail.

- *Sources of Business Information* (University of California Press)—presents an extensive listing of business information sources.
- *Standard and Poor's Standard Corporation Descriptions*—presents detailed financial information relating to many and varied types of firms.
- *Statistical Sources* (Gale Research Co.)—references many sources of statistical information of use to researchers.
- *Wall Street Journal Index*—references data and articles appearing in the *Journal*.

Appendix E

Careers in Marketing

Opportunities in Marketing

The field of marketing offers many career opportunities. In general, marketing has fared better than most disciplines in the past, even during slow economic times.[1,2,3] One publication, *Business Week's Guide to Careers*, has consistently announced that marketing positions account for many of the top entry level jobs for college students.[4,5]

Marketing salaries are very competitive.[6] This is illustrated in Figures E.1 and E.2. The salaries have grown since the data illustrated in the figures were reported but the information is useful to show that marketing positions pay well above the average. Further, marketing positions provide considerable opportunity for upward mobility. Studies show that more advanced-level positions (vice president, president, and chairman of the board) are filled from people in finance and marketing than from any other fields.[7]

Types of Marketing Positions

There are many types of positions available in marketing. Essentially, there are three tiers of job opportunities, based upon the amount of authority and responsibility each commands: entry, intermediate, and advanced. Associated with each tier are various positions such as trainee and operative positions (with normal operating duties, though usually indicating a nonmanagerial situation).

There are also various spheres or general categories into which any of the positions may be classified. These are: industrial or consumer organizations, domestic or international companies, large or small businesses, and profit and not-for-profit organizations. A marketing faculty advisor or a school placement office official can help interested readers explore the opportunities in greater depth.

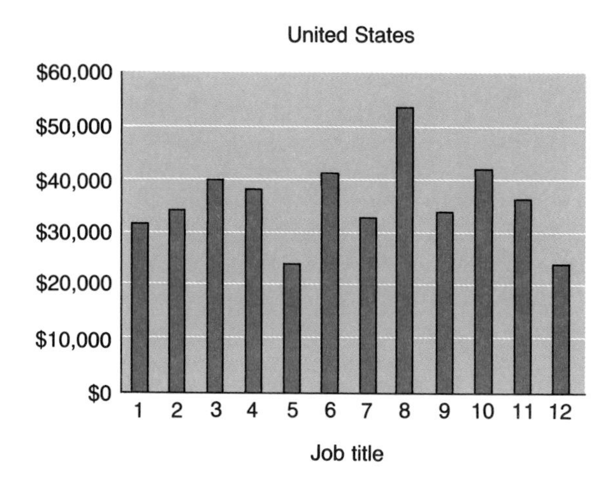

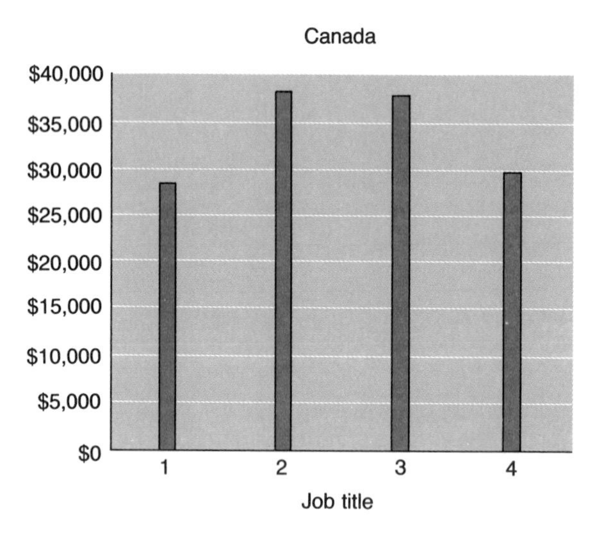

Figure E.1
Average Salary by Job Title
(SOURCE: Based on Gordon McAleer, *An Exploratory Analysis of AMA Members' Salaries for Marketing Educators and Practitioners* (Chicago: American Marketing Association, 1983), p. 17.)

Obtaining a Marketing Job

There are certain strategies and steps that a person should take when searching for a position.[8] Obtaining a job is an exercise in marketing oneself.

- Developing a proper mental attitude is essential to getting all good positions—those with career opportunities. A positive attitude is essential. One who expects to fail generally does.

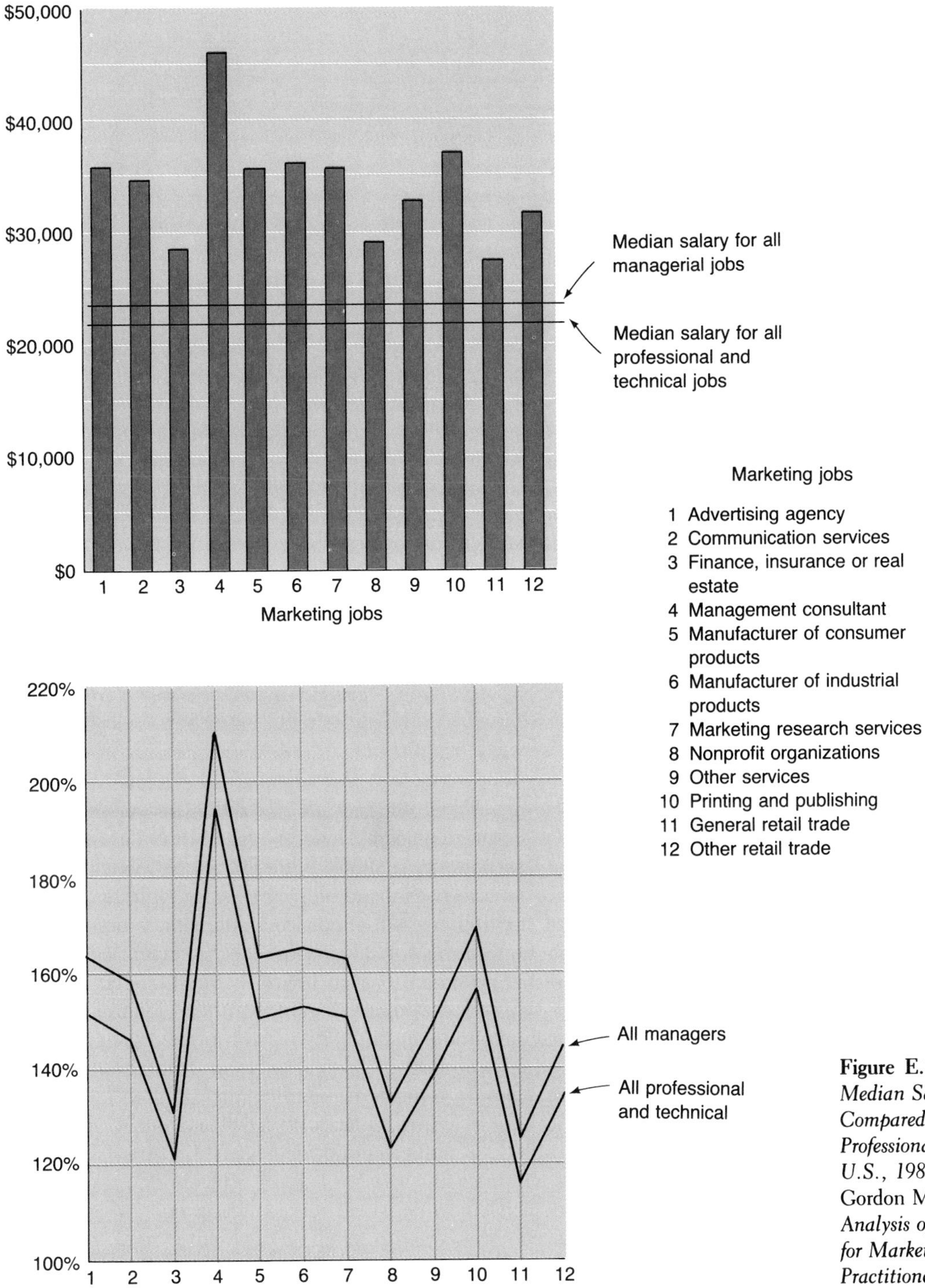

Figure E.2
Median Salaries of Marketing Jobs Compared to All Managerial, Professional and Technical Jobs in the U.S., 1983 (SOURCE: Based on Gordon McAleer, *An Exploratory Analysis of AMA Members' Salaries for Marketing Educators and Practitioners* (Chicago: American Marketing Association, 1983) and *Statistical Abstract of the United States* (Washington, D.C.: U.S. Government Printing Office, 1986), 106th ed.)

- Developing an inventory of one's personal goals is essential because this will provide a clear-cut idea of what one is looking for in a position, which helps to both identify companies with which to seek employment and to evaluate the desirability of positions. The goals should cover all time spans, from one year to ten years or more into the future. Further, they should include both vocational items ("I want to be a sales manager for Westinghouse within ten years") and nonvocational items ("I want to live in a large city, own a condominium, and travel"). The more specific the goals, the more useful they will be in providing targets toward which one can orient the job search. Further, interviewers often look for people who know their own goals.
- Taking inventory of one's capabilities and interests is also important. This should be done in writing (as should goal statements) because this forces a person to think and make these explicit. Knowing one's own capabilities and interests helps in identifying particular companies, industries, and types of jobs to pursue.
- Investigating companies is the next step, which involves identifying those which appear to provide synergy with one's own goals, interests, and capabilities. There are many sources of information about particular companies, including the Job Placement Annual, magazine articles, newspaper ads, publications in the library (such as *Moody's Industrials* and *Standard and Poor's Corporate Records*), conversations with business people in one's home town, professors, parents and friends, and the college placement office.
- Contacting companies that look promising is next on the agenda. One should attempt to segment the marketing in this phase, rather than focusing on all possible companies. There are several ways to do this, including: letters, walk-in interviews, the college placement service, responding to advertisements, personal contacts, and employment agencies. Exhibit E.1 provides a sample letter of introduction to a company. Notice that it does not go into much detail regarding education, experience, and so on. This is the function of the résumé. An example résumé is presented in Exhibit E.2.[9]
- Interviewing is an important aspect of practically every job search. The process is really that of selling oneself to the interviewer.[10] Exhibit E.3 contains several interviewing suggestions.[11]
- Follow-up should take place within a week or two of the interview, which involves contacting the interviewer by telephone, mail, or personally to reaffirm one's interest. It is often a good idea to ask if the person needs further information. Follow-up indicates a genuine interest in the position and that one is a self-starter.

Exhibit E.1
Sample Letter of Introduction

April 2, 1987

Mr. James Loran
Product Manager, Ajax Corporation
2716 Flint Avenue
Chicago, IL 80612

Dear Mr. Loran:

This spring I will receive a B.B.A. degree from Southernmost University with a major in marketing. A family friend, Mr. Thomas Greene, has advised me that you have a traineeship available in product management. My career interest is very definitely in that field, as the attached résumé will attest.

A career opportunity with your company is a very exciting prospect. I am well aware of the Ajax Corporation's excellent performance in the industry and its outstanding reputation as a career choice.

Enclosed is my résumé. It indicates an objective of working in the product management area with an outstanding firm such as yours. My course work includes a number of classes in marketing strategy, marketing research, advertising, and product management, along with a minor in finance. The work experience with several small businesses and the Small Business Institute provided some very useful insights into marketing and management.

In two weeks I will call you and ask for an interview and sincerely hope that you will be able to arrange for one. Thank you for the consideration.

Sincerely,

James Black

Encl.

Exhibit E.2
Sample Résumé

RÉSUMÉ
JAMES BLACK

2846 Whitt Ave.
Southernmost City, Georgia 24916
(404) 555-1918

DATE:	January 1987
WORK EXPERIENCE:	6/86–9/86 Adams Hardware, salesperson 6/85–9/85 Adams Hardware, salesperson 6/84–9/84 Adams Hardware, custodian 6/83–9/83 Acme Sportswear, salesperson 6/82–9/82 Premium Lumber Company, yardman
EDUCATION:	Southernmost University, degree granted 1986 Major: Marketing Minor: Finance G.P.A.: 3.08, G.P.A. in major: 3.35 Consulting in Small Business Institute case: Mervin's Hardware, 1986
EXTRACURRICULAR ACTIVITIES:	American Marketing Association Collegiate Chapter, 1984–1986 (President, 1985–1986) University Outdoors Club, 1985 Beta Beta Beta fraternity, 1983–1986 (Vice President, 1985–1986)
CAREER OBJECTIVES:	Product management in a company that allows opportunity for advancement
PERSONAL DATA:	Date of birth: January 2, 1965 Marital status: single Geographic preference: none Health: Excellent
REFERENCES:	Dr. Raymond Heath, Professor of Marketing Southernmost University Southernmost City Center, GA 24910 Dr. Mary Falmouth, Professor of Marketing Southernmost University Southernmost City Center, GA 24910 Mr. Ralph Carrutheres, President Adams Hardware 9081 Union Square Madford, GA 24873

Exhibit E.3
Interviewing Suggestions

Before the Interview
1. Carefully research the company before the interview.
2. Practice interviewing with a friend prior to the interview.
3. Think of questions to ask the interviewer.
4. Think of how to respond to questions such as: "What interests you about our company?" and "What are your career objectives?"
5. Dress conservatively.
6. Arrive early enough for a few minutes of composure and mental preparation for the interview.
7. Think positively—do not let negative thoughts become self-defeating.
During the Interview
8. Smile, introduce yourself, and shake the interviewer's hand. Remember how to pronounce her or his name.
9. Maintain eye contact and good posture.
10. Use the CANAPE process (discussed in the personal selling chapter).
11. If the interview begins to drag, ask the interviewer questions about the organization and the job.
12. Be a good listener—do not talk too much.
13. Try to differentiate your product (yourself) from the other products (other recruits).
14. Give the interviewer a copy of your résumé.
15. When the interview ends, thank the interviewer for the time and consideration and affirm your interest in the job.

Analyzing a Marketing Case

In the study of business administration, analyzing specific cases is a widely used means of applying theoretical knowledge to practical problems. The idea is to apply textbook materials to realistic situations found in business. The cases themselves are descriptions of real situations. Your task is to project yourself into the role of the decision maker and to decide what the company should do. While additional information would usually be helpful in accomplishing this task, you should restrict your attention to the facts at hand—those presented in the case materials themselves. This simulates most real-world situations, where all of the important information that a decision maker would like to have is seldom available.

The cases we have chosen have been class-tested at several universities to assure that they are interesting, illustrative of points covered in the chapter materials, and that they stimulate class discussions. While the exact solution to a case depends, of course, on the situation, there is a general procedure that you should follow in all cases, as described below.

Step 1. Fact-finding. Read the case as objectively as possible and make a list of the most relevant facts in the situation. Do not use value judgments in this process; for example, avoid listing vague evaluative terms, such as "bad sales results." A better way to describe the situation is to state that sales are down by *x* percent. The purpose of this objectivity is to avoid making premature conclusions.

Step 2. Define the basic problem. State the basic decision that should be made: to remedy an undesirable situation, to take advantage of an opportunity, or to more fully achieve company objectives. Defining the basic problem is often more difficult than it sounds, as there are often many factors to be considered.

Step 3. Define the basic decision alternatives. These are the various courses of action which might be pursued to solve the basic problem. These are related to the problem and specify the major choices that management should consider for problem solving.

Step 4. Analyze the alternatives. Each of the alternatives detailed in Step 3 should be analyzed in detail as carefully as possible. Frequently, it is necessary to make particular assumptions to accomplish this. These assumptions should be explicitly stated to establish the ground rules of the analysis. It is often necessary to use analytical techniques such as break-even or net-present-value analyses. (These techniques are reviewed in various chapters and appendixes.) Generally, the more the quantitative support for the analysis, the better. This does not mean that the qualitative factors should be ignored, however.

Step 5. Recommend a course of action. This is the direct outcome of the analysis done in Step 4. You must select the best alternative, but it is also important to state limitations and other key issues for management to consider when making a recommendation.

This procedure is useful in analyzing the cases. The questions asked at the end of each case are important, but only to direct the discussions; typically, the questions are answered by following the above steps.

Further, the way cases are covered in class will depend on many factors, including the class size, instructor's style, and so on. When class discussion is used, the best way to learn from these cases is to prepare a two- to three-page analysis of each case before class. Then, become active in the class discussion about the case. Being prepared and being active in joint discussions about decisions is important not only in marketing, but in business in general.

Cases

Chapter 1
Atlantic City

Despite the controversy when voters approved legalized casino gambling in 1976, few would doubt the beneficial effects of the resulting inflow of capital to Atlantic City. Prior to that infamous vote, the once-posh seaside resort, renowned for its true-to-life Monopoly game properties of Boardwalk, Atlantic Avenue, and others had become a tattered old town and faced the reality of mundane urban decay that has infected many cities that have outworn their usefulness to the young, affluent, and mobile.

As developers scurried to build their casinos, the influx of investment capital into the city was criticized by many as being of the "wrong type," as it did nothing to help former residents who were displaced by the new buildings and the high rents that reconstruction so often brings. Criticism could be heard from religious factions and others opposed to gambling, as chants damning the Satanical but popular pastime echoed throughout the country.

Regardless, the effects of the decision were obvious. Gone were many of the dingiest of buildings—especially those near the beach since the boardwalk had been rebuilt with new wood void of rotting splinters and missing pieces—and tax revenues were on the rise, meaning better schools, services, and cleaner streets. Most people felt that the glittering lights and "plastic" buildings were good tradeoffs to make.

Aimed at the 50-million-person Northeastern market, gambling in Atlantic City competes head-to-head with Las Vegas, the nation's historic gaming district. With its target population comprising nearly 23 percent of the nation's total income, there was plenty of wealth to sustain business from gamblers who formerly had to travel to Las Vegas, the Caribbean, or Europe to engage in legalized gambling.

The decision by voters to allow gambling resulted in over $2 billion being invested in the city in five years, and for this period, Atlantic City claimed a heady 68 percent compounded growth rate. By 1984, there were 11 casinos operating in the city. In all, their gross win—the amount that the house keeps after paying winners but before expenses—totaled a record $1.95 billion, which exceeded the $1.7 billion mark of Las Vegas' 60 gaming houses.

But all is not totally well in Atlantic City. Revenues are beginning to slow down, as illustrated below:

Casino	*Gross revenues (millions of dollars).* 1984	1983	*Percent change*
Resorts	$ 256.2	$ 252.5	1.5%
Golden Nugget	251.0	262.8	−4.5
Bally's	237.1	230.8	2.7
Caesar's	223.2	213.6	4.5
Tropicana	218.5	199.1	9.7
Harrah's Marina	210.4	201.5	4.4
Sands	159.5	156.4	2.0
Atlantis	147.0	144.0	2.0
Trump Plaza[a]	125.6	—	—
Claridge	123.1	110.2	11.7
Total	$1951.6	$1770.9	10.2%

a. Opened in 1984
Data from New Jersey Casino Control Commission

There are several reasons for the city's problems. In February of 1985, Resorts International barely won renewal of its license because of charges that $341,000 of its money ended up in the hands of the Prime Minister of the Bahamas, where the company has another casino. Another problem has been frequent charges of mob ties. The state's Casino Control Commission refused to grant a gaming license to Hilton Hotels Corp. for its new $308 million casino and hotel, which New Jersey Governor Thomas H. Kean had helped attract. The commission objected partly because of allegations that Hilton had continued to let reputed organized crime figures use the San Francisco Hilton for business meetings even after an internal company investigation in 1976 had identified them.

To many investors, the Hilton decision left an impression that Atlantic City was overregulated. A major problem in attracting gamblers is that there is a shortage of hotel rooms. Big airline carriers refuse to schedule Atlantic City as a stop until there are 10,000 hotel rooms available, a figure that will not be reached until late 1986 at the earliest. Another problem has been the horrendous traffic problems in the city, which is essentially an island along the coast. Finally, the federal government had promised $30 million toward a proposed high-speed rail link to Philadelphia (a system that New Jersey estimated would be used by 3,300 people a day) if the Atlantic County Improvement Authority would chip in another $21 million for a rail terminal. However, the federal money has been put on hold for budgetary reasons.

In the meantime, the city is frequented primarily by "day trippers," people that come into the city for one day of gambling and then leave. Several casinos have begun hotel room expansion plans, but many of these will take up to three years for completion.

But the biggest problem, according to several analysts, is that the gaming companies will have to work harder to get additional business if the city is to remain healthy. "Atlantic City can no longer gamble on easy money if it is to stay prosperous," said one. This view is echoed by Richard Gillman, chairman of the Atlantic City Casino

Association. "The market is there [estimated at $5 billion a year], it's just a question of working harder to get people here." One step in the right direction, according to many observers, is the creation of a new Atlantic City Reinvestment Authority, a group charged with assisting in the development of the city's infrastructure. One result has already been the emerging plans to redevelop the city's aged convention center.

QUESTIONS

1. What factors have hurt further growth in Atlantic City?
2. What can Atlantic City do to market itself better?
3. Should the marketing of Atlantic City be left to the individual casino operators, or should it be a community effort?

The Aurora Swimming Pool System

Ken Bernal is the manager of a swimming pool system owned and operated by Aurora, Illinois; a suburb of Chicago with a population of nearly 100,000. He has served in this capacity for over six years. Ken has often been quoted as saying that he "runs the system like a business." To some extent this is out of necessity, because the city council expects that the operation's revenues should at least cover its costs. Bernal has done better than that: Under his management, revenues have exceeded costs during the last four years, providing a surplus that goes into the city treasury.

The system consists of twelve pools. Eight are 50 meters long and the remaining four are 25 meters in length. Five of the 50 meter pools and one of the 25 meter pools are enclosed and heated, making year-round swimming possible. All pools have high and low diving boards, facilities for the handicapped, dressing rooms, and ample parking. The 50 meter pools are designed for Olympic-style competition and are used for meets between swim teams in addition to public swimming.

According to Bernal, his pools serve several groups. One is the general public, which is mainly interested in recreational swimming. Another group consists of local swim clubs who compete with one another and with out-of-town teams. Another group consists of organizations who sometimes desire swimming parties, those who exercise by swimming, and individuals who use the pools for therapy. The last group is growing rapidly; increasingly, physicians are advising patients to use water as a means of healing.

Pool rates are $2 for adults and $1.50 for children. Special rates are available for groups, competitive teams, senior citizens, and for season passes. The rates have been set at levels that Bernal believes are low enough to attract users yet bring in adequate revenues to the city. Any changes in the rates are subject to approval by the city council. These elected officials have been reluctant to consider any rate increases unless the need for them is clearly indicated.

Bernal is a strong believer in advertising. He utilizes city newspapers and radio stations to attract business by persuading the public that swimming is enjoyable, safe, good exercise, an opportunity to bring the family together, and a way to cool off in summer. Some of the advertisements are offered free by the media as a public service, but over half must be paid for out of Bernal's budget. One of his recent campaigns urged parents to leave their children at the pool for Saturday afternoon swimming lessons and go do something on their own: "We both babysit and teach your children how to swim." Many ads feature a small cartoon duck named Quacker that Bernal has created. Small children often develop a strong identity with the duck and beg their parents to let them go swim with Quacker. Other ads encourage parents to enroll their children in swimming lessons as a safety precaution. The ads are created by Bernal's summer assistant, who teaches advertising at the local community college.

While there are no direct competitors to the municipal pool system, there are many indirect ones. Individuals may engage in other sports, other forms of exercise, and other means of spending leisure time in addition to swimming. Also, health clubs, schools, the YMCA and YWCA, and some homeowners maintain swimming pools. Bernal must consider all of these as potential rivals to his pool system.

QUESTIONS

1. Is Ken Bernal engaged in marketing?
2. What other measures would you suggest that Bernal employ to attract more users to the city's pool?

Chapter 2
Ogden Corp.

Ralph E. Ablon, chairman, president, and chief executive for Ogden Corp., a New York-based conglomerate, decided to look for growth in Ogden's service businesses, which include managing racetracks and airline terminals, maintaining office buildings and industrial plants, and providing catering and housekeeping for remote construction sites and offshore oil rigs. This course has apparently pleased many stock analysts, who recently have added the company to their buy lists. The company also runs a museum aboard the carrier U.S.S. *Intrepid*, berthed in New York, and provides services to New York's Kaufman-Astoria film studios.

Ablon believes that for the rest of this century, at least, customers will want to buy the ends, not the means. He sees the leasing world as confirmation of this belief. In keeping with this strategy, Ogden acquired Allied Maintenance for $1.1 billion in 1982. With this acquisition, the New York company brings in several new enterprises. These include specialized airline-related ventures such as fueling and ground handling at more than 65 airports.

In addition to the acquisition of Allied, Odgen was awarded a $160 million contract to build a hydroelectric power plant in Louisiana. Although Ogden will not be running this particular plant, it could, Ablon says, and indeed he plans both to build and to run such projects as a form of total service.

Ablon also hopes to land a contract to manage a remote U.S. Navy base on an island in the Indian Ocean. The five-year contract will be worth about $150 million.

In the meantime, Ablon is looking hard at Ogden's other two main businesses, transportation and products. The former includes the Avondale shipyards and a fleet of 34 tankers and freighters. The latter includes foods and industrial goods; Ogden manufactures railroad cars, dies and presses, processes ferrous metals, recycles aluminum scrap, and fabricates metal components for high-technology industries.

Ablon says that the future of some operations depends on whether they fit into his strategic concept. He is more optimistic about various industrial businesses (for example, the ongoing truck delivery of molten aluminum to manufacturers of automobile engines) than he is about the future of shipping and food products enterprises.

According to Ablon, the conglomerate's future will depend on its ability to understand the world it faces, and to prepare for the future by "deciding to do the right things, and then doing those things right."

QUESTIONS

1. What is Ogden's strategy? Can marketing help the company? How?
2. Why is it important for a large company like Ogden to have an overriding strategy?

3. Should Ogden keep a business that fits into its overall strategy but is not profitable? What about a business that is highly profitable but does not fit into the overall strategy?

Ponderosa Inc.

Until 1985, Gerald S. Office Jr., the Ponderosa restaurant chain's chairman and president, held fast to offering moderately priced steaks as his company's basic strategy. The strategy worked well in good economic times. In 1979, for example, the company earned over $13 million in profits on sales of a quarter of a billion dollars. The chain's strength in the market, however, largely rested with blue-collar customers. This led to a roller-coaster performance by the company paralleling that of the U.S. economy. To illustrate the boom-and-bust performance of company profits during growth periods and recessions, earnings fell 80 percent in 1974, rose slowly to their peak in 1979, then fell 80 percent again in 1980. Studies indicated that white-collar consumers would not trade down to Ponderosa during bad times and blue-collar consumers steeply reduced their restaurant patronage during recessions.

It became clear to management that it would have to move into new directions if it ever hoped to break the cyclical nature of its business. In 1982, the company launched itself into the Mexican food market by buying the tiny (five unit) Casa Lupita restaurant chain. In 1983, the company spent $21 million to expand its new presence by building ten new outlets and converting five existing Ponderosa restaurants into Casa Lupitas.

Mexican restaurants were expanding at nearly a 20 percent annual pace during the first part of the decade while sales in the restaurant industry were generally flat. In addition, the average Casa Lupita generated about four times the revenue of a Ponderosa due to more seating and an average sales ticket nearly double that of the steak houses. Further, profit margins were much higher because tacos and tortillas were far less expensive than steak. Management felt that ten Casa Lupitas could offer as much profit potential as 80 Ponderosas.

Ponderosa, based in Dayton, Ohio, was far from the first restaurant operation to get into Mexican food chains. The market was dominated by Chi-Chi's and El Torito-La Fiesta, and analysts contended that the industry was poised for a fallout. "There aren't enough cities to support these $3 million restaurants that everyone wants to put up," said one of them. Several new entrants had already run into financial difficulties, such as Garcia's of Phoenix, which had continuously lost money since it began in 1980.

Converting steak houses to Mexican restaurants did offer Ponderosa several advantages. One of them was that costs were less than half as much as a new store. Another was that many of the present Ponderosa sites were considered to be prime locations. But there were also disadvantages. Chief among them was the larger space needs of Mexican restaurants. Officials of Sisco's Mexican restaurants, 13 of which were converted from Cork'n Cleaver Steak Houses (owned by Chart House Inc.), were not completely happy with the results. Another major problem faced by Ponderosa was that none of its management personnel had any experience in running a labor-intensive business such as a Mexican restaurant.

QUESTIONS

1. Why did Mr. Office decide to take Ponderosa in a new direction? Was this a good decision?
2. How do Mexican restaurants mesh with Ponderosa from a synergy perspective?
3. What would you do if you were Mr. Office?

Chapter 3

Smith Bookkeeping

Smith Bookkeeping is a small firm located in a large midwestern city. Its principal business is to provide fundamental bookkeeping services for its clients—mainly small firms in the retailing and service industries.

Smith has been in operation since 1980, when its owner, Brian Smith, a recent accounting graduate of a state university, set it up. Brian wanted to be in business for himself, rather than working for a certified public accountant or another firm. He is well informed about current accounting principles and regulations and has built up a profitable practice. However, he feels that the firm should be larger. In the last year of operation it grossed $240,000.

Brian sets up the accounting records of new clients in a manner that will allow them to fulfill tax obligations and have some financial control over their businesses. Once the books have been set up, he will maintain them for clients who desire this service. In addition, he prepares tax returns for some clients.

Brian's prices are lower than those of CPA firms—20 percent on average. He believes that this allows him to remain competitive in the face of rivalry from both large and small bookkeeping and accounting firms.

The business does no advertising other than a listing in the yellow pages of the local telephone directory. Brian feels that the company cannot afford to advertise, although this might increase revenues enough to justify the expense. Still, he is reluctant to risk such a move.

The business is located in a small office in a shopping center facility. It lacks prestige, but is convenient for many of the company's customers. The office is sufficiently large for Brian to perform his work efficiently. He employs one person who acts as both secretary and computer operator.

Brian has considered segmenting the market. He is not sure if this is advisable, however. One possibility would be benefit segmentation: dividing the customers into groups based upon the kinds of services and associated benefits they want. Another possibility would be volume segmentation. Still another would be demographic or geographic segmentation.

QUESTIONS

1. Should Brian segment the market? Why or why not?
2. What information does he need to determine if segmentation would be advisable?
3. What variables might he use to segment the market?

Lamattina's Bicycle Shop

Frank Lamattina is the owner and manager of a bicycle shop located in Phoenix, Arizona. He has operated the establishment for eight years, since he purchased it from an ex-schoolmate at Arizona State University. His initial investment in the enterprise was $71,500, a sum he believed to be very low at the time of the purchase.

The shop is located in a strip shopping center near one of the city's larger enclosed malls. The surrounding area is primarily residential and commercial, with upper-middle-income consumers dominating the residential sections. Most of the homes and the businesses in the area are relatively new, as this portion of the city was not fully developed until the mid-1970's.

The bulk of Frank's customers are from the surrounding neighborhood and, like the neighborhood, are in upper-middle-income categories. Individuals of all ages frequent the shop. Frank believes that people in almost every age group are motivated to ride bicycles because of a desire to remain healthy and fit, save money, avoid polluting the air, find a new source of recreation, and avoid the traffic problems that plague motorists.

Most of the bicycles in the shop are of good quality and retail for $199 and up. However, Frank has found that extremely expensive bicycles, sold primarily to racers and other enthusiasts, do not provide adequate stock turns. Hence, he avoids the high end of the market. On the other hand, he does not stock the extremely inexpensive models commonly found in discount and other low-end stores. In addition to bicycles, Frank sells accessories and parts and provides a complete repair service.

Frank's prices are slightly higher than those of most of his closest competitors. He believes that this is justified by his liberal return and service policies. As far as he can determine, his prices are approximately 10 percent higher than those of his main competitor, another bicycle shop located in another strip center three miles away.

Most of Frank's advertising appears in a local newspaper and in direct mail pieces sent to customers. The ads feature the high quality of the store's merchandise and service and some of the more appealing policies, such as liberal return privileges. He allocates $200 per month to advertising.

The firm grosses approximately $350,000 per year, producing a profit of around $70,000. In addition, Frank receives an annual salary of $40,000. Both the profit and salary figures have remained stable for the past two years. Revenues of the firm have grown at a rate of about 1 percent per year since 1980.

Frank has considered the possibilities of market segmentation—something he has never attempted before. However, he is uncertain as to whether or not this would be a good idea and, if it is, how to go about it.

QUESTIONS

1. How should Frank Lamattina go about deciding whether or not to segment?
2. If he does decide to segment, what characteristics of the market should he consider?
3. What are the major advantages and disadvantages of segmenting this market?

Chapter 4

Eastman Kodak Co.

Ever since 1884, when George Eastman founded the company in Rochester, New York, Eastman Kodak Co. held fast to its consistent strategy of emphasizing its core technology of film and photographic paper. New markets were targeted over the years, but all of them involved extending the core technology to new markets, such as using its optics to create Ektaprint photocopiers and extending its coated-film chemistry to Ektrachem blood analyzers. Nonetheless, the basic strategy was to avoid introducing any products that could cannibalize or damage the company's basic technology.

This basic strategy served the company well for a century. Kodak's traditional pretax profits were almost unbelievable: 50 percent or more from its sales of film and paper. In film alone, the company controlled 85 percent of the $1.1 billion U.S. market and half of worldwide industry sales.

By the end of fiscal year 1982, however, Kodak began to experience the full effects of stiff competition. Fuji Photo Film Co. had made strong inroads into Kodak's film sales, sales of its year-old disc cameras began to fall, its market share in instant cameras was down (and its presence in the instant camera and film market was being severely challenged by Polaroid in a patent infringement case), and movie film sales were off. As a result, operating profits in 1982 fell 10 percent despite a 5 percent gain in sales to $10.8 billion. Most industry experts anticipated even poorer results in fiscal 1983, when sales were expected to fall to about $10 billion.

On January 4, 1984, Wilbur Prezzano, Kodak's chief marketing executive, announced Kodak's long-rumored entry into the video market. The product was the world's first commercial "Camcorder," an 8-mm combination camera and recorder designed as one integrated small unit.

In 1984, Sony, Panasonic, Sanyo, General Electric, and several other electronics firms were big in the mushrooming video recording market. All of their camera-recorders, however, were quite bulky. Generally they required a separate camera wired to a recorder that used ½-inch tape carried over the shoulder, with the entire outfit weighing more than ten pounds. The new Kodak system weighed only half that much, was integrated into a one-piece system, and had a basic list price of $1,600, which was competitive with the other systems. Much of the miniaturization was made possible by using 8-mm tape, which was about a 37 percent reduction compared to the ½-inch tape used by others. Kodak's tape also was technically advanced and capable of storing 50 percent more data. The resulting videocassette package was small, only slightly bigger than an audiocassette. For playback, customers inserted the camcorder into a special $200 "cradle" that could be wired to any TV set.

Kodak's entry into video recording represented major changes in historic company strategy in several ways. First, instead of making the equipment, Kodak entered into agreement with Japan's Matsushita Electric Industrial Co. to build the new camera. Second, Kodak would neither be the dominant supplier, the technological leader, nor the low-cost producer in the industry. Third, the entry would require Kodak to open a new channel of distribution to appliance, video, and department stores to augment the company's 25,000 U.S. film outlets. Fourth, even if successful, the new cameras and film would compete directly with Kodak's main film technology, where the company had clear technological leadership.

Finally, many industry experts doubted whether Kodak had picked a winner in going after the 8-mm market for several reasons. First, most major video companies had already studied the 8-mm format but had decided to stick with the current size. Second, ½-inch tape sales were booming. Four million VCRs had been sold during the previous year and sales were expected to grow 25 percent the next year. Finally, there was already a huge inventory of movies and film on VHS and Beta formats that would be incompatible with Kodak's new machines.

QUESTIONS

1. What risks does Kodak face by introducing its Camcorder? What risks are involved if it ignores this market?
2. Is Kodak's move a synergistic one?
3. Is it a good idea for Kodak to compete with itself?

Brik Pak, Inc.

In 1977, Tetra Pak International, a $1.5 billion Swedish company that had penetrated 40 percent of the European milk packaging market with its aseptic packaging system, sent Hellmut F. Kirchdorfer to form Brik Pak, Inc., as a subsidiary to duplicate its success in the U.S. The aseptic paper bottles offered several advantages over cans and bottles. Consisting of aluminum foil sandwiched between laminates of paperboard and plastic, the aseptic containers cost about half as much as cans and a third as much as bottles. A more complicated filling process was involved, requiring that both the containers and the contents be sterilized, but nonetheless, the containers offered an overall savings of about 20 percent.

Another major advantage was that the Brik Pak packages required no refrigeration during shipment and storage. Food contents also would remain fresh for several months. Further, because foods were subjected to shorter heating periods than with other containers, their flavors remained more natural.

By 1983, Brik Pak had sold nearly 1 billion aseptic containers, which translated into $50 million in sales. One container, a 250-milliliter (8.4 oz) box complete with drinking straw, became very successful for snacks and lunch boxes. Ocean Spray Cranberries, Inc., became the first fruit juice producer to feature the paper bottles. The early ad campaign focused on the package, its convenience, and the juice's natural taste. Once successful, the focus of Ocean Spray's advertising was on the product and families: they pictured Dad drinking the juice at the office, the kids sipping it at school, and Mom saying, "Now wherever they go, I know they will be drinking something good for them." Ocean Spray's revenues from aseptics were about 7 percent of its $420 million sales in 1983.

A similar story was evident at Coca-Cola Co. Food Division, where aseptic packaging increased Hi-C's sales by nearly 20 percent. Further, executives at Hi-C contended that the sales increase was due almost totally to new business. They believed that the new packaging technology would soon represent about a third of fruit sales.

Attracted by Brik Pak's success, other competitors recently have entered the market. Combibloc Inc., a joint venture of RJR Archer (the packaging subsidiary of R. J. Reynolds) and West Germany's Jagenberg began to market the packages filled with Reynold's Hawaiian Punch. Other packagers, such as Continental, International Paper, X-Cello, and American Can also are thought to be perfecting similar containers.

Aseptic containers are not considered to be feasible for carbonated beverages because they lack the required rigidity, but Brik Pak is developing containers for other liquids such as single servings of wine. Further, Combibloc is developing specialty versions for semisolid and particulate foods such as yogurts, puddings, sauces, and soups.

Milk packaging is a major potential market. In many respects, this application would be ideal for the product. Aseptic containers would eliminate the need for refrigeration, and the long shelf life would enable milk processors to stabilize milk production rather than gear their facilities to handle heavy weekend demand. However, dairy producers have showed the greatest resistance of all to the new containers. One reason is that they tend to resist change in general. Another reason is that many feared consumers would not be willing to trust several-months-old unrefrigerated milk.

QUESTIONS

1. How do you assess the future for aseptic containers in the U.S.? Why?
2. Did Tetra Pak act prematurely by sending Mr. Kirchdorfer to the U.S.? Was it too late?
3. What should Kirchdorfer do now?

Chapter 5
Apple Computers, Inc.

Apple Computers, Inc., was one of the biggest success stories of the late 1970s and early 1980s. In just five years, Steven P. Jobs, Apple's founder, led the company from its origin to over $300 million in sales by 1981. In that year, the company attained more than a 40 percent share of the personal computer (PC) market and profits were nearly 12 percent of sales.

By 1983, however, the situation was much different. While sales were near $1 billion, profits were down to below 8 percent of sales and market share had fallen to 25 percent. IBM, in contrast, entered the PC market in 1981 and by 1983 had attained a 35 percent market share.

IBM's success, according to many industry experts, was due to the company's strong marketing and customer support. This took many forms. IBM's sales staff was the most extensive and perhaps the strongest in the entire computer industry. The company's service and technical support were the most competent. More software was made available to run on the IBM-PC than on any other system and most of the software was considered very "user friendly." The IBM-PC could also be configured in a wide array of specifications to yield a broad family of products. Further, users could readily adapt the computers to communicate with other computers. Within two years, the IBM-PC was well on the way to becoming the industry standard for small business computers.

Apple had long viewed itself as the technological leader in small computers. To counter IBM's entry, Apple introduced the 32-bit Lisa in early 1983. (The bit size of a computer refers to how much binary information can be processed at a time.) At $8,000, Lisa was three times as expensive as the IBM but it had many futuristic features, including a 32-bit processor, a "mouse" (a pointer that makes it easier to tell the computer what to do), and several other advanced features. However, the Lisa would not run any of the software designed for the IBM-PC or any of the other Apples. Further, Lisa was not compatible with other computers and software was practically nonexistent, meaning that users would have to develop their own. Finally, Apple spent little time acquainting dealers and its own sales force with the Lisa.

Initially, Apple targeted the new computer at professionals and managers in large corporations and it got rave reviews from both the press and the technical community. But Apple sold fewer than 20,000 of the systems in 1983—less than half the number management had anticipated.

In early 1984, John Sculley, Apple's new president, announced "this is the year that Apple fights back." Though known as a marketing expert, Sculley stated that Apple's success rests upon the company's continued technological leadership. To augment its line of computers, Apple introduced its IBM-PC competitor, the Macintosh model in January 1984, with a retail price of $1,995. The Macintosh was a less powerful, lower-priced member of the Lisa family with a 32-bit processor and a mouse.

Initially, some software for word processing and financial spreadsheets was to be furnished with the machines. Also, a graphics capability was expected. However, Macintosh was not expected to be compatible with the thousands of software packages available for the IBM-PC, nor would it contain the software necessary to make it communicate with other computers. Further, while many of the independent software producers heralded the Macintosh, few were expected to have software immediately available. Finally, while the Lisa could be compatible with any Macintosh software, the reverse would generally be untrue. And, both the Lisa and the Macintosh were incompatible with Apple II and III machines and software, which were very successful smaller systems in another family and technology.

Many universities proclaimed that the Macintosh was almost exactly the kind of computer they were looking for. Such a market would be consistent with the widespread acceptance Apple had achieved in schools with Apple II and III, but this was a bit different because the Macintosh would most likely be purchased by relatively few universities in large quantities. The company tried to sell the Lisa in large quantities direct to business, which upset the company's extensive retail dealer network. With the Macintosh, Apple executives stated that they were committed to their retail channel because they viewed the product to be attractive mostly to small businesses and individuals.

Many experts felt that Apple's future depended upon the success of the Macintosh and other future innovations. Some critics argued that Apple was missing the mark, however, by spending little money and effort on its own research and development and relying on dated technology developed by universities in the 1970s.

QUESTIONS

1. What are Apple's major strengths and weaknesses?
2. From the information given above, does it appear that Apple will be successful? Why? What about today?
3. What should Apple do?

McDonald's Corporation

The late Ray A. Kroc was known as the "King of the Franchisers." He started in this field in 1955 by expanding two McDonald brothers' hamburger stands. Within two decades his company dominated the fast food industry. By 1983, McDonald's held 42 percent of the $18 billion hamburger segment and 18 percent of the entire fast food industry. But all was not ideal, at least according to many industry experts. Some critics contended that the company's famed golden arches were beginning to show cracks.

Even several McDonald's executives admitted publicly that the chain's high-quality image was slipping. Many critics also contended that the company had lost touch with its customers. In 1983, growth in company per-unit sales slowed to a little over 5 percent, which was down from nearly 10 percent in 1978.

Several events generated severe competition for McDonald's in the early 1980s. First, both Wendy's International Co. and Burger King Corp. began to take on McDonald's directly with intensive promotions. Burger King, with a 16 percent share of the hamburger market segment, began a campaign in 1982 claiming that its Whoppers were bigger and better than Big Macs because they were broiled instead of fried. McDonald's sued Burger King even before the airing of the campaign, which backfired in the eyes of most analysts by drawing public attention to the battle. Wendy's, with a 10 percent share of the market, also began a campaign featuring the competition's oversized bun and lack of meat. Further, McDonald's followed Burger King's lead in reducing the price of plain hamburgers to 39 cents in early 1984. Many argued that emphasizing price only caused further customer concern over quality. "If they were better, why would they have to lower the price?"

Another trend in the industry was that scores of both new and established chains began taking bites out of McDonald's consumer base. With the aging of the population and more two-paycheck families, many restaurant customers were becoming more sophisticated in their tastes and willing to pay a higher price to get more. Ethnic foods were one example of a booming market. The Mexican food segment scored a 21 percent gain in 1983, to become a $1.5 billion market. Chi-Chi's was an upscale restaurant that capitalized on this trend. Its 116 units generated sales of nearly $75 million and $8 million in earnings in six months of 1983. Nearly 35 percent of its revenue came from high-margin alcoholic drinks.

Other kinds of fast-food outlets also were doing quite well. Gourmet hamburger chains such as Chili's Inc., with $3.25 hamburgers cooked to order plus a selection of beers, were proliferating. Upscale chicken outlets, such as Grandy's, a unit of Saga Corp., and Mrs. Winner's Chicken & Biscuits, found profitable niches by serving meals in homey surroundings.

In attempting to attract diverse palettes, Wendy's and Burger King became aggressive in expanding their menus. Wendy's successfully launched its taco salad and baked potatoes in 1983. Burger King was successful with its chicken sandwich. McDonald's, in contrast, failed with its McChicken and McRib sandwiches. While the company's chicken McNuggets were successful, generating 12 percent of company sales, it was the only new offering the company had successfully introduced in five years.

To tap into these booming new segments, several of the successful limited-menu firms begin opening new chains with a different face. Wendy's, for example, launched its Sisters' Chicken & Biscuits units in 1980. By the end of 1984, it was estimated that the company would operate 90 of these stores with per-unit sales averaging about $1 million.

McDonald's, in contrast, did not plan to open any new chains. Further, management did not seem too concerned about the company's not having new menu editions. It was holding fast to its policy of having a consistent national menu, instead of one featuring regional taste preferences such as hush puppies in the south. McDonald's also had difficulty in getting adults into its stores for evening meals. Part of the problem may have been its fixed menu, while another part may have stemmed from the company's strong identity with children. The company had in fact designed many of the restaurants with children in mind, having colorful interiors and playgrounds for their amusement.

Being the largest chain (6,000 domestic and 1,500 foreign units in 1983) held both advantages and disadvantages for the company. The major plus was that it favored patronage by consumers who choose restaurants on the basis of how easy they are to reach. The major drawback was that it was difficult for the company to experiment with its menu and still maintain its consistent quality.

McDonald's promotional strategy was expected to remain relatively constant, with its emphasis on a "good-feeling" image. For expansion, the company focused its attention on barely tapped markets within schools, military installations, and parks. Also, the firm was placing major emphasis upon international expansion where it faced less competition.

During 1983, McDonald's lost four of its key marketing staff. One of the executives was rumored to remark: "They are operations-driven, while the market is consumer-driven. They equate marketing with advertising."

QUESTIONS

1. Which factors led to McDonald's market leadership?
2. What marketing decisions should McDonald's make now?
3. How would you try to compete against McDonald's in the fast-food industry if you were the decision maker for a competitor?

Chapter 6

Pan American World Airways, Inc.

Pan American World Airways was in severe financial difficulty near the end of 1982, but management had a plan: to become the dominant carrier in the Caribbean.

Pan Am, a pioneer in international service, began by serving the islands in 1927. By 1975, however, the company had abandoned these routes for others to the South

Pacific and to Europe. A main reason to abandon the Caribbean was because the company flew 707s, which were fuel hogs when used for island-hopping. By 1982, however, the islands looked more desirable. First, the company now had a fleet of 727s which were more appropriate for typical routes in the Caribbean and the major eastern cities of New York, Orlando, Atlanta, and Miami. Second, island traffic during the winter would significantly counterbalance existing heavy summer usage of company facilities for European departures. Many of these facilities, such as terminals located in New York's J.F.K. Airport, were practically idle during the winter months.

Competition in the Caribbean was rather stiff in 1983, with significant price cutting a common practice on the New York-to-Nassau route. Pan Am's entry increased price cutting in the winter of 1983–1984 and caused all competitors to sharpen their marketing efforts. American Airlines dropped out of the New York-Nassau market after Pan Am's entry because of the route's low profitability. Cyrus S. Collins, American's vice president for the Atlantic/Caribbean, said the company was glad to leave the route due to its low revenue per ticket and was happy that Pan Am "helped us make the decision to leave."

According to Martin Shugrue, Jr., Pan Am's senior vice president for marketing, the company's Caribbean routes were not yet profitable in the full accounting sense. However, "they are making a positive cash contribution and will make money," said Shugrue. In contrast, Collins of American stated that his company's policy was that each route must pay for itself. "We don't think in terms of incremental revenues," said Collins. The remaining 16 of American's routes from New York to the Caribbean were thought to be making money.

Caribbean flights accounted for about 10 percent of American's capacity in 1983. Even during the off-season, American flights averaged 65 percent full. About 40 percent of American's business was sold to wholesalers who largely were responsible for putting together travel packages. Most of the island traffic of Eastern Airlines, based in Miami, was with ethnic travel (instead of pure tourist travel), which tended to be year-round, according to George Lyall, an Eastern vice president for the area. In contrast, Pan Am sold large numbers of seats at rock-bottom wholesale prices to travel package operations in 1983. About 80 percent of Pan Am's passengers were obtained in this way.

By early 1984, Pan Am sought to expand its presence in the Caribbean. Considerable increases in advertising were being budgeted to attract more retail business. In addition, the company wanted to build an "air bridge" between Nassau and Miami, a concept describing hourly service practically around the clock. But there were several obstacles to further penetration.

First, several local governments were concerned about protecting their own carriers, such as Bahamasair and Air France (which flies to the French Islands from Miami). Second, tourism officials remained anxious about Pan Am's commitment. They remembered that when Pan Am's new chairman, C. Edward Acher, ran Air Florida, Inc., that company began serving Bermuda in full force in 1981, only to exit six months later. Finally, Eastern's strength was in many of these markets, and it would not likely give up routes without a major fight.

QUESTIONS

1. What was Pan Am's basic strategy for selecting the Caribbean? Why?
2. Compare and contrast the pricing objectives of Pan Am and American. Why is it possible that there could be such a difference?

3. What can Pan Am do to overcome the major constraints preventing it from gaining further routes?

Central Waterbeds

Central Waterbeds is a retailer of waterbeds and a producer of waterbed frames. Only four years old, the firm has built up a solid sales record. Some of the frames for the beds are purchased from outside manufacturers, but over two-thirds are produced by Central employees in a small building adjoining the retail store. The firm is owned by two partners, Jay Greenwald and David Kenney, who are the managers. They also spend considerable time serving customers and attending to a variety of operative duties. They have two employees in the retail store and five who construct the frames.

The store was opened in 1980 and was successful within a year, providing a good income for both partners. Two years later, Kenney, who was once employed as a cabinet maker, proposed to Greenwald that they produce their own frames. This would allow them to absorb the manufacturer's profit and would enable Central to more effectively control the quality of the products that they sold. Kenney produced several frames, which sold very rapidly. This activity was expanded to the point that Central was producing most of the frames it sold.

The popularity of the Central frames led the partners to consider selling the beds through other retail outlets. The current building and production facilities were large enough to permit hiring more frame makers and expanding output. This would make Central more a producer than a retailer of goods. It was decided to attempt to sell frames to a very successful furniture store in a nearby city. If this venture proved successful, the firm would attempt to sell to other retailers in the region.

Both partners were very optimistic and ambitious persons. Their goal was to become wealthy before they reached the age of 40—about five years in the future. They envisioned Central frames being sold throughout the United States at some time in the future; this did not seem to be unrealistic, since total waterbed sales were expanding at a very fast rate throughout the country. The frames they had developed achieved considerable consumer acceptance and the profit margin was very good.

The furniture retailer that was Central's first target was Mitchell's, a store with 25 employees and over 200,000 square feet of space, 70 percent of which was utilized for display and selling. Currently the store did not stock waterbeds. It was located in a thriving retail center that served primarily upper-middle-income households, who were among Mitchell's primary customers. The store had an image of high-quality merchandise, excellent customer service, and prestige. The store was very sound financially.

Kenney made an appointment to call on the merchandising manager, Karen Timms, who was reputed to be the prime decision maker for purchasing and selling decisions. He was received cordially and felt that Timms displayed considerable interest in the frames he brought for her inspection. She was impressed with the quality of the product and with the sales figures Kenney presented to her. Kenney felt that he had made a good impression and took Timms to lunch to further discuss possibilities of selling the frames through Mitchell's. Timms suggested that Kenney talk to the president of the firm, Pat Hankins. The call on Hankins was less positive. Hankins turned out to be very conservative and needed to be absolutely convinced as to the profitability of an item before she agreed to stock it. She was impressed by the sales and profit figures that Kenney showed her but expressed doubt as to whether waterbeds were appropriate for Mitchell's. In addition, she was concerned that waterbeds might cut into the sales of traditional beds at the store. During the conversation with Kenney, she called in a store sales representative and asked her opinion of the bed frames. The sales representative liked their quality and thought that they might sell well. Hankins suggested that Kenney talk to their operations manager, Mr. O'Brian.

The call on O'Brian was not very satisfactory. Kenney just did not seem to relate well to this manager. He felt that O'Brian was resistant to any major change in the merchandise offerings of Mitchell's, yet he appeared to have the ear of the president.

Kenney got together with Greenwald and discussed what took place during the sales call. They are uncertain as to who really makes buying decisions at the store and what approach to take in selling to them. Kenney has an appointment to make another call on the three next week, when he plans to show them an extensive sample of Central frames.

QUESTIONS

1. Discuss the dynamics of the buying decision of Mitchell's.
2. What actions should Kenney take at the next meeting?
3. What else could Kenney and Greenwald do?

Chapter 7
Videotex

Scores of companies are spending millions of dollars to develop home information systems, electronics-age devices many predict will become the newest home electronics craze. With an initial investment of $50 to $250 to modify their TVs, plus a monthly subscription fee of $20 plus per month, subscribers to videotex would be able to access numerous computer-driven services from their homes, including banking, news, and shopping. Additionally, most videotex services would offer additional in-home features such as monitoring burglar and fire alarms and an electronic message center.

Most previous studies of the market potential for videotex were limited in their ability to predict the future for the service. The cost of doing the research limited sponsors to studying handfuls of consumers in only one or two cities. Further, most of such studies were limited because they did not study people over long periods of time; primarily they involved surveys measuring attitudes at the time consumers filled out the questionnaires.

Booze, Allen & Hamilton, Inc., a major consulting firm, recently completed a major new study on the technology. The inquiry was a $2.5 million effort jointly funded by 28 of the firm's clients, including IBM, AT&T, Xerox, Chase Manhattan Bank, and Metropolitan Life Insurance.

Booze-Allen studied 700 families in depth in Columbia, S.C., Denver, New York, and San Diego. Employees of the firm briefly interviewed each family and then asked them to test a prototype home information system that offered 15 separate videotex services. The most popular package contained nine services: banking, shopping, burglar and fire alarm monitoring, household budgeting, personal calendars, games, education, and electronic messages.

A major surprise was that most people surveyed did not feel that news provided by videotex would be worthwhile. They felt that they received enough news coverage already via television, radio, and newspapers. But the study did reveal that with the right combination of services, there would be a strong demand for videotex. Consumer interest was nearly twice as strong as indicated in other studies. Nearly two-thirds of the people surveyed indicated a strong interest if they could buy their ideal combination of videotex services for $15 per month. Many were willing to pay as much as $50 per month if they could get everything they wanted. One of the most appreciated features of the service was time savings; those surveyed felt videotex would reduce time spent on "chores like banking and shopping." This was especially true in families where both parents worked outside of the home.

Booze-Allen predicted that 17 million to 30 million households in the U.S. would have such a service by 1993, or within 10 years. This was nearly twice the number AT&T had estimated previously. If Booze-Allen was correct, their estimates showed videotex could mean as much as $30 billion in additional revenues to banks, retailers, ad agencies, and cable TV companies.

Some companies, already convinced of the market potential for videotex, did not wait for the results from Booze-Allen. Viewdata Corp. of America, a subsidiary of Knight-Ridder Newspapers Inc., and American Bell were ready to launch Viewtron within months. CBS launched Extravision, a limited-service feature added to its regular TV broadcasts and announced that it was available in limited markets. And Chemical Bank in New York already offers electronic banking to 250 homes with its Pronto home banking system.

Regardless of industry enthusiasm, several experts have warned against taking any survey results as gospel. "Unless we can look at data derived from an extended period of time, we have to be very careful drawing conclusions," warned one. Nonetheless, many companies are fully involved in the new technology.

QUESTIONS

1. Assess the Booze-Allen study discussed above.
2. As a manager, in what circumstances would you decide to spend funds to participate in a multiclient study? When would you avoid such a study?
3. What improvements in the study would you suggest?

Meecham County Hospital

Meecham County Hospital serves a city of over 50,000 people and the surrounding county, made up generally of small towns, ranches, and farms. The institution has been in existence since 1909, when the county constructed a small facility containing only 25 beds. Since that time it has grown steadily, and today it is a modern facility with 350 beds. Financial support comes from patient fees and from the county property tax levy. Thirty-two doctors are currently associated with the organization.

Being a public unit, County serves all residents of the county regardless of their income level, occupation, etc. Median income levels of county residents are slightly below the U.S. and state average levels. The leading employers are two manufacturers, retailers, a university, and agriculture. Unemployment levels tend to be higher than national levels during most periods.

The hospital management attempts to provide residents with as complete a package of services as is financially possible. This includes inpatient and outpatient services, physical therapy, emergency care, maternity care, surgery, and X-ray services. However, county voters turned down a recent bond issue to add 50 beds by a margin of over two to one.

Charges levied by the hospital tend to be lower than national averages. This is because the county subsidizes the services to some extent—reflecting a philosophy that care should be available to local residents who require it, even if they are unable to bear the full costs. Hence, the hospital operates at a deficit. In 1983 this figure was approximately $70,000.

The hospital is located approximately five miles from the city center, in a relatively quiet neighborhood. It is easily accessed by major streets and one freeway. The county has set aside 10 acres of land to utilize for future expansion purposes. To date, however, it has used this land as a city park.

One other hospital is located in the city. Operated by a church, it contains 150 beds and is not as modern as County Hospital. In a larger city approximately 80 miles away, however, more than seven large hospitals exist. These compete with County Hospital, since some county residents believe that they can receive better care or more extensive services in the larger city. The fees at these hospitals, however, are generally higher than County's.

The senior hospital administrator, John Griffith, is concerned about the image of the hospital in the community. He fears that the unit has developed a bad reputation in recent years, one that is reflected in decreasing utilization of the organization's services. The last two years have seen a 10 percent decrease in the occupancy of hospital beds and even larger decreases in other services, particularly surgery and maternity care. Only emergency services have expanded in scope over this time period. Mr. Griffith believes that research should be conducted to determine the organization's image.

Hags and Allen, a local consulting firm, was engaged to administer the study. To keep costs down, students from nearby State University were hired to conduct the actual interviewing and to participate in the research development. After several days of conferring with Mr. Griffith, hospital employees, county officials, doctors, and past patients, the researchers developed a questionnaire, the major portion of which is reproduced here.

Hospital Image Questionnaire

1. Are you a past patient of County Hospital?
   Yes _____
   No _____
2. If you answered yes to question 1 above, during what year did you last use its services?
   ____
3. What is your occupation?
   ____
4. How much before-tax income did your family earn last year?
   ____
5. Where is your home located?
   In the city limits _____
   Beyond city limits _____
6. How many persons reside in your household?
   _____
7. Are you covered by health insurance or other government plans that at least partially pay for hospital care?
   Yes _____
   No _____
8. Please indicate your image of the hospital on the following scales:
   Modern :_____:_____:_____:_____:_____: Old Fashioned
   Helpful :_____:_____:_____:_____:_____: Not helpful
   Expensive :_____:_____:_____:_____:_____: Inexpensive

Convenient	:	:	:	:	: Inconvenient
Dirty	:	:	:	:	: Clean
Careless	:	:	:	:	: Careful
Well staffed	:	:	:	:	: Poorly staffed
Full service	:	:	:	:	: Limited service
Poorly equipped	:	:	:	:	: Fully equipped
Well managed	:	:	:	:	: Badly managed
Unfriendly	:	:	:	:	: Friendly
Competent	:	:	:	:	: Incompetent
Pleasant	:	:	:	:	: Unpleasant
Inefficient	:	:	:	:	: Efficient
Wasteful	:	:	:	:	: Not wasteful

Each student had previously been enrolled in a marketing research class. Once the data had been obtained, the students turned the questionnaires over to Hags and Allen for analysis.

QUESTIONS

1. What are the strengths and weaknesses of the Hags and Allen study?
2. How can John Griffith use the results of the study?
3. What improvements would you suggest for the study's methodology?

Chapter 8
Dart Frames, Inc.

Dart Frames, Inc., produces and markets picture frames by mail throughout the United States. Dart operates a production plant in a free trade zone (a particular geographical area, established by law, to exempt products from certain import or export taxes) of Juarez, Mexico. It constructs picture frames at a low cost, primarily because of inexpensive labor and a ready supply of raw materials. The company's office is located in El Paso, Texas. It advertises the frames in general-interest magazines and takes orders and ships them to customers by mail. A high school art teacher founded the firm in 1978. Previously making frames by hand as a hobby, he decided to go into business for himself and to market his handicrafts by mail. The business flourished, employees were hired to help with construction, and eventually the owner invested in a building and equipment. Total sales in 1983 exceeded $385,000, an increase of 18 percent over the previous year.

The business is a proprietorship, wholly owned and managed by Barry Hamilton. His goal is to continually expand the business. Financially, the firm is on a sound footing. Net profits have exceeded 10 percent of sales ever since the founding of the business and have increased each year. Currently they are 17 percent of sales. The ratio of equity to debt is twelve to one, and return on invested capital is 24 percent. Due to its cautious growth, this company has never experienced a cash flow problem.

There are numerous competitors in the picture frame industry. These products appear in department stores, variety shops, discount outlets, furniture stores, and frame shops. Dart has several other mail-order competitors. The company's main advantage is a quality product at a reasonable price (consumers can buy comparable frames in retail stores only at higher prices) and the convenience of mail order shopping.

Target customers are middle- and higher-income households, both singles and families. These individuals purchase large volumes of frames and tend to be price-conscious. Hamilton believes that they are willing to pay the high prices demanded by many retail stores for quality frames, but want a better product than is available at the low-price end of the line. Hence, Hamilton feels Dart frames are very definitely fulfilling a consumer desire.

The sole means of promoting the frames is through the mail. Hamilton runs advertisements in magazines such as *The Reader's Digest* and *Time* and Sunday newspaper supplements. He has considered purchasing mailing lists and sending out brochures, but has not yet experimented with this medium. Several retailers have approached him and offered to stock the frames, but he has declined, stating that mail order selling has been such a success that he does not want to rock the boat by branching off into new forms of moving goods to target consumers. He has mentioned, however, that if a major retail chain were interested in stocking his products, he would consider their offer, particularly if the chain was a very large one. To date no such offer has materialized, however.

There are some matters that concern Hamilton. One is proposed new postal rate increases, which would increase his costs of doing business and/or customer prices. Another is that competition in the industry has become more formidable; some competitors have lowered their prices and others have increased their promotion expenditures.

Hamilton believes that he can find new opportunities and avoid some of the problems that the firm faces by adding new foreign markets to its targets. He has considered Canada as a very good potential candidate. It has a large middle class, an excellent postal system, and competition does not seem to be as severe as it is in the United States. Accordingly, he has decided to investigate the Canadian market.

QUESTIONS

1. What information does Hamilton need to decide whether or not to enter the Canadian market? How should he get this information? What are the alternatives?
2. Is Hamilton acting too conservatively by avoiding retailers? Should he experiment with them? Are there any relatively safe ways to do this? How about mailing lists?
3. What decisions should Mr. Hamilton make? Why?

Century Stores, Inc.

Century Stores, Inc., is a regional chain of convenience stores located in the southeastern United States. Currently, there are over 40 stores in the chain. It competes with other regional chains, national chains, and with supermarkets for most of its offerings. Century has been in business for 14 years. It has earned returns on investment exceeding industry averages for most of this period.

Each company store offers three major lines. These are groceries and soft drinks, tobacco products, and gasoline. The stores are located at sites nearby suburban neighborhoods, high-traffic streets, schools, and places of employment. The layout and operation of the stores are such that consumers can obtain goods with a minimum of search and waiting time. Most prices are higher than those charged by supermarkets, but consumers are willing to pay these prices in exchange for convenience. Central buying offices do the purchasing for the individual stores.

The company designs all advertising at corporate headquarters in Mobile, although local store managers place the ads with the media. Century uses both radio and newspapers as ad outlets. The ads focus on the convenience and friendly services the company provides.

A trend that worries management is the increasing incidence of consumers who eat out in restaurants, particularly those of the fast-food variety. Growing restaurant patronage reduces amounts spent in convenience stores such as Century, as well as in supermarkets and other grocery stores. Management sees this as a possible barrier to continued sales and profit growth.

One way to take advantage of this trend is to offer takeout food in the stores. Management is considering offering frozen sandwiches that could be easily stored in existing frozen food display cases. A microwave oven could be situated in each store, enabling customers to purchase a sandwich, thaw it in the oven and either consume it in the car or at home. Consumers could obtain the sandwiches even faster than they can in many fast-food restaurants. Further, they could buy soft drinks, coffee, potato chips, etc., stocked by the store.

Century has contacted a food processing firm that can produce the sandwiches and deliver them to company stores at a reasonable price. The firm would furnish beef, turkey, chicken, and ham sandwiches, frozen and attractively packaged. This company has a solid reputation in the industry and could be depended upon for quality products and reliable delivery.

Century management has some reservations about the new product line. Adding sandwiches would use up already scarce frozen food storage space. Further, the firm would have to purchase microwave ovens. Store clerks would be responsible for overseeing the use of the microwaves, taking them away from their other duties. The cooking might create undesirable odors in the stores. Also, stores might become congested with sandwich purchasers, reducing the ability of Century to serve other customers rapidly. Further, addition of the sandwiches might lead to a situation whereby stores become teenage hangouts, upsetting other customers. Finally, Century has had no experience in the fast-food restaurant industry and the addition of the sandwiches would position it there. In the advertising field alone, it has no match for the expertise and large funds expended by such firms as McDonald's, Burger King, and Wendy's.

Despite these reservations, Century management believes that the sandwich product line has considerable potential. According to the company president, "It might revolutionize our business."

QUESTIONS

1. Which demographic and economic trends are important for Century's management to study in determining whether or not sandwiches represent a good opportunity for management to consider?
2. How can management obtain much of this information?
3. What steps can management take to test the potential of the potential product offerings?

Chapter 9
Owens-Illinois Inc.

According to Robert J. Lanigan, president and chief operating officer at Owens-Illinois Inc. (OI), the glass container operation has been taken about as far as a mature business can go. Today, glass accounts for 50 percent of OI's business, whereas by 1988 he predicts that this figure will decrease to only 35 percent. In order to combat this trend, his plans are to expand into plastics and health care, both internally and by acquisition. In order to pay for this expansion Lanigan will use the $50 million per year the glass division is expected to generate, plus profits from OI's forest products division and a $250 million line of credit.

Because of conservative company executives, OI is moving into the new areas slowly and cautiously. This caution is creating an image problem among observers and analysts who feel that the company could be doing things faster and better.

OI enjoys a leadership position in the plastic container market, but this area is no longer growing. Last year this division did $480 million worth of business, supplying manufacturers of household chemicals, toiletries, and cosmetics. Six years ago, OI entered the newer polyethylene terepthalate (PET) beverage bottle market with a separate sales force to push its products. Observers still see OI's move into this area as a hedge against the possibility that plastic will push glass out of the market.

The company is now ready to enter areas of the market with higher-growth, high-technology plastics: flexible packaging for meats and rigid containers that lock out oxygen and moisture for edible oils and fruit juices. Its goal for this area is to double plastic container sales by 1988.

Over the past three years, OI has been getting rid of marginal businesses and cutting costs. It sold its Lily paper and plastic cup business and it has closed four glass container plants. Since 1978, it has invested more than $550 million in new equipment to boost productivity in glass operations. OI has decentralized operations into five autonomous product groups in an effort to foster an entrepreneurial spirit among the managers of these groups.

Edwin D. Dodd, chairman, and Lanigan are confident that OI can reverse ten years of mediocre earnings. In 1980, return on equity peaked at 11.8 percent. They are shooting for a 14 percent return on equity by 1986. This would be a dramatic increase from 1982's meager 6.5 percent level on a net income of $91 million.

According to Lanigan, OI's entry in health care services and supplies has the best new potential for the company. The $225 million division is aiming for a 20 percent return on equity and sales of $1.5 billion by 1988. The most promising health care investment the company has is Health Group Inc. (HGI), a venture capital start up established in 1981 that owns and manages 84 hospitals and nursing homes. HGI sales are expected to top $1 billion by 1988.

QUESTIONS

1. Why is Owens a mature business and what is being done to change this?
2. What is Lanigan doing to reverse Owens' mediocre earnings?
3. What problems lie ahead for the company?

Hyatt Hotels

Jay A. Pritzker, a Chicago financier, started the Hyatt chain of hotels in 1957 with the purchase of an inn near the Los Angeles airport. Stressing quality service, the company grew steadily until 1967. In that year the company opened the Hyatt Regency in Atlanta, with its giant atriums and indoor foliage. The hotel became a regional landmark and a trademark of the Hyatt chain. The Hyatt Regency in Atlanta soon became a huge success, attracting business travelers and conventioneers alike.

Based upon its success in Atlanta, the Hyatt chain took the hotel industry by storm throughout the 1970s. By 1983, the company tripled the scope of its operations, with sales of $1.7 billion. The company operated 70 U.S. and 42 foreign hotels, many of which were designed with airy lobbies and atriums like the one in Atlanta. The focus was on the upper sector of the market, quality service (such as turned-down beds with a mint on the pillow), and a major presence in virtually all large cities.

In mid-1983, however, Hyatt embarked on a new direction. A $10 million ad campaign was launched emphasizing its friendly staff and a "We Wish You Were Here," theme, which replaced ads featuring the chain's splashy architecture and individualized service. The new strategy went far beyond a simple change in promotional tactics, however. Now that Hyatt has saturated all big U.S. cities with convention-size hotels, it is taking aim at secondary cities and suburbs of major cities with smaller-sized projects.

The company also began experimenting with small European-style hotels such as the Park Hyatt in Chicago. These hotels emphasized even greater service and quality. For rates of nearly a one-third premium over a Hyatt Regency, guests of these hotels could expect fresh flowers and bathrobes in each room, apples and cookies, and a concierge service to make all arrangements. After two years of operation, however, such hotels were not yet profitable.

Hyatt also manages 10 U.S. resorts and is expanding in this area. Despite these endeavors, the main thrust of Hyatt's new efforts is on the upper-middle segment of the market.

Hyatt's new direction has produced favorable results, according to company officials. The 1983 occupancy rate was up nearly 4 percent over 1982 and was running about 3 percent ahead of the industry's 68 percent rate.

Many industry experts contend that Hyatt ran the risk of damaging its reputation by downgrading its emphasis, however. In a new campaign, Westin Hotel Co., owners of New York's Plaza Hotel and five other hotels around the country, began to stress excellence and consistent quality. Further, the company is about to enter the market for top-end airport hotels. Stouffer Corporation, which recently opened six new luxury hotels, also has begun a major push to position itself in the luxury end of the market. According to Stouffer management, Hyatt is very vulnerable at the top end of the market.

QUESTIONS

1. What risks did Hyatt take by repositioning itself? What mistakes did Hyatt make?
2. Are the threats posed by Westin and Stouffer strong?
3. What should Hyatt management do?

Chapter 10

J. P. Stevens

J. P. Stevens, although it is the second largest textile producer in the U.S., has the lowest return on equity (2.9 percent) among the ten biggest public textile companies. In 1983, the $2 billion manufacturer unveiled a bold, risky, and novel concept. In conjunction with designer Ralph Lauren, Stevens has created a collection of luxury home furnishings including sheets, crystal stemware, and furniture.

Stevens is demanding that participating stores spend up to $250,000 for construction of 1,000-square-foot boutiques that will carry the new line. Retail prices are high: terrycloth robes cost $195, wine goblets are $35, and a five-piece stainless steel flatware place setting runs $100. Retailers were very enthusiastic about the project and the company was able to choose the stores that best fit the luxurious image.

Stevens' program is an attempt to overcome a history of poor labor relations and at the same time become known as an industry marketing leader. The pursuit of these goals has led Stevens to produce what it calls the first "total home environment." The U.S. textile industry has traditionally been dominated by production- rather than marketing-oriented leaders. Growing competition from foreign manufacturers has led to the shift toward a consumer-first point of view.

Stevens spent 18 months and approximately $5 million developing the collection, and the partnership with Lauren is seen as a move to change the company's stodgy image. The Lauren line will not be available for white sales, the traditional retailing tool, and this has shocked some analysts.

The Lauren line represents a new level of quality and price for J. P. Stevens. Consumers will be courted with high quality and spectacular colors. A 200-thread-per-inch all-cotton twin sheet set will sell for $64; the same size, all-wool blanket will go for $225; while white linen hemstitched sheets will sell for $275 plus $150 for two pillowcases. Lauren will receive about a 5 percent royalty on sales.

The hefty price tags on the goods may prove to be Stevens' biggest problem. Also, in addition to the sizable initial investment the stores must make, J. P. Stevens wants them to buy 28-page full-color mail catalogs even though the brochures contain no price or ordering information. Because the Lauren line would have protected distribution among the selected stores, J. P. Stevens will have to keep its own name off any advertising spreads it plans to run for the line.

Despite these problems, David M. Tracy, vice chairman of the company, is convinced the Lauren goods are changing the J. P. Stevens image. "We want to redefine what decorative home furnishings are," he declares. "Let's not condemn ourselves before we try."

QUESTIONS

1. Why is Stevens attempting to change its image?
2. What problems are involved in such a change?
3. Assess the pros and cons of such a change.

T & R Construction, Inc.

The T & R Construction Company is a corporation solely owned by two men, Bill Timms and Joe Rodriquez. The major business of T & R is to construct warehouse, office, and factory buildings in Nashua, New Hampshire, where the firm is located, and in surrounding communities. The company was founded in 1975 when the two men formed a partnership, merged their business assets, and sought to create a profitable enterprise. By 1986 they realized this goal, as both Timms and Rodriquez were earning $90,000 each in profits and wages.

In addition to his work as an officer in the organization, Rodriquez is an amateur inventor who enjoys tinkering with mechanical things to see what he can create or improve. He had noticed that the fireplace in his home tended to pull out as much or more heat as it contributed to warming the house, an especially undesirable consequence in an era of increasing fuel costs. He knew that there were devices on the market that could blow some of the fireplace heat back into the house, but these were either inefficient or overpriced, in his opinion.

After months of tinkering with various devices he created, Rodriquez came up with one that he thought might have commercial potential. Both he and Timms tried it out in their homes and it seemed to work well. Essentially, it was an improvement on existing products. It consisted of a flat plate which was placed on the fireplace grill and connected electrically to an air pump and six lightweight pipes. The operation was uncomplicated. When a fire in the fireplace reached a critical heat level, the blower (pump system) was activated, resulting in a flow of warm air into the room. This flow would continue so long as the heat level of the fire was sufficiently high. Existing products required that the blower be manually started and stopped. In the case of the T & R prototype, only small amounts of heat, such as that generated by burning a single 2″ × 4″ board, were sufficient to operate the fan and provide surprising warming effects. Further, the fan shut off automatically when a fire died, which was not true of the other systems.

Timms and Rodriquez decided that they should consider marketing the device. They felt that the first step was to obtain a patent. They were not sure how to go about this, however, and patent attorneys were reputed to be very expensive. Also, they believed that the product would not sell without the endorsement of some agency, such as Underwriter Laboratories, stating that the product was safe. Finally, they wondered if the product would actually sell in sufficient volume. To determine the latter, they convinced friends, relatives, and acquaintances to purchase the device for $250 each. All of the purchasers reported favorable results and suggested that T & R go into the market on a large scale.

The two men believed that production of the product would pose no problem. They could easily hire skilled individuals in the immediate area to produce the item for a cost ranging between $50 and $80 (depending upon how many units were constructed). Company cash reserves were sufficient to cover necessary investment costs. In the event that the initial investment was higher than they expected, their relations with a local bank were very good and a loan at an attractive interest rate could be obtained.

There were many unanswered questions in the minds of Timms and Rodriquez during the early months of 1986. How could they go about patenting the product? What about Underwriter Laboratories? Would the product sell well? What types of consumers would most likely purchase the device? How should it be distributed and promoted?

QUESTIONS

1. What information is needed to determine if the product can be introduced?
2. Based on the facts in the case, should the partners introduce the product?

Chapter 11
Atlantic Richfield Co.

By picturing a giant credit card being blown apart in a series of TV ads, Atlantic Richfield (Arco) dramatically announced its cash-only cost- and price-cutting strategy to the public in mid-1982. Within a year, the competition began fuming. Arco followed up its initial ads with a $2 million advertising campaign on West Coast TV and radio stations which claimed that the company's gasoline could save customers up to 30¢ a gallon. Shell Oil's response, along with some of its dealers, was to run full-page newspaper ads denouncing Arco's claims. Arco, in turn, was reported to be thinking of throwing another million dollars into its campaign. Other oil companies that still offered credit cards, including Exxon, Standard Oil, Texaco, and Mobile, were forced into offering discounts for cash-paying customers. Regardless, Arco's market share increased a percentage point to just under 5 percent during the period, which pegged the company as the seventh largest oil seller in the U.S. and fourth largest profit maker ($1.6 billion in 1982).

Eliminating credit and its related costs and then passing the benefits on to customers was just one part of Arco's concerted effort to lower prices and increase market penetration, according to William Kieschnick, Jr., Arco's chief executive officer. The company's basic strategy was to become a high-volume operation by taking actions to become the low-cost producer.

The basic elements of Arco's strategy were formulated after the 1973 Arab Oil embargo. Heavily dependent upon OPEC (Organization of Petroleum Exporting Countries) oil, which was largely Arab-controlled, Arco found itself short of crude oil and with costs for crude higher than many of its competitors. Company sales of gasoline rapidly plunged by 25 percent. In 1975, Arco began taking strategic action by becoming the first major refiner to move heavily into self-service outlets. For the next eight years, the company pruned its distribution back from 30 to 14 states, dropping over 4,000 outlets and cutting its marketing staff from nearly 6,000 to less than 2,000.

The company became heavily involved in Alaskan North Shore exploration and production. By 1983, Arco was pumping nearly 1.5 million barrels a day from these fields. In another move in 1980, the company cut its refinery capacity by over 20 percent and redesigned its operations to handle larger amounts of high-sulfur, heavy crudes that became more widely available and at lower prices on world markets. In another cost-cutting effort, Arco blended much of its unleaded regular gasoline with Oxinol 50, a company-trademarked additive made of methanol and tertiary butyl alcohol. Company executives indicated that the 8 percent blend saved nearly two cents per gallon in cost without a loss in performance.

Many competitors contended that Arco's practices were unfair, however. One complaint was that its ads compared company prices with the full-service credit card prices of only some of its rivals. Another complaint was that the company underpriced nearly a half million barrels a day of Alaskan crude that it sold to itself, thus saving the company hundreds of millions of dollars in taxes and royalties. A spokesman for the Independent Gasoline Marketers Council told a congressional hearing on the issue that Arco "wants to run us out of business to gain monopoly power." If Congress chooses to bar the activities initiated by Arco, the company could face millions of dollars of additional expenses.

Still another major complaint concerned Arco's distribution system. Arco encouraged dealers to invest in company-franchised AM/PM Mini Markets, which were convenience food operations designed to augment self-service gasoline sales. The 800 dealers who owned franchises averaged monthly sales of nearly 160,000 gallons, which was triple the oil industry average. According to one vocal critic, "They can sell gasoline at no profit and still survive."

A major concern to the company's management was the impending decline in production in Prudhoe Bay (Alaska's North Shore). Experts expected that the volumes would start dropping by 1990 and fall in half within five years. The company began an intensive exploration effort to locate more crude, but only the future will tell if its efforts will be fruitful.

QUESTIONS

1. Assess Arco's pricing strategy. What tradeoffs did the company bet that customers would be willing to make?
2. How central were Arco's internal pricing practices, assuming that the charges of critics were correct, to its basic strategy?
3. In what business is Arco defining itself in its recent distribution efforts?

The Circle Pecan Company

The Circle Pecan Company is one of the larger growers and marketers of pecans in the United States. Located in West Texas, the firm was founded by the Murdoch family over 80 years ago. The current owner is Todd Murdoch, a descendant of the original owners. He, his wife, two daughters, and a son are the owners and managers.

Circle pecans are of high quality. The soil and climate on company properties are optimal for growing pecans, and the Murdochs have been thoroughly trained and have considerable experience with pecans. They utilize methods passed down through the family for years, as well as the latest technological innovations from agricultural experiment stations, in order to produce a premium product.

The firm has always sold its nuts directly to companies that use them to produce other food products rather than to either wholesalers or consumers. Currently, the customers are two candy companies and one producer of cookies. The founders of Circle lacked selling experience and felt that the safest course of action would be to sell directly to a limited number of companies—a tradition that has been carried down over the years. One of the candy companies has been a customer for four years. The other two clients have purchased Circle pecans for two years.

Each year, prior to the growing season, Circle enters into negotiations with prospective customers, centered on prices, financing, terms of sale, methods of transportation, and related matters. If the parties can come to terms, they sign one-year contracts. If Circle and the buyer cannot establish a mutually satisfactory agreement a member of the family calls upon another prospective customer. Most of the negotiations with customers are carried on by Todd Murdoch and one of his daughters, Sandy, who work as a sales team.

Circle has only limited descretion in setting prices, since the market determines the basic price of pecans. However, because of the high quality of Circle pecans and because the firm provides fast delivery, prices above those established by the market can usually be negotiated. On average, Circle receives prices that are 5 percent above the market level, although this percentage varies from one year to the next, depending on such factors as the demand for pecans, the quality and quantity of the national crop, and the demand for candies and cookies containing pecans.

Circle does no advertising, relying on personal selling for carrying out the promotion objectives. The Murdochs have considered utilizing ads in several trade magazines read by executives in the confectionary industry, but have never taken the matter very seriously. They suspect, however, that this might be a useful means of uncovering potential customers.

For the past two years the Murdochs have been dissatisfied with their experience with customers. The contracts they have signed were not as favorable to them as in past years, resulting in declines in net income. The family has decided that some changes may be necessary. One alternative would be to seek out new customers, through additional sales calls and perhaps advertising. Another is to attempt to sell pecans to consumers, perhaps through supermarkets, or even through company stores. The other major alternative is to continue with the status quo and do a better job of negotiating contracts with customers. This pattern has worked well in the past. One complicating factor is that the supply of premium quality pecans has increased in recent years, heating up the competition for potential customers. It is expected that this increased competition will continue.

QUESTIONS

1. Assess Circle's marketing strategy thus far.

2. "Basically, pecans are a commodity, which means that the only real decision for management to consider is how much to produce." Discuss.
3. What should Circle's management do?

Chapter 12

American High Speed Rail Corp.

Convinced that no governmental agency would ever be able to raise the required money for high-speed trains, Alan S. Boyd and Lawrence D. Gilson resigned in 1981 as president and vice president, respectively, of Amtrak to form American High Speed Rail Corporation (AHSR). Capitalized with an initial $5 million investment by a Japanese venture capital firm, the company's goal is to develop high-speed routes between certain key U.S. cities, first in California and then in other heavily populated centers.

The idea of high-speed trains is not new. France operates such a system, termed "trains a grande vitess," which at nearly 190 mph is about the fastest available. Another system that operates in Japan, called Shinkansenor, or bullet train, runs at 160 mph. The primary backers of AHSR see the opportunity to establish a North American beachhead for Japanese technology. They are very much interested, therefore, in providing considerable support to AHSR.

AHSR is actively considering two routes for high-speed trains in 1983. The first is between Los Angeles and San Diego, a distance of about 125 miles. AHSR is a primary mover in planning this route. It also is considering another system to race from Los Angeles to Las Vegas, a distance of nearly 275 miles through the desert. This latter system would use a different technology than the bullet trains, employing magnetic levitation devices that would enable the vehicles to float above a single guide rail and be propelled by electronic magnets at dizzying speeds of nearly 250 mph.

Planning is more advanced for the Los Angeles–San Diego route. The corridor's high population density, crowded highways, and almost nonexistent rail service all contribute to the proposed route's desirability, but there is considerable resistance. State officials promised tough environmental and financial reviews. "We're afraid that they will not be able to raise the $3 billion in required capital," said Victor Weisser, California's Public Utilities Commission Director of Transportation. "I fear that they will run out of money halfway through and come running to us for help," Weisser added.

Many local residents also were concerned about the proposed project's potential for noise and vibration. A bill before the California's legislature would require the approval of construction plans by every town and county along the entire route.

If completed, the nonstop trains—80 per day—would run the route in a little less than an hour. Currently the trip takes about 30 minutes by plane and 2½ hours by automobile. AHSR plans to charge $27 for a round trip, less than half of the $60 prevailing airfare but almost double the current Amtrak fee. A study completed by Arthur D. Little Inc., internationally prominent management consultants, estimated that about 100,000 passengers a day would ride the new trains, compared to 3,000 on Amtrak at present.

The Japanese backers of the project are committed to funding 25 percent of all the project's capital needs. First Boston Corp. is another major backer. Together, AHSR and First Boston devised a complex financial plan, including private equity, tax-exempt bonds, bank debt, and supplier credits for total project funding. If the assumptions are correct, said Gilson, "we'll have a positive cash flow from the very first day." First Boston projected pretax profits of $960 million on revenues of $1.6 billion by 1999, or after ten years of full system operation.

As of 1983, AHSR was also studying other lines, including Tampa–Orlando, Dallas–Houston, and a hub for runs between Chicago to St. Louis, Minneapolis, Detroit, and Cincinnati. The builders of France's system were also considering such routes, but they were behind AHSR in developing proposals. The magnetic trains being considered for the Los Angeles–to–Las Vegas route were largely experimental, but officials of the latter city were pushing them heavily. A two-year, $10 million study of the route's feasibility was scheduled to begin late in the year.

AHSR planned more rapid development in California. The goal was to line up financial backing and complete the initial design work by mid-1984. It was thought that the first passengers could be carried by 1987. That is, of course, if AHSR can obtain the approval of California officials.

QUESTIONS

1. What effects, if any, do you think high-speed trains will have on the transportation industry?
2. Outline the scope of AHSR's marketing tasks.
3. What steps can AHSR's management take to get its proposed projects implemented?

National Paper Company

The National Paper Company is a Wisconsin-based manufacturer of paper napkins and towels that it sells to business and nonbusiness organizations for employee and customer use. The company markets its products throughout the eastern half of the United States. It sells the product line directly to large purchasers and through wholesalers to smaller ones.

National is an active price competitor. Management attempts to undercut its rivals whenever possible. It can do this because the firm is able to attain substantial economies of scale in production and in distribution. Its large timber holdings, efficient sawmills, and cost-oriented physical distribution manager have placed company expenses well below those of rivals, making strong price competition feasible.

The napkins and towels National sells to its industrial customers are about average in quality—not much better nor much worse than competitors' offerings. Management believes that most buyers are satisfied with products of this type and are not highly quality-oriented. On the other hand, they do not want to purchase goods that are clearly inferior.

The firm has a sales force of 27 individuals, most of whom have been employed by National for five or more years. Company compensation plans are better than most in the industry, and this plus an attitude of good human relations by the sales manager have led to a highly motivated and skilled sales force. The sales representatives are very familiar with their respective territories and most of their major customers. They are a highly valued asset.

National distributes its products out of two large distribution centers. One, located in Milwaukee, serves the northern part of the market while another in Atlanta serves the southern portion. The firm conveys shipments of finished goods by truck to the Wisconsin warehouse complex and by rail to the Atlanta site. In most cases, the company attains carload and truckload rates.

A problem has developed which is of increasing concern to management. Recently customers have been complaining about unreliable deliveries, especially those emanating from the Atlanta distribution center. Some orders have been arriving as much as three weeks beyond the deadline that National promised. This has happened often enough to cause considerable antagonism among customers. A related problem that has resurfaced is damage in transit, whereby cases of paper products have been torn open and the contents partially damaged. Complaints to the railroad have not produced results, other than a promise by railroad officials to look into the problem.

The traffic manager has proposed that the firm might consider purchasing its own fleet of trucks to serve the Atlanta market. He contends that this could enable the company to overcome the problems that it has experienced in transporting goods to that center. The firm would have full control of distribution to Atlanta and would not be dependent upon outside organizations. The sales manager agrees with this proposal, fearing that some large accounts in the southern region may be lost if the delivery problems are not solved.

QUESTION

1. What would you recommend to management? Defend your answer.

Chapter 13

Benson's Photography

Benson's Photography is located in a suburb of St. Louis. The owner and manager, Diana Benson, has been in business for only six months. The store is located in a large enclosed shopping mall (over 200 stores) that generates considerable pedestrian traffic past her unit. The shop carries a wide line of cameras, supplies, and equipment and provides developing, enlarging, and associated services.

Prior to opening the store, Diana worked as a clerk in another photography shop located in a different mall. Her period of employment was four years. She had the desire to go into business for herself and, using her savings and borrowed capital from relatives, she rented the space and set up the shop. It contains 4,500 square feet of space, 3,600 of which is used for sales, display, and customer service. It is the only photography shop in the mall, although other stores, including department, variety, and drug stores, also carry cameras and equipment and develop films. Diana attempts to provide a wider line of inventory and superior service to compete with these rivals. She realizes, too, that she competes with camera shops and stores located at other sites in the metropolitan area.

Prices Benson charges are about the same as those of other camera shops located in major malls. Periodically, Diana checks her competitors' advertisements and even shops their stores to ensure that her prices are in line. She is especially careful to avoid prices that are above those of other major shops in the area, believing that many consumers shop for prices.

Like her previous employer, Diana allocates 1 percent of each month's sales to next month's advertising. The ads appear in one metro and two suburban newspapers. Their intent is to draw shoppers into the store by describing various specials—items that they can purchase at a low price—and by conveying the idea that the store's services are superior to those of other outlets.

After operating for six months, Diana realized that she needed information to answer some questions that were basic to the operation of her business. What consumers should she seek? What should she do to attract the business of her target market? How should she differentiate the shop from competitors? Diana devised questionnaires and handed them out to customers during one week in April, asking that they complete the questionnaires in the store and return them to her. Approximately 30 percent of the customers complied, providing Diana with a sample of 364 responses.

Analysis provided some interesting facts. Following are some customer characteristics:

Sex/Age	
Men (over age eighteen)	41%
Boys (under age eighteen)	21%
Women (over age eighteen)	29%
Girls (under age eighteen)	9%
Total customers	100%

Location of Residence	
Within one mile of the shopping center	34%
Within five miles of the shopping center	42%
Over five miles from the center	24%
Total	100%

Occupation of Head of Household	
Managers and professionals	11%
White collar workers	19%
Blue collar workers	16%
Self-employed	12%
Student	8%
Military	6%
Retired	10%
Unemployed	5%
Other	13%
Total	100%

Major Reason for Shopping at Benson's	
Convenience	30%
Quality of service	9%
Low prices	24%
Wide product line	20%
Product quality	14%
Other	3%
Total	100%

Number of Visits to Store in Last Month	
1	58%
2–5	33%
6–9	7%
10 or more	2%
Total	100%

Major Problems Associated with Store

Prices too high	39%
Inadequate product line	15%
Inadequate product quality	11%
Poor service	22%
Poor location	10%
Other	3%
Total	100%

Overall Evaluation

Excellent	15%
Good	58%
Average	21%
Not good	4%
Very poor	2%
Total	100%

QUESTIONS

1. Using this information, what would you recommend to Diana in terms of delineating the target consumer and developing marketing strategies?
2. What additional information should she have collected in the survey?

Nabisco Brands, Inc.

Nabisco Brands, Inc., with a 35 percent share of sales in the $2.5 billion cookie industry, is the market leader. For years the main players in the industry have been Nabisco, Keebler, and Sunshine, but some new names have entered the fray for a share of the sweetly profitable cookie domain.

In January 1983, Procter & Gamble began testing a new chocolate chip cookie line in Kansas City under the well-known Duncan Hines name. In a short period of time, their cookies had captured about one fourth of the local market and rumor had it that they would be going national sometime in 1984.

In 1980, PepsiCo, Inc., with its Frito-Lay Division, entered the cookie business by purchasing GrandMa's Inc., a regional manufacturer. One of Frito-Lay's major strengths is its first-rate, direct-to-stores sales system, which permits rapid expansion. The firm distributed GrandMa's to over 30 percent of the U.S. and planned national distribution sometime in 1984.

Foreign companies have also begun to compete for a share of the market by acquiring U.S. enterprises. A leading French company, Groupe Generale Biscuit, purchased Mother's Cake and Cookie Co. in the spring of 1983. They also own an East Coast brand, Burry-Lu Inc., along with a midwest label, Salerno-Megowen Biscuit Co.

Nabisco fought back with more new products. Its strategy was to develop a new line of cookies that would deflect the impact of new entries from P & G and Frito-Lay. This forced competitors to rethink their plans and to spend more on product development and advertising.

Newcomers are drawn to this market because of its size and profitability. Nabisco earned approximately 51 percent of its $440.3 million in 1982 U.S. operating income from cookies and crackers. These numbers undoubtedly have attracted Frito-Lay and P & G.

Procter & Gamble developed a unique cookie with a texture that is crunchy on the outside and chewy on the inside, as well as a six-month shelf life. Estimates are that the company invested $30 million for development of the patented process and test-marketing.

P & G's strategy was to appeal to the retailer, who must be convinced to allot scarce shelf space. The retailer has the option of warehousing the P & G cookies because of their longer shelf life, while rivals usually deliver their brands directly to stores. With the P & G cookie, retailers can set their own prices and margins, while the store-delivered brands are prepriced.

Frito-Lay continued with the store delivery system used for its successful snack foods. It expanded the GrandMa's line to 24 types of both chewy and crispy cookies, but its market share in Kansas City fell from 20 percent to 10 percent after P & G's entry. The morale of company sales representatives fell because time spent with the GrandMa's line took away from the more profitable salty-snack business.

Nabisco countered with a new Almost Home line that featured 15 types of moist and chewy cookies. In an effort to ensure shelf space for the brand, Nabisco offered dealers a 10 percent discount.

Keebler Co., number two in the industry, expanded its operations to include West Coast distribution, in 1982, buying a California baking plant to achieve its distribution push.

Third-place Sunshine Biscuits, Inc. adopted a value strategy. By changing its nine sandwich-type cookies, the company was able to price them below $1 per package. Sunshine was after the customers who don't want to pay $1.50 to $2 for the P & G and GrandMa's brands.

QUESTION

1. Evaluate the performance of each of the cookie producers mentioned above, in terms of their expected success in attracting retailer interest in their brands.

Chapter 14

Kampcraft, Inc.

Kampcraft, Inc., of Butler, Ohio, is a manufacturer of kerosene heaters used by campers, hunters, fishermen, and the like. The firm was founded in the mid-1950s by Byron Vigil, formerly a senior production executive with one of the large U.S. manufacturers of camping equipment. Vigil had always wanted to own and operate his own firm.

By 1986 Kampcraft was earning a return on investment of 19 percent. Company sales during that year exceeded $4 million. Vigil felt that the company was very successful, but his goal was to further increase sales and profits. In his opinion, this could not be accomplished without adding new products.

The firm produces several items. The major line is kerosene heaters, which accounts for two-thirds of the firm's sales and three-fourths of its profits. Other products are portable hand warmers, canteens, and outdoor cooking utensils. The company purchases the canteens and cooking utensils from other firms and places the Kampcraft brand on them.

The target consumers are defined as adult males between the ages of 18 and 65 who engage in camping, hunting, fishing, and other outdoor activities. Some competitors aim at the same target consumers, but one focuses partially on women, an emerging segment in this market.

The firm distributes its products to consumers through sporting goods stores located in larger cities throughout the eastern half of the United States. Six sales representatives serve these stores. Company policy is to appoint one exclusive distributor per 100,000 population. The firm utilizes cooperative newspaper advertising, where it pays for half of the cost of local newspaper ads and the retailer pays the other half.

Kampcraft prices are higher than those of most of its rivals. Management attempts to sell very high quality durable products, and it is felt that consumers are willing to pay more for the premium products. It has attempted, however, to keep prices to retailers no more than 10 percent above industry averages.

In 1986 several of the company operating personnel came up with a new lightweight portable grill that could be used by outdoorsmen as a means of heating food and beverages. The grill is inexpensive to produce and used existing Kampcraft production facilities. It is easily transportable, fits compactly into a portion of an average automobile trunk, and is not difficult to clean. Several company employees have tried out prototypes of the product and are very pleased with the results.

Mr. Vigil feels the product has real potential. He has decided to introduce it not only to outdoorsmen, but to individuals who enjoy backyard cooking but who do not have the space or the inclination to own a standard cooking grill or smoker. Vigil feels that department stores, variety stores, and some discounters would be interested in carrying the product.

Vigil is puzzled as to how to distribute the product to retailers. Should the company usé wholesalers or should it sell directly to retailers? How many channel levels would be needed? If the company utilized wholesalers, how many and what kind should it employ? How might it go about finding desirable wholesales and retailers?

QUESTIONS

1. What should Vigil do?
2. What are the advantages of using wholesalers? What about direct selling?
3. What conflicts do you envision with Kampcraft's current outlets?

American Express Co.

In 1981, the American Express Company acquired Shearson Loeb Rhoades, Inc., for more than $1 billion. To follow up this purchase, Sanford I. Weill, AmEx president, acquired Investors Diversified Services, Inc., (IDS) from Alleghany Corp. for $1.05 billion in 1983.

AmEx's acquisition of IDS was seen as a diversification away from the upper crust of financial services and toward the so-called financial supermarket—the vast, but less profitable, middle market—where Sears, Roebuck and Co., Prudential Insurance Co. of America, and others had been competing for the small, conservative investor.

IDS was founded in 1894 and assembled a large sales staff that sold mutual funds, life insurance, tax shelters and other investments. The firm marketed personal financial planning. By 1983, IDS had a sales force of 4,500 and a customer base of 1.1 million. The company's assets under its own management in 1983 were $17.5 billion, along with $13.5 billion of life insurance in force.

Strategically, the IDS acquisition's impact on AmEx was twofold. It gave AmEx an entry in the middle market while building a stronger distribution chain which would become increasingly important as deregulation increased competition in the financial services sector.

IDS's grass-roots sales force complemented AmEx's more urban network, but this good fit was found in other areas as well. AmEx already had a major share in property and casualty insurance with the Fireman's Fund Insurance subsidiary but it was weak in life insurance. IDS had a large life insurance operation but it was lacking in the areas of property and casualty insurance. IDS also brought strength to AmEx in the management of stock and bond market mutual funds, as well as institutional portfolio management. These are fast-growing areas that were weak spots for AmEx prior to the IDS acquisition.

A merger of this magnitude is likely to create problems. The IDS sales force, though aggressive, is relatively unsophisticated. They may experience difficulty in selling a broad spectrum of complicated new instruments. AmEx has, however, entered the high-stakes bidding war for control of the financial marketplace.

QUESTIONS

1. Describe the positive and negative aspects of the fit between AmEx and IDS.
2. Why do you think AmEx decided to acquire IDS?
3. How has the financial services market changed?

Chapter 15

Hallen, Flaherty, and Jones

George Hallen, managing partner of Hallen, Flaherty, and Jones, a Louisville-based law firm with 32 professionals, complained that he and his partners were so upset over the media popularity of some competing law firms that they were about to hire a press agent. Hallen complained, "We won a major Supreme Court case—a landmark case—involving time-sharing real estate. Timothy, my partner argued it, our staff briefed it, and *we* won it. The *New York Times* wrote up the case. And who did they quote about its significance? Somebody at Branner and Hallis, that's who. They didn't even bother to call us," he fumed. George further added, "This profession is going to the medicine show hucksters and rainmakers."

Much in the legal profession has changed, to the chagrin of many, since the 1977 Supreme Court decision which for the first time allowed lawyers and accountants to advertise. At first, most corporate law firms held back, priding themselves in not being hacks or ambulance chasers. But more and more of them have since turned to media consultants, press agents, and even marketing consultants to help them determine their destinies. "Many of us feel that it is unprofessional to think of prospective clients as prospects," said George.

The legal profession, especially those involved with corporate law, was once most anxious to avoid publicity altogether. Instead, attorneys sought clients through their professional reputation and social contacts. But a tough competitive climate, brought about by many factors including an uncertain economy and a mushrooming number of lawyers, has meant that more and more in the profession are turning to promotion experts to help them present their stories. By 1984, corporate law had become a new game with new rules. In New York, to illustrate, a public relations woman suggested that reporters interview partners of her client, the top law firm of Wood, Hansen, and Blum. The large Richmond, Virginia, law firm of O'Grady, Forest, and Brille published a slick, hardbound eight-page book to tell its story. Three partners of Williams and Rider, one of the country's largest firms, fly periodically from Chicago to New York to lunch with the editor of a legal newspaper, arranged by the law firm's New York agency. In Minnesota's Twin Cities, the nightly business report of the area's public TV station ends with an acknowledgment that it is sponsored by Robbins, Zelle, Larson & Kaplan, one of the state's biggest law firms.

None of the old-line, prestigious firms have gone so far as to buy large displays in the *Yellow Pages* or to run ads on *60 Minutes*. But most of them have begun some form of active promotion. Hill & Knowlton Inc., an international public relations agency, maintains around 20 legal clients on its roster. Agencies around the country have been signing up law firms for retainers that start at about $1,500 a month and hourly rates in excess of $100 per hour.

The activities of the agencies vary. Some provide ghostwriting of bylined articles for trade journals and editorial pages. Most promote court victories and other professional accomplishments. Their main activity, though, is to cajole, chatter, and do whatever necessary to promote their clients as quotable experts to editors and writers of major newspaper and magazine business pages. The jackpot that all of them shoot for is to get their clients to become the subject of glowing feature stories.

Like George Hallen, though, not all lawyers approve. George says, "You never should have to use a flack to sell law the way you sell widgets or cars."

QUESTIONS

1. What roles do PR agents perform for professional services? Can they do this better than the professionals themselves?
2. What other services lend themselves to PR?
3. What should Hallen, Flaherty, and Jones do?

Airship Industries

Alan Bond, the Australian entrepreneur who owns 81 percent of Airship Industries, was confident that the walls surrounding another American institution could be toppled—the airship business. Long dominated by Goodyear Aerospace, competition for airships (blimps) heated up in the early 1980s when Airship brought competition to Goodyear's back door by leasing an airship to Fuji Film for advertising during the 1984 Los Angeles Olympics.

Airship has an interesting history. Begun in the mid-1970s by British naval engineer Roger Munk after a lifelong dream of developing workable airships with improved lift capabilities, Bond bought into the business in the early 1980s because of the potential. Immediate generation of cash flow was created by using the blimps for advertising—in effect, floating billboards. Goodyear had been successful in using its fleet for its own promotion for years, and other companies expressed an interest in doing the same thing. Besides Fuji, McDonald's Corp. franchise holders in the New York metropolitan area had put one up in 1984, suitably emblazoned with Golden Arches, and Resorts International, Inc. began flying an airship to promote its Atlantic City casino.

The use of airships for advertising was seen only as an immediate generator of cash—an interesting one, but only a drop in the bucket. The real potential lay in developing airships for the U.S. Navy.

Modern interest in using blimps as observation posts began in the late 1970s by the U.S. Coast Guard. With a capability of staying aloft for lengthy periods, the Coast Guard saw the ships as a promising means of patrolling waters for safety as well as assisting in its increasing role in fighting the drug trade.

Both Airship and Goodyear fought for Coast Guard attention—Goodyear with a revised version of its traditional blimps, and Airship with its new "vectored thrust propeller" and high-tech, greater lift model. The trials by the Coast Guard were worth $4 million alone, but Goodyear dropped out of the competition. According to Fred Nebiker, vice president of Goodyear Aerospace, "We saw the Coast Guard tests as being a trial only. The eventual design will change if the tests go well and we will be there with our designs at that time." Airship saw Goodyear's withdrawal differently, as more of an admission that its design was obsolete.

Perhaps Goodyear was right since the Coast Guard dropped the project in the early 1980s. But the U.S. Navy did not, as it began to develop plans for airships as radar platforms for its guided missile fleet. "The real market is now developing," according to both Nebiker and Munk. With a potential of several billion dollars, no one was going to take this prospect lightly.

For technical reasons and to establish links with U.S. companies, Airship teamed up with Westinghouse on the Navy project and Goodyear linked with Sperry and Litton for their radar support. Another project was headed by Boeing, which was also active in presenting proposals to the Navy. All three received initial feasibility study grants from the Navy for continued R & D.

Surprising to many, at the Paris Air show (traditionally the trade show where all aircraft firms display their products) was that the airship (a small, nonfunctional model) proposed by Boeing received the greatest attention. It had internal structural supports, unlike the models proposed by either of the two other competitors. Goodyear's model (also small and nonfunctional) also was received well, but Airship did not bring a model. The company had intended to bring a flying version, a real ship, but suffered a setback when one crashed in a Kansas cornfield. As in the development of any new aircraft, such crashes were not unusual.

While developing and testing continued in 1986, an interesting side track was taken by Goodyear. The company filed suit against Fuji in federal court in Lincoln, Nebraska in 1986 and in state court in Fort Lauderdale, Fla., claiming trademark infringement. While Fuji has used blimps for advertising in Europe since 1981 and in the U.S. since the Olympics in 1984, it was the company's use of the blimp shape in printed promotional material during the fall of 1985, including a game called "Blimpo," that raised Goodyear's objections. "We have no intention of trying to keep blimps out of the sky," insisted William L. Newkirk. Goodyear's VP for public relations. "We only want to protect our blimp-shaped symbol," he added.

With his competition against these corporate giants, Bond has a history of playing "David and Goliath." His considerable wealth from many successful business ventures around the world enabled him to finance the Australian yachting team that succeeded in winning the America's Cup in 1983, another American bastion that was impregnable for decades.

QUESTIONS

1. Assess the use of airships as promotional media for companies.
2. How has Airship done in promoting its programs? What role can promotion take in advancing Airship's cause? Outline a promotional program for Airship.
3. Assess Goodyear's actions. Outline a promotional program that Goodyear should take to advance its blimp program.

Chapter 16
Stroh Brewing Co.

As the number 3 brewery in sales, behind the giants Anheuser-Busch and Miller Brewing Co., Detroit-based Stroh lacked the huge advertising budgets of the industry leaders. In 1983, the company spent about $5 million on advertising, less than a quarter of either A-B or Miller. Accordingly, company management was convinced that Stroh's advertising had to "set as many minds in motion as possible" for the company to reach its goals.

Almost every premium beer was targeted at the same market: men in the age range of 18 to 49. Thus, all of the brewers were competing for the attention and money of the same group. Because A-B and Miller could go after the market with numerous repetitions, Stroh management felt that it needed ads that stood out and captured the audience's attention.

Stroh's used humor in its "beer lover campaign," a series of commercials which began years ago and accompanied the company's rapid growth from a regional to a national marketer. Doyle Dane Bernbach, the company's ad agency through the first part of 1983, created most of the ads. Some of DDB's commercials were quite notable. One of the most successful was a parody of Steven Spielberg's movie, "Close Encounters of the Third Kind." A bright light from an alien spaceship surrounds a house. A light ray shoots inside, searching around briefly before finding the refrigerator. The fridge door opens and several bottles float out, apparently into the spaceship. One of the ad's characters says "All that way for a Stroh's." Another looks up as if to watch the spaceship fly away and says, "Don't surprise me none."

"The ads were funny," said one Stroh's executive, "but they did not bring more Stroh's drinkers into the stores." Whether the ads are funny or not, research indicated that beer drinkers enjoy seeing people like themselves in beer commercials. "We strayed too far from the beer drinker's world to get laughter," added the executive.

What shocked many in the advertising industry was that Stroh's took its account away from DDB in 1983 and gave it to Marschalk Co. Until that time, Marschalk's only experience with the company was its design of an uninspiring campaign for Stroh light, "looks like a Stroh light night." But what Marschalk came up with was a series of "Alex the Dog" commercials. The first ad in the series pictures a group of men playing poker. On command, a dog runs into the kitchen. While the camera focuses on the poker players, the audience can hear a refrigerator open, cans clink, cans being opened, and finally a dog drinking. The dog's owner then exclaims "Alex, that better be your water." All of the dog's assumed actions are offscreen, where they are left up to the audience's imagination. The commercial was a big success in getting attention. Further, it received considerable free publicity through newspaper stories and word of mouth.

The second commercial in the series also featured a dog. This time, though, the poker players are camping when they run out of beer. Alex is sent off to buy more. The dog leaves the tent, a car door opens, a seat belt clicks, the car starts, headlights flash across the tent, and the dog's owner shouts, "Alex, you'd better be driving your own car."

A side benefit of the commercials, according to management, was their appeal to younger and more affluent drinkers. All of the beer companies were worried about losing young drinkers to other beverages such as wine and fruit drinks. Humor was considered particularly important in attracting college-aged drinkers who will become tomorrow's major factor in the beer market. Budweiser and Miller also recognized the importance of younger drinkers by developing separate humor-based campaigns designed especially for this audience.

QUESTIONS

1. What are the strengths of the Alex commercials? The weaknesses?
2. What are the implications of changing agencies?

3. What, if any, weaknesses do you see in Stroh's advertising? What would you change?

The Oxford Trust Bank

The Oxford Trust Bank is a large multinational bank that serves business customers in 14 countries throughout the world. In 1983 it had reserves of over $3.1 billion and a retained profit of over $540 million. Headquartered in New York, it has major banking offices in Miami, Chicago, Philadelphia, Boston, Seattle, Los Angeles, London, Paris, Zurich, and Hong Kong. This bank is quite financially secure and has a record of stable growth since its inception in 1922.

Oxford offers many services to its customers. It has correspondent banks located throughout the world. In addition to traditional banking services it offers letters of credit, money transfers, collections, foreign collection systems, advice on domestic and international money markets and on money forecasting, and consulting on how to improve the cost efficiency of customers' treasurer's offices. It has a reputation for solving customers' difficult banking problems.

Mainly, Oxford serves larger businesses, particularly those involved in international operations. These include manufacturers, oil companies, wholesalers, commodity traders, retailers, and law firms. The smaller companies that it does have as customers are mostly subsidiaries of larger firms that it serves.

The bank competes with a number of other large banks, many of which are also headquartered in New York. Other competitors are headquartered in various banking centers such as London and Zurich. Important factors in competition are the sizes of the banks, their financial stability, the bundle of services they offer, and the quality of their services. Many customers want the personal attention of a high-ranking bank officer before entrusting their business to a particular bank. Many of their needs for services are complex, particularly in the case of international business, so a bank is in need of highly trained and experienced officers and technical personnel. In this regard, the Oxford Trust Bank is very strong. It has a cadre of knowledgable personnel with a reputation for outstanding service and considerable knowledge.

In 1983 the bank ran six advertisements in *Business Week* that were similar to others it featured in three other business magazines. The ads showed a senior vice president's photograph and quoted him as saying that the bank was equipped to handle the needs of large customers operating in foreign countries and that personal service was an important objective. The ad went into considerable detail on how the bank provided quality and personalized service throughout the world. It described or listed some of the services. This advertisement appeared in three colors and took up one page in the magazine.

The company scheduled the ads to appear every two months. Each one was slightly different from the others but all carried essentially the same message. The idea, according to the bank's advertising agency, was to obtain impact through repetition, but to change the format of the ads sufficiently so that readers of the magazine did not lose interest.

At the bank's annual meeting, several stockholders who held a substantial amount of company stock objected strongly to the fact that management was spending company funds on advertising. In their view, this was merely a wasteful expense that contributed little or nothing to the well-being of the bank. According to one, "Companies do not make their choice of banks based upon their advertising. Can you imagine a financial officer of a large corporation being so naive as to base its choice of a bank on the advertising messages that it carries? Financial officers are impressed with the reputation of a bank, its personnel, and the quality of its services, based upon these officers' experiences and what they have heard from their peers. Advertising should be used to sell soap, candy bars, and soft drinks, but not banks."

QUESTIONS

1. How should management respond to the stockholders?
2. What else should management do regarding advertising?
3. How should Oxford's advertising differ if the decision were made to target consumers?

Chapter 17

Mary Kay Cosmetics, Inc.

Not many multimillion dollar company chairmen reward top salespeople with furs, jewelry, paid vacations, and pink Cadillacs, much less bake cookies for management trainees. But Mary Kay Ash, founder of Dallas-based Mary Kay Cosmetics, Inc., does, and these inspirations, as well as overall company strategies, have paid off handsomely. Sales of the company's cosmetics rose at a meteoric rate, growing nearly fivefold in as many years, ending in 1982. Even during 1982, a recessionary year in which industry sales flattened at $11 billion, Mary Kay's receipts spurted 30 percent to $305 million. The company's earnings growth was even more impressive, climbing 46 percent from 1981 to $35.5 million.

By 1982, the company had almost 193,000 beauty consultants who sold company products mostly through the party plan. These consultants were directly supervised by about 4,000 full-time sales directors, whose job it was to hire, train, motivate, and replace, if necessary, salespeople—about 99 percent of which were women—in their assigned territories. Everyone in the organization received a uniform appropriate to their job and success. All sales directors, for example, wore grey suits and Haynes Quicksilver pantyhose, accompanied by an amethyst, pink, or strawberry blouse. Salespeople wore mufti until they hit assigned sales targets, when they obtained red blazers. Top performers regularly received company prizes such as diamond stick pins, vacations, and the company's coveted pink Cadillacs.

Regardless of the incentives, however, management recognized that the company would run out of sales recruits before long. Company president Richard Rogers, Ash's 39-year-old son, estimated that the present company sales force design would not be able to allow the company to grow much beyond a doubling from its current levels, a target he felt could be reached in about five years. Despite a lower turnover rate of beauty consultants than Avon Products Inc., the industry's leader with $3 billion in sales, nearly 120,000 sales representatives terminated with Mary Kay—either through firing or voluntary withdrawal—during 1982. Further, only about 60,000 of the present sales force were considered to be significantly productive, with the rest probably leaving in the future.

Regardless of the reason for termination, departure from the company's sales force inevitably led to lost customers for Mary Kay. The party selling concept, pioneered on a large scale by Tupperware, requires sales representatives to invite friends, neighbors, and acquaintances to a party setting, typically in their homes, where they demonstrate the company's skin care products, and take orders and obtain payment for them before the party finishes. Turnover, therefore, led to a break in distribution to some consumers.

Recognizing the inherent limitations caused by the distribution system, Rogers planned a three-pronged strategy to increase growth. The first part involved heavy advertising expenditures which Mary Kay had avoided in the past. The firm budgeted a minimum of $6 million for advertising in 1983, both to promote company cosmetics and to advise consumers that company sales directors are listed in the yellow pages.

Another arm of Rogers' strategy was to expand the number of lines the company handled. Historically, Mary Kay had tied its product strategy to skin care products such as moisturizers that lend themselves to demonstration in a party setting. Rogers planned to add hair care products and body lotions, with an approach that enabled customers to sample the items at home before buying. In a little over six months of testing in limited markets, the new lines seemed to have no effect on total sales. However, Rogers felt that enough time had not elapsed to judge the new lines and that it would take a while to "work out the bugs."

The final part of Rogers' strategy was to expand outside of the U.S. Company efforts in Canada met with initial success but quickly leveled off. Earnings were negligible in Australia, and attempts to launch Mary Kay in Argentina led only to losses. But again, management considered these efforts to be experimental and felt that they had not yet allowed enough time to see whether expansion into other markets could succeed.

QUESTIONS

1. What have been the key decisions leading to Mary Kay's success?
2. Should management decide to expand through retailers?
3. Should Mr. Rogers continue or abandon the new products?

Intertech Corp.

For 26 years Al London has been a sales representative of the Intertech Corp., a manufacturer and marketer of mainframe and personal computers. Al has the reputation of being a star salesman because his sales volumes are consistently one of the top three in the 67-person sales force. At present he is 61 years of age—nearing the retirement point. During 1984, he brought in $1,450,000 of revenue to the company and earned commissions of $83,000.

Intertech is not one of the giants of the computer industry, although its sales are impressive. Last year it earned $29 million in revenues, a 9 percent increase over the previous year. It is locked in rivalry in an intensely competitive industry, made up of giants like IBM, Honeywell, and Tandy on the one hand, and a number of smaller, younger, and very aggressive companies on the other. Profits have declined in the last two years because the firm has been forced to lower prices in the very competitive personal computer market.

Each sales representative has a geographically defined sales territory. Management originally designed these in 1975 and made an attempt to make the territories of roughly equal sales potential, taking into account competition and travel distances in each geographical area. The territory boundaries have not changed since 1975. Al's territory consists of southern Florida and includes the Miami metropolitan area, Fort Lauderdale, Palm Beach, Fort Myers, Hardee, and the Tampa metropolitan area.

For many years Intertech carried only mainframe computers, then in 1978 it branched out into personal computers. It sells the mainframes to businesses, governmental units, and nonprofit organizations, while marketing personal computers to small businesses, some nonprofit organizations, and to consumers through department stores. At present, approximately 60 percent of the company's revenue comes from the sale of personal computers. Management expects this pattern to remain stable for the forseeable future.

Last year, Tracy Loche, Intertech's sales manager, and an assistant conducted an analysis of the sales territories. They found that the potential of some had grown substantially since 1975, while others had remained about the same or had actually declined. Al London's territory was one of those which had grown considerably. It was approximately 80 percent larger than the company average in sales potential and was four times larger than several of the mountain states territories.

When Al was assigned to the territory its potential was about equal to the company average. Over the years he has worked very diligently, making large numbers of calls and constantly striving to serve his prospects effectively. He has developed skills in making sales presentations that are virtually without peer in the company. Further, he has been a very loyal employee, resisting efforts by competitors to lure him to their companies. Al's selling techniques are so excellent that management frequently asks him to act as a trainer for new members of the sales force and for older members who have gone stale. He has been willing to act as a trainer, despite the fact that this takes him away from the field and the opportunity to earn commissions during the training periods.

Over the past two years, Al's sales calls have declined in number. Currently they are only three-fourths of what they were in 1982. The sales manager suspects that he is slacking off a bit, perhaps believing that he has made a substantial contribution to the company and deserves an easier work regimen during his last few years before retirement. Most of Al's current orders are coming from large older customers; he is not spending much time developing new accounts or servicing smaller ones. When the sales manager told him that he should do more prospecting, Al chuckled and said "I did a lot of that way before you were even with the company." Loche is considering splitting up Al's territory. A new sales representative could handle one of the new smaller territories and Al the other. This, he believes, would allow the firm to further penetrate into the southern Florida market. Company sales there are just not growing as fast as the sales manager believes that they might. On the other hand, splitting the territory would probably seriously offend Al, who views the territory as his personal property since he has built it up to a very large revenue producer. Al might retire, go to work for another company, spread ill-will throughout the sales force, or simply cut back in his selling efforts. Further, Loche believes that he has an ethical obligation to promote Al's interests. This man has done so much for the company, and he has unselfishly strived to promote its interests. Surely, this should be taken into account in any decision making.

QUESTIONS

1. Does the sales manager have an ethical obligation to Al?
2. What can Tracy Loche do to increase sales in Al's territory?
3. What can management do to prevent future similar problems?

Chapter 18

L. L. Bean, Inc.

"Whoever's at the head of the L. L. Bean Company," began the letter sent by a Virginia doctor, "I feel that I must write you a love letter, because it's a joy just to know that an organization like yours still exists . . . you act as though you like your customers."

"That's what we like to hear," said Leon A. Gorman, president of Bean. "No amount of progress will displace the way our company feels like a little country store to our customers," he added.

While Bean may have felt like a little country store to shoppers, it certainly did not appear so to industry observers in 1982. Located in Freeport, Maine, the catalog retailer grew from its humble beginnings in the basement of a haberdashery shop to handling nearly 2,000 items and generating $150 million in sales. The focus always has been on quality basics and service, according to Gorman. The company's customer base was spread across the U.S. and foreign countries, but all shared a taste for Bean basics: classic shirts, pants, and shirts in Oxford cloth, chamois, flannel, denim and corduroy, thick sweaters, sturdy footware, and assorted outdoor equipment. Members of the company staff test most of its items and they had to live up to very high expectations.

The company also held fast to a liberal service policy that began in the early 1900s with Leon L. Bean, the company's founder. Mr. Bean invented the idea of bonding leather to rubber and created the first Maine hunting shoes. A total of 90 of his first 100-pair shipment came back because of quality problems. He borrowed $400, corrected the problems, and launched the company on a prosperous voyage that has lasted ever since. Besides a liberal return policy, the company even provides free button replacements for company shirts regardless of how long ago a customer purchased them. The company will even custom-make shoes in unusual sizes for customers so that they can get a proper fit.

Mr. Gorman, grandson of the company's founder, took over as president in the mid-1960s. At the time, company sales had leveled at around $2 million per year. Assuming the presidency provided him the opportunity to make several needed changes and lead the company to dramatic growth. The company converted its mailing list to a computerized application from a hand-typed one, it computerized order entry and inventory management systems, it added credit card service (now about 50 percent of sales), it promoted telephone ordering (now about 25 percent of sales), and it greatly expanded the acquisition and maintenance of mailing lists. By 1980, Bean rented nearly 5 million outside names and maintained its own list of 2.2 million names. Customers, nearly a 50–50 mix of men and women, are mostly upscale and outdoors-oriented.

Names on mailing lists, to whom Bean sends fliers and catalogs, represent the mainstay of the company's marketing effort. The company has avoided the use of TV and newspaper advertising, however. Only recently have officials begun considering the use of toll-free 800 telephone numbers. Management has been reluctant to use any marketing technique that would cause customers to feel that L. L. Bean had lost its country store image.

QUESTIONS

1. What are the major factors accounting for the success of L. L. Bean, Inc.?
2. What steps should management undertake in order to achieve further success?

The East-Side Shelter

The East-Side Shelter is a nonprofit organization that provides temporary housing, food, and counseling advice for homeless itinerants. It is located in a low-income inner-city section of Los Angeles. The shelter has been in operation for over 15 years.

A full-time manager, Harold Holmes, administers East-Side. It has eleven full-time and four part-time employees and several dozen individuals who provide part-time services on a volunteer noncompensated basis. The "clients" or "customers" are individuals, mostly men, who lack housing, food, and often medical care. Some are alcoholics and drug addicts, while others are unemployed persons seeking jobs in the city or on their way to finding jobs elsewhere. During the late 1970s and early 1980s the center operated at full capacity (all 64 beds were continually full and the cafeteria served as many people as resources would allow) primarily due to the recession that affected the city, region, and the country as a whole.

The center engages in limited promotional efforts. Its main tool is word-of-mouth, as those who have utilized its services inform others of their availability. Sometimes police and social workers inform indigents about the facility. In addition, city bus benches contain short messages announcing the existence of the center and its location. Because of the already large demand for its services, the manager does not feel that the center requires substantial promotion efforts. Holmes has indicated that "the truly needy will expend considerable time and energy locating our facilities."

The center provides counseling services for those who request such assistance. One full-time employee is qualified to provide informed advice on alcoholism and drug addiction. Other counselors are part-time volunteers from local hospitals, Alcoholics Anonymous, a psychological counseling center, and two local colleges. The center also furnishes job placement advice, in this case through several center employees and part-time volunteers from local businesses and one college. Limited medical advice is available from one full-time nurse and several volunteers.

East-Side provides all of the services entirely free of charge to clients. The only "price" that center users pay is the time and effort spent waiting in line for the unit to open each day. Crowding is a continual problem, as the demand for services always exceeds the supply.

Fundraising is an all-important activity for East-Side. Some federal grant monies are available, but those are limited. The manager and his employees must engage in what amounts to personal selling and advertising to raise money. Personal selling takes place through presentations by the manager to the city council and various civic organizations in the metropolitan area. The city provides about one-half of the budget of the center. Civic organizations furnish about a sixth. Most of the remainder comes from a direct mail campaign.

Mr. Holmes conducts a direct mail campaign each fall to raise funds. Each target audience member receives a letter and a brochure describing center services, the need for these services, and requesting a contribution from the individual. The mailing list includes all of those who have made a contribution in the past, members of the chamber of commerce, and members of two local college alumni associations who live in the metropolitan area or in nearby towns. The letter also includes a self-addressed postage-paid return letter which contributors can mail, with their check or money enclosed, to the center. East-Side is incorporated as a nonprofit corporation and contributors can deduct their donations from income taxes on both the federal and state levels.

Mr. Holmes designed the brochure and letter. He has had no other experience in developing such creations. The quality of the paper is inexpensive and the brochure is mimeographed at the center. The manager realizes that the resulting mailing package is not impressive, but funds do not permit a more professional presentation.

Holmes has read about the success of many businesses and nonprofit organizations in using similar campaigns. He wonders how his direct mail campaign might be changed in order to make it more successful. In addition, he has thought about utilizing radio, television, and telephone selling. Perhaps the center might even employ magazines and newspapers to raise funds. To date, however, he has not gone beyond the direct mail method.

QUESTIONS

1. What changes, if any, do you think that Mr. Holmes should make in the center's direct mail campaign?
2. Should he consider using other media than direct mail? Which? Why?

Chapter 19

Original Appalachian Artworks, Inc.

"I'm not ready to retire," says Xavier Roberts, founder of Original Appalachian Artworks and a 30-year-old multimillionaire. "Besides, I have a dream—a theme park, a stable of enduring characters and possibly a TV series."

To many, Roberts' visions are more than empty promises. As creator of the Cabbage Patch Kids, those soft, homely dolls that caused stampedes in toy stores during the 1983 Christmas shopping season, Roberts made an indelible mark in the world of children unseen for decades. "I want to be the next Walt Disney," says the self-confident Georgian.

In February 1986, the privately held firm, Original Appalachian Artworks, added four new Furskins teddy bears to the four it introduced in 1985. The freckled bears have names like Boone and Dudley, wear work boots and overalls, and run a general store in mythical Moody Hollow, Georgia. Although sales have been mostly in specialty shops, Roberts sold about 1 million of the $55 bears in 1985. In March 1986, the company contracted with Coleco Industries, Inc., which handles Cabbage Patch, to manufacture, distribute, and market Furskins. Says Roberts, "I see the Cabbage Patch Kids as Mickey Mouse and the Furskins as Donald Duck."

His other dreams are no mere fantasies, either. Roberts has been in an on-again, off-again process of negotiating with ABC Television for a Cabbage Patch cartoon series. And there are plans underway for a multimillion dollar hotel complex in Cleveland, Georgia—Roberts home town, which is 60 miles north of Atlanta.

Initially, the complex will accommodate visitors to Babyland General Hospital, where Cabbage Patch dolls are "born" and "adopted" by buyers. The Spanish-style resort, scheduled to open during the summer of 1986, will spread over 20 of the 500 acres Roberts owns. On the remaining property, there are plans underway to develop an amusement park—another parallel with Disney.

Despite the grand ambitions, Appalachian Artworks faces considerable challenge from the competition. Furskins are the traditional teddy bears—soft and cuddly. High-tech features are used in the competitive versions. Worlds of Wonder, Inc., which introduced the highly successful Teddy Ruxpin storytelling bear in September 1985, has begun to give voices to Snoopy, Charlie Brown, and Mother Goose. Axlon Inc., formed by Atari founder Nolan K. Bushnell, has teamed up with Mattel, Inc. to introduce other talking stuffed animals.

Also, sales of Cabbage Patch Dolls have been slipping. A 25 percent decline in sales were predicted in 1986 by several industry analysts. Original Appalachian—86 percent owned by Roberts—earned about $50 million in royalties from Coleco since the licensing agreement began in 1983. In 1985, Coleco's revenues reached $1.5 billion from Cabbage Patch products.

If there are setbacks ahead for Appalachian, Roberts is too busy to think about them. To respark interest in Cabbage Patch dolls, he plans to introduce Bunny Bee—

who will "pollinate" the mythical Cabbage Patch baby garden—in time for the 1986 Christmas season, and he has begun work on a $25 million Cabbage Patch movie, a project that he plans to personally finance.

QUESTIONS

1. What do you think of the marketing strategies used by Original Appalachian?
2. What pricing strategy should the firm use in setting rates for the hotel complex being planned? Why?
3. What other important issues should Mr. Roberts consider?

Switzer Manufacturing, Inc.

Switzer Manufacturing, Inc., of Crystal Lake, Illinois, is a manufacturer of molded plastic products. The company's founder and president, Tom Jarrell, always has had an interest in motorboat racing and, consequently, Switzer has devoted nearly 25 percent of its capacity to designing and building custom-made high-performance raceboats. Three-quarters of the company's $18.3 million sales come from the manufacture of industrial plastics. The company's boat business was derived from the word-of-mouth reputation that Switzer boats had developed among drivers of high-performance boats on the racing circuit.

Under the direction of Jarrell, Switzer's designers developed a highly efficient hull design for pleasure boats that also allowed high-speed performance. This boat was initially designed for Mr. Jarrell's personal use, but it performed so nicely that the president thought Switzer should enter the pleasure boat market.

The design, called the X–17, would compete with other high-performance pleasure boats in the 30-foot class. The dominant competitors in this market were the boats made by Wellcraft, Cigarette, Donzi, and some of the boats in the Chris Craft line. All of these were pleasurized versions of offshore racing boats with some amenities added for living aboard. The added features plus safety devices made them unsuitable for racing, but they retained high-performance characteristics.

Nationally, there were 876 of these boats sold in 1985, with Wellcraft capturing 61 percent of the market, Cigarette 14 percent, Donzi 10 percent, Chris Craft 9 percent, and the rest being divided among six other companies. The retail prices of these boats ranged between $47,000 and $89,000, plus extra for marine options such as radios and depth finders (electronic devices to tell the water's depth).

The X–17 was considered superior to the competition by company experts. Its top-end speed was 76 mph, compared to about 68 mph for the competitors. Further, because of a patented hull design, the boat could cruise at a fuel consumption rate of 22 gallons per hour, or about a 5 percent improvement over the competition. The primary disadvantage, though, was that the X–17 had a smaller cabin space—about 10 percent smaller. Mr. Jarrell did not feel that this would be a major detriment, however, as all boats in this class had cramped quarters.

Cabins were used primarily for single-tiered bunks, a small galley, and limited head (bathroom) facilities. Because of limited headroom, such boats required all but small children to sit or stoop while moving about the cabins. People spent most of their time in the aft-decks, which were open.

Switzer had already spent $1.3 million in developing the design for the X–17 and another $200,000 for the fiberglass molds, which can be used over and over in the future. Jarrell was anxious to recover these costs. The following additional costs for producing the X–17 were estimated by management.

Manufacturing	
Materials, per unit	$23,725.00
Direct labor, per unit	12,450.00
Allocated overhead, per unit (assuming a 50-unit volume)	8,000.00
Selling and Administrative Costs (Annual)	
Advertising	$325,000.00
Trade shows and other promotional expenses	175,000.00
Other selling expenses	125,000.00
Depreciation	240,000.00

Additionally, an investment of $1.2 million would be required for facility redesign for the X–17s, which is expected to have a five-year life. Switzer would sell through retailers, who traditionally charge a 30 percent markup.

QUESTIONS

1. Assume that the company's policy is to earn a 20 percent return on investment on all projects. What price should it charge for the new boat?
2. What price should it charge to attain a three-year payback?
3. What other important issues should be considered in pricing the X–17?

Chapter 20

Superior Marketing Research, Inc.

Superior Marketing Research, Inc., a Salt Lake City, Utah concern, was about to begin test marketing its new product in the summer of 1986. The product, a can for beverages, was unique. Its design allowed the container's contents to be cooled without refrigeration.

"The principle behind the idea is simple," says Douglas Brown, Superior's 29-year-old president. "When a compressed gas expands, its temperature falls." Inside each can is a metal capsule filled with carbon dioxide under high pressure. A valve outside the can controls the gas, and when opened, the escaping volume cools the container's substance.

Alcoa tinkered with a self-cooling can in the mid-1960s, but abandoned the project because it was unable to keep the costs low enough to make the process economical. Management of Superior feels that it has overcome the cost obstacle by perfecting a way to inject the gas quickly and then vent it slowly so that the gas chills the contents, not just the air outside the can. The carbon dioxide chills the contents by about 30°F. Thus, on an 80°F degree day, and assuming that the contents are at that temperature, the can will chill the product to about 50°F—in about a minute and a half. Depending upon their settings, most home refrigerators operate in the range of 38°F to 48°F. Rights to the initial process were acquired by Superior from two inventors in Little Rock, Arkansas and Hamilton, Alabama.

Laser Arms, a New York City firm, also claims to be in the process of introducing a similar self-cooling can designed by another inventor, but Mr. Brown is doubtful that the claims are valid. "They have not been able to demonstrate a workable product to the public," he stated.

Beverages have come in cans for over 50 years but in all that time, the only major improvement was the pop-top opener introduced in 1962. The self-chilling can could represent a major improvement in the industry. "Replacing beer coolers and emptying acres of shelves in refrigerators . . . is the next logical step in the soft drink and beer wars," says Jesse Meyers, publisher of *Beverage Digest*, a leading industry newsletter.

The container costs Superior more to make than a regular one. When produced in volume, it is anticipated that it will add from 4¢ to 6¢ to the 8¢ cost of a normal pop-top can. But there may be some problems ahead. Making the cans may be easier than selling the idea to soft drink and beer companies. "The beverage companies don't necessarily like us, because we represent change," says Brown. Several of the bottlers think that the idea could fizzle. "The concept might be worth something, but making it practical is another thing," says Jimmy Lee III, president of Buffalo Rock Co. of Birmingham, Alabama, the Pepsi Bottling company that invented the three-liter plastic bottle. "I'd say they've got their work cut out for them. It's not just like moving a product in a bigger package," he added.

Although it is no certain indicator of what is to come, the test marketing plans look promising. In April 1986, Brown was in the final stages of negotiating agreements to test market Superior self-cooling cans with PepsiCo, a Coca-Cola bottler, and two of the top five U.S. brewing companies. "Needless to say, we are incredibly excited about the prospects," said Brown. "The container market for beverages is immense."

QUESTIONS

1. What pricing strategy should Superior use for its new container? Why?
2. What else can Superior do in attempting to market its container?
3. How do you assess Superior's chances for success?

Wechsler Industries, Inc.

In early 1986, Robert Washington, president of Taylor, Michigan-based Wechsler Industries, Inc., faced a big decision for the firm: whether or not to set out in a new direction. Wechsler has been a successful, privately held firm specializing in producing laundry detergents for private labels (a store's own brand, such as Lady Lee) marketed by several supermarket chains, including Kroger, Jewel, Eagle, Dominick's, and Chatham (all based in the Midwest). Sales have been acceptable for the past several years, but management has been concerned about the future.

The bulk of the laundry detergent market is dominated by national brands and heavy advertising. Procter & Gamble leads the list with eight top-selling brands, including Tide, the industry's leader. Other strong competitors included Colgate (seven leading brands) and General Foods (four strong market entries). In total, the leading brands account for 86 percent of the total industry's sales. Advertising budgets also are very large for the national brands, with budgets ranging from $10 million to $65 million for each brand. Advertising expenditures are highly correlated with each brand's market share, although there were a few exceptions. For example, Arm & Hammer has been able to etch out a 3.5 percent share of the market with very little advertising, relying instead on the company's good name and word-of-mouth advertising.

All of the competitors in the industry use a similar pricing structure. Typically, a 20-oz. box of a national brand of laundry detergent sells in the $1.29 to $1.39 range at retail. Retailers typically pay 98¢ for the product. Private labels usually retail in the $1.09 to $1.19 range per 20-oz. box of detergent, and cost the retailers 65¢ a box to acquire. While nearly 85 percent of the average chain store's shelf space is allocated to the national brands, about 10 percent is available for private labels. The remaining shelf space is used for generics and for some specialty products. Independent grocers usually handle only nationally branded detergents.

Wechsler has been quite successful in penetrating the private label business, attaining nearly a 50 percent share of this business in the Midwest. But management was concerned by the fact that sales in the private label business have been flat compared with national brands, which have grown at about 1.5 percent per year over the past three years.

Management has considered three options. First, Wechsler could continue on its current course of action by supplying chains with detergents for private labels and seek some other alternative to fill its excess plant capacity.

Second, it could attempt to market its own national brand. This would be quite costly for several reasons. For one, a sales force would need to be developed to call on retailers. For another, advertising would be required. Because Wechsler is a small firm, especially compared to giants such as Procter & Gamble, management is particularly concerned about this alternative. The very maximum that the firm could possibly allocate to an advertising budget is $1.5 million for 1987.

Finally, Wechsler could try to develop an "in-between" brand: one that had a common label, was sold through several stores (especially independents), but was not heavily advertised. The label would feature the product's phosphate-free contents, which would possibly appeal to people concerned about environmental pollution issues. In total, phosphate-free detergents currently capture about 4.5 percent of the market. The company's promotional message involving its pollution-free contents would be printed on the package and feature the theme "Just as good as the promotional brands." The product would probably sell in the $1.19 to $1.29 range. Wechsler's direct cost for producing the product in volume is estimated at 39¢ for a 20-oz. box.

Washington has held several meetings with food brokers who are very interested in trying to sell the "in-between" product. Brokers are not used by the major detergent manufacturers, as these companies use their own sales forces to call on retailers. The brokers see this new product as a chance to break into the detergent business. Brokers charge a 5 percent commission for their services.

Washington was also convinced that Wechsler would have to spend about $300,000 in promoting the "in-between" product, though not in consumer advertising. The money would be needed to support booths at trade shows, for public relations activities, and for some advertising in trade publications such as *Progressive Grocer*.

QUESTIONS

1. What should Wechsler do?
2. How should Wechsler price its "in-between" product if management selects this alternative? Support your answer.
3. What other marketing issues should management consider?

Chapter 21
General Motors Corp.

"There's going to be a big change in our systems and management style," said GM Chairman Roger B. Smith to the press January 10, 1984. "We're determined to become less bureaucratic and more team-oriented," he added.

GM had operated five automotive divisions since 1916—Chevrolet, Pontiac, Oldsmobile, Buick, and Cadillac. In the 1920s, Alfred P. Sloan, Jr., GM's chairman, was the pioneer of the organizational notion to centralize planning and decentralize operations. Under Sloan's philosophy, divisions were relatively free to make major decisions, including those relating to body styles, and until the 1960s the operation worked rather smoothly, with GM becoming the biggest corporation in the world.

But operations became confused in the 1960s, according to many industry analysts. The number of automobile lines GM produced began to proliferate. By the early 1980s, the number had swollen to 34 lines, compared to five—one for each division—in the 1950s. In order to simplify the resulting enormous engineering job and to reduce costs, the company parceled out tasks across its divisions. To illustrate, Pontiac specialized in rear suspensions while Buick engineered brakes. GM assembly, instead of the divisions, became responsible for assembly operations. Finally, Fisher Body focused on engineering car bodies and making body panels.

The proliferation of responsibility accelerated in the 1970s, when the company began its all-out effort to down-size its vehicles for better gas mileage. GM's approach was to set up "project centers" aimed at coordinating all product development. However, the firm did not control costs very well. No single manager or group had power over all aspects of a project.

Industry analysts contended that GM's sluggishness became obvious. Locking X-car brakes, faulty diesel engines, and lengthy delays in introducing front-wheel drive replacements for full-sized cars embarrassed management. Worse, the company's five car divisions became inundated with lookalike models that confused customers and contributed to declines in market share. According to one analyst, GM "lost the marketing advantage of differentiation without control over product costs."

Management designed the reorganization plan—expected to take about a year to implement—to overcome these problems. The restructuring was to involve many of the company's operations. Under the plan, the company would continue to market autos through the same five car divisions, Chevrolet, Pontiac, Oldsmobile, Buick, and Cadillac, but two new units would develop new models for the divisions. The Chevrolet-Pontiac-GM Canada Group would engineer and build small cars, while the Buick-Oldsmobile-Cadillac Group would develop intermediate and large cars. While the car divisions would exist in the future, they would primarily be marketing arms of the two car groups.

Each group received the responsibility for engineering, manufacturing, and marketing its own cars and would develop its own engineering staff and production facilities from the pool of people, plants, and equipment within the company. In addition to helping to control costs, the reorganization was designed to assist the company in introducing new models on time, boost quality control to enable more effective competition with foreign companies, and enable GM divisions to develop more distinctive models instead of the current lookalikes.

QUESTIONS

1. Describe GM's new organization structure. What are its strengths? Weaknesses?
2. What marketing role does each of the five old divisions play under GM's new structure? The new product groups?
3. What problems do you see ahead for GM's structure?

Consolidated Foods Corp.

In 1981, Consolidated Foods earned $117 million on $6 billion of sales, which represented respective growths of 11 percent and 13 percent over the previous year. The Chicago-based diversified food company's 18 percent return on equity was the best of the major firms in the industry, which averaged 13 percent.

While Consolidated Foods was not exactly a household word, many of its brands were. Sara Lee, Shasta soft drinks, Hanes and L'Eggs hosiery, Bali bras, and Booth Fisheries were among the many well-known brands of Consolidated. The company had recently divested itself of several other divisions, however, such as L'erin cosmetics. Consolidated acquired many of these divisions during a rapid acquisition phase that did not work out as well as management had anticipated. Instead of growth through acquisition, the company's present thrust is to grow by emphasizing its main lines and through new product development.

Joseph Haroldson, Consolidated's new products manager, has just received test results for Italianos, a potential new entry in the frozen pizza market. The firm selected six test markets (Sacramento, Colorado Springs, Spokane, Peoria, Richmond, and Austin) to be representative of the national market. During the nine-month period, market shares for Italianos rose steadily up to the following levels in each of the test cities:

City	*Population*	*Final Month Unit Sales of Italianos*	*Share (%)*
Sacramento	783,381	2,595	9.2
Colorado Springs	215,150	890	11.3
Spokane, WA	341,835	903	7.4
Peoria, IL	124,160	407	8.7
Richmond, VA	219,214	843	10.5
Austin, TX	177,260	705	10.9
Totals	1,861,000	6,343	9.6

The company set the price of Italianos at $2.25 wholesale. With customary markups by retailers, therefore, consumers paid an average of $2.85. The total national market for frozen pizzas was 100,000,000 units annually, and was growing at nearly 7 percent a year. Fixed costs for producing Italianos nationally would be $2.5 million, and variable costs were estimated to be $0.88 per unit. A national advertising program would cost an estimated $2.25 mijllion if the firm ran it at the same level as in the test cities during the test market period. Haroldson estimated that the total investment required to produce Italianos on a national scale would be $6.5 million in plant and equipment. With Consolidated management's goal of a 25 percent return on all projects, Haroldson believed that Italianos could represent a golden opportunity for the company.

QUESTIONS

1. Does Italianos appear to be a desirable opportunity to pursue for Consolidated?
2. How should Haroldson set the budget for the proposed project?

Chapter 22
AT&T and Olivetti

A major link between U.S.-based American Telephone & Telegraph and Italy's Olivetti, announced in late 1983, posed a major threat to IBM both at home and abroad in the multibillion dollar market for the "office of the future." The move was AT&T's second merger, and perhaps most significant one since the divestiture of its telephone operating companies was announced in 1982. The first was a joint venture with the

Dutch electronics giant Philips to develop and market computerized central office switching systems. The new venture with Olivetti did not appear to be associated with the first because it focused on office automation and small private branch exchanges (PBXs).

The alliance between the two companies was a strategic and technological linkage. AT&T spent $260 billion to acquire 25 percent of Olivetti, Europe's number two information processing company (second to IBM). The investment enabled AT&T to offer a complete line of integrated office products without spending years and untold millions of dollars to develop them. Equally important, the link offered AT&T the opportunity to gain a foothold in foreign markets, which the company all but ignored when it was involved in the telephone business exclusively.

Olivetti's chairman and CEO, Carlo De Benedetti, had the image of a marketing giant and strong manager. He had turned Olivetti from a money loser into the largest information processing firm in Europe after IBM. In 1983, the company earned $80 million on worldwide sales of $2.25 billion. Beside European marketing strength, Olivetti has strong design capabilities in data processing and in other office products.

The strength of the partnership between the firms, according to many industry specialists, was the potential link between telecommunications technology and office products. "If AT&T links its telecommunications switches with Olivetti terminals," said one expert, "they can immediately begin selling the office systems concept. And IBM couldn't respond immediately."

While IBM held an unquestioned strength in the design and marketing of computers, it had not yet developed a position in telecommunications. However, the computer giant did not ignore the huge market. IBM had announced a joint venture with Rolm Corp. a year earlier to develop an advanced telephone switch.

Within the first year, AT&T expected to import $250 million in advanced work stations from Olivetti. Olivetti, in turn, would import and market a family of minicomputers that AT&T introduced in mid-1984. Later, in 1985, Olivetti anticipated selling AT&T PBXs in Europe when its contract with Northern Telecom Ltd. expired.

The two companies faced considerable competition, however. In the U.S., IBM and Wang Laboratories were moving ahead to develop a full range of office products. And in Europe, the companies faced IBM, ITT, Nixdorf Computer, Siemens, and CIT-Alcatel. In addition, they had to win approval of nationalistic government authorities for their telecommunications equipment.

QUESTIONS

1. What are the strengths of the link between AT&T and Olivetti? The weaknesses?
2. With all of its financial strength, why would AT&T associate itself with Olivetti instead of developing office products itself?
3. Assess the future of the joint venture.

The Wuxi Project

For many years, the United States government prohibited the exportation of certain technology to China. The result of one such ban led to a lack of equipment necessary for building China's microchip industry.

In 1983, however, the Reagan Administration opened up the way for China to purchase sensitive semiconductor equipment and related technology. The decision enables China to build a microchip industry and gives the country favored export status that is normally reserved for U.S. allies. The Wuxi Project, as it is known, opens the way for other high-tech exports.

On July 30, 1983, the countries worked out a bilateral agreement that allowed significant increases of Chinese textile exports into the U.S. The semiconductor agreements were meant to help build U.S.-China relations. Although China had favored diplomatic status under the Carter Administration, Reagan aides had been reluctant to grant the Chinese the same privileges.

China has benefited in part from U.S. farm belt politics. It signed an agreement only a few days before the textile pact raising the Soviet Union's grain purchases by 50 percent for five years. The Chinese and the Soviets had been withholding purchases of U.S. farm products to pressure the Reagan Administration into concessions. Prior to the textile agreement the U.S. got into trouble by attempting to limit China's textile imports to the levels granted other Asian countries. China's response to this policy cost the U.S. an estimated 4 million metric tons of wheat revenue, as well as sales of cotton, soybeans, and synthetic fibers.

U.S./Chinese trade in the textile and agriculture industries will increase significantly. High-tech exports by American firms are small in comparison, but have great growth potential. Also in the works, and possible only after the semiconductor decision, are talks about weapon sales.

The new agreement changes some of the rules for high-technology exports to China. The U.S. government has categorized a wide range of equipment as unrestricted or "general" for the first time. The agreement also details exactly what technologies firms can sell to China.

New rules governing the Defense Department have also helped pave the way for this agreement. Even though the semiconductors will help China militarily, the new rules disallow the Defense Department from barring sales without explaining why. In all probability, however, China will pose little threat to the fast-changing microchip industry. "National security" was, in the past, a sufficient reason to ban sales of sensitive goods.

Various companies have made other high-technology deals that are awaiting approval by the government. In July, 1983, International Telephone and Telegraph Corp. signed a $1 billion contract to sell the technology and a production line necessary for the manufacture of integrated circuits in China. Semiconductor inspection equipment for wafer-processing is awaiting approval.

The potential market in China for U.S. electronics, particularly manufacturing equipment for large-scale integrated circuits, is vast, and new trading rules have made it happen.

QUESTIONS

1. What tradeoffs are involved in the selling of high-technology capabilities to China?
2. How can U.S. manufacturers influence and prepare for international opportunities?
3. Do you think that it is right to sell equipment that will enhance the military capability of China? of Russia?

Chapter 23
Macklin's Furniture

Macklin's Furniture is a retail store that sells a broad line of household and outdoor furniture. The organization has been in business since 1954 when the owner, Fran Macklin, put together personal savings, loans from relatives, and a bank loan to start the business. Today it grosses about $2,950,000 annually and brings the owner a personal income of $80,000 in a typical year. This business is organized as a proprietorship.

Macklin's stocks a variety of merchandise. Some is top-quality brand name furniture that is in excellent condition. Other items, however, are unbranded or carry brand names that most consumers are not familiar with. Sometimes Fran locates a hotel or motel that is going out of business and purchases large volumes of furniture at a low price, which can be transported to Macklin's, cleaned and reconditioned, and sold as used furniture.

The store is situated in an older portion of the city, just two blocks from the railroad depot. Located on a major traffic artery, its imposing sign attracts many of those who are driving by. The building's interior and exterior are somewhat old but have been well maintained. Within the store, merchandise is arranged according to its function: bedroom furniture is in one section, living room furniture is in another section, etc. The store is carpeted, well lighted, and has a pleasing atmosphere.

Fran uses an interesting pricing policy. Most merchandise, except that which is priced at a low level for promotion purposes, receives a markup of 95 percent, resulting in very high posted retail prices. Sales representatives, however, are allowed to lower the list price to customers by as much as 50 percent. Thus, a sales representative may say (for a kitchen dinette that is priced at $400), "I can give you a special deal if you take that unit home today. You can have it for $200." Approximately 90 percent of the firm's sales are on items that have been "discounted" in this manner.

The store features some products in newspaper advertisements at very low prices. The intention is to lure customers into the store, where they may purchase other products. Fran is careful not to have too many of these items in stock, however, as the store actually suffers on each one sold. In a recent sale, for example, end tables were offered at "a steal—only $19.95." However, only 15 of the tables were in stock and these sold shortly after the store opened on the day of the sale.

Fran is a heavy user of newspaper advertising. He devotes approximately $50,000 annually to this purpose. The ads all feature low prices and make heavy use of terms such as "bargain," "inexpensive," "discount," "special," and "savings." The normal practice is to take out full-page ads, normally on Friday to attract weekend shoppers.

On three occasions during the past ten years Fran has held "going out of business" sales. Large newspaper ads have announced that Macklin's is going out of business and is holding a sale where it will sell merchandise at very low prices. These sales attract large numbers of customers and generate high revenues. After the sale, Fran shuts down the store for several weeks and then reopens under another store name. Fran is aware that he should not use this technique too often, as it could seriously alienate customers and lead to retaliation by competitors. So far, however, these problems have not materialized.

Macklin's sales representatives are well trained in hard-sell techniques—they place considerable pressure on customers to buy items "while they are available," "before prices go up," or "while I'm still able to give you this discount." Fran pays them commissions that encourage them to exert pressure on shoppers whenever possible. The sales representatives are able to earn very attractive incomes from their employment at the store.

QUESTIONS

1. Evaluate Macklin's marketing strategies from an ethical and social responsibility perspective.

2. Would your response to Question 1 change if you learned that there were not an unusually large number of complaints by customers about the store's practices?

Midtown Itinerant Center

The Midtown Itinerant Center (MIC) provides basic short-term room and board for those who are unable to pay for these basic needs. The center is owned and operated by a nonprofit organization that is devoted to aiding the needy. In addition to room and board MIC furnishes limited medical help and some counseling services. It has been able to secure employment for a small percentage of its boarders.

The center is located in one of the low-income areas of Seattle, Washington. It can accommodate 125 persons in beds and can feed over 300 individuals per day. MIC has 5 permanent staff members and 14 other volunteers who work when time permits. One full-time employee serves as the director.

MIC does little advertising. Most of its promotion comes from word-of-mouth from satisfied patrons. It does sponsor a limited number of advertising messages on bus stop benches and in newspapers.

The organization receives 10 percent of its funds from the federal government, 50 percent from the city, and the remainder from a number of fundraising activities. Recently, federal funding was cut by 12 percent so fundraising activities will have to increase unless the center is willing to cut the quality and quantity of its services.

The fundraising to date has involved the director calling on businesses and service clubs and asking for checks and pledges. In effect, the director has conducted sales calls. These have been reasonably effective, but he can only make a limited number of these calls in addition to his other duties. He feels that he cannot increase his selling time much beyond current levels. He has thought about direct mail brochures, radio public service messages, television, and newspaper ads. Another possibility would be to sponsor and charge fees for amateur sporting events such as marathons. However, the director is unsure of what direction to take.

QUESTIONS

1. How can marketing help MIC?
2. What fundraising techniques would you suggest for the director?

Glossary

Accessory equipment Capital items of relative low cost, such as power tools.
Accumulating Building an adequate stock of the items that an intermediary handles.
Action system The component of culture that spells out specific acts society encourages or frowns upon.
Activity reports Written reports of work undertaken by functionaries.
Administered (channel) systems Informal channel arrangements between independent members of a channel system.
Adopter categories Groupings of individuals based upon their relative time of adopting and innovation: innovators, early adopters, early majority, late majority, and laggards.
Advertising Any paid form of nonpersonal promotion of ideas, goods, or services by an identified sponsor.
Advertising agencies Specialists in preparing and placing advertisements that serve advertisers, who are their clients.
Advertising allowances Subsidies, full or partial, paid to intermediaries to reimburse them for advertising the sponsor's product.
Advertising elasticity The sensitivity of total revenue to a change in the amount of advertising expenditure.
Age of mass consumption A type of society where large numbers of consumer goods are available, incomes are high, and the middle class is large.
Aggregating data (data aggregation) Reduction of detailed data to summary measures.
AIDA model Acronym referring to Attention, Interest, Desire, and Action.
Allocating Determining what quantity of items to supply each customer.
Analysis Breaking data down into meaningful categories and studying the differences and relationships between these categories.
Analyzing market opportunity The process of evaluating a particular market's potential.
Antidumping laws Regulations that prohibit foreign firms from selling excess inventory at lower-than-normal prices.
Antimonopoly See *antitrust*.
Antitrust (antimonopoly) laws Laws to inhibit monopolizing and restraining trade.
Approved supplier lists Lists of potential suppliers used and maintained by industrial buyers.
Assorting Collecting a set of heterogeneous goods that will meet the needs of customers.
Attitude tracking Learning whether changes in attitudes are occurring among the target market.
Attitudes Emotional evaluations of beliefs, having a positive or negative affective dimension.
Audience See *receivers*.
Average costs The total costs of some product divided by the volume, in units.

Bait-and-switch Advertising a low-priced item then exerting undue pressure on customers to buy a more expensive one. This is an illegal practice.
Base-point prices Where competitors use a common scheme for charging freight from common zones.
Basing-point pricing See *base-point prices*.

Beliefs A person's set of emotionally neutral cognitions about an entity, real or imagined.
Benefit segmentation Segmentation based upon the types of benefits sought from a product.
Blitz A form of pulsing that also involves rotating the geographical areas that receive the pulses.
Brand extension A strategy of finding new uses for a product.
Brand manager Another name for a product manager.
Branding Giving a unique name to a particular product or class of products offered by a firm.
Breadth (product mix) The number of (noncompeting) product lines offered by a firm.
Break-even The point at which revenues equal costs.
Break-even analysis Determining the volume or price that will result in covering total costs.
Budget The total amount of money to be spent on an activity or activities during a period of time.
Budgeting Expressing plans in financial terms, forming the basis for control.
Bulk-break Shipping a very large quantity to gain favorable transportation rates, then breaking it down into smaller quantities to fill customer (usually retailer) orders.
Business analysis Estimating the magnitude of market opportunity for a new idea, the competitive situation, potential sales, costs, investment requirements, and rate of return.
Business climate A governmental unit's overall attitude toward business.
Buying Bringing together or assembling collections of goods and services.
Buying profiles Listings of characteristics of a firm's customers.
Bypass distribution Using a channel system configuration that differs from those of leading competitors.

Campaign A unified, planned, and organized series of promotion messages.
Cannibalization One company product that takes sales away from another, more profitable, product in a line.
Capital budgeting Budgeting for long-range plans for capital expenditures.
Captain (channel) Primary decision maker (leader) in a channel.
Carload rates Lowered transportation rates that apply to a shipment size that occupies a full railcar.
Cash cow A product with a high market share and a low market growth rate.
Cash discounts Offering of a reduction from the posted price for the rapid payment of cash.
Caveat emptor A Latin phrase meaning let the buyer beware.
Central service One that provides most of the satisfaction when a buyer makes a purchase. (A buyer acquires it for its own sake, see *services*.)
Chain stores Organizations characterized by common ownership of two or more separate units.
Channel of distribution A network of organizations that arrange for changes of title to goods as they move from manufacturer to customers.
Class rates Shipping rates for related groupings of items; high cost in comparison to exception rates.
Cognitive dissonance Lack of equilibrium between two cognitive elements, often relating to a postpurchase decision.
Cognitive processes Mental activities that are geared toward thought processes.
Commercialization The stage where a new item is actually introduced to the market.
Commission Payment, usually to sales reps, as a percentage of their sales volume.
Commodity rates Lowered shipping rates for particular commodities and points.
Common carriers Transporters that accept shipments from all customers; highly regulated.
Communication mix adoption, foreign trade Where the communication mix is altered for a foreign country.
Communications channels Means of carrying messages to receivers.
Competitive conditions Variables related to the intensity and nature of rivals' strategies and tactics (also called *competitor actions*).
Competitor actions Another term for *competitive conditions*.
Complementary products Two or more products whose use is strongly related, such as hamburgers and buns.
Components Industrial supply items that have been more processed than raw materials.
Concept testing Assessing potential buyer reactions to a new product idea beginning in the early stages of idea development.
Consumer protection legislation Laws to promote the well-being of consumers.
Consumer surplus The sum of the differences in what buyers would have been willing to pay for an item and what they finally pay.
Consumerism The demand that customers have increased rights concerning their purchases.
Consumers People, acting as individuals or groups, who buy items for personal use.
Contingency plans Plans written for unforeseen future events.
Continuous annual budget Repeatedly budgeting for one year into the future.
Contract carriers Transporters that make contracts with shippers for their services; less regulated than common carriers.
Contract manufacturing, foreign trade Where a firm retains marketing responsibility in a foreign market, but contracts with a manufacturer to produce items locally.
Contribution gap The difference between a firm's goals and the potential of a product mix toward achieving them.
Contribution margin The difference between the price of an item and its variable costs.
Control information That which permits continuous monitoring of marketing activities.

Controlled exposure A high-pressure sales technique involving placing prospects into situations where they have little choice but to give undivided attention to company-sponsored messages.
Controlling Measuring performance against goals and objectives and taking remedial action when performance is not adequate.
Convenience goods Items for which little shopping effort is spent by buyers who intend to purchase them.
Convenience store A retailer whose primary benefit offered is shopping ease.
Cooperative advertising Where two or more firms, often vertically related in a channel system, combine their advertising efforts.
Cooperatives Independent firms that consolidate their operations in one organization.
Copy An ad's pictures, words, and symbols used to present the theme.
Copyright The exclusive legal right to reproduce, publish, and sell the matter and form of a literary, musical, or artistic work.
Cost-per-thousand (CPM) Price of a single message divided by circulation size in thousands.
Cost-plus pricing Addition of a fixed fee to an item's total cost to establish a price.
CPM See *cost-per-thousand*.
Cross-elasticity The relationship of the change in price of one product to the demand effects on another product. A high cross-elasticity means that the products are highly related in this regard, and vice versa.
Culture All activities that are repeated somewhat consistently among a given population. Its three components are the normative, action, and symbolic and material products systems.

Data Pieces of information.
Decentralization Where managers formally delegate authority and responsibility to subordinate managers.
Decentralized market-based divisions Where major subunits of an organization are created to operate much like separate companies that focus on different segments or different markets entirely.
Deception Misleading customers by making false claims.
Decline (stage) Final stage of the product life cycle; marked by declining profits and sales.
Decode The receiver's transformation of messages into meaning.
Delphi technique A means of eliciting expert opinions by concealing the identity of each other's individual responses.
Demarketing Using marketing actions to deliberately restrict demand or shift demand to some other product because of shortages.
Demographic characteristics Objective and measurable characteristics of human populations, such as age, sex, race, and so forth.
Dependent variable A variable, usually one of primary research interest, whose value is presumed to be a function of specific independent variables.
Depth (product line or mix) The number of substitutes that a company offers within a line.
Derived demand Demand that is predicated upon what the customers of producers (and eventually consumers) seek for need satisfaction.
Description (buying) Ordering items on the basis of specifications, grades, or brands.
Development (new product) Engaging in concept testing, prototype construction, branding decisions, and packaging decisions.
Diffusion of innovations The time sequence by which various groups (innovators, early adopters, early majority, late majority, and laggards) in a population adopt an innovation.
Direct distribution A producer that sells its output to final customers with no intermediaries involved.
Direct investment, foreign trade Committing capital to developing company-owned foreign facilities.
Direct mail Where products are ordered through a catalog or other form of advertising media and shipped to the customer by mail.
Direct marketing The total of activities by which products and services are offered to market segments in one or more media for informational purposes or to solicit a direct response from a present or prospective customer or contributor by mail, telephone, or other access.
Diversification Entering new markets with new types of product offerings.
Diversion-in-transit A privilege granted by carriers where the point of destination is changed while the shipment is in transit.
Dog A product with a low market growth rate and a low market share.
Draw Payment to a sales rep as a loan against forthcoming commissions.
Drive to maturity (society) A type of society where a middle class exists plus a large number of foreign advisors and technicians.
Drives Mental elements that incite a person's behavioral acts.
Dual adaptation, foreign trade Where both the product and the communication mix are altered for a foreign country.
Dual distribution Marketing a product to the same or a closely related market segment through two or more competing channel structures.

Early adopters The second group of people (13.5%) of a society that adopt a new innovation.
Early majority The third group of people (34%) who adopt a new innovation.
Economic factors Variables related to the material welfare of society.
Economic man See *marginal utility model*.
Economic order quantity (EOQ) An amount calculated by formula which represents the number of units of an item that should be ordered at a time to maintain an inventory in the most economical way.

Economies of scale Reduced costs with increased volumes from being able to use larger and more efficient plants and equipment.
Elastic A condition where the demand for a product is sensitive to a price change; when a reduction in price causes total revenue to increase (or an increase in price causes total revenue to fall).
Encode The source's transformation of ideas into messages.
Environmental monitoring Keeping track of environmental forces, such as the government's monetary policies, employment levels, and growth patterns.
Equilibrium price The price where the quantity demanded of an item is equal to the quantity supplied at that price.
Ethics Standards or conduct that are moral or demonstrate personal integrity.
Evaluation of potential opportunity Financial assessment of expected revenues and costs associated with a future product or service.
Evoked set (of brands) A subset of brands within an overall set of a generic product class that buyers choose when making a related product buying decision.
Exception rates Negotiated reductions in shipping rates from class rates.
Exchange A process whereby two parties trade goods, services, or claims to goods and services (such as money) with one another for profit.
Exchange facilitators Organizations that do not take title to goods. They serve to bring about purchases by acting as a go-between among buyers and sellers.
Exchanges in a chain (chain of exchanges) An interwoven web of exchanges beginning with a set of resources and ending with the production and sale of some final good or service.
Exclusive distribution Providing channel members with exclusive rights to sell a product line in a certain territory.
Exploratory (technological) forecasting Forecasting future developments in technology by examining anticipated future production capabilities.
Exporting Selling domestically produced output abroad.
Expropriation When a government seizes an investment, with no remuneration at all.

F.O.B. (Free-on-board) The point to which the seller pays transportation costs.
Facilitation The process of finding ways to make it easy for others to adopt some behavior.
Facilitative functions Specialized activities that aid marketers in performing particular functions.
Facilitator An agent helping in the development of some activity or exchange process.
Fair trade A legally enforceable agreement that restricts an intermediary from selling an item below a certain price set by the manufacturer or agreed upon by another intermediary (also called *resale price maintenance*).
Family brands Where more than one of a firm's products have the same name.
Feedback Getting information about how messages were received by an audience.
Fiscal policy Government spending and taxing activities to buy operating items and to bring about economic stability.
Fixed costs Those costs that do not vary in total as a company's operating volume changes.
Flexible break-even pricing A combination of break-even analysis with judgment to attempt to determine an optimal price for a product.
Flights Another name for *pulsing*.
Floor planning A financial inducement to get intermediaries to maintain an adequate stock by offering free or discounted financing of the item while in inventory, usually for a limited period of time.
Forecast An estimate of the future value of some variable or the occurrence of some event.
Format Advertising layout specifications.
Franchising A form of organization where a central business organization—a franchisor—grants privileges to independently owned outlets called franchisees.
Frontal strategy Using a channel system configuration paralleling those of leading competitors.
Full-service stores Retailers offering numerous supplementary customer services and generally high margins.
Function A type of work that needs to be done.
Functional organization Where all specialists within a given function, such as sales, report to a central position.

Gap between producers and consumers (end users) A break, caused by specialization, in the linkage between buyers and sellers.
GATT (General Agreement on Tariffs and Trade) The first modern trade agreement among numerous trading nations.
Generic product A type or class of item designed to satisfy some basic need.
Geographic segmentation Subdividing the market into geographic areas and orienting a marketing mix to those potential buyers located in each area.
Goals More concretely defined, measurable statements of the company's intended position, usually with a shorter time span than objectives.
Growth (stage) Second stage of the product life cycle; marked by rapid expansion of sales and profits.

Heterogeneous Having dissimilar elements or parts. The opposite of homogeneous.
High-involvement situations A decision setting where the outcome is considered to be of great importance and there is heavy personal involvement.
High-profile strategy A strategy of high levels of promotion and high price, especially during product introduction.
Homogeneous Like in nature or kind, similar structure and composition.

Horizontal marketing system Alliances between two or more companies to jointly tap a market opportunity.
House accounts Customers that are handled by management rather than by a sales rep.
Hypothesis An operational extension of a research problem theory that can be tested and measured.

In-store retailing Where consumers visit a retailer's place of business to buy items.
Independent retailers Single operations that are not affiliated with other units in the same or similar type of business.
Independent variable A variable that presumably affects the value of a dependent variable.
Index A percentage determined by the proportion that one entity has to another entity, such as a target market characteristic in proportion to that characteristic in the overall population.
Individual brands Unique names given to individual items.
Industrial (and other producer) buyers Institutional purchasers that buy items so that they can perform their major organizational tasks.
Industry potential (forecast) Estimate of future total sales in an industry.
Inelastic A condition where the demand for a product is not very sensitive to a price change; when a reduction in price does not cause total revenue to appreciably increase (or an increase in price does not cause total revenue to decline appreciably).
Innovators The first group of people (2.5%) of a society that adopt a new innovation.
Inspection A procedure of examining each item upon delivery of a purchase.
Installations Major capital items, such as buildings.
Institutional buyers Organizational buyers (see *industrial buyers*).
Intensity (distribution) The width of a channel, referring to the scope of the market served.
Intensive distribution Making an item available at all locations where customers expect to find it.
Intermediaries Specialists who typically perform similar marketing activities for several producers or other intermediaries.
Interpretation (in research) Determining and reporting the meaning of particular research to management.
Intrapreneurship An entrepreneurial spirit within large organizations; one where individual effort is not stifled by lengthy lists of rules and procedures.
Introduction stage Initial stage of the product life cycle.
Inventory A quantity of materials, supplies, or finished units maintained on hand to smooth production levels and to enable the supply of uneven demand.
Inventory holding costs The costs associated with maintaining units in inventory.
Inventory stock-out costs The lost profit potential from lost sales due to being out of inventory of an item.

Joint decisions Buying decisions that involve two or more persons.
Joint projects, foreign trade Partnerships between domestic and foreign firms for the purpose of carrying out business operations.
Joint venturing Where two companies agree to form a legal partnership for some project.
Joint venturing, foreign trade Where an exporter and nationals in a foreign country join together in establishing a business in which they are legal partners.

Laggards The fifth and final group of people (last 16%) that adopt a new innovation.
Late majority The fourth group of people (24%) that adopt a new innovation.
Leader prices Items sold at reduced prices, but at a slight profit, to attract additional customers, who might buy other items at regular prices.
Learning An outcome of reinforcement that changes the probability that a behavior will recur the next time that the need arises.
Learning curve effect See *learning effect*.
Learning effect Reduced costs from becoming more experienced with an operation with practice.
License A permission granted by competent authority to engage in a business, occupation, or activity otherwise restricted.
Licensing Entering into an agreement with another company where it has the right to use some name, patent, technological process, or some other item of value in exchange for a fee.
Lifestyle characteristics Psychological and sociological differences in the patterns of a person's way of life.
Lifestyle Everyday behaviorally oriented facets of people's activities, as well as their feelings, attitudes, and opinions.
Lifestyle segmentation Segmentation by psychological and sociological differences in the patterns of a person's way of life (also called *psychographic segmentation*).
Limited-service stores Retailers offering very limited supplementary customer services and generally lowered margins.
Logistics See *physical distribution*.
Loss leaders Items sold below cost (resulting in a negative contribution to overhead) for the purpose of attracting additional customers to buy other items that are sold at a profit.
Low-involvement cases (situations) A decision setting where the outcome is not considered to be of great importance and there is little personal involvement.
Low-profile strategy A strategy of low promotion and low price, especially during product introduction.

Macro forecasts Forecasts of broad levels of economic activity, such as gross national product.
Macro marketing Marketing from the perspective of the overall economy. It includes the nature of marketing institutions and their interplay within a socioeconomic system.
Mailing list List containing names and addresses of individuals who are to receive direct mail.

Mailing list brokers Specialists in renting mailing lists.
Management by exception A style of management that involves focusing attention primarily on troublesome areas; the reporting of information concerning troublesome areas that interfere with the attainment of company goals.
Management contracting, foreign trade Where an exporter agrees to provide management skills to a foreign company that provides capital.
Manufacturer's sales branches Sales branches that are owned and operated by manufacturers. The Bureau of the Census reports them as wholesalers.
Margin The difference between the price and the cost of an item, or between revenues and costs.
Marginal cost The additional cost involved with producing one more unit of some item.
Marginal revenue The incremental revenue earned from selling one more unit of some item.
Marginal utility model A hypothetical consumer who chooses between alternatives in a manner that is consistent with evaluations of how the alternatives will affect the consumer's self interests (also called the *economic man model*).
Markdown The measure of a price reduction from an item's stated price.
Market development Trying to satisfy new markets with essentially the same product as is used to satisfy old markets.
Market entry Attempting to improve company performance by expanding the scope of operations through penetrating an additional market.
Market expansion Attempting to more fully penetrate an existing target, as opposed to selecting new or additional ones.
Market niche A position of market strength among one or more segments of a market.
Market potential Estimate of a total market's volume.
Market segmentation Dividing a total market into two or more groups of potential buyers so that each group reflects customers having similar needs, but so that the needs of each group differ from other groups.
Market-centered organization Where market managers are created to develop and coordinate specific marketing mixes for each of a company's products being targeted at a particular market.
Market-structured organization Structuring a marketing department around major target markets.
Marketing The process of planning and executing the conception, pricing, promotion, and distribution of ideas, goods, and services to create exchanges that satisfy individual and organizational objectives.
Marketing concept See *marketing orientation*.
Marketing information system (MIS) A formal system (usually part of a general management information system) for routinely collecting and reporting information to aid marketing decision making.
Marketing management Analysis, planning, implementation, and control of all of those business activities that are designed to facilitate desired exchanges between a firm and its selected group of customers.
Marketing mix The various marketing activities used by a given firm to serve a target market.
Marketing mix modification A strategy of locating new segments, changing the marketing mix to stimulate growth, or product modification, especially during product maturity.
Marketing orientation A firm's emphasis on attaining its objectives, usually including profit, by organizing and integrating all activities toward satisfying the needs and wants of a selected group of customers (often called the *marketing concept*).
Marketing research Systematically obtaining and analyzing information about a market, such as what buyers want, need, think, and feel.
Markon See *markup on cost*.
Markup The margin charged for an item over its cost.
Markup on cost A markup calculated with the cost of the item used as the base number (also called *markon*).
Markup on selling price A markup calculated with the price of the item used as the base number (sometimes simply called *markup*).
Markup pricing Establishing the price of an item by increasing the amount by a fixed percentage over the item's total cost.
Materials management Receiving and storing raw materials for continuous production and storing finished goods and then moving them in a way that allows efficient transportation.
Maturity (stage) Third stage of the product life cycle; marked by stagnating sales and mixed profits.
Media Communication channels (or vehicles) to use in advertising, such as television and newspapers.
Merchant wholesalers Organizations that take title to the goods they sell. They may be full-service or limited-service firms.
Merge/purge Combining two or more mailing lists and eliminating duplicated names.
Message A communication that is encoded by managers and decoded by an audience.
Metropolitan statistical areas (MSA) Integrated social and economic units having 50,000 or more inhabitants in an identifiable city or area.
Micro forecasts Forecasts of company sales, either in total or for particular categories (product groups, geographic areas, types of customers).
Micro marketing Marketing decision making within a firm.
Milking strategy A strategy of cutting all costs to the bone, including marketing.
Mission A statement that establishes the general direction a firm intends to take in the marketplace.
Model An abstraction of the phenomenon that it intends to represent.
Modified rebuy A repetitive buying situation where moderate effort is made to evaluate new supply sources.
Monetary policy Deliberate exercise of the government's power to expand or contract the money supply.
Monopolistic competition A market that is composed of many buyers and sellers who transact over a range of prices because of differentiation.
Monopoly See *pure monopoly*.
MSA See *metropolitan statistical area*.

Multiple channel system Using a separate channel in each of two or more market segments.
Multivariate analysis The study of two or more variables at a time and their interrelationships.

Nationalization When a government forcibly buys out an operation run by foreigners.
Need Physical or mental state arising within a person resulting from some felt deficiency.
Negotiated contracts (buying) Purchasing in a way so that the specifications may be changed during production, usually relating to major capital items.
Net present value analysis A method of using compound interest calculations to discount future cash flows to equal their current financial worth.
New idea generation Developing potential new product or service ideas.
New product or service idea Untested product or service concepts that may become a new offering if it appears to have the potential to fulfill company goals.
New tasks (buying) Buying situations that are original experiences.
Niche See *market niche.*
Nonprofit marketing See *not-for-profit marketing.*
Nonprofit organization A term used interchangeably with *not-for-profit organization.*
Nonstore retailing Where the seller's operation is not confined to the fixed premises normally associated with retailing (also called *direct marketing*).
Normative (technological) forecasting Forecasting future developments in technology by examining needs, under the assumption that they will trigger new developments.
Normative system The component of culture that spells out the duties, responsibilities and privileges of society membership.
Not-for-profit marketing Applying marketing concepts to not-for-profit organizations.
Not-for-profit organizations Institutions whose mission is to provide some service, but not to earn a profit.

Objective stimuli The real attributes of an object, such as a product.
Objectives Broadly defined statements of the company's intended position, usually encompassing a long-range time horizon.
Odd-number prices Setting prices to end with odd numbers, such as 99¢ and $7.95.
Oligopolistic competition A market that consists of a few sellers who are highly sensitive to each other's pricing and other marketing strategies.
Organization An administrative and functional structure of work interactions among people within an economic unit.
Organizational buyers Institutional purchasers such as businesses, government agencies, and nonprofit organizations that buy items to enable them to perform their organizational tasks.
Organizational decisions Determining the formal structure of the work interactions among people in an organization.

Patent Rights secured to the inventor of an item granting exclusive control over the item for a period of years.
Patronage motives Reasons why shoppers choose a particular retailer.
Payback period analysis A method of estimating the number of periods, usually years, that it will take to recover the investment cost of a venture.
Payback period pricing Setting a price so that it will enable the covering of all costs and capital investment within a specified time period.
Penetration pricing Establishing beginning low prices to encourage rapid adoption by the market to get average product costs down.
Perception The act of becoming aware, through the senses, of objects, qualities, and relationships existing in the environment.
Personal selling Personal communication with one or more prospective buyers for the purpose of making sales.
Personality That which establishes and maintains a consistency of attitudes and beliefs that characterize a person's unique behavioral orientations.
PERT An acronym for *Program Evaluation Review Technique,* a statistical method for evaluating and controlling projects.
Phantom freight Charging for freight that exceeds the actual transportation charge.
Phases of commitment Stages that industrial buyers go through in the purchasing process, ranging from need recognition to performance feedback and evaluation.
Physical distribution Activities involved in efficiently and effectively moving products across space and time from producers to customers.
Piggyback Truck trailers that are loaded, placed on railroad flatcars, transported, and driven to the final destination by truck (also called *trailer on flatcar* or *TOFC*).
Planning Determining the activities intended to accomplish a company's goals as well as the utilization of the funds needed to implement them.
Planning information Information used for developing marketing strategy.
Political variables Those factors created by actions of governmental authorities.
Pooling effects Synergy resulting from combining competencies.
Population The complete set of a defined group, including all members, people, or objects of that group.
Postsale activities Activities performed by a sales rep after a sale to nurture full customer satisfaction.
Posttests Assessments of how well advertising messages were received by an audience after the fact.
Pretests Assessments of whether or not intended messages will be effective.
Preconditions for takeoff (society) A type of society where science is applied in agriculture and extractive industries. Characterized

by a small percentage of wealthy landowners and a large majority of poor people.
Preemptive penetration A strategy of high levels of promotion and low price, especially during product introduction.
Premiums Items offered for free or at substantial discounts to stimulate the sale of another item.
Presale preparation Sales reps becoming familiar with the company's and its competitor's products, as well as learning about customer needs and how well they are being met.
Prestige pricing Selling premium products at high prices to engender prestige for the items.
Price discrimination Charging different prices to different buyers for items of the same kind and grade.
Price elasticity The sensitivity of total revenue to a change in price.
Pricing Setting prices high enough to cover costs and earn a profit, yet low enough to attract buyers.
Primary data Data originated for a particular study.
Primary source-generated data The primary data generated for a particular study.
Private carriers Shippers who maintain their own fleets of transportation equipment.
Problem child A product with a high market growth rate and a low market share.
Processing-in-transit The privilege of processing goods while in transit at a lower rate than if the goods were unloaded, processed, and then moved to the point of destination.
Product adaptation, foreign trade Where the product that the firm markets is altered for a foreign country.
Product development Attempting to further satisfy a current target through major modification of a total product offering.
Product invention, foreign trade Designing a new product and communication mix for a foreign country.
Product life cycle An orderly pattern over time of a product's introduction, growth, maturity, and decline in sales and profits.
Product line A group of closely related products that are offered for sale by a company.
Product manager A manager who is responsible for managing the marketing efforts for one or a group of products. (See *product-centered organization.*)
Product mix The complete set of products offered for sale by a company.
Product modification A strategy of slightly changing the product to tap new market opportunities.
Product orientation See *production orientation.*
Product portfolio The categorization, for strategic marketing purposes, of products according to current or expected market growth rate and market share.
Product positioning Placing the product uniquely, in the minds of customers, when compared to rival offerings.
Product-centered organization Where authority for a particular product is assigned to a particular manager, called a product manager or brand manager.
Production orientation A perspective holding that the key to business success lies in solving technologically related problems (also called *product orientation*).
Promoting (promotion) Communication with potential buyers about an item's existence and uses to stimulate sales.
Promotions mix The combination of promotion types used by a firm.
Prospecting Developing a list of potential customers to contact who, because of their needs and abilities, are most likely to become converted to customers.
Prototype A model of a new product, used in testing, that exhibits the features of the version that will later be produced in quantity.
Pruning The elimination of a product from the product mix.
Psychographic (factors) Another term for lifestyle variables.
Psychographic segmentation See *lifestyle segmentation.*
Public relations Function of evaluating public attitudes, identifying the policies and procedures of an individual organization with the public interest, and executing a program of action to earn public understanding and acceptance.
Publicity Nonpersonal unpaid promotion resulting from planting commercially significant news in a published medium or on radio, television, or stage.
Pulling (an item) Developing strong demand among final buyers, who exert pressure on their suppliers to stock the item.
Pulsing An advertising tactic where very large amounts of money are spent during a short time period followed by a absence of advertising (also called *flights*, or *waves*). (Also see *blitz.*)
Pure competition A market that is composed of many buyers and sellers, each of whom has no individual effect on the market, and who trade in an undifferentiated commodity.
Pure monopoly A market that is made up of only one seller.
Push money Special payments offered to intermediaries to encourage their aggressive efforts to sell a particular product.
Pushing (an item) Marketing efforts to intermediaries, who are then expected to promote the item to final customers.

Quantity discounts Offering discounts from stated prices for sizable orders.
Quota (sales) A formally expressed goal for a sales rep, stated either in dollars or in units.
Quotas (trade) Limits on the quantity or volumes of goods that can be imported into or exported from a country.

Raw materials Natural and farm products.
Receivers Members of the group that intercepts a communication message (also called *audience*).
Reciprocity Agreement to buy from a supplier if the supplier also buys some other products from the first company.
Recruiting Determining which persons to hire and convincing them to join the organization.

Recycle strategy An attempt to restimulate demand through heavy promotion.
Reference groups Groups to whom individuals refer in setting standards of proper conduct.
Reinforcement The effects of behavior on need satisfaction.
Reliability The degree to which study results are consistent with the underlying phenomena being measured; repeatability.
Reps Salespeople.
Resale price maintenance See *fair trade*.
Research information (basic) A base of information, generally secondary, that provides a springboard or starting point for marketing researchers for their studies.
Resident buyers Independent buying organizations, located in major wholesale markets, that make purchases for multiple customers—normally small retailers.
Retailers Intermediaries who receive the majority of their sales from consumers, not businesses or other organizations.
Retrenchment Withdrawing from peripheral market segments to a position where the firm has its strongest niche.
Route Sales rep's itinerary schedule for calling on customers.

Safety stock Inventory levels maintained in reserve to meet unexpected demand.
Sales analysis Periodic examination of all marketing activities for the purpose of identifying who is buying the company's products.
Sales force A company's set of salespeople.
Sales force structure Deciding how sales reps should be deployed among potential accounts.
Sales orientation An emphasis on persuading potential customers to buy the firm's products.
Sales presentation The process of delivering a sales message to a prospective customer.
Sales promotion Promotional activities other than personal selling, advertising, or publicity that stimulate customer purchasing and dealer effectiveness.
Salespeople People hired to stimulate customer sales through personal communication. Successful ones are usually problem solvers. (Also called *salesworkers, sales representatives*, and *reps*.)
Sample A subset of a population that is examined in a study and used to make inferences about the entire population.
Sampling (shipments) Inspecting a portion of a total order.
Screening Separating new ideas into those that warrant further consideration and those that deserve immediate rejection.
Secondary data Data already existing and collected for some other purpose, often by some other party.
Secondary sources (of data) Places where existing data already collected may be obtained (also see *secondary data*).
Segmetation by market attribute Placing buyers into groups based on who is attracted by the same element of a marketing mix.
Selective distribution Stocking an item in a relatively small number of outlets.
Selective penetration A strategy of low promotion and high price, especially during product introduction.
Selective perception Perception that is controlled by a person's desires and other cognitions, causing control of his or her perceptual attention and exposure to stimuli.
Self-liquidating premium A premium for which the price covers the associated variable cost of the item.
Selling intermediaries Those who engage in making actual sales, thereby linking producers and final customers.
Services Intangible goods, such as legal advice and dry cleaning.
Shipping intermediaries Those who engage in transportation.
Shopping goods Items for which buyers spend considerable amount of shopping time for purchase to allow comparisons of competing attributes, such as for refrigerators, TV sets, and furniture.
Shopping store A retailer whose primary benefit offered is a broad mix of products ideal for browsing.
SIC codes See *standard industrial classification codes*.
Skimming Establishing beginning prices at high levels, and then lowering them over time.
Social class See *social stratification*.
Social communication The advertising and promotion of social causes.
Social marketing The use of marketing principles to advance a social cause or issue.
Social orientation Striving to satisfy various publics, such as society at large, employees, and minorities, in addition to target customers.
Social responsibility A concept that suggests that businesses have the need to be concerned about the well-being of society in general when they make their decisions, not just the needs of their customers or their own profits.
Social stimuli Information a person receives from other people concerning the attributes of an object, such as a product.
Social stratification Systems whereby members of various groups are differentiated from other groups, often relating to economic position.
Societal marketing Applying marketing concepts directly to social issues and causes and not-for-profit organizations.
Societal orientation See *social orientation*.
Sorting Receiving bulk shipments from different suppliers and grouping them into bundles of related items.
Specialty goods Items that buyers insist upon by brand or type and will go to great lengths to acquire.
Specialty store A retailer whose primary benefit is a very deep mix of products within one or a few lines.
Specific market factors Unique characteristics relating to a particular market.
Specific product A subclass of a generic product with distinguishable attributes that set it apart from other items within the same generic class.
Stages of adoption Mental states that people pass through before adopting a new innovation: awareness, interest, evaluation, trial, and adoption.
Standard industrial classification (SIC) codes Means of categorizing industrial buyers by the types of products they produce.

Standardizing and grading Categorizing products according to a system of types and measures such as weights, sizes, colors, names, etc.

Star A product with a high market share and a high market growth rate.

Status quo strategy A strategy of continuing the marketing thrust as usual.

Stimuli Entities that trigger a person's mental processes.

Stock-out Lost sales because finished goods are not on hand when customers want them.

Storing (storage) Collecting a quantity of an item at various places, such as a store or warehouse.

Straight extension, foreign trade Where a company uses the same product and promotion mix in a foreign market as is used domestically.

Straight rebuy A very repetitive buying situation where a reorder is simply made to a past supplier.

Structure An entity's organizational arrangements.

Substitute products Closely related products, such as in a line, which serve as alternatives to each other.

Supplemental service That which is provided to augment the sale of some central service or a tangible good, such as gift wrapping and free delivery.

Supplies Items not part of a producer's final product but which are required for operation, such as lubricants.

Symbiotic marketing Another term for *horizontal marketing systems.*

Symbolic stimuli A person's subjective perceptions, either real or imagined, of an object's attributes, such as a product.

Symbols and material products system The component of culture involving its widely used goods, institutions, ideas, and similar entities.

Symmetry effects Synergy resulting from relationships between current activities and activities required for a proposed new venture.

Synergy A situation that exists when, because of a combination of activities, the value of the combined effort is greater than the value of the sum of the parts.

Systems approach to physical distribution Minimizing total PD costs, subject to enabling the channel system to maintain a desired level of service.

Testing (product) Assessing an actual prototype, along with its planned package and brand.

The takeoff (society) A type of society where a middle class exists plus a large number of foreign advisors and technicians.

Theme Overall information to be conveyed by advertising.

Total consumption system All buyer-related needs, not just those pertaining to physical attributes.

Total costs The combination of fixed plus variable costs.

Total product A set of specific product physical attributes, plus all other elements of the marketing mix.

Trade agreements Narrower statements than treaties, covering only economic issues; their effect is to regulate intercountry trade. Also called *trade alliances.*

Trade alliance See *trade agreements.*

Trade discounts Price allowances offered to channel members to compensate them for the activities that they perform.

Trade show Periodic meetings of an industry's members to display new product offerings and to learn trends in the business.

Trademark Legally protected words, numbers, letters, and pictorial designs relating to specific brands that are legally protected for the holder.

Trading up Developing substitute products that are more desirable and profitable than others in a line, and convincing customers that they should purchase the more profitable ones.

Traditional societies A type of society where most people exist at low levels of poverty and are illiterate.

Trailer on flatcar See *piggyback.*

Transportation management Administration of the physical movement of goods from point of origin to point of destination.

Transporting (transportation) Moving a product from one location to another, as by truck, rail, boat, or plane.

Treaties Formal statements of alliance between two or more countries.

Trials The number of repetitions involving a need and a resulting behavior response.

Truckload rates Lower transportation rates that apply to a shipment size that occupies a full truck trailer.

Two-step flow of communication The process of using formal communications techniques to influence opinion leaders who, in turn, influence others through conversations and other informal means.

Target customers See *target market.*

Target market A set of customers that the firm is attempting to satisfy (also called *target customers*).

Target-return pricing Setting a price in anticipation of earning a target rate of return on investment.

Tariffs Taxes on imports or exports.

Technological considerations Scientific advancements and their effects on markets.

Telemarketing The use of telephones for direct marketing.

Territory design The method of assigning prospects to sales representatives.

Uniform delivered prices Charging one common price to buyers of an item regardless of their location.

Unit pricing Posting prices in terms of commonly accepted unit volume measures, such as the price per ounce.

Unitary elasticity An elasticity coefficient of 1.0; a point in a demand curve where a price cut yields the same total revenue as the original price.

Univariate analysis The study of one variable at a time, also called *monovariate analysis.*

Unsought goods Items that most buyers will not seek out, such as cemetery plots.

Utility A product's total value for producing satisfaction.

Validity The extent to which a study measures what is intended.
Value analysis An approach used by institutional buyers to reduce costs by carefully analyzing components of items to see if they can be standardized, redesigned, or made by less expensive means.
Variable costs Costs which vary in total in proportion to volume changes.
Vertical integration Purchasing firms located either forward or backward in a channel.
Volume segmentation Segmentation according to the extent to which customers use a particular product.

Waves Another name for pulsing.
Wheel of retailing New types of retailers make their initial inroads by offering low prices with few services. Later they increase their services to attract more customers, resulting in higher prices and leaving room for a new breed of retailer to enter.
Wholesalers Marketing intermediaries that receive the bulk of their revenue from producers, other wholesalers, retailers, or non-profit organizations.

Zone prices Charging uniform prices to all buyers within a stated zone.

Notes

Chapter 1

1. American Marketing Association Board, "AMA Board Approves New Marketing Definition," *Marketing News* 19, no. 5 (March 1, 1985): 1.
2. Gregory D. Upah and Richard E. Wokutch, "Assessing Social Impacts of New Products: An Attempt to Operationalize the Macromarketing Concept," *Journal of Public Policy and Marketing* 4 (1985): 166–78.
3. Shelby D. Hunt, "General Theories and the Fundamental Explanada of Marketing," *Journal of Marketing* 47, no. 4 (Fall 1983): 14.
4. Most basic economics texts elaborate on the utility theory and how society's overall utility is increased through exchange. For example, see Ryan C. Amacher and Holley H. Ulbrich, *Principles of Economics* (Cincinnati: South-Western Publishing Co., 1986), Chapter 20. Most authors do not distinguish awareness as a utility dimension. For instance, see Robert F. Hartley, *Marketing Fundamentals* (New York: Harper & Row 1983), Chapter 1. Further, some reviewers have indicated that awareness is implicit among the other components. It is separately identified here, however, to highlight the fact that exchange will not take place unless buyers are made aware of an item.
5. For further discussion of a system, see D. R. Anderson, D. J. Sweeney, and T. A. Williams, *An Introduction to Management Science: Quantitative Approaches to Decision Making*, 4th ed. (St. Paul: West, 1985), Chapter 1.
6. For an excellent discussion of the rationale of modern business activity, including profit, see Richard H. Leftwich and Ansel M. Sharp, *Economics of Social Issues* (Plano, Texas: Business Publications, Inc., 1986), Chapter 7.
7. The marketing functions are just as necessary during periods of shortages as they are in more abundant times. See Nicholas G. Papodopoulos, "Shortage Marketing: A Comprehensive Framework," *Journal of the Academy of Marketing Science* 11, no. 1 (Winter 1983): 40–60; and Douglas J. Dalrymple and Leonard J. Parsons, *Marketing Management: Strategy and Cases* (New York: John Wiley & Sons, 1986): 2–5.
8. See "Towards a Socialist Marketing Concept—The Case of Romania," *Journal of Marketing* 50, no. 1 (January 1986): 28–39. Also see Richard A. Connor, Jr. and Jeffrey P. Davidson, "A Strategic Client Centered Marketing Approach for Professional Service Firms," *Journal of Professional Services Marketing* 1, no. 2 (Winter 1986): 21–33.
9. Philip Kotler, "A Generic Concept of Marketing," *Journal of Marketing* 36, no. 2 (April 1972): 46–54; and Benson P. Shapiro, "Marketing for Nonprofit Organizations," *Harvard Business Review* 36, no. 4 (September/October 1973): 123–32. Also see Johan Arndt, "How Broad Should the Marketing Concept Be?," *Journal of Marketing* 42, no. 1 (January 1978): 101–3; and Michael J. Houston, "The Marketing of Higher Education: A Multimarket, Multiservice Approach" in *Marketing of Services*, ed. John H. Donnelly and William R. George (Chicago: American Marketing Association, 1981): 138–43. Also see Brent Knight and Dennis Johnson, "Marketing in Higher Education," *Educational Record* 62, no. 4 (Winter 1981): 28–31.
10. See "Brian F. Harris and Roger A. Strang, "Marketing Strategies in the Age of Generics," *Journal of Marketing* 49, no. 4 (Fall 1985): 70–81.
11. Theodore Levitt, "Marketing Myopia," *Harvard Business Review* 23, no. 3 (July/August 1960): 45–56. Also see Robert Ball, "Volkswagon Rabbit Back to Prosperity," *Readings in Marketing Strategy*, Jean Claude Larouche & Edward C. Strong, eds. (Palo Alto: The Scientific Press, 1982): 41–48.
12. General Electric Company, *1952 Annual Report* (New York: General Electric Co., 1952): 20–21.
13. See Franklin S. Houston, "The Marketing Concept: What It Is and What It Is Not," *Journal of Marketing* 50, no. 2 (April 1986): 81–87.
14. Ibid.
15. Studies indicate that marketing receives the major emphasis of management attention in all types of firms. "Marketing: The New Priority," *Business Week*, November 21, 1983: 96–99, 102–4, 106. Also see P. W. Haserot, "Developing a Marketing Mindset," *Executive Female*, May/June 1985: 26–28.

16. Adapted from Philip Kotler, *Marketing Management: Analysis, Planning, and Control*, 4th ed. (Englewood Cliffs, N.J.: Prentice-Hall, 1980): 9.
17. S. W. Sohn and R. S. Smith, "Countries Are Like Corporations [Mexico and W. T. Grant]," *U.S. Banker* 95 (January 1984): 40–42.
18. Victor J. Cook, Jr., "Understanding Marketing Strategy and Differential Advantage," *Journal of Marketing* 49, no. 2 (Spring 1985): 137–42.
19. See E. Jerome McCarthy and William Perreault, *Basic Marketing*, 8th ed. (Homewood, Ill.: Richard D. Irwin, 1984): 46.
20. Some have argued that planning is implied in the 4 Ps. We discuss it separately to emphasize its importance, but note that it relates to all of the other Ps, as Figure 1.5 suggests.

Chapter 2

1. See Anthony J. Pingitore, Jr., "New Product Success Is Not a Process; It must coincide with corporate strategies," *Marketing News* 18, no. 14 (July 6, 1984): 9.
2. Frank Harrison, *Policy, Strategy, and Managerial Action* (Boston: Houghton-Mifflin Co., 1986): 46–52.
3. J. Clifton Williams, Andrew J. DuBrin, and Henry Sisk, *Management and Organization* (Cincinnati: South-Western Publishing Co., 1985), Chapter 4.
4. Theo Haimann, William G. Scott, and Patrick E. Conner, *Management* (Boston: Houghton-Mifflin Co., 1985), Chapter 25.
5. James L. Gibson and James H. Donnely, Jr., *Organizations: Behavior, Structure, Processes* (Plano, Texas: Business Publications, Inc., 1985), Chapter 14.
6. George A. Steiner, *Strategic Planning* (New York: The Free Press, 1983): 106–9.
7. For example, see William J. Baumol, *Business Behavior, Value and Growth* (New York: Harcourt, Brace & World, 1966); Robin Marris (with a foreword by J. K. Galbraith), *The Economic Theory of Managerial Capitalism* (New York: Basic Books, 1968); R. A. Gordon, *Business Leadership in the Large Corporation*, 2d ed. (Berkeley: University of California Press, 1961); and Raymond Aron, *The Industrial Society* (New York: Simon & Schuster, 1981).
8. For further discussion, see Richard J. Schonberger, *Operations Management: Planning and Control* (Plano, Texas: Business Publications, Inc., 1981): 211.
9. Some argue that marketers should exert more control. See Carl P. Zeithaml and Valerie A. Zeithaml, "Environmental Management: Revising the Marketing Perspective," *Journal of Marketing* 48, no. 2 (Spring 1984): 46–53.
10. For example, see U.S. Bureau of the Census, *Annual Survey of Manufacturers, Census of Retail Trade, Census of Wholesale Trade, and Census of Selected Service Industries.*
11. J. Bohn, "Eaton, Dana Sighting Broader Market Focus," *Automotive News*, August 12, 1985: 16–17.
12. "Picture This: Kodak Wants to Be a Biotech Giant Too," *Business Week*, May 26, 1986: 88, 90.
13. "Mac Booth Aims to Put Some Flash into Polaroid," *Business Week*, April 7, 1986: 83.
14. Lloyd M. Levin, "Ecomores, New Marketing Research Field Pursues Economic Implications of Changing Sexual Mores," *Marketing News* 9, no. 2 (January 16, 1976): 6.
15. See Robert D. Buzzell and Frederick D. Wierseman, "Successful Share-Building Strategies," *Harvard Business Review* 59, no. 1 (January/February 1981): 135–44.
16. See "Vie De France: A Baker That Rose Too Fast," *Business Week*, July 21, 1986: 107.
17. "Motor Scooters Finally Make a Dent in the U.S. Market," *Business Week* (July 16, 1984): 31, 35.
18. For further discussion of institutional rigidity and the effects of strategy change see John B. Miner, Tim Singleton, and Vincent P. Luchsinger, *The Practice of Management: Text, Readings, Cases* (Columbus, Ohio: Charles E. Merrill Publishing Co., 1985), Chapter 10.
19. See Wroe Alderson, *Marketing Behavior and Executive Action: A Functionalist Approach to Marketing Theory* (Homewood, Ill.: Richard D. Irwin, 1957): 102–4.
20. Joseph M. Winski and Christy Marshall, "Concept, Not Economy, Said Fatal to 'Families'," *Advertising Age* 53, no. 19 (May 3, 1982): 84.
21. The discussion of synergy is based upon H. Igor Ansoff, *Corporate Strategy: An Analytic Approach to Business Policy for Growth and Expansion* (New York: McGraw-Hill, 1965), Chapter 5.
22. "E Systems: Gunning for a Maker of Offensive Electronic Weaponry," *Business Week*, September 13, 1982: 78.
23. Bill Kuzbyt, "Dataproducts, Exxon Set Joint Venture," *Electronic News*, June 3, 1985: 16–17.
24. "Canteen Puts on a White Collar," *Business Week*, March 28, 1983: 141, 143, 147.
25. See Rajendra K. Srivastava, Mark I. Alpert, and Allan D. Shocker, "A Customer-Oriented Approach for Determining Market Structures," *Journal of Marketing* 48, no. 2 (Spring 1984): 32–45.
26. Some large multiproduct firms position their offerings relative to other items produced by the same firm.
27. John H. Shain, "Strategic Positioning in Operations Management," *Bankers Magazine*, March/April 1985: 11–14.
28. For further discussion of procedures for evaluating preferences, see V. Srinivasan, "A General Procedure for Estimating Consumer Preference Distributions," *Journal of Marketing Research* 12, no. 3 (November 1975): 377–89; Roger J. Best, "The Predictive Aspects of a Joint-Space Theory of Stochastic Choice," *Journal of Marketing Research* 13, no. 2 (May 1976): 198–204; and Robert A. Westbrook, "Intrapersonal Affective Influences on Consumer Satisfaction with Products," *Journal of Consumer Research* 7, no. 2 (June 1980): 49–54.
29. Richard M. Johnson, "Market Segmentation: A Strategic Marketing Tool," *Journal of Marketing Research* 8, no. 1 (February 1971): 13–18.
30. For further insights on strategy, see Robin Wensley, "Strategic Marketing: Betas, Boxes, or Basics," *Journal of Marketing* 45, no. 3 (Summer 1981): 173–82.
31. Gay Jervey, "Lipton Jumps into Fray with Decaffeinated Tea," *Advertising Age* 54, no. 19 (May 2, 1983): 1–70.
32. "A Blend of Tobacco and Life Insurance," *Business Week*, April 22, 1977: 26–27.
33. J. Bohn, "Robotics Sales Rise as Imports Squeeze Profits," *Business Marketing*, August 1985: 12–13.
34. Terry Haller, "An Organization Structure to Help You in the '80's," *Advertising Age* 51, no. 29 (August 25, 1980): 45–46.
35. Peter Finch, "Xerox Bets All on New Sales Groups," *Business Marketing*, July 1985: 3–9.

Chapter 3

1. Rajendra K. Srivastava, Mark I. Alpert, and Allan F Shocker, "A Customer-Oriented Approach for Determining Market Structures, *Journal of Marketing* 48, no. 2 (Spring 1984): 32–45.

2. N. Travers, "Kent Price Aims High at Citibank," *Banker*, May 1985: 26–28.
3. See Morris B. Holbrook and Douglas V. Holloway, "Marketing Strategy and the Structure of Aggregate, Segment-Specific, and Differential Preferences," *Journal of Marketing* 48, no. 1 (Winter 1984): 62–67.
4. Peter Doyle and John Saunders, "Market Segmentation and Positioning in Specialized Industrial Markets," *Journal of Marketing* 49, no. 2 (Spring 1985): 24–32.
5. Jagdish N. Sheth and Gary L. Frazier, "A Margin-Return Model for Strategic Planning," *Journal of Marketing* 47, no. 2 (Spring 1983): 100–109 and A. Hoffman, "The Segmentation Challenge: How to Assess the Response," *Direct Marketing*, June 1985: 93–94.
6. "What's Wrong at IBM?" *Business Week*, March 17, 1986: 48–49.
7. "Betting on a Computer System for Managers," *Business Week*, June 18, 1984: 134–35 and "Information Retrieval System Designed for Marketing Uses," *Marketing News*, May 24, 1985: 1–2.
8. Gay Jervey, "Kodak Widens Office Market Exposure," *Advertising Age* 56, no. 45 (June 10, 1985): 40.
9. "Six Demographic Variables Shape Consumer Demand," *Marketing News* 18, no. 25 (December 7, 1984): 11, 14.
10. For an excellent discussion of benefit segmentation, see Russell I. Haley, *Developing Effective Communications Strategy: A Benefit Segmentation Approach* (New York: Ronald Press, John Wiley & Sons, 1985).
11. Kent L. Granzin and Donald M. Jensen, "Market Segmentation in the Professional Basketball Market," *1984 Marketing Educators' Proceedings* (Chicago: American Marketing Association, 1984): 239–43.

Chapter 4

1. "Mickey Mouse Haunts Miami Beach Hotels," *Business Week*, August 1, 1977: 24–26. See also "Miami Beach Targets Young Professionals," *Sales and Marketing Management*, January 13, 1986: 34–35.
2. For a discussion of projected business climate in the late 1980s see James O'Toole, "What's Ahead for the Business-Government Relationship?" *Harvard Business Review* 57, no. 2 (March/April 1979): 94–105. See also "Antitrust Policy: Big Ain't So Bad After All," *Economist*, January 25, 1986: 28.
3. See "The Upheaval in Health Care," *Business Week*, June 20, 1984: 44–48. See also A. A. Ullman, "The Impact of the Regulatory Life Cycle on Corporate Political Strategy," *California Management Review* 28, no. 4 (Fall 1985): 140–54.
4. See Joel Bleeke, "Deregulation: Riding the Rapids," *Business Horizons* 23, no. 3 (May/June 1983): 15–25.
5. The Media Institute, *Crooks, Conmen and Clowns* (New York: The Media Institute, 1981).
6. John A. Jennings, "Myth Believers: Many Have Inflated Notion on Profits," *The Detroit News*, November 3, 1975: 3–B.
7. "New Protectionism in Foreign Trade: Forms and Causes," *EFTA Bulletin* (October/December 1985): 14–16.
8. For an excellent discussion, see "Cracking the China Market," *Industry Week* (February 17, 1985): 35–36.
9. The *Congressional Record* is a good source of information regarding pending trade and other political actions by the federal government.
10. For further discussion of government assistance, see Evan J. Douglas, *Managerial Economics: Theory, Practice, and Problems* (Englewood Cliffs, N.J.: Prentice-Hall, 1983), Chapter 12.
11. Roy J. Harris, Jr. "Back from the Bank: Lockheed Shows Signs of Prospering Again," *Wall Street Journal* 58, no. 93 (May 12, 1983): 1.
12. "Headquarters: The Right Sites," *Advertising Age* 54, no. 51 (December 5, 1983): M–16. See also "Houston at the Crossroads," *Economy* (October 26, 1985): 30.
13. "Take Stock in Syracuse," *Business Week*, March 28, 1983: 54.
14. Ernest F. Cooke, "The Sun Belt Myth," *Developments in Marketing Science*, vol. VI (Miami: Academy of Marketing Science, 1983), 328–33. See also "*Inc's* Fifth Annual Report on the States," *Inc.* (October 1985): 90–104.
15. Robert G. Harris and James M. Cannon, "Public Regulation of Marketing Activity, Part I: Institutional Typologies of Market Failure," *Journal of Macromarketing* 3, no. 3 (Spring 1983): 49–58.
16. Sallie Gaines, "Santa Fe Merger Derailed: Ruling May Sink Southern Pacific, Cut Service," *Chicago Tribune*, July 25, 1986, Sec. 3, pp. 1–2.
17. Ray O. Werner, "Legal Developments in Marketing," *Journal of Marketing* 46, no. 3 (Summer 1982): 109–10.
18. Robert E. Baldwin, *Economic Development and Growth* (Melbourne, Florida: Krieger Publishing Co. Inc., 1980), Chapter 7.
19. Ibid.: 418.
20. *U.S.* v. *U.S. Steel Corp.*, 251 U.S. 247 (1920).
21. *U.S.* v. *Aluminum Company of America*, 148 F. 2d 416 (2d Cir. 1945). Also see Ray O. Werner, "Marketing and the United States Supreme Court (1975–1981)," *Journal of Marketing* 44, no. 3 (Summer 1980): 80.
22. Fred W. Morgan and Karl A. Boedecker, "The Role of Personal Selling in Products Liability Litigation," *Journal of Personal Selling & Sales Management* 1, no. 1 (Fall/Winter 1980–81): 34–40.
23. For further detail of acts discussed here, along with numerous other pieces of important legislation, see Laurence P. Feldman, *Consumer Protection: Problems and Prospects* (St. Paul: West Publishing, 1980).
24. Upton Sinclair, *The Jungle* (Pasadena, California: Published by Upton Sinclair, 1935): 117.
25. *Warner-Lambert Co.* v. *Federal Trade Commissions*, F.T.C. Dkt. 77–855 and 77–1118 (April 1978).
26. Dorothy Cohen, "The FTC's Advertising Substantiation Program," *Journal of Marketing* 44, no. 1 (Winter 1980): 26–35.
27. Scott Hume, "RC Uncaps Legal Battle," *Advertising Age* 55, no. 40 (July 9, 1984): 12.
28. For a discussion of small business adaptations to technology see R. Eugene Hughes, "Responding to Changes in Process Technology: Strategies for the Small Business," *Journal of Small Business Management* 22, no. 1 (January 1984): 8–15.
29. "America Can Beat Anyone in High Tech, Just Ask Bruce Merrifield," *Business Week*, April 7, 1986: 94, 96.
30. William W. Burke, "NASA's Partnership with Industry," *Management Review*, December 1985: 30–32.
31. Alvin Toffler, *Future Shock* (New York: Random House, 1970), p. 14.
32. See, for example, "Publishers Go Electronic," *Business Week*, June 11, 1984: 84–87, 90, 92, 97.
33. John G. Myers, "Marketing Management: An Assessment," *Journal of Marketing* 43, no. 1 (January 1979): 17–29.
34. "A New Strategy for No. 2 in Computers," *Business Week*, May 2, 1983: 66–70.
35. For further discussion see Edwin B. Flippo and Gary M. Munsinger, *Management* (Boston: Allyn and Bacon, Inc., 1982), Chapter 6.
36. "The Shape of Energy Markets to Come," *Public Utilities Fortnightly*, January 9, 1986: 21–28.
37. "The Great Arctic Energy Rush," *Business Week*, January 24, 1983: 52.
38. For example, see George Leland Bach, *Economics* (Englewood Cliffs, N.J.: Prentice-Hall, 1980).

39. *Statistical Abstract of the United States* (Washington, D.C.: U.S. Government Printing Office, 1986), 106th ed.
40. Ibid.
41. "The Climate Is Right for Forest Products Again," *Business Week*, January 13, 1986: 82.
42. Technically, the Treasury Department can also affect the money supply. For further discussion, see Bach, *Economics*, Chapter 7.

Chapter 5

1. For an interesting discussion of viewing a buying situation from the perspectives of a sociologist, a psychologist, a consumer advocate, an economist, and a marketing expert, see James F. Engel, David T. Kollat, and Roger D. Blackwell, *Consumer Behavior*, 2d ed. (New York: Holt, Rinehart, and Winston, 1973): 3–5.
2. See, for instance, "The Consumer Drives R. J. Reynolds Again," *Business Week*, June 4, 1984: 92–95, 99.
3. See C. Glen Walters, "Consumer Behavior: An Appraisal," *Journal of the Academy of Marketing Science* 7, no. 4 (Fall 1979): 273–84.
4. *Statistical Abstract of the United States* (Washington, D.C., U.S. Government Printing Office, 1986): 5.
5. *Statistical Abstract of the United States* (Washington, D.C.: U.S. Government Printing Office, 1986).
6. George J. Stolnitz, "Our Main Population Patterns: Radical Shifts, Cloudy Prospect," *Business Horizons* 25, no. 2 (July/August 1982): 91–99. Also see "Households Changing Constantly," *Advertising Age*, August 29, 1985: 32.
7. Kenneth Dreyfack, William J. Hampton, and John A. Byrne, "When Companies Tell B-Schools What to Teach," *Business Week* (February 10, 1986): 60–61. Also see Robin Peterson and Donald A. Michie, "Strategic Elements of the Nontraditional Education/Marketing Interface," *American Marketing Association Educators' Proceedings* (Chicago American Marketing Association, 1983): 133–38.
8. See Gerald Albaum and Del I. Hawkins, "Geographic Mobility and Demographic and Socioeconomic Market Segmentation," *Journal of the Academy of Marketing Science* 11, no. 2 (Spring 1983): 97–113. Also see "Aberation Across the Nation," *Sales and Marketing Management*, September 9, 1985: 23.
9. *Statistical Abstract of the United States* (Washington, D.C.: U.S. Government Printing Office, 1984): 896. Also see *A Guide to Consumer Markets* (New York: The Conference Board, most recent edition).
10. Raymond W. LaForge, Richard M. Reese, and Wilbur Stanton, "Identifying and Attracting Consumer Outshoppers," *Journal of Small Business Management* 22, no. 1 (January 1984): 22–29.
11. Harold W. Berkman and Christopher Gilson, *Consumer Behavior: Concepts and Strategies* (Boston: Kent Publishing Co., 1986): 19–20.
12. See, for instance, Mariea Grubbs Hoy and Raymond P. Fisk, "Older Consumers and Services: Implications for Marketers," *1985 American Marketing Association Educators' Proceedings* (Chicago: American Marketing Association, 1985): 50–55.
13. W. Thomas Anderson, Jr., Eli P. Cox III, and David G. Fulcher, "Bank Selection Decisions and Marketing Segmentation," *Journal of Marketing* 40, no. 1 (January 1976): 40–45. For a nonprofit organization example, see Scott M. Smith and Leland L. Belk, "Market Segmentation for Fund Raisers," *Journal of the Academy of Marketing Science* 10, no. 3 (Summer 1982): 208–16.
14. See "Today's Army Relying on Marketing Research to Attain Recruitment Goals," *Marketing News* 18, no. 14 (July 6, 1984): 1–16.
15. See "Coffee Companies Pitch to a More Discerning Drinker," *Business Week*, May 28, 1984: 72–73.
16. James F. Engel and Roger D. Blackwell, *Consumer Behavior* (New York: Dryden Press, 1982): 17, 18.
17. Ryan C. Amacher and Holly H. Ulbrich, *Principles of Economics* (Cincinnati: South-Western Publishing Co., 1986), Chapter 20.
18. John A. Carlson and Robert J. Gieseke, "Price Search in a Product Market." *Journal of Consumer Research* 9, no. 4 (March 1983): 357–65. Also see Ann Keely, "Consumers Also Plan Strategies," *Marketing News* 20, 13 (June 20, 1986): 6, 10.
19. Gerald Zaltman and Melanie Wallendorf, *Consumer Behavior: Basic Findings and Management Implications* (New York: John Wiley & Sons, 1983): 15–17.
20. Franco M. Nicosia, *Consumer Decision Processes: Marketing and Advertising Implications* (Englewood Cliffs, N.J.: Prentice-Hall, 1966).
21. James F. Engel, David T. Kollat and Roger D. Blackwell, *Consumer Behavior* (New York: Holt, Rinehart & Winston, 1968). The model was revised in the second edition (1973) and then again in the third edition (1978).
22. John A. Howard and Jagdish N. Sheth, *The Theory of Buyer Behavior*, (New York: John Wiley & Sons, 1968). Some details of the model were revised in John U. Farley, John A. Howard, and L. Winston Ring, *Consumer Behavior Theory and Application*, (Boston: Allyn & Bacon, 1974).
23. For a detailed discussion of the many models, see Gerald Zaltman and Melanie Wallendorf, *Consumer Behavior: Basic Findings and Management Implications* (New York: John Wiley & Sons, 1983), Chapter 22.
24. See Richard L. Oliver, "A Cognitive Model of the Antecedents and Consequences of Satisfaction Decisions," *Journal of Marketing Research* 17, no. 3 (November 1980): 460–69. See also Robert A. Westbrook, "A Rating Scale for Measuring Product/Service Satisfaction," *Journal of Marketing* 44, no. 2 (Fall 1980): 68–72, and Solveig Wikstrom, "Another Look at Consumer Dissatisfaction as a Measure of Market Performance," *Journal of Consumer Policy* 6, no. 1 (1983): 19–36.
25. James Engel, Roger Blackwell, and Paul Miniard, *Consumer Behavior* (New York: The Dryden Press, 1985): Chapter 4.
26. Marsha L. Richins, "Negative Word-of-Mouth by Dissatisfied Consumers: A Pilot Study," *Journal of Marketing* 47, no. 1 (Winter 1983): 68–78.
27. Jack A. Lesser and Marie Adele Hughes, "The Generalizability of Psychographic Market Segments Across Geographic Locations," *Journal of Marketing* 50, no. 1 (January 1986): 18–27.
28. Pat Sloan, "New Clearasil Line Faces up to Adult Acne," *Advertising Age* 55, no. 43 (July 19, 1984): 3, 49.
29. Jean Houston, *Life Force* (Pine Brook, N.J.: Dell Books, 1986): 48–51.
30. Chester R. Wasson, "Consumer Choice Processes Search or Automatic Response?," *Journal of the Academy of Marketing Science* 7, no. 4 (Fall 1979): 350–73.
31. William J. McGuire, "Some Internal Psychological Factors Influencing Consumer Choice," *Journal of Consumer Research* 3, no. 2 (March 1976): 302–19.
32. Because memory cannot be observed directly, theorists are in disagreement as to whether two parts of the brain are used for memory or whether active and long-term memory are two functions of the same part.
33. For a detailed summary see James R. Bettman, "Memory Factors in Consumer Choice: A Review," *Journal of Marketing* 43, no. 2 (Spring 1979): 37–53. Also see David W. Nylen, *Advertising: Planning, Implementation, and Control* (Cincinnati: South-Western Publishing Co., 1985): 104–7.

34. Forgetting about satisfactions received from particular items or stores often leads to buying competing products or patronizing competing stores. See Klaus Peter Kaas, "Consumer Habit Forming, Informational Acquisition, and Buying Behavior," *Journal of Business Research* 10, no. 2 (March 1982): 3–15.
35. See Herbert E. Krugman, "The Impact of Television Advertising: Learning without Involvement," *Public Opinion Quarterly* 29, no. 2 (Fall 1965): 349–56.
36. Leon G. Schiffman and Leslie Lazar Kanuk, *Consumer Behavior* (Englewood Cliffs, N.J.: Prentice-Hall, 1983): 199–201.
37. For more extensive coverage, see Flemming Hansen, "Psychological Theories of Consumer Choice," *Journal of Consumer Research* 3, no. 3 (December 1976): 132–37.
38. Terrell G. Williams, *Consumer Behavior: Fundamentals & Strategies* (St. Paul: West Publishing, 1982): 165–66.
39. For a comprehensive discussion of changing attitudes, see Engel, Blackwell and Miniard, *Consumer Behavior*, Chapter 16.
40. See Raymond L. Horton, *Buyer Behavior: A Decision Making Approach* (Columbus, Ohio: Charles E. Merrill Publishing Co., 1985): Chapter 13.
41. D. L. Sparks and W. T. Tucker, "A Multivariate Analysis of Personality and Product Use," *Journal of Marketing Research* 8, no. 1 (February 1971): 67–70. Also see Ugar Yvas and Glen Riecken, "Personality, Organization—Specific Attitude and Socioeconomic Correlates of Charity Giving Behavior," *Journal of the Academy of Marketing Science* 9, no. 1 (Winter 1981): 52–65.
42. Terrell G. Williams, *Consumer Behavior: Fundamentals & Strategies*, 108.
43. For a comprehensive discussion of various approaches to lifestyle and an extensive list of references to both theory and application, see William D. Wells, "Psychographics: A Critical Review," *Journal of Marketing Research* 12, no. 2 (May 1975): 196–213. See also Russell W. Belk, Kenneth D. Bahn, and Robert N. Mayer, "Developmental Recognition of Consumption Symbolism," *Journal of Consumer Research* 9, no. 2 (June 1982): 4–17.
44. Christie H. Paksoy, "Life Style Analysis of Major Bank Credit Card Users," *Journal of Marketing* 39, no. 3 (July 1975): 17–34.
45. Joseph T. Plummer, "The Concept and Application of Life Style Segmentation," *Journal of Marketing* 38, no. 1 (January 1974): 33–37.
46. Del I. Hawkins, Roger J. Best, and Kenneth A. Coney, *Consumer Behavior: Implications for Marketing Strategy* (Plano, Texas: Business Publications, Inc., 1983): 388–89.
47. Joseph T. Plummer, "Life Style Patterns and Commercial Bank Credit Card Usage," *Journal of Marketing* 35, no. 2 (April 1971): 41.
48. James U. McNeal, *Consumer Behavior: An Integrative Approach* (Boston: Little, Brown, 1982): 144.
49. Herbert Krugman, "What Makes Advertising Effective?" *Harvard Business Review* 31, no. 2 (March/April 1975): 96–102.
50. Neil Bidman and Milton Rokeach, "Archie Bunker's Bigotry: A Study in Selective Perception and Exposure," *Journal of Communication* 45, no. 3 (Winter 1974): 36–47.
51. Diane Mermigas, "Opinions Splinter over Zap's Sting," *Advertising Age* 55, no. 44 (July 23, 1984): 3.
52. See Jack Z. Sissors and William B. Goodrich, *Media Planning Workbook* (Lincolnwood, Ill.: Crain Books, 1985).
53. Brian Moran, "CBN's $5 Million to Back the Book," *Advertising Age* 55, no. 40 (July 9, 1984): 10.
54. Naresh K. Malhotra, Aran K. Jain, and Stephen W. Legakos, "The Information Overload Controversy: An Alternative Viewpoint," *Journal of Marketing* 46, no. 2 (Spring 1982): 27–30.
55. See E. E. Jones and H. D. Gerard, *Foundations of Social Psychology* (New York: Wiley, 1967), Chapter 7. See also Pradeep K. Korgaonkar and George P. Moschis, "An Experimental Study of Cognitive Dissonance, Product Involvement, Expectations, Performance and Consumer Judgement of Product Performance," *Journal of Advertising* 11, no. 3 (1982): 32–44.
56. Engel, Kollat, and Blackwell, *Consumer Behavior*: 356.
57. Ibid.: 356–57.
58. Most psychologists in the U.S. ascribe to theoretical precepts termed *behaviorism*, of which reinforcement is a central part. Other theoretical systems also exist, such as field theory. For further discussion of various theories, see Del I. Hawkins, Kenneth A. Coney, and Roger J. Best, *Consumer Behavior: Implications for Marketing Strategy* (Plano, Texas: Business Publications, 1983), Chapter 11.
59. See Dorothy Cohen, *Consumer Behavior* (New York: Random House, 1981): 209–11.
60. For further discussion of learning, see Engel, Blackwell, and Miniard, *Consumer Behavior*, Chapter 17. See also Kass, "Consumer Habit Forming: 3–15.
61. For further discussion of culture see Charles M. Schaninger, Jaques C. Bodugeois, and Christian Buss, "French-English Subcultural Consumption Differences," *Journal of Marketing* 49, no. 2 (April 1985): 82–92.
62. See "Baby Boomers Push for Power," *Business Week*, July 2, 1984: 52–58, 62.
63. These examples plus additional ones are in David A. Ricks, J. S. Arpan, and M.Y. Fu, *International Business Blunders* (Columbus: Grid Publishing, 1975).
64. Daniel Yankelovich, *The Yankelovich Monitor* (New York: Daniel Yankelovich Inc.)
65. W. L. Warner, with Marchia Meeker and Kenneth Eels, *Social Class in America* (New York: Harper & Row, 1960). Social class is an important determinant of consumption for nonprofit organizations. See, for example, John E. Robbins and Stephanie S. Robbins, "Museum Marketing: Identification of High, Moderate, and Low Segments," *Journal of the Academy of Marketing Science* 9, no. 1 (Winter 1981): 66–77.
66. W. Lloyd Warner and Paul Lunt, *The Social Life of a Modern Community* (New Haven: Yale University Press, 1941). Also, W. Lloyd Warner, Marchia Meeker, and Kenneth Eels, *Social Class in America* (Chicago: Science Research Associates, 1949). This same system of social class classification has been employed in numerous marketing research projects and has developed into the foundations of marketing theory. For example, see Engel, Blackwell, and Miniard, *Consumer Behavior*, Chapter 5.
67. Pierre Martineau, "Social Classes and Spending Behavior," *Journal of Marketing* 29, no. 3 (October 1958): 121–30.
68. George P. Mochis and Gilbert A. Churchill, Jr., "An Analysis of the Adolescent Consumer," *Journal of Marketing* 43, no. 3 (Summer 1979): 40–48.
69. Brian Sternthal and C. Samuel Craig, *Consumer Behavior: An Information Processing Perspective* (Englewood Cliffs, N.J.: Prentice-Hall, 1982): 220.
70. Paul S. Hugstad, "A Re-examination of the Concept of Privilege," *Journal of Marketing* 44, no. 3 (Summer 1980): 12–19.
71. For further discussion see Gerald Zaltman and Melanie Wallendorf, *Consumer Behavior* (1983): 136–37.
72. Engel, Kollat, and Blackwell, *Consumer Behavior*, Chapter 6; and Richard C. Becherer, Fred W. Morgan, and Lawrence M. Richard, "Informal Group Influence Among Situationally/Dispositionally-Oriented Consumers," *Journal of the Academy of Marketing Science* 10, no. 2 (Summer 1982): 269–80.

73. For further discussion, see James F. Engel and Roger D. Blackwell, *Consumer Behavior* (1982): 169–72. For an alternate approach, see Patrick E. Murphy and William A. Staples, "A Modernized Family Life Cycle," *Journal of Marketing Research* 16, no. 2 (June 1979): 12–22.
74. Gerald Zaltman and Melanie Wallendorf, *Consumer Behavior* (1983): 169–70.
75. Rosann L. Spiro, "Persuasion in Family Decision-Making," *Journal of Consumer Research* 9, no. 4 (March 1983): 393–402.
76. For an interesting discussion of influence strategies, see C. Whan Park, "Joint Decisions in Home Purchasing: A Muddling-Through Process," *Journal of Consumer Research* 9, no. 3 (September 1982): 151–62.
77. See Peter C. Wilton and Edgar A. Pessemier, "Forecasting the Ultimate Acceptance of an Innovation: The Effects of Information," *Journal of Consumer Research* 8, no. 3 (September 1981): 162–71.
78. Trudy Lieberman, "How Mr. Coffee Captured U.S. Kitchens Recent Gadgetry Coup," *Detroit Free Press*, May 12, 1976: 1C–3C.
79. Janet Neiman, "Frozen Breakfast Foods Seen As Sleeper," *Advertising Age* 53, no. 18 (April 26, 1982): 20.
80. Everett M. Rogers, *Diffusion of Innovations* (New York: The Free Press, 1962). Further findings were elaborated upon in E. M. Rogers and F. Lloyd Shoemaker, *Communication of Innovations* (New York: The Free Press, 1971).
81. Duane L. Davis and Ronald S. Rubin, "Identifying the Energy Conscious Consumer: The Case of the Opinion Leader," *Journal of the Academy of Marketing Science* 11, no. 2 (Spring 1983): 169–87.
82. Rogers, *Diffusion of Innovations*: 81.
83. Vijay Mahajan and Eiton Muller, "Innovation Diffusion and New Product Growth Models in Marketing," *Journal of Marketing* 43, no. 4 (Fall 1979): 55–68.

Chapter 6

1. See, for instance, A. Coskun Samli and John T. Mentzer, "An Industrial Analysis Market Information System," *Industrial Marketing Management* 9, no. 4 (July 1980): 237–45.
2. For more information, see *Facts for Marketers*, U.S. Department of Commerce, Business and Defense Services Administration. Also see *Industry Profiles*, 1958–1983 (same administration source).
3. New York, New Jersey, Pennsylvania, Ohio, Indiana, Illinois, Wisconsin, Michigan, and California. From U.S. Bureau of the Census, *Statistical Abstract of the United States* (Washington, D.C.: U.S. Government Printing Office, 1986).
4. Ibid.
5. John M. Browning, Noel B. Zabriskiei, and Alan B. Huellmantel, "Strategic Purchasing Planning" *Journal of Purchasing and Materials Management* 19, no. 2 (Spring 1983): 19–24.
6. John L. Forbis and Nitin T. Mehta, "Value Based Strategies for Industrial Products," *Business Horizons* 24, no. 3 (May/June 1981): 32–42.
7. Robert G. Cooper, "New Product Success in Industrial Firms," *Industrial Marketing Management* 11, no. 3 (July 1982): 215–23.
8. E. R. Corey, *Industrial Marketing: Cases and Concepts* (Englewood Cliffs, N.J.: Prentice-Hall, 1980): v.
9. See Peter Doyle and John Saunders, "Market Segmentation and Positioning in Specialized Industrial Markets," *Journal of Marketing* 49, no. 2 (Spring 1985): 26–31.
10. See, for instance, "How Two Hospital Suppliers Are Facing a Penny-Pinching Eve," *Business Week*, June 18, 1984: 54–56.
11. See David R. Rink and H. Robert Dodge, "Industrial Sales Emphasis Across the Life Cycle," *Industrial Marketing Management* 9, no. 4 (October 1980): 305–10.
12. Kiran Shah and Peter J. LaPlaca, "Assessing Risks in Strategic Planning," *Industrial Marketing Management* 101, no. 3 (April 1981): 77–91.
13. See Paul F. Anderson and Terry M. Chambers, "A Reward/Measurement Model of Organizational Buying Behavior," *Journal of Marketing* 49, no. 2 (Spring 1985): 9–12.
14. Joseph A. Bellizzi, "Organization Size and Influence," *Industrial Marketing Management* 10, no. 1 (February 1981): 17–21.
15. See Joseph Cherian and Rohit Deshpande, "The Impact of Organizational Culture in the Adoption of Industrial Innovations," *1985 Marketing Educators' Conference Proceedings* (Chicago: American Marketing Association): 30–33.
16. "Goodyear Takes the Pain Out of Selling Tires," *Marketing Communications* 10 (September 1985): 74–76.
17. Walter Guzzardi, Jr., "The Fight for 9/10 of a Cent," *Fortune* 24, no. 5 (April 1961): 152.
18. See Barbara Bund Jackson, *Winning and Keeping Industrial Customers* (Lexington, Mass.: Lexington Books, 1985): 65–91.
19. For further reference, see H. Verma and C. Gross, *Introduction to Quantitative Methods: A Managerial Emphasis* (Santa Barbara: Wiley/Hamilton, 1978), Chapter 11.
20. For further discussion, see Leenders, Fearon, and England, *Purchasing and Materials Management*, Chapter 2.
21. See Donald W. Fogarty and Thomas R. Hoffmann, *Production and Inventory Management* (Cincinnati: South-Western Publishing, 1983): 385–89.
22. Ibid.
23. See Dan H. Robertson and Danny N. Bellenger, *Sales Management* (New York: MacMillan, 1980), Chapter 12.
24. Ibid.
25. See Christopher P. Puto, Wesley E. Pattou III, and Ronald H. King, "Risk Handling Strategies in Industrial Vendor Selection Decisions," *Journal of Marketing* 49, no. 1 (Winter 1985): 89–98.
26. See Paul H. Scharr and Bobby J. Calder, "Psychological Effects of Restaurant Meetings on Industrial Buyers," *Journal of Marketing* 50, no. 1 (January 1986): 87–97.
27. Jagdish N. Sheth, "A Model of Industrial Buying Behavior," *Journal of Marketing* 37, no. 3 (October 1973): 50–56.
28. See Robert E. Krapfel, Jr., "An Advocacy Behavior Model of Organizational Buyers' Vendor Choice," *Journal of Marketing* 49, no. 4 (Fall 1985): 51–59.
29. See David R. Lambert, Paul D. Boughton, and Gary R. Bouville, "Conflict Resolutions in Organizational Buying Centers," *Journal of the Academy of Marketing Science* 14 (Spring 1986): 57–62.
30. *Statistical Abstract of the United States* (Washington, D.C: U.S. Government Printing Office, 1986).
31. See William P. Browne, *Politics, Programs, and Bureaucrats* (Port Washington, N.Y.: Associated Faculty Press, 1980): 212–49.
32. Larry Croghan, "Pitching the Pentagon: A Game for Well-Armed Shops," *Ad Week* 27 (February 24, 1986): 27–30.
33. See Michael D. Hutt and Thomas W. Speh, *Industrial Marketing Management* (New York: Dryden Press, 1981): 39–40.

Chapter 7

1. "The Fast-Food Stars: Three Strategies for Fast Growth," *Business Week*, July 11, 1977: 56–57.
2. See William D. Danko and James M. MacLachlan, "Research to

Accelerate the Diffusion of a New Invention," *Journal of Advertising Research* 23, no. 3 (June/July 1983): 39–43.

3. See Ronald L. Zallocco, Donald W. Scotton, and David A. Jeresko, "Strategic Planning in the Commercial Airline Industry," *Journal of the Academy of Marketing Science* 11, no. 4 (Fall 1983): 404–16.
4. "1986: A Challenging Year for Advertising Budgets, Media Got Scrutiny," *Advertising Age* 57 (January 13, 1986): 1–2.
5. See D. R. Anderson, D. J. Sweeney, and T. A. Williams, *An Introduction to Management Science: Quantitative Approaches to Decision Making*, 4th ed. (St. Paul: West, 1985), Chapter 16.
6. Raymond McLeod, Jr. and John Rogers, "Marketing Information Systems: Uses in the Fortune 500," *California Management Review* 25, no. 3 (Fall 1983): 106–18. Also see "Electronic Information Gives Competitive Edge," *Marketing News* 20 (January 3, 1986): 20.
7. Donald S. Tull and Del I. Hawkins, *Marketing Research: Measurement and Method* (New York: MacMillan, 1980): 12. Also see "Fourth Generation Systems Soothe End Users," *Data Management* 136 (January 13, 1986): 28–29.
8. "Marketing's Back, and GE's Got It in Its Business Information Center," *Marketing News* 19 (October 25, 1985): 17–18.
9. "McKesson to the Rescue," *Sales and Marketing Management* 136 (January 13, 1986): 28–29.
10. See Gilbert A. Churchill, Jr., *Marketing Research: Methodological Foundations* (Hinsdale, Ill.: Dryden Press, 1981): 127. Also see Harper W. Boyd, Jr., Ralph Westfall, and Stanley F. Stasch, *Marketing Research: Text and Cases*, (Homewood, Ill.: Richard D. Irwin, 1981), Chapter 6.
11. For example, see "A Guide to Consumer Markets," most recent edition (N.Y.: The Conference Board).
12. Arnold Amstutz, "The Marketing Executive and Management Information Systems," *Proceedings of the 1966 Fall Conference of the American Marketing Association* (Chicago: American Marketing Association, 1966): 76.
13. "Can John Young Redesign Hewlett Packard?" *Business Week*, December 6, 1982: 72–74, 76–78.
14. James I. Cash, Jr., F. Warren McFarlan, and James L. McKenney, *Corporate Information Systems Management: Text and Cases* (Homewood, Ill.: Richard D. Irwin, 1983), Chapter 5.
15. See Robert A. Peterson, *Marketing Research* (Plano, Texas: Business Publications, Inc., 1982): 37–44.
16. See A. Charnes, W. W. Cooper, D. B. Learner, and F. Y. Phillips, "Management Science and Marketing Management," *Journal of Marketing* 49, no. 2 (Spring 1985): 93–105.
17. See "Management Warms Up to Computer Graphics," *Business Week*, August 13, 1984): 96–97, 101–2.
18. Rohit Deshpande, "The Organizational Context of Market Research Use," *Journal of Marketing* 46, no. 4 (Fall 1982): 91–101.
19. See A. Parasuraman, *Marketing Research* (Reading, Mass.: Addison-Wesley Publishing Co., 1986): 5–8.
20. See Dick Warren Twedt, *1978 Survey of Marketing Research* (Chicago: American Marketing Association, 1978). Also see Rohit Deshpande and Gerald Zaltman, "Factors Affecting the Use of Marketing Research Information: A Path Analysis," *Journal of Marketing Research* 19, no. 1 (February 1982): 14–31.
21. See R. Craig Endicott, "Agency Income Surges 15.3%," *Advertising Age*, (March 27, 1986): 1–6; K. T. Higgins, "Competition Intensifies as Nielson, AGB Jockey for Audience Measurement Lead," *Marketing News*, (November 22, 1985): 1; also see Jack J. Honomichl, "Marketing Research Big Business in Dollars, Not Publicity," *Advertising Age* 50, no. 17 (May 16, 1979): 58.
22. Robert F. Hartley, *Marketing Mistakes* (Columbus, Ohio: Grid, 1976): 67–68.
23. See Johan Arndt, "On Making Marketing Science More Scientific: Role of Orientations, Paradigms, Metaphors, and Puzzle Solving," *Journal of Marketing* 49, no. 3 (Summer 1985): 11–23.
24. See *Report of a Definitions Committee of the American Marketing Association* (Chicago: American Marketing Association, 1961).
25. For further discussion, see Boyd, Westfall, and Stasch, *Marketing Research, Text and Cases*, Chapter 2. Also see William F. O'Dell and Stanley Stasch, "Theory of Research for the Marketing Decision-Maker?" *Journal of Marketing* 30, no. 2 (April 1966): 52–55.
26. For a discussion of areas that marketing researchers feel need more effort, see Calvin P. Duncan and Charles M. Lillis, "Directions for Marketing Knowledge Development: Opinions of Marketing Research Managers," *Journal of the Academy of Marketing Science* 10, no. 1 (Winter 1982): 20–36.
27. Hartley, *Marketing Mistakes*: 62.
28. See Gil Mosard, "Problem Definition: Tasks and Techniques," *Journal of Systems Management* 34, no. 3 (June 1983): 16–21.
29. See David A. Aaker and George S. Day, *Marketing Research* (New York: John Wiley & Sons, 1986): 29–37.
30. Lawrence M. Lamont and William J. Lundstrum, "Identifying Successful Industrial Salesmen by Personality and Personal Characteristics," *Journal of Marketing Research* 14, no. 4 (November 1977): 517–29.
31. William G. Zickmond, *Exploring Marketing Research* (New York: The Dryden Press, 1985), Chapter 2.
32. Lamont and Lundstrum, "Identifying Successful Industrial Salesmen," p. 521.
33. This definition follows Boyd, Westfall, and Stasch, *Marketing Research: Text and Cases*: 14–15.
34. Hartley, et al., *Essentials of Marketing Research*, pp. 80–81.
35. Zickmond, *Exploring Marketing Research*, Chapter 7.
36. Joseph R. Hochstim, "Practical Uses of Sampling Surveys in the Field of Labor Relations," *Proceedings of the Conference of Business Application of Statistical Sampling Methods* (Monticello, Ill.: Bureau of Business Management, Univ. of Illinois, 1950): 181–82.
37. Peterson, *Marketing Research*, Chapter 7.
38. For further discussion see David F. Groebner and Patrick W. Shannou, *Business Statistics: A Decision Making Approach* (Columbus, Ohio: Charles E. Merrill Publishing Co., 1985), Chapter 5.
39. For further discussion of ways to determine a sample's size see Philip G. Enns, *Business Statistics* (Homewood, Ill.: Richard D. Irwin, 1985), Chapter 8.
40. Evidence also exists that too large a sample only increases sampling error. See Benjamin Lipstein, "Bigger Sample No Proof of More Accuracy: Lipstein," *Marketing News* 11, no. 10 (May 20, 1977): 1.
41. Henry Assael and John Keon, "Nonsampling v. Sampling Errors in Survey Research," *Journal of Marketing* 46, no. 2 (Spring 1982): 114–23.
42. For further discussion of observation techniques see James M. Siukula, "Status of Company Usage of Scanner Based Research," *Journal of the Academy of Marketing Science* 14, no. 2 (Spring 1986): 63–71.
43. Surveys are even used as legal evidence in the courtroom. See Fred W. Morgan, "The Admissibility of Consumer Surveys as Legal Evidence in Courts," *Journal of Marketing* 43, no. 4 (Fall 1979): 33–40.
44. For further discussion of survey types see Aaker and Day, *Marketing Research*.
45. See Boyd, Westfall, and Stasch, *Marketing Research: Text and Cases*, Chapter 3.

46. For example, see Gerald J. Gorn, "The Effects of Music in Advertising on Choice Behavior: A Classical Conditioning Approach," *Journal of Marketing* 46, no. 1 (Winter 1982): 94–101.
47. Cutting in with New Pack," *Advertising Age* 53, no. 18 (April 26, 1982): 2.
48. For an expanded, comprehensive discussion, see Peterson, *Marketing Research*, Chapter 5.
49. See Robert N. Zelnio and Jean P. Gagnon, "The Construction and Testing of an Image Questionnaire," *Journal of the Academy of Marketing Science* 9, no. 3 (Summer 1981): 288–99.
50. Peterson, *Marketing Research,* Chapter 8.
51. For a discussion of various kinds of scales, see Russell I. Haley and Peter B. Case, "Testing Thirteen Attitude Scales for Agreement and Brand Discrimination," *Journal of Marketing* 43, no. 4 (Fall 1979): 20–32.
52. Boyd, Westfall and Stasch, *Marketing Research*, p. 310.
53. Lipstein, "Bigger Samples No Proof," p 1.
54. See, for instance, Kevin F. McCrohan & Larry S. Lowe, "A Cost/Benefit Approach to Postage Used on Mail Questionnaires," *Journal of Marketing* 45, no. 1 (Winter 1981): 130–33.
55. John J. O'Connor, "L&M Back with Cigaret Brand Tests," *Advertising Age* 54, no. 25 (June 13, 1983): 1, 62.
56. For a discussion of possible errors at this stage, see Henry Assael and John Keon, "Nonsampling vs. Sampling Errors in Survey Research," *Journal of Marketing* 46, no. 2 (Spring 1982): 114–23.
57. Aaker and Day, *Marketing Research* (New York: John Wiley and Sons, 1986): 406–19.
58. For further discussion of these techniques, see Anderson, Sweeney, and Williams, *An Introduction to Management Science: Quantitative Approaches to Decision Making.*

Chapter 8

1. Pioneer Electronic: Still Committed to Videodiscs after a Wobbly Start," *Business Week*, January 24, 1983: 38–39.
2. "Where Frontier Lost Its Way," *Business Week*, February 7, 1983: 120. Also see "A New Frontier for People Express," *Economist* 297, October 12, 1985: 80–81.
3. Carol Jouzaitis, "People Express for Sale," *Chicago Tribune* (June 24, 1986): Sec. 3, pp. 1, 7.
4. See "Gillette: When Being No. 1 Just Isn't Good Enough," *Business Week*, August 13, 1984: 126–31. Also see R. O. Bennett and L. F. Cunningham, "Determining Profitable Products/Market Segments," *Journal of Retail Banking* 7 (Fall 1985): 53–62.
5. For further discussion, see C. W. Gross and R. T. Peterson, *Business Forecasting*, 2d ed. (Boston: Houghton Mifflin, 1983), Chapter 1.
6. "The Prophets of Doom Have a Dismal Record," *Business Week*, January 27, 1986: 22.
7. "The Booming Conservation Industry," *Business Week*, April 6, 1981: 59.
8. "Studies Are Greatly Underestimating Size of Sporting Goods Market, Company Finds," *Marketing News* 18, no. 13 (June 22, 1984): 9.
9. Spyros Makridakis, Steven C. Wheelwright, and Victor C. McGee, *Forecasting Methods and Applications* (New York: John Wiley & Sons, 1983): 4, 5.
10. See George C. Michael, *Sales Forecasting* (Chicago: American Marketing Association, 1979) and Gross and Peterson, *Business Forecasting.*
11. Wroe Alderson and Paul E. Green, *Planning and Problem Solving in Marketing* (Homewood, Ill.: Richard D. Irwin, 1964): 420.
12. For further discussion of exponential smoothing, see E. S. Gardner and D. G. Dannenbring, "Forecasting with Exponential Smoothing: Some Guidelines for Model Selection," *Decision Sciences* 11, no. 2 (1980): 370–83. Also several standardized computer programs are available for calculating optimal alpha values; see, for instance, H. V. Verma and C. W. Gross, *Introduction to Quantitative Methods: A Managerial Emphasis* (Santa Barbara, Ca.: Wiley/Hamilton, 1978): 105–15, 604–6.
13. Michael D. Geurts and I. B. Ibrahim, "Comparing the Box-Jenkins Approach with the Exponential Smoothed Forecasting Model Application to Hawaii Tourists," *Journal of Marketing Research* 12, no. 2 (May 1975): 182–88.
14. See David A. Aaker and George S. Day, *Marketing Research* (New York: John Wiley & Sons, 1986): 507–22, 526–30.
15. For further discussion of time series, see Gross and Peterson, *Business Forecasting*, Chapter 5. Also see Robert T. Green and Arthur W. Allaway, "Identification of Export Opportunities: A Shift-Share Approach," *Journal of Marketing* 49, no. 1 (Winter 1985): 83–88.
16. *Sales and Marketing Management* typically publishes its "Survey of Buying Power" in October.
17. For further discussion of judgmental methods, see Gross and Peterson, *Business Forecasting*, Chapter 2.
18. Richard M. Burton, John S. Chandler, and H. Peter Holzer, *Quantitative Approaches to Business Decision Making* (New York: Harper & Row Publishing Co., 1985), Chapter 11.
19. Alan Glasser, *Research and Development Management* (Englewood Cliffs, N.J.: Prentice-Hall, 1982), Chapter 10. Also see Justin G. Longenecker and Charles D. Pringle, *Management* (Columbus, Ohio: Charles E. Merrill Publishing Co., 1985), Chapter 7.
20. See, for example, Makridakis, Wheelwright, and McGee, *Forecasting*: 653–55. See also Mark P. McElreath, *Priority Research Questions in Public Relations, Key Results from a Delphi Survey* (Lawrence, Kan.: Association for Education in Journalism, 1980). See also Jean-Claude Larreche and Reza Moinpour, "Managerial Judgment in Marketing: The Concept of Expertise," *Journal of Marketing Research* 20, no. 2 (May 1983): 110–21.
21. For an interesting case study of the oil embargo's impact on one tourist industry, see "Holiday Inns, Inc.," in William F. Glueck, *Business Policy: Strategy Formulations and Executive Action*, 2d ed. (New York: McGraw-Hill, 1976): 389–404.
22. For further discussion of conditional events, see Verma and Gross, *Introduction to Quantitative Methods*: 24–26.
23. For further discussion see Raymond Neveu, *Fundamentals of Managerial Finance* (Cincinnati: South-Western Publishing Co., 1985), Chapter 11.
24. For further discussion, see G. David Quirin and John C. Wiginton, *Analyzing Capital Expenditures: Private and Public Perspective* (Homewood, Ill.: Richard D. Irwin, 1981), Chapter 7.

Chapter 9

1. Edgar A. Pessemier, *Product Management: Strategy and Organization* (New York: John Wiley & Sons, 1982): 4, and Robert D. Hisrich and Michael P. Peters, *Marketing Decisions for New and Mature Products: Planning, Development, and Control* (Columbus, Ohio: Charles E. Merrill Publishing Co., 1984), Chapter 1.
2. "Measured Risk-Taking Augments Marketing Science to Create Sweet Smell of Success," *The Marketing News* 16, no. 13 (December 24, 1982): 3.
3. An exception is the C. F. Mueller Company, which in 1982 brought out a new pasta product—its first addition in 117 years. "Mueller Cooks Up First New Product in 117 Years," *Advertising Age* 53, no. 43 (October 16, 1982): 52.

4. Theodore Levitt, "Marketing Success Through Differentiation of Anything," *Harvard Business Review* 58, no. 1 (January/February 1980): 83–91.
5. For further discussion, see Yoram J. Wind, *Product Policy: Concepts, Methods, and Strategy* (New York: Addison-Wesley, 1982): 252–55.
6. Michael H. Mescon, Michael Albert, and Franklin Khedouri, *Individual and Organizational Effectiveness* (New York: Harper & Row, 1985), Chapter 2.
7. These definitions are based on *Marketing Definitions: A Glossary of Marketing Terms*, compiled by the Committee on Definitions of the American Marketing Association, Ralph S. Alexander, Chairman, (Chicago: American Marketing Association, 1960).
8. See P. "Rajan" Varadarajan, "Product Diversity and Firm Performance: An Empirical Investigation," *Journal of Marketing* 50, no. 3 (July 1986): 43–57.
9. Robert U. Ayers and Wilber A. Steger, "Rejuvenating the Life Cycle Concept," *Journal of Business Strategy* 6 (Summer 1985): 66–76. Also, for an excellent discussion of alternative life-cycle shapes, see David R. Rink and John E. Swan, "Product Life Cycle Research: A Literature Review," *Journal of Business Research* (September 1979): 218–42.
10. William Qualls, Richard W. Olshavsky, and Ronald E. Michaels, "Shortening of the PLC—An Empirical Test," *Journal of Marketing* 45, no. 4 (Fall 1981): 76–80.
11. Martin G. Letscher, "Distinguishing Fads from Trends with 6 Research Guidelines," *The Marketing News* 17, no. 2 (January 21, 1983): 3, 15.
12. Ilkka A. Ronkainen, "Criteria Changes Across Product Development Stages," *Industrial Marketing Management* 14 (August 1986): 171–78.
13. See Stanley R. Schultz and S. R. Rao, "Product Life Cycles of Durable Goods for the Home," *Journal of the Academy of Marketing Science* 14 (Spring 1986): 7–12.
14. Philip Kotler, *Marketing Management: Analysis, Planning and Control*, 3d ed. (Englewood Cliffs, N.J.: Prentice-Hall, 1980): 240–41.
15. Michael E. Porter, "How Competitive Forces Shape Strategy," *Harvard Business Review* 57, no. 2 (March/April 1979): 139.
16. See "Games' Action Colors Teaching in New Software," *Advertising Age* 55, no. 32 (June 11, 1984): 3, 96. Also see "The Schoolyard Brawl Breaking Out in Classroom Computers, *Business Week*, April 7, 1986: 90–91.
17. Theodore Levitt, "Exploit the Product Life Cycle," *Harvard Business Review* 43, no. 6 (November/December, 1965): 81–94.
18. Hans B. Thorelli and Stephen Burnett, "The Nature of Product Life Cycles for Industrial Goods Businesses," *Journal of Marketing* 45, no. 4 (Fall 1981): 97–108.
19. See Valarie S. Folkes and Barbara Kostos, "Buyers' and Sellers' Explanations for Product Failure: Who Done It?" *Journal of Marketing* 50, no. 2 (April 1986): 74–80.
20. "Seagram Antes $40 Million," *Business Week*, August 27, 1977: 68.
21. "Abbott: Profiting from Products that Cut Costs," *Business Week*, June 18, 1984: 56, 60.
22. "Korvette's Selling Off Chicago Stores," *Advertising Age*, (August 22, 1977): 32.
23. See William Qualls, Richard W. Olshavsky, and Ronald E. Michaels, "Shortening of the PLC—An Empirical Test."
24. See "Life Cycle for Brands? Forget It," *Advertising Age* 57 (March 17, 1986): 18–20.
25. George S. Day, "Diagnosing the Product Portfolio," *Journal of Marketing* 41, no. 3 (April 1977): 29–38. See also Derek F. Abell, *Defining the Business: The Starting Point for Strategic Planning* (Englewood Cliffs, N.J.: Prentice-Hall, 1980). Also see Timothy M. Devinney, David W. Stewart, and Allan D. Schocker, "A Note on the Application of Portfolio Theory: A Comment on Cardozo and Smith," *Journal of Marketing* 49, no. 4 (Fall 1985): 107–12.
26. William K. Hall, "SBU's: Hot New Topic in the Management of Diversification," *Business Horizons* 26, no. 1 (February 1978): 17. Also see Kenneth Davidson, "Strategic Investment Theories," *Journal of Business Strategy* 6 (Summer 1985): 16–28.
27. See George Day, "The Product Life Cycle: Analysis and Applications Issues," *Journal of Marketing* 45, no. 4 (Fall 1981): 60–67.
28. Robin Wensley, "Strategic Marketing: Betas, Boxes, or Basics," *Journal of Marketing* 45, no. 3 (Summer 1981): 173–82.

Chapter 10

1. Edgar A. Pessemier, *Product Management: Strategy and Organization* (New York: John Wiley & Sons, 1982): 8, 9. Also see "Products Need Share of Heart," *Advertising Age* 57 (January 27, 1986): 18, 19.
2. Ralph Biggadike, "The Risky Business of Diversification," *Harvard Business Review* 57, no. 3 (May/June 1979): 103–11. See also "International Flavors: Funding Far-Out Ideas for Future Growth," *Business Week*, no. 2868 (November 1984): 129, 133.
3. Leigh Lawton and A. Parasuraman, "The Impact of the Marketing Concept on New Product Planning," *Journal of Marketing* 44, no. 1 (Winter 1980): 20.
4. See for instance "Better Reaps Big Bucks," *Venture* 7 (December 1985): 112.
5. Laurie Freeman and Patricia Winters, "Franchise Players: Brand Expansion Preferred Route," *Advertising Age* 57, no. 44 (August 18, 1986): 3, 61.
6. Michael Morris and William Lundstrum, "Product Innovation and the Strategic Impact of the Marketing Concept," *1984 American Marketing Association Educators' Conference Proceedings* (Chicago: American Marketing Association, 1984): 226–30.
7. Peter Drucker, "Creating Strategies of Innovation," *Planning Review* 13 (November 1985): 8–11.
8. "When Boeing Gets into the Streetcar Business," *Business Week*, September 12, 1977: 130.
9. "Look, Ma, No Dials: More Major Appliances Go Digital," *Business Week*, November 12, 1984: 97, 100, 101.
10. "U.S. Bars Sears Bait-Switch Strategy in Appliance Sales," *Detroit News*, October 21, 1976: 7A.
11. For review of new product conceptual models, see Chakravarthi Narasimhan and Subrata K. Sen, "New Product Models for Test Market Data," *Journal of Marketing* 47, no. 1 (Winter 1983): 11–24.
12. For an excellent discussion of idea generating techniques, see Philip Kotler, *Marketing Management: Analysis, Planning and Control*, 4th ed. (Englewood Cliffs, N.J.: Prentice-Hall, 1980): 202–5. Also see Ashok K. Gupta, S. P. Raj, and David Wilemon, "A Model for Studying R&D—A Marketing Interface in the Product Innovation Process," *Journal of Marketing* 50, no. 2 (April 1986): 7–17.
13. For a discussion on screening, see C. Merle Crawford, *New Products Management* (Homewood, Ill.: Richard D. Irwin, 1983), Chapter 4.
14. Crawford, *New Products Management*: 366–83.
15. For further discussion, see Everett Rogers, *Diffusion of Innovations* (New York: The Free Press, 1962), Chapter 5. Also see Thomas S. Robertson, *Innovative Behavior and Communication* (New York: Holt, Rinehart & Winston, 1971): 46–49. See also Michael L. Rothschild and William C. Gaidis, "Behavioral Learning Theory: Its Relevance to Marketing and Promotions," *Journal of Marketing* 45, no. 2 (Spring 1981): 70–78.

16. For further discussion, see Douglas J. Dalrymple and Leonard J. Parsons, *Marketing Management* (New York: John Wiley & Sons, 1983), Chapter 12.
17. See Robert Peterson, *Marketing Research* (Plano, Texas: Business Publications, 1983), Chapter 14.
18. Various attitude measurement models that relate preferences and multiattributes of product concepts are also useful in concept testing. For an excellent technical discussion of several models, see Joel Huber, "Predicting Preferences on Experimental Bundles of Attributes: A Comparison of Models," *Journal of Marketing Research* 12, no. 3 (August 1975): 290–97.
19. Edward M. Tauber, "Reduced New Product Failures: Measure Needs as Well as Purchase Interest," *Journal of Marketing* 37, no. 3 (July 1973): 61–64.
20. "Picking Panel Members to Pass Judgment," *Advertising Age* 57 (February 13, 1986): 12–13.
21. See Chapter 7 for a more extensive treatment of these tests.
22. Nancy Giges, "Baking Soda May Put Teeth in Dental Care," *Advertising Age* 55, no. 74 (November 1, 1984): 2.
23. For a discussion of these techniques, see Subhash C. Jain, *Marketing Planning and Strategy* (Cincinnati: South-Western Publishing, 1983), Chapter 5.
24. See Ronald F. Bush, Peter H. Bloch, and Claude F. Reynaud, "The Brand Trademark: A Valuable and Vulnerable Resource," *1984 American Marketing Association Educators' Proceedings* (Chicago: American Marketing Association, 1984): 276–79.
25. Based on Committee on Definitions, *Marketing Definitions, A Glossary of Marketing Terms* (Chicago: American Marketing Association, 1960): 18–20.
26. The Lanham Act of 1946 specifies the types of marks that can be protected and makes provision for registration records. However, registration is not compulsory and registering a mark does not automatically grant full rights. It is necessary to show that the firm was the first to use a trademark and that the product has been offered for sale on a continuing basis.
27. See William S. Sachs and George Benson, *Product Planning and Management* (Tulsa: Penwell Books, 1981): 298–301. Also see "Courts Penalize Trademark Misdeeds," *Advertising Age* 57 (January 6, 1986): 34.
28. "Wither Generics," *Advertising Age* 57 (March 3, 1986): 17.
29. Robert F. Hartley, *Marketing Mistakes* (Columbus, Ohio: Grid, 1976): 59–70.
30. James U. McNeal and Linda M. Zeren, "Brand Name Selection for Consumer Products," *Business Topics* 34, no. 2 (Spring 1981): 35–39.
31. Charles Jennings, "How to Protect a Trade Mark," *Industrial Marketing Digest* 8, no. 4 (Fourth quarter, 1983): 67–71.
32. "CE Retailers' Brand Loyalty Is Fading," *Chain Store Age* 62 (January 1986): 34–36.
33. For a discussion of branding terminology, see Thomas F. Shutte, "The Semantics of Branding," *Journal of Marketing* 33, no. 2 (April 1969): 5–11. Also, for a discussion of legal regulations governing labeling, see Warren A. French and Hiram C. Barksdale, "Food Labeling Regulations: Efforts Toward Full Disclosure," *Journal of Marketing* 38, no. 3 (July 1974): 14–19. See also Meir Statman and Tyzoon T. Tyebjee, "Trademarks, Patents, and Innovation in the Ethical Drug Industry," *Journal of Marketing* 45, no. 3 (Summer 1981): 71–81, and Arthur W. Weil, "50,000 OTC Drug Products Face FDA Label Review," *Product Marketing* 9, no. 3 (October 1980): 1, 14.
34. For a detailed example of this pressure on a national bakery, see Robert D. Buzzell and Charles C. Slater, "Decision Theory and Marketing Management," *Journal of Marketing* 26, no. 3 (July 1962): 7–16. See also Michael Levy, John Webster and Roger A. Kerin, "Formulating Push Marketing Strategies: A Method and Application," *Journal of Marketing* 47, no. 1 (Winter 1983): 25–34.
35. As told to one of the authors by the comptroller of Koepplinger's Bread Co. Also see "Here's How to Get the Most Value Out of Your Packaging Buys," *Purchasing* 100 (January 16, 1986): 27.
36. A. E. Gallo and J. M. Connor, "Packaging in Food Marketing," *National Food Review* (Spring 1981): 10–11.
37. Jack Milgram and Aaron Brody, *Executive Summary: Packaging in Perspective; a Report to the Ad Hoc Committee on Packaging* (Cambridge, Mass.: Arthur P. Little, 1974), C–75831, p. S–2. For additional reference, see Dik Warren Twedt, "How Much Value Can Be Added Through Packaging," *Journal of Marketing* 32, no. 1 (January 1968): 58–61.
38. Thomas F. Pillon, "Contract Packaging: One Answer to Many Needs," *Purchasing* 89, no. 4 (November 20, 1980): 66–68.
39. A novel suggestion is to utilize a vice president of new products, who would operate on the same level as the vice president of marketing. According to proponents of this approach, it would reflect the importance of new product development, provide sufficient expertise and leverage, and coordinate all of the efforts of the firm to developing new products. See James H. Myers, "An Organization Design Approach to Improving the Effectiveness of New Product Introduction," *Annual Proceedings, Marketing Educators' Conference* (Chicago: American Marketing Association, 1982): 247. Also see "New Product Gurus: Who Needs Them?" *Marketing Communications* 11 (February 1986): 21–24.
40. For a discussion of product manager authority, see Victor P. Buell, "The Changing Role of the Product Manager in Consumer Goods Companies," *Journal of Marketing* 39, no. 3 (July 1975): 3–11; and Carl McDaniel and David A. Gray, "The Product Manager," *California Management Review* 23, no. 3 (Fall 1980): 89.

Chapter 11

1. Pat Sloan, "Chesebrough Tightens Belt for More Growth in Fast Lane," *Advertising Age* 54, no. 10 (March 7, 1983): 4, 51.
2. Leah Rozen, "Murder Inc. (Bug Div.) Is Healthy Business," *Advertising Age* 46, no. 31 (August 15, 1977): 71.
3. See "Fire a Buyer, Hire a Seller," *Chain Store Age* 62 (March 1986): 28.
4. See C. Glenn Walters, *Marketing Channels* (Glenview, Illinois: Scott, Foresman, 1982), Chapter 1.
5. Some experts extend the notion of a channel beyond customers, all the way to trash disposal centers. Thus, in this view, trash collectors and recycling centers are considered as channel members. See William G. Zikmund and William J. Stanton, "Recycling Solid Wastes: A Channels-of-Distribution Problem," *Journal of Marketing* 35, no. 3 (July, 1977): 34–39. See also Alf H. Walle, "A Preliminary Investigation of the Quadrants of Recycling Model," *Developments in Marketing Science* (Miami: Academy of Marketing Science, 1983): 38–40.
6. See Frank Meissner, "Farmers' Markets Have Merchandising Image Which Is Not Supported by Reality," *Marketing News* 18, no. 22 (October 26, 1984): 17.
7. Philip Kotler, *Marketing Decision Making: A Model Building Approach* (New York: Holt, Rinehart & Winston, 1980): 288. Also see Pat Sloan, "Retailers Ready for Change," *Advertising Age* 57 (January 27, 1986): 38.

8. Also see James Constantin, Rodney Evans, and Malcolm Morris, *Marketing Strategy and Management* (Dallas: Business Publications, 1976): 268.
9. See "CompuServe Unveils 'The Electronic Mall,' " *Marketing News* 18, no. 23 (November 9, 1984): 3.
10. See the discussion of sorting in Wroe Alderson, *Marketing Behavior and Executive Action: A Functionalist Approach to Marketing Theory* (Homewood, Ill.: Richard D. Irwin, 1957), Chapter 7.
11. For a more extensive discussion, see Ronald D. Michman, "Trends Affecting Industrial Distributors," *Industrial Marketing Management* 9, no. 2 (July 1980): 213–16.
12. See "Northrop's Campaign to Get a New Fighter Flying in the Third World," *Business Week*, June 18, 1984: 24–28.
13. For an extensive discussion of legal constraints on interorganizational arrangements, see Rogene A. Bucholz, *Business Environment and Public Policy* (Englewood Cliffs, N.J.: Prentice-Hall, 1983), Chapter 9.
14. "Will IBM Climb to the Top in Software Too?" *Business Week*, October 22, 1984: 100–1.
15. Based on A. L. Munsell, "Evaluating Channels of Distribution," in *Allocating Field Sales Resources* (New York: The Conference Board, 1970): 45–47.
16. See the surrogate indicators of profitability used by intermediary buyers, Chapter 14.
17. Karl H. Vesper, *New Venture Strategies* (Englewood Cliffs, N.J.: Prentice-Hall, 1980): 218–20.
18. Ralph C. Noeber, J. David Reitzel, Donald P. Lyden, Nathan J. Roberts, and Gordon B. Severance, *Contemporary Business Law: Text and Cases* (New York: McGraw-Hill Book Company, 1982): 1092–93.
19. For example, see "Industrial Building Materials, Inc., *v*. Inter-Chemical Corp.," *Journal of Marketing* 35, no. 3 (July, 1971): 76. See also Kresl Power Equipment *v*. Acco Industries," *Journal of Marketing* 45, no. 2 (Spring 1981): 138.
20. Landis Hand, *Competition in Industry* (New York: Forman Books, 1983): 348–49.
21. Bucholz, *Business Environment*, Chapter 9.
22. Seymour H. Fine, "Industrial Marketing Strategy: Distribution Oriented," *1984 Proceedings: American Marketing Association Educators' Conference* (Chicago: American Marketing Association, 1984): 167–70.
23. Research indicates that integrated systems are often far superior vis-à-vis streamlining activities and decisions. See Michael Etgar, "Effects of Administrative Control on Efficiency of Vertical Marketing Systems," *Journal of Marketing Research* 13, no. 1 (February 1976): 12–24. Also see Nancy Giges, "Kentucky Fried Chicken Coup for PepsiCo," *Advertising Age* 57 (July 28, 1986): 3, 66.
24. For an interesting discussion of integration, see C. Glen Walters, *Marketing Channels* (Glenview, Illinois: Scott, Foresman, 1982), Chapter 7.
25. "The Consumer Drives R. J. Reynolds Again," *Business Week*, June 4, 1984: 94.
26. Joseph P. Guiltinan, Ismail B. Rajab, and William C. Rogers, "Factors Influencing Coordination in a Franchise Channel," *Journal of Retailing* 56, no. 2 (Fall 1980): 41–58.
27. "Apple's New Crusade," *Business Week*, November 26, 1984: 149.
28. Bert Rosenbloom, *Marketing Channels: A Management View*, 2d ed. (Hinsdale, Ill.: Dryden, 1983). See also Stanley D. Sibley and Donald A. Michie, "An Exploratory Investigation of Cooperation in a Franchise Channel," *Journal of Retailing* 58, no. 4 (Winter 1982): 23–45.
29. For a discussion of channel conflict, see Ian F. Wilkinson, "Power and Satisfaction in Channels of Distribution," *Journal of Retailing* 55, no. 2 (Summer 1979): 79–94.
30. "Winnebago Industries: Gambling on Two Hybrids to Win Back Lost Inventory," *Business Week*, November 15, 1982: 147.
31. James Brown, "Channel Cooperation: Its Relationship to Channel Performance," in Robert F. Lusch and Paul H. Zinszer, eds., *Contemporary Issues in Marketing Channels* (Norman: The University of Oklahoma, 1979): 87–101.
32. Peter Petre, "How to Keep Customers Happy Captives," *Fortune* 112 (September 2, 1985): 42–46.
33. Donald A. Michie and Stanley D. Sibley, "Channel Member Satisfaction: Controversy Resolved," *Journal of the Academy of Marketing Science* 13 (Spring 1985): 188–205.
34. Gene Siskel, "Five Powerful Pieces Set into Place," *Chicago Tribune*, Feb. 23, 1975, Sec. 6, p. 2.
35. For further discussion see Douglas J. Dalrymple and Leonard J. Parsons, *Marketing Management: Strategy and Cases* (New York: John Wiley & Sons, 1986): 519–24.
36. Robert F. Dwyer, "Channel Member Satisfaction: Laboratory Insights," *Journal of Retailing* 56, no. 2 (Summer 1980): 45–65. Also see Barbara Bund Jackson, *Winning and Keeping Industrial Customers* (Lexington, Mass.: Lexington Books, 1986): 166–76.
37. John R. Nevin and Robert W. Raukert, "The Influence of Exercising Power Sources in a Channel of Distribution," in Michael G. Harvey and Robert F. Lusch, eds., *Proceedings: Distribution Conference* (Norman: The University of Oklahoma, 1982): 75–80.
38. Donald W. Jackson, Jr. and Bruce J. Walker, "The Channel's Manager: Marketing's Newest Aide," *California Management Review* 23, no. 3 (Winter 1980): 52–58. Also see Donald W. Jackson, Janet E. Keith, and Bruce J. Walker, "Who Is Responsible for Managing Marketing Channels in Manufacturing Firms?" *1985 American Marketing Association Educators' Proceedings* (Chicago: American Marketing Association, 1985): 215–21.

Chapter 12

1. Earl M. Guelzo, *Introduction to Logistics Management* (Englewood Cliffs, N.J.: Prentice-Hall, 1985): 4–5.
2. Bert Rosenbloom, unpublished correspondence with the authors.
3. Ronald H. Ballou, *Business Logistics: Management, Planning, and Control* (Englewood Cliffs, N.J.: Prentice-Hall, 1985): 16–17.
4. "Foremost-McKesson: The Computer Moves Distribution to Center Stage," *Business Week*, December 7, 1981: 116–17. Also see "McKesson's Profits Rise 58 Percent in 1985 in Drugs and Health Care," *Chemical Marketing Reporter* 229 (February 24, 1986): 9–12.
5. *Statistical Abstract of the United States* (Washington, D.C.: U.S. Government Printing Office, 1986): 492.
6. See R. Eric Reindenbach and Terence A. Oliva, "General Living Systems Theory and Marketing: A Framework for Analysis," *Journal of Marketing* 45, no. 4 (Fall 1981): 30–37.
7. "JIT Delivery Good, Not Good Enough," *Purchasing* 100 (March 27, 1986): 19–24.
8. "Creativity Is the Key," *Traffic Management* 23 (January 1986): 35–37.
9. For an excellent discussion of selecting the appropriate service level, including numerous references, see Bert Rosenbloom, "Using Physical Distribution Strategy for Better Channel Management," *Journal of the Academy of Marketing Science* 7, no. 1 (Winter 1979): 61–70.
10. Robert C. Lieb, *Transportation* (Reston, Virginia: Reston Publishing Co., 1985): 18–19.

11. Larry Harrington, "How Push Distribution Cuts Inventory Costs," *Traffic Management* 25 (January 1986): 18–21.
12. See David B. Montgomery and Charles B. Weinberg, "Toward Strategic Intelligence Systems," *Journal of Marketing* 43, no. 4 (Fall 1979): 41–52.
13. For discussion see Philip B. Schary, *Logistics Decisions: Text and Cases* (New York: Dryden Press, 1984), Chapter 4.
14. See "Detroit's Latest Problem Is Booming Sales," *Business Week*, September 17, 1984: 45, 48.
15. See Donald B. Rosenfield and Mart T. Pendrock, "The Effects of Warehouse Configuration Design on Inventory Levels and Holding Costs," *Sloan Management Review* 21, no. 2 (Summer 1980): 21–33.
16. To better understand the complexities of inventory problems, see Harvey M. Wagner, *Principles of Operations Research: With Applications to Managerial Decisions*, 2d ed. (Englewood Cliffs, N.J.: Prentice-Hall, 1981), Chapters 9, 19, and Section II.
17. See "Computer-to-Computer Ordering Passes Test by Wholesale Grocers' Association," *Marketing News* 18, no. 23 (November 9, 1984): 36.
18. For an extensive coverage of these techniques, see Douglas M. Lambert and James R. Stock, *Strategic Physical Distribution Management* (Homewood, Ill.: Richard D. Irwin, 1983): 319–21.
19. Janet Neiman, "P&G's Cookie Monster on Kansas City Rampage," *Advertising Age* 54, no. 13 (March 21, 1983): 3, 54.
20. "Warehousing Review," *Distribution* 84 (March 1986): 81–99.
21. Breaking bulk consists of transmitting large shipments to markets and breaking these down into individual orders for customers.
22. Steven B. Oresman and Charles D. Scudder, "A Remedy for Maldistribution," *Business Horizons* 22, no. 3 (June 1974): 61.
23. Transportation Association of America, *Transportation Facts and Trends* (Washington, D.C: Transportation Association of America, July 1980): 4.
24. "U.S. Rail Rates for Coal Raise Tempers Abroad," *Business Week*, November 21, 1983: 43, 44.
25. Craig Endicott, "Distributors Are Water's Driving Force," *Advertising Age* 55, no. 67 (October 8, 1984): 52, 54.
26. "The ICC's Chief Swerves from Deregulation," *Business Week*, November 9, 1981: 74. Also see "Shippers, Carriers Argue Merits of Further Trucking Deregulation," *Traffic Management* 24 (October 1985): 13–15.
27. "A Painful Transition for the Transport Industry," *Business Week*, November 28, 1983: 83–84.
28. "Eastern Fights for Life," *Fortune* 113 (February 17, 1986): 8–12.
29. "Braniff's Bumpy Flight," *Financial World* 154 (December 11, 1985): 17–19. Also see "World Airways to End Its Passenger Service," *The Boston Globe*, September 4, 1986: 41.
30. "Eastern Airlines: Borman's Battle at the Brink," *Economist* 298 (February 1, 1986): 66–69.
31. John J. Coyle, Edward J. Bardi, and Joseph L. Cavinato, *Transportation* (St. Paul: West Publishing Co., 1986): 40–44.

Chapter 13

1. Danny R. Arnold, Louis M. Capella, and Garry Dismith, *Strategic Retail Management* (Menlo Park, Calif.: Addison-Wesley, 1983), Chapter 15.
2. For an example of a test system, see Jeffrey L. Seglin, "Screen Test," *Inc.* 6, no. 7 (July 1984): 114, 116, 117, 119.
3. *Prime Time Sunday*, NBC, September 30, 1979.
4. See Robert E. O'Neill, "EFT Update: Familiarity Breeds Acceptance," *Progressive Grocer* 60, no. 2 (March 1981): 133–41.
5. See the discussion of sorting in Wroe Alderson, *Marketing Behavior and Executive Action: A Functionalist Approach to Marketing Theory* (Homewood, Ill.: Richard D. Irwin, 1957), Chapter 7.
6. *Statistical Abstract of the United States*, 106th ed. (Washington, D.C.: U.S. Government Printing Office, 1986): 772, 774.
7. See William B. Franklin and James C. Cooper, "Its Sluggish Growth—But Its Growth," *Business Week* August 4, 1986: 19–20.
8. *The State of Small Business: A Report to the President* (Washington, D.C.: U.S. Government Printing Office, 1983): 201.
9. See Nancy Giges, "Nabisco Shakes Units, Rattles Shops," *Advertising Age* 55, no. 88 (December 24, 1984): 2.
10. Stanley C. Hollander, "Retailing: Cause or Effect?" in William F. Decker, *Emerging Concepts in Marketing* (Chicago: American Marketing Association, 1962): 220–30.
11. *Statistical Abstract of the United States*, 106th ed., pp. 774–75.
12. "Investigating the Collapse of W. T. Grant," *Business Week*, July 19, 1976: 60–62. Also see S. W. Sohn and R. S. Smith, "Countries Are Like Corporations [Mexico and W. T. Grant]," *U.S. Banker* (January 1984): 40–42.
13. "Allied Stores: Shift Back to Hard Goods," *Stores* 65, no. 4 (April 1983): 41.
14. Alvin D. Star and Michael Z. Mossel, "Survival Rates for Retailers," *Journal of Retailing* 57, no. 2 (Summer 1981): 87–99.
15. David Schulz, "Selling the Newest Trendy Pastime: Exercise," *Stores* 65, no. 2 (February 1983): 5, 9–12.
16. "Why Profits Shrink at a Grand Old Name," *Business Week*, April 11, 1977: 66–78.
17. J. Barry Mason and Morris L. Mayer, *Modern Retailing* (Plano, Texas: Business Publications, Inc., 1985), Chapter 4.
18. For an excellent discussion of retail gravitation, see Lawrence G. Golden and Donald A. Zimmerman, *Effective Retailing* (Boston: Houghton Mifflin Co., 1986), Chapter 12.
19. See Kenneth C. Schneider and Rolf O. Christiansen, "Energy, Retailing and Customer Shopping Strategy: A Time Dimensioned Analysis," *Journal of Retailing* 58, no. 3 (Fall 1982): 27–45.
20. For further discussion, see Robert F. Hartley, *Marketing Mistakes* (Columbus, Ohio: Grid, 1976): 7–17.
21. *Statistical Abstract of the United States*, 106th ed., p. 274.
22. Based on *The Census of Retailing, 1982* (U.S. Department of Commerce).
23. "Retailers Know They Belong," *Advertising Age* 54, no. 25 (June 13, 1983): M–28.
24. For a good discussion of franchising, see W. M. Greenfield, *Calculated Risk: A Guide to Entrepreneurship* (Lexington, Mass.: D. C. Heath and Co., 1986), Chapter 10.
25. *Statistical Abstract of the United States*, 106th ed., p. 18.
26. Ronald W. Hasty, *Retailing* (Philadelphia: Harper & Row, 1983): 107–10.
27. Barry Berman and Joel R. Evans, *Retail Management: A Strategic Approach* (New York: Macmillan, 1986): 67–72.
28. See Stanley R. Sondeno, *Small Business Management* (Plano, Texas: Business Publications, Inc., 1985), Chapter 6.
29. See Howard H. Stevenson, Michael J. Roberts, and H. Irving Grousbeck, *New Business Ventures and the Entrepreneur* (Homewood, Ill.: Richard D. Irwin, Inc., 1985), Chapter 5.
30. James R. Lowry, *Retail Management* (Cincinnati: South-Western Publishing Co., 1983): 106–7.
31. Robert F. Lusch, *Management of Retail Enterprises* (Belmont, Calif.: Wadsworth, 1982): 88–90.

32. Shelby D. Hunt, "The Socioeconomic Consequences of the Franchise System of Distribution," *Journal of Marketing* 36, no. 3 (July 1972): 32–38.
33. Gregory P. Stone, "City Shoppers and Urban Identification: Observations on the Social Psychology of City Life," *American Journal of Sociology* 60 (1954): 36–45. A more recent verification was reported by William R. Darden and Fred D. Reynolds, "Shopping Orientation and Product Usage Rates," *Journal of Marketing Research* VIII, no. 4 (November 1971): 505–8.
34. John J. Burnett, Shelby D. Hunt, and Robert Amason, "Feminism: Implications for Department Store Strategy and Salesclerk Behavior," *Journal of Retailing* 57, no. 4 (Winter 1981): 71–85.
35. Bruce T. Mattson, "Situational Influences on Store Choice," *Journal of Retailing* 58, no. 3 (Fall 1982): 46–58.
36. The Stone Study has been replicated and its essential findings well-justified. See Louis E. Boone, David L. Kurtz, James C. Johnson, and John A. Bonno, "City Shoppers and Urban Identification Revised," *Journal of Marketing* 38, no. 2 (July 1974): 67–69. See also Robin Peterson and David Lill, "Shopping Orientation Concept and Small Business," *American Journal of Small Business* 5, no. 2 (July 1980): 39–43; and "Big Things in Small Packages," *Progressive Grocer* (Februray 1986): 26.
37. Canteen Corporation, *Annual Report*, 1985.
38. "Location Is Everything: Near-Scientific Site Formula Yields Success," *Chain Store Age* (January 1986): 64–72.
39. Jacob Hornik and Laurence P. Feldman, "Retailing Implications of the Do-It-Yourself Consumer Movement," *Journal of Retailing* 58, no. 2 (September 1982): 44–63.
40. "Apple's New Crusade," *Business Week*, November 26, 1984: 154.
41. Stanley C. Hollander, "Notes on the Retail Accordian Theory," *Journal of Retailing* 16, no. 2 (Summer 1966): 29–40. See also Danny N. Bellenger and Jac L. Goldstucker, *Basic Retailing* (Homewood, Ill.: Richard D. Irwin, 1982): 326–40.
42. "What Attracts Shoppers to a Retailer?" *Chain Store Age* (March 1986): 9–19.
43. J. Patrick Kelly and William R. George, "Strategic Management Issues for the Retailing of Services," *Journal of Retailing* 58, no. 2 (Summer 1982): 26–43. Also see "Market Share Tactics," *Stores* (February 1986): 56.
44. Malcolm P. McNair, "Significant Trends and Developments in the Postwar Period," in *Competitive Distribution in a Free, High Level Economy and Its Implications for the University*, ed. A. B. Smith (Pittsburgh: University of Pittsburgh Press, 1958): 1–25. For a critical discussion, see Stanley C. Hollander, "The Wheel of Retailing," *Journal of Marketing* 34, no. 3 (July 1960): 37–42. Also see "Mass Appeals," *Forbes* (May 5, 1986): 56.
45. "K mart: The No. 2 Retailer Starts to Make an Upscale Move—At Last," *Business Week*, (June 4, 1984): 50–51.
46. "This process is also sometimes called institutional trading up. For an excellent discussion and appraisal, see Arieh Goldman, "The Role of Trading Up in the Development of the Retailing System," *Journal of Marketing* 39, no. 1 (January 1975): 54–62.
47. In 1980, 140 banks offered VISA debit cards and held 800,000 accounts. Walter Kiechel, "Explosion in the Bank Card Cafeteria," *Fortune* 26, no. 9 (September 8, 1980): 18.
48. "Department Stores: Threats and Opportunities," *Chain Store Age* (January 1986): 24–25.
49. Pierre Martineau, "The Personality of the Retail Store," *Harvard Business Review* 31, no. 1 (January/February 1958): 47. See also Ronald W. Hasty, *Retailing*: 545.
50. Lorraine Baltera, "Neiman's Biggest Seller Is Image," *Advertising Age* 48, no. 37 (June 6, 1977): 3ff.
51. See "Merchandising Image Affected by Clutter, Research," *Marketing News* 18, no. 25 (December 7, 1984): 16, 18.
52. See Delbert J. Duncan, Stanley C. Hollander, and Ronald Savitt, *Modern Retail Management* (Homewood, Ill.: Richard D. Irwin, 1983): 245.
53. "There Are Two Kinds of Supermarkets: The Quick and the Dead," *Business Week* (August 11, 1986): 62–63.
54. Louis Bucklin, "Retail Strategy and the Classification of Consumer Goods," *Journal of Marketing* 27, no. 1 (January 1963): 50–55.
55. Janet Wallach, "Fashion Furs," *Stores* 65, no. 3 (March 1983): 10.
56. "Hartmarx: Cashing in on Discount Suits without Losing Its Upscale Image," *Business Week* (May 14, 1984): 200.
57. Leonard J. Berry, "The Components of Department Store Image: A Theoretical and Empirical Analysis," *Journal of Retailing* 45, no. 2 (Spring 1969): 5, 7–9.
58. "Programmed Service Builds Competitive Edge," *Progressive Grocer* 34, no. 8 (September 1972): 62–68.
59. These firms often markdown items for a special promotion; however, see Pat Sloan, "Retailers Trimmin' More Than Trees," *Advertising Age* 55, no. 86 (December 17, 1984): 2, 56.
60. "How Long Can Cabbage Patch Kids Keep Coleco Afloat?", *Business Week*, October 22, 1984: 41–42.

Chapter 14

1. *Statistical Abstract of the United States*, 106th ed. (Washington, D.C.: U.S. Government Printing Office): 1986, 783, 784.
2. Wholesalers are particularly suited to perform sorting activities. For further discussion, see Wroe Alderson, *Dynamic Marketing Behavior* (Homewood, Ill.: Richard D. Irwin, 1965), Chapter 1. Also see "Back to the Future," *Progressive Grocer* (February 1986): 61–62.
3. Kevin Higgins, "Searle Plots a Dual Marketing Strategy for NutraSweet Brand," *Marketing News* 2, no. 9 (December 1984): 6, 7.
4. "An Auto Parts Company Running in High Gear," *Business Week*, April 16, 1984: 112. Also see "Magna—A Unique Heavyweight in Tough World of Auto Parts," *Automotive News*, April 14, 1986: 1–3.
5. See Mary Ann Lederhaus, "Improving Marketing Channel Control through Power and Exchange," *Journal of the Academy of Marketing Science* 12, no. 13 (Summer 1984): 18–34. Also see "What to Do When Distributors Merge," *Purchasing*, December 5, 1985: 84–85.
6. R. Faletra, "Distributor Wars: Davids vs. the Goliaths," *Purchasing*, January 16, 1986: 58A-28–58A-29.
7. Donald A. Ball and Wendall H. McCulloch, Jr., *International Business: Introduction and Essentials* (Plano, Texas: Business Publications, Inc., 1985): 411–12.
8. "Ore-Ida Turns Tatters into Taters," *Advertising Age* 55, no. 77 (November 12, 1984): 4, 58, 60.
9. "Working the Field," *Industrial Distribution* 74 (October 1985): 81–83.
10. Wendy Kimbrell, "Ambassador Joins Office Equipment Fray," *Advertising Age* 55, no. 80 (November 26, 1984): 60.
11. For an excellent discussion of wholesaling, see Louis W. Stern and Adel I. El-Ansary, *Marketing Channels* (Englewood Cliffs, N.J.: Prentice-Hall, 1982), Chapter 4.
12. James R. Brown and Sherman A. Timmins, "Substructural Dimensions of Interorganizational Relations in Marketing Channels," *Journal of the Academy of Marketing Science* 9, no. 3 (Summer 1981): 168–

71. Also see "Wholesaling Ignored Despite Modernization," *Marketing News* (February 14, 1986): 35.

13. Louis P. Bucklin, *Competition and Evolution in the Distributive Trades* (Englewood Cliffs, N.J.: Prentice-Hall, 1972): 203.
14. *Statistical Abstract*, 1986: 784.
15. "Manufacturer Relations," *Progressive Grocer* (February 1986): 37–39.
16. See James P. Forkan, "My Little Pony's Furlongs Ahead of the Toy Pack," *Advertising Age* 55, no. 86 (December 17, 1984): 3.
17. For a more extensive treatment, see Gerald Pintel and Jay Diamond, *Retailing* (Englewood Cliffs, N.J.: Prentice-Hall, 1983), Chapter 9. Also see Douglas J. Dalrymple and Leonard J. Parsons, *Marketing Management: Strategies and Cases* (New York: John Wiley & Sons, 1986): 554–60.
18. Lewis A. Spalding, "Buying Offices: A Changing Business," *Stores* 65, no. 4 (April 1983): 18–21.
19. See M. G. Kolchin, "The Role of Structure in the Performance of Department Store Purchasing Agents," *Journal of Purchasing Materials Management* 22, no. 2 (Spring 1986): 7–12.
20. Evidence exists that an individual buyer is most instrumental in making purchase decisions even if a buying committee exists. Buyers exercise considerable influence because they determine what information is to be presented to the committee. Thus, focusing on satisfying the buyer is usually the key to success. See Barry Berman and Joel R. Evans, *Retailing Management: A Strategic Approach* (New York: Macmillan, 1986): 275–90. Also see "Offshore Buying Specialists Do Exist," *Purchasing* (January 30, 1986): 36.
21. Robert W. Mueller and Franklin H. Graf, "New Items in the Food Industry, Their Problems and Opportunities," a special report to the Annual Convention of the Super Market Institute, Cleveland, Ohio, May 20, 1968: 2.
22. "The Big News at AT&T Isn't Its Personal Computer," *Business Week*, July 9, 1984: 80–81.
23. Danny N. Bellenger and Jac I. Goldstucker, *Retailing Basics* (Homewood, Ill.: Richard D. Irwin, 1983): 150–51. See also Brian Moran, "Computerland Sells Labeled Line," *Advertising Age* 55, no. 67 (September 6, 1984): 3, 34.
24. "Grand Union: Jimmy Goldsmith's Maverick Plan to Restore Profitability," *Business Week*, May 14, 1984: 188, 191, 193. Also see John Schwartz, "Beef a Natural for Grand Union's Strategy," *Advertising Age* (Feburary 28, 1986): 54.
25. David B. Montgomery, "New Product Distribution: An Analysis of Supermarket Buyer Decisions," *Journal of Marketing Research* 12, no. 3 (August 1975): 255–64.
26. Roger A. Dickinson, *Buyer Decision Making* (Berkeley, Calif.: Institute of Business and Economic Research, 1967): 14–17. See also Stern and El-Ansary, *Marketing Channels*, Chapter 3; and "Levi's The Jeans Giant Slipped as the Market Shifted," *Business Week*, November 5, 1984: 79, 82.
27. "The VCR Boom Puts Blank Tapes into Fast Forward," *Business Week*, August 6, 1984: 92–93.
28. See "Display Makers Serve Two Masters," *Marketing News* 18, no. 25 (December 7, 1984): 15, 19.

Chapter 15

1. *Statistical Abstract of the United States*, 106th ed. (Washington, D.C.: U.S. Government Printing Office, 1986).
2. R. Craig Endicott, "P & G Retains Ad Spending Crown," *Advertising Age* 71 (September 26, 1985): 1.
3. Raymond Serafin, "Stroh Signature Signs Off TV for Launch," *Advertising Age* (March 17, 1986): 92 and ibid.
4. See Edward W. Wheatley, "Theory of Marketing—The Practice of Law," *Journal of Professional Services Marketing* 2 (Winter 1985): 79–88.
5. Many studies have reported these results. For classics, see J. M. Bowles, Jr. and N. H. Pronko, "Identification of Cola Beverages: II. A Further Study," *Journal of Applied Psychology* 22, no. 3 (May 1948): 55–59. "Does the Label Change the Taste?" *Printers Ink* 16, no. 12 (March 1962): 59–63; and James C. Makens, "Effect of Brand Preference Upon Consumers' Perceived Taste of Turkey Meat," *Journal of Applied Psychology* 49, no. 4 (1969): 261–63.
6. Raymond L. Horton, *Buyer Behavior: A Decision Making Approach* (Columbus, Ohio: Charles E. Merrill, 1985): 218.
7. " '84 Elections and Olympics Top List Of Stories to Come," *Advertising Age* 55, no. 1 (January 2, 1984): 26.
8. Janet Neiman, "All-Bran Ads May Inspire Health Trend," *Advertising Age* 55, no. 73 (October 29, 1984): 6, 12.
9. Robert Raissman, "Sports Shoe Endorsement Wars Settled," *Advertising Age* 54, no. 21 (May 16, 1983): 24.
10. See Kenneth G. Hardy, "Key Success Factors for Manufacturers' Sales Promotions in Package Goods," *Journal of Marketing* 50 (July 1986): 13–23.
11. Marji Simon, "Survey Probes Strengths, Weaknesses of Promotions," *Marketing News* 18, no. 12 (June 8, 1984): 3, 4.
12. Laurie Freeman, "Consumers Avert K-C Tissue," *Advertising Age* 56, no. 4 (January 17, 1985): 32.
13. Adapted from *Marketing Definitions: A Glossary of Marketing Terms*, compiled by the Committee on Definitions of the American Marketing Association, Ralph S. Alexander, Chairman (Chicago: American Marketing Association, 1960).
14. See Terence A. Shimp and M. Wayne DeLozier, *Promotion Management and Marketing Communications* (New York: The Dryden Press, 1986), Chapter 6.
15. William G. Nickels, *Marketing Communication and Promotion* (Columbus, Ohio: Grid Publishing, 1984): 72, 73. See also "How Do You Make Software Sound Sexy?" *Business Week*, January 21, 1984: 110, 112.
16. Jacob Jacoby and Wayne D. Hoyer, "Viewer Miscomprehension of Televised Communication: Selected Findings," *Journal of Marketing* 46, no. 4 (Fall 1982): 12–26.
17. "How Do You Make Software Sound Sexy?"
18. For further discussion of this section's topics, see Leon Shiffman and Leslie Kanuk, *Consumer Behavior* (Englewood Cliffs, N.J.: Prentice-Hall, 1983), Chapter 9. Also see Jean Perrieu, Christian Dussart and Paul Francoise, "Advertisers and the Factual Content of Advertising," *Journal of Advertising* 14 (March 1985): 30–35.
19. For a further discussion of fear appeals, see John J. Burnett and Richard L. Oliver, "Fear Appeal Effects in the Field: A Segmentation Approach, *Journal of Marketing Research* 16, no. 2 (May 1979): 181–90; Homer E. Spence and Reza Moinpour, "Fear Appeals in Marketing—A Social Perspective," *Journal of Marketing* (July 1972): 39–43. Also see John S. Wright, Willis L. Winter, Jr., and Sherilyn E. Zeigler, *Advertising* (New York: McGraw-Hill, 1982): 237–38.
20. For a discussion of factors influencing whether a one- or a two-sided argument should be used, see C. I. Hovland, A. A. Lumsdaine, and F. D. Sheffield, *Experiments on Mass Communication*, vol. 3 (Princeton, N.J.: Princeton University Press, 1948), Chapter 8. See also Henry Assael, *Consumer Behavior and Marketing Action* (Boston: Kent Publishing, 1981): 489–90.
21. B. Sternthal, R. Dholakia, and C. Leavitt, "The Persuasive Effects of Source Credibility: Test of Cognitive Response," *Journal of Con-*

sumer Research 4, no. 4 (December 1978): 252. Also see Paul H. Schurr and Julie L. Ozanne, "Influences on Exchange Processes: Buyers' Preconceptions of a Seller's Trustworthiness and Bargaining Toughness," *Journal of Consumer Research* 11 (March 1985): 939–53.

22. Helena Czepiec, "Are Foreign Products Still Seen as National Stereotypes?" *1984 AMA Educators' Proceedings* (Chicago: American Marketing Association, 1984): 49–51.
23. In 1983, SRI Research Center conducted a nationwide telephone survey, asking consumers which celebrities they were most aware of and to whom their reactions were favorable. The largest number of mentions was given to Bill Cosby. Following him were Chrysler chairman Lee Iacocca, Victoria Principal (actress), Bob Hope, Don Meredith, Robert Young, Jaclyn Smith, Lauren Bacall, and James Garner. See Scott Hume, "Stars Are Lacking Luster As Ad Presenters," *Advertising Age* 54, no. 47 (November 7, 1983): 3, 92.
24. Robert Raisssman, "Sports Shoe Endorsement Wars Settled," *Advertising Age* 54, no. 21 (May 16, 1983): 24.
25. See Robert R. Harmon and Kenneth A. Coney, "The Persuasive Effects of Source Credibility in Buy and Lease Situations," *Journal of Marketing Research* 19, no. 2 (May 1982) 255–60; Maurice I. Mandell, *Advertising* (Englewood Cliffs, N.J.: Prentice-Hall, 1980): 534–35.
26. Janet Neiman, "Super Challenges Making Peanut Butter Market Sticky," *Advertising Age* 54, no. 20 (May 9, 1983): 34.
27. Advertising rates are published. Perhaps the best known sources are the monthly publications of Standard Rate and Data Service, Inc., Skokie, Ill. This firm publishes separate data books for media categories, including *Business Publications Rates and Data* (or trade magazines), *Spot Radio Rates and Data, Spot Television Rates and Data, Consumer Magazines and Farm Publications Rates and Data, Print Media Production Data*, and *Transit Advertising Rates and Data* (on the sides of busses, cabs, etc.). Also, *Advertising Age* is an invaluable source for keeping current with advertising trends, including rates.
28. Peggy J. Kreshel, "How Leading Advertising Agencies Perceive Effective Reach and Frequency," *Journal of Advertising* 14 (September 1985): 32–38.
29. Ruth Stroud, "Nike Weighing Ad Promo Budget Cuts," *Advertising Age* 56, no. 5 (January 21, 1985): 6.
30. See "Datril Again Tries Price vs. Tylenol," *Advertising Age* 54, no. 13 (March 21, 1983): 2, 52.
31. B. G. Yovovich, "Stepping into a New Era," *Advertising Age* (August 22, 1983): M31.
32. Roger A. Strang, "Sales Promotion—Fast Growth, Faulty Management" *Harvard Business Review* (July/August 1976): 115–24 and Kenneth G. Hardy, "Key Success Factors for Manufacturers' Sales Promotions in Package Goods," *Journal of Marketing* 50 (July 1986): 13–23.
33. *Consumer Promotion Report* (monograph) (New York: Dancer, Fitzgerald, Sample, 1982).
34. Yovovich, "Stepping into a New Era," p. M9.
35. P. Rajan Varadarajan, "Coupon Fraud: A $500 Million Dilemma," *Business* 35 (July/September 1985): 23–29.
36. William F. Gloede, "Postal Probe Clips $1M-a-week Coupon Scam," *Advertising Age* (March 31, 1986): 10.
37. John H. Holmes and John D. Lett, Jr., "*Journal of Advertising Research*, October 1977: 35–40.
38. *Ibid.* Also see Donn J. Tilson and Donald Vance, "Corporate Philanthropy Comes of Age," *Public Relations Review* 11 (Summer 1985): 26–33.
39. Bertrand R. Canfield and Frazier Moore, *Public Relations: Principles, Cases, and Problems*, 6th ed. (Homewood, Ill.: Richard D. Irwin, 1973): 4.
40. Robert S. Mason, "What's a PR Director for Anyway?" *Harvard Business Review* 52 (September/October 1974): 120–26.
41. "Marathon Sponsorship Is Promotional Centerpiece for Xerox Photocopier Line," *Marketing News* 18, no. 4 (February 17, 1984): 1, 40.
42. Julie Franz, "News Spotlight Powers Tylenol Ad Recall: Visibility Increases after Poisoning," *Advertising Age* (March 31, 1986): 4.

Chapter 16

1. See S. Watson Dunn and Arnold M. Barban, *Advertising: Its Role in Modern Marketing* (New York: The Dryden Press, 1985), Chapter 2.
2. Kevin Higgins, "Japanese Buyout Fuels Scripto's Campaign for Dominance in Lighter, Writing Instrument Markets," *Marketing News* 19, no. 4 (February 15, 1985): 1, 15.
3. Ronald B. Marks, "Consumer Response to Physicians' Advertisements," *Journal of the Academy of Marketing Science* 12, no. 3 (Summer 1984): 35–52.
4. Julie Franz, "Name's the Game in Beatrice Car Deal," *Advertising Age* 56, no. 9 (February 4, 1985): 64. Also see Terence A. Shimp and M. Wayne DeLozier, *Promotion Management and Marketing Communications* (New York: The Dryden Press, 1986): 211–14.
5. For further discussion, see Paul F. Lazarsfelt, Bernard R. Berelson, and Hanzel Gaudlet, *The Peoples Choice* (New York: Columbia University Press, 1948): 151. For a more recent discussion, see Henry Assael, *Consumer Behavior and Marketing Action* (Boston: Kent Publishing, 1984): 372–74.
6. David W. Nylen, *Advertising Planning, Implementation, and Control* (Cincinnati: South-Western, 1986): 257–59.
7. See George P. Moschis and Roy L. Moore, "Anticipatory Consumer Specialization," *Journal of the Academy of Marketing Science* (Fall 1985): 109–23.
8. Numerous marketing researchers have studied opinion leadership. For example see Naresh K. Malhotra, "A Scale to Measure Self-Concepts, Person Concepts, and Product Concepts," *Journal of Marketing Research* 18, no. 4 (November 1981): 456–64, and Leon G. Schiffman and Vincent Gaccione, "Opinion Leader in Institutional Markets," *Journal of Marketing* 38, no. 2 (April 1974): 49–53; Arch G. Woodside and Wayne DeLozier, "Effects of Word-of-Mouth Advertising on Consumer Risk Taking," *Journal of Advertising* 5, no. 2 (Fall 1976): 12–19.
9. Jesse Snyder, "K mart says 'Come On Down," *Advertising Age* 56, no. 11 (February 11, 1985): 1, 84.
10. Scott Hume, "Midway Campaign Built on 'Achieve,' " *Advertising Age* 56, no. 10 (February 7, 1985): 51.
11. See James M. McNeal and Stephen W. McDaniel, "An Analysis of Needs-Appeals in Television Advertising," *Journal of the Academy of Marketing Science* 12, no. 2 (Winter 1984): 176–90.
12. See Vincent J. Blasko and Charles H. Patti, "The Advertising Budgeting Practices of Industrial Marketers," *Journal of Marketing* 48, no. 4 (Fall 1984): 104–10.
13. See Leo Bogart, *Strategy in Advertising* (Lincolnwood, Ill.: NTC Business Books, 1986): 184–87.
14. "Advertisers Give High Grades to Their Co-op Programs," *Marketing News* 19, no. 4 (February 15, 1985): 15.
15. See Stanley E. Moldovan, "Copy Factors Related to Persuasion Scores," *Journal of Advertising Research* 24 (January 1985): 16–22.

16. For further discussion of creativity and message development, see James F. Engel, Martin R. Warshaw, Thomas C. Kinnear, *Promotion Strategy: Managing the Marketing Communications Process* (Homewood, Ill.: Richard D. Irwin, 1983), Chapter 11.
17. Philip Kotler, *Marketing Management: Analysis, Planning, and Control*, 3d ed. (Englewood Cliffs, N.J.: Prentice-Hall, 1980): 324–27.
18. For a conceptual discussion of the utilization of humor in advertising, see Thomas J. Madden and Marc G. Weinberger, "The Effects of Humor on Attention in Magazine Advertising," *Journal of Advertising* 11, no. 3 (1982): 8–14.
19. "Ads Tackle Teen Drunk Driving," *Advertising Age* 54, no. 45 (October 24, 1983): 32.
20. Robert A. Swerdlow, "Star Studded Advertising: Is It Worth the Effort?" *Journal of Marketing Science* 12, no. 3 (Summer 1984): 89–102.
21. Craig Reiss, "Living Campaign Has Powerful Pull," *Advertising Age* 55, no. 1 (January 2, 1984): 1, 34.
22. Ronald L. Earl and William M. Pride, "Do Disclosure Attempts Influence Claim Believability and Perceived Advertiser Credibility?" *Journal of the Academy of Marketing Science* 12, no. 1 (Spring 1984): 23–27.
23. Abdul G. Azhari and Joseph M. Kamen, "Study Shows Billboards Are More Effective Than Recall, Attitude-Change Scores Indicate," *Marketing News* 18, no. 29 (November 23, 1984): 11.
24. See "Magazines That Zero in on the Super Rich," *Business Week*, May 23, 1983: 46.
25. Chris Woodward, "Northeast Gives Courant New Direction," *Advertising Age* 56, no. 5 (January 24, 1985): 38.
26. William F. Gloede, "Yuppies—Last Hope for Cigars?" *Advertising Age* 56, no. 8 (January 31, 1985): 3, 41.
27. See Peggy J. Kreshel, Kent M. Lancaster, and Margaret A. Toomey, "How Leading Advertising Agencies Perceive Effective Reach and Frequency," *Journal of Advertising* 14, no. 3 (September 1985): 32–38.
28. For further discussion, see Kenneth E. Runyon, *Advertising* (Columbus, Ohio: Charles E. Merrill, 1984): 422–45.
29. Scott Hume, "La-Z-Boy Ads Reach for Spread-Out Sales," *Advertising Age* 55, no. 31 (June 7, 1984): 37.
30. Gay Jervey, "Candy Makers Sweet on Adults," *Advertising Age* 56, no. 10 (February 7, 1985): 45.
31. Mandell, *Advertising*, Chapter 17.
32. Runyon, *Advertising*: 426–27.
33. Jay W. Forrester, "Advertising: A Problem in Industrial Dynamics," *Harvard Business Review* 26, no. 2 (March/April 1959): 102.
34. Thomas F. Garbett, "Researching Corporate Advertising," *Journal of Advertising Research* 23, no. 1 (February/March 1983): 33–38. Also see Murphy A. Sewall and Dan Sarel, "Characteristics of Radio Commercials and Their Recall Effectiveness," *Journal of Marketing* 50 (January 1986): 52–60.
35. See Ronald M. Gwynn, "Tracking Advertising Through to Sales," *Business Marketing* 70 (February 1985): 90–98.
36. For discussion and comparison of several techniques, see Del Hawkins, Kenneth A. Coney, and Roger J. Best, *Consumer Behavior: Implications for Marketing Strategy* (Dallas: Business Publication, 1980), Chapter 14.
37. Don E. Schultz and Dennis G. Martin, *Strategic Advertising Campaigns* (Chicago: Crain Books, 1979), Chapter 9.
38. Gay Jervey, "Nabisco's Parkson Folding into Ohlmeyer," *Advertising Age* 54, no. 25 (June 13, 1983): 2, 64.
39. See Stewart Alter, "Bates OKs Saatchi Talks," *Advertising Age* (May 5, 1985): 1, 90; and Stewart Alter, "Biggest Global Agency: DDB-Needham-BBDO," *Advertising Age* (April 28, 1986): 1, 94.
40. See "New Account-Shift Wave Hits Megashops," *Advertising Age* (June 23, 1986): 1, 80 and "Saatchi, Omnicom Losses Mount," *Advertising Age* (June 30, 1986): 1, 70.
41. See Mary K. Hotz, John K. Ryans, Jr., and William K. Shanklin, "Agency/Client Relationships as Seen by Influentials on Both Sides," *Journal of Advertising* II, no. 1 (1982): 37–44.
42. Debra C. Scamman and Richard J. Semenik, "The FTC's Reasonableness Basis for Substantiation of Advertising," *Journal of Advertising* 12, no. 1 (1983): 4–11.
43. Jacob Jacoby, Margaret C. Nelson, and Wayne D. Hoyer, "Corrective Advertising and Affirmative Disclosure Statements: Their Potential for Confusing and Misleading the Consumer," *Journal of Marketing* 46, no. 1 (Winter 1982): 61–72.
44. Japhet H. Nkonge, "How Communications Medium and Message Format Affect Corrective Advertising," *Journal of the Academy of Marketing Science* 12, no. 1 (Spring 1984): 63.
45. Gary M. Armstrong, George R. Franke, and Frederick A. Russ, "The Effects of Corrective Advertising on Company Image," *Journal of Advertising* 11, no. 4 (1982): 39–47.
46. Vance Packard, *The Hidden Persuaders* (New York: Pocket Books, 1957).
47. John Kenneth Galbraith, *Economics and the Public Purpose* (Boston: Houghton Mifflin, 1973): 140.
48. Johnathan Alter, "FTC Relaxing Its Tight Grip," *Advertising Age* 53, no. 12 (May 3, 1982): M14.
49. Eric J. Zanot, J. David Pineus, and E. Joseph Lamp, "Public Perceptions of Subliminal Advertising," *Journal of Advertising* 12, no. 1 (1983): 39–45.
50. "A New View of Advertising's Economic Impact," *Business Week*, December 22, 1975: 49–54. See also Mark S. Albion and Paul W. Farris, *Appraising Research on Advertising's Economic Impact* (Cambridge, Mass.: Marketing Science Institute, 1979).
51. James M. Ferguson, "Comments on the Impact of Advertising on the Price of Consumer Products," *Journal of Marketing* 46, no. 1 (Winter 1982): 102–5.
52. John M. Scheidell, *Advertising, Prices, and Consumer Reaction: A Dynamic Analysis* (Washington, D.C.: American Enterprise Institute for Public Policy Research, 1978): 21–29.

Chapter 17

1. See Joseph A. Bellizzi and Ronald W. Hasty, "Student Perceptions of Questionable Personal Selling Practices," *Journal of the Academy of Marketing Science* 12, no. 2 (Spring 1984): 218–25. Also see Lucette B. Commer and Marvin A. Jolson, "Sex-Labeling of Selling Jobs and Their Applicants," *Journal of Personal Selling and Sales Management* 5 (May 1985): 15–22.
2. *Statistical Abstract of the United States* (Washington, D.C.: U.S. Government Printing Office, 1986).
3. See "100 Leading National Advertisers," *Advertising Age* 56, (August 24, 1985): 2, 181.
4. Joseph A. Bellizzi, A. Frank Thompson, and Lynn J. Loudenback, "Cyclical Variations of Advertising and Personal Selling," *Journal of the Academy of Marketing Science* 11, no. 2 (Spring 1983): 142–55.
5. Charles W. Stryker, "The Power of the Sales Information System: How to Harness the Information Revolution and Boost Your Sales Productivity," *Business Marketing* 70 (June 1985): 120–28.
6. Joseph A. Bellizzi and Paul A. Kline, "Technical or Nontechnical Salesmen?" *Industrial Marketing Management* 14 (May 1985): 69–74.

7. Carlton A. Pederson, Milburn D. Wright, and Barton A. Weitz, *Selling: Principles and Methods* (Homewood, Ill.: Richard D. Irwin, 1984): 24–27.
8. See Gilbert A. Churchill, Jr., Neil M. Ford, Steven W. Hartley, and Orville C. Walker, Jr., "The Determinants of Salesperson Performance: A Meta-Analysis," *Journal of Marketing Research* 22 (May 1985): 103–18.
9. Barbara Bund Jackson, *Winning and Keeping Industrial Customers* (Lexington, Mass.: Lexington Books), Chapter 4.
10. For an extended discussion of prospecting, see Robin Peterson, *Personal Selling: An Introduction* (Santa Barbara, Calif.: Wiley, 1978), Chapters 5 and 6.
11. Roy Price, "Sales Productivity Rises 80 Per Cent at Rank Xerox France," *Industrial Marketing Digest* 8, no. 4 (Fourth Quarter 1983): 39–43.
12. See Jon B. Freiden and Douglas S. Bible, "The Home Purchase Process: Measurement of Evaluative Criteria Through Pairwise Measures," *Journal of the Academy of Marketing Science* 10, no. 4 (Fall 1982): 359–76.
13. "Huffy Peddles a New Line," *Sales and Marketing Management* 130, no. 4 (March 14, 1983): 16.
14. W. J. Tobin, "Do You Want to See Your Volume Grow and Grow? *Printer's Ink* 21, no. 9 (February 16, 1951): 54.
15. Paul H. Schurr and Bobby J. Calder, "Psychological Effects of Restaurant Meetings on Industrial Buyers," *Journal of Marketing* 50 (January 1986): 87–97.
16. Ralph E. Anderson and Joseph F. Hair, Jr., *Sales Management: Text with Cases* (New York: Random House, 1983): 201–4. See also Arthur Meidon, "Optimizing the Number of Industrial Salespersons," *Industrial Marketing Management* 11, no. 1 (February 1982): 63–74.
17. Walter J. Semlow, "How Many Salesmen Do You Need?" *Harvard Business Review* 32, no. 3 (May/June 1959): 126–32.
18. Walter J. Talley, Jr., "How to Design Sales Territories," *Journal of Marketing* 25, no. 1 (January 1961): 7–13.
19. For a discussion of various means of determining sales force size, see Meidon, "Optimizing the Number of Industrial Salespersons," pp. 53–62.
20. Rayna Skolnik, "Olympia Girds for the Next Round," *Sales and Marketing Management* 130, no. 7 (May 16, 1983): 37–40.
21. T. A. Cates, E. James Randall, and Ernest F. Cooke, "Job Analysis: The First Step in Selecting and Training Sales People," in *Developments in Marketing Science*, John Rogers, ed. (Logan Utah: Academy of Marketing Science, 1983): 192–96. Also see Anderson and Hair, Jr., *Sales Management*, Chapter 7 and E. James Randall, Ernest F. Cooke, and Lois Smith, "A Successful Application of the Assessment Center Concept to the Salesperson Selection Process," *Journal of Personal Selling and Sales Management* 5 (May 1985): 53–61.
22. W. J. Tobin, "What Are Good Salesmen Like?" *Printer's Ink* 23, no. 16 (June 11, 1954): 35ff.
23. Bradley D. Lockeman and John H. Hallaq, "Who Are Your Successful Sales People?" *Journal of the Academy of Marketing Science* 10, no. 4 (Fall 1982): 457–72. Also see Alan J. Dubinsky and Steven W. Hartley, "A Path-Analytic Study of a Model of Salesperson Performance," *Journal of the Academy of Marketing Science* 14 (Spring 1986): 36–46.
24. John E. Swan and Robert T. Adkins, "The Image of the Salesperson: Prestige and Other Dimensions," *Journal of Personal Selling and Sales Management* 1, no. 1 (Fall/Winter 1980–81): 48–56.
25. See Alan J. Dubinsky, "Perceptions of the Sales Job: How Students Compare with Industrial Salespeople," *Journal of the Academy of Marketing Science* 9, no. 4 (Fall 1981): 352–67.
26. David L. Kurtz and Jay E. Klompmaker, *Professional Selling* (Plano, Texas: Business Publications, 1985): 47–48.
27. See, for instance, "Scrutiny for the Bounty," *Sales and Marketing Management* 131, no. 3 (August 15, 1983): 59.
28. See Gilbert A. Churchill, Jr., Neil M. Ford, and Orville Walker, *Sales Force Management: Planning, Implementation, and Control* (Homewood, Ill.: Richard D. Irwin, 1985): 307–12.
29. Ram C. Rao and Ronald E. Turner, "Organization and Effectiveness of the Multi Product Salesforce," *Journal of Personal Selling and Sales Management* 10, no. 1 (May 1984): 24–31.
30. Thayer C. Taylor, "The Sales Cost Barometer Declines," *Sales and Marketing Management* 130, no. 3 (February 21, 1983): 8, 9.
31. "St. Regis Divides to Conquer," *Sales and Marketing Management* 131, no. 5 (October 10, 1983): 39–42.
32. See Derek A. Newton, *Sales Force Management: Text and Cases* (Plano, Texas: Business Publications, 1985): 216–21.
33. Arthur J. Bragg, "What Have You Done for Your Sales Force Lately?" *Sales and Marketing Management* 129, no. 3 (December 6, 1982): 30–31.
34. "Compensation," *Sales and Marketing Management* 130, no. 3 (February 21, 1983): 70.
35. "Worthington Sees a Light," *Sales and Marketing Management* 130, no. 2 (February 7, 1983): 13.
36. "Hyster Lifts the Stakes," *Sales and Marketing Management* 129, no. 7 (November 15, 1982): 53–56.
37. Robert L. Berl, Nicholas C. Williamson, and Terry Powell, "Industrial Salesforce Motivation: A Critique and Test of Maslow's Hierarchy of Needs," *Journal of Personal Selling and Sales Management* 4, no. 1 (May 1984): 32–39.
38. Neil M. Ford, Orville C. Walker, Jr., and Gilbert A. Churchill, Jr., "Differences in the Attractiveness of Alternative Rewards Among Industrial Salespersons: Additional Evidence," *Journal of Business Research* 13 (April 1985): 123–38.
39. Pradeep K. Tyagi, "Relative Importance of Key Job Dimensions and Leadership Behaviors in Motivating Salesperson Work Performance," *Journal of Marketing* 49 (Summer 1985): 76–86.
40. "Steely Industrial Marketer Proves His Mettle," *Sales and Marketing Management* 130, no. 1 (January 17, 1983): 19.
41. A. Parasuraman and Charles M. Futrell, "Demographics, Job Satisfaction, and Propensity to Leave of Industrial Salesmen," *Journal of Business Research* 11, no. 2 (March 1983): 33–48.
42. R. Kenneth Teas, "Selling Task Characteristics and the Job Satisfaction of Industrial Salespeople," *Journal of Personal Selling and Sales Management* 1, no. 9 (Spring/Summer 1981): 18–26.
43. Leonard M. Lodish, "CALLPLAN: An Interactive Salesman's Call Planning System," *Management Science* 12, no. 4 (December 1971): 25–40. Also see Raymond La Forge and David W. Cravens, "Steps in Selling Effort Deployment," *Industrial Marketing Management* 11, no. 3 (July 1982): 183–94.
44. For a conceptual analysis of optimal salesperson routes, see S. Robert Anderson, *Professional Sales Management* (Englewood Cliffs, N.J.: Prentice-Hall, 1981), Chapter 7.
45. See H. L. Verma and C. W. Gross, *Introduction to Quantitative Methods: A Managerial Emphasis* (Santa Barbara, Calif.: Wiley/Hamilton, 1978), Chapter 13.
46. See Otto A. Davis and John U. Farley, "Allocating Sales Force Effort with Commissions and Quotas," *Management Science* 12, no. 4 (December 1971): 55–63.
47. For an excellent detailed discussion, see Gordon R. Storholm, *Sales Management* (Englewood Cliffs, N.J.: Prentice-Hall, 1982), Chapter 9.

48. For a discussion of a model approach to evaluating performance, see Rene Y. Darmon, "Identifying Profit-Producing Salesforce Members," *Journal of Personal Selling and Sales Management* 2, no. 2 (November 1982): 14–23.

Chapter 18

1. "Electronic Shopping: All Systems Go," *Business World Magazine* 1, no. 1 (January 1984): 17.
2. Kenneth C. Otis II, "Introduction to Direct Marketing," *Direct Mail Marketing Manual* (New York: Direct Mail Marketing Association, Inc., 1981): 1–1.
3. For an excellent discussion of direct marketing see Bob Stone, *Successful Direct Marketing Methods* (Chicago: Crane Books, 1979) and William A. Cohen, *Direct Response Marketing: An Entrepreneurial Approach* (New York: John Wiley & Sons, 1984). Also see Dave Galanti, Joanne Y. Cleaver, Sewell Whitney, and Mark Trost, "Direct Marketing," *Advertising Age* 56 (March 7, 1985): 26–51.
4. Paul L. Edwards, "Mailers Join Campaign to Find Missing Children," *Advertising Age* 56, no. 29 (April 15, 1985): 68. Also see Trey Rider, "Direct Marketing Is the Key of Professional Services," *Direct Marketing* 48, no. 4 (September 1985): 24–31.
5. *Membership Roster 1982–1983*, Direct Mail/Marketing Association, Inc., New York, July 1982. Also see David W. Nylen, *Advertising: Planning, Implementation and Control* (Cincinnati: South-Western, 1986), Chapter 15.
6. *1981 Fact Book in Direct Response Marketing, Statistical Update* (New York: The Direct Mail/Marketing Association, Inc., 1981), p. 1.
7. See Liz Murphy, "Market or Perish," *Sales and Marketing Management* 34 (May 13, 1985): 50–53.
8. Terry Trucco, "Catalogs Gain with Changing Japan Shopper," *Advertising Age* 54, no. 50 (November 28, 1983): M32, M34.
9. " 'True Marketing' Can Help Direct Marketers Prosper," *Marketing News* 20, no. 8 (April 11, 1986): 13.
10. *Ibid.*
11. Paul L. Edwards, "Links with General Shops Boost DM Agency Billings," *Advertising Age* (March 24, 1986): 100.
12. "Wise Telemarketing Produces Sales, Committed Customers," *Direct Marketing* 49, no. 3 (July 1986): 80.
13. Cecelia Reed, "KKB Takes Bottom Line for Health Club," *Advertising Age* (August 18, 1986): 52, 56.
14. Jim Kobs, *Profitable Direct Marketing* (Chicago: Crain Books, 1980).
15. *1981 Fact Book*: 11.
16. *1981 Fact Book*: 19.
17. *1981 Fact Book*: 31–32.
18. " 'True Marketing' Can Help Direct Marketers Prosper." Also see S. Watson Dunn and Arnold M. Barbau, *Advertising: Its Role in Modern Marketing* (New York: The Dryden Press, 1985), Chapter 24.
19. *1981 Fact Book*: 12.
20. "Survey: Business Calls Costing $229.70," *Marketing News* 20, no. 16 (August 1, 1986): 1.
21. *1981 Fact Book*, p. 5. Also see John McIlquham, "Insurer's Research Leads to Products and $1 Billion," *Direct Marketing* 47, no. 2 (March 1985): 48, 71.
22. Many mailing lists and other pertinent customer data are stored in computers. See John Moore, "Computer Integral Part of Mail Order Operations," *Direct Marketing* 59, no. 11 (March 1983): 62–63, 66.
23. "Allstate Campaign Increases Motor Club Membership," *Direct Marketing* 44, no. 7 (November 1981): 28.
24. Lauren B. Januz, "Merge/Purge Can Be a Helpful Tool But Look Before Leaping In," *The Marketing News* 17, no. 23 (November 11, 1983): 15.
25. Lauren B. Januz, "These Production Guidelines Will Ease the Mailing Process," *The Marketing News* 17, no. 5 (March 4, 1983): 14.
26. "U.S. Army Generates 450,000 Leads," *Direct Marketing* 44, no. 7 (November 1981): 65.
27. Lauren B. Januz, "Making the Offer Fit the Goal Can Make a Mailing a Winner," *The Marketing News* 17, no. 7 (April 1, 1983): 14.
28. " 'True Marketing' Can Help Direct Marketers Prosper."
29. John Hawkins, "Dow Pharmaceuticals Proves Doctors Open Their Mail," *Direct Marketing* 45, no. 11 (March 1983): 88–89.
30. J. A. Quelch and H. Tareuchi, "Non-Store Marketing: Fast Growth or Slow?" *Harvard Business Review* 59, no. 3 (July/August 1981): 75–84.
31. "The Boom in Catalog Sales," *Business Year* 1, no. 1 (April 1985): 8, 9.
32. Laurie Freeman, "Bissell Directs Self-Help Pitch," *Advertising Age* 56, no. 17 (March 4, 1985): 74.
33. Tony Cole, "Which Lists?" *Industrial Marketing Digest* 10 (Third quarter, 1985): 87–100.
34. Lawrence G. Chait, "Checkpoints for Catalog Success—Part Two," *Direct Marketing* 45, no. 10 (February 1983): 30. Also see Pete Hoke, "Mail Order: Continuing Its Maturation, Competitiveness," *Direct Marketing* 48 (July 1985): 64–86.
35. See "Thirst for Business News Quenched by Fountain of Regional Publications," *Marketing News* 19, no. 7 (March 29, 1985): 12, 15.
36. Herschell Gordon Lewis, "Add Strength to Your Copy: Choose Your Words with Care," *Direct Marketing* 45, no. 10 (February 1983): 38.
37. Robert J. Cohen, "Next Year's Cost Increases May Average Only 6%," *Advertising Age* 54, no. 47 (November 7, 1983): M-10. Also see Trey Rider, "Direct Marketing Is the Key of Professional Services."
38. "Magazines React to Copy Sales Slamo," *Advertising Age* 56, no. 17 (March 4, 1985): 66.
39. Lynn Reiling, "Kids and Collegians Targeted by New Networks," *Marketing News* 19, no. 8 (April 12, 1985): 14. Also see Christine Dugas, "A Harder Sell for Madison Avenue," *Business Week* (August 26, 1985): 28–29.
40. John I. Coppett and Roy Dalevoorhees, "Telemarketing: Supplement to Field Sales," *Industrial Marketing Management* 14 (August 1985): 213–16. Also see "Real Estate Broker Sells with LORA," *Advertising Age* 57 (March 24, 1986): 103W.
41. John W. Arnold, "What Exactly Is Telemarketing?" *Sales and Marketing Management* 26 (April 1985): 14–16.
42. Richard Edel, "Companies Find Marketing Answer in Telephone," *Advertising Age* 56, no. 18 (March 7, 1985): 14, 15.

Chapter 19

1. See "OPEC's Small Miracle," *Business Week*, August 18, 1986: 34–45.
2. Jon Udell, "How Important Is Pricing in Competitive Strategy?" *Journal of Marketing* 28, no. 1 (January 1964): 44–48. Also see Robert G. Cooper, "Overall Corporate Strategies for New Product Programs," *Industrial Marketing Management* 14 (August 1985): 179–93.
3. See "Airlines in Turmoil," *Business Week*, October 10, 1983: 98–102.
4. See Michael Kranish, "Texas Air Would Be Logan's Top Gun," *Boston Globe*, September 16, 1986: 59, 62.
5. See Ryan C. Amacher and Holley H. Ulbrich, *Principles of Microeconomics* (Cincinnati: South-Western, 1986), Chapter 5.

6. Arnold C. Harberger, *The Demand for Durable Goods* (Chicago: University of Chicago Press, 1960): 3–14 and Scott A. Neslin and Robert W. Schoemaker, "Using a Natural Experiment to Estimate Price Elasticity: The 1974 Sugar Shortage and the Ready-to-Eat Cereal Market," *Journal of Marketing* (Winter 1983): 44–57. Also see Ram C. Rao and Frank M. Bass, "Competition, Strategy, and Price Dynamics: A Theoretical and Empirical Investigation," *Journal of Marketing Research* 22 (August 1985): 283–96.
7. Lawrence Southwick, Jr., *Managerial Economics* (Plano, Texas: Business Publications, 1985), Chapter 8.
8. For a description of one approach to estimating demand, see Gordon A. Wyner, Lois H. Benedetti, and Bart M. Trapp, "Measuring the Quantity and Mix of Product Demand," *Journal of Marketing* 48, no. 1 (Winter 1984): 101–9. Also see Birger Wernerfelt, "The Dynamics of Prices and Market Share Over the Product Life Cycle," *Management Science* 31 (August 1985): 928–39.
9. A.D.H. Kaplan, Joel B. Dirlam, and Robert F. Lanzillotti, *Pricing in Big Business* (Washington, D.C.: Brokings Institute, 1958).
10. For insights in analyzing competition, see Bruce D. Henderson, "The Anatomy of Competition," *Journal of Marketing* 47, no. 2 (Spring 1983): 7–11. Also see Joe F. Goetz, Jr., "The Pricing Decision: A Service Industry's Experience," *Journal of Small Business Management* 23 (April 1985): 61–67.
11. "Three Computer Makers and Chapter 11: Trying to Write a Happy Ending," *Business Week*, March 4, 1985: 112, 113.
12. "Aluminum Prices Just Keep Plunging," *Business Week*, August 27, 1984: 36.
13. Albert L. Page, "A Test of the Share/Price Market Planning Relationship in One Retail Environment," *Journal of the Academy of Marketing Science* 7, no. 1 (Winter 1979): 25–39.
14. Tom Bayer, "Air War Ads Draw Battle Lines," *Advertising Age* 55, no. 58 (September 10, 1984): 2, 102.
15. "American Tries to Muscle in on the Low-Cost Carriers," *Business Week*, February 4, 1985: 33, 36.
16. P. Ronald Stephenson, William L. Cron, and Gary L. Frazier, "Delegating Pricing Authority to the Sales Force: The Effects on Sales and Profit Performance," *Journal of Marketing* 43, no. 2 (Spring 1979): 21–28. Also see Alvin J. Williams and John Seminerio, "What Buyers Like from Salesmen," *Industrial Marketing Management* 14 (May 1985): 75–78.
17. For further discussion of such models, see R. Stark, "Competitive Bidding: A Comprehensive Bibliography," *Operations Research* 14, no. 2 (March/April 1971): 484–90; and Herbert Maskowitz and Gordon P. Wright, *Operations Research Techniques for Management* (Englewood Cliffs, N.J.: Prentice-Hall, 1979), Chapter 15. See also Purnell Benson, "Price Quotations for Sale of Individual Contract Projects," *1984 AMA Educators' Proceedings* (Chicago: American Marketing Association, 1984): 80–82. Also see Ronald A. Shill, "Managing Risk in Contract Bidding with Multiple Incentives," *Industrial Marketing Management* 14 (February 1985): 1–16.

Chapter 20

1. For an excellent discussion of contemporary pricing practices and other pricing issues, see Kent B. Monroe, *Pricing: Making Profitable Decisions* (N.Y.: McGraw-Hill, 1979), Chapter 1. ALso see Michael Hutt and Thomas Speh, *Industrial Marketing Management* (New York: The Dryden Press, 1985), Chapter 14.
2. Bruce Allen and David R. Lambert, "Searching for the Best Price: An Empirical Look at Consumer Search Effort," *Journal of the Academy of Marketing Science* 6, no. 4 (Fall 1978): 245–57 and Robert U. Ayres and Wilber A. Steger, "Rejuvenating the Life Cycle Concept," *Journal of Business Strategy* 6 (Summer 1985): 66–76. Also see "People Is Plunging But Burr Is Staying Cool," *Business Week* (July 17, 1986): 31–32.
3. "Why Santa's Bag Will Be Short on Home Computers," *Business Week*, December 19, 1983: 66.
4. Gary M. Erickson and Johnny K. Johansson, "The Role of Price in Multi-Attribute Product Evaluations," *Journal of Consumer Research* 12, no. 2 (September 1985): 195–99 and Eitan Gerstner, "Do Higher Prices Signal Higher Quality?" *Journal of Marketing Research* 22, no. 2 (May 1985): 209–15.
5. Charles A. Ingene and Michael Levy, "Cash Discounts to Retail Customers: An Alternative to Credit Card Sales," *Journal of Marketing*, 46, no. 2 (Spring 1982): 92–103.
6. Ashok Rao, "Quantity Discounts in Today's Markets," *Journal of Marketing* 44, no. 4 (Fall 1980): 44–51. Also see Rajiv Lal and Richard Staelin, "An Approach for Developing an Optimal Discount Pricing Policy," *Management Science* 30, no. 4 (December 1984): 1524–39.
7. William T. Cummings and Lonnie L. Ostrom, "Measuring Price Thresholds Using Social Judgment Theory," *Journal of the Academy of Marketing Science* 10, no. 4 (Fall 1982): 395–409. Also see "Florida Bank Group Cuts Charges to Keep Customers," *Marketing News* 20 (August 17, 1986): 20.
8. For a discussion of unit pricing, see J. Paul Peter and James H. Donnelly, Jr., *A Preface to Marketing Management* (Plano, Texas: Business Publications, 1985), Chapter 10.
9. "What's Giving Some Ski Resorts a Lift," *Business Week*, January 14, 1985: 32.
10. Harry Nystrom, Hans Tamsons, and Robert Thams, "An Experiment in Price Generalization and Discrimination," *Journal of Marketing Research* (May 1975): 177–181. Also see Benson P. Shapiro, "Rejuvenating the Marketing Mix," *Harvard Business Review* 63 (September/October 1985): 28–34.
11. Mark Moriarty, "Feature Advertising-Price Interaction Effects in the Retail Environment," *Journal of Retailing* 59, no. 2 (Summer 1983): 80–98. Also see Stewart A. Washburn, "Establishing Strategy and Determining Costs in the Pricing Decision," *Business Marketing* 70 (July 1985): 64–78.
12. Joseph P. Guiltinan, "Risk-Aversion Pricing Policies: Problems and Alternatives," *Journal of Marketing* 40, no. 1 (January 1976): 15. See also Barry Berman and Joel R. Evans, *Retail Management: A Strategic Approach* (New York: Macmillan, 1983), Chapter 14.
13. For an example of failure to analyze these factors, see Thomas S. Robertson and Scott Ward, "Management Lessons from Airline Deregulation," *Harvard Business Review* 61, no. 1 (January/February 1983): 40–41.
14. "Panelists Offer Pricing Strategy Advice for Consumer and Industrial Products," *Marketing News* 19, no. 3 (Feb. 1, 1985): 1, 10, 11.

Chapter 21

1. Thomas V. Bonoma, "Market Success Can Breed 'Marketing Inertia'," *Harvard Business Review* 59, no. 3 (September/October 1981): 115–21. Also see Fredrick W. Gluck, "Big Bang Management," *Journal of Business Strategy* 6 (Summer 1985): 59–64.
2. See J. Clifton Williams, Andrew J. DuBrin, and Henry Sisk, *Management and Organization* (Cincinnati: South-Western Publishing, 1985), Chapter 9.
3. See E. Frank Harrison, *Policy and Managerial Action* (Boston: Houghton-Mifflin, 1986).

4. Geoffrey Calvin, "The Bigness Cult's Grip on Beatrice Foods," *Fortune* 106, no. 6 (September 20, 1982): 129.
5. For further discussion, see the classic: Peter F. Drucker, *Concept of the Corporation* (New York: John Day, 1946): 47–48. Also see John C. Camillus, *Strategic Planning and Management Control* (Lexington, Mass.: Lexington Books, 1986), Chapter 7.
6. Lloyd L. Byars, *Strategic Management: Planning and Implementation—Concepts and Cases* (New York: Harper & Row, 1985): 409–21.
7. Some managers feel that this system has major weaknesses. See Fredrick E. Webster, Jr., "Top Management's Concerns about Marketing Issues for the 1980s," *Journal of Marketing* 45, no. 3 (Summer 1981): 12, 13. Also see Bertran J. Hansotia, Mazaffar A. Saikh, and Jagdish N. Sheth, "The Strategic Determinancy Approach to Brand Management," *Business Marketing* 70 (February 1985): 66–83.
8. For extensive discussions of product management, see David W. Cravens, Gerald E. Hills, and Robert B. Woodruff, *Marketing Decision Making: Concepts and Strategy* (Homewood, Ill.: Richard D. Irwin, 1980), Chapter 11; and Sabbash C. Jain, *Marketing, Planning, and Strategy* (Cincinnati: South-Western Publishing, 1985), Chapter 11.
9. See Linda Richardson, "Profit System Improves Product Manager-Salesforce Communication," *Marketing News* 17, no. 6 (March 18, 1983): 21.
10. See "Intrapreneurship Now Favorite Weapon of Corporate Strategists," *Marketing News* 20, no. 12. (June 6, 1986): 23, 26.
11. James S. Atmann, "Coordinating Product Managers Essential for Success," *The Marketing News* 17, no. 5 (March 4, 1983): 9.
12. For a classic discussion, see Alfred D. Chandler, Jr., *Strategy and Structure* (Cambridge, Mass.: M.I.T. Press, 1962; Doubleday Edition, 1966). Also see Douglas Dalrymple and Leonard Parsons, *Marketing Management: Strategy and Cases* (New York: John Wiley & Sons, 1986), Chapter 3.
13. Standard Rate and Data Service.
14. Craig Reiss, "Hefty Net Rate Hikes Forecast," *Advertising Age* (March 14, 1983): 76.
15. "Leading National Advertisers," *Advertising Age* (September 26, 1985): 122 and *Statistical Abstract of the United States*.
16. See Henry L. Tosi, John R. Rizzo, and Steven J. Carroll, *Managing Organizational Behavior* (Cambridge, Mass.: Ballinger Publishing, 1986), Chapter 16.
17. See John B. Miner, Tim Singleton, and Vincent P. Luchsinger, *The Practice of Management: Text, Readings, and Cases* (Columbus, Ohio: Charles E. Merrill, 1985), Chapter 11.
18. "Smith Corona Is Typing in Black Ink Again," *Business Week* (June 9, 1986): 70–71.
19. Charles W. Gross and Robin T. Peterson, *Business Forecasting* (Boston: Houghton Mifflin Company, 1983): 3–11.
20. See Rudolph Schaffke and Howard G. Jensen, *Managerial Accounting* (Rockleigh, N.J.: Allyn and Bacon, 1981), Chapters 10 and 15.
21. This style corresponds with an autocratic managerial style (Theory X). See the classic: Douglas McGregor, *The Human Side of Enterprise* (New York: McGraw-Hill, 1960). Also see Robert N. Anthony, Glen A. Welsch, and James S. Reece, *Fundamentals of Management Accounting* (Homewood, Ill.: Richard D. Irwin, 1985), Chapter 16.
22. This style corresponds with a democratic style of management (Theory Y). See McGregor ibid. Also see J. Clifton Williams and George P. Hubar, *Human Behavior in Organizations* (Cincinnati: South-Western Publishing, 1986), Chapter 16.
23. Robert M. Fulmer, *The New Management* (New York: Macmillan, 1982), Chapter 13. See also R. Henry Migliore and Robert E. Stevens, "A Marketing View of Management by Objectives," *Managerial Planning* 28, no. 2 (March/April 1980): 16–19.
24. For an interesting futuristic look at research, including simulation, see Paul E. Green, "Science in Marketing: Quick View of Its Present, Future," *Advertising Age* 48, no. 24 (July 11, 1977): 117–20.
25. For examples of techniques and additional reference, see David A. Aaker, "ADMOD: An Advertising Decision Model," *Journal of Marketing Research* 12, no. 1 (February 1975): 37–45; Darral G. Clarke, "Econometric Measurement of the Duration of Advertising Effect on Sales," *Journal of Marketing Research* 13, no. 3 (November 1976): 345–57; and Richard M. Helmer and Johny K. Johansson, "An Exposition of the Box-Jenkins Transfer Function Analysis with an Application to the Advertising Sales Relationship," *Journal of Marketing Research* 14, no. 2 (May 1977): 227–39.
26. Leonard M. Lodish, "Call Plan: An Interactive Salesman's Call Planning System," *Management Science* 19, no. 4 (December 1971): 25–40.
27. Lary Galledge, "Audits Can Salvage Promotion," *Marketing News* 17, no. 17 (August 18, 1983): 4.
28. See Theo Haimann, William G. Scott, and Patrick E. Conner, *Management* (Boston: Houghton Mifflin, 1985), Chapter 21.
29. For further discussion, see Charles T. Horngren, *Introduction to Financial Accounting* (Englewood Cliffs, N.J.: Prentice-Hall, 1984): 328–35.
30. "GE Generates Service Business by Shifting Dollars; From Advertising to Order-Capturing," *Marketing News* 17, no. 13 (June 24, 1983): 12, 13.
31. See Diane Mermigas, "NBC Scores Big Gains, May Sweep End in Tie," *Advertising Age* 54, no. 23 (May 30, 1983): 2.
32. See George E. Pinches, *Essentials of Financial Management* (New York: Harper & Row, 1985), Chapter 7.
33. See J. Irwin Peters and Robert D. O'Keefe, "Sales and Customer Analysis for Sales Management," *Journal of Personal Selling and Sales Management* 11, no. 2 (Spring/Summer 1981): 44–48.
34. Unfortunately, many firms experience difficulty in identifying real problems. See Dana Smith Morgan and Fred W. Morgan, "Marketuring Cost Controls: A Survey of Industry Practice," *Industrial Marketing Management* 9, no. 3 (July 1980): 217–21.

Chapter 22

1. "Hallmark Expands Overseas," *The Marketing News* 13, no. 19 (July 12, 1980): 20.
2. Elizabeth Guider, "WW Is Getting Fat on Italy's Diet Craze," *Advertising Age* 52, no. 44 (November 23, 1981): 66.
3. See "Heinz Struggles to Stay at the Top of the Stack," *Business Week*, March 11, 1985: 49.
4. Most comprehensive economics texts contain discussions of the rationale for trade. For example, see William P. Albrecht, Jr., *Economics* (Englewood Cliffs, N.J.: Prentice-Hall, 1983), Chapter 20.
5. Jerry Demuth, "Exporting's Hard Sell," *Venture* 7, no. 1 (January 1985): 72, 73.
6. See, for example, "A Seattle Steel Plant Heads for New Life in Shanghai," *Business Week*, December 12, 1983: 32, 33. Also see Kathleen K. Wiegner, "Progressive Partner," *Forbes*, April 29, 1985: 55–56.
7. *Annual Report, R. J. Reynolds Industries, 1982* (Winston-Salem, North Carolina: R. J. Reynolds Industries, 1982): 6.
8. Dagmar Mussey, "Euro Slump Key to Carnation Dairy Buy," *Advertising Age* 52, no. 19 (November 23, 1981): 68.
9. *Annual Report, Electrolux Corporation, 1985* (Stockholm: Electrolux Corporation, 1985).

10. *Annual Report, H. J. Heinz Company 1985* (Pittsburg, 1985).
11. *Annual Report, Fruehauf Corporation* (Detroit: Fruehauf Corporation, 1983).
12. See Raymond Vernon and Louis T. Wells, *Economic Environment of International Business* (Englewood Cliffs, N.J.: Prentice-Hall, 1981), Chapter 1 and Ken Gofton, "How Mattel Plays to Win," *Marketing* 22 (July 11, 1985): 22–26.
13. See Louis Kraar, "Inside Japan's 'Open' Market," *Fortune* 104, no. 10 (November 5, 1981): 118–26. Also see Alkarim Jivani, "Where Global Obstacles Lie," *Marketing* 22 (July 4, 1985): 20–26.
14. "U.S. Cigarette Makers Try to Open a Market," *Business Week*, March 22, 1982: 42.
15. Jack Barton, "Japanese Turning Away from West," *Advertising Age* 56, no. 15 (February 25, 1985): 46.
16. "The Red Tycoons," *Newsweek*, April 17, 1978: 84–89.
17. Philip R. Cateora and John M. Hess, *International Marketing*, 3d ed. (Homewood, Ill.: Richard D. Irwin, 1975): 403.
18. Price Waterhouse & Co., *Information Guide for Doing Business in Korea* (United States: Price Waterhouse & Co., 1986): 6.
19. Robert T. Green and Arthur W. Alloway, "Identification of Export Opportunities: A Shift-Share Approach," *Journal of Marketing* 49, no. 1 (Winter 1985): 83–88.
20. For a comprehensive series of reports on multinational activities in the Middle East, see "Special Report: Marketing to the Arab World," *Advertising Age* (January 30, 1986).
21. For an excellent discussion of floating currency rates and their potential impact on foreign marketing, see "What's Keeping the Dollar Aloft," *Business Week*, December 19, 1983: 56. See also "Who Will Pay for Brazil's Devaluation?" *Business Week*, March 7, 1983: 27–28.
22. For an excellent discussion of world transportation routes, see *Oxford Economic Atlas of the World*," 4th ed. (England: Oxford University Press, 1982): 82ff.
23. "The Frustrations behind Penney's Cutback," *Business Week*, November 16, 1981: 60.
24. "The New China, A Special Report," *Newsweek*, February 5, 1979. Also see Richard H. Holton, "Marketing and the Modernization of China," *California Management Review* 27 (Summer 1985): 33–45.
25. David H. Blake and Robert T. Walters, *Politics of Global Economics Relations* (Englewood Cliffs, N.J.: Prentice-Hall, 1983), Chapter 4.
26. "Phone Market: Japan Keeps Hanging Up on the U.S.," *Business Week*, March 11, 1985: 67.
27. "A Bid to Expand Free Trade with the U.S.," *Business Week*, January 16, 1984: 42, 44. Also see "A Grey Market for Cars Fades Away," *Business Week*, August 18, 1986: 54–55.
28. For example, see "U.S. Oil Companies Feel the Heat," *Business Week*, June 13, 1970: 42–43, and "Libya Takes 52 Percent of Oxy, Chops Amoseas Production," *The Oil and Gas Journal*, August 20,1973: 24–25.
29. Raymond Vernon and Louis T. Wells, Jr., *Manager in the International Economy* (Englewood Cliffs, N.J.: Prentice-Hall, 1981), Chapter 13.
30. See Vern Terpstra, *International Marketing* (New York: The Dryden Press, 1983), Chapter 5. See also "Economic Reform Survives the Assassination," *Business Week*, December 12, 1983: 50–51.
31. See GATT: *General Trade Agreement on Tariffs and Trade* (Washington, D.C.: U.S. Department of Commerce, 1964).
32. Recently, GATT principles have been placed under stress by pressures on industrial nations to protect workers, industries and communities from trade competition through greater cartelization, although GATT still permeates basic groundrules for international trade. For further discussion, see "Europe: The Currency Crunch May Crimp Growth," *Business Week*, August 22, 1983: 44–45. See also "Latin America Could Add to U.S. Trade Woes," *Business Week*, January 16, 1984: 16.
33. OPEC has lost some of its former power due to oil gluts and dissension among members. See, for instance, "What Oil Glut?" *Business Week*, February 11, 1985: 29.
34. See "Levitt: Global Companies to Replace Dying Multinationals," *Marketing News* 19, no. 6 (March 16, 1985): 15.
35. See "Europe a Different Game," *Advertising Age* 54, no. 43 (October 10, 1983): 6.
36. See "Levi Strauss Plans to Close Plants in U.K., France," *Advertising Age* 56, no. 19 (March 11, 1985): 55.
37. "U.S. Department of Commerce, *Statistical Abstract of the United States* (Washington, D.C.: U.S. Government Printing Office, 1986). Also see Wesley J. Johnston and Michael R. Czinkota, "Export Attitudes of Industrial Manufacturers," *Industrial Marketing Management* 14 (May 1985): 123–32.
38. For an interesting discussion of business blunders in international marketing, see David A. Ricks, Marilyn Y.C. Fu, and Jeffrey S. Aspan, *International Business Blunders* (Columbus, Ohio: Grid Publications, 1974).
39. See Phillip Niffenegger and John White, "How European Retailers View American Imported Products: Results of a Product Image Survey," *Journal of the Academy of Marketing Science* 10, no. 3 (Summer 1982): 281–82.
40. Ruel Kahler, *International Marketing* (Cincinnati: South-Western Publishing Co., 1983), Chapter 5. Also see Herschel Peak and George Kulstad, "Don't Just Do Something, Sit There—Conquering Cross-Cultural Challenges," *Business Marketing* 70 (October 1985): 138–46.
41. "A U.S. Trade Pact: This Could Be the Year," *Business Week*, January 23, 1984: 52.
42. See Philip Barnard, "Conducting and Coordinating Multi-Country Quantitative Studies Across Europe," *Journal of the Market Research Society* 24, no. 1 (January 1982): 46–64.
43. See Gunter A. Pauli, "Some Advice on Marketing Foreign Products in Japan," *Industrial Management* 40 (September 1985): 121–27.
44. For further discussion, see Kahler, *International Marketing*: 172–74.
45. When U.S. advertising agencies desire to do business abroad, they often take on foreign partners. See "BBDO Links with Major Japan Shop," *Advertising Age* 55, no. 4 (January 25, 1984): 2, 80.
46. See "Olivetti and AT&T: An Odd Couple That's Flourishing," *Business Week*, March 4, 1985: 44, 45.
47. "Will Mexico Make It?" *Business Week*, October 1, 1984: 74, 75.
48. Warren J. Keegan, "Multinational Product Planning: Strategic Alternative," *Journal of Marketing* (January, 1969): 58–62. Also see Norman W. McGuinness and Blair Little, "The Influence of Product Characteristics on the Export Performance of New Industrial Products," *Journal of Marketing* 45, no. 2 (Spring 1981): 110–22; and Saul Sands, "Can You Standardize International Marketing Strategy?" *Journal of the Academy of Marketing Science* 7, no. 2 (Spring 1979): 117–32.
49. Richard J. Barnet and Ronald E. Muller, *Global Reach: The Power of the Multinational Corporations* (New York: Simon and Schuster, 1974): 15.
50. "The Multinational Corporate Colossus," *The Center Report*, April 1974: 3. See also "AMA Launches Push on International Front," *Advertising Age* 54, no. 43 (October 10, 1983): 1, 87.
51. Geoffrey Shields, "The Multinationals," *World Issues*, December 1977/January 1978, p. 5.

52. Ibid.: 5.
53. West Germany still enforces a sixteenth-century law preventing preservatives in beer. The law has the effect of preventing beer imports. See "European Court to Strike Down German Beer Restriction," *Advertising Age* 55, no. 4 (January 23, 1984): 56.
54. "Trying to Outwit the French: The Multinationals Plot to Slip Through France's Taut Controls," *Business Week*, September 12, 1977: 108.
55. Ibid.

Chapter 23

1. Valarie A. Zeithamal, A. Parasuraman, and Leonard L. Berry, "Problems and Strategies in Services Marketing," *Journal of Marketing* 49, no. 2 (Spring 1985): 33–46. Also see Connie A. Fox, "The Seven Myths of Service Marketing," *Bank Marketing* 17 (June 1985): 24–32.
2. Kevin Higgins, "Comprehensive Reform Legislation Needed to Build Confidence of Marketplace in Financial Institutions," *Marketing News* 19, no. 12 (June 7, 1985): 1. Also see Terry Paul and John Wong, "The Retailing of Health Care," *Journal of Health Care Marketing* 4 (Fall 1984): 23–24.
3. Zeithamal, Parasuraman, and Berry, "Problems and Strategies in Services Marketing." Also see Edward W. Wheatley, "Theory of Marketing—The Practice of Law," *Journal of Professional Services Marketing* 1 (Winter 1986): 79–88.
4. J. Donald Weinranch and Janie R. Pierce, "Strategic Marketing in Small Hospitals: Confronting the Challenges and Opportunities," *Developments in Marketing Science* (Miami: Academy of Marketing Science, 1983): 187–91. Also see Paul K. McDevitt and Lisa A. Shields, "Tactical Hospital Marketing: A Survey of the State of the Art," *Journal of Health Care Marketing* 5 (Winter 1985): 9–16.
5. A. Parasuraman, Valarie A. Zeithamal, and Leonard L. Berry, "A Conceptual Model of Service Quality and Its Implications for Future Research," *Journal of Marketing* 49, no. 4 (Fall 1985): 41–50.
6. Andrew Leckey, "HMOs Riding Popular Wave," *Chicago Tribune*, July 4, 1986, Sec. 3, p. 1.
7. August J. Aguila, "Marketing of Accounting Services Hinges on Referrals, Service Expansion, Communications," *Marketing News* 18, no. 9 (April 27, 1984): 3. Also see D. W. (Wes) Balderson, "Pro Teams Correlate Their Marketing Efforts with Performance on the Field," *Marketing News* 20 (August 15, 1986): 1.
8. Colleen Milligan and Judith O'Keefe Vindici, "Stressing Existing Services Leads to Growth," *Marketing News* 19, no. 13 (June 21, 1985): 1, 20. Also see Tim M. Henderson, "No-Frills Marketing of Community-Based Primary Care," *Journal of Health Care Marketing* 5 (Winter 1985): 47–50.
9. Kevin Higgins, "Impresarios Nurture Professional Karate into a Salable Sport," *Marketing News* 18, no. 13 (June 22, 1984): 1, 20.
10. Gary M. Erickson, "Competition for HMO Enrollments: The Importance of Price, Federal Qualification, and Individual Practice," *1984 AMA Educators' Proceedings* (Chicago: American Marketing Association, 1984): 235–38.
11. Michael R. Solomon, Carol Surprenant, and Evelyn G. Gataman, "A Role Theory Perspective on Dyadic Interactions: The Service Encounter," *Journal of Marketing* 49, no. 1 (Winter 1985): 99–111.
12. Ibid. Also see William A. Flexner, "Evaluating a Marketing Consultant: A Consultant's Viewpoint," *Journal of Health Care Marketing* 4 (Summer 1984): 55–58.
13. Harvey W. Rubin, "The Promotion of the 'State-of-the-Art' Life Insurance Products," *Developments in Marketing Science* (Miami Academy of Marketing Science, 1985): 312–14.
14. Frederick W. Langrehr, "Consumer Images of Two Types of Competing Financial Service Retailers," *Journal of the Academy of Marketing Science* 13, no. 3 (Summer 1985): 248–64.
15. Philip Kotler and Gerald Zaltman, "Social Marketing: An Approach to Planned Social Change," *Journal of Marketing* 34, no. 3 (July 1971): 3. Also see S. Prakash Seth, *Handbook of Advocacy Advertising* (Cambridge, Mass.: Ballinger Publishing, 1986).
16. Scott M. Smith and Leland L. Beik, "Market Segmentation for Fund Raisers," *Journal of the Academy of Marketing Science* 10, no. 3 (Summer 1982): 208–16. Also see Lois R. Smith and S. Tamer Cavusail, "Marketing Planning for Colleges and Universities," *Long Range Planning* 17 (December 1984): 104–17.
17. An impediment is the tendency of some not-for-profit organizations to liken marketing to some function such as promotion. See Irvin A. Zaenglein, "Lack of Understanding of What Marketing Is Impedes Its Application by Many Institutions," *Marketing News* 17, no. 15 (July 22, 1983): 6.
18. For example, see William Lazer and Eugene J. Kelley, *Social Marketing Perspectives and Viewpoints* (Homewood, Ill: Richard D. Irwin, 1973) and Gene R. Laczniak, Robert F. Lusch, and Patrick E. Murphy, "Social Marketing: Its Ethical Dimensions," *Journal of Marketing* 43, no. 2 (Spring 1979): 29–36.
19. See Karen F. A. Fox and Philip Kotler, "The Marketing of Social Causes: The First 10 Years," *Journal of Marketing* 44, no. 4 (Fall 1980): 24–33.
20. For example, see Janice R. Nall and Parks B. Dimsdale, "Civic Group Adopts Marketing Technique," *Marketing News* 19, no. 13 (June 21, 1985): 13.
21. This discussion is based on Michael L. Rothschild, "Marketing Communications in Non Business Situations or Why It's So Hard to Sell Brotherhood Like Soap," *Journal of Marketing* 43, no. 2 (Spring 1979): 11–20.
22. Today's patients have inputs in the hospitals they select. See Steven R. Steiber and Joseph A. Boscavino, "Positioning Opportunities Abound as Hospital Patients Become Consumers," *Marketing News* 17, no. 4 (February 18, 1983): 5. Also see David Andrus, "Factors Affecting Rural Consumers' Satisfaction with Medical Care," *Journal of Health Care Marketing* 14 (Summer 1984): 7–15.
23. See R. Bruce Hutton, "Advertising and the Department of Energy's Campaign for Energy Conservation," *Journal of Advertising* 11, no. 2 (1982): 27–39.
24. Philip Kotler, "Strategies for Introducing Marketing into Nonprofit Organizations," *Journal of Marketing* 43, no. 2 (Spring 1979): 37–44.
25. Gene R. Laczniak, Robert F. Lusch, and Patrick E. Murphy, "Social Marketing: Its Ethical Dimensions," *Journal of Marketing* 43, no. 1 (January 1979): 12–17.
26. Ibid.: 34.
27. Richard M. Durand and Subhash Sharma, "Conservation or Energy Development: Consumer Perceptions of Alternate Solutions to the Energy Crisis," *Journal of the Academy of Marketing Science* 10, no. 4 (Fall 1982): 410–31.
28. See Chris T. Allen, "Self-Perception Based Strategies for Stimulating Energy Conservation," *Journal of Consumer Research* 7, no. 2 (March 1982): 381–90.
29. Nicolas G. Papadopoulos, "Shortage Marketing: Comprehensive

Framework:" *Journal of the Academy of Marketing Science* 11, no. 1 (Winter 1983): 40–60.

Appendix C

1. For further discussion, see Harold Bierman, Jr., Charles Bonini, and Warren Hausman, *Quantitative Analysis for Business Decisions*, 4th ed. (Homewood, Ill.: Richard D. Irwin, 1973), Chapters 3 and 4.
2. Other criteria than the expected value may be used to reflect the risk associated with a potential negative outcome (ibid., Chapter 4).
3. Virtually all cost and managerial accounting texts contain discussions of break-even analysis. For example, see Ray H. Garrison, *Cost Accounting: Concepts for Planning, Control, and Decision Making* (Plano, Texas: Business Publications, 1982), Chapter 18.
4. Many types of fixed costs, such as advertising, vary with volume changes—at least from year to year. Within a particular time period, however, such costs are budgeted at a fixed level and may be considered fixed.
5. In some cases, fixed costs jump in total as volume increases, such as with the addition of a new machine. This has the effect of creating a steplike increase in total fixed costs. The basic solution procedure, however, is basically the same as illustrated, except that each step is considered.
6. Practically all finance texts include detailed discussions of methods involving the present value of funds. For example, see Raymond P. Nevin, *Fundamentals of Managerial Finance* (Cincinnati: South-Western Publishing, 1981), Chapter 14.
7. Ibid., Chapter 10.

Appendix E

1. David Burstein, "When the Smoke Clears, the Jobs Will Appear," *Advertising Age* 55, no. 1 (January 2, 1984): M–9, M–20.
2. "Job Opportunities for Marketing Show a 32% Gain in the Second Half of 1983," *The Marketing News* 18, no. 3 (February 3, 1984): 1.
3. Kevin Higgins, "Economic Recovery Puts Marketers in Catbird Seat," *The Marketing News* 17, no. 21 (October 14, 1983): 1, 8.
4. Steven S. Ross, "Entry-Level Jobs with a Future," *Business Week's Guide to Careers* 2, no. 1 (February/March 1984): 36, 37.
5. John Stodden, "Jobs with a Future," *Business Week's Guide to Careers* (1986 Edition): 36–40.
6. Gordon McAleer, *An Exploratory Analysis of AMA Members' Salaries for Marketing Educators and Practitioners* (Chicago: American Marketing Association, 1983).
7. See *Careers in Marketing* (Chicago: American Marketing Association, 1983): 16.
8. See Susan Bernard, "Strategies that Work," *Business Week's Guide to Careers* (1986 Edition): 14–18. Also see Susan Bernard and Gretchen Thompson, "How to Approach the Job Search," *Business Week's Guide to Careers* 2, no. 3 (October/November 1984): 63–65.
9. See Sandra Grundfest, "A Cover Letter and Résumé Guide," *Business Week's Guide to Careers* (1986 Edition): 8–13.
10. See Shirley Sloan Fraser, "Those Intimidating Interview Questions," *Business Week's Guide to Careers* 2, no. 3 (October/November 1984): 26–29.
11. Also see *Careers in Marketing* (Chicago, American Marketing Association, 1983): 25–26.

Name Index

Subject Index

Photo/Advertisement Credits (continued)

Chapter 13 **297** Courtesy Triple Five Corporation Ltd.; **298** Courtesy The Price Company; **301** Courtesy Montgomery Ward; **310** Courtesy The Southland Corporation; **315** Courtesy Triple Five Corporation Ltd.; **318** Courtesy Polaroid Corporation. Designer/Art Director: Vartus Artinian; Writer: Brian Flood; Product Manager: Rick Colson; **319** Jeffrey D. Smith/Woodfin Camp & Associates

Chapter 14 **323** The Granger Collection; **324** Peter Tenzer/Wheeler Pictures; **327** Courtesy McKesson Corp.; **330** Courtesy IGA, Inc., Chicago, IL; **335** James B. Sanderson/The Stock Market; **337** Joel Gordon; **339** Robert Frerck/Odyssey Productions

Chapter 15 **343** Courtesy RC Cola; **344** Courtesy Yankee Publishing Incorporated; **346** Courtesy Denny's, Inc., and Foote, Cone & Belding; **348** Courtesy United Technologies/Pratt & Whitney; **353** Courtesy U.S. West and Fallon McElligott, Inc.; **356** Courtesy E. & J. Gallo Winery; **362** Courtesy The Irwin Company, Wilmington, Ohio, and Lord, Sullivan & Yoder, Inc.

Chapter 16 **366** The Granger Collection; **367** Reprinted with permission, *Advertising Age,* March 24, 1986, copyright Crain Communications Inc.; **368** The Granger Collection; **372** The Granger Collection; **375** Courtesy Tahiti Tourism Promotion Board/UTA French Airlines and Cunningham & Walsh; **378** Courtesy The Minnesota Zoo and Fallon McElligott, Inc.; **379** Courtesy Johnston & Murphy and Weitzman, Dym & Associates, Inc.; **383** Courtesy Polo/Ralph Lauren and Geers Gross Advertising; **388** Courtesy Michelin Tire Corporation

Chapter 17 **393** Michael Melford/Wheeler Pictures; **394** Courtesy Cray Research, Inc.; **396** Frank Fournier/Woodfin Camp & Associates; **401** Courtesy Selling Solutions, Inc.; **409** Jon Feingersh/Stock, Boston; **414** Craig Hammell/The Stock Market; **415** Courtesy ITT Life Insurance Corporation

Chapter 18 **420** Courtesy Knoll International. Designed by: Knoll Graphics; Art Directors: Harold Matossian and Takaaki Matsumoto; Photographer: Mike Sekita; **421** Lester Sloan/Woodfin Camp & Associates; **422** Courtesy Montgomery Ward; **423** Courtesy Jetro; **427** Courtesy AT&T; **432** Courtesy Sears; **434** Courtesy Comark, Inc.

Chapter 19 **438** Courtesy Hyundai Motor America and Backer & Spielvogel; **439** Gerald Davis; **440** Michael Quackenbush/The Image Bank; **442** Michael Melford/Wheeler Pictures; **451** Reprinted by permission of Rolls-Royce Motors Inc.; **454** John Marmaras/Woodfin Camp & Associates; **456** Nicholas Foster/The Image Bank

Chapter 20 **461** Courtesy Gumpertz/Bentley/Fried Advertising, Los Angeles, for Palm Springs Convention and Visitors Bureau; **462** Courtesy United Airlines; **466** Courtesy Denny's Restaurants; **467** Courtesy Tiffany & Co.; **468** Walter Bibikow/The Image Bank; **477** Mieke Maas/The Image Bank; **480** ARCO Petroleum Products Company, courtesy Kresser, Craig/D.I.K. Advertising. Production Company: Papenek & Young; Director: Barry Young; Producer: Paul Papenek; Agency Producer: Len Levy; Copywriter: Cameron Day; Art Director: Ron Goodwin

Chapter 21 **485** Bob Straus/Woodfin Camp & Associates; **486** Courtesy Ashton-Tate. Ashton-Tate is a registered trademark and the Ashton-Tate logo is a trademark of Ashton-Tate; **488** Courtesy WFLD-TV, Metromedia Chicago, and Fallon McElligott, Inc.; **498** Courtesy *The Wharton Magazine*; **503** Reprinted with permission from February 1982 *Savings & Loan News*, a publication of the United States League of Savings Institutions. Copyright 1982 United States League of Savings Institutions; **506** Courtesy Shade and Fallon McElligott, Inc.

Chapter 22 **510** Loren McIntyre courtesy East/West Network; **511** Courtesy IBM; **512** Courtesy American Airlines and Bozell, Jacobs, Kenyon & Eckhardt, Inc.; **519** Courtesy New Zealand Tourist and Publicity Office and Lowe Marschalk, Inc.; **522** Owen Franken; **526** Milton & Joan Mann; **532** *left* Robert Frerck/Odyssey Productions; **532** *right* CameraMann Int'l., Ltd.

Chapter 23 **535** Courtesy Foote, Cone & Belding; **539** Courtesy AT&T Communications and N W Ayer Incorporated; **541** Courtesy North Carolina Travel & Tourism and McKinney Silver & Rockett. Art Director: Michael Winslow; Writer: Jan Karon; Photographer: Harry DeZitter; **543** Courtesy San Diego Zoo and Phillips-Ramsey; **546** Courtesy United Way Services; **549** Courtesy Texaco Inc.; **553** Courtesy Richmond Metropolitan Authority and Finnegan & Agee